THE THEOLOGY OF PAUL THE APOSTLE

The Theology of
Paul the Apostle

James D. G. Dunn

WILLIAM B. EERDMANS PUBLISHING COMPANY
GRAND RAPIDS, MICHIGAN / CAMBRIDGE, U.K.

© 1998 Wm. B. Eerdmans Publishing Co.
2140 Oak Industrial Drive N.E., Grand Rapids, Michigan 49505 /
P.O. Box 163, Cambridge CB3 9PU, U.K.
All rights reserved

Paperback edition 2006

Printed in the United States of America

13 12 11 10 09 08   14 13 12 11 10 9 8

Library of Congress Cataloging-in-Publication Data

Dunn, James D. G., 1939-
The Theology of Paul the Apostle / James D. G. Dunn.
p.   cm.
Includes bibliographical references and index.
ISBN 978-0-8028-4423-1 (pbk.: alk. paper)
1. Bible. N.T. Epistles of Paul — Theology.
2. Paul, the Apostle, Saint.   I. Title.
BS2651.D84   1998
227′.092 — dc21   97-23189
                                                CIP

www.eerdmans.com

To
Stephen Barton, Loren Stuckenbruck,
Walter Moberly, Mark Bonnington
and John Arnold
who fill the term "collegiality"
with such rich meaning,
and the other members of the
New Testament Postgraduate Seminar,
my weekly pride and delight.

Contents

Chapter 8. How Should Believers Live?   625

Chapter 9. Epilogue 713

Preface

My fascination with Paul began about forty years ago. Even as a schoolboy I could not help being impressed by Paul's missionary achievements, particularly his extensive travels and his success in establishing Christianity in Europe. In my student days the fascination deepened as I began to appreciate something of Paul the theologian. The combination of profound theological reflection and sensitive grappling with all too real human problems, of outspoken argument and pastoral insight, "found me" at many points. As a University teacher I have lectured on Paul and his theology for more than twenty-five years, constantly drawn back to him as I tackled a series of different subjects, the lectures, I hope, becoming steadily richer as I probed more and more aspects of Paul's theology.

The dialogue with Paul's theology became increasingly serious in the mid-70s and early 80s. My work on *Jesus and the Spirit* (1975), *Unity and Diversity in the New Testament* (1977), and *Christology in the Making* (1980) all forced me to encounter Paul's thought at ever deeper levels. "The new perspective on Paul" introduced by E. P. Sanders in his *Paul and Palestinian Judaism* (1977) made a complete rethink necessary and led me through a close study of the Antioch incident (Gal. 2.11-14) in 1980 into a sustained reassessment of Paul's attitude to and relationship with his fellow Jewish Christians and his ancestral religion, which is ongoing. Preparation for my first major commentary, on *Romans* (1988), made it necessary to engage fully with Galatians, reflected in my *Jesus, Paul and the Law* (1990) and the subsequent commentary on *Galatians* (1993). And working on my commentary on *Colossians and Philemon* (1996) likewise increased my detailed familiarity with later Pauline thought. Briefer treatments of 1 Corinthians and Ephesians have helped ensure a breadth of detailed knowledge of the Pauline corpus. All this was repeatedly stimulated by classroom exchanges, postgraduates working on Paul, and sustained involvement with annual seminars at the annual meetings of the Society of

New Testament Studies and the Society for Biblical Literaure — to all of whom I owe immeasurable debts.

I had long hoped to work up my much revised lecture notes into a full-scale study of Paul's theology. But an imminent radical syllabus revision provided the final spur, with a study leave (Easter through summer 1996) giving the needful occasion. As the time approached to begin the research leave, my feelings evoked in my mind the image of a river which had been fed by many streams, but whose flow had been restricted so that volume and pressure were building up. I felt at times as though the dam might burst, and the opening paragraphs (§2) were composed in my mind long before I finally sat down at home at my old Mac Plus. Six months of highly concentrated drafting enabled me to complete the first draft (less §1 and §25) and have given, I hope, the text a degree of consistency and coherence which would otherwise have been hard to achieve.

In that drafting I had to make various hard decisions. One was the decision, foreshadowed long before, to use Romans as a kind of template on which a fuller exposition of Paul's whole theology should be attempted. I try to explain and justify that decision in the Prologue (§1). The value of this method is that it has allowed sustained exposition of the themes which Paul himself develops in Romans. But it has also meant that the treatment of other letters has been more broken and to that extent less satisfactory. This is unavoidable in a thematic treatment of Paul's theology. The alternative procedure of analysing each letter in turn has its own drawbacks.

A second important decision was to treat the subjects in sufficient detail for (Paul's) theological and (my) exegetical rationale to be clear. Treatments of particular themes which assumed awareness of older discussion would have made for a shorter book, but it would not have been so self-contained. For the same reason I have included the key texts themselves, on some occasions in quite extensive quotations. As one whose book reading has to be squeezed into all sorts of occasions, I am very conscious that readers will not always have a text of Paul's letters to hand. The danger then is that the text as remembered may not match the point being made and the force of the latter may then be lost. In this case reader convenience and authorial desire to persuade made a compelling case (and not all that many extra pages).

A third decision was on the extent of engagement with fellow scholars on points of substance and detail. Obviously such discussion can be endless (as the increasing size of commentaries reminds us), and the book was already in danger of becoming overlong. Hard choices had to be made and discussion limited to documenting the range of discussion on the points being developed. Inevitably the decisions on what to include, whom to refer to, and so on were personal and often arbitrary, and I can only apologize to those who think I have ignored some important aspects or contributions. Hopefully reviews will highlight any important omissions which can subsequently be remedied.

A fourth question was what to call the book. In the narrowness of our focus (or arrogance) we students of the New Testament or of Christianity's beginnings tend to think that a reference to "the theology of Paul" is self-explanatory. But such a title would help ensure that the appeal of the book remained limited to circles of biblical scholarship and church. Outside these circles "The Theology of Paul" would more likely evoke the response What is theology? and Who is Paul? — if they evoked anything. "The Theology of St. Paul" would be more recognizable. But the old Protestant in me still doubts whether a Paul who addressed all Christians as saints would welcome the term being used to designate a Christian elite. There was, however, an obvious solution. Paul himself had one title which he prized above all others and which indeed he insisted on as his most regular self-designation when introducing himself to the recipients of his letters. That was "apostle." The term was also distinctive within Christianity, and sufficiently well known beyond. And thus the matter was resolved. Only one title would do: *The Theology of Paul the Apostle.*

The first draft was dispatched to Eerdmans at the end of September 1996, and within a week I had multiple copies loose bound for use in class and seminar. I am most grateful to Bill Eerdmans for making this possible, and subsequently to John Simpson for masterminding the subediting. I was therefore able to dispatch various copies to colleagues who had kindly agreed to read the first draft, to use it in my undergraduate lectures (which did not really work), and to provide enough copies for my postgraduate NT seminar to work with throughout the first term (autumn 1996).

I am more grateful than I can say to those who were able to respond in these different ways. I have in mind especially Professors Paul Achtemeier, Bob Jewett, and John Reumann in the US, Professor Eduard Lohse in Germany, and Professor Graham Stanton in the UK. In particular, my Doctor-father from days of yore, Charlie Moule, read through every page and in a sequence of tightly packed letters picked up my typos, improved my English, and bade me think again on numerous points. It was good to resume the old teacher-pupil relationship and to find it still as beneficial as in those well-remembered Cambridge days of the mid-60s. The postgraduate seminar spent ten weeks putting the first draft under the microscope and forced me to clarify the obscure and to better defend (sometimes to abandon) the more idiosyn-cratic. To my colleagues in other institutions who have not experienced the exquisite sensation of week-by-week being put through the ringer, I can commend it wholeheartedly. Other members of the seminar will not be sur-prised if I make particular mention of my immediate colleague, Walter Moberly. The seminar soon began to follow a particular ritual, with the opening pause broken by Walter's gentle voice announcing that he had "only three minor points and two points of major substance to raise."

To all of the above I can only say a heartfelt "Thank you." I am very conscious of the very many ways in which the content and presentation of the following pages have been improved. Their contributions have undoubtedly saved me from several embarrassments and have no doubt enhanced the value of the whole. Needless to say the remaining blemishes and more questionable judgments are wholly my own.

I have made a point of drawing in as much comment and discussion on the first draft as I can, not simply to weed out the more obvious flaws, but because I want to give as much body as possible to the idea of doing theology as a cooperative venture, or dialogue (to use the preferred "model" in the following pages). I have no illusions that the present book (or any book) is or could be "the last word" on Paul's theology. It is intended rather as a contribution to the ongoing dialogue or discussion regarding what Paul's theology was/is and what its continuing relevance is to the study and practice of religion and theology. Any comments or critiques which help improve any subsequent revision will be gratefully received in the same spirit.

Last but not least I want to express my appreciation to my dear wife, Meta, my rock and wise counsellor, without whom the project would have been impossible from the beginning.

James D. G. Dunn
January 25, 1997
(Conversion of St. Paul and Birthday of Rabbie Burns)

N.B. Unless otherwise indicated, the full titles for all works cited in the footnotes can be found either in the General Bibliography or in the bibliography of the first footnote of the section (§). Reference works are included in the Abbreviations.

Bibliography

General Bibliography

J. Ådna, et al., eds., *Evangelium–Schriftauslegung–Kirche,* P. Stuhlmacher FS (Göttingen: Vandenhoeck und Ruprecht, 1997); **J.-N. Aletti**, *Comment Dieu est-il juste? Clefs pour interpréter l'épître aux Romains* (Paris: Seuil, 1991); **L. Baeck**, "The Faith of Paul," *Judaism and Christianity* (New York: Harper, 1966) 139-68; **W. Barclay**, *The Mind of St Paul* (London: Collins/New York: Harper, 1958); **C. K. Barrett**, *Essays on Paul* (London: SPCK/Philadelphia: Westminster, 1982); *Freedom and Obligation: A Study of the Epistle to the Galatians* (London: SPCK/Philadelphia: Westminster, 1985); "Paulus als Missionar und Theologe," *ZTK* 86 (1989) 18-32; *Paul: An Introduction to His Thought* (London: Chapman/Louisville: Westminster/John Knox, 1994); **M. Barth**, "St. Paul — A Good Jew," *HBT* 1 (1979) 7-45; **M. Barth**, et al., *Foi et Salut selon S. Paul* (AnBib 42; Rome: Biblical Institute, 1970); **J. M. Bassler**, ed., *Pauline Theology 1: Thessalonians, Philippians, Galatians, Philemon* (Minneapolis: Fortress, 1991); **F. C. Baur**, *Paul: The Apostle of Jesus Christ* (1845; 2 vols.; London: Williams and Norgate, 1873, 1875); *Vorlesungen über neutestamentliche Theologie* (1864; Darmstadt: Wissenschaftliche Buchgesellschaft, 1973) 128-207; **J. Becker**, *Paul: Apostle to the Gentiles* (Louisville: Westminster, 1993); **J. C. Beker**, *Paul the Apostle: The Triumph of God in Life and Thought* (Philadelphia: Fortress, 1980); "Paul's Theology: Consistent or Inconsistent?" *NTS* 34 (1988) 364-77; **S. Ben-Chorin**, *Paulus. Der Völkerapostel in jüdischer Sicht* (Munich: DTV, 1980); **K. Berger**, *Theologiegeschichte des Urchristentums. Theologie des Neuen Testaments* (Tübingen/Basel: Francke, 1994); **H. D. Betz**, *Paulinische Studien. Gesammelte Aufsätze III* (Tübingen: Mohr, 1994); **W. Beyschlag**, *New Testament Theology* (2 vols.; Edinburgh: Clark, 1895) 2.1-281; **J. Blank**, *Paulus. Von Jesus zum Christentum* (Munich: Kösel, 1982); **J. Bonsirven**, *Theology of the New Testament* (London: Burns and Oates/Westminster: Newman, 1963) 193-368; **G. Bornkamm**, *Early Christian Experience* (London: SCM/New York: Harper and Row, 1969); *Paul* (London: Hodder and Stoughton/New York, Harper and Row, 1971); **M. Bouttier**, *Christianity according to Paul* (London: SCM/Naperville: Allenson, 1966); **D. Boyarin**, *A Radical Jew: Paul and the Politics of Identity* (Berkeley: University of California, 1994); **F. F. Bruce**, *Paul: Apostle of* *the Free Spirit* (Exeter: Paternoster,1977) = *Paul: Apostle of the Heart Set Free* (Grand Rapids: Eerdmans, 1977); **C. Buck and G. Taylor**, *Saint Paul: A Study in the Development of His Thought* (New York: Scribner, 1969); **R. Bultmann**, *Theology of the New Testament* I (London: SCM/New York: Scribner, 1952); **G. B. Caird**, *New Testament Theology* (Oxford: Clarendon/New York: Oxford University, 1994); **W. S. Campbell**, *Paul's Gospel in an Intercultural Context: Jew and Gentile in the Letter to the Romans* (Frankfurt: Lang, 1992); **H. Cancik**, et al., eds., *Geschichte–Tradition–Reflexion,* M. Hengel FS, *Band I Judentum* (ed. P. Schäfer), *Band III Frühes Christentum* (ed. H. Lichtenberger) (Tübingen: Mohr, 1996); **B. S. Childs**, *Biblical Theology of the Old and New Testaments* (London: SCM/Minneapolis: Fortress, 1992); **H. Conzelmann**, *An Outline of the Theology of the New Testament* (London: SCM/New York: Harper and Row, 1969) 155-286; **C. H. Cosgrove**, *The Cross and the Spirit: A Study in the Argument and Theology of Galatians* (Macon: Mercer University, 1988); **N. A. Dahl**, *Studies in Paul* (Minneapolis: Augsburg, 1977); **G. N. Davies**, *Faith and Obedience in Romans: A Study in Romans 1–4* (JSNTS 39; Sheffield: JSOT, 1990); **W. D. Davies**, *Paul and Rabbinic Judaism* (London: SPCK/Philadelphia: Fortress, 1948, [4]1981); *Jewish and Pauline Studies* (Philadelphia: Fortress, 1984); **C. A. Davis**, *The Structure of Paul's Theology: "The Truth Which Is the Gospel"* (Lewiston: Mellen, 1995); **A. Deissmann**, *Paul: A Study in Social and Religious History* (1912, [2]1926; New York: Harper, 1957); **M. Dibelius and W. G. Kümmel**, *Paul* (London: Longmans, 1953); **C. H. Dodd**, *The Meaning of Paul for Today* (London: Allen and Unwin/New York: Meridian, 1920); *The Bible and the Greeks* (London: Hodder and Stoughton, 1935); **K. P. Donfried**, ed., *The Romans Debate* (Peabody: Hendrickson, [2]1991); **K. P. Donfried and I. H. Marshall**, *The Theology of the Shorter Pauline Letters* (Cambridge: Cambridge University, 1993); **J. Drane**, *Paul: Libertine or Legalist?* (London: SPCK, 1975); **J. D. G. Dunn**, *Jesus and the Spirit: A Study of the Religious and Charismatic Experience of Jesus and the First Christians as Reflected in the New Testament* (London: SCM/Philadelphia: Westminster, 1975 = Grand Rapids: Eerdmans, 1997); *Christology in the Making: A New Testament Inquiry in the Origins of the Doctrine of the Incarnation* (London: SCM, [2]1989 = Grand Rapids: Eerdmans, 1996); *Jesus, Paul and the Law: Studies in Mark and Galatians* (London: SPCK/Louisville: Westminster, 1990); *Unity and Diversity in the New Testament* (London: SCM/Philadelphia: TPI, [2]1990); *The Partings of the Ways between Christianity and Judaism* (London: SCM/Philadelphia TPI, 1991); *The Theology of Paul's Letter to the Galatians* (Cambridge/New York: Cambridge University, 1993); *1 Corinthians* (Sheffield: Sheffield Academic, 1995); **G. Ebeling**, *The Truth of the Gospel: An Exposition of Galatians* (Philadelphia: Fortress, 1985); **H.-J. Eckstein**, *Verheißung und Gesetz. Eine exegetische Untersuchung zu Galater 2.15–4.7* (WUNT 86; Tübingen: Mohr, 1996); **G. Eichholz**, *Die Theologie des Paulus im Umriß* (Neukirchen-Vluyn: Neukirchener, 1972); **N. Elliott**, *The Rhetoric of Romans: Argumentative Constraint and Strategy and Paul's Dialogue with Judaism* (JSNTS 45; Sheffield: JSOT, 1990); *Liberating Paul: The Justice of God and the Politics of the Apostle* (Maryknoll: Orbis, 1994); **E. E. Ellis**, *Paul and His Recent Interpreters* (Grand Rapids: Eerdmans, 1961); **M. S. Enslin**, *Reapproaching Paul* (Philadelphia: Westminster, 1972); **T. Engberg-Pedersen**, ed., *Paul in His Hellenistic Context* (Minneapolis: Fortress, 1995); **P. Feine**, *Theologie des Neuen Testaments* (Leipzig: Hinrichs, 1910) 230-549; **J. A. Fitzmyer**, *To Advance the Gospel* (New York: Crossroad, 1981); *Paul and His Theology: A Brief Sketch* (Englewood Cliffs: Prentice Hall, ²1989); *According to Paul: Studies in the Theology of the Apostle* (New York: Paulist, 1993); **R. T. Fortna and B. R. Gaventa**, *The Conversation Continues: Studies in Paul and John*, J. L. Martyn FS (Nashville: Abingdon, 1990); **A. Fridrichsen**, *The Apostle and His Message* (Uppsala: Almqvist and Wiksells, 1947); **D. B. Garlington**, *Faith, Obedience and Perseverance: Aspects of Paul's Letter to the Romans* (WUNT 79; Tübingen: Mohr, 1994); **D. Georgi**, *Theocracy in Paul's Praxis and Theology* (Minneapolis: Fortress, 1991); **H. Gese**, *Essays on Biblical Theology* (Minneapolis: Augsburg, 1981); **J. Gnilka**, *Theologie des Neuen Testaments* (Freiburg: Herder, 1994) 16-132; *Paulus von Tarsus. Zeuge und Apostel* (Freiburg: Herder, 1996); **M. Goguel**, *L'Apôtre Paul et Jésus-Christ* (Paris: Librairie Fischbacher, 1904); **E. J. Goodspeed**, *Paul* (Nashville: Abingdon, 1947, 1980); **L. Goppelt**, *Theology of the New Testament 2: The Variety and Unity of the Apostolic Witness to Christ* (Grand Rapids: Eerdmans, 1982) 31-150; **M. Grant**, *Saint Paul* (London: Weidenfeld and Nicolson/New York: Scribner, 1976); **A. J. Guerra**, *Romans and the Apologetic Tradition: The Purpose, Genre and Audience of Paul's Letter* (SNTSMS 81; Cambridge: Cambridge University, 1995); **D. Guthrie**, *New Testament Theology* (Leicester: Inter-Varsity/Downers Grove: InterVarsity, 1981); **D. A. Hagner and M. J. Harris**, eds., *Pauline Studies,* F. F. Bruce FS (Exeter: Paternoster/Grand Rapids: Eerdmans, 1980); **D. M. Hay**, ed., *Pauline Theology 2: 1 and 2 Corinthians* (Minneapolis: Fortress, 1993); **D. M. Hay and E. E. Johnson**, eds., *Pauline Theology 3: Romans* (Minneapolis: Fortress, 1995); **R. B. Hays**, *The Faith of Jesus Christ: An Investigation of the Narrative Substructure of Galatians 3.1–4.11* (Chico: Scholars, 1983); *Echoes of Scripture in the Letters of Paul* (New Haven: Yale University, 1989); **M. Hengel**, *Between Jesus and Paul* (London: SCM/Philadelphia: Fortress, 1983); *The Pre-Christian Paul* (London: SCM/Philadelphia: TPI, 1991); **M. Hengel and U. Heckel,** eds., *Paulus und das antike Judentum* (WUNT 58; Tübingen: Mohr, 1991); **M. Hengel and A. M. Schwemer**, *Paul between Damascus and Antioch* (London: SCM, 1997); **O. Hofius**, *Paulusstudien* (WUNT 51; Tübingen: Mohr, 1989); "Paulus — Missionar und Theologe," in Ådna, et al., eds., *Evangelium* 224-37; **H. J. Holtzmann**, *Lehrbuch der neutestamentlichen Theologie* (Tübingen: Mohr; 1911) 2.1-262; **M. D. Hooker**, *Pauline Pieces* (London: Epworth, 1979); *From Adam to Christ: Essays on Paul* (Cambridge/New York: Cambridge University, 1990); **M. D. Hooker and S. G. Wilson**, eds., *Paul and Paulinism,* C. K. Barrett FS (London: SPCK, 1982); **D. G. Horrell**, *The Social Ethos of the Corinthian Correspondence* (Edinburgh: Clark, 1996); **G. Howard**, *Paul: Crisis in Galatia: A Study in Early Christian Theology* (SNTSMS 35; Cambridge/New York: Cambridge University, 1979, ²1990); **H. Hübner**, "Paulusforschung seit 1945. Ein kritischer Literaturbericht," *ANRW* II.25.4 (1987) 2649-2840; *Biblische Theologie des Neuen Testaments 2: Die Theologie des Paulus* (Göttingen: Vandenhoeck, 1993); *Biblische Theologie als Hermeneutik. Gesammelte Aufsätze* (Göttingen: Vandenhoeck, 1995); **A. J. Hultgren**, *Paul's Gospel and Mission: The Outlook from His Letter to the Romans* (Philadelphia: Fortress, 1985); **A. M. Hunter**, *The Gospel According to St Paul* (London: SCM/Philadelphia: Westminster, 1966); **J. C. Hurd**, *The Origin of 1 Corinthians* (London: SPCK, 1965); **E. Käsemann**, *Essays on New Testament Themes* (London: SCM/Naperville: Allenson, 1964); *New Testament Questions of*

Today (London: SCM/Philadelphia: Fortress, 1969); *Perspectives on Paul* (London: SCM/Philadelphia: Fortress, 1971); **R. D. Kaylor**, *Paul's Covenant Community: Jew and Gentile in Romans* (Atlanta: John Knox, 1988); **L. E. Keck**, *Paul and His Letters* (Philadelphia: Fortress, 1982); **H. A. A. Kennedy**, *The Theology of the Epistles* (London: Duckworth, 1919) 13-160; **K. Kertelge**, *Grundthemen paulinischer Theologie* (Freiburg: Herder, 1991); **J. Knox**, *Chapters in a Life of Paul* (1950; Macon: Mercer University, ²1987); **W. L. Knox**, *St Paul and the Church of the Gentiles* (Cambridge: Cambridge University, 1939); **H. Koester**, *Introduction to the New Testament* 1: *History, Culture, and Religion of the Hellenistic Age,* 2: *History and Literature of Early Christianity* (Berlin: de Gruyter/Philadelphia: Fortress, 1982); **L. Kreitzer**, *2 Corinthians* (Sheffield: Sheffield Academic, 1996); **W. G. Kümmel**, *Heilsgeschehen und Geschichte. Gesammelte Aufsätze 1933-1964* (Marburg: Elwert, 1965); *The Theology of the New Testament* (Nashville: Abingdon, 1973) 137-254; *Introduction to the New Testament* (revised ed., Nashville: Abingdon, 1975); **O. Kuss**, *Paulus. Die Rolle des Apostels in der theologischen Entwicklung der Urkirche* (Regensburg: Pustet, 1975); **T. Laato**, *Paulus und das Judentum. Anthropologische Erwägungen* (Åbo: Academy, 1991); **G. E. Ladd**, *A Theology of the New Testament* (Grand Rapids: Eerdmans, ²1993) 397-614; **K. Lake**, *The Earlier Epistles of St Paul* (London: Rivingtons, 1911); **J. Lambrecht**, *Pauline Studies* (BETL 115; Leuven: Leuven University, 1994); **P. Lapide and P. Stuhlmacher**, *Paul: Rabbi and Apostle* (Minneapolis: Augsburg, 1984); **A. T. Lincoln and A. J. M. Wedderburn**, *The Theology of the Later Pauline Letters* (Cambridge: Cambridge University, 1993); **E. A. Livingstone**, ed., *Studia Biblica 1978 Vol. 3* (JSNTS 3; Sheffield: JSOT, 1980); **W. von Loewenich**, *Paul: His Life and Work* (Edinburgh: Oliver and Boyd, 1960); **E. Lohse**, *Die Einheit des Neuen Testaments. Exegetische Studien zur Theologie des Neuen Testaments* (Göttingen: Vandenhoeck, 1973); *Die Vielfalt des Neuen Testaments. Exegetische Studien zur Theologie des Neuen Testaments* 2 (Göttingen: Vandenhoeck, 1982); *Paulus. Eine Biographie* (Munich: Beck, 1996); **L. De Lorenzi**, ed., *Paul di Tarse: Apôtre du notre temps* (Rome: Abbaye de S. Paul, 1979); **G. Lüdemann**, *Paulus und das Judentum* (Munich: Kaiser, 1983); *Paul, Apostle to the Gentiles: Studies in Chronology* (Philadelphia: Fortress, 1984); *Opposition to Paul in Jewish Christianity* (Minneapolis: Fortress, 1989); **S. Lyonnet**, *Études sur l'épître aux Romains* (AnBib 120; Rome: Biblical Institute, 1989); **J. G. Machen**, *The Origin of Paul's Religion* (Grand Rapids: Eerdmans, 1925); **A. J. Malherbe**, *Paul and the Popular Philosophers* (Minneapolis: Fortress, 1989); **T. W. Manson**, *On Paul and John* (London: SCM/Naperville: Allenson, 1963) 11-81; **S. B. Marrow**, *Paul: His Letters and His Theology* (Mahwah: Paulist, 1986); **U. Mauser**, "Paul the Theologian," *HBT* 11 (1989) 80-106; **W. A. Meeks**, *The First Urban Christians: The Social World of the Apostle Paul* (New Haven: Yale University, 1983); **W. A. Meeks**, ed., *The Writings of St. Paul* (New York: Norton, 1972); **O. Merk**, "Paulus-Forschung 1936-1985," *TR* 53 (1988) 1-81; **H. Merklein**, *Studien zu Jesus und Paulus* (WUNT 43; Tübingen: Mohr, 1987); **P. S. Minear**, *The Obedience of Faith: The Purposes of Paul in the Epistle to the Romans* (London: SCM/Naperville: Allenson, 1971); **M. M. Mitchell**, *Paul and the Rhetoric of Reconciliation: An Exegetical Investigation of the Language and Composition of 1 Corinthians* (Louisville: Westminster/John Knox, 1993); **C. G. Montefiore**, *Judaism and St. Paul: Two Essays* (London: Goschen, 1914); **O. Moe**, *The Apostle Paul: His Message and Doctrine* (1928; Minneapolis: Augsburg, 1954);

R. **Morgan**, *Romans* (Sheffield: Sheffield Academic, 1995); L. **Morris**, *New Testament Theology* (Grand Rapids: Zondervan, 1986) 19-90; C. F. D. **Moule**, *Essays in New Testament Interpretation* (Cambridge/New York: Cambridge University, 1982); J. **Munck**, *Paul and the Salvation of Mankind* (London: SCM/Richmond: John Knox, 1959); "Pauline Research since Schweitzer," in J. P. Hyatt, ed., *The Bible in Modern Scholarship* (Nashville: Abingdon, 1965) 166-77; J. **Murphy-O'Connor**, *Becoming Human Together: The Pastoral Anthropology of St. Paul* (Wilmington: Glazier, 1982); *The Theology of the Second Letter to the Corinthians* (Cambridge: Cambridge University, 1991); *Paul: A Critical Life* (Oxford: Clarendon/New York: Oxford University, 1996); J. **Murphy-O'Connor and J. Charlesworth**, eds., *Paul and the Dead Sea Scrolls* (New York: Crossroad, 1990); M. D. **Nanos**, *The Mystery of Romans: The Jewish Context of Paul's Letter* (Minneapolis: Fortress, 1996); J. H. **Neyrey**, *Paul in Other Words: A Cultural Reading of His Letters* (Louisville: Westminster, 1990); G. W. E. **Nickelsburg with G. W. MacRae**, eds., *Christians among Jews and Gentiles*, K. Stendahl FS (Philadelphia: Fortress, 1986); K.-W. **Niebuhr**, *Heidenapostel aus Israel: Die jüdische Identität des Paulus nach ihrer Darstellung in seinen Briefen* (WUNT 62; Tübingen: Mohr, 1992); A. D. **Nock**, *St. Paul* (London: Oxford University/New York: Harper, 1938); E. H. **Pagels**, *The Gnostic Paul: Gnostic Exegesis of the Pauline Letters* (Philadelphia: Fortress, 1975); C. M. **Pate**, *The End of the Ages Has Come: The Theology of Paul* (Grand Rapids: Zondervan, 1995); D. **Patte**, *Paul's Faith and the Power of the Gospel: A Structural Introduction to the Pauline Letters* (Philadelphia: Fortress, 1983); S. **Pedersen**, ed., *The Pauline Literature and Theology* (Aarhus: Aros/Göttingen: Vandenhoeck, 1980); R. **Penna**, *Paul the Apostle 1: Jew and Greek Alike, 2: Wisdom and Folly of the Cross* (Collegeville: Liturgical/Glazier, 1996); O. **Pfleiderer**, *Paulinism: A Contribution to the History of Primitive Christian Theology* (2 vols.; London: Williams and Norgate, 1877); S. E. **Porter and C. A. Evans**, eds., *The Pauline Writings* (Sheffield: Sheffield Academic, 1995); F. **Prat**, *The Theology of Saint Paul* (2 vols.; London: Burns, Oates, and Washbourne, 1926, 1927); H. **Räisänen**, *Jesus, Paul and Torah: Collected Essays* (JSNTS 43; Sheffield Academic, 1992); K. H. **Rengstorf**, ed., *Das Paulusbild in der neueren deutschen Forschung* (Darmstadt: Wissenschaftliche Buchgesellschaft, 1964); A. **Richardson**, *An Introduction to the Theology of the New Testament* (London: SCM/New York: Harper, 1958); P. **Richardson and J. C. Hurd**, eds., *From Jesus to Paul*, F. W. Beare FS (Waterloo: Wilfrid Laurier University, 1984); P. **Richardson with D. Granskou**, *Anti-Judaism in Early Christianity 1: Paul and the Gospels* (Waterloo: Wilfrid Laurier University, 1986); H. **Ridderbos**, *Paul: An Outline of His Theology* (Grand Rapids: Eerdmans, 1975); R. **Riesner**, *Die Frühzeit des Apostels Paulus: Studien zur Chronologie, Missionsstrategie und Theologie* (WUNT 71; Tübingen: Mohr, 1994); J. A. T. **Robinson**, *Wrestling with Romans* (London: SCM/Philadelphia: Westminster, 1979); C. J. **Roetzel**, *The Letters of Paul: Conversations in Context* (Atlanta: John Knox, 1975, ²1982); R. L. **Rubenstein**, *My Brother Paul* (New York: Harper, 1972); A **Sabatier**, *The Apostle Paul: A Sketch of the Development of His Doctrine* (London: Hodder and Stoughton/New York: Pott, 1906); E. P. **Sanders**, *Paul and Palestinian Judaism* (London: SCM/ Philadelphia: Fortress, 1977); *Paul* (London: Oxford University, 1991); "Paul," in J. Barclay and J. Sweet, eds., *Early Christian Thought in Its Jewish Context*, M. D. Hooker FS (Cambridge: Cambridge University, 1996) 112-29; S. **Sandmel**, *The Genius of Paul* (1958; Philadelphia: Fortress, 1979); K. O.

Sandnes, *Paul — One of the Prophets?* (WUNT 2.43; Tübingen: Mohr, 1991); **K. H. Schelkle**, *Theology of the New Testament* (4 vols.; Collegeville: Liturgical, 1971-78); *Paulus. Leben — Briefe — Theologie* (Darmstadt: Wissenschaftliche Buchgesellschaft, 1981); **A. Schlatter**, *Die Theologie der Apostel* (Stuttgart: Calwer, 1922) 239-432; **H. Schlier**, *Grundzüge einer paulinischen Theologie* (Freiburg: Herder, 1978); **W. Schmithals**, *Paul and the Gnostics* (Nashville: Abingdon, 1972); *Theologiegeschichte des Urchristentums. Eine problemgeschichtliche Darstellung* (Stuttgart: Kohlhammer, 1994); **H. J. Schoeps**, *Paul: The Theology of the Apostle in the Light of Jewish Religious History* (London: Lutterworth/Philadelphia: Westminster, 1961); **G. Schrenk**, *Studien zu Paulus* (Zurich: Zwingli, 1954); **A. Schweitzer**, *Paul and His Interpreters: A Critical History* (London: Black/New York: Macmillan, 1912); **E. Schweizer**, *Neotestamentica: German and English Essays 1951-1963* (Zurich: Zwingli, 1963); *Beiträge zur Theologie des Neuen Testaments. Neutestamentliche Aufsätze (1955-1970)* (Zurich: Zwingli, 1970); *A Theological Introduction to the New Testament* (Nashville: Abingdon, 1991) 55-95; **C. A. A. Scott**, *Christianity according to St Paul* (Cambridge: Cambridge University, 1927); **R. Scroggs**, *Paul for a New Day* (Philadelphia: Fortress, 1977); **A. F. Segal**, *Paul the Convert: The Apostolate and Apostasy of Saul the Pharisee* (New Haven: Yale University, 1990); **J. N. Sevenster and W. C. van Unnik, eds.**, *Studia Paulina in honorem Johannis de Zwaan septuagenarii* (Haarlem: Bohn, 1953); **M. L. Soards**, *The Apostle Paul: An Introduction to His Writings and Teaching* (New York: Paulist, 1987); **E. Stauffer**, *New Testament Theology* (London: SCM/New York: Macmillan, 1955); **K. Stendahl**, *Paul among Jews and Gentiles* (Philadelphia: Fortress, 1976/London: SCM, 1977); *Final Account: Paul's Letter to the Romans* (Minneapolis: Fortress, 1995); **G. B. Stevens**, *The Theology of the New Testament* (Edinburgh: Clark/New York: Scribner, [2]1918) 325-482; **J. S. Stewart**, *A Man in Christ: The Vital Elements of St. Paul's Religion* (London: Hodder and Stoughton/New York: Harper, 1935); **S. K. Stowers**, *A Rereading of Romans: Justice, Jews and Gentiles* (New Haven: Yale University, 1994); **G. Strecker**, *Eschaton und Historie. Aufsätze* (Göttingen: Vandenhoeck, 1979); *Theologie des Neuen Testaments* (Berlin: de Gruyter, 1996) 11-229; **Studiorum Paulinorum Congressus Internationalis Catholicus 1961** (2 vols.; Rome: Pontifical Biblical Institute, 1963); **P. Stuhlmacher**, *Reconciliation, Law and Righteousness: Essays in Biblical Theology* (Philadelphia: Fortress, 1986); *Biblische Theologie des Neuen Testaments 1: Grundlegung von Jesus zu Paulus* (Göttingen: Vandenhoeck, 1992) 221-392; **G. Theissen**, *The Social Setting of Pauline Christianity* (Philadelphia: Fortress/Edinburgh: Clark, 1982); *Psychological Aspects of Pauline Theology* (Philadelphia: Fortress/Edinburgh: Clark, 1987); **W. Trilling**, *A Conversation with Paul* (London: SCM/New York: Crossroad, 1986); **A. Vanhoye**, ed., *L'Apôtre Paul. Personnalité, style et conception du ministère* (BETL 73; Leuven: Leuven University, 1986); **J. C. Walters**, *Ethnic Issues in Paul's Letter to the Romans: Changing Self-Definitions in Earliest Roman Christianity* (Valley Forge: TPI, 1993); **F. Watson**, *Paul, Judaism and the Gentiles* (SNTSMS 56; Cambridge: Cambridge University, 1986); **A. J. M. Wedderburn**, *The Reasons for Romans* (Edinburgh: Clark/Minneapolis: Fortress, 1988); **H. Weinel**, *St Paul: The Man and His Work* (London: Williams and Norgate/New York: Putnam, 1906); *Biblische Theologie des Neuen Testaments* (Tübingen: Mohr, [3]1921) 261-436; **B. Weiss**, *Biblical Theology of the New Testament* (2 vols.; Edinburgh: Clark, 1882, 1883) 1.274–2.149; **D. E. H.**

Whiteley, *The Theology of St Paul* (Oxford: Blackwell, 1964); **U. Wilckens**, *Rechtfertigung als Freiheit: Paulusstudien* (Neukirchen-Vluyn: Neukirchener, 1974); **B. Witherington**, *Paul's Narrative Thought World* (Louisville: Westminster/John Knox, 1994); **W. Wrede**, *Paul* (London: Philip Green, 1907); **N. T. Wright**, *The Messiah and the People of God* (University of Oxford D. Phil. thesis, 1980); *The Climax of the Covenant: Christ and the Law in Pauline Theology* (Edinburgh: Clark, 1991); **F. Young and D. F. Ford**, *Meaning and Truth in 2 Corinthians* (London: SPCK/Grand Rapids: Eerdmans, 1987); **D. Zeller**, *Juden und Heiden in der Mission des Paulus: Studien zum Römerbrief* (Stuttgart: Katholisches Bibelwerk, ²1976); **J. A. Ziesler**, *Pauline Christianity* (Oxford/New York: Oxford University, ²1990).

Commentaries on the Pauline epistles consulted

Romans

C. K. Barrett, *The Epistle to the Romans* (BNTC/HNTC; London: Black/New York: Harper and Row, 1975, ²1991); **K. Barth**, *The Epistle to the Romans* (1919, ²1922, ⁶1929; ET London/New York: Oxford University, 1933); **M. Black**, *Romans* (NCB; London: Oliphants/Grand Rapids: Eerdmans, ²1989); **F. F. Bruce**, *The Epistle of Paul to the Romans* (TNTC; London: Tyndale/Grand Rapids: Eerdmans, 1963); **C. E. B. Cranfield**, *The Epistle to the Romans* (ICC, 2 vols.; Edinburgh: Clark, 1975, 1979); **C. H. Dodd**, *The Epistle to the Romans* (MNTC; London: Hodder and Stoughton/New York: Harper, 1932); **J. D. G. Dunn**, *Romans* (WBC 38, 2 vols.; Dallas: Word, 1988); **J. A. Fitzmyer**, *Romans* (AB 33; New York: Doubleday, 1993); **E. Käsemann**, *An die Römer* (HNT 8a; Tübingen: Mohr, 1973) = *Commentary on Romans* (Grand Rapids: Eerdmans/London: SCM, 1980); **O. Kuss**, *Der Römerbrief* (3 vols.; Regensburg: Pustet, 1957, 1959, 1978); **M.-J. Lagrange**, *Épitre aux Romains* (ÉB; Paris: Gabalda, ²1922, ⁶1950); **F. J. Leenhardt**, *L'Épitre de Saint Paul aux Romains* (CNT; Neuchâtel: Delachaux, 1957) = *The Epistle to the Romans* (London: Lutterworth/Cleveland: World, 1961); **H. Lietzmann**, *An die Römer* (HNT 8; Tübingen: Mohr, 1906, ⁴1933, ⁵1971); **O. Michel**, *Der Brief an die Römer* (KEK; Göttingen: Vandenhoeck, ¹⁰1955, ¹⁴1978); **D. Moo**, *The Epistle to the Romans* (NICNT; Grand Rapids: Eerdmans, 1996); **L. Morris**, *The Epistle to the Romans* (Pillar; Grand Rapids: Eerdmans/Leicester: Inter-Varsity. 1988); **J. Murray**, *The Epistle to the Romans* (NICNT, 2 vols.; Grand Rapids: Eerdmans, 1959, 1965); **A. Nygren**, *Commentary on Romans* (London: SCM/Philadelphia: Muhlenberg, 1952); **W. Sanday and A. C. Headlam**, *The Epistle to the Romans* (ICC; Edinburgh: Clark, 1895, ⁵1902); **H. Schlier**, *Der Römerbrief* (HTKNT 6; Freiburg: Herder, 1977); **W. Schmithals**, *Der Römerbrief* (Gütersloh: Gütersloher, 1988); **P. Stuhlmacher**, *Der Brief an die Römer* (NTD 6; Göttingen: Vandenhoeck, 1989) = *Paul's Letter to the Romans* (Louisville: Westminster/John Knox, 1994); **U. Wilckens**, *Der Brief an die Römer* (EKK 6, 3 vols.; Zürich: Benziger/Neukirchen-Vluyn: Neukirchener, 1978, 1980, 1982); **T. Zahn**, *Der Brief des Paulus an die Römer* (Leipzig: Deichert, 1910, ³1925); **D. Zeller**, *Der Brief an die Römer* (RNT; Regensburg: Pustet, 1985); **J. Ziesler**, *Paul's Letter to the Romans* (London: SCM/Philadelphia: TPI, 1989).

1 and 2 Corinthians

C. K. Barrett, *The First Epistle to the Corinthians* (BNTC/HNTC; London: Black/ New York: Harper, 1968); *The Second Epistle to the Corinthians* (BNTC/HNTC; London: Black/New York: Harper, 1973); **H. D. Betz**, *2 Corinthians 8 and 9* (Hermeneia; Philadelphia: Fortress, 1985); **F. F. Bruce**, *1 and 2 Corinthians* (NCB; London: Oliphants, 1971 = Grand Rapids: Eerdmans, 1980); **R. Bultmann**, *Der zweite Brief an die Korinther* (KEK; Göttingen: Vandenhoeck, 1976) = *The Second Letter to the Corinthians* (Minneapolis: Augsburg, 1985); **H. Conzelmann**, *Der erste Brief an die Korinther* (KEK; Göttingen: Vandenhoeck, 1969) = *1 Corinthians* (Hermeneia; Philadelphia: Fortress, 1975); **E. Fascher**, *Der erste Brief des Paulus an die Korinther 1-7* (THKNT; Berlin: Evangelische, 1975); **G. D. Fee**, *The First Epistle to the Corinthians* (NICNT; Grand Rapids: Eerdmans, 1987); **V. P. Furnish**, *2 Corinthians* (AB 32A; New York: Doubleday, 1984); **J. Héring**, *The First Epistle of Saint Paul to the Corinthians* (London: Epworth, 1962); *The Second Epistle of Saint Paul to the Corinthians* (London: Epworth, 1967); **P. E. Hughes**, *Paul's Second Epistle to the Corinthians* (NICNT; Grand Rapids: Eerdmans, 1961); **H.-J. Klauck**, *1 Korintherbrief* (Wurzburg: Echter, 1984); **H. Lietzmann**, *An die Korinther I/II* (HNT 9; Tübingen: Mohr, 1949); **R. P. Martin**, *2 Corinthians* (WBC 40; Waco: Word, 1986); **J. Moffatt**, *The First Epistle of Paul to the Corinthians* (MNTC; London: Hodder and Stoughton/New York: Harper, 1938); **A. Plummer**, *Second Epistle of St Paul to the Corinthians* (ICC; Edinburgh: Clark, 1915); **A. Robertson and A. Plummer**, *First Epistle of St Paul to the Corinthians* (ICC; Edinburgh: Clark, 1911); **W. Schrage**, *Der erste Brief an die Korinther* (EKK 7, 2 [of 3] vols.; Zürich: Benziger/Neukirchen-Vluyn: Neukirchener, 1991, 1995); **M. E. Thrall**, *2 Corinthians 1-7* (ICC; Edinburgh: Clark, 1994); **J. Weiss**, *Der erste Korintherbrief* (KEK: Göttingen: Vandenhoeck, 1910); **H. D. Wendland**, *Die Briefe an die Korinther* (NTD 7; Göttingen: Vandenhoeck, 1964); **H. Windisch**, *Der zweite Korintherbrief* (KEK; Göttingen: Vandenhoeck, 1924); **C. Wolff**, *Der erste Brief des Paulus an die Korinther 8-16* (THKNT; Berlin: Evangelische, 1982).

Galatians

J. Becker, *Der Brief an die Galater* (NTD 8; Göttingen: Vandenhoeck, 1990); **H. D. Betz**, *Galatians* (Hermeneia; Philadelphia: Fortress, 1979); **P. Bonnard**, *L'Épitre de Saint Paul aux Galates* (CNT; Neuchâtel: Delachaux, 1953); **U. Borse**, *Der Brief an die Galater* (RNT; Regensburg: Pustet, 1984); **F. F. Bruce**, *The Epistle to the Galatians* (NIGTC; Grand Rapids: Eerdmans/Exeter: Paternoster, 1982); **E. de W. Burton**, *The Epistle to the Galatians* (ICC; Edinburgh: Clark, 1921); **G. S. Duncan**, *The Epistle of Paul to the Galatians* (MNTC; London: Hodder and Stoughton/New York: Harper, 1934); **J. D. G. Dunn**, *The Epistle to the Galatians* (BNTC; London: Black/Peabody: Hendrickson, 1993); **R. Y. K. Fung**, *The Epistle to the Galatians* (NICNT; Grand Rapids: Eerdmans, 1988); **M.-J. Lagrange**, *Saint Paul Épitre aux Galates* (ÉB; Paris: Gabalda, [2]1925); **H. Lietzmann**, *An die Galater* (HNT 10; Tübingen: Mohr, [4]1971); **J. B. Lightfoot**, *Saint Paul's Epistle to the Galatians* (London: Macmillan, 1865); **R. N. Longenecker**, *Galatians* (WBC 41; Dallas: Word, 1990);

D. Lührmann, *Der Brief an die Galater* (ZBK; Zurich: Theologischer, 1988); **F. Mussner**, *Der Galaterbrief* (HTKNT; Freiburg: Herder, [3]1977); **A. Oepke**, *Der Brief des Paulus an die Galater* (THKNT; Berlin: Evangelische, [3]1973, edited by J. Rohde); **J. Rohde**, *Der Brief des Paulus an die Galater* (THKNT; Berlin: Evangelische, 1989); **H. Schlier**, *Der Brief an die Galater* (KEK; Göttingen: Vandenhoeck, [4]1965); **T. Zahn**, *Der Brief des Paulus an die Galater* (Leipzig: Deichert, 1905).

Philippians:

F. W. Beare, *The Epistle to the Philippians* (BNTC/HNTC; London: Black/New York: Harper, 1959); **P. Bonnard**, *Épitre de Saint Paul aux Philippiens* (CNT; Neuchâtel: Delachaux, 1950); **G. B. Caird**, *Paul's Letters from Prison (Ephesians, Philippians, Colossians, Philemon)* (Oxford: Clarendon, 1976); **J.-F. Collange**, *The Epistle of Saint Paul to the Philippians* (London: Epworth, 1979); **J. Ernst**, *Die Briefe an die Philipper, an Philemon, an die Kolosser, und an die Epheser* (RNT; Regensburg: Pustet, 1974); **G. D. Fee**, *Paul's Letter to the Philippians* (NICNT; Grand Rapids: Eerdmans, 1995); **J. Gnilka**, *Der Philipperbrief* (HTKNT 10.3; Freiburg: Herder, 1968); **G. F. Hawthorne**, *Philippians* (WBC 43; Waco: Word, 1983); **J. H. Houlden**, *Paul's Letters from Prison: Philippians, Colossians, Philemon and Ephesians* (Harmondsworth: Penguin/Philadelphia: Westminster, 1970); **J. B. Lightfoot**, *Saint Paul's Epistle to the Philippians* (London: Macmillan, 1868); **E. Lohmeyer**, *Die Briefe an die Philipper, Kolosser und an Philemon* (KEK; Göttingen: Vandenhoeck, [8]1929, [13]1964); **R. P. Martin**, *Philippians* (NCB; London: Oliphants, 1976 = Grand Rapids: Eerdmans, 1980); **P. T. O'Brien**, *The Epistle to the Philippians* (NIGTC; Grand Rapids: Eerdmans, 1991); **M. R. Vincent**, *Philippians and Philemon* (ICC; Edinburgh: Clark, 1897).

Colossians and Philemon:

J.-N. Aletti, *Saint Paul Épitre aux Colossiens* (ÉB; Paris: Gabalda, 1993); **M. Barth and H. Blanke**, *Colossians* (AB 34B; New York: Doubleday, 1994); **H. Binder**, *Der Brief des Paulus an Philemon* (THKNT 11.2; Berlin: Evangelische, 1990); **F. F. Bruce**, *The Epistle to the Colossians, to Philemon, and to the Ephesians* (NICNT; Grand Rapids: Eerdmans, 1984); **G. B. Caird** (see Philippians); **M. Dibelius**, *An die Kolosser, Epheser, an Philemon* (HNT 12; Tübingen: Mohr, [3]1953); **J. D. G. Dunn**, *The Epistles to the Colossians and to Philemon* (NIGTC; Grand Rapids: Eerdmans/Carlisle: Paternoster, 1996); **J. Ernst** (see Philippians); **J. Gnilka**, *Der Kolosserbrief* (HTKNT 10.1; Freiburg: Herder, 1980); *Der Philemonbrief* (HTKNT 10.4; Freiburg: Herder, 1982); **J. H. Houlden** (see Philippians); **J. B. Lightfoot**, *The Epistles of St Paul: Colossians and Philemon* (London: Macmillan, 1875); **A. Lindemann**, *Der Kolosserbrief* (ZBK; Zurich: Theologischer, 1983); **E. Lohmeyer** (see Philippians); **E. Lohse**, *Die Briefe an die Kolosser und an Philemon* (KEK; Göttingen: Vandenhoeck, 1968) = *Colossians and Philemon* (Hermeneia; Philadelphia: Fortress, 1971); **R. P. Martin**, *Colossians and Philemon* (NCB; London: Oliphants, 1973 = Grand Rapids: Eerdmans, 1981); **C. Masson**, *L'Épitre de Saint Paul aux Colossiens*

(CNT 10; Neuchâtel: Delachaux, 1950); **C. F. D. Moule**, *The Epistles to the Colossians and to Philemon* (Cambridge: Cambridge University, 1957); **P. T. O'Brien**, *Colossians, Philemon* (WBC 44; Waco: Word, 1982); **P. Pokorný**, *Der Brief des Paulus an die Kolosser* (THKNT 10.1; Berlin: Evangelische, 1987) = *Colossians: A Commentary* (Peabody; Hendrickson, 1991); **E. Schweizer**, *Der Brief an die Kolosser* (EKK 12; Zürich: Benziger/Neukirchen-Vluyn: Neukirchener, 1976) = *The Letter to the Colossians* (London: SPCK, 1982); **P. Stuhlmacher**, *Der Brief an Philemon* (EKK; Zürich: Benziger/Neukirchen-Vluyn: Neukirchener, 1975); **M. Wolter**, *Der Brief an die Kolosser. Der Brief an Philemon* (ÖTK 12; Gütersloh: Mohn, 1993); **N. T. Wright**, *The Epistles of Paul to the Colossians and to Philemon* (TNTC; Leicester: IVP/Grand Rapids: Eerdmans, 1986).

1 and 2 Thessalonians:

E. Best, *The First and Second Epistles to the Thessalonians* (BNTC/HNTC; London: Black/New York: Harper, 1972); **F. F. Bruce**, *1 and 2 Thessalonians* (WBC 45; Waco: Word, 1982); **E. von Dobschütz**, *Die Thessalonicher-Briefe* (KEK; Göttingen: Vandenhoeck, 1909, 1974); **J. E. Frame**, *The Epistles of St. Paul to the Thessalonians* (ICC; Edinburgh: Clark, 1912); **T. Holtz**, *Der erste Brief an die Thessalonicher* (EKK 13; Zürich: Benziger/Neukirchen-Vluyn: Neukirchener, 1986); **I. H. Marshall**, *1 and 2 Thessalonians* (NCB; London: Oliphants/Grand Rapids: Eerdmans, 1983); **B. Rigaux**, *Saint Paul. Les Épitres aux Thessaloniciens* (ÉB; Paris: Gabalda, 1956); **W. Trilling**, *Der zweite Brief an die Thessalonicher* (EKK 14; Zürich: Benziger/Neukirchen-Vluyn: Neukirchener, 1980); **C. A. Wanamaker**, *The Epistles to the Thessalonians* (NIGTC; Grand Rapids: Eerdmans/Exeter: Paternoster, 1990).

Abbreviations

AB	Anchor Bible
ABD	*Anchor Bible Dictionary,* ed. D. N. Freedman (6 vols.; New York: Doubleday, 1992)
Aland[26]	*Novum Testamentum Graece,* ed. K. Aland, et al. (Stuttgart: Deutsche Bibelstiftung, [26]1979)
AnBib	Analecta Biblica
ANRW	*Aufstieg und Niedergang der Römischen Welt*
Apoc. Abr.	*Apocalypse of Abraham*
Apoc. Elij.	*Apocalypse of Elijah*
Apoc. Mos.	*Apocalypse of Moses*
Apoc. Zeph.	*Apocalypse of Zephaniah*
AV	Authorized Version = KJV
b.	Babylonian Talmud
BAGD	W. Bauer, *A Greek-English Lexicon of the New Testament and Other Early Christian Literature,* ET and ed. W. F. Arndt and F. W. Gingrich. 2nd ed. revised by F. W. Gingrich and F. W. Danker (Chicago: University of Chicago, 1979)
BAR	*Biblical Archaeology Review*
BCE	Before the Christian era
BDB	F. Brown, S. R. Driver, and C. A. Briggs, *Hebrew and English Lexicon of the Old Testament* (Oxford: Clarendon, 1907)
BDF	F. Blass, A. Debrunner, and R. W. Funk, *A Greek Grammar of the New Testament* (University of Chicago/University of Cambridge, 1961)
BETL	Bibliotheca ephemeridum theologicarum lovaniensium
Bib	*Biblica*
BibRes	*Biblical Research*

BJRL	*Bulletin of the John Rylands University Library of Manchester*
BNTC	Black's New Testament Commentary
Bousset/Gressmann	W. Bousset and H. Gressmann, *Die Religion des Judentums im späthellenistischen Zeitalter* (HNT 21; Tübingen: Mohr, 1925, ⁴1966)
BR	*Biblical Research*
BU	Biblische Untersuchungen
BWANT	Beiträge zur Wissenschaft vom Alten und Neuen Testament
BZ	*Biblische Zeitschrift*
BZNW	Beihefte zur *ZNW*
CBQ	*Catholic Biblical Quarterly*
CE	Christian era
cf.	*confer,* compare
ch(s).	chapter(s)
CIJ	*Corpus Inscriptionum Judaicarum*
CNT	Commentaire du Nouveau Testament
ConB	Coniectanea biblica
ConNT	*Coniectanea neotestamentica*
CRINT	Compendia Rerum Iudaicarum ad Novum Testamentum
Daube, *Rabbinic Judaism*	D. Daube, *The New Testament and Rabbinic Judaism* (London: Athlone, 1956)
Deissmann, *Biblical Studies*	A. Deissmann, *Bible Studies* (Edinburgh: Clark, 1901)
Deissmann, *Light*	A. Deissmann, *Light from the Ancient East* (New York: Doran, 1927)
DJD	Discoveries in the Judaean Desert
Dodd, *Bible*	C. H. Dodd, *The Bible and the Greeks* (London: Hodder and Stoughton, 1935)
DPL	*Dictionary of Paul and his Letters,* ed. G. F. Hawthorne, et al. (Leicester: Iner-Varsity/Downers Grove: InterVarsity, 1993)
DSS	Dead Sea Scrolls
ÉB	Études bibliques
ed(s).	edited by, editor(s)
EDNT	*Exegetical Dictionary of the New Testament,* ed. H. Balz and G. Schneider (3 vols.; Grand Rapids: Eerdmans, 1990-93)
e.g.	*exempli gratia,* for example

EKK	Evangelisch-katholischer Kommentar zum Neuen Testament
Ep. Arist.	*Epistle of Aristeas*
ET	English translation
et al.	*et alii,* and others
ETL	*Ephemerides theologicae lovanienses*
Eusebius	
HE	*Historia Ecclesiastica*
EvT	*Evangelische Theologie*
ExpT	*Expository Times*
FRLANT	Forschungen zur Religion und Literatur des Alten und Neuen Testaments
FS	Festschrift, volume written in honour of
García Martínez	F. García Martínez, *The Dead Sea Scrolls Translated: The Qumran Texts in English* (Leiden: Brill/Grand Rapids: Eerdmans, ²1996)
GLAJJ	M. Stern, *Greek and Latin Authors on Jews and Judaism* (3 vols.; Jerusalem: Israel Academy of Sciences and Humanities, 1976, 1980, 1984)
GNB	Good News Bible
hap. leg.	*hapax legomenon,* sole occurrence
HBT	*Horizons in Biblical Theology*
Hengel, *Judaism*	M. Hengel, *Judaism and Hellenism* (2 vols.; London: SCM/Philadelphia: Fortress, 1974)
HeyJ	*Heythrop Journal*
HKNT	Handkommentar zum Neuen Testament
HNT	Handbuch zum Neuen Testament
HNTC	Harper's New Testament Commentaries
HTKNT	Herders theologischer Kommentar zum Neuen Testament
HTR	*Harvard Theological Review*
ICC	International Critical Commentary
IDB	G. A. Buttrick, ed., *Interpreter's Dictionary of the Bible* (4 vols.; Nashville: Abingdon, 1962)
IDBS	*IDB Supplementary Volume,* ed. K. Crim (Nashville: Abingdon, 1976)
Int	*Interpretation*
JAAR	*Journal of the American Academy of Religion*
JBL	*Journal of Biblical Literature*
JJS	*Journal of Jewish Studies*
JLW	*Jahrbuch für Liturgiewissenschaft*

Josephus	
Ant.	*Jewish Antiquities*
Ap.	*Contra Apionem*
War	*The Jewish War*
JR	*Journal of Religion*
JSJ	*Journal for the Study of Judaism*
JSNT	*Journal for the Study of the New Testament*
JSNTS	*JSNT* Supplement Series
JSOT	*Journal for the Study of the Old Testament*
JSP	*Journal for the Study of the Pseudepigrapha*
JSPS	*JSP* Supplement Series
JSS	*Journal of Semitic Studies*
JTC	*Journal for Theology and the Church*
JTS	*Journal of Theological Studies*
Jub.	*Jubilees*
KEK	H. A. W. Meyer, Kritisch-exegetischer Kommentar über das Neue Testament
KJV	King James Version (1611) = AV
KuD	*Kerygma und Dogma*
Loeb	Loeb Classical Library
Long/Sedley	A. A. Long and D. N. Sedley, *The Hellenistic Philosophers* (2 vols.; Cambridge: Cambridge University, 1987)
LSJ	H. G. Liddell and R. Scott, *A Greek-English Lexicon,* rev. H. S. Jones (Oxford: Clarendon, ⁹1940) with Supplement (1968)
LXX	Septuagint
m.	Mishnah
Metzger	B. M. Metzger, *A Textual Commentary on the Greek New Testament* (London: United Bible Societies, 1975)
MM	J. H. Moulton and G. Milligan, *The Vocabulary of the Greek Testament* (London: Hodder, 1930)
MNTC	Moffatt New Testament Commentary
Moore, *Judaism*	G. F. Moore, *Judaism in the First Three Centuries of the Christian Era: The Age of the Tannaim* (3 vols.; Cambridge: Harvard University, 1927-30)
Moule, *Idiom Book*	C. F. D. Moule, *An Idiom-Book of New Testament Greek* (Cambridge: Cambridge University, 1953)
Moulton, *Grammar*	J. H. Moulton, *Grammar of New Testament Greek* (2 vols.; Edinburgh: Clark, 1906-29)
ms(s).	manuscript(s)

MT	Masoretic text (of the Old Testament)
NCB	New Century Bible (new edition)
NDIEC	G. H. R. Horsley, *New Documents Illustrating Early Christianity* (North Ryde: The Ancient History Documentary Research Centre, 1981-)
NEB	New English Bible (NT 1961; OT and Apoc. 1970)
NICNT	New International Commentary on the New Testament
NIGTC	New International Greek Testament Commentary
NIV	New International Version (1978)
NJB	New Jerusalem Bible (1985)
NovT	*Novum Testament*
NovTSup	Supplement to *NovT*
NRSV	New Revised Standard Version (1989)
NT	New Testament
NTD	Das Neue Testament Deutsch
NTS	*New Testament Studies*
NTTS	New Testament Tools and Studies
OCD	N. G. L. Hammond and H. H. Scullard, eds., *Oxford Classical Dictionary* (Oxford: Clarendon, 1970)
OT	Old Testament
ÖTKNT	Ökumensicher Taschenbuchkommentar zum Neuen Testament
OTP	*The Old Testament Pseudepigrapha,* ed. J. H. Charlesworth (2 vols.; London: Darton/Garden City: Doubleday, 1983, 1985).
pace	with due respect to, but differing from
par(s).	parallel(s)
passim	elsewhere
PG	*Patrologia graeca,* ed. J. P. Migne
Philo	
Abr.	*De Abrahamo*
Aet. Mund.	*De Aeternitate Mundi*
Cher.	*De Cherubim*
Conf.	*De Confusione Linguarum*
Cong.	*De Congressu Quaerendae Eruditionis Gratia*
Decal.	*De Decalogo*
Det.	*Quod Deterius Potiori Insidiari Soleat*
Ebr.	*De Ebrietate*
Fuga	*De Fuga et Inventione*
Gigant.	*De Gigantibus*
Heres	*Quis Rerum Divinarum Heres*

Immut.	*Quod Deus Immutabilis Sit*
Leg. All.	*Legum Allegoriae*
Legat.	*Legatio ad Gaium*
Migr.	*De Migratione Abrahami*
Mos.	*De Vita Mosis*
Mut.	*De Mutatione Nominum*
Opif.	*De Opificio Mundi*
Plant.	*De Plantatione*
Post.	*De Posteritate Caini*
Praem.	*De Praemiis et Poenis*
Prob.	*Quod Omnis Probus Liber Sit*
Qu. Exod.	*Quaestiones et Solutiones in Exodum*
Qu. Gen.	*Quaestiones et Solutiones in Genesin*
Sac.	*De Sacrificiis Abelis et Caini*
Som.	*De Somnis*
Spec. Leg.	*De Specialibus Legibus*
Virt.	*De Virtutibus*
Vit. Cont.	*De Vita Contemplativa*
Pss. Sol.	*Psalms of Solomon*
QD	Quaestiones Disputatae
RB	*Revue biblique*
REB	Revised English Bible (1989)
rev.	revised by
RGG	*Die Religion in Geschichte und Gegenwart. Handworterbuch für Theologie und Religionswissenschaft*, ed. K. Galling, et al. (3rd ed., 7 vols.; Tübingen: Mohr, 1957-65)
RNT	Regensburger Neues Testament
RSV	Revised Standard Version (NT 1946, OT 1952, Apocrypha 1957)
RTR	*Reformed Theological Review*
Sanders, *Judaism*	E. P. Sanders, *Judaism: Practice and Belief 63 BCE– 66 CE* (London: SCM/Philadelphia: TPI, 1992)
SANT	Studien zum Alten und Neuen Testament
SBL	Society of Biblical Literature
SBLDS	SBL Dissertation Series
SBLMS	SBL Monograph Series
SBLSP	*SBL Seminar Papers*
SBM	Stuttgarter biblische Monographien
SBS	Stuttgarter Bibelstudien
SBT	Studies in Biblical Theology
Schneemelcher	W. Schneemelcher, *New Testament Apocrypha*, ET

	ed. R. McL. Wilson (2 vols.; Cambridge: Clarke/Louisville: Westminster/John Knox, ²1991, 1992)
SEÅ	*Svensk exegetisk årsbok*
Sib. Or.	*Sibylline Oracles*
SJT	*Scottish Journal of Theology*
SNT	Studien zum Neuen Testament
SNTSMS	Society for New Testament Studies Monograph Series
SNTU	*Studien zum Neuen Testament und seiner Umwelt*
SPCIC	*Studiorum Paulinorum Congressus Internationalis Catholicus 1961* (AnBib 17-18; Rome: Biblical Institute, 1963)
SR	*Studies in Religion/Sciences Religieuses*
ST	*Studia Theologica*
Str-B	H. Strack and P. Billerbeck, *Kommentar zum Neuen Testament* (4 vols.; Munich: Beck, 1926-28)
SUNT	Studien zur Umwelt des Neuen Testaments
Schürer	E. Schürer, *The History of the Jewish People in the Age of Jesus Christ,* rev. and ed. G. Vermes and F. Millar (4 vols.; Edinburgh: Clark: 1973-87)
T. Abr.	*Testament of Abraham*
T. Ben.	*Testament of Benjamin*
T. Dan	*Testament of Dan*
T. Iss.	*Testament of Issachar*
T. Job	*Testament of Job*
T. Jos.	*Testament of Joseph*
T. Jud.	*Testament of Judah*
T. Levi	*Testament of Levi*
T. Naph.	*Testament of Naphthali*
T. Reub.	*Testament of Reuben*
T. Zeb.	*Testament of Zebulun*
TDNT	G. Kittel and G. Friedrich, eds., *Theological Dictionary of the New Testament* (ET 10 vols.; Grand Rapids: Eerdmans: 1964-76)
TDOT	G. J. Botterweck and H. Ringgren, eds., *Theological Dictionary of the Old Testament* (ET Grand Rapids: Eerdmans, 1974-)
THKNT	Theologischer Handkommentar zum Neuen Testament
ThQ	*Theologische Quartalschrift*
ThViat	*Theologia Viatorum*

TLZ	*Theologische Literaturzeitung*
TNTC	Tyndale New Testament Commentaries
TQ	*Theologische Quartalschrift*
TR	*Theologische Rundschau*
TRE	*Theologische Realenzyklopadie,* ed. G. Krause and G. Müller (Berlin/New York: de Gruyter, 1976-)
TS	*Theological Studies*
t.t.	technical term
TU	Texte und Untersuchungen
TynB	*Tyndale Bulletin*
TZ	*Theologische Zeitschrift*
UBS	*The Greek New Testament,* ed. K. Aland, et al. (New York: United Bible Societies, ¹1966, ³1975)
Urbach, *Sages*	E. E. Urbach, *The Sages: Their Concepts and Beliefs* (2 vols.; Jerusalem: Magnes, 1979)
USQR	*Union Seminary Quarterly Review*
VC	*Vigiliae christianae*
Vermes	G. Vermes, *The Dead Sea Scrolls in English* (London: Penguin, ⁴1995)
VF	*Verkündigung und Forschung*
v.l.	*varia lectio,* alternative reading
viz.	*videlicet,* namely
vol.	volume
v., vv.	verse, verses
WBC	Word Biblical Commentary
WMANT	Wissenschaftliche Monographien zum Alten und Neuen Testament
WTJ	*Westminster Theological Journal*
WUNT	Wissenschaftliche Untersuchungen zum Neuen Testament
ZBK	Zürcher Bibelkommentare
ZNW	*Zeitschrift für die neutestamentliche Wissenschaft*
ZTK	*Zeitschrift für Theologie und Kirche*

CHAPTER I

Prologue

§1 Prolegomena to a theology of Paul[1]

1. **Bibliography: P. J. Achtemeier**, "The Continuing Quest for Coherence in St. Paul: An Experiment in Thought," in Lovering and Sumney, eds., *Theology and Ethics* (§23 n. 1) 132-45; **A. K. M. Adam**, *Making Sense of New Testament Theology: 'Modern' Problems and Prospects* (Macon: Mercer University, 1995); **Berger**, *Theologiegeschichte* 440-47; **H. Boers**, *What Is New Testament Theology?* (Philadelphia: Fortress, 1979); **H. Braun**, "The Problem of a New Testament Theology," *JTC* 1 (1965) 169-85; **R. E. Brown**, *Biblical Exegesis and Church Doctrine* (London: Chapman, 1982 = New York: Paulist, 1985); *The Critical Meaning of the Bible* (London: Chapman, 1986 = New York: Paulist, 1981); **R. Bultmann**, *Theology* 2.237-51; "Is Exegesis without Presuppositions Possible?" *Existence and Faith* (London: Collins Fontana, 1964; New York: Meridian, 1960) 342-51; **B. S. Childs**, *The New Testament as Canon: An Introduction* (Philadelphia: Fortress, 1985); **C. Dohmen and T. Söding**, eds., *Eine Bibel — zwei Testamente. Positionen Biblischer Theologie* (Paderborn: Schöningh, 1995); **J. R. Donahue**, "The Changing Shape of New Testament Theology," *TS* 50 (1989) 314-35; **J. D. G. Dunn**, *The Living Word* (London: SCM/Philadelphia: Fortress, 1987); "Prolegomena to a Theology of Paul," *NTS* 40 (1994) 407-32; "In Quest of Paul's Theology: Retrospect and Prospect," in D. M. Hay and E. E. Johnson, eds., *Pauline Theology* 4 (Atlanta: Scholars, 1997) 95-115; **J. D. G. Dunn and J. Mackey**, *New Testament Theology in Dialogue* (London: SPCK/ Philadelphia: Westminster, 1987); **V. P. Furnish**, "On Putting Paul in His Place," *JBL* 113 (1994) 3-17; **F. Hahn**, *Historical Investigation and New Testament Faith* (Philadelphia: Fortress, 1984); **G. F. Hasel**, *New Testament Theology: Basic Issues in the Debate* (Grand Rapids: Eerdmans, 1978); **J. L. Houlden**, *Patterns of Faith: A Study in the Relationship between the New Testament and Christian Doctrine* (London: SCM/Philadelphia: Fortress, 1977); **H. Hübner**, "Pauli Theologiae Proprium," *NTS* 26 (1979-80) 445-73; *Biblische Theologie des Neuen Testaments* I: *Prolegomena* (Göttingen: Vandenhoeck, 1990); **R. Jewett**, "Major Impulses in the Theological Interpretation of Romans since Barth," *Int* 34 (1980) 17-31; **E. Käsemann**, "The Problem of a New Testament Theology," *NTS* 19 (1972-73) 235-45; **L. E. Keck**, "Toward the Renewal of New Testament Christology," *NTS* 32 (1986) 362-77; **K. Kertelge**, "Biblische Theologie im Römerbrief," in S. Pedersen, ed., *New Directions in Biblical Theology* (NovTSup 76; Leiden: Brill, 1994) 47-57; **E. Lohse**, "Changes of

1

§1.1 Why a theology of Paul?

Paul was the first and greatest Christian theologian. From the perspective of subsequent generations, Paul is undoubtedly the *first* Christian theologian. Of course, all who think about and express their faith as Christians can quite properly be called "Christian theologians," or at least be described as functioning theologically. But Paul belongs to that group of Christians who have seen it as part of their calling to articulate their faith in writing and to instruct others in their common faith, and who have devoted a considerable portion of their lives to so doing. And, so far as we today are concerned, Paul was effectively the first Christian to commit himself to this calling. Others functioned theologically from the beginning. There were a good many apostles, prophets, teachers, and pastors in the earliest Christian churches. But from the first Christian generation we have only one firsthand testimony, the theologizing of only one man — Paul the apostle, who had been Saul the Pharisee. Only with the letters of Paul can we be fully confident that we are in touch with the first generation of Christianity and of Christian theologizing as such.[2]

Moreover, Paul was "first" in the other sense of being preeminent among Christian theologians. He belonged to that generation which was more creative and more definitive for Christianity's formation and theology than any other since. And within that generation it was he more than any other single person who ensured that the new movement stemming from Jesus would

---

Thought in Pauline Theology? Some Reflections on Paul's Ethical Teaching in the Context of his Theology," in Lovering and Sumney, eds., *Theology and Ethics* (§23 n. 1) 146-60; **O. Merk**, *Biblische Theologie des Neuen Testaments in ihrer Anfangszeit* (Marburg: Elwert, 1972); **R. Morgan**, *The Nature of New Testament Theology* (London: SCM/Naperville: Allenson, 1973); "New Testament Theology," in S. J. Kraftchick, et al., eds., *Biblical Theology: Problems and Perspectives,* J. C. Beker FS (Nashville: Abingdon, 1995) 104-30; **J. Plevnik**, "The Center of Pauline Theology," *CBQ* 51 (1989) 461-78; **H. Räisänen**, *Beyond New Testament Theology* (London: SCM, 1990); **T. Söding**, "Inmitten der Theologie des Neuen Testaments. Zu den Voraussetzungen und Zielen neutestamentlicher Exegese," *NTS* 42 (1996) 161-84; **G. Strecker**, ed., *Das Problem der Theologie des Neuen Testaments* (Darmstadt: Wissenschaftliche Buchgesellschaft, 1975); **P. Stuhlmacher**, *How to Do Biblical Theology* (Allison Park: Pickwick, 1995); **A. J. M. Wedderburn**, "Paul and 'Biblical Theology,' " in S. Pedersen, ed., *New Directions in Biblical Theology* (NovTSup 76; Leiden: Brill, 1994) 24-46; **N. T. Wright**, *The New Testament and the People of God* (London: SPCK/Minneapolis: Fortress, 1992).

2. This, of course, is not to dispute that the memories of Jesus' teaching and ministry were already subject to considerable theological reflection during the first generation of Christianity. But who was doing the theologizing, who were the theologians, is not at all clear. And if other NT writings are as early as Paul's letters (possibly James), they have hardly been as significant as Paul's letters.

become a truly international and intellectually coherent religion. Paul has indeed been called the "second founder of Christianity," who has, "compared with the first, exercised beyond all doubt the stronger . . . influence."[3] Even if that should be regarded as an overblown assessment of Paul's significance, the fact remains that Paul's influence and writings have shaped Christianity as the writings/theology of no other single individual have. The Synoptic Gospels certainly take us back closer to the teaching of Jesus. John's Gospel has had an immeasurable influence on subsequent perception of Jesus Christ in particular and on Christian spirituality in general. Without Acts we would have little clear idea how Christianity first spread. But if theology is measured in terms of articulation of Christian belief, then Paul's letters laid a foundation for Christian theology which has never been rivaled or superseded.

Hence also the claim that he is the *greatest* Christian theologian of all time. In effect, this is simply to restate the traditional Christian affirmation of the canonical status of Paul's letters. For that status was in itself simply the recognition of the authority which these letters had been accorded more or less since they were first received. They were evidently valued by the churches to which they were addressed, cherished as of continuing value for instruction in Christian faith, worship, and daily living, and circulated to other churches in an ever widening circle of authority until their canonical status (as providing an official rule of faith and life) was acknowledged in the second century.[4] So Paul's status within the New Testament canon in itself gives Paul's theological writings a preeminence which overshadows all the Christian theologians who followed.

This is not to say that Paul's authority as a theologian has been merely formal. For what has been most noticeable down through the centuries is not so much respect for Paul the canonized church founder,[5] as the impact of Paul's theology itself. Nor is it to claim that Paul's theology has been as influential, particularly in the early church, as it deserved to be. But even in the patristic period his influence on Clement, Ignatius, and Irenaeus is clear enough. And in late antiquity, Augustine restated Christian theology as, it could be said, a form of Pauline theology which came to dominate most of the Middle Ages. In turn, few will need reminding that it was preeminently the influence of Paul's theology which shaped the Reformation. And in the modern period the diverse testimonies of F. C. Baur and Karl Barth attest the

---

3. Wrede, *Paul* 180; see further Meeks, *Writings* Part V.

4. We need not go into more detail on these processes. On the early influence of Paul see particularly E. Dassmann, *Der Stachel im Fleisch. Paulus in der frühchristlichen Literatur bis Irenäus* (Münster: Aschendorff, 1979), and A. Lindemann, *Paulus im ältesten Christentum. Das Bild des Apostels und die Rezeption der paulinischen Theologie in der frühchristlichen Literatur bis Marcion* (Tübingen: Mohr, 1979).

5. In formal terms Peter has been much the more influential.

same continuing formative influence of the first great apostle-theologian. Perhaps we should add that it is not a question of whether Paul himself was a *better* theologian than any of these, or than others from East and West, past and present, who might be named. It is rather that Paul's theology inevitably provides an indispensable foundation and serves as a still flowing fountainhead for the continuing stream of Christian theologizing. So that even those who have wanted to critique Paul's theology or to build their own theologies on a different basis have found it necessary to interact with Paul and where possible to draw support from his writings.

It is important, therefore, for each generation of Christian theology to reflect afresh on Paul's theology. And over the generations there has been no dearth of such attempts.[6] But in the past fifty years, since Bultmann's epochal exposition of NT theology,[7] there have been only a handful of full-scale attempts to restate or to wrestle with Paul's theology at sustained depth. There have been several briefer treatments as part of a New Testament theology,[8] or at a more popular level.[9] Various individual studies have been collected into partial theologies.[10] There have been several combination treatments of Paul's life and theology.[11] With these may be associated developmental schemas, which trace the development of Paul's theology through or from his conversion and over the course of his mission and letter writing — an important alternative model for grappling with Paul's theology.[12] But in comparison

6. As the General Bibliography and subsequent section bibliographies amply attest.

7. Bultmann, *Theology.*

8. E.g., Conzelmann, *Outline;* Kümmel, *Theology;* Goppelt, *Theology;* and Gnilka, *Theologie.* Even the recent nicely compact treatments of Stuhlmacher, *Biblische Theologie,* and Strecker, *Theologie,* are overly compressed or cut corners at various points. And Schlier's evocative study *(Grundzüge)* rather tails off.

9. Particularly popular have been Keck, *Paul,* and Ziesler, *Pauline Christianity* — as earlier Dodd, *Meaning.* Barrett's *Paul* may fill a similar role for the next generation. Somewhat more substantial is Witherington, *Paul's Narrative Thought World.*

10. Particularly influential have been Käsemann's essays *(Perspectives; Essays; New Testament Questions).* See also especially Kertelge, *Grundthemen;* Hofius, *Paulus-studien;* Penna, *Paul the Apostle.*

11. A sudden flood in 1996, with Gnilka, *Paulus* (the theological section drawing heavily on his *Theologie*); Lohse, *Paulus;* Murphy-O'Connor, *Paul.* The earlier treatment by Bornkamm, *Paul,* remains popular.

12. E.g., Sabatier, *Paul;* Buck and Taylor, *Saint Paul;* Bruce, *Apostle;* and Becker, *Paul.* Note also the attempt made by Pauline Theology group of the SBL to discuss the theologies of Paul's letters in sequence (the *Pauline Theology* volumes edited by Bassler, Hay, and Hay and Johnson). The other alternative, a thematic study of NT theology as a whole, as by Richardson, *Introduction;* Guthrie, *New Testament Theology;* and Caird, *New Testament Theology,* makes it difficult to gain a sustained grasp of the coherence of Paul's theology or of its distinctive features. For example, it is not possible to gain a clear impression of the role of the law in Paul's theology from Caird's *Theology.*

with the larger scale treatments of earlier generations,[13] there have been remarkably few thoroughgoing attempts to restate Paul's theology as a coherent, self-consistent, and self-sustaining whole. The important treatments of W. D. Davies, Johannes Munck, Christiaan Beker, and Hans Hübner have pursued particular theses — Davies setting Paul as fully as possible within the context of Rabbinic Judaism,[14] Munck giving a sustained critique of the continuing influence of Baur's reconstruction of earliest Christianity, Beker developing his coherence and contingency thesis, and Hübner expounding the task of his *Biblische Theologie* as a working up *(Aufarbeitung)* of the theological conversation *(Umgang)* of the NT authors with the OT.[15] Of recent studies, probably only Herman Ridderbos's *Paul* fully rivals the older treatments in scope, though the remarkably durable English language study by D. E. H. Whiteley should not go unmentioned.[16]

A fresh attempt at a full restatement of Paul's theology is made all the more necessary in the light of what is now usually referred to as "the new perspective on Paul."[17] The lack of substantial systematic treatments of Paul's theology in the past generation or two is probably best explained by the fact that restatements of Paul's theology had become so predictable. With little fresh to be said, there was little call for another book which simply repeated the same old material or shuffled the same old pieces around in search of new patterns. Into this quiet cul-de-sac of NT study and Christian theology, however, Ed Sanders's *Paul and Palestinian Judaism* entered and brought a rude awakening. What he drew attention to was not so new in itself — the character of Palestinian Judaism as a religious system postulated on the initiative of divine grace. But he did it with such effect that nobody who entertained serious aspirations to understand Christian beginnings generally or Pauline theology in particular could any more ignore the sharp contrast he drew between his restatement of Palestinian Judaism and the traditional reconstructions of Judaism within Christian theology. Nothing less became necessary than a complete reassessment of Paul's relationship with his ancestral religion, not to mention all the considerable consequences which were bound to follow for our contemporary understanding of his theology.

That reassessment is still in process of unfolding. It has reinvigorated the study of Paul's theology in a way which seemed impossible only twenty-five

---

13. One thinks of Baur, *Paul;* Pfleiderer, *Paulinism;* B. Weiss, *Biblical Theology;* Feine, *Theologie;* Prat, *Theology,* or the three volumes by Cerfaux (§10 n. 1, §14 n. 1, §20 n. 1).

14. In reaction to the then dominant interest in setting Paul within the context of Hellenistic religion and culture.

15. Hübner, *Biblische Theologie* 1.28.

16. Whiteley, *Theology.*

17. See further below §14.1.

years ago and has set off several fresh rounds of controversy. A particularly pleasing aspect of the new phase has been the fresh and creative dialogue which has now opened up with Jewish students of the Jewish Paul.[18] The foundational and pivotal role of Paul in Christian theology as a whole makes such a reassessment all the more important — and all the more sensitive and controversial for long-established restatements of Paul's gospel based on the older paradigm. What follows is intended as a positive and eirenic contribution to that reassessment.

§1.2 What is a "theology of Paul"?

Unpacking the very term "theology" is itself a challenge. Many definitions have been offered, and several layers of refinement are possible.[19] But the more complex or refined the definition, the less support it is likely to command. At first sight it might seem adequate to at least begin with a simple working definition. Thus, for example, "theology" as talk *(logos)* about God *(theos),* and all that is involved in and follows directly from such talk, particularly the coherent articulation of the religious faith and practise thereby expressed. But problems quickly arise when we ask how one can or should "talk about God," or when the word "theology" is linked with other words or differentiated in its scope.

In particular, there are several issues which come immediately to the surface as soon as the word "theology" is qualified by the terms "New Testament" or "biblical." They emerge not least because of the problematic of these qualifying terms: in what sense can or should one speak of a *"New Testament* theology" or of a *"biblical* theology"? Our focus on Paul means that we will escape some of these problems and may even point the way to possible solutions for them. There are other problems, however, which, in contrast, arise immediately from the character of Paul's own ministry and self-perception. Was he first and foremost a theologian or a missionary, church founder, and pastor? Is a focus on the *theology* of Paul inevitably too restrictive? Or again, there are problems which relate to the character of Paul's communication — as letters and not theological treatises. Does a focus on Paul's theology not skew our perception of the communication he sought to achieve and of the continuing communicative potential of these letters?

---

18. Particularly Segal, *Paul the Convert;* Boyarin, *A Radical Jew;* and Nanos, *Mystery.* Montefiore, *Judaism,* Schoeps, *Paul,* and Sandmel, *Genius,* represent earlier phases of the dialogue. In contrast, H. Maccoby's *The Mythmaker: Paul and the Invention of Christianity* (London: Weidenfeld and Nicholson/New York: Harper and Row, 1986) is a regrettable reversion to older polemics.

19. See, e.g., the review of some recent definitions in my "In Quest of Paul's Theology."

A brief review of the way in which such problems have arisen and been addressed over the past two centuries and of the various critiques to which the concept of a biblical theology has been subjected should be sufficient to highlight the main issues.

a) *Description or dialogue?* Few if any who are familiar with NT theology will need to be reminded that its character as a distinctive and distinguishable discipline only stretches back a little over two hundred years — to J. P. Gabler's initial attempt to distinguish biblical theology from dogmatic theology in 1787.[20] The distinction he pressed for then, between biblical theology with its essentially *historical* character and dogmatic theology with its *didactic* character, set up or brought to focus a tension which was unavoidable for any post-Enlightenment textual study. It is a tension which underlies every attempt to speak of the theology of the NT or the theology of any NT writing, a tension which surfaces repeatedly whenever the viability and methodology of NT theology are discussed. One need only invoke the names of William Wrede, Krister Stendahl, and now also Heikki Räisänen on the one side, as representative of those who insist that NT theology (if that is even a proper title) can never be more than descriptive — a form of Religious Studies phenomenology, we might say, rather than theology properly so called.[21] On the other side we could just as easily range Adolf Schlatter and Alan Richardson, who would not accept that biblical theology's historical character cut it off from dogmatic theology,[22] Karl Barth and Rudolf Bultmann with their insistence that the word of God, the kerygma, still sounds through the words of Paul,[23] or now the restatements of biblical theology by Hans Hübner and Peter Stuhlmacher with the expressly Christian standpoint implicit in the very title.[24]

---

20. *On the Proper Distinction between Biblical and Dogmatic Theology and the Specific Objectives of Each;* ET by J. Sandys-Wunsch and L. Eldredge in *SJT* 33 (1980) 134-44 (commentary and summary 144-58); the key extract may also be consulted in W. G. Kümmel, *The New Testament: The History of the Investigation of Its Problems* (London: SCM/Nashville: Abingdon, 1973) 98-100.

21. W. Wrede, "The Task and Methods of 'New Testament Theology,' " in Morgan, *Nature of New Testament Theology* 68-116; K. Stendahl, "Biblical Theology," *IDB* 1.418-32; Räisänen, *Beyond New Testament Theology.*

22. A. Schlatter, "The Theology of the New Testament and Dogmatics," in Morgan, *Nature of New Testament Theology* 117-66; Richardson, *Introduction.* The latter is subjected to trenchant critique by L. E. Keck, "Problems of New Testament Theology," *NovT* 7 (1964) 217-41.

23. Barth, *Romans,* Preface to the second edition (2-15); R. Bultmann, "The New Testament and Mythology," in H.-W. Bartsch, ed., *Kerygma and Myth* I (London: SPCK/New York: Harper and Row, 1953) 1-44; also his *Theology* 2.251.

24. Hübner, *Biblische Theologie;* Stuhlmacher, *Biblische Theologie.* On some of the problems in the conception of "biblical theology" see my "Das Problem 'Biblische Theologie,' " in Dohmen and Söding, *Eine Bibel* 179-93.

Of course the debate has moved far beyond Gabler's straightforward distinction. We know now that a purely objective description of anything, least of all someone else's thought, is simply not possible. We are all conscious of the "two horizons" in reading texts and of the hermeneutical task of fusing them together *(Horizont-verschmelzung)*.[25] But with Paul the challenge is slightly different — easier in one way, more difficult in another. For by their very nature, Paul's letters are highly personal communications, not dispassionate treatises. And in them he is dealing again and again with matters of fundamental significance, which he clearly thought of as issues of life and death for his readers. In one degree or other his letters are all defence and exposition of "the truth of the gospel" (Gal. 2.5, 14). It is impossible to take Paul seriously, therefore, even as a descriptive exercise, without recognizing this inner intensity and claim for the existential significance of his message. It is impossible to enter into his thought world even briefly, let alone to engage in interpretation of what he says, without making at least some theological assessment of the arguments he offers and the opinions he expresses. The hermeneutical model, in other words, needs to be more that of the dialogue with a living respondent than the clinical analysis of a dead corpse.[26] A theology of Paul cannot be content unless it encounters the "real presence" within the text.[27]

In the case of Paul in particular, therefore, I would wish to restate the tension of a theological hermeneutic as a tension between *critical disinterestedness* and *personal involvement* with the subject matter; that is, between a disinterestedness which finds all outcomes of the analysis of Paul's thought equally acceptable in principle, none of which need make any difference to one's own theology or commitments; and a personal involvement which, while still seeking as much historical objectivity as possible, recognizes that the findings may have personal consequences, requiring some adaptation or shift, however small, in one's own overall ideological standpoint and lifestyle.[28] On this understanding, the test of a good theology of Paul will be the degree to which it enables the reader and the church not only to enter into the thought world of Paul but also to engage theologically with the claims he makes and

25. The term is Gadamer's; see particularly A. C. Thiselton, *The Two Horizons* (Exeter: Paternoster/Grand Rapids: Eerdmans, 1980) 15-16.

26. I have attempted a brief elaboration of what I mean by this model of hermeneutical dialogue in Dunn and Mackey, *New Testament Theology in Dialogue* ch. 1. See further below §1.5.

27. The allusion is to G. Steiner, *Real Presences* (London: Faber and Faber/Chicago: University of Chicago, 1989).

28. Such personal involvement will normally include participation in (or reaction against!) a particular faith (Christian) tradition and worshiping community, and the preunderstanding which such participation (or reaction) involves.

the issues he addresses, driven thereby afresh to the text itself, informed by what is to be read there, and stimulated to join in the resulting debate about what Paul has said and with Paul, on issues of ongoing theological concern.[29]

b) *Theology or religion?* A second important and relevant development in the history of NT study has been the *religionsgeschichtlich* recognition that a focus on theology understood as doctrine is far too narrow an understanding of the hermeneutical enterprise known as "NT theology."[30] This again is particularly true, it need hardly be said, in the case of Paul. The typical structure of his letters, with their combination of theological argument and paraenesis, is almost sufficient in itself to make the point for us. To attempt an engagement with Paul's theology which focused exclusively, for example, on Romans 1–11 and ignored 12–16, or on Galatians 1–4 and ignored 5–6, would be self-condemned as lopsided and incomplete. The outworking of what he believed in daily life and in the gatherings of his churches was fundamental to Paul's understanding of the gospel.

The point has assumed a fresh importance in the recent reassessment of Paul's relationship with his own Jewish heritage and past. For it remains a continuing question as to whether "theology" is the best label to describe Jewish faith and life; the centre of gravity in traditional Judaism seems to be so much more on praxis, on *Torah,* instruction or direction, on *Halakhah,* how to walk, than on belief. Consequently a focus on what Paul believed, his *faith,* has probably prejudiced the analysis of how Paul's theology related to his Jewish heritage by starting from an implicit dichotomy between Paul and his parent religion.

Consequently, it may be that some will prefer to speak of our larger enterprise as a study of the *religion* of Paul. I prefer, however, to understand the term "theology" in a more rounded way, as talk about God and all that is involved in and follows directly from such talk, including not least the interaction between belief and praxis. The old liberal Protestant restatement of the classic Christian conviction, that ethics and relationships are the test bed on which dogmas are either destroyed or proven, needs to be dusted off and examined afresh, within theology and not simply as a critique of it. A theology remote from everyday living would not be a theology of Paul.

As the History of Religions practitioners recognized, such a broader focus inevitably brings the theology of Paul into closer relationship with the

---

29. For the wider issues here, more appropriately discussed under the heading of "New Testament Theology," see, e.g., R. Morgan, "Theology (NT)," *ABD* 6.473-83, particularly 480-83; and W. G. Jeanrond, "After Hermeneutics: The Relationship between Theology and Biblical Studies," in F. Watson, ed., *The Open Text: New Directions for Biblical Studies* (London: SCM, 1993) 85-102, particularly 92-98.

30. The classic statement was by Wrede, "Task and Methods" (above n. 21).

other religious and, as we would say now, social forces of the day. Paul's theology, properly speaking, was itself one of the religious factors and social features of the first-century eastern Mediterranean world, with all the potential for interaction and mutual influence hinted at particularly in the Corinthian correspondence. As a succession of insightful studies has brought home to us,[31] it is no longer realistic to write a theology of Paul which ignores these factors, which assumes, for example, that the problems addressed in 1 Corinthians were purely "theological" (that is, doctrinal) in character. The influence of patrons, networks of power, social standing, the character of slavery, food as a system of communication, ritual as defining group boundaries, and so on, must be taken into account in any theological analysis of Paul's arguments and exhortations.[32] Such recognition should not be seen as compromising the theological enterprise. On the contrary, it is such recognition of its rootedness in and relatedness to the all too real social relationships of the time which helps to bring out the living character of Paul's theology.

c) *Theology or rhetoric?* A third phase in contemporary biblical studies with possible implications for a theology of Paul in particular are the developments in literary criticism. The impact here, however, is less obvious. With so many of the other NT documents we are forced to deal in effect only with the *implied* author, since the real author is unknown to us (beyond perhaps a name and a detail or two). In such circumstances, speculation as to author and occasion of composition is always likely to create more heat than light and to be less fruitful for a theological appreciation of the document than a careful study of the text itself; the greater the speculation the less weight can be put on any theological corollaries drawn from it. Moreover, since the Gospels are *sui generis* in the ancient world we need to depend on the Gospels themselves for an appreciation of their message. We cannot draw immediate illumination from close genre parallels in the ancient world, so that for the task of interpretation we are locked in much more tightly to the world of the Gospel itself. In the case of Acts, on the other hand, we have to take account of narrative theory, of the ancient skills involved in a story well told, able to be retold effectively in a whole variety of circumstances and occasions, each retelling depending for its effectiveness on the drama of the story line, on the vividness of characterization, on the quality of the speeches, and so on — so that to that extent again Acts is a document self-contained, self-sustained.

---

31. I am thinking particularly of Theissen, *Social Setting;* Holmberg, *Paul and Power* (§21 n. 1); Meeks, *First Urban Christians;* N. R. Petersen, *Rediscovering Paul* (§21 n. 57); and Neyrey, *Paul.*

32. See the recent reviews by S. R. Garrett, "Sociology (Early Christianity)," *ABD* 6.89-99; S. C. Barton, "Social-Scientific Approaches to Paul," *DPL* 892-900; and the critique by Horrell, *Social Ethos* ch. 1.

With Paul's letters, however, it is impossible to escape their character as *letters,* communications from a *known* author to *specific* people in *particular* circumstances. They have an intensely personal character which makes it, if not impossible, at least unwise to abstract what is said from the person and personality of the author.[33] One of the principal fascinations of these letters, indeed, is their self-revelatory character — Paul as a persuader of great forcefulness and (judging by the fact that his letters have been preserved) great effectiveness, Paul as an irascible protagonist, and above all (in his own eyes at least), Paul as apostle commissioned by God through Christ, whose missionary work itself was an embodiment and expression of his gospel.[34] Likewise, Paul's arguments and exhortations focus so frequently on the situations of his audiences and the views of those who disagreed with him that it becomes impossible to understand these arguments and exhortations fully without some awareness of these situations and of the views opposed by Paul[35] — a point to which we must return. In short, the theological force of Paul's letters is again and again inextricably related to their character as dialogue with their recipients, indeed, as one side of a sequence of specific dialogues whose terms in large part at least have been determined by the situations addressed.

A theology of Paul is therefore tied to historical analysis and contextualization to a degree neither possible nor necessary to achieve in the case of most other earliest Christian writings. Where a Pauline argument was dictated with another group in view, on a particular issue posed in particular terms, the argument angled to achieve a particular effect, we simply cannot hope to do that argument justice in our appreciation of it unless we have grasped enough of these particularities to follow the line of argument and to pick up the nuances intended by Paul. In this case the "world" of the text and the "social world" of Pauline Christianity substantially overlap in the historical context within which and for which the letter was written.

At this point literary and rhetorical analyses have been helpful in highlighting some of the letters' particularities as literary products of the first

---

33. This became particularly clear to me in recent work on Galatians; see my *Theology of Galatians* 1-6.

34. See further below §21 n. 35.

35. See, e.g., J. P. Sampley, "From Text to Thought World," in Bassler, *Pauline Theology* 7: "Because Paul focuses so frequently on the position of his opponents our capacity to understand Paul is directly proportionate to our ability to understand Paul's opponents." The point can, however, be overstated; for example, my colleague Walter Moberly observes that the theological force of Paul's theology of the cross, in 2 Corinthians in particular, is much more dependent on the internal coherence of Paul's exposition in 2 Corinthians than on a detailed knowledge of who Paul's opponents were.

century. Not least, they have alerted us to the distinctive features of the openings and closings of Paul's letters as compared with epistolary practice of the time and have made us more aware of the rhetorical techniques by means of which Paul sought to persuade his readers.[36] On this point, too, students of Paul's theology need constantly to remind themselves of and make allowances for the fact that his letters were not dispassionate theological treatises any more than the Gospels were dispassionate portrayals of Jesus. At the same time they need to remember that persuasive rhetoric is vulnerable to a counter-rhetoric of denial or a hostile hermeneutic of suspicion. If genuine engagement with Paul's theology takes on a dialogical character, it should also be noted that the most fruitful dialogues depend on a degree of sympathy of the one dialogue partner for the concerns of the other.

Rhetorical anaysis can also beget its own scholasticism. In particular it seems to me fairly pointless to argue about whether Paul's letters are "epideictic" or "deliberative" or something else, when most are agreed that Paul's creative genius has adapted to his own ends whatever model he may have borrowed and has done so to such an extent that the parallels are as likely to be misleading as helpful.[37] And as for some of the elaborate structures which have been proposed for Paul's letters, one might simply observe that there seems to be an inverse ratio between the length of proposed chiasms in an individual letter and the light they shed on either the argument or its point. The vigour of Paul's theology evidently did not allow it to be easily contained within regular grammatical and compositional structures!

In short, the various phases of discussion regarding the character and task of a "New Testament theology" over the last two hundred years have helped clarify the task of writing a theology of Paul: a dialogue with Paul and not merely a description of what he believed; a recognition that Paul's theology embraced Christian living as well as Christian thinking; and a willingness to hear Paul's theology as a sequence of occasional conversations. But this last observation simply raises a further question.

---

36. H. D. Betz led the way, particularly his *Galatians*. On the diatribe, note particularly S. K. Stowers, *The Diatribe and Paul's Letter to the Romans* (SBLDS 57; Chico: Scholars, 1981). See also the essays by H. D. Betz, "The Problem of Rhetoric and Theology according to the Apostle Paul," and by W. Wuellner, "Paul as Pastor: The Function of Rhetorical Questions in First Corinthians," in Vanhoye, ed., *L'Apôtre Paul* 16-48, 49-77 and particularly R. D. Anderson's fuller critique of contemporary use of ancient rhetorical theories in *Ancient Rhetorical Theory and Paul* (Kampen: Kok Pharos, 1996).

37. See, e.g., the critique of Betz, *Galatians,* by Longenecker, *Galatians* cxi-cxiii.

§1.3 Can a theology of Paul be written?

Given our distance from Paul in time and culture, this is by no means an idle question. In fact, however, we seem to be in a better position to write a theology of Paul than the theology of anyone else for the first hundred years of Christianity. In contrast, though a theology of Jesus would be more fascinating, we have nothing firsthand from Jesus which can provide such a secure starting point. The theologies of the Evangelists are almost equally problematic, since their focus on the ministry and teaching of Jesus makes their own theologies that much more allusive. Moreover, in two at least of the four cases we have only one document to use; we can speak with some confidence of the theology of that document, but the theology of its anonymous author remains tantalizingly intangible. So too with the other NT letters. Either we have only one letter from a particular pen, or the author is unknown, or the letter is too short for us to get much of a handle on its theology, or all three. A theology of 1 Peter is never going to have the depth and breadth of a theology of Paul. Within the first century of Christianity the closest parallel is Ignatius, where, arguably, there are as many genuine letters. But even so we are talking about seven letters written over a very short period, all but one to a relatively small area, in similar circumstances and on a limited range of themes.[38]

In the case of Paul, however, we have a variety of letters, seven at least, whose authorship by Paul is virtually unquestioned — plus what we might call an afterwave or tail of the comet or, better, the school or studio of Paul, which is still able to tell us something about what went before.[39] They were written to a variety of churches in the northeast quadrant of the Mediterranean — from Galatia in the east to Rome in the west — relating to at least three different regions and so also to a variety of local situations. And they were written over a longer period of probably six to eight years, possibly longer. That is to say, we have the possibility of building up a stereoscopic picture of Paul's theology, a picture in depth. Or, to vary the metaphor, we have the possibility of gaining a degree of "fix" in plotting Paul's position

---

38. See W. R. Schoedel, *Ignatius of Antioch* (Hermeneia; Philadelphia: Fortress, 1985).

39. I refer of course to Romans, 1 Corinthians, 2 Corinthians (two or more letters?), Galatians, Philippians, 1 Thessalonians, and Philemon. There is a roughly even split among critical commentators on Colossians and 2 Thessalonians (I regard the latter as written by Paul and the former as probably written by Timothy before Paul's death; see below §11 n. 7 and §12 n. 23), while the majority regard Ephesians and the Pastorals as definitely post-Pauline (I side with the majority). But the last named should not be wholly disregarded when the attempt is made to describe the theology of the apostle whose name they bear. Here weight can be properly given to Childs's plea for a canonical reading of the individual texts *(New Testament as Canon)*.

on some subjects by means of a sort of triangulation — something not possible for other Christian writers of the first three generations of Christianity.

This makes the task of writing a theology of Paul all the more challenging and crucial as a test case. For if we cannot write a theology of Paul, when so much seems to be in favour of the enterprise, then the hope of writing a theology of the New Testament, or a theology of the first generations of Christianity, is likely to prove even further beyond our powers. If the task proves beyond our competence in the case of Paul, for any one of a number of reasons which we will consider, then talk of a or the theology of the NT will become virtually meaningless.

All these observations, however, simply clear the ground for the more challenging issue. The problem of writing a theology of Paul can be restated thus: when we talk of "Paul's theology" are we talking about the theology of any particular letter as such, or the theology of all the individual letters aggregated into a whole? More pressingly, by the "theology of Paul" do we mean the theology of the Paul who stands behind the letters, or Paul the actual letter-writer as such? — bearing in mind in both cases that not every letter which he wrote has been preserved. It is a wholly justified assumption that Paul himself had a much richer theology than he ever actually put on paper. By "Paul's theology" do we therefore mean that larger, fuller, richer theology, which we can assume lay behind the letters and from which he drew the particular elements and emphases of each letter? By the "theology of Paul" do we mean the cistern or stream of what we might call Paul's theological consciousness, or do we mean the particular buckets of theology which he drew from that cistern or stream?[40]

The answer to which I have found myself forced is that a theology of Paul cannot be more than the sum of the theology of each of the individual letters, and yet has to be more than simply the sum of the letters' theologies. Such a riddle requires some explanation.

The theology of Paul cannot be more than the sum of the theology of each of the individual letters for the obvious reason that these letters are the only firm evidence we have of Paul's theology.[41] Consequently we are bound to them and bound by them, and if we try to dispense with them in any degree we simply lose touch with our primary and only real sources.

40. Cf. particularly Keck, *Paul* ch. 2; Hultgren, *Paul's Gospel* ch. 1. This was the problem which dominated the early years of the SBL Pauline Theology group (see Bassler, ed., *Pauline Theology;* Hay, ed., *Pauline Theology*). A similar problem was raised by one or two of those invited to contribute to the Cambridge University Press series on the theology of the individual writings of the NT (The Theology of the New Testament), for which I have served as Editor. How could a theology of one letter fail to draw in Paul's other letters? How could a theology of Galatians, say, fail to become a theology of Paul?

41. The evidence of Acts can never be more than secondary and supportive.

At the same time, however, a theology of Paul has to be more. Why? Because the letters themselves indicate the need to go behind the letters themselves, and they do so in such a way that we will never be able to explicate them as fully as we can without taking that fuller theology into account. The letters are somewhat like the sections of an iceberg above water: we can deduce from what is visible a good deal of what is invisible. Alternatively, Paul's letters are like the embossed marks on paper made by an irregular shape behind the paper; these marks are sufficiently clear to enable us to gain a coherent picture of the underlying irregular shape.

I have in mind here the great number of allusions and echoes which are the inevitable feature of any lively dialogue or correspondence and which are clearly evident in Paul's letters, forming a vital link between the text and its historical context. In the following chapters I will be referring to such allusions and reflecting on the character of allusion at several points.[42] Here all that is necessary is to indicate the range and importance of such allusions.

In the first place we have to recognize the allusively referential character of Paul's language itself. Paul wrote in an ancient language. That language only makes sense as koine Greek, understood in the light of the usage of koine Greek in the first century of the common era. The marks on the pages of Greek NTs can only be read as communication by those who attend to all the long-established skills of NT grammarians in reference to accidence and word-formation, syntax and style. This most basic of facts should be sufficient in itself to remind exegetes that the texts composed by Paul are inextricably rooted in the speech context of their time, linked by myriad roots and shoots to the meanings and metaphors which such language commonly conjured up in the minds of the recipients of Paul's letters. The point is too obvious to require any elaboration. But since too casual talk of the autonomy of a text sometimes seems to forget this basic character of a historical text — as though a historical text translated into English could properly be described as "autonomous" — it needs at least to be restated.[43] Anyone who tries to dispense with or to ignore the boundaries indicated by grammarian and lexicographer only confuses invention with understanding.

Secondly, part of that common currency of language was evidently shared knowledge of the Jewish scriptures, presumably in most cases in their

---

42. See below particularly §8.3, §11.4, and §23.5. On the importance and recognition of such allusions or "intertextual echoes" see Hays, *Echoes of Scripture* ch. 1.

43. See further my "Historical Text as Historical Text: Some Basic Hermeneutical Reflections in Relation to the New Testament," in J. Davies, et al., eds., *Words Remembered, Texts Renewed,* J. F. A. Sawyer FS (JSOTS 195; Sheffield: Sheffield Academic, 1995) 340-59. Adam's proposal for a "non-modern New Testament theology" *(Making Sense)* hardly takes account of this unavoidably basic historical work in NT interpretation.

Greek (LXX) form. In C. H. Dodd's appropriate metaphor, the scriptures were "the substructure" of Paul's theology, the metaphor reminding us that what was in mind was not simply Paul's explicit quotations of scripture, but the way in which scriptural terminology, idiom, and imagery shaped and determined so much of what Paul wrote.[44] Unless we are to suppose that Paul was quite unconcerned whether the recipients of his letters appreciated the force carried by such allusions, we have to take it that Paul felt able to assume a considerable knowledge of the LXX on the part of his converts — a knowledge gained in many cases at least, presumably, by previous exposure to the Jewish scriptures prior to their conversion as well as by intensive teaching thereafter.[45] For example, we will note later how much Paul seems able to have taken for granted that his readers would know what he meant by such key terms as "righteousness" and "works of the law."[46]

Thirdly, Paul's allusive taken-for-granted references include much of the faith already common to Paul and his readers. This is why it is so difficult to reconstruct Paul's evangelistic preaching — simply because he did not feel it necessary to repeat it in letters to his converts. Instead he could refer to it briefly[47] or allude to it by using brief formulae — usually summarized as "kerygmatic tradition."[48] He did so knowing, we may confidently assume, that even such brief formulations would evoke knowledge of a substantial range of basic teaching which he had passed on, when he preached to his readers the gospel of Jesus Christ and established them as a new church. Such allusions should not be evaluated simply by the brevity of their reference. To reconstruct Paul's theology as measured by the proportions of his explicit treatment would certainly result in a statement whose disproportions would have been pointed out at once by both Paul and the recipients of his letters. We do not "weigh" Paul's theology simply by counting the number of words he used.

Fourthly, we may cite the more controversial case of allusions to Jesus tradition, particularly within the paraenetic sections of Paul's letters. As we shall see subsequently, much the best way to make sense of the allusiveness

---

44. See below §7 nn. 34, 37; cf. now particularly Hübner, *Biblische Theologie*.

45. I remain strongly of the opinion that the main body of initial Gentile converts came into Christianity via the synagogue, as proselytes or God-fearers; see, e.g., my *Partings* 125-26; and on God-fearers see now Hengel and Schwemer, *Paul between Damascus and Antioch* 61-76 (357-70), 107-8. The fact that the LXX was unknown to wider Greco-Roman circles confirms that such familiarity as Paul clearly assumes must have come in many cases at least from lengthy exposure to the scriptures in a synagogue context.

46. See below §§14.2, 14.4-5

47. Obvious examples are 1 Cor. 2.2; Gal. 3.1; and 1 Thes. 1.9-10.

48. See further particularly §7.3.

of Paul's use of Jesus tradition is that substantial amounts of this tradition were already part of the earliest churches' store of foundation tradition. It was rarely necessary to cite it as tradition stemming from Jesus himself since it was already known as such in the common discourse and worship of the churches. Here again Paul's theological counsel could be most effective precisely by being allusive.[49] And here again any attempt to reconstruct Paul's theology has to give weight to what both he and his readers could take for granted.

Finally, within Paul's letters there are many passages where Paul is clearly alluding to issues and topics which lay between Paul and his readers, above all the particular matters at dispute between Paul and some of his readers — the reasons why he wrote to them in the first place. In such cases it was obviously not necessary for Paul to spell out the arguments or considerations which he was countering. His readers knew them only too well! The problem for us who wish to write a theology of Paul, however, is that in his replies Paul evidently angled his own exposition or argument to counter these views, at least in part. But this means that we will not really be able to understand the "why" of a line of argument or of a particular emphasis without having some awareness of the arguments being thus countered.[50] As we shall see in due course, 1 Corinthians is a particularly good case in point.[51]

To sum up. In enquiring after the theology of Paul, it is simply not realistic to attempt to confine ourselves to the theologies of Paul's individual letters. At best that would give us the theology of Paul's controversies rather than the theology of Paul. More important, however, the letters themselves, by their very character as one side of a dialogue and by the very frequency of allusions in them, leave us no choice but to inquire after the fuller theology on which the particular letters draw, the fuller theology and context which surely informs the light and shade, the emphasis and lack of emphasis of the individual passages in the letters, and thus enables us to build up a picture with both depth of focus and width of angle. Such a dialogue within a dialogue — that is, the dialogue between text and historical context within the larger hermeneutical dialogue — is not easy to carry through with success, but the skill to engage in that dialogue is part of what the professional expertise of the NT specialist is all about.

The basic point regarding the multilayered character of Paul's theology as it comes to us in his letters can be put another way, using the currently

49. See further below §8.3 and §23.5.
50. See also above §1.2c.
51. See below especially §24. On Romans see particularly Donfried, ed., *The Romans Debate*. And on Galatians see J. M. G. Barclay, "Mirror Reading a Polemical Letter: Galatians as a Test Case," *JSNT* 31 (1987) 73-93.

popular language of narrative theology. As Richard Hays, one of the main proponents of this approach to Paul's theology, has put it: "the framework of Paul's thought is constituted neither by a system of doctrines nor by his personal religious experience but by a 'sacred story,' a narrative structure"; "the story provides the foundational substructure on which Paul's argumentation is constructed."[52] In fact, Paul's theology can be said to emerge from the interplay between several stories, his theologizing to consist in his own participation in that interplay.

As the structure of the following chapters indicates, we could readily speak of the substructure of Paul's theology as the story of God and creation, with the story of Israel superimposed upon it. On top of that again we have the story of Jesus, and then Paul's own story, with the initial intertwining of these last two stories as the decisive turning point in Paul's life and theology. Finally, there are the complex interactions of Paul's own story with the stories of those who had believed before him and of those who came to form the churches founded by them.

In more general terms we could distinguish three phases or levels in any theologizing. The *first* or deepest level is that of inherited convictions or traditional life patterns. At this level we are dealing with axioms and presuppositions, often hidden and undeclared. An important part of theological education is to enable and facilitate critical self-reflection on these presuppositions. In Paul's case these include particularly the first two stories (of God and Israel) mentioned above. The *second* is the sequence of transformative moments in the individual's (or community's) growth and development. These window-opening experiences usually generate other insights and corollaries and can shape attitudes and determine important life choices. They will be much nearer the surface of the person's theology and more obvious to the onlooker. In Paul's case we would think most immediately of his conversion. But his early interaction with those who were Christians before him, and particularly his confrontation with Peter in Antioch (Gal. 2.11-18), were probably also very formative in his theology.[53] The *third* level is, of course, that of immediate issues and current reflections. This will be the level nearest the surface, by which I mean the level most accessible to the onlooker, which is not the same as saying that it is a superficial level. In Paul's case, of course, that is the level of the letters themselves, the level of the particular questions addressed and objectives pursued by Paul in his different letters.

The reality of Paul's theology, then, is the interaction between the

---

52. Hays, *Faith* 5, 6. See also Wright, *Climax*, and Witherington, *Narrative*, who speaks of four stories — (1) the story of a world gone wrong, (2) the story of Israel, (3) the story of Christ, and (4) the story of Christians, including Paul himself.

53. See further below §14.5a.

different stories or levels which his letters evidence. It is that interaction which gives Paul's theology its dynamic character; a static "theology of Paul" would not be the theology of Paul. The more we can recognize these allusions, be conscious of how the particular point functions within the larger stories, alert to the presuppositions and taken-for-granteds, sensitive to statements angled to particular audiences, then the more hope we can have of writing a theology of Paul deserving of the title. Not least of value in the talk of different narratives and levels is the likelihood that the interaction among them will help explain the tensions which continually surface in explorations of Paul's theology. For many at least of these are the tensions between the different stories and levels. Paul himself, as Pharisaic Jew become apostle of Jesus Christ to the Gentiles, embodied one of the most painful of these tensions within himself.[54] Little wonder, then, that his theologizing should consist to such an extent of the attempt to hold these tensions together in a coherent whole.

It will be sufficiently clear, therefore, what my answer to the third question is. Can a theology of Paul be written? The answer is Yes. It is possible to recognize the allusions, to hear the different stories, to probe below the surface to the different levels.[55] Of course the recognition will be incomplete, the hearing imperfect, the probing often uncertain. But that is true in the attempt to reconstruct the thought and thinking of any person — living or dead. And the character of Paul's writings as letters to churches gives us better hope of success than with most other figures from the ancient past. The theology of Paul is too important for the challenge to be ducked.

§1.4 How to write a theology of Paul?

If then we can speak about the *theology* of Paul, and not just his doctrine or religion or rhetoric, and about the theology of *Paul,* and not just the theology of his letters, that still leaves us with the question: How to go about writing that theology?

For some the chief object of search should be the *centre,* or more explicitly, the organizing centre of Paul's theology. This evokes an old discussion, which still rumbles on, particularly in German scholarship, with

---

54. See particular §19 below.

55. It is the atomistic exegesis of H. Räisänen in his *Paul and the Law* (§6 n. 1) which prevents him from recognizing the coherence of Paul's thought, since that coherence lies so much in the flow of the argument of his letters and in the below-the-surface taken for granteds of the argument. Contrast also Sanders, "Paul" 124: "As a religious genius, he was free of the academic requirement of systematic consistency."

older alternatives still posed and defended.[56] Does the central dynamism of Paul's theology lie in the tension between Jewish Christianity and Gentile Christianity (as Baur originally suggested)? Is the centre of Paul's theology "justification by faith" (as Bultmann and Ernst Käsemann continued to insist with tremendous conviction)?[57] Or should the central feature be found in "participation in Christ" or some form of "Christ-mysticism" (one thinks particularly of Albert Schweitzer)?[58] Or is it rather the theology of the cross which stands firmly at the centre (as, for example, in Ulrich Wilckens).[59] Alternatively, should we be looking for some underlying unifying principle, perhaps in last generation's terms of Paul's anthropology,[60] or salvation history,[61] or in the more recent idea of an underlying narrative of covenant or Christ?[62]

The problem with the imagery of centre or core or principle, however, is that it is too fixed and inflexible. It encourages the impression from the start that Paul's theology was static and unchanging.[63] Would a different imagery help — such as substratum, master symbolism, basic grammar, or the like? In recent discussions on Paul's theology in North America the image of "lens" was, in the event, the most popular — though what the lens was and what passed through it were more a matter of dispute. For Edgar Krentz, "apocalyptic was the theological lens."[64] For Hays, the objective was "to trace the contours of the hermeneutical lens through which Paul projects the images of the community's symbolic world onto the screen of the community's life."[65] And for Jouette Bassler, the lens was Paul's experience through which

---

56. See also V. P. Furnish, "Pauline Studies," in E. J. Epp and G. W. MacRae, eds., *The New Testament and Its Modern Interpreters* (Atlanta: Scholars, 1980) 333-36; for the larger debate on a centre in New Testament theology, see Hasel, *New Testament Theology* ch. 3; Plevnik, "Center."

57. As is well known, "justification by faith" was the theological basis for Bultmann's demythologizing programme and provided Käsemann with his "canon within the canon" (see below §14 nn. 4-5). See also, e.g., Hübner, "Pauli Theologiae Proprium."

58. Schweitzer, *Mysticism* (§15 n. 1); see also Sanders, *Paul* 453-63, 502-8.

59. Wilckens, *Römer,* index "Sühnetod (Christi)"; see also J. Becker (below n. 78).

60. As Braun, "Problem"; also below §3 n. 7.

61. See the volumes by O. Cullmann (below §18 n. 1).

62. See above n. 52. Some would regard this as simply a refurbishing of the older salvation history model.

63. Achtemeier prefers to speak of a "generative center," which he finds in Paul's "conviction that God raised Jesus from the dead" ("Continuing Quest" 138-40).

64. E. Krentz, "Through a Lens: Theology and Fidelity in 2 Thessalonians," in Bassler, ed., *Pauline Theology* 1.52-62 (here 52).

65. R. B. Hays, "Crucified with Christ: A Synthesis of the Theology of 1 and 2 Thessalonians, Philemon, Philippians and Galatians," in Bassler, ed., *Pauline Theology* 1.227-46 (here 228).

the "raw material of Paul's theology" passed *(sic).*[66] But even with these few examples, the image is becoming laboured and artificial. And whether it captures or evokes the dynamism of Paul's theologizing in sufficient degree is most doubtful. In fact, it was the dynamic character of Paul's theology which made one of the lasting impressions of the ten-year-long discussions in the SBL Pauline Theology group — the sense that Paul's theology was an "activity," was always interactive,[67] the sense that Paul was never simply theologian per se, but was always at one and the same time Paul the theologian, missionary, and pastor, or, in a word, Paul the apostle.[68]

The most obvious alternative is to recognize the changing character of Paul's theology and to attempt a description of it in terms of its *development* through Paul's letters. That "dynamic" means "development" has usually been taken for granted in such treatments. The example most commonly cited has been that of Paul's eschatology, the usual assumption being that the delay of the parousia weakened Paul's imminent expectation or changed his understanding of the process by which transformation into the resurrection body took place.[69] The problems here are well known: we cannot be sure enough of the relative datings of the letters to draw any firm lines of chronological development between them,[70] and we do not know enough of the circumstances of each letter to be able to determine how much the particularities of the formulations were a reflection of changing circumstances rather than of changing theology.[71]

In recent years the issue has been more the question of whether we need to speak of development *before* Paul even wrote his letters.[72] So far as

66. J. M. Bassler, "Paul's Theology: Whence and Whither?" in Hay, ed., *Pauline Theology* 2.3-17 (here 11).

67. Bassler (n. 66), *Pauline Theology* 2.10-11, 16-17. See also Furnish, cited by C. B. Cousar, "The Theological Task of 1 Corinthians," in Hay, ed., *Pauline Theology* 2.90-102 (here 91); D. M. Hay, "The Shaping of Theology in 2 Corinthians," in Hay, ed., *Pauline Theology* 2.135-55 (here 135-36); S. J. Kraftchick, "Death in Us, Life in You: The Apostolic Medium," in Hay, ed., *Pauline Theology* 2.156-81 (here 157).

68. Cf. B. R. Gaventa, "Apostle and Church in 2 Corinthians," in Hay, ed., *Pauline Theology* 2.193-99; R. Jewett, "Ecumenical Theology for the Sake of Mission: Romans 1.1-17 + 15.14–16.24," in Hay and Johnson, eds., *Pauline Theology* 3.89-108.

69. See below §12 and n. 81. On the relation between 1 Corinthians 15 and 2 Corinthians 5 in particular see, e.g., Martin, *2 Corinthians* 97-99.

70. See, e.g., P. J. Achtemeier, "Finding the Way to Paul's Theology," in Bassler, *Pauline Theology* 1.27.

71. See Moule (§12 n. 1); and further J. Lowe, "An Examination of Attempts to Detect Development in St. Paul's Theology," *JTS* 42 (1941) 129-42; V. P. Furnish, "Developments in Paul's Thought," *JAAR* 38 (1970) 289-303; Beker, "Paul's Theology" 366-67.

72. Note particularly the recent flurry of attempts to fill out a distinctive Antiochene theology (Berger, *Theologie;* E. Rau, *Von Jesus zu Paulus: Entwicklung und Rezeption der*

Paul himself was concerned, the key question would be: To what extent did Paul's conversion result in a transformation of the old fixed points of his ancestral religion — completely, or only partially? In coming to faith in Jesus Christ did he leave "Judaism" behind (as Gal 1.13-14 seems to suggest)? Or should we hesitate even to speak of "conversion," at least in the sense of a change from one religion to another?[73] Again, assuming that Paul's persecuting activities had been directed primarily against the Hellenists, as most do, had the Hellenists already made a decisive breach with the law, and was Paul simply converted to this view?[74] Or is it necessary rather to assume that either Paul's sense of commissioning to the Gentiles, or his antagonism to "works of the law," or both, only developed in the years between the Damascus road christophany and his earliest letter?[75] The debate here is ongoing and no breadth of consensus has yet been achieved.

What might be called mediating attempts between the static imagery of centre and the changing imagery of development have sought to identify a particular moment or principle which remains relatively stable within the flux or which became the decisive determinant in the development. The most obvious candidate is, once again, Paul's conversion itself. It can even be argued that Paul's theology as a whole was simply an unfolding of the significance of the initial christophany.[76] Or the christophany itself can be seen as providing, in E. P. Sanders' terms, the solution from which Paul's whole theology of human plight and divine redemption can be deduced.[77] Among recent studies, Jürgen Becker[78] has attempted to combine a developmental schema with a search for the centre. He argues in effect for three principal phases in Paul's theological writing: first, his theology of election (*Erwählungstheologie* — 1 Thessalonians);[79] second, a theology of the cross (*Kreuzestheologie* — Corinthians); and third, his message of justification (*Rechtfertigungsbotschaft* — already in Galatians). Of these three the second is the real centre; the

---

antiochenischen Theologie im Urchristentum [Stuttgart: Kohlhammer, 1994]; Schmithals, *Theologiegeschichte,* index "Antiochien"). But see now Hengel and Schwemer, *Paul between Damascus and Antioch* 279-91.

73. See below §7.4.

74. See further below §14.3.

75. See, e.g., the theses of Watson, *Paul,* and N. Taylor, *Paul, Antioch and Jerusalem* (JSNTS 66; Sheffield: Sheffield Academic, 1992).

76. Particularly Kim, *Origin* (§7 n. 1).

77. Sanders, *Paul* 442-47. See also below §7.5 and n. 101.

78. J. Becker, *Paulus. Der Apostel der Völker* (Tübingen: Mohr, 1989) = *Paul.*

79. There have been repeated attempts to distinguish an earlier stage of Paul's theology in 1 Thessalonians; see, e.g., T. Söding, "Der Erste Thessalonicherbrief und die frühe paulinische Evangeliumsverkündigung. Zur Frage einer Entwicklung der paulinischen Theologie," *BZ* 35 (1991) 180-203; Schulz, *Neutestamentliche Ethik* (§23 n. 1) 301-33; and §16 n. 35 below; but see also Lohse, "Changes of Thought."

theology of the cross is the "canon" by which the theology of election is defined; the message of justification is the language in which the theology of the cross is clothed.

However, of all the attempts in this area, the most sophisticated and influential has probably been Beker's advocacy of a model of *coherence within contingency,* where for him "the coherence of the gospel is constituted by the apocalyptic interpretation of the death and resurrection of Christ."[80] The strength of this model is precisely that the coherence does not reduce to some static formulation or unalterable structure of thought, and so cannot be easily broken by the shifting currents of contingency. Rather, the coherence is that stable, constant element which expresses what Beker calls "the convictional basis of Paul's proclamation," or what Paul himself refers to as "the truth of the gospel" (Gal. 2.5, 14).[81]

Certainly students of Paul's theology would be wise to adopt some such model. It is simply a matter of respect for our subject matter and for the sheer stature of the man that we should assume an essential coherence to his thought and praxis, unless proved otherwise. And it is simply a matter of common sense that any such coherence will have taken a variety of forms, some of which may be defined in developmental terms, but all of which will be contingent in greater or less degree. At all events, it is the more flexible model which is most likely to prove fruitful as a tool in analysis of Paul's theology.[82]

§1.5   Toward a theology of Paul

In the light of the preceding discussion, readers should know that two methodological decisions have shaped my own attempt to write a theology of Paul.

a) As has been hinted at several points in the preceding pages, my own preferred model is that of dialogue. Dialogues (not just theological dialogues) between people are the primary means by which individuals learn about others and learn to understand others. It is precisely in dialogue that we learn to appreciate allusions. It is precisely through dialogue that one becomes more aware that the stories of the dialogue partner are different from one's own. It

---

80. Beker, "Paul's Theology" 364-77; also "Recasting Pauline Theology," in Bassler, ed., *Pauline Theology* 1.18, reflecting on his earlier *Paul the Apostle.*

81. Beker, "Paul's Theology" 368; also "Recasting" 15.

82. Childs' criticism of Beker (*Introduction* 310) seems to misunderstand Beker's agenda; where the canon preserves the contingency of the letters, it bears testimony to the same tension between contingency and coherence and necessitates the same dialogue between historical inquiry into each letter's allusive character and the themes deemed to be of continuing importance on a canonical reading.

is not least in thus truly encountering another that we become more sharply conscious of the different levels at which our own principles and values are based and of the different levels which form and determine our own thinking and decision making.

Of course to speak of a dialogue with a man long dead is an extension of the metaphor. But here again we benefit from the fact that Paul comes to us as a letter writer, that is, as one side or partner in a sequence of dialogues. This means that we can enter into a theological dialogue with Paul in several ways.

For one thing, we can overhear his own historical dialogue with those to whom and for whom he wrote. All students of Paul would be more or less agreed that we can reconstruct the other sides of the dialogue, at least to some extent, both by setting Paul's letters in their historical context and by listening for the allusions to the other sides of the dialogue. To that extent, then, we can appreciate what Paul says as dialogue.

For another, we can enter some way into Paul's own dialogue with himself. To be taken seriously are the observations made above about the allusive character of Paul's letter writing, including allusions to the different stories in which he was caught up, or, alternatively put, the different levels within Paul's own story. In which case, our ability to recognize these allusions is also our ability in effect to wrestle with Paul through the tensions set up by the interaction between these different stories and levels. That is to say, we can empathize in at least some measure with Paul's own theologizing.

And for another, we naturally bring our own questions and traditions to our scrutiny of what Paul has said. That is to say, to the extent that we can hear Paul in his own terms we can begin genuinely to dialogue with him on our own part. Despite the intervening centuries it can be a genuine dialogue rather than a monologue. For the questions we pose can only be properly answered in Paul's terms. And if useful answers are to emerge, then the questions themselves must be rephrased in the light of the dialogue until they are formulated in such terms as Paul can give real answers to.

I make no apology, then, for pursuing my task along these lines. In particular, I am not concerned to reconstruct the theology of Paul as a historical artifact of primarily antiquarian or curiosity value. Theology wrestles with the supreme questions of reality and human existence. And as already noted, from the perspective of Christian theology, Paul's contribution to the ongoing dialogue on these questions is unsurpassed. So my endeavour in the following pages is, first of all, so far as possible, to get inside the skin of Paul, to see through his eyes, to think his thoughts from inside as it were, and to do so in such a way as to help others to appreciate his insight and subtlety and concerns for themselves. At the same time I wish to theologize *with* Paul, to engage in mutually critical dialogue with him, as one would hope a maturing student would engage critically with the thought of his or her teacher. Of course, a one-to-one dialogue will hardly draw out the full riches of Paul's theology. And despite the numerous footnotes on the following pages the attempt to draw other voices into the dialogue remains limited. On the other hand, the model of the one-to-one tutorial remains an invaluable tool for teaching and learning — even if it is fast disappearing in British universities at under-graduate level! And I treasure the hope that the dialogue will continue through and beyond the critical interactions of reviewers with this book.

b) One final point needs to be decided before embarking on the enter-prise. That is, where one should best locate oneself within the flow of Paul's thought in order to begin the dialogue with it. Such a decision will be neces-sary. For if we dialogue with Paul freely across the range of his reminiscences and letters we may simply end up with a mishmash — not the theology of Paul as he would have owned it at any particular time. A theology of Paul which gives an account of his faith just after the Damascus road christophany will not be quite the same as the theology of Paul between the Jerusalem consultation and the incident at Antioch, which will not be quite the same as the theology of Paul before and after he heard the news from Galatia, which will not be quite the same as the theology of Paul during his exchanges with the church at Corinth, and so on.

In fact, however, the decision is easy to make. For there is one letter of Paul's which is less caught in the flux and developing discourse of Paul with his churches than the others. And that is Romans.[83] In the movement and dialogue of Paul's theologizing, his letter to the Romans is a relatively (I stress relatively) fixed feature. It was written to a church which was not his own founding. It was written at the end of a (or, better, the) major phase of Paul's missionary work (Rom. 15.18-24), which included most of the other undisputed letters. It was written under probably the most congenial circum-stances of his mission, with time for careful reflection and composition. And, above all, it was clearly intended to set out and defend his own mature understanding of the gospel (Rom. 1.16-17) as he had thus far proclaimed it and as he hoped to commend it both in Jerusalem and beyond Rome in Spain. In short, Romans is still far removed from a dogmatic or systematic treatise on theology, but it nevertheless is the most sustained and reflective statement of Paul's own theology by Paul himself.

How to write a theology of Paul, then? Paul's letter to the Christians in Rome is the nearest thing we have to Paul's own answer to that question. Which is also to say that Romans provides us with an example of the way Paul himself chose to order the sequence of themes in his theology. If, there-

---

83. Cf. the subtitle of Hultgren's *Paul's Gospel;* not to mention Melanchthon's *Loci Communes* (1521).

fore, we wish to grasp at and dialogue with the mature theology of Paul we cannot do better than take Romans as a kind of template on which to construct our own statement of Paul's theology, a dominant chord by which to tune our own lesser instruments. A theology of Paul which sets out to describe and discuss the theology of Paul at the time he wrote Romans and by constant reference to Romans as prompter and plumb line is surely headed in the right direction. Now read on.

CHAPTER 2

God and Humankind

§2 God[1]

1. **Bibliography: E. Baasland**, "Cogitio Dei im Römerbrief," *SNTU* 14 (1989) 185-218; **M. N. A. Bockmuehl**, *Revelation and Mystery in Ancient Judaism and Pauline Christianity* (WUNT 2.36; Tübingen: Mohr, 1990 = Grand Rapids: Eerdmans, 1997); **G. Bornkamm**, "The Revelation of God's Wrath (Romans 1–3)," *Early Christian Experience* 47-70; **Childs**, *Biblical Theology* 351-412; **R. Bultmann**, "What Does It Mean to Speak of God?" *Faith and Understanding: Collected Essays* (London: SCM/New York, Harper and Row, 1969) 53-65; **N. A. Dahl**, "The One God of Jews and Gentiles (Romans 3.29-30)," *Studies* 178-91; "The Neglected Factor in New Testament Theology," in D. H. Juel, ed., *Jesus the Christ: The Historical Origins of Christological Doctrine* (Minneapolis: Fortress, 1991) 153-63; **G. Delling**, "MONOS THEOS," and "Geprägte partizipiale Gottesaussagen in der urchristlichen Verkündigung," *Studien zum Neuen Testament und zum hellenistischen Judentum. Gesammelte Aufsätze 1950-1968* (Göttingen: Vandenhoeck, 1970) 391-400, 401-16; **J. D. G. Dunn**, "Biblical Concepts of Revelation," in P. Avis, ed., *Divine Revelation* (London: Darton/Grand Rapids: Eerdmans, 1997) 1-22; **J. Dupont**, *Gnosis. La connaissance religieuse dans les Épitres de Saint Paul* (Louvain: Nauwelarts/Paris: Gabalda, 1949); **Feine**, *Theologie* 296-343; **Fitzmyer**, *Paul* 41-49; **Gnilka**, *Paulus* 193-201; **R. M. Grant**, *Gods and the One God* (Philadelphia: Westminster, 1986); **F. Hahn**, "The Confession of the One God in the New Testament," *HBT* 2 (1980) 69-84; **T. Holtz**, "Theo-logie und Christologie bei Paulus," in E. Grässer and O. Merk, eds., *Glaube und Eschatologie*, W. G. Kümmel FS (Tübingen: Mohr, 1985) 105-21; **P.-G. Klumbies**, *Die Rede von Gott bei Paulus in ihrem zeitgeschichtlichen Kontext* (FRLANT 155; Göttingen: Vandenhoeck, 1992); **A. Lindemann**, "Die Rede von Gott in der paulinische Theologie," *Theologie und Glaube* 69 (1979) 357-76; **D. Lührmann**, *Das Offenbarungsverständnis bei Paulus und in paulinischen Gemeinden* (WMANT 16; Neukirchen-Vluyn: Neukirchener, 1965); **R. MacMullen**, *Paganism in the Roman Empire* (New Haven: Yale, 1981) 73-94; **Morris**, *Theology* 25-38; **H. Moxnes**, *Theology in Conflict: Studies in Paul's Understanding of God in Romans* (Leiden: Brill, 1980); **R. M. Ogilvie**, *The Romans and Their Gods* (London: Chatto and Windus/New York: Norton, 1969); **Schlier**, *Grundzüge* 25-54; **H. J. Wicks**, *The Doctrine of God in the Jewish Apocryphal and Apocalyptic Literature* (New York: Ktav, 1915, reissued 1971).

§2.1 *God as axiom*

A systematic study of Paul's theology has to begin with his belief in God. This is not simply because the term "theology" may be said to have "speech about God" as its primary meaning.[2] It is much more because God is the fundamental presupposition of Paul's theology, the starting point of his theologizing, the primary subtext of all his writing. The word "God" itself occurs 548 times in the Pauline corpus, 153 in Romans alone. Only two chapters of the extensive Pauline writings lack any explicit mention of "God." As a rule in the Pauline letters God is mentioned at once as the primary legitimating factor behind Paul's life work — "Paul, called to be an apostle . . . through God's will" (1 Cor. 1.1), "Paul, apostle . . . through God the Father" (Gal. 1.1), and the one which becomes almost stereotypical thereafter, "Paul, apostle of Christ Jesus through God's will."[3] The regular greeting in his letters is of "grace to you and peace from God our Father," followed by a thanksgiving to God. In Romans itself the attentive reader cannot but be struck by the steady sequence of genitive phrases which marks the first chapter — "gospel of God," "son of God," "beloved of God," "the will of God," "power of God," "righteousness of God," "wrath of God," "what may be known of God," "the glory of God," "the truth of God," "the judgment of God." Whatever else Paul's theology was, it was talk "of God." Nor is it coincidental that the thematic statement of Romans is an affirmation of "God's righteousness" (1.17), that the first main section begins as an assertion of "God's wrath" (1.18), and that the starting point of his indictment is "what may be known of God" (1.19, 21).

The problem for us, however, is that Paul's convictions about God are all too axiomatic. Because they were axioms, Paul never made much effort to expound them. They belong to the foundations of his theology and so are largely hidden from view. Consequently it is not possible for us to read off Paul's theology of God from any particular passage in Paul, as one can with his understanding of justification and faith from Romans 3–4 or his understanding of the resurrection of the dead from 1 Corinthians 15. It is presumably for this reason that many analyses of Paul's theology forego a section on "God" and jump at once into other aspects or even presuppositions, usually an analysis of the human condition.[4] In so doing, by staying

---

2. Bultmann's misgivings on the point need to be recalled ("What Does It Mean to Speak of God?").

3. 2 Cor. 1.1; Eph. 1.1; Col. 1.1; 2 Tim. 1.1.

4. In this century see Holtzmann, Prat, Scott, Bultmann, Whiteley, Ridderbos, Eichholz, Kümmel, Ladd, Goppelt, and Berger. Feine, Schlier, Morris, whose first section on the Pauline writings is entitled "God at the Center" (25-38), Fitzmyer, and Becker, *Paul* 379-82 are exceptions. Hence the title of Dahl's essay, "The Neglected Factor in New

closer to the explicit level of Paul's written thought, they reflect the character of that writing. But they also run the danger of missing some of the (theo)logical connections which help explain the slants and turns of Paul's theology but which lie below the surface, in the foundational substructure of Paul's theology.

Fortunately the same phenomenon works to our advantage. For to put the same point another way, Paul did not need to explain his beliefs about God because they were already common to and shared with his readers. His "speech about God" was part of the shared speech of the first Christian congregations, already a fundamental "taken-for-granted" of their common discourse. So, for example, an appeal to the "will of God" could be effective without elaboration simply because the importance of doing God's will was equally axiomatic for them also. If then we are to fill out Paul's repeated references and allusions to God into a more coherent or at least connected "speech about God" we have to set them into the context of the beliefs about God which Paul shared with his readers. Here, in other words, we have the first example of the need to set Paul's individual statements into historical context — in this case into the context of the beliefs about God which Paul could have expected to inform and motivate his readers' own faith.

As will quickly become evident, these shared beliefs were Jewish through and through. One of the reasons why Paul did not have to explain or defend his belief in God was because it was the fundamental belief of his own tradition, the belief in which he himself had been instructed from his youth, and out of which he had lived his life for as long as he could remember. Thus in Romans his language again and again falls into the rhythm of traditional Jewish affirmations about God — "God who is blessed forever" (1.25), "God will judge the world" (3.5), "God who gives life to the dead" (4.17), God "who searches the hearts" (8.27), and so on.[5] In other words, Paul's conversion had not changed his belief in and about God. It was the Creator God of Genesis who had also enlightened him (2 Cor. 4.6, echoing Gen. 1.3). It was the God who had called Jeremiah who had also chosen him (Gal. 1.15, echoing Jer. 1.5). It was the grace of this God which had made him what he was (1 Cor. 15.10). In short, his most fundamental taken-for-granted remained intact.

At the same time, the impact of this God-given "revelation of Christ" did not leave his fundamental belief in God unaffected. Indeed, one of the most fascinating aspects of a study of Paul's theology is the exploration of

---

Testament Theology," which is "*theo*-logy in the strict sense of the word" (153). Dahl's criticism (154) of Cullmann's statement that "early Christian theology is in reality almost exclusively Christology" (*Christology* 2-3) has much wider application.

5. See further Moxnes, *Theology in Conflict* 15-31.

the ways in which Paul's belief in Christ impacted on his theology of God.[6] But for the moment we need focus only on the principal features of Paul's speech about God which he inherited from his forefathers.

This recognition of the essentially Jewish character of Paul's "speech about God" is not challenged by the fact that the majority of those in Paul's congregations were Gentiles. For Paul's Gentile converts probably were drawn largely, in the first instance at least, from among those Gentiles who seem to have frequented, even crowded, many a diaspora synagogue at this time.[7] The fact that they were called "God-worshipers" *(sebomenoi ton Theon)* suggests in itself that the Jewish belief in God was one of Judaism's main attractions.[8] As noted before,[9] Paul's assumption of his readers' familiarity with and respect for the LXX presupposes a prior knowledge of the LXX which can only have been gained in the synagogue and in the new gatherings in the name of Jesus Messiah. As for preaching to Gentiles unfamiliar with Jewish traditions, it will be no accident that Luke portrays Paul's two "Gentile sermons" as devoted almost entirely to the proclamation of God — hardly at all of Jesus.[10] In so doing Luke simply expresses the logic of a Jew preaching to non-Jews: turning to God meant turning to the God confessed by Jews.[11] And Paul confirms that he followed just that logic in his own preaching to Gentiles, when he reminds his Thessalonian converts "how you turned to God from idols, to serve a living and true God" (1 Thes. 1.9).[12]

If then we are to lay bare the substructure of Paul's thought, to hear the taken-for-granteds which link his allusions to God into a fuller "speech

6. This has been the main consideration in most studies which bring Paul's theology of God to focus (Klumbies, *Rede* 13-33), summed up in such phrases as "talk of God determined by the confession of Christ's cross and resurrection" (Lindemann, "Rede von Gott" 362), "the christologically determined theology of the New Testament" (Rahner and Thüsing, *New Christology* [§10 n. 1] 85), christology "within the horizon of monotheism" (Holtz, "Theo-logie" 108), "the christological interpretation of God," "the christologically defined God" (Klumbies, *Rede* 237, 247), and Paul's "christological monotheism" (Wright, *Climax* 99, 129); see further below §10.5.

7. Cf. Acts 13.43, 50; 16.14; 17.4, 17; 18.7.

8. One of the most explicit non-Jewish, non-Christian descriptions is that of Juvenal: the God-fearers who "worship nothing but the clouds, and the divinity of the heavens" (*Satires* 14.96-97). The idea that Jews identified God with heaven goes back to Hecataeus of Abdera (c. 300 BCE; see *GLAJJ* 1.28, 305-6). On God-fearers see, e.g., Schürer, *History* 3.160-71, and J. Reynolds and R. Tannenbaum, *Jews and Godfearers at Aphrodisias* (Cambridge: Cambridge Philological Society, 1987) 48-66.

9. See above §1.3 and n. 45.

10. Acts 14.15-17; 17.22-31.

11. Acts 14.15; 15.19; 26.18, 20.

12. Klumbies unjustifiably maintains that Paul sets "the Christian God in contrast to the idols *and* to the God of the Jews" (*Rede* 143-44).

about God," we must spell out his Jewish presuppositions in a little detail. The most obvious aspects to focus on are Jewish monotheism, the belief in God as creator, as sovereign, and as final judge, and on God as the God of Israel.

§2.2 *God as one*

The most fundamental Jewish belief was in the oneness of God. Paul had no doubt been taught to say the *Shema* from his youth, probably as a daily confession: "Hear O Israel: The Lord our God is one Lord" or ". . . the Lord our God, the Lord is one" (Deut. 6.4). On the basis of Deut. 6.7 a devout Jew, as Paul evidently had been, would say the *Shema* twice a day. Similarly, the decalogue, the basic statement of Jewish obligation, begins with the unequivocal charge: "You shall have no other gods besides or before me" (Exod. 20.3). It is not surprising then that works of Jewish apologetic take this as their starting point. The *Letter of Aristeas,* written probably in the second half of the second century BCE, begins its exposition of the law "first of all by demonstrating that God is one" (*Ep. Arist.* 132). Philo equally reflects the primacy of the first commandment for diaspora Jews of Paul's day in his exposition of it:

> Let us, then, engrave deep in our hearts this as the first and most sacred of commandments, to acknowledge and honour one God who is above all, and let the idea that gods are many never even reach the ears of the man whose rule of life is to seek for truth in purity and goodness (*Decal.* 65).

And for Josephus, too, "the first word [of the decalogue] teaches us that God is one" (*Ant.* 3.91).[13]

Tied into this was the conviction that God is invisible, or, more precisely, is un-image-able (Exod. 20.4) and unlookable-on (Exod. 33.20). Hence the implacable hostility in Judaism from earliest days to idolatry.[14] Josephus, Paul's younger contemporary, in his most succinct apologia for Jewish religion expresses his people's conviction on this point in refined terms:

---

13. Further data and bibliography in Rainbow, "Jewish Monotheism" (§10 n. 1) 81-83.

14. Classically in Isa. 44.9-20; Wisdom 11–15; Epistle of Jeremiah. Livy's report that no image was found in the Jerusalem temple, "since they do not think the God partakes of any figure," made this feature of Jewish religion more widely known (*GLAJJ* 1.330-31; 2.353).

He [Moses] represented him [God] as one, uncreated and immutable to all eternity; in beauty surpassing all mortal thought, made known to us by his power, although the nature of his real being passes knowledge. . . . By his works and bounties he is plainly seen, indeed more manifest than aught else; but his form and magnitude surpass our powers of description. No materials, however costly, are fit to make an image of him; no art has skill to conceive and represent it. The like of him we have never seen, we do not imagine, and it is impious to conjecture (*Ap.* 2.167, 190-91).

We may observe in passing that such critique foreshadows the modern critique of Feuerbach and Freud of the notion of God itself as an outward projection of inner sensations. Significant, then, is the fact that traditional Jewish theology both recognized the dangers of such self-projection and distinguished their own convictions from it.

It is clear that Paul shared both these distinctively Jewish beliefs.[15] In his discussion of food offered to idols (1 Cor. 8.1), his first instinct was to affirm his ancestral faith in God as one: "we know that an idol is nothing in the world and that there is no God except one" (1 Cor. 8.4). He confessed the *Shema* (similarly Eph. 4.6). Equally axiomatic was the proposition of God's oneness in Gal. 3.20: "God is one." So, too, early in Romans he bases his rebuttal of justification by works on the Jewish confession "God is one" (Rom. 3.30). Somewhat surprisingly, it was to be 1 Timothy, one of the latest members of the Pauline corpus, which would affirm Jewish monotheism most fully: "the only God" (1.17); "there is one God" (2.5); "the blessed and only Sovereign, the King of kings and Lord of lords, who alone has immortality" (6.15-16). Paul did not write the letter, but the confessions are his. Perhaps from the same hand, and equally in character with Paul's own faith, is the concluding doxology early on added to Romans: "to God, only, wise" (Rom. 16.25).[16]

Paul's antipathy to idolatry is equally clear and expressed with characteristic Jewish fear, dismay, and scorn. Luke portrays Paul in Athens as "deeply distressed to see that the city was full of idols" (Acts 17.16) and as quick to denounce idolatry (17.29). The picture is borne out by Paul's own recollection of how his Thessalonian readers had "turned to God from idols" (1 Thes. 1.9). In contrast to dead idols God is "the living and true God" (1 Thes. 1.9).[17] In

---

15. See also Hahn, "Confession."

16. Cf. particularly 2 Macc. 1.24-25 ("O Lord, Lord God, Creator of all things . . . you alone are king and are kind, you alone are bountiful, you alone are just and almighty and eternal"); Sir. 1.8 ("There is one who is wise"); Philo, *Fuga* 47 ("the only wise"), *Pseudo-Phocylides* 54 ("the only God is wise"). See further Delling, *"MONOS THEOS."*

17. "Living God" — also Rom. 9.26 (citing Hos. 1.10 LXX 2.1); 2 Cor. 3.3; 6.16; 1 Tim. 3.15; 4.10. The phrase is frequent in the OT — e.g., Deut. 2.26; Josh. 3.10; 1 Sam. 17.26, 36; Ps. 84.2; Isa. 37.4, 17.

Romans the first charge he brings against human impiety (1.18) takes for granted God's invisibility (1.20)[18] and follows closely the traditional Jewish condemnation of idolatry: "they changed the glory of the incorruptible God for the mere likeness of corruptible humanity, birds, beasts, and reptiles" (1.23).[19] And elsewhere Paul's condemnation of idolatry is as forthright as that of any of his Jewish predecessors: "flee from idolatry" (1 Cor. 10.14).[20]

Thus it is all too clear that Jewish monotheism was one of the primary presuppositions and starting points in Paul's thought about God and about the appropriate and inappropriate ways in which humans conceived of and worshiped God.

§2.3 Other gods?

This all too clear picture of a sharp antithesis between Paul's Jewish monotheism and Gentile polytheism and idolatry may, however, be too clear. The misgivings arise on three fronts: from recognition of a form of monotheism in Greco-Roman religion; from a questioning of the strictness of Jewish monotheism; and from some of Paul's own statements related to the issue.

a) The distinctiveness of Jewish belief in the oneness of God should not be exaggerated. Most of the old religions and religious cults of the time envisaged a supreme god at the head of a divine hierarchy,[21] and the more philosophically minded could readily conceive of God as one, with "all 'gods' simply his will at work in various spheres of action."[22] Nevertheless, this was hardly the radical monotheism of the Jews. For typical of the liberal tolerance of the Hellenistic period was precisely this readiness to recognize the deity in many manifestations.[23] Piety, understood as honouring the

---

18. Note also Col. 1.15 ("the invisible God") and 1 Tim. 1.17 ("incorruptible, invisible, only God").

19. The language is drawn from Ps. 106.20 and Jer. 2.11, and vv. 22-23 contain echoes of Isa. 44.9-20 and Wisdom 11–15 (note particularly 11.15; 12.24; 13.10, 13-14; 14.8; 15.18-19); cf. also *Ep. Arist.* 138. See also §5.4.

20. See also 1 Cor. 5.10-11; 6.9; 10.7; Gal. 5.20; cf. Col. 3.5 and Eph. 5.5. The term itself, *eidōlolatria,* "worship of idols," may indeed be a Pauline formation, since it occurs elsewhere in biblical Greek only in 1 Pet. 4.3, though it does appear also in *T. Jud.* 19.1 and 23.1 (both v.l.) and in *T. Ben.* 10.10.

21. MacMullen, *Paganism* 7, notes that in inscriptions in Asia Minor Zeus is invoked two and a half times as often as any other.

22. MacMullen, *Paganism* 87; see also, e.g., H. Chadwick, *Origen: Contra Celsum* (Cambridge: Cambridge University, 1953) xvi-xx.

23. For example, we regularly find Zeus hyphenated with what was seen as the local variation — Zeus Sarapis, Zeus Dionysus, Zeus Ammon, Zeus Baal, even Zeus

divinity according to local ancestral custom, called for genuine respect for other gods and their cults. In contrast, it was the intolerance of Judaism in refusing to recognize these other gods as manifestations of Yahweh (or Yahweh as the manifestation of Zeus)[24] which provoked the charge of atheism against Jews — refusal to recognize the reality of other gods (Josephus, *Ap.* 2.148).[25]

Greek philosophy could be equally critical of idolatry, as Celsus was quick to remind the second-century Christians (*Contra Celsum* 1.5, citing Heraclitus). That the gods were incorporeal, lacked human feelings, and needed no sacrifices was a philosophical commonplace.[26] Later Christian criticism of anthropomorphism was as much indebted to Greek criticism of the traditional gods as to Jewish polemic against idolatry.[27] Nevertheless, despite the fine-grained conceptuality of the philosophic discussion about the gods, the importance to city and state of thriving cults was not in dispute. The fading glory of the Athenian intellectual tradition sat comfortably in a city which was "full of idols" (Acts 17.16). In contrast, Jewish refusal to imag(in)e the form of God and antipathy to worship characterized by devotion to humanly crafted images was a matter of some bewilderment to most Greeks and Romans. The Roman poet Juvenal, writing early in the second century, was probably typical when he satirized the nebulous character of his judaizing compatriots, "who worship nothing but the clouds and the *numen* of heaven" (*Satires* 14.97).

It is the exclusiveness of Israel's monotheism, therefore, which marked it out in the ancient world, and the intolerance of its attack on idolatry. We need not doubt that Paul shared that intolerance of all such debasement of the image of God: "claiming to be wise they became fools, and changed the glory of the incorruptible God for the mere likeness of corruptible humanity, birds, beasts, and reptiles" (Rom. 1.22-23).

b) Some would find another qualification of Jewish monotheism from the Jewish side, particularly in the explosion of intermediary figures which seem to be interposed between God and the cosmos in the Second Temple period[28] and in the hints of Jewish syncretism which have been detected in

---

Ahuramazda, and the triple form Zeus Helios Sarapis (LSJ, *Zeus* II; H. Kleinknecht, *theos, TDNT* 3.76; MacMullen, *Paganism* 83-84, 90).

24. Augustine recalls that Varro (2nd century BCE) "thought the God of the Jews to be the same as Jupiter" (*GLAJJ* 1.209-10).

25. This is the root of the popular prejudice against Christians as atheists, already in *Martyrdom of Polycarp* 3.2; 9.2.

26. MacMullen, *Paganism* 76.

27. Grant, *Gods* 76-77. See also the extracts in Long/Sedley, §23.

28. Bousset/Gressmann, 319; Hengel, *Judaism* 1.155. Most extreme is M. Barker, *The Great Angel: A Study of Israel's Second God* (London: SPCK, 1992).

diaspora Judaism.[29] But although there does seem to have been a rapid expansion in the angelic population in the two hundred years before Paul, this does not constitute any real threat to Jewish monotheism.[30] It was, after all, one way for Jewish apologists to conceptualize the gods of other nations — to regard them as part of Yahweh's heavenly retinue[31] or as angels appointed by Yahweh to rule over these nations.[32] At the same time there is a repeated warning in Jewish writings of the period that angels are not to be regarded as gods or to be worshiped.[33] So, too, within Judaism, the figure of divine Wisdom[34] is not a divine being independent of God, however vigorous the poetic imagery used of her. She is in fact another vivid way of speaking of God's immanence, without detracting from his transcendence. For example, in Wisdom 10ff. Wisdom is portrayed as Yahweh's care for the patriarchs and for Israel.[35] Less vivid, but playing the same role as the wisdom of God, were similar circumlocutions like the spirit of God and the glory of God.[36]

As for the tradition of syncretistic Judaism in the diaspora, once we have discounted extreme cases like Elymas in Cyprus, the "false prophet and magus" (Acts 13.6-8), and the seven sons of Sceva, "a Jewish high priest" (Acts 19.14), the evidence is very slight and at best ambiguous. In particular, despite the long-running speculation of a syncretistic Jewish worship of angels in Asia Minor, the data are probably better explained in terms of pagan

29. Particularly in reference to the "false teaching" at Colossae; see, e.g., my *Colossians* 27-28; also *GLAJJ* 1.359; C. E. Arnold, *The Colossian Syncretism: The Interface between Christianity and Folk Belief at Colossae* (WUNT 2.77; Tübingen: Mohr, 1995). Contrast Hengel and Schwemer, *Paul between Damascus and Antioch* 76-80.

30. Wicks, *Doctrine of God* 122-28; "in each century the clear doctrine of the majority of the authors, whatever their angelology, is that of a God who is in unmediated contact with His creation" (124). See further Hurtado, *One God* (§10 n. 1) 17-39.

31. E.g., Exod. 15.11; Pss. 29.1; 82.1; 89.6-7; 95.3; 103.21; 148.2. See further Caird, *Principalities* (§5 n. 1) 1-4, 11-12; Wink, *Unmasking* (§5 n. 1) 109-11.

32. Deut. 32.8-9; Dan. 10.13, 20-21; Sir. 17.17; *Jub.* 15.31; *1 Enoch* 89.59-60; 90.22-25; Targum Pseudo-Jonathan on Gen. 11.7-8. The idea was taken over into the Christian era; so, e.g., Emperor Julian in his oration against the "Galileans": "over each nation is a national god, with an angel acting as his agent . . ." (MacMullen, *Paganism* 82); other examples in Wink, *Unmasking* (§5 n. 1) 92.

33. *Apoc. Zeph.* 6.15; *Apoc. Abr.* 17.2; Philo, *Fuga* 212; *Som.* 1.238. See further L. T. Stuckenbruck, *Angel Veneration and Christology: A Study in Early Judaism and in the Christology of the Apocalypse of John* (WUNT 2.70; Tübingen: Mohr, 1995).

34. Prov. 8.22-31; Sir. 24.1-22; Bar. 3.9-37; Wis. 6.12–11.1; *1 Enoch* 42; Philo, in several passages (see my *Christology* 169, 171, 173-74).

35. Dunn, *Christology* 168-76, 215-30. See further below §11.1.

36. See also Kleinknecht, *TDNT* 3.98-99; Casey, *Jewish Prophet* (§10 n. 1); Hurtado, *One God* (§10 n. 1) ch. 2.

borrowing of only half-understood Jewish concepts.[37] Such a thesis certainly fits best with the consistent evidence of Jewish communities eager to maintain their ethnic identity and ancestral customs. The sounder testimony, then, is that of Josephus, who affirms without qualification that "to acknowledge God as one is common to all the Hebrews" (*Ant.* 5.112). And Tacitus, the most savage of Roman critics of the Jews, writing early in the second century, equally is in no doubt and notes with grudging respect:

> The Jews conceive of one god only, and that with the mind only; they regard as impious those who make from perishable materials representations of gods in man's image; that supreme and eternal being is to them incapable of representation and without end. Therefore they set up no statues in their cities, still less in their temples; this flattery is not paid their kings, nor this honour given to the Caesars (*Hist.* 5.5.4).

Paul, too, evidently had no doubts about Jewish monotheism in his own continued affirmation of the *Shema*. The issue of how he saw Jesus, now exalted as Lord, fitting into this monotheism, and particularly how he made use of the figure of divine Wisdom in speaking of Jesus as Lord, are questions to which we must return.[38] For the moment we need only speak of Paul as heir of a consistently affirmed and clearly perceived Jewish faith in God as one.

c) Within the context of such discussions Paul's own allusions to wider beliefs about God are fascinating and at times puzzling. Thus he carries on from his confession of God as one in 1 Corinthians 8 with the ambivalent comment: "for, even if there are so-called gods, whether in heaven or on earth, as indeed there are gods many and lords many, yet for us there is one God, the Father" (1 Cor. 8.5-6). Paul's language leaves unclear whether he intends to carry over the qualification ("so-called gods") into the following clause or wishes to affirm the existence of other gods as such. Earlier he was more forthright: "every so-called god" (2 Thes. 2.4); the gods worshiped by Gentiles were "beings that by nature are no gods" (Gal. 4.8).[39] His ambiguity in 1 Corinthians 8 may therefore be deliberate, either because he himself was

---

37. See particularly A. R. R. Shepherd, "Pagan Cults of Angels in Roman Asia Minor," *Talanta* 12-13 (1980-81) 77-101 (here 94-99); P. Trebilco, *Jewish Communities in Asia Minor* (SNTSMS 69; Cambridge: Cambridge University, 1991) 137; S. Mitchell, *Anatolia: Land, Men and Gods in Asia Minor,* 2 vols. (Oxford: Clarendon, 1993) 2.46. Arnold (above n. 29) ignores the characteristically traditional Jewish features in the letter which indicate how mainstream was the Jewish threat to the Christian house church(es) of Colossae; see further my "The Colossian Philosophy: A Confident Jewish Aplogia," *Bib* 76 (1995) 153-81.

38. See below particularly §10.5.

39. A characteristically Jewish assertion (2 Chron. 13.9; Isa. 37.19; Jer. 2.11; 5.7; 16.20; Wis. 12.27; Ep. Jer. 23, 29, 51-52, 64-65, 69, 72).

uncertain how much to concede or because he wrote out of pastoral sensitivity, *ad hominem,* to give as much weight as he could to the fears of the "weak" in Corinth.[40] Certainly he could hardly but be aware of the many gods worshiped in the cities he visited. His intention, however, seems to have been to maximize the force of the confession of God as one, which he shared with the Corinthians, by affirming it boldly in the face of these other more common beliefs. So what if others so believe! It does not affect the truth given to us that "God is one"!

Equally ambivalent is the implication in the latter stages of the same discussion that idols are indwelt by demons (1 Cor. 10.20-21). Again we have to ask: was Paul simply reflecting the real fears of the "weak" members of the Corinthian church,[41] naming realities of which he himself was less than certain? Or indeed, was his use of the term "demons" simply the result of his deliberate echo of Deut. 32.17, with the further echo in 10.22 of Deut. 32.21 implying that the idol is "no god" (Deut. 32.21)? In this connection it should not escape notice that "demons" are never mentioned again in the undisputed letters of Paul,[42] nor does Paul anywhere speak of exorcism.[43] Evidently, then, he could leave ambiguous the status of other gods/demons, for what mattered were two things most of all: (1) The one ultimate reality is God; so *anything* which detracts from that, even as an empty "nothing" (idol) still detracts from the one ultimate reality of God. (2) Idols/demons have an all too real *existential* reality — whether merely the human projections of other gods (above §2.2), or objectively real demons — and that existential reality can be so crippling and enslaving that it must be given no place.[44]

"The Satan" appears more frequently.[45] But the consistent use of the

---

40. See, e.g., the discussion in Conzelmann, *1 Corinthians* 143, and Fee, *1 Corinthians* 372-73. Paul "is not interested in the ontological existence of other gods, but in the existential fact that whatever is worshiped is indeed, for that person, a god" (Wink, *Unmasking* [§5 n. 1] 113; also 125).

41. In Ps. 96.5 the LXX (95.5) translates Hebrew *'elilim* ("idols") as *daimonia* ("demons"). Cf. Philo: "It is Moses' custom to give the name of angels to those whom other philosophers call demons (or spirits), souls, that is, which fly and hover in the air. . . . So if you realize that souls and demons and angels are but different names for the same underlying object, you will cast from you that most grievous burden, the fear of demons or superstitition" (*Gigant.* 6, 16). On demons in popular religion of the time see MacMullen, *Paganism* 79-80; and further at §5.1.

42. But note 1 Tim. 4.1.

43. Though cf. Acts 16.18; 19.13.

44. See further below §24.7.

45. Rom. 16.20; 1 Cor. 5.5; 7.5; 2 Cor. 2.11; 11.14; 12.7; 1 Thes. 2.18; 2 Thes. 2.9; also 1 Tim. 1.20; 5.15. Note also "the god of this age" (2 Cor. 4.4), "Beliar" (2 Cor. 6.15), "the evil one" (2 Thes. 3.3; Eph. 6.16), "the ruler of the power of the air" (Eph. 2.2), and "the devil" (Eph. 4.27; 6.11; 1 Tim. 3.6-7; 2 Tim. 2.26).

definite article probably reflects the continuing influence of the original concept, that of a force hostile to God but permitted so to act by God to serve his will.[46] Hence the inference of 1 Cor. 5.5 — a member of the congregation handed over to the Satan, for the salvation of his spirit (similarly 1 Tim. 1.20);[47] and of 2 Cor. 12.7 — "a messenger of the Satan," giving Paul occasion to learn one of his most valuable lessons (12.9-10). In Romans the only reference is the confident hope that "the God of peace will crush the Satan under your feet speedily." Earlier in Romans Paul mentions other hostile heavenly powers only to assert their powerlessness before God in Christ (Rom. 8.38-39).

There are matters here to which we will have to return when we consider Paul's conception of evil.[48] For the moment it is enough to note that whatever reality such forces had for Paul, they evidently did not compromise his monotheism. Paul's confidence in God as one remained unshaken.

§2.4 God and the cosmos

It is clear from the early verses of Romans that God's role as creator is another fundamental taken-for-granted of Paul's theology: God has been knowable "from the creation of the world" (Rom. 1.20); he is the creator (1.25).[49] This was a less controversial aspect of Paul's theism. The concept of creation and of a creator, or at least a divine architect, could easily hold its place within the range of Greco-Roman religion and philosophy.[50] Paul thus had no difficulty in making use at this point of what should probably be regarded as Stoic terminology — in particular, the contrast of the invisible discerned by the mind (1.20). The terms "eternal" and "deity" (1.20) had already been drawn from Stoic thought into the Jewish wisdom tradition by the Wisdom of Solomon and Philo.[51] And the talk of creation using the prepositions "from," "through," and "to" (as in Rom. 11.36) was again

46. Job 1–2; Zech. 3.1-2; 1 Chron. 21.1 as an interpretation of 2 Sam. 24.1.
47. Wink, *Unmasking* (§5 n. 1) — "Satan is the means of his deliverance!" (16).
48. See further below §5.
49. See also Rom. 8.19-22, 39; 1 Cor. 11.9; Col. 1.15-16, 23; 3.10; Eph. 3.9; and the matching concept of "new creation" (2 Cor. 5.17; Gal. 6.15).
50. Plato's *Timaeus* was a fundamental text in Greek intellectual thought. See also Kleinknecht, *TDNT* 3.73-74 and H. Sasse, *kosmos, TDNT* 3.874-80. Philo's portrayal of creation in *De Opificio Mundi* was heavily influenced by middle Platonic thought. See further J. Dillon, *The Middle Platonists* (London: Duckworth/Ithaca: Cornell University, 1977) 155-78.
51. *Aidios* — cf. Wis. 2.23 and 7.26; *theiotēs* — in LXX only in Wis. 18.19. See further Lietzmann, *Römer* 31-32; W. Michaelis, *aoratos, TDNT* 5.368-69.

typically Stoic.[52] Even here, however, we should probably recognize distinctively Jewish influence in the exclusive use of "create/creation" for the act and fact of *divine* creation, reflecting the same exclusiveness in the use of the Hebrew *bara'* ("create"), in contrast to the less discriminating usage of Greek thought.[53]

A sharper contrast can be seen between the characteristically Greek view of the cosmos and the characteristically Jewish view. In the former, the fundamental Platonic distinction between the visible world accessible to the senses and the world of ideas accessible only through the mind was of widespread influence.[54] The tendency was for the two to be set in sharp antithesis, the material world in all its corruptibility regarded as much inferior to the imperishable world of the mind. It was but a step for the physical to be despised, the material to be regarded as a burden and a downward drag, and salvation to be understood as an escape from materiality.[55] There is something of the same instinct in the Jewish antithesis between creator and creation, in the abandoning of the anthropomorphism of the early Pentateuchal traditions, and in the classic utterance of Isa. 31.3 — "The Egyptians are human, and not God; their horses are flesh, and not spirit."[56] And Paul is not uninfluenced by this antithesis himself — a subject to which we must return in §3.

What is significant at this point, however, is Paul's essentially Jewish conception of a cosmos which was created good (Gen. 1.26-31). Humankind is still the image of God (1 Cor. 11.7). "The earth is [still] the Lord's, and everything in it" (1 Cor. 10.26, citing Ps. 24.1). "Nothing is profane/unclean in itself" (Rom. 14.14). Even more explicit is 1 Timothy: "Everything created by God is good" (1 Tim. 4.4). So the created realm still speaks of God (Rom. 1.19-20),[57] and, despite its present subjection to futility, it will share in the final redemption (Rom. 8.19-23). It is no surprise, then, that God's act in raising from the dead, the climax of his salvation, is of a piece with his act

---

52. E.g. Pseudo-Aristotle, *De Mundo* 6; Philo, *Cher.* 125-26; Seneca, *Epistle* 65.8. See further my *Romans* 701.

53. See my *Romans* 57-58.

54. The influence is particularly clear in Philo's *Opif.* 16-44.

55. Classically in the tag *sōma sēma,* "the body a tomb (of the soul)," and in the much-quoted saying of Empedocles about "the alien garb of the flesh" *(allognos chiton sarkos)* cited by E. Schweizer, *TDNT* 7.1026 and 1027 respectively.

56. Wis. 9.15 ("a perishable body weighs down the soul, and this earthly tent burdens the thoughtful mind") illustrates well how far Greek perception penetrated Hellenistic Judaism.

57. Echoing Wis. 13.1, but also a common perception in Stoic thought; see, e.g., Pseudo-Aristotle, *De Mundo* 6 and Philo, *Spec. Leg.* 1.35; and further Bornkamm, "Revelation" 50-53.

in creating: "he who gives life to the dead"[58] is "he who calls things that have no existence into existence" (Rom. 4.17).[59] Subsequently the Pauline thought is developed in terms of a still clearer integration of creation and salvation (Col. 1.15-20; v. 20 — "all things" reconciled to God),[60] and of a renewal in accordance with the image of the creator (3.10; similarly Eph. 4.24).

Also characteristically Jewish is Paul's conception of the divine ordering of the cosmos and of human society (Rom. 13.1-5).[61] As already noted, the will of God was a determining factor in Paul's own life and plans (Rom. 1.10; 15.32).[62] With the devout "Jew," it was of the highest importance for Paul to "discern the will of God" (Rom. 2.18; 12.2). To be sure, the pious qualification "God willing" was in widespread use.[63] But whereas Greek tradition allowed for the arbitrary and inexplicable with its notion of fate, Paul, as with Jewish thought generally, courted the problem of theodicy by attributing all to the divine "purpose" (Rom. 8.28-30; 9.11)[64] and "will" (9.19). Nor did he flinch from the harshness of the corollary: the divine potter has the "right" "to make from the same lump of clay one vessel for honourable use and another for dishonourable use" (9.19-22).[65] His final solution to such a puzzling riddle of history and experience was the apocalyptic conviction that God's purpose was a "mystery," hidden from the ages and revealed to only a privileged few (Rom. 11.25).[66] Within that mystery is held together an original call which is "irrevocable" (11.29) and an ultimate purpose of mercy (11.30-32).

58. The language echoes the second of the Eighteen Benedictions: "you make the dead alive." In Paul note its repeated use in 1 Cor. 15.22, 36, 45.

59. Both elements of the latter phrase are distinctively Jewish: creation as an effective "calling" (Isa. 41.4; 48.13; Wis. 11.25; *2 Baruch* 21.4); belief that God created *ex nihilo* (2 Macc. 7.28; Philo regularly, e.g., *Opif.* 81 and *Leg. All.* 3.10; *Joseph and Aseneth* 12.2; *2 Baruch* 21.4; 48.8; *2 Enoch* 24.2). Paul in fact echoes Philo here: "he called things that have no existence into being" (*Spec. Leg.* 4.187). And the thought of both phrases echoes *Joseph and Aseneth* 8.9.

60. Cf. Isa. 11.6-9; 65.17, 25; *Jub.* 1.29; 23.26-29; *1 Enoch* 91.16-17; Philo, *Spec. Leg.* 2.192. See further L. Hartman, "Universal Reconciliation (Col. 1.20)," *SNTU* 10 (1985) 109-21.

61. See below §24.2.

62. See also 2 Cor. 8.5; Gal. 1.4; Col. 4.12; 1 Thes. 4.3; 5.18; also Eph. 1.5, 9, 11; 5.17; 6.6.

63. See Deissmann, *Bible Studies* 252; BAGD, *thelō* 2.

64. Note the frequency of *pro-* ("before") words attributed to God in this section — Rom. 8.28-29; 9.11, 23; 11.2; also 1 Cor. 2.7; Gal. 3.8; Eph. 1.5, 11; 2.10; 3.11.

65. The imagery was popular in Jewish tradition (see particularly Isa. 29.16; 45.9; Jer. 18.1-6; Sir. 33.13); Paul no doubt had Wis. 15.7 in mind; see further my *Romans* 557.

66. See further my *Romans* 678.

Bound up with this was a different view of time. The Greeks more typically thought of time as cyclical,[67] the relation of the material world and the world of the mind as more fixed.[68] In contrast, Jews saw time more naturally as a progression of ages, and looked for the age to come to release them from the evils of the present. Paul shared the latter view. He thought naturally of "this age" as something inferior: "do not be conformed to this age" (Rom. 12.2); "the wisdom of this age" is folly beside the wisdom of God (1 Cor. 2.6); the present age is evil (Gal. 1.4).[69] Implicit is the thought of an age to come, as his benedictions also indicate: God as blessed "into the age," or "into the ages," or "into the ages of the ages,"[70] echoing the prayer of the psalmist.[71] So also the process of salvation is in accord with God's timetable. Christ has come at "the fullness of time" (Gal. 4.4). "The appointed time has been shortened" (1 Cor. 7.29). "The end(s) of the ages" has come upon him and his readers (1 Cor. 10.11).[72] Inevitably, then, the climax of all things will be "God, the all in all" (1 Cor. 15.28).

Of a piece with all this is the thought of a final judgment for the cosmos, presumably to bring "the present evil age" to a close, and of God as final judge. The concept was familiar in Greek thought, but particularly prominent in the Jewish tradition.[73] For Paul it was simply axiomatic, as the opening chapters of Romans bear ample testimony: "we know that the judgment of God is in accordance with truth" (2.2-3); there will be a day of wrath when God will judge the secrets of humankind (2.5-8, 16); judgment will be in accordance with the law (2.12-15); all the world is liable to God's judgment (3.19). Not least of importance for Paul at this point are two fundamental axioms of the Jewish concept of divine justice: that God "will render to each according to his works" (2.6)[74] and that God's judgment will be impartial

---

67. I refer particularly to the Stoics' conception of everlasting recurrence (see Long/Sedley 1.308-13), but also to the cycle of the seasons mythicized in the mystery cults.

68. Particularly in the various forms of Platonism.

69. See also Rom. 8.18; 1 Cor. 1.20; 2.8; 3.18-19; 2 Cor. 4.4; Eph. 2.2; 5.16.

70. Rom. 1.25; 9.5; 11.36; (16.27); 2 Cor. 9.9; 11.31; Gal. 1.5; Phil. 4.20; also 1 Tim. 1.17 and 2 Tim. 4.18. The contrast between a present age dominated by evil and an age to come is explicitly drawn only in the later Jewish apocalypses *4 Ezra* and *2 Baruch,* but it is a natural development of such seminal passages as the visions in Daniel 2 and 7, was implicit in Qumran's talk of "the time of wickedness" (CD 6.10, 14; 12.23; 15.7; 1QpHab 5.7), and was probably already part of the Jesus tradition (Matt. 12.32; Mark 10.30; Luke 20.34-35).

71. Pss. 41.13; 72.19; 88.52; 106.48.

72. Cf. particularly 1QpHab 7; *4 Ezra* 6.7; 11.44. But the plural "ends" in 1 Cor. 10.11 causes some puzzlement.

73. See documentation in my *Romans* 80, 84.

74. Ps. 62.12 and Prov. 24.12; but also Job 34.11; Jer. 17.10; Hos. 12.2; Sir. 16.12-14; *1 Enoch* 100.7; elsewhere in Paul 2 Cor. 5.10; Col. 3.25; also 2 Tim. 4.14.

(2.11).[75] God's wrath must be just, "otherwise how will God judge the world?" (3.5-6).[76]

Correlated with this also is the first big idea which Paul expounds in Romans: that the wrath of God is already being revealed from heaven (1.18). The concept was again familiar in the ancient world: divine indignation as heaven's response to human impiety or as a way of explaining communal catastrophes or unlooked-for tragedy.[77] But for Paul, as for his Jewish forbears,[78] "the wrath of God" here is hardly different from the wrath of final judgment, just and true.[79] And from the indictment which explains 1.18, it is clear that for Paul "the wrath of God" denotes the inescapable, divinely ordered moral constitution of human society,[80] "God's reaction to evil and sin."[81] God's righteousness as creator, the obligations appropriate to him as creator, has determined that human actions have moral consequences.[82] Thus the consequence of disowning the dependence of the creature on the creator has been a futility of thought and a darkening of experience (1.21). Focusing reverence on the creature rather than the creator has resulted in idolatry, debased sexuality, and the daily nastiness of disordered society (1.22-31). God's wrath, we might say, is his handing over of his human creation to themselves. Hence the threefold repeated judgment, "wherefore God handed them over" — "in the desires of their hearts" (1.24), "to disgraceful passions" (1.26), "to a disqualified mind" (1.28).[83] Evidently for Paul this is the same divine wrath which will be manifest in the day of judgment: we know

75. Deut. 10.17; 2 Chron. 19.7; Sir. 35.12-13; *Jub.* 5.16; 21.4; 30.16; 33.18; *Pss. Sol.* 2.18; elsewhere in Paul Col. 3.25 and Eph. 6.9. See further particularly J. Bassler, *Divine Impartiality: Paul and a Theological Axiom* (SBLDS 59; Chico: Scholars, 1982).

76. Elsewhere in Paul: a "day" of judgment (1 Cor. 1.8; 5.5; Phil. 1.6, 10; 2.16; 1 Thes. 5.2, 4); a day of "wrath" (Rom. 5.9; 9.22; 1 Thes. 1.10; 5.9).

77. H. Kleinknecht, et al., *orgē, TDNT* 5.383-409.

78. See, e.g., J. Fichtner, *orgē, TDNT* 5.401.

79. It is the same term which is repeated consistently through the opening chapters of Romans — 1.18; 2.5, 8; 3,5; 4.15; 5.9.

80. Cf. Dodd, *Romans* 20-24; G. H. C. Macgregor, "The Concept of the Wrath of God in the New Testament," *NTS* 7 (1960-61) 101-9 (here 105); A. T. Hanson, *The Wrath of the Lamb* (London: SPCK, 1957) 85, 110; Whiteley, *Theology* 61-72; Ridderbos, *Paul* 108-10. But the thought should not be reduced to a deist view: God is active in sustaining this moral structure of his creation. See further below §18.6.

81. Fitzmyer, *Paul* 42.

82. Note the deliberate parallel between the revelation of God's righteousness (1.17) and the revelation of his wrath (1.18). For the meaning of "God's righteousness" see below §14.2.

83. This understanding of God's wrath as consequence and outworking of disobedience helps explain the otherwise difficult 1 Thes. 2.16. Feine, *Theologie* 307-8, compares Pss. 79.5; 103.9 and Isa. 57.16 and notes that Rom. 9.22 is qualified by 11.32. See also Col. 3.6 and my *Colossians* 216-17.

the character of God's final judgment from the moral constitution of the world he has created.

Here, too, then, even though Greek and Jewish thought overlapped considerably in their conceptions of God's relation to the world, Paul's theism is typically Jewish. And not as an abstract theory about God, but as a practical way of understanding and prescribing human responsibility towards creation, towards others, and towards oneself.

§2.5 The God of Israel

Implicit in all that has been said so far is the fact that this one God, creator and judge of all, was also understood to be the God of Israel. It is not simply that the one God was confessed by Israel (in the *Shema*). The point is rather that Israel believed itself chosen by God to be his own (classically in Deut. 7.6-8). This was a major part of the offence of Jewish monotheism: that Yahweh was not simply the national manifestation of the supreme God such as *all* peoples could claim for themselves. On the contrary, Israel alone had the true perception of God because the one God had given Israel the special revelation of himself through the fathers and Moses and because of all the nations God had taken only Israel as his own. The claim was classically rendered in Deut. 32.8-9:[84]

> When the Most High gave each nation its heritage,
>   when he divided humankind,
> he fixed the boundaries of the peoples
>   according to the numbers of the sons of God;
> but the LORD's own portion was his people,
>   Jacob his allotted share.

This claim naturally set up a tension in Israel's theology, an unavoidable tension between particularism (God of Israel) and universalism (only one God). It is evident in such prophecies as Amos 9.7 ("Did I not bring Israel up from Egypt, and the Philistines from Caphtor, the Arameans from Kir?"), and Jonah (the God of Israel equally concerned for the people of Nineveh).[85] We could also mention John the Baptist: "Do not think to say among yourselves, 'We have Abraham as our father'; for I say to you that God is able from these stones to raise up children for Abraham" (Matt.

---

84. For the thought of Israel as God's inheritance see, e.g., 1 Kings 8, 51, 53; Pss. 33.12; 74.2; Isa. 6.17; Jer. 10.16; Mic. 7.18; Sir. 24.8; *Pss. Sol.* 9.8-9.

85. For God as the God of all nations, see also Ps. 145.9; Wis. 11.22-24; *1 Enoch* 84.2.

3.9/Luke 3.8). It was implicit also in the tension between the obligations of God both as creator and as Israel's God and in the claim that the God of Israel judged impartially. The point to be noted here, however, is that Paul was fully aware of that tension and was able to exploit it with effect at a key point in his argument in Romans: "Is God the God of Jews only? Is he not also God of Gentiles? Yes, of Gentiles too, since, after all, 'God is one' " (Rom. 3.29-30). That was not a proposition from which most Jews of Paul's time would have dissented: too much Christian apologetic has assumed an unjustified antithesis between Jewish particularism and Christian universalism.[86] In this case it was the immediate corollary drawn by Paul, exploiting that same tension, which was more controversial: that this one God of all justifies Jew and Gentile alike by faith (3.30).

It was equally important for Paul that the same claim could be expressed alternatively: Gentiles were now coming to share in the blessings promised by God particularly to (and through) Israel (Gal. 3.6-14); Gentiles who have not known God[87] have now been given share in Israel's knowledge (4.8-9).[88] Hence Paul's readiness to address the largely Gentile congregations in Rome and elsewhere as "beloved by God,[89] called to be saints,"[90] "God's elect,"[91] that is, using epithets which had marked out the distinctiveness of

86. Dahl's protest at this point has been too much ignored: "No Jew or Jewish Christian would deny that God, being one, is not only the God of the Jews but also the God of the Gentiles. . . . both Jewish and Christian monotheism are particular as well as universal" ("One God" 189, 191). See also A. F. Segal, "Universalism in Judaism and Christianity," in Engberg-Pedersen, ed., *Paul in His Hellenistic Context* 1-29. On the final acceptability of Gentiles as "righteous Gentiles" see particularly T. L. Donaldson, "Proselytes or 'Righteous Gentiles'? The Status of Gentiles in Eschatological Pilgrimage Patterns of Thought," *JSP* 7 (1990) 3-27; and below §6 n. 50. See also §24 n. 35 below.

87. Cf. also 1 Thes. 4.5; 2 Thes. 1.8. That the nations do not know God is a classically Jewish perception (Job 18.21; Ps. 79.6; Jer. 10.25; Wis. 13.1; 14.22). See further Dupont, *Gnosis* 1-8.

88. The theme is best expressed in the summary of Pauline thought which is Ephesians: no longer "alienated from the commonwealth of Israel, strangers to the covenants of promise" and "without God in the world," but "fellow citizens with the saints and members of the household of God" (Eph. 2.12, 19).

89. E.g., Deut. 32.15; 33.26; Pss. 60.5; 108.6; Isa. 5.1, 7; 44.2; Jer. 12.7; 31.3; Bar. 3.36; the LXX renders "Jeshurun" as *ēgapēmenos* ("beloved"). Elsewhere in Paul note Rom. 9.25; 11.28; 1 Thes. 1.4; 2 Thes. 2.13.

90. "The saints" = Israel (e.g., Pss. 16.3; 34.9; 74.3; Isa. 4.3; Dan. 7.18, 21-22; Tob. 8.15; Wis. 18.9; 1QSb 3.2; 1QM 3.5; 10.10) — a characteristic feature of Paul's address (1 Cor. 1.2; 2 Cor. 1.1; Phil. 1.1; Col. 1.2; also Eph. 1.1).

91. Rom. 1.7; 8.33; Col. 3.12. Cf., e.g., 1 Chron. 16.13; Ps. 105.6; Isa. 43.20; 65.22; Tob. 8.15; Sir. 46.1; Wis. 4.15; *Jub.* 1.29; *1 Enoch* 1.3, 8; 5.7-8; CD 4.3-4; 1QM 12.1; 1QpHab 10.13. See further my *Romans* 502. It is a primary concern of Paul's argument in Romans 9–11 to clarify what Israel's election means for Israel; see further below §19.

Israel's self-understanding. Gentiles share in God's blessings by sharing in the special status God gave to Israel.

In effect this becomes the Pauline version of the tension within Israel's theology between particularism and universalism. How could God be the God of Israel and the God of Gentile and Jew alike at one and the same time? The tension is evident in Paul's use of what seems to have already become a traditional formulation — "inherit the kingdom of God."[92] For the language of inheritance inevitably evokes the promise to the patriarchs foundational to Israel's self-understanding (the inheritance of the land of Israel).[93] But the concept of God's kingdom as it appears in Paul seems to lack all national features and to have become a universal expression of God's rule.[94] Perhaps we may see here an echo of what was Jesus' central theme (the kingdom of God), in view particularly of traditions like Matt. 8.11-12/Luke 13.28-29 and Mark 12.9, in which the adaptation of the Jewish tension is already evident.[95]

In Romans the tension comes to poignant expression in one of the main subthemes of the letter: the "faithfulness of God." It was the question posed immediately by Paul's indictment of the "Jew" in Romans 2: "What then is the advantage of the Jew? . . . Has their unfaithfulness rendered null and void the faithfulness of God?" (3.1-3). In other words, could Paul only defend his gospel for Gentiles by denying that God remained committed to Israel? His denial was, as usual, emphatic: *mē genoito* — "By no means. God forbid." But the tension remained. Indeed, the theological argument of the letter reaches its climax precisely as the attempt to square the circle: that God is both a God who elects one and rejects the other (9.6-13) and the God who will have mercy on all (11.25-32). The God of Israel is the one God, is the God of all. And in his concluding summary Paul seeks to maintain the tension by declaring that "Christ became servant of circumcision for the sake of God's faithfulness" (Rom. 15.8).[96] Christiaan Beker is thus justified in seeing in this resolution a

---

92. Matt. 25.34; 1 Cor. 6.9-10; 15.50; Gal. 5.21; also Eph. 5.5; Jas. 2.5.

93. Gen. 15.7-8; 28.4; Deut. 1.39; 2.12; etc.; see further J. Herrmann and W. Foerster, *TDNT* 3.769-80.

94. Contrast the fact that in Daniel 7 the kingdom is given to "the saints of the Most High," to Israel (7.25-27). Is there an echo of this in Col. 4.11, where Paul seems to associate Jews particularly with the kingdom (cf. Acts 28.23, 31)?

95. For Matt. 8.11-12/Luke 13.28-29, cf. particularly Ps. 107.3; Isa. 43.5-6; 49.12; Mal. 1.11; Bar. 4.37. For Mark 12.9, cf. Isa. 5.1-7.

96. The fact that the same Hebrew concept, "faithfulness" *(emet, emunah)*, underlies *alētheia* (truth) and *pistis* (faithfulness) obscures the importance of the theme for Romans: *alētheia* (Rom. 1.18, 25; 2.2, 8, 20; 3.7; 15.8); *pistis* (Rom. 1.17; 3.3, 25). See my *Romans* 44, 133, 847 and on 15.11 (850); see also below on "the righteousness of God" (§14.2). For the "faithfulness of God" elsewhere in Paul see 1 Cor. 1.9; 10.13; 2 Cor. 1.18; 1 Thes. 5.24; cf. 2 Thes. 3.3 and 2 Tim. 2.13.

key to the coherent theme of Paul's gospel, which he postulates as the final triumph of God.[97]

§2.6 God in experience

The ancient philosophical debates about the existence and nature of God/the gods were much like philosophical debates ever since.[98] The ancient Hebrew convictions, however, had always been rooted more deeply in experience of revelation — God experienced in summons and call (archetypically of Abraham and Moses), in prophetic inspiration, in the emotion-stirring imagery of the psalmist, and in the wisdom given from on high, not to mention the visions and mystical experiences of the apocalypses.

Paul too was familiar with such debates. Luke's portrayal of his speeches in Acts 14.15-17 and 17.24-29 is often questioned because they indicate a more positive "natural theology" than the indictment of Rom. 1.18-32 implies. But arguments from the natural order were as much Jewish as Greek,[99] and Romans 1 shows a similar willingness to use characteristically Stoic categories. We have already noted "eternal" and "deity" in 1.20;[100] and in 1.26 and 28 the ideas of living "in accordance with nature" and of actions which are "fitting" are characteristically, even distinctively, Stoic.[101] Nevertheless, it is true that even here Paul proceeds from a "knowability of God" which is primarily dependent on divine revelation: "what can be known about God is evident in them [unrighteous humankind], for God has shown it to them" (1.19).[102]

The very term "knowledge" brings out the point being made here. For whereas in Greek thought the term characteristically denotes a rational perception, the Hebrew concept also embraced the knowing of personal relationship. Bultmann put it in his own terms: the Hebrew usage "is much broader

97. Beker, *Paul* 77-89, 328-37. But Klumbies persists in setting Paul's Christ-grounded talk of God in "diametrical contrast to the Jewish understanding of God" (*Rede* 205; see also his conclusion — 245-46, 251-52). Moxnes's treatment is more balanced (*Theology in Conflict*).

98. See particularly the debates in Cicero, *On the Nature of the Gods*.

99. As the Jewish character of the Acts 17 speech indicates: vv. 24-25 — Exod. 20.11; Ps. 145.6; Isa. 42.5; 57.15-16; Wis. 9.1-3, 9; vv. 26-27 — Gen. 1.14; Deut. 32.8; Ps. 74.17; Wis. 7.18; vv. 27-28 — Ps. 145.18; Jer. 23.23.

100. See above §2.4.

101. *Physis* ("nature") is not a Hebrew concept, but primarily Greek and typically Stoic: "to live in accordance with nature" was the Stoic ideal. And "what is fitting" is a Stoic phrase, a technical term in philosophy (see further H. Köster, *physis, TDNT* 9.263-66 and H. Schlier, *kathēkō, TDNT* 3.438-40).

102. See further Dupont, *Gnosis* 20-30.

than the Greek, and the element of objective verification is less prominent than that of detecting or feeling or learning by experience."[103] So with the knowledge of God. It is not merely a theoretical acknowledgment that theism is a viable intellectual position. To know God is to worship him (1.21).[104] As Paul had noted earlier: human wisdom is inadequate to achieve that knowledge (1 Cor. 1.21); to know God is to be known by him, a two-way relationship of acknowledgment and obligation (Gal. 4.9). As in the (Jewish) scriptures,[105] the "knowledge of God" includes experience of God's dealings,[106] the two-way knowing of personal relationship.[107]

At this point we should recall how fundamental to Paul's theology was the experience of his conversion. For Paul remembered it as an experience of revelation. The gospel came to him "through revelation," when God chose "to reveal his son in (or to) me" (Gal. 1.12, 16). "The God who said, 'Out of darkness shall light shine' has shone in our hearts to bring the illumination of the knowledge of the glory of God" (2 Cor. 4.6).[108] This sense of knowledge from God as personal revelation is clearly present also in 1 Cor. 2.7-13 — the hidden wisdom of God "revealed to us through the Spirit," on the analogy of individual self-knowledge and inspiration. And something of this will no doubt be implicit in the double reference to divine revelation with which Paul, no doubt deliberately, begins his theological exposition in Romans (Rom. 1.17, 18).

In the Corinthian correspondence Paul also recalled that he was no stranger to "visions and revelations of the Lord," including the mystical experience of a heavenly journey (2 Cor. 12.1-7). It is possible, indeed, that Paul had practised a form of Jewish mysticism prior to his conversion.[109] And his conception of the process of salvation as personal and bodily transformation[110] is not unrelated to ideas present in Jewish apocalypses and mystical practise, whose principal motivation was the knowledge of God and of heavenly mysteries.[111] At the same time, we should also observe that Paul had made a point of discounting just such experiences (12.6-10).

103. R. Bultmann, *ginōskō*, *TDNT* 1.697; see further 690-92, 696-98.

104. See particularly Bornkamm, "Revelation" 56; Schlier, *Grundzüge* 34-40.

105. E.g., 1 Sam. 3.7; Ps. 9.10; Isa. 43.10; Mic. 6.5. See further Dupont, *Gnosis* 74-81. See also above n. 87.

106. Rom. 1.28; Eph. 1.17; Col. 1.10; cf. Phil. 1.9; Col. 3.10; Phm. 6.

107. 1 Cor. 8.3; 13.12; Gal. 4.9.

108. On Paul's conversion see further below §7.4 and §14.3.

109. J. Bowker, " 'Merkabah' Visions and the Visions of Paul," *JSS* 16 (1971) 157-73.

110. See below §18.2.

111. See particularly Segal, *Paul* ch. 2; C. R. A. Morray-Jones, "Transformational Mysticism in the Apocalyptic-Merkabah Tradition," *JJS* 43 (1992) 1-31; J. M. Scott, "The Triumph of God in 2 Cor. 2.14: Additional Evidence of Merkabah Mysticism in Paul," *NTS* 42 (1996) 260-81.

More typical of Paul's experience of God was a sense of the grace and power which were transforming and sustaining his daily living. The grace of God to (or into) him (on the Damascus road) was not in vain, but was with him in the effectiveness of his ministry (1 Cor. 15.10). The same sense of God's grace is emphasized elsewhere, as the transforming power of his own conversion[112] and as the force explaining his missionary success.[113] That "grace" and "power" are nearly synonymous in Paul's thought is confirmed by his similar talk of his experience of the transforming power of God — the gospel as the power of God which effects salvation (Rom. 1.16), God's power transcending his all too human weakness,[114] and subsequently in Ephesians, "the gift of the grace of God given me in accordance with the working of his power" (Eph. 3.7).[115]

Paul also lived his life consciously "before God," "in the sight of God."[116] He speaks freely of confidence in and from God (2 Cor. 3.4-6). He saw his preaching bring conviction which he could only attribute to God.[117] He experienced comfort as from God (2 Cor. 1.3-7).[118] The three great fruits of the Spirit, love, joy, peace — whose emotional dimension should not be ignored — he naturally attributed to God. "We have peace with God" (Rom. 5.1). "The love of God has been poured out in our hearts" (Rom. 5.5). "May the God of hope fill you with all joy and peace in believing, that you may overflow in hope, in the power of the Holy Spirit," is the prayer which climaxes the body of his letter to Rome (Rom. 15.13). The grace and peace from God the Father with which he greeted all his readers were no mere convention.[119]

The same sense of experienced relationship with God is evident in Paul's prayer. Not simply in the fact of his characteristic opening thanksgiving, which was fairly conventional.[120] But partly in the regular assurance of his constancy in prayer (he makes the claim under oath in Rom. 1.9-10),[121] which

112. Gal. 1.15 and 2.21.
113. Rom. 15.15; 1 Cor. 3.10; Gal. 2.9.
114. 2 Cor. 4.7; 13.4.
115. See also 1 Cor. 1.18; 2.5; 2 Cor. 6.7; 12.9; Col. 1.29. See further below §13.2.
116. 1 Thes. 1.3; 3.9; 2 Cor. 2.17; 12.19. See further Schlier, *Grundzüge* 27. To call on God as witness (Rom. 1.9; 2 Cor. 1.23; Phil. 1.8; 1 Thes. 2.5, 10) was common in both Greek and Jewish literature (see my *Romans* 28).
117. 1 Cor. 2.4-5; 1 Thes. 1.5.
118. See also Rom. 15.5; 1 Cor. 14.3, 31; 2 Cor. 7.6, 13; Col. 2.2; 1 Thes. 3.7; 2 Thes. 2.16; Phm. 7.
119. See further Feine, *Theologie* 297-98.
120. W. G. Doty, *Letters in Primitive Christianity* (Philadelphia: Fortress, 1973) 31-33.
121. Rom. 1.9-10; 1 Cor. 1.4; Phil. 1.3-4; Col. 1.3; 1 Thes. 1.2-3; 2.13; 2 Thes. 1.3, 11; 2.13; Phm. 4; also Eph. 1.16.

suggests a life lived out of a prayerful relationship with God. Partly also in the occasional addition of "my" — giving thanks to "my God,"[122] indicating a relationship apprehended in personal terms. And partly in his regular opening reference to God as "our Father,"[123] whose sense of personal intimacy is confirmed by the reference to the "Abba! Father!" cry distinctive of Christian discipleship in Rom. 8.15 and Gal. 4.6. In Rom. 8.16 Paul speaks explicitly of a sense of sonship to God as Father borne in upon believers as they pray the "Abba" prayer.[124]

We should simply note here the extent to which Christ is bound up with Paul's sense of personal knowledge of and relationship with God. The transforming revelation of the Damascus road was of God's son in (or to) him (Gal. 1.16). The knowledge of God came to him "in the face of Christ" (2 Cor. 4.6). It was the grace of the Lord (Christ) which he experienced as power in weakness (2 Cor. 12.9). The grace and love of God came to their definitive and climactic expression in Christ (Rom. 5.8, 15; 8.39). The grace and peace with which he greeted his readers he attributes to the Lord Jesus Christ as much as to God our Father (Rom. 1.7).[125] His prayers were offered to God through Christ (Rom. 7.25). The implications of all this we will, of course, return to.[126] For the moment it suffices to note the experiential dimension of his belief in God.[127]

§2.7 Conclusion

(a) God was the base rock and foundation of Paul's theology. The frequent references to God show just how fundamental this conviction was, just as Paul's failure to expound this primal belief in any detail indicates its taken-for-granted character. (b) Theism was almost universal in the ancient world and equally taken-for-granted by most whom Paul would have encountered. But part of the axiomatic character of Paul's belief was his inherited Jewish conviction that God is one. And this he sustained resolutely in the face of

---

122. Rom. 1.8; 1 Cor. 1.4 v.l.; Phil. 1.3; Phm. 4.

123. The regular greeting in Paul's letters (Rom. 1.7; 1 Cor. 1.3; 2 Cor. 1.2; Gal. 1.3; Phil. 1.2; Col. 1.2; 2 Thes. 1.1-2; Phm. 3; also Eph. 1.2; the Pastorals lack the characteristic "our" — 1 Tim. 1.2; 2 Tim. 1.2; Tit. 1.4). Similarly in benedictions (Phil. 4.20; 1 Thes. 3.11, 13; 2 Thes. 2.16; also Eph. 6.23). Also in prayer (Col. 1.3, 12; 3.17; 1 Thes. 1.3; 3.9-10; Eph. 5.20).

124. For Paul the experience of glossolalia evidently included a sense of speaking to God (1 Cor. 14.2, 28).

125. See n. 123 above.

126. See below particularly §10.5.

127. See further below particularly §16.4.

the characteristic polytheism of the Greco-Roman world. (c) Similarly taken for granted was the conviction that this one God was the creator of the cosmos and would be final judge. The integration of creation and salvation in Paul's theology derives directly from his understanding of God. (d) That this one God was also God of Israel is in effect the central tension in the theology of Paul, the Jew who understood himself to be called to serve as apostle to the Gentiles. (e) Paul's theology of God was no abstract speculation but sustained and informed by his own experience in conversion and mission and prayer. It is the integration of intellectual rigour, missionary and pastoral effectiveness, and personal experience which makes his speech about God so compelling.

§3 Humankind[1]

§3.1 Anthropological presuppositions

Still more hidden from view in Paul's theology are his ideas on what it means to be human. This is perfectly understandable. Which of us writing to friends or treating some aspect of theology would feel the need to explain what we mean when we speak, for example, of the human "mind" or "spirit"? Even more than with his theistic presuppositions, Paul's anthropological presuppositions hardly called for analysis and discussion in his letters. But we who attempt to listen in to Paul's theological dialogue with the recipients of his letters will never begin adequately to appreciate Paul's theology unless we understand his anthropology. For the heart of his theology, as of his religion as a whole, was the impact of divine revelation and grace on the human being. And in writing of that impact Paul presupposed things about the human being which we need to understand if we are to grasp how revelation and grace "worked" for Paul in his theology and religion. In this case, more so than

1. **Bibliography**: **Barrett**, *Paul* 65-74; **Boyarin**, *Radical Jew* ch. 3; **E. Branden-burger**, *Fleisch und Geist. Paulus und die dualistische Weisheit* (WMANT 29; Neukir-chen-Vluyn: Neukirchener, 1968); **P. Brown**, *The Body and Society: Men, Women and Sexual Renunciation in Early Christianity* (New York: Columbia University, 1988/London: Faber and Faber, 1989); **Bultmann**, *Theology* 1.191-246; **Conzelmann**, *Outline* 173-84; **J. D. G. Dunn**, "Jesus — Flesh and Spirit: An Exposition of Romans 1.3-4," *JTS* 24 (1973) 40-68; *Paul for Today* (Ethel M. Wood Lecture; London: University of London, 1993); **Gnilka**, *Theologie* 43-57; *Paulus* 205-20; **R. H. Gundry**, SOMA *in Biblical The-ology with Emphasis on Pauline Anthropology* (SNTSMS 29; Cambridge: Cambridge University, 1976); **R. Jewett**, *Paul's Anthropological Terms: A Study of Their Use in Conflict Settings* (Leiden: Brill, 1971); **E. Käsemann**, "On Paul's Anthropology," *Per-spectives* 1-31; **W. G. Kümmel**, *Man in the New Testament* (1948; London: Epworth, 1963); **D. B. Martin**, *The Corinthian Body* (New Haven: Yale, 1995); **Ridderbos**, *Paul* 115-21; **H. W. Robinson**, *The Christian Doctrine of Man* (Edinburgh: Clark, [3]1926); **J. A. T. Robinson**, *The Body: A Study in Pauline Theology* (London: SCM, 1952 = Philadelphia: Westminster, 1977); **A. Sand**, *Der Begriff "Fleisch" in den paulinischen Hauptbriefen* (Regensburg: Pustet, 1967); **Schlier**, *Grundzüge* 97-106; **U. Schnelle**, *Neu-testamentliche Anthropologie* (Neukirchen-Vluyn: Neukirchener, 1991); **W. D. Stacey**, *The Pauline View of Man in Relation to Its Judaic and Hellenistic Background* (London: Macmillan, 1956); **Strecker**, *Theologie* 132-36; **Stuhlmacher**, *Theologie* 1.273-78; **Whiteley**, *Theology* 31-44.

with Paul's theology of God, we will have to step back from our attempt to follow the logical sequence of Paul's theological exposition in Romans in order to fill in some of the less obvious links in his thought as a whole.[2]

The degree to which Paul's anthropology is interwoven into his theology can be illustrated from the two most important terms in Paul's anthropology — "body" and "flesh." For the former extends across the whole of Paul's theology and can serve as an unexpected link motif.[3] Paul uses it to speak of the human body (see below), ominously of "the body of sin" and "the body of death" (Rom. 6.6; 7.24), of Christ's body of flesh (Col. 1.22; 2.11) and of the resurrected body (1 Cor. 15.44), of the sacramental bread (1 Cor. 10.16-17) and of the church as the body of Christ.[4] The range of usage in Colossians is particularly striking — the body of the cosmos (1.18), the human body (2.23), Christ's body of flesh (1.22; 2.11), Christ as the embodiment of the divine fullness (2.9), Christ the final "reality" (2.17), and the body the church (1.18, 24; 2.19; 3.15).[5] As for "flesh," the term is obviously crucial for Paul's understanding of how the gospel operates. Apart from anything else it clearly describes the force field opposed to the Spirit of God: to live "according to the flesh" is the antithesis to Christian living (Rom. 8.4-13); the flesh is a soil which produces corruption (Gal. 6.8). And yet, as we shall see, few terms have been more misunderstood and seldom has Paul's meaning been more misrepresented than in translations of *sarx*, "flesh."

The importance of Paul's anthropology, however, has sometimes been overstated. In a famous passage Bultmann claimed that "Every assertion about God is simultaneously an assertion about man and vice versa. For this reason and in this sense Paul's theology is, at the same time, anthropology."[6] Unfortunately, this statement lent itself all too easily to a kind of anthropological reductionism, as we see in the corollary claim of one of Bultmann's pupils, Herbert Braun, that christology is the "variable" whereas "the essentially Christian element, the constant . . . in the New Testament" is the "self-understanding of faith."[7] Nevertheless, Bultmann's observation is important at two points.

2. Even in the first main theme of Paul's exposition in Romans, however, all the most relevant anthropological terms occur — *sōma* (1.24), *sarx* (2.28; 3.20), *kardia* (1.21, 24; 2.5, 15, 29), *nous* (1.28), *psychē* (2.9), *pneuma* (2.29), and *syneidēsis* (2.15).

3. This was the starting point for John Robinson's study: "the concept of the body forms the keystone of Paul's theology. In its closely inter-connected meanings, the word *sōma* knits together all his great themes" (*Body* 9). Robinson's *Body* has proved remarkably popular.

4. Rom. 12.4-5; 1 Cor. 12.12-27; Col. 2.19; Eph. 4.12-16.

5. See my "The 'Body' in Colossians," in Schmidt and Silva, eds., *To Tell the Mystery* (§12 n. 1) 163-81.

6. Bultmann, *Theology* 1.191.

7. H. Braun, "Der Sinn der neutestamentlichen Christologie," *ZTK* 54 (1957) 341-77 (here 371) = "The Meaning of New Testament Christology," in *God and Christ: Existence and Providence, JTC* 5 (1968) 89-127 (here 118).

First, he underscores the extent to which Paul's theology is practical and not merely speculative. Paul wrote as a missionary and pastor, and not as an academic theologian; or to be more precise, he wrote as a missionary-pastor theologian. Paul spoke of God and Christ because the reality of God and Christ impinged directly on himself and his churches. Bultmann was simply putting into his own terms the famous epigram of Melanchthon: "to know Christ [is] to know his benefits."[8]

Second, despite Bultmann's own existentialist individualism, his statement underscores the interdependence of the different facets of Paul's theology. Or to put it differently, Paul's theology is *relational*. That is to say, he was not concerned with God in himself or humankind in itself. The classical Greek philosophical debates about existence and subsistence and the later church debates about the natures of Christ are remote from Paul. As the opening of his exposition of the gospel in Rom. 1.16ff. clearly shows, his concern was rather with humankind in relation to God, with men and women in their relationships with each other, and subsequently with Christ as God's response to the human plight. In other words, Paul's anthropology is not a form of individualism; persons are social beings, defined as persons by their relations. In Pauline perspective, human beings are as they are by virtue of their relationship to God and his world. His gospel is of God in Christ reconciling the world to himself. His doctrine of salvation is of man and woman being restored to the image of God in the body of Christ. And so on. This context is vital to a proper understanding of Paul's anthropology.

Such a clarification of Paul's conception of the human being is all the more important, since much of Paul's anthropology is inevitably strange to modern self-perception. The danger here is worth noting: that we will come to Paul with our own equally unexamined presuppositions about how the person is constituted and read them into what Paul says.[9] Failure to ask what it means to be a human being in our own time may prevent us from recognizing how different and distinctive was Paul's understanding. Failure to ask what it meant to be a human being in Paul's thought may prevent us from hearing how his theology can challenge our own understanding. The ancient oracle inscribed on the temple of Apollo at Delphi, "*gnōthi seauton,* Know thyself" (Plato, *Protagoras* 343b), and the famous maxim of Socrates, "The unexamined life is not worth living" (Plato, *Apology* 38a), can have wider application than at first appears.

---

8. *Loci Communes* 1521 — the starting point for Hultgren, *Christ and His Benefits* (§9 n. 1).

9. Note particularly Martin's warning against reading Paul in terms of Cartesian ontological dualism — between, on the one side, body, matter, nature, and the physical, and, on the other, soul, nonmatter, the supernatural, and the spiritual (*Corinthian Body* 3-37). Cf. Robinson, *Body* 12-13.

Still more confusing has been the long-running debate on whether Paul's anthropology was influenced more by Hellenistic or by Jewish categories and to apportion Paul's ideas accordingly.[10] There is indeed a distinction in broad terms which has some merit and value. That is, in simplified terms, while Greek thought tended to regard the human being as made up of distinct parts, Hebrew thought saw the human being more as a whole person existing on different dimensions. As we might say, it was more characteristically Greek to conceive of the human person "partitively," whereas it was more characteristically Hebrew to conceive of the human person "aspectively." That is to say, we speak of a school *having* a gym (the gym is part of the school); but we say I *am* a Scot (my Scottishness is an aspect of my whole being).[11]

However, the complexity and diversity of the evolving debate within Greek philosophy on physics can hardly be adequately grasped by such distinctions.[12] And the influence of Hellenistic thought particularly on diaspora Judaism diminishes the distinction anyway — as Philo always demonstrates. In actual usage the overlap between particular writers and schools across the spectrum is extensive. Paul himself, as a man living in both worlds, to some extent straddles the so-called divide. For example, few would dispute that Paul's use of *psychē* ("soul") is in direct continuity with the Hebrew *nephesh,* and the same can be argued for *sarx* ("flesh") and *pneuma* ("spirit").[13] At the same time, it is well known that *sōma* ("body") has no direct equivalent in Hebrew,[14] that *nous* ("mind") is a concept much more characteristically Greek than Hebrew,[15] and that Paul draws the concept of *syneidēsis* ("conscience") from Greek usage.[16] But it would be foolish to read Paul's meaning straight from the diverse Hebrew and Greek use of these terms. It is the way Paul used them, whatever their origin, which has to be determinative for us.

10. The debate goes back to H. Lüdemann, *Die Anthropologie des Apostels Paulus und ihre Stellung innerhalb seiner Heilslehre* (Kiel, 1872) and focused particularly on the *pneuma-sarx* ("spirit-flesh") antithesis in Paul. It entered a new phase in the discussion of possible Gnostic influence on Paul which dominated the middle decades of the twentieth century. The debate is reviewed, e.g., by Stacey, *Man* 40-55, and for individual terms by Jewett, *Anthropological Terms.*

11. The distinction "aspectivally/partitively" is drawn from Whiteley, *Theology* 36. See further 41-44, and cf., e.g., Robinson, *Body* 14; E. Jacob, *psychē, TDNT* 9.630-31; Stuhlmacher, *Theologie* 1.274.

12. We need only refer to the extracts provided by Long/Sedley.

13. See below §§3.3 and 3.6.

14. In the LXX *sōma* translates a number of different Hebrew words; see F. Baumgärtel, *sōma, TDNT* 7.1044-45.

15. See below §3.5.

16. The concept (if not the experience) is almost wholly lacking in Jewish writings (first in Wis. 17.11 in the sense "[bad] conscience"), but was well established in popular Greek usage by the first century BCE (see C. Maurer, *synoida, TDNT* 7.902-4, 908-13).

Or again, we might start with Bultmann's famous observation that by "body" Paul means "the whole person"; "man does not *have* a *sōma;* he *is sōma.*"[17] In context that can be easily read as an assertion of Hebraic influence over against more typical Greek usage. But it is well known that in Greek usage frequently and from earliest times *sōma* can stand for the whole person or function in effect as a reflexive pronoun.[18]

Instead of trying to play off Hebrew and Greek influence against each other, then, or to spend time looking for particular parallels in Greek or Hebrew thought, as though that might fully explain Paul's anthropology, the more promising approach will be to look for the coherence of Paul's thought in itself and only to draw attention to points of possible influence where they are relevant to our better understanding of Paul.

We begin by trying to clarify the force of Paul's two principal anthropological terms, *sōma,* "body," and *sarx,* "flesh."

§3.2 Sōma

Sōma is one of the two most important Pauline terms in his talk of humankind. It occurs more than 50 times in the undisputed Paulines in what we might call the normal usage, that is, in reference to the human body of everyday existence. Romans contains some striking usage, but almost always in isolated verses,[19] which makes it difficult to gain a proper handle on Paul's conceptuality. Fortunately, however, 1 Corinthians contains more intensive usage, in which the scope of Paul's understanding of the body becomes clearer.

By way of preliminary clarification, we should note that the term "body" itself well illustrates the difficulties in correlating twentieth-century thought with that of Paul and in resolving the question of Greek or Hebrew influence. For in English usage the first meaning of the term "body" is usually the individual "material organism" or corpse.[20] So English speakers may find it hard to free themselves from the identification body = physical body. That sense in fact reflects early and continuing Greek usage; in Homer *sōma* always

---

See further particularly C. A. Pierce, *Conscience in the New Testament* (London: SCM/Chicago: Allenson, 1955); H.-J. Eckstein, *Der Begriff Syneidesis bei Paulus* (WUNT 2.10; Tübingen: Mohr, 1983). See also below §6.3 and §24.7.

17. Bultmann, *Theology* 1.192, 194; the latter is cited as an approved axiom by Conzelmann, *Outline* 176; Bornkamm, *Paul* 130; and Stuhlmacher, *Theologie* 1.274.

18. See, e.g., E. Schweizer, *sōma,* *TDNT* 7.1026 (Euripides), 1028 (Plato), 1030 (Xenophon), 1032 (Lycurgus), and 1040 (Plutarch).

19. Though note the 3 occurrences in 8.11-13.

20. *Concise Oxford Dictionary,* "body."

means "dead body, corpse."[21] And the connotation enters biblical usage in the LXX and the non-Pauline NT,[22] reflecting the more "partitive" Greek conception of the person, the *sōma* as not integral to the person. But as already noted, the LXX is diffident in its use of *sōma,* since the Greek term has no immediate equivalent in Hebrew. And, as we shall have to clarify later, it is not the overlap between "body" and "flesh" which is likely to express distinctive Hebraic notions so much as those passages where *sōma* is a more tentative rendering of other Hebrew terms. More to the immediate point is the fact that Paul never uses *sōma* in the sense "corpse." We are thus warned again that reading Paul's anthropology in the light of modern usage or of ancient Greek usage is likely to distort our appreciation of Paul's thought from the outset.

In Paul's own usage *sōma,* like so many of his terms, has a spectrum of meaning. The focus on physicality is only one end of the spectrum. As we shall see in a moment, *sōma* as denoting human body includes the physical body but is more than that. A better word to use — it would also help us break away from our twentieth-century preconceptions — is the alternative term *"embodiment" — sōma* as the embodiment of the person. In this sense *sōma* is a relational concept. It denotes the person embodied in a particular environment. It is the means by which the person relates to that environment, and vice versa. It is the means of living in, of experiencing the environment. This helps explain the degree of overlap with the narrower sense "physical body," for the environment of everyday experience is a physical environment. But *sōma* as embodiment means more than my physical body: it is the embodied "me," the means by which "I" and the world can act upon each other.[23]

Alternatively, we could use a term like "corporeality" or even "corporateness." For it is precisely "bodiness" (corporeality, corporateness) which enables individuals as bodies to interact with each other, to cooperate with one another.[24] The body is the medium of that interaction and cooperation.

21. LSJ, *sōma.*
22. See again Baumgärtel, *TDNT* 7.1045; also BAGD, *sōma* 1a.
23. Robinson, *Body* 28, goes too far in suggesting that "*sōma* is the nearest equivalent to our word 'personality,' " introducing a still more problematic modern category. Gundry, SOMA, on the other hand, critically weakens his case (that *sōma* always means the physical body) by focusing too narrowly on this end of the spectrum in biblical usage, by concentrating his critique on Bultmann's suggestion that *sōma* means "the whole person," and by thus failing to engage with a more nuanced statement (as here in terms of "embodiment").
24. This was the point at which Käsemann broke with Bultmann's more individualistic conception of body in terms of "relationship to oneself" by defining body as the human "capacity for communication" ("Anthropology" 21; "we are always what we are in the mode of belongingness and participation"; more fully 18-22; see also Stuhlmacher,

To reduce that simply to a physical exchange, say of handshake or of physical goods, would reduce a multidimensional collaboration of persons to something more one-dimensional. It is precisely the interaction of individuals bodily which makes it meaningful to speak of a corporate body or corporation, that is, of individuals as bodies working together in harmony for a common purpose. If "body" meant simply "physical body," such a usage would be quite discrete and at some remove from the basic meaning. But body understood to denote corporeality leads directly into the idea of the body corporate.

These points can be readily illustrated from Paul's body language. It is true that he often speaks of the body where the thought is primarily of physical function or physical presence. Fallen humanity, given over to the desires of their hearts, dishonour their bodies among themselves (Rom. 1.24). Husband and wife "have authority" over each other's bodies (1 Cor. 7.4), though presumably Paul does not think of their lovemaking as a purely "physical" act.[25] Paul will be present "by the Spirit," though absent "by the body" (1 Cor. 5.3). Presence "in the body" means absence from the Lord, and vice versa (2 Cor. 5.6, 8).[26] He recalls an "out of the body" experience (2 Cor. 12.2-3), though, noticeably, he is not sure whether it happened "in the body" or "outside the body." He speaks of bearing the marks of Christ on his body (Gal. 6.17), presumably thinking particularly of the scars and physical effects of the various beatings and severe hardships he endured; though the similar thought in 2 Cor. 4.10 ("carrying the death of Jesus in our body") puts us in touch with a much richer conception of "sharing Christ's sufferings."[27] Even the more partitive sounding trichotomy of "spirit, soul, and body" in 1 Thes. 5.23 comes in a context emphasizing "wholeness,"[28] where the enumeration is more like that of Deut. 6.5, denoting completeness of commitment.[29]

Theologie 1.275; but Becker, *Paul* 385, warns that Käsemann's view may be equally ideological in origin). In similar vein the starting point for Robinson's study of Pauline usage is "the vast solidarity of historical existence" (*Body* 8); "the flesh-body was not what partitioned a man off from his neighbour; it was rather what bound him in the bundle of life with all men and nature" (*Body* 15). Schweizer finds this sense already in LXX use of *sōma;* "it is used for man in confrontation with others" (*TDNT* 7.1048).

25. Cf. Gnilka, *Theologie* 44.

26. Jewett's comment that Paul's use of *sōma* here "is thoroughly gnostic" (*Anthropological Terms* 276) illustrates the datedness of his study, written as it was when the Gnostic hypothesis to explain the problems at Corinth was at the height of its influence.

27. See further below §18.5.

28. *Holotelēs, holoklēron,* both meaning "whole, complete." See also Schnelle, *Anthropologie* 123.

29. Robinson, *Man* 108; Stacey, *Man* 123; contrast the suggestion of Jewett, *Anthropological Terms* 175-83, that Paul here resists a libertinist "attempt to divide man into higher and lower parts."

Elsewhere, however, the richer meaning of "embodiment" is clearer. The spectrum of meaning is particularly evident in 1 Cor. 6.13-20, where Paul uses *sōma* eight times. We could be content with the meaning "physical body" when he talks about sexual relationships with a prostitute (6.13, 16, 18). But Paul also reminds the Corinthians that "your bodies are members of Christ" (6.15), where narrowing the meaning to physical bodies would assuredly diminish Paul's meaning. What he was reminding the Corinthians of was that they *themselves* ("us" — 6.14) were members of Christ — but they themselves precisely as embodied beings, whose bodily engagements indicated the quality and character of their commitment and discipleship.[30] So the concept of body is larger than physical body. Moreover, as bodies they were inevitably in corporate relationships which determined their identity, and it was the corporate relationship as members of Christ's body which should be decisive and render unthinkable a bodily relationship with a prostitute, representative of another corporate order.[31] In the concluding two references, the body as "temple of the Holy Spirit" is another way of saying "the Holy Spirit in you" (6.19), that is, not just in the physical body, as though the body was something distinct from the whole person, but the body as the embodiment of the whole person. And the final call to "glorify God in your body" is the deduction drawn from the fact that "you were bought with a price" (6.20). That is, it is a call not merely for a disciplining of the physical body, but for disciplined social (corporate) relationships.

The importance of body as personal embodiment is also clear in Rom. 12.1. When Paul exhorts the Roman believers "to present your bodies a sacrifice," he assuredly does not call upon them to offer up arms and legs on a sacrificial altar! His summons is rather that they should offer up *themselves*. The parallel with 6.13 and 16 puts the point beyond dispute: "to hand over your bodies" (12.1) = "to hand over yourselves" (6.13, 16).[32] But what they were to offer up was themselves precisely as bodies, themselves in their corporeality, in the concrete relationships which constituted their everyday living. The equivalent to Israel's commitment in cultic sacrifice was the dedication expressed in their embodied relationships.[33]

---

30. Cf. Bultmann, *Theology* 1.195 (but then with existentialist gloss — 195-96, 199); Barrett, *1 Corinthians* 147-49; Jewett, *Anthropological Terms* 260-61.

31. Cf. the differently angled discussion of Martin, *Corinthian Body* 176-77. To bring out the point Paul rephrases Gen. 2.24 as "he who unites with a prostitute is one *body*" (6.16).

32. The middle term here is "hand over your members" (the same word as in 1 Cor. 6.15, also in Rom. 6.13, 19) — *sōma* denoting the collectivity of the "members" (see further my *Romans* 337, 709).

33. See further particularly E. Käsemann, "Worship in Everyday Life" (§20 n. 1), and below §20.3.

The implications are the same, if not so immediately clear, in other passages. When Paul notes that Abraham's body "was already dead" (Rom. 4.19), he means that Abraham was impotent. When Paul says "I treat my body roughly" (1 Cor. 9.27), he presumably refers not simply to an ascetic physical severity,[34] but to a strict discipline of life and conduct.[35] When he envisaged even a loveless martyrdom, he says "I may hand over my body in order that I might boast (or be burned)" (1 Cor. 13.3); in the variant reading at least, the "I" who hands over his body is the "I" of the burned body.[36] When he talks of each receiving judgment "according to what each has done through or by means of the body" (2 Cor. 5.10),[37] he evidently was thinking of the body as the medium of (as we would say) self-expression.[38] When Paul speaks of his "bodily presence as weak" (2 Cor. 10.10), he certainly has in mind not just his physical strength or appearance, but the impression which his whole manner and presentation of the gospel made on his hearers (1 Cor. 2.3). Or when he expresses his heartfelt desire "that Christ might be magnified in my body" (Phil. 1.20), he again no doubt had more than the physicality of his appearance or actions in mind, but the character of his witness as embodied. We can hardly think that Paul wanted to glorify Christ through only part of his existence, the body as a subset of his whole being. He wanted rather to glorify Christ through his whole life, despite the fact that he was being held prisoner in a Roman jail.

Bearing in mind what was said above about the body corporate, we should further note that in the second large cluster of body terms in 1 Corinthians (17 in 12.12-27) Paul makes extensive use of the body as a model of human cooperation and interrelationships. We will have to return to this theme later in another connection.[39] Here the point is merely to underscore the social dimensions which are consequent upon and the inevitable corollary of bodiness. It is the interplay between body corporate and body corporeal, between church as body and mutual (bodily, that is, also social) relationships, which provides the linkage earlier, in 1 Cor. 11.29-30. Because believers are em-

---

34. Cf. Col. 2.23 — "severe treatment of the body, not of value to anyone in regard to the gratification of the flesh."

35. For this verse and the following two verses, contrast Gundry, SOMA 36-37, 47-48.

36. The variant is taken as original by NIV, NJB, and NRSV; but see Fee, *1 Corinthians* 629 n. 18 and 633-34.

37. On the phrase itself *(dia tou sōmatos)* see, e.g., Furnish, *2 Corinthians* 276.

38. Even Gundry agrees here that "the *sōma* is the man himself" (SOMA 47). Similarly in Rom. 8.13 "the deeds of the body" is not a distancing phrase by which the perpetrator might distance himself from his actions, but an alternative way of speaking of "the evil which I do" (7.19).

39. See below §§20.4-5.

bodied beings, whose embodiment is what makes it possible for them to function collectively as a body, failure to "discern the body" has bodily consequences (many ill and weak, some even dead).[40]

In some way most striking of all is the distinction Paul makes between the present body and the resurrection body in 1 Cor. 15.35-44, the third large cluster of body terms in 1 Corinthians (9 occurrences). Evidently confronted by some incredulity that there could be a resurrection of the body (15.12, 35),[41] Paul responds by rebuking the implication that the only body which could be conceptualized is the unsatisfactory present body. "You fool! What you sow does not come to life unless it dies. And what you sow is not the body which is to be, but bare seed. . . . But God gives it a body as he has chosen, and to each kind of seed its own body" (15.36-38). Paul proceeds to distinguish heavenly bodies from earthly bodies (15.40), his unusual use of *sōma* for sun, moon, and stars[42] already indicating that Paul was ploughing his own furrow at this point. The analogy is applied (15.42-44): the present body (the embodiment of the soul) ends in corruption, dishonour, weakness; the resurrection body (the embodiment of the Spirit — 15.45) is raised in incorruptibility, glory, power. The soulish body takes after Adam, of the earth, made of dust; the spiritual body will be patterned after Christ's resurrection body (15.45-49).[43] Evidently, the soulish body, the present body as such, cannot share in the kingdom of God; it is also corruptible flesh and blood, and only the incorruptible, the spiritual body, is capable of inheriting God's kingdom (15.50).[44]

40. There are more dimensions to this rich passage. I focus only on the social dimensions which G. Theissen first brought effectively to wider notice (see below §22.6). Here note particularly Martin, *Corinthian Body* 194-96: "By opening Christ's body to schism, they open their own bodies to disease and death" (194); but see also §22 n. 66 below.

41. To be noted is the fact that the theme of the chapter is the resurrection *of the dead* (the phrase is repeated 13 times); see particularly M. de Boer, *The Defeat of Death: Apocalyptic Eschatology in 1 Corinthians 15 and Romans 5* (Sheffield: JSOT, 1988). For the debate on what the Corinthian position referred to here was, see, e.g., R. A. Horsley, " 'How Can Some of You Say That There Is No Resurrection of the Dead?' Spiritual Elitism in Corinth," *NovT* 20 (1978) 203-31, and A. C. Thiselton, "Realized Eschatology at Corinth," *NTS* 24 (1977-78) 510-26.

42. The more typical common term between human beings and stars would be *psychē* ("soul") — Martin, *Corinthian Body* 126, who also reminds us (one of his principal themes) that the distinction would not be between material and immaterial (127).

43. I remain puzzled how it is that some exegetes fail to recognize the reference here to Christ's resurrected embodiment (see my *Christology* 107-8); compare after all Rom. 8.11 and Phil. 3.21. See further below §11.5a.

44. Cf. Martin's stimulating treatment (*Corinthian Body* 123-29), though he allows the whole-ism of Paul's concept to be too much determined by his previous analysis of what he calls the "hierarchy of essences" in Greek thought. Paul does not say that "the immortal and incorruptible part of the human body will be resurrected" (128), but envisaged the transformation of the whole person in his or her embodiment.

The point for us could scarcely be clearer. Redemption for Paul was not some kind of escape from bodily existence, but a transformation into a different kind of bodily existence (15.51-54). "Body" is the common term. But not fleshly body, or body made of dust, or corruptible body, or mortal body. That is only the present embodiment, the embodiment appropriate to a physical world subject to decay and death.[45] The embodiment of the resurrection body will be different, an embodiment appropriate to the world of Spirit, beyond death. Quite what Paul envisaged we can hardly begin to say. Quite possibly he himself was simply using these distinctions heuristically, to indicate the fact (the "that") of the distinction rather than its "what." The point for us here, however, is precisely the fact of the distinction. For it is that which underlines the character of Paul's concept of "body," and precisely as embodiment within a larger corporate and social whole.

To sum up, then, *sōma* expresses for Paul the character of created humankind — that is, as embodied existence. It is precisely as embodied, and by means of this embodiment, that the person participates in creation and functions as part of creation. The body, the body corporeal and not just the body corporate, is what makes possible a social dimension to life, is what enables the individual to participate in human society, or, alternatively expressed, is what prevents the individual from opting out of this world or constructing a religion which denies social interdependence and responsibility. Here we may simply observe how the exhortation of Rom. 12.1-2 runs on at once into the exposition of the church's corporate responsibility as one body in Christ (12.3-8), and on into the wider social responsibilities outlined in 12.9–13.14.[46] It is also this somatic character of Paul's anthropology which prevents Paul's theology from falling into any real dualism between creation and salvation. For it is precisely as part of creation and with creation that Paul the individual and his fellow believers share in the birth pangs of creation, groaning with the rest of creation as they await the redemption of their bodies (Rom. 8.22-23). In short, *sōma* gives Paul's theology an unavoidably social and ecological dimension.

---

45. Contrast Gundry: "a *pneumatikon sōma* . . . is a physical body renovated by the Spirit" (SOMA 165-66). But a "physical body" which is not subject to decay and death is hardly the "normal meaning" of *sōma* for which Gundry has pressed throughout his study, given not least his starting point in *sōma* = corpse. The emphasis in the passage is more on discontinuity and transformation than on continuity (Käsemann, "Anthropology" 8-10).

46. See further below §24.2.

§3.3 Sarx

Sarx ("flesh") is the other most prominent Pauline anthropological term. It occurs 91 times in the Pauline letters, 26 times in Romans alone.[47] It is also the most controversial term. This is principally because of the range of usage, since it seems to span from the innocuous sense of the physical material of the body to the sense of "flesh" as a force hostile to God. The simple question which has generated immense discussion is how the one term can encompass such a range.

The dominant view over the past century or so[48] has been that Paul's spread of usage reflects a combination of Jewish and Hellenistic influences, in one measure or another. That is, the idea of flesh as material body reflects the typical Hebrew sense of *basar,* whereas the idea of flesh as antagonistic to God is more Hellenistic in character. But which is the dominant influence, and which emphasis is the more significant for an understanding of Paul's theology? And does the tension caused by this diverse usage make Paul's theology incoherent? The differing views on such questions have caused more confusion on this subject than in almost any other area of Paul's theology.

(a) The theological issues are posed most sharply by those who regard *sarx* in Paul as a cosmic power like, but hostile to, *pneuma* ("s/Spirit"),[49] *sarx* as a "principle of sin,"[50] or *sarx* as "something like a Gnostic aeon."[51] Bultmann, for example, analyses *sarx* not in his section on "anthropological concepts" but together with sin and death — "flesh and sin as powers to which man has fallen victim."[52] Coming at the question from his own distinctive angle, but equally impressed by the antithesis of flesh and spirit, Albert Schweitzer concluded that the two were not merely hostile but mutually exclusive: "being in Christ" as a state of existence had taken the place of the physical "being in the flesh"; being "in the Spirit" meant no longer being

47. No other NT author uses the term so much — John 13 times (8 of them in John 6.51-63), Hebrews 6 times, 1 Peter 7 times, Revelation 7 times (5 of them in Rev. 19.18).

48. Referring back again to Lüdemann (above n. 10); see Jewett, *Anthropological Terms* 52-54.

49. This view goes back to F. C. Baur (Jewett, *Anthropological Terms* 51); similarly, e.g., J. Weiss (Jewett 63), Brandenburger, *Fleisch* 45, and Strecker, *Theologie* 133.

50. The definition has also recurred regularly since Baur (Sand, *Begriff* 7), e.g., Pfleiderer (Sand 29-31) and A. Oepke (Sand 216); "radically evil" (Sand 63, describing Bousset's view). Even Ridderbos regards flesh as "a description of sin itself," as a description of "the sinful-in-itself" (*Paul* 103-4).

51. Käsemann, *Leib* (§20 n. 1) 105.

52. Bultmann, *Theology* 1.245 (also 197-200); but he does point out that it is not "realistic mythology," but "figurative, rhetorical language."

"in the flesh."[53] The issue here, then, is whether Paul regarded *sarx* as a substance or force field which is irredeemably evil and from which the believer has already been removed, or a hostile cosmic power whose authority over the believer has already been broken.

(b) Others have found sufficient explanation for the problem of *sarx* in Paul in more psychological than cosmological terms. The idea of *sarx* as the seat of sensuality, summed up in the phrase "the pleasures of the flesh," goes back to ancient times.[54] The overtone of frailty and corruptibility which attaches so closely to the Hebrew *basar* has been strengthened by the usage in the DSS.[55] But is that sufficient to explain the more negative uses of *sarx* in Romans 7–8? A popular solution has been to distinguish the two Pauline phrases: *en sarki* ("in the flesh") and *kata sarka* ("according to the flesh"). The former denotes simply life on earth; the latter denotes "the conscious spiritual orientation of life on the earthly level."[56] *Sarx* "becomes bad only when man builds his life on it."[57] But once again the question arises: Can the two usages be held together, or are we left in effect with two neatly discrete senses — a neutral sense of *sarx* distinct from a more characteristically negative sense?[58]

(c) A third aspect of the confusion caused by Paul's use of *sarx* is the more practical question of how *sarx* should be translated. For the translation "flesh" seems to be largely unacceptable to most contemporary English language translators of the Pauline letters.[59] Possibly, we may presume, because

---

53. Schweitzer, *Mysticism* (§15 n. 1) 127, 167. Cf. even Schweizer, *TDNT* 7.135 — "The man who has come to faith in the Son of God is no longer in the *sarx*, for he believes, and he has thus ceased to build his life on the *sarx*, which is to sin."

54. Schweizer, *TDNT* 7.104-5; Jewett, *Anthropological Terms* 50.

55. Particularly Gen. 6.3; 2 Chron. 32.8; Job 34.15; Pss. 56.4; 78.39; Isa. 31.3; 40.6-7; Jer. 17.5 (see BDB, *basar*); in DSS see, e.g., 1QS 11.9, 12; 1QH 4.29; 15.21. See also R. Meyer, *TDNT* 7.110-14.

56. Schweizer, *TDNT* 7.130-31, though he goes on to note that when *sarx* thus functions as a norm "by which a man directs his life [it] becomes a power which shapes him" (132).

57. Schweizer, *TDNT* 7.135.

58. Whiteley, *Theology* 39 — "flesh . . . used in a moral sense . . . does not necessarily have any physical meaning"; Davies, *Paul* 19 (65 cases of "a purely material sense"; 35 cases of "ethical significance"). Davies then attempts to explain the more negative usage in terms of the rabbinic idea of the *yetzer ha-ra,* "evil impulse" (20-27). While the link to Paul's own usage is less than clear, no doubt the rabbinic usage was an alternative attempt to describe the experience of human fallibility.

59. The problems caused by modern translations of *sarx* can be illustrated from two important contemporary translations. REB translates *sarx* in Romans variously as "human" (1.3), "flesh" (2.28), "natural descent" (4.1), "mere human nature" (7.5), "unspiritual self" (7.18), "unspiritual nature" (7.25), "nature" (8.3), and "old nature" (8.4-5). NIV translates the same sequence as "human nature" (1.3), "physical" (2.28), untranslated (4.1), "sinful nature" (7.5, 18, 25; 8.3), "sinful man" (8.3), and "sinful nature" (8.4-5).

"flesh" in English has a somewhat old-fashioned ring. But probably also because, consciously or unconsciously, its negative usage seems to carry unacceptable dualistic overtones (materiality as evil). Even the problems of translation, then, pose issues of some moment in any attempt to understand Paul's theology and how Paul envisaged the life of faith and the process of salvation.

Given the confusion caused by Paul's theology at this point, any attempt to grasp Paul's concept of *sarx* is bound to review his actual usage, however briefly. Here it quickly becomes apparent that the usage can be set out, without contrivance,[60] in something of a spectrum.[61]

(i) At one end of the spectrum there is indeed a more or less neutral usage, denoting the physical body, or physical relationship or kinship, without any negative connotation.[62]

(ii) Still with primary reference to the physical, *sarx* embraces the typically Hebraic thought of weakness (Rom. 6.19). *Sarx* cannot inherit the kingdom of God because it is perishable and mortal (1 Cor. 15.50).[63] It is "mortal" (2 Cor. 4.11), subject to affliction and weariness (2 Cor. 7.5) — "the weakness of the flesh" (Gal. 4.13-14).

(iii) In some passages this sense of weakness gains a further overtone of inadequacy in contrast to a superior realm or mode of being: "flesh and blood" in contrast to God (Gal. 1.16); a life lived "in the flesh" in contrast to "Christ in me" (Gal. 2.20); Onesimus a brother not merely "in the flesh" but, more importantly, "in the Lord" (Phm. 16); the "thorn in the flesh" underlining human weakness in contrast to the power of God (2 Cor. 12.7-9). Or more sharply, life "in the flesh" stands in contrast to being "with Christ, which is far better" (Phil. 1.22-23).

(iv) In other passages this weakness gains a moral connotation. It is precisely as *sarx* that no person is justified before God (Rom. 3.20; Gal. 2.16), precisely as *sarx* that no one can boast before God (1 Cor. 1.29). The flesh weakens and incapacitates the law (Rom. 8.3). "Those who are in the flesh are not able to please God" (Rom. 8.8).

(v) Still more alarming, *sarx* is the sphere of sin's operations. "When we were in the flesh the sinful passions were in operation" (Rom. 7.5). "No good thing dwells in me, that is, in my flesh" (Rom. 7.18). "With my flesh

---

60. Jewett, *Anthropological Terms* 4-6, rightly warns against the danger of abstracting usage from context and against a purely lexical study. But the following analysis is alert to context, without making it depend on such an elaborate reconstruction of the various contexts as offered by Jewett.

61. I follow here for the most part the analysis of my "Jesus — Flesh and Spirit" 43-49.

62. Rom. 11.14; 1 Cor. 6.16; 15.39; Eph. 5.29, 31; Col. 2.1; cf. 2 Cor. 7.1.

63. See further below §3.4.

I serve the law of sin" (Rom. 7.25). God "sent his own Son in the very likeness of sinful flesh *(sarkos hamartias)* . . . and condemned sin in the flesh" (Rom. 8.3).

(vi) The negative force of *sarx* becomes most apparent as not only mortal but also defective, disqualifying, or destructive, when set in antithesis to *pneuma* ("Spirit"). To think of circumcision only as a rite "performed visibly in the flesh" is to misunderstand it; the circumcision which God wants is "of the heart, in Spirit and not in letter" (Rom. 2.28). "The flesh's way of thinking is death, whereas the Spirit's way of thinking is life and peace" (Rom. 8.6). "Having begun with the Spirit," Paul asks his Galatian converts somewhat despairingly, "are you now made complete with the flesh?" (Gal. 3.3). Later he bids them "Walk by the Spirit and you will not satisfy the desires of the flesh. For the flesh desires against the Spirit . . ." (5.16-17). Then he sets "the works of the flesh" (a list of social vices) over against "the fruit of the Spirit" (5.19-23). Similarly to the Philippians he asserts boldly, "It is we who are the circumcision, who worship by the Spirit of God . . . and who put no confidence in the flesh" (Phil. 3.3).

(vii) Consequently *sarx* itself can be characterized as a source of corruption and hostility to God. "The flesh's way of thinking is hostility to God" (Rom. 8.7). "Make no provision for the flesh to satisfy its desires" (Rom. 13.14). "Those who belong to the Christ Jesus have crucified the flesh with its passions and desires" (Gal. 5.24). "Those who sow to their own flesh shall from the flesh reap corruption" (Gal. 6.8).[64]

(viii) Not least of interest is the way in which the phrase *kata sarka* ("according to the flesh") mirrors the same spectrum.[65] At one end it can denote simply physical kinship — "Israel *kata sarka*" (1 Cor. 10.18). But it also lends itself to a contrast with a relationship considered more significant: Jesus Son of David *kata sarka,* but Son of God in power *kata pneuma* (Rom. 1.3-4; cf. 9.5);[66] Abraham as "our forefather *kata sarka*," in implied contrast to Abraham as "father of all who believe" (Rom. 4.1, 11; cf. 9.3);[67] and later

---

64. See also Gal. 5.13; Eph. 2.3; Col. 2.13, 18, 23.

65. Cf. also *sarkikos* and *sarkinos:*

	more neutral but nevertheless in some contrast	more negative
sarkikos	Rom. 15.27; 1 Cor. 9.11	1 Cor. 3.3; 2 Cor. 1.12; 10.4
sarkinos	2 Cor. 3.3	Rom. 7.14; 1 Cor. 3.1

BAGD, *sarkikos,* defines the difference between the terms as *sarkikos,* "belonging to the flesh, fleshly"; *sarkinos,* "consisting of flesh, fleshy."

66. Though I would still wish to say there may be something in my earlier thesis regarding Rom. 1.3-4 in particular ("Jesus — Flesh and Spirit"), I do not want to press it here. But see also §8 nn. 8 and 37 below.

67. Cf. Schweizer, *TDNT* 7.127 — *sarx* in Rom. 4.1 "is not viewed negatively, but it is also not the decisive sphere for salvation."

kata sarka denotes the slave's relationship with his earthly master as set against the more important relationship with his heavenly master (Col. 3.22-24; Eph. 6.5-6). Moral overtones enter with the disparagement of social status as judged *kata sarka* — "not many wise *kata sarka*" (1 Cor. 1.26). Paul's perspective is no longer *kata sarka,* that is, inferior and inadequate to a perspective *kata pneuma* (2 Cor. 1.17; 5.16). He no longer acts *kata sarka* (2 Cor. 10.2-3). He denounces boasting *kata sarka* (2 Cor. 11.18). Sharper still is the warning: "if you live *kata sarka* you will certainly die, but if by the Spirit you put to death the deeds of the body you will live" (Rom. 8.13). And an almost dualistic note enters in the antithesis between those born *kata sarka* and those born *kata pneuma* (Gal. 4.23, 29), and between "those who exist *kata sarka* [and who] take the side of the flesh" and "those who exist *kata pneuma* [and who] take the side of the Spirit" (Rom. 8.5).

At first glance the spectrum of Paul's usage of *sarx* seems to be continuous, without obvious break. The facts that each usage on the spectrum seems to merge into the next, that several of the texts cited above could easily have been put at different points in the spectrum, and that Galatians in particular contains such a range of usage help make the point. This suggests that there is a common link throughout, namely, *sarx* denoting what we might describe as human mortality. It is the continuum of human mortality, the person characterized and conditioned by human frailty, which gives *sarx* its spectrum of meaning and which provides the link between Paul's different uses of the term. The spectrum runs from human relationships and needs, through human weakness and desires, through human imperfection and corruption, to the fully deprecatory and condemnatory tone of the *sarx-pneuma* antithesis.[68] This first impression hypothesis, however, needs to demonstrate that it can encompass the features in Paul's usage which caused earlier commentators to speak of *sarx* as a cosmic power, to hold neutral and negative usages as distinct, or to translate *sarx* so diversely.

(a) First, despite the sharpness of some of Paul's antitheses, there is no good reason to see in Paul's usage a concept of flesh as a principle of sin or as a hostile cosmic power. In his fullest discussion of the relation between flesh and sin (Romans 7–8) Paul makes two things abundantly clear. One is that the sinning "I" cannot distance itself from the flesh. The problem which has caused the law's failure is not the law itself, but the fact that "I (myself) am fleshly *(sarkinos)*" (7.14); "I myself with my mind serve the law of God and with my flesh the law of sin" (7.25). In other words, the flesh is not something separable from the person, any more than the mind or the body is.

---

68. This conclusion accords with the dominant view among British scholars that Paul's complete range of usage grows out of the Hebrew *basar* (see, e.g., Robinson, *Man* 111-22; Stacey, *Man* 154-73).

As Paul could say, "I am body," rather than "I have a body,"[69] so he would more naturally say, "I am flesh," rather than "I have flesh" (that is, flesh which I could somehow dispense with).[70]

The other thing that Paul makes clear in Romans 7–8 is that the real culprit is neither the law nor the "I" but sin (7.17, 20). The problem with flesh is not that it is sinful *per se* but that it is vulnerable to the enticements of sin — flesh, we might say, as "the desiring I" (7.7-12).[71] It is the all too human/fleshly need to satisfy appetites which leaves the individual exposed to the wiles of sin (7.8) and indeed, or so it would seem, impotent before the power of sin at work within the "I" (7.23).[72] It is the interaction between the law and the flesh which weakens and disables the law (8.3), not because the flesh is conceived of as itself a malicious or hostile principle, but simply because the flesh is inadequate to the task (8.7-8). So also the *kata sarka* language of verses 4-5 indicates not an orientation inspired *by* a malevolent power, but an orientation *to* what is transient and perishable (8.6), a life lived solely at the animal level of satisfying merely human appetites and desires (also 8.12-13).

In short, Paul walks quite a fine line between regarding flesh as irredeemably flawed and treating it as actively antithetic and hostile to God. In the flow of his rhetoric and diversity of his expression he seems at times to veer more to the one than to the other. But the connecting thread throughout is the weakness and corruptibility of the flesh, so that a life lived on that level or characterized by that level is headed inescapably for death (8.6, 13).

In the light of the same discussion (Romans 7–8), it makes no better sense to conceptualize flesh as a cosmic power. Romans 7's clear distinction between the fleshly "I" and sin, in terms of responsibility for breach of the law, counts decisively against it. As we shall see,[73] sin itself can certainly be described as a cosmic power in Paul's thinking. But it would be more accurate to speak of sin making its headquarters in the flesh, or using and abusing the flesh, than to speak of the flesh as such as likewise a cosmic power.[74] One could indeed speak of flesh as a kind of sphere or character of existence, but to envisage that as a cosmic dimension or force field is unnecessary.[75] *Kata sarka* denotes simply life lived at the level of decaying materiality, where the

---

69. See above §3.2.

70. That "flesh" denotes the whole person (that is, in her/his fleshliness) is one of Sand's main conclusions (*Begriff* 217).

71. On the relation of "desire" to "flesh" and "sin," see below §4.7, §5.5, and §§18.3-4.

72. On the "inner person" of 7.22 see below §18.3.

73. Below §5.3.

74. As, e.g., by Robinson, *Man* 117 and Davies, *Paul* 19.

75. Cf. Schnelle, *Anthropologie* 73-75.

satisfaction of human appetite and desire is the highest objective — "whose god is their belly" (Phil. 3.19).[76]

Nor is it any more justified to speak of flesh as a power, or condition, which in Paul's view the believer has escaped. Certainly Paul talks of a being "in the flesh" which is no longer true of the believer (7.5; 8.8-9).[77] But he also talks elsewhere of the life of faith lived "in the flesh" (Gal. 2.20; Phil. 1.22), even "in our mortal flesh" (2 Cor. 4.11). Within the context of human living, conduct cannot be other than "in the flesh" (2 Cor. 10.3); it would be as impossible as a bodiless existence. The more consistent contrast, in fact, would be between life lived *en sarki, "in* the flesh," and life lived *kata sarka, "according to* the flesh" (as in 2 Cor. 10.3), the former understood as the inescapable condition of human existence ("in the flesh"), the latter understood as a morally culpable quality of social living "according to the flesh"). But Paul evidently did not think it necessary to maintain such a clear-cut distinction, varying his usage in Romans 7–8 between *en sarki* and *kata sarka* in a confusing way. His usage elsewhere, however, suggests that the variation in Romans 7–8 was more rhetorical or stylistic than anything else. The basic fact remains that Paul can and does use *en sarki* to speak *both* of a lifestyle which has been left behind *and* of the inescapably fleshly character of human existence.[78] But in Romans 7–8 *kata sarka* more consistently denotes a lifestyle at odds with God.

(b) Even if Paul's usage did not go to such extremes (designating *sarx* as a cosmic power), the transition in his usage from *sarx* as human frame to *sarx* as opposed to God (Rom. 8.7; Gal. 5.17) remains problematic in terms of the continuity of the spectrum. This was compounded by a shift in interpretation which Bultmann also inaugurated. For sixty years previously, the usual assumption was that Paul's preconversion experience had been of the weakness of the flesh and consequent inability to keep the law.[79] But sixty years ago the idea that Romans 7 testifies to Paul's preconversion sense of moral failure began to be abandoned.[80] The more explicit self-testimonies of Gal. 1.13-14 and Phil. 3.5-6 expressed rather a consciousness of effective law-keeping on the part of the pre-Christian Paul. The result was a reversal of emphasis: that the root of Paul's failure, as of the failure of his fellow Jews

76. Thus when Paul describes the list of vices in Gal. 5.19-21 as "the works of the flesh," he presumably means flesh surrendered to its weakness and/or manipulated by sin.

77. See further below §18.2.

78. Later we will see how this confusion may be resolved in terms of "the eschatological tension" (§18).

79. Jewett, *Anthropological Terms* 51-52, 56, traces this back to C. Holsten.

80. W. G. Kümmel, *Römer 7 und die Bekehrung des Paulus* (Leipzig: Hinrichs, 1929).

generally, was not the weakness of the flesh, but rather their "confidence in the flesh."

The problem was that this confidence was understood in classic Reformation terms as confidence in human ability to keep the law, "flesh" defined in Bultmann's classic terms as "the self-reliant attitude of the man who puts his trust in his own strength and in that which is controllable by him."[81] It is this assumption which in effect causes the disjunction in the spectrum, since human presumption of ability to please God seems somewhat remote from the more obvious range of *sarx*. What had been lost sight of, however, was the fact that in the immediate context, "confidence in the flesh" for Paul was confidence in belonging to the people of Israel, confidence in a national identity marked out by physical kinship, by circumcision in the flesh (Phil. 3.3-4).[82] As we shall see later,[83] it is precisely the fact that circumcision is "in the flesh," physical and visible (Rom. 2.28),[84] denoting a religious identity conceived in such terms (Gal. 6.12-13), which explains Paul's hostility to it.[85]

It follows then that it is *sarx* as denoting membership of Israel which provides the middle link in the spectrum of Paul's usage. Thus Paul can speak of Israel *kata sarka* where the usage is more neutral in character (1 Cor. 10.18, or even Rom. 4.1). But the same language is strongly negative in Gal. 4.23 and 29. The point is that the physical/sarkical relationship with Abraham was both something to be cherished (Rom. 9.3, 5) and also a source of misplaced confidence (9.8). It is precisely the interlocking of physical descent and spiritual acceptability to God, religious confidence "in the flesh," against which Paul reacted in his conversion to faith in Jesus the Christ (Phil. 3.3-4).

In other words, to turn the point completely around, it was precisely

81. Bultmann, *Theology* 1.240.

82. Contrast Bultmann, *Theology* 1.242-43: " 'confidence in the flesh' is the supposed security which a man achieves out of that which is worldly and apparent, that which he can control and deal with . . . is nothing else than man's confidence in himself."

83. Below §14.5.

84. Contrast Sand, *Begriff* 132, who at once links circumcision to the thought of one's own power and the danger of self-reliance and self-praise. Cf. Bultmann's similar jump at this point (Rom. 2.28-29) through the idea of the outward and visible to "all that has its nature in external 'appearance' " to an equation of "flesh" with the "world" (*Theology* 1.234-35). Here again he ignores the emphasis on national identity as marked out by circumcision in the flesh — as indicated by the next verse: "What then is the advantage of the Jew, or what is the value of circumcision?" (3.1).

85. Jewett, *Anthropological Terms* 95-101, recognizes the importance of Gal. 6.12-13 as a clue to Paul's most controversial usage, but in the event persists with the view that what Paul was warning against was "man's . . . trusting in that which his own flesh can accomplish" (101), "boasting in one's own flesh" as self-righteousness (114); similarly 145-47 (on Rom. 7.5). Similarly Schweizer, *TDNT* 7.133. Boyarin, however, has seen and develops the point (*Radical Jew,* particularly 67-70, 81-85).

because there was *no* clear distinction between neutral and moral usage of "flesh" that the category was so problematic for Paul. *Sarx* in its character as weak and corruptible was always an ambiguous category for Paul, both at the individual level and at the corporate level. To mark off a neutral sense, "flesh" denoting ethnic identity, as clearly distinct from a moral sense, "flesh" the ally of sin, would obscure the fact that for Paul it was precisely "flesh" denoting ethnic identity which was at the root of his own people's failure to appreciate the gospel.

(c) The consequences for translation of *sarx* in Paul are also worthy of note. For one thing, the range of translations for the same term destroys any sense that Paul had an integrated concept of *sarx,* whose spectrum of meaning might have a coherence and integration which helped explain that spectrum. For another, translations like "unspiritual nature" and "sinful nature" give a misleading[86] and falsely dualistic overtone to Paul's usage. Flesh for Paul was neither unspiritual nor sinful. The term simply indicated and characterized the weakness of a humanity constituted as flesh and always vulnerable to the manipulation of its desires and needs as flesh. And for another, such translations tend to individualize *sarx* (despite using the term "nature") and to lose sight of *sarx* as denoting a corporate or national identity. In so doing they also lose sight of the important theological point that humankind as *sarx* in this sense is equally vulnerable to manipulation by nationalist demagogery of all kinds. A much more satisfactory rule of translation would be to recognize that *sarx* is an important technical and linking term in Paul's letters and is therefore best translated consistently by the same term, "flesh."[87]

§3.4 Sōma *and* sarx

We are now in a position to clarify the relationship between these two terms in Paul. This is of no less importance, since the overlap and difference between them in Paul's theology makes his usage highly distinctive. Surprisingly, however, the significance of his anthropology at this point, as also its potential ramifications, have been largely ignored in subsequent theology — at considerable cost.

The first point of distinctiveness is the very fact that Paul did make a distinction between *sōma* and *sarx.* In contrast, Hebrew thought simply had the one word *basar,* which usually means "flesh." As already noted, there is no direct equivalent for *sōma* in Hebrew. On the other hand, in Greek thought

---

86. As though "nature" were a less problematic term than "flesh"!
87. Barrett makes a similar protest (*Paul* 69).

sōma and *sarx,* "body" and "flesh," were much closer synonyms than in Paul. Hence, once again, the more dualistic *Tendenz* of Greek anthropology, with the terms "body" and "flesh" able to express, more nearly as equivalents, a sense of imprisonment in the material world.[88]

Paul, however, made a much clearer distinction between the two words. In simplifying terms, the spectrum of meaning for *sōma* is for the most part morally neutral, whereas the spectrum of meaning for *sarx* is for the most part morally negative. The analysis of each term in §§3.2 and 3.3 above should sufficiently document the point. The two analyses will also show how each spectrum overlaps with the other to some extent. Paul does use *sōma* with a strongly negative overtone when he speaks of "the body of sin" (Rom. 6.6) and "the body of this death" (7.24), or when he talks of "putting to death the deeds of the body" (8.13). So too *sarx* can be used quite neutrally (as in 1 Cor. 10.18). That there is some overlap between the two terms is also indicated by the substitution of *sōma* for *sarx* in Rom. 8.13 and 1 Cor. 6.16.[89] But the negative note when it attaches to *sōma* is usually given by a qualifying phrase or adjective — "body *of sin*" (Rom. 6.6), "*mortal* body" (8.11). Whereas *sarx* is more regularly negative *without* any qualifying phrase or adjective. Interesting here are the two phrases in Col. 1.22 and 2.11, unique in the Pauline letters, which speak of Christ's "body of flesh" — *sarx* itself functioning as the qualifying term to emphasize the crude physicality of Jesus' bodily death.[90]

As with the term *sōma,* however, the most revealing passage is, once again, 1 Cor. 15.35-50. Here the point of significance is the clear distinction between a "flesh and blood [which] cannot inherit the kingdom of God" (15.50) and a *body* which will (15.44).[91] "Body," the more neutral term, can be transformed and raised again.[92] "Flesh" cannot.[93] There is redemption for

88. See above §2.4.

89. Cf. also 1 Cor. 7.34 ("body and spirit") with 2 Cor. 7.1 ("flesh and spirit") and 2 Cor. 4.10 with 4.11.

90. Cf. the similar phrases in 1QpHab 9.2 and 4QpNah/4Q169 2.6. The phrase *(sōmati sarkos)* also occurs in the Greek of Sir. 23.17 and *1 Enoch* 102.5. On Col. 2.11 as a reference to Christ's death see my *Colossians* 157-58.

91. Paul does use *sarx* in this connection (15.39), but we should note that whereas he uses *sōma* for heavenly bodies, his use of *sarx* is limited to the "lower" beings: humans, animals, birds, and fish (Martin, *Corinthian Body* 125).

92. Note the implication (but it is no more than that) of 2 Cor. 4.16–5.5 that there is a continuity of process of transformation and renewal through death to resurrection (the Spirit given as the first stage of the process; see further below §18.6). Possibly, therefore, Paul assumed the transmutation of Jesus' dead body into a spiritual body.

93. Gnilka, *Theologie* 46. The common assumption today that 15.50 begins a new paragraph (e.g., Aland[26], NRSV, NIV, REB; Fee, *1 Corinthians* 797-98) should not be allowed to obscure the still implicit antithesis between body and flesh. The common terms are *phthora,* "dissolution, corruption" (15.42, 50), and *aphtharsia,* "incorruptibility, im-

the body (Rom. 8.23), but salvation in the last day involves the dissolution or destruction of the flesh (1 Cor. 5.5). In short, and again in somewhat oversimplying terms, "body" denotes a *being in the world,* whereas "flesh" denotes a *belonging to the world.*[94] For Paul, human beings will always be embodied beings, by definition. But the climax of salvation is the final leaving behind of the flesh with all its inherent weakness and corruptibility.

If all this is correct, then the relationship of *sōma* and *sarx* for Paul can be visualized diagrammatically:

FLESH BODY

negative neutral

What is the theological significance of this somewhat contrived but nevertheless clear distinction between *sōma* and *sarx* in Paul? The answer is probably that he was combining elements of Hebrew and Greek anthropology into a new synthesis. On the one hand he affirmed the more holistic Hebrew understanding of human embodiment, with what that meant for the corporeality and corporateness of human existence as integral to being human. At the same time he recognized something of importance in the more negative Greek attitude to existence "in the flesh," which he also wanted to affirm. For Paul, however, the negative factor was not simply bodily existence itself but the ephemeral character of human existence as existence in desiring, decaying flesh which, as it is focused on and clung to, subverts that existence as existence before and for God. The point is that he could affirm both, the double affirmation preventing both a simplistic overvaluation of the physical and a simplistic undervaluation of the physical. Moreover, as a matter of apologetic and missionary strategy, he had common ground with both Jew and Greek in their diverse perspectives on reality and could hope thereby to win from both a hearing for the gospel as it related to existence in this age.

In broader terms we could say that Paul's distinction between *sōma*

---

mortality" (15.42, 50, 53-54). The former refers to both "flesh and blood" and "body," but the latter only to "body" (Schweizer, *TDNT* 7.128-29; Fee 798-99; Plevnik, *Paul and the Parousia* (§12 n. 1) 147-55; *pace* J. Jeremias, "Flesh and Blood Cannot Inherit the Kingdom of God," *NTS* 2 [1955-56] 151-59).

94. Cf. Robinson, *Body* — "*sarx* as neutral is man living in the world, *sarx* as sinful is man living for the world: he becomes a 'man of the world' by allowing his being-in-the-world, itself God-given, to govern his whole life and conduct" (25); "while *sarx* stands for man, in the solidarity of creation, in his distance from God, *sōma* stands for man, in the solidarity of creation, as made for God" (31).

and *sarx* made possible a positive affirmation of human createdness and creation and of the interdependence of humanity within its created environment. Sadly, however, this potential in Paul's theology was soon lost as the distinction itself was lost to sight. Already with Ignatius the need to oppose Gnostic dualism called forth the insistence that it was the *flesh* of Jesus which had been resurrected (*Smyrneans* 3).[95] And subsequently in the "Hellenization" of Christian thought the negative overtones of fleshliness became more and more attached to human bodiness, and not least to the creative function of sexuality. What Paul had objected to — the denigration of sexual relations per se[96] — became a feature of Christian spirituality in late antiquity.[97] Concupiscence, sexual desire, came to be regarded by definition as wicked. Virginity was exalted above all other human conditions. Original sin was thought to be transmitted by human procreation. The results of such denigration of sexuality continue to distort Christian attitudes to gender till this day. A recovery of Paul's distinction between human bodiness, to be affirmed and rejoiced in, and human fleshliness, always to be guarded about and against, could be a major contribution to ongoing theological reflection in such areas.

§3.5 Nous *and* kardia

We have focused the discussion of Paul's anthropology on the two key words *sōma* and *sarx*. The other terms he uses are not so important, but they do deserve some consideration. Fortunately their significance has also been less contentious. Not least of interest is the fact that, like *sōma* and *sarx,* the other most prominent terms fall into natural pairs. The first of these is *nous* and *kardia,* "mind" and "heart."

Nous occurs 21 times in the Pauline letters, most of them in Romans (6 occurrences) and 1 Corinthians (7). In the NT it is almost exclusively a Pauline concept (the term appears only 3 other times). Its infrequency and irregularity in the LXX as a translation equivalent indicates that it was not a concept which fitted naturally to Hebrew thought, whereas in Greek thought

95. Cf. Stuhlmacher, *Theologie* 1.277. Worth noting is the observation of Beker, *Paul* 153: "A resurrection of the flesh signals a loss of Paul's apocalyptic thinking; it underscores the continuity between the old age and the new age to such an extent that the spiritual transformation of the new age is ignored."

96. With most modern scholars I regard 1 Cor. 7.1 ("It is well for a man not to touch a woman") as a quotation from the Corinthians (in the letter they had sent him) which Paul seeks to counter (e.g., REB, NRSV; Barrett, *1 Corinthians* 154; Fee, *1 Corinthians* 273-74). See further below §24.5.

97. See Brown, *Body,* particularly 397, 399-400, 406-8, 416-19, 422; cf. his earlier comment on Paul (48).

nous was the highest part of the person. This reflects the typically Greek evaluation of reason or rationality as that which relates to the divine, as of a piece with the divine, as the divine in humanity.[98] The influence of such perception on Paul is most obvious at Rom. 1.20. There he clearly trades on the commonplace of Greek philosophy: that the human mind perceives the existence and nature of God rationally as more or less an axiom of human reason and indeed an unavoidable corollary of the fact of human rationality itself. In this Paul was simply using the apologetic bridge to non-Jewish religious philosophy which had earlier been constructed within Hellenistic Judaism.[99]

The importance of "mind" for Paul is easily documented. It is with his mind that he approves the law of God (Rom. 7.23, 25). The transformation of Christian existence comes through "the renewal of the mind" (12.2; Eph. 4.23). Full conviction at the rational level was important in making ethical decisions (Rom. 14.5). In contrast, the Galatians' disregard for the gospel preached by Paul was *anoētos,* "senseless, foolish" (Gal. 3.1, 3). So, too, it was of the highest importance that his mind conformed to that of Christ (1 Cor. 2.16). Worship should engage the mind as well as the spirit (1 Cor. 14.14-15). In some instances the language appears almost dualistic — mind over against flesh (Rom. 7.25) or spirit (1 Cor. 14.15). But such a deduction would misrepresent a Paul who saw offering of the body as of a piece with renewal of the mind (Rom. 12.1-2). As it is more accurate to speak of the human *sōma* as the embodied "I,"[100] so it would be more accurate to speak of the *nous* as the rational person, the perceiving, thinking, determining "I," the "I" not simply at the mercy of outside powers but able to respond and to act with understanding.[101] In which case "renewal of the mind" (Rom. 12.2) means not a new capacity to discern God's will by rational means, but the integration of rationality within the total transformation of the person, the recovery of the mind's proper function from its "disqualified" state and the undue regard and disregard for it which was the consequence of human presumption (Rom. 1.28).

Kardia, "heart," occurs 52 times in Paul (one-third of the NT usage), 15 times in Romans. It is more characteristically Hebrew, but equally Greek, in both cases denoting the innermost part of the person, the seat of emotions,

---

98. See J. Behm, *noeō, TDNT* 4.954-57.

99. See further, e.g., Bornkamm, *Early Christian Experience* 50-53, and my *Romans* 57-58.

100. See above §3.2.

101. Jewett, *Anthropological Terms,* presses needlessly for two more limited and distinct senses: *nous* as "a complex of thoughts and assumptions which can make up the consciousness of a person" (378), and *nous* as "the agent of self-control and rational communication" (380). The idea of individual thoughts is carried more by the characteristically plural use of *noēma* (2 Cor. 3.14; 4.4; 10.5; 11.3; Phil. 4.7).

but also of thought and will.[102] Paul's usage reflects this range of meaning. God is "he who searches the heart" (Rom. 8.27).[103] The law and circumcision must penetrate to the heart (Rom. 2.15, 29). Likewise obedience and belief need to be "from the heart" (Rom. 6.17; 10.9-10). The emotive dimension is apparent in talk of "the love of God poured out in our hearts" (Rom. 5.5), "the anguish of my heart" (9.2; 2 Cor. 2.4), "the desire of my heart" (Rom. 10.1), the peace of God garrisoning the heart (Phil. 4.7; Col. 3.15), and God encouraging/comforting the heart.[104] And the heart as the organ of decision-making is evident in 1 Cor. 7.37 and 2 Cor. 9.7.[105] Alongside *nous,* denoting "the thinking I," we may say that *kardia* denotes "the experiencing, motivating I." It was important for Paul that the experience of God's grace penetrated to the innermost depths of a person[106] and that the corresponding faith was an expression of deeply felt commitment.

Not least of interest is the fact that both terms were thought to be necessary — even though the range of usage of each overlapped with the other.[107] In other words, it was important, for Paul as well, that the human being was not just rational and not just a bundle of feelings, but both. "Mind" certainly distinguished humanity from the brute beast; but in the human person, rationality, emotion, and volition were all united in the concept of "heart." Perhaps it is significant that Paul spoke of the latter ("heart") so much more often than the former ("mind") and could speak of a peace from God "which surpasses understanding" (Phil. 4.7). It would probably not be straining the evidence too much to say that Paul thus in effect refused to reduce the wholeness of the person to rationality, but sought rather to maintain a balance between the rational, the emotional, and the volitional.[108] In which case here too Paul provides some precedent for a western European culture which holds the heritage of the Enlightenment and of the Romantic Revival in uneasy tension.

---

102. Robinson, *Man* 106; F. Baumgärtel and J. Behm, *kardia, TDNT* 3.606-9.

103. Echoing a classic theme — 1 Sam. 16.7; 1 Kgs. 8.39; Pss. 17.3; 44.21; 139.1-2, 23; Prov. 15.11; Jer. 11.20; 12.3. See also 1 Cor. 4.5; 14.25; 1 Thes. 2.4; and contrast 2 Cor. 5.12.

104. Col. 2.2; 4.8; 2 Thes. 2.17; Eph. 6.22. Note also Phil. 1.7-8, where *kardia* parallels *splanchna,* "(feeling of) affection."

105. Note also 2 Cor. 8.16 ("eager concern") and Col. 3.22/Eph. 6.5 ("single-mindedness"). Talk of a "clean heart" in 1 Tim. 1.5 and 2 Tim. 2.22 has a more stereotyped ring.

106. 2 Cor. 1.22; 3.2-3; 4.6; Gal. 4.6; Eph. 1.18; 3.17.

107. *Nous* could have an emotive overtone in Greek thought (LSJ, *noos* 3), just as it could occasionally (6 times) translate Hebrew *leb,* "heart" (as against the 723 occasions in which *leb* is translated as *kardia*). See also above n. 102.

108. Contrast Philo and Josephus, and in more recent times, Pfleiderer and Holtzmann, who all subordinate *kardia* entirely to *nous* (noted by Jewett, *Anthropological Terms* 306-8).

§3.6 Psychē *and* pneuma

The only other pairing[109] which calls for some attention is *psychē,* "soul," and *pneuma* in the sense of "(human) spirit." Both terms are little used by Paul, but their usage has some significance for our appreciation of his anthropology and of how Paul conceived of the interface between the divine and the human.

Paul uses *psychē* just 13 times, 4 of them in Romans. This itself is in striking contrast to the regular use of the term in classical Greek and of *nephesh* in the OT (756 times).[110] The difference between Hebraic and Greek anthropology becomes as clear here as anywhere. For in classical Greek usage the *psychē* is "the essential core of man which can be separated from his body and which does not share in the body's dissolution."[111] Here is the origin of the concept of "the immortality of the soul," as the continuing existence of an inner, hidden part of the human person after death. In contrast, in Hebrew thought, *nephesh* denotes the whole person, the "living *nephesh*" of Gen. 2.7.[112]

Paul's usage clearly echoes the typical Hebraic mind-set.[113] *Psychē* denoting the person is clear in several passages.[114] Elsewhere the sense slides into "life," or *psychē* as the focus of human vitality.[115]

The number of uses of *pneuma* denoting human spirit in Paul is uncertain, since it is unclear in several passages whether the divine Spirit or the human spirit is referred to.[116] In any case, it will be significant that the number of references to the (Holy) Spirit far outweigh those to the (human) spirit.[117] The immediate inference which can fairly be drawn is that for Paul the gospel is not about an innate spirituality awaiting release, but about the divine Spirit acting

109. On "conscience" and "inner person" see above n. 16 and below §18.3.

110. Stacey, *Man* 121.

111. Jacob, *TDNT* 9.611.

112. BDB, *nephesh* 4. Striking here is the fact that *nephesh* can be used of the dead person shortly after death, while the corpse still has the person's distinguishing features (see Jacob, *TDNT* 9.620-21).

113. So most; e.g., Stacey, *Man* 124; Conzelmann, *Outline* 179.

114. Rom. 2.9; 13.1; 16.4; 1 Cor. 15.45 (citing Gen. 2.7); 2 Cor. 1.23; 12.15; 1 Thes. 2.8.

115. "Life" — Rom. 11.3; Phil. 2.30; "vitality" — Col. 3.23; Eph. 6.6; cf. Phil. 1.27 ("with one *psychē*"), 2.2 (*sympsychos,* "united in soul") and 2.20 (*isopsychos,* "of like soul"). Contrast the more partitive sounding 1 Thes. 5.23; but see p. 57 above.

116. Particularly 1 Cor. 4.21; 14.15, 32; 2 Cor. 4.13; Gal. 6.1; Eph. 1.17; Phil. 1.27; see also §16 n. 89 below.

117. Reference to the human spirit is clear enough in nineteen cases (Rom. 1.9; 8.16; 1 Cor. 2.11; 5.3-5; 7.34; 1 Cor. 14.14; 16.18; 2 Cor. 2.13; 7.1, 13; Gal. 6.18; Eph. 4.23; Phil. 4.23; Col. 2.5; 1 Thes. 5.23; 2 Tim. 4.22; Phm. 25), though three at least of these could be added to the previous note (Rom. 1.9; 1 Cor. 5.3; 14.14). Of the 146 references to *pneuma* in the Pauline letters, well over 100 refer to the Spirit of God.

upon and in a person from without. More to the point here, the spirit is evidently that dimension of the human person by means of which the person relates most directly to God. Hence passages like Rom. 1.9 ("I serve God with my spirit") and 8.16 ("the Spirit bears witness with our spirit"), the analogy between the Spirit of God and the human spirit in 1 Cor. 2.11,[118] and the idea that the person "who is united with the Lord is one spirit" (1 Cor. 6.17), not to mention the ambiguous references noted above (n. 116). Indeed there has been a persistent view that for Paul the human spirit is but a manifestation of the divine Spirit.[119] This could well reflect the influence of Hebraic thought.[120] And though it would not be inconsistent with Stoic (and subsequently Gnostic) anthropology in particular, it marks a further difference between characteristic Hebraic and Hellenistic thought in that it is the *pneuma* which is the highest (or deepest) dimension of the person rather than the *nous*.[121]

As with the two previous anthropological pairs there is evidently an overlap of meaning in the respective usage ranges of *psyche* and *pneuma*. This reflects the origins of both terms in Greek and Hebrew usage, but in Paul's developed usage the influence is predominantly from Hebrew anthropology. For both terms (*psyche/nephesh* and *pneuma/ruach*) express an original identification of "breath" as the life force.[122] In the Hebrew scriptures the overlap is evident in a number of texts.[123] Most striking is Gen. 2.7 — "God breathed into his nostrils the breath (*n^esamah*) of life; and man became a living *nephesh*" — since *n^esamah* and *ruach* are close synonyms (e.g., Job 27.3; Isa. 57.16). But in the interval between that earlier usage and Paul a distinction becomes clearer — *pneuma* denoting more the Godward dimension of the human being, *psyche* limited more to the vital force itself.[124] We need not attempt to trace the development.[125] Its outcome is clear enough in Paul's own usage, which is all

---

118. See also Moule, *Holy Spirit* (§16 n. 1) 7-11.

119. Robinson, *Man* 110; Bultmann, *Theology* 1.206-9; Schweizer, *TDNT* 6.435-36; Jewett, *Anthropological Terms* 182-200; Fee, *Empowering Presence* (§16 n. 1) 24-26. Contrast Stacey, *Man* 133-36.

120. For the human spirit as divine Spirit see Gen. 6.3; Job 27.3; 32.8; 33.4; 34.14-15; Ps. 104.29-30; Eccl. 12.7; Isa. 42.5; Ezek. 37.5, 6, 8-10. Contrast Stacey, *Man* 137: "the Pauline usage of spirit for the 'godward side of man' is not found in the Old Testament."

121. Cf. A. Dihle, *psyche, TDNT* 9.634. Compare the data collected by Baumgärtel and Kleinknecht in *TDNT* 6.360-62 and 357-59. Contrast the older view of Pfleiderer and Holtzmann that the *nous* is the "Anknüpfungspunkt" for the divine spirit (Jewett, *Anthropological Terms* 359).

122. Jacob, *TDNT* 9.609, 618-19; Kleinknecht and Baumgärtel, *TDNT* 6.334-37, 360.

123. BDB, *nephesh* 2; *ruach* 4.

124. Robinson, *Man* 19-20, 109.

125. The hypothesis of Gnostic influence is unnecessary to explain the *pneumatikos/psychikos* distinction in 1 Cor. 2.13–3.1 (the hypothesis pioneered by Richard

that need concern us here. I refer once again to 1 Cor. 15.44-46, but also 2.13-15. For in 15.44-46 *psychē* and *psychikos* clearly denote the living person, but one limited to the present bodily existence (in contrast to the *sōma pneumatikon,* the "spiritual body"). And in 2.14 the *psychikos* person is by definition one who is unable to receive or appreciate the things of the *pneuma.*

Where this observation may be of wider relevance is in the insight that for Paul the human being is more than "soul." *Psychē* is not sufficient to describe the depths of the individual. Persons exist on and are related to fuller dimensions of reality than just the psychical. At the end of a century which has grown to appreciate the insights of Freud and Jung, then, Paul's anthropology may carry a salutary lesson for us. That lesson would be to warn against thinking that the psyche can reveal everything of importance about the inner life of a person. Paul, once again in line with his Jewish heritage, also speaks of the human spirit, a still deeper depth or higher reality of the person. Moreover, he both implies and teaches that it is only by functioning at that level and by opening the human spirit to the divine Spirit that the human being can be whole. At least, that is an important feature of his theology and gospel — as we shall see.

§3.7 *Summary*

In sum, Paul's conception of the human person is of a being who functions within several dimensions. As embodied beings we are social, defined in part by our need for and ability to enter into relationships, not as an optional extra, but as a dimension of our very existence. Our fleshness attests our frailty and weakness as mere humans, the inescapableness of our death, our dependence on satisfaction of appetite and desire, our vulnerability to manipulation of these appetites and desires. At the same time, as rational beings we are capable of soaring to the highest heights of reflective thought. And as experiencing beings we are capable of the deepest emotions and the most sustained motivation. We are living beings, animated by the mystery of life as a gift, and there is a dimension of our being at which we are directly touched by the profoundest reality within and behind the universe. Paul would no doubt say in thankful acknowledgment with the psalmist: "I praise you, for I am fearfully and wonderfully made" (Ps. 139.14).

Reitzenstein in 1909). What is in view are two levels of spirituality ("mature/infant" — 2.6/3.1; "wise/foolish — 1.25-27) rather than two classes of persons. Sufficient explanation can be found in the Jewish Wisdom tradition; see particularly R. A. Horsley, "Pneumatikos vs. Psychikos: Distinctions of Spiritual Status among the Corinthians," *HTR* 69 (1976) 269-88; *pace* Jewett, *Anthropological Terms* 343-44.

CHAPTER 3

Humankind under Indictment

§4 Adam[1]

§4.1 The dark side of humanity

An analysis of Paul's theology following the outline he himself provided in Romans has little choice on where to begin. For the first main section of his exposition quickly unfolds as *an indictment of humankind* (Rom. 1.18–3.20). So, having given some indication of his assumptions regarding God and about the way human beings are constituted, we turn at once to his doleful analysis of the human condition.

In fact, this next stage (for us) of Paul's theology follows on immediately from the last. It simply completes the portrayal of Paul's anthropology.

1. **Bibliography**. **C. K. Barrett**, *From First Adam to Last: A Study in Pauline Theology* (London: Black/New York, Scribner, 1962); **G. Bornkamm**, "Sin, Law and Death: An Exegetical Study of Romans 7," *Early Christian Experience* 87-104; **E. Brandenburger**, *Adam und Christus. Exegetisch-religionsgeschichtliche Untersuchungen zu Röm. 5.12-21 (1 Kor. 15)* (WMANT 7; Neukirchen: Neukirchener, 1962); **Gnilka**, *Paulus* 201-5; **M. D. Hooker**, "Adam in Romans 1," *NTS* 6 (1959-60) 297-306; "A Further Note on Romans 1," *NTS* 13 (1966-67) 181-83; **J. Jervell**, *Imago Dei: Gen. 1.26f. im Spätjudentum, in der Gnosis und in den paulinischen Briefen* (FRLANT 76; Göttingen: Vandenhoeck, 1960); **Laato**, *Paulus* ch. 4; **J. R. Levison**, *Portraits of Adam in Early Judaism From Sirach to 2 Baruch* (JSPS 1; Sheffield: Sheffield Academic, 1988); **B. J. Malina**, "Some Observations on the Origin of Sin in Judaism and St. Paul," *CBQ* 31 (1969) 18-34; **R. Scroggs**, *The Last Adam: A Study in Pauline Anthropology* (Philadelphia: Fortress/Oxford: Blackwell, 1966); **Strecker**, *Theologie* 63-69; **F. R. Tennant**, *The Sources of the Doctrines of the Fall and Original Sin* (Cambridge: Cambridge University, 1903); **A. J. M. Wedderburn**, "The Theological Structure of Romans 5.12," *NTS* 19 (1972-73) 339-54; "Adam in Paul's Letter to the Romans," in E. A. Livingstone, ed., *Studia Biblica 1978* III (Sheffield: JSOT, 1980) 413-30; **Whiteley**, *Theology* 48-58; **N. P. Williams**, *The Ideas of the Fall and of Original Sin* (London: Longmans, 1927).

For a striking feature of Paul's understanding of humankind is the number of times a negative sign is attached to the various key terms described in §3. This we saw is particularly true of *sarx* ("flesh"), the human person belonging to the world, weak and corruptible. Life in the world cannot be lived except "in the flesh." But life lived *kata sarka,* "in accordance with the flesh," where animal appetites and desires dominate existence, is a life hostile to God, unable to please God (Rom. 8.7-8). *Sōma* ("body") is the more neutral term, but it too could be used in a strongly negative sense — "the body of sin" (6.6), "this body of death" (7.24). At best this body is still the mortal body, the dead body yet to be redeemed (6.12; 8.10-11). So too the *nous* ("mind"), though similarly neutral, has been corrupted: the Pauline letters speak of the "disqualified mind" (Rom. 1.28), the "futility of the mind" (Eph. 4.17), the "mind of flesh" (Col. 2.18). Rom. 1.21 and 24 speak in turn of humanity's "foolish heart darkened," and of humans being "handed over in the desires of their hearts to uncleanness." The human person as *psychē* ("soul") is also earthbound. *Psychē* is indeed the principle of life, but life incomplete, circumscribed, transitory — humanity on its own level, not God's. The *psychikon sōma* needs to be redeemed (Rom. 8.23), needs to become the *pneumatikon sōma* (1 Cor. 15.44-49). Even the human *pneuma* ("spirit") can, in one place, be spoken of as needing to be cleansed from "defilement" (2 Cor. 7.1).

Equally striking is the language Paul uses when he recalls the opening indictment of Romans in summary terms — Rom. 5.6-10:

> While we were still *weak,* yet Christ at that time died for the *ungodly.* For only rarely will someone die for a *righteous* man; for perhaps someone will dare to die for the *good* man. But God demonstrates his love to us in that while we were *sinners* Christ died for us. . . . For if when we were *enemies* we were reconciled to God. . . .

The human condition Paul had in mind was marked not only by weakness (the condition of the *sarx*), but by ungodliness *(asebeia),* the term he had used in the opening of the indictment (1.18).[2] They were literally "without worship,"[3] lacking in reverence. They were marked by unrighteousness *(adikia)* and absence of goodness, the former term again echoing the opening indictment of 1.18 (the wrath of God "revealed from heaven against all impiety and unrighteousness of human beings who suppress the truth in unrighteousness").[4] There was

---

2. Paul uses *asebeia,* "ungodliness," only in Rom. 1.18 and 11.26 and the corresponding adjective *asebēs,* "ungodly," only in Rom. 4.5 and 5.6. But they appear also in 1 Tim. 1.9; 2 Tim. 2.16; and Tit. 2.12.

3. *Sebomai,* "worship."

4. *Adikia,* "unrighteousness," is the more prominent term in the indictment (Rom. 1.18 [twice], 29; 2.8; 3.5).

something fundamentally unjust in their relationships.[5] Worst of all, in a clearly intended climax to the sequence, human beings were "sinners" and "enemies" of God. To clarify what Paul had in mind in this sweeping criticism will be one of the tasks of this chapter.

Subsequently the author of Ephesians described the human condition in even starker terms (Eph. 2.1-3):

> . . . you were dead in your trespasses and sins, in which you once walked, in accordance with this world, in accordance with the ruler of the power of the air, the spirit which is now at work in the sons of disobedience; among whom we all also once conducted ourselves in the passions of our flesh, following the desires of flesh and senses, and we were by nature children of wrath, like the rest [of humankind].

Here again powerful imagery is used to characterize humankind, which echoes Paul's earlier language and whose meaning and implications we will have to tease out in the course of this chapter.

In these passages (Rom. 5.6-10; Eph. 2.1-3) Pauline theology recognizes in its own terms what all religious philosophies have recognized in theirs: that there is a dark side to the human character, which must be taken into account, otherwise it may destroy humanity. Whatever forces there are outside individuals which bear upon them in an adverse, oppressive way (below §5), there is also a virulent toxin within, whose poison, if allowed to spread unchecked, will slowly kill the whole organism. The rabbis described it as the *yetser hara,* "the evil impulse" within, to explain the mad, self-damaging choices we all make. The Gnostics, Manichees, and Cathars attempted to explain it in terms of the evilness of matter, requiring a strict asceticism in response. Shakespeare characterizes it as a fatal flaw within his tragic heroes. Robert Louis Stevenson depicted its frightening potential in *Dr Jekyll and Mr Hyde.* Oscar Wilde warned of the degeneration which can unfold behind outward appearance in *The Picture of Dorian Gray.* And Jonathan Swift simply followed out its outworking in the most pitiless portrayal of human debasement in the Yahoos of *Gulliver's Travels.*

Paul's attempt to explain this dark side of humanity focuses on the figure of *Adam* and the account of "man's first disobedience"[6] in Genesis 2–3 — what has traditionally been described as "the Fall."[7]

---

5. *Adikia,* indicating the lack of order, right *(dikē),* lack of righteousness, justice *(dikaiosynē).*

6. Milton, *Paradise Lost* 1.1.1.

7. The Bible does not use the term "fall" itself in referring to the account of Adam and Eve. But the imagery was strengthened by the parallel "falls" of the king of Babylon and the king of Tyre described in Isa. 14.12-15 and Ezek. 28.16-17 (cf. Luke 10.18),

§4.2 Adam in Jewish scripture

Where did Paul draw his Adam theology from? The most obvious answer is: from Genesis 1–3 itself and the theological themes opened up already there. The key themes which we find in Paul are distinctively Jewish, and there is no obvious alternative source in the wider religious thought of the time. The nearest contender, the Hermetic tractate *Poimandres,* itself shows clear evidence of influence from the Genesis narratives.[8] If we are to understand Paul's teaching on the subject, therefore, it would be well to familiarize ourselves with the traditions of theological reflection with which Paul himself was no doubt familiar and which he could assume would inform in some degree his readers' reception of his own writing on the subject.

There are several notable features in Genesis 1–3 which bear directly on Paul's own use of the passage. First, the use of the term *adam. Adam* is widely used throughout the Hebrew scriptures in the sense "humankind, human being."[9] The same is true in Genesis 1–2, as is clear from 1.26-28 and 2.7. At the same time, there is in the account an ambivalence between *adam* as an individual and *adam* representing humankind as a whole. But this only really begins at 2.18;[10] and in 2.23-24 the Hebrew shows awareness of this ambivalence by using *ish* ("man") with *ishah* ("woman, wife"). The confusion is caused by the story format, by the fact that the double story serves to explain both marriage and the harshness of human labour, and by the merging of myth with history (so also in Gen. 5.1-2, 3-5). Paul also displays the same ambivalence. He speaks of "man" *(anēr,* not *anthrōpos)* as the "image and glory of God," whereas "the woman/wife is the glory of man/husband" (1 Cor. 11.7). And he implies that the initial failure in Eden was that of Eve (2 Cor. 11.3; much starker in the later 1 Tim. 2.14).[11] Nevertheless, the sense that the Genesis account is the account of humankind, whether represented

---

although the imagery of Genesis 3 itself is of disobedience and consequent expulsion from the presence of God. O. S. Wintermute translates *Jub.* 12.25 as a reference to "the day of the Fall" (*OTP* 2.82), but R. H. Charles (revised by C. Rabin) takes the reference to "the day of the collapse (of the tower of Babel)" (H. F. D. Sparks, ed., *The Apocryphal Old Testament* [Oxford: Clarendon, 1984] 49), which makes better sense in context. In *4 Ezra* 7.118 the Latin term *casus* is translated by NRSV and *OTP* as "fall"; but it could denote a moral calamity (the Syriac has "misfortune, evil"); see Levison, *Adam* 123.

8. Dodd, *Bible* especially 145-69. The same is true of Gnostic tractates found at Nag Hammadi, particularly *The Apocryphon of John, The Hypostasis of the Archons,* and *The Apocalypse of Adam.*

9. BDB, *adam* 2.

10. The LXX translates *adam* as *anthrōpos* up to 2.18, but thereafter (and in 2.16) as *Adam.*

11. 2 Cor. 11.3 simply follows the Genesis story line; it is 1 Tim. 2.14 which makes a theological point of the story.

as a single person or as male and female, never leaves Genesis 1–3. And, as we shall see, Paul's own use of the narratives shares the same sense. When Paul speaks of or alludes to "Adam" he speaks of humankind as a whole.

Second, we may note also the deliberate play in the Hebrew of Gen. 2.7 between *adam* and the material from which *adam* was made, *adamah* ("ground, earth") — "the LORD God formed the *adam,* dust from the *adamah.*" The tie-in was no doubt deliberate: the *adam* was formed to till the *adamah* (2.5-9); and subsequently the *adamah* is caught up in *adam*'s penalty for his disobedience (the ground cursed and its produce necessitating hard labour), a penalty which will last till *adam* returns to the *adamah* (3.17-19).[12] Paul clearly had this passage in mind when he speaks of the futility of creation in its subjection to corruption in Rom. 8.20-22. But we might also note that the theme ties in closely to what was said above (§3.2) regarding the implications of Paul's *sōma* language, as indicating the human bond to the rest of creation.

Third, "the tree of the knowledge of good and evil" (Gen. 2.9), from which the *adam* was sternly ordered not to eat (2.17), has caused endless discussion. The most obvious understanding is not that the fruit would give Adam an awareness of right and wrong which he would otherwise have totally lacked; the command itself presupposes that Adam already knew the difference between obedience and disobedience.[13]. Rather what seems to be in view is the issue of moral autonomy. The fruit of the tree would make Adam think he knew best, wise in his own eyes, no longer needing to depend on God for direction and moral boundaries. Hence the temptation of the serpent: "You will be like God, knowing good and evil" (3.5). And the attractiveness of the tree to Eve: "the tree was to be desired to make one wise" (3.6).[14]

Fourth, the warning is that disobedience on this point will result in death (2.17 — "in the day that you eat of it you shall die"). In the event the result is exclusion from the other named tree, "the tree of life" (2.9, 22, 24), and by implication from the presence of God in the garden. Adam chooses to know for himself, independent of God. The result, however, is indeed independence from God; but that means also being cut off from access to life.

---

12. See further Gen. 4.11-12; 5.29; 8.21-22.

13. Tennant, *Fall* 12-13; Lyonnet, "Sin" (§5 n. 1) 5-6.

14. That this was the understanding of the passage in early Judaism is probably confirmed by the strong echo of the Genesis 2–3 narrative in Ezekiel 28, which describes how the king of Tyre was expelled from Eden (28.13, 16) because he compared his mind with the mind of God and claimed (divine) wisdom (28.2-10). Also by the subsequent renderings of the story: Josephus, *Ant.* 1.37, paraphrases Gen. 2.17 as the tree "of the wisdom *(phronēsis)* by which might be distinguished what was good and what evil"; and Targum Neofiti translates similarly, "the tree of knowledge, from which everyone who eats will know to distinguish between good and evil." See discussion in G. J. Wenham, *Genesis 1–15* (WBC 1; Waco: Word, 1987) 63-64.

The obverse implication is that it was the divine intention for Adam to have access to the tree of life as part of the human share in and responsibility for creation. The explicit permission, "You may eat from every tree in the garden" (2.16), with only the tree of the knowledge of good and evil forbidden (2.17), clearly includes permission to eat of the tree of life. Which also implies the divine intention that humankind should "live for ever" (3.22). Yet it is left entirely unclear whether eternal life was to be gained by a regular eating from the tree (as the former verses may imply), or could be gained from a single eating (as 3.22 may imply). This further ambiguity in the Genesis mythic story probably reflects an enduring uncertainty as to the origin of death. Was death always part of the created order, as we today inevitably must take it to be? Or does the fact of death indicate some flaw or failure in creation? These ambiguities and questions remain part of Paul's theologizing at this point, derived, no doubt, directly from the original Adam stories.

Granted then that Paul was directly influenced by the Genesis narratives (Genesis 1–3), as we shall see, can we detect other influence from the long pre-Christian Jewish theological tradition? Since the passage has been so central to Christian theology of "the fall" (and in Christian iconography), it comes as a salutary caution to note that the Hebrew scriptures in fact take little notice of the Adam story, although there are allusions at a number of places,[15] and there is certainly a concept of universal sinfulness.[16] It is not really possible, therefore, to speak of a Jewish scriptural tradition of "the fall," and this should be noted in assessing where Jewish influences on Paul's theology are to be identified. The situation changes, however, in the Jewish writings of the postbiblical (so-called "intertestamental") period.

§4.3 Adam in post-biblical Jewish tradition

Ben Sira, the most important of the deuterocanonical Jewish writings, does not change the picture much. Indeed, at first sight it does not seem to have a real concept of anything approximating a fall. Sir. 15.14 — God "from the beginning made humankind and left him in the power of his inclination (diaboulion)." But as 15.15 makes clear (and despite Gen. 6.5 and 8.21), the inclination (yetser) is not regarded as evil.[17] Sir. 17.1 rehearses the creation

---

15. 1 Chron. 1.1; Deut. 4.32; Job 31.33; Ezek. 28.12-15; Hos. 6.7; also Tob. 8.6. But see also Tennant, Fall 15-16 n. 7.

16. Gen. 6.5; 8.21; Tennant, Fall 101-2, refers to 1 Kgs. 8.46; 2 Chron. 6.36; Job 4.17; 14.4; 25.4; Pss. 51.5; 130.3; 143.2; Prov. 20.9; Eccl. 7.20; Jer. 17.9. See also Fitzmyer, Paul 71-72; Merklein, "Paulus und die Sünde" (§5 n. 1) 139-42, with bibliography in n. 46.

17. Tennant, Fall 111-17; Levison, Adam 34-35. In what follows, cf. Levison 35-48.

of humankind "out of the earth," but adds "and turned him back to it again" in echo of Gen. 3.19, without any hint that this was originally a word of judgment. Ben Sira simply notes that the life created by God was of limited duration (17.2) and repeats that God "made them [plural] in his image" (17.3). But the "inclination" (Greek) is again something positive (17.6). Without more ado, ben Sira notes that God himself "showed them good and evil" (17.7) and "bestowed knowledge upon them, and allotted to them the law of life. He established with them an eternal covenant" (17.11-12). It is not that ben Sira had no conception of human sin. Quite the contrary, as the very next passage clearly demonstrates (17.25–18.14): humans are all too sinful and mortal. It is simply that this human condition is not traced back to a primeval act of disobedience and consequent punishment.[18] Even in 40.1-11, the echo of Gen. 3.19 seems to be drawn in simply to service the thought that hard work and expectation of death are the common lot. Death is simply "the Lord's decree for all flesh" (41.1-4).

There is, however, one exception to this predominant emphasis in ben Sira: Sir. 25.24 — "From a woman sin had its beginning, and because of her we all die."[19] The parallel to Wis. 2.23-24 (cited below)[20] and 2 Cor. 11.3 and 1 Tim. 2.14 (referred to above) can hardly be accidental.[21] Ben Sira knew (and at least drew upon) the tradition that death was the consequence of an original sin.[22]

Of greater importance is the Wisdom of Solomon. Its particular relevance for us lies in the fact that Paul certainly knew and seems deliberately to echo it in his opening indictment (Rom. 1.19–2.6).[23] There are clear refer-

18. Similarly in 24.28; 33.10-13; and 49.16, the last of which provides an early expression of the subsequently prominent theme of Adam's glorification.

19. The Hebrew reads: "Because of her we die *yhd*," which could be translated ". . . communally"; that is, death is our common lot.

20. Note also *Life of Adam and Eve — Vita* 44 and *Apoc. Mos.* 14 and 32; also *2 Enoch* 30.17.

21. *Pace* J. R. Levison, "Is Eve to Blame? A Contextual Analysis of Sir. 25.24," *CBQ* 47 (1985) 617-23; also *Adam* 155; followed uncritically by Stowers, *Rereading* 89, 92 (he makes no reference to Wis. 2.23-24 whatsoever); dismissed by P. W. Skehan and A. A. Di Lella, *The Wisdom of Ben Sira* (AB 39; New York: Doubleday, 1987) 348-49.

22. Tennant, *Fall* 119-21, 244.

23. See particularly H. Daxer, *Römer 1.18–2.10 im Verhältnis zu spätjüdischen Lehrauffassung* (Naumburg: Pätz'sche, 1914); C. Bussmann, *Themen der paulinischen Missionspredigt auf dem Hintergrund der spätjüdisch-hellenistischen Missionsliteratur* (Bern/Frankfurt: Lang, 1975) 108-22; briefly set out in Sanday and Headlam, *Romans* 51-52. For the strong echo of Wis. 15.1-4 in Rom. 2.4 see my *Romans* 82-83. The evidence is all the more interesting since the date of the Wisdom of Solomon is so uncertain — variously set between about 220 BCE and 50 CE. D. Winston dates it to the reign of Gaius Caligula (37-41 CE; *ABD* 6.122-23). The later it is dated, and the more likely to an Alexandrian provenance,

ences in Wisdom to the creation of the first human formed from the earth (Wis. 7.1) and given rule over the creatures (9.2-3), and to the first-formed father of the world's transgression (*paraptōma* — 10.1). Notable also is the echo of Gen. 3.19 in Wis. 15.8 and the accusation in 15.11 that the human fashioned from clay "failed to know the one who formed him" (cf. Rom. 1.19-21).[24] Most noteworthy of all is Wis. 2.23-24:

> For God created humankind for incorruption,
> and made him/her the image of his own eternity;
> But through the devil's envy death entered into the world,
> and those who are of his party experience it.

The vocabulary and ideas here form an echo chamber for several of Paul's own theological assertions in this area.[25] So here, too, we can be confident that Paul was aware of such theological reflection and probably drew on it.[26]

Other postbiblical texts indicate that by Paul's time the role of Adam's disobedience had become a major factor in generating explanations for the human condition. We may simply note the retelling of the story of Adam's disobedience and expulsion in *Jub.* 3.17-25, with its striking though also characteristic elaboration in 3.26-31.[27] The beasts cease to speak a common language and are expelled with Adam.[28] But to Adam alone is it "granted . . .

---

the more striking is Paul's knowledge of it. The facts suggest either a widespread circulation of the text in diaspora synagogues or that Paul came upon it in his postconversion rethinking of his Jewish heritage, not least in its interface with Gentile culture and need.

24. As well as the echo of 15.1-4 in Rom. 2.4, note the shared image and language of the potter in Wis. 15.7 and Rom. 9.21. As Levison notes (*Adam* 53), the anthropology of 15.11 is more Greek than Hebrew, since it speaks of a soul being breathed into the clay figure, rather than of the clay figure becoming a living soul (similarly Philo, *Virt.* 203-4; cf. *Plant.* 42 — the mind is the true *anthrōpos* in us).

25. "Incorruption" *(aphtharsia)* — Rom. 2.7; 1 Cor. 15:42, 50, 53-54.
"Image" *(eikōn)* — Rom. 1.23; 1 Cor. 11.7; 15.49; 2 Cor. 3.18; 4.4; Col. 1.15; 3.10.
"Eternity" *(aïdiotēs)* — Rom. 1.20 *(aïdios)*.
"Death entered into the world," the same words as in Rom. 5.12.

26. Levison, *Adam* 51-52, argues that 2.24 is a reference to Cain. But *diabolos* was already established as a reference to God's heavenly opponent: it is the regular translation for *satan* (the heavenly "accuser") in the LXX (2 Chron. 21.1; Job 1–2; Zech. 3.1-2) and appears also for "Mastema, the chief of the spirits" hostile to God in the Greek fragment of *Jub.* 10.8. The theme of "envy" is part of the serpent's temptation in *Apoc. Mos.* 18.4, and "envy" is the explanation for the serpent's malice in Josephus, *Ant.* 1.41. And if the death is thought of as eternal death (Tennant, *Fall* 124-26; Levison), then it fits the idea of death as exclusion from the tree of life (Genesis 3) rather than as a reference to Cain's murder of Abel.

27. *Jubilees* is usually dated to the mid-2nd century BCE.

28. The motif is picked up in Philo, *Conf.* 6-8; *Qu. Gen.* 1.32; and Josephus, *Ant.* 1.41.

that he might cover his shame" (referring to Gen. 2.25; 3.10-11, 21). Hence the law's requirement that its practitioners "should cover their shame and they should not be uncovered as the Gentiles are uncovered" (*Jub.* 3.31). The implication of promiscuity as characteristic of Gentiles is reflected in Rom. 1.24-27. However, that more likely reflects a broader Jewish tradition[29] than simply *Jubilees*.

Philo seems to have thought that human failure is the inevitable result of the human constitution. The two creation stories speak of "two kinds of humans, the one, those who live by reason, the divine inbreathing, the other those who live by blood and the pleasure of the flesh. The latter is a moulded clod of earth, the other is the faithful impress of the divine image" (*Heres* 56-57). But the double allusion to the second creation story (Gen. 2.7) indicates that Philo was also thinking of each human being (*Leg. All.* 1.31-32). Consequently it is *aisthēsis* ("sense perception") and the pleasure of the senses which bring reason into slavery (*Opif.* 165-66). This is Philo's interpretation of the temptation through the woman. For as mind corresponds to the man, sense perception corresponds to the woman (*Opif.* 165). And thus "woman becomes for him the beginning of blameworthy life," and "bodily pleasure *(hē tōn sōmatōn hēdonē)* is the beginning of wrongs and violations of the law" (*Opif.* 151-52).[30] The result is the defiling of the divine image (*Virt.* 205). It was being given knowledge of their nakedness that was for humans "the beginning of evil" (*Qu. Gen.* 1.40). Zeal for pleasure brings about spiritual death, by causing the earth-born creature to give himself over to the earth from which he was compounded and to turn away from heaven (the soul) back to the earth (physical death) (*Qu. Gen.* 1.51).[31]

The *Life of Adam and Eve* emerged probably a little after Paul,[32] but it shows some striking parallels with Paul. Most notable are the passages

29. See further below §5.5.

30. See also with reference to *epithymia*, "desire," Philo, *Decal.* 142, 150, 153, 173; *Spec. Leg.* 4.84-85. In *Heres* 294-95 Philo describes how the unformed soul in the child "closely resembles smooth wax and has not yet received any impression of good or evil." Similarly in *Praem.* 62 he maintains that "all we human beings, before the reason in us is fully grown, lie in the borderline between vice and virtue with no bias to either side."

31. Philo's reuse of the Genesis 1–3 material is, of course, much more complex (see Levison, *Adam* 63-88). I select only a few pertinent points here.

32. The text comes down to us in two recensions, Greek *(Apoc. Mos.)* and Latin *(Vita Adae et Evae),* which may, however, both stem from an original Hebrew text. Such an original cannot be dated more accurately than between 200 BCE and 100 CE, but there may well have been a version prior to Paul, and its midrashic rather than allegorical treatment suggests a provenance within the land of Israel (M. D. Johnson in *OTP* 2.252). Our current texts could therefore reflect traditions and speculations about Adam and Eve known to Paul.

which bear upon our present theme:[33] Satan's transformation of himself into the brightness of an angel;[34] the location of Paradise in the third heaven;[35] the identification of *epithymia* ("desire") as the root of all sin;[36] and the theme of "death gaining rule over all our race" as a result of Adam and Eve's transgression.[37] It is also of relevance to note that the image of God seems to remain unaffected by the expulsion from Paradise,[38] whereas Adam laments "that I have been estranged from my glory with which I was clothed" (*Apoc. Mos.* 20.2; 21.6). In view of the reflections above on Genesis 2–3, we may also note that, according to the *Apocalypse of Moses,* "the throne of God was made ready where the tree of life was" (22.4) and that the promise to a faithful Adam was of resurrection and renewed access to the tree of life,[39] "and you shall be immortal forever" (28.4).[40]

The two classic Jewish apocalypses, *4 Ezra* and *2 Baruch,* both emerged in the period following the destruction of Jerusalem in 70 CE, that is, a generation after Paul. But the degree of continuity with motifs already developed suggests that in our immediate area of interest they may reflect themes already current in Jewish theologizing at the time of Paul. Thus we note that in Ezra's words in *4 Ezra* 3.7-10 there is something of the same ambivalence as in Rom. 5.12-14 on the responsibility for universal death. Adam transgressed the commandment "and immediately you [God] appointed death for him and his descendants" (*4 Ezra* 3.7). But the subsequent flood and its destruction was the consequence of the ungodly things and disobedience of the inhabitants of the world of that time (3.8-10).

More striking is Ezra's attribution of Adam's sin to his "evil heart" (3.21-26):

> The first Adam, burdened with an evil heart, transgressed and was overcome, as were also all who were descended from him. Thus the disease became permanent; the law was in the hearts of the people along with the

---

33. *OTP* 2.255 (M. D. Johnson).

34. *Vita* 9.1 = *Apoc. Mos.* 17.1; 2 Cor. 11.14. We should also note that 2 Cor. 11.13 emphasises "deceit," a characteristic motif (using a different word) in the echoes of the serpent's success in deceiving Eve (2 Cor. 11.3; Rom. 7.11).

35. *Apoc. Mos.* 37.5; 2 Cor. 12.2-4. In *Vita* 25.1-3 Adam is also taken up to the heavenly Paradise. *Paradeisos* had become established in Greek as the term for the garden of Eden (Gen. 2.8-10, 15-16; 3.1-3, 8, 10, 23-24; BAGD, *paradeisos*).

36. *Apoc. Mos.* 19.3; Rom. 7.7. See further below §§4.7 and 5.5.

37. *Apoc. Mos.* 14; Rom. 5.12, 14; 7.9-11. See further below §4.6.

38. *Apoc. Mos.* 10.3; 12.1-2; 33.5; 35.2; *Vita* 37.3; 39.2-3.

39. Adam asked to be allowed to eat of the tree of life before being cast out (*Apoc. Mos.* 28.2).

40. "The resurrection of the dead at the last day is repeatedly taught" (Johnson, *OTP* 2.254).

evil root; but what was good departed, and the evil remained. . . . The inhabitants of the city [Jerusalem] transgressed, in everything doing just as Adam and all his descendants had done, for they also had the evil heart.

Here we see a similar ambivalence: there is no "original sin"; the "evil heart" is an unexplained part of humanity. If anyone is to be blamed it is God, for failing to take away the evil heart (3.20)![41] At the same time, the angel Uriel's alternative image speaks of "a grain of evil seed sown in Adam's heart from the beginning; and how much ungodliness it has produced until now — and will produce until the time of threshing comes" (4.30).[42] Both "the evil heart" and the "grain of evil seed" are presumably equivalent to the "inclination" of Gen. 6.5 and 8.21, the rabbis' evil *yetser.*[43]

Most striking of all is Ezra's lament in 7.118: "O Adam, what have you done? For though it was you who sinned, the fall *(casus)* was not yours alone, but ours also who are your descendants." To be noted, however, is the fact that this is presented as Ezra's own view, which the angel Uriel qualifies by affirming human responsibility (7.127-31).[44] What comes out clearly, then, in the debate between Ezra and Uriel is precisely the problem of fairly apportioning responsibility for human failure.

2 Baruch reflects a similar agonizing about responsibility for the disaster which befell Jerusalem in 70 CE. Adam was guilty of deliberate transgression (4.3).[45] "The darkness of Adam" (18.2) brought brevity of life and death for those who were born from him (17.3). "Death was decreed against those who trespassed" from the first day (19.8), "against those who were to be born" (23.4).[46] "When he [Adam] transgressed, untimely death came into being" (56.6). The question of responsibility is explicitly posed: "O Adam, what did you do to all who were born after you? And what will be said of the first Eve who obeyed the serpent, so that this whole multitude is going to corruption?" (48.42-43). But it is answered in terms of individuals being

41. Levison, *Adam* 117-18.

42. See further A. L. Thompson, *Responsibility for Evil in the Theodicy of IV Ezra* (SBLDS 29; Missoula: Scholars, 1977); and the brief "Excursus on Adam's Sin" in M. E. Stone, *Fourth Ezra* (Hermeneia; Minneapolis: Fortress, 1990) 63-67. Other references to Adam in *4 Ezra* are 7.11-14 (reflecting on the physical hardship consequent on Adam's transgression); 7.62-74; 8.44-45 (people are still properly called God's own image).

43. Cf. particularly the now famous passage about the two spirits which determine the natures of all humanity (1QS 4.15-26); see, e.g., O. J. F. Seitz, "The Two Spirits in Man: An Essay in Biblical Exegesis," *NTS* 6 (1959-60) 82-95.

44. It is important throughout *4 Ezra* to observe who is the speaker, since the whole is presented as in effect a debate between Ezra and Uriel, in which Uriel's view has to be given more weight. See again Levison, *Adam* 123-24.

45. Levison, *Adam* 130-31. Other references are in 14.17-19.

46. But there is a prospect of resurrection for "all who sleep in hope" (30.1).

repaid for their own transgressions (48.47).[47] The point is made explicitly in 54.14, 19:

> For, although Adam sinned first and has brought death upon all who were not of his own time, yet each of them who has been born from him has prepared for himself the coming torment. . . . Adam is, therefore, not the cause, except only for himself, but each of us has become our own Adam.

The failure, whether of Adam or of humankind generally, is categorized as transgression of the law (48.47), failure to love the law (54.14), and failure to acknowledge God from his creation (54.18).

We need not pursue the inquiry further into rabbinic traditions.[48] Their relevance to the first century CE is too disputed. We clearly have enough evidence to indicate that there was considerable reflection on the Adam tradition, and in several strands of late Second Temple Judaism. Within them there is a striking unity of perspective on two points in particular. The first is that Genesis 1–3 invites an interpretation which takes seriously the play between Adam and *adam* ("humankind"). The second is that Genesis 2–3 provides some sort of explanation for the reality of death in human experience.[49] Beyond that there is an open and unresolved debate: whether death is simply the consequence of humanity's composition from the dust of the earth, or an unlooked-for outcome of creation (hence the need for resurrection); and whether Adam's transgression triggers the transgressions of those born after him, or all should be held wholly responsible for their own sins.[50] Some also reflect on the nature of that transgression — pleasure (Philo), desire *(Apocalypse of Moses)*, with sexual connotations (as in *Jub.* 3.31), failure to acknowledge God as creator *(2 Baruch)*. It should be evident from all this that Paul was entering into an already well-developed debate and that his own views were not uninfluenced by its earlier participants.

§4.4-9 Adam in Paul's theology

The simplest way to proceed is again to follow Paul's own train of thought on the subject. For one of the most striking features of Romans is the fact

---

47. Levison, *Adam* 135-36.

48. But see Scroggs, *Adam* 32-58. On Pseudo-Philo see C. T. R. Hayward, "The Figure of Adam in Pseudo-Philo's Biblical Antiquities," *JSJ* 23 (1992) 1-20.

49. See further Scroggs, *Adam* 19.

50. See also M. de Boer, "Paul and Jewish Apocalyptic Eschatology," in Marcus and Soards, eds., *Apocalyptic* (§12 n. 1) 169-90 (here 177-80).

that Paul repeatedly calls upon Genesis 1–3 to explain his understanding of the human condition.

§4.4 Romans 1.18-32

It is noteworthy how Paul immediately begins his indictment of humankind in Romans by referring to the relation of creature to Creator. In this he was little different from the tradition just reviewed. He starts with the axiom that God has made himself known, or at least knowable through what he has made (1.19). The echo of Wis. 13.1-9 is particularly strong. From the things made, God's character ought to have been discernible (1.20) — the common religious axiom of the time.[51] But human beings failed to glorify God as God or to give him thanks (1.21). Paul clearly assumes that the only appropriate attitude for the creature towards the Creator is one of worship and gratitude. Any real sense of God's majesty (glory), his eternal power and deity (1.20), would surely bring home the human creature's finite weakness and corruption — a very Jewish perception.[52] "Knowledge of God is a lie if it is not acknowledgement of him."[53] Hence, as in Wis. 13.8-9, they are without excuse (1.20).[54] And the consequence, again as in Wis. 13.1 — futility of thinking and a foolish heart darkened (1.21).

> Paul's implication is plain: where life is not experienced as a gift from God it has lost touch with reality and condemns itself to futility. . . . man's whole ability to respond and function not least as a rational being has been damaged. Without the illumination and orientation which comes from the proper recognition of God his whole centre is operating in the dark, lacking direction and dissipating itself in what are essentially trifles.[55]

Lurking behind this we should probably see the figure of Adam, the archetypal human who deliberately refused to give God his due, by refusing to obey God's one command (Gen. 2.17).[56] But in Rom. 1.22 the echo becomes stronger. The claim to be wise, which in direct contrast plunged into folly, recalls the current understanding of the tree of the knowledge of good and

---

51. See above §2.6. See further my *Romans* 57-58.

52. E.g. Exod. 24.15-17; 20.18-20; Isa. 6.1-5; Ezekiel 1; see also G. von Rad, *doxa, TDNT* 2.238-42.

53. Bultmann, *Theology* 1.213.

54. Cf. also particularly *4 Ezra* 7.22-24 and 8.60.

55. Dunn, *Romans* 60.

56. So particularly Hooker, "Adam" 300-301; Wedderburn, "Adam" 413-19. The view does not command widespread support; see, e.g., Fitzmyer, *Romans* 274.

evil.[57] To covet wisdom, independent of God, was itself the temptation to become like God (Gen. 3.5-6), which resulted in Adam's debarment from life. It is the same reaching beyond oneself, resulting only in damage to oneself, as with the king of Tyre (Ezekiel 28), the "vaulting ambition, which o'erleaps itself, and falls on the other."[58] The implication is that humankind is dependent for wisdom from on high, and when it claims such wisdom in itself or in its own resources, that is simply a recipe for folly, darkened counsel, and disaster.[59] The temptation is to become like God. The outcome is that humans are less able to function effectively even as humans. Claiming to have "come of age" and no longer to need God, they become not godlike and independent but futile and confused. The tragedy is that humankind apart from God can no longer properly know itself or recognize its true nature. It thinks it is godlike and cannot grasp that it is only God-breathed earth.

Paul then proceeds to document this folly by indicating what humankind has exchanged God for — for human-made idols,[60] the desires of their own human hearts, and sexual immorality (1.23-24). "They exchanged the truth of God for falsehood and worshiped and served the creature rather than the Creator" (1.25). The echoes of the already running Jewish theological reflection are clear — not least the sustained polemic against idolatry in Wisdom 11–15, the implication that "desire" was at the root of the primal sin,[61] and the characteristic Jewish polemic against Gentile sexual license.[62] On the last of these we need to recall that Jewish attempts to account for the origin of sin also drew in Gen. 6.1-4 (the sin of the "sons of God" in having sexual relations with earthly women).[63] The point is that human creatures need their gods. As creatures they will always be dependent on someone or something for their fulfilment as creatures. If not God, then something altogether baser. Without God they become subservient to their own desires. It is their relation to God (bearing his image) which makes them "like God." Without that they have only substitutes and copies.

57. See above n. 14.

58. Shakespeare, *Macbeth* Act I Scene 7.

59. Scroggs, *Adam* 8: "the primary cause for man's present predicament is . . . his refusal to remain under God's guidance."

60. In 1.23 the influence of Gen. 1.20-25 may be detected in the choice of the last three nouns (N. Hyldahl, "A Reminiscence of the Old Testament at Romans 1.23," *NTS* 2 [1955-56] 285-88).

61. See also below on Rom. 7.7 (§4.7).

62. For details see my *Romans* 61, 65-66. Stowers, despite recognizing an element of Jewish polemic against Gentiles here (*Rereading* 92-97), gives too little weight to the echoes and parallels with Wisdom 11–15, familiar in scholarship for the past hundred years (see above n. 23 and further below §§5.4-5).

63. E.g. *Jub.* 4.22; 5.1-10; 7.21; *1 Enoch* 6–11; 86; *T. Reub.* 5; *T. Naph.* 3.5; CD 2.18-21.

An important aspect of Paul's indictment here is the way in which he draws in Israel's traditional indictment of its own idolatry and descent into promiscuity in the episode of the golden calf in the wilderness.[64] The critique of human futility (1.21) draws on Jer. 2.5-6: the fathers in the wilderness "went far from me, went after worthlessness, and became worthless."[65] The language of Rom. 1.23 is largely determined by Ps. 106.20: in making the golden calf "they exchanged the glory of God for the image of an ox that eats grass."[66] This blending of traditions can hardly be accidental. It must rather reflect a view already established, but which we find clearly expressed only in later rabbinic tradition: that the exodus and giving of the law at Sinai was like a new creation (or start), and that the idolatry with the golden calf was like a new fall.[67] If so, the point is that Paul already had in mind a *twofold* indictment. One draws on the characteristic Jewish condemnation of *Gentile* religion and sexual practice. The other, less overt, contains the reminder that *Israel* itself falls under the same indictment. It is this which makes the indictment truly universal — "on all human impiety and unrighteousness" (Rom. 1.18), "Jew first and Gentile as well" (2.9-10).

§4.5 *Romans 3.23*

Romans 3.23 deserves a brief mention. Paul gives an explanation of why the righteousness of God is for all, without distinction. The reason is, once again, axiomatic; it needs no elaboration or justification. "For all have sinned and lack the glory of God." The axiom is presumably the same as that which governed Jewish theologizing about Adam: that all humankind are caught in the nexus of sin and death. The echo of that theological tradition is twofold. First, the thought of Adam's sin resulting in his deprivation of the glory of God is already present in *Apoc. Mos.* 20.2 and 21.6.[68] Correspondingly, the hope of the age to come could be expressed in terms of the restoration or enhancement of the original glory (*Apoc. Mos.* 39.2-3).[69] Second, the ambiguity as to whether the reference is to a glory lost or to a glory fallen short

---

64. Exod. 32.25-28; Deut. 9.13-21; 1 Kgs. 12.28-30; Neh. 9.18; Ps. 106.19-23; Acts 7.39-41.

65. *Emaitōthēsan* ("became futile") is used by both texts.

66. And again Jer. 2.11 — "my people have exchanged their glory for that which does not profit."

67. Details in Wedderburn, "Adam" 414-15.

68. Cited above §4.3. See further Scroggs, *Adam* 26, 48-49, 73-74.

69. See also *4 Ezra* 7.122-25; *2 Baruch* 51.1, 3; 54.15, 21. Other references in my *Romans* 168.

of[70] probably reflects the ambiguous role of the tree of life in the garden: did the primal pair lose something they already possessed (Gen. 2.16), or were they deprived of the *opportunity* of attaining eternal life (Gen. 3.22)? At all events, humankind in seeking to grasp for God's glory (to be like God) had lost even the share in that glory which they had originally been given.

§4.6 Romans 5.12-21

Only in the conclusion to the first complete section of his argument in Romans[71] does Paul introduce an explicit reference to Adam. Conscious, perhaps, of the narrower focus of much of the intervening discussion, Paul deliberately steps back to sum up and set the whole discussion within a universal perspective. In this way, no doubt, he intended the conclusion to the section to match the universal sweep of its opening (1.18-32). We may note at once, therefore, Paul's awareness that Adam *(adam)* denotes humankind. For in these verses Paul encapsulates all human history under the two archetypal figures (note the double "all" of 5.18) — Adam and Christ — as embodying, in effect, the only two alternatives which the gospel opens to humankind.[72] This, we may say, is his own version of the epochal choice between death and life laid before Israel in the climax to the Deuteronomic covenant (Deut. 30.15-20). As will become clear, even with Paul's distinctive input, the thought is quite of a piece with the Jewish tradition sketched above.[73]

Whether Paul also thought of Adam as a historical individual and of a historical act of disobedience is less clear. Philo should remind us that the ancients were more alert to the diversity of literary genres than we usually give them credit for.[74] And Paul's very next use of the Adam story (Rom. 7.7-11) is remarkably like *2 Baruch* 54.19 in using Adam as the archetype of "everyman." Be that as it may, the use Paul makes of Genesis 1–3 here is entirely of a piece with the tradition of Jewish theologizing on Adam in using the Genesis account to make sense of the human experience of sin and death.

70. The Greek *hystereō*, "lack," carries the double sense.
71. For 5.12-21 within the structure of Romans see my *Romans* 242-44.
72. The point is even clearer in 1 Cor. 15.21-22: "through a human being came death . . . in Adam all die." It is unnecessary to elaborate 1 Cor. 15.21-22 further here.
73. Contrast Strecker: "The Pauline anthropological dualism stands closer to the Gnostic systems than perhaps to genuine Judaism" (*Theologie* 68). The difference from the later Gnostic systems is evident particularly in Paul's treatment of sin and death as quasi-cosmic powers and in his emphasis on human responsibility in sinning; see further Wedderburn, "Romans 5.12" 342-44, 348-49, and below §5.
74. See above §4.3.

And his concern and point are not dependent on the resolution of any tension between questions of history or myth.[75]

> [12]Therefore as through one person sin entered into the world and through sin, death — and so death came to all, in that all sinned. [13]For until the law, sin was in the world, but sin is not accounted in the absence of the law. [14]Nevertheless death reigned from Adam to Moses, even over those who did not sin in the very manner of Adam's transgression — he who is the type of the one to come (Rom. 5.12-14).

The allusion to Genesis 3 is clear, as the parallel with Wis. 2.23-24 (cited above §4.3) not least confirms. The theme is familiar to us from the above review: how it is that death became such an inescapable part of the human lot. Paul draws the obvious implication from the function of the tree of life in Genesis 2–3, that death was not part of the original divine intention in creation. "Death," which initially had no place within the world, "entered the world." But ambiguity remains, and Paul's own distinctive contribution to the debate only partly clarifies that ambiguity, and partly underlines its complexity. Paul's more distinctive ideas become evident at five points.

First, he makes it clear that so far as he was concerned, death is not simply the natural consequence of the created state. It is the consequence of sin. Death entered the world "through sin" (5.12). "Death came to all, in that all sinned" (5.12). "Sin reigned in death" (5.21). The nexus of sin and death is very strong in Paul, and we will have to look at it afresh from a different angle later (§5.7).

Second, is each individual responsible for his or her own death? On the one hand, death for all Adam's race is the result of Adam's transgression. On the other, all die because all sin (5.12).[76] Death has ruled continuously from Adam, even over those who did not sin like Adam (5.14). Alternatively expressed, through Adam's disobedience "the many were made sinners" (5.19). But the causal connection implied here by "made" *(katestathēsan)* may be nonspecific and very loose, "made" functioning simply as equivalent to "became" *(egenonto)*.[77] In other words, Paul asserts a continuum of life ending in death which stretches from Adam to the present. What precisely

---

75. "What sin entered was the world of human beings, of human experience . . . rather than creation. This is the language of universal experience, not of cosmic speculation" (Dunn, *Romans* 272).

76. The dominant consensus is that *eph' hō* in "*eph' hō* all sinned" (5.12) is best taken as "for this reason, because"; see particularly Cranfield, *Romans* 274-81. However, Ridderbos, *Paul* 96-99, still presses for a "corporate sense," and Fitzmyer, *Romans* 413-17, argues for a consequential sense ("with the result that"); similarly Ladd, *Theology* 443.

77. A. Oepke, *kathistēmi, TDNT* 3.445; see further my *Romans* 284.

first constituted that continuum remains unclear. But that it began with Adam (was in operation effectively from the beginning) is clear enough. And that it is continuing human sin which maintains that continuum is also clear.

Third, it thus becomes evident that Paul was operating with a double conception of death. In this case it is the distinction between the death of humanity as an *outcome* of Adam's first transgression and death as a *consequence* or even penalty for one's own individual transgressions. Presumably this ties in with some sort of equivalent distinction between natural death and spiritual death (as in Philo?). In other words, the attempt to correlate the universal fact of mortality with the talk of death immediately consequent upon eating from the tree of knowledge of good and evil (Gen. 2.17; 3.3) was bound to lead to some such distinction.

Fourth, Paul works with a very complex notion of sin. He introduces the notion of "sin" *(hamartia)* as a personified power: "sin entered the world" (5.12); "sin ruled in death" (5.21). "Sin" in effect takes the role of the serpent/Satan, though as a much more significant figure than the serpent. But "sin" is also "reckoned," like an attribute or statistic (5.13);[78] and sin also increases or grows (5.20 — *epleonasen*), perhaps more like a fruit (cf. Phil. 4.17).[79] In the same context the equivalent verb is used *(hamartanō)* to denote particular acts of sin (5.12, 14, 16). This complexity requires further analysis in §5 below.

Fifth, Paul also uses three further terms for Adam's sin — *parabasis,* "overstepping, transgression" (5.14), *paraptōma,* "false step, transgression" (6 times in 5.15-20), and *parakoē,* "disobedience" (5.19). These are all stronger words than *hamartia* ("sin" as failure) and allow a point of clarification. "Sin" is only "counted" where there is law (5.13). "Transgression," on the other hand, is the conscious breach of a known law; Adam disobeyed the explicit command of the Creator (Gen. 2.17; 3.1-6). In other words, "transgression" is "sin counted." This helps so far. It allows a concept of guilt to be attached solely to "transgression," deliberate breach of divine command. But it still leaves an uncomfortable question: why do those still die who only commit "sin" but not "transgression"? The fact that Paul continues to use the verb *hamartanō* as equivalent to the noun *parabasis/paraptōma* in 5.14 and 16 does not help.

What Paul seems to be saying is something like this. (1) All humanity

---

78. Paul draws here on the idea of heavenly books in which human deeds are recorded, an idea already current elsewhere in Judaism (see particularly Dan. 7.10; *Jub.* 30.17-23; *1 Enoch* 89.61-64, 70-71; 104.7; 108.7; *2 Baruch* 24.1); see further my *Colossians* 164 (on Col. 2.14).

79. There may be an echo of Sir. 23.3, where the subject is plural ("sins") — ". . . that my sins may not increase *(pleonasōsin).*"

shares a common subserviency to sin and death. This is not merely a natural fleshness, a created mortality. Sin is bound up with it, a falling short of God's intended best. Death is the outcome of a breakdown within creation. (2) There is a two-sidedness to this state of affairs, involving both sin as a given of the social fabric of society and sin as an accountable action of individual responsibility.[80] It is precisely this merging of the one into the other which makes it so difficult to determine the precise lines of responsibility — in contemporary society as well. (3) Overall, however, this state is the consequence of humanity's refusal to acknowledge God, of the creature's attempt to dispense with the Creator. When humankind declared its independence from God, it abandoned the only power which can overcome the sin which uses the weakness of the flesh, the only power which can overcome death. (4) Nevertheless, guilt only enters into the reckoning with the individual's own transgression.[81] Human beings are not held responsible for the state into which they are born. That is the starting point of their personal responsibility, a starting point for which they are not liable.[82] In short, Paul's analysis shares something of the same ambiguity which plagued earlier Jewish theological reflection on the subject. Nonetheless, it is a bold attempt to make sense of the harsh reality of sin and death in human experience.

Finally, we should note that here again (as in 1.18-32) Paul meshes the particular experience of Israel into the universal experience of humankind. For it is the introduction of the law which transforms non-guilty sin into guilty transgression (5.13). And by "law" Paul naturally refers to the Mosaic law. Thus he can even presuppose a period without law from Adam to Moses (5.14).[83] And the "law" which "came in" (5.20) is again, no doubt, the Mosaic law, but introduced onto a universal stage of sinners (5.19 — "the many") and sin's rule (5.21). Here is another player (the law) in the drama of human history whose complex role will require further analysis (§6). For the moment, however, we need simply note that here again Paul sees Israel's own experience of sin and death as in some sense paradigmatic for humanity as a whole.

---

80. Cf. Bultmann's handling of Rom. 5.13-14 (*Theology* 1.252-53).

81. Cf. Whiteley: "St. Paul does believe in Original Sin, but not in Original Guilt" (*Theology* 51).

82. A useful illustration in the 1970s was Rhodesia's "unilateral declaration of independence" from the British crown. In consequence, that was a British colony properly speaking in rebellion against Britain. A baby born in Rhodesia (now Zimbabwe) in those days would, of course, not have been held responsible for the state of rebellion. But had the rebellion continued, that child, when it came of age, would have had to assume some personal responsibility for maintaining or ending the rebellion.

83. But see also below n. 89.

§4.7 Romans 7.7-13

Paul reverts yet again to the Adam narratives in another passage in which the law is a key player. Indeed the whole point of the passage is to defend the law from any implication that the law should bear the primary responsibility for the experience of death.[84] In terms of the previous argument, death was a factor before the law came on the scene (5.13-14). Here the concern is clearly to pin the blame for human subjection to death firmly on the power of sin.

> [7]What then shall we say? That the law is sin? Certainly not! Nevertheless, I would not have experienced sin except through the law; for I would not have known covetousness unless the law had said "You shall not covet." [8]But sin, seizing its opportunity through the commandment, stirred up all manner of covetousness in me. For in the absence of the law sin is dead. [9]And in the absence of the law I was alive once upon a time. But when the commandment came, sin became alive, [10]and I died. The commandment intended for life proved for me a means to death. [11]For sin, seizing its opprtunity through the commandment, deceived me and through it killed me. . . . [13]Did that which is good, then, become death to me? Certainly not! But sin. . . .

The reference to Adam is not immediately apparent. The key, however, has already been given to us in the above review of Jewish theological reflection on Adam's disobedience. It is the recognition that wrong desire, lust, or covetousness *(epithymia)* had already been widely recognized to be the root of all sin. We noted the point in Philo[85] and particularly in *Apoc. Mos.* 19.3: *"epithymia is the origin of every sin."*[86] And the most Jewish document in the NT, James, makes precisely the same affirmation: "desire *(epithymia)* conceives and gives birth to sin" (Jas. 1.15). This provides sufficient explanation why Paul should focus on the tenth commandment of the Decalogue: "You shall not covet *(ouk epithymēseis)*" (Exod. 20.17; Deut. 5.21).[87] In other words, Paul shared the wider belief that the primal sin was

---

84. For Rom. 7.7-25 as an apologia for the law, see below §6.7.

85. See above n. 30.

86. See also *Apoc. Abr.* 24.9.

87. A reference to sexual desire is possible: it was a natural corollary to draw from the talk of nakedness and consequent shame (Gen. 2.25; 3.7, 10), as *Jubilees* and Philo indicate (see further R. H. Gundry, "The Moral Frustration of Paul before His Conversion: Sexual Lust in Romans 7.7-25," in Hagner and Harris, eds., *Pauline Studies* 80-94; Boyarin, *Radical Jew* ch. 7), but the primary Pauline emphasis is on the estrangement of God and Adam (cf. *Apoc. Mos.* 19-21; and further J. A. Ziesler, "The Role of the Tenth Commandment in Romans 7," *JSNT* 33 [1988] 41-56).

wrong desire, that what the serpent appealed to in the garden was Adam's coveting of divine status: "You shall be like God" (Gen. 3.5).[88]

Once this point has been taken, the semi-allegorical reading of Genesis 2–3 in Rom. 7.7-11 becomes clear. The command not to eat of the tree of the knowledge of good and evil (Gen. 2.17) is read as a particular expression of the commandment, "You shall not covet."[89] The serpent is identified as the representation of "sin." And the "I" is an existential self-identification with Adam, *adam,* "Everyman," humankind (cf. *2 Baruch* 54.19).[90] Paul's interpretation of the story then follows straightforwardly, displaying some sharp psychological insight.[91] All is well with human society when no law needs to be applied; humankind enjoys life (Gen. 2.7; Rom. 7.9), and sin is disempowered, ineffective (7.8 — *nekra*). But sin seizes the opportunity provided by the law to whet humankind's curiosity as to what the commandment may be forbidding. In this way desire for the forbidden is stirred up and becomes an insatiable force, whose final outworking is death. Given the warning, "In the day you eat of it you will die" (Gen. 2.17), and the serpent's rebuttal, "You will not die" (3.4), there is a particularly striking echo of the woman's complaint: "The serpent deceived me, and I ate" (Gen. 3.13); "sin . . . deceived me and through it [the commandment] killed me" (Rom. 7.11).[92] Thus it was that the commandment which had been intended to regulate life (Gen. 2.16-17) became the means of death (Rom. 7.10, 13).

The use of the Adam story once again to speak of the general condition of humankind seems clear beyond dispute. At the same time, however, we should note that Paul may once again have been deliberately meshing in the story of Israel. For the experience of the "I" here also mirrors that of Israel

---

88. To interpret *epithymia* as "zeal for keeping the Law" (Bultmann, *Theology* 1.265), or "zeal for one's own righteousness" (Bornkamm, "Sin" 90; Hübner, *Law* [§6 n. 1] 72) is entirely tendentious and without justification in the text (recognized by Ridderbos, *Paul* 145-46, and Theissen, *Psychological Aspects* [§18 n. 1] 208; see particularly H. Räisänen, "The Use of *epithymia* and *epithymein* in Paul," in *Jesus, Paul and Torah* 95-111).

89. It becomes a commonplace in later rabbinic tradition that the law as such was already in force at the time of Adam. Already in *4 Ezra* 7.11 it is stated that Adam transgressed God's statutes (plural). Note Paul's equation of "the law" and "the commandment" in 7.8, 9 and 12. See further my *Romans* 379.

90. For the debate on the significance of "I" see my *Romans* 381-83; Fitzmyer, *Romans* 462-65; J. Lambrecht, *The Wretched "I" and Its Liberation: Paul in Romans 7 and 8* (Louvain: Peeters/Grand Rapids: Eerdmans, 1992) — all with further bibliography.

91. In the following sentences I use the present tense, but the point would be the same if a historic tense were used.

92. Cf. also 2 Cor. 11.3 and 1 Tim. 2.14. The "I" here echoes *Eve's* words.

in significant measure.[93] On a view that the law was only given later, through Moses,[94] it was *Israel* which experienced sin provoking covetousness by means of the commandment given on Mount Sinai.[95] The thought will once again be of Israel's decline into idolatry and surrender to unbridled lust at the foot of Sinai itself. The death, or better, slaughter which followed was burned deeply into Israel's folk memory.[96] In this way Paul would not let his Jewish or Jewish-influenced readers forget that Israel too was bound up in the solidarity of human frailty and failure and was as firmly caught in the nexus of sin and death as any Gentile.

§4.8 Romans 8.19-22

For the sake of completeness we should include also Paul's final allusion in Romans to the Genesis 3 narrative. This comes in the section where Paul lifts his eyes to give a more sustained forward look to the final hope of a completed salvation. What is striking is the way he includes creation within that hope. "Creation was subjected to futility *(mataiotēs)*" (8.20). *Mataiotēs* denotes the futility of an object which does not function as it was designed to, or, more precisely, an object which has been given a role for which it was not designed and which is unreal or illusory. The allusion is clearly to Gen. 3.17-18. The equivalent verb was used in Rom. 1.22 to describe the vacuousness of the thinking which does not start from an acknowledgment of God. Creation has been caught up in the futility of human self-deception. For humankind to think that it stands in relation to the rest of creation as creator to creation ("You shall be like God") imposes futility as much on creation as on humankind itself. There is thus an out-of-joint-ness about creation which its human creatures share (8.22-23).[97] But as creation shares in humankind's futility, so it will share in humankind's liberation from "the slavery of corruption" (8.21).

The point to be underlined here is the solidarity of humankind with

---

93. See particularly D. J. Moo, "Israel and Paul in Romans 7.7-12," *NTS* 32 (1986) 122-35; Wright, *Climax* 197. I am more sympathetic to this view now than I was in my *Romans* 383.

94. Rom. 5.13-14, 20; Gal. 3.17-19.

95. To press for an inconsistency between Rom. 5.13-14 and 7.9 (Räisänen, *Law* (§6 n. 1) 147; Wedderburn, "Adam" 424) is unnecessarily pedantic.

96. Exod. 32.25-28; and again in the plague consequent on the idolatry of Baal Peor (Num. 25.1-9; 1 Cor. 10.7-10). 1 Cor. 10.6 attributes the calamity to evil desire.

97. The imagery is vivid: creation groaning like a wounded animal and like a woman in labour to bring forth the new creation. Such vivid personification of nature is typical of the more poetic strains of Jewish writing. The classic parallel is Virgil, *Eclogue* 4.50-52. For fuller details see my *Romans* 470-73.

the rest of creation, of *adam* with the *adamah* from which *adam* was made.[98] In other words, the conviction is a corollary drawn directly from Genesis 2–3. At first the thought here seems to go beyond that of 1 Cor. 15.42, 50, which speaks only of humans sharing the transformation of resurrection. But here we need to recall again the significance of *sōma*, as the embodiment appropriate to the environment. The recognition of the nature of humankind as a corporeal species leads directly to the confident hope that God will provide also an appropriate environment for embodiment in the age to come.

§4.9 Summary

In sum, humankind in the world is not just weak and corruptible. There is an inescapable dimension of sin, of failure and transgression, also involved. Humans were created for relationship with God, a relationship which is the essence of human life, a relationship which gives humankind fulfilment of being, as creature (in relation to God) and as human (in relation to the rest of the world). But humankind has made the mistake of thinking it could achieve a more satisfying relation with the world if it freed itself from its relation with God. It has turned from God and focused attention exclusively on the world, revolting against its role as creature and thinking to stand as creator in its own right. In consequence humankind has fallen when it thought to rise, has become foolish not wise, baser not superior. It has denied its likeness to God and preferred the likeness of beasts and things (§4.4). It has lost its share in the majesty of divinity, and now falls far short of what it might have become (§4.5). Instead of sharing eternal life, it has become dominated by death (§4.6), a "sucker" for sin (§4.7). It shares in a pervasive out-of-joint-ness, frustration, and futility with the rest of creation (§4.8).

Such is Paul's indictment of humankind as first laid out in Rom. 1.18ff. and elaborated subsequently in the letter. Its inspiration comes primarily from Genesis 2–3, but also from his own experience within the world of women and men. And though the imagery and biblical language is stranger now to modern ears, the point of Paul's critique remains sharp and continues to probe the conscience of a society in whose ears the subtly deceptive whisper still entices: "You shall be like God."

---

98. W. Schmithals, *Die theologische Anthropologie des Paulus: Auslegung von Röm 7.17–8.39* (Stuttgart: Kohlhammer, 1980) 158, notes how *un*dualistic is the thought of sighing *with* rather than to escape *from* creation.

§5 Sin and death[1]

§5.1 The power of evil

The sense of dis-ease within humanity can be analysed from another angle. The negative signs which appear so often in Paul's talk of humankind (§4.1) can be assigned another cause. Cassius might insist that "The fault, dear Brutus, is not in our stars, but in ourselves, that we are underlings."[2] But Shakespeare does not imply thereby that the source of social malaise lies solely within individuals. Human relationships, wealth and poverty, power and powerlessness in their interactions within society are also a major factor. And in addition, the fear that the stars may indeed be involved has been a recurring suspicion or nightmare in all ages. And if not the stars, then supramundane forces of some sort or kind.

Generation after generation has known what it is to be merely the flotsam and jetsam swept along on some floodtide of human history. There

1. **Bibliography**. **Barrett**, *Paul* 56-64; **Beker**, *Paul* 213-34; **H. Bietenhard**, *Die himmlische Welt im Urchristentum und Spätjudentum* (WUNT 2; Tübingen: Mohr, 1951); **C. C. Black**, "Pauline Perspectives on Death in Romans 5-8," *JBL* 103 (1984) 418-33; **Bultmann**, *Theology* I, 246-59; **G. B. Caird**, *Principalities and Powers: A Study in Pauline Theology* (Oxford: Clarendon, 1956); **W. Carr**, *Angels and Principalities: The Background, Meaning and Development of the Pauline Phrase* HAI ARCHAI KAI HAI EXOUSIAI (SNTSMS 42; Cambridge: Cambridge University, 1981); **Conzelmann**, *Outline* 192-98; **Eichholz**, *Theologie* 63-100; **Elliott**, *Rhetoric* particularly 167-223; **Gnilka**, *Theologie* 62-69; *Paulus* 220-23; **T. Ling**, *The Significance of Satan* (London: SPCK/New York: AMS, 1961); **S. Lyonnet**, "The Notion of Sin," in S. Lyonnet and L. Sabourin, *Sin, Redemption, and Sacrifice: A Biblical and Patristic Study* (AnBib 48; Rome: Biblical Institute, 1970) 3-57; **G. H. C. MacGregor**, "Principalities and Powers: The Cosmic Background of Paul's Thought," *NTS* 1 (1954-55) 17-28; **H. Merklein**, "Paulus und die Sünde," in H. Frankemölle, ed., *Sünde und Erlösung im Neuen Testament* (Freiburg: Herder, 1991) 123-63; **G. Röhser**, *Metaphorik und Personifikation der Sünde. Antike Sündenvorstellungen und paulinische Hamartia* (WUNT 2.25; Tübingen: Mohr, 1987); **H. Schlier**, *Principalities and Powers in the New Testament* (Herder: Freiburg, 1961); *Grundzüge* 64-77, 107-21; **Strecker**, *Theologie* 136-42; **W. Wink**, *The Powers* 1: *Naming the Powers: The Language of Power in the New Testament* (Philadelphia: Fortress, 1984); 2: *Unmasking the Powers: The Invisible Forces That Determine Human Existence* (Philadelphia: Fortress, 1986); 3: *Engaging the Powers: Discernment and Resistance in a World of Domination* (Minneapolis: Fortress, 1992).

2. Shakespeare, *Julius Caesar* Act I Scene 2.

have been many Jean Valjeans and countless Dr. Zhivagos.[3] And even a postreligious world reaches instinctively for religious language when confronted with the reality of evil whose malignity and captivating power goes far beyond human comprehension. A twentieth century which had hoped that the Holocaust of the early 1940s was a horrific throwback to barbarous precivilization has been appalled by the genocidal massacres ("ethnic cleansing"!) of Bosnia and Rwanda fifty years later. One could easily speak of demonic forces of nationalism and tribalism let loose in these countries without being accused of overstatement — so hard to comprehend are the forces which compel so many to rape, torture, and murder apparently without compunction. When in early 1996 a gunman went berserk in a primary school in the Scottish country town of Dunblane, killing sixteen youngsters and their teacher, the headmaster said that evil had visited his school. And who could deny the fittingness of his description?

The ancient world had its own stock of explanations. The old myths portrayed the gods as acting within the world in ways quite as malicious and capricious as any earthly beings. From earliest times too, and usually understood as the more ultimate explanation, was the appeal made to inescapable fate *(heimarmenē),* a theme much taken up by poet, playwright, and philosopher.[4] This included both the rationalization that actions set in train unavoidable consequences[5] and attempts to square the circle of moral responsibility for actions performed.[6] When a less specific term was wanted, the talk would as often be of some *daimōn,* a term which could simply denote an unknown superhuman determinant of destiny, particularly misfortune and distress.[7] Already in Hesiod the souls of the deceased of the Golden Age are described as *daimones,*[8] a usage extended later to departed souls generally.[9] And by the time of Paul it would have been common to think of *daimones* as spiritual or semidivine beings inferior to the gods, especially evil spirits. A familiar social practice was to drink a toast after dinner to the "good genius"

3. Referring to the heroes of Victor Hugo's *Les Miserables* and Boris Pasternak's *Dr. Zhivago.*

4. See *OCD* 430-32; Long/Sedley, Glossary under "fate."

5. See, e.g., Cicero, *On Divination* 1.125-26 (Long/Sedley 337).

6. A classic example is provided by Diogenes Laertius 7.23: "The story goes that Zeno was flogging a slave for stealing. 'I was fated to steal,' said the slave. 'And to be flogged,' was Zeno's reply" (Long/Sedley 389).

7. W. Foerster, *daimōn, TDNT* 2.1-6. It is worth using *daimōn* rather than "demon" since the earlier Greek concept was much broader and less definite than the Judeo-Christian concept of evil spiritual beings under the direction of Satan.

8. *Opera et Dies* 122 (LSJ *daimōn* II; *OCD* 310).

9. Foerster, *TDNT* 2.6-8. See also above §2 n. 41. On Jewish demonology see, e.g., Ling, *Satan* 3-11.

(agathos daimōn).[10] In turn, the prevalence of magical practices, both "white magic" and "black magic,"[11] indicates the breadth of concern to find means, by incantantations and amulets, to ward off the ill effects or to gain the protection of such mysterious powers and forces.[12] The account in Acts 19.18-19 certainly reflects a level of popularity of magical practices such as Paul must have encountered on more than one occasion.[13]

At first sight, in the indictment in Rom. 1.18–3.20, Paul does not seem to look in this direction for an explanation of human failure and transgression. But the climactic paragraph of the indictment begins by summing up the indictment as a charge against both Jews and Greeks that they are all alike "under sin" (3.9). This is the first mention of "sin" in the letter, and it first appears as a power "under" which all humankind labours. We have also already noted that in 5.12 and 7.8-9 personified "sin" appears on the world stage from offstage to wreak its havoc in the world and in humanity. Furthermore, in §2.3(c) we have observed that on a number of occasions (particularly in the Corinthian correspondence) Paul has previously spoken of other gods (1 Cor. 8.5-6), of demons *(daimonia)* which could evidently act on or in people (1 Cor. 10.20-22), and of "the god of this world [who] has blinded the minds of the unbelievers" (2 Cor. 4.4). Not least, in Rom. 8.38-39 he speaks of various spiritual beings who apparently have the potential to separate believers from the love of God. Such references open up a dimension of Paul's analysis of the human condition which we can hardly ignore.

§5.2 *The heavenly powers*

What were the heavenly powers which Paul envisaged as threatening believers? It would be as well, first, to clarify the actual terms he uses. Apart from the references noted in §2.3(c), there are a number of passages in the Pauline letters where several such "powers" are listed. Only two come in the undisputed Paulines (Rom. 8.38-39; 1 Cor. 15.24). But in the other lists (in Colossians and Ephesians), there is sufficient overlap with terms and ideas elsewhere

---

10. LSJ, *daimōn*.

11. Here again we need to beware of the wholly negative connotations which now attach to the word. Philo could speak of "true magic . . . a fit object for reverence and ambition" (*Spec. Leg.* 3.100).

12. *OCD* 637-38.

13. H. D. Betz, *The Greek Magical Papyri in Translation* (Chicago: University of Chicago, 1986) contains abundant illustrations from a later period but no doubt reflecting beliefs and practices going back to Paul's time and beyond. See also Arnold, *Colossian Syncretism* (above §2 n. 29) Part I.

in Paul that we can include the later lists without fear of any significant misrespresentation of Paul's own views.[14]

> I am convinced that neither death nor life nor angels nor rulers, neither things present nor things to come nor powers, neither height nor depth, nor any other creature will be able to separate us from the love of God which is in Christ Jesus our Lord (Rom. 8.38-39).

> Then comes the end, when he [Christ] hands over the kingdom to God the Father, after he has destroyed every ruler and every authority and power (1 Cor. 15.24).

> For in him were created all things in the heavens and on the earth, the visible and the invisible, whether thrones or dominions or principalities or authorities (Col. 1.16).

> God raised him [Christ] from the dead and seated him on his right in the heavenly places, far above every ruler and authority and power and dominion and above every name that is named, not only in this age but in the age to come (Eph. 1.20-21).

> Our struggle is not against flesh and blood, but against the rulers, against the authorities, against the cosmic powers of this darkness, against the spiritual forces of evil in the heavenly places (Eph. 6.12).

14.	Rom.	1 Cor.	Phil.	Col.	Eph.	1 Pet.
angeloi	8.38					3.22
archai	8.38	15.24		1.16; 2.10, 15	1.21; 3.10; 6.12	
archōn		2.6, 8			2.2	
bathos	8.39			cf. 3.18		
dynameis	8.38	15.24			1.21	3.22
enestōta	8.38	3.22			cf. 1.21	
exousia	13.1	15.24		1.16; 2.10, 15	1.21; 2.2; 3.10; 6.12	
zōē	8.38	3.22	1.20			
thanatos	8.38	3.22	1.20			
kosmokratōr					6.12	
ktisis	8.39			cf. 1.16		
kyriotēs				1.12	1.21	
mellonta	8.38	3.22			cf. 1.21	
pneumatika					6.12	
hypsōma	8.39				cf. 3.18	

angeloi ("angels"), *archai* ("principalities"), *archōn* ("ruler"), *bathos* ("depth"), *dynameis* ("powers"), *enestōta* ("things present"), *exousia* ("authority"), *zōē* ("life"), *thanatos* ("death"), *kosmokratōr* ("cosmic power"), *ktisis* ("creature"), *kyriotēs* ("dominion"), *mellonta* ("things to come"), *pneumatika* ("spiritual forces"), *hypsōma* ("height").

In every case what seems clearly to have been in mind were heavenly beings, subordinate to God and his Christ, with the potential to intervene between God and his creation, and hostile to his purposes and people.[15] The most common terms are *archai* and *exousiai,* "rulers and authorities." The full sequence of references confirms their status as supramundane powers.[16] Rom. 8.38 also speaks of *angeloi,* "angels," again obviously thought of as agents of heaven or intermediaries between heaven and earth.[17] Since the assurance is that they cannot come between God and his people, the thought is presumably of hostile angels.[18] Three lists add *dynameis* ("powers"), another term familiar in Greek and biblical literature.[19] Since 1 Cor. 15.24 has in view Christ's lordship over and destruction of "every ruler and every authority and every power," again a power hostile to God must be in view.

The most intriguing feature of the Rom. 8.38-39 list is the reference to "neither height nor depth." The terms are probably astronomical. *Hypsōma* ("height") denotes the apogee of the planets, the highest point in the heavens reached by the heavenly body.[20] *Bathos* ("depth") is not the normal antithesis to *hypsōma,*[21] but usually denotes the space below the horizon from which

---

15. In the case of Col. 1.16 we need simply refer forward to Col. 2.15 (see below §9.8). Carr, *Angels,* argues consistently for the tendentious thesis that the powers were not conceived of by Paul as evil or hostile, but his thesis has won very little support. Characteristic is the strained treatment of Rom. 8.38-39 (112-14). Carr meets the challenge of Eph. 6.12 by arguing that the verse was inserted into the letter in the first half of the second century (104-10).

16. 1 Cor. 15.24; Col. 1.16; 2.10, 15; Eph. 1.21; 3.10; 6.12. The reference to the *archonta* in 1 Cor. 2.6, 8 is more open to debate: heavenly or earthly rulers; see, e.g., Wink, *Naming* 40-45. There is no example of *exousia* = heavenly power in pre-Christian usage (Wink, *Naming* 157-58); but for *archē* we can refer to *1 Enoch* 6.8 (Greek); *T. Job* 49.2; *T. Abr.* B 13.10 (ms E).

17. See Bietenhard, *Welt* ch. 5.

18. Typical is a reference to Gen. 6.1-4; see, e.g., *1 Enoch* 6–8; *Jub.* 5.1; *T. Reub.* 5.6; further BAGD, *angelos;* Wink, *Naming* 23-26; and above §4.4 n. 63. In Paul note also 1 Cor. 6.3; 11.10; 2 Cor. 11.14; Col. 2.18. On Gal. 3.19 see below §6.4.

19. BAGD, *dynamis* 5, 6; see also 1 Pet. 3.22. It was natural to conceive of heavenly beings as characterized by power (e.g., 2 Kgs. 17.16 LXX; *4 Macc.* 5.13; Philo, *Conf.* 171; *Spec. Leg.* 1.209; Matt. 24.29; Mark 14.62; Acts 8.10). The LXX often translates "the Lord of hosts" as "the Lord of powers." See further Wink, *Naming* 159-60. But Wink finds only *1 Enoch* 20.1 (one Greek ms) as an example of *dynamis* = evil power (162); A.-M. Denis and Y. Janssens, *Concordance grecque des pseudépigraphes d'Ancien Testament* (Louvain-la-Neuve: Université Catholique de Louvain, 1987), cite also *1 Enoch* 18.14.

20. W. L. Knox, *Gentiles* 106-7; G. Bertram, *TDNT* 8.613.

21. That would be *tapeinōma* = the lowest point in the planet's course (LSJ, *tapeinōsa*).

the stars arise.[22] Even so, however, not very far away is the thought that the heavenly bodies might influence human conduct, or at least the thought that the forces which influence planets and stars may also influence human destiny.

The Rom. 8.38-39 list of potentially threatening powers begins with "death and life." That "death" is well conceived as a hostile power will become evident later (below §5.7), but here the pair probably simply denote every conceivable condition of humankind (cf. Phil. 1.20). *Nothing* can separate the believer from the love of God. The same is probably true of the "things present" and "things to come" (Rom. 8.38). No conceivable eventuality can separate the believer from the love of God. Nothing created ("nor any creature") — and that means *nothing*.

In the Colossians list some have suggested that the "thrones" and "authorities" parallel "visible," referring, that is, to earthly powers.[23] But that is unlikely. What is probably envisaged is a hierarchy of heavenly powers, with "thrones" as the topmost rank.[24] This is most likely how anyone familiar with the Jewish-Christian apocalyptic tradition would read the term. So, for example, in *T. Levi* 3.8 "thrones" are heavenly beings located with "authorities" in the seventh heaven.[25] Likewise the parallel with Eph. 1.21 strongly suggests that *kyriotētes* ("dominions") refers to heavenly powers.[26] *Kosmokratores* ("cosmic powers") and *pneumatika,* "spiritual forces of evil in the heavenly places" in Eph. 6.12, need no further comment.[27]

Among the most interesting of the names used for heavenly powers is *stoicheia* in Galatians and Colossians. Paul speaks of enslavement "under the *stoicheia* of the world" (Gal. 4.3) and warns the Galatians about returning to slavery to "the weak and beggarly *stoicheia*" (4.9). Colossians warns similarly of being captivated "through philosophy and empty deceit . . . in accordance with the *stoicheia* of the world" (Col. 2.8) and reminds the believers in Colossae that they have "died with Christ from[28] the *stoicheia* of the world"

---

22. Lietzmann, *Römer* 88-91; BAGD, *bathos.* Wink, *Naming* 49-50, suggests alternatively that the two terms refer "to the top and bottom of the pillars that support the firmament of heaven."

23. E. Bammel, "Versuch zu Kol. 1.15-20," *ZNW* 52 (1961) 88-95. For Wink, *Naming* 11, the parallelism indicates that they are "both earthly *and* heavenly, both visible *and* invisible."

24. See particularly Lightfoot, *Colossians* 151-52; also Wink, *Naming* 19.

25. See also *2 Enoch* 20.1 (also located in the seventh heaven) and *Apoc. Elij.* 1.10-11 (hostile to the faithful; "thrones of death"), and cf. Rev. 13.2. The usage presumably derives from the vision of Dan. 7.9, echoed in Rev. 4.4. See further Bietenhard, *Welt* ch. 4.

26. See also *1 Enoch* 61.10 and again *2 Enoch* 20.1, though these do not constitute evidence of pre-Christian use.

27. See, e.g., A. T. Lincoln, *Ephesians* (WBC 42; Dallas: Word, 1990) 444-45.

28. The preposition "from" *(apo)* is surprising here but presumably denotes that "from" which death has set them free (cf. Rom. 9.3; BDF §211).

(2.20). The long debate about the reference of *stoicheia* should almost certainly be regarded as settled in favour of the elemental substances of which the cosmos was usually thought to be composed (earth, water, air, and fire).[29] The point here is that these substances were also commonly divinized (mythologized or personified) as divine spirits or deities.[30] Philo, for example, speaks of the four elements *(stoicheia)* as having in them "transcendent powers" *(Aet. Mund.* 107), and of those who revere the elements and identify them with different gods *(Vit. Cont.* 3).[31] And in Gal. 4.3, 8-9 slavery to the *stoicheia* is equated with slavery to other (non-)gods.

The picture, then, seems to be very clear. Paul shared a common belief that there were several heavens;[32] he had even experienced a heavenly journey to the third heaven (2 Cor. 12.2-4).[33] More to the point he shared what was presumably also a common belief that the lower heavens[34] were populated by various hostile powers or that the hostile heavenly powers mounted a kind of roadblock to prevent access to the higher heavens (paradise being in the third heaven — 2 Cor. 12.3). If this meant that they also hindered or could even prevent access to God (cf. Rom. 8.38-39), that would be serious indeed.[35]

What is puzzling, however, is that Paul says so little about the heavenly powers. The two references in the undisputed Paulines (Rom. 8.38-39; 1 Cor. 15.24) look as though they were added almost for effect. Moreover, the lists are very varied, with only "rulers and authorities and powers" appearing with any regularity. The suspicion begins to mount, therefore, that Paul himself did not have a very strong, or at least very clear, belief regarding these heavenly

29. This is by far the most common usage in literature prior to Paul. See further J. Blinzler, "Lexikalisches zu dem Terminus *ta stoicheia tou kosmou* bei Paulus," in *SPCIC* 2.429-43; E. Schweizer, "Die 'Elemente der Welt.' Gal. 4.3, 9; Kol. 2.8, 20," in O. Böcher and K. Haacker, eds., *Verborum Veritas,* G. Stählin FS (Wuppertal: Brockhaus, 1970) 245-59, reprinted in Schweizer, *Beiträge* 147-63; D. Rusam, "Neue Belege zu den *stoicheia tou kosmou* (Gal. 4.3, 9; Kol. 2.8, 20)," *ZNW* 83 (1992) 119-25. Further details in my *Colossians* 149-50.

30. "The divinization of the elements was a commonplace in the whole Graeco-Roman period" (Wink, *Naming* 74). Wink 76-77, however, thinks that the reference in Col. 2.20 and Gal. 4.3, 9 is different (referring to basic religious practices and beliefs); see also his *Unmasking,* particularly 133-34, 148-49.

31. "Can we compare those who revere the elements *(stoicheia),* earth, water, air, fire, which have received different names from different peoples who call fire Hephaestus because it is kindled *(exaptō),* air Hera because it is lifted up *(airō)* and exalted on high. . . ?" *(Vit. Cont.* 3).

32. H. Traub, *ouranos, TDNT* 5.511-2; Bietenhard, *Welt* 8-10, 14, 37-42, 96, 215-19.

33. Most assume that Paul is testifying to his own experience here (cf. 12.7a).

34. The "heavenly places" in Ephesians seems to be a description used of both the lower (3.10; 6.12) and the higher heavens (1.3, 20; 2.6).

35. This is presumably why the heavens need to be renewed as well (Rev. 21.1).

powers.[36] That there were real powers, supraindividual, suprasocial forces, spiritual realities which influenced events and conduct, he had no doubt. But he never thought it of relevance to describe or define these powers in any detail.

In other words, the position is very similar to what we found above when we asked whether Paul believed there were other gods (§2.3c). Even with the more regularly referred to "Satan" (and equivalent terms),[37] the outline of Paul's conceptualization becomes more blurred when examined more closely. As already noted (§2.3c), the retention of the definite article ("the Satan") probably reflects the continuing influence of the original concept — "the Satan" as the name given to the spiritual force which tests and tries the servants of God.[38] Notable also is the way the concept of "evil" and of "the evil one" merge into one another,[39] an existentially real power cohered in a single focus — experienced as malevolent and therefore conceived of as personal. And "the ruler of the power *(exousia)* of the air" (Eph. 2.2) is not so far in conceptuality from "the authority *(exousia)* of darkness" (Col. 1.13) or indeed "the spirit of the world" (1 Cor. 2.12), which in turn is no great distance from the modern phrase "the spirit of the age."[40]

In each case it would seem that Paul refers to such heavenly beings as opposed to God's purposes, not so much because he had clear beliefs about them himself, but because he needed terms to speak of the all too real supraindividual, suprasocial forces of evil which he experienced and saw at work, and because these were the terms which expressed widely held current beliefs. That is to say, the assurances at the points cited above were probably largely *ad hominem,* with a view to reassuring those for whom such heavenly powers were all too real and inspired real fear. This would explain, for example, the vagueness of the term *stoicheia.* Paul used the term as a convenient reference for all the nameless forces (like "fate" and malicious *daimones*) that kept people awake at night in fearful trepidation. It was the powers that his converts experienced and still feared which had been overcome and rendered ineffective. Rather, as with the final items on the list of Rom. 8.38-39, Paul was covering all possibilities. No eventuality, no dimension of reality, no created being, however heavenly, however powerful, could defeat God's purpose in Christ.

36. Cf. Schlier, *Principalities* 13-14.
37. See above §2 n. 45.
38. Caird observes how often in Paul's epistles "the law duplicates those functions which we have seen elsewhere attributed to Satan" (*Principalities* 41-43). But see further below §6.
39. Rom. 12.9; 1 Cor. 5.13; 2 Thes. 3.3; Eph. 6.16.
40. Ling, *Satan* 48, 51-53; cf. also 60-61, 78-84.

All this should be borne in mind when assessing the relevance of Paul's conceptualization of the heavenly powers. For nearly two hundred years this whole area of ancient belief has regularly been identified as a prime example of the problem of "myth," and since Bultmann it has been a prime candidate for his programme of demythologization.[41] But Paul's relative detachment from the issue, or lack of commitment to it as of pressing urgency, suggests that in this case the mythological gap is much narrower. Indeed, perhaps we have to say that Paul himself engaged in his own demythologization at this point. For he did believe in spiritual powers and treated the subject with immense seriousness.[42] But the spiritual powers he focused his theological and pastoral concern on were not the "rulers and authorities," but the powers of sin and death.[43] And these are existential more than ontological realities, the personifications or reifications, or, better, recognition of powers which were (and are) nevertheless all too real in human experience.[44]

---

41. "New Testament and Mythology," in H. W. Bartsch, ed., *Kerygma and Myth* (London: SPCK, 1953) 1-44.

42. Wink argues that the "principalities and powers" are best interpreted as "the inner and outer aspects of any given manifestation of power. As the inner aspect they are the spirituality of institutions, the 'within' of corporate structures and systems, the inner essence of outer organizations of power. As the outer aspect they are political systems, appointed officials, the 'chair' of an organization, laws — in short, all the tangible manifestations which power takes" (*Naming* 5; see also, e.g., 10, 100-101, 109, 118, 139-40, 146). Thus *archē* he defines as "the presociological word for the institutionalization and continuity of power through office, position, or role" (13); *exousia* refers "to the legitimations, sanctions, and permissions that undergird the everyday exercise of power" (17); and "Satan is the real interiority of a society that idolatrously pursues its own enhancement as the highest good" (*Unmasking* 25). Even if Wink overpresses his argument, the main thrust of his interpretation needs to be taken with utmost seriousness. Cf. Ling, *Satan* 89-92; Schlier, *Principalities* 19-20, 25-27, 30-33.

43. Contrast Wink, who follows Beker in suggesting that Paul demythologized the powers in terms of wisdom and law. "As the structures of value and normative behavior in this age, wisdom and law are the powers that regulate existence for Gentile and Jew respectively" (*Naming* 62-63). A different line of thought might have treated "time" as a constrictive "power," enabling a potential critique of attempts to restrict concepts like resurrection, new creation, and final judgment within its narrow bounds.

44. Note also Wink's caution about undue use of the term "personification": "the spirituality of an institution" is something real (*Naming* 105); "personification means illusion" (136). Likewise his warning about the danger of thinking myth can be dispensed with: "all our 'explanations' of myths are dispensable and time-bound and will soon be forgotten [Wink no doubt means us to include his own], but the myth lives on, fed by its continual interplay with the very reality it 'presents'" (142-43); "we have no other form of access to this realm" (145).

§5.3 Sin

Much of what needs to be said about "sin" has already been covered in §4. But given the importance of the term in Paul's exposition of his theology in Romans, it deserves a separate treatment, into which the findings of the earlier discussion can be meshed. It is also appropriate to treat the topic here. For although Paul brings "sin" into the picture fully only from Rom. 5.12 onwards, we have already seen that it is a prominent feature of his analysis of the human condition based on Genesis 1–3. Indeed, given the prominence of the term in the two most explicit uses of the Adam narrative (5.12-14; 7.7-13), its absence in 1.18-32 is of little moment. If anything, the absence of "sin" in Romans 1 simply reflects Paul's technique of focusing his analysis in any one section on only one or two factors at a time. Moreover, as already noted (§5.1), Paul sums up the indictment of his opening section (1.18–3.20) in 3.9 with the words: "we have now charged both Jews and Greeks as all alike under sin," that is, "under the power of sin." So Paul himself was certainly assuming that what he had described in the preceding paragraphs, from 1.18 on, were the varying manifestations of the power of sin.

In focusing on the term "sin" itself, then, two remarkable features should be noted at once. The first is the astonishing predominance of the term in Romans. Of 64 occurrences in the Pauline letters, no less than three-fourths appear in Romans. Putting the point the other way round, *hamartia* occurs three times as often in Romans as in the rest of the Pauline corpus as a whole. Moreover, 41 of the 48 Romans occurrences occur in 5.12–8.3 — an extraordinary intensity of usage. The second feature worthy of preliminary note is the fact that the striking personification of "sin" in Romans is almost equally as unusual in the rest of the Pauline corpus, where the plural usage ("sins") predominates.[45] The only passages outside Romans which correlate closely with the dominant Romans usage are the epigrammatic 1 Cor. 15.56 ("The sting of death is sin, and the power of sin is the law") and Gal. 2.17 and 3.22. We will pick up the first half of 1 Cor. 15.56 below (§5.7) and the second in §6. The two Galatians references anticipate the personification of sin in Romans, with their talk of Christ as a "servant of sin" (2.17) and of everything confined "under sin" (3.22). These references, however, are sufficient to show that the Romans usage, though exceptional in intensity, is not at odds with Paul's theology expressed elsewhere in his letters.

In Rom. 5.12–8.3, however, "sin" appears repeatedly as a personified

---

45. "Sins" — Rom. 3.25 *(hamartēmata);* 4.7 (a quotation); 7.5; 11.27 (a quotation); 1 Cor. 15.3, 17; Gal. 1.4; Eph. 2.1; Col. 1.14; 1 Thes. 2.16; 1 Tim. 5.22, 24; 2 Tim. 3.6. For some analysis of the various relevant Hebrew and Greek terms and conceptions in the Hebrew Bible and the LXX see Lyonnet, *Sin* 12-19, 24-26.

power.[46] It entered the world "through one man" (5.12). It has reigned in or by means of death (5.21). It can rule or lord it over a person (6.12, 14). In 6.16-23 the metaphor of enslavement to sin is the dominant motif, sin likened to a master who pays wages (6.23). In 7.8-11 sin is likened to a living being (the serpent of Genesis 3) or a cunning enemy which seizes its opportunity and builds a bridgehead within weak humanity.[47] And in 7.14 Paul's "I" laments that he is "fleshly, sold under sin," like a defeated captive in war, sold into slavery.[48] Such a persistent personification of sin is also exceptional for the time. Given its prominence in the context of Paul's use of Genesis 1–3, Paul may have derived it from the closely related but enigmatic personification in Gen. 4.7 — sin crouching (like a wild beast) at Cain's door (cf. Sir. 27.10).[49] And parallels in Greek usage have been indicated.[50] But the usage of Romans is primarily a Pauline creation. It must, therefore, indicate a tremendous sense on Paul's own part of sin as a power bearing down upon himself and upon humankind generally.

Putting together our earlier findings, then, we can summarize Paul's understanding of "sin" as a power. "Sin" is the term Paul uses for a compulsion or constraint which humans generally[51] experience within themselves or in their social context, a compulsion towards attitudes and actions not always of their own willing or approving. If Paul made anything of its root meaning, *hamartia* would denote that power which draws men and women back from the best and keeps causing them to miss the target.[52] In particular, sin is that power which makes human beings forget their creatureliness and dependence on God, that power which prevents humankind from recognizing its true nature, which deceives the *adam* into thinking he is godlike and makes him unable to grasp that he is but *adamah*. It is that power which turns humankind in upon itself in preoccupation with satisfying and compensating for its own weakness as flesh.[53] It is that power which has caused countless

46. Of the forty-one references in 5.12–8.3 only a handful clearly have in view the sinful act (5.13b; 7.5; 7.13b; 8.3b). See also above §4.6.

47. BAGD, *aphormē;* see my *Romans* 380.

48. Note also 6.6; 7.23, 25; 8.3, 10.

49. Lyonnet, *Sin* 27-28, maintains that in Judaism there was "a tendency to consider sin . . . as a power which governs men and inspires their conduct." But his best reference is to "sin" (singular?) as characterizing the "angel of darkness" in 1QS 3.17-23.

50. BAGD, *hamartia* 3.

51. He knew well that he could generalize, "for all have sinned" (3.23), "all are under sin" (3.9). On the universality of sin see §4 n. 16.

52. Schlier, *Grundzüge* 64-65. Aristotle defined *hamartia* as a "missing of virtue, the desired goal, whether out of weakness, accident or defective knowledge" (*Ethica Nicomachea* 1106b; cited by G. Stählin, *TDNT* 1.294).

53. Ling observes that in 1 Cor. 5.5 and 2 Cor. 12.7 "the sphere of Satan's operations is the *sarx*" (*Satan* 40-42).

individuals of good will but inadequate resolve to cry out in despair: "I can't help it," "I can't fight it."

Paul does not devote any attention to the question of sin's origin: where did this power come from? The issue was widely reflected upon among both Greek and Jewish ethicists.[54] But all that concerned Paul was the reality of human experience — as the poignant testimony of the "I" in Rom. 7.7-25 so clearly attests.[55] "Sin" simply "entered the world" (5.12); it "came to life" (7.9). That was all Paul felt he need say.[56] The issue of personal responsibility he tried to resolve by depicting "sin" as a power which fully masters the fleshly "I" (7.14), without really denying the "I"'s part in the evil it does or exculpating its failure to do the good (7.14-23).[57] And the question of guilt he resolved in terms of the law. The power of sin constrains humankind to think and act in certain ways, but guilt attaches only to a conscious or deliberate breach of a known command (5.13; 7.9).

Nor should we think that Paul envisaged the power of sin in only individualistic terms. The indictment of Rom. 1.18-32 is all about relationships. The summary reference to the power of sin in 1 Cor. 15.56 no doubt sums up the reality of the social constraints and circumstances which were major factors in the problems confronted in 1 Corinthians 1–14. To be sure, Paul did not think in terms of the modern idea of "institutional sin," the power of sin (injustice and manipulation) entrenched in social institutions.[58] But he would have recognized the point. It was the point he was making in his own way in 1 Cor. 1.26-29: it is the world as an organized system of social values which did not recognize God.[59] It was the social mores and practices of the time against which he was battling in 1 Corinthians 5–6 and 8–11. This, we may also speculate, is why he focused so much attention on sin as a power, in disregard for the heavenly powers he refers to so briefly elsewhere. For, as Wink has seen, the very fluidity and intangibility of the imagery (and now

---

54. See n. 5 above and ben Sira and *4 Ezra* in §4.3.

55. Note 7.7 — "know sin" in the sense "experience sin" (see my *Romans* 378).

56. Bultmann tries to pull the two images together: "sin came into the world by sinning" (similarly Conzelmann, *Outline* 195); the commandment "woke the sin slumbering in him" (*Theology* 1.251). Is it sufficient to define Paul's personification of sin as nothing other than "the essence of human failings *(der Inbegriff menschlicher Tatverfehlungen)*" (Röhser, *Metaphorik* 177)?

57. Cf. Stuhlmacher, *Theologie* 279 — "sin is guilt and destiny at one and the same time." Already Eph. 2.3 sees things in more ontological terms: "we were by nature children of wrath, like everyone else."

58. R. Niebuhr, *Moral Man and Immoral Society: A Study in Ethics and Politics* (New York: Scribner, 1932).

59. Note also *kosmos* ("world") in 1 Cor. 3.19; 4.9, 13; 5.10; 7.31-34; 11.32; and the tie-in to "the *stoicheia* of the world" (above §5.2). Cf. Bultmann, *Theology* 1.254-57; Ladd, *Theology* 437-39.

for "sin" also) suggests that Paul had in mind the invisible (spiritual) power structures which actually do condition, constrain, and control social living in ways no individual or state can master.[60]

In short, Paul's theology at this point is both experiential and practical. And since he refers to "sin" as a power so little elsewhere we may assume that he would have been little concerned about the name itself. What mattered to him was the reality of this dimension of evil, breaking through into individual and social living, entrapping and driving individuals and communities like a pitiless slave owner, entwining its tentacles ever more tightly around persons and their circumstances in an embrace of death. Paul could afford to be so dramatic and so brutally frank in his personification of this power of sin simply because he was convinced that in the gospel he had the means to counter it.

§5.4 The effects of sin — misdirected religion

Paul's indictment of humankind is that in declaring independence from the power of God, human beings have simply put themselves under the power of sin. That power manifests itself for Paul in three characteristic ways. They are already indicated in Rom. 1.18-32, as the description unfolds of the human condition consequent upon human failure to acknowledge God as God.

The first we may describe as *misdirected religion*. It is no doubt a deliberate irony on Paul's part that the first outcome of the refusal to worship God (1.21) is the worship of images of humans and animals (1.23, 25).[61] It is a claim and insight worth pondering. That the substitute for appropriate honouring of God is religion![62] What it implies is a sense on Paul's part that the basic instinct of the creature to invest ultimate significance in God's creative power cannot be wholly suppressed, only perverted. God can be replaced by gods of human contriving. Instead of attributing ultimate significance to God, human beings can readily give that significance to what they more easily define or attain or control. The temptation to become like God (Gen. 3.5) takes effect when human beings bring religion under their control, when it becomes a means of glorifying themselves. The will to become like

60. See above n. 42.
61. On Paul's hostility to idolatry elsewhere see above §2 n. 20.
62. Cf. Karl Barth's famous critique of "religion as unbelief" (*Church Dogmatics* 1.2 [Edinburgh: Clark, 1956] 297-325): "From the standpoint of revelation religion is clearly seen to be a human attempt to anticipate what God in His revelation wills to do and does do. It is the attempted replacement of the divine work by a human manufacture" (302), with reference to Rom. 1.18-32 (306-7).

God is the will to power, to shape lives and determine destinies. The basic urge which drives human beings to gain power over others is a perversion of the creature's basic instinct to acknowledge God and to acknowledge dependence on God.[63]

Most striking here is the fact that Paul attempts to bring his own ancestral religion under the same indictment. The accusation of decline into idolatry, as we have already noted, was not simply a rerun of the standard Jewish condemnation of Gentile idolatry. For Israel too had often enough fallen into the same trap.[64] Even so Paul felt it necessary to devote Rom. 2.1–3.19 to ensuring that his own kinsfolk were not exempted from his indictment. This should be clear enough in the way Romans 2 develops. In it Paul attacks with increasing explicitness what he evidently regarded as a typically Jewish conviction that they had a favoured status before God which would exempt them from judgment on their own sinful actions.[65] His attack, in other words, is upon a confidence falsely based on their religion. Since Paul devotes so much space to making this critique it must have been important for him. So it is worth tracing his indictment through in some detail.[66]

(1) Paul begins by rounding on an imagined interlocutor: "therefore you are without excuse, you sir, whoever you are who act as judge" (2.1). The interlocutor can hardly be other than the self-identified "Jew" of 2.17.[67]

---

63. See also Eichholz, *Theologie* 70-76. Cf. Ling, *Satan* 42: "The conception of Satan which emerges from these Pauline references is that of a spirit characterized by an insatiable appetite for power and self-aggrandizement."

64. See above §4.4.

65. Cf. Beker, *Paul* 80: "What is argued is the equal status of Jew and Gentile under sin; what is presupposed is the self-evident character of the Gentile under sin."

66. For fuller detail in what follows see my *Romans* 76-160. Elliott, *Rhetoric*, attempts to undermine this whole line of exegesis: (1) Elliott writes that Paul gives no clue at the start that 1.18–3.20 is an indictment and that this only becomes clear at 3.9 and 20 (106-7) — a most odd reading of 1.18ff. (2) Although he recognizes that 1.18-32 "is aimed particularly at the Gentile world" in the language of Hellenistic Jewish propaganda (173-74), Elliott thinks it "arbitrary" (125-26) to deduce that the interlocutor of 2.1ff. who affirms the indictment of 1.18-32 is most obviously intended to be the voice of such propaganda (see below n. 67). (3) He ignores the fact that the issue addressed in Romans 2 is "the advantage of the Jew" (3.1), that is, over the non-Jew, and that this issue is clearly to the fore as much in 2.1-16 as in 2.17-29 (the evidence is about to be marshaled). It is hardly the case that at 2.17 "there is an obvious shift to a new conversation partner" (127; cf. 174-90, 284). See further below (nn. 75 and 79). Elliott's thesis is an example of exegesis doing service to rhetorical theory.

67. The modern consensus (e.g., Eichholz, *Theologie* 83-85; Ziesler, *Romans* 81; G. P. Carras, "Romans 2.1-29: A Dialogue on Jewish Ideals," *Bib* 73 [1992] 183-207; Fitzmyer, *Romans* 297; Stuhlmacher, *Romans* 39-40; Boyarin, *Radical Jew* 86-95; Thielman, *Paul* [§6 n. 1] 168-70; others in Elliott, *Rhetoric* 174-75). Stowers' attempt to read

Anyone who was familiar with the scathing critique of Gentile religion in Wisdom 11–15, which Rom. 1.18-32 so clearly echoes,[68] could scarcely have failed to recognize that Paul's indictment was characteristic of a diaspora Judaism conscious of its moral superiority over typical Gentile religion. In other words, the judging interlocutor is in effect the "Jew" who speaks in the Wisdom of Solomon.[69]

(2) The clear implication of 2.1-6 is not that the interlocutor thinks he commits no sin. Rather, what Paul criticizes is the interlocutor's sense that, even though he does commit the very things he condemns in Gentiles, he himself "will escape the condemnation of God" (2.3). He has failed to realize his own need for deep repentance (2.4-5). But this is an attitude which we find again in Jewish writings of the time. *The Psalms of Solomon* are confident that "those who act lawlessly[70] will not escape the condemnation of the Lord" (the same phrase as in Rom. 2.3). At the same time they are equally confident that their own sins are atoned for (*Pss. Sol.* 3.8), that they will be forgiven (9.6-7), that the Lord will spare his holy ones (13.10), that God will support them and grant them mercy (16.11-15). Equally striking is the echo of Wis. 15.1-4 in Rom. 2.4:

> But you, our God, are kind and true, patient [cf. Rom. 2.4]. . . . For even if we sin, we are yours, knowing your power [cf. Rom. 1.19-20]; but we will not sin, knowing that we are reckoned yours. For to know you is complete righteousness [cf. Rom. 1.17], and to know your power [cf. Rom. 1.19-20] is the root of immortality. For neither has the evil intent of human art misled us, nor the fruitless toil of painters . . . [leading into the polemic against idolatry — cf. Rom. 1.23-25].

Given the echoes back and forth between Romans 1–2 and Wisdom 11–15 it is hard to doubt that the attitude critiqued by Paul in Rom. 2.4 was just the one expressed in Wisdom. Once again the interlocutor is in effect the "Jew" who speaks in the Wisdom of Solomon. Also indicative of the mind-set of

---

2.1-16 as directed to the pretentious Gentile at times seems to assume that the issue hangs on the rhetorical device itself (*Rereading* 13, 101), whereas it hangs primarily on the fact that the preceding critique was so characteristically Jewish, particularly of Gentile idolatry and sexual practice, a feature that Stowers ignores completely at the crucial point (27-29, 100-104). Despite 102, the one who "judges" in 14.3-4 is most likely the Jewish believer who refrains from eating "unclean" food (14.14); see below §24.3.

68. See above §2.4, §4.3 n. 23, and below (2).

69. See Laato, *Paulus* 109-12, 118-19.

70. Literally "those who do *anomia* (lawlessness)." *Anomia* is the mark of the enemy Gentiles and those who sided with them and acted like them (*Pss. Sol.* 1.8; 2.3, 12; 15.8, 10; 17.11, 18). In contrast the group behind the *Psalms of Solomon* regarded themselves as "the righteous" in opposition to "the sinners" (1.1-3; 2.1-2, 16, 34-35; 3.3-12, etc.).

both *Psalms of Solomon* and Wisdom of Solomon is the distinction they make between the way God deals with them and the way he deals with "sinners." Israel is disciplined; the others are punished. Israel is chastised; the others are scourged. Israel is tested; the ungodly are condemned. Israel expects mercy; their opponents can look only for wrath.[71]

(3) The same confidence seems to be more openly critiqued in the following two paragraphs. God's judgment will be completely evenhanded (2.6-11): "Jew first and Gentile as well, for there is no partiality with God" (2.9-11). Similarly 2.12-16. So far as final judgment is concerned, the critical difference is not between being "outside the law" *(anomos)* and being "within the law" (*en nomō*, 2.12), between "Gentiles who do not have the law" and Jews who do (2.14). The measure of judgment will be the same in both cases: whether they did what the law requires (2.13-14).[72]

(4) It is the very same confidence which comes at last clearly to expression in the final two paragraphs (2.17-24, 25-29). The "Jew" relies on the law and boasts in God (2.17). He is confident that having the law and being instructed in the law put him in a position of religious superiority over the other nations (2.18-20). He regards his circumcision as a kind of talisman, a prophylactic against serious sin, whose very presence in his flesh marks him out as belonging to the people chosen by God and secure in God's favour (2.25, 28).[73] In reality, says Paul, a breach of the law was as serious if committed by a Jew (2.21-24),[74] just as fulfilment of the law was as valid if performed by the uncircumcised (2.26-29).

(5) That this interpretation is on the right lines is surely indicated by Paul's very next sentence. "What then is the advantage of the Jew, or what

71. *Pss. Sol.* 3.4-12; 7.1-10; 8.23-34; 13.5-12; Wis. 11.9-10; 12.22; 16.9-10.

72. See also §6.3 below.

73. "They understand their election, their circumcision, God's revelation to Israel as something which more or less protects them against the consequences of the nonfulfilment of the law" (Schlier, *Grundzüge* 76). "The Jew whom Paul is addressing and attacking here is a Jew who does not successfully keep the Law, *and relies on God's grace to the Jews to save her at the last judgment.* Paul's adversary is covenantal grace, not good works" (Boyarin, *Radical Jew* 211, his emphasis). For the significance of circumcision see my "What Was the Issue between Paul and 'Those of the Circumcision'?" in Hengel and Heckel, *Paulus und das antike Judentum* 295-313 (especially 306-21); also below §14.4.

74. That Paul "pretends to be speaking of things that are characteristic of 'Judaism *as a whole* and of *every* individual Jew without exception,'" "a piece of propagandist denigration" (Räisänen, *Law* [§6 n. 1] 100-101) is a gross exaggeration. Paul engages in a rhetorical rebuke and exhortation familiar at the time in Stoic as well as Jewish writings, which may include allusion to one or two well-known cases (see, e.g., my *Romans* 113-15), to warn that such breaches of the law by Jews should be regarded in quite as serious (or still more serious) a light as breaches by Gentiles.

is the value of circumcision?" (3.1).[75] Paul himself clearly saw his indictment in 2.1-29 as directed against his ancestral religion — that is, against the overconfident religious identity it had given his Jewish contemporaries and against an overreliance on its praxis which their appreciation of the law seems to have engendered. To that extent Paul regarded his own people's religion as misdirected. It was his own people's discounting of their breaches of the law and their characteristic overvaluation of their status as God's chosen people[76] which Paul saw as proof sufficient that Jews as well as Greeks were "all alike under sin" (3.9).[77]

(6) The final catena of texts in 3.10-18 simply drives the point home more deeply. For all the Psalm citations presuppose an antithesis between the righteous (the faithful member of the covenant people) and the unrighteous.[78] Paul thus calls upon texts which would have seemed at first to bolster Israel's sense of distinctiveness from Gentiles and sense of privilege over against Gentiles. But by now he has thoroughly undermined that presupposition of favoured status before God. Consequently, these same scriptures can serve as a condemnation of *all* humankind. The point becomes explicit in 3.19: the law speaks to those "within the law," that is, to those whose confidence before God and over against other nations rested in their possession of the law as the mark of God's favour. It is only when such scriptures are seen to include the Jewish people as well that *every* mouth can be stopped and *all* the world become liable to God's judgment (3.19).[79]

For Paul, then, the power of sin has manifested itself characteristically

---

75. The question has clearly been raised by Paul's preceding argument and therefore is posed rhetorically *to* Paul. Elliott, *Rhetoric* 139-41, however, makes the surprising proposal that the questioner in 3.1-8 is *Paul* interrogating the interlocutor, so that it is the *interlocutor* who first makes the characteristic Pauline response, *mē genoito* ("Certainly not!" 3.4, 6; but see also 3.31; 6.2, 15; 7.7, 13; 9.14; 11.1, 11; 1 Cor. 6.15; Gal. 2.17; 3.21). On Stowers' only partially more plausible reading (see now *Rereading* ch. 5), see Penna, *Paul* 1.111-16. And on the degree of distinctiveness of Paul's *mē genoito* formula, see Malherbe, "*Mē Genoito* in the Diatribe and Paul," *Paul and the Popular Philosophers* 25-33.

76. Jewish "unfaithfulness" (3.3) will certainly have the indictment of ch. 2 in view; the argument here does not require the further thought of their failure to believe in Christ — despite, e.g., C. H. Cosgrove, "What If Some Have Not Believed? The Occasion and Thrust of Romans 3.1-8," *ZNW* 78 (1987) 90-105.

77. That the summary in 3.9 implies an indictment focused on Greeks (1.18-32) and Jews (2.1–3.8) is recognized, e.g., by Beker, *Paul* 79 (following "most scholars"), and Fitzmyer, *Romans* 270-71.

78. Pss. 14.1-3; 53.2-3; 5.9; 140.3; 9.28; 35.2; see my *Romans* 150-51.

79. Cf. Merklein, "Paulus und die Sünde" 129. Elliott, *Rhetoric* 145, again misses the force of 3.19: the indictment is so largely (not exclusively) directed against Paul's fellow Jews (3.19a) precisely in order to demonstrate that *all* are liable to God's judgment (3.19b).

in misdirected religion. And that included not just Gentile idolatry, but also the idolatrous misplaced confidence of his own people in their own God-given religion and status before God. The critique at this point is easily misunderstood and requires careful statement.[80] In one of the most famous expositions of this century Bultmann rightly recognized that Paul identifies religious "boasting" as a primary expression of sin. However, he further identified the boasting of Rom. 2.17, 23 as the "extreme expression . . . of the attitude of sinful self-reliance."[81] In turning Paul's critique of religion into a critique of self-reliance Bultmann grasped only part of Paul's argument — and the part directed more against Gentile idolatry[82] than that directed against Jewish religious self-understanding. For the "boasting" language of Rom. 2.17 and 23 in context hardly suggests an attitude of *self*-reliance. Rather, it expresses clearly a *national* reliance — a confidence that God is Israel's God, that possession of the law puts the possessors in a position of advantage over all others, that the people marked out by circumcision are secure in God's praise.[83] These are issues to which we must return later.

§5.5 The effects of sin — self-indulgence

It is no coincidence that Paul traces the outworking of human independence from God through idolatry to "the desires of their hearts" as expressed in unclean and dishonouring sexual activity (Rom. 1.23-24, 25-27). For the link between idolatry and sexual license was well established both in Jewish folklore[84] and in Jewish apologetic,[85] and carries over into Christianity.[86] The critique reveals a penetrating psychological insight. For if the instinct to serve

---

80. Caird, *Theology* 91, is too strong: "For Paul the Jew there was a lie at the root of the Jewish religion."

81. Bultmann, *Theology* 1.242; followed, e.g., by Eichholz, *Theologie* 90, 116; Ladd, *Theology* 444-45; Schlier, *Grundzüge* 76-77; Hübner, *Law* [§6 n. 1] 113-16; Westerholm, *Law* [§6 n. 1] 170 (but see n. 73 above).

82. The interpretation here advocated also fits better with Paul's warning against Greeks boasting in their wisdom (1 Cor. 1.29, 31), since the opposite there, "boasting in the Lord" (1 Cor. 1.31), is equivalent to the opposite here, "glorifying God as God and giving him thanks" (Rom. 1.21).

83. The same is true of Paul's contrast between appropriate "boasting" and his pre-Christian "confidence in the flesh" (Phil. 3.3) and of his critique of his Galatian opponents for seeking to "boast in your [the Galatians'] flesh" (Gal. 6.12-13); see further above §3.3b and below §14.5e.

84. We recall again the sin of the golden calf and of Baal Peor (above §4.4 and §4.7).

85. Here we may note again particularly Wis. 14.12-27. See also Hos. 4.12-18; Ep. Jer. 43; *2 Enoch* 10.4-6; *T. Ben.* 10.10.

86. 1 Cor. 5.11; 6.9; Gal. 5.20; Col. 3.5; 1 Pet. 4.3; Rev. 21.8; 22.15; *Didache* 5.1.

a greater than oneself (a greater being or cause) is deeply rooted in the human psyche, the instinct to reproduce (the sex drive) is also fundamental to all living species. And as the one can be misdirected, so can the other; the more fundamental the drive, the more profoundly disorienting its distortion. The obsessional preoccupation with sex which is such a feature of contemporary society and which in differing degrees underlies so much literature and art of earlier generations bears witness to the validity of Paul's and earlier Jewish insight on the point. Independence from God can quickly become commitment to self-indulgence, or rather slavery to self-indulgence (cf. Rom. 6.15-23).

We must be careful, however, lest we overstate Paul's point here. The immediate manifestation of sin Paul names as *epithymia* (1.24), a term we met several times in §4.[87] *Epithymia* can be used in a neutral or good sense, meaning "desire." Thus Paul elsewhere expresses "a great desire to see you face to face" (1 Thes. 2.17) and a "desire to depart and be with Christ" (Phil. 1.23). But more typically Paul uses *epithymia* in a bad sense, as desire for something forbidden, "covetousness" or "lust." This is the immediate effect of sin in the next two references in Romans: sin provokes the desires of the mortal body (6.12); it was sin that stirred up covetousness (7.7-8). In 1.24 there is probably an allusion to Ps. 78.29 ("God gave them their *epithymia,* what they craved for"), referring back to the episode of the quails in the wilderness (Num. 11.31-35).[88] On a number of other occasions Paul speaks of the "desire(s) of the flesh," again in a similarly negative way.[89] The implication is of a life lived habitually in terms of satisfying natural or animal appetites as the be-all and end-all. Boldly asserted "freedom" can all too soon become freedom simply to indulge one's own desires (Gal. 5.13, 16).[90] The later Paulines speak of an "old self corrupt and deluded by its lusts" (Eph. 4.22), of "senseless and harmful desires which plunge people into ruin and destruction" (1 Tim. 6.9), of enslavement to various passions and pleasures (Tit. 3.3).[91] Sin, we may say, is that power which transforms *epithymia* from something neutral or positive into something harmful, from "desire" into "lust." It is the power which turns desire in upon itself in destructive self-indulgence.[92]

---

87. See above particularly §4.7.

88. Note also Ps. 106.14-15: "They had a wanton craving in the wilderness, and God put them to the test in the desert; he gave them what they asked, but sent a wasting disease among them."

89. Rom. 13.14; Gal. 5.16, 24; also Eph. 2.3. Rom. 6.12 — "the desires of the mortal body."

90. Cf. "walking in accordance with the flesh"; see above §3.3 and Phil 3.19 — "whose god is their belly."

91. See also 2 Tim. 2.22; 3.6; 4.3; Tit. 2.12.

92. As already noted (§4.3), Paul here draws on a longer tradition of Jewish analysis.

Within this larger picture, one of the most characteristic expressions of self-indulgent desire is sexual activity.[93] This is the clear implication of Rom. 1.24: "God handed them over in the desires of their hearts to the uncleanness of dishonouring their bodies among themselves." "Uncleanness, impurity" (*akatharsia*) typically denotes sexual immorality;[94] and "dishonouring their bodies among themselves" likewise presumably refers to sexual activities in which people treated themselves (their bodies) with lack of respect. But the sense of "desire" as sexual lust is also obvious in the association of *epithymia* with *pathos* ("passion") in both 1 Thes. 4.5 and Col. 3.5. In each case what is in view is unspecified sexual indulgence. And it ties in with Paul's (and Jewish) antipathy to *porneia*, "sexual immorality," which probably covers the whole range of unlawful sexual intercourse.[95] Paul's concern regarding *porneia* as a constant danger for many of his converts is indicated by repeated references to it, summed up in the exhortation, "Flee *porneia*" (1 Cor. 6.18).[96]

Perhaps it needs to be added again that this was not an antipathy to all sexual activity as such. On the contrary, Paul shows realistic appreciation of the strength of sexual desire in 1 Cor. 7.9 — "better to marry than to be consumed [with passion]." And his assertion of conjugal rights as a mutual responsibility in 7.3-4 was very progressive for the time. To be noted not least is the fact that in 7.5 it is enforced abstinence which gives Satan scope for temptation rather than the delights of the marital bed.[97] Nevertheless, Paul was surely right to recognize the power of the sex drive, which if not appropriately channeled can quickly diminish individuals (who no doubt still think of themselves as "wise") and distort relationships and responsibilities.

In his listing of the effects of human turning from God in Romans 1 Paul next notes a particular kind of sexual irregularity — homosexual practice among both women and men[98] — the fruit of "disgraceful passions" (Rom.

---

93. "Desire" = lust was familiar in the ancient world — e.g., Plutarch, *Moralia* 525AB; Susanna (Theodotion) 8, 11, 14, 20, 56; Josephus, *Ant.* 4.130, 132.

94. BAGD, *akatharsia;* e.g., *1 Enoch* 10.11; *T. Jud.* 14-15; *T. Jos.* 4.6. In the NT *akatharsia* is almost exclusively a Pauline term (nine ocurrences in the Pauline corpus), on several occasions linked with *porneia* ("sexual immorality") (2 Cor. 12.21; Gal. 5.19; Eph. 5.3; Col. 3.5).

95. BAGD, *porneia;* see also below §24.4 and n. 74. For the more relaxed views of Greek society on the subject see below §24 n. 80.

96. See also 1 Cor. 5.1; 6.13; 7.2; 2 Cor. 12.21; Gal. 5.19; Col. 3.5; Eph. 5.3. Note again the link between idolatry and *porneia* assumed in the first version of the "apostolic decree," in Acts 15.20. Jewish and Christian concern on the subject is well illustrated by similar warnings in the *Testaments of the Twelve Patriarchs* — particularly *Testament of Reuben* and *Testament of Judah*.

97. Ling, *Satan* 38, 61-62; Wink, *Unmasking* 20.

98. My colleague Mark Bonnington points out how unusual it was that Paul should speak of male and female homosexual practice in the same terms (1.26-27).

1.26-27).[99] This is a point at which Jewish and early Christian tradition stood out against contemporary Greco-Roman culture, where homosexual practice was quite acceptable and even highly regarded.[100] In contrast Jewish reaction to it as a perversion, a pagan abomination, is consistent,[101] and not least among diaspora Jews who would have been most familiar with Gentile mores.[102] Paul's reaction stands firmly in the Jewish tradition, as 1 Cor. 6.9 confirms.[103] He regards homosexual practice as "contrary to nature" (Rom. 1.26),[104] as itself the consequence of a life which has wandered away from God (1.27).[105] This is the "wrath of God": to grant humans their desires when their desires

99. To be noted is the fact that Paul speaks only of homosexual acts. He says nothing about a homosexual orientation itself, only about the indulgence of "desires" (1.24), "passions" (1.26), and "sexual desire" (1.27).

100. See particularly Plato's *Symposium* and Plutarch's *Lycurgus;* bibliography in Fitzmyer, *Romans* 275; and further below §24.4 nn. 80 and 89. Greco-Roman views of homosexual practice, however, were not uniformly approbative; see D. F. Greenberg, *The Construction of Homosexuality* (Chicago: University of Chicago, 1988) 141-60, 202-10.

101. Particularly Lev. 18.22; 20.13. See further my *Romans* 65.

102. Wis. 14.26; *Ep. Arist.* 152; Philo, *Abr.* 135-7; *Spec. Leg.* 3.37-42; *Sib. Or.* 3.184-86, 764; *Pseudo-Phocylides* 3, 190-92, 213-14; Josephus, *Ap.* 2.273-75.

103. In 1 Cor. 6.9 three terms are used in a list of unacceptable lifestyles — "adulterers, effeminate *(malakoi),* and practising homosexuals *(arsenokoitai)*." *Malakos* means "soft, smooth" and probably refers to effeminate men, such as Philo describes in *Spec. Leg.* 3.37-42 *(malakia,* "effeminacy" — 3.39, 40; cf. *Som.* 1.122-23; 2.9; see further D. B. Martin, "*Arsenokoitēs* and *Malakos:* Meanings and Consequences," in R. L. Brawley, ed., *Biblical Ethics and Homosexuality: Listening to Scripture* [Louisville: Westminster/John Knox, 1996] 117-36, here 124-28). *Arsenokoitēs* (also in 1 Tim. 1.10) is a hitherto unknown term, which may well have been a new coinage (by Paul?). If so, it was most obviously derived directly from the condemnation of homosexual practice in Lev. 18.22 and 20.13 (LXX — . . . *meta arsenos koitēn gynaikos*; D. F. Wright, "Homosexuals or Prostitutes? The Meaning of Arsenokoitai [1 Cor. 6.9; 1 Tim. 1.10]," *VC* 38 [1984] 125-53; *pace* Martin, "*Arsenokoitēs*" 118-23). Pederasty in particular (homosexual intercourse with a boy) may be in view (cf. again Philo, *Spec. Leg.* 3.39; see particularly R. Scroggs, *The New Testament and Homosexuality* [Philadelphia: Fortress, 1983] here 106-8; Furnish, *Moral Teaching* [§24 n. 1] 69-70). But had Paul wished to be so specific, the term "pederast" *(paiderastēs)* itself lay close to hand. Nor does the list in 1 Cor. 6.9 imply a particular link between any two items in the list. And Scroggs's attempt to limit Paul's critique to pederasty in Rom. 1.26-27 (117) ignores the fact that the condemnation implies a similarity in the desire *(orexis)* of the male partners for each other (1.27) and includes lesbian relationships (1.26); see further B. J. Brooten, *Love between Women: Early Christian Responses to Female Homoeroticism* (Chicago: University of Chicago, 1996) 239-66.

104. Using the typically Stoic concept; see above §2.6. Cf. the use of the same phrase *(para physin)* in Plato, *Republic* 5.13; *Laws* 6.26b-c; Philo, *Spec. Leg.* 3.39. See further R. B. Hays, "Relations Natural and Unnatural: A Response to John Boswell's Exegesis of Romans 1," *Journal of Religious Ethics* 14 (1986) 184-215; also *Moral Vision* (§23 n. 1) ch. 16.

105. There is probably an allusion to Wis. 12.23-24 here.

are lusts, to grant women and men their self-indulgent choices — and the consequences of these choices.[106]

Paul thus sees the effects of sin principally in the distortion of humankind's two principal instinctual drives. It is not the sexual drive which is most fundamental. But just as the sexual drive can be sublimated and redirected into other channels, so the instinctive urge to surrender oneself to a greater can be sublimated and redirected. When it is thus cut loose from the truth of God, it becomes more a destructive than a creative force. And when it combines with the instinctive urge to create new life, the power for distortion of life and subversion of society becomes almost uncontrollable.

§5.6 The effects of sin — sins

Although Paul says relatively little about "sins" (plural) in Romans,[107] the corollary that (the power of) sin lies behind or comes to expression in (individual) sins is unavoidable.[108] And although he does not use the term in Romans 1, it is hardly misrepresenting Paul to say that the sequence of sin begetting sins begetting sins ("God handed them over") continues till the end of the chapter. The consequence of thinking God unfit for human knowing is that the organ of human knowing, understanding, and evaluating is itself rendered unfit (1.28).[109] Left to itself, "free" of God, the human mind is incapable of exercising adequately the discernment and discrimination on which decision making depends. The result is inappropriate and "unfitting"[110] judgments. Paul then illustrates the effect of this in the vice list in 1.29-31:

> [29]unrighteousness, wickedness, greed, badness, jealousy, murder, rivalry, deceit, spite, rumour-mongers, [30]slanderers, God-haters, insolent, arrogant, braggarts, contrivers of evil, disobedient to parents, [31]senseless, faithless, loveless, merciless.

106. See above §2.4 on "the wrath of God."

107. See above n. 45. Most of the references echo soteriological formulae. *Parabasis* ("transgression") is used in Rom. 2.23; 4.15; 5.14; Gal. 3.19; 1 Tim. 2.14. *Paraptōma* ("transgression") is used in Rom. 4.25; 5.15-20 (six times); 11.11-12; 2 Cor. 5.19; Gal. 6.1; Eph. 1.7; 2.1, 5; Col. 2.13 (again mainly in soteriological formulae).

108. See particularly Schlier, *Grundzüge* 67-69.

109. Note the wordplay: "they did not think fit *(edokimasan)* to keep God in mind (so) God handed them over to a disqualified *(adokimon)* mind." *Dokimazō* has the sense of "test, examine, prove by testing, accept as proved": their disapproval of God simply demonstrated that they had failed the test as thinking beings and were functioning one dimension short of reality.

110. See §2 n. 101 above.

Such vice lists were common in ancient ethics. They were particularly popular among the Stoics, but common also in Judaism. Paul uses the technique on a number of occasions.[111] For example,

> 1 Cor. 5.10-11 — sexually immoral, greedy, robber, idolater, slanderer, drunkard
> 1 Cor. 6.9-10 — [9]sexually immoral, idolaters, adulterers, effeminate, practising homosexuals, [10]thieves, greedy, drunkards, slanderers, swindlers
> Gal. 5.19-21 — [19]sexual immorality, impurity, debauchery, [20]idolatry, sorcery, hostility, strife, jealousy, displays of anger, selfish ambition, dissension, factions, [21]envyings, drunkenness, excessive feasting.

The diversity in the items in these lists indicates that Paul was not simply taking over a standard catalog each time but varied them at least on some occasions to speak more directly to particular concerns in the communities written to.[112] We need not comment further on particular items. But two features are worth noting. One is that the bulk of the vices listed are social. The effect of sin is seen at its most serious not so much in secret vices practised in private, but in the breakdown of human relationships. The other is that so many of the vices are petty — the petty acts of envy and deceit, of jealousy and conceit, of gossip and backbiting, of greed and spite, of heartlessness and ruthlessness. But it is precisely such petty vices which undermine a community of trust and poison society. The repeated "God handed them over" (Rom. 1.24, 26, 28) suggests a power of sin gaining an ever tighter stranglehold on humanity. If so, it is worth noting that for Paul the evidence of sin's most pervasive effect is to be seen not so much in idolatry or in sexual license as in the pettiness which disfigures collegiality and community.

§5.7 Death

As with "sin," we have already dealt quite fully with Paul's conception of death (above §4). Here we need simply to draw the various threads of the earlier discussion together and to underline its status as a power bearing down

---

111. See further below §23.7b.
112. Hence the emphasis in the 1 Corinthian lists. Likewise the bulk of the Galatians 5 list seems to be directed against the factional tensions which the coming of the "troublemakers" had occasioned within the Galatian churches (see my *Galatians* 302, 304-6). In Rom. 1.29-31 the list is more stylized, beginning with four words ending with *-ia (adikia, ponēria, pleonexia, kakia)* and ending with four beginning with *a- (asynetous, asynthetous, astorgous, aneleēmonas)*.

upon humankind, constituting a form of slavery from which the gospel brings release.

First, it should be observed that Paul speaks of "death" with a spectrum of usage similar (and related) to that of flesh. At the more "neutral" end he can contemplate death with some equanimity.[113] But the predominant usage (almost always in Romans) is of death in a more negative sense: as a due punishment (Rom. 1.32 — for the kind of sins outlined in 1.29-31), as the forfeiture of life (7.10), and as an official sentence (*apokrima* — 2 Cor. 1.9).[114]

In particular, death is the outcome of life lived "in the flesh" under the sway of sinful passions (Rom. 7.5), the outcome of the flesh's "mind-set" (8.6), the outcome of life lived "in accordance with the flesh" (*kata sarka* — 8.13).[115] Paul thus recognized the "naturalness" of death. But as with the predominant weight in his talk of "flesh,"[116] so it is the sense of death as a negating force which predominates — death, we might say, as the end of a process of decay, the final destruction of the corruptible (1 Cor. 15.42, 50). The total perishing of the flesh is all that the life devoted to feeding its desires can look forward to. "Those who sow to their own flesh will from the flesh reap corruption" (Gal. 6.8).[117]

Even more striking is the intimate link between sin and death.[118] As with "sin," the main weight of Paul's talk of "death" in Romans falls in 5.12–8.2 (18 occurrences). Death entered the world through sin (5.12). "By one man's transgression the many died" (5.15). "Sin reigned in death" (5.21). Death is the end result, the *telos,* the climactic expression and completion of sin (6.16, 21).[119] "The wages of sin is death" (6.23). The fruit of sinful passions is death (7.5). Sin's life means humankind's death (7.9-10). Sin produces death (7.13). Believers have been "freed from the law of sin and death" (8.2).[120] In other words, death is the last and worst effect of sin. The

---

113. Rom. 14.8; 1 Cor. 3.22; 9.15; 15.31-32; 2 Cor. 6.9; 11.23; Phil. 1.20-21.

114. Lyonnet, *Sin* 7, cites Augustine: "When it is asked with what death God threatened the first men . . . , whether it was the death of the soul or of the body or of the whole man, or that which is called the second death, the answer is: all of them" (*City of God* 13.12).

115. See also 2 Cor. 2.16; 3.7; 7.10.

116. See above §3.3.

117. "He who derives life out of the transitory must, himself, perish with the perishing of the transitory" (Bultmann, *Theology* 1.247).

118. Cf. particularly Schlier, *Grundzüge* 108-11.

119. Consequently, "he who has died is declared free from sin" (6.7), and "the death he [Christ] died, he died to sin once and for all" (6.10).

120. The kaleidescope of metaphors in this paragraph is typical of Paul (see below §13.4). It is no criticism to observe that they cannot be harmonized (cf. Bultmann, *Theology* 1.249). They are metaphors!

same point emerges from the similarly close link between Adam and death: death is the lot of Adamic humanity.[121]

This confirms what we saw above (§4.6): for Paul, death is not the intended outcome for humankind; it is the result of sin. The point is that life in this age can no more escape death than it can escape flesh, can no more escape death than it can escape sin. The influence of these intermeshed factors is all-pervasive. Even the individual who seeks to avoid the vices listed above (§5.6) is still caught in the network of corporate "flesh," of the structures of "sin."[122] There is no escape, except through death — the death of the other "one man," which "the many" can share, just as they share in Adam's susceptibility to sin and death.[123] This must be what Paul meant when he described sin as the "sting *(kentron)* of death" (1 Cor. 15.56). Sin is the poison which gives death its final effect, the goad which makes death so painful. Were there no sin, would there be no death, or would it be simply that death was no longer painful? Paul does not address that question. It is sufficient for him that the existential reality is that death is inescapable as the end of this life.

For the same reason Paul can think of death as a dominating power, like sin. It exercises rule like a king (Rom. 5.14, 17). It lords it over the living (6.9). It is one of the powers which might intervene between God and those he loves (8.38). It is "the last enemy" (1 Cor. 15.26). Who has stood by the coffin of a loved one and has not experienced that sense of a battle lost, that feeling of irreplaceable loss? And what person of moral resolve has not at times resonated with the anguished cry of Rom. 7.24: "Who will deliver me from the body of this death?" The cosmos itself longs for an existence no longer dominated by death as the end (Rom. 8.20-21).

In short, part of the strength of Paul's theology is that it takes seriously the reality of death. Here again we need not become caught up in questions about the value or viability of the particular imagery he used. It is the brute fact that life ends in death which has to be accepted — and dealt with in a theology which offers hope. Paul's theology does so. And in doing so it poses the existential question: will death be a release from fleshliness and sin — or their final triumph?

---

121. Rom. 5.12, 15, 17; 1 Cor. 15.21; Phil. 2.8.

122. Paul Achtemeier, in a private communication, suggested that this is what Paul had in mind in using such terms as "body of sin" (Rom. 6.6) and "body of death" (Rom. 7.24), which are therefore to be set in direct contrast with the church as "body of Christ," that is, as a new community in which a different set of social and moral forces is in operation.

123. Rom. 5.6-10; 6.2-10; 7.6; 2 Cor. 4.11; 5.15; Col. 2.20; 3.3; Phil. 3.10. Cf. Cranfield's analysis of the four senses in which Paul speaks of dying (*Romans* 299-300; taken up by Fitzmyer, *Romans* 432-33). See further Black, "Pauline Perspectives."

§5.8 *In sum*

Whatever we make of Paul's talk of spiritual powers, several points in his treatment are clear and worthy of note. (1) However conceptualized, there are real forces for evil operative in the world. (2) These are not to be reduced simply to human willfulness or individual selfishness. There are also constraints and pressures operating within and upon human society which combine with human weakness to corrupt both individual and community. (3) Paul's assessment of this human condition in terms of the power of "sin," of what this power produces in individual and society, and of how it interlocks with the reality of death and gives death its frightening and negative character has relevance not simply for personal spirituality but also for other analyses of society and all strategies towards community building. (4) Not least of importance for a theology of Paul is the claim of Paul's gospel that in Christ the power of these powers to dominate individual and community has been decisively broken. But that is to anticipate what follows.

§6 The law[1]

1. **Bibliography**. **Barrett**, *Paul* 74-87; **Becker**, *Paul* 392-98; **Beker**, *Paul* 235-54; **P. Benoit**, "The Law and the Cross according to St Paul: Romans 7.7–8.4," *Jesus and the Gospel* II (London: Darton, Longman, and Todd, 1974) 11-39; **Bornkamm**, *Paul* 120-29; **Boyarin**, *Radical Jew* ch. 6; **Bultmann**, *Theology* I, 259-69; **Conzelmann**, *Outline* 220-35; **Cranfield**, *Romans* 845-62; **W. D. Davies**, "Paul and the Law: Reflections on Pitfalls in Interpretation," *Jewish and Pauline Studies* 91-122; **C. H. Dodd**, "The Law," *Bible* 25-41; **A. van Dülmen**, *Die Theologie des Gesetzes bei Paulus* (Stuttgart: Katholisches Bibelwerk, 1968); **J. D. G. Dunn**, "Was Paul against the Law? The Law in Galatians and Romans: A Test-Case of Text in Context," in T. Fornberg and D. Hellholm, eds., *Texts and Contexts: Biblical Texts in Their Textual and Situational Contexts*, L. Hartman FS (Oslo: Scandinavian University, 1995) 455-75; **J. D. G. Dunn**, ed., *Paul and the Mosaic Law* (WUNT 89; Tübingen: Mohr, 1996); **Finsterbusch**, *Thora* (§23 n. 1) 39-55; **Fitzmyer**, "Paul and the Law," *To Advance the Gospel* 186-201; *Paul* 75-82; **L. Gaston**, *Paul and the Torah* (Vancouver: University of British Columbia, 1987); **Gnilka**, *Theologie* 69-77; *Paulus* 224-28; **K. Haacker**, "Der 'Antinomismus' des Paulus in Kontext antiker Gesetzestheorie," in Cancik, et al., eds. *Geschichte Band III Frühes Christentum* 387-404; **S. J. Hafemann**, *Paul, Moses, and the History of Israel* (WUNT 81; Tübingen: Mohr, 1995); **F. Hahn**, "Das Gesetzesverständnis im Römerbrief und Galaterbrief," *ZNW* 67 (1976) 29-63; **I.-G. Hong**, *The Law in Galatians* (JSNTS 81; Sheffield: Sheffield Academic, 1993); **Howard**, *Paul* ch. 4; **H. Hübner**, *Law in Paul's Thought* (Edinburgh: Clark, 1984); **K. Kertelge**, ed., *Das Gesetz im Neuen Testament* (Freiburg: Herder, 1986); **Kümmel**, *Theology* 181-85; **Ladd**, *Theology* 538-54; **Merklein**, "Paulus und die Sünde" (§5 n. 1); "Der (neue) Bund" (§19 n. 1); **H. Räisänen**, *Paul and the Law* (WUNT 29; Tübingen: Mohr, 1983); *Jesus, Paul and Torah: Collected Essays* (JSNTS 43; Sheffield: Sheffield Academic, 1992); **P. Richardson and S. Westerholm**, *Law in Religious Communities in the Roman World: The Debate over* Torah *and* Nomos *in Post-Biblical Judaism and Early Christianity* (Waterloo: Wilfrid Laurier University, 1991); **Ridderbos**, *Paul* 130-58; **E. P. Sanders**, *Paul, the Law and the Jewish People* (Philadelphia: Fortress, 1983); **Schlier**, *Grundzüge* 77-97; **Schoeps**, *Paul* 168-218; **T. R. Schreiner**, *The Law and Its Fulfillment: A Pauline Theology of Law* (Grand Rapids: Baker, 1993); **R. B. Sloan**, "Paul and the Law: Why the Law Cannot Save," *NovT* 33 (1991) 35-60; **Strecker**, *Theologie* 150-56; **Stuhlmacher**, *Theologie* 253-68; **F. Thielman**, *Paul and the Law: A Contextual Approach* (Downers Grove: InterVarsity, 1994); **S. Westerholm**, *Israel's Law and the Church's Faith: Paul and His Recent Interpreters* (Grand Rapids: Eerdmans, 1988) particularly ch. 9; **Whiteley**, *Theology* 76-86; **U. Wilckens**, "Zur Entwicklung des paulinischen Gesetzesverständnisses," *NTS* 28 (1982) 154-90; **M. Winger**, *By What Law? The Meaning of* Nomos *in the Letters of Paul* (SBLDS 128; Atlanta: Scholars, 1992); **Ziesler**, *Pauline Christianity* 107-15.

§6.1 Sin, death, and the law

According to Paul's analysis, then, humankind lives out its life in the service of sin, whose payoff is death (Rom. 6.23).[2] Or to change the metaphor: sin is the spider which succeeds in entrapping humankind in the web of death. Or again, taking up the vivid metaphor of 1 Cor. 15.56: sin is the sting which provokes humanity into the frenzied tarantella which can end only in death. But is there not another agent involved, another partner in the dance of death, the enticing substance which draws the insect into the flytrap? "I would not have experienced sin except through the law," says Paul (Rom. 7.7). "In the absence of the law sin is dead. And in the absence of the law I was alive once. But when the commandment came, sin became alive, and I died" (7.8-10). Likewise in other striking passages Paul indicates that sin and death find a partner in the law, where law also seems to be a power, forming a fearful triumvirate with the other two. "The *law* came in to increase the trespass; . . . [and so] *sin* increased . . . and reigned in *death*" (Rom. 5.20-21).[3] "The sting of *death* is *sin,* and the power of *sin* is the *law*" (1 Cor. 15.56). And one passage draws together all the elements which combine to bring humanity down: "For when we were in the *flesh,* the passions of *sins* which operate through the *law* were effective in what we are and do[4] to bear fruit for *death*" (Rom. 7.5).

It is noteworthy that Paul recognizes the logic of his own argument by himself posing the question: "What then shall we say? That the law is sin?" (Rom. 7.7). The question is, of course, a rhetorical technique in which he moves his argument forward by posing questions to himself or by imagining an interlocutor in debate or a heckler in the crowd firing questions at him.[5] Nevertheless the rhetorical tactic would not work if the question made no sense at this point. It is Paul himself who has invited that question. It is Paul's own teaching which has implied, as an immediate corollary, that the law itself is sin, a power equally as terrible as sin itself.

In addition, the Pauline commentator can hardly avoid noting the regularly negative attitude Paul displays towards the law. For example, his indictment in Rom. 1.18–3.20 concludes with the sweeping assertion: "by

2. "Le continuel ouvrage de votre vie, c'est bâtir la mort" (Montaigne).

3. Others would add Gal. 3.19 here; but see below §6.4.

4. Literally "in our members *(melesin),*" or "in our constituent parts." But the "members/parts" (understood as active members) constitute the body (Rom. 12.4-5; 1 Cor. 12.12, 14, 27; Eph. 4.25). So we could also translate "in our bodies" (REB). And later in the same chapter "in our members" (Rom. 7.23) is equivalent to "in me" (7.17, 20); see above §3.2.

5. On Paul's "diatribe" style see particularly S. K. Stowers, *The Diatribe and Paul's Letter to the Romans* (SBLDS 57; Chico: Scholars, 1981).

works of the law shall no flesh be justified before him [God]" (3.20). In the passage just cited above he continues: "Now we have been released from the law, having died[6] to that by which we were confined" (7.6). And in a much-cited passage later in the letter he maintains that "Christ is the end *(telos)*[7] of the law as a means to righteousness for all who believe" (Rom. 10.4). Again, in 2 Cor. 3.6-9 Paul refers to "the old covenant" of Moses (3.14-15) as a "ministry of death" and a "ministry of condemnation." In Gal. 2.19 he gives his assessment of his own conversion: "Through the law I died to the law, in order that I might live to God." In 3.10-13 he speaks of Christ's redemption from "the curse of the law." In 4.8-10 he implies that to observe the law is to come under the power of the *stoicheia*.[8] And in 5.4 he warns the Galatians: "You have been estranged from Christ, you who are seeking to be justified by the law; you have fallen away from Christ."

It is on the basis of such teaching that the fundamental gospel/law dialectic of Reformation theology has been established: gospel and law stand in sharpest antithesis. And contemporary commentators have not hesitated to conclude that for Paul the law is indeed a hostile or even demonic power, a tyrant like sin, with a function similar to that of Satan.[9] Or again, a common conclusion has been that in Paul's view the law never had any positive role in the process of salvation. On the contrary, by the law humankind is led or driven into sinning.[10]

Yet at the same time it cannot escape notice that Paul also speaks of the law in positive terms, particularly in Romans. The saving righteousness of God[11] is attested by the law and the prophets (Rom. 3.21). "Do we make the law invalid through faith?" Paul asks. "Not at all," he replies. "On the contrary, we establish the law" (3.31). "The law is holy, and the command-ment holy and just and good. . . . The law is spiritual" (7.12, 14). "God sent his own Son . . . in order that the requirement of the law might be fulfilled in us who walk not in accordance with the flesh but in accordance with the Spirit" (8.3-4). "Owe nothing to anyone except to love one another; for he who loves the other has fulfilled the law" (13.8). On the basis of such teaching other commentators insist with equal vigor that the law remained a positive force for Paul and had not been abrogated by Christ.[12]

---

6. A variant textual tradition (D F G it vg[cl]; Or[mss] Ambst) reads: "Now we have been released from the law of death by which we were confined" (cf. Rom. 8.2).

7. On the precise force of *telos* see below §14.6b and n. 143.

8. Similarly in Col. 2.8, 20-21. On the *stoicheia* see above §5.2.

9. Caird, *Principalities* (§5 n. 1) 41-53; Hübner, *Law* 26-36.

10. Bultmann, *Theology* 1.264; Conzelmann, *Outline* 226-27; similarly Kümmel, *Theology* 184; Westerholm, *Law* 196.

11. See below for this rendering §14.2.

12. So particularly Cranfield, *Romans* 852-61; Finsterbusch, *Thora* ch. 5.

How is such diverse teaching to be explained? How should we react to such contrasting interpretations? One possibility is that Paul changed or developed his views between the writing of Galatians and the later writing of Romans.[13] That is always possible, though the time gap between the two letters is not all that long.[14] And the talk of love of neighbour fulfilling the law in Gal. 5.14 sounds very much like the talk of love of neighbour fulfilling the law in Rom. 13.8-10.[15] Others have been content to find and to leave Paul's teaching inconsistent and irreconcilable in its contradictions.[16]

The subject is obviously important and the issues sensitive.[17] For an attempt to analyse Paul's theology at the time he wrote Romans it cannot but hold a central place. Apart from anything else, *nomos* ("law") is itself a major theme in Romans — the main subplot, in fact.[18] Between 2.12 and 8.7 the word appears no less than 66 times. Given, then, the importance of the theme, its historic importance in theology, and the continuing disagreement on what was Paul's own theology of the law, we shall have to pay it some considerable attention. In the event it will prove most convenient to divide the discussion into three sections.[19]

But first, a few ground-clearing preliminaries.

§6.2 *Torah,* nomos, *and* ho nomos

First, there is an old claim that the Hebrew *torah* is a much broader category than the Greek *nomos,* and that Paul's rendering of the former by the latter (following the LXX) distorted the Jewish concept of *torah* and gave unjustified foundation

---

13. Drane, *Paul,* e.g., 61-77, 132-36; Hübner, *Law,* e.g., 55-57, 63-65, 136-37. Cf. the "contingency" thesis of Beker, *Paul* ch. 6.

14. There is a general consensus that Romans was written sometime in the period 55-58 (see, e.g., my *Romans* xliii-xliv). Estimates of the date of Galatians range from 48/49 to the mid-50s. My own estimate is between late 50 and mid-51 (see my *Galatians* 8, 19).

15. See further below §23.5.

16. Particularly Sanders, *Law* 35-36, 68-69, 77-81, 86, 123, 138, 144-48; and Räisänen, *Law* 9, 11-15 and *passim* — "contradictions and tension have to be *accepted* as *constant* features of Paul's theology of the law" (11).

17. By "sensitive issues" I have two in particular in mind. One is the issue of traditional Christian misrepresentation of Judaism as legalist in character; we must return to this later (§14.1). Raising that issue (the misrepresentation of Judaism within the tradition of Christian NT scholarship) in turn often seems to touch raw nerves within the Christian community. I presume this is because the law/gospel issue affects personal faith more directly than most other Pauline controversies.

18. Of 119 occurrences of *nomos* throughout the Pauline corpus, 72 are in Romans and 32 in Galatians.

19. See also §14.5 and §§23.3-5 below.

to the accusation of Jewish legalism.[20] However, while it is certainly true that "Torah" is a broader category than "law,"[21] the overlap between the two terms is substantial from the first. The focus of "covenant" on "commandment" goes back to Exod. 24.7, where the "the book of the covenant" is the term used for what is primarily a collection of ordinances (20.1–23.33). In Exod. 34.28 "the words of the covenant" are "the ten commandments."[22] In Deuteronomy *torah* denotes the collection of ordinances/commandments/statutes which are Israel's covenantal obligations — "all this *torah*" (4.8), "all the words of this *torah*" (32.46). And in Deut. 30.10 "this book of the *torah*" likewise refers primarily to the commandments and statutes written in it. Moreover, in the Aramaic portion of Ezra, the Hebrew *torah* becomes the Aramaic *dath* ("law," 7.12, 14, 21, 26). And in other Second Temple literature both *torah* and *nomos* continue to be used to denote divine commands which have to be "done."[23] This does not provide any support for a further link, *nomos* = legalism. But it does mean that Paul's subsequent use of *nomos* to sum up Israel's covenantal obligations, as set out by Moses (the Mosaic law), is not in itself a distortion or misrepresentation of his Jewish heritage.

Second, does the presence or absence of the article make any difference? Should we translate "the law," that is, the Jewish law, only when the article appears?[24] And should we take at least some of the occurrences without the article as references to "a law," or law in general, or some legal principle? This issue was thoroughly discussed in an earlier generation, and little more need be said here.[25] The consensus is that no firm rule can be established on

20. S. Schechter, *Aspects of Rabbinic Theology* (1909; New York: Schocken, 1961) 117; R. T. Herford, *Judaism in the New Testament Period* (London: Lindsey, 1928) 30-32; Dodd, "The Law" 25-41; cf. Schoeps, *Paul* 216-18.

21. Paul also recognizes this broader reference when he uses *nomos* more in the sense of "scripture" (Rom. 3.19, referring to quotations principally from the Psalms; 1 Cor. 14.21, quoting from Isaiah; 14.34). In what sounds more like a "generic" sense (Rom. 4.15b; 5.13; 7.1a; Gal. 5.23 — Fitzmyer, *Paul* 75), however, the thought focuses almost exclusively on the Mosaic law (cf. Rom. 8.15b).

22. Schoeps, *Paul* 214.

23. Westerholm, "Torah, *Nomos* and Law," in Richardson and Westerholm, *Law* 45-56, citing 1QS 8.15, 21-22; *Pss. Sol.* 14.1-2; Sir. 45.5; Bar. 4.1; 1 Macc. 2.67-68; 2 Macc. 7.30 (48-49). See earlier S. Westerholm, "Torah, Nomos and Law: A Question of 'Meaning,' " *Studies in Religion* 15 (1986) 327-36; also *Law* 136-40; A. F. Segal, "Torah and *nomos* in Recent Scholarly Discussion," *Studies in Religion* 13 (1984) 19-28; and the protest to the same effect in Urbach, *Sages* 288-90.

24. Origen suggested the rule that only *ho nomos* refers to the Mosaic law (Sanday and Headlam, *Romans* 58).

25. Sanday and Headlam, *Romans* 58; Burton, *Galatians* 447-60; BDF §258(2); Moule, *Idiom-Book* 113; Moulton, *Grammar* 3.177; Räisänen, *Law* 17; Winger, *Law* 44-46, 67-68, 76-77; Schreiner, *Law* 33-34.

the basis of the article's presence or absence.[26] Context is a surer guide. So, for example, in the first mention of "law" in Romans, it is clear enough that 2.17, 23a, and 25 refer to the law of Moses (despite *nomos* lacking the article). And the same must apply in 2.12-14, even though it could be argued that Paul deliberately speaks simply of "law" precisely because he wants to claim that (some) Gentiles have sufficient knowledge of what God has laid down in the Torah (without having "the law").[27] Similarly one could argue that the absence of the article in 5.13 is Paul's way of indicating that what he says has wider reference (to Adamic humanity) than simply to Israel, even though 5.14 confirms that it is the Mosaic law he had in mind. The alternation of *ho nomos* and *nomos* in 7.7-12 seems to make no difference; it is the same law throughout, "the holy law" of Moses. And in 1 Cor. 9.20-21 the distinction between "those under law" and those "without law *(anomoi)*" is clearly equivalent to the distinction between Jews and Gentiles.[28] In short, we may have to retain awareness that Paul wanted to make universal claims at various points, even when speaking of the Torah, the law of Moses as such. But as a rule we can assume that when Paul spoke of *nomos* and *ho nomos* he was thinking of the Torah.

This raises one last issue which we need to mention here for completeness, but which we will take up only later. That is the question whether at certain key points in his argument[29] Paul uses the word *nomos* in the sense of "order" or "principle."[30] This has a crucial bearing on whether Paul regarded the law as a positive force in the gospel and in the Christian life,[31] but it does not affect the present discussion of the law as a negative factor in Paul's indictment of humanity.

§6.3 *The measure of God's requirement and judgment*

A study of the role of law in Paul's theology could start at several different points. But as we move through Romans the most immediately obvious

---

26. For example, in Galatians *ho nomos* 10 times, *nomos* 22 times.

27. See below §6.3.

28. See further Gal. 3.23 below (§6.4) and Gal. 4.4.

29. Rom. 3.27 ("*nomos* of faith"); 7.21 ("I find it to be the *nomos* . . ."); 7.23 ("I see another *nomos* in my members"); 8.2 ("the *nomos* of the Spirit of life").

30. So most. See particularly H. Räisänen, "The 'Law' of Faith and the Spirit," in *Jesus* 48-68; also *Paul* 50-52. Räisänen has demonstrated such a range of usage for *nomos* from a search of Greek literature — "Paul's Word-Play on *nomos:* A Linguistic Study," *Jesus, Paul and Torah* 69-94. See also Winger, *Law;* and Schreiner, *Law* 37-38 for critique of Winger.

31. See below §§23.3-5. On Rom. 7.23 see below §18.3 and n. 58, and §23.4 and n. 102.

function of the law is that of defining and measuring sin and trangression. This role is explicitly mentioned for the first time as the very last clause of the indictment and then is alluded to three further times in the next four chapters.

3.20 — . . . through the law comes the knowledge of sin;

4.15 — . . . where there is no law there is also no transgression;

5.13 — . . . sin is not accounted in the absence of law;

7.13 — . . . that it might appear as sin, through that which is good . . . in order that sin through the commandment might become utterly sinful.

Two features are worthy of note. One is that Paul said nothing of this function of the law in Galatians, where his talk of the law is equally as intense as in Romans.[32] And yet he can hardly have thought of it for the first time between the two letters. Presumably, then, it was something he took for granted and simply had no occasion to mention in the particular polemic of the earlier letter. In contrast, we can equally presume that when he set his hand to the more systematic exposition of his gospel in Romans this function of the law was simply too fundamental to be missed out. This is confirmed by the other feature, which is the taken-for-granted way Paul alludes to this function in Romans: 3.20 — almost an afterthought; 4.15 and 5.13 — the reader is invited to respond with "of course." In each case Paul is able to refer to this function as something axiomatic, as a fundamental and agreed datum on the basis of which other arguments could be built and from which firm conclusions could be drawn.

We need hardly ask from where it was that Paul learned this role of the law in defining transgression and making people conscious of transgression. It is implicit in the law codes as a whole, not least in their warning against deliberate sin and in their provision for the unwitting sin.[33] It is implicit in the psalmist's delight in the law and lament over his sins.[34] It is classically illustrated in the account of the grief and penitence of King Josiah when he heard the newly rediscovered book of the law read (2 Kgs. 22.3–23.25) and in the account of the response made by the exiles returned to Jerusalem when they heard the book of the law read out to them over a sequence of days (Nehemiah 8–10). Paul would have learned it well in his schooling as a Jewish youth and in his training and practice as a Pharisee.[35] It needed no elaboration from him.

32. The 27 occurrences of *nomos* in Gal. 2.16–5.4 are equivalent to the 66 occurrences in Rom. 2.12–8.7.

33. See, e.g., R. C. Cover, "Sin, Sinners (OT)," *ABD* 6.34-38.

34. Classic examples in Psalms 19, 32, 51, and 119.

35. Gal. 1.13-14; Phil. 3.5-6.

This also means, a point to be noted, that it was not a function of the law which he now questioned or wished to abandon. It remained axiomatic for him as a believer in Messiah Jesus.[36] It was not a point of controversy between Paul and his fellow Jews, Christian or otherwise. The law's function in defining sin and making people conscious of sin was not an issue.

Recognition of this function of the law also helps us recognize the importance of another aspect of the same function — the law as measure of divine judgment.[37] For Paul this again was axiomatic. The link is implicit in the passages just cited. Knowledge of sin through the law means also that all the world is liable to God's judgment (3.19-20). "The law brings about wrath, and where there is no law there is also no transgression" (and thus also no wrath; 4.15). The judgment of death is linked with sin defined by the law as transgression (5.13-14; 7.13). This, we should recall, is the note on which Paul first introduces *nomos* into his indictment — Rom. 2.12-13:

> For as many as have sinned without the law shall also perish without the law; and as many as have sinned within the law shall be condemned by the law. For it is not the hearers of the law who are righteous before God, but the doers of the law will be counted righteous.

And Paul himself uses the Decalogue repeatedly as a measure of God's requirement throughout Romans.[38] In other words, Paul took it for granted that the law was given to be obeyed; submission to the law was what God expected (Rom. 8.7).

This too is straight from Paul's Torah textbook. The warning of the divine curse for failure to observe God's commandments was fundamental to Israel's understanding of the terms of their covenant relationship with God: "Cursed is everyone who does not abide by all that has been written in the book of the law to do it" (Gal. 3.10; Deut. 27.26).[39] The exile to Babylon and the continued dispersion of the majority of Israel's people outside the boundaries of the promised land was proof of God's continued wrath.[40] That final judgment would be in accord with the law could be taken for granted.[41] So too recognition of the need actually to *do* the law was characteristic of historic

---

36. "Insofar as the law is an expression of the divine will, it remains of unrestricted validity" (van Dülmen, *Theologie* 218).

37. But note O. Hofius's debate with E. Jüngel and U. Wilckens ("Die Adam-Christus-Antithese und das Gesetz: Erwägungen zu Röm. 5.12-21," in Dunn, ed., *Paul and the Mosaic Law* 192-99).

38. Rom. 2.21-22; 7.7-8; 13.9.

39. For the quotation see my *Galatians* 170; further discussion below §14.5c.

40. Thielman, *Paul* 51-55, notes how much Josephus makes use of the biblical theme of divine retribution for covenant breaking.

41. Stuhlmacher, *Theologie* 260. On judgment see above §2.4.

Judaism,[42] and exhortations similar to Rom. 2.13 can readily be documented from near contemporary Jewish sources.[43] Paul's logic here is no different in substance from the multifarious exhortations and pleas of Israel's prophets.

Not least of interest and importance here is the fact that Paul evidently regarded the law as a standard of *universal* judgment. Gentiles would be subject to judgment in accordance with the same standard. This is implicit in the summation of his critique of human decline from the knowledge and acknowledgment of God (1.19, 21) at the end of Romans 1: "having known the just decree *(dikaiōma)* of God, that those who practise such things are worthy of death, they not only do them but give approval to those who practise them" (1.32).[44] As we have seen, the critique was largely modeled on traditional diaspora Jewish condemnation of Gentile idolatry and sexual license.[45] So the presupposition is that humankind in general had not only some knowledge of God (1.19, 21) but also some spiritual and moral awareness of what was appropriate and inappropriate in human conduct.[46] The same corollary follows from the description of final judgment in 2.6-11: that God "will render to each in accordance with his works" (2.6) without partiality (2.11).[47]

Above all 2.12-15 is largely directed to demonstrating that Gentiles who are "without the law" (2.12), and "who have not the law," nevertheless can be said to be "the law for themselves" (2.14). The grounds Paul gives for this assertion are that they "by nature do what the law requires . . . [and] demonstrate the business of the law written in their hearts" (2.14-15). Their active consciences (usually understood as denoting a painful or disturbing awareness of personal wrongdoing)[48] also bear the same testimony of a more universal moral sensibility (2.15). What precisely Paul had in mind in these verses has been a subject of much debate.[49] But the point for us is clear enough. Gentiles could be said to have some knowledge of what God expected

---

42. E.g., Deut. 4.1, 5-6, 13-14; 30.11-14; 1 Macc. 2.67; 13.48.

43. E.g., Philo, *Cong.* 70; *Praem.* 79; Josephus, *Ant.* 20.44; *m. Abot* 1.17; 5.14. See further my *Romans* 97.

44. Thielman, *Paul* 169, notes that *dikaiōma* used in the sense of "regulation" or "commandment" elsewhere in the NT always refers to the Mosaic law (Luke 1.6; Rom. 2.26; 8.4; Heb. 9.1, 10).

45. See above §5 n. 68. Note also 4.15: "the law brings about wrath" — presumably also, therefore, the "wrath" of 1.18ff.

46. Hence the appropriateness of drawing on a more widespread (Stoic) sense of what was "in accord with nature" and "fitting" (1.26-28; see above §2 n. 101). This assertion of a more widespread consciousness of moral law as a "decree of God" is the other side of Paul's understanding of divine wrath (see above §2.4). See further my *Romans* 69, and below §23.7b.

47. See above §2.4 nn. 74 and 75.

48. On "conscience" see above §3 n. 16.

49. See further my *Romans* 98-102; Fitzmyer, *Romans* 309-11.

of humanity; and since the law was (for Jews generally) the highest and clearest expression of God's will, it could also be said that Gentiles were aware of the law.[50] The law could thus be said to stand as the measure of God's requirement and judgment for the world of humankind as a whole (2.16; 3.6).[51] And Paul could wind up his indictment appropriately: the law stops every mouth and makes all the world liable to God's judgment (3.19) — Jew first, and also Gentile.

This, then, is the first function of the law which emerges from a study of Romans — the law in its function of defining sin, bringing sin to conscious awareness in its character as transgression, and serving as the measure of divine judgment on such transgression.

§6.4 Israel under the law

Although Paul introduces the law in Romans in the broadest possible terms, the fact remains, however, that for Paul the law was first and foremost the Jewish law, the Mosaic Torah. Even in the first mention of *nomos* in Rom. 2.12 he presupposes the distinction between those who are "outside the law" and those "in(side) the law" (2.12), between "the Gentiles who do not have the law" and (by implication) the Jews who "have the law" (2.14). We have already argued that Romans 2 as a whole is directed against a sense of Jewish privilege over the Gentiles — a sense of privilege which focused almost entirely in or derived almost entirely from having the law (2.18-20, 23). And in the climax of his indictment it is clear from 3.19 that the preceding catena of condemnatory texts was likewise particularly directed against "those within the law."[52] As we shall also see in due course,[53] Paul alludes to this same sense of privilege later in Romans. But in Romans he does not spell out this

50. The Jewish Wisdom writers and Philo in effect argued in the same way: the heavenly wisdom which was sought by all people of good will was to be found preeminently in the Torah (particularly Sir. 24.1-23; Bar. 3.9–4.4; already implicit in Psalm 19); Philo assumes both that "right reason *(logos)*" is the rule of life (e.g., *Opif.* 143; *Leg. All.* 1.46, 93) and that divine *logos* and the law are identical (explicitly *Migr.* 130). Subsequently the rabbis often debated the issue of the righteous Gentile (see, e.g., Moore, *Judaism* 1.278-79 and 2.385-86). See also Stowers, *Rereading* 113-17, 120-21. J. C. Poirier, "Romans 5.13-14 and the Universality of Law," *NovT* 38 (1996) 344-58, extends the argument to include 5.13-14. See also §2 n. 86; and on 7.7-11 see above §4 n. 89.

51. Whether this means that Paul here makes salvation dependent on obedience to the law, so that Romans 2 "cannot be harmonized with any of the diverse things which Paul says about the law elsewhere" (Sanders, *Law* 123, 132; he therefore treats Romans 2 in an appendix), is an issue to which we will have to return below in §18.6.

52. See again above §5.4(6).

53. See below §14.5e and §14.6b.

function of the law in any detail. Fortunately, however, he had already done so in the earlier Galatians. So it is possible to fill out some of the assumptions made in Romans on this point from the earlier letter, which is so much dominated by the same subject.

In Galatians Paul actually poses the question: "Why then the law?" (Gal. 3.19). The answer will obviously be crucial for any understanding of Paul's theology of the law. And though the question comes well into the main argument of the letter, the section it introduces is sufficiently independent of the preceding context for us to break into Paul's argument at this point without distorting his meaning. All we need to note is that the question is introduced as part of a contrast between the promise(s) of blessing given to Abraham, and the law which appeared on the scene fully 430 years later.[54] His point has been that the later law could not nullify the primary promise (3.15-18). "For if the inheritance is from law, it is no longer from promise; but to Abraham God gave it freely through promise" (3.18). Paul then proceeds:

> [19]Why then the law? It was added for the sake of transgressions, until the coming of the seed to whom the promise was made, having been ordered through angels by the hand of an intermediary. [20]Now an intermediary means that there is not just one party; but God is one. [21]Is then the law against the promises [of God]? Not at all! For if the law had been given which could make alive, then righteousness certainly would be from the law. [22]But the scripture confined everything under the power of sin, in order that the promise might be given from faith in Jesus Christ to those who believe. [23]However, before the coming of this faith we were held in custody under the law, confined till the faith which was to come should be revealed, [24]so that the law became our custodian to Christ, in order that we might be justified from faith. [25]But with faith having come, we are no longer under the custodian. . . .

The passage has some notorious difficulties, and precisely what Paul's answer was to his question is unfortunately much disputed. That he is elaborating the contrast between the promise (to Abraham) and the law (through Moses) is clear enough.[55] But just how negative was his attitude to the law?[56] We can best answer our question by taking the key parts of Paul's answer to his question in turn.

---

54. The figure of 430 years is presumably based, as also Josephus, *Ant.* 2.318, on the figure given in Exod. 12.40 for the length of time the people of Israel dwelt in Egypt.

55. Cf. G. N. Stanton, "The Law of Moses and the Law of Christ: Galatians 3.1–6.2," in Dunn, ed., *Paul and the Mosaic Law* 113.

56. Eckstein's concluding note is that only in relation to the promise can we speak of an "inferiority" of the law (*Verheißung* 255).

"It was added because of transgressions" (3.19). What does Paul mean? Most commentators turn almost at once to the passage in Romans which sounds like a close parallel: "the law came in to increase the trespass" (Rom. 5.20). In other words, the law was added in order to produce transgressions, to bring about more wickedness![57] However, the parallel between the two texts is more superficial than substantial. In fact, the text of Gal. 3.19 is quite different from that of the later Rom. 5.20. What Paul says in Gal. 3.19 is that the law "was added *for the sake of* transgressions." The preposition, *charin,* is a special prepositional usage of *charis* ("grace") and so strikes a much more positive note than any parallel with Rom. 5.20 might suggest.[58] If the law was added "for the sake of transgressions," then the more obvious inference to draw is that the law was added *in order to deal with* transgressions[59] — "for the sake of transgressions" in the sense of providing a solution to the problem caused by the breach of the law on the part of those to whom and for whom the law had been given. The allusion, in other words, is probably to that major function of the law in the provision of the sacrificial system, which was at the heart of the law for religious Israel — as we might say, the provision of the shedding of blood without which there was no remission of sins (Heb. 9.22). That is certainly a more positive role than the one indicated in Rom. 5.20, and without knowledge of the later Romans text it must be judged doubtful whether any Galatian believer would have heard Gal. 3.19 as a criticism of the law.

The law "was ordained through angels by a mediator" (3.19). The mediator was obviously Moses.[60] And there is clearly a negative contrast

57. See Lietzmann, *Galater* 21; Bultmann, *Theology* 1.265; Schlier, *Galater* 152-54; Conzelmann, *Outline* 227; van Dülmen, *Theologie* 42; Ridderbos, *Paul* 150; Betz, *Galatians* 165-67 — "wholly negative . . . due to a later state of depravation in the Jewish religion"; Beker, *Paul* 56; Hübner, *Theologie* 2.83 ("for the one who relies on it, the law is a nihilistic power" — 2.85); Räisänen, *Law* 144-45; Bruce, *Galatians* 175-76; Westerholm, *Law* 178, 185-86; Hong, *Law* 150-52; Barrett, *Paul* 81. Hübner notes that "this has a very cynical note about it" (*Law* 26; cf. also 80).

58. LSJ, *charis* VI.1 — "for the sake of, on behalf of, on account of."

59. Sanders, *Law* 66, agrees that this is the simplest reading of 3.19a, citing also Keck, *Paul* 74; Finsterbusch, *Thora* 40. Cranfield, *Romans* 857, reads the phrase more in the light of Rom. 5.13: "to give to men's wrong-doing the character of conscious disobedience"; similarly Merklein, "Paulus und die Sünde" 135, citing Wilckens, *Römer* 177. Schreiner, *Law* 74-77, 127, assumes that the alternative to "provoke transgressions" is "restrain transgressions," neither of which can be derived easily from the Greek.

60. There is little dispute on this point. See particularly Longenecker, *Galatians* 140-43. Gaston, *Paul* 43, glosses the phrase as "in the hand of each of the seventy mediators" (angels of the nations)! Cf. Penna, *Paul* 2.73.

intended with the promise given directly to Abraham by God himself.[61] But what is the point of adding that the law was given "through angels"? Once again some have seen here "a categorical denial of the divine origin of the Torah"[62] — even that the law is here presented as "the product of demonic angelic powers."[63] But this ignores entirely the well-established Jewish tradition that at Mount Sinai God was accompanied by angels. The tradition is already present in the LXX of Deut. 33.2: "angels from his right hand were with him." It is alluded to by other Jewish authors of the period[64] and is present in other NT passages.[65] The language is evidently the familiar imagery of God as an oriental potentate dispensing law, his majesty enhanced by the magnificence of his courtly retinue.[66] This is almost certainly the tradition on which Paul was here trading.[67] So here again the reference is much more positive than has often been assumed.

"Before faith came, we were held in custody, confined under the law" (3.23).[68] Here again the role of the law seems to be depicted in negative terms: the law as a kind of jailor or prison warder.[69] Notable is (probably) the first occurrence in the Pauline letters of the phrase "under

---

61. Hence the puzzling 3.20, which has occasioned literally hundreds of interpretations — 250 to 300, said Lightfoot, already in 1865 (*Galatians* 146). But the basic contrast is clear enough.

62. Drane, *Paul* 34, 113; similarly Zahn, *Galater* 171; Lagrange, *Galates* 83; Hays, *Faith* 227; Sanders, *Law* 68; cf. Räisänen, *Law* 130-31. Rightly disputed by Stuhlmacher, *Theologie* 265, and Eckstein, *Verheißung* 200-202.

63. Hübner, *Law* 26, 29-31. The interpretation can be traced back as far as *Barnabas* 9.4 — "they erred because an evil angel was misleading them." Cf. Bultmann, *Theology* 1.268 — "the Gnostic myth of the giving of the Law by angels"; Schlier, *Galater* 158 — "on the way to a Gnostic understanding of the law"; Beker, *Paul* 53-54, 57 — "the utter negation of the law . . . the enemy of faith"; Sloan ties Gal. 3.19 in with Israel's zeal for the law as opening up to (even provoking) "the onslaught of the powers of sin" ("Paul and the Law" 55-56, 59).

64. E.g., *Jub.* 1.29–2.1; Philo, *Som.* 1.143; *Apoc. Mos.* preface; Josephus, *Ant.* 15.136. See further T. Callan, "Pauline Midrash: The Exegetical Background of Gal. 3.19b," *JBL* 99 (1980) 549-67.

65. Acts 7.38, 53; Heb. 2.2.

66. See above §2.3b.

67. Gaston, *Paul* 35-37, disputes an allusion to this tradition as not containing the idea of the law given *through* angels, despite Philo's talk of angels who "convey the biddings of the Father to his children" and as "mediators" (*Som.* 1.141-3) and the use of the very phrase ("through angels") in this connection in both Josephus, *Ant.* 15.136 and Heb. 2.2.

68. We will return to 3.21 later (§6.6).

69. Cf. NIV — "held prisoners by the law, locked up." "The two statements seem to use *enclose* metaphorically to mean that no escape was possible from the condemnation that the law pronounced on those who sinned" (Thielman, *Paul* 132).

the law."[70] The implication seems to be that the law for Paul was indeed a kind of power — indeed a power just like sin.[71] Yet, once again, equally significant is probably the fact that the first verb used ("held in custody") probably denotes what is best described as *protective* custody."[72] The function envisaged for the law in Gal. 3.23, in other words, is to be understood not so much as oppressive and subjugative, but as a protective oversight. At the same time the second verb ("confined") certainly indicates a purpose and period of restriction, even if the implication is of a temporary restriction ("till the coming faith should be revealed").[73]

The same mixed message is given in the very next image used — that of the *paidagōgos*. "The law was our *paidagōgos*" (3.24). As is well known, the *paidagōgos* was a slave who conducted the son of the household to and from school. Here again commentators have been impressed by the negative image of the *paidagōgos* in various ancient reminiscences: the *paidagōgos* remembered by his charges as greedy, intemperate, and harsh. Consequently the same conclusion is regularly drawn, that the law is here being presented in strongly hostile terms.[74] On the other hand, it would be unwise to build too much on the unpleasant memories of childhood of various Greco-Roman authors. Many Victorians had bad memories of tutors or governesses. But that did not mean that the role of tutor or governess was in principle something negative and repressive. The persons responsible for discipline in a child's upbringing will inevitably evoke some uncomfortable recollections in their charge's later memory. And no doubt there were bad tutors and bad *paida-*

---

70. The argument of Gaston, *Paul* 29-30, and Stowers, *Rereading* 112 (citing Howard, Sanders, and Hübner), that Paul refers to Gentiles as *hypo nomon,* is unconvincing (see also 4.4). The apparent anomaly that Gentiles will also be judged in terms of the law (cf. Räisänen, *Law* 18-23) is explained in Rom. 2.12-16 (above §6.3), where Gentile liability before the law is clearly distinct from "having the law," or being "within the law."

71. Note the parallel between "under sin" (3.22) and "under law" (3.23) — emphasized by Hong, *Law* 156-58.

72. Its principal sense is "guard, watch over," like a city garrison (as in 2 Cor. 11.32; BAGD, *phroureō*); or, "protect, keep," as in the only other two NT examples — Phil. 4.7 ("The peace of God, which passes all understanding, will *keep* your hearts and your minds in Christ Jesus") and 1 Pet. 1.5 ("You who by God's power are being *protected* through faith for a salvation ready to be revealed in the last time"). So also, e.g., Oepke, *Galater* 120; Bonnard, *Galates* 75; Borse, *Galater* 137.

73. The only two other occurrences in Paul probably have the same sense — here Gal. 3.22, but also Rom. 11.32. We might compare *Ep. Arist.* 139, 142, cited below §14.3.

74. Schlier, *Galater* 168-70; van Dülmen, *Theologie* 47-48; Betz, *Galatians* 177-78 — "the pedagogue . . . an ugly figure," "the radical devaluation of the law"; Westerholm, *Law* 196 — "a period of unpleasant restraint"; Hong, *Law* 160 — "the enslavement of the law."

gōgoi. But the role as such was essentially positive — to instruct in good manners, to correct as appropriate, to protect as necessary.[75] In Galatians 3, then, Israel is likened to a child growing up in an evil world (cf. 1.4), needing protection from that evil and discipline to bring it safe to the maturity of adulthood. And that protective, disciplining role was the role of the law, likened to a *paidagōgos.*

In this important passage, therefore, where Paul actually attempts to set out the role of the law, his answer is fairly clear. In the sequence of Israel's history,[76] the law was given as an act of God's magnanimity for Israel's benefit, probably as a means of dealing with Israel's sins, and certainly with constrictive consequences, but basically to protect, instruct, and discipline. This fits also with what is in effect the continuation of the imagery into the beginning of chapter 4.[77] There, clearly, Israel is likened to a child under age, under the protection and administration of guardians and stewards (4.1-2). Again the role is basically positive, however harsh the child's upbringing might be.[78] And again, as is clearly implied (cf. 4.4), that is the role of the law. The picture here sketched by Paul, we should also note, is one which other Jewish writers recognized and drew confidence from.[79] And, correspondingly, it is almost certainly the relationship between Israel and the law which Paul was presupposing in Romans 2.

In this second function of the law we can indeed speak of the law as a kind of power — a power set over Israel, so that Israel could be said to be "under the law." Indeed, Paul may be playing here on the well-established

75. See D. J. Lull, " 'The Law was our Pedagogue': A Study in Galatians 3.19-25," *JBL* 105 (1986) 481-98; N. H. Young, "*Paidagōgos:* The Social Setting of a Pauline Metaphor," *NovT* 29 (1987) 150-76; T. D. Gordon, "A Note on *PAIDAGŌGOS* in Galatians 3.24-25," *NTS* 35 (1989) 150-54; Longenecker, *Galatians* 146-48.

76. In context, the "we" in 3.23-25 must be Israel, Jews at large, or Jews who had believed in Christ in particular. The switch to "you (Galatians)" in 3.26-29 confirms a switch from thought of Jews to thought of Gentiles between 3.25 and 26. So also Ramsay, *Galatians* 381, and T. L. Donaldson, "The 'Curse of the Law' and the Inclusion of the Gentiles: Galatians 3.13-14," *NTS* 32 (1986) 94-112 (here 98). The possibility of confusion arises because in the end Paul believes Jew and Gentile are both in the same boat (hence 3.13-14; 4.3-6).

77. 4.1-7 in effect constitutes a recapitulation of the argument of 3.23-29 (see my *Galatians* 210).

78. Paul was no doubt thinking of the *patria potestas* in Roman law, by which absolute power was vested in the head of the family and children technically regarded as property of the father with legal status little different from that of slaves (*OCD,* "patria potestas"). Note, however, that the child is still the heir. Nor does the imagery here imply a denigration of Jewish status in favour of Gentile or Christian status (4.5-6), since in a later image the latter are thought of as still in the womb (4.19)! The full inheritance is outstanding for both (4.1-2; 5.21).

79. On the protective role of the law see again *Ep. Arist.* 139-42, cited in §14.3.

Jewish conviction that the one God had appointed angels to rule over other nations, while keeping Israel for himself, as his own portion.[80] The point then would be that God had appointed the law to function as a kind of guardian angel over his own people. This would help explain what otherwise is a somewhat puzzling twist in Paul's argument, in which he likens Israel under the law to Gentiles under the *stoicheia,* enslaved to no-gods (4.1-5, 8-10). Israel under the law was equivalent to other nations, each under its guardian angel. But this point is tied into the more important critique of the relationship between Israel and the law in which Paul was engaged in both Galatians and Romans and to which we now turn.

§6.5 A relationship whose time is past

Were §6.4 the whole story, so far as this second function of the law was concerned, we would be left with something of a puzzle. For in Galatians Paul does number the law with "the weak and beggarly *stoicheia.*" He does regard the relationship as a kind of slavery (4.3-5). And he is adamant against any thought of Gentile believers entering into the same relationship (4.8-11). In Romans Paul is equally adamant about his readers not being "under the law" (Rom. 6.14-15). On the contrary, they have been freed from the law (7.1-6). This affirmation of the law's special relationship with Israel therefore has a negative side. That negative sign is immediately evident in the same Galatians material, and also underlies the developing argument of Romans.

a) The first point which stands out is Paul's argument in Galatians 3–4 that Israel's special relation under the law was only *temporary.*[81] The guardian angel role of the law was a kind of interregnum between the giving of the promise and its fulfilment (3.16-25). The law was a sort of regent during the time of Israel's minority (4.1-5). But that also means that this role was intended to end with the coming of "the faith" (3.23-25),[82] with the arrival of the promised seed (3.16), with the sending of God's Son (4.4). Coming to expression here is a fundamental feature of Paul's perspective — his sense that the coming of Christ marked a climax and completion in God's overarching purpose. Here Christ is the promised seed: a new epoch in the fulfilment of God's promise to Abraham is underway. The sending of God's Son indicates

80. Deut. 32.8-9; Sir. 17.17; *Jub.* 15.30-32; cf. Howard, *Paul* ch. 4; see also §2 n. 32 above.

81. Emphasized also by Schreiner, *Law* 77-80, and D. Boyarin, "Was Paul an 'Anti-Semite'? A Reading of Galatians 3–4," *USQR* 47 (1993) 47-80.

82. That is, "the faith" just referred to — "faith in Jesus Christ" (3.22); see also below §14.8b.

that God's long-standing intention has reached its fulfilment at the appointed time (4.4),[83] at the date set (4.2).

The implication is clear. The fulfilment of the promise meant that Israel no longer needed the special protection of the law, no longer needed the law as its guardian angel. It was time once again for an immediacy between the promiser and those for whom the promise had been given (3.6-9, 15-18, 25-29), without the intervention of the law (3.19-24). It was time for the heirs to enter upon their inheritance, to leave behind the slavelike status of the underage child (4.1-7). In contrast, their clinging to the law was a clinging to an underprivileged status. And the attraction of the law to Gentile believers was the attraction of the detention room, equivalent to putting themselves under their old no-gods, the *stoicheia* (4.8-10).[84]

b) A further strand is bound up with this eschatological critique of the datedness of Israel's special relationship to the law. That is the breadth of the promise to Abraham. Whereas the law, at least in this second, protective function, had particular reference to Israel, the promise was also for Gentiles. Paul plays on different facets of this argument in his two great chapters dealing with the promise to Abraham (Romans 4 and Galatians 3). We can reexpress the main thrust of the Galatians 3 exposition in this way. The promise was not simply of land (cf. Rom. 4.13) and of seed (both Romans 4 and Galatians 3). It was also of blessing, and of blessing to the Gentiles through Abraham: "In you [Abraham] shall all the nations/Gentiles be blessed" (Gal. 3.8).[85] This third element of promise, of blessing for the nations, Paul clearly regarded as a fundamental feature of the promise to Abraham (hence 3.14).[86]

The critique at this point, then, is that Paul's kinsfolk were failing to recognize that the time for fulfilment of the third element of the promise had arrived together with the promised seed. Instead they were concentrating too much on the law. They were assuming, in effect, that the later-coming law had somehow qualified or annulled the promise (3.17), that is, on this point of blessing to the nations. They were, in effect, too concerned to maintain their privileged position under the law. Their failure to acknowledge Jesus as

83. See further §7.5 and §18.1. The sense of eschatological climax was a feature of earliest Christianity (cf. Mark 1.15; Eph. 1.10; Heb. 1.2; G. Delling, *TDNT* 6.305) and was evident also in Qumran (cf. particularly 1QpHab. 7.2).

84. That 4.10 has in view the Jewish Sabbath and other festivals is clear beyond reasonable doubt. See, e.g., my *Galatians* 227-29. Jewish festivals were evidently very attractive to many Gentile sympathizers then (Philo, *Mos.* 2.21; Josephus, *Ap.* 2.282; Juvenal, *Satires* 14.96) and subsequently (see my "Two Covenants or One? The Interdependence of Jewish and Christian Identity," in Cancik, et al., eds., *Geschichte Band III Frühes Christentum* 97-122 (here 99-107).

85. Gen. 12.3, 7; 13.15-16; 15.5, 18; 17.7-8, 19; 18.18; 22.17-18; 26.4; 28.14.

86. We will return to the much contested passage 3.10-14 later (see below §14.5c).

the fulfilment of the promise and to recognize the immediate corollary that the time had come for the rest of the promise to be fulfilled meant that they were behind the times. Their evaluation of the law was doubly outdated.

c) This we may assume lies behind the critique of Israel and the law in Romans 2–3, already outlined in §5.4 above.[87] An appreciation of Galatians 3–4 enables us to hear some of the overtones in and recognize some of the assumptions behind Romans 2–3. A significant part of Paul's criticism in Romans 2–3 was directed against Israel's continued assumption that it enjoyed a favoured nation status before God.[88] The Jewish interlocutor boasted in the law (Rom. 2.23) because he saw the law as marking his privileged relation with God (2.17-20). Israel boasted because the law gave it advantages over other nations, set it in relation to the nations as "a guide of the blind, a light for those in darkness, an instructor of the foolish, a teacher of the young/immature, having the embodiment of knowledge and of truth in the law" (2.19-20).[89] In so doing, in continuing to assert this position of privilege, Israel was focusing on the outward and visible and defining privilege in terms of the flesh.[90] But the promised Spirit was rendering all such evaluations outdated, in Rome (2.28-29) as in Galatia (Gal. 3.1-5, 14).

In Romans too, therefore, the first criticism of the law is not a criticism of the law as such. It is a criticism of Paul's fellow Jews for assuming that their historic status of privilege under the law still held good, even after the coming of their Messiah. It is an eschatological criticism: that a privilege, which Paul continued to acknowledge (Rom. 3.1-2; 9.4), had been abused by being still asserted after its time was past. The mistake was all the worse since Gentiles were being persuaded to follow suit. They were being persuaded that they too had to enter inside Israel's protective boundary when the promised blessing was already more freely available outside.[91]

d) We should not underestimate the significance at this point of Paul's assumption that the coming of Christ marked an eschatological division of time. If there was indeed a new (and Paul would say final) phase of God's purpose, then the role of the law in relation to Israel belonged to the old phase.

---

87. Contrast Fitzmyer, *Paul* 78-79, who assumes that Paul must have realized the inadequacy of the earlier (Galatians) argument and decided to offer a different explanation in Romans; but see §6.5d below.

88. See above §5.4.

89. Each phrase, particularly the first two, echoes sentiments familiar in Jewish literature of the time; see my *Romans* 112.

90. See above §3.3b. Cf. N. T. Wright, "The Law in Romans 2," in Dunn, ed., *Paul and the Mosaic Law* 131-50 (here 142; though Wright's exposition is distorted by his "Israel in exile" *idée fixe*).

91. On Rom. 10.4 see below particularly §14.6b; cf. also Eph. 2.14-15 — the law "done away with" *(katargeō)* as an excluding barrier.

It was passé. In marking out the depth of the contrast and its consequences Paul uses some of his most negative and hostile language in relation to the law. The fact that a similar contrast is drawn in no less than three of his principal writings indicates how fundamental it was in Paul's theology.

In Romans the contrast of epochs (between, we may say, Moses and Christ) is overshadowed by the more universal contrast between Adam and Christ (Rom. 5.12-21). But we have already noted that Paul was unable to refrain from allying the law with the powers of sin and death. Some time after the first two actors in the tragedy of humanity "entered" the world stage with Adam (5.12), the third actor "slipped in" (5.20)[92] with Moses (5.13-14) to join them. "The law came in to increase the trespass," increasing, that is, sin's sway through death (5.20-21).[93] Here the law is not simply an insertion between Abraham and Christ, as in Galatians 3. The sweep of God's purpose under review in Romans 5 is from Adam to Christ, from creation to salvation. So here also there is no thought of the law's protective role vis-à-vis Israel. When the Moses to Christ phase of God's purpose is set within the Adam to Christ epoch, the more positive function of the law in relation to Israel falls out of sight. Within the larger comparison of epochs (Adam and Christ) it is the more negative role of the law in relation to sin which commands attention. Just what Paul's critique of the law at this point amounts to is a question to which we shall have to return below (§6.7).

In Paul's earlier letters the contrast of epochs (before and after Christ) was drawn in even sharper terms than in Romans 5. In Gal. 4.21-31 Paul transposes the epochal contrast between promise and law into an apocalyptic contrast between two covenants (4.24).[94] The one is represented by Abraham's slave Hagar and her son Ishmael, the other by Abraham's freeborn wife Sarah and her son Isaac (4.22).[95] The former represents Sinai, that is, the law, and present Jerusalem and the slavery of the children of the flesh (4.23, 25). The latter represents the Jerusalem above and the freedom of the children of promise (4.23, 26). The simpler contrast between epochs does not fit easily into an apocalyptic contrast between an earthly and a heavenly Jerusalem.[96]

---

92. The choice of verb may be deliberate *(pareisēlthen)* to give a more negative note. Its only other NT usage is in Gal. 2.4.

93. See above §5.7.

94. These should not be understood as "old covenant" and "new covenant" (cf. 1 Cor. 11.25; 2 Cor. 3.6). Only one covenant is at issue here — the promise to Abraham of seed. Hagar represents the covenant misconceived. Only the free woman represents the covenant of promise. See further my *Galatians* 249-50.

95. The reference is to Gen. 16.15 and 21.2 and to the promises in Gen. 15.5 and 17.15-19.

96. For this apocalyptic understanding of the Jerusalem of God's purpose in heaven, see particularly *2 Baruch* 4.2-6 and *4 Ezra* 7.26 and 13.36 (further material in my *Galatians* 253-54).

But the implication is more or less the same: a divine intention (represented by God's promise to Abraham and the Jerusalem of God's purpose) has not been achieved in the present Jerusalem and her people. The slavery motif introduced at the beginning of 4.1 now dominates the representation of an epoch which held sway until the fulfilment of the promise.[97] But now the tables are completely turned.[98] In this new epoch Israel is less like Isaac (the child of promise) and more like Ishmael (the slave child). And by clear implication, the law belongs in the passé, fleshly column.[99] Or to be more precise, the law which the Galatians wanted to be under (4.21) belongs to the inferior column. To want to be under the law is to want to go back to an incomplete and misunderstood phase of God's purpose, to want to be a child *kata sarka* and not *kata pneuma*.[100]

Paul's sharpest contrast between epochs, however, is drawn in 2 Cor. 3.1-18. Here the two covenants are indeed old and new (3.6, 14), and the old is clearly identified with the "tablets of stone" at Sinai (3.3).[101] The contrast is with the "new covenant" (3.6), which, given the parallel reference to the Sinai covenant (3.3),[102] can hardly be other than an allusion to Jer. 31.31.[103] What is striking is the very negative language used of the old covenant.[104] "The *gramma* (letter) kills" (3.6), where the *gramma* clearly represents the ministry of the old covenant in contrast to that of the new. "Stone (tablets)" and "letter" are then described as the medium of "the ministry of death" (3.7), "the ministry of

97. The slavery motif is represented by the verb *douleuō* ("be a slave" — 4.25), the nouns *douleia* ("slavery" — 4.24) and *paidiskē* ("slave-girl" — 4.22, 23, 30-31), and the contrasting adjective *eleutheros* ("free" — 4.22, 23, 26, 30-31). Note also how 5.1 picks up the theme.

98. C. K. Barrett's argument that Paul was forced to take up this particular scriptural material and to expound it in such a contentious way because the agitators moving among the Galatian churches had first used it to prove their case (to be a son of Abraham it was necessary to be circumcised, like Isaac), has been widely accepted ("The Allegory of Abraham, Sarah, and Hagar in the Argument of Galatians," *Essays* 118-31).

99. On the two columns (4.25) see particularly J. L. Martyn, "Apocalyptic Antinomies in Paul's Letter to the Galatians," *NTS* 31 (1985) 410-24; also my *Galatians* 252.

100. On the significance of the relationship to Abraham being conceived in terms of "flesh," see above §3.3b.

101. An allusion to Exod. 31.18 and 32.15 (cf. Deut. 9.10-11) can hardly be doubted.

102. "Living/life-giving Spirit" stands in antithesis to both the "tablets of stone" in 3.3 and the *gramma* in 3.6.

103. Cranfield, *Romans* 854; Furnish, *2 Corinthians* 183; Wright, *Climax* 176; Thielman, *Paul* 110-11; Hafemann, *Paul* 120, 122, 127-48. Since "fleshly" is usually a negative term for Paul, the positiveness of the reference to "tablets which are fleshly hearts" must be determined by an allusion to Ezek. 11.19 and 36.26, where the same phrase ("fleshly heart") is used.

104. On "the old covenant" see Furnish, *2 Corinthians* 208-9.

condemnation" (3.9). The point of these forceful negatives, however, is to substantiate the principal claim: that the old covenant has been surpassed and replaced by something better. In other words, the midrashic exposition of Exod. 34.29-35 of which 2 Cor. 3.7-18 consists[105] is simply a further variation on Paul's conviction that the coming of Christ marked a new and eschatological epoch in God's overall purpose. In the midrash the character of the old ministry is represented by the glory shining on Moses' face (3.7; Exod. 34.29-30). Paul assumes[106] that that glory was "fading" (*katargoumenēn* — 3.7),[107] and sees in that fading glory an indication that the whole epoch is passé (*to katargoumenon* — 3.11),[108] at an end (*to telos tou katargoumenou* — 3.13).[109]

At the same time, we should note several qualifying factors in Paul's midrashic analysis in 2 Cor. 3.7-18. (1) The contrast is primarily between the ministries of Moses and of Paul.[110] (2) Paul affirms that Moses' ministry was one of "glory" (3.7-11), albeit a lesser glory now set aside;[111] and Moses' going into the presence of the Lord (Exod. 34.34) is seen as a type of Christian conversion (2 Cor. 3.16).[112] (3) Strictly speaking, Israel is not blamed for

105. Windisch, *2 Korinther* 115; J. D. G. Dunn, "2 Corinthians 3.17 — 'The Lord is the Spirit,' " *JTS* 21 (1970) 309-20; others in L. L. Belleville, *Reflections of Glory: Paul's Polemical Use of the Moses-Doxa Tradition in 2 Corinthians 3.1-18* (JSNTS 52; Sheffield: Sheffield Academic, 1991) 172 n. 1, with critique of the use of the term ("midrash") in n. 2.

106. This is Paul's gloss on the Exodus account. Belleville (above n. 105) finds evidence of some reflection of the impermanence or deterioration of the glory in 1QH 5.32 (46-47), Philo, *Mos.* 2.271, 280 (33), Pseudo-Philo 19.16 (41), and rabbinic and kabbalistic traditions (67, 75); but see Hafemann, *Paul* 287-98.

107. "Fading" is probably too weak a translation for *katargoumenon* here; e.g., NRSV replaces RSV's "fading as this was" with "a glory now set aside." See further Hafemann, *Paul* 301-9; Hafemann prefers "was being rendered inoperative," drawing particular attention to its passive form (310). See also n. 108.

108. Paul's use of the same verb is striking. It is a favourite verb of his (25 of the 27 NT occurrences are in the Pauline corpus), with a range of meaning indicating the effective end of what is referred to (BAGD, *katargeō* — "make ineffective, nullify, abolish, wipe out, set aside").

109. The use of the neuter in 3.11 and 13 indicates "the entire ministry of the old covenant symbolized by Moses" (Furnish, *2 Corinthians* 205; Thielman, *Paul* 113, 115, 117).

110. *Diakonia* ("ministry") is the key concept in 2 Corinthians 3 (3.3, 6, 7-9), linking the passage to its context (4.1; cf. 2.14-17). See further K. Kertelge, "Buchstabe und Geist nach 2 Kor. 3," in Dunn, ed., *Paul and the Mosaic Law* 118-30; Hafemann, *Paul* Part One.

111. The idea of a dispensation which both *kills* and yet is *glorious* is an example of the unresolved tension between two contrasting convictions which Sanders, *Law* 138, finds in Paul's theology. The resolution lies in recognizing that the contrast is relative, not absolute.

112. "Moses is actually, here, in one sense a *precursor* of the new covenant people in 3.18, since he, alone among the Israelites, is able to look at the divine glory with unveiled face" (Wright, *Climax* 180).

failing to recognize that the old covenant is at an end: "their minds have been hardened" (3.14), "blinded" (4.3-4);[113] they simply have not realized the epochal shift brought about by Christ (3.14).

(4) Not least of significance for us here is the fact that the word "law" *(nomos)* is never used. What Paul places on the passé side of the antithesis is *gramma* (3.6-7). The point is that *gramma* is not simply a synonym for *nomos*.[114] It focuses rather on the law as written, visible to sight in the written letter. This obviously ties in to Israel's inability to understand Moses properly, that is, to grasp the limited and temporary scope of the epoch represented by Moses (3.15-16).[115] And presumably it is this shortfall in understanding which gives the "letter" its killing character, in contrast to the writing of the Spirit in the human heart (3.3, 6-7). This correlates in turn and most closely with Rom. 2.28-29, where the same contrast is drawn, and *gramma* is explicitly associated with an understanding of Jewish identity too determined by the visible and the fleshly. And in Rom. 7.6 the contrast is between "oldness of letter" and "newness of Spirit," the "old-new" antithesis being the same as in 2 Cor. 3.6 and 14. Moreover, we should recall that the promise of the new covenant in Jer. 31.33 was of the law *(nomos)* "written on their hearts." That is to say, the more the identification of *gramma* is with the law written on tablets of stone, the more it stands in distinction from the law written in the heart.[116]

In short, the law as *gramma* in 2 Corinthians 3 matches the Sinai of slavery in Galatians 4 and the law as the ally of sin in Romans 5. In each case the focus is on the negative side of the law's role in the epoch which stretched from Moses to Christ. And in each case the implication is that that epoch has

113. Presumably the thought is of a piece with Rom. 11.7, the only other occasion where Paul uses the verb "hardened," likewise implying divine overruling, as the following OT quotations confirm (11.8-10; cf. 11.25, 32). But see further Hafemann, *Paul* 365-81.

114. *Pace* Schreiner, *Law* 81-83, 130; Thielman, *Paul* 110-12. See further Kertelge (n. 110 above).

115. To be noted is the fact that it is not so much a hermeneutical shortfall as an eschatological shortfall which Paul has in mind; the Spirit/letter contrast is between epochs and the experiences characteristic of these epochs, rather than between a "spiritual" and a "literal" meaning of scripture (see, e.g., Furnish, *2 Corinthians* 199-200). Nevertheless a new hermeneutical principle does emerge, as Hafemann, *Paul,* repeatedly argues; see also Hays, *Echoes* ch. 4, and Boyarin, *Radical Jew* 97-105. Nor does *gramma* = legalism, as Räisänen, *Law* 45, rightly notes.

116. Cranfield, *Romans* 855-56, therefore has grounds for saying that "there is here no suggestion that the law is done away." See further Hafemann, *Paul* 156-73: "the letter/Spirit contrast is between *the Law itself without the Spirit,* as it was (and is! cf. 3:14-15) experienced by the majority of Israelites under the Sinai covenant, and *the Law with the Spirit,* as it is now being experienced by those who are under the new covenant in Christ" (171, his emphasis); Merklein, "Der neue Bund" 293-99.

come to an end. In the other treatments of the same theme (§6.5a-c) the point of the critique was that Israel in clinging to its position of privilege, marked by the law, had failed to realize that that time of favoured nation status was past. But in the more radical expositions of the contrast between the epochs (§6.5d) the implication of Israel's privilege is lost to sight. As Paul looked back from his sense of experiencing the promised eschatological Spirit,[117] it was the contrast with the old epoch which most struck him and which marked out the old era as one of comparative slavery, focused too much on the visible and the fleshly.

This second function of the law, then, in its special relation to Israel, is a complex one in Paul's theology. Discussion of it naturally leads into the profoundest feature of all, the alliance of the law with the power of sin and death. It will be convenient to take the latter first (death), since it stands in tension with another aspect of the law's function vis-à-vis Israel which we have left on one side till this point.

§6.6 A law for life? — or death?

The fact that the law makes a trio with sin and death in Paul's theology can cause the commentator to ignore another trio — law, *life,* and death. The interplay of the latter three, however, is a further important facet of Paul's understanding of the law's function in relation to Israel. And it is one to which he reverts as often as the former. Particularly notable, of course, is Rom. 7.10: "the commandment intended for life proved for me a means of death." And we should recall the passage just examined — 2 Cor. 3.6, 7: "the letter kills . . . the ministry of death, chiseled in letters on stones." A more outright denial of the law's relation to life comes in two passages in Galatians. Paul gives his own testimony: "Through the law I died to the law, that I might live to God" (Gal. 2.19). And subsequently in Gal. 3.21 Paul seems to go out of his way to deny that "the law has been given which could make alive." We should also note the description of the function of the law drawn from Lev. 18.5, used in both Gal. 3.12 and Rom. 10.5: "the one who does them [God's ordinances and statutes] shall live by them." In both cases, however, this function of the law is set in some contrast to faith: "the law is not from faith" (Gal. 3.12); Lev. 18.5 expresses "the righteousness which is from the law" in contrast to "the righteousness from faith" (Rom. 10.5-6). At the same time we should not forget that in Rom. 8.2 Paul speaks of "the *nomos* of the Spirit of life" as

117. It is this contrast (with the Spirit) which determines the sharpness of the negative in the passages examined (Gal. 4.29; 2 Cor. 3.3, 6, 8, 16-18; cf. Rom. 7.4-6).

well as of "the law of sin and death." How does this law-life-death strand fit within Paul's theology of the law?

Rom. 7.10 provides the obvious starting point. As already noted,[118] the allusion to Genesis 2–3 is plain. And Paul's interpretation of Genesis 2–3 is also plain. The commandment not to eat from the tree of the knowledge of good and evil was intended to regulate Adam's life in the garden (Gen. 2.17). Alternatively expressed, the commandment was intended to regulate Adam's access to the tree of life: obedience to the commandment ensured continued access to the source of life. In contrast, disobedience was threatened with immediate death (2.17) and in the event resulted in the primal pair being debarred from the tree of life (3.22). To be noted is the fact that the dual sense of death (cut off from the source of life and consequent physical death)[119] is matched by a dual sense of life. Access to the tree of life was part of daily living for obedient Adam. But to eat of the tree of life also meant living forever (3.22).

As we have seen, however, Paul's use of the Adam narratives is also bound up with allusions to Israel's parallel experience.[120] Here thought turns immediately to the terms of the covenant as laid out in Deuteronomy, particularly the great climax at the end of Deuteronomy 30:

> [15]See, I have set before you today life and prosperity, death and adversity. [16]If you obey the commandments of the LORD your God that I am commanding you today, by loving the LORD your God, walking in his ways, and observing his commandments, decrees, and ordinances, then you shall live and become numerous, and the LORD your God will bless you in the land you are entering to possess. [17]But if your heart turns away and you do not hear, but are led astray to bow down to other gods and serve them, [18]I declare to you today that you will perish; you shall not live long in the land that you are crossing the Jordan to enter and possess. [19]I call heaven and earth to witness against you today that I have set before you life and death, blessings and curses. Choose life so that you and your descendants may live, [20]loving the LORD your God, obeying him, and holding fast to him; for that means life to you and length of days, so that you may live in the land that the LORD swore to give to your ancestors, to Abraham, to Isaac, and to Jacob (NRSV).

Here, clearly, the life promised is length of days and Israel's continued life in the promised land through successive generations.[121] Failure to observe the

---

118. See above §4.7 and §5.3.
119. See above §5.7.
120. See above §§4.4, 6, 7.
121. So also Deut. 4.1; 6.24; 8.1; 11.8 (LXX); 16.20; 30.6; cf. 12.1; 31.13.

commandments will result in death — both physical death of the disobedient and expulsion from the land.[122] The parallel with Genesis 3 is not accidental (physical death and expulsion from the garden).

Within the context of covenant theology, the meaning of Lev. 18.5, addressed to the people already chosen by God, becomes clearer: "You shall keep my statutes and my ordinances, which by doing them a person shall live in/by them *(bahem)*"; "You shall keep all my commandments and all my decrees and shall do them, by doing which a person shall live in/by them" (LXX). What is in view is the way life is lived within and by the community of Israel, the covenant people. As in Genesis 2–3 and Deuteronomy 30, the law (commandment) is the way of ordering and regulating the life of those chosen by God. Obedience to the law is the way to ensure continued life, to maintain the life of the covenant. That this includes the thought of a community life stretching through future generations is implicit. Whether it includes the thought of the individual's eternal life is less clear. But it should also be clear that there is no thought of obedience earning or meriting life or of obtaining a life not previously experienced.[123] Failure to keep the commandments will, by implication, forfeit life. But the life is a gift, and keeping the law is thought of primarily as the way of living appropriate to the covenant and its continuance.

This understanding of Lev. 18.5 is confirmed by what may be regarded as the first commentary on it — Ezek. 20.5-26. God gave Israel his statutes and ordinances "which by doing them a person shall live in/by them *(bahem)*" (20.11, 13, 21).[124] There again the act of divine initiative in choosing Israel is plain (20.5-6, 9-10). Equally plain is the fact that God gave Israel his ordinances as a means of living. Here again the thought is neither of first attaining life by obedience, nor of a life first attained after death (eternal life), but of a covenant status first given by God and of life therein lived out or preserved or maintained by doing the law (God's statutes and ordinances). Subsequently the thought of sharing in the life of the world to come becomes more prominent;[125] but still the understanding of Lev. 18.5

---

122. The double warning reflects the preceding warnings both of a cursed existence in the land (28.15-62; 29.20-27) and of exile from the land (28.63-68; 29.28).

123. *Pace* the usual interpretation of Rom. 10.5; e.g. Bultmann: "the keeping of it [the Law] would bestow life" (*Theology* 1.262); Westerholm, *Israel's Law* 147; Schreiner, *Law* 111; Stuhlmacher, *Romans* 156 ("will obtain life"); Fitzmyer, *Romans* 589 ("the way to life"; similarly *Paul* 76). Better is Stuhlmacher, *Theologie* 260: "The Torah is bestowed on Israel so that it can remain alive *(am Leben)* before God."

124. The Lev. 18.5 clause is repeated each time. Note also 20.25 — "I gave them statutes that were not good and ordinances by which they could not live." The critique of the preexilic cult in 20.25-26 (Stuhlmacher, *Theologie* 256) does not affect the point here.

125. The concept of "eternal life" as such appears only in later Jewish writings (Dan. 12.2; 2 Macc. 7.9; 1QS 4.7; *4 Macc.* 15.3).

as speaking of a way of life, and not of a life yet to be achieved or attained, is retained.[126]

Against this background something at least of the puzzle of Paul's use of Lev. 18.5 becomes clear,[127] and also his seeming disparagement of the law in Gal. 3.21. For if the law was given primarily to *regulate* life within the people of God, then indeed its role is properly speaking secondary. The primary role in first establishing the covenant relation is the initiative of God — the promise to Abraham (in Paul's terms), the deliverance from Egypt (in Deuteronomy, Leviticus, and Ezekiel). The corresponding response on the human side to such divine initiative is faith, the trust which Adam did not display[128] but which Abraham supremely exemplifies (Gal. 3.6-9; Romans 4). Strictly speaking, the law has no role at that point. Strictly speaking, "the law is not from faith" (Gal. 3.12). Its role comes in as the secondary phase — to regulate life for those already chosen by God (Gal. 3.12 = Lev. 18.5). Paul's complaint is that his fellow Jews have put too much emphasis on that secondary stage (Rom. 10.5); but that is not in itself a criticism of the law. Nor is it a criticism of the law to assert that "the law is not from faith," simply an assertion that they have different functions within the divine dispensation of grace. The two have been brought into confrontation, but the implication of Lev. 18.5 rightly understood is that their roles should properly be regarded as complementary.[129]

A similar clarification can be brought to Gal. 3.21, where Paul seems at first glance to be criticizing the law by denying that "the law had been

126. See, e.g., Prov. 3.1-2; 6.23; Neh. 9.29; Bar. 4.1; 1QS 4.6-8; *Pss. Sol.* 14.2-3; *Ep. Arist.* 127; Philo, *Cong.* 86-87 — Philo's exposition of Lev. 18.5: "The true life is the life of him who walks in the judgements and ordinances of God, so that the practices of the godless must be death." Hence the description of the law as "the law of life" (Sir. 17.17), "the commandments of life" (Bar. 3.9). The point was recognized by Ladd, *Theology* 540 n. 3. H. Lichtenberger, "Das Tora-Verständnis im Judentum zur Zeit des Paulus," in Dunn, ed., *Paul and the Mosaic Law* 7-23, sums up the Torah theology of the Qumran texts neatly as "Weisung zum Leben und Lebens-Weise" (11), and refers further to the 1996 Tübingen dissertation of F. Avemarie, *Tora und Leben. Untersuchungen zur Heilsbedeutung der Tora in der frühen rabbinischen Literatur* (Tübingen: Mohr, 1996). Cf. G. E. Howard, "Christ the End of the Law: The Meaning of Romans 10.4ff.," *JBL* 88 (1969) 331-37: "Tannaitic Judaism interpreted Lev. 18.5 not in terms of perfection but rather in terms of making Yahweh's law the foremost aspect of one's life" (334).

127. I would normally not wish to discuss Gal. 3.12 and Rom. 10.5 out of their contexts, but the issue here can in fact be treated independently of the arguments of these passages.

128. See above §4.4.

129. See further my *Romans* 601 and *Galatians* 175-76. We shall have to return to this theme later (below §14.7b and §23.4). But the critique has already been clarified sufficiently above in §6.5.

given which could make alive." In fact, there is no criticism of the law implied here, simply a recognition that its function was different. The role of "making alive" in biblical usage is almost exclusively that of God[130] or of his Spirit,[131] whereas, as we have now seen, the role of the law was to *regulate* life already given, not to *give* life where none was before.[132] That is why the law is not against the promises (Gal. 3.21). The promises refer to the primary establishment of relationship by God with God. In the case in point, the promise refers to God's life-giving act in the fulfilment of the promise of seed for Abraham (Rom. 4.17), to which the only possible response was one of faith (4.16-21).[133] It was only at the next stage and as the next stage that the law came in. There is no hint here of an implication on Paul's part that his Galatian opponents thought of the law as life-*making*.[134] But even if there were, he would still be criticizing a false evaluation of the law's function, not the law itself.

Here then we can speak of a third function of the law (in addition to those discussed in §6.3 and §6.4 above): to regulate and prosper life for the people chosen by God.[135] Presumably that function was also distorted by Israel's clinging to the special relationship with God which the law thus was intended to protect and prosper (§6.5). And presumably this helps explain why Paul thought he had had to die to the law in order to live to God (Gal. 2.19). But this third function also ties in to the first function identified above (§6.3). For it is as a guide to life/living that the law functions also as a measure of what God looks for in his people. This leaves open, then, the further question whether this function is synonymous with the law's role in protecting and disciplining Israel (§6.4), that is, whether it is exclusive to Israel. Or whether there is a continuing role of the law for life (and so judgment) which outlasts the period of Israel's special relationship with God. This is a question to which we will also have to return later.[136]

<hr>

130. 2 Kgs. 5.7; Neh. 9.6; Job 36.6; Ps. 71.20; *Joseph and Aseneth* 8.3, 9; 12.1; 22.7; *Ep. Arist.* 16; John 5.21; Rom. 4.17; 1 Cor. 15.22.

131. A particularly NT emphasis (John 6.63; Rom. 8.11; 1 Cor. 15.45; 2 Cor. 3.6; 1 Pet. 3.18).

132. This is not quite the same as saying that for Paul "the law never had any salvific purpose" (e.g., Räisänen, *Law* 150), which can lead to an unjustified conclusion that Paul thus denigrated the law.

133. The parallel to Gal. 3.21 in Romans 4 is 4.13: "the promise to Abraham was not through the law . . . but through the righteousness of faith."

134. We have no texts which would give any real support to such a view in Jewish circles current at the time of Paul.

135. Recognition of this feature of Paul's teaching goes some way to meeting Schoeps's criticism that Paul's picture of the role of the Torah "was a complete travesty" (*Paul* 200).

136. See below §23.

More to the point here, it is this function of the law which, according to Paul's own testimony, proved not to be for life but for death (Rom. 7.10). It is this final aspect of Paul's analysis of the law's relation to sin and death to which we must now turn.

§6.7 Is the law sin?

So far the criticism of the law seems to have been relatively mild. In the indictment in Rom. 1.18–3.20 the criticism focused more or less entirely on a Jewish sense of privilege over the Gentiles, marked by boasting in possession of the law and the benefits it provided (§6.4). In contrast Paul reasserted the more fundamental role of the law in defining sin, bringing it to consciousness as transgression, and judging it (§6.3). In overemphasizing Israel's special relation with God through the law, the "Jew" of 2.17 had failed to give enough weight to this more fundamental role of the law and so had failed to appreciate that those who did not keep the law (2.21-27), even if they were "within the law," were equally "under judgment to God" (2.12; 3.19). This we should note was the extent of Paul's critique at the end of his opening indictment.[137] But we have already noted that a more sombre note is struck in Rom. 5.20. For if "the law came in to increase the trespass," that implies a much more negative criticism of the role of the law as such than anything we have so far dealt with in this section (§6).[138] Certainly the antithesis between law and grace which marks the two following references to the law (6.14-15) would seem to run quite counter to any evaluation of the law as a gracious gift to protect Israel and to order Israel's life as God's covenant people.[139] Is it the case, then, that the alliance of the law with sin and death takes us to a much deeper and sharper criticism of the law?[140]

---

137. In 3.20, of course, he foreshadows the critique of "justification from works of the law," but that properly belongs to a later phase of the exposition of his theology in Romans (see further below §14.5). It is a feature of Paul's style that he introduces a new topic when drawing the previous topic to conclusion; see my *Romans* 271.

138. But to see the increase of the trespass as an increase of legalism and self-righteousness, legalistic zeal, egotistic satisfaction (e.g., Bultmann, *Theology* 1.265; Cranfield, *Romans* 293-94, 847-48) has no more justification here than in 7.8 (see above §4 n. 88); the suggestion is rightly rejected by Wilckens, *Römer* 329 n. 1104; Räisänen, *Law* 144 n. 81; Merklein, "Paulus und die Sünde" 125-26, 160-61.

139. Some commentators emphasize the "where" in 5.20 ("where sin increased") and interpret it as "in Israel" (Cranfield, *Romans* 293; Thielman, *Paul* 192; and particularly Wright, *Climax* 39).

140. As particularly Hofius (above n. 37) 202-3.

It is only with chapter 7 that Paul really engages with these issues.[141] At first the analogy of two marriages (7.1-4) looks simply like a further statement of the epochal change brought by Christ. "The law exercises lordship over a person for as long as that person lives" (7.1). That looks like another assertion of the law functioning as a power.[142] But the focus is actually on the limitation of the law's lordship over the wife become widow. The married woman is under the law of her husband, bound both to her husband and by the law. Only when her (first) husband dies can she marry again. Only then "is she released from the law of her (first) husband" (7.2).[143] Here it would appear that, despite talk of being "bound by the law" and "released from the law," there is no real criticism of the law as such implied in the first three verses. There is no suggestion that the marriage law governing the first marriage was harsh or unfair to the wife. Paul would hardly have called for the abolition of the basic law forbidding adultery as unjust constraint! If anything, he would have numbered that function of the law more as part of its protective role.[144] The point is simply that the situation changes when death intervenes.[145] The law has not changed, but its relevance as the law of the husband, and consequently also its binding power on the wife now become widow, has ceased. The wife now become widow is released from that law.

A much more negative note, however, enters in the application in 7.4-6. The first marriage is paralleled to life "in the flesh," in which the sinful passions operated through the law to produce death (7.5).[146] It is that old life from which Paul and his readers have been released, from the constraint of law as used by sin (7.6). It is precisely this line of thought which causes Paul himself to ask the question: "What then shall we say? That the law is sin?" (7.7). As pointed out at the beginning of §6, the deduction that the law *is* sin seems to follow from Paul's own argument.

What needs to be remembered at this point, however, is that the question

141. *Nomos* occurs 23 times in Romans 7 alone.

142. In these chapters the verb *kyrieuō* is used three times in reference to the lordship of death (6.9), sin (6.14), and the law (7.1).

143. The same verb ("released") is used in the application of 7.6.

144. Paul addresses the analogy explicitly to "those who know the law" (7.1), that is, the Torah. The analogy presupposes the Jewish law on marriage and is much less applicable to Roman law (see my *Romans* 359-60). So the parallel between the woman under the law of her first husband and Israel under the law (§§6.4-5 above) is at least suggested. The image of being "constrained" by the law (7.6) also echoes Gal. 3.23-25 and 4.1-3.

145. In 7.1-3 the death in view is clearly that of the first husband. But in the application it is the readers' death, permitting their remarriage to Christ, which is in view (7.4-6).

146. Rom. 7.5, we may recall, is the verse which most explicitly links the roles of flesh, sin, law, and death (§6.1 above).

in 7.7 is Paul's rhetorical introduction to a section which actually constitutes *a defence of the law* (7.7–8.4).[147] The first line and indeed main burden of this defence is that human failure is *not* the law's fault. The real culprit is sin. The law simply gave sin the occasion to strike home and wrap its tentacles round a person's flesh (7.7-13).[148] This may be all that Paul meant by the law's coming in "to increase the trespass" (5.20). For on this analysis, the result of the law coming into force was indeed to give occasion for a breach of the commandment (7.7-8).[149] Alternatively, or in addition, the commandment had something of the character of a stalking horse: it brought sin out into the open and showed up its true nature (7.13). In that sense too it "increased the trespass."[150] In the light of this first stage in Paul's defence of the law, then, even the criticism in 5.20 appears less as an attribution of malicious intent to the law and more as an indication of its complex role in relation to sin.[151]

The defence of the law is extended and deepened in 7.14-25. For there is another factor in the drama besides sin, death, and the law. And that is me! — me as fleshly (7.14), that is, weak and corruptible, easy prey to the blandishments of sin.[152] Consequently blame for sin's death-dealing has to be apportioned with still greater care. Paul does this first by exposing the divided nature of the typical person in the face of sin's power. The "I" is divided. "I" want to do what is right, but "I" fail to do so. "I" want to avoid what is evil, but still "I" do it. "I" am on both sides of the division. Here again it is the power of sin, exploiting my fleshly weakness, which is the real culprit (7.14-17).

How does this help defend the law? What has been too little appreciated at this point is that in the second part of this argument (7.18-23), Paul maintains in effect that the law shares the same plight as the "I."[153] As the "I" is divided,

---

147. Recognized, e.g., by Kümmel, *Römer 7* (above §3 n. 80) 9-10; Stendahl, *Paul* 92; Beker, *Paul* 105.

148. See further above §4.7 and §5.3.

149. One of the contradictions seen by Räisänen (above n. 16) is between 5.13-14 and 7.8 (*Law* 147). But it is simply a case of variant metaphors, and to look for consistency among metaphors is the pursuit of pedantic minds; contrast below n. 152.

150. Several commentators understand 5.20 in the sense of the law identifying sin as transgression (e.g., Whiteley, *Theology* 80; Bornkamm, *Paul* 125; Cranfield, *Romans* 293; Thielman, *Law* 192, 199); see also the careful statement of Merklein, "Paulus und die Sünde" 135-37.

151. *Pace* Hofius (n. 140 above) 205-6, too profound a conclusion should not be drawn from 5.20 in isolation from Paul's further argument.

152. The inconsistency which Sanders, *Law* 77-78, finds with statements elsewhere in Paul regarding the fulfillability of the law is explained by the fact that in Romans 7 the focus is precisely on the human person *as flesh*. Romans 8 opens up a different perspective.

153. The repetition of Paul's complaint (7.15, 19) indicates not simply repetition for sake of emphasis (7.17, 20), but a development in the argument (7.21-23); see further below §18.3.

so also is the law.[154] There is "the law of God" cherished by the "I" (7.22), approved by the mind (7.23, 25), even when sin conspires with human weakness to prevent compliance. And there is the law used by sin (in the way described in 7.7-13) to bind the "I" ever more tightly to death. This must be what Paul means by "the law of sin" (7.23, 25) and "the law of sin and death" (8.2).[155] The weakness of the flesh means that the law on its own is unable to counteract the power of sin (8.3).[156]

The defence of the law is clear, therefore. It is not the law that is at fault. Its role in defining and measuring sin remains unaffected. Its role in protecting Israel and in ordering Israel's life, and any abuse of that role by Israel, is not in view here. Moreover, we have still to examine the other side of the divided law and whether it had any continuing role for Paul.[157] But so far as its alliance with the power of sin and death is concerned, the law is defended by Paul rather than condemned. That alliance he represents as effected by force majeure, by the power of sin, on an unwilling "I" and an unwitting law. And even then, the alliance is effective only because the weakness of the flesh gives the power of sin such scope and so disables the law.

One could say, then, that the weakness of the law is simply the obverse and unavoidable corollary of its role as the measure of God's will and yardstick of judgment. For, given the weakness of human nature, the statement of what is forbidden was always likely to incite desire, just as the statement of what was required was always likely to incite defiance. If there are laws to guide

154. Similarly, Hahn, "Gesetzesverständnis" 46; and more recentlyWright, *Climax* 197, and Boers, *Justification* (§14 n. 1) 87-88, 93-94, 120-32 (see further below §18.3 n. 58 and §23.4), but generally dismissed (see, e.g., Fitzmyer, *Paul* 75; Thielman, *Paul* 200 and n. 23).

155. Paul's choice of language would be very strange if he did not want or expect his readers to associate the *nomos* of sin and death with the *nomos* abused by sin to bring about death in 7.7-13 (*pace* particularly Räisänen [n. 30 above]). Those who think *nomos* means "principle" in 7.23 include Ziesler, *Romans* 197-98; Moo, *Romans* 462-65; Stuhlmacher, *Theologie* 262; Fitzmyer, *Romans* 131; Schreiner, *Law* 34-35. But see also my *Romans* 392-95, 416-18; Schlier, *Grundzüge* 84-85; and cf. Wright, *Climax* 198. Winger, *Law* 91, makes the odd comment that he "can see nothing in the texts to support or elucidate the division of Jewish *nomos* into (for example) that part which is 'of God' and that part which is 'of sin and death.'" Hence he finds four different *nomoi* ("laws") in 7.23 (185-89). But Paul's point is that sin has been able to abuse the law as such. Paul is certainly playing with the word *nomos,* but in the event "law perverted by sin to bring about death" is little different from "law of sin" and "law of sin and death."

156. This would not be a criticism of the law's provision of atonement (through repentance and sacrifice; cf. Gal. 3.19; §6.4 above), but of the law's inability to prevent sin from inciting the desire which the law forbade.

157. See below §23.

human endeavour and rules to ensure the most fruitful cooperation, it seems to be an inescapable feature of human society that there will be lawbreakers and rule-ignorers. Does that disqualify the laws and render the rules pointless? Is the law, used by sin and betrayed by human weakness in consequence, itself sin? "Certainly not!" replies Paul (7.7). The law, even though used by the power of sin, is still holy; the commandment of God is still "holy and just and good" (7.12).

We could perhaps press the theological logic one step further at this point.[158] For the law can thus be seen also as the bond which ties sin and death together (1 Cor. 15.56). Death is painful (it has a sting) because of sin (it is a punishment). But what gives sin its power to make death so painful is the law, since it is the law which condemns sin to death. The law thus is God's clear indication that there is no end to sin except death. Insofar as the human "I" is "sinful flesh," God's judgment is that the "I" must die. God's purpose to break the power of sin in the flesh is accomplished through the destruction of the sinful flesh.[159] The law, then, was, as it were, a calculated risk on God's part. If it leads humans to death then it brings about the believer's deliverance from the power of sin and the weakness of the flesh. But it also hastens the total destruction (death) of those who live their lives solely in terms of the flesh. The religious, trusting in other than God, perish with what they trusted in. The self-indulgent perish with that in which they took pleasure. Whereas those who acknowledge God trust in the Creator to remake them in his own image through and beyond death. But here we anticipate too much.

§6.8 Conclusions

The role which Paul sees the law playing within his indictment of human weakness and transgression should thus be clear.[160]

(1) The law has a role in defining sin, bringing it to consciousness as transgression, and condemning that transgression. It also plays the same role, in a less explicit way, with Gentiles, through an innate knowledge of God and

---

158. This last line of reflection was stimulated by Bultmann, *Theology* 1.267, but differs from him. Cf. Westerholm, *Law* 189-92; and contrast Sanders, *Law* 73-75, 79, who sees a criticism of God lurking behind 7.10, 13, 14-25.

159. We here foreshadow the exposition of Rom. 8.3 (below §9.3).

160. And thus far a good deal more consistent than Sanders and Räisänen (above n. 16) allow. Their finding is based on too atomistic (Räisänen) and superficial an analysis of Paul's key arguments. Contrast Stuhlmacher, *Theologie* 262 — "an astonishing coherence and constancy of his thought"; and cf. the critique of Sanders and Räisänen in Schreiner, *Law* 87-90, 136-37.

God's requirements, not least through conscience. That role seems to be largely unaffected by the discussion of the law's other functions.[161] It is this function of the law which provides the basis of the indictment which forms the first main section of Paul's exposition in Romans (1.18–3.20). All humanity, Jew as well as Gentile, is guilty before God because all have fallen short of what God intended humanity for and have transgressed the commandments of God known to be such.

(2) The law had a special relationship with Israel, particularly to protect and discipline Israel in the period from Moses to Christ. But that was a temporary role. It should not be assumed, however, that this is the only function of the law and therefore that the coming of Christ means the abolition of the law.[162]

(3) Israel's inability to recognize the temporary nature of this role of the law is reflected in its continued assumption of privileged relation with God, as indicated not least by its having been given the law of God. The privilege thus misunderstood leaves Israel more, not less, vulnerable to the indictment in Rom 1.18–3.20. The fulfilment of God's purpose in the coming of Christ, the eschatological shift in the ages, means that Israel is now "behind the times" and is mistaking the significance of the law as Israel's law. There are aspects here (particularly "works of the law") which we have still to analyse.

(4) The law was given to Israel primarily to give direction to Israel's living and as the terms on which Israel's covenant status and life were to be maintained. Whether this function of the law coincided wholly with the law's function in protecting Israel, or can be regarded as distinct from the law as peculiarly Israel's, thus far remains unclear. Similarly unclear is the extent to which the life-prospering-become-death-dealing function of the law, law become letter, is bound up with Paul's critique of Israel's failure to recognize the eschatological shift in the ages, or continues to be an integral part of the law's function. We will have to return to this question also later.[163]

(5) The law is used by the power of sin to entrap the human weakness of the flesh. If we relate this to Israel's misjudgment regarding the law (3), we could say that for Paul Israel's clinging to its privileged position was itself a classic example of how sin abuses the law and uses the weakness of the

---

161. Bultmann can even say, "The will of God revealed to the Christian is identical with the demand of the Law" (*Theology* 1.262); see further the thesis of van Dülmen, *Theologie* 85-230; and cf. Hahn, "Gesetzesverständnis" 60-62.

162. As, e.g., Räisänen, *Law* 56-57, Becker, *Paul* 395, and Thielman, *Paul* 134, seem to assume.

163. See further §14 and §23.

flesh to tie humankind into the nexus of sin and death.[164] As sin turns "desire" into "lust," so it was sin which transformed the law into *gramma* for Israel. It was the law focused in the requirement of circumcision in the flesh which gave sin the opportunity to bind Israel to a fleshly perspective.

(6) The law as the ally of the powers of sin and death should not be regarded as itself a cosmic power. It is rather the instrument of God's determination to expose sin for what it is. In thus giving the law, God seems to have surrendered it to the power of sin and death, since sin uses and abuses the law to bring about death. But at a deeper level God's purpose may have been to bind sin to death and thus to exhaust the power of sin in death. It may appear to be the tragedy of the law that it condemns sin and sinner to death. But it may also be the triumph of the law that it transforms death from a final judgment on the sinner to the final destruction of sin itself.

164. If the "I" of Rom. 7.14-25 reflects anything of the "I" = Israel of 7.7-12 (see above §4.7), then Paul may have had particularly in mind Israel's continuing reliance on the flesh (cf. Rom. 2.28; 3.20; Gal. 2.16; 6.12-13; Phil. 3.3-4) as the occasion for sin's trapping it within its old age mind-set (see again above §3.3).

CHAPTER 4

The Gospel of Jesus Christ

§7 Gospel[1]

1. **Bibliography**: §7.1 — **J. A. Fitzmyer**, "The Gospel in the Theology of Paul," *To Advance the Gospel* 149-61; **Goppelt**, *Theology* 2.110-18; **L. A. Jervis and P. Richardson**, eds., *Gospel in Paul: Studies on Corinthians, Galatians and Romans*, R. N. Longenecker FS (JSNTS 108; Sheffield: Sheffield Academic, 1994); **E. Lohse**, "*Euangelion Theou*: Paul's Interpretation of the Gospel in His Epistle to the Romans," *Bib* 76 (1995) 127-40; **Merklein**, "Zum Verständnis des paulinischen Begriffs 'Evangelium,'" *Studien* 279-95; **P. T. O'Brien**, *Gospel and Mission in the Writings of Paul* (Carlisle: Paternoster, 1995); **Penna**, "The Gospel as 'Power of God' according to 1 Corinthians 1.18-25," *Paul* I, 169-80; **Strecker**, "Das Evangelium Jesu Christi," in *Eschaton* 183-228; **P. Stuhlmacher**, *Das paulinische Evangelium* (Göttingen: Vandenhoeck, 1968); "The Pauline Gospel," in Stuhlmacher, ed., *The Gospel and the Gospels* (Grand Rapids: Eerdmans, 1991) 149-72; *Theologie* 311-26.

§7.2 — **J. W. Aageson**, *Written Also for Our Sake: Paul and the Art of Biblical Interpretation* (Louisville: Westminster/John Knox, 1993); **Dunn**, *Unity* ch. 5; **E. E. Ellis**, *Paul's Use of the Old Testament* (Grand Rapids: Eerdmans, 1957); **C. A. Evans and J. A. Sanders**, eds., *Paul and the Scriptures of Israel* (JSNTS 83; Sheffield: JSOT, 1993); **A. T. Hanson**, *Studies in Paul's Technique and Theology* (London: SPCK/Grand Rapids: Eerdmans, 1974); **Hays**, *Echoes of Scripture;* **M. D. Hooker**, "Beyond the Things That Are Written? St Paul's Use of Scripture," *Adam* 139-54; **D. Juel**, *Messianic Exegesis: Christological Interpretation of the Old Testament in Early Christianity* (Philadelphia: Fortress, 1988); **D.-A. Koch**, *Die Schrift als Zeuge des Evangeliums* (Tübingen: Mohr, 1986); **B. Lindars**, *New Testament Apologetic* (London: SCM, 1961); **H.-J. van der Minde**, *Schrift und Tradition bei Paulus* (Paderborn: Schöningh, 1976); **Penna**, "Paul's Attitude toward the Old Testament," *Paul* 2.61-91; **D. M. Smith**, "The Pauline Literature," in D. A. Carson and H. G. M. Williamson, eds., *It Is Written: Scripture Citing Scripture*, B. Lindars FS (Cambridge: Cambridge University, 1988) 265-91; **C. D. Stanley**, *Paul and the Language of Scripture: Citation Techniques in the Pauline Epistles and Contemporary Literature* (SNTSMS 74; Cambridge: Cambridge University, 1992).

§7.3 — **Dunn**, *Unity* ch. 4; **Gnilka**, *Theologie* 16-30; also *Paulus* 229-37; **A. M. Hunter**, *Paul and His Predecessors* (London: SCM/Philadelphia: Westminster, revised 1961); **W. Kramer**, *Christ, Lord, Son of God* (London: SCM/Naperville: Allenson, 1966);

§7.1 Euangelion

Paul's indictment has been fierce. All humanity lives its life on earth under the power of sin. All humanity finds itself drawn inexorably, whether by some primeval instinctive disposition or by its own will to self-destruction, into a policy of gratifying the flesh, disregarding what it knows to be right, and disowning God. All humanity, Jew as well as Gentile, stands under the condemnation of God's law and consequently is liable to God's judgment. As a statement of charges against humankind, that is a bleak prospectus. Paul spends as much time as he does on drawing it up in Romans (1.18–3.20) not simply because his view of humankind is pessimistic. To such an accusation, Paul would no doubt reply that, on the contrary, he was simply being realistic, and that failure to recognize this reality is the fatal flaw in all idealistic or utopian visions. And reviewing the history of "man's inhumanity to man" and abuse of creation, who could blame him? But the main reason that Paul could be so devastatingly critical of humankind was no doubt his conviction that he knew the appropriate response to that indictment. A response, not a defence. A response of grace which fully dealt with the charges. "Just as sin ruled in death, so also grace [will] reign through righteousness to eternal life" (Rom. 5.21).

That response is summed up in the word "gospel *(euangelion)*." This is another word which is predominantly Pauline in the NT (60 of the 76 occurrences).[2] He has already indicated its importance in the setting out of his

---

V. H. Neufeld, *The Earliest Christian Confessions* (NTTS 5; Grand Rapids: Eerdmans, 1963); **Schlier**, *Grundzüge* 122-28; **P. Stuhlmacher**, "Recent Exegesis on Romans 3.24-26," *Reconciliation* 94-109; *Theologie* 168-75, 179-96; **K. Wengst**, *Christologische Formeln und Lieder des Urchristentums* (Gütersloh: Gütersloher, 1972).

§§7.4-5 — **C. Dietzfelbinger**, *Die Berufung des Paulus als Ursprung seiner Theologie* (WMANT 58; Neukirchen: Neukirchener, 1985); **J. D. G. Dunn**, " 'A Light to the Gentiles,' or 'The End of the Law'? The Significance of the Damascus Road Christophany for Paul," *Jesus, Paul and the Law* 89-107; "Paul's Conversion — A Light to Twentieth-Century Disputes," in Ådna, et al., ed., *Evangelium* 77-93; **P. Fredriksen**, "Paul and Augustine: Conversion Narratives, Orthodox Traditions, and the Retrospective Self," *JTS* 37 (1986) 3-34; **J. Jeremias**, *Der Schlüssel zur Theologie des Apostels Paulus* (Stuttgart: Calwer, 1971); **S. Kim**, *The Origin of Paul's Gospel* (WUNT 2.4; Tübingen: Mohr, 1981 = Grand Rapids: Eerdmans, 1982); **H. Räisänen**, "Paul's Call Experience and His Later View of the Law," *Jesus, Paul and Torah* 15-47; **Segal**, *Paul the Convert;* **P. Stuhlmacher**, " 'The End of the Law': On the Origin and Beginnings of Pauline Theology," *Reconciliation* 134-54; **U. Wilckens**, "Die Bekehrung des Paulus als religionsgeschichtliches Problem," *Rechtfertigung* 11-32.

2. *Euangelion* ("gospel") — Matthew (4 occurrences), Mark (8), Acts (2), Romans (9), 1 Corinthians (8), 2 Corinthians (8), Galatians (7), Ephesians (4), Philippians (9), Colossians (2), 1 Thessalonians (6), 2 Thessalonians (2), 1 Timothy (1), 2 Timothy (3), Philemon (1), 1 Peter (1), Revelation (1). *Euangelizomai* ("preach [gospel]") — Matthew (1 occurrence), Luke (10), Acts (15), Romans (3), 1 Corinthians (6), 2 Corinthians (2),

theology in Romans. He has introduced himself as "called to be an apostle, set apart for the gospel of God" (Rom. 1.1). One of his reasons in writing the letter was his "eagerness to preach the gospel to you who are in Rome as well" (1.15) — presumably in line with his commission as "apostle to the Gentiles" (11.13), even if it stood in some tension with his "aim to preach the gospel where Christ has not been named" (15.20).[3] And *euangelion* has been one of the key words in the thematic statement which the rest of Romans was intended to expound: "For I am not ashamed of the gospel, since it is the power of God for salvation . . ." (1.16). It is also significant that in 2.16 Paul had made a point of noting that the final judgment would be "in accordance with my gospel through Christ Jesus." The gospel which responded to his indictment of humankind did not run counter to God's judgment in accordance with his law (2.12-15).

In his earlier letters Paul had given equal indication of the importance of "the gospel." At the beginning of 1 Corinthians he emphasizes that his commission was to preach the gospel, not to baptize (1 Cor. 1.17). It was "through the gospel" that Paul had "become father" to the Corinthians (4.15). "Woe to me if I preach not the gospel," he cries (9.16). Effective preaching of the gospel was always his primary concern (9.23).[4] So too the letter to the Galatians was evidently provoked by his considerable alarm at the prospect of their turning away from the gospel and of the gospel being turned into something else (Gal. 1.6-9). The revelation of Christ on the Damascus road had been given him "in order that I might preach (the good news of) him among the Gentiles" (1.16). His top priority was "the truth of the gospel" (2.5, 14).[5] More than any other of Paul's key themes, this concern for the gospel remains constant throughout Paul's written ministry — as prominent in what was probably his first letter (1 Thessalonians)[6] as in what may well have been his final imprisonment (Philippians).[7]

Galatians (7), Ephesians (2), 1 Thessalonians (1), Hebrews (2), 1 Peter (3), Revelation (2); (the Paulines have 21 of 54). *Kērygma* ("proclamation") — Rom. 16.25; 1 Cor. 1.21; 2.4; 15.14; 2 Tim. 4.17; Tit. 1.3 (the Paulines have 6 of 8). On "the word of the cross" (1 Cor. 1.18) and "the word of reconciliation" (2 Cor. 5.19) see Stuhlmacher, *Theologie* 318-26.

3. Too much can be made of this tension: e.g., Elliott, *Rhetoric,* builds too much on 1.15, just as G. Klein builds too much on 15.20 ("Paul's Purpose in Writing the Epistle to the Romans" [1969], in Donfried, ed., *Romans Debate* 29-43). The combination of pastoral concern (1.11), sensitivity to possible offence (1.12), somewhat lame-sounding excuses (1.13), and eagerness to visit (1.13, 15) indicates a tentativeness in formulation which should make the modern commentator hesitant to build very much on any particular element in the section. See also my *Romans* 33-34 and 865, and below §7.4. The principle of 15.20 is spelled out more fully in 2 Cor. 10.13-16 (see further §21.2d).

4. A repeated theme in the Corinthian correspondence — 1 Cor. 9.12-18; 2 Cor. 11.7-11.

5. So also Col. 1.5.

6. 1 Thes. 1.5; 2.2, 4, 8, 9; 3.2.

7. Phil. 1.5, 7, 12, 16, 27 (twice); 2.22; 4.3, 15.

The motif of the gospel as the power of God for salvation is given a remarkably rich elaboration in the Corinthian epistles. There the straightforward understanding of the power of God, as manifested most obviously in resurrection,[8] is complemented and qualified by the repeated assertion that the power of God is expressed most characteristically (in this age) on the cross and in the weakness and foolishness of preaching and ministry.[9]

Another feature of Paul's usage is his readiness to speak of "the gospel of God"[10] almost as much as of "the gospel of (the) Christ."[11] Most notable is the fact that he introduces the subject, and his exposition of it in Romans, as "the gospel of *God*" (Rom. 1.1), to be balanced a little later by reference to "the gospel of his [God's] *Son*" (1.9). This is one of a sequence of balancing statements Paul makes in the opening of Romans and suggests that Paul was deliberately indicating (but not in a trumpet-blowing manner) that his christology, and so also his understanding of "the gospel of Christ," was wholly consistent with and indeed part and parcel of his understanding of God. The point is the same in 2.16: the judgment is God's, but it will be "in accordance with my gospel,[12] through Jesus Christ."[13] It should occasion no surprise for Paul's readers, therefore, when they come to Paul's response to his indictment and find that the centrality of Christ Jesus is fully matched by emphasis on God as the initiator (3.21-26).[14] The gospel of *Christ* vindicates the faithfulness of *God*.[15]

Given the importance of the term for Paul, it is worth clarifying

8. 1 Cor. 6.14; 15.43; 2 Cor. 13.4; cf. 1 Cor. 4.20.

9. 1 Cor. 1.18, 24; 2.4-5; 2 Cor. 1.8; 4.7; 6.4-10; 12.9; 13.4. Cf. Penna, *Paul* 1.169-80.

10. Rom. 1.1; 15.16; 2 Cor. 11.7; 1 Thes. 2.2, 8, 9.

11. Rom. 15.19; 1 Cor. 9.12; 2 Cor. 2.12; 9.13; 10.14; Gal. 1.7; Phil. 1.27; 1 Thes. 3.2; "the gospel of his Son" (Rom. 1.9); "the gospel of our Lord Jesus" (2 Thes. 1.8).

12. "In accordance with" must mean that Paul sees the gospel as the criterion for either the assertion being made or the judgment itself (or both). See further below §21.2a.

13. "Through Christ Jesus" should probably be taken with the verb "judge" (as most agree). For Christ as future judge see below §§12.2-3.

14. Rom. 3.21-26 —

. . . the righteousness of
God has been revealed

. . . the righteousness of God	through faith in Christ Jesus . . .
They are justified by his grace	through the redemption which is in Christ Jesus,
whom God set forth as an expiation	through faith, in his blood,
to demonstrate his righteousness . . .	
in the forbearance of God, to demonstrate	
his righteousness . . . that he might be just	
and the one who justifies	him who believes in Jesus.

15. See above §2.5 and further below §19.

166

where it came from. A striking feature is the absence of the singular noun in the LXX (and of any Hebrew equivalent) and the unfamiliarity of the singular form in Greek texts of the period.[16] Evidently, then, we are faced with a neologism, or at least the adaptation of a term to new uses. To explain this, some[17] have suggested that Paul, or his Greek-speaking Christian Jewish predecessors, adapted the singular form from the more familiar plural form, "good tidings," particularly as used within the context of the Caesar cult.[18] But where the thought is of "the gospel of God," a much more likely background is the quite common theme in the LXX (expressed by the verb *euangelizomai*) of proclaiming good news from God and about God.[19]

Particularly significant is Isaiah's consistent message of encouragement in a sequence of prophecies.[20] Isa. 40.9 calls on "the preacher of good news"[21] to proclaim to the cities of Judah, "Behold your God!" Similarly Isa. 52.7 praises the one "who preaches the good news *(euangelizomenou)* of peace, who preaches *(euangelizomenos)* good things, who announces salvation *(sōtēria)*, who says to Zion, 'Your God reigns.' " 60.6 envisages the returning exiles preaching the good news *(euangelizountai)* of "the LORD's salvation *(sōtērion)*." Most striking of all is Isa. 61.1-2:

> The Spirit of the Lord GOD is upon me,
>   because the LORD has anointed me;
> he has sent me to bring good news *(euangelisasthai)* to the poor,
>   to bind up the brokenhearted,
> to proclaim *(kēryxai)* liberty to the captives,
>   and release to the prisoners,
> to proclaim the year of the LORD's favour. . . .

We know that this Isaianic theme was influential in Jewish theological reflection around the time of Jesus. *Pss. Sol.* 11.1 clearly echoes Isa. 52.7: "Sound in Zion the signal trumpet of the sanctuary; announce *(kēryxate)* in Jerusalem the voice of one bringing good news *(euangelizomenou)*." And there are several allusions to Isa. 61.1 in the Qumran scrolls. 11QMelch

---

16. The few references have the meaning "reward of good tidings" given to the messenger (LSJ, *euangelion*).

17. Particularly Strecker, *Eschaton* 183-228; also *euangelion*, *EDNT* 2.71; *Theologie* 355-57.

18. References in LSJ, *euangelion*; cf. *NDIEC* 3.12-15.

19. Pss. 40.9; 68.11; 96.2; Isa. 40.9; 52.7; 60.6; 61.1; Joel 2.32; Nah. 1.15.

20. In each case the LXX differs from the Hebrew, but not significantly for our present purposes.

21. Either Zion itself, or one who preaches "to Zion."

2.15-24 is an explicit exposition of Isa. 52.7 and 61.1-3, applied to the sect's own situation.[22]

It is hardly surprising, then, that we have a strong tradition of Jesus also drawing on Isa. 61.1-2 as providing some sort of blueprint for his own mission.[23] And a tradition of using Isa. 52.7 and 61.1 in exposition of the gospel evidently developed quite quickly in earliest Christianity,[24] as Paul's own quotation of Isa. 52.7 in Rom. 10.15 confirms.

The most obvious explanation for Paul's use of *euangelion,* therefore, is that the singular noun was drawn into play in the early Greek-speaking mission as the appropriate noun to match the use of these texts in talking about the good news proclaimed by and about Jesus.[25] To be more precise, it is quite probable that it was Paul himself who coined the usage as a new technical term for his own proclamation.[26] Adaptation of old vocabulary to new usage to express the rich newness of the Christian message is something Paul is well known for.[27] In which case we could further speculate that it was due to the influence of Paul that the term came into use in Mark,[28] where it is distinctive,[29] and thus came to stand for the written gospel.[30] Be that as it may, Paul was certainly the first, so far as we know, to sum up the Christian message as the "gospel." And his use of the term certainly established its

22. See also 1QH 18.14; 4Q521 12; cf. CD 2.12. Collins, *Scepter* (§8 n. 1) 132 n. 89, reckons that the hymnist in 1QH 18.14 applies the prophecy of Isaiah 61 to himself. For 4Q521 see Collins, *Scepter* 117 or García Martínez 394. Collins 11 has CD 2.9 instead of 2.12.

23. Matt. 11.5/Luke 7.22; Luke 4.16-21; cf. Luke 6.20/Matt. 5.3. The parallel between Matt. 11.5/Luke 7.22 and 4Q521 is particularly striking: "he will heal the wounded, give life to the dead, and preach good news to the poor . . ." (4Q521 12); ". . . the lame walk, the lepers are cleansed, the deaf hear, the dead are raised, and the poor have good news preached to them" (Matt. 11.5/Luke 7.22).

24. Acts 4.27; 10.36, 38 (alluding to Isa. 52.7 and 61.1 in sequence); Eph. 2.17; 6.15; Rev. 1.6 and 5.10 probably echo Isa. 61.6. The Acts references are best explained as Luke drawing on older tradition.

25. See further Stuhlmacher, *Evangelium;* also "Gospel" 149-72; Goppelt, *Theology* 2.111-12; Wilckens, *Römer* 1.74-75; cf. O'Brien, *Gospel* 77-81.

26. In talking about the gospel in Rom. 1.16 ("I am not ashamed of the gospel") Paul may indeed be echoing the words of Jesus himself, preserved in Mark 8.38/Luke 9.26 (C. K. Barrett, "I Am Not Ashamed of the Gospel," *New Testament Essays* [London: SPCK, 1972] 116-43).

27. The other most striking examples are "grace" *(charis)* and "love" *(agapē)*; see below §13.2.

28. Mark 1.1, 14, 15; 8.35; 10.29; 13.10; 14.9.

29. Of the four Matthean uses, 24.14 and 26.13 were drawn directly from Mark, and 4.23 and 9.35 were probably modeled on Mark 1.14-15.

30. The transition is more or less visible in Mark 1.1; see particularly R. A. Guelich, "The Gospel Genre," in Stuhlmacher, ed., *Gospel* 173-208. See further §9.9(6) below.

significance and centrality in Christian theology.[31] So his understanding of the "gospel" is of particular interest.

§7.2 "In accordance with the scriptures"

A second striking feature of Paul's talk of the gospel of Jesus Christ is his concern to insist that this gospel was not a *novum* or unexpected turn in God's purposes. Quite the contrary. His opening statement in Romans immediately defines "the gospel of God" as that "which was promised beforehand through his [God's] prophets in the holy scriptures" (Rom. 1.1). When he announces the theme of the letter (1.16-17) — the gospel as "the power of God for salvation to *all* who believe, Jew first and also Greek; for in it the righteousness of God is revealed from faith to faith" — he immediately adds "as it is written" and proceeds to cite his scriptural authorisation (Hab. 2.4).[32] And when he turns from his indictment (1.18–3.20) to indicate the response of the gospel ("But now apart from the law the righteousness of God has been revealed"), once again he immediately adds, "as attested by the law and the prophets" (3.21). So too, as the argument of Romans unfolded, it was obviously of first importance to Paul to be able to expound Gen. 15.6 in a way which documented his gospel (Romans 4). The theological climax of the letter's exposition is the attempt to maintain the proposition that the word of God had *not* failed (Rom. 9.6).[33] And the final catena of scriptures (15.9-12) was for Paul no doubt the most fitting way to round off his whole argument.

Equally important was it for Paul to be able to say in Galatians that "scripture preached the gospel beforehand to Abraham" (Gal. 3.8). In both these letters (Galatians and Romans) three texts stand at the heart of his exposition of the gospel — Gen. 15.6; Lev. 18.5; and Hab. 2.4.[34] And Paul

---

31. Goppelt, *Theology* 2.114: "No witness of the New Testament . . . established the limits of the message of Christ as the one gospel theologically more precisely over against the distortions that arose under Jewish and Hellenistic influences than did Paul."

32. Hab. 2.4 is not the "text" for the letter, as though the letter was set out as an exposition of this text in particular: *kathōs gegraptai* ("as it is written") has more the character of a validation formula (see below n. 43).

33. On the prominence of scripture in Romans 9–11 in particular see H. Hübner, *Gottes Ich und Israel. Zum Schriftgebrauch des Paulus in Römer 9–11* (Göttingen: Vandenhoeck, 1984); J. W. Aageson, "Scripture and Structure in the Development of the Argument in Romans 9–11," *CBQ* 48 (1986) 265-89; "Typology, Correspondence and the Application of Scripture in Romans 9–11," *JSNT* 31 (1987) 51-72.

34. Gen. 15.6 (Rom. 4.3-23; Gal. 3.6-9); Lev. 18.5 (Rom. 10.5; Gal. 3.12); Hab. 2.4 (Rom. 1.17; Gal. 3.11). That just these texts appear in both letters in which Paul seeks to define his gospel in relation to its Jewish matrix is significant. On Paul's exposition of Hab. 2.4 and Gen. 15.6 see below §14.7. On Lev. 18.5 see above §6.6.

would hardly regard it as simply a matter of form to be able to remind the Corinthians that the central claims of the gospel he had preached to them were "in accordance with the scriptures" (1 Cor. 15.3-4).

Two features call for comment here. The first has already been indicated: the degree to which Paul considered it important and necessary to base his gospel (and so also his theology) on the scriptures of his people. There are about one hundred explicit quotations from scripture in the Pauline corpus.[35] More than ninety percent of them come from the four *Hauptbriefe* (Romans, 1 and 2 Corinthians, Galatians), but since Paul's theological arguments are most thoroughly sustained in just these letters, that should not surprise us unduly. And when we add the number of allusions which form the warp of Paul's theological weaving, the picture balances up considerably.[36] In other words, Paul's theological language was, by and large, the language of scripture. Scripture formed "the substructure of his theology."[37]

The theological logic of Paul's concern is also clear. These texts were "scripture,"[38] "the holy scriptures" (Rom. 1.2),[39] "the oracles of God" (Rom. 3.2).[40] As such they had already been recognized as divinely authorized statements or oracles in writing,[41] a status which Paul simply took for granted.

---

35. These are conveniently listed in Koch, *Schrift* 21-24, and Smith, "Pauline Literature" 268-72.

36. Probable allusions are conveniently indicated in the margins of Aland[26]. Ellis's list (*Paul's Use* 153-54) is fairly modest (contrast, e.g., my "Deutero-Pauline Letters," in J. Barclay and J. Sweet, eds., *Early Christian Thought in Its Jewish Context* [Cambridge: Cambridge University, 1996] 130-44). But it indicates the balance. Hays, *Echoes,* has demonstrated the importance of recognizing such allusions for the better appreciation of Paul's arguments.

37. I deliberately echo the subtitle of C. H. Dodd, *According to the Scriptures: The Substructure of New Testament Theology* (London: Nisbet, 1952 = New York: Scribner, 1953). Ellis, *Paul's Use* 116, observes how much of the sweep of Paul's theology can be linked to specific use of OT texts (see also 125); similarly Koch, *Schrift* 285-99. Hanson finds Paul in effect writing midrashim at several points in his letters (*Studies* 167 — referring to Rom. 6.7; 8.19-21, 33-34, 34-39; 11.17-24; 1 Cor. 5.6-8; 10.14-21; 2 Cor. 4.13-15; 5.19–6.2; Gal. 3.18-20; Col. 2.14-15). He defines a "midrash" as "written meditation on the significance of a passage of Scripture with a view to bringing out its full meaning" (*Studies* 205). See further Aageson, *Written Also for Our Sake,* and Hübner, *Theologie* Band 2.

38. The singular is used 8 times in the Pauline corpus (see nn. 42 and 44 below) and was already in use elsewhere for the collectivity of the scriptures (Philo, *Mos.* 2.84; *Ep. Arist.* 155, 168).

39. Cf. Philo, *Fuga* 4; *Spec. Leg.* 1.214; *Heres* 106, 159.

40. Paul echoes earlier LXX usage here (Num. 24.4[B]; 24.16; Deut. 33.9; Pss. 12.6 [LXX 11.7]; 18.30 [LXX 17.31]; 107[LXX 106].11; 119[LXX 118].11, 103, 148; Wis. 16.11). See further my *Romans* 131.

41. The scriptures in view would be more or less the books contained in our OT (cf. Sirach prologue; Josephus, *Ap.* 1.37-42; *4 Ezra* 14.37-48), though the concept of a

Hence the appeals to "the scripture,"[42] the use of the formula, "(as) it is written,"[43] and the inference that scripture speaks as a living voice of God.[44] It is important for an appreciation of Paul's theology to realize that none of this was changed by Paul's conversion. On the contrary, it became all the more important to him to be able to say that his gospel was "in accordance with the scriptures."

The other feature, however, seems to run somewhat counter to the first. That is the liberty Paul evidently felt in citing scripture, his apparent readiness to put what his contemporaries might have regarded as a forced or strained construction on a scriptural text. This feature itself has two aspects.

On the one hand, there is the issue of the text form used by Paul, an issue somewhat confused by uncertainty as to the text form(s) available to Paul.[45] However, the recent study by Christopher Stanley has provided a definitive treatment by focusing solely on this issue. It certainly confirms that Paul must have engaged in deliberate manipulation of the text form[46] and provides a valuable analysis of the kinds of adaptation.[47] But it also notes that the great bulk of the modifications would have had little effect on the meaning of the original text: they were simply adaptations in grammar or syntax or wording to fit the text cited most appropriately to the syntax and rhetoric of the letter.[48] And, more to our present point, it shows that such adapted (even

---

fixed and closed canon as such was not yet clearly evident, as the larger scope of the LXX indicates. In any case, the bulk of Paul's references (80%) are to the Pentateuch, Isaiah, and the Psalms (Smith, "Pauline Literature" 273).

42. Rom. 4.3; Gal. 4.30.

43. Rom. 1.17; 2.24; 3.4, 10-12; 4.17; 8.36; 9.13, 33; 10.15; 11.8, 26-27; 12.19; 14.11; 15.3, 9, 21; 1 Cor. 1.19, 31; 2.9; 3.19; 9.9; 10.7; 14.21; 15.45; 2 Cor. 4.13; 8.15; 9.9; Gal. 3.10, 13; 4.27. But he uses other introductory formulae (see again Smith, "Pauline Literature" 268-72).

44. Rom. 9.17; 10.11; 11.2; Gal. 3.8, 22; also 1 Tim. 5.18. In other passages God is the one who speaks the scriptural text (Rom. 9.25; 2 Cor. 6.2, 16). See also Koch, *Schrift* 258-73, on "the argumentative function of the scriptural citations."

45. His primary text was what we today call the LXX (Smith, "Pauline Literature" 272-73).

46. But this was already a familiar finding; see, e.g. Ellis, *Paul's Use.*

47. Stanley finds 112 different readings "where it can be affirmed with reasonable confidence that Paul has indeed adapted the wording of the biblical text" (*Paul* 259). He lists six categories (260-61): (a) changes in word order (17); (b) alterations in grammar (16); (c) omissions (46); (d) additions (11); (e) substitutions (22); (f) limited selection (9). Cf. Koch's somewhat different statistics (*Schrift* 186-90); but the substantive point is the same.

48. Stanley, *Paul* 262-63; see further 342-46. He also notes that "Paul takes no pains to conceal from his audience the fact that he has incorporated interpretive elements into the wording of his quotations"; for example, "in Rom. 10.11, Paul quotes Isa. 28.16 in a form different from that which he had used only twelve verses earlier in Rom. 9.33" (264; see further 346-48).

tendentiously adapted) citations would have been wholly characteristic for the time. Both Greco-Roman and Jewish literature provide "strong evidence for a general cultural and literary ethos in which incorporating interpretive elements into the wording of a quotation was considered a normal and acceptable means of advancing one's argument."[49]

On the other hand, however, there is the use to which Paul put his quoted text, the interpretation he drew from it. In a number of cases, where the text is key to the claims Paul makes, Paul's exposition of the text must have sounded strange. Some of these would probably have raised few eyebrows — strange, but not improper use of a scriptural text.[50] In others, although the exegetical techniques may have been familiar, the conclusions would certainly have been controversial.[51] We will see later how this bears upon two of his key texts — Gen. 15.6 and Hab. 2.4.[52] And we have already observed the exegetical turnaround Paul attempts in his catena of texts in Rom. 3.10-18.[53] He tries to pull off the same feat later in Romans. In particular we could note 9.25-26 — texts about Israel's restoration applied to the Gentiles; 10.6-8 — a text about the do-ability of the law applied to "the word of faith"; and 10.13 — "the Lord" on whom Joel anticipated the remnant calling understood as Christ.[54] In Galatians similar issues arise with the exegetical claims in Gal. 3.8, 10, and 16.[55] And the most astonishing turnaround of all, the "allegory" in Gal. 4.21-30,[56] ends with Sarah's counsel to cast out Hagar and Ishmael (Gen. 21.10) transformed most provocatively into the equivalent counsel that Jewish persecutors of Christians should be equivalently ejected.[57]

In evaluating this material we should distinguish the issue of the

---

49. Stanley, *Paul* 337; see also his conclusions on 291, 337, and his final section on "Form and Freedom" (350-60). E.g., " 'Interpretive renderings' are thus an integral part of every public presentation of a written text" (352); and his approval of a phrase used by Shemaryahu Talmon, "controlled freedom of textual variation" (354). Such a finding renders superfluous earlier discussion (as, e.g., in Hanson, *Studies* 145-49).

50. See, e.g., Rom. 10.18; 11.8-10; 12.19; 1 Cor. 9.9 (and 1 Tim. 5.18); 1 Cor. 14.21; 2 Cor. 8.15; Gal. 4.27; and possibly even the *way* in which texts are used (albeit in the service of christology) in 1 Cor. 10.4; 15.45; and Eph. 4.8-10.

51. Not surprisingly the chief examples come from the two letters where Paul is in most intensive debate with his Jewish heritage (Galatians and Romans).

52. See below §14.7. But contrast his relatively traditional understanding of Lev. 18.5 — if I am right (see above §6.6).

53. See above §5.4(6).

54. On the last two texts see further below §23.3 and §10.4d.

55. On 3.10 in particular see below §14.5c.

56. On the significance of Paul's use of the term "allegorically" in Gal. 4.24 and parallels with Philo, see my *Galatians* 247-48; on the larger discussion regarding typology and allegory, see, e.g., my *Unity* 85-87, 89-91.

57. See above §6.5d; and further my *Galatians* 256-59.

hermeneutical principle behind such usage from that of the exegetical techniques used. In the latter, "Paul was in every respect a man of his world."[58] In the former the principle is clear and can be summed up in the phrase: Jesus as the Christ. It was the conviction that God's purposes had been and were being fulfilled in Messiah Jesus which gave Paul the hermeneutical clue to read and understand the scriptures.[59] That this was the effective and definitive principle for Paul is clear enough from such passages as Rom. 9.33; 10.13; 15.3; 1 Cor. 10.4; and Gal. 3.16. But only in one passage does he actually spell it out explicitly. That is in the midrash of 2 Cor. 3.7-18 and most explicitly in 3.14: "up until the present day the same veil remains unlifted over the reading of the old covenant, because (only) in Christ is it taken away." Whether the subject of the final verb is "the old covenant" or "the veil,"[60] the effective point is the same: that it is only "in Christ" that the veil is lifted which prevents the proper understanding of the old ministry (of Moses) as *old* covenant.[61]

It only needs to be added that this was not an arbitrarily chosen principle, or one which encouraged or permitted arbitrary interpretative techniques.[62] We have already observed that Paul's citation of texts was wholly in accord with contemporary practice. And to recognize that Paul had a particular hermeneutical perspective is simply to put him alongside careful readers (as distinct from casual hearers) of all generations. So our earlier conclusion can stand: as a believer in Messiah Jesus, Paul continued to respect and to use the Jewish scriptures as God's word. Nor, we should perhaps add, can the hermeneutical principle Paul applied (or lens through which he read) be fairly described as anti-Jewish.[63] For one Jew to acknowledge another Jew as Messiah and to interpret Jewish scripture accordingly can hardly be so designated. But once again we begin to move beyond the immediate subject and indicate wider issues to which we must return.[64]

58. I use here the words of Stanley, *Paul* 291.

59. Often cited is the undeveloped comment of Hooker: "For him [Paul] it is axiomatic that the true meaning of scripture has been hidden, and is only now made plain in Christ" ("Beyond" 151).

60. On the dispute see, e.g., Furnish, *2 Corinthians* 210, and Hafemann, *Paul* (§6 n.1) 380-81.

61. See further Koch, *Schrift* 335-41, 344-53; Hays, *Echoes* 140-49; also Hanson, *Studies* ch. 11 (though his "doctrine of the pre-existent Christ" tends to skew his discussion); and Aageson, *Written*.

62. See further my *Unity* 93-102.

63. I have in mind here the much cited thesis of R. Ruether, *Faith and Fratricide: The Theological Roots of Anti-Semitism* (New York: Seabury, 1974), that anti-Judaism is the "left hand" of classical christology. However justified that critique became, it can hardly be used against the first Christians.

64. See below §§14, 19, and 23.

§7.3 *Kerygmatic and confessional formulae*

A third notable feature of Paul's introductory talk of the gospel in Romans is his immediate use of earlier Christian tradition. In Rom. 1.1-4 he continues to disrupt the normal epistolary greeting by inserting what most regard as a pre-Pauline formula (1.3-4):[65]

> [1]. . . the gospel of God, [2]which was promised beforehand through his prophets in the holy scriptures, [3]concerning his Son
>> Who was descended from the seed of David in terms of the flesh,
>> [4]and who was appointed Son of God in power in terms of the
>> Spirit of holiness as from the resurrection of the dead.

And in turning from his indictment of humankind (1.18–3.20) to his exposition of the gospel's response, we find the same feature: Paul reaches almost instinctively, or so it would appear, for a formulation which others would recognize and acknowledge (3.21-26):[66]

> [21]. . . the righteousness of God has been revealed, as attested by the law and the prophets. . . . [24] They are justified as a gift by his grace through the redemption which is in Christ Jesus,
>> [25]whom God set forth as an expiation (through faith) in his blood,
>> to demonstrate his righteousness in passing over the sins
>>> committed in former times,
>> [26]in the forbearance of God. . . .

Intensive work on the question of pre-Pauline formulae was carried out in the 1960s and early 1970s, and the substantive findings of these studies still stand.[67] Several variations of formulae which presumably served as summaries or even liturgical responses can be detected simply by the regularity of their form and the frequency with which they are repeated.[68]

---

65. There is a considerable consensus in favour of recognizing the use of a pre-Pauline formula, though its precise content and wording are disputed; see my *Romans* 5-6; Fitzmyer, *Romans* 229-30.

66. Again there is substantial consensus on the use of preformed material (3.25-26a), though again there is dispute over the detail and particularly whether v. 24 should also be regarded as part of the earlier tradition. See, e.g., Stuhlmacher, *Reconciliation* 96-97; also *Romans* 163-64; Kraus, *Tod Jesu* (§9 n. 1) 15-20; Fitzmyer, *Romans* 342-43; otherwise Campbell, *Rhetoric* (§9 n. 1) 37-57.

67. Kramer, *Christ* 19-44; Neufeld, *Confessions* 42-68; Wengst, *Formeln* 27-48, 55-104; see also the earlier A. Seeberg, *Der Katchismus der Urchristenheit* (Leipzig, 1903; reprinted Munich: Kaiser, 1966); Hunter, *Paul* 15-35.

68. In addition, some think that 2 Cor. 5.19 incorporates a pre-Pauline formula (see below §9 n. 125).

(1) Resurrection formulae — "God raised him from the dead."[69] (2) "Died for" formulae — "Christ died for us."[70] (3) "Handed over *(paradidōmi)*" formulae — "he was handed (or handed himself) over (for our sins)."[71] (4) Combined formulae — "Christ died and was raised."[72] (5) Confessional formulae — "Jesus is Lord."[73]

Some dispute the existence of such formulae. And it is true that they cannot be demonstrated conclusively to be any more than the characteristic speech of an author. But three factors weigh in favour of recognizing such snatches as indeed formulae which Paul instinctively echoes. One is the expectation that the first churches would inevitably develop such summaries in their preaching, catechesis, and worship. That is simply the almost universal experience of good homiletics, pedagogy, and liturgical practice. So, for example, Rom. 10.9 almost invites us to recognize it as echoing a baptismal confession: "If you confess with your mouth 'Jesus is Lord,' and believe in your heart that God raised him from the dead, you will be saved."[74] In that sentence we could almost put "God raised him from the dead" in quotation marks also, as echoing the core of the preaching or catechesis which the baptisand personally appropriated and confessed in the words "Jesus is Lord." That the confession can be identified in contexts of worship (1 Cor. 12.3), evangelism (2 Cor. 4.5), and paraenesis (Col. 2.6) strengthens the expectation outlined above. And the presence of "faithful sayings" in the Pastorals[75] and what appear to be liturgical chants in

69. Rom. 4.24-25; 7.4; 8.11; 10.9; 1 Cor. 6.14; 15.4, 12, 20; 2 Cor. 4.14; Gal. 1.1; Col. 2.12; 1 Thes. 1.10; Eph. 1.20; 2 Tim. 2.8; 1 Pet. 1.21; Acts 3.15; 4.10; 5.30; 10.40; 13.30, 37.

70. Rom. 5.6, 8; 14.15; 1 Cor. 8.11; 15.3; 2 Cor. 5.14-15; 1 Thes. 5.10; Ignatius, *Trallians* 2.1.

71. Rom. 4.25; 8.32; 1 Cor. 11.23; Gal. 1.4; 2.20; Eph. 5.2, 25; 1 Tim. 2.6; Tit. 2.14; *1 Clement* 16.7. See Wengst, *Formeln* 55-77; V. P. Furnish, " 'He Gave Himself (Was Given) Up . . .': Paul's Use of a Christological Assertion," in A. J. Malherbe and W. A. Meeks, eds., *The Future of Christology*, L. E. Keck FS (Minneapolis: Fortress, 1993) 109-21.

72. Rom. 4.25; 8.34 (14.9); 1 Cor. 15.3-4; 2 Cor. 5.15; 13.4; 1 Thes. 4.14. Only in 1 Thes. 4.14 does it say that Jesus rose; elsewhere the formula speaks of Jesus' resurrection as the action of God.

73. Rom. 10.9; 1 Cor. 8.6; 12.3; 2 Cor. 4.5; Phil. 2.11; Col. 2.6; Eph. 4.5; Acts 2.36; 10.36; John 20.28.

74. This may be the earliest Christian confession that we have (see Neufeld, *Confessions* 51; and further my *Romans* 607-8). Other confessions can be identified (Neufeld, *Confessions* chs. 4-7; Wengst, *Formeln* Kap. 2) but not easily in the undisputed Paulines.

75. Kerygmatic tradition — 1 Tim. 1.15; 2 Tim. 2.11; Tit. 3.5-8; church tradition — 1 Tim. 3.1; cf. Tit. 1.9; ethical tradition — 1 Tim. 4.8-9; 2 Tim. 2.11-13.

Revelation (no doubt used on earth as much as in heaven!)[76] confirms the same broad picture.

A second consideration in favour of recognizing Paul's use of preexisting formulae is the point already noted — the fact that these phrases appear so regularly, and not solely in the Pauline literature. This suggests a commonality of faith and of expression of that faith. Which in turn suggests that summary formulations like these were indeed in fairly widespread use in the earliest Christian churches.

The third consideration is one which brings us back to our present point in following out Paul's theological exposition in Romans. That is the brevity of the central passage, Rom. 3.21-26. It really is astonishing that, after such an elaborate and extensive indictment (1.18–3.20), Paul could be content to give the heart of his response to it in a mere six verses. The obvious reason for this is that he was able to quote a summary statement which was noncontroversial (for Christian readership). By building his response around a widely recognized formulation describing the efficaciousness of Jesus' death in displaying God's saving righteousness as it deals with sins, Paul was able to make his point both briefly and effectively. This is all the more striking since he was writing to congregations (in Rome) which he did not know personally. In other words, Paul could take it for granted that such a formula, or indeed this particular formula, was one to which his readers would assent. This must mean, in turn, that in using the formula Paul was not adding anything which significantly altered or qualified it;[77] otherwise he could not have made that assumption and would have had to argue his point more circumspectly and in more detail.

All this emphasizes Paul's conviction that the central christological claims of his gospel were in direct continuity with the gospel already being preached before his conversion. The point is not simply that he could make this claim (a claim which others might dispute). It is rather that he could and did assume that such summary formulations would be both recognized and acknowledged as expressions of a shared faith in all the churches to which he wrote. He makes the point explicitly in 1 Cor. 15.1-3: that

---

76. Rev. 4.8, 11; 5.9-10, 12, 13; 7.10, 12; 11.15, 17-18; 15.3-4. We could also mention the early hymns preserved in Luke 1–2 (1.46-55, 68-79; 2.14, 29-32) and those identified elsewhere in the Pauline corpus (Phil. 2.6-11; Col. 1.15-20; 1 Tim. 3.16). But the point does not depend on their being so identified.

77. See the brief discussion in my *Romans* 163-64. Would an insertion of "through faith" (3.25) or the addition of v. 26 to extend a narrower concept of divine righteousness (to Israel past and present) to believers in Jesus generally (e.g., Stuhlmacher, *Reconciliation* 103-5; Martin, *Reconciliation* 85-88; others cited in my *Romans* 175) be regarded as such a modification? Cf. the discussion in Fitzmyer, *Romans* 342-43, and see further below §9.2(1).

the gospel which I preached *(euēngelisamēn)* to you, which you also received *(parelabete),* in which you have taken your stand, through which you are also being saved . . . [is the gospel] which I also received *(parelabon)* . . .

The continuity of and authority behind his gospel was not simply that of the scriptures. It was also that of the earliest formulations of the common faith in Christ. Whether that also meant continuity with Jesus' own proclamation is a point to which we will return in §8.

§7.4 *The apocalypse of Jesus Christ*

All the above points have been drawn from the remarkably parallel way in which Paul both opens Romans (1.1-4) and pronounces the key statement of the gospel (3.21-26): (1) reference to the gospel (1.1; 3.21-22); (2) scriptural confirmation (1.2; 3.21); and (3) use of already established Christian tradition (1.3-4; 3.25-26). The last point in particular, however, seems to stand in some tension (some would no doubt say "contradiction") with Paul's explicit claims in his most polemical letter — Galatians. There he insists "that the gospel preached by me is not of human origin. For it was not from a human being that I received it, neither was I taught it, but through a revelation *(apokalypsis)* of Jesus Christ" (Gal. 1.11-12). How could Paul both deny that he had received the gospel through human mediation and yet also affirm that his gospel was in accord with the tradition he received?

Unless we are content to conclude that Paul was wholly unscrupulous in his shifts and manoeuvres (a judgment we should hesitate before passing on anyone), the answer has to be something along the following lines. What Paul received and preached, and echoed in his letters, was indeed the common Christian conviction that "Christ died (for us) and was raised (from the dead)." That remained the shared confession and bond which held together the first Christian churches, despite all their diversity, in one gospel. What Paul was convinced of on the Damascus road, however, was not simply this central confessional claim but also that this Jesus was now to be preached to the Gentiles. It is this latter point which Paul focuses on in his own most explicit reference to his conversion: God revealed "his Son in me, in order that I might preach *(euangelizomai)* him among the Gentiles" (Gal. 1.15-16).[78] It

---

78. This is why several commentators have preferred to speak of Paul's "commission" rather than his "conversion" (particularly Stendahl, *Paul* 7-23). On this point the evidently deliberate echo of the prophetic call of Jeremiah (Jer. 1.5) and of the Servant of Yahweh (Isa. 49.1, 6) in Gal. 1.15-16 should be noted. See also below §14.3d.

is the primary point in other references (1 Cor. 9.1; 15.8-11). And it is confirmed by the same emphasis in the three Acts accounts of Paul's conversion.[79]

It was this interpretation of the shared gospel which Paul saw as his primary responsibility to carry out and proclaim. The risen Christ had appointed him apostle (1 Cor. 9.1; 15.8). That is, not to some general apostleship, but specifically as "apostle to the Gentiles" (Rom. 11.13). It was evidently this understanding of the gospel to be preached by him as apostle which he attributed directly to God, through Jesus Christ (Gal. 1.1). It was the gospel so received and so understood that he was so anxious to sustain and defend in the passionate denials of Gal. 1.16-22 and 2.3-6. Just as it was this gospel whose affirmation (at last) by the Jerusalem leadership he had been so anxious about on his second trip to Jerusalem following his conversion (2.1-2).[80] The awkwardness of Rom. 1.15 (Paul's "eagerness to preach the gospel to you who are in Rome as well")[81] is to be explained precisely by this fact: that it was of the essence of his gospel that it should be preached to the Gentiles. *That* was why he was "not ashamed of the gospel, since it is the power of God for salvation, for *all* who believe, Jew first *but also Gentile*" (1.16).[82]

The resolution of the tension between Galatians 1 and 1 Cor. 15.1-7 confirms that Paul's sense of commission as apostle to the Gentiles was a distinctive feature of Paul's understanding of the gospel from the first. This is usually questioned by those who deduce that the revolution in Paul's theology occasioned by his Damascus road encounter focused more immediately on the law.[83] The theological logic then runs: if the law is no longer a means to salvation, then the gospel may be offered freely to the Gentiles. Paul nowhere says anything like that. A different logic is suggested by three factors. (1) His own emphasis on his prophet-like commissioning "to the nations."[84] (2) The implication that his "zeal" as a persecutor had been directed against (Hellenist) Jews preaching Jesus to Gentiles, so that he was converted (turned about) to follow the course to which he had been so

---

79. Acts 9.15; 22.15; 26.16-18.

80. See further my "The Relationship between Paul and Jerusalem according to Galatians 1 and 2," *Jesus, Paul and the Law* 108-28.

81. By "awkwardness" I refer to the seeming conflict with 15.20; see above at n. 3.

82. See also the thesis of S. Mason, " 'For I Am Not Ashamed of the Gospel' (Rom. 1.16): The Gospel and the First Readers of Romans," in Jervis and Richardson, *Gospel* 254-87: "that Paul was the first Christian to use *euangelion*-language, and that he used it with particular bearing on his Gentile mission . . ." (287, referring to his discussion from 277).

83. E.g. Wilckens, "Bekehrung" 15, 18, 23-25; a repeated emphasis of Stuhlmacher, "The End of the Law," *Reconciliation* 139-41; "The Law as a Topic of Biblical Theology," *Reconciliation* 110-33 (here 124); *Theologie* 285, 313; Kim, *Origin* 3-4 and *passim;* Dietzfelbinger, *Berufung* 90, 105-6, 115, 118, 125, 144-45.

84. See above n. 78.

violently opposed.[85] (3) His continued recognition of the law, *not* as a life-giver, but as an orderer of life for the people of God.[86] These factors suggest a somewhat different theological logic: if the gospel is for the Gentiles, what does that mean for the continuing role of the law for the now expanding people of God? However, whether immediately or as a corollary which became clearer over time, it remains true that his conversion was the light which brought fresh illumination to Paul in regard to the law. And that is a subject to which we will have to return.[87]

More to our immediate point, Paul's conversion was a conversion for Paul the theologian. Not a conversion from one religion to another. He remained a Jew and an Israelite, though we can speak of a conversion from one form (or sect) of the religion of his people (Pharisee) to another (Nazarene).[88] But certainly Paul's conversion must be seen as a fulcrum point or hinge on which his whole theology turned round. And certainly it was the encounter with the risen Christ (as he perceived it) which formed that fulcrum and hinge. It was no doubt the total reversal of some very basic theological axioms (about Israel's status and the importance of preserving it) and previous conclusions (Jesus as a false claimant to messiahship rejected by God) which was at the heart of the theological reconstruction which must have followed. All this is implicit in 2 Cor. 4.4-6, where Paul speaks explicitly of his gospel, and Phil. 3.7-8 in particular. How quickly that process of reconstruction followed and how much followed directly or immediately from the conversion experience itself are questions we need not pursue here.[89]

What should not be ignored, however, is the evidence that Paul's own experience played a vital role in the reconstruction of his theology as a Christian and apostle. The theology of Paul was neither born nor sustained by or as a purely cerebral exercise. It was his own experience of grace which lay at its heart.[90]

§7.5 The eschatological "now"

A final point is of sufficient importance to deserve separate mention. Paul's conversion was for him not simply a turning around on a continuous road or unbroken surface. It was much more a transition to a different plane. It was

---

85. See below §14.3c.
86. See above §6.6.
87. See below §14.
88. Segal, *Paul* xii-xiv, 6-7, 11, 117.
89. Kim, *Origin,* however, substantially overstates his case. See Räisänen, "Call Experience" *passim;* Dunn, "Light" 95-100.
90. Rom. 1.5; 3.24; 5.2, 15, 17, 20-21; 1 Cor. 3.10; 15.10; Gal. 1.15; 2.9, 21.

a breakthrough from one age to another, in some sense a "rescue from the present evil age" (Gal. 1.4). It was for him the beginning of the "new creation."[91] The rupture with Paul's past was traumatic. He speaks of being unnaturally hastened (aborted) in his birth into a new life (1 Cor. 15.8).[92] He consigns all that he had previously cherished to the rubbish heap (Phil. 3.7-8).[93] The same sense of eschatological transformation is expressed in the "But now" with which Paul begins his exposition of the core of the gospel in Rom. 3.21. This "eschatological now" is a feature of his writing in Romans and elsewhere.[94] And the use of "revelation" terminology in the opening statements of his gospel in Romans is equally notable.[95]

In such language, of course, we hear the language of the convert — the black-and-white sharpness of distinctions which the new perspective brought, the shadows into which the new brightness cast the old assumptions. Anyone who can use the word "revelation" of a breakthrough in intellectual or religious insight will know something of what Paul experienced and why he so expressed himself. And of course the sharpness of the sense of apocalyptic disjunction has to be meshed into the very real continuities which nevertheless were maintained.[96] It would be theologically unsophisticated and rhetorically naive to take Paul's apocalyptic hyperbole simply at face value without reference to other features of his theology. Nevertheless, it is of major importance to appreciate the sense of eschatological newness which transformed and continued to sustain Paul's theology and not to let it be wholly discounted in favour of theological convictions easier to translate into modern terms. For it was clearly this "revelation" which formed the new perspective from which Paul would henceforth read the holy scriptures.[97] And it was clearly this new perspective which gave his theology its cutting edge, both in successful mission and in provocation to so many of his Christian Jewish contemporaries.

---

91. 2 Cor. 5.17; Gal. 6.15.

92. See below §13 n. 87.

93. Here again we may need to recognize the rhetoric of hyperbole (that is, a legitimate way of stressing a point), in character somewhat like the apparently "over the top" challenge of Jesus' call to discipleship (Luke 9.59-62; 14.26).

94. Rom. 3.26; 6.22; 7.6; 11.30; 1 Cor. 15.20; 2 Cor. 5.16; Eph. 2.13; Col. 1.22, 26; 3.8; 2 Tim. 1.10; similarly the "now" in Rom. 5.9-11; 8.1; 11.30-31; 13.11; 2 Cor. 6.2; Gal. 2.20; 4.9; Eph. 3.5, 10; 5.8;

95. 1.17, 18 (*apokalyptetai* repeated); 3.21 *(pephanerōtai)*. Cf. K. Snodgrass, "The Gospel in Romans: A Theology of Revelation," in Jervis and Richardson, *Gospel* 288-314, who provides a complete list of revelation terms used in Romans (291-92) and concludes: "Revelation does not merely bring the gospel; the gospel *is* revelation" (314).

96. We have already noted substantial continuities above, not only in §§2 and 3, but also in §§4-6.

97. See above §7.2.

An inevitable corollary is that Paul could no longer view his Pharisaic past in dispassionate (let alone enthusiastic) terms. Whether this means that his view of his native Judaism was now distorted, as has often been deduced, is another question we will have to take up later.[98] It does mean that in some sense at least Paul did reconstruct his theology "from solution to plight."[99] That is to say, it is an unavoidable conclusion that from his conversion onwards Paul theologized in the light of the fundamental "revelation of Jesus Christ" given him on the Damascus road.[100] It does not mean, however, that in order to rationalize his solution he had to invent a plight.[101] All it need mean is that as a believer in Jesus Messiah he now recognized serious faults in his previous theology, that the gospel of Jesus Christ showed up the flaws in his previous "zeal for his ancestral traditions" (Gal. 1.14). But hopefully these aspects will become clearer as we proceed.

The point to be emphasized in conclusion, however, is that Paul's gospel, the divine response to the divine indictment, was centred wholly on Jesus Christ. It was the encounter with Christ on the Damascus road which revolutionized Paul's whole faith and life. Christ became the key to understanding God's purpose for humankind, and indeed God himself. Christ was the light which expelled his darkness and illuminated the scriptures. Encountering this Christ turned his whole system of values upside down, and coming to know Christ became his supreme passion (Phil. 3.10). What then was the Christ content of Paul's gospel, the christological substance of his theology?

98. See below particularly §19.
99. Sanders, *Paul* 442-43.
100. Cf. Segal, *Paul* 28-30, 79, 117-18.
101. As Sanders, *Law* (§6 n. 1) 68, implies. Contrast F. Thielman, *From Plight to Solution: A Jewish Framework for Understanding Paul's View of the Law in Romans and Galatians* (NovTSup 61; Leiden: Brill, 1989), written to refute Sanders. The argument of Romans 2 presupposes that Jews like the pre-Christian Paul had to be convinced of a need for more far-reaching repentance.

§8 Jesus the man[1]

1. **Bibliography**: **R. Bultmann**, "The Significance of the Historical Jesus for the Theology of Paul," *Faith and Understanding: Collected Essays* (London: SCM/New York: Harper and Row, 1969) 220-46; **J. D. G. Dunn**, "Jesus Tradition in Paul," in B. Chilton and C. A. Evans, eds., *Studying the Historical Jesus: Evaluation of the State of Current Research* (Leiden: Brill, 1994) 155-78; **J. W. Fraser**, *Jesus and Paul* (Abingdon: Marcham Manor, 1974); **V. P. Furnish**, *Jesus According to Paul* (Cambridge: Cambridge University, 1993); **E. Jüngel**, *Paulus und Jesus. Eine Untersuchung zur Präzisierung der Frage nach dem Ursprung der Christologie* (Tübingen: Mohr, [3]1967); **J. Klausner**, *From Jesus to Paul* (London: Allen and Unwin, 1943); **H.-W. Kuhn**, "Der irdische Jesus bei Paulus als traditionsgeschichtliches Problem," *ZTK* 67 (1970) 295-320; **Kümmel**, "Jesus und Paulus," *Heilsgeschehen* 439-56; **Ladd**, *Theology* 448-55; **O. Michel**, "Der Christus des Paulus," *ZNW* 32 (1933) 6-31; **E. Reinmuth**, "Narratio und argumentatio — zur Auslegung der Jesus-Christus-Geschichte im ersten Korintherbrief. Ein Beitrag zur mimetischen Kompetenz des Paulus," *ZTK* 92 (1995) 13-27; **R. Riesner**, "Paulus und die Jesus-Überlieferung" in Ådna et al., eds., *Evangelium* 347-65; **Strecker**, *Theologie* 102-12; **P. Stuhlmacher**, "Jesustradition im Römerbrief," *Theologische Beiträge* 14 (1983) 240-50; *Theologie* 300-305; **M. Thompson**, *Clothed with Christ: The Example and Teaching of Jesus in Romans 12.1–15.13* (JSNTS 59; Sheffield: Sheffield Academic, 1991); **A. J. M. Wedderburn**, ed., *Paul and Jesus: Collected Essays* (JSNTS 37; Sheffield: Sheffield Academic, 1989); **D. Wenham**, *Paul: Follower of Jesus or Founder of Christianity?* (Grand Rapids: Eerdmans, 1995); **S. G. Wilson**, "From Jesus to Paul: The Contours and Consequences of a Debate," in Richardson and Hurd, eds., *From Jesus to Paul* 1-21.

§8.4-5 — **J. H. Charlesworth**, ed., *The Messiah: Developments in Earliest Judaism and Christianity* (Minneapolis: Fortress, 1992); **J. J. Collins**, *The Scepter and the Star: The Messiahs of the Dead Sea Scrolls and Other Ancient Literature* (New York: Doubleday, 1995); **N. A. Dahl**, "The Messiahship of Jesus in Paul" and "The Crucified Messiah," *Jesus the Christ: The Historical Origins of Christological Doctrine* (Minneapolis: Fortress, 1991) 15-25 and 27-47; **J. A. Fitzmyer**, "The Christology of the Epistle to the Romans," in A. J. Malherbe and W. A. Meeks, eds., *The Future of Christology*, L. E. Keck FS (Minneapolis: Fortress, 1993) 81-90; **I. Gruenwald** et al., eds., *Messiah and Christos: Studies in the Jewish Origins of Christianity*, D. Flusser FS (Tübingen: Mohr, 1992); **F. Hahn**, *Christologische Hoheitstitel* (Göttingen: Vandenhoeck, [5]1995), earlier ET, *The Titles of Jesus in Christology* (London: Lutterworth, 1969) 136-239; **M. Hengel**, " 'Christos' in Paul," *Between Jesus and Paul* 65-77, 179-88; **M. Karrer**, *Der Gesalbte. Die Grundlagen des Christustitels* (FRLANT 151; Göttingen: Vandenhoeck, 1991); **J. E. Keck**, " 'Jesus' in Romans," *JBL* 108 (1989) 443-60; **S. V. McCasland**, " 'Christ Jesus,' " *JBL* 65 (1946) 377-83; **J. Neusner** et al., eds., *Judaisms and Their Messiahs at the Turn of the Christian Era* (Cambridge: Cambridge University, 1987); **Wright**, *Climax* 41-55.

§8.1 How much did Paul know or care about the life of Jesus?

The gospel for Paul was preeminently the gospel of Christ.[2] What did that
mean for Paul? The most obvious answer is that it was Christ's *death* which
gave the proclamation of Christ its character as "gospel." Paul's immediate
response to the indictment of Rom. 1.18–3.20 centres on Jesus' sacrificial
death (3.24-25). The divine response to human weakness, failure, and rebellion
had been the same (5.6-10). It was the obedience of Christ, that is, in death
(cf. Phil. 2.7), which answered the death-bringing disobedience of Adam
(Rom. 5.18-19). Grace has come to effect in believers by their being baptized
into Christ's death (6.3-4). God has dealt with the problem and power of sin
by condemning sin in the flesh, that is, in Christ's death (8.3). Similarly
elsewhere, for example, it is Christ's death "for all" which provided the
motivation for and the message of Paul's mission of reconciliation (2 Cor.
5.14-15, 18-21). And the formulae which he cites so often (§7.3) all focus on
Jesus' death and resurrection.

Many deduce from such data that Jesus' death (and resurrection) was
the only part of Jesus' historic mission that was important for Paul's theology.[3]
His gospel was a gospel of salvation, a gospel of rescue. So it would be natural
if Jesus was only significant for Paul's theology as saviour and for his rescue
act on the cross.

That initial deduction seems to be borne out by what we find elsewhere
in Paul. For when we search out what Paul actually does say about Jesus'
ministry, the gleanings are indeed remarkably sparse. He mentions that Jesus
was "born of a woman" (Gal. 4.4), a typical Jewish circumlocution for a
human person.[4] In the same context he mentions that Jesus was "born under
the law" (Gal. 4.4); that is, Jesus was born as a Jew. This ties in with the first
line of the confessional formula cited in Rom. 1.3-4: "descended from the
seed of David in terms of the flesh." It is of interest to note that this opening
confession is balanced (an *inclusio*) by the concluding declaration "that Christ
has become servant of the circumcised for the sake of God's truth" (Rom.
15.8). Jesus had brothers.[5] But beyond that we have nothing. Allusions to
Christ's "meekness and gentleness" (2 Cor. 10.1), to his "compassion" (Phil.
1.8), and to the fact that "Christ did not please himself" (Rom. 15.3) could
be read as allusions to his passion. And the tradition of the institution of the
Lord's Supper (cited in 1 Cor. 11.23-26) is already part of the passion and
also focuses on Christ's death.

2. See above §7 n. 11.
3. See, e.g., below §23 n. 114.
4. Job 14.1; 15.14; 25.4; 1QS 11.20-21; 1QH 13.14; 18.12-13, 16; Matt. 11.11.
5. 1 Cor. 9.5; Gal. 1.19.

In short, Paul tells us next to nothing about the life and ministry of Jesus apart from its climactic finale. Had we possessed only Paul's letters, it would be impossible to say much about Jesus of Nazareth, let alone even to attempt a life of Jesus. Paul makes it clear that Jesus was a Jew. And that is a crucially important fact. But beyond that the life of Jesus seems to be little more than an assumed and hidden antecedent to the all-important record of his death. What are we to make of this for an appreciation of Paul's gospel and theology?

In a famous debate on 2 Cor. 5.16 — "if indeed we knew Christ according to the flesh, now we no longer know him in that way" — it was argued that Paul was referring to "Christ according to the flesh." Paul had once known about (as persecutor?) or even known the earthly Jesus. But now he had wholly abandoned that knowledge; the earthly Christ was no longer important or relevant to him. The Christ of his theology as a Christian ("now") was Christ risen from the dead.[6] However, that exegesis no longer carries weight. Almost certainly in 5.16 *kata sarka* ("according to the flesh") should be taken with the verb rather than the noun: "even though we once knew Christ from a human point of view" (NRSV).[7] Even so, the sentence indicates a substantial transformation in Paul's evaluation of Christ. And since the new evaluation focuses so much on the death of Christ (5.14-15), it is still possible that the old evaluation had made more of Jesus' life. After all, Paul did reckon "the Christ insofar as the flesh is concerned" as one of Israel's blessings (Rom. 9.5). So 2 Cor. 5.16 could still indicate a conversion from an earlier evaluation of Jesus simply as "the Christ."[8] In other words, it could help

6. E.g. J. Weiss, *Paul and Jesus* (London: Harper, 1909) 41-53; Bousset, *Kyrios* (§10 n. 1) 169: "as a pneumatic, the apostle boldly breaks all the historical connections that are burdensome to him, rejects the authorities in Jerusalem, and intends no longer to know *Iēsous kata sarka*"; Bultmann, *2 Corinthians* 155-56: "The *Christos kata sarka* is Christ as he can be encountered in the world, before his death and resurrection. He should no longer be viewed as such . . ." (cf. his *Theology* 1.238-39). See the brief review of views in Fraser, *Jesus* 46-48, 51-55; C. Wolff, "True Apostolic Knowledge of Christ: Exegetical Reflections on 2 Corinthians 5.14ff," in Wedderburn, ed., *Paul* 81-98 (here 82-85).

7. See, e.g., Fraser, *Jesus* 48-50; Furnish, *2 Corinthians* 312-13, 330; Wolff (above n. 6) 87-91; Thrall, *2 Corinthians* 412-20. "2 Cor. 5.16 refers to the turnabout in the apostle's own understanding of Christ" (Stuhlmacher, *Theologie* 301).

8. Here the parallel with Rom. 1.3 may have some significance. In accordance with its usual weight in Paul (especially in contrast with *kata pneuma*), the *kata sarka* qualifying phrase could possibly indicate some hesitation about emphasizing Jesus' Davidic messiahship. To proclaim a royal messiah was more provocative (and politically dangerous) than proclaiming a suffering messiah (see further my *Romans* 13; and below n. 37). The issue here does not hang on such a reading; but cf. Denney, Plummer, and Bruce on 2 Cor. 5.16, cited by Furnish, *2 Corinthians* 330.

explain Paul's apparent lack of interest in Jesus' ministry apart from its climactic events.[9]

And yet there is something exceedingly odd about such a conclusion. Paul knew and cared little about Jesus' life? Could that indeed be the case? Such a sharp disjunction between earthly Jesus and exalted Lord might go down well in the European lecture halls of nineteenth-century liberal theology. But that was principally because of nineteenth-century life of Jesus research, with its reaction against "the Christ of faith" (Paul) and fascination with "the historical Jesus" (the Synoptic Gospels).[10] Is there not a danger of reading a modern agenda into Paul's silences? Is there not a danger of mistaking what he took for granted and of hearing his silences as ignorance or disinterest? "Taken-for-granted" does not mean "couldn't care less."

§8.2 Some a priori considerations

It would be astonishing indeed if a movement which focused so intensively on one known as Jesus Christ, which marked itself out by baptism in his name, and which took its own name from that same individual ("Christians")[11] was as uninterested in this Jesus as Paul's letters seem to imply. Even for any who were converted from mystery cults, the very bare form of the kerygmatic outline, such as we find in 1 Cor. 15.3-4, would hardly provide equivalent gratification. For cultic myths, and so also the corresponding initiation rites, were usually a good deal more elaborate and complex.[12] Is it conceivable, then, that the first believers in Christ would find sufficient liturgical (we might add emotional and spiritual) satisfaction simply in the repetition of such formulae as we noted before (§7.3)?

Moreover, whether or not the kerygma could be seen as equivalent to a mystery cult myth, the fact remains that the Jesus on whom the gospel centred had lived and ministered for a number of years within the lifetime of

---

9. But see below §8.5.

10. See, e.g., the classic exposition in A. Harnack, *What Is Christianity?* (New York: Putnam/London: Williams and Norgate, 1901).

11. It is likely that the name was already coming into currency; cf. Acts 11.26; 26.28; 1 Pet. 4.16.

12. As is indicated, e.g., in the famous wall paintings in the "villa of mysteries" at Pompeii. It should be remembered that the "mysteries" included public rites and processions as well as secrets for the initiates (note particularly Apuleius, *Metamorphoses* 11; see further below §17.1). See Wedderburn, *Baptism* (§17 n. 1) 98; also "Paul and the Story of Jesus," in Wedderburn, ed., *Paul* 161-89, who prefers "story" to "myth" (for what was celebrated or reenacted by the first Christians) since the former can include those parts of the narrative better classed as "historical accounts" (166).

the first-generation converts. And we can also speak without exaggeration of a universal curiosity regarding the prominent or hero figure, which is as evident in ancient writings as it is today.[13] So it would be altogether surprising if those who claimed to have put their faith in this Christ were not a little curious about the character and content of his life and ministry prior to his death.

We may add a further line of reflection.[14] It starts from the sociological insight that the emergence of a new sect or religious community is bound to depend in one degree or other on the formulation and preservation of some *de facto* sacred tradition by which it defines itself and by which it marks itself off from other similar or related movements or groupings. Certainly the kerygma of the death and resurrection of Jesus would have been at the heart of this sacred tradition for the first Christians. But again it would be most surprising if the first Christians' identity-defining texts (oral or written) did not include traditions about the earlier phase of Jesus' ministry and teaching. This would constitute an indispensable stock of material which they could rehearse in their communal gatherings, draw on for their worship, refer to for wisdom in dealing with ethical and theological issues of daily life, communicate in instruction of new converts, and use in evangelistic, apologetic, or polemical exchange with outsiders.

The evidence which we have is wholly consistent with this a priori picture and confirms its strong credibility. I have in mind the emphasis which we find, not least in Paul's letters, on teaching and tradition. We know from a number of passages[15] that Paul saw it as a fundamental part of his apostolic role in founding a new church to bequeath it with the traditions *(paradoseis)* which gave the new church its identity and which would distinguish it from synagogue, collegium, and mystery cult.

The central role of teachers in the churches associated with Paul[16] points to the same conclusion. This must mean that the first Christian gatherings recognized the need to maintain and pass on their characteristic and distinctive traditions. What other role would "teachers" have? In an oral community the treasury of sacred tradition would have to be entrusted to those whose special gift and responsibility it was to retain and retell the tradition on the community's behalf.

Nor do we have to look far for examples of that tradition. For it is

13. Note, e.g., the degree of biographical interest evident in Dio Chrysostom in the life and teaching of Diogenes, or, on the Jewish side, in Jeremiah preserved (by his disciples) in "The Words of Jeremiah" (Jer. 1.1, i.e., canonical Jeremiah).

14. In this section I am drawing on my "Jesus Tradition" 156-59.

15. 1 Thes. 4.1; 2 Thes. 3.6; 1 Cor. 11.2; 15.3; Col. 2.6 — all using the words denoting the transmission and reception of tradition *(paradidōmi* and *paralambanō).*

16. Acts 13.1; 1 Cor. 12.28; Gal. 6.6.

there in the Synoptic Gospels. As is now becoming more clearly recognized, the Gospels themselves *do* display a biographical interest in Jesus. That is, they can be classified as "biographies," not in terms of modern biographical concerns,[17] but in terms of ancient biography. In other words, they display a didactic concern to portray the character of their subject matter by recounting what he did and said.[18] Luke, for instance, was clearly determined to portray Jesus in an edifying way as an example of one who lived by prayer.[19] Matthew has grouped so much material, for example, in the "Sermon on the Mount" (Matthew 5–7), no doubt for didactic and catechetical reasons. And Acts 10.36-39 at least suggests that a current form of early preaching/teaching included an outline of Jesus' ministry.[20]

Of course the Gospels were not yet written. But where was the material on which Mark and the others drew to construct their Gospels? It can hardly be assumed that it was lying forgotten in participants' memories or mouldering in some box or back room before Mark heroically dug it out. The primary thesis of form-critical study of the Gospels[21] points in quite the opposite direction. It would be wholly arbitrary to assume that the process studied by form criticism (the transmission, grouping, and interpretation of the "forms" of Jesus tradition) was confined to certain select individuals and churches in the land of Israel. It would be still more ludicrous to assume that all the Pauline churches were wholly ignorant of such material until they received their copy of Mark's Gospel. In short, it would be utterly astonishing if the congregations to which Paul wrote did not possess their own stock of Jesus tradition, much of which Paul himself probably supplied.

And if we wish to know where Paul first encountered such material, Paul provides an obvious and inviting answer. He could, of course, have been familiar with much of the Jesus tradition at second (hostile) hand. For as a neophyte Pharisee he could hardly have gained his considerable knowledge of the "ancestral traditions" (Gal. 1.13-14) elsewhere than in Jerusa-

---

17. This was Bultmann's mistake in judging the canonical Gospels in terms of modern biographical interest in the inner life and development of the subject.

18. See further D. E. Aune, *The New Testament in Its Literary Environment* (Philadelphia: Westminster, 1987); R. A. Burridge, *What Are the Gospels? A Comparison with Graeco-Roman Biography* (SNTSMS 70; Cambridge: Cambridge University, 1992).

19. Luke 3.21; 5.16; 6.12; 9.18, 28-29; 11.1; 22.41-45. See further B. E. Beck, *Christian Character in the Gospel of Luke* (London: Epworth, 1989).

20. Cf. G. N. Stanton, *Jesus of Nazareth in New Testament Preaching* (SNTSMS 27; Cambridge: Cambridge University, 1974) ch. 3. Wenham, *Paul* 338-72, 388-91, elaborates the suggestion of Hays, *Faith* (§14 n. 1) 85-137, 257, that Paul knew an outline of Jesus' story. See also above n. 13.

21. *Formgeschichte* — investigation of the history of the forms which constitute the building blocks from which the Gospels were constructed.

lem itself.[22] Of course, we cannot be sure when Paul spent this time in Jerusalem, but the most probable chronology of his life certainly makes it possible, even likely, that Saul of Tarsus was in Jerusalem during some at least of Jesus' ministry. In which case he could hardly have been ignorant of reports and rumours about Jesus' teaching and activities.[23] But even if we cannot build too much on such speculation, there is the probability that Paul would have received some instruction (from the Damascus believers) following his conversion (cf. 1 Cor. 15.1). And still more to the point, we have Paul's own testimony that he spent a fortnight in Jerusalem "getting to know Cephas [Peter]" (Gal. 1.18). This happened some two or three years after Paul's conversion,[24] that is, only about five years after the close of Jesus' ministry. Once again we can hardly assume that their conversations never or only rarely touched on Jesus' pre-passion ministry.[25] On the contrary, "getting to know" Peter must surely have included "getting to know" Peter's role as Jesus' leading disciple during Jesus' ministry in Galilee.[26] Not least of importance would it have been for Paul, if he had previous knowledge of Jesus, to "set the record straight," informed by the most authoritative witness.[27]

From all this we can conclude with a high degree of probability that Paul must have both known and cared about the ministry of Jesus prior to Jesus' "handing over" and death. The case is built on circumstantial evidence, but as such it must be accounted a strong case. Nevertheless, it is quite proper

22. The evidence of Pharisees operating beyond Judea, even into Galilee, is sparse enough. It is unrealistic to hypothesize that Paul could have trained as a Pharisee in Tarsus. And if he had to travel to realize that ambition, he would certainly have looked nowhere other than Jerusalem. The ambiguous testimony of Gal. 1.22 cannot provide a sufficient counter to that inherent probability. See further Hengel, *Pre-Christian Paul* ch. 2 (particularly 27), and Murphy-O'Connor, *Paul* 52-62.

23. G. Theissen, *Shadow of the Galilean* (London: SCM/Philadelphia: Fortress, 1987) paints a plausible picture of someone in the land of Israel building up a picture (shadow) of Jesus' ministry solely from such reports.

24. In "after three years" (1.18) the year from which counting began would be reckoned as the first year, so the time scale could be anything over two years.

25. Much quoted is the nicely English observation of C. H. Dodd: "we may presume they did not spend all the time talking about the weather." (*The Apostolic Preaching and its Developments* [London: Hodder & Stoughton, 1936] 16).

26. See further my debate with O. Hofius in "Relationship" (§7 n. 80) and "Once More — Gal. 1.18: *historēsai Kēphan*," *Jesus, Paul and the Law* 127-28, the latter responding to Hofius, "Gal. 1.18: *historēsai Kēphan*," *ZNW* 75 (1984) 73-85 = *Paulusstudien* 255-67.

27. Recognition of such dependency would no more contradict Paul's repeated claim in the same chapter that he received his gospel directly from God "through a revelation of Jesus Christ" (Gal. 1.11-12; see further above §7.4), though it is probably the case that Paul's opponents put a different construction on the visit (cf. Acts 9.26-30).

to ask whether there are no further indications within the Pauline letters that
Paul had such knowledge and valued it.

§8.3 *Echoes of Jesus tradition in Paul*

In seeking to draw Paul's theology from his letters we must always bear in
mind two important qualifying factors.[28] One is the probability that Paul
already shared a good deal in common with the recipients of his letters, in
this case of information and teaching about Jesus. This follows from the
argument just outlined above, and we will have to take it up again later on.[29]
Here we might simply observe once again the significance of the fact that
Paul could assume knowledge and acceptance of such shared tradition even
in the case of churches which he himself had not established (in Rome).

The other is that Paul was not attempting to "reinvent the wheel" every
time he wrote. In other words, he would not have been trying to cover every
aspect of his theology every time he dictated another letter. On the contrary,
as the letters themselves make quite clear, they were occasional documents
(including Romans). Their content was determined principally by Paul's perception of the needs of the recipient churches. That inevitably means gaps
and silences which modern commentators naturally find frustrating, but which
they must nevertheless allow for in their reconstructions of Paul's theology.
Put another way, Paul obviously did not regard his letters as the means of
communicating Jesus tradition to his churches. But if that task had already
been carried out when the church was first established, then Paul did not need
to repeat it. And if nothing in the Jesus tradition was at issue, then we should
not expect Paul to have written about it.[30]

In short, it is important for us to recall that readers of Paul's letters enter
upon a conversation which was already well under way and that we can hardly
expect Paul (as it were) to rehearse the earlier stages in the conversation for our
benefit. Like someone sitting down to a film some time after its beginning, we
have to try to deduce the earlier progress of the plot from the allusions made to
it and to use them to make more sense of what unfolds before our own eyes. In
this case it is possible to detect a number of such allusions, though, like the

28. See above §1.3.
29. See below §23.5.
30. As we will note more fully later (§23.5), Paul cites Jesus' words explicitly only
three times (1 Cor. 7.10-11; 9.14; 11.23-25). In each case some controversy was involved:
a relaxation of Jesus' ruling (7.12-15), Paul's refusal to follow Jesus' counsel (9.15-18),
and the disorder of the Lord's Supper in Corinth (11.17-22). Thompson, *Clothed* 70-76,
has briefly summarized the various reasons suggested in the past for Paul's lack of explicit
reference to Jesus tradition.

late-starting film watcher (or conversation overhearer), it is not possible to deduce from them how much weight to give them in reconstructing (as far as we need to) the earlier part of the plot (or conversation).

(1) One reference we have already alluded to in §7.1 above, the inference we drew from Paul's use of *euangelion* ("gospel"). We may note again the uniqueness of the coinage (singular *euangelion*) and the possible allusion to Jesus' words in Rom. 1.16 ("I am not ashamed of the gospel").[31] Together these observations make quite a strong case for the conclusion that wrapped up in Paul's use of the term was a memory of Jesus as the one "who preaches the good news *(euangelizomenou)* of peace" (Isa. 52.7), one who was sent "to bring good news *(euangelisasthai)* to the poor" (Isa. 61.1), and that Paul was at least sometimes aware of this (Rom. 1.16).

(2) A second allusion can be recognized in the rather striking but not much commented on parallel between Jesus' and Paul's teaching on the kingdom (of God). That the kingdom of God was the central feature of Jesus' preaching is well known.[32] We would expect anyone who knew or cared about Jesus' ministry to be aware of this. Paul, however, says very little about the kingdom. Where the term does occur, it usually appears in the formulaic talk of "inheriting the kingdom,"[33] or with similar future eschatological reference.[34] This suggests that the category of "the kingdom of God" lay to hand in the common stock of early Christian tradition. Paul took it up as occasion demanded, as an obviously familiar theme. In contrast to Jesus, however, Paul made much more of the term "righteousness." Indeed, the inverse ratio between the two uses[35] has suggested to some[36] that Paul, with some deliberateness, replaced Jesus' emphasis on the kingdom with his own emphasis on righteousness.[37]

31. See above §7.1 and n. 26.

32. See, e.g., G. R. Beasley-Murray, *Jesus and the Kingdom of God* (Grand Rapids: Eerdmans/Exeter: Paternoster, 1986).

33. 1 Cor. 6.9-10; 15.50; Gal. 5.21; cf. Eph. 5.5. In the Jesus tradition cf. particularly Matt. 5.5 and 19.29.

34. 1 Thes. 2.12; 2 Thes. 1.5; cf. Col. 4.11; 2 Tim. 4.1, 18. Of Jesus' eschatological but present reign (1 Cor. 15.24; cf. Col. 1.13).

35.

	Jesus-Synoptics	Pauline corpus
kingdom	ca. 105	14
righteousness	7	57

36. Particularly Jüngel, *Paulus* 266-67; cf. also A. J. M. Wedderburn, "Paul and Jesus: The Problem of Continuity," in Wedderburn, ed., *Paul* 99-115 (here 102-10).

37. Is this perhaps another indication that Paul was careful not to promote the idea of Jesus as a king? It would be a politically risky emphasis, given the formal charge on which Jesus was executed and the fact that Paul's mission concentrated on several of the most important Roman cities of the empire (cf. Acts 17.6-7; Mark 15.26 pars.). See also above n. 8. Similarly Wenham, *Paul* 78-79.

In fact, however, the more striking inverse ratio is between kingdom and Spirit.[38] For Paul does also say something about the kingdom in the present, and as manifested in the Holy Spirit: Rom. 14.17 — "the kingdom of God does not consist of eating and drinking, but of righteousness, peace, and joy in the Holy Spirit."[39] And the reference reflects a quite closely equivalent emphasis in the Jesus tradition: that God's eschatological rule was already being manifested in the present, particularly through the Spirit.[40] In both cases it was the powerful activity of the Spirit which was regarded as the manifestation of God's final rule. Hence Paul's thought of the Spirit as the first part of the inheritance which is the kingdom.[41] For both Jesus and Paul, in other words, the Spirit *is* the presence of the kingdom still to come in its fullness.[42] To find such an awkward tension — between a kingdom already present and yet still to come — and some resolution of the tension in the experience of the Spirit in two teachers related to the degree that Jesus and Paul were can hardly be pure coincidence. More likely Paul was both aware of and influenced by the Jesus tradition at this point.[43]

(3) The same text (Rom. 14.17) points up another feature in Paul where we may again see influence from the Jesus tradition. That is in relation to a restrictiveness in Jewish practice of table fellowship against which both Jesus and Paul protested. For the kingdom also featured both in Jesus' protest against the restrictiveness of Pharisaic table fellowship[44] and in Paul's equivalent protest against a practice of table fellowship too much determined by concerns

---

38.

	Jesus-Synoptics	*Pauline corpus*
kingdom	ca. 105	14
Spirit	13	110+

39. Cf. 1 Cor. 4.20 — "the kingdom of God is not a matter of word but of power."

40. Matt. 12.28/Luke 11.20.

41. 1 Cor. 6.9-11; Gal. 4.6-7; also Eph. 1.13-14. See further below §18.2.

42. See further my "Spirit and Kingdom" (§18 n. 45 below); also *Unity* 213-14; so also Thompson, *Clothed* 206. The significance of this point is insufficiently recognized by G. Haufe, "Reich Gottes bei Paulus und in der Jesus tradition," *NTS* 31 (1985) 467-72, and N. Walter, "Paul and the Early Christian Jesus-Tradition," in Wedderburn, ed., *Paul* 51-80 (here 63).

43. See also Kümmel, "Jesus und Paulus," *Heilsgeschehen* 439-56 (here 448-49); G. Johnston, " 'Kingdom of God' Sayings in Paul's Letters," in Richardson and Hurd, eds., *From Jesus to Paul* 143-56 (here 152-55); Witherington, *End* (§12 n. 1) 74; Wenham, *Paul* 71-78, who in his ch. 2 rather ambitiously tests other points of possible correlation around the kingdom theme.

44. Luke 14.12-24/Matt. 22.1-10. By general consent, "Pharisees" is a nickname designating the Pharisees as "the separated ones" (see Schürer, *History* 2.395-400), and it was in the matter of clean and unclean and other purity rules regulating the consumption of food (so table fellowship) that their "separateness" was most noticeable. See further my *Partings* 41-42, 107-11; and below §14 n. 100. Luke reminds us, however (7.36; 11.37; 14.1), that there were different levels of observance among those designated as Pharisees.

about clean and unclean (14.14, 20).[45] The triple link (kingdom, Spirit, table fellowship) is rather striking.[46]

All the more so when it is correlated with a further table fellowship parallel between Jesus and Paul. One of the features of Jesus' ministry which provoked most hostile comment was his willingness to eat with "sinners."[47] And one of the most significant events in Paul's early ministry was his confrontation with Peter over the latter's "separation" from table fellowship with "Gentile sinners" (Gal. 2.12, 14-15). Paul's outrage would be all the more understandable if there was a known and shared tradition of Jesus having discounted the laws of clean and unclean (Mark 7.15). The tradition was evidently understood with differing force.[48] But the sudden insertion into the context (Gal. 2.15, 17) of the term which focused the offence in both cases ("sinner") is again striking. The implication may well be that Paul was deliberately alluding to the Jesus tradition of Jesus' table fellowship with sinners, in the knowledge that Peter would recognize the allusion and in the hope that Peter would be shamed accordingly.[49]

Taken together, then, these episodes certainly strengthen the likelihood that Paul both knew and was significantly influenced by his knowledge of the life and ministry of Jesus as one who ate with "sinners" and who saw the kingdom foreshadowed in such table fellowship.

(4) A further feature has again not been given the attention it deserves. This is the obvious inferences to be drawn from Rom. 8.15-17 and Gal. 4.6-7.

45. The use of the terms *koinos* ("profane, unclean") and *katharos* ("clean") in 14.14 and 20 is a sure indication that the scruples addressed in Romans 14 were Jewish in character. *Koinos* in Greek means simply "common." It only gains the sense "profane, unclean" from its use to render the equivalent Hebrew terms *(tame', chol)* in the Maccabean and post-Maccabean period (1 Macc. 1.47, 62; Mark 7.2, 5; Acts 10.14; 11.8). See further my *Romans* 818-19 and 825-26; and below §20.3 and §24.3 n. 45.

46. Stuhlmacher, "Jesustradition" 246, also points out a possible echo of Luke 15.2 in Paul's appeal to the Romans to "accept" one another (Rom. 14.1, 3; 15.7); despite the use of different verbs, the common context of table fellowship, linked to the theme of Jesus' servant ministry (Rom. 15.8; cf. Mark 10.42-45/Luke 22.25-27), is again noteworthy (see also Thompson, *Clothed* 231-33).

47. Mark 2.15-17 pars.; Matt. 11.19/Luke 7.34; Luke 7.39; 15.1-2; 19.7. For the significance of the term "sinner" see below §14.5a and n. 101.

48. The implication of Rom. 14.14 is that Paul knew the more antithetical Markan version and would have agreed with Mark's gloss in Mark 7.19 ("thus declaring all foods clean"). But Matthew's version is significantly softer (Matt. 15.11, 17-18). See further my "Jesus and Ritual Purity: A Study of the Tradition-History of Mark 7.15," *Jesus, Paul and the Law* 37-60. Matthew's version and Peter's conduct in Antioch (Gal. 2.12) are consistent with the Acts portrayal of Peter as one who (despite having been Jesus' principal disciple) had "never eaten anything profane or unclean" (Acts 10.14; 11.8). See also Thompson, *Clothed* 185-99; Wenham, *Paul* 92-97.

49. Dunn, "Jesus Tradition" 171; A. J. M. Wedderburn, "Paul and Jesus: Similarity and Continuity," in Wedderburn, ed., *Paul* 117-43 (here 124, 130-43).

The similarity of the passages indicates that Paul was referring to a common experience among early Christians — that is, the experience of the Spirit crying "Abba! Father!" through them. From this shared experience he draws two important points. First, that the experience attests their standing as children of God. And second, that the experience is of the Spirit of Christ, the Spirit of God's Son (Gal. 4.6), and thus attests that they share in some sense in Christ's sonship — "heirs together with Christ" (Rom. 8.17).

This must mean that Paul saw the experience and practice of the Abba prayer as something distinctive for the first Christians. He could hardly have drawn such a far-reaching conclusion from the prayer if it had been in common use in Jewish pietistic circles in the land of Israel or elsewhere.[50] And what would point him to that conclusion? The most obvious answer is that the Abba prayer was remembered in Christian circles as a characteristic feature of Jesus' own prayer. In other words, it was probably Jesus' own practice which stamped the Aramaic term with its character as a quasi-sacred prayer form. And it was probably the memory of Jesus thus hallowing the address which ensured that the Aramaic term was preserved into the Greek-speaking churches. This accords with one of the most widely accepted conclusions of modern critical study of the Jesus tradition: that Jesus' prayer life was indeed characterized and distinguished by his use of Abba to address God.[51] In which case the conclusion is hard to avoid that Paul was aware both of the practice of the Abba prayer in early Christian circles and of its origin.[52]

(5) There is still further evidence to be considered regarding possible echoes of Jesus' teaching. But that is better left for later discussion.[53] And hopefully enough has been set out already to give added significance to other less specific allusions. In particular, if indeed there was fair knowledge of Jesus' ministry "below the surface" of Paul's dialogue with his churches, then texts like 2 Cor. 10.1[54] and Phil. 1.8[55] (referred to at the beginning of §8) can

50. This consideration has been given too little weight in evaluating the historicity of the Gospel traditions regarding Jesus' own prayer practice.

51. This despite the infrequency of references and the difficulty of establishing the case by the criterion of dissimilarity (see further my *Christology* 26-28; also *Romans* 453-54).

52. Wenham, *Paul* 277-80, deduces from the use of "Abba" in Romans 8 (cf. Mark 14.36) that Paul knew the Gethsemane story. It could be argued equally, on the basis of the close link between Spirit and sonship in Rom. 8.15-17 and Gal. 4.6-7, that Paul knew an account of Jesus' baptism and anointing (Mark 1.10-11 pars.).

53. See below §23.5.

54. Cf. particularly C. Wolff, "Humility and Self-Denial in Jesus' Life and Message and in the Apostolic Existence of Paul," in Wedderburn, ed., *Paul* 145-60.

55. *Splanchna Christou Iēsou* ("the compassion of Christ Jesus") may echo a term *(splanchnizomai)* characteristically and distinctively used of Jesus' emotional response at various points during his ministry — Mark 1.41; 6.34/Matt. 14.14; Mark 8.2/Matt. 15.32; Mark 9.22; Matt. 9.36; 20.34; Luke 7.13; also Matt. 18.27; Luke 10.33; 15.20.

be identified more readily as references not only to his self-giving death but also to the character of his ministry as a whole.[56]

This last suggestion becomes all the more weighty if we allow a greater element of *imitatio Christi* in Paul's exhortation than is usually acknowledged. I refer here particularly to Rom. 13.14: "put on the Lord Jesus Christ." The reference is not simply to a once-for-all change of clothing at baptism,[57] since the exhortation is to those long since baptized. What is envisaged, therefore, is something which can be repeated. The more probable allusion is to the stage: an actor playing the role of a character "put on" that character, assumed that character for the length of the play.[58] What Paul implies, then, is the intensity of dedication and application in living out the life of Christ (cf. Gal. 2.20) which the actor shows in "living the part."[59]

Another indication of some sort of *imitatio Christi* is Rom. 15.1-5: we ought "not to please ourselves . . . for the Christ too did not please himself," with the final plea "to live in harmony among yourselves in accordance with Christ Jesus *(kata Christon Iēsoun)*." The reference is primarily to the passion (15.3). But in a context of community fellowship,[60] where it is "the Christ" who is referred to (15.3) and with an echo of his being "servant of the circumcised" (15.8), it is unlikely that many would think solely of Jesus' death.[61] Such an appeal to Jesus as an antidote to communal disaffection is explicit in two other passages: 1 Cor. 11.1 ("Be imitators of me as I am of Christ") and Phil. 2.5 ("Let this mind be in you which was also in Christ Jesus").[62] It is hardly straining either evidence or probabilities to infer that Paul's readers would give content to such exhortations by recalling stories about and teaching of Jesus.[63]

---

56. On Rom. 15.3 see further below §23.5. The same could be argued for 2 Cor. 8.9 and Phil. 2.5, but the point depends on later argument (§§11.4, 5c).

57. As can be argued for Gal. 3.27. See further below §17.2.

58. Dionysius of Halicarnassus 11.5 attests this use for the first century BCE: "to put on Tarquin" = to play the role of Tarquin (LSJ, *endyō;* A. Oepke, *TDNT* 2.320).

59. See further Thompson, *Clothed* 149-58, who draws in the subsequent talk of "putting on the new nature, which is being renewed in knowledge in accordance with the image of him who created it . . ." (Col. 3.10-11, which also echoes Gal. 3.27-28; see my *Colossians* 220-23; cf. Eph. 4.24).

60. See above (2) and (3).

61. See further my *Romans* 838, 840 and Thompson, *Clothed* 221-25, 228-29.

62. Note how each exhortation climaxes an appeal for communal harmony (1 Cor. 10.31–11.1; Phil. 2.1-5). Although the christology of Phil. 2.5-11 is disputed, the appeal of the passage is, in part at least, to Jesus the man, whose obedience to death characterized his whole life. On 2.5 see further below and §11.4 n. 66.

63. Paul's other reference to being "imitators of the Lord" (1 Thes. 1.6) refers solely to his passion.

Rom. 6.17 may also be more significant here than has usually been realized. Paul reminds his readers "that when you were slaves of sin you gave your obedience from the heart to the one to whom you were handed over as a pattern of teaching" (Rom. 6.17). The clause is awkward, but its general meaning clear enough. Less certain is the meaning of the final phrase, *typos didachēs,* "pattern of teaching." Most think it refers to a fixed catechetical form, already well enough known for Paul to allude to it without further detail.[64] But *typos* in the Pauline corpus almost always has a personal reference — a particular individual (or individuals) providing a pattern or example of conduct.[65] The appositional syntax here ("to whom as a pattern") is the same as in two of these other cases.[66] The verb ("hand over," *paradidōmi*) is most common in Paul in reference to the handing over of a person to another authority or power.[67] And we have no other clear evidence of extensive catechetical teaching as already regarded as a necessary precondition of baptism.[68] The nearest parallel is Col. 2.6: "as you received the tradition of Christ Jesus as Lord, walk in him." And that also suggests a Christian conduct to be modeled on the traditions of Jesus passed on to new converts.[69]

In short, once grant the likelihood that Paul and the churches to which he wrote shared a good deal of common Jesus tradition, familiar enough on both sides to be a matter of allusion and implicit reference, the probability becomes strong that Paul would have naturally and without contrivance referred to that tradition in just that way. Against that plausible background several passages in Paul gain additional illumination and resonance. And the conclusion becomes increasingly persuasive that knowledge of and interest in the life and ministry of Jesus was an integral part of his theology, albeit referred to only *sotto voce* in his written theology.

---

64. See, e.g., Käsemann, *Romans* 181; Moo, *Romans* 400-402; Fitzmyer, *Romans* 449-50. Nanos, *Mystery* 212-8, suggests that the reference is to the apostolic decree (Acts 15.29).

65. Rom. 5.14; Phil. 3.17; 1 Thes. 1.17; 2 Thes. 3.9; 1 Tim. 4.12; Tit. 2.7; so also 1 Pet. 5.3; Ignatius, *Magnesians* 6.2; otherwise only 1 Cor. 10.6.

66. Phil. 3.17; 2 Thes. 3.9 ("us/ourselves as a pattern").

67. Rom. 1.24, 26, 28; 1 Cor. 5.5; 13.3; 15.24; 2 Cor. 4.11. Of Jesus' being handed over see above §7 n. 71. The same verb is a t.t. for the transmission of tradition (1 Cor. 11.2, 23; 15.3), but the imagery here is of a slave being "handed over" to a new master, whereas the idea of being "handed over" to a catechetical pattern is rather strained.

68. See further below §17.2.

69. See further my *Colossians* 138-41.

§8.4 Jesus

An initially attractive possibility is that the use of the personal name "Jesus" on its own would also indicate an interest in the human person Jesus of Nazareth as such. For the references to Jesus in Paul are so overwhelmingly to "Jesus Christ," or "Christ Jesus," or "the Lord Jesus," or some combination of all three titles,[70] that the relatively few references to "Jesus" alone could suggest an allusion to the person behind the "titles of exaltation." However, the line of inquiry does not in fact advance the present discussion in any significant degree.

The name "Jesus" (alone) appears in the Pauline corpus 16 times.[71] But the great majority of these refer to Jesus' death and resurrection.[72] In 1 Cor. 12.3, "Jesus is accursed" is set in antithesis to "Jesus is Lord." A reference to some disparagement of the earthly Jesus cannot be entirely excluded,[73] but in context any disparagement is as likely to have been directed against the exalted Lord (also "Jesus"). Similarly in 2 Cor. 11.4 the "other Jesus" preached could refer to a differently interpreted Jesus tradition. But most assume that what the "false apostles" (11.13) were preaching was more likely a "theology of glory" focusing on the exalted Jesus.[74] In 2 Cor. 4.5 Paul says, "we proclaim Jesus Christ as Lord, and ourselves as your slaves for Jesus' sake." The unusual phrase "for Jesus' sake" could refer to the earthly Jesus, but a Paul who made no distinction between earthly and exalted Jesus (both were "Jesus") is hardly making such a point obvious. And Phil. 2.10 has in view a universal obeisance before the exalted Jesus ("at the name of Jesus, every knee should bend . . ."). Hardly expressive of a particular interest in the life of Jesus.

Only Rom. 3.26 may be of some relevance. It refers to a person as "of the faith of Jesus" (literally). Many now assume that the last two words *(pistis Iēsou)* denote "the faith(fulness) of Jesus." That would read the text as referring to a person whose identity or status was derived from the faithful way in which Jesus discharged his ministry up to and particularly in his death on the cross. The interpretation is unlikely, in my judgment, though the preceding reference to "the faith" (probably added to the formula in 3.25)

---

70. "Jesus Christ" (23), "Christ Jesus" (48), "Lord Jesus" (27), "Lord Jesus Christ" (52) — excluding Ephesians and the Pastorals. The figures are inexact since there are many variant readings (most often "Jesus Christ" for "Christ Jesus" and vice versa).

71. Rom. 3.26; 8.11; 1 Cor. 12.3; 2 Cor. 4.5b, 10 (twice), 11 (twice), 14; 11.4; Gal. 6.17; Phil. 2.10; 1 Thes. 1.10; 4.14 (twice); also Eph. 4.21.

72. Rom. 8.11; 2 Cor. 4.10-11, 14; Gal. 6.17; 1 Thes. 1.10; 4.14.

73. See those cited in my *Jesus and the Spirit* 234-35 and 420 n. 177.

74. Hence Paul's emphasis throughout the letter on sharing Christ's sufferings. See below §18.5.

could give it more weight in this instance. That is an issue to which we will have to return.[75] Without that interpretation, however, we simply have a variant for the fuller phrase "the faith of Jesus Christ" (3.22), and no particular reference to Jesus' ministry prior to his death can be deduced — not from a text whose focus is on Christ's sacrificial death, at any rate.

§8.5 Messiah

If the name "Jesus" adds nothing to the present discussion, what about the name "Christ"? To describe "Christ" as a "name" is to acknowledge the almost universally accepted fact that "Christ" has become more or less equivalent to a proper name in Paul's letters.[76] That in itself is an astonishing fact. For it means that at the time of Paul's writing, the Christian claim that Jesus was Messiah[77] was no longer controversial. No longer was it necessary for Paul to argue the case that Jesus was indeed Israel's long-awaited Davidic Messiah.[78]

To be sure, 1 Cor. 1.23 does indicate that the proclamation of a crucified Jesus as Messiah/Christ was an offence to Jews: "we proclaim Christ crucified, to Jews a stumbling block *(skandalon)*."[79] But what the image of the "stumbling block" portrays is not simply someone grieved at or hostile to a particular teaching. For the *skandalon* denotes an obstacle over which someone might actually trip (not simply disapprove of).[80] That is to say, what is in view in 1 Cor.

75. See below §14.8.

76. So, e.g., Goppelt, *Theology* 2.67; M. Hengel, "Christos"; "Christological Titles in Early Christianity," in Charlesworth, ed., *Messiah* 425-48 (here 444). Jesus is referred to simply as Christ (or the Christ) nearly 180 times in the undisputed Paulines (i.e., apart from Ephesians and the Pastorals). See also n. 70 above.

77. *Christos* ("Christ"), of course, is simply the Greek for the Hebrew *Mashiah* ("Messiah").

78. Rom. 1.3 ("descended from the seed of David") is already a formula (see above §7.3) which Paul can simply cite without making anything of it. That we can indeed speak of such a general expectation within Israel, and as the dominant form of the expectation within the different strands of messianic hope, is one of the main findings of both The Messiah Symposium (Charlesworth, ed., *Messiah* xv) and Collins, *Scepter*. This finding gives added weight to Dahl's earlier observations in "Crucified Messiah" 38-40. Collins also reviews the evidence for messiah as "son of God" (particularly 4Q246 and 4Q174) and concludes that "the notion that the messiah was Son of God in a special sense was rooted in Judaism" (*Scepter* ch. 7, here 169).

79. Similarly Rom. 9.33 (citing Isa. 8.14) and Gal. 5.11. Note also Trypho's comment in Justin's *Dialogue:* "It is just this that we cannot comprehend, that you set your hope on one crucified" (*Dialogue* 10.3; also 90.1), cited by Hengel, "Titles" (above n. 76) 426-27.

80. Rom. 14.13, 21 (note 14.23); 1 Cor. 8.13 (note 8.10-11).

1.23 is the offence most Jews took at being invited actually to believe in and commit themselves to this crucified Christ.[81] For the rest, we may take it, they were not so much concerned about or interested in the new Jewish sect centred on this Jesus. That presumably is why the Nazarenes who remained in Judea were able to flourish there relatively undisturbed (Acts 21.20!). And presumably it was for the same reason that Paul felt no need to instruct his converts on how to meet any challenges from the local synagogues on the point.

If this were all there was to the use of "Christ" in Paul's speaking of Jesus, we would be no further forward in our present quest. For it would mean that any memory of Jesus' messiahship as a feature of or an issue during Jesus' ministry would have been lost to sight and forgotten.[82] However, there is more to Paul's usage than most recognize. In fact, there are quite a number of passages in Paul where *Christos* seems to retain something at least of its more titular sense and where we should more properly translate "the Christ."[83]

In Romans we may refer particularly to 9.3 and 5.[84] In a context where Paul's thought was entirely taken up with questions of Jewish identity and privilege it makes very obvious sense to translate:

> I could pray that I myself be anathema from the Christ for the sake of my brothers, my kinsmen in terms of the flesh . . . theirs are the fathers and from them came the Christ insofar as the flesh is concerned (Rom. 9.3-5).

That it was the fleshly relationships of "the Christ" which Paul had particularly in mind simply strengthens the point. A similar case could be put for Rom. 15.3 and 7: "Let each of us please his neighbour. . . . For the Christ too did not please himself" (15.2-3); "Therefore welcome one another, as the Christ also welcomed you." The possibility is strengthened if we accept that "pleasing the neighbour *(plēsion)*" is Paul's way of recalling the love command — "love your neighbour *(plēsion)*" (13.9, 10).[85] For that in turn

---

81. See further my "How Controversial Was Paul's Christology?" in M. C. de Boer, ed., *From Jesus to John: Essays on Jesus and New Testament Christology,* M. de Jonge FS (JSNTS 84; Sheffield: Sheffield Academic, 1993) 148-67 (here 154-55).

82. I remain strongly of the opinion that messiahship was in fact an issue during Jesus' ministry; see my "Messianic Ideas and Their Influence on the Jesus of History," in Charlesworth, ed., *Messiah* 365-81.

83. Dahl notes "messianic connotations" in 1 Cor. 10.4; 15.22; 2 Cor. 5.10; 11.2-3; Eph. 1.10, 12, 20; 5.14; Phil. 1.15, 17; 3.7 ("Messiahship" 17 and 24 n. 11). The case, of course, does not rest on the presence (or absence) of the definite article; on the article with proper names see BDF §260.

84. Rom. 9.5 is the only generally recognized example (e.g., Dahl, "Messiahship" 17; Fitzmyer, "Christology" 83; *Romans* 111).

85. Apart from the equivalent text in Gal. 5.14, Rom. 15.2 is the only other time that *plēsion* appears in the undisputed Paulines.

sounds like an echo of Jesus' teaching, and with 15.2-3, an echo also of
Jesus' own implementation of his neighbour-love teaching.[86] Rom. 15.19
could also be mentioned as one of a number of references to "the gospel of
the Christ,"[87] references which also gain more weight in light of the earlier
discussion (§8.3(1)).[88] And it is just possible that the distinctively Pauline
use of the double name "Christ Jesus" (as against "Jesus Christ") is a direct
translation equivalent of "Messiah Jesus," with *Christos* still bearing titular
force.[89]

        We need not press the point any further. It would be surprising if Paul
the Jew showed no interest whatsoever in the messiahship of Jesus. Certainly
it remains a striking fact that the titular significance has almost disappeared.
Nevertheless, allusions such as those above suggest that "Messiah/Christ"
had not entirely lost its titular significance for Paul. More to the immediate
point, such references also suggest that the role of Messiah recalled by Paul
in his use of "Christ" included Jesus' ministry before the cross as well as that
of "Christ crucified." When we add in the initial observation that Paul also
regarded the fact of Jesus' Jewishness as important,[90] the point gains still more
significance.

§8.6 Adam

We have gleaned a good deal more about Paul's knowledge of and interest in
the life and ministry of Jesus, prior to his passion, than has usually been
recognized. Overall, however, the harvest has been fairly meagre — hardly
enough to provide a square "life of Jesus" meal, let alone a harvest home
banquet. However, there is still one other aspect of Paul's christology which
needs to be taken into account at this point. That is what we might call the
representative significance of Jesus in Paul's theology.

---

        86. See further below §23.5.
        87. Rom. 15.19; 1 Cor. 9.12; 2 Cor. 2.12; 9.13; 10.14; Gal. 1.7; Phil. 1.27; 1 Thes.
3.2.
        88. Other "Christ" references in Romans where there may still be an overtone of
"*the* Christ" are 7.4; 8.35; 14.18; 16.16. In Galatians we might also mention 3.16; 5.2, 4
(both anarthrous), 24; 6.12. See also n. 83 above. Given its emphasis on "according to the
scriptures" we should add 1 Cor. 15.3 (Hengel, "Titles" [above n. 76] 444-45). Wright,
Climax 41-55, has been a lone voice in arguing that "*Christos* in Paul should regularly be
read as 'Messiah,' " particularly because of the term's "incorporative" significance (41);
but note also Hahn's earlier protest (*Titles* 182, 186).
        89. McCasland, "Christ Jesus" 382-83; Cranfield, *Romans* 836-37. Dahl had
already observed that *Iēsous* remains Jesus' proper name: "The confession reads: 'Jesus
is Lord' . . . or 'Jesus Christ is Lord' . . . , but not 'Christ is Lord' " ("Messiahship" 16).
        90. Rom. 1.3; 15.8; Gal. 4.4.

This comes out most explicitly in what can properly be called Paul's Adam christology.[91] Quite explicitly in two important passages, Paul deliberately sets Jesus alongside Adam, as the one who answers to the clamant and long-standing emergency brought about for humankind by Adam's first disobedience. The two passages are Rom. 5.12-21 and 1 Cor. 15.20-22.[92]

> [15]Not as the trespass, so also the effect of grace; for if by the trespass of the one, the many died, how much more the grace of God and the gift in grace, which is of the one man Jesus Christ, has overflowed to the many. . . . [17]For if by the trespass of the one death reigned through the one, how much more those who receive the abundance of grace and of the gift of righteousness shall reign in life through the one, Jesus Christ . . . (Rom. 5.15-19).
>
> [20]For since death came through a human being, the resurrection of the dead has come also through a human being. [21]For as in Adam all die, so also in Christ shall all be made alive (1 Cor. 15.21-22).

The point for us here is the fact that Adam is clearly understood in some sort of representative capacity. Adam is humankind, an individual who embodies or represents a whole race of people.[93] But in that case, so also does Christ. Adam "is the type of the one to come" (Rom. 5.14), that is, Christ. That is to say, Christ is the eschatological counterpart of primeval Adam. Adam is the pattern or "prototype"[94] of Christ in that each begins an epoch, and the character of each epoch is established by their action. Hence all who belong to the first epoch are "in Adam," and all who belong to the second are "in Christ" (1 Cor. 15.22).

All this refers most directly to Jesus' death and resurrection, understood as an epochal act equivalent to Adam's primeval transgression. Does it have any bearing on our present concern? The answer probably lies in the use made in early Christian reflection of another Adam/humankind passage — Ps. 8.4-6:[95]

---

91. In what follows, see also my *Christology* 108-13.
92. We will take up the further text, 1 Cor. 15.45, later (§10.2).
93. See above §§4.2, 6.
94. Käsemann, *Romans* 151.
95. In order to maintain the psalm's reference to the representative human individual and the force of the phrase "son of man" I have retained the anachronistic traditional rendering of "man" for the Hebrew *enosh* ("man, mankind" — BDB; Greek *anthrōpos*) and "son of man" for Hebrew *ben adam* (Greek *huios anthrōpou*). NRSV's rendering, "human beings" and "mortals," makes the argument of Heb. 2.6-9 (see below) much less cogent and loses the parallel "son of man" = "man," which is so important for understanding the use of "son of man" *(huios anthrōpou)* in the Gospels.

> ⁴What is man that you remember him,
>   or the son of man that you care for him?
> ⁵You made him a little lower than the angels,
>   and crowned him with glory and honour.
> ⁶You put him in charge over the works of your hands,
>   and put everything in subjection under his feet.

We know that this text was the subject of some early Christian reflection, in Paul but also elsewhere. In three cases in the Pauline corpus it is the last line of the passage (Ps. 8.6b) which is either quoted or echoed.[96] That is to say, Paul and others evidently found in Ps. 8.6b an appropriate description of Jesus' exaltation (most clearly in 1 Cor. 15.27).

The logic of this use of Ps. 8.4-6 is plain. The psalmist was assumed to have described God's purpose in creating humankind. God's intention had been to give his human creation authority over the rest of his creation. The reference will no doubt have been primarily to Gen. 1.28: God created human male and female as the climax of his creation, and said to them, "Be fruitful and multipy, fill the earth and subdue it, and have dominion over the fish of the sea and over the birds of the air and over every living thing that moves upon the earth." By referring Ps. 8.6b to Jesus the clear implication is that this divine purpose was seen to have been fulfilled in the exaltation of Christ. In his exaltation to God's right hand Christ (at last) fulfilled human destiny. All things were at last being put in subjection under the feet of God's representative man.

Of course, the reference in this use of Ps. 8.6 is still to the Christ who died and was raised. But the implication of its use is that Jesus was being described as one who had fulfilled the *complete* divine plan for humankind. His work could be seen through the lens not only of Ps. 8.6, but also of the whole passage (Ps. 8.4-6). Jesus only fulfilled the role of Ps. 8.6b because he could be said to have come to it via Ps. 8.4-6a. This logic is not evident in any of the references to Psalm 8 in the Pauline letters. But it is clear in the use made of Ps. 8.4-6 in Heb. 2.5-9. There the point is very clear. It was not to angels that the coming world was subjected (2.5). Nor yet at this stage to humans. "As it is, we do not yet see everything put in subjection to man/humankind. But we do see Jesus, who 'for a little was made lower than the angels,'[97] now 'crowned with glory and honour' . . . ." In other words, the divine programme for humankind had failed to achieve its goal: humankind was not exercising the intended dominion over the rest of creation. But in Jesus God had "run the programme through again." And in him it *had* achieved its goal: all things were at last under the feet of God's man.

96. 1 Cor. 15.27; Phil. 3.21; Eph. 1.22.
97. Heb. 2.9 follows the LXX at this point.

It is likely that Hebrews has simply demonstrated the logic of the early use made of Ps. 8.4-6 and that Paul's briefer allusions reflect the same logic. In which case we can say that Paul's Adam christology embraced not only Jesus' death and resurrection. It also embraced his life as a whole. It was not simply that his death and resurrection were somehow representative. It was rather that his death was the death of a representative person, a representative life. In other words, in his Adamic role Jesus first shared the actual destiny of the first Adam (death) before he achieved the intended goal for Adam (dominion over all things). In this highly symbolic christology, Jesus first represented old Adam before he became last Adam (1 Cor. 15.45).[98]

This line of theological reflection may seem a little speculative and insufficiently grounded in Paul's own writings. But the idea that Jesus shared all the negative features of the human condition, life under the powers of sin and death (also "under the law"), is in fact well founded elsewhere in Paul.

Most striking is Rom. 8.3: "What the law was unable to do in that it was weak through the flesh, God did by sending his own Son in the very likeness of sinful flesh and as a sin offering and condemned sin in the flesh." This is a text to which we will have to return more than once.[99] Here we focus simply on the key phrase — "in the very likeness of sinful flesh (en homoi-ōmati sarkos hamartias)." There is considerable debate as to what precisely homoiōma signifies. But probably it denotes a likeness which embodies the reality "enlikened" so far as that is possible, as we would say, "a mirror image," an exact replica.[100] What is thus "enlikened"? The answer is, "sinful flesh" — that is, as we have seen, flesh not sinful in itself, but flesh in its weakness and corruptibility, vulnerable to and in the event dominated by the power of sin.[101] "Sinful flesh" is (in the event) sin-committing humankind, enslaved by human desire, on the way to death. The phrase as a whole ("in the very likeness of sinful flesh") seems to be designed to stress closeness of identity with the human condition, which the power of sin so ruthlessly exploits and which ends in death, without implying that Jesus himself actually succumbed to that power (cf. 2 Cor. 5.21).[102] The theological logic is obviously that God could only deal with the problem of "sinful flesh" by sending

98. See further below §§9.1 and 10.2.
99. See below §§9.2(2), 9.3, 11.3a.
100. See discussion in my *Romans* 316-17 and "Paul's Understanding" (§9 n. 1) 37-38.
101. See above §§3.3, 5.3-5, 6.7.
102. Here we need to recall the ambiguity of Paul's concept of death — both as a consequence of human state and as punishment of transgression, and the distinction between "sin" and "transgression" (see above §§4.6 and 5.7).

his Son in complete solidarity and identity with humankind in its existence under the powers of sin and death.[103]

The same point emerges in the parallel passage in Gal. 4.4-5: "God sent his Son, born of woman, born under the law, in order that he might redeem those under the law, in order that we might receive the adoption." As we noted above, "born of woman" means simply "a human person."[104] And "born under the law" indicates Jesus the Jew, that is, in a state of tutelage (Gal. 4.1-3).[105] In other words, Jesus from birth functioned in a representative capacity, representing humankind in general and his fellow Jews in particular.[106] Paul could even claim that Jesus alone is Abraham's "seed" (Gal. 3.16), not as a narrowing of the promise, but precisely so that all Abraham's seed could be included, so that all might share in Abraham's inheritance in him and through him (3.28-29). Only as the Christ fulfilled this representative role could he redeem those "under the law" and bring to humankind the effective status of God's children.[107]

We could perhaps add here Phil. 2.6-8. The Philippian hymn (2.6-11) seems to be impregnated with Adam christology.[108] Here we might simply note the second part of 2.7: "being (or becoming) in the likeness of humans *(homoiōmati anthrōpōn)*, and being found in form as humankind *(hōs anthrōpos)*." The parallel to Rom. 8.3 is quite striking. And whatever it means precisely, it seems to denote that Christ in his life, prior to his death, was reckoned to be representative of humankind. It was this fact which gave his death its significance, as a death which broke the power of sin and death for humankind.

To sum up. There does seem to have been abroad in first generation Christianity an already quite sophisticated Adam christology. This was used not only in reference to Christ's death (and resurrection), but also to the presupposition of his death. The presupposition was that Jesus' life was also Adamic in character. That is to say, the first stage of Adam christology was Jesus running through the first part of God's programme for humanity. Jesus' representative capacity included humankind in its weakness under sin and

---

103. The nuance of the phrase is so subtle that there is always likely to be debate on its precise force; in recent discussion see V. P. Branick, "The Sinful Flesh of the Son of God (Rom. 8.3): A Key Image of Pauline Theology," *CBQ* 47 (1985) 246-62, and F. M. Gillman, "Another Look at Romans 8.3: 'In the Likeness of Sinful Flesh,' " *CBQ* 49 (1987) 597-604. See further my *Romans* 421-22.

104. See above n. 4.

105. See above §6.4.

106. Note again the intermeshing of the story of humankind with that of Israel, precisely in Jesus himself (see above §§4.4, 6, 7). See further my *Galatians* 215-17.

107. Again see further below §9.3.

108. The claim is much disputed; see further below §11.4.

subjection to death, as also Israel in its confinement under the law. Jesus' representative capacity in the first instance was solidarity with the Adam who dies. The theological logic of this is already summed up in the early centuries in the classic formulation of Gregory of Nazianzus: "What has not been assumed cannot be healed" (*Epistle* 101.7). Or in the alternative formulation of Irenaeus: "Christ became what we are in order that we might become what he is" (*Adversus Haereses* 5 preface), and Athanasius: "He became man that we might become divine" (*De Incarnatione* 54).

§8.7 The incarnate Son?

In the light of subsequent discussion (§11) it may be appropriate to speak also of a concept of incarnation, as at least implicit in Paul's christology. In particular, if an active Wisdom christology (as well as Adam christology) lies behind the talk of God sending his Son (Gal. 4.4; Rom. 8.3), then the sending is from heaven and the mission of the sent Son presumably starts from birth.[109]

Any implicit thought of incarnation comes to more explicit expression within the most important statement of Wisdom christology, in what may well have been the last Pauline letter written before his death — Col. 1.15-20. For in the great Wisdom hymn of 1.15-20, or its extension into a second matching stanza,[110] we read: "in him all the fullness [of God] was pleased to dwell" (1.19). The key term is "fullness" *(plērōma)*, a term which in itself denotes completeness.[111] What its precise reference is here has been the subject of considerable debate. But the growing consensus now is that it expresses the conviction that God's power and presence fill the universe, a conviction which comes to expression quite regularly in earlier Jewish writing.[112] We should further note that the idea of divine indwelling human beings (using the same verb) is also present in Jewish writing.[113] Likewise the verb "pleased" is regularly used in the LXX with God as the subject to describe his good pleasure.[114] Consequently we can assume that the ambiguity of the text cloaks the thought of the full presence of God being pleased to dwell in Christ.[115]

---

109. See below §11.3, though note the hesitations voiced there.

110. See below §11 n. 41.

111. Hence its regular Greek use for the full complement of a ship's crew (LSJ, *plērōma* 3).

112. E.g., Jer. 23.24; Wis. 1.6-7; *Ep. Arist.* 132; Philo, *Leg. All.* 3.4; *Gigant.* 47; *Conf.* 136; *Mos.* 2.238.

113. Wis. 1.4; *T. Zeb.* 8.2; *T. Ben.* 6.4; *1 Enoch* 49.3.

114. E.g., Ps. 68.16 — "God was pleased to dwell in it [Zion]"; *3 Macc.* 2.16; other examples in G. Schrenk, *TDNT* 2.738.

115. See the fuller discussion in my *Colossians* 99-102.

The point is strengthened by its repetition in 2.9: "in him [as usual, Christ] dwells all the fullness of the deity in bodily form." Two of the key words are repeated from 1.19 — "fullness *(plērōma)*" and "dwells *(katoikeō)*." There is no reason why either should be given a different reference from that in 1.19. Two additional terms, however, help sharpen the thought, both of them, oddly enough, *hapax legomena* in biblical Greek.

One is "in bodily form," the adverb *sōmatikōs*. We have already seen that *sōma* ("body") indicates the bodiness of a person, what enables the person to encounter other embodied persons.[116] So the obvious significance of *sōmatikōs* is to emphasize the encounterable reality of the divine indwelling in Christ. "*Sōmatikōs* underscores the accessibility (come-at-ableness) of the divine epiphany."[117] But that thought can hardly have reference to anything other than Jesus' life on earth, or at least to his ministry,[118] even if the thought goes on to focus on Christ's death (2.11-15). In this too any thought of incarnation is tied closely to the Adam theology also present in Gal. 4.4-5 and Rom. 8.3. The present tense ("continues to dwell") presumably indicates that this function of the earthly Jesus is ongoing. That is to say, Christ in his historical embodiment still brings the character of deity most fully into focus.

The second rare term used in 2.9 is "deity *(theotēs)*." The term would presumably have been known as denoting the nature or essence of deity, that which constitutes deity.[119] In effect the thought is the same as that of 1.19, the more abstract phrase "fulness of divine nature" being preferred here to the phrase "all the [divine] fulness."[120] What is noticeable is that in neither passage does the writer actually say that "the fulness of *God*" dwelled in Christ. In 1.19 the unspecified "all the fulness" is preferred. In 2.9, the unusual *theotēs* ("deity") is preferred to *theos* ("God").

At any rate, the thought of incarnation is very close, if not already present, particularly in Col. 2.9. The uniqueness of the language is simply a reminder that a thought was struggling to come to expression and having to draw upon unusual terminology to express the unprecedented claim. One other point of significance worth noting is that in three of the four texts mentioned in this section, the subject referred to is God's "Son."[121] This feature, together

116. See above §3.2.

117. Dunn, *Colossians* 152; see the fuller discussion there.

118. Given the parallels between 1.19 and Ps. 139.7 and Wis. 1.7, on the one hand, and the account of Jesus' baptism (Mark 1.11) on the other, there could be an allusion to the tradition of the Spirit's descent at Jordan. The *sōmatikōs* of 2.9 may weaken the link (as being less restricted in its reference) and almost certainly rules out the view that only resurrection is in view. For bibliography on both points see my *Colossians* 102 n. 42.

119. BAGD, *theotēs*.

120. Again see further my *Colossians* 151.

121. Rom. 8.3; Gal. 4.4; Col. 1.13.

with the unusual term *theotēs* ("divine nature" — Col. 2.9), was to become a principal building block of subsequent christology.

§8.8 Conclusion

It can be demonstrated with a fair degree of probability, then, that Paul both knew and cared about the ministry of Jesus prior to his passion and death; that he recalled, alluded to, and was himself influenced in his own theology and conduct by important features of the Jesus tradition; that Jesus' Jewishness and messiahship remained important aspects of Paul's christology; that he regarded Jesus' representative significance as a fundamental feature of his theology's overview of history and salvation; and that the thought of God's actual presence in the earthly Jesus comes to clear expression in his later theology.

The theological importance of these findings should also be noted. (1) Paul regarded continuity between Jesus' teaching and his own gospel as a matter of substantive fact. He neither saw his theology as taking off solely from a kerygma of Jesus' death and resurrection,[122] nor could he have been content to affirm the bare "that-ness" *(Daß)* of Jesus' historical ministry and crucifixion,[123] nor would he have accepted that his own understanding of the gospel constituted a departure from or perversion of Jesus' own teaching.[124]

(2) In that continuity between Jesus' teaching and Paul's theology, the fact of Jesus' Jewishness was something to be affirmed and celebrated, and the claim that Jesus had fulfilled his people's hopes for a Messiah was something not to be forgotten. This continuity was evidently counted as of first importance, even though the concept of "Messiah" itself underwent radical reinterpretation. The continuity through Jesus, precisely as Jesus the Jew and Messiah, reaffirmed and undergirded the continuity between the Israel of old and the new movement which took Israel's Messiah as its own name.

(3) At the same time the continuity which Jesus embodied was not only with Israel, but with humankind (Adam) as a whole. The gospel *(euangelion)* which stemmed from and focused on this Jesus could therefore speak not simply to the Israel of old, but to the world at large. Which also means that for Paul salvation was intended to fulfill the purpose of creation. And to achieve that, God had reached down to the depths of human impotence under the powers of sin and death and had identified himself in an unprecedented way (incarnation?) with the man Jesus.

---

122. See above §8.1.

123. Cf. particularly Bultmann, "Historical Jesus" 237-38.

124. I have in mind the debate in life of Jesus research from Reimarus to Harnack (alluded to at the end of §8.1 above).

§9 Christ crucified[1]

1. **Bibliography**: **G. Aulén**, *Christus Victor: An Historical Study of the Three Main Types of the Idea of Atonement* (London: SPCK, 1931, new edition 1970); **Barrett**, *Paul* 114-19; **G. Barth**, *Der Tod Jesu Christus im Verständnis des Neuen Testaments* (Neukirchen-Vluyn: Neukirchener, 1992); **M. Barth**, *Was Christ's Death a Sacrifice?* (Edinburgh: Oliver and Boyd, 1961); **Becker**, *Paul* 399-411; **Beker**, *Paul* 182-212; **C. Breytenbach**, *Versöhnung. Eine Studie zur paulinischen Soteriologie* (WMANT 60; Neukirchen-Vluyn: Neukirchener, 1989); "Versöhnung, Stellvertretung und Sühne. Semantische und traditionsgeschichtliche Bemerkungen am Beispiel der paulinischen Briefe," *NTS* 39 (1993) 59-79; **Bultmann**, *Theology* I, 292-306; **D. A. Campbell**, *The Rhetoric of Righteousness in Romans 3.21-26* (JSNTS 65; Sheffield: Sheffield Academic, 1992); **J. T. Carroll and J. B. Green**, *The Death of Jesus in Early Christianity* (Peabody: Hendrickson, 1995) 113-32; **Cerfaux**, *Christ* (§10 n. 1) 118-60; **C. B. Cousar**, *A Theology of the Cross: The Death of Jesus in the Pauline Letters* (Minneapolis: Fortress, 1990); **R. J. Daly**, *Christian Sacrifice* (Washington: Catholic University of America, 1978); **Davies**, *Paul* ch. 9; **G. Delling**, "Der Tod Jesu in der Verkündigung des Paulus," *Studien zum Neuen Testament und zum hellenistischen Judentum* (Göttingen: Vandenhoeck, 1970) 336-46; **Dodd**, "Atonement," *Bible* 82-95; **J. D. G. Dunn**, "Paul's Understanding of the Death of Jesus as Sacrifice," in S. W. Sykes, ed., *Sacrifice and Redemption: Durham Essays in Theology* (Cambridge/New York: Cambridge University, 1991) 35-56; **J. A. Fitzmyer**, "Reconciliation in Pauline Theology," *To Advance the Gospel* 162-85; *Paul* 54-55, 62-66; **G. Friedrich**, *Die Verkündigung des Todes Jesu im Neuen Testament* (Neukirchen-Vluyn: Neukirchener, 1982); **Gese**, "Atonement," *Biblical Theology* 93-116; **Goppelt**, *Theology* II, 90-98; **K. Grayston**, *Dying, We Live: A New Inquiry into the Death of Christ in the New Testament* (London: Darton/New York: Oxford University, 1990); **R. G. Hamerton-Kelly**, *Sacred Violence: Paul's Hermeneutic of the Cross* (Minneapolis: Fortress, 1992); **M. Hengel**, *The Atonement: The Origins of the Doctrine of Atonement in the New Testament* (London: SCM/Philadelphia: Fortress, 1981); **D. Hill**, *Greek Words and Hebrew Meanings: Studies in the Semantics of Soteriological Terms* (London: Cambridge University, 1967) 23-81; **Hofius**, "Sühne und Versöhnung. Zum paulinischen Verständnis des Kreuzestodes Jesu," *Paulusstudien* 33-49; **M. D. Hooker**, "Interchange in Christ" and "Interchange and Atonement," *Adam* 13-25, 26-41; *Not Ashamed of the Gospel: New Testament Interpretations of the Death of Christ* (Carlisle: Paternoster/Grand Rapids: Eerdmans, 1994) 20-46; **A. J. Hultgren**, *Christ and His Benefits: Christology and Redemption in the New Testament* (Philadelphia: Fortress, 1987); *Paul's Gospel* 47-81; **B. Janowski**, *Sühne als Heilsgeschehen* (Neukirchen-Vluyn: Neukirchener, 1982); **Käsemann**, "The Saving Significance of the Death of Jesus in Paul," *Perspectives* 32-59; **K. Kertelge**, "Das Verständnis des Todes Jesu bei Paulus," in Kertelge, ed., *Der Tod Jesu. Deutungen im Neuen Testament* (Freiburg: Herder, 1976) 114-36; **W. Kraus**, *Der Tod Jesu als Heiligtumsweihe. Eine Untersuchung zum Umfeld der Sühnevorstellung in Römer 3.25-26a* (WMANT 66; Neukirchen-Vluyn: Neukirchener, 1991); **Ladd**, *Theology* 464-77; **J. D. Levenson**, *The Death and Resurrec-*

§9.1 As one died

There can be no doubt as to where the centre of gravity of Paul's theology is to be found. It lies in the death and resurrection of Jesus. We have already noted how Paul, having completed his indictment in Romans (1.18–3.20) turned at once, not to Jesus' life or teaching, but to his function as the God-provided "expiation" for sins past and present (Rom. 3.25).[2] In Galatians Gal. 3.13-14, Christ accursed on the cross plays this same role as the decisive resolution to the problem of how the blessing of Abraham might come to the Gentiles for whom it was also intended. And subsequently in Colossians the same emphasis is much elaborated with a vivid series of metaphors at the centre of the theological exposition (2.6-23) to describe the effectiveness of Christ's death (2.11-15): circumcision (2.11), burial and resurrection (2.12), death and (new) life (2.13), expunging of the record (2.14), and stripping off and public triumph (2.15).[3]

tion of the Beloved Son (New Haven: Yale University, 1993); **E. Lohse**, *Martyrer und Gottesknecht* (Göttingen: Vandenhoeck, [2]1963); **S. Lyonnet and L. Sabourin**, *Sin, Redemption, and Sacrifice* (AnBib 48; Rome: Biblical Institute, 1970) 61-296; **B. H. McLean**, *The Cursed Christ: Mediterranean Expulsion Rituals and Pauline Soteriology* (JSNTS 126; Sheffield: Sheffield Acadamic, 1996); **I. H. Marshall**, "The Development of the Concept of Redemption in the New Testament" (1974) and "The Meaning of 'Reconciliation' " (1978), *Jesus the Saviour: Studies in New Testament Theology* (London: SPCK, 1990) 239-57, 258-74; **R. P. Martin**, *Reconciliation: A Study of Paul's Theology* (London: Marshall, Morgan and Scott/Atlanta: John Knox, 1981) Part II; **Merklein**, *Studien* 15-39; **L. Morris**, *The Apostolic Preaching of the Cross* (3rd ed.; Grand Rapids: Eerdmans/London: Tyndale, 1965); *The Cross in the New Testament* (Exeter: Paternoster/Grand Rapids: Eerdmans, 1965); *Theology* 66-74; **Moule**, *Origin* (§10 n. 1) 111-26; **Penna**, "The Blood of Christ in the Pauline Letters," *Paul* II, 24-22; **S. E. Porter**, Katallassō *in Ancient Greek Literature, with Reference to the Pauline Writings* (Córdoba: Ediciónes El Almendro, 1994); **Ridderbos**, *Paul* 182-97; **Schlier**, *Grundzüge* 128-40; **D. Seeley**, *The Noble Death: Graeco-Roman Martyrology and Paul's Concept of Salvation* (JSNTS 28; Sheffield: JSOT, 1990); **G. S. Sloyan**, *The Crucifixion of Jesus: History, Myth, Faith* (Mineapolis: Fortress, 1995); **Strecker**, *Theologie* 112-18; **P. Stuhlmacher**, "Eighteen Theses on Paul's Theology of the Cross," *Reconciliation* 155-68; "Sühne oder Versöhnung," in U. Luz and H. Weder, eds., *Die Mitte des Neuen Testaments,* E. Schweizer FS (Göttingen: Vandenhoeck, 1983) 291-316; *Theologie* 294-300; **V. Taylor**, *The Atonement in New Testament Teaching* (London: Epworth, [3]1958); **R. de Vaux**, *Studies in Old Testament Sacrifice* (Cardiff: University of Wales, 1964); **H. Weder**, *Das Kreuz Jesu bei Paulus. Ein Versuch, über den Geschichtsbezug des christlichen Glaubens nachzudenken* (FRLANT 125; Göttingen: Vandenhoeck, 1981); **Whiteley**, *Theology* 130-51; **S. K. Williams**, *Jesus' Death as Saving Event: The Background and Origin of a Concept* (Missoula: Scholars, 1975); **Witherington**, *Narrative* 160-68; **F. M. Young**, *Sacrifice and the Death of Christ* (London: SPCK/Philadelphia: Westminster, 1975); **Ziesler**, *Pauline Christianity* 91-95.

2. See further above the opening of §8.1.

3. See my *Colossians* 146.

To be sure, as we have just demonstrated, Paul's theology certainly had a significant place for the pre-passion Jesus (§8). But the point remains that his gospel, and so also his theology, focused on the cross. Even where Paul's christology embraced the whole story of Jesus, the whole story was significant primarily because it brought out more fully the significance of the saving event of the cross and resurrection.

So with the messiahship of Jesus. Evidently a claim that Jesus, as teacher or prophet, was Messiah would have caused few problems for Paul's Jewish contemporaries. Possibly the claim that Jesus of Nazareth had been raised from the dead would in itself have not occasioned any great theological difficulty for most of Paul's fellow Jews. It was the claim that Jesus had been crucified *as Messiah*,[4] that crucifixion was the heart and climax of Jesus' messianic role, which was so offensive (1 Cor. 1.23). Already it could be said in Jewish factional polemic that a crucified man was under God's curse. Deut. 21.23, "Cursed is everyone who has been hanged on a tree," had been applied to other such victims of capital punishment.[5] And Gal. 3.13 suggests that the same text was applied to the crucified Jesus in very early polemic against the Nazarenes, quite possibly by Paul himself in his days as persecutor. A crucified/cursed Messiah was no doubt for most Jews a contradiction in terms.[6] To make a crucified man the focal point of proclamation ("openly proclaimed as crucified" — Gal. 3.1) was equally foolish to Gentiles (1 Cor. 1.23), since crucifixion was generally regarded as the most degrading and shameful of deaths in the Roman repertoire of execution.[7] In response, the first Christians had not attempted to defend the claim for Jesus' messiahship independent of the cross.[8] Nor did Paul, though the

---

4. It is hardly feasible to argue that Jesus was recognized as Messiah only *after* his crucifixion (despite the seeming implication of Acts 2.36, and Hahn, *Titles* [§8 n. 1] 161-62). See particularly the conclusion of Dahl, "Crucified Messiah" [§§ n. 1] 39-40: "the title 'Messiah' was inseparably connected with the name of Jesus because Jesus was condemned and crucified as a messianic pretender."

5. 4QpNah 1.7-8 — referring clearly to the crucifixion ("hanged alive on the tree" — Deut. 21.22-23) of his Pharisaic opponents ("those who seek smooth things"; see line 2) by Alexander Jannaeus (Josephus, *Ant.* 13.380-81 displays a similar shock); 11QT 64.2-13 (a restatement and elaboration of Deut. 21.18-23 in which "hanging on a tree" [lines 8-11] is the means of execution [= crucifixion]). See further J. A. Fitzmyer, "Crucifixion in Ancient Palestine, Qumran Literature and the New Testament," *CBQ* 40 (1978) 493-513. McLean, *Cursed* 133, argues that these Qumran texts did not have crucifixion in view. But note also Acts 5.30 and 10.39.

6. Trypho challenges Justin: "Prove to us that he [the Messiah] had to be crucified and had to die such a shameful and dishonourable death, cursed by the law. We could not even consider such a thing" (*Dialogue* 90.1).

7. M. Hengel, *Crucifixion* (London: SCM/Philadelphia: Fortress, 1977).

8. The earliest stage in Christian apologetic is probably indicated by such passages as Luke 24.25-27, 46; Acts 8.32-35; 17.2-3; 1 Cor. 15.3; 1 Pet. 1.11.

battle was seemingly well past by the time he wrote his letters. Jesus was Messiah as the crucified one, or he was no Messiah at all. The only Christ Paul knew or cared about was "Christ crucified" (1 Cor. 1.23; 2.2).

The same is true for the Adam christology sketched out above (§8.6). There is no thought of a salvific moment which is prior to the cross. The Son being sent "in the very likeness of sinful flesh" (Rom. 8.3) is not an event of significance independent of what follows. He was sent thus, as we shall see, to deal with sin, that is, by his death.[9] Similarly in the parallel Gal. 4.4-5: he was sent, "born of woman, born under the law, in order that he might redeem those under the law . . ." — that is, precisely by his death.[10] The Philippian hymn likewise does not envisage a role for the one "become man" except in the obedience which answers Adam's disobedience — "death, the death of the cross" (Phil. 2.7-8).[11] The Adam-Christ interplay is the interplay of death and life (1 Cor. 15.22); or to be more precise, the interplay of a life which ends only in death and a life which dies but which also conquers death in resurrected life. Even in the case of Heb. 2.5-9, if we may regard that as a fuller exposition of the Adam christology lying behind Paul's use of Ps. 8.4-6,[12] the vital link between "being made a little lower than the angels" and the achievement of the Adamic goal ("all things in subjection to him") is "the suffering of death." Christ retraces Adam's steps "in order that by the grace of God he might taste death for everyone" (Heb. 2.8-9).

Probably the single most evocative statement of this theme in Paul is 2 Cor. 5.14: "the love of the Christ constrains us, because we have reached the conclusion, that one has died on behalf of all *(hyper pantōn),* therefore all have died." As so often, an epigram is enigmatic in its precise force and relies for its effect more on impression than on precision. But almost certainly the epigram ("one died for all, therefore all died") is an expression of Adam christology,[13] that is, in the intermediate stage just indicated. "The Christ" here is once again a representative figure. But here again he doubles for the dying Adam. "As in Adam all die" (1 Cor. 15.22), so here Jesus' death is the death of all humanity.

What is Paul saying? It would diminish the power of the epigram to translate it into a sequence of logical propositions. The exposition should reflect in some measure at least the astounding visionary claim being made

9. See below §9.2(2).

10. See below §9.3c.

11. That "the death of the cross" was part of the original hymn and central to it has been well argued by Hofius, *Christushymnus* (§11 n. 1) 7-12, 63-67.

12. See above §8.6.

13. Cf. Windisch, *2 Korintherbrief* 182-83; Kertelge, "Verständnis" 121-22. See the analysis of various alternatives in Thrall, *2 Corinthians* 409-11.

and not be afraid to "reflect" accordingly.[14] Presumably, then, Paul invited his readers to theologize somewhat along the following lines. If Jesus dies, then all are dead. If *the Christ* dies, then no one can escape death. When Paul says the "one" (eschatological Adamic figure) died, he means that there is no other end possible for all human beings. All humankind dies, as he died, as flesh, as the end of sinful flesh (Rom. 8.3). Had there been a way for sinful flesh to overcome its downward drag, to escape its subjection to the power of sin, God's representative man need not and would not have died. The one would have demonstrated to the all how the sinful flesh could be overcome. But Christ died, the one man died, because there is no other way for humankind, for every man and woman, to go. The death of the one signifies that there is no way out for weak and corrupted flesh except through death, no answer to the power of sin working in and through the flesh except its destruction in death. As Karl Barth put it, "Man could not be helped other than through his annihilation."[15]

If we may press the line of reflection a little further, the point is that this is true of *all* humankind. Whether they acknowledge God (Rom. 1.21) or not, whether they choose to live life without reference to God (or his Christ) or not, they die. They may think of it as peculiarly their own death, as it is. But it is death, the death that everyone dies. The death of the one is the death of the all.[16] The key question which Paul's gospel answers is whether that is all there is to it. Is death the end, the end of the story, finis? Paul's answer is that it need not be so. Those who in faith identify themselves with Christ find that Christ's death has a further significance. For the moment, however, the point is that Christ's identification with humankind means that his death spells out the death of all. The one's identification with the all means that the death of the one is the death of all. Only if the all identify with the death of the one can the story go forward.[17]

This Pauline theology of the cross, then, is somewhat enigmatic. In fact

---

14. Contrast what follows with Hamerton-Kelly's typical interpretation: "once we conclude that one has died representing all, then it follows that all have died, because they see in his death the effects of their mimetic rivalry and can therefore freely renounce it by choosing to mime the nonacquisitive desire of the victim, and thus 'crucify the flesh with its passions and desires' (Gal. 5.24)" (*Sacred Violence* 70).

15. Cited by G. C. Berkouwer, *The Triumph of Grace in the Theology of Karl Barth* (Grand Rapids: Eerdmans, 1956) 135.

16. It would be a mistake to confine the "all" of 2 Cor. 5.14 to "believers" (*pace* Martin, *Reconciliation* 100-101; *2 Corinthians* 131). Christ's representative capacity before resurrection ("sinful flesh" — Rom. 8.3) is different from his representative capacity after resurrection (1 Cor. 15.45; see below §10.6). Cf. Furnish, *2 Corinthians* 327.

17. This was the insight which Irenaeus took forward with his concept of "recapitulation"; see, e.g., J. N. D. Kelly, *Early Christian Doctrines* (London: Black, [3]1960) 170-74.

that reflects a repeated feature of most of Paul's theology of the death of Jesus. For, as we have already observed,[18] Paul never felt it necessary to expound his theology of Christ crucified in any detail. All his references are either creedal or kerygmatic formulae or brief allusions.[19] This, we deduced, was because it was not a matter of unclarity or controversy between Paul and his readers. Formulaic or allusive references were sufficient to recall a central theme in their shared faith.[20] The problem for us is that such compressed teaching is often difficult for us to unfold. However, although the theology of these passages contains numerous problems and is among the most contested elements of Paul's theology, the actual images used are rather more explicit.

§9.2 A sacrifice for sins

One of the most powerful images used by Paul to explicate the significance of Christ's death is that of the cultic sacrifice, or more precisely the "sin offering" which could be offered up by individuals or groups in the Jerusalem temple (Leviticus 4) and the annual Day of Atonement sacrifices (Lev. 16.11-19). Equally, it has been one of the most repellent features of Paul's (and early Christian) theology for modern readers. The idea of bloody sacrifice and of divine-human relationships being somehow dependent on it is generally abhorrent to post-Enlightenment culture, something to be consigned to a more primitive and cruder period of conceptualization of divine-human relationships. Consequently, some scholars have used the fact that Paul's references are so formulaic and allusive to argue, unjustifiably, that the sacrificial imagery is not part of Paul's own distinctive theology and is secondary to it.[21] And

18. See above §7.3.

19. We should note, however, that Paul's theology of suffering in 2 Corinthians (particularly his own suffering as an apostle) is in effect an extended theology of the cross (see further below especially §18.5).

20. The fact that such formulae existed, however, indicates that the theme was central, the formulae being the product of sustained "repeat teaching" when new churches were founded. Here again this degree of "taken-for-grantedness" undermines the argument of, e.g., Seeley, *Noble Death,* that certain features are unimportant to Paul because he makes such brief reference to them.

21. E.g., Käsemann, *Perspectives* 42-45: "The idea of the sacrificial death is, if anything, pushed into the background" (45); Hengel, *Atonement* 45: "He himself was no longer much concerned with this cultic vocabulary"; Friedrich seems to go out of his way to play down any sacrificial significance in the key passages (*Verkündigung* 42, 66, 70-71, 75, 77). But see Cousar's critique of Käsemann (*Theology* 16-18), and Stuhlmacher's critique of Friedrich ("Sühne," especially 297-304). In Eph. 5.2 the imagery is explicit: "Christ loved us and gave himself up for us, a fragrant offering *(prosphora)* and sacrifice *(thysia)* to God."

others have attempted to cut more drastically at the root by arguing that any theology based on violence or on the idea of redemptive suffering is fundamentally misconceived.[22] However, it does not seem possible to deny either Paul's use of sacrificial imagery or its centrality to his gospel (however briefly stated). What *we* make of it is a question which can be tackled only when the data of Paul's conceptuality are clear.

(1) *Romans 3.25.* The obvious starting point is the brief response to the indictment of Rom. 1.18–3.20 which Paul provides in Rom. 3.21-26. Having reiterated the key concept, "the righteousness of God" (3.21-22),[23] and recalled the conclusion of the universal indictment (3.22-23 — "there is no distinction, for all have sinned . . ."), Paul then states what can hardly be regarded as other than the core of his own as well as of his shared gospel (3.24-26):[24]

> [24]They are justified as a gift by his grace through the redemption which is in Christ Jesus,
>> [25]whom God presented as an expiation (through faith) in his blood,
>> to demonstrate his righteousness in passing over *(paresin)* the sins committed in former times,
> [26]in the forbearance of God, to demonstrate his righteousness in the present time, that he might be just and the one who justifies him who believes in Jesus.

The key term here is "expiation," *hilastērion.* This must have a sacrificial reference, for the term is used almost exclusively in LXX for the lid of the ark, the "mercy seat,"[25] the place where, on the Day of Atonement, atonement was made for the holy place and for all the assembly of Israel (Lev. 16.16-17).

The passage has provoked several debates, none of which are particularly consequential at this point.[26] (a) Should *hilastērion* be understood as

---

22. So particularly Hamerton-Kelly, *Sacred Violence,* who reads Paul through the spectacles provided by René Girard, *Violence and the Sacred* (Baltimore: Johns Hopkins University, 1977) and *The Scapegoat* (Baltimore: Johns Hopkins University, 1986); see, e.g., his interpretation of Gal. 3.13 (below n. 107). See also those cited by Sloyan, *Crucifixion* 190-92.

23. See below §14.2.

24. For the view that 3.24-26 contains pre-Pauline formulation see above §7.3 and n. 66. Hultgren, *Paul's Gospel* 71, describes 3.21-25 as "the Pauline gospel in miniature."

25. See particularly Exod. 25.6-21 (7 occurrences) and Lev. 16.2, 13-15 (7 occurrences) translating *kapporeth;* similarly Ezek. 43.14, 17, 20 (5 occurrences) translating *azarah;* also Amos 9.1 (not in all mss.). Note also Heb. 9.5 (the only other occurrence of *hilastērion* in the NT). McLean, *Cursed* 43-46, seems to be in error when he denies that the LXX uses *hilastērion* for *kapporeth* (43). See also Philo, *Cher.* 25; *Heres* 166; *Fuga* 100, 101; *Mos.* 2.95, 97; and further Kraus, *Tod Jesu* 21-32.

26. Kraus, *Tod Jesu* 4-6, contains lengthy bibliography.

the *place* or the *means* of expiation? The former is most fully supported.[27] But the one sense easily elides into the other, as subsequent usage demonstrates.[28]

(b) Should we translate "expiation" or "propitiation"?[29] The problem with the latter is that it invariably evokes the idea of appeasing God, whereas in Rom. 3.25 Paul explicitly states that it is God himself who provided the *hilastērion*. More to the point, Hebrew usage contrasts markedly with common Greek usage on this precise point. Characteristically in Greek usage the human being is the active subject and God is the object: the human action propitiates God.[30] But in Hebrew usage God is never the object of the key verb *(kipper)*. Properly speaking, in the Israelite cult, God is never "propitiated" or "appeased." The objective of the atoning act is rather the removal of *sin* — that is, either by purifying the person or object, or by wiping out the sin. Atonement is characteristically made "for" a person or "for sin."[31] And it can be said that it is God himself who expiates the sin (or for the sin).[32] Of course, the atoning act thus removes the sin which provoked God's wrath,[33] but it does so by acting on the sin rather than on God.[34] The imagery is more of the removal of a corrosive stain or

27. Particularly Davies, *Paul* 237-41; Stuhlmacher, *Reconciliation* 96-103; *Theologie* 194; Lyonnet and Sabourin, *Sin* 155-66; Janowski, *Sühne* 350-54; Hultgren, *Paul's Gospel* 55-60, who speculates that Rom. 3.23-26a was the conclusion to a homily delivered by Paul on the Day of Atonement in a synagogue in Ephesus (62-64).

28. *4 Macc.* 17.22; Josephus, *Ant.* 16.182. See, e.g., L. Morris, "The Meaning of *hilastērion* in Romans 3.25," *NTS* 2 (1955-56) 33-43; Cranfield, *Romans* 214-17; Williams, *Jesus' Death* 39-40; Fitzmyer, *Paul* 64; Cousar, *Theology* 63-64; Campbell, *Rhetoric* 107-13, 130-33; Hooker, *Not Ashamed* 43-44. In a paper delivered at the NT Conference in Aberdeen (September 1996), D. Bailey pointed out that in biblical Greek (and in Philo and Josephus) the appositional object in a double accusative construction (here "whom as an expiation") is almost always anarthrous (without definite article); *pace* particularly Seeley, *Noble Death* 20-21.

29. This classic debate in English-speaking scholarship was occasioned by Dodd's study of the *hilaskesthai* word group ("Atonement"), to which Morris replied (*Apostolic Preaching* chs. 5-6). See also Hill, *Greek Words* 23-36; Ladd, *Theology* 470-74.

30. *Exilaskomai* (the normal LXX translation for *kipper*) is used in this way in Zech. 7.2 (cf. 8.22 and Mal. 1.9); but these are the only three LXX passages where *exilaskomai* translates *chalah* ("appease, entreat").

31. E.g., Exod. 32.30; Lev. 4.35; 5.26; Ezek. 45.17. See further Lyonnet, *Sin* 124-46.

32. E.g., 2 Kgs. 5.18: "May the Lord expiate (for) your servant"; Ps. 24.11 (LXX) — the Psalmist prays, "Expiate (for) my sin"; Sir. 5.5-6: ". . . he will expiate the multitude of my sins." See further Dodd, "Atonement"; F. Büchsel, *TDNT* 3.315-17, 320-21 (on Rom. 3.25); B. Lang, *kipper, TDOT* 7.290-92.

33. So also occasionally in the OT (Num. 16.46; 25.11-13).

34. This point is not really taken by Witherington, *Narrative* 163-64.

the neutralization of a life-threatening virus than of anger appeased by punishment.[35]

(c) Is the background more that of martyr theology than of the cult? The question is provoked by the use of *hilastērion* to describe the atoning significance of the Maccabean martyrs in *4 Macc.* 17.21-22.[36] But again it makes little difference. The martyr theology in view is itself simply the application of the same sacrificial metaphor (see also Dan. 3.40 LXX).[37] If anything, the thought that it is God who presented Christ as *hilastērion* points back directly to the cult. For the sacrificial system, after all, was provided by God in the Torah, whereas such a thought is missing in Jewish martyr theology.[38]

A more consequential issue is the puzzle of what Paul (and the formula) meant in talking of "the passing over *(paresin)* of the sins committed in former times." *Paresis,* which occurs only here in the Greek Bible, means "passing over," but not in the sense of "overlooking, disregarding." Rather, it had a more strictly legal sense of "letting go unpunished, remission of penalty."[39] What is clear is that God's righteousness was expressed in such "passing over" of sin. Such withholding of penalty ("God's forbearance") was part of God's covenant obligation.[40] It is also clear that this righteousness was "demonstrated" by the *hilastērion:* the sacrificial act was, as it were, God's legal justification for remitting due penalty. What is unclear, however, is whether Paul regarded the *hilastērion* of Jesus as validating the sacrificial system or as indicating its merely provisional character. Or whether it was the sacrificial system which validated Jesus' death as a *hilastērion,* at least in effecting remission of penalty — with the implication that Jesus' death and resurrection were more effective. The brevity of Paul's formulation leaves these questions unresolved. Whatever the concern of the

35. See further my "Paul's Understanding" 48-50. Contrast again Hamerton-Kelly: "it is not God who needs to be propitiated, but humanity" (*Sacred Violence* 80).

36. See particularly Hill, *Greek Words* 41-45. Williams, *Jesus' Death* 135, disputes that there was an established martyr theology in pre-70 Judaism; but see also Seeley, *Noble Death* ch. 5, and below n. 127.

37. H. Riesenfeld, *TDNT* 8.511. Lohse, *Martyrer* 71, suggests that diaspora Judaism developed this theology precisely because it served as a substitute for the sacrificial cult in faraway Jerusalem. Similarly, but more nuanced, Kraus, *Tod Jesu* 42-44.

38. Kertelge, "Verständnis" 118-19.

39. BAGD, *paresis.* Against W. G. Kümmel, *"Paresis und endeixis,"Heilsgeschehen* 260-70, who presses too hard for the sense "forgiveness" (262-63), see particularly Kraus, *Tod Jesu* 95-104. C. F. D. Moule, in a private communication, prefers "(what looked like) divine ignoring" of sin.

40. On the phrase "in the forbearance of God" see especially Kraus, *Tod Jesu* 112-49. On God's righteousness, see below §14.2.

older formula, his primary concern was with the second "demonstration of God's righteousness, in the now time" (3.26).[41]

Before we attempt to tease out more of the highly compressed theology of atonement in Rom. 3.24-26,[42] we should consider the other sacrificial texts in Paul.

(2) *Romans 8.3.* We have already considered part of this verse — "God sent his own Son in the very likeness of sinful flesh."[43] Here we take up the immediately following phrase — "and as a sin offering *(peri hamartias)* and condemned sin in the flesh." Here again there is some dispute. Some think *peri hamartias* should be translated less precisely as "for sin."[44] But the phrase is used quite often in the LXX to translate the Hebrew *(le)chatta'th* ("as a sin offering").[45] Given the centrality of cultic imagery in the key gospel statement of 3.21-26, it must be judged highly likely that Paul intended a similar allusion here.[46] Since the phrase also leads into the next clause ("and condemned sin in the flesh"), it is likely that the *peri hamartias* indicates the means by which this condemnation was carried out. As we saw with 3.25, it was precisely the sin offering which had been provided by God to deal with sin.

(3) *1 Cor. 5.7.* Paul explicitly states, "Christ, our paschal lamb, has been sacrificed." This is rather striking, since the Passover lamb was not strictly speaking a sacrifice.[47] However, the Passover is already associated with atonement in Ezek. 45.18-22. And this link was probably already forged in the double association of the Last Supper with the Passover and with Jesus'

41. See also my *Romans* 173-74; Fitzmyer, *Romans* 351-52.

42. Below §9.3; since God's righteousness is also a central theme in 3.21-26 we will have to return to the passage in §14.2.

43. See above §8.6.

44. See, e.g., Lietzmann, *Römer* 79; Barrett, *Romans* 147; Cranfield, *Romans* 382; and further Friedrich, *Verkündigung* 68-71. Grayston, *Dying* 110, prefers "with authority concerning sin."

45. E.g., Lev. 5.6-7, 11 and 16.3, 5, 9; Num. 6.16 and 7.16; 2 Chron. 29.23-24; Neh. 10.33 (2 Esd. 20.34 LXX); Ezek. 42.13; 43.19. In Isa. 53.10 the phrase translates Hebrew *asham* ("guilt offering"). For the debate on the distinction between *chatta'th* and *asham* see D. Kellermann, *asham, TDOT* 1.431-35.

46. Wilckens, *Römer* 2.127; Michel changed his mind in favour of this view in the fifth edition of his *Römer;* Hengel, *Atonement* 46; Kraus, *Tod Jesu* 191-93; Becker, *Paul* 410; Stuhlmacher, *Theologie* 291; see further Wright, "The Meaning of *peri hamartias* in Romans 8.3," *Climax* 220-25. Against those who think a sacrificial reference would be too abrupt within the train of thought, Campbell claims with some justification "that a theme of Levitical and sacrificial imagery runs, partly submerged, throughout the text of Romans" (*Rhetoric* 18, 132).

47. G. B. Gray, *Sacrifice in the Old Testament* (London: Oxford University, 1925) 397: "the Paschal victim was not a sin-offering or regarded as a means of expiating or removing sins."

"blood poured out *(ekchunnomenon)* for many" (Mark 14.24 pars.). There
the language is unavoidably sacrificial and signifies atonement.[48] The same
tendency to run together different metaphors and descriptions of Jesus' death,
thereby blurring older distinctions, is clearly evident elsewhere in the early
churches.[49] Paul's language here suggests that the same evolution of imagery
was already well advanced in his theology.

(4) *2 Cor. 5.21* — "He who knew no sin, God made sin for our sake."
The antithesis "sinless/made sin" makes it difficult to doubt that Paul had in
mind the cult's insistence on clean and unblemished animals for sacrifice.[50]
The allusion is not so much to the sin offering as such, but to the function of
the sin offering — "made sin," not *peri hamartias* (as in Rom. 8.3).[51] A more
specific allusion to the Day of Atonement's scapegoat is likely (Lev. 16.21).[52]
An allusion to the servant of Isa. 53.4-6 is also possible.[53] But Isaiah 53 in
turn is studded with sacrificial terminology and imagery and, like the martyr
theology of *4 Maccabees* 17, is simply an application of the theology of
sacrifice to the Servant.[54]

(5) Similarly, the several passage in the Paulines which use the phrase
"in/through his blood"[55] cannot be adequately understood except as a reference
to Christ's death as a sacrifice. The emphasis on blood can hardly have come
from the tradition of Jesus' death, since it was not remembered as particularly
bloody. The only obvious allusion is to Jesus' death understood as a sacrifice,
since it was precisely the manipulation of the victim's blood which was the
decisive act of atonement.[56] Likewise Paul's talk of Jesus' death as "for sins,"[57]

---

48. Jeremias, *Eucharistic Words* (§22 n. 1) 222-26.

49. 1 Pet. 1.18-19; John 1.29.

50. Stuhlmacher, *Reconciliation* 59; *Theologie* 195; Hengel, *Atonement* 46; Daly,
Sacrifice 237, 239. This is a minority view (see, e.g., Furnish, *2 Corinthians* 340; Breytenbach, *Versöhnung* 202-3; Thrall, *2 Corinthians* 439-41). But see below n. 82.

51. But note that LXX translates the Hebrew of Lev. 4.24 and 5.12 ("it is
chatta'th") as "it is sin *(hamartia)*." See further Sabourin in Lyonnet and Sabourin, *Sin*
248-53, and below §9.3.

52. Windisch, *2 Korintherbrief* 198.

53. E.g., Cullmann, *Christology* (§10 n. 1) 76 (McLean, *Cursed* 108, misquotes
Cullmann); Martin, *2 Corinthians* 140, 157. With reference to n. 50 above, both Furnish
and Thrall acknowledge that Isaiah 53 may be in Paul's mind (Thrall 442) or that the
language is clarified against the background of Isaiah 53 (Furnish 351; he also compares
1 Pet. 2.24).

54. Note not least the *peri hamartias* in Isa. 53.10. So, e.g., Taylor, *Atonement*
190; M. Barth, *Sacrifice* 9-10.

55. Rom. 3.25; 5.9; Eph. 1.7; 2.13; Col. 1.20.

56. Lev. 4.5-7, 16-18, 25, 30, 34; 16.14-19. See, e.g., Davies, *Paul* 232-37;
Schweizer, *Erniedrigung* (§ 10 n. 1) 74; Lohse, *Martyrer* 138-39; Penna, *Paul* 2.24-44.

57. Rom. 4.25; 8.3; 1 Cor. 15.3; Gal. 1.4.

or "for us" (or equivalent),[58] presumably reflects the same imagery, even if in the latter case it may have been mediated through martyr theology.[59]

§9.3 Paul's theology of atoning sacrifice

Granted then that Paul saw Jesus' death as an atoning sacrifice, what light does that shed on Paul's understanding of Jesus' death? How did Jesus' death "work" to deal with the power of sin entrenched in human flesh? The obvious way to find an answer would be to inquire into the Jewish theology of sacrifice. But here we run into a considerable problem. For there is no clear rationale in scripture or in Second Temple Judaism concerning sacrifice. We can hardly doubt that the daily burnt offering[60] was of profound meaning to the devout and penitent worshipper in Israel, and still more the Day of Atonement sacrifices. But just how the sacrifice effected atonement remains an unsolved riddle.[61]

Our case is not altogether hopeless, however. For in the light of the passages reviewed above (§9.2) it seems likely that Paul himself had a fairly well-defined theory of sacrifice. Moreover, whereas Jewish theologians may already have recognized other means of expiation,[62] Paul seems to have been content to retain an important place for the category of atoning sacrifice in describing the effect of Jesus' death. It may therefore be possible to correlate Paul's language with what we know of the sin offering ritual in particular, and thereby to deduce at least Paul's own theology of atonement. The exercise is unavoidably speculative, but if a clear correlation offers itself, as I believe it does, the results can be given some weight.[63]

a) First, the starting point is bound to be that the sin offering was "for sin" *(peri hamartias),* that is, intended somehow to deal with sin. As the flow of thought in Rom. 8.3 indicates, the intention was to pass effective judgment on the sin. In some way or other, the ritual of killing the sacrifice removed the sin from the sinner. It is true, of course, that the sin offering dealt only

---

58. Rom. 5.6-8; 8.32; 2 Cor. 5.14-15, 21; Gal. 2.20; 3.13; 1 Thes. 5.9-10; also Eph. 5.2, 25.

59. Martyr theology certainly lies in the background of Rom. 5.7. See further H. Riesenfeld, *TDNT* 8.508-11; Schlier, *Grundzüge* 134-35.

60. Exod. 29.38-46; Num. 28.1-8; Josephus, *Ant.* 3.237; detailed regulations as recalled in the *m. Tamid* 4.1–7.4.

61. Barth, *Sacrifice* 13: "It seems necessary to admit that we do not know or understand what the Old Testament and 'Judaism' really believed and taught about the mystery of expiating sacrifice." Davies goes further: "It is doubtful if there was any rationale of sacrifice in the first century" *(Paul* 235). See also Moore, *Judaism* 1.500.

62. Davies, *Paul* 253-59; Lohse, *Martyrer* 21-25; but see also n. 36 above.

63. In what follows I elaborate the key points of my "Paul's Understanding."

with inadvertent or unwitting sins;[64] for deliberate sins, for deliberate and unrepented breach of the covenant, properly speaking, there was no atonement. At the same time, however, the fact that a death was necessary to compensate for even an inadvertent sin signified the seriousness of even these sins in a cult-centred community. The others were too serious for any compensation to be made. In such cases, strictly speaking, the sinner's covenant status was forfeit. No other life could expiate for the sin.[65]

An important aspect of the ritual, particularly on the Day of Atonement, was the purification of the altar and sanctuary.[66] It is doubtful, however, whether this should be regarded as the primary or sole purpose of the sin offering.[67] The more consistently emphasized objective of the sin offering is the removal of sin and the consequent forgiveness of the sinner.[68] And the "mechanism" whereby a purification ritual of the sanctuary achieved that end is more speculative and less rooted in the text than the one suggested here.[69]

b) Second, we can tie in what we have already seen of Paul's Adam christology in this connection (§9.1). For, as Jesus somehow embodied "sinful flesh" in order to deal with sin in the flesh (Rom. 8.3), so presumably Paul saw the sin offering as somehow embodying the sin of the one who offered it ("made sin" — 2 Cor. 5.21). This would probably be the significance for Paul of that part of the ritual where the offerer laid a hand on the beast's head. Thereby the sinner identified himself with the beast, or at least indicated that the beast in some way represented him.[70] That is to say, the

---

64. Lev. 4.2, 22, 27; 5.15, 18; Num. 15.24-29.

65. De Vaux, *Sacrifice* 94-95; Lyonnet and Sabourin, *Sin* 178. But the Day of Atonement did deal with "all the inquities of the people of Israel, and all their transgressions, all their sins" (Lev. 16.21). For the later rabbinic ruling see *m. Yoma* 8.8.

66. Lev. 8.15; 16.16, 18-20; see Lang, *TDOT* 7.296.

67. So particularly McLean, *Cursed* 37-38, following J. Milgrom, who prefers to translate *kipper* as "purge, purify (ritually)" (see, e.g., "Atonement," "Day of Atonement," *IDBS* 78-83; similarly Lyonnet and Sabourin, *Sin* 175-80; and Kraus, *Tod Jesu* 45-70, citing also particularly Ezek. 43.13-27; other bibliography in McLean 37 n. 50); hence McLean prefers to translate *chatta'th* as "purification offering" rather than "sin offering." Stowers, *Rereading* 206-13, also follows Milgrom and McLean.

68. Hence the repeated formula in Leviticus 4–5: "the priest will make atonement for him/for his sin and he will be forgiven" (4.20, 26, 31, 35; 5.6, 10, 13, 16, 18).

69. Cf. Lang's critique of Milgrom (*TDOT* 7.294). McLean's observation that the blood of the sin offering is never applied to a person (*Cursed* 38) would seem to tell more against the "purification" thesis than for it.

70. E.g., H. H. Rowley, *Worship in Ancient Israel* (London: SPCK/Philadelphia: Fortress, 1967) 133; Gese, "Atonement" 105-6; Janowski, *Sühne* 199-221; Merklein, *Studien* 25-8; Hofius, "Sühne" 35-36; K. Koch, *chata,"TDOT* 4.317 ("the animal becomes sin in the literal sense, i.e., the sphere of *chatta'th* becomes concentrated in the animal. . . . Through the imposition of hands . . . the act of transfer is made manifest"); cf. Lang, *TDOT* 7.294-95, 296-97.

animal represented the offerer *qua sinner,* so that the offerer's sin was somehow identified with the animal and its life stood in for his. The only difference in Christ's case is that the initiative came from God rather than from the sinner (Rom. 8.3; 2 Cor. 5.21).

This reading of the action of the offerer laying a hand on the offering is by no means generally accepted. The action is usually regarded as a less significant part of the ritual, signifying simply whose animal is being offered.[71] But this hardly seems an adequate explanation of the importance attached to this action in the detailed instructions of Leviticus 4. And if that were all the action meant, we would have expected it to be repeated in all sacrifices, non-bloody ones as well, whereas, in fact, it occurs only as part of the ritual for sacrifices involving blood.[72] Again, where the same action is used outside the sacrificial ritual (the verb is the same: *samach*), identification seems to be the chief rationale.[73] Nor does there seem to be any significant distinction between laying on one hand or two.[74]

The only place where the significance of laying hands on a sacrificial animal is explained is Lev. 16.21. There the High Priest lays both hands on the second goat in the Day of Atonement ceremony and thereby "puts them [the sins just confessed] upon the head of the goat." The fact that it is the first goat which is described as the sin offering and not the second is probably not a decisive consideration.[75] For the two goats were probably understood as two sides or two portrayals of the one reality: the goat which carried the sins physically out of the camp was a vivid alternative representation of what the sin offering was intended to accomplish.[76] This is certainly the implication

71. W. Eichrodt, *Theology of the Old Testament* (London: SCM/Philadelphia: Westminster, 1961) 1.165-66; de Vaux, *Sacrifice* 28, 63; McLean, *Cursed* 28, (with other bibliography n. 23), 79.

72. McLean, *Cursed* 28-32, plays down the atoning significance attached to the burnt offering, despite Lev. 1.4: "he shall lay his hand upon the head of the burnt offering, and it shall be accepted for him to make atonement for him."

73. Num. 27.18, 23 and Deut. 34.9 — Joshua becomes another Moses; Num. 8.10 — the Levites become representatives of the people who lay hands on them; Lev. 24.14 — the witnesses identify the defilement, which they have experienced by hearing the blasphemy, with the blasphemer (Daube, *Rabbinic Judaism* 226-27).

74. Num. 27.18 — Moses is commanded to "lay your hand (singular) on Joshua"; in the event (27.23) "he laid his hands (plural) upon him." In Num. 8.10 and Lev. 24.14 (see n. 73) the plural "hands" probably represents the single hands of many individuals. McLean, *Cursed* 28, queries the description of the ritual attached to the burnt offering in Philo, *Spec. Leg.* 1.198, but it speaks quite clearly of the offerer laying hands (plural) on the head of the victim. However, he does note that the Mishnah assumed the laying on of both hands for sacrifices (e.g., *Menahoth* 9.7-8).

75. *Pace* Janowski, *Sühne* 219-20.

76. See also Stuhlmacher, *Theologie* 192-93.

of texts from near Paul's time where the language of expiation/atonement is used for both goats.[77] Rom. 8.3 and 2 Cor. 5.21 strongly suggest that Paul too had in mind such a composite picture of Jesus' death as sacrifice.

Nor is it a decisive objection that a sin-laden animal would be rendered unholy (so unable to function in the cult), or that the priests could eat the meat left over from the sin offerings.[78] The animal had to be holy, without defect, precisely so that both priest and offerer could be confident that the death it died was *not its own*. As 2 Cor. 5.21 clearly implies, only the sinless could effectively make atonement for the sinful. And what happened to the flesh of the animal was not important, since, as is well known, the life of the animal was its blood.[79] All the more significant is it, then, that the blood was wholly used up in the ritual. Indeed, the blood played a more important role in the sin offering than in any other sacrifice.[80] And it is explicitly stated that "it is the blood, that is, the life, that makes expiation" (Lev. 17.11). In other words, the equivalence between offerer and sacrifice lay exclusively in the *blood* of the victim, not in the whole victim. And its role as atoning sacrifice was completed in the blood ritual.

c) Third, we can make a further deduction from Rom. 8.3 and 2 Cor. 5.14, 21. Paul saw the death of the sacrificial animal as the death of the sinner qua sinner. This is still clearer in Rom. 6.6: "our old nature has been crucified with him [Christ], in order that the body of sin might be done away with/destroyed *(katargēthē)*." In other words, the way in which the sacrifice dealt with sin was by the destruction of the sin-laden sacrifice. The sprinkling, smearing, and pouring away of the sacrificial blood in the sight of God indicated that the life was wholly destroyed, and with it the sin of the sinner.

---

77. 11QT 26-27 — the High Priest "shall expiate with it for all the people of the assembly (the sin offering goat) and it shall be forgiven to them . . . [and he shall expiate] for all the children of Israel (the scapegoat) and it shall be forgiven to them" (Vermes); *m. Shebuoth* 1.7 — "*As the blood of the goat that is sprinkled within (the Holy of Holies) makes atonement for the Israelites,* so does the blood of the bullock make atonement for the priests; *and as the confession of sin recited over the scapegoat makes atonement for the Israelites,* so does the confession of sin recited over the bullock make atonement for the priests" (emphasis added). Note the assumption that sins are confessed also over the bullock which serves as sin offering for the priests (as in *m. Yoma* 3.8). This evidence calls in question the sharp distinction between the functions of the two goats, maintained, e.g., by Kraus, *Tod Jesu* 45-59.

78. Eichrodt, *Theology* (above n. 71) 1.165 n. 2; de Vaux, *Sacrifice* 94; McLean, *Cursed* 41, 80-81.

79. Lev. 17.10-12; Deut. 12.23.

80. Davies, *Paul* 235-36, citing A. Büchler, *Studies in Sin and Atonement* (London: Jews' College, 1928) 418-19; R. de Vaux, *Ancient Israel* (London: Darton/New York: McGraw-Hill, 1961) 418; *Sacrifice* 92; Daly, *Sacrifice* 108.

One can hardly fail to recognize here what we may call the sacrificial chiasmus, or what Morna Hooker has described as "interchange."[81]

> By the sacrifice the *sinner* was made *pure* and lived *free of that sin;*
> By the sacrifice the *pure* animal *died.*

And we can hardly fail to fill out the rest of the second line by adding:

> By the sacrifice the *pure* animal was made *impure* and *died for that sin* —

by its death destroying the sin. As the sin was transferred one way, bringing death to the sacrificial animal, so its purity and ongoing life were in effect transferred in reverse. This certainly seems to be how Paul thought of it. The clearest expression of the sacrificial chiasmus/interchange is 2 Cor. 5.21:[82]

> For our sake God made the *sinless one* into *sin,*
> so that in him *we* might become the *righteousness* of God.

So too Rom. 8.3:

> [God] sent his Son in the very image of sinful flesh and condemned *sin* in the flesh [of *Jesus*],
> in order that *the just requirement of the law* might be fulfilled in *us.*

So too Gal. 4.4-5:

> God sent forth his *Son,*
> > born of woman,
> > > born *under the law,*
> > > > in order that he might redeem those *under the law,*
> in order that we might receive the *adoption.*

The same theology is operative in Gal. 3.13, although the metaphor is not directly sacrificial:[83]

> *Christ* redeemed us from the *curse* of the law,
> having become a *curse* for *us.*

---

81. See Hooker, *Adam* 13-41. McLean, *Cursed* 143, uses the same term with reference to Rom. 8.3; 2 Cor. 5.21; and Gal. 3.13.

82. For those who doubt whether there is a sacrificial allusion here, the alternative of Christ's Adamic solidarity/identification with sinful humanity is an attractive alternative (Furnish, *2 Corinthians* 340 and Thrall, *2 Corinthians* 441-42); see above §9.2(4).

83. See further below §9.5; and note also 2 Cor. 8.9 (below §11.5c).

In short, to say that Jesus died as representative of Adamic humankind and to say that Jesus died as sacrifice for the sins of humankind was for Paul to say the same thing. And even if the rationale cannot be traced back firmly to a Hebrew theology of sacrifice, it certainly seems to be the theological logic of Paul's own thought. Jesus' death was the end of humankind under the power of sin and death, the destruction of man and woman as sinner (cf. Rom. 7.4). This evidently, so far as Paul was concerned, was the only way God could deal with the power of sin and death. The sentence of death on the infected portion of humanity was the means to life for the rest of humanity.

This was the good news of Paul's gospel: those who identified with Christ in his death were saved from dying their own death as the outcome of their subservience to sin. By identifying with Christ in his death, the death they could experience was his death. Death was still inescapable (2 Cor. 5.14), but by virtue of their sharing in his death, neither sin nor death would have the last word.

We will have to return to this strand of theological reflection and follow it further.[84] For the moment, however, we may observe one corollary. That is, the inadequacy of the word "substitution" to describe what Paul was teaching in all this. Despite its much favoured pedigree,[85] "substitution" tells only half the story. There is, of course, an important element of Jesus taking the place of others — that, after all, is at the heart of the sacrificial metaphor. But Paul's teaching is *not* that Christ dies "in the place of" others so that they *escape* death (as the logic of "substitution" implies).[86] It is rather that Christ's sharing *their* death makes it possible for them to share *his* death. "Representation"[87] is not an adequate single-word description, nor particularly "participation" or "participatory event."[88] But at least they help convey the sense of a continuing identification with Christ in, through, and beyond his death, which, as we shall see, is fundamental to Paul's soteriology.

---

84. See below particularly §18.5.

85. See, e.g., those cited by McLean in relation to 2 Cor. 5.21 (*Cursed* 110-13); also Ridderbos, *Paul* 188-91; Witherington, *Narrative* 168.

86. See, e.g., Ladd, *Theology* 468-70.

87. As, e.g., Taylor, *Atonement* 85-90, 196-200, 206; Hooker, *Not Ashamed* 30, 36; cf. the German term *Stellvertretung* (e.g., Merklein, "Tod," and Strecker, *Theologie* 114).

88. As in Whiteley, *Theology* 145, 147; Cousar, *Theology* 74. Becker speaks of "inclusive substitution," "substantial union and identification" (*Paul* 409-10).

§9.4 The beloved Son

One possible variation on the sacrificial theme is the death of the beloved Son. "Son of God" is a way of referring to Jesus which Paul uses surprisingly rarely.[89] Distinctive of his usage, however, is an association between Jesus as God's Son and his death on the cross. Rom. 5.10: ". . . we were reconciled to God through the death of his Son." Rom. 8.3: "God sent his Son in the very likeness of sinful flesh and as a sin offering. . . ." Gal. 2.20: "the Son of God who loved me and gave himself for me." Gal. 4.4-5: "God sent his Son . . . in order that he might redeem those under the law. . . ."

This feature of Paul's theology may be the result simply of the strong tradition of Jesus as God's Son which can be traced back to Jesus himself.[90] In particular, Paul may possibly have intended an allusion to the parable of the vineyard tenants (Mark 12.1-9 pars.), where the death of the "beloved son" (Mark 12.6-8) is given some emphasis.[91] But it may also reflect Paul's awareness and use of the tradition of Isaac, Abraham's "beloved son" offered up in sacrifice by his father (Gen. 22.1-19), the Aqedah.[92] Certainly, in Rom. 8.32 Paul seems deliberately to echo Gen. 22.16:

> Rom. 8.32 — "he did not spare his own son";
> Gen. 22.16 — "you did not spare your son, your only (MT) / beloved (LXX) one."

To what extent the Aqedah tradition had been developed and was already conceived in vicarious terms is disputed.[93] But the possibility that Paul himself is a witness to an already vicarious interpretation of the binding of Isaac must at least be reckoned with.[94]

---

89. Only 17 occurrences in the Paulines.

90. See my *Christology* 22-33, and above §8.3(4).

91. See further below §11.3a; note also the "beloved son" in Mark 1.11 pars. and 9.7 pars., and cf. §8 n. 52 above.

92. This is the term by which the tradition of Jewish reflection on "the binding" of Isaac (Gen. 22.9) is generally known.

93. On the one side see P. R. Davies and B. D. Chilton, "The Aqedah: A Revised Tradition History," *CBQ* 40 (1978) 514-46. On the other see R. Hayward, "The Present State of Research into the Targumic Account of the Sacrifice of Isaac," *JSS* 32 (1981) 127-50; and A. F. Segal, " 'He Who Did Not Spare His Own Son . . .': Jesus, Paul and the Akedah," in Richardson and Hurd, eds., *From Jesus to Paul* 169-84. The debate turns on such points as the significance of Philo, *Abr.* 172, and the dating of traditions in Pseudo-Philo (note 18.5; 32.2-4; 40.2) and in the Targums. See also the discussion by Penna, "The Motif of the 'Aqedah Against the Background of Romans 8.32," *Paul* 1.142-68.

94. See, e.g., Schoeps, *Paul* 141-49; R. le Déaut, "La présentation targumique du sacrifice d'Isaac et la sotériologie paulinienne," *SPCIC* 2.563-74; Hengel, *Atonement* 61-63.

However, the principal dynamic in Paul's interaction with the Abraham traditions probably points to a different conclusion. For Abraham's offering of Isaac was a matter of considerable importance in pre-Pauline Jewish reflection — but as a demonstration of Abraham's faithfulness.[95] If Paul was making a point in Rom. 8.32, therefore, it was not in terms of the atonement being a reward for the Aqedah.[96] The point was rather that the Aqedah served more as a type of *God's* faithfulness (in the sacrifice of Christ) rather than of Abraham's (in the sacrifice of Isaac).[97] Anyway, the soteriological weight lies more on the following clause: "he did not spare his own Son *but gave him up for us all.*"

Whatever the background of this motif in Paul, the powerful imagery of the father offering up his son in sacrifice adds a note of particular poignancy to Paul's theology of the death of Jesus. The tradition of the death of the beloved Son, and Rom. 8.32 in particular, therefore, like the suffering Servant of Isaiah 53 and the martyr theology of *4 Maccabees* 17, provides a further variation on the sacrificial metaphor as a way of comprehending the meaning of Christ's death.

§9.5 The curse of the law

Sacrifice is not the only metaphor used by Paul to elucidate the significance of Christ's death. It remained the most important one, as we see from his frequent allusion to kerygmatic formulae referring to Christ's blood or his death "for our sins."[98] But he did use others, and we cannot do justice to his theology without at least dealing with them briefly.

The starkest is one already mentioned: Gal. 3.13 —

> Christ redeemed us from the curse of the law, having become a curse on our behalf, because it is written, "Cursed is everyone who has been hanged on a tree" (Deut. 21.23).

Here the plight of humankind is put in terms of curse rather than of being under the power of sin and death. But it comes to the same thing.

---

95. Already implied in Neh. 9.8 and Sir. 44.20, and developed particularly in 1 Macc. 2.52 and *Jub.* 17.15-16. Jas. 2.23 attests the same tradition of interpretation. For the development of the tradition in Second Temple and early rabbinic thought, by association with Passover and martyr theology, see Levenson, *Death* 173-99. See also below §14.7c and n. 167.

96. *Pace* N. A. Dahl, "The Atonement — An Adequate Reward for the Akedah? (Rom. 8.32)," in E. E. Ellis and M. Wilcox, eds., *Neotestamentica et Semitica,* M. Black FS (Edinburgh: Clark, 1969) 15-29.

97. Levenson, *Death* 222-23, notes that the allusion gives more weight to the assurance of 8.28: as Abraham remained faithful, and yet Isaac lived, so God's willingness to hand over his son eventuated not in his death but in his postmortem life. See further below §10.3.

98. See above §9.2(5).

The curse in view is twofold. First, Paul has altered the wording of
Deut. 21.23 to include an allusion back to the curse text cited in Gal. 3.10,
"Cursed is everyone who does not abide by all that has been written in the
book of the law to do it" (Deut. 27.26).[99] So the curse falls on those who fail
to obey the law,[100] that is, on Jews, though we should note that Gentiles are
also in effect included. For Gentiles by definition are outside the law (*anomoi,*
"those without law, outlaws"), and so also fail to obey the law.[101] But the
primary thought is of a curse on Jewish sin.[102]

This is clearer in the second curse text, Deut. 21.23. For what is in
view there is the Israelite who has committed a crime punished by death (Deut.
21.22).[103] His body hung on a tree is accursed by God and therefore constitutes
a defilement of the land;[104] so it must be removed without delay. This ties in
with the understanding of curse as implying rejection and expulsion;[105] and
in a Deuteronomistic setting particularly with the warning of the divine curses
on covenant breakers, which entails their expulsion from the land of covenant
inheritance (Deut. 29.27-28; 30.1).[106] The point is, however, that the covenant-
breaking Israelite thus cursed and expelled from the covenant land has in
effect been expelled from the covenant. That is to say, he is placed in the
same position as the one already outside the covenant, the Gentile. The cursed
Israelite is like the uncovenanted Gentile.[107]

99. Paul modifies Deut. 21.23 to include *epikataratos* ("cursed"), the repeated
term of Deut. 27.21-26 and 28.16-19. See also McLean, *Cursed* 134-36.

100. What Paul means by that is a subject to which we will return; see below
§14.5c.

101. See my *Galatians* 132-33 (on "Gentile sinners"); also below §14 n. 101.

102. Cf. the slight tangle in which Paul finds himself in Rom. 2.7-16 (above
§§5.4[3] and 6.3).

103. Note that the preceding ruling referred to the "stubborn and rebellious son,"
whose death was necessary to "purge the evil from your midst" (Deut. 21.18-21).

104. Note the concern for purity, the holiness of the land (*tame* [piel], *miainō,*
"defile, render unclean").

105. McLean, *Cursed* 125, refers to Gen. 3.16-19 with 23-24; 4.11-14; 49.7; Deut.
29.27-28; Jer. 17.5-6.

106. Cf. Bruce: "The curse of Deut. 27:26 was pronounced at the end of a
covenant-renewal ceremony and had special reference therefore to the covenant-breaker"
(*Galatians* 164); "The penalty of being hanged on a tree until one dies is prescribed in
the Temple Scroll for an Israelite who . . . has been guilty of breaking the covenant-bond.
To be exposed 'in the sun' was judged in Old Testament times to be a fitting punishment
for Israelites who were guilty of covenant violation" ("The Curse of the Law," in Hooker
and Wilson, eds., *Paul and Paulinism* 31). Cf. Grayston, *Dying* 80.

107. Cf. Eckstein, *Verheißung* 152. Contrast again Hamerton-Kelly: Gal. 3.13
meant "that the whole system of sacred vengeance based on Law was undermined, because
the curse is not divine vengeance at all but rather human violence dissembled through the
Sacred into the vengeance of the god" (*Sacred Violence* 79).

The theological logic in Gal. 3.13, therefore, seems to be that the cursed Christ[108] has been in effect put out of the covenant. In his death[109] he identified with sinning Jew and Gentile alike. Thus he brought the blessing of Abraham to Gentiles and made it possible for all to receive the promised Spirit (3.14).[110] For "in Christ" the blessing was no longer restricted to those who "abide by all that has been written in the book of the law to do it" (Gal. 3.10).[111] Nor were Gentiles (as *anomoi*) cut off from it by the barrier of the law. That was why the gospel could be good news to Gentiles,[112] as also for Jews who did not cling to covenant prerogatives.[113]

§9.6 Redemption

Among the range of metaphors used in the Pauline literature for the effectiveness of Christ's death, "redemption" *(apolytrōsis)* occurs a few times, and not least as part of Paul's central statement in Rom. 3.24 — ". . . justified as a gift by his grace through the redemption which is in Christ Jesus."[114] The image is of the ransoming of a captive or prisoner of war from slavery.[115] It could be used for sacral manumission of a slave,[116] a relevant consideration given Paul's extensive use of the slave metaphor subsequently in Romans 6.[117] But the stronger influence was almost certainly that of Israel being

108. "Become a curse" is, of course, simply a more vivid way of saying "become accursed" (Mussner, *Galater* 233, compares Jer. 24.9; 42.18; Zech. 8.13). The thought is close to that of 2 Cor. 5.21 — God "made him sin"; see above §9.3.

109. We recall that Deut. 21.23 had already been referred to crucifixion; see above n. 5.

110. The ambiguity of the "us" in Gal. 3.13 is a well-known problem (see, e.g., my *Galatians* 176-77) but accords with the way Paul seems deliberately to mesh (or even merge) the story of Israel with that of Adam (see above §§4.4, 6, 7).

111. The sense of "substitution" is stronger here (McLean, *Cursed* 126-27, with bibliography), but the "in Christ" of Gal. 3.14, 26-29 also underlines the sense of participation or representation.

112. Levenson, *Death* 210-13, relates the thought forward to the replacement of Isaac by Christ in 3.16, and thus finds a further echo of the Aqedah (see above §9.4). The fact that the promise of blessing to the nations is repeated (Gen. 22.18) as a direct consequence of Abraham's offering of Isaac (22.16) gives added plausibility to the suggestion.

113. See above §5.4 and below §§14.4-5.

114. See 1 Cor. 1.30; Col. 1.14; also Eph. 1.7 ("through his blood"), 14; Rom. 8.23 refers to "the redemption of the body."

115. *Ep. Arist.* 12, 33; Philo, *Prob.* 114; Josephus, *Ant.* 12.27; see further BAGD, *apolytrōsis*.

116. See Deissmann, *Light* 320-31. The typical form was "N.N. sold to the Pythian Apollo a male slave named X.Y. at a price of . . . minae, for freedom" (322).

117. Campbell, *Rhetoric* 126-30, draws particular attention to "the context of slavery."

ransomed (from slavery) in Egypt, prominent in Paul's principal quarry for scriptural texts (Deuteronomy, Psalms, and Isaiah).[118] The old debate on whether the concept of "redemption" included the idea of paying a price[119] was occasioned more by the subsequent Anselmian interpretation[120] than by the image itself or the scriptural background evoked by Paul.

It is less clear whether the verb "buy" *(agorazō),* or "buy from/back" *(exagorazō),*[121] has similar redemptive overtones. But while it is true that the verbs themselves do not necessarily carry such an implication,[122] the contexts carry overtone enough. The sequence of 1 Cor. 7.21-23 is all about slavery: "You were bought with a price; do not become slaves of human beings" (7.23). The price in view, in other words, was the purchase price whereby slaves were transferred from one owner to another — purchased to be set free (7.22).[123] And in Gal. 3.13 — "Christ has purchased us from the curse of the law" — the contextual thought is obviously of those who have been slaves "under the law" (4.1-3, 8-10). In a slave-owning society the imagery of manumission and liberation was one which could hardly fail to appeal to gospel proclaimers.

§9.7 Reconciliation

An alternative image used by Paul, and only by the Paulines in the NT, is that of reconciliation.[124] It is particularly prominent in 2 Cor. 5.18-20:[125]

118. E.g., Deut. 7.8; 9.26; 15.15; Pss. 25.22; 31.5; Isa. 43.1, 14; 44.22-24; 51.11; 52.3 (fuller details in my *Romans* 169). See also Lyonnet and Sabourin, *Sin* 105-15; Fitzmyer, *Paul* 66-67.

119. See, e.g., Morris, *Apostolic Preaching* 41-46; Hill, *Greek Words* 73-74; and further K. Kertelge, *EDNT* 1.138-40. Marshall, "Development" 251-52 n. 4, makes a helpful clarification of the distinction between "price" and "cost." See also Lyonnet and Sabourin, *Sin* 79-103.

120. Anselm, *Cur Deus Homo?* — Christ made the satisfaction which God's justice required (see Aulén, *Christus Victor* 84-92); but note Bultmann, *Theology* 1.297 — "paid to those powers who lay claim to man, who has fallen into their grasp, primarily the Law."

121. *Agorazō* — 1 Cor. 6.20; 7.23; *exagorazō* — Gal. 3.13; 4.5.

122. McLean, *Cursed* 127-31.

123. In this context we must of course include the imagery of "liberation" — Rom. 6.18-22; 8.2; 1 Cor. 7.22; Gal. 5.1 (see further below §§14.9d, 16.5a, and 23.6).

124. *Katallassō* — Rom. 5.10; 2 Cor. 5.18-20 (3 occurrences); also 1 Cor. 7.11; *katallagē* — Rom. 5.11; 11.15; 2 Cor. 5.18-19; *apokatallassō* — Col. 1.20, 22; Eph. 2.16. Porter's *Katallassō* demonstrates that Paul's use of *katallassō* and derivatives, with God as subject and sinners as object, is unattested prior to Paul.

125. On the issue of how best to translate *hōs hoti* at the beginning of v. 19 see Furnish, *2 Corinthians* 317-18, and Thrall, *2 Corinthians* 431-32. Thrall translates the

[18][God] reconciled us to himself through Christ and gave us the ministry of reconciliation. [19]As indeed, that God was in Christ reconciling the world to himself, not counting their transgressions against them, and has entrusted to us [literally, put within us] the message of reconciliation. [20]On Christ's behalf, therefore, we are ambassadors, as God makes his appeal through us. We beseech you on Christ's behalf: be reconciled to God.

The imagery is obvious. It presupposes a state of estrangement or hostility between God and humankind.[126] The idea that a death can bring about reconciliation may in itself evoke the idea of martyr theology (as implied also in Rom. 5.7).[127]

There are several notable features in the text. (a) One is the strong insistence that the reconciliation is between God and the world.[128] It is the fundamental Creator/creature relationship which is being restored here. Christ is the medium of the reconciliation, not the one who is reconciled.[129] (b) Another is the equally strong insistence that God was involved in the act of reconciliation — "through Christ" (v. 18), "in Christ" (v. 19). The emphasis is equivalent to what we have seen already in Rom. 3.25, not to mention 2 Cor. 5.21. The image is not of God as an angry opponent having to be cajoled or entreated, but of God, the injured partner, actively seeking reconciliation.[130] (c) Equally striking is the correlated or alternative metaphor — "not counting their transgressions against them."[131] The image of forgiving or choosing to ignore active hostility can be as effective as that of sacrifice for sins. (d) Not least is the confirmation that the message of reconciliation, focused in the cross (5.21), is the heart of the gospel. If Christ is the representative of God in effecting the reconciliation ("God was in Christ"), the

---

second *hōs* in v. 20 ("as") by "with the conviction that" (437). Furnish numbers himself with those who think Paul is drawing on a traditional formulation here, at least for the first part of v. 19 — "God was in Christ . . . transgressions against them" (334-35, 351; so also, e.g., Martin, *Reconciliation* 93-97).

126. Explicitly in Rom. 5.10; Col. 1.21; Eph. 2.16.

127. Cf. particularly the use of the term in 2 Maccabees (1.5; 5.20; 7.33; 8.29), where the context of martyr theology is strong (5.20; 7.33-38; 8.3-5), though the thought there is of *God* being reconciled (cf. *1 Clement* 48.1). But note Breytenbach's insistence that in biblical tradition the concepts of reconciliation and atonement do not belong together and that the former does not contain the latter (*Versöhnung,* but with some qualification on 215 and 221).

128. Similarly Rom. 11.15 and Col. 1.20.

129. The periphrastic "was reconciling" may imply that the process of reconciliation will not be complete till the final consummation (cf. Rom. 8.19-23; 1 Cor. 15.26; Col. 1.22).

130. See also Martin, *Reconciliation* 99, 103-7.

131. Probably an echo of Ps. 32.2, as in Rom. 4.8.

apostles are the representatives of God in proclaiming it ("God makes his appeal through us").

We should just note that subsequently, in Col. 1.20, the thought of God reconciling the world through Christ is elaborated — "through him to reconcile all things to him, making peace through the blood of his cross (through him), whether the things on the earth or the things in the heavens."[132] The reconciliation of individuals to God (1.22), as particularly also the reconciliation of Jew and Gentile (Eph. 2.16), are stages in a grander cosmic plan. That is presumably why the church in both these epistles can (or should) function as the locus of (and pattern for!) the reconciled world (Col. 1.18; Eph. 1.22-23).[133]

§9.8 Conquest of the powers

There is at least one other image we should note, particularly as it became an important theme in subsequent theology — *Christus victor*.[134] The theme is implicit in Rom. 8.31-39. Clearly envisaged is the heavenly court where final judgment shall be dispensed (8.33-34). Any accusations brought against God's elect will fail. Christ's death (8.32, 34) and resurrection (8.34) provide sufficient answer. Indeed, nothing can separate them from the love of Christ (8.35), the love of God which is in Christ (8.39). Christ's death and resurrection mean that any and all heavenly powers have lost any effective power over those who belong to Christ and any effective say in their destiny.

The same theme is implicit earlier in reference to the particular powers of sin and death. Christ having died, neither sin nor death has any more hold over him (Rom. 6.7-10). The corollary for those "in Christ" is obvious (6.11).

Where the theme of Christ's victory over the powers becomes explicit in the undisputed Paulines (1 Cor. 15.24-28) the reference is more to Christ's exaltation than to his death (15.27). And the conquest of death itself is an event awaiting the final consummation of all things (15.26, 28). This reminder that the process has begun but has still a good way to run is important, as we shall see later.[135]

Here, however, we should note how, once again in Colossians, the theme is focused in the cross in one of the most vivid metaphors ever coined in the

---

132. That cosmic reconciliation is in view (and not just human creation) is implied by the thematic *ta panta* ("all things"). Cf. Rom. 8.19-23 and Phil. 2.10-11. See further particularly Gnilka, *Kolosserbrief* 74-76.

133. See further my *Colossians* 96, 103-4.

134. Echoing Aulén.

135. See below §18.

Paulines — Col. 2.15: "He stripped off the rulers and the authorities, exposing them to public disgrace, leading them in triumph in him." The final image is that of the public triumph, in which the defeated foes are led captive in the train of the triumphant general.[136] The transformation of values, from the cross as the most shameful of deaths,[137] to the cross as a chariot leading the defeated powers in chains behind it, is about as audacious as one could imagine. For such a metaphor to be coined, the sense of release from oppressive powers now enjoyed by newly converted Christians must have been almost palpable.

§9.9 Conclusions

(1) Paul uses a rich and varied range of metaphors in his attempt to spell out the significance of Christ's death.[138] We have highlighted the most important ones — representation, sacrifice, curse, redemption, reconciliation, conquest of the powers. It is important to recognize their character as metaphors: the significance of Christ's death could be adequately expressed only in imagery and metaphor. As with all metaphors, the metaphor is not the thing itself but a means of expressing its meaning. It would be unwise, then, to translate these metaphors into literal facts, as though, for example, Christ's death were literally a sacrifice provided by God (as priest?) in the cosmos, conceived as a temple.[139]

(2) The point is underlined by the variety of these metaphors. Paul does not hesitate to run them together — redemption and sacrifice (Rom. 3.25), representation, reconciliation, (not) reckoning, and sacrifice (2 Cor. 5.14-21), redemption and curse (Gal. 3.13), and the sweep of images in Col. 2.11-15. Presumably the point is that no one metaphor is adequate to unfold the full significance of Christ's death. The fact that they do not always fit well together (Col. 2.11-15!) makes the same point. It would be unwise, therefore, to make one of these images normative and to fit all the rest into it, even the predominant metaphor of sacrifice.[140]

(3) A common theme running through the plurality of metaphors, though particularly stressed in that of reconciliation, is the initiative of God: "God sent,"

---

136. Cf. 2 Cor. 2.14, where, however, it is probably the apostles who are depicted as the prisoners of Christ; see further my *Colossians* 168-69.

137. See above n. 7.

138. Cf. Becker, *Paul* 407-11; Carroll and Green, *Death* 125-26.

139. Hebrews is an imaginative extension of the metaphor in that direction.

140. Martin is in danger of doing this with the metaphor of "reconciliation": "Paul's thought can best be captured in the omnibus term "reconciliation"; " 'Reconciliation' is the way Paul formulated his gospel in communicating it to the Gentiles" (*Reconciliation* 46, 153).

"God put forward," "God made," "God gave up," "God in Christ." Jesus does not act in any way independently of God or in opposition to God. The act of Jesus is the act of God. Nor does the cross of Jesus constitute the basis of a religion different from that of Israel, even if it does become for Christians the climactic expression of the provision made by God for the sins of his people.[141]

(4) The variety of metaphors also attests the impact of the proclamation of the cross on Paul and through his gospel. They would hardly have been living and fruitful metaphors had they not corresponded to experiences of conscience set at rest, of release and liberation, of reconciliation, and so on. From the beginning, we may well infer, the doctrine of atonement was not independent of the experience of atonement. From the first Christ was known by his benefits.[142]

(5) All this serves to underline the centrality of the death of Jesus in Paul's gospel and decisively undercuts any attempt to derive an alternative scheme of salvation from Paul. Paul does not present Jesus as the teacher whose teaching is the key to saving knowledge and wisdom. Nor does he argue that Jesus' incarnation was a saving event, that the Son, by taking flesh, healed it.[143] As the passages demonstrate, where overtones of a theology of incarnation are most readily heard, the soteriological moment focuses entirely on the cross (and resurrection).[144]

(6) It may very well have been Paul who thus gave the gospel its focus in the death of Jesus, who stamped the "cross" so firmly on the "gospel."[145] And we may speculate that it was Paul's influence which caused Mark to shape his "gospel" (Mark 1.1) to climax in the cross — a passion narrative with extended introduction.[146] And since Matthew and Luke incorporated

---

141. Cf., e.g., Taylor, *Atonement* 75-77. "God in Christ" is the basis of J. Moltmann's *Crucified God* (New York: Harper and Row/London: SCM, 1974).

142. Echoing again Melanchthon (cited above §3.1). See also S. B. Marrow, "Principles for Interpreting the New Testament Soteriological Terms," *NTS* 36 (1990) 268-80.

143. Observing that the Fathers "juxtaposed the two theories on salvation (that is, salvation through the incarnation and through the resurrection)," Cerfaux notes that "Paul's position never varies: the starting point of his soteriology, which is the death and resurrection, and his conception of Christ according to the flesh, always prevent him from attributing to the incarnation a positive and efficacious action in the order of salvation" (*Christ* 171).

144. Rom. 8.3; 2 Cor. 5.19; Gal. 4.4-5; Phil. 2.6-8.

145. See above §7.1. The point here does not relate to the idea itself of Christ's death as an atonement for sins, which, of course, was already developed before Paul, as 1 Cor. 15.3 sufficiently indicates; see, e.g., the discussion in Hengel, *Atonement* 33-75, and above §7.3.

146. Echoing the well-known description given by M. Kähler, *The So-Called Historical Jesus and the Historic Biblical Christ* (1896; Philadelphia: Fortress, 1956) 80 n. 11.

other Jesus tradition (Q) by fitting it into Mark's gospel framework, we may say that it was Paul who first shaped and determined Christianity's distinctive category of "gospel."

(7) Certainly it will be important to note also that in Paul's theology the cross becomes determinative for his whole perspective, a criterion by which he measures other would-be gospels, a *point d'appui* from which he sallies forth to engage opposing theologies.[147] This is evident from such varied passages as 1 Cor. 1.18-25; 2 Cor. 12.1-10; and Gal. 6.12-15, where again it is important to note that the fulcrum point, the central soteriological moment, is the cross.

(8) Consequently it is also doubtful whether the death of Christ can be dispensed with in any theology calling itself Christian — as docetism attempted. It is equally doubtful whether such a central metaphor as "sacrifice" can be discarded. It remains a difficult metaphor for contemporary commentators. But its application in martyr theology and in evoking a spirit of self-sacrifice indicates how fruitful it could be. And its power in expressing the seriousness of sin and the alienation experienced in a fractured society remains largely undiminished.[148] As the debate about myth and demythologizing has demonstrated, the outdated metaphor has to be remetaphored rather than simply discarded if the potency of its message for Paul and the first Christians is not to be lost.

(9) At the end of all discussion, Paul's message as God's ambassador on Christ's behalf is stark. Christ's death offers an effective response to the power of death and its sting (sin). That response is itself death. Those who ignore that response will find that their death is their own, as they choose, and that's that — finis. But for those who find in Christ's death the answer to sin and death, who identify with him in his death, there is the prospect of sharing with him also in his resurrection beyond death.

---

147. Cf. particularly Käsemann, "Saving Significance," with its typically trenchant statements: e.g., "the cross leads us back from illusory heroism to the humanity of creatureliness" (41); "before the God who humbles himself, self-transcending man comes to an end" (45-46); "we cannot say *crux nostra theologia* (Luther) unless we mean that this is the central and in a sense the only theme of Christian theology" (48); "the cross is the ground and test of Christology" (54). Also Stuhlmacher, "Eighteen Theses."

148. See further Young, *Sacrifice* ch. 6.

§10 The risen Lord[1]

1. **Bibliography**: **Beker**, *Paul* 135-81; **W. Bousset**, *Kyrios Christos* (1921; Nashville: Abingdon, 1970) chs. 3-4; **R. E. Brown**, *Introduction to New Testament Christology* (London: Chapman/New York: Paulist, 1994); **Bultmann**, *Theology* I, 121-33; **D. B. Capes**, *Old Testament Yahweh Texts in Paul's Christology* (WUNT 2.47; Tübingen: Mohr, 1992); **P. M. Casey**, *From Jewish Prophet to Gentile God: The Origins and Development of New Testament Christology* (Cambridge: James Clarke/Louisville: Westminster/John Knox, 1991); **L. Cerfaux**, *Christ in the Theology of St. Paul* (Freiburg: Herder, 1959); **O. Cullmann**, *The Christology of the New Testament* (London: SCM, 1959); **C. J. Davis**, *The Name and Way of the Lord: Old Testament Themes, New Testament Christology* (JSNTS 129; Sheffield: Sheffield Academic, 1996); **J. D. G. Dunn**, "1 Corinthians 15.45 — Last Adam, Life-Giving Spirit," in B. Lindars and S. S. Smalley, eds., *Christ and Spirit in the New Testament,* C. F. D. Moule FS (Cambridge: Cambridge University, 1973) 127-42; "Christology as an Aspect of Theology," in A. J. Malherbe and W. A. Meeks, eds., *The Future of Christology,* L. E. Keck FS (Minneapolis: Fortress, 1993) 202-12; **G. D. Fee**, "Christology and Pneumatology in Romans 8.9-11," in J. B. Green and M. Turner, eds., *Jesus of Nazareth, Lord and Christ: Essays on the Historical Jesus and New Testament Christology,* I. H. Marshall FS (Grand Rapids: Eerdmans/Carlisle: Paternoster, 1994) 312-31; **J. A. Fitzmyer**, "The Semitic Background of the New Testament *kyrios*-Title," *A Wandering Aramean: Collected Aramaic Essays* (Missoula: Scholars, 1979) 115-42; *Paul* 51-58; **Goppelt**, *Theology* 2.79-87; **Hahn**, *Titles* (§8 n. 1) 68-135; **M. J. Harris**, *Jesus as God: The New Testament Use of Theos in Reference to Jesus* (Grand Rapids: Baker, 1992); **M. Hengel**, *The Son of God: The Origin of Christology and the History of Jewish-Hellenistic Religion* (London: SCM, 1976); *Studies in Early Christology* (Edinburgh: Clark, 1995); **I. Hermann**, *Kyrios und Pneuma. Studien zur Christologie der paulinischen Hauptbriefe* (Munich: Kösel, 1961); **L. W. Hurtado**, *One God, One Lord: Early Christian Devotion and Ancient Jewish Monotheism* (Philadelphia: Fortress, 1988); **K. T. Kleinknecht**, *Der leidende Gerechtfertigte. Die alttestamentlich-jüdische Tradition vom "leidenden Gerechten" und ihre Rezeption bei Paulus* (WUNT 2.13; Tübingen: Mohr, 1984); **L. J. Kreitzer**, *Jesus and God in Paul's Eschatology* (JSNTS 19; Sheffield: Sheffield Academic, 1987); **D. R. de Lacey**, " 'One Lord' in Pauline Theology," in H. H. Rowdon, ed., *Christ the Lord: Studies in Christology,* D. Guthrie FS (Leicester: Inter-Varsity, 1982) 191-203; **Morris**, *Theology* 46-50; **C. F. D. Moule**, *The Origin of Christology* (Cambridge: Cambridge University, 1977); **C. F. D. Moule**, ed., *The Significance of the Resurrection for Faith in Jesus Christ* (London: SCM/Naperville: Allenson, 1968); **G. W. E. Nickelsburg**, *Resurrection, Immortality, and Eternal Life in Intertestamental Judaism* (Cambridge: Harvard University, 1972); **G. O'Collins**, *Christology: A Biblical, Historical and Systematic Study of Jesus* (London: Oxford University, 1995); **P. Pokorný**, *The Genesis of Christology: Foundations for a Theology of the New Testament* (Edinburgh: Clark, 1987); **K. Rahner and**

§10.1 The resurrection of the crucified

If the cross of Jesus stands at the centre of Paul's theology, so also does the resurrection of Jesus. Christ crucified is also he whom God raised from the dead. More to the point, the significance of the one cannot be grasped in isolation from that of the other. Without the resurrection, the cross would be a cause for despair. Without the cross, the resurrection would be an escape from reality. Unless the one died the death of all, the all would have little to celebrate in the resurrection of the one, other than to rejoice in his personal vindication.

Certainly, as we have seen, we have to take seriously the fact that Paul focuses the response of the gospel to the indictment of Rom. 1.18–3.20 in the death of Christ (3.21-26), without any immediate reference to his resurrection. Certainly Paul recalls his gospel preaching to the Galatians simply as the open portrayal of Jesus Christ as crucified (Gal. 3.1). Certainly he focuses his withering critique of human wisdom in 1 Corinthians in the folly of the preaching of the cross (1 Cor. 1.18-25).[2]

But we need also to recall that Paul's opening statement in Romans already spoke of Jesus as "appointed Son of God in power . . . as from the resurrection of the dead" (Rom. 1.4). And his subsequent formulaic echo brought the resurrection of Christ to the centre of the redemptive process: as Abraham believed him "who gives life to the dead" (4.17),[3] so the first Christians believed in "him who raised Jesus our Lord from the dead, who was handed over for our transgressions and raised for our vindication" (4.24-25). The distinction between "handed over on account of our transgressions" and "raised on account of our vindication"[4] is rhetorical. Paul hardly intended

---

W. Thüsing, *A New Christology* (London: Burns and Oates, 1980); **P. A. Rainbow**, "Jewish Monotheism as the Matrix for New Testament Christology: A Review Article," *NovT* 33 (1991) 78-91; **N. Richardson**, *Paul's Language about God* (JSNTS 99; Sheffield: Sheffield Academic, 1994); **Schlier**, *Grundzüge* 140-54; **E. Schweizer**, *Erniedrigung und Erhöhung bei Jesus und seinen Nachfolgern* (Zurich: Zwingli, [2]1962), earlier ET, *Lordship and Discipleship* (London: SCM/Naperville: Allenson, 1960); **D. M. Stanley**, *Christ's Resurrection in Pauline Soteriology* (AnBib 13; Rome: Pontifical Biblical Institute, 1961); **Strecker**, *Theologie* 87-98, 118-24; **Stuhlmacher**, *Theologie* 305-11; **V. Taylor**, "Does the New Testament call Jesus 'God'?" *New Testament Essays* (London: Epworth, 1970) 83-89; **W. Thüsing**, *Per Christum in Deum. Studien zum Verhältnis von Christozentrik und Theozentrik in den paulinischen Hauptbriefen* (Münster: Aschendorff, 1965); **Whiteley**, *Theology* 99-123; **Witherington**, *Narrative* 169-85; **Wright**, "Monotheism, Christology and Ethics: 1 Corinthians 8," *Climax* 120-36; **Ziesler**, *Pauline Christianity* 35-48.

2. See further above §9.9.

3. See above §2 nn. 58, 59.

4. The term used here, *dikaiōsis* ("vindication, justification, acquittal") is an

to imply that there were two distinct and independent judgments made on the basis of the two events.[5] But it is notable that he did not regard the effect of the sacrificial death of Christ as complete in itself. The first part required the ratification of the second. The vindication of Christ was also the vindication of those whom he represented.

Similarly in 5.9-10, in the first two of his repeated *pollō mallon* ("how much more") phrases,[6] Paul twice puts the resurrection on the "how much more" side of the equation:

> [9]How much more, then, having now been justified by his blood, we shall be saved through him from wrath. [10]For if when we were enemies we were reconciled to God through the death of his Son, how much more, having been reconciled, we shall be saved by his life.

So also in Rom. 6.3-11, the "both-and" of death and resurrection is determinative as much for Christ (6.7, 9-10) as for those united "with him" (6.3-6, 8, 11). The application of the analogy of the married woman envisages a similarly two-phase change of status — a death which frees from the law by widowing, "in order that you might become another's, the one who was raised from the dead" (7.1-4).[7] In the climactic vision of the heavenly court sitting in final judgment, the death of Jesus conjointly with his resurrection is what provides the definitive answer to any charges which may be brought against "the elect of God": "Who is there to condemn? It is Christ Jesus who died, rather was raised . . ." (8.34). And in the echo of the (probably) earliest baptismal confession, "Jesus is Lord," the saving faith thus confessed is simply "that God raised him from the dead" (Rom. 10.9-10).[8]

Elsewhere we may particularly recall the summary of the gospel as Paul first received it and which he continued to pass on to the churches he founded: "that Christ died for our sins in accordance with the scriptures, and that he was buried and that he was raised on the third day in accordance with the scriptures" (1 Cor. 15.3-4). The expansion which then follows is

---

unusual member of the *dikai-* word group. Paul uses it elsewhere only in Rom. 5.18, probably as a stylistic variation, to avoid undue repetition (*dikaiosynē* — 5.17, 21; *dikaiōma* — 5.16, 18). Cranfield, *Romans* 251-52, notes possible influence from Isa. 53.11, where LXX uses *dikaiōsai* (differing from the Hebrew).

5. See further my *Romans* 224-25. The two parallel *dia* ("on account of") phrases highlight the formulaic character of the verse but at some cost to precision of meaning. Cf. Rom. 8.10.

6. Rom. 5.9, 10, 15, 17; elsewhere 1 Cor. 12.22; 2 Cor. 3.9, 11; Phil. 1.23; 2.12.

7. The analogy is strained, of course, but its application clear; see my *Romans* 361-62.

8. See above §7.3.

taken up exclusively with the resurrection appearances of Christ (15.5-8),[9] and the subsequent exposition exclusively with "the resurrection from the dead" as proved by the resurrection of Christ (15.13-20).[10] Paul can even say: "if Christ has not been raised, then our preaching is empty, and your faith is empty" (15.14); "and if Christ has not been raised, your faith is futile, you are still in your sins" (15.17). There could hardly be a clearer statement that, so far as the gospel is concerned, Christ's death alone is no gospel. If we press the logic of the sacrificial rationale suggested above (§9.3), we could say that the sinner's destruction is no gospel without resurrection. Alternatively, that the slave set free from the power of sin must have another master, else the old one will resume ownership (Rom. 6.12-23). Or that the woman of the Rom. 7.1-3 analogy needs not only to be widowed but also to be married again (7.4). It is not only the power of sin that has to be overcome, but death. And only the risen one (1 Cor. 15.25-26), and only resurrection (15.51-57) can do that.

There can be no question, then, of the centrality of Jesus' resurrection for Paul,[11] that is, the resurrection of Jesus as God's act.[12] Once again, it is not simply a matter of how often Paul speaks explicitly on the theme.[13] It is more that the references he does make to it show how fundamental it was to his gospel and to his faith.[14]

And not just to Paul's own theology. This was the bedrock on which the common faith of the first Christians was built. The resurrection of Christ by God was where and how it all began.[15]

Already, prior to Paul's conversion, the claim had been established as of creedal veracity that Christ had been "raised on the third day" "in accordance with the scriptures *(kata tas graphas)*" (1 Cor. 15.4). What scriptures were in view has always been something of a puzzle. The first *kata tas graphas* (15.3) has always been easier to explicate than the second (15:4). The most

9. Despite, e.g., Conzelmann, *Outline* 204, there can be little doubt that Paul thought of the resurrection of Jesus as an event which had happened, however much we may wish to quibble over its character as "historical"; even if the risen one had as it were exited from time, Paul still thought of him as interacting with those still caught in the toils of time.

10. See further above §3.2.

11. As for NT theology as a whole (Stuhlmacher, *Theologie* 169-75).

12. Schlier, *Grundzüge* 142-43.

13. *Anastasis* ("resurrection") of Christ — Rom. 1.4; 6.5; 1 Cor. 15.21; Phil. 3.10; *anistēmi* ("rise, resurrect") — 1 Thes. 4.14; *egeirō* ("raise up") — Rom. 4.24, 25; 6.4, 9; 7.4; 8.11(2), 34; 10.9; 1 Cor. 6.14; 15.4, 12, 13, 14, 15(2), 16, 17, 20; 2 Cor. 4.14; 5.15; Gal. 1.1; Eph. 1.20; Col. 2.12; 1 Thes. 1.10; 2 Tim. 2.8.

14. See further Stanley, *Christ's Resurrection*.

15. See particularly Pokorný, *Genesis*.

likely candidates for the second are Hos. 6.1-2 and Jon. 1.17–2.2 (the latter prompted by Matt. 12.40):

> Come, let us return to the LORD;
> for it is he who has torn, and he will bind us up,
> that we may live before him.
> After two days he will revive us;
> and on the third day he will raise us up (LXX *anastēsometha*),
> that we may live before him (Hos. 6.1-2).

> Jonah was in the belly of the fish three days and three nights. Then Jonah prayed to the LORD his God from the belly of the fish, saying, "I called to the LORD out of my distress, and he answered me; out of the belly of Sheol I cried, and you heard my voice" (Jon. 1.17–2.2).

Since neither text particularly invited a messianic interpretation, it is probable that "the third day" came initially from earliest Christian testimony (the first resurrection appearances),[16] and that it was "the third day" which provided the clue to interpreting the Hosea and Jonah texts.[17] More to the point here, these texts could be seen as part of a substantial theme running through the scriptures, which consistently promised vindication to the righteous following their suffering.[18] In other words, an important background to Paul's twin emphases on cross and resurrection came with the first Christians' merging of the twin themes of the crucified Messiah and the vindicated righteous. In each case, the unexpected element (*crucified* Messiah, *already resurrected* righteous) confirms that the impulse behind the theological development came from the *novum* which Good Friday and Easter Sunday unfolded, and not from traditional Jewish expectation. But it is equally evident that this primal datum of Christian faith quickly drew various scriptures to it and became the core around which the new (Christian) apologia and kerygma were soon constructed.

---

16. See, e.g., Lindars, *Apologetic* (§7 n. 1) 59-63; Hahn, *Titles* 180. We may compare the way in which in the Synoptic tradition a vaguer expectation of vindication ("after three days" — Mark 8.31; 9.31; 10.34) seems to have been given greater precision in the course of transmission ("on the third day" — Matt. 16.21/Luke 9.22; Matt. 17.23; Matt. 20.19/Luke 18.33), presumably also on the basis of events as remembered.

17. For a review of alternative explanations see Fee, *1 Corinthians* 727-28. Contrast Pokorný: "As interpretation it may indeed contain a historical reminiscence, but this is only a hypothetical possibility. The statement about the third day has above all a theological function" (*Genesis* 145-46).

18. Including not least Job, Psalms 18 and 30, Isaiah 53, Daniel 7, Wisdom 1–5, and 2 Maccabees 7. See further Nickelsburg, *Resurrection,* and Kleinknecht, *Gerechtfertigte.* Note also Acts 2.23-24; 3.13-14; 4.10; 5.30; 8.32-35; 13.27-30.

The creedal formulae already noted (§7.3) also confirm that the resurrection of Christ was part of the distinguishing (creedal) faith of the Nazarenes well before Paul dictated his first letter. An important factor in the shaping of Paul's own theology, we may presume, was the correlation of his own experience on the Damascus road with the creedal testimonies he was then taught.[19] Of Paul's own testimony we might simply note 1 Thes. 4.14 in particular — "we believe that Jesus died and rose again." For this is probably Paul's first recorded statement of faith, and he presents it precisely as already a common confession, which he could simply assume his readers shared with him.

Paul's theological reflection on this subject, then, takes the resurrection of the crucifed as a given fact of faith, and reflects accordingly — most obviously in 1 Corinthians 15. This means that we should not look in Paul for philosophical discussion as to whether and how such a thing is possible. It is not that such discussion would have been foreign to the age. For in Platonic philosophy the world of the senses was as much disjoined from noumenal reality as the world of cause and effect of Newtonian physics was closed to the divine. It is rather that Paul, like the first Christians, assumed a reality in which spiritual and material interacted, not least in human beings, in which death was not the end of everything, and in which embodiment was intrinsic to human existence.[20] The resurrection of Christ was therefore not an unthinkable thought for them.

Nevertheless, it came to Paul (as no doubt to those before him) with the force of revelation.[21] As the central presupposition of his conversion experience, it became the key term which redefined all his language, the paradigmatic event by which all reality was to be conjugated — first the death of Jesus, and then everything else in the light of the resurrection of the crucified. Without some appreciation of that givenness of the resurrection of the crucified for Paul it will hardly be possible to appreciate either his gospel or his theology.

---

19. Paul's addition of "and last of all . . . he appeared also to me" (1 Cor. 15.8), to the sequence of testimonies he thereafter learned (15.5-7), and in the same format (*ōphthē*, "he appeared to") must have been acceptable to his predecessors in faith. The agreement of Gal. 2.7-9 (cf. 1 Cor. 15.9-11) would have been impossible otherwise. We have no hint of Paul's testimony being questioned prior to Pseudo-Clement, *Homily* 17.18-19 (see Schneemelcher 2.535-37).

20. See above §3.2.

21. See above §7.4. As one probably experienced in visionary states (2 Cor. 12.7; see above §2.6), Paul had no doubts that the appearance on the Damascus road was different in kind — "last of all" (1 Cor. 15.8). The passive *ōphthē*, ("was seen by, appeared to") also indicates an understanding of the givenness of the vision and of something/someone there to be seen.

Most amazing of all, the resurrection of Jesus was understood by Paul (also those before him) as ushering in a new age, even the last days.[22] In the formula quoted in Rom. 1.4 Jesus' resurrection is spoken of as "the resurrection *of* the dead" rather than "his resurrection *from* the dead."[23] And in 1 Cor. 15.20 and 23 Jesus' resurrection is referred to as "the firstfruits" of the general resurrection, that is, the first sheaf of the ongoing harvest of dead humanity (15.22).[24] This eschatological significance was not dependent on an assumed shortness of "the last days."[25] What was important was that the last days had begun. And not simply that the resurrection of Christ marked a quantum shift into a new epoch or era, but that this new era was marked as final, climactic, in the unfolding purpose of God.[26] What meaning such a belief can have two thousand years later is an issue which will remain with us through subsequent chapters, since it is not resolvable in terms of christology alone but depends also in large part on the soteriology and ecclesiology still to be discussed.[27]

The theological significance of the pivotal fact of Christ's resurrection unfolded for Paul in two directions. First, in its bearing on Christ himself. The resurrection was never less than the resurrection of Jesus, something which had happened to *him*.[28] Second, in its bearing on those who committed themselves to this risen Jesus. The two are interwoven, as we shall see,[29] but it is the former on which we focus at this point.

22. Cf. Acts 2.17 (a surprising phrase in Acts); Heb. 1.2; Jas. 5.3; 1 John 2.18. In Paul the thought is less explicit. But note 1 Cor. 4.9 (apostles as the last act in the amphitheater); 10.11 ("the ends of the ages"); 15.45 (see below §10.2); 1 Thes. 2.16 ("to the end"?). See further below §§12.4 and 18.1.

23. This understanding of the phrase is questioned by Fitzmyer, *Romans* 236-37. But elsewhere Paul invariably speaks of Christ's resurrection as "from the dead" (Rom. 4.24; 6.4, 9; 7.4; 8.11[2], 34; 10.7, 9; Gal. 1.1; Col. 1.18; 2.12; 1 Thes. 1.10; Eph. 1.20; 2 Tim. 2.8). Not least of note is the careful way in which in 1 Corinthians 15 Paul distinguishes "the resurrection *of* the dead" (when speaking of the general resurrection, 15.12, 13, 21, 42) from Christ's resurrection "*from* the dead" (15.12, 20). Note also Acts 4.2.

24. On the metaphor of firstfruits see below §13.4 n. 68.

25. See below §12.4. Already some twenty years from Christ's death and resurrection, the metaphor of firstfruits was still very much alive.

26. Cf. particularly Beker, *Paul:* "The cross . . . is the apocalyptic turning point of history" (205); "The death and resurrection of Christ in their apocalyptic setting constitute the coherent core of Paul's thought" (207); "According to Paul, the cosmic dimensions of the death and resurrection of Christ signify that the cross is God's judgment of the world and that the resurrection is the beginning of the ontological renewal of creation that will come to completion in God's new age" (211). See also above §2.4 and below §18.6.

27. See also §12.5 and §18 below.

28. Rightly stressed by O'Collins, *Christology* 87-90.

29. Particularly §18.

§10.2 The last Adam

We begin our analysis of the christological significance of the resurrection of Jesus with Paul's Adam christology. This is the third part of the theme already discussed in §8.6 and §9.1. The point is simply stated: in and by the resurrection, Christ became "last Adam." As we saw in §8.6, the theological logic of Adam christology could be extended back to include Jesus' whole life. But the focus of Adam christology lies clearly in Christ's death and resurrection. And if the exposition of the theme in Romans 5 centres on the death of Christ (5.15-19),[30] the exposition of 1 Corinthians 15 certainly centres on the resurrection of Christ. As Adam stands for death, so Christ stands for resurrection — 1 Cor. 15.21-22:

> [21]For since death came through a human being, the resurrection of the dead has come also through a human being. [22]For as in Adam all die, so also in Christ shall all be made alive.

In this case we could combine thought of death and resurrection without strain: as Adam represents humankind through life to death, so Christ represents humankind through death to life.

Similarly with the use of Ps. 8.4-6 in the further Adam christology of 15.27: God "has subjected everything under his feet" (Ps. 8.6). Although an allusion to Ps. 8.4-5 may also be implied in reference to Christ's life (as in Heb. 2.6-9),[31] the thought in 1 Cor. 15.27 is exclusively on the exaltation of the resurrected Christ. It is the risen and exalted Christ who fulfills and completes the divine plan for humankind (humankind's responsibility to rule over the rest of creation).

Most striking of all is Paul's third recourse to Adam christology within the same chapter — 1 Cor. 15.45:[32]

> [44]If there is a soulish body, there is also a spiritual body. [45]Thus also it is written: "the first man Adam became a living soul"; the last Adam [became] life-giving spirit.

The scriptural text cited is obviously Gen. 2.7: "the LORD God formed man of dust from the ground, and breathed into his nostrils the breath of life; and man

30. Also Rom. 8.3 and Gal. 4.4-5.

31. See again above §8.6. Note how the Adam christology of Heb. 2.6-9 is expounded in terms of Jesus' suffering as both representative and as "pioneer" leading many sons to glory through death to liberty (2.9-15).

32. In the following text I translate *psychikos* as "soulish" to bring out the allusion to Gen. 2.7 — "became a living soul *(psychē)*" — and *anthrōpos* as "man," since the thought is of Adam and Christ as two representative individuals.

became a living soul."[33] It should be recalled that the text is cited as part of Paul's discussion of the resurrection body, part of his distinction between the present body and the different body of postmortem resurrection (1 Cor. 15.35-50). The former is the body vitalized and characterized by *psychē* ("soul"), so *psychikos* ("soulish"); the latter by *pneuma* ("spirit/Spirit"), so *pneumatikos* ("spiritual"). Adam represents the former — the race of humanity which ends in death, the embodiment which cannot make the transition through death without transformation. Christ represents the latter — the race of humanity which begins from the resurrection of the dead, the embodiment of resurrection. As there is a disjunction between the seed which dies and the life of the new plant which "comes to life" the next spring (15.36), so there is more of a disjunction between Adam and Christ here than in Romans 5. The first Adam stands for humankind from creation up to death. The last Adam stands for eschatological humankind, the life of the new creation, from resurrection onwards.[34] Strictly speaking, then, as the first Adam began ("became") with creation (Gen. 2.7), so "the last Adam" began ("became" implied) with the resurrection of Jesus.[35]

The resurrection of Christ, therefore, opens up a whole new reality of existence, equivalent to the existence which Adam represents. In the event, Adam's has been an existence dominated by sin and death. In contrast, the existence embodied by the resurrected Christ is one where death has expended its sting and is now stingless (1 Cor. 15.54-57). Between them Adam and Christ span the whole of history from "first" to "last." But where the effectiveness of the first is marked by universal death, the effectiveness of the last really begins from Christ's resurrection. What this highly mythological or symbolical language means in actuality is something to which we must return.[36]

§10.3 Son of God in power

We have already noted that Paul speaks relatively seldom of Jesus as God's Son.[37] Here we should simply observe that in a number of instances it is the resurrected and exalted Christ who is in view.

Notable is the first christological statement in Romans: the gospel of

---

33. It is inconsequential whether Paul added "first" and "Adam" to Gen. 2.7: they are merely explicative elaborations; and Adam was "first" man independently of whether Christ was "last." Nor does it matter whether v. 45b is treated as part of the text quoted or as Paul's elaboration of it. For discussion see Koch, *Schrift* 134-37, and Stanley, *Paul* 207-9 (both in §7 n. 1).

34. See further Scroggs, *Adam* (§4 n. 1) 82-100.

35. See further below §§11.4-5 and 10.6.

36. See below §§12.5 and 15.5.

37. Above §9.4.

God "concerns his Son, who was descended from the seed of David in terms of the flesh, and who was appointed Son of God in power in terms of the spirit of holiness as from the resurrection of the dead" (Rom. 1.3-4). The formula, at least as used by Paul, seems to envisage a divine sonship which embraced the whole of Jesus' life (as son of David as well), but a sonship which was also enhanced by the resurrection ("appointed Son of God in power").[38] We should not speak here of an "adoptionist" christology, for "adoptionism" properly speaking affirms a taking into sonship of one who was not previously "son."[39] But we can hardly avoid seeing the resurrection of Christ itself as a christological moment of significance. To be sure, the text speaks only of a freshly empowered sonship ("in power, with power"). But it also speaks of an "appointment,"[40] and affirms that Jesus entered upon a position or status or role which he had not previously enjoyed or exercised.

Almost certainly what is reflected here is the impact of the resurrection of Jesus.[41] Jesus had not simply died — end of story! He had been raised again. Something quite new and hitherto unprecedented had happened to him. Jesus, and not just his disciples, had entered upon a new chapter, a new epoch, a new existence. How could that not be expressed in terms of a new status and role?

This line of reflection helps explain Paul's use of "Son" language when speaking of his own conversion. It was a "revelation," and a revelation of God's Son (Gal. 1.16). The same sense of a quantum shift of perspective on reality is thus tied in to the understanding of Christ as God's Son. Similarly, in what is usually regarded as Paul's summary of his preaching to Gentiles (1 Thes.

---

38. The argument that "in power" was an addition by Paul to a preformed formula can be safely rejected: it was partly dependent on the idea that the Davidic messiah was not thought of as God's son (a thesis now decisively undermined by the DSS — see above §8 n. 78) and ignored the unlikelihood of Paul significantly modifying a shared formula quoted to demonstrate his "good faith" to unknown churches. The suggestion that "in power" should be taken with the verb rather than the object ("declared with power to be the Son of God by his resurrection from the dead" — NIV) involves something of a distortion of the Greek syntax (cf., e.g., Fitzmyer, *Romans* 235).

39. The term can be used too lightly (as by Gaston, *Paul* [§6 n. 1] 113; Gnilka, *Theologie* 25), a stricture which applies also to the pre-Pauline formula which Paul attached to his own phrase "concerning his Son." But the questioning of the term's applicability does not depend on presupposing a preexistence christology here (as Stuhlmacher, *Theologie* 187-88). See further my *Christology* 34-35; *Romans* 6, 14.

40. The participle "appointed" (*horisthentos,* the only instance of the verb *horizō* in Paul) is frequently taken in the sense "designated" (NJB), "declared" (NRSV), "proclaimed" (REB). But "appointed" better expresses the force of the verb as denoting an act which brought Jesus to his status ("Son of God in power"), as commentators strongly agree (in addition to those cited in my *Romans* 13, see, e.g., Fitzmyer, *Romans* 235, and Moo, *Romans* 47-48).

41. "The confession 'Son of God' is primarily an explicit expression of Jesus' *exaltation*" (Hengel, *Son* 66).

1.9-10),[42] the primary thought is of God's Son, raised by him from the dead, his coming from heaven awaited by those who have believed in him.

Somewhat different in emphasis is the thought of Christ's heavenly rule as Son in 1 Cor. 15.28. The context again envisages a role and status which began with Christ's resurrection (15.25). But, unusually, it is a temporary role, to be climaxed in the Son's own subjection to God, "that God might be all in all" (15.28). Correlated in some way is presumably the later theology of Col. 1.13 — God "has transferred us into the kingdom of the son of his love" — where once again the thought is of the beloved son.[43] The resurrection was no doubt understood as Christ's appointment to kingship, though we should recall that the motif of the beloved son relates more to Christ's death[44] than to his resurrection.

No more need be said at this point. Another strand of the same motif focuses more on the idea of Christ's sonship as something shared with his followers,[45] and to that we will have to return.[46] For the moment, however, it is enough to note that for Paul, Jesus' divine sonship was in some sense a function of his resurrection.

§10.4 The Lord

Insofar as christological titles are concerned, and insofar as usage is the measure, the most significant way of speaking about Christ for Paul is indicated by the title *kyrios*, "Lord."[47] The great bulk of the occurrences of this

---

42. E.g., Bruce, *1 and 2 Thessalonians* 18.

43. "Son of his love" is best seen as a Semitic form equivalent to "beloved son" (BDF §165).

44. See above §9.4.

45. Rom. 8.29; Gal. 4.6-7; Col. 1.18b; cf. Heb. 2.10-17.

46. See below §§16.5c and 18.2.

47. In the undisputed Paulines (excluding Ephesians and the Pastorals) *kyrios* is used of Jesus about 200 times. The statistics cannot be precise because of textual variations and uncertainty as to the reference (God or Christ).

Lord Jesus Christ (in varying order)	55
Lord Jesus	21
in the Lord Jesus	2
Lord Christ	2
the Lord	82
in the Lord	33
kyrios = God (OT quotations)	19
kyrios = God or Jesus?	6

The six texts referred to in the last line are Rom. 10.12-13; 1 Cor. 1.31; 2.16; 2 Cor. 10.17-18, discussed below.

word are simply references to Christ, the theology of lordship almost as implicit as the theology of messiahship. But the fact that "Lord" is so regularly appended to "Jesus Christ," particularly in the formal language of letter openings and closings, is a reminder that the *kyrios* title is what denotes the Lord Jesus Christ's special status and dignity.[48] Likewise the fact that Paul speaks so often of Christ simply as "the Lord"[49] indicates an already ingrained attitude to the exalted Christ as simply "the Master," for Paul as for all Christians.

That Jesus' lordship was central for Paul and his gospel is sufficiently indicated by various passages. He summarizes his gospel as the preaching of "Jesus Christ as Lord" (2 Cor. 4.5).[50] Very similar is the recollection of the gospel proclamation in Col. 2.6 — "as you received the tradition of Christ Jesus as Lord. . . ."[51] And in 1 Cor. 12.3 he uses the confession "Jesus is Lord" as the decisive test of whether inspiration is from the Holy Spirit or not.[52]

In passages where the theology of Jesus' lordship becomes explicit, it is clear that the resurrection was understood as the decisive event in his becoming Lord.[53] Exaltation to lordship, we might say, was the other side of the coin of the appointment to sonship "in power" (Rom. 1.4).[54] Thus Rom. 10.9: the confession that "Jesus is Lord" was the public expression of belief that "God raised him from the dead." "Jesus is Lord" by virtue of his resurrection from the dead. Or again, Rom. 14.9: "it was for this purpose that Christ died and lived again *(ezēsen),* in order that he might be Lord over both dead and living."

Most striking is the climax of Phil. 2.6-11, usually regarded as a pre-Pauline hymn quoted by Paul:

---

48. E.g., Rom. 1.4, 7; 16.20; 1 Cor. 1.2, 3; 2 Cor. 1.2, 3; 13.13; Gal. 1.3; 6.18.

49. This usage is particularly prominent in the Corinthian and Thessalonian epistles, which contain 67 of the 82 references. Contrast Romans (5), Galatians (1), Philippians (2), and Philemon (0). Why this should be the case is a minor puzzle. We should also recall that Paul refers to Jesus simply as "Christ" (or "the Christ") more often (above §8 n. 76) and that "in Christ" or "in Christ Jesus" is more common than "in the Lord" (see further below §15 nn. 29 and 37).

50. See, e.g., Furnish, *2 Corinthians* 223.

51. See my *Colossians* 139-40.

52. See further below §§16.4 and 21.6a.

53. References to the earthly Jesus as "the Lord" (as in 1 Cor. 9.14 and 11.23) do not constitute counterevidence; it was natural to use the now familiar title while referring back to earlier phases (as in Britain people might speak of "the Queen" when referring to her childhood).

54. Hence what looks like Paul's rounding off the quoted formula (Rom. 1.4) by adding "Jesus Christ our Lord."

[9]Wherefore God has exalted him to the heights
    and bestowed on him the name which is over every name,
[10]so that at the name of Jesus every knee should bow,
    in heaven and on the earth and under the earth,
[11]and every tongue confess that Jesus Christ is Lord
    to the glory of God the Father.

The name bestowed is presumably "Lord," since it is the confession of that lordship which constitutes the climactic worship of all creation.[55] Although resurrection as such is not mentioned here, the exaltation follows upon and is the divine answer to the cross (2.8). So the thought is effectively the same: Christ was given the status of "Lord" by God as the formal title of his vindication following his obedient death. This at least is a variation on the vindication of the suffering righteous, or, more clearly, a variation on the third phase of Adam christology (§10.1). But the latter is a thesis which will call for some further reflection.[56]

The affirmation of Jesus' lordship is one which we can trace back at least to the earliest days of Christian reflection on Christ's resurrection.[57] One of the scriptures which quickly became luminous for the first believers was evidently Ps. 110.1: "The LORD said to my Lord, 'Sit on my right until I make your enemies a footstool for your feet.'" The first Christians now knew who "my Lord" was who was thus addressed by the Lord God. It could only be Messiah Jesus.[58] He was now "God's vice-regent."[59] The text was clearly in mind in several Pauline passages.[60] In each case the installation to lordship

---

55. So most; see, e.g., Hawthorne, *Philippians* 91-92. Moule, "Further Reflexions" (§11 n. 1), suggests that the name is "Jesus" (270); but it is difficult to see in what sense this was "given" to Jesus at his exaltation. O'Brien, on the other hand, argues that the name is "Yahweh" (*Philippians* 237-38); but such subtlety is hardly suggested by the final phrase ("to the glory of God the Father"); whereas the relation of Jesus to God as "Lord" to "God" is regular in Paul (see below §10.5a).

56. See further below §11.4.

57. See below on 1 Cor. 16.22 (n. 66).

58. For a full discussion of the use of Ps. 110.1 in Christian apologetic, including its initial application to Jesus, see particularly D. M. Hay, *Glory at the Right Hand: Psalm 110 in Early Christianity* (SBLMS 18; Nashville: Abingdon, 1973); M. Gourgues, *À la droite de Dieu. Résurrection de Jésus et actualisation du Psaume 110.1 dans le Nouveau Testament* (ÉB; Paris: Gabalda, 1978); M. Hengel, " 'Sit at My Right Hand!' The Enthronement of Christ at the Right Hand of God and Psalm 110.1," *Studies* 119-225.

59. Cerfaux, *Christ* 466. "The right (hand)" denotes power (e.g., Exod. 15.6, 12; Deut. 33.2; Job 40.9; Pss. 17.7; 18.35, etc.). Hence a seat at the right hand is a seat of special honour (1 Kgs. 2.19; Ps. 45.9).

60. Rom. 8.34; 1 Cor. 15.25; Col. 3.1; also Eph. 1.20. Outside the Pauline corpus — Mark 12.36 pars.; 14.62 pars.; Acts 2.34-35; Heb. 1.3, 13; 8.1; 10.12; 12.2; 1 Pet. 3.22.

61. BAGD, *kyrios;* Lietzmann, *Römer* 97-101; W. Foerster, *TDNT* 3.1041-58; Hahn, *Titles* 68-70.

is coincident with or the immediate corollary to Christ's resurrection. "It is Christ who died, rather was raised, who also is on God's right" (Rom. 8.34). The resurrection (1 Cor. 15.23) evidently began Christ's reign as Lord (15.24-25). Resurrection meant being raised to a seat on God's right (Col. 3.1). God "raised him from the dead and made him sit on his right in the heavenly places" (Eph. 1.20).

The significance of this ascription of lordship to the risen Christ is also fairly clear, though it can be exaggerated. (a) At the very least, *kyrios* denoted an asserted or acknowledged dominance and right of disposal of superior over inferior — whether simply master over slave, king over subject, or, by extension, god over worshiper.[61] To confess someone as one's "lord" expressed an attitude of subserviency and a sense of belonging or devotion to the one so named.[62] And if the confession was used in baptism (as seems likely in Rom. 10.9), it would also indicate a transfer of allegiance and change in acknowledged ownership. At the very least, then, the confession of Jesus as Lord betokened a life now committed to his service.

(b) There is a fair amount of evidence that the title *kyrios* was already a principal way of speaking of the god or goddess of particular cults — particularly of Egyptian or other gods from the east (notably Isis). Also of deified rulers in Egypt (for example, Ptolemy XIV and Cleopatra). The Roman emperors were also spoken of as *kyrioi*.[63] To what extent the last had cultic overtones is unclear. The emperor cult at this stage was still only spreading through the empire from the east, and it fulfilled a primarily political rather than religious function.[64] In Hellenistic culture, different lordships could be acknowledged in different spheres without implying conflict of loyalties. The sharp antithesis between "Caesar is Lord" and "Christ is Lord" *(Kyrios Kaisar* and *Kyrios Christos),* indicated later in *Martyrdom of Polycarp* 8.2, is not yet in evidence in Paul's time.

Whatever the precise facts, however, it is clear that Paul was aware of "many lords" honoured in many cults of his day (1 Cor. 8.5).[65] It is also clear that the attribution of lordship to Jesus could not have been derived from or modeled on the cultic worship of his Hellenistic environment. Apart from anything else, the evidence of 1 Cor. 16.22 shows clearly enough that Jesus

62. Paul makes important use of this point in Rom. 14.4-8.

63. For the data see LSJ, *kyrios* B; BAGD, *kyrios* 2cg; *NDIEC* 3.33, 35-36. In Acts 25.26 the emperor is referred to simply as "the Lord."

64. See also Cullmann, *Christology* 215, 220, Hahn, *Titles* 111-12, and Moule, *Origin* 35-43, against the older idea that the *kyrios* title was applied to Jesus in opposition to the emperor cult.

65. The context of 1 Cor. 8.5 is clearly that of cultic worship. We have good archaeological evidence of many shrines in Corinth — Apollo, Athena, Aphrodite, Asclepius, etc. See, e.g., Murphy-O'Connor, *Corinth* (§22 n. 8).

had already been designated Lord *(mar)* in Aramaic.[66] And the carryover of the Aramaic form into Greek-speaking churches indicates their own awareness of its origin.[67] More to the point, and in direct opposition to the tolerant pluralism of Hellenism, Paul affirms, "But for us . . . there is one Lord, Jesus Christ" (8.6). For Paul the risen Christ was quite simply *the* Lord. And he was personally convinced that this lordship would eventually be acknowledged by all.[68] As 1 Cor. 8.5-6 itself implies, this was an expression not so much of intolerance[69] as of belief in the uniqueness of Christ (in consequence of his resurrection), and a corollary of the equivalent uncompromising Jewish monotheism. Jesus is the *one* Lord just as, and indeed just because, God is the *one* God. What all this meant for the cultic-liturgical veneration of the Lord Jesus is an issue to which we must return below.[70]

(c) An interesting feature of the use of Ps. 110.1 in reference to Jesus' resurrection is the way in which it seems to have been combined with Ps. 8.6. We have indicated the use of both above.[71] The point here is that the thought of Ps. 110.1b ("until I make your enemies a footstool for your feet") seems to have been merged with that of Ps. 8.6b ("having subjected everything under his feet"). Either Ps. 8.6b is drawn in to complement Ps. 110.1 (as in 1 Cor. 15.25-27),[72] or the citation of Ps. 110.1b is modified by incorporating the phrasing of Ps. 8.6b.[73] Whether this happened consciously or unconsciously makes little difference. Either way the point is that the lordship of Christ was understood also as the fulfilment of God's purpose in creating Adam/humankind. Jesus as Lord is also last Adam. Whereas the lordship of Christ is unqualified in relation to other "lords many" (1 Cor. 8.5-6), his lordship in relation to God as Creator is qualified.

---

66. This formulation preserved in Aramaic *(maranatha)* in Greek-speaking churches was the Achilles' heel of Bousset's thesis *(Kyrios Christos)* that the title "Lord" only came into usage in the Hellenistic churches (followed by Bultmann, *Theology* 1.124-25). Fitzmyer argues that the hymn of Phil. 2.6-11 originated in Aramaic (*According to Paul* 89-105). The fact that the confession in Rom. 10.9 has the form "Jesus is Lord" rather than "Jesus Christ is Lord" suggests that lordship was first ascribed to the historically remembered individual, Jesus, before "Jesus Christ" became the more established referent.

67. See also the early use of Ps. 110.1 outlined above.

68. 1 Cor. 15.24-27; Phil. 2.9-11.

69. We recall that Paul seems to leave the status of the other gods and lords deliberately ambiguous (above §2.3c).

70. See further below §10.5c.

71. See above n. 60 (Ps. 110.1) and §8 n. 96 (Ps. 8.4-6).

72. 1 Cor. 15.25-27; Eph. 1.20-22; Heb. 1.13–2.8.

73. Mark 12.36/Matt. 22.44; 1 Pet. 3.22. The fact that the feature (the merging of Pss. 110.1 and 8.6) is so widespread in the NT suggests that it was not first created by Paul himself, but that he reflects an already established feature of early Christian apologetic (Dunn, *Christology* 109).

This presumably helps explain why Paul's fullest statement of Christ's lordship (1 Cor. 15.24-28) climaxes in the Lord subjecting himself to the one God of all (15.28).[74]

(d) The greatest significance in Paul's use of the term *kyrios* for Jesus lies in the fact that "(the) Lord" was already a customary way of speaking of God in Jewish circles. This can certainly be established in Aramaic usage for the preceding two centuries.[75] The point is less clear in Greek translations of the scriptures, since *kyrios* appears for the Hebrew *YHWH* only in later Christian copies of the LXX. In pre-Christian copies *YHWH* itself is either written out or transcribed in Greek letters.[76] But almost certainly *kyrios* would be the spoken term when such texts were *read* in diaspora synagogues. This is confirmed not only by Paul's use of *kyrios* in scriptural quotations,[77] but also by the usage of Philo and Josephus.[78]

What is most striking in Paul's *kyrios*-christology, however, is the fact that he refers some of the scriptural *kyrios* = Yahweh references to *kyrios* Jesus. The sequence in Rom. 10.9-13 is particularly notable:

> [9]If you confess with your mouth, "Jesus is Lord," and believe in your heart that God raised him from the dead, you will be saved. . . . [11]For the scripture says, "Everyone who believes in him shall not be put to shame" (Isa. 28.16). [12]For there is no distinction between Jew and Greek, for the same one is Lord of all, rich to all who call upon him. [13]For "everyone who calls upon the name of the Lord shall be saved" (Joel 2.32).

Since Paul has just emphasized the confession "Jesus is Lord" (10.9), it would be surprising if he did not mean his readers to understand the "Lord" of 10.12

74. Kreitzer, *Jesus* 152-53, finds a contrast between 1 Cor. 15.27-28 (emphasizing God's role in subjecting all things) and Phil. 3.21 (it is Christ himself who subjects all things) — "a tremendous step" (153). But 1 Cor. 15.25 shows that Paul could speak of Christ doing the subjecting (Ps. 110.1) without evidently detracting from the primary role of God. Nor should we speak of an "interim kingdom" or of a kingdom of Christ distinct from that of God; God shares his kingly rule with Christ who in the end "hands over the kingdom of *God* to the Father" (15.24).

75. See Fitzmyer, "Semitic Background," particularly 119-23; briefly in *EDNT* 2.330 and *Romans* 112-13.

76. See particularly G. Howard, "The Tetragram and the New Testament," *JBL* 96 (1977) 63-83.

77. Rom. 4.8; 9.28, 29; 10.16; 11.3, 34; 12.19; 14.11; 15.11; 1 Cor. 3.20; 10.26; 14.21; 2 Cor. 3.16, 17(twice), 18(twice); 6.17, 18. On 2 Cor. 3.16-18 see below §16.3 and n. 51.

78. Philo, *Leg. All.* 1.48, 53, 88, 90, 95-96; 2.1, 47, 51-53, 71, 78, 88, 94, 101, 106, etc. Josephus, *Ant.* 13.68; in *Ant.* 5.121 Josephus notes that "*Adoni* in the speech of the Hebrews means 'lord *(kyrios).*' " See also Moule, *Origin* 39-41; de Lacey, "One Lord" 191-95; Capes, *Yahweh Texts* 39-43.

and 13 as Jesus also. To "believe in him" (10.11) is evidently equivalent[79] to "calling upon him" (10.12). So the Lord whose name is called upon in 10.13 could hardly be other than the Lord Jesus. But 10.13 quotes Joel 2.32 (3.5 in Hebrew), where the remnant of Israel is envisaged as calling upon God.[80] The Lord Jesus is now envisaged as fulfilling the role of the Lord God.[81] In short, Paul seems to have had no qualms about transferring God's role in eschatological salvation to the risen Jesus.[82]

Paul may be doing something similar in other passages.[83] In 1 Cor. 2.16: " 'Who has known the mind of the Lord, who has instructed him?' (Isa. 40.13). But we have the mind of Christ." Precisely what the overlap amounts to in this case is unclear. Paul could be implying that "the mind of Christ" *is* "the mind of the Lord."[84] But he could equally be implying that "the mind of Christ" is the next best thing. The answer to Isaiah's question is, of course, "No one!" But the mind of Christ gives a clearer insight into the mind of God than otherwise would be possible (cf. Phil. 2.5). This would fit well with the immediate context, where the role in making known "the depths of God" is attributed to the Spirit (1 Cor. 2.9-12),[85] and also with the revelatory role attributed to the crucified and risen Christ elsewhere in the Corinthian epistles.[86] Given that in Paul's scriptural quotations *kyrios* usually denotes God, and also that Isa. 40.13 is again cited in Rom. 11.34, where the reference to God is incontrovertible, not too much should be made of 1 Cor. 2.16 in the present discussion.

There is a similar ambiguity in 2 Cor. 10.17-18. The quotation, "Let him who boasts, boast in the Lord" (Jer 9.24 [LXX 9.23]), is itself an adap-

---

79. Note the explanatory "for." The "in him" in the quotation of Isa. 28.16 does not appear in the Hebrew, but is attested in Greek versions, and so should not be regarded as a Pauline addition (see my *Romans* 583; Stanley, *Paul* [§7 n. 1] 124).

80. Joel 2.32 was quite widely used in early Christian self-understanding, both with christological modification (1 Cor. 1.2; Acts 9.14, 21; 22.16) and without (Acts 2.17-21, 39; with other echoes in Rom. 5.5; Tit. 3.6; Mark 13.24 pars.; Rev. 6.12).

81. Fitzmyer, *Romans* 593, observes that the title "Lord of all" (10.12) is a Jewish formula, used of Yahweh in 1QapGen 20.13 and 4Q409 1.6; cf. Josephus, *Ant.* 20.90.

82. To conclude from the reuse of the text that Paul "identified Jesus with Yahweh" (Capes, *Yahweh Texts* 123) oversimplifies Paul's hermeneutics; see further below §10.5.

83. In addition to those discussed below Capes, *Yahweh Texts* 140-49, cites 1 Cor. 10.26 and 2 Tim. 2.19. See also Whiteley, *Theology* 107-8.

84. Cf. Kreitzer, *Jesus* 19, 224 n. 68.

85. The Hebrew of Isa. 40.13 reads "Spirit *(ruach)* of the Lord"; LXX "the mind *(nous)* of the Lord."

86. 1 Cor. 1.23-24, 30; 2 Cor. 4.4-6. *Pace* Capes, *Yahweh Texts* 134-35, 138-40, if Christ is the "*wisdom* of God" (1.24), then the parallel is with "the *mind* of the Lord," rather than with "the mind of *the Lord*" (2.16a).

tation of both Hebrew and Greek.[87] Otherwise the usual rule would presumably apply straightforwardly (in quotations *kyrios* refers to God). But Paul then adds, "For it is not the one who commends himself that is approved, but the one whom the Lord commends." And the normal rule is that outside scriptural quotations "the Lord" is Christ. Paul evidently saw no problem in leaving that ambiguity unresolved. This in turn leaves the question open as to whether Paul's citation of the same text (in the same form) in 1 Cor. 1.31 had Christ in mind.[88]

Most striking of all is Phil. 2.9-11, already cited at the beginning of this section: "at the name of Jesus every knee shall bow . . . and every tongue confess that Jesus Christ is Lord" (2.10-11). No one who knew their scriptures could fail to recognize the allusion to Isa. 45.23: "to me every knee shall bow and every tongue confess."[89] What is astonishing, however, is that these words in Isaiah are spoken by God, and in one of the most unyielding monotheistic passages in the whole Bible.

> [21]There is no other god besides me,
>   a righteous God and a Saviour;
>   there is no one besides me.
> [22]Turn to me and be saved,
>   all the ends of the earth!
>   For I am God, and there is none other.
> [23]By myself I have sworn,
>   from my mouth has gone forth in righteousness
>   a word that shall not return:
> "To me every knee shall bow,
>   every tongue shall swear" (LXX adds "to God").

At the very least we have to recognize that the Philippian hymn (2.6-11) envisaged acclamation of and reverence before Christ which, according to Isaiah, God claimed for himself alone. On any count that is an astounding transfer for any Jew to make or appropriate.[90]

Yet, at the same time, we have to note the final line of the hymn: "every tongue confess that Jesus Christ is Lord, to the glory of God the Father" (2.11). This means that the acclamation of Jesus Christ as Lord involved no heavenly coup or takeover, no replacement of God by Christ. On

---

87. "In the Lord" has replaced "in this"; Stanley, *Paul* (§7 n. 1) 187-88, attributes the adaptation to Paul himself.

88. Bousset, *Kyrios Christos* 149; Furnish, *2 Corinthians* 474; Fee, *1 Corinthians* 87; Capes, *Yahweh Texts* 134-36.

89. The wording is in complete agreement with the LXX.

90. Of recent studies cf., e.g., Kreitzer, *Jesus* 116, and Capes, *Yahweh Texts* 159.

the contrary, it was *God* who would be glorified in the confession of *Jesus*. And not because the one was identified with the other (Jesus is Lord, God is Father). But, most obviously, because the one God (of Isaiah 45) had chosen to share his sovereignty with the exalted Christ. In other words, we are back once again in the scenario of 1 Cor. 15.24-28. The universal lordship of Jesus Christ has been determined and effected by God, but the supreme glory is God's.[91]

The exaltation to lordship which the resurrection brought Jesus could hardly be stated in more fulsome terms than Phil. 2.10-11. But that only opens up for us the still more intriguing issue of whether Paul in fact assumed that the risen Christ had been deified, or, if that formulation of the issue jars, whether the risen Christ had been recognized as divine.

§10.5 Jesus as God?

The issue here is best discussed under three heads: (a) the significance of Christ's lordship in relation to God as one;[92] (b) whether Paul ever spoke of Jesus as *theos* ("God/god"); (c) the significance of the veneration offered to the exalted Christ. A fourth aspect, the preexistence of Christ, we will treat separately in §11.

(a) *The significance of Christ's lordship within a context of monotheism.* Within Jewish thought there was a fair amount of speculation about exalted heroes. For example, Enoch and Elijah had been translated to heaven.[93] The righteous martyrs of Wisdom 5 fully expected to be numbered with the sons of God/angels (5.5, 15-16). A generation after Paul, Jewish writings could speak of Ezra and Baruch as having been taken up to heaven.[94] According to Sir. 45.2 God made Moses "equal in glory to the holy ones (angels)."[95] Such exalted figures were sometimes spoken of as sharing in divine functions not least in judgment. Enoch's role in the final judgment was a subject of some speculation.[96] In *T. Abr.* (A) Adam is depicted as sitting on a glorious throne

---

91. Cf. Thüsing, *Per Christum* 46-60.

92. The issue does not arise in the same way with "Son of God," for obvious reasons, even though it emphasizes the closeness of the bond between Jesus and God (Hengel, *Son* 10, 63).

93. Gen. 5.24; 2 Kgs. 2.11.

94. *4 Ezra* 14.9; *2 Baruch* 13.3, etc.

95. Josephus also reports speculation as to whether Moses had been taken (or had returned) to "the deity" (*Ant.* 3.96-97; 4.326; cf. Philo, *Sac.* 8-10; *Mos.* 2.290).

96. *Jub.* 4.22-23; *1 Enoch* 12–16; *T. Abr.* (B) 11. In the *Similitudes of Enoch* the Son of Man "will judge the secret things" (*1 Enoch* 49.4; 61.9) and is apparently identified subsequently as Enoch (71.14).

(ch. 11) and then Abel is depicted as exercising judgment over the entire creation (13.2-3).[97] And there is a later rabbinic tradition in which the famous rabbi Akiba (two generations after Paul) speculated that the other throne (implied in the plural of Dan. 7.9) was for the Messiah.[98]

This material is cited not as evidence of parallels to Christ's exaltation or to demonstrate the source of Christian reflection on the subject. It is cited rather to indicate that Jewish monotheistic faith could accommodate the idea of one highly exalted, without (apparently) any thought that Jewish mono-theism was compromised or would have to be rethought.[99]

This ties in to the fact that Paul evidences no sense of strain in speaking both of Christ's lordship and of God as one in the same breath. So particularly 1 Cor. 8.5-6:

> For, even if there are so-called gods, whether in heaven or on earth, as indeed there are gods many and lords many,
>> yet for us there is one God, the Father,
>>> from whom all things and we for him,
>> and one Lord Jesus Christ,
>>> through whom all things and we through him.

In an astonishing adaptation of the *Shema* (Deut. 6.4),[100] Paul attributes the lordship of the one God to Jesus Christ. And yet his confession of God as one is still affirmed. Evidently the lordship of Christ was not thought of as any usurpation or replacement of God's authority, but expressive of it. The one Lord attests the one God. This also ties in with Phil. 2.10-11. As noted above, the universal confession of Jesus' lordship is understood as glorifying God the Father.

---

97. In Recension B only Abel features (*T. Abr.* 11). Note also the role attributed to the mysterious Melchizedek figure in 11QMelch (below n. 120).

98. *b. Ḥagigah* 14a; *b. Sanhedrin* 38b. See further my *Partings* 186-87, 224; Casey, *Jewish Prophet* 81-82; Hurtado, *One God* ch. 3. Rainbow's critique of Hurtado falls back on the suggestion that Jesus himself may have convinced his followers "that he as the Messiah would participate in the incomparable status of the one God" ("Jewish Monotheism" 90); but see below §11 n. 34.

99. The sense of threat to the basic conviction of God's oneness is first evident in the Johannine traditions (John 5.18; 10.30-33) and the so-called "two powers" heresy (A. F. Segal, *Two Powers in Heaven: Early Rabbinic Reports about Christianity and Gnosticism* [Leiden: Brill, 1977]; see further my *Partings* 215-29).

100. Dunn, *Christology* 180; also *Partings* 180, 182; Wright, *Climax* 121, 128-32 ("christological monotheism" — fullest statement in 114-18). Rainbow, "Jewish Mono-theism" 83, notes the remarkable step of Jews using a "one" formula for any other than God. But is it correct to say that "to Paul, Jesus' lordship can almost threaten the Father's godship" (de Lacey, "One Lord" 200-201)? On Jewish monotheism see above §§2.2-3.

Equally striking is the repeated formula in the Pauline letters in which God is spoken of as "the God and Father of our Lord Jesus Christ."[101] The striking feature is that Paul speaks of God not simply as the God of Christ, but as "the *God . . .* of our *Lord* Jesus Christ." Even as Lord, Jesus acknowledges his Father as his God. Here it becomes plain that *kyrios* is not so much a way of *identifying* Jesus with God, but if anything more a way of *distinguishing* Jesus from God. We may note also 1 Cor. 3.23 — "You are Christ's, and Christ is God's"; and 11.3 — "the head of Christ is God."[102] And again 1 Cor. 15.24-28: the Lord of all (cf. Rom. 10.12)[103] has been given his lordship by God. It is a lordship which fulfills God's purpose in making humankind (to be responsible in ruling over the rest of creation).[104] And it is a lordship which will in the end be wholly subject to God.

The only obvious resolution of the tension set up by Paul's talk of Jesus as Lord, then, is to follow the logic suggested by his reference of Yahweh texts to Jesus as Lord (§10.4d). That is, that Jesus' lordship is a status granted by God, a sharing in his authority. It is not that God has stepped aside and Jesus has taken over. It is rather that God shared his lordship with Christ, without it ceasing to be God's alone.[105]

In this light it becomes a matter of little surprise that Paul can speak both of "the judgment seat of God" (Rom. 14.10) and equivalently of "the judgment seat of [the] Christ" (2 Cor. 5.10). Christ is envisaged as acting as God's representative.[106] In the final day God will judge the secrets of humankind "through Jesus Christ" (Rom. 2.16). Alternatively expressed, the Lord at his coming "will bring to light the things hidden in darkness and will disclose the purposes of the heart"; but the resulting commendation will be from God (1 Cor. 4.5).[107] Similarly Paul's talk of "the day of the Lord" is obviously modeled on traditional eschatological expectation.[108] But Paul evidently regarded that as focusing on Christ. Hence the variations, "the day of

---

101. Rom. 15.6; 2 Cor. 1.3; 11.31; Col. 1.3; Eph. 1.3, 17; also 1 Pet. 1.3.

102. On 3.23 and 11.3 see also Thüsing, *Per Christum* 10-29.

103. See above n. 81.

104. See above §10.4c.

105. In Paul, however, it is always God who is described as the one who gives the Spirit (1 Cor. 2.12; 2 Cor. 1.21-22; 5.5; Gal. 3.5; 4.6; 1 Thes. 4.8; Eph. 1.17; cf. the "divine passives" of Rom. 5.5 and 1 Cor. 12.13), in some contrast to Acts 2.33 and the original expectation of the Baptist (Mark 1.8 pars.). The point is missed by Turner, *Holy Spirit* (§16 n. 1) 174-78.

106. This is a more substantial share in final judgment than that accorded to Enoch or Abel above. At the same time we should note the tradition that the saints would also be given roles in the final judgment (Matt. 19.28/Luke 22.30; 1 Cor. 6.2-3).

107. See also 2 Thes. 1.7-10; 2 Tim. 4.1; and further below §§12.2-3.

108. Amos 5.18-20; Joel 2.1-2, 11, 31; Zeph. 1.7, 14, 18, etc.

our Lord Jesus Christ," "the day of the Lord," "the day of Jesus Christ," "the day of Christ."[109] It is in Christ that God's purpose reaches its climax.[110] Similarly in Rom. 11.26, the hope of a final deliverer (Isa. 59.20) is transferred from Yahweh to Christ, though the focus in the remaining verses is solely on God (Rom. 11.28-36).[111] This "christologizing" of traditional theistic eschatology is the best example of a more diffuse phenomenon in which "God-language" becomes implicitly christological,[112] without the christology ceasing to be theocentric.[113]

In all this it is clear that Paul's understanding of God's purpose and of God's revelation has been radically altered, but not his understanding of God as one and finally sovereign. Jesus as Lord shares in that sovereignty and exercises it at least in part. If at least the exalted Christ is conceived of as God's vice-regent, it is not clear what the implied "more than (vice-regent)" amounts to.

(b) *Does Paul speak of Jesus as "God/god"?* The debate here revolves round one text in particular — Rom. 9.5. The list of blessings granted to Israel (9.4-5) climaxes in "the Christ":

> [4]Theirs is the adoption, the glory and the covenants, the law, the service and the promises; [5]theirs are the fathers and from them came the Christ insofar as the flesh is concerned. God who is over all, may he be blessed for ever. Amen.

109. "The day of our Lord Jesus (Christ)" — 1 Cor. 1.8; 2 Cor. 1.14
   "the day of the Lord" — 1 Cor. 5.5; 1 Thes. 5.2; 2 Thes. 2.2
   "the day of Jesus Christ" — Phil. 1.6
   "the day of Christ" — Phil. 1.10; 2.16
   "the day" — Rom. 2.5, 16; 1 Cor. 3.13; 1 Thes. 5.4; 2 Thes. 1.10; 2 Tim.
   1.12, 18; 4.8

110. Kreitzer, *Jesus* ch. 2, focuses on the theme of parousia and final judgment in arguing that there is a "conceptual overlap between God and Christ with respect to the execution of Final Judgment" (93, 111). In the Thessalonian epistles he draws particular attention to 1 Thes. 3.13; 4.14; and 2 Thes. 1.7-10 as all alluding to Zech. 14.5, also 2 Thes. 1.6-12 (Isa. 66.4-6, 15) and 2 Thes. 1.9 (Isa. 2.10; *Jesus* 117-22). See further below §12.2.

111. To be noted is the fact that later rabbinic tradition saw no difficulty in referring the passage to the Messiah (*b. Sanhedrin* 98a). See further below §19 n. 140.

112. This is the principal thesis of Richardson, *Paul's Language*. But he also observes that "Paul's *Christos*-language is grammatically subordinate to his *theos*-language" (304-5, 311). "If it is true that Paul uses God-language in order to interpret and 'define' Christ, it is also true that language about Christ in turn redefines the identity of God" (307).

113. Thüsing's thesis, in summary: "The Pauline christocentricity is intrinsically directed towards God *(von innen heraus ausgerichtet auf Gott)*, because already the christology of Paul is theocentric" (*Per Christum* 258).

What is at issue is whether the final clause would be more fairly translated: "from them, according to the flesh, comes the Messiah, who is over all, God blessed for ever. Amen" (NRSV).[114] This is stylistically the most natural reading,[115] and it accords with Paul's style elsewhere.[116] And in an independent doxology we would expect "Blessed" to come first.[117]

On the other hand, the theology implied in referring the benediction to the Messiah would almost certainly jar with anyone sensitive to the context. The list is a sequence of Israel's blessings and would naturally end with a benediction to the God of Israel (cf. Rom. 1.25), just as the whole discussion (Romans 9–11) climaxes with a doxology to God alone (11.33-36). Similarly, the juxtaposition of "the Messiah" and "he who is over all, God" would most obviously suggest different referents, rather than the same person in different status.[118] To be sure, Paul later in the same section speaks of Jesus as "Lord of all" (10.12). But "Lord," as we have seen, is not to be equated *simpliciter* with "God." And it is equally notable that it is precisely the other Pauline benedictions which bless "the God and Father of our Lord Jesus (Christ)."[119]

In other words, to infer that Paul intended Rom. 9.5 as a benediction to Christ as "God" would imply that he had abandoned the reserve which is such a mark of his talk of the exalted Christ elsewhere. And this would be no insignificant matter. For it would not allow any of the qualification outlined above in terms of God sharing his sovereignty with the exalted Christ. For

114. NRSV is a revision here of RSV. So also NIV and NJB. See further particularly Cranfield, *Romans* 464-70; B. M. Metzger, "The Punctuation of Rom. 9.5," in B. Lindars and S. S. Smalley, eds., *Christ and Spirit in the New Testament*, C. F. D. Moule FS (Cambridge: Cambridge University, 1973) 95-112; and Harris, *Jesus as God* 143-72. The alternative rendering is ". . . the Christ according to the flesh. God who is over all, may he be blessed for ever." This is the reading of manuscripts A, B, and C. REB has not revised NEB on this point. See further Kuss, *Römer* 678-96; Dunn, *Romans* 528-29; and O'Collins, *Christology* 144. As Fitzmyer's listing of the contrasting opinions shows, commentators are almost equally divided on the subject.

115. The intervention of *to kata sarka* between the antecedent ("the Christ") and the relative pronoun ("who") is less problematic than beginning a separate sentence with "who."

116. Rom. 1.25; 2 Cor. 11.31; Gal. 1.5; also 2 Tim. 4.18. We may note that in 2 Cor. 11.31 "he who is blessed for ever" is also poorly articulated to its context.

117. As in 2 Cor. 1.3; Eph. 1.3; also 1 Pet. 1.3 and Luke 1.68. In the LXX of Ps. 67.19 (Hebrew 68.18), however, we have "The Lord God be blessed"; but see Fitzmyer, *Romans* 549.

118. Kümmel, *Theology* 164. If *kata sarka* invites some contrast — but that is by no means certain (cf. Rom. 4.1; 9.3; 1 Cor. 1.26; 10.18) — it would more naturally be given in a contrasting phrase, usually *kata pneuma*. Cf. 2 Cor. 10.3-4 *(ou sarkika alla dynata tō theō)*.

119. 2 Cor. 1.3; 11.31; also Eph. 1.3; 1 Pet. 1.3.

"he who is over all, God" can hardly be other than the one God, the Creator,[120] elsewhere described by Paul (in his benedictions!) as "the God and Father of our Lord Jesus Christ." Paul's formulation is certainly loose, and a construal of the text as a benediction to Christ can hardly be disallowed as a reading legitimated by the wording. It is even possible that Paul's own reserve on the issue slipped at this point. But if so, in terms of reconstructing Paul's theology, we would be wiser to hear the benediction as a moment of high exultation (for Israel's blessings) and not as a considered expression of his theology.

We need not discuss other possible references in the Pauline corpus. They either depend on contentious or little supported readings of the text,[121] or are later.[122] So far as Paul's own theology is concerned, the issue hangs on Rom. 9.5.

(c) *The significance of the veneration offered to the exalted Christ.* The use of *kyrios* for Christ in itself suggests that veneration was indeed offered to the exalted Lord in earliest Christian worship.[123] There is certainly evidence that Jesus was invoked or besought in Christian worship and prayer.[124] 1 Cor. 1.2 and Rom. 10.13 indicate that from very early on believers identified

120. Cf. particularly Eph. 4.6. Otherwise the absence of the definite article *(theos* and not *ho theos)* could invite a distinction easily expressed in English between "god" and "God." But that in turn would suggest more of an angel christology, the Messiah exalted as the supreme angel ("over all"). Cf. particularly 11QMelch (Melchizedek is described as *elohim)* and particularly the *Prayer of Joseph,* where the historical Jacob/Israel is identified as "an angel of God," "firstborn of every living thing," "archangel of the power of the Lord and the chief captain among the sons of God," and "the first minister before the face of God." But the latter is almost certainly later than Paul (see my *Christology* 21). In Acts 8.9-10 Luke reports that the Samaritans regarded Simon as "the Great Power," that is, as some sort of manifestation or embodiment of divine or supreme angelic power. But we are now at some remove from Rom. 9.5.

121. Gal. 2.20; Col. 2.2; 2 Thes. 1.12. See Cullmann, *Christology* 313; Brown, *Introduction* 177, 179-80; Harris, *Jesus as God* 259-68.

122. Particularly Tit. 2.13 — "awaiting the blessed hope and appearance of the glory of our great God and Saviour, Jesus Christ." This is the most probable rendering, though it could be taken differently; see, e.g., Cullmann, *Christology* 313-14; Harris, *Jesus* 185; Brown, *Introduction* 181-82; J. D. Quinn, *The Letter to Titus* (AB 35; New York: Doubleday, 1990) 155-57. At the same time we should recall the strong monotheistic affirmations in the Pastorals, particularly 1 Timothy (1 Tim. 1.17; 2.5; 6.15-16). And is "Jesus Christ" in apposition to "our great God and Saviour" or to "the glory of our great God and Saviour" (cf. particularly John 1.14 and 12.41)?

123. "The address of Jesus as Lord has its life-situation . . . in the cult"; Phil. 2.9-11 makes it "necessary to speak of a worship of Jesus" (Hahn, *Titles* 102, 110). Hurtado's central thesis is that it was "the cultic veneration of Jesus as a divine figure" (and religious experience) which occasioned the Christian "mutation" of Jewish monotheism *(One God* 11, 123-24).

124. Hurtado, *One God* 104-8; "this regularized place of Christ in such prayer is without parallel in Jewish groups" (107).

themselves as "those who call upon the name of the Lord (Jesus Christ)."[125] As already noted, 1 Cor. 16.22 is obviously an already well-established invocation, set and retained in Aramaic: "*Maranatha* (Our Lord, come!)."[126] And Paul testifies that he himself "besought the Lord three times" for the thorn in the flesh to be removed (2 Cor. 12.8). The implication of the last at least is that the exalted Lord could effect an alteration of Paul's personal circumstances. Similar in significance is the way in which the regular format of Paul's greeting refers to "God our Father and the Lord Jesus Christ" as the joint bestowers of grace and peace.[127] The closing benedictions likewise assume a conjoint authority, particularly 1 Thes. 3.11-13: "Now may our God and Father himself, and our Lord Jesus, direct our way to you; and may the Lord make you increase and abound in love to one another. . . ."[128] All this at least accords with a high christology of Jesus as highly exalted Lord.

At the same time an equivalent caution to that noted in (a) and (b) above must also be observed here. This is indicated in the care which Paul seems to take in his use of the normal worship terms. His thanks *(eucharistein, eucharistia)* are always addressed to God and never to Christ or "the Lord."[129] This is not simply because traditional formulation is being used, for Paul modifies the formulation on several occasions by adding "through Jesus Christ" or "through him."[130] The point, then, is that Christ is neither simply the content of the thanksgiving,[131] nor its recipient. In his exalted state he is envisaged as somehow mediating the praise to God. It is equally notable that the normal prayer terms *(deomai, deēsis)* are usually addressed to God and never to Christ.[132] So too with the term *doxazō*,

---

125. Davis, *Name* 129-39 (note the earlier conclusion on 106); Strecker, *Theologie* 94-95. But the formula "in the name of" as such does not imply a necessarily exalted authority (cf. 1 Cor. 1.13, 15).

126. See above n. 66.

127. Rom. 1.7; 1 Cor. 1.3; 2 Cor. 1.2; Gal. 1.3; Eph. 1.2; Phil. 1.2; 2 Thes. 1.2; Phm. 3.

128. Directing a person's way is a divine prerogative (Bruce, *1 and 2 Thessalonians* 71, referring to Pss. 32.8; 37.23; Prov. 3.6b; 16.9). Note also 2 Cor. 13.14: "The grace of our Lord Jesus Christ and the love of God and the fellowship of the Holy Spirit be with you all"; and 2 Thes. 2.16. Davis, *Name* 153, notes that "there are no examples of such binitarian prayer within pre-Christian monotheism."

129. *Eucharisteō* — Rom. 1.8; 7.25; 14.6; 1 Cor. 1.4 (and 14); 14.18; Phil. 1.3; Col. 1.3, 12; 3.17; 1 Thes. 1.2; 2.13; 2 Thes. 1.3; 2 Thes. 2.13; Phm. 4; *eucharistia* — 1 Cor. 14.16; 2 Cor. 4.15; 9.11, 12; Phil. 4.6; 1 Thes. 3.9; also 1 Tim. 2.1-3; 4.3-5.

130. Rom. 1.8; 7.25; Col. 3.17.

131. The phrase is *dia* with the genitive ("through"), not *dia* with the accusative ("on account of").

132. *deomai* — Rom. 1.10; 1 Thes. 3.10; *deēsis* — Rom. 10.1; 2 Cor. 1.11; 9.13-14; Phil. 1.4, 19; 4.6; also Eph. 6.18; 1 Tim. 2.1; 5.5; 2 Tim. 1.3.

"glorify."[133] For Paul, properly speaking, only God is to be glorified.[134] The same is true of *latreuō,* "serve (religiously, cultically)," and *latreia,* "service, worship," and the one use of *proskyneō,* "worship, reverence" in Paul (1 Cor. 14.25).[135] It is equally noticeable that Christ is absent from the passage which speaks most explicitly about worship in the Pauline churches. In 1 Corinthians 14, the speaker in tongues speaks "to God" (14.2, 28); thanks are given to God (14.18); the worship is to God (14.25). Such uniformity in Paul's usage should certainly make us hesitate before asserting that Paul "worshiped" Christ, since the evidence more clearly indicates otherwise.

Elsewhere the thought is more of Jesus as the content of the worship. This is implicit in any use made of passages (hymns) like Phil. 2.6-11 and Col. 1.15-20, for they are not addressed *to* Christ, but give praise to God *for* Christ.[136] Jesus' death is similarly the theme of the Lord's Supper in 1 Cor. 11.26. Likewise, Paul serves God in the gospel of his Son (Rom. 1.9). To acknowledge the gospel of Christ is to glorify God (2 Cor. 9.13). The confession of Jesus Christ as Lord is to the glory of God the Father (Phil. 2.11). The thought of God's "riches in glory in Christ Jesus" evokes the doxology "To our God and Father be glory for ever and ever" (Phil. 4.19-20). And in Col. 3.16-17 "the word of Christ" provides the subject matter for worship, and worship is offered "in the name of the Lord Jesus," but the thanks are given to God.[137] Not least of interest is Paul's talk of thanksgiving before a meal in Rom. 14.6: the one who eats or does not eat "does so to the Lord and gives thanks to God." And in Rom. 15.5-6, the climactic glorification of

---

133. Rom. 1.21; 3.7; 4.20; 11.36; 15.6, 7, 9; 1 Cor. 6.20; 10.31; 2 Cor. 1.20; 4.15; 9.13; Gal. 1.5, 24; Phil. 1.11; 2.11; 4.20; Eph. 1.6; 3.21; 1 Tim. 1.17. Note also 2 Cor. 4.4 — "the glory of Christ who is the image of God"; 2 Cor. 8.19 — "for the glory of the Lord"; Eph. 1.12, 14; 2 Tim. 4.18.

134. As Beker points out (*Paul* 362-63), *doxa* in Paul refers overwhelmingly to the glory of God (Rom. 1.23; 3.23; 5.2; 6.4; 9.23; 15.7, etc.). The relatively fewer references to the "glory of Christ" (1 Cor. 2.8; 2 Cor. 4.4; cf. 2 Cor. 3.18; 8.19, 23; 2 Thes. 2.14) are to be taken either as anticipations of the final glory of God or in terms of Christ manifesting what of God is perceptible to human sight (cf. Tit. 2.13 and n. 122 above). Note, e.g., 2 Cor. 1.20 — "we say the 'Amen' through him [Jesus Christ] to the glory of God"; Phil. 1.11; and the addition of "through Jesus Christ" in Rom. 16.27.

135. *latreuō* — Rom. 1.9; Phil. 3.3; 2 Tim. 1.3; *latreia* — Rom. 12.1.

136. The Colossian hymn (1.15-20) is an extension of the thanksgiving to the Father begun in 1.12. Hengel speaks too casually of "hymns to Christ" ("Hymns and Christology," *Between Jesus and Paul* 78-96).

137. Note, however, the adaptation of Col. 3.16-17 in Eph. 5.19-20: "singing and making melody in your hearts to the Lord," as well as the later hymns in Revelation (Hurtado, *One God* 102-3).

"the God and Father of our Lord Jesus Christ" is to be "in accord with Christ Jesus," not shared by him.[138]

All this suggests that we need a more carefully nuanced formulation in speaking about the cultic veneration of Jesus in earliest Christianity. If we observe the ancient distinction between "worship" and "veneration,"[139] we would have to speak of the veneration of Christ, meaning by that something short of full-scale worship. Or if we observe the equivalent distinction between "worship" and "adoration,"[140] we could say that Jesus was worshiped, meaning by that something short of the adoration reserved for God alone.[141] Either way, hindsight shows us that Paul's reserve was soon lost to sight.[142] Whether Paul himself was conscious of a steady transition in worship and whether this was a trend which Paul would have approved of, we cannot tell. But the upshot is that the degree of caution noted in (a) and (b) above is strengthened rather than diminished, and assessment of Paul's christology as we find it in his principal letters has to be couched accordingly.

§10.6 The life-giving Spirit

The final feature of Paul's resurrection christology which calls for consideration appears in only one passage — 1 Cor. 15.45:

"The first man Adam became a living   soul" (Gen. 2.7);
  the last   Adam [became] life-giving spirit."

Clearly the second clause (45b) is intended as a corollary to or expression of Paul's Adam christology. The risen Christ is the eschatological equivalent of the earthly Adam.[143] What is surprising here, however, is the parallel or

---

138. Note also how both sections climax (14.10-12; 15.9-13); see Thüsing, *Per Christum* 30-45. And cf. again Phil. 2.11 and 1 Cor. 15.24-28.

139. The second Council of Nicaea (787) ruled that worship *(latreia, adoratio)* should be offered to God alone. To the saints veneration *(douleia, veneratio)* was due. For the cult of Mary, the concept of *hyperdouleia* (without Latin equivalent) came to be used (K. Hausberger, "Heilige/Heiligenverehrung," *TRE* 14.651).

140. See my *Partings* 318 n. 69.

141. Harris is uninhibited on the point: in the Pauline letters Jesus "is the object of human faith and adoration" *(Jesus as God* 171).

142. John 20.28; Pliny, *Epistles* 10.96.7.

143. The "became" may be implicit and determined by Gen. 2.7, just cited (Fee, "Christology" 321), but it presumably refers once again to the "becoming" which happened in the resurrection/exaltation (cf. §§10.3-4 above). See further below §11.5a.

antithesis which Paul chooses to Gen. 2.7's "living soul." In the context we might have expected *sōma pneumatikon,* "spiritual body," for that is the theme in verse 44, picked up also in verse 46. Or we could have expected *pneuma zōn,* "living spirit," for that would have made a better parallel/antithesis with verse 45a. But Paul writes instead, *pneuma zōopoioun,* "life-giving spirit."

What did Paul mean by using this phrase? As already noted (§6.6), the role of "making alive" in biblical usage is almost exclusively that of God or of his Spirit.[144] Accordingly, Paul could hardly expect the well-informed reader to think of anything other than the life-giving power of God himself. Here, in other words, the thought is not so much of last Adam as the *pattern* of existence, as though all spiritual bodies of which Christ was the "firstfruits" (15.23) would be similarly "life-giving." The thought is more of the last Adam as the *progenitor* of a new kind of humanity — resurrected humankind. It is the *uniqueness* of the risen Christ's role as "life-giver" which is in view.

Should we then use the facility given us by English usage to translate "life-giving Spirit," rather than "life-giving spirit"? That is, did Paul intend his readers to think of the Holy Spirit? That indeed would be the reading which the term itself *(zōopoioun pneuma)* invited. For the Spirit of God is the obvious manifestation of the life-giving power of God. And although *zōopoieō* as such is not used of the Spirit in Jewish scriptures, an association between "(God's) Spirit" and "life" was bound up with the word itself, since Hebrew *ruach,* like Greek *pneuma,* denotes also "breath," the breath of life. The association goes back to Gen. 2.7 itself: "God breathed into the *adam*'s nostrils the breath of life." But it is clearer in other passages: notably Job 33.4 — "The Spirit of God has made me, and the breath of the Almighty gives me life"; Ps. 104.29-30 — "When you take away their breath, they die and return to their dust. When you send forth your Spirit, they are created"; and the wonderful vision in Ezekiel 37, where the prophet prophesies to the *ruach* to breathe upon the slain (representing Israel) "that they may live" (37.9-10). Not least we should note that in Rom. 8.11 and 2 Cor. 3.6 Paul himself speaks of the life-giving *(zōopoieō)* function of the Spirit and in Rom.8.2 speaks of the Spirit as "the Spirit of life."[145]

144. See the references in §6 nn. 130 and 131. See also Penna, "Adamic Christology and Anthropological Optimism in 1 Corinthians 15.45-49," *Paul* 1.206-31 (here 218-22).

145. Consequently I find it difficult to imagine that any reader of this text, well informed in the biblical tradition and in Paul's usage elsewhere, would read *pneuma zōopoioun* as other than a reference to or at least an allusion to the Spirit of God (*pace* Fee, "Christology" 321). Fee's argument would logically lead to distinguishing "the Spirit of Christ" from "the Spirit of God."

146. See my earlier more boldly stated "1 Corinthians 15.45."

The implication, then, is that Paul intended to represent the risen Christ as in some sense taking over the role of or even somehow becoming identified with the life-giving Spirit of God.[146] The idea is hardly far-fetched. There are other ways of speaking of God's active presence and self-manifestation, like glory and wisdom, which Paul elsewhere identifies with Christ.[147] And we have already observed the impact of the resurrection in bringing about radical revision in earliest Christian understanding of how God interacted with his world. But the Spirit was one of the most prominent ways of envisaging that interaction. So it is hardly surprising that Paul's bringing of these self-manifestations of God into focus in Christ should include an identification of the Spirit also with Christ.

At the same time, 1 Cor. 15.45 is unique in the Pauline writings.[148] Indeed, it would be as unique as Rom. 9.5, if that should be read as a benediction to the Christ as "God over all" (§10.5b). Consequently, we should treat it with similar reserve.

Paul himself displays a certain reluctance elsewhere in speaking of the relation of the Spirit to the resurrection of Christ. He has no qualms in attributing the future resurrection of the body to the Spirit: God "will give life to your mortal bodies through his Spirit, which dwells in you" (Rom. 8.11).[149] But he almost seems to fall over backward in the same text to avoid saying that God raised Jesus from the dead through the Spirit.[150] Jesus' resurrection life was not simply to be understood as a creation of the Spirit, any more than the last Adam was to be understood simply as a spiritual body or living spirit. This presumably ties in with another probably relevant fact: that whereas the identification with divine Wisdom for Paul reaches back to eternity,[151] the identification suggested in 1 Cor. 15.45 is from the resurrection. Evidently the transition of resurrection involved some sort of realignment of God's interaction with his world as well as of his rule in heaven.

147. "Glory" — see 1 Cor. 2.8; 2 Cor. 4.4, 6; Col. 1.27; "Wisdom" — see below §11.2.

148. *Pace,* e.g., Hermann, *Kyrios,* and Strecker, *Theologie* 97, I do not regard 2 Cor. 3.17 as equivalent; see my "2 Corinthians 3.17 — 'The Lord is the Spirit,'" *JTS* 21 (1970) 309-20, and below §16.3.

149. Fee prefers the reading "*because of* his Spirit which dwells in you" (*Empowering Presence* [§16 n. 1] 543); but Paul thought of the Spirit more as the means of salvation than as the reason for it.

150. Rom. 8.11 is a very cumbersome sentence. It would have been much easier to say simply "If the Spirit that dwells in you gave life to Jesus, the Spirit will also give life to you." See further my *Christology* 144, referring also to Rom. 1.4; 6.4; 1 Cor. 6.14; 2 Cor. 13.4.

151. See below §§11.1-2.

Another relevant factor is the way in which the Spirit in Paul's theology seems now to be determined by relation to Christ or defined by Christ. The Spirit's presence is indicated by the cry "Abba! Father!" in distinctive echo of Jesus' prayer and indicative of a sharing in his sonship (Rom. 8.14-17).[152] The Spirit's inspiration is marked by the confession "Jesus is Lord" (1 Cor. 12.3). The work of the Spirit is to transform Christians into the divine likeness (2 Cor. 3.18), which is Christ (4.4).[153] Hence also the Spirit is now known as "the Spirit of Christ" (Rom. 8.9), "the Spirit of [God's] Son" (Gal. 4.6), "the Spirit of Jesus Christ" (Phil. 1.19).[154] What is implied, presumably, is that the Spirit of God, hitherto a somewhat nebulous concept, was now being understood as related to Christ. Jesus Christ had come to be seen as the definition of the Spirit. And since Paul was so reluctant to attribute the resurrection of Jesus to the Spirit, the Spirit of Christ in view must be the Spirit which distinguished his whole ministry. In other words, the character of Jesus' ministry had become the defining character of the Spirit. In a tradition which had learned to be wary in attributing inspiration to the Spirit of God, this would have provided an invaluable test: only that power was to be recognized as the Spirit of God which manifested the character of Jesus.[155]

Other texts which need to be borne in mind are the "triadic" texts where Paul speaks of God, Christ, and the Spirit as acting conjointly or as equivalent ways of denoting the source and character of divine grace.[156] The degree to which Paul could assume Christ as functioning within the traditional conception of God immanent in his people through or as Spirit is a further striking indication of the transformation wrought on Paul's (and early Christian) theology by the resurrection.[157]

In the light of all this we can perhaps be a little clearer on the significance of 1 Cor. 15.45 for Paul's theology. The point presumably is that Paul saw all of God's purpose for humankind, and the means to effecting it, as focused in the resurrection of the crucified and given its definition by the resurrection of the crucified. As the Adam of God's purpose is the risen Christ, so he also focuses the life-giving power of the Spirit, by which that

152. See above §8.3(4).
153. See further below §18.2.
154. This is not simply Paul. See also Acts 16.7 and 1 Pet. 1.11.
155. See further below §16.4; also §21.6.
156. Particularly Rom. 8.9-11; 1 Cor. 12.4-6; 2 Cor. 1.21-22; 13.13; Gal. 4.6; 2 Thes. 2.13; cf. 1 Cor. 1.4-7; subsequently Eph. 4.4-6.
157. Cf. Schlier, *Grundzüge* 181-83: the Spirit is "the power of the self-expression of God in Jesus Christ." Fee is overconfident that Paul was "presuppositionally trinitarian" and made clear "distinctions between . . . the specific roles of the three divine persons" ("Christology" 330-31), importing analytic categories which took several centuries of sophisticated debate even to formulate.

purpose is to be extended to embrace those represented by the last Adam. This would mean, in turn, that, so far as giving life is concerned, Christ is not conceived of as working separately from the Spirit. On the contrary, Christ is experienced in and through, even *as* the life-giving Spirit, just as the Spirit experienced other than as the Spirit of Christ is for Paul not the Spirit of God. Alternatively expressed, using a different image, man and woman in marriage become one flesh, so believer and Lord in the union of commitment are one Spirit (1 Cor. 6.17). The Spirit is the medium of Christ's union with his own.[158] Once again, however, we begin to transgress into a different topic.

One possible and interesting corollary is nevertheless worth highlighting before we conclude. For this line of reflection begins to suggest that early Christian experience may have played a significant part in the development of a trinitarian conception of God. For it was by the Spirit that believers cried "Abba! Father!" (Rom. 8.15). And by the same Spirit that they confessed "Jesus is Lord" (1 Cor. 12.3). In other words, the believers in Paul's churches experienced worship as a double relationship — to God as Father and to Jesus as Lord — and attributed this experience to the Spirit.

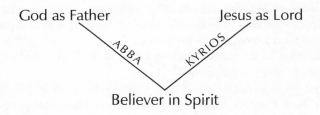

purpose God as Father   Jesus as Lord

ABBA   KYRIOS

Believer in Spirit

Add to this Paul's somewhat puzzling talk of the risen Lord's relationship to God (closely correlated, but distinct) and Paul's similarly puzzling conception of the risen Christ's relationship with the Spirit (closely identified, but not completely), and we can see something at least of the dynamic in conceptuality and worship (or, we might say, conceptuality in worship), which in the event found its most lasting expression in a trinitarian understanding of God.[159]

158. However much the phrasing is determined by the Gen. 2.24 template ("one flesh," "one spirit"), Paul seems to be saying more than simply "that the Spirit has forged a 'uniting' relationship between the believer and the Lord" (Fee, "Christology" 322). I do not see a problem with my formulation, given also that Paul can speak both of the Spirit indwelling the believer and of the believer "in the Spirit" (see below §15.4e).

159. Cf. Fee, *Empowering Presence* (§16 n. 1) 841-45.

§10.7 Conclusions

The fuller conclusions will have to await the completion of §11. But we can already draw some provisional conclusions which begin to integrate the findings of the various sections above.

(1) In terms of Jesus' own status and the place which he consequently holds within Paul's theology, there can be no doubt that Paul understood the resurrection of Jesus to be decisive. It was through and by means of the resurrection that Christ became last Adam, Son of God in power, Lord, conjoint with God in veneration, life-giving Spirit.

(2) It would be difficult to make any real distinction between Jesus' resurrection and his exaltation in Paul's thought.[160] The resurrection was itself the exaltation which installed Jesus into his new status. Within the NT, Paul is not alone in this; it is only Acts 1 which offers a different schema.

(3) Paul already establishes the two-sidedness of subsequent and classic christology. For on the one hand the risen Christ is last Adam, prototype of God's new human creation, in accord with the original blueprint. On the other, he is on the side of God, co-regent with God, co-lifegiver with the Spirit. And in between he is God's Son, whose sonship is shared with those who believe in him, the elder brother of a new family, firstborn from the dead. Yet he is also Son of God in power. And he is Lord, whose lordship both completes the intended dominion of Adam and exercises divine prerogatives.

(4) In this somewhat confusing welter of imagery, of terminology being transformed, of conceptuality being stretched, of vision being both enlarged and clarified, we should recognize not simply the importance of creative thought but also the impact of experience. The experience was primarily of Christ as one risen — an experience of dramatic and profound significance for Paul himself. But also in view was the ongoing experience of this Lord in worship, in daily life as a constant point of reference, and in and through the Spirit.

(5) At the same time, the christological reflection evident within Paul's theology is held within the bounds of his inherited monotheism. Jesus as Lord does not infringe on God as one, and even the highest accolade given to the exalted Christ is "to the glory of God the Father."

(6) All these factors, and the tugging to and fro of the different strands involved, help explain how Paul could at times express himself in unprecedented language, make astonishing associations, and suggest astonishing links or equations. Here not least the impact of the resurrection is evident, both as liberating older structures of theology and as indicating new forms.

---

160. See, e.g., Schlier, *Grundzüge* 144-47.

§11 The preexistent one[1]

1. **Bibliography**: **Barrett**, *Paul* 105-14; **Cerfaux**, *Christ* (§10 n. 1) 247-74, 419-38; **F. B. Craddock**, *The Pre-Existence of Christ in the New Testament* (Nashville: Abingdon, 1968); **C. E. B. Cranfield**, "Some Comments on Professor J. D. G. Dunn's *Christology in the Making*," in L. D. Hurst and N. T. Wright, eds., *The Glory of Christ in the New Testament*, G. B. Caird FS (Oxford: Clarendon, 1987) 267-80; **Davies**, *Paul* ch. 7; **J. D. G. Dunn**, *Christology;* "Pauline Christology: Shaping the Fundamental Structures," in R. F. Berkey and S. A. Edwards, eds., *Christology in Dialogue* (Cleveland: Pilgrim, 1993) 96-107; "Why 'Incarnation'? A Review of Recent New Testament Scholarship," in S. E. Porter, et al., eds., *Crossing the Boundaries: Essays in Biblical Interpretation*, M. D. Goulder FS (Leiden: Brill, 1994) 235-56; **Eichholz**, *Theologie* 132-63; **A. Feuillet**, *Le Christ sagesse de Dieu d'apres les épîtres Pauliniennes* (ÉB; Paris: Gabalda, 1966); **S. E. Fowl**, *The Story of Christ in the Ethics of Paul: An Analysis of the Function of the Hymnic Material in the Pauline Corpus* (JSNTS 36; Sheffield: Sheffield Academic, 1990); **R. H. Fuller**, *The Foundations of New Testament Christology* (London: Lutterworth/ New York: Scribner, 1965); **D. Georgi**, "Der vorpaulinische Hymnus Phil. 2.6-11," in E. Dinkler, ed., *Zeit und Geschichte*, R. Bultmann FS (Tübingen: Mohr, 1964) 263-93; **Goppelt**, *Theology* 2.72-79; **J. Habermann**, *Präexistenzaussagen im Neuen Testament* (Frankfurt: Lang, 1990); **R. G. Hamerton-Kelly**, *Pre-Existence, Wisdom, and the Son of Man: A Study of the Idea of Pre-Existence in the New Testament* (SNTSMS 21; Cambridge: Cambridge University, 1973); **A. T. Hanson**, *The Image of the Invisible God* (London: SCM, 1982); **O. Hofius**, *Der Christushymnus Philipper 2.6-11* (Tübingen: Mohr, 1976, [2]1991); **M. D. Hooker**, "Philippians 2.6-11," *Adam* 88-100; **M. de Jonge**, *Christology in Context: The Earliest Response to Jesus* (Philadelphia: Westminster, 1988); **J. Knox**, *The Humanity and Divinity of Christ* (Cambridge: Cambridge University, 1967); **Kümmel**, *Theology* 151-72; **K.-J. Kuschel**, *Born before All Time? The Dispute over Christ's Origin* (London: SCM, 1992); **Ladd**, *Theology* 457-63; **E. Larsson**, *Christus als Vorbild. Eine Untersuchung zu den paulinischen Tauf- und Eikontexten* (Uppsala: Almqvist and Wiksells, 1962) 2. Teil; **H. von Lips**, *Weisheitliche Traditionen im Neuen Testament* (WMANT 64; Neukirchen-Vluyn: Neukirchener, 1990); **J. Macquarrie**, *Jesus Christ in Modern Thought* (London: SCM/Philadelphia: TPI, 1990) 48-68; **I. H. Marshall**, "Incarnational Christology in the New Testament," *Jesus the Saviour: Studies in New Testament Theology* (London: SPCK, 1990) 165-80; **R. P. Martin**, *Carmen Christi: Philippians 2.5-11 in Recent Interpretation and in the Setting of Early Christian Worship* (SNTSMS 4; Cambridge: Cambridge University, 1967); **Merklein**, "Zur Entstehung der urchristlichen Aussage vom präexistenten Sohn Gottes," *Studien* 247-76; **Morris**, *Theology* 42-46; **C. F. D. Moule**, "Further Reflexions on Philippians 2.5-11," in W. W. Gasque and R. P. Martin, *Apostolic History and the Gospel*, F. F. Bruce FS (Exeter: Paternoster/Grand Rapids: Eerdmans, 1970) 264-76; **J. Murphy-O'Connor**, "Christological Anthropology in Phil. 2.6-11," *RB* 83 (1976) 25-50; "1 Cor. 8.6: Cosmology or Soteriology?" *RB* 85 (1978) 253-67; **C. C. Newman**, *Paul's Glory-Christology: Tradition and Rhetoric* (NovTSup 69; Leiden: Brill, 1992);

266

§11.1 Divine Wisdom

There is another important aspect of Paul's christology which requires separate treatment. This is partly because it can only partially be contained under the heading of resurrection. It is also somewhat uncertain whether it appears in Romans, our principal matrix for setting out Paul's theology. That need be given little weight for our purposes — although presence or absence of a theme in what Paul certainly saw as his most carefully wrought exposition of the gospel is always worthy of some consideration in ranking the relative importance of various elements in his theology, especially when there is any tension among them.

The theme in view is the preexistence of Christ. Some sort of preexistence certainly seems to be envisaged in a number of passages. Of these, two in particular make the point clearly enough — 1 Cor. 8.6 and Col. 1.15-20. 1 Cor. 8.6 —

> For us there is one God the Father,
>> from whom are all things and we for him,
> and one Lord Jesus Christ,
>> through whom are all things and we through him.

We have already looked at this verse in other connections.[2] Here it is the second half which calls for attention. There can be little doubt that it is talking of creation. "All things" *(ta panta)* was a familiar way of speaking about "everything, the universe, the totality of created entities."[3] And the sequence of prepositions, "from whom," "to whom," and "through whom," was equally familiar in talk of God and the cosmos.[4] Paul's readers could have

---

O'Collins, *Christology* (§10 n. 1); **J. A. T. Robinson**, *The Human Face of God* (London: SCM/Philadelphia: Westminster, 1973); **J. T. Sanders**, *The New Testament Christological Hymns: Their Historical Religious Background* (SNTSMS 15; Cambridge: Cambridge University, 1971); **E. J. Schnabel**, *Law and Wisdom from Ben Sira to Paul* (WUNT 2.16; Tübingen: Mohr, 1985); **E. Schweizer**, "Zum religionsgeschichtlichen Hintergrund der 'Sendungsformel' Gal. 4.4f., Röm. 8.3f., John 3.16f., 1 John 4.9," *ZNW* 57 (1966) 199-210 = *Beiträge* 83-95; **Stuhlmacher**, *Theologie* 287-93; **C. A. Wanamaker**, "Philippians 2.6-11: Son of God or Adamic Christology?" *NTS* 33 (1987) 179-93; **B. Witherington**, *Jesus the Sage: The Pilgrimage of Wisdom* (Minneapolis: Fortress/Edinburgh: Clark, 1994); *Narrative* 94-128; **N. T. Wright**, "Jesus Christ Is Lord: Philippians 2.5-11," and "Poetry and Theology in Colossians 1.15-20," *Climax* 56-98, 99-119.

2. See above §§2.3 and 10.5a.

3. BAGD, *pas* 2a*d* and 2b*b*. In the NT cf., e.g., 1 Cor. 15.27-28; Eph. 3.9; and John 1.3.

4. The usual examples are pseudo-Aristotle, *De mundo* 6; Seneca, *Epistles* 65.8; Marcus Aurelius, *Meditations* 4.23; Philo, *Cher.* 125-26. In Paul note Rom. 11.36 and Col. 1.16 below; also Heb. 2.10.

little doubt that Paul was attributing a role in creation to the "one Lord Jesus Christ."[5] What is notable here is that the sequence of prepositions has been divided between the one God and the one Lord. Just as Paul in effect split the *Shema* between the one God and the one Lord,[6] so the same formula has split God's role as Creator between the Father and Jesus Christ. The "one Lord Jesus Christ, through whom are all things," clearly existed before the creation of the "all things *(ta panta).*"

The point is even clearer in Col. 1.15-20. The letter falls at the end of the undisputed Paulines,[7] but the passage is widely regarded as a hymn quoted and adapted by the writer.[8] And anyway, its principal theme, so far as we are concerned here, was already stated in 1 Cor. 8.6. So it can be regarded as an expression of Pauline theology without straining the point. The hymnic passage is introduced by a relative pronoun, "who"; but it is quite clear that the antecedent is "the Son of his [God's] love" (1.13):[9]

> [15]who is the image of the invisible God,
>> the firstborn of all creation.
> [16]For in him were created all things
>> in the heavens and on the earth,
>> the visible and the invisible
>
> . . . .
>
> all things were created through him and for him.
> [17]He himself is before all things,
>> and all things hold together in him.

Again we note the repeated "all things *(ta panta),*" and the similar prepositional "in him," "through him," "for him" sequence. That creation is in view is explicitly stated (1.16). And though "firstborn of all creation" (1.15) could be taken as equivalent to first created being, the context makes it fairly clear that the primary sense is that of precedence over creation. He in whom and through whom all things were created is evidently thought of as "before all

---

5. *Pace* Murphy-O'Connor, "1 Cor. 8.6," followed by Kuschel, *Born* 285-91, who see only a reference to the new creation. The fact that the confession is made of Jesus Christ as the exalted Lord does not alter the content of the confession.

6. See above §10.5a.

7. See, e.g., my *Colossians* 35-39. An appropriate comment is that of E. Käsemann — "The dating of the epistle presents two alternatives: If genuine, then because of content and style as late as possible; if not genuine, then as early as conceivable" ("Kolosserbrief," *RGG*[3] 1728, cited in my *Colossians* 19).

8. The discussion is briefly reviewed, with further bibliography, in my *Colossians* 83-86.

9. The second half of the passage also refers clearly to Christ's resurrection (1.18 — "firstborn from the dead") and reconciling death on the cross (1.20).

things," that is, prior to all things.[10] Again, there is little doubt that the hymn praises the exalted Christ; the theological logic works back from end to beginning, from salvation to creation.[11] But again there can be little doubt that a role in the original creation of the cosmos is attributed to God's Son, the Christ Jesus.

What are we to make of this? How can this language be used of Christ? What are its christological implications? Fortunately we do not need to look far, at least for the initial answer. Indeed, few issues in recent NT theology have commanded such unanimity of agreement as the source of the language and imagery used in these two passages.[12] By common consent, it was drawn from earlier Jewish reflection on divine Wisdom. The language appealed to the first Christians because it had been so much used of the figure of heavenly Wisdom. What we have in these passages, in other words, are classic expressions of Wisdom christology.[13]

We can illustrate the point briefly. Wisdom is the "image of God."[14] That is, the invisible God has made himself visible in and through his wisdom (Col. 1.15). Wisdom is God's "firstborn" in creation.[15] God "made all things by wisdom,"[16] "through whom the universe *(to pan)* was brought to completion."[17] Wisdom was "before all things,"[18] and "holds all things together."[19] Such a sequence of correlation can hardly be a matter of coincidence. Even in the case of the briefer 1 Cor. 8.6, we are not surprised to read Philo making a similar division in the "by, from, and through" formulation, between the

---

10. See discussion and bibliography in my *Colossians* 90 and 93 n. 24.

11. See, e.g., Kuschel, *Born* 331, 335, and those cited in my *Colossians* 879 n. 16. Habermann, *Präexistenzaussagen* makes the point repeatedly (e.g., 260, 421).

12. See particularly the three most recent studies, by Habermann, *Präexistenzaussagen,* 86-87, 169-71, 240-51; von Lips, *Traditionen* 295-97, 299-301, 306-7; and Kuschel, *Born* 291, 331-33.

13. Other NT passages include at least Heb. 1.1-4 and John 1.1-18; and see below §11.3.

14. Wis. 7.26; Philo, *Leg. All.* 1.43. Philo speaks similarly of the divine Logos, his more favoured image; see my *Colossians* 88.

15. Prov. 8.22, 25; Philo, *Ebr.* 30-31; *Qu. Gen.* 4.97; "a commonplace of the Hellenistic synagogue" (Knox, *St Paul* 159 n. 3).

16. Ps. 104.24; Prov. 3.19; Wis. 9.2; "Wisdom that effects all things *(ta panta)*" — Wis. 8.5. Note the equivalence of wisdom and word in Wis. 9.1-2, and of word of God and Spirit/breath of God in Ps. 33(LXX 32).6. The "in him" (Col. 1.16) probably reflects the Hellenistic Jewish idea of the Logos as the "place" in which the world exists (particularly Philo, *Som.* 1.62-64); see my *Colossians* 91 n. 20.

17. Philo, *Det.* 54; similarly *Heres* 199 and *Fuga* 109.

18. Sir. 1.4; Aristobulus (second century BCE) in Eusebius, *Praeparatio Evangelica* 13.12.11 (*OTP* 2.841).

19. Wis. 1.6-7. Also of the divine word (Sir. 43.26) and Logos in Philo (*Heres* 23, 188; *Fuga* 112; *Mos.* 2.133; *Qu. Exod.* 2.118).

originating role of God ("by whom"), God as ultimate cause, and the instrumental role of the Logos ("through whom") (*Cher.* 125-27). We can be quite confident, then, that those who wrote such language and at least many of their readers would recognize where it came from. It was drawn from a wide strand of Jewish reflection on God's work as Creator through the medium of his wisdom or word.

Clearly, then, Paul was attributing to *Christ* the role previously attributed to divine Wisdom. Indeed, it is entirely consistent with the evidence to conclude that Paul was tacitly identifying Christ with Wisdom, indeed, *as* Wisdom. In thinking of preexistent Wisdom Paul now thought of Christ. But what did that mean? Who or what was Wisdom? Before we can ask about the christological implications of the language in its application to Christ we have to clarify the identity of divine Wisdom.[20]

At this point, unfortunately, the consensus begins to fragment. Opinion has divided, broadly, in three ways.[21] Some assume that the language must be taken straightforwardly as an indication that Jewish monotheism was not so clearly delimited as the *Shema* and Second Isaiah imply. That is a view we have already dismissed.[22] An important point here is that the same language would function differently and be understood differently within a monotheistic system as against a polytheistic or syncretistic system. In the latter, Wisdom could be readily conceived as a divine being and given divine honours. But in Judaism, Wisdom had no temple, no priests. In a Judaism sensitized to the constant threat of surrounding polytheism and syncretism, there is never any hint that Wisdom was thought to pose any kind of threat to Israel's confession of God as one.[23]

The opposite solution is to read the talk of Wisdom as an extension of Israel's use of vivid metaphor and personification in speaking of God's interaction with the world and his people.[24] For example, Ps. 85.10-11 pictures

20. Failure to pursue such questions is the principal weakness of Habermann, *Präexistenzaussagen* 87-89, 178-80, 219, 420-21. To observe that the NT passages show no speculative interest in the character of Wisdom's preexistence (246, 416) simply ducks the issue.

21. In what follows I draw summarily on my fuller discussions in *Christology* 168-76 (also 230-39) and *Partings* 197-99.

22. See above §2.3b.

23. Consequently in recent debate this has been the least favoured option of the three. See also Casey, *Jewish Prophet* (§10 n. 1) 88-90; Hurtado, *One God* (§10 n. 1) 42-50; Kuschel, *Born* 20-27. See also above §2.3b.

24. E.g., B. L. Mack and R. E. Murphy, "Wisdom Literature," in *Early Judaism and Its Modern Interpreters,* ed. R. A. Kraft and G. W. E. Nickelsburg (Atlanta: Scholars, 1986) 377 ("a poetic personification for God's intimate activity and for his personal summons"), citing J. Marböck, *Weisheit im Wandel. Untersuchungen zur Weisheitstheologie bei ben Sira* (Bonn: Hanstein, 1971); others in my *Christology* 326 n. 22.

"righteousness" and "peace" as kissing each other. Isa. 51.9 calls upon the arm of the Lord to "awake [and] put on strength." In *Joseph and Aseneth* 15.7-8, "Repentance" is depicted as "the Most High's daughter . . . the guardian of all virgins . . . a virgin, very beautiful and pure and chaste and gentle." Wisdom may be seen, therefore, as simply a more sustained way of focusing the thought that all God's dealings with creation and Israel are wise, God's wisdom in action. This is particularly clear in Wisdom of Solomon 10–11, where it is God's protection of Israel as Wisdom that is rehearsed and God alone who is praised accordingly (10.20; 11.10, 13, 17, 21-26) and where God's "hand" and "Spirit" are alternative images (11.17; 12.1).

Such alternation of imagery also accords with what we find elsewhere, with the Wisdom of God functioning in ways similar to the Word of God, the Spirit of God, the Glory of God, and the Name of God.[25] These were all means of speaking about the wholly other God who is yet near. Early Jewish thought evidently resolved the problem of holding together the transcendence of God and the immanence of God by using these circumlocutions for the latter. Thus the Word of God denotes what we would call the rationality of God's dealings with humankind, just as Wisdom denotes their wisdom. The Spirit of God expresses the dynamic vitality of God's presence. The Glory of God is that of God which may be seen by human eye. And so on. In short, the Wisdom of God is not something other than God, but God's wisdom, God in his wisdom.[26]

The principal alternative to this second view is to regard Wisdom as a "hypostatization" of divine attributes, that is, something occupying "an intermediate position between personalities and abstract beings" or, as we might say, halfway between a person and a personification.[27] This has proved attractive to those who remain impressed by all that is attributed to Wisdom as such and who find talk of "personification" too wooden and inadequate.[28] On the latter point it can be readily conceded that "personification" is inadequate to describe the vividness of Israel's poetry and imagery. But "hypostasis" introduces a concept which only gained the technical theological nuance (for which its use is proposed here) in the third and fourth centuries of the Christian era, and only as a device to resolve a peculiarly

25. E.g. Wis. 18.15; Ps. 139.7; *1 Enoch* 39.7, 9, 13; *m. Aboth* 3.2. On the glory of God see my *Christology* 315 n. 10; and on the name of God cf. Davis, *Name* (§10 n. 1) 110-18.

26. E.g., Prov. 2.6; Sir. 1.1; Wis. 7.15.

27. I allude to the classic definition of "hypostasis" provided by W. O. E. Oesterley and G. H. Box, *The Religion and Worship of the Synagogue* (London: Pitman, [2]1911) 195.

28. See, e.g., Craddock, *Pre-existence* 32-33; Gese, *Biblical Theology* 192-93; Hengel, *Judaism* 1.153-55, 2.98 n. 294; others in my *Christology* 325 n. 21.

Christian dilemma.[29] Its use in the present discussion is anachronistic and imports a distinction which, so far as we can tell, never occurred to first-century Jews.

Would it be fair, then, to argue that the substance of "hypostatization" was already present in early Jewish talk of Wisdom, even if an appropriate technical term was not yet to hand? Perhaps.[30] But when one appreciates the vigour of Jewish metaphor and is willing to recognize that Wisdom functions as an extended metaphor — and when one observes that the bulk of Jewish opinion sees no difficulty in identifying talk of God's glory and God's wisdom as talk of God's immanence[31] — is recourse to a term like "hypostatization" really necessary? If "personification" is unsatisfactory, let us talk simply of the "metaphor" of Wisdom. But above all, whatever term is used, the point is hard to escape that, according to the evidence available to us, Wisdom was universally understood within early Judaism as God's wisdom, as the immanent God in his wise engagement with his creation and his people.

With this degree of clarification, such as it is, we can pose the question again: What are the christological implications of applying such Wisdom language to Christ? What did it mean in effect to identify Jesus as Wisdom?

§11.2 Jesus as Wisdom

What did this mean for Paul? If answer there be, it is most likely to be found in the two passages already quoted — 1 Cor. 8.6 and Col. 1.15-17.

a) *1 Cor. 8.6.* One obvious answer might be that Paul simply assumed that the Christ who was crucified had been with God in and from the beginning of all things. Certainly the idea of the Messiah as preexistent is one which Jewish thought was to embrace subsequently, and texts were already in cur-

---

29. I echo the protests of G. F. Moore, "Intermediaries in Jewish Theology," *HTR* 15 (1922) 41-85 (here 55), and G. L. Prestige, *God in Patristic Thought* (London: SPCK, [2]1952; 1964) xxviii. Similarly Marböck, *Weisheit im Wandel* (above n. 24) 129-30, and Kuschel, *Born* 195-96.

30. Witherington suggests that the thought of Proverbs and ben Sira never goes beyond personification (*Sage* 38-43, 92-93), but that in the Wisdom of Solomon "one sees the beginnings of a groping beyond just personification of an attribute of God to a hypostasis" (*Sage* 109). Cf. Whiteley, *Theology* 111-12. Von Lips opts for a resolution involving both personification and hypostasis (*Traditionen* 153-66), without asking whether "hypostasis" is an appropriate term to describe, for example, the depiction of "repentance" or "wisdom" as a woman.

31. See, e.g., those cited, *inter alios,* in my *Christology* 315 n. 10 and 326-27 nn. 22, 37-41; add de Jonge, *Christology* 197, and Kuschel, *Born* 192-99, 205-7, with further bibliography. Kuschel sums up: "Personification and pre-existence are poetic, stylistic means for giving form to that which has no form, for making the intangible tangible, for portraying that which has no image: God himself in his revelation for human beings" (*Born* 207).

rency which could readily be interpreted in that sense.[32] But the thought here is not simply of a historical figure whose historical role was predetermined by God, so that he could be said to have been apocalyptically preexistent with God.[33] It was probably in this way that conceptuality developed from ideal preexistence to real preexistence.[34] But here the thought is of participation in the acts of creation, and the identification, if anything, is with divine Wisdom. And while Wisdom as a way of speaking of God's creating act, as the means through which he created, seems to have been wholly sensible in Jewish Wisdom theology, it is more questionable whether the earliest expressions of the Messiah's preexistence would have gone so far.

A more obvious parallel is the identification of divine Wisdom with the Torah. This identification is already made and made with much greater explicitness in Sir. 24.23 and Bar. 4.1. Ben Sira's great hymn to Wisdom (Sir. 24.1-22) is a classic expression of Jewish Wisdom theology, and well demonstrates the richness of visual imagery involved in talk of Wisdom.[35] But clearly for ben Sira the climax comes in the identification with the Torah:

> All these things [the varying descriptions of Wisdom] are the book of the covenant of the Most High, the law which Moses commanded us, as an inheritance for the assemblies of Jacob. It fills with wisdom like the Pishon. . . .

Very similar is the great hymn in Bar. 3.9-37, which climaxes with the thought of Wisdom's appearance on earth and, again, immediate identification with the Torah. "Afterward she appeared upon the earth and lived among humans. She is the book of the commandments of God, the law which endures for ever . . ." (3.38–4.1).[36]

32. See my *Christology* 70-72.

33. The obvious model for this would be Exod. 25.40.

34. For the issue of ideal preexistence see, e.g., J. Klausner, *The Messianic Idea in Israel* (New York: Macmillan, 1955 = London: Allen and Unwin, 1956) 460: "That the Messiah himself existed before creation is nowhere stated in Tannaitic literature . . . 'the name of the Messiah' is the *idea* of the Messiah, or, more exactly, *the idea of redemption through the Messiah*. This idea did precede creation." For the rabbinic belief in seven things "created before the world was created," including the name of the Messiah, see *b. Pesahim* 54a; *Nedarim* 39b; Targum Pseudo-Jonathan Zech. 4.7. Stuhlmacher takes too much for granted an already established concept of the preexistent Son of Man/Messiah (*Theologie* 187), assuming that the *Similitudes of Enoch* were already well known. See further Davies, *Paul* 158-63, and my *Christology* 69-81, 294 n. 37, and 296 n. 64.

35. Wisdom is likened to a sequence of trees and spices, to sweet honey and refreshing drink (Sir. 24.13-21).

36. See further Schnabel, *Law and Wisdom* 69-92 (Sirach), 98-99 (Baruch), 109-12 *(1 Enoch)*, 117-18 *(Pss. Sol.)*, 122-24 *(Ep. Arist.)*, 127-28 *(Sib. Or.* 3), 132-34 (Wisdom), 136-38 *(4 Macc.)*, 149-51 *(4 Ezra)*, 158-61 *(2 Baruch)*, 206-26 (DSS).

In both cases it would be equally easy to speak of the preexistence of the Torah, and many do.[37] But it would be more accurate to say that the hidden wisdom of God had been made available to Israel in and through the law. Israel now had access to the wisdom which had been God's mode of working from the beginning (Sir. 24.9), the wisdom which was the secret of good living (Bar. 3.14; 4.4). It was there in the law. It was the law. In other words, it was not so much that the law was preexistent as that preexistent Wisdom was now to be recognized as the law.

In effect what Paul and the other first Christians were doing was putting Christ in this equation in place of the Torah. And the rationale was probably the same: not so much that Christ as Jesus of Nazareth had preexisted as such, but that preexistent Wisdom was now to be recognized in and as Christ. Linked into the theology of a lordship which shared in some way in the one God's sovereignty, the combination was astounding and category-shattering, whatever the concept of preexistence involved.

At this point we need to recall that Paul had in fact already explicitly identified Christ as God's Wisdom — in 1 Cor. 1.24 and 30: "Christ the power of God and the wisdom of God" (1.24); "who has become wisdom for us from God, righteousness, holiness, and redemption" (1.30). In context, it will be recalled, Paul has been contrasting human wisdom with divine wisdom (1.17-31). The claim being made, then, is the astonishing one that the foolishness of the cross, the proclamation of Christ crucified, is the real measure of divine wisdom (1.21-25). The thought is probably very similar to that in ben Sira and Baruch and implicit in 1 Cor. 8.6: that Jesus Christ is the clearest exposition and explanation of divine Wisdom, that the cross is the fullest embodiment of the wisdom which created the universe and which humans need if they are to live the good life.[38] As we have already seen (§10.6), Paul in effect does the same thing with the Spirit later in the same letter (1 Cor. 15.45). The life-giving Spirit can be most clearly recognized now through identification with the last Adam, the risen Christ. So the creating Wisdom of God can be most clearly recognized now through identification with the crucified Christ.

Is there then a thought of preexistence in 1 Cor. 8.6, not to mention 1.24 and 30? Of course there is. But it is the preexistence of divine Wisdom.

---

37. A rabbinic tradition attests the idea of the Torah's role in creation already for Rabbi Akiba in the generation or so after Paul; but it was not important for the rabbis, nor does it seem to rise beyond the idea that God predetermined the Torah's role (see, e.g., Craddock, *Pre-existence* 47-53).

38. Von Lips's disjunction between 1 Cor. 1.24, 30 and 8.6 (*Traditionen* 349-50) again makes too much of the "hypostatic" character of the Wisdom imagery in 8.6 and ignores the likelihood that whoever made the Wisdom connection in 8.6 could hardly fail to recall that it was precisely the *crucified* Christ who had been explicitly identified as God's wisdom in 1.24 and 30.

That is, the preexistence of God. And should we speak here of the "incarnation" of divine Wisdom in Christ? Paul does not do so, but in the light of the later John 1.14 it would be wholly appropriate as an interpretation of Paul's theology. Whether the subtlety of the theology is best expressed as "the preexistence of Christ" *simpliciter*[39] is another question. However, continuing debate about the appropriateness of the phrase and its theological outworking should not be allowed to obscure the central points above: that Paul's Wisdom christology is wholly consistent with the continued confession of God's oneness (1 Cor. 8.6) and that for Paul the mystery of divine wisdom has been revealed as never before in Christ and in his cross (1 Cor. 1.24).

(b) *Col. 1.15-20.* Much the same can be said of the more explicit creation language of Col. 1.15-17.[40] Here, however, the interesting additional feature is the fact that the hymn continues into a second stanza (1.15-18a, 18b-20) and that this second stanza is clearly set out in parallel to the first.[41] At this point we can speak quite properly of a balance between old creation and new. As Christ was "the image of God" in the first creation, so he is "the beginning" of the new (1.15, 18). As Christ was "the firstborn of all creation," so he is "the firstborn from the dead" (1.15, 18). As all things were created "in him," so "in him all the fullness of God was pleased to dwell" (1.16, 19). As "all things were created through him and to him," so the divine intention was that "all things" should be reconciled "through him" and "to him" (1.16, 20). Here is another parallel with 1 Cor. 15.45, since the sequence here, in fact, is equivalent to the one there between first Adam and last Adam. The Adam christology, we may say, spelled out the means by which God brought into existence the eschatological form of humankind equivalent to the original humankind. So here the Wisdom christology spells out the means by which God continued to exercise his sovereignty to bring about the reconciliation of the old in the creation of the new through cross and resurrection.

---

39. As by Schnabel, *Law and Wisdom* 258. My cautionary notes about the "limited horizon" of author and first readers and regarding "conceptuality in transition" have been paid insufficient attention (see particularly my *Christology,* xi-xxxix, particularly xiv-xvi).

40. Exposition here does not depend on a particular theory regarding the Colossian "philosophy" (Col. 2.8) which Paul saw as some sort of threat to the Colossian believers; see my "Colossian Philosophy" (above §2 n. 37); also *Colossians* 23-35.

41. 1.15 "who is the first born"   1.18b
    1.16 "because in him"   1.19
    1.16 "all things, through him, to him"   1.20

Note also the thematic repetition of "all things" (twice each in vv. 16 and 17, once each in vv. 18 and 20) and the movement from the creation of "all things in the heavens and on the earth" (1.16) to a climax of reconciliation of "the things on the earth and the things in the heavens" (1.20). For our purposes it does not matter whether the second stanza was part of the original hymn or added subsequently as a reflective elaboration.

What is noteworthy here is that the christological moment of the resurrection is given equivalent weight to that of the preexistent agent in creation. "He is the beginning" — that is, the new beginning of resurrection. He is "firstborn from the dead," not just as the first of the new order, but "in order that he might be in all things preeminent" (1.18). This is further explained as coming about, "because in him all the fullness of God was pleased to dwell" (1.19), where the movement to preeminence begins from the (bodily — 2.9) indwelling of the divine fullness in the earthly Jesus.[42] In other words, the postresurrection preeminence was not simply that of divine Wisdom, but involved, as we might say, a second birth (resurrection). Clearly in view here is a kind of two-stage becoming.[43] In the balanced, two-stanza form of the passage, it cannot be said that the one becoming is more important than the other. The second was evidently as necessary for the completion of Christ's preeminence and his work of reconciliation (1.20) as the first was for creation. Creation and reconciliation are the work of the one God through the same Christ, but each required its own birth and becoming.

Here again we observe the overlapping character of what we have described as Paul's Adam christology and Wisdom christology. Both emphasize the divine purpose of creation as embodied in Christ, the one in terms of the humanity God created, the other in terms of his creative plan and power. Both emphasize a purpose realized only in and through Christ and through his death and resurrection, as a decisive new moment both for Christ and for the new kind of humanity he both represented and brought about.

It would of course be pedantic and unjustified to play off the double emphases of the two stanzas against each other. The lesson to be learned, rather, is that the two stanzas embody different extended metaphors and that neither should be pressed at the expense of the other.[44] The tensions inherent in setting such different metaphors alongside each other are inevitable in the expression of themes so difficult to conceptualize. That the metaphors and images do not fit neatly together is simply a function of the way metaphors "work." A hymnic passage, constructed to set off a sequence of allusion and association and structured to bring out some pleasingly rhetorical parallels, is not to be treated as a dogmatic or legal document. But neither should theology refrain from speaking in that language just because it is so highly figurative.

---

42. On Col. 1.19 and 2.9 see above §8.7. There it is observed that a concept of "incarnation" is close to hand; but it is the "incarnation" of "God in all his fullness" (1.19), "all the fullness of the deity" (2.9), not of a separate "being."

43. Or incorporating an intermediary stage in the indwelling at Jordan or incarnation (see above §8 n. 118).

44. Those so minded could equally well press for an Arian interpretation of "firstborn of all creation" (1.15) and for an Adoptionist or Nestorian interpretation of 1.18-19; see my *Christology* 189, 191-92.

Once again, then, we can hardly fail to speak of Christ's preexistence expressed in this passage.[45] But once again it is the preexistence of God, of the divine Wisdom by means of which God created and sustains the universe.[46] It is the preexistence of the divine fullness whereby God's presence fills the universe and which is now embodied (incarnate?) in Christ, above all in his cross and resurrection.

§11.3 Other possible Wisdom passages

There are other passages in Paul where the thought of Christ as divine Wisdom may be implicit. Because of their allusiveness they add little to the discussion, except to show that a Wisdom christology might well have been more characteristic of Paul's theology than the passages just reviewed indicate on their own. But they should at least be noted and the value of their testimony weighed.

a) *Gal. 4.4 and Rom. 8.3* — "God sent his Son." Since the influential study of Eduard Schweizer, it has been widely accepted that this brief clause expresses a Wisdom christology.[47] The principal argument in favour is the fact that in Gal. 4.4-6 God's sending forth *(exapesteilen)* of his Son (4.4) is set in parallel to God's sending forth *(exapesteilen)* of the Spirit of his Son (4.6). The closest parallel to this thought of a double sending is in Wis. 9.10 and 17:

> [10]Send *(exaposteilon)* her [Wisdom] forth from the holy heavens,
> and from the throne of your glory send *(pempson)* her.
> . . . .
> [17]Who has known your counsel, except you have given wisdom
> and sent *(epempsas)* your Holy Spirit from on high?

The thought of Rom. 8.3-4 is similar, using the verb *pempō,* but not mentioning a second sending of the Spirit. Nevertheless, the language is close, and even to a degree stereotyped.[48] So the underlying theology is presumably the same.

---

45. But would Paul have spoken of "the preexistence of *Jesus*" (as Stuhlmacher, *Theologie* 288)? Contrast Kümmel: "Perhaps it is also not accidental that Paul does not use 'Jesus' for the pre-existent One, because his taking seriously the historical concreteness of the man Jesus forbids the projection of this name back into the pre-existence" (*Theology* 155). Note O'Collins's more careful critique in *Christology* 238-43. I do not recognize my earlier analysis *(Christology)* in the polemic of Hanson, *Image* 74-75.

46. "The plain meaning of the words used" (Morris, *Theology* 45 n. 24) depends on what meaning the imagery conveys.

47. Schweizer, "Hintergrund."

48. Note the close parallel between Gal. 4.5-7 and Rom. 8.14-17.

When this language is correlated with the similar motif in the Johannine writings,[49] the plausible thesis emerges that talk of "God sending his Son" became quite quickly established in early Christianity. And since in the Johannines there is no doubt that the sending was from heaven, it can readily be deduced that the same thought was implicit in the earlier Pauline formulation, as the parallel with Wis. 9.10 suggests.[50]

The problems here are the dangers of reading too much into such a brief phrase, of assuming that the imagery of Son would have been integrated so quickly with that of female Wisdom,[51] and of reading back the obviously much developed Johannine theology into a letter written nearly fifty years earlier. Moreover, against the single reference to the sending of Wisdom (Wis. 9.10) the much more established theme of the sending of a prophet has to be considered.[52] Jesus also used this motif.[53] In particular if a precedent for the idea of God sending his Son is sought, it is most obviously to be found in Jesus' own sending parable (Mark 12.1-9 pars.).[54] For there the thought is at its most explicit: God sent his only Son (12.6) "last of all" (cf. Gal. 4.4) as the climax of his sending of the prophets (Mark 12.2-5) and in pursuit of his inheritance (cf. Gal. 4.1, 7).[55]

49. Note particularly the parallel language in John 3.16-17 and 1 John 4.9, 10, 14.

50. Those who see the language of preexistence in Gal. 4.4 and Rom. 8.3 include Fuller, *Foundations* 231; Conzelmann, *Outline* 200; Goppelt, *Theology* 2.74; Hengel, *Son* (§10 n. 1) 10-11; Hanson, *Image* 59-62; Cranfield, "Comments" 271; Longenecker, *Galatians* 167-70; Stuhlmacher, *Theologie* 289-90; Fitzmyer, *Romans* 484-85; Gnilka, *Theologie* 24-25; O'Collins, *Christology* 127-28.

51. But note the later Col. 1.13, 15-17; see above §8.7.

52. Moses (Exod. 3.12-15[A]; Ps. 105.26; Mic. 6.4), Gideon (Judg. 6.14), and usually the prophets (Judg. 6.8; 2 Chron. 36.15; Jer. 1.7; 7.25; Ezek. 2.3; 3.5-6; Mic. 6.4; Obad. 1; Hag. 1.12; Mal. 3.1; Luke 4.26; 20.13); also Paul himself (Acts 22.21). Though note also the sending of angels (Gen. 24.40; Ps. 151.11 [LXX]; Acts 12.11) and spirit/Spirit (Judg. 9.23; Zech. 7.12; Wis. 9.17; Luke 24.49).

53. Mark 9.37/Luke 9.48 *(apostellō);* Mark 12.2-5 pars. *(apostellō* — 3 times of the owner sending; Luke uses *pempō* twice); Matt. 15.24; Luke 4.18; 10.16. J. A. Bühner, *Der Gesandte und sein Weg im 4. Evangelium* (Tübingen: Mohr, 1977), has demonstrated that the Johannine sending christology was developed from the motif of God sending his prophets.

54. Cerfaux, *Christ* 447; R. H. Fuller and P. Perkins, *Who Is This Christ? Gospel Christology and Contemporary Faith* (Philadelphia: Fortress, 1983) 46-47; de Jonge, *Christology* 43, 190-91. See also Ziesler, *Pauline Christianity* 43; Kuschel, *Born* 274-76, 300-301, 305.

55. See further my *Christology* 38-44. Marshall, "Incarnational Christology" 171, however, thinks that "born of woman" and "in the very likeness of sinful flesh" suggest a different "field of meaning" for "sent" from that in Mark 12.6 (similarly de Jonge, *Christology* 191); though the further question should be asked whether the different field of meaning is that of Adam christology (see above §8.6, and also below §11.4).

When the unpacking of such a brief phrase depends so much on allusion, it would be unwise to put too much weight on the conclusions drawn. Exegesis cannot exclude the possibility that the sending of Wisdom from heaven stands in the background. But the sending of various human agents, including Jesus hailed as God's own Son, can hardly be excluded either. In the event, with a preexistent Wisdom christology already established (§11.2), the verdict here can be left open.

(b) *1 Cor. 10.4.* In 1 Cor. 10.1-4 Paul uses a sort of allegory to warn his readers. The Israelites in the wilderness experienced a kind of baptism in their crossing of the Red Sea (10.1-2). They enjoyed a kind of spiritual food and drink, referring to the Exodus traditions of the manna and quails (Exod. 16.13-15), and of the water brought miraculously from the rock (Exod. 17.6). Paul describes this rock as "following them" and then identifies it: "the rock was Christ" (1 Cor. 10.4). And then Paul goes on to apply his warning. These events were typical (10.6). For despite such blessings, the Israelites had been rejected in the wilderness (10.5). Those who had experienced the real baptism into Christ (12.13) and the spiritual food and drink of the Lord's Supper (10.16) should take appropriate notice.

With reference to 1 Cor. 10.4 in particular, the inference is attractive that Paul had in mind a range of reflection which these traditions stimulated in Jewish thought closely contemporary with Paul. In particular, pseudo-Philo already attests the idea that the source of the wilderness water "followed them [the people of Israel] in the wilderness forty years."[56] Still more interesting is the fact that Wis. 11.4 already thought of the "water given them from the flinty rock" as part of Wisdom's protection of Israel in the wilderness (11.1ff.).[57] And Philo simply crystallized what was already implicit in the Wisdom of Solomon by identifying the rock allegorically with Wisdom.[58]

Paul looks as though he is doing something similar. "The rock was Christ" is at least the interpretative key by which Paul makes clear the significance of the episode (and resulting legend). "Baptized into Moses" was a clear enough allusion to "baptized into Christ." "Spiritual food and drink" likewise. But the rock: what could that refer to? Paul indicates his answer: Christ. The fact that he uses the past tense, however — "the rock was Christ" rather than "the rock is Christ" — suggests that he may have intended a

56. Pseudo-Philo 11.15 (probably late first century CE). The reference is to the water of Marah (Exod. 15.25). But Num. 21.17-18 invited meditation on all the sources of divinely supplied water (as CD 6.3-11 already demonstrates). For the developed legend in rabbinic haggadah see, e.g., Fee, *1 Corinthians* 448 n. 34.

57. Note also the possible allusion in 1 Cor. 10.1-2 to Wis. 10.17-18 and 19.7-8 (Habermann, *Präexistenzaussagen* 206-7).

58. Particularly *Leg. All.* 2.86: "the flinty rock is the wisdom of God . . . from which he satisfies the thirsty souls that love God."

historical rather than a typological equation.[59] In which case the logic is little different from that earlier in the same letter (1 Cor. 8.6): perhaps in dependence on Wis. 11.4, like Philo, Paul simply transferred what was said about Wisdom to Christ. Like the divine wisdom behind creation, now recognized in and as Christ, so the divine wisdom which oversaw Israel in the wilderness can now likewise be recognized in and as Christ.

c) *Rom. 10.6-8* should also be given brief mention. Paul cites Deut. 30.12-14 and interprets it:

> Do not say in your heart, "Who will go up into heaven?"
> that is, to bring Christ down;
> or "Who will go down into the abyss?"
> that is, to bring Christ up from the dead. . . .

The talk of "bringing Christ down [from heaven]" is frequently taken as a reference to incarnation,[60] and the relevance of the passage to the present discussion is heightened by the fact that Bar. 3.29-30 uses the same passage (Deut. 30.12-14) in its hymn to Wisdom.[61] The implication could be, then, that key events in the programme of salvation do not need to be repeated (incarnation, resurrection); once performed, their effect is now embodied in "the word of faith" (Rom. 10.8). But the thought here is all on the resurrection (10.9-10) and exaltation of him who is now Lord of all (10.12-13). And the parallel with Baruch 3 suggests rather that there is no need to pursue Christ to the heavens since he/(Wisdom) is accessible through "the word of faith"/(the Torah — Bar. 4.1).

59. This observation is generally regarded as fatal to my earlier suggestion that a typological equation is sufficient explanation of the phrase (*Christology* 330 n. 78). See particularly Hanson, *Image* 72 — part of his much more extensive thesis that Christ existed as "an eternal being beside God the Father," "the form in which God was known to Israel of old . . . the form of a man" (81-82), and that Christ is referred to as such much more frequently in the NT than is generally recognized today (*Jesus Christ in the Old Testament* [London: SPCK, 1965]), including here the pillar of cloud (1 Cor. 10.1-2), "the medium or means by which the then present Christ exercised his supernatural power" (*Image* 71, 86; also Wolff, *1 Korinther 8–16* 42-43; Habermann, *Präexistenzaussagen* 213; Fee, *1 Corinthians* 448 n. 36; Witherington, *Sage* 317-18). On the other hand, note Hays, *Echoes* 91: "Paul's metaphors should not be pressed. He does not mean, at the level of literal statement, that Moses passed out baptismal certificates or that theologians should debate whether Christ was igneous, metamorphic, or sedimentary." Those who favour a typological equation include E. Schweizer, "Jesus Christ," *TRE* 16.687; Kuschel, *Born* 280-85. E. E. Ellis, "*Christos* in 1 Corinthians 10.4, 9," in M. C. De Boer, ed., *From Jesus to John: Essays on Jesus and New Testament Christology,* M. de Jonge FS (JSNTS 84; Sheffield: Sheffield Academic, 1993) 168-73, sees both typology and preexistence. See also §§22.5 and 7 below.

60. E.g., Hanson, *Image* 73-74; Cranfield, "Comments" 273-74; Fitzmyer, *Romans* 590.

61. See further my *Romans* 603-5; and further below §§19.4b and 23.3.

The order of the clauses does not constitute evidence to the contrary, since it is determined by the order of clauses in Deut. 30.12-14.[62] At all events, even if a preexistent Wisdom reference is to be seen here, it does not take us any further.

In short, the passages just cited may indeed strengthen the conclusion that Paul worked with a lively Wisdom christology and that he readily embraced the thought of Christ as preexistent Wisdom. But because the language is allusive and includes typological identification, the theological force of the christology implied is not very clear. It may confirm the findings of §11.2, but is hardly clear enough to extend them. The theological weight of Paul's Wisdom christology still lies essentially in 1 Cor. 1.24; 8.6 and Col. 1.15-20.[63]

§11.4 Phil. 2.6-11

The other most important passage in discussion regarding the preexistent Christ is the other great hymn (as it is generally regarded)[64] within the Pauline letters — Phil. 2.6-11. Its importance can hardly be overestimated. Martin Hengel, in particular, regards it as primary evidence that the most significant developments in christology had already taken place within the first twenty years of Christianity's beginnings.[65]

As usual the context is important. In making his appeal to the Philippians for harmony and active concern one for another (2.1-4), Paul calls on his readers to cultivate a habit of mind "which [was] also in Christ Jesus" (2.5).[66] And then he continues:

62. See further my *Christology* 184-86.

63. We need not go further here into such passages as Eph. 1.3-14 and 4.8-10; see my *Christology* 186-87 and 234-39.

64. For most of this century Phil. 2.6-11 has been designated a pre-Pauline hymn. The description is fitting, but the issue does not greatly affect us, since Paul presumably made use of it as an appropriate expression of his own theology. The translation in the text is set out to indicate the passage's rhythmic or hymnic character rather than to propose a particular structure, on which nothing in the present discussion really depends. The most common inference drawn is that "the death of the cross" (2.8c) was added by Paul, but see Hofius, *Christushymnus* (above §9 n. 11). For the debate on literary form and authorship, see, e.g., Martin, *Carmen* 24-62; O'Brien, *Philippians* 188-93, 198-202.

65. Hengel, *Son* (§10 n. 1) 1-2; also "Hymns" (§10 n. 136) 94-95; also "Christological Titles in Early Christianity," in Charlesworth, ed., *Messiah* (§8 n. 1) 425-48 (here 440-44) = *Studies* (§10 n. 1) 359-89 (here 379-83).

66. For this translation see Martin, *Carmen* 84-88; Moule, "Further Reflexions" 265-66; O'Brien, *Philippians* 205; Hawthorne, *Philippians* 79-81; Fee, *Philippians* 200-201. Fowl, *Story* 89-101, while following the alternative rendering ("within the realm of Christ"), proceeds to argue that "2.6-11 functions as an *exemplar* within Paul's argument" (92). See also L. W. Hurtado, "Jesus as Lordly Example in Philippians 2.5-11," in Richardson and Hurd, eds., *From Jesus to Paul* 113-26 (especially 120-25).

> 6who, being in the form of God,
>   did not reckon to be equal with God
>   as something to be grasped,
> 7but emptied himself,
>   took the form of a slave,
>   and became in the very likeness of humankind.
> And being found in likeness as a human being,
>   8he humbled himself
>   and became obedient unto death,
>   the death of the cross.
> 9Wherefore, God has exalted him to the heights
>   and bestowed on him the name
>   which is over every name,
> 10that at the name of Jesus
>   every knee should bow,
>   in heaven and on the earth and under the earth,
> 11and every tongue confess
>   that Jesus Christ is Lord
>   to the glory of God the Father.

A vigorous debate still continues around this hymnic passage.[67] However, the suggestion that the hymn has been constructed with strong allusion to Adam or even modeled on the template of Adam christology is still persuasive.[68]

Before elaborating the claim and dealing with the strong critique

67. The bibliographies of Hawthorne, *Philippians* 71-75, and O'Brien, *Philippians* 186-88, contain nearly 170 and nearly 100 items respectively.

68. Other suggestions for allusive background are not necessarily alternatives — especially the Servant of Isaiah 53, particularly in 2.7ab (J. Jeremias, "Zu Phil. 2.7: *HEAUTON EKENŌSEN*," *NovT* 6 [1963] 182-88; M. Rissi, "Der Christushymnus in Phil. 2.6-11," *ANRW* 2.25.4 [1987] 3314-26), martyr theology (Schweizer, *Erniedrigung* [§10 n. 1] 93-99; followed by Martin, *Carmen* 191-96, and Fowl, *Story* 73-75), Wisdom theology (Georgi, "Hymnus"; followed by Kuschel, *Born* 255-66, and Witherington, *Sage* 261-63), and Son of God christology (Wanamaker, "Philippians 2.6-11"). We have already noted how Paul runs different imagery together in passages like Rom. 8.3 and Gal. 4.4-7 (see also Hofius, *Christushymnus* 67-74). But a Wisdom allusion is far harder to hear in this case than in the creation language of 1 Cor. 8.6 and Col. 1.15-17 (cf. Sanders, *Hymns* 72-73). Still more so a Son of Man allusion (Larsson, *Christus* 237-42, 247-49; see my *Christology* 312 nn. 86, 87). And as with most of the search for a pre-Christian Gnostic redeemer myth, the search here has also proved fruitless (see, e.g., Hengel, *Son* [§10 n. 1] 25-41 [also §20 n. 97 below]; my *Christology* ch. 4; E. Schweizer, "Paul's Christology and Gnosticism," in Hooker and Wilson, eds., *Paul and Paulinism* 115-23; Kuschel, *Born* 248-50; O'Brien, *Philippians* 193-94; *pace* Bultmann, *Theology* 1.131, 298 and particularly E. Käsemann, "A Critical Analysis of Philippians 2.5-11," *JTC* 5 [1968] 45-88); preoccupation with Käsemann's thesis diminishes the value of Sanders, *Hymns,* and Hamerton-Kelly, *Pre-Existence.*

leveled against it, an important preliminary point needs to be made. That is on the nature of allusion. For the fact of the matter is that too much of the debate on the exegesis of this passage has displayed rather crass artistic or literary insensitivity. As we have occasion to observe more than once in the present study,[69] allusions by their nature are not explicit. Poets or literary critics who had to spell out every allusion and echo would undermine their art and deprive their more perceptive readers of the moment of illumination, the thrill of recognition. Their artistic skills would be reduced to the level of high school examination cribs. For example, it is fairly clear in the last movement of Brahms's first symphony, with its echo of Beethoven's ninth, that Brahms is laying claim to be Beethoven's successor. Whereas Dvorak's ninth, "from the new world," contains echoes of American folk tunes, without actually quoting any. In literature, it would generally be recognized that the works of poets like John Milton and T. S. Eliot are full of allusions,[70] and one cannot begin adequately to appreciate the compositions of a hymnwriter like Charles Wesley without being aware that they are shot through with scriptural allusions. Scholars and students will hardly need reminding that at the back of the usual NT Greek texts there is a whole catalogue of allusions to the (Jewish) scriptures, which far exceed the number of explicit quotations.[71]

So with Paul in particular, we have already suggested a number of allusions to Jesus traditions (§8.3).[72] And in his use of Adam motifs we noted the allusions (hardly explicit) in Rom. 1.18-25 and 7.7-13.[73] Indeed, if our earlier analysis of Paul's christology is at all justified, then Adam was a figure who lay behind a great deal of Paul's theologizing.[74] To make recognition of such allusions depend on precision of meaning in individual terms would run counter to the art of allusion. On the contrary, it is often the imprecision of meaning of a term or the multifaceted imagery of a metaphor that enables the interconnection or imaginative jump[75] which is the stuff of allusion. The importance of the point justifies its reiteration: exegesis of particular terms which insists on only one referential meaning for each term and denies all the

69. See especially above §1.3 and below §23.5.

70. Hays, *Echoes* 18-21, refers particularly to J. Hollander, *The Figure of Echo: A Mode of Allusion in Milton and After* (Berkeley: University of California, 1981). My postgraduate student Stephen Wright referred me particularly to H. Bloom, *A Map of Misreading* (New York: Oxford University, 1975).

71. See also above §1.3 and §7 n. 36.

72. See also below §23.5.

73. See above §§4.4, 7.

74. See §§8.6, 9.1, and 10.2.

75. The technical term is "trope," defined by Quintilian, *Institutes* 8.6.1, as the artistic alteration of a word or phrase from its proper meaning to another.

other possible meanings will often be wrong exegesis because it unjustifiably narrows meaning ("either-or" exegesis) and rules out associations which the author may have intended to evoke precisely by using a sequence of such evocative terms.[76] It need hardly be pointed out that such hermeneutical considerations have particular relevance when the passage is a poem or a hymn. The relevance of these reflections in this case should become clear as we proceed.

In assessing Phil. 2.6-11 it is not too difficult to identify four or five points of contact with Adam tradition and Adam christology as we have now become familiar with it.[77]

2.6a — in the form of God;[78]
2.6bc — tempted to grasp equality with God;[79]
2.7 — took the form of a slave [to corruption and sin];[80]
2.8 — obedient to death;[81]
2.9-11 — exalted and glorified.[82]

But four points in particular can be brought against this exposition.

First, the hymn uses the term "form *(morphē)*" rather than the term used in Gen. 1.27, "image *(eikōn)*." In a discussion of allusion, however, the argument carries little weight. The terms were used as near synonyms,[83] and it would appear that the writer preferred "form of God" because it made the appropriate parallel and contrast with "form of a slave."[84] Such

76. Cf. Hays, *Echoes* 20: "When a literary echo links the text in which it occurs to an earlier text, the figurative effect of the echo can lie in the unstated or suppressed (transumed) points of resonance between the two texts."
77. I have yet to see any alternative framework of thought into which the hymn "fits" at so many points (*pace* Rissi, "Christushymnus" [above n. 68] 3318 n. 18). The discussion here makes no attempt to cover all the ground covered in my *Christology* xviii-xix, 114-21, but focuses on the issues which responses to these earlier expositions provoked.
78. Cf. Gen. 1.27 — "in his own image."
79. Cf. Gen. 3.5 — "you will be like God."
80. Cf. Wis. 2.23; Rom. 8.3, 18-21; 1 Cor. 15.42, 47-49; Gal. 4.3-4; Heb. 2.7a, 9a, 15.
81. Cf. Gen. 2.17; 3.22-24; Wis. 2.24; Rom. 5.12-21; 7.7-11; 1 Cor. 15.21-22.
82. Cf. Ps. 8.5b-6; 1 Cor. 15.27, 45; Heb. 2.7b-8, 9b.
83. Martin, *Carmen* 102-19; Kim, *Origin* (§7 n. 1) 200-204. As O'Brien observes, "most exegetes recognize that the semantic fields of the two terms overlap considerably" (*Philippians* 263). What more could one look for in making an effective allusion?
84. That any explanation of "form of God" must make reasonable sense of this contrast is rightly emphasized by Habermann, *Präexistenzaussagen* 110, 113-16, and Wanamaker, "Philippians 2.6-11" 181-83. But they both use "either-or" exegesis, in particular ignoring the fact that Gal. 4.4-5 and Rom. 8.3 can also be seen as expressing an Adam interchange theme (see above §9.3).

a double function of a term is precisely what one might expect in poetic mode.[85]

Second, a strong case has been made that the much discussed term in 2.6c, *harpagmos* ("something to be grasped"), has the extra precision of denoting something grasped in retention, to be taken advantage of, rather than something to be grasped at.[86] But to press for one meaning to the exclusion of the other is an either-or exegesis which ill befits the word's range of usage, the poetic style of the passage, and indeed the lengthy debate on the meaning of the word. In fact, there is no real evidence for the claim that the sense "retaining" inheres in the word itself.[87] *Harpagmos* is better taken with less precision as "act of robbery"[88] or as equivalent to the English gerund usage "seizing, grasping" — hence here, "as a matter of seizing, something to be grasped." Since the object of this action, "the being like God" (literally), is a clearer echo of Gen. 3.5,[89] the contrast with Adam's attempt to be like God[90] would hardly be missed by many who were familiar with Paul's Adam theology.[91]

The third objection to recognition of an Adam allusion is in effect that

---

85. Cf. Cullmann: "Without the background of Paul's doctrine of the two Adams, either these words can scarcely be understood, or we become lost in tangential theological speculations foreign to early Christianity" (*Christology* [§10 n. 1] 177).

86. In recent scholarship note particularly Habermann, *Präexistenzaussagen* 118-27; Wright, *Climax* 77-83. For the earlier debate, see Martin, *Carmen* 134-53.

87. Moule, "Further Reflexions" 266-68, 271-76; J. C. O'Neill, "Hoover on *Harpagmos* Reviewed, with a Modest Proposal Concerning Philippians 2.6," *HTR* 81 (1988) 445-49. For example, in the two disputed cases from Eusebius, *HE* 5.2.2-4 and 8.12.1-2 (in the first of which Phil. 2.6 is explicitly cited), the critical point is surely that death was not something already possessed by the would-be martyrs, but something they eagerly grasped at (*pace* Wright, *Climax* 85).

88. LSJ, *harpagmos;* BAGD, *harpagmos.*

89. The Hebrew *ke'lohim* (Gen. 3.5) could be translated by *isa theǭ* (Phil. 2.6) equally as well as by *hōs theoi* (Gen. 3.5 LXX). Hebrew *k* ("like") is translated by *isa* on a number of occasions in the LXX (Job 5.14; 10.10; 13.28, etc.; Isa. 51.23; cf. Deut. 13.6; Wis. 7.3). As usual, the article with the infinitive *(to einai)* indicates something either previously mentioned or otherwise well known. The earlier discussion of the Adam motif suggests that the Adamic temptation "to be like God" *(to einai isa theǭ)* would have been well enough known in Jewish and early Christian circles (above §§4.2-7). "It is hard to doubt that *to be on equality with God* was intended to evoke the story of Adam. It recalls much too clearly the temptation to which Adam fell" (Barrett, *Paul* 108).

90. That Adam christology works by antithetic parallelism is evident from Rom. 5.15-19.

91. The ambiguity of the relation between "form of God" and "being like God" closely echoes the ambiguity of the relation between "image of God" in Gen. 1.27 and "like God" in 3.5, as indeed also the ambiguity of the function of the tree of life in the garden prior to Adam's expulsion (see above §4.2).

the hymn seems to split the failure of Adam and its outcome into two phases. First, the refusal to grasp equality with God (2.6) has as its converse the act of "emptying" (in contrast to "grasping"),[92] "taking the form of a slave" (in contrast to "being in the form of God"), and becoming like humankind (possibly an allusive contrast to the serpent's temptation, "You shall be like God") (2.7). But then the further act of "obedience to death" (2.8) is presumably set in contrast to the "disobedience" which brought sin and death (as in Rom. 5.19). This interesting feature, however, could be explained simply by the fact that the Adam analogy is here stretched out to cover the whole life of Jesus rather than only his death (as in Rom. 5.15-19).

A fourth objection is that the latter half of the hymn ill fits an Adam christology, given the high exaltation envisaged in 2.9-11.[93] But this neglects the obvious parallel between Phil. 2.10-11 and 1 Cor. 15.24-28, the latter in direct continuity with the Adam-Christ contrast in 15.21-22, and itself embodying the clear allusion to Ps. 8.6 (15.27). It also ignores the fact that Jewish reflection on Adam seems already to have embraced the thought of Adam's exaltation to heaven and glorification.[94]

In short, the case for hearing a deliberate allusion to and contrast with Adam in Phil. 2.6-11 remains strong.[95] Given the number and sequence of allusions[96] it could indeed be said that the Philippians hymn is, after Heb. 2.5-9, the fullest expression of Adam christology in the NT.

Where does that leave the issue of the preexistent Christ? Here it needs to be stated again that the issue is independent of finding an Adam christology

---

92. Cf. particularly Moule, "Further Reflections" 272. The prominence given to the verb *ekenōsen* ("emptied himself") is another example of the danger of treating the hymn as a dogmatic statement ("what did he empty himself of?"; see Hawthorne, *Philippians* 85, for the traditional range of answers). The function of the term is more to characterize than to define. Note Fee's helpful comment in *Philippians* 210: "this is metaphor, pure and simple."

93. Kreitzer, *Jesus* (§10 n. 1) 224 n. 72: vv. 9-11 "breaks the mould of any Adamic motif"; Witherington, *Sage* 259.

94. *Vita Adae et Evae* 25/*Apoc. Mos.* 37; *T. Abr.* A 11; cf. the subsequent exaltation of Adam in rabbinic literature (Scroggs, *Adam* [§4 n. 1] 38-58).

95. See also C. H. Talbert, "The Problem of Pre-Existence in Philippians 2.6-11," *JBL* 86 (1967) 141-53; Ladd, *Theology* 460-61; Hooker, "Philippians 2.6-11"; Murphy-O'Connor, "Anthropology"; G. Howard, "Phil. 2:6-11 and the Human Christ," *CBQ* 40 (1978) 368-87; H. Wansbrough in NJB; Macquarrie, *Jesus Christ* 56-59; Ziesler, *Pauline Christianity* 45; Barrett, *Paul* 107-9; (earlier bibliography in Martin, *Carmen* 161-64). The critique of my earlier treatment by L. D. Hurst, "Re-Enter the Pre-Existent Christ in Philippians 2.5-11," *NTS* (1986) 449-57, is a good example of failure to appreciate how allusion works, equivalent to the old confusion between parable and allegory.

96. Wright speaks of multiple intertextual echoes (*Climax* 58).

in the Philippians passage.[97] Given the two-stage contrast with Adam just noted, an obvious understanding of the first stage would be from preexistence to existence (2.6-7) and from existence to death (2.8) — all the more obvious, indeed, given the aorist tenses and language of 2.7.[98] "Emptied himself and took the form of a slave" (2.7ab) could possibly be understood as some act of self-abasement during Jesus' life.[99] But "became in the very likeness of humankind" (2.7c) is more naturally read as a reference to birth ("was born in the very likeness of humankind").[100]

An alternative possibility may be that the first stage envisaged is the mythic stage of prehistory, in which Adam himself makes the transition from *adam* = humankind to *adam* = the progenitor of Seth and other children (Gen. 5.1-5).[101] Or again, in our earlier forays into reflection about Adam, we have noted the awkwardness of the double conception of death. Adam's grasping disobedience had a two-stage outcome: he was banished from the presence of God (and the tree of life, Gen. 3.22-24)[102] — the first death (2.17); and he was thereafter subject to corruption and physical death (5.5).[103] Is it possible, then, that the hymn's intention was to reflect that two-stage outworking of Adam's transgression? In each case, the Adam-Christ, by his own choice, freely embraced the outcome which Adam's grasping and disobedience brought upon humankind. He freely embraced the lot of humankind as slave to sin and death, which was the consequence of Adam's

97. In critiques of my earlier treatment of this theme, it has been insufficiently observed that this point had already been made (*Christology* 119-20). Cf. Kuschel, *Born* 262-63; Wright, *Climax* 91-92, 95-97.

98. So most; e.g., Hanson, *Image* 65; Marshall, "Incarnational Christology" 170; Morris, *Theology* 44; Habermann, *Präexistenzaussagen* 147; O'Brien, *Philippians* 223-37, 267; Fee, *Philippians* 203 n. 41 (O'Brien and Fee with bibliography); Witherington, *Sage* 261; O'Collins, *Christology* 35-36.

99. As an allusion to the Servant or suffering righteous (above n. 68) the thought would already embrace that of Jesus' death (see, e.g., Rissi, "Christushymnus" [above n. 68] 3319-21; O'Brien, *Philippians* 220-24).

100. So NRSV — "being born in human likeness"; NIV — "being made in human likeness." But also NJB — "becoming as human beings are"; REB — "bearing the human likeness." The parallel with Rom. 8.3 is particularly noticeable ("in the very likeness of"); see above §§8.6 and 9.2(2). In his critique of my earlier study Witherington, *Sage* 263, and *Narrative* 102-3, ignores the significance of both Rom. 8.3 (". . . of sinful flesh") and Gal. 4.4 ("under the law").

101. See above §4.2. But at least the passage (Gen. 5.1-5) reflects an early awareness of some sort of transition in the narrative into human history as such (see also §4 n. 10).

102. See further above §4.2.

103. The same two phases are echoed in Rom. 8.3 ("in the very likeness of sinful flesh, and as a sin offering") and Gal. 4.4-5 ("born under the law, in order that he might redeem those under the law").

grasping.[104] And he freely accepted the death which was the consequence of Adam's disobedience. In consequence, he was super-exalted (reversing Adam's double subjection to death) to the status and role originally intended for Adam (Ps. 8.6).[105]

It is precisely the function of such allusive poetry to set in motion such a sequence of reflections and parallels. But the fact remains that it has also set in motion the thought of Christ's preexistence. And a commentator could hardly draw out the one while disallowing the other. The problem would then remain of filling out that thought of preexistence. Is Christ Jesus then to be envisaged as making an Adamic choice at some time (!) in eternity? A choice in effect to become man? That is the almost inevitable corollary.[106] The only qualification which needs to be made is once again that this is an extended metaphor. In the parallel Wisdom christology we observed that it was not simply Christ, God's Son, who was being spoken of in the Wisdom christology, but Christ as Wisdom. So here it is not simply Christ Jesus as such of whom the hymn speaks, but Christ Jesus in the role of Adam, the Adam that God intended. Wisdom's preexistence allowed amazing language to be used of Christ. So also Adam's prehistory allowed similarly amazing language to be used of Christ. The mistake would be to collapse the metaphor into a straightforward statement of historical fact. To dispense with the metaphor would be to lose sight of and hold on what it expresses. The metaphor *is* the message.

Whatever the actual (range of) imagery, however, the basic message of the hymn is clear enough. As a continuation of the appeal of 2.1-4, Christ is presented as one who did not stand on status but emptied himself, as one whose whole life speaks of serving not grasping, as one whose way to exaltation was only through death.

§11.5 Other possible preexistent Adam passages

As with the Wisdom christology, so here, three other passages deserve at least brief consideration.

---

104. Cf. Hooker: "At this point the one who is truly what man is meant to be — in the form and likeness of God — becomes what other men *are,* because they are in Adam" ("Philippians 2.6-11" 98-99).

105. To argue that the exaltation or hyperexaltation *(hyperypsōsen)* of 2.9 was a resumption of the divine mode of existence already enjoyed in 2.6 ("the pre-existent was already *Kyrios*" — Fuller, *Foundations* 230) ignores not only the Adam motif (cf. Ps. 8.5-6), but also the consistent emphasis that *kyrios* was bestowed on Jesus at exaltation (see §10.4 above) and the more likely implication of the verb *hyperhypsoō* (cf. O'Brien, *Philippians* 236).

106. See particularly Wright's exposition (*Climax* 90-98).

(a) The first is once again 1 Corinthians 15, this time the full sequence 15.44-49, with particular reference to "the second human being from heaven," "the heavenly one" (15.47-49). In his exposition regarding the resurrection body, Paul holds out the prospect that "we shall bear the image of the heavenly one" (15.49). In fact, however, it is difficult to see why this passage should come into consideration. The reason is probably the old hunt for evidence of a pre-Christian Gnostic redeemer concept, wedded to the popular hypothesis of the 1950s to 1970s that Paul's opposition in Corinth was Gnostic in character. Within that context a reference to "a heavenly man" was too inviting to be neglected: the reference must be to the preexistent "man"! The fact that Philo interpreted the two creation narratives (Genesis 1 and 2) as referring to "two types of men, the one a heavenly *(ouranios)* man, the other an earthly" *(Leg. All.* 1.31) has encouraged some to deduce that Paul's heavenly *(epouranios)* man must be equivalent to Philo's and must therefore have been conceived of as preexistent.[107]

But such an interpretation runs completely counter to the thrust of the passage. What is in view throughout is the spiritual body of the resurrection. In the contrast between "psychical body" (the body of the old creation) and "spiritual body" (the resurrection body), it is explicitly stated that the psychical was first, not the spiritual (15.46). That in turn is an exposition of 15.45, the contrast between the first Adam, the "living *psychē*," and the last Adam, that is, eschatological humanity. Consequently "the heavenly one" can hardly be other than the resurrected Christ.[108] As the race of earthly humanity was patterned on the earthly Adam (Gen. 2.7), so the race of resurrected humanity would be patterned on the risen Christ (1 Cor. 15.21-22). "As we have borne the image of the earthly one, we shall also bear the image of the heavenly one" (15.49). In other words, in terms of Adam christology, this is the Christ of the third phase (resurrection, last Adam), not of any prior phase which preceded that of the earthly Adam. Not even a reading of Phil. 2.6-7 as speaking of preexistent Adam-Christ can justify a reading of "the second human being from heaven" as the preexistent Christ.[109]

(b) The second passage is 2 Cor. 4.4-6:

---

107. Bousset, *Kyrios Christos* 195-98; Hanson, *Image* 63-64, 80; R. P. Martin, *The Spirit and the Congregation: Studies in 1 Corinthians 12–15* (Grand Rapids: Eerdmans, 1984) 153-54. We should note, however, that Philo's heavenly man "was an image or type or seal, an object of thought (only), incorporeal . . ." (*Opif.* 134, Loeb translation).

108. See above §10.6.

109. See also, e.g., Ladd, *Theology* 462-63; Macquarrie, *Jesus Christ* 62-63; Fee, *1 Corinthians* 792-93.

[4]. . . the light of the gospel of the glory of the Christ, who is the image of God. . . . [6]For it is God, who said "Let light shine out of darkness," who has shined in our hearts to give the light of the knowledge of the glory of God in the face of Jesus Christ.

An attractive reading of the passage is that Paul was thinking in Wisdom terms, that is, of Christ as the image of God (cf. Col. 1.15). The clear echo of Gen. 1.3 ("Let there be light") strengthens an allusion to Wisdom's role in creation (cf. 1 Cor. 8.6). If there is also an allusion to Paul's Damascus road experience, the inference would be that Paul equated the light from heaven, which struck him down,[110] with the glory of God. His recognition of the glorious heavenly figure as Christ could then be said to have been the basis of his subsequent Wisdom christology.[111]

An allusion to Paul's conversion experience is indeed likely,[112] though we should also note that there is nothing in the text to indicate that all this was evident to Paul from the first.[113] More to the point, however, the structure of thought seems to be more that of Adam christology than of Wisdom christology. Talk of the gospel and of the death and life of Jesus (4.10-11) suggests reference to the risen Christ rather than to the more typical creation context of Wisdom christology.[114] The shift in thought from "the Lord" as "the Spirit" (3.16-18)[115] to "Jesus Christ as Lord" (4.5) parallels the thought of the risen Lord as "life-giving Spirit" in 1 Cor. 15.45.[116] And the passage is nested within a sequence of thought involving believers' transformation into glory (3.18; 4.17) — elsewhere in Paul a motif of Adam christology.[117] As with 1 Cor. 15.47-49, therefore, the glory and image are best understood as that of the Christ who has been raised and who thus fulfills the divine plan for humankind, made in God's image and sharing his glory.[118]

(c) The third passage appears in Paul's plea to the Corinthians to take part in the collection for the poor Christians in Jerusalem. Paul urges upon them the example of Christ — 2 Cor. 8.9:

110. At least according to Acts 9.3-4; 22.6-7, 11; 26.13-14.

111. So particularly Kim, *Origin* ch. 6; cf. Segal, *Paul* ch. 2; and Newman, *Paul's Glory-Christology*.

112. Cf. the "in me" of Gal. 1.16 with the "in our hearts" here.

113. "The gospel of the glory of the Christ" sounds like Paul's later reflection on the event, when his conception of the gospel had become more elaborate theologically.

114. See above §§7.3, 9.1, and 10.1.

115. See below §16.3.

116. See above §§10.4 and 10.6.

117. Rom. 8.29-30; 1 Cor. 15.49; Phil. 3.21; Col. 3.9-10; Eph. 4.22-24. Contrast Hamerton-Kelly, *Pre-Existence* 147: "The soteriology implied throughout 3.18–4.18 is based on the idea of Christ as the pre-existent image of God" (also 155).

118. So also Kuschel, *Born* 294. On Adam's loss of glory see above §4.5.

> For you know the grace of our Lord Jesus Christ, that, although he was rich, on your account he became poor, in order that by his poverty you might become rich.

The passage is usually seen as a statement equivalent to Phil. 2.6-11 — that is, as denoting the preexistent Christ's self-abasement in incarnation.[119] The reading is certainly stronger than in the case of 1 Cor. 15.47-49. And the very possibility of reading the verse in this way constitutes in itself an argument in favour of the reading. In which case the considerations above come into play only in part, since the statement itself is fairly bald and unmetaphorical. But this corollary in its turn puts something of a question mark against reading it that way. For all the other passages which have spoken of Christ's preexistence, as we have seen, have been allusive and strongly metaphorical (Jesus as Wisdom, Jesus as Adam).

To this has to be added the fact that what is in view here is evidently a one-stage act of abasement. Elsewhere the one stage is always the cross and resurrection. And even with passages like those reviewed above (§11.2-3), the thrust has been towards the obedience of the cross (Phil. 2.9), the action which redeems (Gal. 4.5), the sacrifice which condemns sin in the flesh (Rom. 8.3). This suggests that the one stage here also, the rich becoming poor, is more likely to be a reference to the "interchange" of cross and resurrection.

This is confirmed by the fact that when Paul speaks elsewhere of the "grace" of Christ, his thought is always of Christ's death and resurrection.[120] Elsewhere also formulations structured to indicate "interchange" have likewise been focused on Christ's death.[121] And elsewhere too the contrast between poverty and riches is regularly the contrast between spiritual wealth and material poverty.[122] This last is also the most obvious thought in the immediate context, where the interchange between spiritual benefit and material need is close to hand, as in the other most important collection context (Rom. 15.27). It would also fit here with the tradition of Jesus' own relative poverty during his own ministry[123] and the contrast between his consciousness of sonship ("Abba" — Mark 14.36) and apparent sense of spiritual abandonment in the cry of desolation from the cross (Mark 15.34).[124]

---

119. E.g., A. Oepke, *TDNT* 3.661: "The best commentary [on Phil. 2.6-7] is to be found in the par. 2 Cor. 8.9"; Craddock, *Pre-Existence* 100-106; Furnish, *2 Corinthians* 417; O'Collins, *Christology* 127.

120. See particularly Rom. 5.15, 21; Gal. 2.20-21; Eph. 1.6-7.

121. 2 Cor. 5.21; Gal. 3.13. See above §9.3.

122. Tob. 4.21; 2 Cor. 6.10; Jas. 2.5; Rev. 2.9; cf. 1 Cor. 1.5; 4.8; 2 Cor. 9.11. Cf. Kuschel, *Born* 296-97. Despite Marshall, "Incarnational Christology" 170-71, does Phil. 4.19 (heavenly riches) provide a counterparallel?

123. Cf. Mark 10.28-30 and Matt. 8.20/Luke 9.58.

124. Such points were ignored by Hanson, *Image* 65-66.

In other words, the most obvious way to take 2 Cor. 8.9 is as a vivid allusion to the tremendous personal cost of Jesus' ministry and particularly the willing sacrifice of his death. It was as a result of this self-impoverishment that the first Christians had experienced the richness of God's grace. That Paul intended an allusion to the preexistent Christ's self-abasement in incarnation must be judged unlikely.

§11.6 Conclusions

(1) Paul does have a conception of the preexistent Christ. But it is the preexistence of Wisdom now identified by and as Christ. It is the prehistorical existence of Adam as a template on which a vivid Adam christology begins to be drawn. That there is no clear thought of Christ's preexistence independent of such imagery (Wisdom and Adam) is a factor of considerable importance in determining the significance to be given to subsequent statements of Christ's preexistence.[125]

(2) When we add in the identification with the Spirit in 1 Cor. 15.45, we have a striking sequence. Wisdom and Spirit were primary ways of speaking of God's interaction with his world and his people. That Christ should "absorb" their roles to the extent that he does is very striking. What an impact it was that Christ made by his life and death and resurrection that such identifications should be thus expressed!

(3) How much of this is directly attributable to the resurrection of Christ itself? We have seen how much of the Adam christology is deduced backward from the thought of Christ as the eschatological equivalent to Adam (§8.6). We have seen how the equation with the life-giving Spirit is formulated only with respect to the resurrected Christ (§10.6). In some degree also it must be significant that it is the exalted Lord who is described in terms of Wisdom's role in creation in 1 Cor. 8.6 and the exalted Christ who is hymned in Col. 1.15-20. Even with the thought of preexistence, then, the primary christological moment continues to be focused on the death and resurrection of the Christ.

125. Too many seem content to conclude "preexistence" without asking what that would have meant to Paul and his generation (e.g., Marshall, "Incarnational Christology"; Habermann, *Präexistenzaussagen;* Witherington, *Sage* 270). It is to the credit of earlier studies (Craddock, Hamerton-Kelly) that they recognized an issue here (ideal or actual preexistence, etc). Cf. Hengel, *Son* (§10 n. 1) 72: "The problem of 'pre-existence' necessarily grew out of the combination of Jewish ideas of history, time, and creation with the certainty that God had disclosed himself fully in his Messiah Jesus of Nazareth. . . . Only in this way was *the unsurpassibility and finality of God's revelation* in Jesus of Nazareth expressed in a last, conclusive way."

(4) When we inquire more closely into the relation of the thus exalted Christ with God, an interesting feature emerges. On the one hand, when the theme is soteriological, Paul seems relatively unconcerned to particularize or distinguish the source of grace, whether God or Christ or indeed the Spirit. Christ is understood as the focus of that grace and as characterizing it. But when Paul speaks with some view to the relation of Christ with God, of christology or theology per se, then it is made quite clear that the christology is held within the theology, that the reflection on Christ is held firmly within a sustained and confessed monotheistic framework. If God as Father can no longer be understood without Jesus as Son, he is still the one God, "the God and Father of our Lord Jesus Christ." And if this is a functional christology, it is not yet clear what the ontological corollaries are. In assessing Paul's christology at this point and in theologizing further on the basis of it, a central fact remains primary: that Paul's christology was not seen as a threat to Israel's inherited monotheism by his Jewish contemporaries, nor was it intended by Paul himself as a complete redefinition of that monotheism.[126] The continued Christian confession that God is one depends more than is generally appreciated on being able still to affirm that conclusion. As does the viability of any real rapprochement between historic Judaism and Christianity in their central confessions.

(5) The fundamental structure of Paul's christology in its overlap and tension between Adam and Wisdom christology also points the way forward to the subsequent agonizing of Christian theologians over how Jesus could be seen as both God and human being. In Christ God's original design for humanity finally takes concrete shape. In Christ the infinite gap between the "image" which is God's creative wisdom and the "image" which is created humanity is bridged, both image which stamps and image which is stamped. Here, as elsewhere, this revelatory insight is subjected to the law of diminishing definition, as theologians attempt to conceptualize the inconceivable and lose the wonder in endless refinement.

126. This presumably applies also to Wright's talk of "christological monotheism" being modified by being set within the framework of Jewish "creational monotheism" (*Climax* 117); see also above §2 n. 6.

§12 Until he comes[1]

§12.1 The coming (parousia) of Christ

We have strayed some distance from the course of Paul's own exposition in Romans. But it was necessary to do so if we are to gain a clear impression of the coherence of Paul's christology. And at least most of what we have so far looked at was evidently in the back of his mind as he wrote his letter to Rome. Here again is underlined the importance of allusion in filling out what need not be explicitly elaborated.[2]

There is one other element in Paul's christology which takes us still

1. **Bibliography**: **W. Baird**, "Pauline Eschatology in Hermeneutic Perspective," *NTS* 17 (1970-71) 314-27; **J. Baumgarten**, *Paulus und die Apokalyptik* (WMANT 44; Neukirchen-Vluyn: Neukirchener, 1975); **J. C. Beker**, *Paul* 135-81; *Paul's Apocalyptic Gospel: The Coming Triumph of God* (Philadelphia: Fortress, 1982); **V. P. Branick**, "Apocalyptic Paul?" *CBQ* 47 (1985) 664-75; **Cerfaux**, *Christ* (§10 n. 1) 31-68; **C. H. Dodd**, "The Mind of Paul," *New Testament Studies* (Manchester: Manchester University, 1953) 67-128; **J. D. G. Dunn**, "He Will Come Again," *Int* 51 (1997) 42-56; **W. Harnisch**, *Eschatologische Existenz. Ein exegetischer Beitrag zum Sachanliegen von 1 Thessalonischer 4.13–5.11* (FRLANT 110; Göttingen: Vandenhoeck, 1973); **R. Jewett**, *The Thessalonian Correspondence: Paul's Rhetoric and Millenarian Piety* (Philadelphia: Fortress, 1986); **E. Käsemann**, "The Beginnings of Christian Theology" (1960), *New Testament Questions* ch. 4; **L. E. Keck**, "Paul and Apocalyptic Theology," *Int* 38 (1984) 229-41; **R. N. Longenecker**, "The Nature of Paul's Early Eschatology," *NTS* 31 (1985) 85-95; **J. Marcus and M. L. Soards**, eds., *Apocalyptic and the New Testament*, J. L. Martyn FS (JSNTS 24; Sheffield: Sheffield Academic, 1989); **A. L. Moore**, *The Parousia in the New Testament* (NovTSup 13; Leiden: Brill, 1966); **C. F. D. Moule**, "The Influence of Circumstances on the Use of Eschatological Terms," *Essays* 184-99; **J. Plevnik**, *Paul and the Parousia: An Exegetical and Theological Investigation* (Peabody: Hendrickson, 1996); **Ridderbos**, *Paul* 486-537; **J. A. T. Robinson**, *Jesus and His Coming: The Emergence of a Doctrine* (London: SCM/New York: Abingdon, 1957; Philadelphia: Westminster, 2,1979); **T. E. Schmidt and M. Silva**, eds., *To Tell the Mystery: Essays in New Testament Eschatology*, R. H. Gundry FS (JSNTS 100; Sheffield: Sheffield Academic, 1994); **Schweitzer**, *Paul and His Interpreters;* **G. Vos**, *The Pauline Eschatology* (Grand Rapids: Eerdmans, 1961); **B. Witherington**, *Jesus, Paul and the End of the World: A Comparative Study of New Testament Eschatology* (Exeter: Paternoster/Downers Grove: InterVarsity, 1992); *Narrative* 186-204.

2. So Rom. 4.24-25; 5.14, 19; 6.9-10; 7.4; 8.3, 9-11, 32-34, 39; 9.5, 33; 10.9-13; 14.9; 15.8.

further from the course of Romans. That is the coming (again) of the exalted Christ. But it is equally necessary that we look at it here and thus round out our picture of Paul's christology. More to the point, there would be something theologically incomplete in leaving the analysis of Paul's christology after analysing the significance of Jesus' resurrection and Christ's preexistence. For in Paul's theology the coming (again) of Christ answers to both and completes both. As the resurrection of Jesus began a new age, a new humanity, so his coming again will bring that age to a climax and complete the work of salvation which was then begun.[3] And as the assertion of Christ's preexistence was a way of saying that God in Christ was also God in creation, so the assertion of Christ's coming again is a way of saying that God in Christ is also God in final judgment. The climactic end point of both creation and salvation is one and the same. The resurrection sheds light not only on the beginning and character of creation, but also on the eschatological future. In Pauline perspective Christ is the key to both.

The distinctiveness of this early Christian belief in the coming again of the Christ should not be underrated. The thought of Elijah's reappearance on earth was already well established.[4] And already Enoch was probably linked with Elijah in this role.[5] But that was less surprising. After all, neither Enoch nor Elijah had died. Instead, they had been translated to heaven[6] and were being held in reserve there, as it were, for the last phase before the end. There was also clear expectation that the righteous would be vindicated in heaven following their oppression and death.[7] But that was a vindication which those still on earth could only see in vision or by undertaking a heavenly journey.[8] There was no thought yet clearly expressed, so far as we can tell, of the vindicated righteous returning in triumph to earth or of their vindication being displayed on earth. Here, then, we can speak of a striking advance in conceptuality which can be traced back to the earliest postresur-

---

3. 1 Cor. 15.23; Phil. 1.6. Cf. Cerfaux, *Christ:* "in Christian thought the parousia will always remain the point towards which the whole movement begun by the resurrection tends" (85); "the parousia is foreshadowed in Christ's resurrection, and his resurrection and second coming are both implicit in his death" (152).

4. Mal. 3.1-3; 4.5; Sir. 48.10-11; Mark 6.15 par.; 8.28 pars.; 9.11-12 par.; John 1.21; see also *Sib. Or.* 2.187-89; Justin, *Dialogue* 49. In Pseudo-Philo, Elijah is identified with Phinehas preserved "in Danaben" until he comes down as Elijah (48.1); see R. Hayward, "Phinehas — the Same Is Elijah: The Origin of a Rabbinic Tradition," *JJS* 29 (1978) 22-38.

5. *1 Enoch* 90.31; Rev. 11.3; *4 Ezra* 6.26; *Apoc. Elij.* 4.7. See further my *Christology* 92-94.

6. Gen. 5.24; 2 Kgs. 2.11.

7. See, e.g., my *Partings* 185-87.

8. Dan. 7.21-22; *T. Abr.* 11; Rev. 6.9-11.

rection days,[9] if not to Jesus' own parables and interpretation of the "son of man" vision in Daniel 7.[10] As the formulation of Jesus' vindication in terms of "resurrection" was an astonishing "first" in Christian theologizing, so the claim that their vindicated Messiah would come again (to earth) was likewise something hitherto unheard of in the theologizing of Second Temple Judaism.[11] At the same time, the idea of the coming again of a great hero was quite compatible with Jewish reflection in this area.[12] It is no great suprise, then, that the thought and talk of Christ's coming again as such seem to have occasioned little controversy within Jewish synagogues (or elsewhere). Rather, we should see this very early line of Christian reflection as part of the developing theological reflection within Second Temple Judaism and a contribution to it.[13]

Given the new theological departure which it constituted, it is somewhat surprising that the coming *(parousia)* of Christ is a topic which has commanded relatively little attention among NT scholars in the past few decades. This is in marked contrast with the themes just examined (§§9-11) — and despite the popular interest inevitable at the end of a millennium. The contrast is even stronger with the opening decades of the twentieth century, when the impact of Albert Schweitzer's portrayal of Jesus the apocalyptic prophet rippled throughout the whole of NT study for half a century. For most students of Christian beginnings through the middle of the century it was simply to be taken for granted that "the delay of the parousia" was a major factor to be called on in explanation of a whole variety of features: particularly in tracing development in Paul's and earliest Christian theology, in explaining the emergence of "early Catholicism," and in accounting for the burst of Christian writing (not least the Gospels) in the final

---

9. A classic essay is J. A. T. Robinson, "The Most Primitive Christology of All?" *Twelve New Testament Studies* (SBT; London: SCM/Naperville: Allenson, 1962) 139-53.

10. The theme of "return" is quite prominent in some of Jesus' parables (e.g., Matt. 25.1-12; Mark 13.34-36; Luke 19.12-27), as also the "coming" *(erchomenos)* of the Son of Man (Mark 13.26; 14.62). It is not entirely clear why the idea of Christ's *return* (not actually necessary to complete the process of salvation) would otherwise have emerged. Contrast the thesis of Robinson that the parousia belief did not derive from the teaching of Jesus, but was an adaptation of his teaching to meet the uncertainty of whether *the Christ* had come or not *(Coming* ch. 7).

11. This applies to the term *parousia* itself, since in the NT the term is never used for Jesus' first coming (on earth), with the possible exception of 2 Pet. 1.16, and the term itself never has the sense of "return."

12. See above n. 4.

13. P. G. Davis, "Divine Agents, Mediators and New Testament Christology," *JTS* 45 (1994) 479-503, notes that it is the *combination* of different patterns of mediation which really marks out the distinctiveness of NT christology.

decades of the first century.[14] But interest in such questions seems to be in (temporary?) abeyance.

With particular reference to Paul's christology, eschatology invited a neat developmental schema. The phase of interest in christological titles as such drew attention to two notable features of the Thessalonian epistles, generally reckoned to be the earliest of Paul's letters. One was the appearance of a distinctive "Son of God" reference in a second coming context (1 Thes. 1.10) — Paul's Thessalonian converts characterized as those who await God's Son from heaven. The other was that *kyrios* ("Lord") is such a prominent title in the two Thessalonian letters, dominated as they are by eschatology.[15] The data invited the thesis that the earliest stage of christology was future oriented.[16]

It would not be true to say that interest in the issues raised by Schweitzer has been lacking in the last quarter of the century. In particular, the term "apocalyptic" has repeatedly been drawn back into the centre of discussion — despite a continuing lack of clarity as to the meaning and appropriate use of the term.[17] Ernst Käsemann responded to Bultmann's existentialist finesse of Schweitzer[18] by insisting that "apocalyptic was the mother of all Christian theology"[19] and set off a fresh round of debate.[20] And "apocalyptic" has been a crucially central term and concept for the perspectives and schemas of J. L. Martyn and J. C. Beker in their interpretation of Paul, the former focusing on the cross,[21] the latter on the parousia. But in both cases "apocalyptic" has served more as a hermeneutical key than as necessitating a focus on the parousia itself.[22] The theme of Christ's (second) coming as

14. The most systematic attempt was that of M. Werner, *The Formation of Christian Dogma* (1941; London: Black/New York: Harper, 1957).

15. *Kyrios* — 24 occurrences in 1 Thessalonians and 22 in 2 Thessalonians — a higher proportion than in any of Paul's other letters.

16. So particularly Hahn, *Titles* (§10 n. 1) 89-103 (emphasizing 1 Cor. 16.22), 284-88.

17. See, e.g., the reviews by R. E. Sturm, "Defining the Word 'Apocalyptic': A Problem in Biblical Criticism," in Marcus and Soards, eds., *Apocalyptic* 17-48; and the somewhat self-indulgent treatment by R. B. Matlock, *Unveiling the Apocalyptic Paul: Paul's Interpreters and the Rhetoric of Criticism* (JSNTS 127; Sheffield: Sheffield Academic, 1996).

18. Cf. Baumgarten's unsuccessful attempt *(Paulus)* to argue that Paul "de-eschatologized" apocalyptic tradition.

19. Käsemann, "Beginnings" 102.

20. See again n. 17.

21. "The focus of Paul's apocalyptic lies not on Christ's parousia, but rather on his death" (Martyn, "Apocalyptic Antinomies" [§6 n. 99] 420.

22. Martyn's thesis goes back to his earlier article ("Epistemology at the Turn of the Ages: 2 Corinthians 5.16," in W. R. Farmer, et al., eds., *Christian History and Interpretation,* J. Knox FS [Cambridge: Cambridge University, 1967] 269-87), where he finds

such continues to command little interest in scholarly writing on Paul — possibly because the embarrassment at a mistaken imminent expectation and at talk of a literal descent from heaven (1 Thes. 4.16) continues to afflict Christian scholarship.

What then of Paul's own theology at this point? Without forgetting that the coming again is part of a larger eschatological scenario, our present christological interest determines that we should focus primarily on the parousia and its concomitant features.

§12.2 The parousia hope in the Thessalonian letters

Our concern, it should be recalled, is not to reconstruct a theology of Paul composed of elements drawn equally from all his letters and given weight proportional to the space allocated to explicit treatments of themes. Our concern is rather to gain a picture of Paul's theology at the time he wrote Romans, the most mature statement of his theology. Nevertheless, in this case the most obvious procedure is to start with what are usually regarded as the earliest of Paul's letters — 1 and 2 Thessalonians.[23] For the simple fact is that the parousia theme dominates these letters, as it does none of Paul's other letters. Here not least the issue is posed whether Paul's theology amounts to nothing more than his theologizing on particular occasions and issues. Other-wise expressed, it is possible that the early prominence of the theme might slant or distort the picture emerging from the later letters. And overall we have to allow the possibility that in the wake of the Thessalonian epistles Paul's theology shifted or developed in emphasis. Hopefully these issues will become clearer as we proceed.

The preoccupation with the parousia hope in the Thessalonian letters

---

"an inextricable connexion between eschatology and epistemology" (272) and redefines "apocalyptic" as a new way of knowing, not *kata sarka* ("according to the flesh") but *kata stauron* ("according to the cross"). In contrast, for Beker it is the apocalyptic theme of God's imminent triumph which alone gives Paul's theology its fundamental coherence (so particularly *Paul* 143, 176-81); but see also §18 n. 18 below.

23. There is a wide consensus of opinion that 1 Thessalonians is the first of Paul's letters (see, e.g., Kümmel, *Introduction* 257). The authorship of 2 Thessalonians is much debated. Scholarship is divided on whether it can be attributed to Paul or should be ascribed to a later disciple (contrast, e.g., Kümmel 264-69 and Koester, *Introduction* 2.242-46). In my own view, the differences in style and theological emphasis are of little account in contrast to those which mark the later Paulines. In particular, the differences between 1 and 2 Thessalonians on our present theme are no greater than the shifts in tactics or switches in emphasis which occur in many a debate and argument. Paul must not be judged by yardsticks of theoretical consistency. Genuine engagement with people of diverse views in changing situations will inevitably call forth statements of differing emphases.

is certainly striking. The theme is prominent early on. Paul reminds the Thessalonians "how you turned to God from idols to serve the living and true God and to await his Son from the heavens, whom he raised from the dead, Jesus who delivers us from the coming wrath" (1 Thes. 1.9-10).[24] They are soon reminded also of the exhortation Paul left with them: "to lead a life worthy of God who calls you into his own kingdom and glory" (2.12). They themselves are his "hope, joy, and crown of boasting before our Lord Jesus at his coming *(parousia)*" (2.19). Paul's prayer is that their hearts will be established "blameless in holiness before our God and Father at the coming *(parousia)* of our Lord Jesus with all his angels" (3.13).[25]

We reach the heart of 1 Thessalonians, and probably the principal reason for Paul's writing, in 4.13–5.11. Here Paul addresses what had evidently become a serious problem quite soon after his departure from Thessalonica. Some of the Thessalonian believers had died. The implication is that the other Thessalonian believers feared that those who had died would therefore be disadvantaged or even missed out at the parousia (4.15).[26] Paul's response provides the single clearest statement of his parousia belief:

> [13]We do not want you to be ignorant, brothers, concerning those who are asleep, lest you grieve like others do who have no hope. [14]For if we believe that Jesus died and rose again, so also God will bring with him those who have fallen asleep through Jesus. [15]For this we declare to you by a word of the Lord, that we who are alive, who are left until the coming *(parousia)*

---

24. Note also 2.16 — "wrath has come upon them [the Jews of Judea in particular] *eis telos* [in full, completely]"; see Bruce, *1 and 2 Thessalonians* 48, and above §2 n. 83; note also J. M. Court, "Paul and the Apocalyptic Pattern," in Hooker, ed., *Paul and Paulinism* 57-66. To treat this as a specifically anti-Jewish comment ignores the fierceness of the expectation regarding "those who do not know God and upon those who do not obey the gospel of our Lord Jesus" in 2 Thes. 1.8-9 (that is, Gentiles as well as Jews); see above §2.5 and n. 87; also discussion in Wanamaker, *1 and 2 Thessalonians* 227-28; and C. J. Schlueter, *Filling Up the Measure: Polemical Hyperbole in 1 Thessalonians 2.14-16* (JSNTS 98; Sheffield: Sheffield Academic, 1994), particularly chs. 8 and 9.

25. The *parousia* imagery here and in the subsequent passages is probably that of the visit of a high-ranking official or ruler to a city, with his entourage, when he would be met on his approach by a deputation of leading citizens and escorted into the city (A. Oepke, *TDNT* 5.859-60; Bruce, *1 and 2 Thessalonians* 57). See also n. 53 below. Plevnik, *Parousia* 6-10, is unduly critical of this inference and fails to ask what Paul's imagery would most naturally evoke in the minds of his readers.

26. It is difficult to be more precise; see, e.g., the review of interpretations in Wanamaker, *1 and 2 Thessalonians* 164-66. There is no hint in the letter that the problem was partly caused because Paul had taught a realized eschatology and now felt the need to correct "an exaltation theology of present glory" (*pace* C. L. Mearns, "Early Eschatological Development in Paul: The Evidence of 1 and 2 Thessalonians," *NTS* 27 [1980-81] 137-57 [here 141]).

of the Lord, will by no means precede those who have fallen asleep. [16]Because the Lord himself, with a word of command, with the archangel's call, and with the sound of God's trumpet, will descend from heaven. And the dead in Christ will rise first; [17]then we who are alive, who are left, will be caught up together with them on the clouds to meet the Lord in the air. And so we shall be always with the Lord. [18]So then, comfort one another with these words.

Needless to say, this vivid portrayal of the Lord descending from heaven and being met by both living and resurrected[27] saints (halfway?), "caught up[28] on the clouds,[29] in the air," presumably to escort him to the earth,[30] has captured Christian imagination through the centuries. More attention, however, should have been paid to the preceding imagery: the primary actor is God, who "will bring with him [Jesus] those who have fallen asleep through Jesus."[31] Quite how the two are to be correlated remains unclear.[32]

The "word of the Lord" leads at once[33] into a reminder of the Jesus tradition, that "the day of the Lord comes like a thief in the night" (5.2, 4),[34]

27. Here the active voice, "will rise (*anastēsontai*) first" (4.16) echoes the unusual active voice of 4.14 (Jesus "rose [*anestē*] again"). The more common formula uses the passive ("was raised [*egerthē*]"; see above §7 n. 72); but cf. Rom. 14.9.

28. The verb *harpazein* ("snatch or take away") normally implies the use of force (BAGD, *harpazō*), but had evidently become a regular term for rapture to heaven in both Jewish (Gen. 5.24 LXX; *Apoc. Mos.* 37.3; *Joseph and Aseneth* 12.8; *Greek Apocalypse of Ezra* 5.7; 2 Cor. 12.2, 4; Rev. 12.5; cf. Acts 8.39; see further A. W. Zwiep, *The Ascension of the Messiah in Lukan Christology* [NovTSup 87; Leiden: Brill] ch. 2) and Greek thought (see BAGD, *harpazō* 2b, and *nephelē*).

29. For clouds as indicating mode of heavenly transport and triumphal procession see particularly Isa. 19.1; Ezek. 1.4-28; Dan. 7.13; Mark 13.26 pars.; 14.62 par.; Acts 1.9, 11; Rev. 1.7. Plevnik notes that the clouds are mentioned as transporting the resurrected and living saints, not Christ in this case (*Parousia* 60-63). For the other imagery (the cry of command, the archangel's call, and the trumpet) see Plevnik 45-60, 84-88.

30. See Bruce, *1 and 2 Thessalonians* 102-3, and again n. 25 above.

31. The two phrases "with him" and "through Jesus" should not both be taken with the verb "will bring" (as NRSV; REB changes the sense); see Bruce, *1 and 2 Thessalonians* 97-98; otherwise Best, *1 and 2 Thessalonians* 188-89. Quite what dying "through Jesus" (rather than "in Christ" — 4.16) means is also uncertain; see below §15.4c.

32. For similar tensions in the background of apocalyptic thinking see A. F. J. Klijn, "1 Thessalonians 4.13-18 and Its Background in Apocalyptic Literature," in Hooker, ed., *Paul and Paulinism* 67-73 (here 69).

33. The *peri de* of 5.1 indicates a further but obviously related topic, presumably also raised by the Thessalonians for clarification (cf. 4.9, 13).

34. This is one of the clearest examples of a paraenetic tradition (passed on by Paul in founding a new church) whose echoes of a distinctive parable of Jesus (Matt. 24.43/Luke 12.39) are best explained if Paul had repeated the parable to them as part of their foundational Jesus tradition. See further above §8.3 and below §23.5.

and thence into a sustained exhortation to wakefulness — again echoing a characteristic theme of Jesus' parables of crisis.[35] The development is notable for its use of classic prophetic imagery and apocalyptic contrast — labour pains, children of light/darkness, asleep/awake, day/night, sober/drunk (5.3-8).[36] The climax is the assurance that "God has not set us for wrath but to obtain salvation through our Lord Jesus Christ who died for us, in order that whether we wake or sleep we might live with him" (5.9-10). The final benediction ensures that they will not easily be able to forget the main thrust of the letter: "May the God of peace himself sanctify you wholly, and may your spirit, soul, and body be kept sound and blameless at the coming of our Lord Jesus Christ. He who calls you is faithful, and he will do it" (5.23-24).

The evidence of 2 Thessalonians confirms the importance of the parousia christology at this stage of Paul's theologizing. Even more quickly than in the first letter, the subject is soon taken up in one of the most powerful of all Paul's statements on the theme (2 Thes. 1.7-10). The Thessalonians will be granted rest from their present suffering,

> [7]in the revelation *(apokalypsei)* of the Lord Jesus from heaven with his powerful angels [8]in flaming fire. He will inflict punishment on those who do not know God and on those who do not obey the gospel of our Lord Jesus. [9]They will suffer the penalty of eternal destruction and exclusion from the presence of the Lord and from the glory of his might, [10]when he comes on that day to be glorified among his saints and to be wondered at among all who have believed, because our testimony to you was believed.

As with 1 Thessalonians, the letter has been occasioned by a particular crisis. There it was the problem of unexpected events prior to the parousia. In this case it is the problem of escalating expectation, overheated eschatological enthusiasm. The Thessalonians had been given to believe "that the day of the Lord has come," that it was already present (2.2).[37] Paul's response was to damp down the fires of enthusiasm by insisting that crucial events were yet to intervene before the end (2.3-12):

35. Matt. 24.42-43; 25.13; Mark 13.34-37; Luke 12.37. Also Mark 14.34-38 par.
36. On the imagery see again Plevnik, *Parousia* 105-6, 108-10; Dunn, *Romans* 786-88 (on the parallel Rom. 13.11-12).
37. Paul's formulation, "neither through spirit[-inspired utterance], nor through word, nor through letter . . ." (2.2), envisages a continuing ferment, with various communications contributing to the confusion. On this difficult text, see particularly Jewett, *Thessalonian Correspondence* 97-100. Jewett has abandoned his earlier description of the Thessalonians in terms of "enthusiastic radicalism," in favour of "millenarian radicalism" (142-47, 161-78). "The day of the Lord" here probably denotes the final short period climaxing in the coming of Christ, so that an element of imminent expectation was still involved.

³That day will not come unless the rebellion comes first and the lawless person, the son of destruction, is revealed *(apokalyphthē)*. ⁴He opposes and raises himself over every so-called god or object of worship, so that he takes his seat in the temple of God, claiming himself to be God. . . . ⁶And you know what is now restraining him, so that he may be revealed *(apokalyphthēnai)* in his own time. ⁷For the mystery *(mystērion)* of law-lessness is already at work; only he who restrains him will do so until he is out of the way. ⁸And then the lawless one will be revealed, whom the Lord Jesus will do away with by the breath of his mouth and destroy at the appearance of his coming *(parousia)*, ⁹whose coming *(parousia)* is by the activity of the Satan, in every miracle and sign and wonder that is false, ¹⁰and with every deceit of injustice for those who are perishing, because they did not receive the love of the truth so as to be saved. ¹¹Therefore God sends them an effective delusion so that they believe the lie, ¹²in order that all may be condemned who did not believe the truth but took pleasure in injustice.

After that powerful depiction the rest of the letter is something of an anticli-max, made up of disconnected themes and (unlike 1 Thessalonians) without further reference to our theme.

This sustained emphasis on eschatology and its particular character raises many issues. Here we will concentrate on the christological features.

First, with such evidence it is hard to avoid drawing an obvious infer-ence: that Paul had given prominence to the theme of Christ's parousia during his preaching in Thessalonica (1 Thes. 1.10). Noticeable also is the fact that he continued to reiterate that emphasis throughout the first letter and did not hesitate to elaborate it in the second. Should we then deduce that this was a prominent feature of all Paul's missionary preaching and teaching, at least in the early phases of his missionary work? Not necessarily. Galatians refers to preaching which preceded that in Thessalonica, and an imminent parousia would have been a powerful motivation in bringing the Galatian churches "to heel." But as we shall see, of all Paul's major letters, Galatians seems least interested in the theme. On the other hand, the letters to cities geographically closest to Thessalonica contain the closest parallels to the emphasis of 1 Thes-salonians. Both 1 Thessalonians and Philippians speak of "the day of Christ/the Lord,"³⁸ and both speak of believers as "awaiting or expecting" Jesus' return "from heaven."³⁹ 1 Corinthians is the only other letter which consistently shows that the subject had a place of significance in Paul's theology. And the talk in 2 Cor. 3.14-15 and 4.3-4 of minds veiled (by God) and of "those who are perishing" being prevented by another heavenly being

38. 1 Thes. 5.2; Phil. 1.6, 10; 2.16.
39. 1 Thes. 1.10; Phil. 3.20.

302

from seeing the truth is one of very few passages in the rest of Paul which begins to approach the harsh pessimism of 2 Thes. 2.9-12.[40]

We have to envisage the possibility, then, that the theme of Christ's coming again featured quite prominently in Paul's preaching during the early phase of his Aegean mission. It was not particularly picked up by the Philippians, but events in Thessalonica (the early death of some of Paul's converts) evidently brought it to the fore there, and Paul responded without retracting or qualifying what he had said. The letter only succeeded in stoking the fires of imminent expectation,[41] and Paul responded with a still more forthright statement of eschatological expectation, but qualified as regards the imminence of the day of the Lord. Since the letters were most probably written during the earlier phase of Paul's association with Corinth, it is not surprising that 1 Corinthians in particular reflects something of that preoccupation.

Second, we can hardly avoid noting the strikingly distinctive features of the two letters. What marks out the first is the "word of the Lord" (1 Thes. 4.15). The central section of the letter in effect revolves around it. Although many continue to assume that Paul is drawing here on some word from the Jesus tradition,[42] that can hardly provide the complete explanation. The language itself is characteristic of earliest Christian eschatological reflection in the light of Christ's exaltation as "Lord."[43] And the "word" is very closely related to the problem in Thessalonica, more or less echoing their concern: that those who had died would be left behind at the parousia in comparison with those still alive.[44] It is more likely, then, that the "word of the Lord" was an inspired utterance or prophecy given to Paul (privately or in the Christian assembly, perhaps drawing on earlier Jesus tradition) as he meditated prayerfully on the Thessalonians' distress.[45] It is also quite likely that vv. 16-17 were part of the prophetic word.

40. But cf. also Rom. 9.19-23 and 11.7-10.

41. See n. 37 above.

42. See, e.g., those cited by Wanamaker, *1 and 2 Thessalonians* 170.

43. "The coming of the Lord" — see below n. 57. The imagery of those who have died as "sleeping" was familiar in both Jewish and Greek thought (see, e.g., R. Bultmann, *TDNT* 3.14 n. 60). In the NT see 1 Cor. 7.39; 11.30; 15.6, 18, 20, 51; also Matt. 27.52; Acts 7.60; 13.36. It is notable, however, that the NT does not use that image in referring to Jesus' death.

44. I am among the first to wish to acknowledge allusions to Jesus tradition, but the fact that the language is closer to the Thessalonians' situation than to anything in the Jesus tradition should be given more weight. Of course, it is quite possible that a prophetic word might take up and elaborate an earlier, less specific element of the Jesus tradition. See also below n. 47.

45. See, e.g., Best, *Thessalonians* 189-93; Plevnik, *Parousia* 78-81, 90-94; others in my *Jesus and the Spirit* 418 n. 154, and Wanamaker, *1 and 2 Thessalonians* 170. Perhaps it is unfamiliarity with the phenomenon of (inspired) prophetic utterance which has made this less obvious or attractive as an option for so many commentators. But neither Paul nor the Thessalonians were strangers to the experience of prophecy (note particularly 1 Thes. 5.19-22;

The wording continues to echo that of the Thessalonians' concern (4.17a), the imagery is that of visionary exultation ("caught up in the clouds" — 4.17b), and 4.18 refers back to 4.15-17 as a whole.[46] In which case it is of some interest to note that Paul was content simply to pass on the "word of the Lord" without further comment. In some contrast, it is the image of the day of the Lord coming "like a thief in the night" (5.2 — probably echoing familiar Jesus tradition) on which Paul draws in the following exhortation (5.1-11).[47]

At all events, we should note that the "word of the Lord" was very specific and directed to a specific issue in the Thessalonian church. That could help explain why Paul does not take it up or echo it[48] in his later letters.

Thirdly, two striking features of the two main passages in 2 Thessalonians are their vivid visionary character and harsh note of vengefulness.[49] Nothing in the Pauline letters is closer to the genre of apocalypse.[50] Characteristic of such literature is that it has been written out of crisis and persecution[51] and indulges its hopes and fears, its resentments and antagonisms, in inflated symbolism and assurance of God's vindication and vengeance. So here we observe the repeated use of the language of "revelation" (1.7; 2.3, 6), talk of the "mystery" (2.7),[52]

---

see below §21.5c). And it should be remembered that the letter was most probably written from Corinth, where charismatic phenomena, including not least words of wisdom and prophecies, were part of the regular worship (1 Cor. 12.8-10; ch. 14; in 1.7 note the close association of rich spiritual gifts and awaiting the revelation of the Lord Jesus Christ).

46. Alternatively, 4.16-17 could also be Paul's own elaboration of an earlier inspired utterance, though if the whole word was actually delivered during the worship of the Corinthian church it would be hard to tell what was inspired and what was exultant commentary.

47. D. Wenham tries to demonstrate the existence of a pre-Synoptic eschatological discourse which circulated in the early churches and which Paul may have used (*Gospel Perspectives* 4: *The Rediscovery of Jesus' Eschatological Discourse* [Sheffield: JSOT, 1984]; more qualified in his *Paul* (§8 n. 1) 305-28 (328 n. 89).

48. Possibly in the reference to the trumpet in 1 Cor. 15.52. But the sounding of a trumpet in theophanies and in proclamation of the end was an established feature of Jewish imagery; see particularly G. Friedrich, *TDNT* 7.80, 84, 86-88.

49. The "vengeance" of God is, of course, an established idea in Jewish eschatology (see particularly Isa. 59.17-18; and further my *Romans* 749-50).

50. Cf. Jewett, *Thessalonian Correspondence* 168; Krentz, "Through a Lens" (above §1 n. 64).

51. See, e.g., J. J. Collins, *The Apocalyptic Imagination* (New York: Crossroad, 1984) 31; L. L. Thompson, *The Book of Revelation: Apocalypse and Empire* (New York/Oxford: Oxford University, 1990) 25-26; but note also Thompson's own qualification of this generalisation (particularly 175-76). I do not mean to imply that "apocalyptic" and "eschatology" should be used as synonyms (see my *Unity* 310).

52. The unveiling of the "mystery" was a characteristic feature of apocalyptic writing and perspective from Daniel on (Dan. 2.18-19, 27-30; see also, e.g., 1QS 3.23; 4.18; 1QpHab 7.5; 1Q27; *1 Enoch* 103.2; 106.19; *2 Enoch* 24.3; *4 Ezra* 10.38; 14.5; Rev. 10.7). See further

the vision of the Lord coming with his angels,[53] final tribulation and opposition embodied in a single powerful individual,[54] and the climactic denouement bringing vindication and due recompense to enemies.[55]

In other words, in 2 Thessalonians Paul speaks with the voice of an apocalyptic visionary. The language is exaggerated, and the feelings it both expresses and provokes are powerful, echoing similar frustrations and longings of the past. As with so much apocalyptic imagery, it has an element of the grotesque about it and evokes something of the atmosphere of a Hieronymus Bosch painting. To assert this is by no means to suggest that such passages can be discarded or disregarded. It is simply to say that their character needs to be recognized, along with the degree to which their literary medium has shaped the message they give.[56] But it is also to observe that the integration of such passages into Paul's overall theology will be as difficult as the integration of the Revelation of John into the overall theology of the NT. At the same time, the fact that Paul nowhere reverts to such imagery in his subsequent letters may suggest that Paul, while content to use it occasionally, did not regard it as a constant feature of his gospel and theology.

§12.3 Christ's role in the end events in the later letters

In contrast to the Thessalonian letters, Paul's later writings do not have much to say, at least explicitly, on the coming (again) of Christ. The data can be

---

R. E. Brown, *The Semitic Background of the Term "Mystery" in the New Testament* (Philadelphia: Fortress, 1968); and below §19 n. 132. For "the mystery of lawlessness" (2.7), cf. particularly Ps. 88.23 LXX ("son of lawlessness") and 1Q27 1.2, a fragment containing the phrase "the mystery of sin"; also "the man of lies" in 1QpHab 2.1-2 and 5.11.

53. For the heavenly entourage in theophanies see Deut. 33.2; Ps. 68.17; Dan. 7.10; *1 Enoch* 1.9 (quoted in Jude 14-15). An echo of Zech. 14.5 LXX may be intended. See also n. 25 above.

54. Various prototypes would spring to mind: Antiochus IV (2.4a echoes Dan. 11.36-37), the king of Tyre (2.4b echoes Ezek. 28.2), the king of Babylon (Isa. 14.4-20), and Pompey, conqueror of Judea in 63 BCE (*Pss. Sol.* 17.11 — "the lawless one"). Caligula's attempt to have his statue erected in the Jerusalem temple (40 CE) would be a recent memory (Bruce, *1 and 2 Thessalonians* 168-69). The deceitful attractiveness of this antichrist figure was a theme of earliest Christian eschatology (Mark 13.22/Matt. 24.24; Revelation 13, particularly vv. 13-14). Cf. the earlier discussion by Vos, *Eschatology* ch. 5.

55. The fierceness of the expectation of judgment is characteristic of a more violent age; cf., e.g., Ps. 79.6; Isa. 2.19-21; Matt. 25.41, 46. Isa. 66.15-16 (judgment executed "with flames of fire") may be echoed in 2 Thes. 1.8. 2.8 certainly echoes Isa. 11.4 ("with the breath of his lips he [the Davidic messiah] will do away with the wicked").

56. Cf. particularly Ridderbos, *Paul* 520-21; though the imagery also makes it dubious whether Paul's expectation should be focused too tightly on "*the man* of lawlessness" (515-19).

marshaled quite straightforwardly. Of the seven references to Christ's *parousia* ("coming"), six occur in 1 and 2 Thessalonians[57] and only one elsewhere: 1 Cor. 15.23, referring to the sequence of resurrections, "Christ the firstfruits, then those who are Christ's at his *parousia.*"

However, 1 Corinthians, the only other letter where the theme is at all prominent, has four other references. In the opening thanksgiving Paul reminds the Corinthians of the richness of their spiritual endowment "as you eagerly await the revelation *(apokalypsin)* of our Lord Jesus Christ, who will also sustain you till the end, irreproachable in the day of our Lord Jesus Christ" (1.7-8). In the fullest reference (4.4-5) Paul warns against precipitate judgment:

> [4]It is the Lord who judges me. [5]So then, do not pass judgment on anything before the time, before the Lord comes, who will bring to light the hidden things of darkness and make manifest the purposes of the heart. Then praise will come to each from God.

Also to be considered are 11.26, Paul's note appended to his description of the Lord's Supper: "for as often as you eat this bread and drink the cup, you announce the Lord's death until he comes," and the final invocation of the letter: "*Maranatha* (Our Lord, come!)" (16.22).

Elsewhere the pickings are slimmer. In Romans, Paul's most fully elaborated theological statement, the parousia is explicitly mentioned only once. And not as the climax of his statement of Christian confidence (Rom. 8.31-39); there it is the thought of Christ's continuing intercession in heaven on behalf of his own which serves as that climax (8.34). But as the climax of his hope for Israel's eventual salvation (11.26-27):[58]

> [26]and so all Israel shall be saved, as it is written:
> "Out of Zion will come the deliverer;
> he will turn away ungodliness from Jacob.
> [27]And this will be my covenant with them,
> when I take away their sins."

The slight modification of the text ("out of Zion")[59] presumably indicates the continuing assumption that Jerusalem would be the focus of the eschatological climax (cf. 2 Thes. 2.4, 8). But Paul could conceivably have had the

---

57. 1 Thes. 2.19; 3.13; 4.15; 5.23; 2 Thes. 2.1, 8.

58. The quotation is mixed, the first three lines from Isa. 59.20-21, the fourth probably drawn from Isa. 27.9. But there are also echoes of other scriptural themes, particularly Jer. 31.33-34. See further my *Romans* 682-84, and below §19 nn. 138, 140.

59. MT reads "to Zion," and LXX "for the sake of Zion."

heavenly Jerusalem in mind (cf. Gal. 4.26) — that is, a direct descent from heaven (1 Thes. 4.16) rather than via Jerusalem.

There are no explicit references to the parousia in 2 Corinthians or Galatians. But in Philippians there is a rare indication of how Paul held together different elements in his expectation — Phil. 3.20-21:

> 20Our citizenship is in heaven, from which we eagerly await a saviour, the Lord Jesus Christ, 21who will transfigure our body of humiliation so that it may be conformed to his glorious body, by the power which enables him also to subject all things to himself.

Here we have the three motifs — coming again, final resurrection modeled on Christ's, and Christ's own reign in glory[60] — clearly correlated only here in Paul's letters.

Finally, in Col. 3.3-4, there is the equally unusual reference to the (final) "revelation" of Christ as a revelation in glory: ". . . your life has been hidden *(kekryptai)* with Christ in God. Whenever the Christ, who is our life, has been revealed *(phanerōthē)*, then you also will be revealed with him in glory."[61] The use of the traditional apocalyptic contrast of something hitherto hidden, now to be revealed, forms an effective bracket with the idea of "the mystery which has been hidden *(apokekrymmenon)* from the ages and from the generations . . . now revealed *(ephanerōthē)* to his saints . . . which is Christ in you, the hope of glory" (1.26-27). Despite the more common view that Colossians displays a loss of future eschatology,[62] these two passages show more clearly than anywhere else in Paul that the second coming matches and completes the significance of the first. The revelation which for Paul in particular distinguished Christ's first appearing (the unveiling of the ages-old mystery)[63] only achieves completion in Christ's second appearing.[64]

The analysis, of course, should not focus exclusively on explicit ref-

---

60. We may note that Phil. 3.21 is the only NT allusion to Ps. 8.6 which is independent of Ps. 110.1 (see above §10.4c).

61. In speaking of final "revelation" Paul usually prefers *apokalyptō* ("reveal" — Rom. 8.18; 1 Cor. 3.13; 2 Thes. 2.3, 6, 8; also *apokalypsis* — Rom. 2.5; 8.19; 1 Cor. 1.7; 2 Thes. 1.7). But its near synonym, *phaneroō*, is used in this connection elsewhere in early Christian tradition (1 Pet. 5.4; 1 John 2.28; 3.2; the matching noun is not *phanerōsis* but *epiphaneia* — see n. 64 below). See further my *Colossians* 207-8.

62. See those cited in my *Colossians* 201 n. 1.

63. For Paul the mystery which Christ revealed focused in God's eternal plan to bring Gentile to share equally with Jew in God's purposes of salvation (see further my *Colossians* 121-23; and above n. 52).

64. Subsequently, in the Pastorals, it is the concept of a final "appearing" *(epiphaneia)*, rather than of a second *parousia*, which predominates (1 Tim. 6.14; 2 Tim. 1.10; 4.1, 8; Tit. 2.13; already 2 Thes. 2.8).

erences to Christ's *parousia* or "appearing." The *parousia,* arguably, belongs to a complex of motifs, any one of which may evoke the whole.[65] In Romans, in particular, it presumably is implicit in talk of judgment "through Christ Jesus" (2.16). Also in the two expressions of the "how much more" hope: that "having now been justified by his blood, we shall be saved through him from wrath"; "having been reconciled [to God through the death of his Son], we shall be saved by his life" (Rom. 5.9-10). No doubt the parousia hope is likewise implied in 8.19-21, in the talk of "the revelation of the sons of God" and of the future being set free "into the liberty of the glory of the children of God" (cf. 8.29-30). Also in the talk of "our salvation nearer than when we believed" (13.11), with the correlative exhortation to "put off the works of darkness" and to "put on the Lord Jesus Christ" (13.12-14). And again in the confidence that "the God of peace will crush the Satan under your feet speedily" (16.20).[66] Nor should we forget how in Paul "the day of the Lord" has "taken over" from "the day of Yahweh" and how God has evidently chosen to share his judgment seat with the Lord Jesus.[67]

What is notable, however, is that Paul seems for the most part to have been willing to leave the different aspects of his eschatological expectation uncorrelated. In Romans, Christ comes into talk of final judgment only in the somewhat enigmatic Rom. 2.16 — judgment by God "in accordance with my gospel through Christ Jesus."[68] In Romans 8 the failure to mention Christ's parousia as a fundamental feature of the climax to the salvation process remains surprising. And the question remains open whether the talk of Christ's intercession in 8.34 is a random element drawn in from the Jewish idea of angel-spirit intercessors (cf. 8.26),[69] or the tip of a larger submerged motif which elsewhere in the NT surfaces only in Hebrews.[70]

1 Cor. 4.4-5 does integrate second coming and final judgment. But in 1 Corinthians 15 the risen Christ is simply the template for the final resurrection. No attempt is made to indicate how the parousia fits into the scenario of 15.24-28 — presumably prior to Christ's subjection of the last enemy, death, and his own subjection to God. And no clear account is given of the role of the last Adam in the final transformation (15.47-57), unless it is indicated in his role as "life-

---

65. The reference in 1 Cor. 11.26 (and 16.22) also suggests that the coming of the Lord was a regular theme in worship. See also n. 86 below.

66. Cf. 2 Thes. 2.8. The motif of the final binding or defeat of evil is a strong feature of Jewish eschatological expectation (see, e.g., *Jub.* 5.6; 10.7, 11; 23.29; *1 Enoch* 10.4, 11-12; 13.1-2, etc.; see further my *Romans* 905).

67. See Vos, *Eschatology* 79-80, and above §10.5a.

68. See again §10.5a above.

69. E.g., Job 33.23-26; Tob. 12.15; *1 Enoch* 9.3; 15.2; 99.3; 104.1; *T. Levi* 3.5; 5.6-7; *T. Dan* 6.2; see further J. Behm, *TDNT* 5.810-11, and my *Romans* 478.

70. Heb. 7.25 (using the same verb); but see also 4.16; 6.20; 7.19; 9.24; 10.19-22.

giving Spirit" (15.45),[71] or implicit in the reference to "the last trumpet" (cf. 1 Thes. 4.16), or alluded to in the final thanksgiving "to God who gives us the victory through our Lord Jesus Christ" (15.57).

In 2 Corinthians, the principal eschatological section (2 Cor. 4.7–5.10) brackets a description of the process of salvation-transformation with two intriguing references (4.14 and 5.10). In 4.14 the prospect is held out that God "who raised the Lord Jesus will also raise us with Jesus and present us with you." Here again the future share in Christ's resurrection completes what began in Christ's own resurrection. But is Christ thought of as otherwise "involved"? Some think the "presentation" is by God in Christ's court or at Christ's judgment seat (5.10). That would be a unique feature within Paul's theology, though consistent with the idea of God subjecting all things to Christ.[72] But the thought could be rather of God presenting the trophies of his saving purpose (completed in resurrection) to his (own) heavenly court.[73]

In Galatians the failure to refer at all to Christ's coming and judgment is also surprising, given, not least, the apocalyptic character of the opening reference to rescue "from the present evil age" (1.4), the talk of "new creation" (6.15), and the final warnings of eschatological retribution (6.7-9). And the more explicit Philippians[74] rounds off with the abrupt and enigmatic "The Lord is near" (4.5), leaving it unclear whether a temporal or spatial "nearness," or both, is in view.

The picture which has emerged from the main body of Paul's letters, then, is rather "bitty" and fragmented. The clearest theme is that of Christ's reign consequent upon his resurrection-exaltation.[75] In only one passage does Paul allude to the idea of Christ's intercession (Rom. 8.34). The reign (and the intercession) will presumably continue until Christ's lordship is complete. Death has still to be finally defeated (1 Cor. 15.26). Satan has still to be (finally) crushed (Rom. 16.20). Believers are to "inherit the kingdom of God"[76] and to be finally "presented."[77] All creation is still to give climactic

---

71. Cf. Fee, *1 Corinthians* 789; but contrast Rom. 8.11 with Phil. 3.21.

72. See above §10.4c on the use of Pss. 110.1 and 8.6; also Col. 2.15.

73. See discussion in Furnish, *2 Corinthians* 259. The motif of "presentation" in Paul remains curiously ambiguous. In Rom. 14.10 the "presentation" is before the judgment seat of God. In 2 Cor. 11.2 Paul's intention was "to present [his converts] as a pure virgin to Christ." In Col. 1.22 the grammar is unclear, but the parallel with Eph. 1.4 suggests a presentation by Christ before himself (so explicitly in Eph. 5.27). In Col. 1.28, however, the thought is of the Christian missionaries presenting their converts "in Christ" (to God?).

74. Phil. 1.6; 2.16; 3.20-21.

75. See above §10.4a.

76. 1 Cor. 6.9-10; 15.50; Gal. 5.21; cf. 1 Thes. 2.12; 2 Thes. 1.5; Eph. 5.5; 2 Tim. 4.1, 8.

77. Rom. 14.10; 2 Cor. 4.14; 11.2; Col. 1.22, 28; Eph. 5.27.

acclamation to Jesus as Lord (Phil. 2.11). At some point Christ will come again — "the day of the Lord."[78] As deliverer — from what? — "to turn away ungodliness from Jacob" (Rom. 11.26). To transform and conform believers' bodies to his own (Phil. 3.20-21). To exercise final judgment.[79] And then, presumably, the grand finale will be the handing over of the kingdom to God and the subjection of Christ himself to God, so that God will be all in all (1 Cor. 15.24, 28).

So the elements of Paul's hope and expectation are clear enough. What remains unclear is how he correlated them all, why the apocalyptic character of the Thessalonian letters appears relatively isolated, and why Paul did not set out his theology on this point with greater coherence in the later letters, not least the more carefully laid-out Romans. What was his mature theology of the coming again of Christ? This brings us to the old puzzle, the delay of the parousia, the inference that Paul did indeed modify his eschatology over the years.

§12.4 The delay of the parousia

The suggestion that the delay of the parousia was a significant factor in the development of Paul's theology has a fair degree of plausibility. For one thing, it fits with the picture which has emerged above — that is, of an early emphasis on the Lord's imminent return (1 and 2 Thesalonians), with only briefer reference to the parousia subsequently. In the light of the distress and confusion caused by such teaching among the Thessalonian believers, Paul could have "drawn in his horns" on this subject in later preaching, teaching, and writing. And for another, it is possible to trace some development in Paul's own personal expectations. We need simply compare the "we who are alive" of 1 Thes. 4.15[80] with the expectation or hope of departure (in death) in Phil. 1.19-23.[81] As Paul himself grew older, and given the strenuous character of his life (2 Cor. 11.23-27), the intervention of his own death before the coming

---

78. Rom. 2.16; 1 Cor. 1.8; 5.5; 2 Cor. 1.14; Phil. 1.6, 10; 2.16; 1 Thes. 5.2; 2 Thes. 2.2; see further Plevnik, *Parousia* 11-39.

79. 1 Cor. 4.4-5; 2 Cor. 5.10.

80. Also 1 Cor. 15.51-52.

81. In one of the more famous hypotheses, C. H. Dodd suggested that Paul's perspective was changed by the severe crisis suffered between the writing of 1 Corinthians and 2 Corinthians, referred to in 2 Cor. 1.8-10 ("Mind of Paul" 109-18). See also Buck and Taylor, *Saint Paul* ch. 14. Hence, e.g., in 2 Cor. 4.14 Paul now seems to include himself with those who (will) have died and will be raised at the end. But too much should not be built on the "we" of all these passages; it would be as natural for Paul to identify himself with those who had died as with those who were still alive.

of the Lord must have become an increasingly pertinent factor in his own forward thinking.

Yet this reading of the Pauline letters is seriously flawed. It may be overplaying the significance of the Thessalonian letters, but it may also be overplaying the relative silence on the parousia subsequently. Put another way, such a reading is probably giving too little weight to the circumstantial factors which determined the emphases of the different letters.[82] As we have seen, it was the particular response of the Thessalonian believers to Paul's original preaching of the parousia, and the particular circumstances of unexpected death and overheated enthusiasm, which drew out the emphases of 1 and 2 Thessalonians. In contrast, the fact that Paul said so little on the subject subsequently at least indicates that the problems in the other churches, which stimulated his further letter writing, were rather different. On this point, neither the early nor the later letters can be treated as universal statements of Paul's eschatological expectation. As the one may need to be discounted in the light of circumstances, so the other may need to be enhanced in the light of different circumstances.[83]

In fact, there is a striking consistency in imminence of expectation throughout the undisputed letters of Paul.[84] Paul's sense of "eager expectation" *(apekdechomai)* of the final denouement is as fresh in the later letters as in the early.[85] He rounds off 1 Corinthians by echoing the Aramaic invocation "Our Lord, come" (1 Cor. 16.22) in a way which suggests it was well established in Paul's Greek-speaking churches.[86] Earlier in the same letter, in somewhat enigmatic sentences, Paul asserts both that "the time has been shortened"[87] and that "the form of this world is passing away" (7.29, 31). If he were thinking of "the time" as still lengthy or of the passing of the world's form as a lengthy process, he could hardly draw out the corollary that earthly ties should now be disregarded (7.29-31).[88] Similarly with the assertions in Rom. 13.11-12 that "now is our salvation nearer than when we [first] believed" and that "the night is far advanced, the day is at hand." Here again it is hard to ignore the overtone of heightened imminence, particularly in the use of the comparative in v. 11 ("nearer") and of the aorist in v. 12 ("has

---

82. See particularly Moule, "Influence of Circumstances," and above §1 n. 69.

83. It also needs to be recalled that "the tension between near-expectation and accommodation to delay in fulfilment of the hope" is characteristic of biblical eschatology (C. L. Holman, *Till Jesus Comes: Origins of Christian Apocalyptic Expectation* [Peabody: Hendrickson, 1996]).

84. So also Plevnik, *Parousia* 158-60, 276-81.

85. Gal. 5.5; 1 Cor. 1.7; Rom. 8.19, 23, 25; Phil. 3.20.

86. Note also how the formula is repeated in Rev. 22.20 and *Didache* 10.6.

87. See below §24 n. 95.

88. See further below §24.5.

advanced" = is well advanced).[89] Nor should the confidence that "the God of peace will crush Satan under your feet *speedily (en tachei)*" (16.20) be speedily discounted.[90] Even in Phil. 4.5, Paul can still give as motivation for confident conduct the assurance that "the Lord is near," where it would be unjustifiably arbitrary to exclude a note of temporary imminence.[91]

There is also the often noted point that Paul assumed various events had to happen before the day of the Lord would come. According to 2 Thes. 2.5, Paul insists that this had been part of his teaching, even where his eschatological expectation had been least inhibited.[92] And we should recall that it was the Thessalonians, not Paul, who were surprised when some of their fellow believers "fell asleep." On the other hand, we should not exaggerate the length of time which Paul expected to elapse before the Lord's return. His hope for "the reconciliation of the world" (Rom. 11.15) and his hope to evangelize personally in Spain are sometimes proffered in this connection (15.24, 28).[93] But here we need to recall that Paul saw his apostolic ministry in eschatological terms. He likened himself and his fellow missionaries to the last act in the arena watched by a gallery of angels and human beings (1 Cor. 4.9). He seems to have envisaged his role as apostle to the Gentiles (Rom. 11.13) as potentially decisive in bringing in the full number of the Gentiles (11.25) and in thus provoking his fellow Jews to jealousy (11.14). Their resulting acceptance would mean nothing less than "life from the dead," that is, the final resurrection (11.15). The end of history was only a mission away.[94] Even in Col. 1.24, Paul could envisage that his own sufferings would somehow "fill up what is lacking of the afflictions of the Christ in my flesh for the sake of the body." The implication is that his own missionary sufferings would complete the entail of eschatological tribulation expected before the new age could be fully ushered in.[95]

The conclusion which should be drawn from the different weights of

89. Cf. G. Stählin, *TDNT* 6.716 n. 85. NJB — "the night is nearly over."

90. *En tachei* — cf. Luke 18.8; Rev. 1.1; 22.6-7.

91. *Pace* Moore, *Parousia* 124. Cf. 1 Cor. 16.22; Rev. 22.20. The parallel with Rom. 13.11-14 (on eschatological imminence as a motive for conduct) also suggests that a soon-coming nearness is in view. See the discussion in O'Brien, *Philippians* 488-90.

92. What Paul means by "what is now restraining him [the lawless one]" (2.6) and "he who restrains him" (2.7) has been the subject of unending debate (see, e.g., Wanamaker's review, *1 and 2 Thessalonians* 250-52). The enigmatic character of the reference is typical of such apocalyptic symbolism and claims.

93. E.g., Vos, *Eschatology* 87-91; Witherington, *End* 19, 32 — "possible but not necessary imminence of the end" (47-48).

94. See further my *Romans* 657-58. It is quite possible that the collection was part of the same strategy; see particularly Munck, *Paul* 303-4, and Aus, "Paul's Travel Plans" (§24 n. 1 and §19 n. 153).

95. See further my *Colossians* 114-17, and below §18.5.

emphasis given to the parousia in Paul's letters, therefore, is not that his theology underwent a marked development. Even in what can best be regarded as the last of Paul's letters (Colossians), the expectation of Christ's final "appearing" is as calm and as confident as ever it was (Col. 3.4). More to the immediate point, there is no real hint in Paul's letters of any crisis caused by "the delay of the parousia." On the evidence as we have it, "the delay of the parousia" can almost wholly be discounted as a factor in explaining any development in Paul's own theology.

§12.5 Conclusions

(1) It can be claimed with confidence that the coming again of Christ was a firm part of Paul's theology, maintained consistently from first to last in our written sources. Paul's conviction that the parousia was imminent and becoming ever closer also seems to have remained remarkably untroubled by the progress of events and passing of time.[96]

(2) It is just possible that the teaching of 1 and 2 Thessalonians was only an early expression of Paul's maturing theology — except that he had been already preaching and teaching for a decade or more. A more appropriate conclusion is that 1 and 2 Thessalonians indicate Paul's willingness on occasion to reach for traditional apocalyptic symbolism to make an appropriately visionary statement.[97] Either way, the effectiveness of apocalyptic language, in reassuring by means of its somewhat surreal imagery rather than by conveying factual information, needs to be borne in mind.[98] The distinctiveness of the Thessalonian statements within the Pauline corpus should also be given some weight. Did Paul regard the "word of the Lord" in 1 Thes. 4.15(-17) as particular to the Thessalonians in their bewilderment and distress? Were the more extreme apocalyptic depictions in 2 Thessalonians 1 and 2 stirred by the crisis in Thessalonica and of particular relevance only to them in their crisis of confidence? At the same time, we should recall that both Jewish and Christian tradition is accustomed to context-particular prophecies being subsequently accorded scriptural status.

---

96. But Schweitzer went too far when he maintained that "from his first letter to his last Paul's thought is *always uniformly dominated* by the expectation of the immediate return of Jesus . . ." (*Mysticism* [§15 n. 1] 52, emphasis added). Better is Ridderbos, *Paul* 487-92; Beker, *Apocalyptic Gospel* 48-49, cited also by Witherington, *End* 34-35.

97. In later letters note particularly the repeated use of the *mystērion* theme — 1 Cor. 2.1, 7; 4.1; 15.51; Rom. 11.25; Col. 1.26-17; 2.2; 4.3 (as well as 2 Thes. 2.7).

98. As the history of the interpretation of Revelation reminds us, to treat apocalyptic writing as detailed prophecy or coded timetable is to court hermeneutical (not to say pastoral) disaster.

(3) The overall picture of Paul's expectation regarding Christ, then, is that the parousia hope was an integral part of his theology, as the end point to which the decisive events of Jesus' death and resurrection were building up. But it did not form the centre of gravity of his christology. Unlike the cross and resurrection, parousia hope did not gain confessional status.[99] Moreover, the particulars of that hope and their inner coherence were not clearly formulated, nor was it deemed necessary that they should be. The hope could be given expression in lurid apocalyptic colors, but they were not central or essential to it. The fulfilment of the hope in a particular way or within a specified time frame was not part of the hope. The possibility or prospect of the hope not being realized before Paul's own death evidently did not trouble him. Beside the centrality of Christ's death and resurrection in Paul's theology, the hope of his coming again could be left relatively undefined.[100]

(4) Finally, in relating the present analysis to those preceding, what can we say about the conception of Christ which Paul held in his theology? The range of imagery is remarkable. The most straightforward image is that of the individual seated on God's right, sharing God's kingly rule. It is not difficult to integrate with this the complementary imagery of heavenly intercession, subjection (or destruction?) of enemies (defeat of death, that is, by resurrection),[101] royal parousia to earth (before or after? and where?), judgment ("the day of the Lord"), and final submission to God.[102] But Paul also envisages the exalted Christ in the image of the last Adam, the prototype of resurrected human beings, the elder brother of the new family, the firstborn from the dead.[103] As we shall see later,[104] the Adam aspect of this latter imagery correlates with the "in Christ" "mysticism" of Paul's soteriology, where Christ is envisaged as a corporate person "in" whom believers can find themselves. More difficult to integrate is the Wisdom strand of Paul's christology. For preexistent Wisdom is less a person and more a way of speaking of God's universal self-expression, and if the exalted Christ is to be thought of in an analogous way,[105] the problems of integrated conceptuality become still more difficult. The same applies to the seeming equation of last Adam

---

99. *Pace* Gnilka, *Theologie* 21-22, 1 Thes. 4.15 should not be cited in this context (see above §12.2 and n. 45).

100. We will return to the question of the resurrection and judgment from a soteriological perspective later; see below §18.6.

101. Plevnik, *Parousia* 256-59.

102. The reign of Christ evidently *precedes* his parousia. Paul has no thought of a millennial reign *following* Christ's parousia (Plevnik, *Parousia* 129), or of a kingdom of Christ distinct from the kingdom of God (§10 n. 74 above).

103. See above §10.2.

104. See below particularly §15.2.

105. As would appear to be the case in Eph. 1.23.

with life-giving Spirit (1 Cor. 15.45) and to the thought of Christ indwelling his own.[106]

The obvious conclusion to draw from all this is that the different imagery is not in fact mutually consistent, and any attempt to integrate it in a single portrayal would be conceptually confusing, to say the least. We would be better advised to recognize it *all* as imagery and not to overemphasize or concentrate exclusively on one or another metaphor. The common theme to all the imagery — God's purpose for salvation, now and in the future, as focused in and explicated by Christ — is what matters. The ramifications of this for contemporary restatements of Paul's parousia hope have not been given sufficient attention.[107]

106. As in Rom. 8.10 and Gal. 2.20.
107. See further my "He Will Come Again," and below §15.5.

CHAPTER 5

The Beginning of Salvation

§13 The crucial transition[1]

§13.1 A new epoch

The structure of Paul's theology so far has been quite clear. The key to a right understanding of the human condition is of humankind as a creation of the one creator God. But a fleshly creature is inevitably weak. The need to satisfy natural desires is a point of strength if it reinforces creaturely dependence on God. But humankind as a whole has turned its back on God, seeking to live out of its own wisdom. And what should have been a point of strength has become a means of enslavement. For typical human experience is of a force ("sin") turning women and men in upon themselves in increasing forgetfulness of God, where satisfaction of desire has become the be-all and end-all and where even religion has become a substitute for God. Life, intended to be lived before God as regulated by God, has become an ever more anxious — and vain — attempt to escape the power of death. Under the twin powers

1. **Bibliography**: **Barrett**, *Paul* 87-91; **Bultmann**, *Theology* 1.288-92; **D. J. Doughty**, "The Priority of *CHARIS*," *NTS* 19 (1972-73) 163-80; **B. R. Gaventa**, *From Darkness to Light: Aspects of Conversion in the New Testament* (Philadelphia: Fortress, 1986); **Gnilka**, *Paulus* 248-55; **M. Goodman**, *Mission and Conversion: Proselytizing in the Religious History of the Roman Empire* (Oxford: Clarendon, 1994); **J. R. Harrison**, *Paul's Language of Grace* (charis) *in Its Graeco-Roman Context* (Macquarie University Ph.D. thesis, 1996); **S. McKnight**, *A Light among the Gentiles: Jewish Missionary Activity in the Second Temple Period* (Minneapolis: Fortress, 1991); **W. Manson**, "Grace in the New Testament," in W. T. Whitely, ed., *The Doctrine of Grace* (London: Hodder and Stoughton, 1932) 33-60; **J. Moffatt**, *Grace in the New Testament* (London: Hodder and Stoughton, 1931); **A. D. Nock**, *Conversion* (London: Oxford University, 1933); **M. Theobald**, *Die überströmende Gnade. Studien zu einen paulinischen Motivfeld* (Würzburg: Echter, 1982); **G. P. Wetter**, *Charis. Ein Beitrag zur Geschichte des ältesten Christentums* (Leipzig: Brandsetter, 1913).

317

of sin and death, even God's good law has been manipulated and corrupted, and the result is human enslavement and social factionalism and embitterment.

Paul's answer was the gospel of Jesus Christ, a gospel which focused particularly on Christ's death and resurrection. In some sense Jesus both summed up what humankind was and in his death drew a final line under that humankind. Sinful flesh could be dealt with only by killing it. The power of sin could exhaust itself only in death. Jesus' death embodied and enacted that fact. His resurrection meant a new beginning, a life no longer under the power of sin, no longer under the shadow of death. This was gospel, good news, because if it was true for Jesus it could be true for others. But how do individual people become part of this new humanity? How do they enter the new family of which Christ is firstborn and eldest brother? Or alternatively, how do they escape the power of sin and death? Such questions provide the subject matter which will dominate the rest of this study.

Three aspects need to be noted at the outset. First, it is important to grasp the epochal character of Paul's (and the first Christians') claim. Through Christ there had been a decisive shift in the possibilities confronting humankind. An epoch characterized by the power of sin and death had been overtaken by a new epoch, one marked by grace and faith. An epoch characterized by Jewish privilege and protection under the law had reached its goal in the fulfilment of ancient promise and the possibility of a new maturity before God for Gentile as well as Jew. An epoch characterized by human envy and deceit, injustice and ungodliness, could be left behind by those who responded to the gospel of Jesus Christ in a new possibility of the old creaturely trust in the life-giving God. Human history is familiar with talk of transitions from one age to another. We speak of the stone age, the Middle Ages, the age of empire, the nuclear age, the electronic age, and so on. Paul's claim is much more far-reaching. What he envisaged was a transition not only from BC to AD, but the most fundamental of all transitions, within which all others must be evaluated, a transition capable of affecting every age and transforming each individual existence.

Second, and central to the gospel, was the conviction that the epochal transition from first Adam to last Adam, from death to life, must be echoed in human lives, that the transition made by Christ himself must be mirrored in individuals (and communities) themselves making or experiencing a similar transition. Romans, for example, conceptualizes the personal transition in sharply antithetical terms: not just an Adam epoch replaced by a Christ epoch (Rom. 5.12-21), but one expressed in terms of individual experience of death followed by life (6.3-4), of widowhood making possible remarriage (7.1-4), of night giving way to day (13.11-13). In Galatians Paul talks of a "rescue" "from the present evil age" (1.4), of his own experience of conversion as a "revelation" (1.12, 16), of the new condition as a "new creation"

(6.15). And we have already noted the importance of "the eschatological now" for Paul.[2] This certainly involved a wholly transformed perspective — a new awareness of God (1 Cor. 14.25), a veil taken away (2 Cor. 3.14-18), a complete reassessment of values and priorities (Phil. 3.7-11).[3] But also moral transformation, as those who have lived lives of immorality now live with a new ethic and a new sense of responsibility for others (e.g., 1 Cor. 6.9-11).[4] And also transformation of social identity and community (baptism, the body of Christ).[5] These are all points which will become more luminous as we proceed.

Third, the transition from one epoch to another had a double aspect for Paul. It did not happen all in one moment. It took place in two stages. It had a beginning, but it was also a continuing process. This is mirrored in the two tenses of Paul's Greek — the aorist, denoting a decisive event in the past, and the present, denoting an ongoing process. In classical theological terms it has been expressed, misleadingly, as the distinction between "justification" (once for all) and "sanctification" (ongoing process).[6] Language more representative of Paul's own way of putting the point would be his description of believers as "those who are [in process of] being saved,"[7] of salvation as a process of "being transformed."[8] An alternative ritual expression of the same point is the balance between the two principal Christian sacraments — the once-for-allness of baptism and the repeated celebration of the Lord's Supper. However expressed, it is important for an understanding of Paul's theology to recognize that both aspects are equally fundamental. Both tenses must be experienced and worked through if we are to understand how it is for Paul that Jesus Christ is indeed gospel. In this chapter we will concentrate on the aorist tense, "the beginning of salvation," and return to the present continuous tense, "the process of salvation," in chapter 6.

13.2 Grace as event[9]

It is important to grasp that for Paul, behind the whole salvation process always lay the initiative of God. No other word expresses his theology so

2. See above §7.5.
3. See further below §§14 and 16.
4. See further below §23.
5. See further below §§17 and 20.
6. See further below §§14 and 18.
7. 1 Cor. 1.18; 15.2; 2 Cor. 2.15.
8. Rom. 12.2; 2 Cor. 3.18; note also 2 Cor. 4.16; Col. 3.10. See further below §18.2.
9. I borrow Bultmann's section title at this point.

clearly on this point as "grace" *(charis).*[10] For it summed up not only the epochal event of Christ itself ("the grace of our Lord Jesus Christ")[11] but also the grace which made the vital breakthrough in individual human experience (the grace "received," "given," "accepted").[12] And it defined not only the past act of God initiating into a life of faith, but also present continuing experience of divine enabling ("this grace in which we stand," "under grace," grace sufficient),[13] as well as particular enablings and commissionings ("grace and apostleship," "charisms which differ in accordance with the grace given to us").[14] In short, *charis* joins *agapē* ("love") at the very centre of Paul's gospel.[15] More than any other, these two words, "grace" and "love," together sum up and most clearly characterise his whole theology.

Why this word? Why "grace"? Part of the explanation can be found in its OT background. There were two words of relevance here, *chen* ("grace, favour") and *chesed* ("gracious favour, loving kindness, covenant love").[16] Both denoted the generous act of a superior to an inferior. But the former was more one-sided, might be given for a specific situation only, and could be withdrawn unilaterally.[17] The latter was a more relational term. In its secular usage that implied a degree of reciprocity: the one who received an act of

---

10. See also Doughty, "Priority of *CHARIS*"; Barrett, *Paul* 87-91. The Pauline letters use *charis* 100 times as against 55 for the rest of the NT.

11. 2 Cor. 8.9; cf. Rom. 5.15; Gal. 2.21; Eph. 1.6-7.

12. Rom. 3.24; 5.15, 17, 20; 1 Cor. 1.4-5; 15.10; 2 Cor. 6.1; Gal. 1.6, 15; 2.21; Eph. 2.5, 8.

13. Rom. 5.2, 21; 6.14, 15; 2 Cor. 1.12; 8.1; 9.8, 14; 12.9; Gal. 5.4; Col. 3.16; Eph. 1.7-8. Hence also the standard greeting of Paul's letters — "Grace to you and peace from God our Father and our Lord Jesus Christ" (Rom. 1.3; 1 Cor. 1.3; 2 Cor. 1.2; Gal. 1.3-4; etc.) — and the regular benediction with which he closed his letters — "the grace of our Lord Jesus Christ be with you all" (Rom. 16.20; 1 Cor. 16.23; 2 Cor. 13.13; Gal. 6.18, etc.).

14. Rom. 1.5; 12.3, 6; 15.15; 1 Cor. 3.10; Gal. 2.9; Eph. 3.2, 7-8. Also "grace (gracious action)" as the particular outworking or manifestation of grace — 1 Cor. 16.3; 2 Cor. 1.15; 8.1, 4, 6-7, 19; Eph. 4.29.

15. Note particularly Paul's emphasis on the love of God (Rom. 5.5, 8; 8.37, 39; 2 Cor. 13.13; 2 Thes. 2.16; 3.5) and the love of Christ (Rom. 8.35; Gal. 2.20; 2 Cor. 5.14; Eph. 3.19; 5.2, 25). *Agapē* ("love") is another word, like "gospel," which early Christianity and Paul minted afresh to express the richness and vitality of their experience of divine acceptance. It appears only exceptionally in nonbiblical Greek prior to the second and third century CE, and most of the 20 LXX occurrences refer to conjugal love (Wis. 3.9 is an exception). Contrast the 116 occurrences in the NT, of which 75 appear in the Pauline corpus (see further my *Romans* 739).

16. *Chen* 67 times; *chesed* 245 times.

17. H.-J. Fabry, *TDOT* 5.24-25. The word appears most often in the phrase "find favour in the eyes of" (BDB, *chen*).

chesed responded with a similar act of *chesed*.[18] But in its religious usage the recognition was deeply rooted that God's initiative was a lasting commitment which excluded from the outset the possibility of any comparable response.[19]

What is of interest here is the contrast between the LXX's translation of these terms and Paul's use of *charis*. In LXX *charis* is almost always the translation for *chen*,[20] whereas *eleos* ("mercy") was the usual translation for the more common and richer *chesed*. In Paul, however, the position is reversed, with *eleos* used only four times in the undisputed Paulines.[21] It would appear, then, that Paul preferred *charis*, presumably because in its usage he could combine the most positive features of the two Hebrew words: *charis* denotes, as it were, the unilateralness of *chen* and the lasting commitment of *chesed*.

Part of the explanation for Paul's choice of *charis* may also be found in the contemporary wider Greek usage. Although common in Greek in a range of senses ("beauty, goodwill towards, favour, gratitude for, delight in"), *charis* did not have a particularly theological or religious connotation.[22] However, an important context of Greek usage has not been given sufficient attention until recently. This is the context of benefaction, the benefactions of the gods or of individuals to cities or institutions — *charis* as "favour" done, and regularly in the plural, *charites*, "favours" bestowed or returned.[23] In this context the term would have been familiar to Paul and his readers, visible to daily sight in the numerous inscriptions which adorned any Greek city commemorating and honouring previous benefactors. When his converts read the word *charis*, the language of benefaction would usually have been the most immediate context of meaning for their understanding of the term.

---

18. H.-J. Zobel, *TDOT* 5.47-50, citing, e.g., Gen. 21.23; Josh. 2.12, 14; 2 Sam. 2.5-6.

19. Zobel, *TDOT* 5.62-63 — most notably in the oft-repeated confession of the Lord as "a God merciful and gracious, slow to anger, and abounding in steadfast love and faithfulness" (Exod. 34.6; Num. 14.18; Neh. 9.17; Pss. 86.15; 103.8). See also W. Zimmerli, *TDNT* 9.376-87. The claim that "the word *charis* is almost totally unknown in Jewish religious literature" (Doughty, "Priority of *CHARIS*" 170) is too lightly made; contrast K. Berger, *EDNT* 3.457-58; particularly interesting is Philo's brief discussion in *Immut.* 104-8.

20. Only in Esth. 2.9, 17 does *charis* translate *chesed*.

21. Rom. 9.23; 11.31; 15.9; Gal. 6.16; that Paul was well aware of the strong overtones of covenant love for Israel in *eleos* is indicated by the prominence of the verb *eleeō*) in Rom. 9.15-18 and 11.30-32.

22. LSJ, *charis;* H. Conzelmann, *TDNT* 9.373-76.

23. See particularly Harrison, *Paul's Language of Grace*, who notes that the theme has been almost wholly neglected since Wetter's pioneering study. Both draw attention especially to the role of the Caesars as bestowers of divine *charis* (Wetter, *Charis* 15-19; Harrison §2.5). *Res Gestae Divi Augusti* 15-24 record the magnitude of Augustus' largesse, which would have been well known not least to the readers of Paul's letter to Rome (Harrison §6.1.2.4).

Against this double background several features of Paul's grace theology call for comment. (1) First, a common feature in the usages outlined above is the idea of spontaneous kindness and generous giving. As with the *chesed* theology of ancient Israel, Paul rooted his understanding of divine-human relations in the conviction that God's purpose for humankind was one of generous initiative and sustained faithfulness from start to finish. A striking characteristic of Paul's usage is that the terms *dōrea* ("gift") and *dōrean* ("as a gift, undeservedly") are usually linked with the concept of *charis*.[24] God's grace is always gift. Hence the most common verbal phrase with *charis* is "grace given (by God)."[25]

(2) A second common feature is the sense of "grace" as *action*. It denoted not simply an attitude or a disposition but also the act which expressed the attitude;[26] the actual favour(s) bestowed by the benefactor were what the laudatory inscriptions commemorated. So with Paul, "grace" was a dynamic concept, the powerful action of God,[27] overlapping with the concepts of "power" and "Spirit" in Paul's usage.[28] As the references already surveyed indicate clearly enough, "grace" described the dynamic experience of being grasped and engraced by God. For example, 2 Cor. 12.9: "My *grace* is sufficient for you; my *power* is made perfect in weakness."

Several features of Paul's usage, however, mark it out from the contemporary parallels. (3) In the latter, *charis* is regularly used in the plural — the favours or benefactions bestowed. But Paul's usage is consistently singular; the singularity of grace is a feature of Paul's theology. This will be due partly to the influence of the underlying Hebrew concept: in the OT *chen* is never used in the plural, and *chesed* only rarely.[29] But it also presumably reflects the fact that for Paul grace had a single source (God) and a single focal expression (the redemptive act of Christ). All grace was an expression of divine grace; every gracious act was only "gracious" to the extent that it reflected the grace of God in Christ. All grace was the same grace.

(4) In Paul's letters the unilateral nature of this grace is given even more emphatic expression. The idea of mutuality which was attached to human

---

24. *Dōrea* — always (5.15, 17; 2 Cor. 9.15; Eph. 3.7; 4.7); *dōrean* 2 of 4 occurrences (Rom. 3.24; Gal. 2.21).

25. Rom. 12.3, 6; 15.15; 1 Cor. 1.4; 3.10; Gal. 2.9; Eph. 3.8; 4.7; 2 Tim. 1.9.

26. See also Wetter, *Charis* 37-94; Moffatt, *Grace* 25-29; Zobel, *TDOT* 5.51.

27. "Grace is *God's eschatological deed*" (Bultmann, *Theology* 1.289).

28. See further Wetter, *Charis*, e.g., 40-41, 71-72, 96-97, 104-5; Bultmann, *Theology* 1.290-91; Dunn, *Jesus and the Spirit* 202-5.

29. Fabry, *TDOT* 5.24; Zobel notes that the plural of *chesed* appears only 18 times (out of 245) (*TDOT* 5.45). But the plural of *chesed* is more common in the DSS (Zobel, *TDOT* 5.64), as also the plural of *charis* in Philo (e.g., Conzelmann, *TDNT* 9.389-90).

chesed in the OT, and the importance of reciprocity which was such a central feature of the benefaction ideology of the Greco-Roman world, are both left behind in Paul, even more than in the OT's concept of divine *chesed*. Typical of Paul's theology of grace is the use of terms like "overflow" *(perisseuō),* "abound" *(pleonazō),* "surpassing/extraordinary" *(hyperballō),* and "riches" *(ploutos);*[30] "grace overflowed in abundance" *(hypereperisseusen)* (Rom. 5.20). No room is left for any thought that the human recipient of divine grace can somehow repay it.[31] The one to whom *charis* has been given should return *charis* indeed, but always in the sense of "thanks,"[32] never in the sense of a "favour" returned. "Grace" remains God's wholly generous and undeserved action from beginning to end.

(5) At the same time we can say that for Paul grace begets grace. As we shall see later, *charis* bestowed comes to expression in *charisma*.[33] The reception of God's grace in Christ results in gracious acts — as evident most strikingly in Paul's exhortations regarding the collection for the Jerusalem church.[34] The point here is that Paul saw the action of grace not merely in the reciprocal giving and returning of grace; even the return of *charis* in the sense of "thanks" did not complete the Pauline circle of grace. *Charis* came to fuller expression in *charisma* as a gift to the community, a benefit for the common good (1 Cor. 12.7). The character of divine grace in Christ was fully recognized and responded to when the recipient became a vehicle of that same grace to others (2 Corinthians 8–9). The grace of God came to characteristic expression not only in the salvation of the individual but also in the building of the community.

§13.3 The new beginning

Paul had no concept of the unconscious or unintentional Christian. He did not think of all men and women as willy-nilly "in Christ," whether they want to be or not, whether they know it or not. The given of humankind's condition is membership of Adam, sharing in Adam's humanity, under the power of sin, on the way to death. But membership of the last Adam, sharing in Christ's

---

30. *Perisseuō/perisseia* — Rom. 5.15, 17; 2 Cor. 4.15; 8.7; 9.8. *Pleonazō* — Rom. 6.1; 2 Cor. 4.15. *Hyperballō* — 2 Cor. 9.14; Eph. 2.7. *Ploutos* — Eph. 1.7; 2.7; cf. 2 Cor. 8.9; Col. 3.16; Eph. 3.8. See further Theobald, *Gnade.*

31. As Harrison observes, key terms in benefaction ideology, like *amoibē* ("return, recompense") and *apodidōmi* ("to return, recompense"), are missing from Paul's vocabulary of grace.

32. "Thanks be to God" — Rom. 6.17; 7.25; 1 Cor. 15.57; 2 Cor. 2.14; 8.16; 9.15.

33. See below §20.5.

34. See below §24.8a.

resurrected humanity, beyond the power of sin and death, was not a given in the same way. It had to come about. A transition was involved, an ending and a beginning, a step across a chasm, a jump to a new plane, the experience of new life. And that did not happen automatically. As we shall see, Adam's initial creaturely faith had to be recovered and expressed again from the side of humankind. The Spirit had to be bestowed afresh by God, in a new beginning as decisive as the first bestowal by which the dust of the earth became humankind (Gen. 2.7).

Of course, Paul speaks throughout not only as a theologian, but as an apostle, as a missionary. And his preaching was not simply the impartation of information ("knowledge") that his hearers were spiritual beings who only needed to know the facts for their destiny to be secure. Paul preached for a decision, "with a view to the obedience of faith among all the nations" (Rom. 1.5). He lays out his understanding of the normal procedure on more than one occasion: the gospel as "the power of God for salvation to all who believe" (1.16); the preacher must be sent to preach so that the hearers may believe (10.14-17); the foolishness of preaching saves those who believe (1 Cor. 1.21); "so we preach and so you believed" (15.11); the ambassador must plead on behalf of Christ, "Be reconciled to God" (2 Cor. 5.20); the Spirit is received by hearing with faith (Gal. 3.2); "you received the word of God which you heard from us" (1 Thes. 2.13). The summons to believe was a fundamental part of Paul's gospel.[35] The "call" of God must be responded to.[36] People had to receive what God offered through him if the process of salvation was to begin.[37] If we are to represent Paul's theology adequately, this point must be given a place of some prominence.

A particularly striking feature of Paul's letters is the frequency with which he refers his audiences back to their beginnings, to the decisive hearing, the act of commitment, the initial experience of grace. Paul's aorists again and again recall his readers to that initial stage and to its character as determinative for their ongoing discipleship.

---

35. *Pisteuō* ("believe"): aorist — Rom. 10.9, 14, 16; 13.11; 1 Cor. 3.5; 15.2, 11; 2 Cor. 4.13; Gal. 2.16; Eph. 1.13; 2 Thes. 1.10; 1 Tim. 3.16; present (= "believer" or the act of believing) — Rom. 1.16; 3.22; 4.5, 11, 24; 9.33; 10.4, 10, 11; 15.13; 1 Cor. 1.21; 14.22; 2 Cor. 4.13; Gal. 3.22; Eph. 1.19; Phil. 1.29; 1 Thes. 1.7; 2.10, 13; 4.14; 1 Tim. 1.16; perfect — 2 Tim. 1.12; Tit. 3.8.

36. *Kaleō* ("call") — a prominent theme in the Paulines (Rom. 4.17; 8.30; 9.11, 24; 1 Cor. 1.9; 7.15-24; Gal. 1.6, 15; 5.8, 13; Eph. 4.1, 4; Col. 3.15; 1 Thes. 2.12; 4.7; 5.24; 2 Thes. 2.14; 1 Tim. 6.12; 2 Tim. 1.9).

37. *Dechomai* ("receive") — 2 Cor. 6.1; 11.4; 1 Thes. 1.6; 2.13. *Paralambanō* ("receive [traditions about]") — 1 Cor. 15.1, 3; Gal. 1.9; Phil. 4.9; Col. 2.6; 1 Thes. 2.13.

Are you unaware that all we who were baptized into Christ Jesus were baptized into his death? So then we were buried with him through baptism into death . . . (Rom. 6.3-4).

Thanks be to God that when you were slaves of sin you gave your obedience from the heart to the one to whom you were handed over as a pattern of teaching. Having been set free from sin you became enslaved to righteousness (6.17-18).

So then, my brothers, you also were put to death in relation to the law through the body of Christ, in order that you might become another's. . . . But now we have been released from the law, having died to that by which we were confined, so that we might serve in newness of Spirit and not in oldness of letter (7.4, 6).

You did not receive a spirit of slavery, falling back into fear; but you received the Spirit of adoption (8.15).

Our salvation is nearer than when we believed (13.11).

I give thanks to my God everywhere concerning you for the grace of God which was given to you in Christ Jesus, that in every way you have been enriched in him . . . (1 Cor. 1.4-5).

We have received not the spirit of the world but the Spirit which is from God, in order that we might know what has been granted to us by God (2.12).

You were washed, you were sanctified, you were justified in the name of the Lord Jesus Christ and in the Spirit of our God (6.11).

In one Spirit we were all baptized into one body . . . and were all drenched with the one Spirit (12.13).

. . . the gospel which you received, in which you stand, through which you are being saved, if you hold fast to the word which I preached to you, unless you believed in vain (15.1-2).

God has anointed us, who also has sealed us and given the Spirit as guarantee in our hearts (2 Cor. 1.21-22).

You show that you are a letter of Christ delivered by us, written not with ink but with the Spirit of the living God (3.3).

It is God who said "Out of darkness light will shine" who has shone in our hearts to give the light of the knowledge of the glory of God in the face of Jesus Christ (4.6).

I am astonished that you are so quickly turning away from the one who called you in the grace of Christ to another gospel (Gal. 1.6).

. . . we have believed in Christ Jesus, in order that we might be justified by faith in Christ and not by works of the law . . . (2.16).

This only I want to learn from you: was it by works of the law that you received the Spirit, or by hearing with faith? Are you so foolish?

> Having begun with the Spirit are you now made complete with the flesh?
> (3.2-3).
>
> For freedom Christ has set us free. Stand firm, therefore, and do not
> be subject again to a yoke of slavery. . . . You were called to freedom,
> brothers; only not the freedom for opportunity to the flesh, but through
> love serve one another (5.1, 13).

These listings are by no means exhaustive and could be continued into the
other Pauline letters. But the point should be clear enough. We are talking
about an event, decisive in character, determinative for the future, transforming
all loyalties. For Paul the process of salvation had to have a beginning. Without
conscious commitment it could not proceed.

Should we speak of this necessary beginning as a "conversion"? The
idea of conversion, of a turning from an old allegiance to a new, was well
enough known in the ancient world, whatever the term used.[38] And the term
is as appropriate as a general description of what Paul sought by means of
his preaching as it is to describe Paul's own beginning in faith.[39] But there
are hesitations about its appropriateness similar to those regarding Paul's
"conversion" — two in particular.

First, Paul does use the term "convert, turn round" *(epistrephō)* in this
connection. Most notably in 1 Thes. 1.9, where he recalls the much retold
story of how the Thessalonians "turned to God from idols to serve a living
and true God." A similar "turning" is implied in Gal. 4.9, where Paul expresses
his concern lest the Galatians "turn [back] to the weak and beggarly elemental
forces." But he uses the term in only one other passage (2 Cor. 3.16), where
he modifies a scriptural allusion (Exod. 34.34) by incorporating another familiar scriptural phrase, "turn to the Lord."[40] This suggests that "convert"
was not Paul's customary language and imagery in talking about his readers'

---

38. The point should not be overdone. Cult membership was not usually exclusive
of other loyalties. But there were no doubt some dramatic cases of "turning round," of
which the classic literary case is that of Lucius in Apuleius, *Metamorphoses* 11; the study
of Nock, *Conversion,* is itself a classic (ch. 9 on Lucius). And for Gentiles to become
proselytes would involve a major transition and new social persona. But the new Christian
sect was distinctive within Judaism in its evangelistic concern; see McKnight, *Light,* and
Goodman, *Mission* ch. 4; Hengel and Schhwemer, *Paul between Damascus and Antioch*
75-76.

39. See above §§7.4-5 and below §14.3.

40. Exod. 34.34 LXX — "whenever Moses went in *(eiseporeueto)* before the Lord
he would remove *(periereito)* the veil"; 2 Cor. 3.16 — "whenever he turned *(epestrepse)*
to the Lord the veil was taken away *(periaireitai).*" "Turn to the Lord" occurs in Deut.
4.30; 1 Sam. 7.3; 1 Kgs. 8.33; 2 Chron. 24.19; 30.9; Ps. 22(LXX 21).27; Isa. 6.10; 19.22;
Jer. 24.7; Joel 2.12-14; Zech. 1.3; Tob. 14.6; Sir. 5.7; 17.25 (Furnish, *2 Corinthians* 211;
Gaventa, *Darkness* 50 n. 58).

coming to faith. And while it made good sense in describing a Gentile once for all turning from idolatry, its regular use in scripture for repeated returning to God[41] may have made it a less appropriate image for the decisive, once-for-all act which Paul had in mind.[42]

Second, Paul is just as shy of using the obviously related language of "repentance" and "forgiveness." Despite the relative prominence of verb and noun ("repent, repentance") in the Synoptic tradition and in Acts,[43] Paul speaks of "repentance" only once in what we might call a conversion situation (Rom. 2.4).[44] Even more striking is the fact that the usual term for "forgiveness" appears only in a scriptural quotation in Paul's principal letters,[45] and otherwise only in the later Col. 1.14 — "in whom we have redemption, the forgiveness of sins."[46] For some reason not altogether clear to us, Paul evidently preferred not to talk in these terms.[47] The reason may possibly be because such terms were so characteristic of his own former theology and practice.[48] What he wanted was a different emphasis, and possibly a more positive summons. He found it in the call to faith — by far the more prominent theme in his gospel preaching and theology. It was less the "turning away from" which Paul emphasized and more the "commitment

41. See BDB, *shub* 6c, d; G. Bertram, *TDNT* 7.724-25. The point is made more complex since Yahweh can also be said to "turn back, repent, convert" — Exod. 32.12; Deut. 32.17; Josh. 7.26; 2 Kgs. 23.26; Jonah 3.9 (BDB, *shub* 6f).

42. Here, as with baptism, the influence of the memory of John the Baptist on the new sect may have to be recognized: his call for "repentance/conversion," linked to a once-for-all baptism (Mark 1.4 pars.), was probably something new in Jewish tradition.

43. "Repent" — Matt. 5, Mark 2, Luke 9, Acts 5. "Repentance" — Matt. 2, Mark 1, Luke 5, Acts 6. "Forgiveness" — Matt. 1, Mark 2, Luke 5, Acts 5. It is equally noticeable, however, that John's Gospel uses none of these terms.

44. In 2 Cor. 7.9-10 his hope is for his readers' repentance, and in 12.21 for his (Christian) opponents' repentance; cf. 2 Tim. 2.25. Equally lacking is the idea of "conviction (of sin?)" — 1 Cor. 14.24; Eph. 5.11, 13; 1 Tim. 5.20; 2 Tim. 4.2; Tit. 1.9, 13; 2.15.

45. Rom. 4.7, citing Ps. 32.1.

46. The character of Colossians raises the question whether this was Paul's choice of wording, on which Eph. 1.7 seems to have been modeled; see my *Colossians* 81, and 35-39 on the question of authorship. But *charizomai* is also used in the sense "forgive," as among believers (2 Cor. 2.7-10), and again in Col. 2.13 and 3.13 (followed by Eph. 4.32) for divine forgiveness.

47. The testimony of Acts is noticeably different on this point (Acts 13.38; 17.30; 20.21; 26.18, 20).

48. Traditional Christian caricaturing of early Judaism assumed that the Baptist's and Jesus' call for repentance and their offer of forgiveness was something new. The assumption caused great puzzlement and offence to scholars of early Judaism, as did also Paul's surprising failure to express such a scriptural emphasis within his own gospel and theology (see, e.g., Moore, *Judaism* 3.151; Sanders, *Paul* 1-12, 33-59).

to." There is matter for reflection here in contemporary gospel preaching and theologizing.[49]

Whatever questions remain regarding the use of the term "conversion" in Paul's theology, however, the key point remains that the Christian life for him had a clear beginning. In writing to the churches he founded, and to others, he simply took it for granted that his audiences were made up of individuals who had gone through a significant transition in their experience. They had responded to Paul's (or his team's) preaching, made some kind of confessional commitment to Jesus as Lord, and been baptized in Jesus' name. They had experienced God's grace and had become members of a group whose mutual interdependence and ethos were expected to characterize their whole lives. We can hardly doubt that most of his original audiences would be well able to recall the day when they became "Christian."

§13.4 Metaphors of salvation

Another noteworthy feature of Paul's talk of the crucial transition and new beginning is the wide variety of metaphors he draws on to describe it and its significance. It is worth categorizing them briefly.

Paul draws on metaphors from the customs of his time. "Justification" is a legal metaphor; to be justified is to be acquitted.[50] In the same area we may note the image of expunging a record of debt or criminal guilt (Col. 2.14).[51] "Redemption" we have already looked at — the buying back of a slave or a war captive.[52] "Liberation" and "freedom" were important words and, more to the point, were important experiences for Paul and his converts.[53] "Reconciliation" we have also looked at above — the bringing together of two parties at enmity with each other into a new peace and cooperation.[54] Another is the image of enjoying citizenship, or community membership, within but different from that of the surrounding city or region (Phil. 3.20).[55]

---

49. Gaventa also makes the point that whereas "convert" and "repent" imply the action of the person to rectify the relationship with God, in Paul's letters God is the one who acts. "It is not believers who turn, but God who turns believers" (*Darkness* 44).

50. See further below §14.2.

51. For details see my *Colossians* 164-66.

52. See above §9.6.

53. *Eleutheria* ("freedom") — Rom. 8.21; 2 Cor. 3.17; Gal. 2.4; 5.1, 13; *eleutheroō* ("to free") — Rom. 6.18, 22; 8.2, 21; Gal. 5.1; *eleutheros* ("free") — Rom. 7.3; 9.1; Gal. 4.31.

54. See above §9.7.

55. See Schürer, *History* 3.88-89. As a Roman colony, Philippi itself had a special constitution, governed as though it was on Italian soil and thus enjoying rights not available to other cities of the region.

The imagery of being transferred into another kingdom in Col. 1.13 probably reflects the origins of the Jewish communities in Asia Minor, established by Antiochus the Great when he settled two thousand Jewish families in Lydia and Phrygia to help stabilize the region.[56]

Paul also draws on metaphors from everyday life. One of Paul's favourite terms is "salvation,"[57] which has become such an established technical term in theology that its force as a metaphor can easily be forgotten. *Sōtēria* ("salvation") would have been familiar in the sense of "rescue, a bringing safely or to safety." In a Jewish context, thought of the exodus from Egypt or the return from exile in Babylon would be prominent.[58] But the term would no doubt have been familiar to Paul's readers also in the everyday sense of "bodily health, preservation." We have papyrus letters from the period in which the writer inquires anxiously about the *sōtēria* of children or friends.[59] "Salvation" for Paul, we might say, denoted the wholeness of the healthy person. The metaphor of "inheritance" is another crucial theme for Paul.[60] Others occasionally used are the more humdrum metaphors of waking up,[61] night giving way to day,[62] "putting off or on" clothes, including putting on armour,[63] receiving an invitation,[64] and writing a letter.[65]

Paul drew equally from agriculture — sowing and watering (1 Cor. 3.6-8), irrigation (1 Cor. 12.13c)[66] and the pitcher of water poured out (Rom. 5.5), grafting (Rom. 11.17-24),[67] and harvest (Rom. 8.23).[68] Likewise from

56. Josephus, *Ant.* 12.147-53; see also my *Colossians* 77.

57. Rom. 1.16; 10.1, 10; 11.11; 13.11; 2 Cor. 1.6; 6.2; 7.10; Phil. 1.19, 28; 2.12; 1 Thes. 5.8, 9; 2 Thes. 2.13; also Eph. 1.13; 2 Tim. 2.10; 3.15.

58. E.g., Exod. 14.13; 15.2; Isa. 46.13; 52.7, 10.

59. MM, *sōtēria*. Worth recalling is the number of times in the Gospels when someone healed is told, "Your faith has saved you" (particularly Luke — 8.48; 17.19; 18.42; but note also 7.50). Note how the imagery is exploited in Acts 4.9-12.

60. *Klēronomia* ("inheritance") — Gal. 3.18; Col. 3.24; Eph. 1.14, 18; 5.5; *klēronomeō* ("inherit") — 1 Cor. 6.9-10; 15.50; Gal. 5.21; *klēronomos* ("heir") — Rom. 4.13-14; 8.17; Gal. 3.29; 4.1, 7; Tit. 3.7.

61. Rom. 13.11; Eph. 5.14.

62. Rom. 13.12; cf. 1 Thes. 5.5-8.

63. Rom. 13.12, 14; Col. 3.8, 12; 1 Thes. 5.8; Eph. 4.22, 25; 6.11, 14-17. On the last three notes see further my *Romans* 785-88.

64. *Kaleō* — see above n. 22.

65. 2 Cor. 3.3.

66. See further below §16 n. 27.

67. The medical imagery of the fusion of the two ends of a broken bone in Rom. 6.5 *(symphytos)* is closely parallel (Dunn, *Baptism* [§16 n. 1] 141).

68. The dominant image in *aparchē*, "firstfruits," is the harvest, the firstfruits of the wine press and the threshing floor (Exod. 22.29; 23.19; Lev. 2.12; 23.10; Num. 15.20; 18.12, 30; Deut. 26.2, etc.); see further my *Romans* 473.

commerce. The "seal" stamped on an item was a visible mark of ownership.[69] The *arrabōn* constituted the first instalment and guarantee of what was still to come.[70] The phrase "into the name of," used in baptism (1 Cor. 1.13-15), occurs frequently in papyrus records of transfer of ownership — equivalent to the modern signing of a cheque, whereby ownership of the funds stated is transferred "to the account of" the person named.[71] The image of conveying is probably drawn upon in the term *bebaioō*, "confirm."[72] Paul alludes with equal facility to the result of the process of refining — *dokimos*, "tested and approved"[73] — and to building (1 Cor. 3.10-12).

We should note that Paul also drew his images from religion. One of his favourite ways of referring to the members of his churches was as "saints" *(hagioi)*,[74] those who had been set apart and dedicated to the service of God. Here we may note that while the noun *hagiasmos* ("sanctification") was used for the process of salvation,[75] the verb in Paul usually denotes the beginning action, whereby individuals were set apart to discipleship.[76] On one occasion he uses the related image of anointing (2 Cor. 1.21). We have already noted how important the metaphor of sacrifice is for Paul's understanding of the death of Jesus (§§9.2-3). Paul also uses the imagery of priestly service for his own ministry,[77] as indeed for all Christian commitment and other acts of service in the gospel.[78] All the justified have "access" to the inner sanctum of the cult (Rom. 5.2). Their bodies are themselves temples enshrining God's presence.[79] It is noticeable, however, that he never uses the image of "priest" as such, for his own work or for that of others.[80] Most interesting is the way in which Paul, despite his strong hostility to Gentile converts being circumcised, nevertheless transfers the image "circumcision" to the event of the cross and its outworking.[81] Given the importance of ritual cleansing within

69. 2 Cor. 1.22; Eph. 1.13; 4.30; cf. Rom. 4.11; 15.28; see MM, *sphragizō, sphragis*.

70. 2 Cor. 1.22; 5.5; Eph. 1.14; see MM, *arrabōn;* A. J. Kerr, *"ARRABŌN," JTS* 39 (1988) 92-97, limits the sense to "first instalment." See also §18 n. 43 below.

71. MM, *onoma* (5).

72. 1 Cor. 1.6, 8; 2 Cor. 1.21; Col. 2.7. The noun *bebaios* (used in Rom. 4.16 and 2 Cor. 1.7) was a t.t. to denote legally guaranteed security in property transfers (MM, *bebaios*).

73. Rom. 14.18; 16.10; 1 Cor. 11.19; 2 Cor. 10.18; 13.7; 2 Tim. 2.15.

74. "The saints" *(hoi hagioi)* 39 times in Paul (examples in §2 n. 90 above).

75. Rom. 6.19, 22; 1 Cor. 1.30; 1 Thes. 4.3, 4, 7; 2 Thes. 2.13; 1 Tim. 2.15.

76. Rom. 15.16; 1 Cor. 1.2; 6.11; Eph. 5.26; 2 Tim. 2.21.

77. Rom. 1.9; 15.16; Phil. 2.17.

78. Rom. 12.1; 15.27; 2 Cor. 9.12; Phil. 2.25, 30; see further §20.3 below.

79. 1 Cor. 3.16-17; 6.19; 2 Cor. 6.16; cf. Eph. 2.21.

80. Contrast 1 Pet. 2.5, 9; Rev. 1.6; 5.10; 20.6, but these passages refer to all believers.

81. Phil. 3.3; Col. 2.11; but see my *Colossians* 154-58 for discussion of the latter verse.

the Jewish tradition,[82] it is not surprising that Paul draws on the image of washing and purifying.[83] It is likely also that he used the Christian adaptation of this ritual cleansing tradition (baptism) as a metaphor, powerful in its imagery of plunging below the surface and emerging to a new life;[84] but the metaphorical force of this last usage is disputed.[85] Nor should we forget the most powerful imagery of all — that of "new creation."[86]

Finally in this brief categorization we can refer to metaphors drawn from the major events of life. Paul speaks of his own conversion as an "abortion" (1 Cor. 15.8),[87] of "becoming your [the Corinthians'] father through the gospel" (1 Cor. 4.15), of giving birth to the Galatians (Gal. 4.19), of the Galatians as "born in accordance with the Spirit" (4.29). An important alternative family image for Paul was that of adoption.[88] Elsewhere he likens becoming a Christian to an engagement with Christ (2 Cor. 11.2), and being a Christian to marriage with Christ (1 Cor. 6.17). And not least of his powerful images is that of death, likening the crucial transition to a dying, even a crucifixion.[89]

Two lines of reflection emerge from consideration of such a kaleidoscope of images. One is that these metaphors bring out the *reality* of the experience of the new beginning for Paul. Evidently they all described something in the experience of his readers with which they could identify. Something had happened in their lives, something of major importance. Underlying all these metaphors was some tremendously significant event, a turning point of great moment. One does not use images like birth, marriage, and death for everyday occurrences. They only function as images for events which are literally life-changing.

---

82. See, e.g., my *Partings* 38-42, with reference particularly to E. P. Sanders, *Jewish Law from Jesus to the Mishnah* (London: SCM/Philadelphia: TPI, 1990) 29-42, 184-236.

83. Particularly 1 Cor. 6.11; also Eph. 5.26; cf. Tit. 3.5.

84. Rom. 6.3; 1 Cor. 10.2; 12.13; Gal. 3.27.

85. See below §17.2.

86. 2 Cor. 5.17; Gal. 6.15; cf. Rom. 8.19-23; Col. 3.10; Eph. 2.10, 15; 4.24.

87. The term *ektrōma* denotes "premature birth." Since it could imply the deformity often involved in such a birth, it may have originated as a jibe against Paul by opponents ("freak, monstrosity"). Paul probably took it up to indicate that his birth (as a believer) was premature, forced ahead of time, in order that he might be included within the circle of apostles before it closed ("last of all"). See further my *Jesus and the Spirit* 101-2; Fee, *1 Corinthians* 732-34; and below §21 n. 31. H. W. Hollander and G. E. van der Hout see the term rather as an expression of Paul's own sense of insufficiency ("The Apostle Paul Calling Himself an Abortion: 1 Cor. 15:8 within the Context of 1 Cor. 15:8-10," *NovT* 38 [1996] 224-36). My colleague Loren Stuckenbruck notes that the Qumran *Book of Giants* may have understood the *nephalim* of Gen. 6.4 as "abortions" (4Q530 2.6; 4Q531 5.2).

88. Rom. 8.15, 23; Gal. 4.5; Eph. 1.5.

89. Rom. 6.3-6; 7.4, 6; Gal. 2.19; Col. 2.20; 3.3.

This has a corollary worthy of some attention. For it means that many of Paul's first readers experienced the gospel as acceptance, liberation, or rescue, as cleansing and new dedication, as a dying to an old life and beginning of a new. There is little evidence that Paul preached for conviction of sin or to stir up feelings of guilt. Nevertheless, for so many of his converts the gospel was received and experienced as an answer to unresolved riddles, as a solution to their plight.[90] In a word, Paul's gospel met real and felt needs.

Second, the very different metaphors Paul drew upon were presumably attempts to express as fully as possible a reality which defied a simple or uniform or unifaceted description. There was something so rich and real in the various experiences of conversion which Paul's gospel brought about that Paul had to ransack the language available to him to find ways of describing them. The vitality of the experience made new metaphors necessary if the experience was to be expressed in words (as adequately as that is possible) and to be communicated to others.

This in turn points up another corollary of some interest. For the wide variety of metaphors presumably reflects a wide variety of experiences. Given that variety, it would be a mistake to take any one of Paul's metaphors and to exalt it into some primary or normative status so that all the others must be fitted into its mould. Something like this has indeed happened with the metaphor of justification in classic Protestant theology. In popular evangelism it has happened with the metaphors of salvation and new birth. In such cases there is an obvious danger. The danger is that the event of new beginning in faith comes to be conceptualized as of necessity following a particular pattern, the same for everyone. Equally dangerous is the assumption often made that the same language or imagery must always be used, that experience of individuals must conform to the language which describes it. Instead of diversity of experience and imagery there can be pressure to reduplicate both pattern and jargon, in effect to mass reproduce believers according to a standard formula.[91] Not so with Paul. For him the crucial transition was a many-sided event, and not necessarily the same for any two people. And it required a whole vocabulary of words and metaphors to bring out the richness of its character and the diversity of individual cases.

Underlying both lines of reflection is a more fundamental point — the indispensability of metaphors to express such experiences. We are familiar with the fact that rational description is often inadequate to capture the real

90. The allusion is to Sanders's claim that for Paul "solution" came before "plight"; see above §1 n. 77 and §7 n. 101.

91. Hence the importance of noting that the language of repentance and forgiveness has so little place in Paul's theological reflections, even though they would generally be thought to be central in most traditional preaching of the gospel.

quality of aesthetic or deeply moving experiences. The impact of a piece of music or the distinctions among different wines can often be so intensely personal and intangible as to be beyond communication in terms of logic. Still more so with regard to experiences which are so life-transforming. To attempt to dispense with metaphors or to reduce their poetry to the prose of clinical analysis would be as great a disservice as any that theology could be guilty of.[92]

Within this diverse way of speaking of the crucial transition, however, there are three or four aspects which deserve special mention, partly because they bring out the central features of the new beginning for Paul and partly because of their significance in the history of Christian theology. We will look at them in turn:[93] justification by faith (§14), participation in Christ (§15), and the gift of the Spirit (§16).[94]

92. Fitzmyer, *Paul* 65-66, quotes Richardson's *Introduction* 222-23 with effect: Paul offers us "not theories but vivid metaphors, which can, if we let them operate in our imagination, make real to us the saving truth of our redemption by Christ's self-offering on our behalf. . . . It is an unfortunate kind of sophistication which believes that the only thing to do with metaphors is to turn them into theories."

93. Cerfaux, *Christian* (§14 n. 1) Part III, deals with the same three aspects in reverse order.

94. "Or four," since it might be appropriate to include baptism (§17) as a separate category.

§14 Justification by faith[1]

1. **Bibliography**: **Barrett**, *Paul* 91-103; **Becker**, *Paul* 279-304, 356-72; **Beker**, *Paul* 255-71; **Berger**, *Theologiegeschichte* 491-97; **H. Boers**, *The Justification of the Gentiles: Paul's Letters to the Galatians and Romans* (Peabody: Hendrickson, 1994); **Bornkamm**, *Paul* 135-56; **Bultmann**, *Theology* I, 270-87; **L. Cerfaux**, *The Christian in the Theology of St. Paul* (London: Chapman, 1967) 373-466; **Conzelmann**, *Outline* 171-73, 213-20; **H. Cremer**, *Die paulinische Rechtfertigungslehre im Zusammenhange ihrer geschichtlichen Voraussetzungen* (Gütersloh: Bertelsmann, [2]1900); **A. von Dobbeler**, *Glaube als Teilhabe. Historische und semantische Grundlagen der paulinischen Theologie und Ekklesiologie des Glaubens* (WUNT 2.22; Tübingen: Mohr, 1987); **van Dülmen**, *Theologie* (§6 n. 1); **J. D. G. Dunn**, "The Justice of God: A Renewed Perspective on Justification by Faith," *JTS* 43 (1992) 1-22; "Paul and Justification by Faith," in R. N. Longenecker, ed., *The Road from Damascus: The Impact of Paul's Conversion on His Life, Thought and Ministry* (Grand Rapids: Eerdmans, 1997) 85-101; **Eckstein**, *Verheißung*; **Fitzmyer**, *Paul* 59-61; **Gnilka**, *Theologie* 78-96; *Paulus* 237-47; **Goppelt**, *Theology* 2.124-41; **F. Hahn**, "Gibt es eine Entwicklung in den Aussagen über die Rechtfertigung bei Paulus?" *EvT* 53 (1993) 342-66; **Howard**, *Paul* ch. 3; **E. Käsemann**, " 'The Righteousness of God' in Paul," *New Testament Questions* 168-82; *Perspectives* 60-101; **K. Kertelge**, *"Rechtfertigung" bei Paulus* (Münster: Aschendorff, 1967, [2]1971); **Kümmel**, *Theology* 193-203; **R. Liebers**, *Das Gesetz als Evangelium. Untersuchungen zur Gesetzeskritik des Paulus* (Zürich: Theologischer, 1989); **E. Lohse**, "Die Gerechtigkeit Gottes in der paulinischen Theologie, wieder abgedruckt," *Einheit* 209-27; *Paulus* 199-214; **Martin**, *Reconciliation* (§9 n. 1) 127-54; **A. E. McGrath**, *Iustitia Dei: A History of the Christian Doctrine of Justification,* 2 vols. (Cambridge: Cambridge University, 1986); **Merklein**, *Studien* 39-64; **C. Müller**, *Gottes Gerechtigkeit und Gottes Volk. Eine Untersuchung zu Römer 9–11* (Göttingen: Vandenhoeck, 1964); **Penna**, "The Problem of the Law in Paul's Letters," *Paul* 2.115-34; **J. Reumann**, *Righteousness in the New Testament* (Philadelphia: Fortress/New York: Paulist, 1982); **Ridderbos**, *Paul* 159-81; **Sanders**, *Paul, the Law and the Jewish People* (§6 n. 1); **Schlier**, *Grundzüge* 48-50, 158-73; **M. A. Seifrid**, *Justification by Faith: The Origin and Development of a Central Pauline Theme* (NovTSup 68; Leiden: Brill, 1992); **K. R. Snodgrass**, "Justification by Grace — to the Doers: An Analysis of the Place of Romans 2 in the Theology of Paul," *NTS* 32 (1986) 72-93; **K. Stendahl**, "The Apostle Paul and the Introspective Conscience of the West," *HTR* 56 (1963) 199-215 = *Paul among Jews and Gentiles* (London: SCM/Philadelphia: Fortress, 1977) 78-96; **Strecker**, "Befreiung und Rechtfertigung," *Eschaton* 229-59; *Theologie* 147-66; **P. Stuhlmacher**, *Gerechtigkeit Gottes bei Paulus* (Göttingen: Vandenhoeck, 1965); "The Apostle Paul's View of Righteousness," *Reconciliation* 68-93; *Theologie* 326-48; **Whiteley**, *Theology* 156-65; **S. K. Williams**, "The 'Righteousness of God' in Romans," *JBL* 99 (1980) 241-90; **M. Winninge**, *Sinners and the Righteous: A Comparative Study of the Psalms of Solomon and Paul's Letters* (ConB New Testament Series 26; Stockholm: Almqvist and Wiksell, 1995); **Witherington**, *Narrative* 245-72; **M. Wolter**,

§14.1 A new perspective on Paul

"What was the gospel of Christ, according to Luther and all subsequent Protestants?" asks Patrick Collinson.[2] He answers:

Rechtfertigung und zukünftiges Heil. Untersuchungen zu Röm. 5.1-11 (BZNW 43; Berlin: de Gruyter, 1978); **J. A. Ziesler**, *The Meaning of Righteousness in Paul: A Linguistic and Theological Inquiry* (SNTSMS 20; Cambridge: Cambridge University, 1972); *Pauline Christianity* 87-91, 103-7.

§14.3 — see the bibliography on §§7.4-5 (§7 n. 1).

§§14.4-5 — **M. Bachmann**, *Sünder oder Übertreter. Studien zur Argumentation in Gal. 2.15ff.* (WUNT 59; Tübingen: Mohr, 1992); "Rechtfertigung und Gesetzeswerke bei Paulus," *TZ* 49 (1993) 1-33; **C. Burchard**, "Nicht aus Werken des Gesetzes gerecht, sondern aus Glauben an Jesus Christus — seit wann?" in Cancik, et al., eds., *Geschichte Band III Frühes Christentum* 405-15; **C. E. B. Cranfield**, " 'The Works of the Law' in the Epistle to the Romans," *JSNT* 43 (1991) 89-101; **M. Cranford**, "Abraham in Romans 4: The Father of All Who Believe," *NTS* 41 (1995) 71-88; **J. D. G. Dunn**, "Works of the Law and the Curse of the Law (Gal. 3.10-14)," *Jesus, Paul and the Law* 215-41; "Yet Once More — 'The Works of the Law': A Response," *JSNT* 46 (1992) 99-117; "4QMMT and Galatians," *NTS* 43 (1997) 147-53; **Finsterbusch**, *Thora* (§23 n. 1) ch. 4; **D. Flusser**, "Die Gesetzes werke in Qumran und bei Paulus," in Cancik, et al., eds., *Geschicht Band I Judentum* 395-403; **Hahn**, "Gesetzesverständnis" (§6 n. 1); **C. Heil**, *Die Ablehnung der Speisgebote durch Paulus* (Weinheim: Beltz Athenäum, 1994); **R. Heiligenthal**, *Werke als Zeichen* (WUNT 2.9; Tübingen: Mohr, 1983); **Hübner**, *Law* (§6 n. 1); **C. G. Kruse**, *Paul, the Law and Justification* (Leicester: Apollos, 1996); **D. J. Moo**, " 'Law,' 'Works of the Law,' and Legalism in Paul," *WTJ* 45 (1983) 73-100; **Räisänen**, *Paul* (§6 n. 1), particularly ch. 5; **Sanders**, *Law* (§6 n. 1); **Schreiner**, *Law* (§6 n. 1) chs. 2 and 4; **Thielman**, *Paul* (§6 n. 1); **Westerholm**, *Israel's Law* (§6 n. 1), particularly ch. 8.

§14.8 — **J. D. G. Dunn**, "Once More, *PISTIS CHRISTOU*," in D. M. Hay and E. E. Johnson, eds., *Pauline Theology* 4 (Atlanta: Scholars, 1997) 61-81; **R. A. Harrisville**, "*PISTIS CHRISTOU:* Witness of the Fathers," *NovT* 36 (1994) 233-41; **R. Hays**, *Faith of Jesus Christ;* "*PISTIS* and Pauline Christology: What Is at Stake?" in D. M. Hay and E. E. Johnson, eds., *Pauline Theology* 4 (Atlanta: Scholars, 1997) 35-60; **M. D. Hooker**, "Pistis Christou," *Adam* 165-86; **G. Howard**, "On the 'Faith of Christ,' " *HTR* 60 (1967) 459-65; **A. Hultgren**, "The Pistis Christou Formulations in Paul," *NovT* 22 (1980) 248-63; **L. T. Johnson**, "Romans 3.21-26 and the Faith of Jesus," *CBQ* 44 (1982) 77-90; **I. G. Wallis**, *The Faith of Jesus Christ in Early Christian Traditions* (SNTSMS 84; Cambridge: Cambridge University, 1995); **S. K. Williams**, "Again Pistis Christou," *CBQ* 49 (1987) 431-47.

2. P. Collinson, "The Late Medieval Church and Its Reformation (1400-1600)," in J. McManners, *The Oxford Illustrated History of Christianity* (New York: Oxford, 1990) 258-59. McGrath expresses the point in characteristic Protestant terms: "The Christian doctrine of justification . . . constitutes the real centre of the theological system of the Christian church. . . . There never was, and there never can be, any true Christian church without the doctrine of justification . . . the *articulus stantis et cadentis ecclesiae* (*Iustitia Dei* 1-2).

That man enjoys that acceptance with God called "justification," the beginning and end of salvation, not through his own moral effort even in the smallest and slightest degree but entirely and only through the loving mercy of God made available in the merits of Christ and of his saving death on the Cross. This was not a process of gradual ethical improvement but an instantaneous transaction, somewhat like a marriage, in which Christ the bridegroom takes to himself an impoverished and wretched harlot and confers upon her all the riches which are his. The key to this transaction was faith, defined as a total and trustful commitment of the self to God, and in itself not a human achievement but the pure gift of God. "Faith cometh by hearing and hearing by the word of God": *fides ex auditu.*

The consequences of Luther's rediscovery of justification by faith were dramatic, not just in theology and church but also in their social and political, their literary and cultural outworkings. By no means all in the interval since then will have agreed that justification was "the main doctrine of Christianity."[3] But in the twentieth century there can be little doubt that the theme has stood at the centre of Pauline theology, reinforced in particular by the fuller significance attached to it by two of the most important Protestant NT scholars. In Bultmann's case, for example, it provided the theological basis for his demythologizing programme.[4] And for Ernst Käsemann, "justification by faith" was the "canon within the canon," the primary test by which we may discern the spirits and recognize the word of God today.[5] A mark of ecumenical rapprochement in the scond half of the century, in biblical scholarship at least, is the degree to which the importance of justification by faith is recognized by Catholic as well as Protestant.[6]

The negative side of this emphasis was an unfortunate strain of anti-Judaism. Paul's teaching on justification was seen as a reaction against and in opposition to Judaism. As Luther had rejected a medieval church which

3. *Apology of the Augsburg Confession* (1531) 4.2, cited by Reumann, *Righteousness* 3.

4. R. Bultmann, in H. W. Bartsch, ed., *Kerygma and Myth* (London: SPCK, 1957) 210-11; Bultmann, *Jesus Christ and Mythology* (New York: Scribner, 1958 = London: SCM, 1960) 70.

5. E. Käsemann, *Das Neue Testament als Kanon* (Göttingen: Vandenhoeck, 1970) 405.

6. E.g., H. Küng, *Justification* (London: Burns and Oates, 1964); Kertelge, *"Rechtfertigung";* Reumann, *Righteousness;* the Lutheran-Roman Catholic 1983 Consultation agreement in *Justification by Faith* (Minneapolis: Augsburg, 1985); and the agreed statement by the second Anglican–Roman Catholic International Commission, *Salvation and the Church* (Anglican Consultative Council and the Secretariat for Promoting Christian Unity, 1987).

offered salvation by merit and good works, the same, it was assumed, was true of Paul in relation to the Judaism of his day.[7] Judaism was taken to have been the antithesis to emerging Christianity: for Paul to react as he did, it must have been a degenerate religion, legalistic, making salvation dependent on human effort, and self-satisfied with the results. The assumption was reinforced at the beginning of the modern period of NT study as Judaism and Christianity were cast in still sharper antithesis. According to F. C. Baur, commenting on Galatians, "the essential principle of Christianity first attained a decided place in its struggle with Judaism."[8] And for most of the present century Judaism still functioned as the negative foil for Paul's positive theology. Bultmann's characterization of Paul's polemic against "boasting" as directed against the Jew who puts confidence in himself and in what he achieves[9] has continued to influence two generations of Pauline scholarship (and preaching).[10]

In all this time the discussion of justification by faith in Christian theology has still been principally determined by the issues posed by the Reformation and the consequent debate between Catholic and Protestant. The principal exegetical debates have been whether the verb "justify" meant "*make* righteous" (Catholic) or "*reckon as* righteous" (Protestant), whether "justified" denoted transformation or status,[11] and whether "the righteousness of God" was subjective genitive (righteousness as a property or activity of God) or objective genitive ("righteousness as a gift bestowed by God").[12]

---

7. Luther made an explicit link: the church was tarnished with "Jewish legalism"; the Catholics' "rules and regulations remind me of the Jews, and actually very much was borrowed from the Jews"; on faith and works, the doctrine of the church was a variation of the Jewish error that mere acts can win favour in God's sight (cited by M. Saperstein, *Moments of Crisis in Jewish-Christian Relations* [London: SCM/Philadelphia: TPI, 1989] 30).

8. Baur, *Paul* 1.267.

9. Bultmann, *Theology* 1.243; earlier, "Romans 7 and the Anthropology of Paul" (1932), *Existence and Faith* (New York: Meridian, 1960 = London: Collins, 1964) 173-85 (here 178-79). But note Seifrid's clarification of Bultmann's position (*Justification* 33).

10. See, e.g., those referred to in my *Romans* 185; and further G. F. Moore, "Christian Writers on Judaism," *HTR* 14 (1922) 197-254; C. Klein, *Anti-Judaism in Christian Theology* (London: SPCK/Philadelphia: Fortress, 1978); Boyarin, *Radical Jew* 209-19.

11. See, e.g., Fitzmyer, *Paul* 61. Ziesler's analysis revolves around this question (*Meaning*).

12. This debate crosses confessional lines (see the brief surveys in Reumann, *Righteousness* 66, and Fitzmyer, *Romans* 258-63); Fitzmyer himself presses for the subjective sense (*Romans* 105-7). In the modern period the objective genitive has been maintained with greatest force — a righteousness which comes from God (Rom. 10.3; Phil. 3.9). See, e.g., Bultmann, *Theology* 1.285; Ridderbos, *Paul* 163; Cranfield, *Romans* 96-99; Strecker, *Theologie* 160-63. Käsemann's influential redefinition of "the righteousness of

But behind the Catholic-Protestant debate, and obscured by it, was the more fundamental issue of Christianity's relation to Judaism, in particular the relation of Paul's gospel and theology to his ancestral religion. Two factors made it impossible for that situation to persist. One was Vatican II, and in effect the removal of most of the old Catholic-Protestant agenda as no longer at issue. The other was the Holocaust and its continuing reverberations in Christian theology. If post-Vatican II theology could no longer simply restate the old debate between Protestant and Catholic in the traditional terms, post-Holocaust theology could no longer stomach the denigration of historic Judaism which had been the dark-side-of-the-moon corollary to the Christian doctrine of justification.

Twenty years ago the picture began to change, and Pauline studies, which had been in something of a trough, regained new vitality. This was principally due to "the new perspective" provided by E. P. Sanders.[13] He exposed the element of caricature (and worse) in much Protestant portrayal of Second Temple Judaism more effectively than any previous protests.[14] He demonstrated that Judaism has always been first and foremost a religion of grace, with human obedience understood as response to that grace. The covenant had been given by divine initiative, and the law provided the framework for life within the covenant. Doing the law was a means of staying in the covenant, not of getting into it in the first place. For Sanders a key descriptive phrase for Judaism's "pattern of religion" was "covenantal nomism." He defined it thus:[15]

> covenantal nomism is the view that one's place in God's plan is established on the basis of the covenant and that the covenant requires as the proper response of man his obedience to its commandments, while providing means of atonement for transgression. . . . *Obedience maintains one's*

God" as a gift which has "the character of power" ("Paul knows no gift of God which does not convey both the obligation and the capacity to serve" and which is "at any time separable from its Giver") was a bold attempt to transcend debates which had become rather sterile ("Righteousness," here 170, 174); followed, e.g., by Bornkamm, *Paul* 147; Kümmel, *Theology* 197-98; and Hübner, *Law* 130-34.

13. Sanders, *Paul and Palestinian Judaism*. See my "The New Perspective on Paul" (Manson Memorial Lecture, 1982), *Jesus, Paul and the Law* ch. 7.

14. Unfortunately his overtly polemical style has not helped many of his readers to hear what he has been saying.

15. Sanders, *Paul and Palestinian Judaism* 75, 420, 544. Worth noting is the fact that J. Neusner, though fiercely critical of Sanders' methodology, nevertheless accepted Sanders' understanding of Judaism in terms of "covenantal nomism" as valid ("Comparing Judaisms," *History of Religions* 18 [1978-79] 177-91), and that despite some criticism Sanders feels justified in continuing to regard the phrase as an appropriate summary of Jewish covenant theology (*Judaism* 262-78, 377-78, 415-17).

position in the covenant, but it does not earn God's grace as such. . . .
Righteousness in Judaism is a term which implies the *maintenance of status* among the group of the elect.

Not least among the values of Sanders's work is that it allowed the fundamental problem of the relation of Christianity to Judaism and of Paul's theology to his Jewish heritage to reemerge on centre stage. The Protestant Paul had always been a puzzle to Jewish scholars who tried to take him seriously,[16] and equally to those from the Christian side who immersed themselves in Jewish tradition.[17] The Judaism which NT scholarship posed as the foil to Paul's theology was not one they recognized. The best solution they could think of was that Paul must have been reacting against a form of Judaism of which no real trace now remains, except in his letters — a diaspora Judaism, different from Palestinian Judaism.[18] Variations of this hypothesis (that Paul was reacting against some form of Judaism which taught justification by good works) continue to be offered by those who find the evidence of Paul's own polemic to be explicable in no other terms.[19] Sanders himself did not offer much help here, since in the light of the new perspective on Second Temple Judaism he could only see an incoherent and inconsistent Paul.[20]

An alternative approach was pioneered by those who followed up the other aspect of Baur's thesis: that Christianity was shaped by the conflict between Jewish and Gentile Christianity, that is, by the conflict of Jewish and

16. See S. Schechter, Schoeps, and S. Sandmel, cited by Sanders, *Paul and Palestinian Judaism* 4-8.

17. Mention should be made particularly of Moore, *Judaism* 3.151 (cited in my *Romans* 206-7); see also R. T. Herford, *Judaism in the New Testament Period* (London: Lindsey, 1928); J. Parkes, *The Conflict of the Church and the Synagogue: A Study in the Origins of Antisemitism* (London: Soncino, 1934).

18. The point is argued differently by Montefiore, *Judaism and St. Paul* 81-82, 92-100, and Schoeps, *Paul* 27-32, 213 ("a Diaspora Jew who had become alienated from the faith-ideas of the fathers" — 262). Westerholm, *Israel's Law* 34-46, gives a good summary of their views.

19. E.g., Westerholm, *Israel's Law* ch. 8, particularly 148; "the notion of it [the Jewish religion of Paul's day] as perverted anthropocentric legalism turns out to be a vicious caricature" (Räisänen, *Paul* 167-68, 188; but note also 168 n. 39); Laato, *Paulus* ch. 5 (extending his overdrawn contrast between "Jewish optimism" and "Pauline pessimism"); Schreiner, *Law* ch. 4, who attempts to argue the difficult "have your cake and eat it" thesis that "although the term *works of law* does not denote legalism, Paul condemns legalism when he says righteousness is not by works of law" (94). Contrast Beker: "The common portrayal of Jews anxiously striving for merits in order to obtain credit with God is simply false, for it confuses God's confirmation of faithful behavior with egocentric striving and a perverted conception of God and his righteousness" (*Paul* 268).

20. This was my own early criticism of Sanders ("New Perspective," *Jesus, Paul and the Law* 202).

Gentile partisans, but within Christianity. Again and again this point has had to be repeated in exegesis particularly of Galatians: that Paul was not arguing against Jews as such or Judaism as such but against other Christian (Jewish) missionaries.[21] The underlying issue is still the same: how the gospel relates to Israel's heritage in terms of continuity and discontinuity. But the slant of the discussion and its implications are significantly different.

Where this came to bear on justification by faith was the persistent, but minority, view through the century that the doctrine of justification by faith was formulated within and as a result of the early mission to Gentiles. It was a polemical doctrine, hammered out in the face of Jewish Christian objections to that mission as law-free and not requiring circumcision. "Justification by faith" was Paul's answer to the question: How is it that Gentiles can be equally acceptable to God as Jews?[22] "The new perspective on Paul," by forcing a reassessment of what Paul was reacting against, has given fresh impetus to this line of inquiry. What was at issue between Paul and "those of the circumcision"? Can we continue to speak in terms of Jewish boasting in self-achieved merit? What is it about "works of the law" to which Paul objects so strenuously?[23]

We enter, then, upon one of the most vigorous debates in current NT studies, all the more important because of its central significance for formulating the gospel, testing theology, and reappraising Christianity's Jewish roots and heritage. The doctrine of justification by faith, which has proved so luminous over four centuries of Protestant theology in particular, has the capacity to provide fresh illumination in the present (and no doubt future) reassessments of Paul's theology.

§14.2 The righteousness of God

For the theology of Paul as expressed particularly in Romans, this phrase, "the righteousness of God," is the obvious place to start. For it is just this phrase which provides the focus for the thematic statement defining his gospel in Rom. 1.16-17:

> [16]For I am not ashamed of the gospel, since it is the power of God for salvation to all who believe, Jew first but also Gentile. [17]For the righteous-

21. A point of consensus in Dunn, ed., *Paul and the Mosaic Law* 310.
22. Particularly Wrede, *Paul* 122-28; Stendahl, *Paul* 1-7; Howard, *Paul* ch. 3.
23. These are issues which have been at the centre of my own contribution to the current debate — particularly "Works," "Yet Once More," and "Justice." There have been numerous reviews of the debate occasioned by "the new perspective"; Thielman, *Paul* ch. 1, is one of the most recent and most useful.

ness of God is being revealed in it from faith to faith — as it is written,
"He who is righteous by faith shall live."

That Paul's use of the phrase here is not accidental is confirmed by the
thematic repetition of it throughout the crucial argument in Rom. 3.21-26.
In 3.21 he resumes the main thrust of his exposition by calling it to the fore:
"But now, apart from the law, the righteousness of God has been revealed. . . ." And it is the theme of God's righteousness which dominates
the rest of that key paragraph (3.22, 25, 26). Elsewhere Paul makes less use
of the phrase. But its recurrence at key points in the statement of his gospel
reaffirms its importance for Paul's theology.[24] And the wider use of
dikaiosynē ("righteousness") and *dikaioō* ("justify") in the Pauline corpus
confirms the centrality of the concept for Paul.[25] But what is the relation of
"righteousness" to "justification"?

As is well known, discussion of the subject suffers from some termino-
logical problems. I refer in part to the fact that English uses two different
words, "justify" and "righteousness," to translate what are cognate terms in
Greek *(dikaioō, dikaiosynē)*, thus causing some unavoidable confusion for
those who think in English.[26] More to the theological point, "righteousness"
is a good example of a term whose meaning is determined more by its Hebrew
background than by its Greek form. The point is that the underlying Hebrew
thought in both cases is different from the Greek.

In the typical Greek worldview, "righteousness" is an idea or ideal
against which the individual and individual action can be measured. Contemporary English usage reflects this ancient mind-set when it continues to
use such expressions as "Justice must be satisfied." In contrast, in Hebrew
thought "righteousness" is a more relational concept — "righteousness" as
the meeting of obligations laid upon the individual by the relationship of
which he or she is part.[27] A classic example is 1 Sam. 24.17: King Saul was

---

24. Rom. 10.3; 2 Cor. 5.21; Phil. 3.9.

25.	Paul	Romans	NT as whole
dikaiosynē	57	33	91
dikaioō	27	15	39
dikaiōma ("requirement, righteous deed")	5	5	10
dikaiōsis ("justification")	2	2	2
dikaiokrisia ("righteous judgment")	1	1	1

26. The issue is nicely pointed by Sanders, *Paul* 44-47; see also Fitzmyer, *Romans*
258.

27. See Schrenk, *TDNT* 2.195; G. von Rad, *Old Testament Theology* 1 (Edinburgh:
Oliver and Boyd, 1962) 370-76; Bultmann, *Theology* 1.272, 277; Conzelmann, *Outline*
216; E. R. Achtemeier, "Righteousness in the OT," *IDB* 4.80-85; Kertelge, *"Rechtfertigung"* 38-43; Ziesler, *Righteousness* 34-43; Goppelt, *Theology* 2.138; McGrath, *Iustitia
Dei* 8. The credit for realigning the debate on "righteousness" to its Hebrew background,

unrighteous in that he failed in his duty as king to his subject; David was more righteous because he refused to lift his hand in violence against the Lord's anointed. That is, in a relationship of mutual obligation, David was to be reckoned more righteous than Saul because he fulfilled his obligation to Saul, whereas Saul failed in his obligation to David.[28] This recognition that the thought world which comes to expression in the English term ("justification") is through and through Hebraic/biblical/Jewish in character is a key factor in gaining a secure hold on Paul's teaching on justification. Despite formal recognition of the relational character of Hebrew "righteousness," the ramifications of the insight have been too little appreciated in much discussion of Paul's teaching.

The relevance of this observation begins to become clear when we recall Paul's thematic statement about justification, in Rom. 1.16-17, as "the righteousness of God . . . from faith to faith." For the righteousness of God, in line with the understanding of "righteousness" above, denotes God's fulfilment of the obligations he took upon himself in creating humankind and particularly in the calling of Abraham and the choosing of Israel to be his people. Fundamental to this conception of God's righteousness, therefore, is the recognition of the prior initiative of God, both in creation and in election.[29] As Deuteronomy repeatedly points out, it was nothing that Israel was or had done which caused God to choose them as his people, to enter into covenant with them; it was only his love for them and his loyalty to the oath which he had promised to the fathers.[30] It should be equally evident why God's *righteousness* could be understood as God's *faithfulness* to his people.[31] For his righteousness was simply the fulfilment of his covenant obligation as Israel's God in delivering, saving, and vindicating Israel, despite Israel's own failure.[32] The Qumran covenanter gave voice to a

---

with the resulting emphasis on relationship, is rightly to be given to Cremer, *Rechtfertigungslehre.* The point first came home to me many years ago in reading Paul Achtemeier's article on "Righteousness in the NT," *IDB* 4.91-99.

28. Similarly Judah's verdict on his relationship with Tamar (Gen. 38.26).

29. For the emphasis on God's righteousness as Creator see particularly Müller, *Gerechtigkeit,* and Stuhlmacher, *Gerechtigkeit* 228-36; also Reumann, *Righteousness* 13-14, 20.

30. Deut. 4.32-40; 6.10-12, 20-23; 7.6-8, etc.

31. See also above §2.5 and two paragraphs below.

32. Particularly in the Psalms (e.g., Pss. 51.14; 65.5; 71.15) and second Isaiah (Isa. 46.13; 51.5-8; 62.1-2). In Pss. 51.14 and 65.5 NRSV translates *tsedhaqah* as "deliverance"; in the others God's "righteousness" parallels his "salvation"; and in Isa. 62.2 NRSV translates *tsedhaqah* as "vindication." Elsewhere, e.g., in Mic. 6.5 and 7.9 NRSV translates God's *tsedhaqah* as his "saving acts" and his "vindication." See further BDB, *tsedhaqah* 2 and 6a. Stuhlmacher notes particularly Hos. 11.8-9 (*Theologie* 331). Contrast Ridderbos, *Paul* 164, who sees "an absolute antithesis between the Pauline and the synagogical

personal consciousness of this grace in moving terms which would no doubt
have resonated with Paul (1QS 11.11-15):

> As for me, if [12]I stumble, the mercies of God shall be my eternal salvation.
> If I stagger because of the sin of the flesh, my justification *(mshpti)* shall
> be by the righteousness of God which endures for ever. [13]. . . He will draw
> me near by his grace, and by his mercy will he bring [14]my justification
> *(mshpti)*. He will judge me in the righteousness of his truth and in the
> greatness of his goodness he will pardon *(ykipper)* all my sins. Through
> his righteousness he will cleanse me of all the uncleanness of [15]man and
> of the sins of the children of men (Vermes).

The illumination which this background sheds on Paul's usage is immediate. It explains why he could simply announce his theme as "the revelation of the righteousness of God" (Rom. 1.16-17) without further ado. He
was able to assume that "the righteousness of God" was "the power of God
for salvation," and that even an unknown church would recognize this effective equation without further explanation. Only so would his language have
made sense (particularly in Rome), since otherwise *dikaiosynē* was a purely
legal concept ("justice").[33] Only so could he have set "the righteousness of
God" evidently in some contrast with "the wrath of God" (1.18).[34] Only so
could he elaborate "the righteousness of God" so briefly in 3.21-26 as expressed in God's "forbearance," showing God to be not only "just" but also
"the one who justifies the one who believes in Jesus" (3.26). That God's
righteousness here (as in 2 Cor. 5.21) consists in his provision of sacrifice for
sin could likewise be assumed.[35] For Gentile as well as Jew in the Roman

---

doctrine of justification," the latter "not to be spoken of other than in a future-eschatological
sense," and only the former "a present reality already realized in Christ." In view of the
documentation just cited, the quest for technical usage of the complete phrase as such is
unnecessary if not misguided; see particularly Seifrid, *Justification* 99-108, in relation to
Käsemann's claim that Paul took up the phrase as a t.t.

33. LSJ, *dikaiosynē*. In view of the insistence on the forensic or forensic-
eschatological force of the term (particularly Bultmann, *Theology* 1.273, 276, and
Ridderbos, *Paul* 163), the covenantal context within which the concept of God's
righteousness is used needs to be given equal if not more stress.

34. Strictly speaking, "God's righteousness" includes God's wrath, since wrath is
the appropriate response to human failure to acknowledge God (see above §§2.4 and 4.4).
But God's righteousness was seldom used in this way in the OT (Stuhlmacher, *Theologie*
327-29), and it is the character of God's righteousness as "saving righteousness" which
is clearly to the fore in 1.17. See further, e.g., Reumann, *Righteousness* 68.

35. The implication of 3.25-26 is that Jesus' sacrificial death demonstrates both
God's justice, in that he deals with sin (in the destruction of the sin-embodying life of the
sacrifice), and also his (saving) righteousness, in that he justifies the sinner; see further
above §§9.2-3. Note the integration of judicial and sacrificial metaphors.

congregations, Paul could take it for granted that "the righteousness of God" would be understood as God's action on behalf of human beings. In so doing he drew directly upon Christianity's heritage of Israel's covenant faith.

It should also be clearer how one of Paul's principal secondary themes emerges within Romans. For as we noted earlier, Paul was concerned in this letter to explain and vindicate the faithfulness of God.[36] But as we have now also seen, "the righteousness of God" overlaps with that of God's faithfulness to Israel — righteousness as remaining true to his obligation to the people he had chosen as his own. Hence the close link between God's "faithfulness," God's "truth," and God's "righteousness" in Rom. 3.3-7. Likewise the final reprise of the theme in 9.30–10.13, as central to his argument in chs. 9–11 that God's word has not failed (9.6) with regard to Israel (11.25-32). The heart of Paul's theology of justification was the dynamic interaction between "the righteousness of God" as God's saving action for *all* who believe and "the righteousness of God" as God's faithfulness to *Israel,* his chosen people.

The recognition of the essentially relational character of Paul's understanding of justification also speaks with some immediacy to the traditional debates of post-Reformation theology. In fact, it largely undercuts them and leaves much of the dispute pointless. The debate on whether "the righteousness of God" was subjective or objective genitive, "an activity of God" or "a gift bestowed by God," can too easily become another piece of either-or exegesis.[37] For the dynamic of relationship simply refuses to conform to such analysis. In contrast, Paul took it for granted that God's righteousness was to be understood as God's activity in drawing individuals into and sustaining them within the relationship, as "the power of God for salvation."

The other dispute, as already noted, was whether the verb *dikaioō* means "*make* righteous" or "*reckon as* righteous." But once again the basic idea assumed by Paul was of a relationship in which God acts on behalf of his human partner, first in calling Israel into and then in sustaining Israel in its covenant with him. So once again the answer is not one or the other but both. The covenant God counts the covenant partner as still in partnership, despite the latter's continued failure. But the covenant partner could hardly fail to be transformed by a living relationship with the life-giving God.[38]

Here again the clarification and displacement of these older issues allows the more pressing issue to emerge more fully into the light. That is the issue of

36. See above §2.5.

37. See above n. 12. Cf. the mediating "genitive of authorship" — righteousness which goes forth from God" (Reumann, *Righteousness* 66). Seifrid's discussion is somewhat confusing (*Justification* 214-18). Stuhlmacher properly sees "the righteousness from God" in Phil. 3.9 as "a saving demonstration of God's righteousness going out from God" (*Theologie* 337).

38. Cf. Barrett, *Paul* 99; Strecker, *Theologie* 164-66. See also below §24.8.

whether Paul's theology of justification constituted a decisive rebuttal and disowning of Judaism. The progress we have so far made on that issue can be summed up in three points. First, Paul's teaching on justification was drawn immediately from the scriptural understanding of God's righteousness outlined above. That the language of Romans stems directly from such OT usage is well appreciated and is not in dispute.[39] Second, and fundamental to Jewish self-understanding and covenant theology, was the recognition and affirmation that Israel's standing before God was due entirely to the initiative of divine grace. The same point is implicit in a covenantal system which provided atonement for sin through repentance and sacrifice. This point is gaining ground in the current discussion of Paul's theology, but it has not yet gained complete acceptance.[40] Third, it should be equally clear from where Paul derived his emphasis on the initiative of divine grace within his teaching on justification. That is to say, it did not first emerge as a reaction against Paul's Pharisaic past or in response to his "judaizing" oppponents. In its essence it was simply a restatement of the first principles of his own ancestral faith. This third point is the most controversial and carries over into the next phase of the discussion.

From the line of exposition developed in §14.2 a question emerges crying out for an answer. If Paul's theology of justification was so Hebraic in character, what was he reacting against in his polemical formulation of the teaching? The more we stress the continuity between Paul's teaching on justification and his Jewish heritage, the more pressing becomes the issue: why then his classic rebuttal of "justification by works" in favour of "justification by faith"? This, we recall, is how he sums up his gospel at key points in his letters both to Rome and Galatia:

> By works of the law shall no flesh be justified before him, for through the law comes the knowledge of sin. . . . We reckon that a person is justified by faith, apart from works of the law (Rom. 3.20, 28).

> Knowing that no human being is justified by works of the law but only through faith in Jesus Christ, we have believed in Christ Jesus, in order that we might be justified by faith in Christ and not by works of the law, because by works of the law shall no flesh be justified (Gal. 2.16).

Here we find ourselves once again back into the issue of Paul and the law.[41] And since so many have assumed that the answer to the above questions lies

---

39. In recent studies see particularly Williams, "Righteousness" 260-63; see also my *Romans* 40-42.

40. For an example of the older view of Judaism's "calculus of merits" see Whiteley, *Theology* 163-64.

41. For the first part of the analysis see above §6.

in Paul's conversion, that is where we will have to pick up the debate.[42] Twice in defending his own gospel Paul himself found it necessary to begin at that point.[43]

§14.3 The impact of Paul's conversion

The most influential interpretation of Paul's conversion is that it transformed not simply his view of Jesus but also his view of the law. He converted from a zealous practitioner of the law to someone who warned his Gentile converts vehemently against the law (Gal. 5.1-12). We need only think of Paul's description of what he had been — "exceedingly zealous for my ancestral traditions" (Gal. 1.14), "so far as righteousness (with)in the law was concerned, blameless" (Phil. 3.6) — and of his turnaround in counting "loss" what he had previously counted "gain" (3.7) — for the point to be clear. We recall also his assertion that (presumably in his conversion) "I through the law died to the law that I might live to God" (Gal. 2.21). If a single text has summed up a strong consensus position at this point, it is Rom. 10.4: what Paul concluded from his Damascus road encounter was that "Christ is the end of the law."[44]

Usually as part of the argument it is maintained that Paul persecuted the Hellenists because they had already abandoned the law. This assumes, as I do, that Paul's persecution was directed principally against fellow diaspora rooted, Greek-speaking Jews who had become baptized disciples of Messiah Jesus and to whom Stephen had provided leadership.[45] The exegetical grounding is then provided by Phil. 3.6 — "as to zeal a persecutor of the church" — since "zeal" is most naturally understood as "zeal for the law."[46] The argument then proceeds smoothly: Paul was converted to the position he had persecuted; he abandoned the law like those he had persecuted. If Paul's rationale is sought it can be readily guessed at: the law had approved the

---

42. See particularly Kim, *Origin* (§7 n. 1); Seifrid, *Justification* ch. 3.

43. Gal. 1.13-16; Phil. 3.3-9.

44. See above §7 n. 83.

45. On the Hellenists see particularly Hengel, *Between Jesus and Paul* 1-29; *Pre-Christian Paul* 68-79. C. C. Hill, *Hellenists and Hebrews: Reappraising Divisions within the Earliest Church* (Minneapolis: Fortress, 1992), attempts a rebuttal of this view, but ignores or plays down too many of the cumulative arguments behind it. Contrast, e.g., S. G. Wilson, *The Gentiles and the Gentile Mission in Luke-Acts* (SNTSMS 23; Cambridge: Cambridge University, 1973) ch. 5.

46. Cf. Gal. 1.14 — "being exceedingly zealous for my ancestral traditions"; Acts 21.20 — "zealots for the law." See, e.g., O''Brien, *Philippians* 375-76 and those cited by him.

punishment of Jesus by death; but the Damascus road encounter revealed to Paul that God had vindicated this Jesus; therefore the law is a fool[47] and should now be discarded.[48] "Christ is the end of the law!"

The interpretation is obviously a strong one, and we need not discuss all its elements here. It is questionable, for example, whether the little we know of the Hellenists actually does support the view that they had broken with the law.[49] And any thesis to the effect that Paul regarded Christ as "the end of the law" must take account of the remarkably positive view of the law Paul continued to maintain in his letters.[50] But the more pressing question at this point is whether the interpretation gives sufficient account of Paul's other most explicit testimony to the before and after of his conversion — Gal. 1.13-16, which in fact matches the details of the more commonly referred to Phil. 3.3-6 in a significant measure. Four features of the former passage are worthy of note.[51]

a) Paul clearly regarded his conversion as a turning from his "way of life previously in Judaism" (Gal. 1.13). It is insufficiently appreciated that the use of the term "Judaism" here (and in v. 14) is highly distinctive. We know of only a handful of uses of the term prior to this, and the two occurrences in these verses are the only times the term appears in the NT. The earlier uses also give us some flavour of the term. For it first appears in 2 Maccabees, and in each case it denotes the national religion of Judea, "Judaism," presented as a rallying point for resistance to the Syrians and for maintenance of national identity as the covenant people of the Lord.[52] Alternatively expressed, "Judaism" was coined as a title to express opposition to "Hellenism" (2 Macc. 4.13).[53]

---

47. I originally wrote "the law is an ass," but then realized that the allusion to the words of Mr. Bumble in *Oliver Twist* was likely to be missed.

48. See, e.g., those cited by Räisänen, *Paul* 249 n. 112, and Eckstein, *Verheißung* 162-63.

49. See, e.g., H. Räisänen, "The 'Hellenists': A Bridge between Jesus and Paul?" *Jesus, Paul and Torah* 177; C. K. Barrett, *Acts 1–14* (ICC; Edinburgh: Clark, 1994) 337-38.

50. See, e.g., Rom. 3.31; 8.4; 1 Cor. 7.19; Gal. 5.14. See further below §§23.3-5.

51. In what follows I draw on my "Paul's Conversion" (§7 n. 1).

52. 2 Macc. 2.21 ("fought bravely on behalf of Judaism"); 8.1 ("enlisted those who had remained within Judaism"); 14.38 (the martyr Razis "had been accused of Judaism and had risked body and soul with all earnestness on behalf of Judaism"); also *4 Macc.* 4.26. See also S. J. D. Cohen, "Ioudaios: 'Judean' and 'Jew' in Susanna, First Maccabees, and Second Maccabees," in Cancik, et al., eds., *Geschichte Band I Judentum* 211-20 (here 219).

53. The only other occurrence of "Judaism" which is probably from our period is a funerary inscription from Italy which praises a woman "who lived a gracious life in(side) Judaism" (*CIJ* 537) — the same phrase (*en tō Ioudaismō,* "within Judaism") which we find also in 2 Macc. 8.1 and Gal. 1.13-14.

In other words, the term "Judaism" seems to have been coined as a means of giving focus to the determination of the Maccabean patriots to defend the distinctive national identity given them by their ancestral religion. It was not simply a neutral description of "the religion of the Jews," as we might wish to use it today.[54] From its earliest usage it carried overtones of a religious identity shaped and hardened in the fires of persecution, of a religion which identified itself by its determination to maintain its distinctiveness and to remain free from the corruption of other religions and peoples. It is wholly understandable that this confrontation between Judaism and Hellenism came to particular focus in key test cases, distinctively Jewish laws and traditions which the Syrians were determined to suppress and which therefore became rallying points for the loyalists and the make-or-break points at which the confrontation would be won or lost. In 2 Maccabees 6 these are indicated in sequence as the temple and therefore the traditional feasts, circumcision, and eating swine's flesh.[55]

An important point emerges from this: "Judaism" defined itself over against the wider Hellenism, including Hellenizing Jews. In several of these references there is expressed a consciousness of being "within Judaism" as a kind of protected or fenced-off area and of looking out from within. This ties in very closely with what we have already noted about the role of the law in relation to Israel (§6.4). The self-understanding is rather close to what we find in *Ep. Arist.* 139, 142:

> In his wisdom the legislator [Moses] . . . surrounded us with unbroken palisades and iron walls to prevent our mixing with any of the other peoples in any matter. . . . To prevent our being perverted by contact with others or by mixing with bad influences, he hedged us in on all sides with strict observances connected with meat and drink . . . after the manner of the Law.

In other words, "Judaism," as we find it in our sources, defined itself by separating itself from the wider world and understood the Torah in part at least as reinforcing and protecting that separateness.

If it is proper to speak of Paul converting from "Judaism," this was the Judaism he had in mind.

In Phil. 3.3-6 the corresponding emphasis is Paul's previous "confidence in the flesh," that is, his physical and ethnic identity as a Jew. This he spells out

---

54. I have reflected elsewhere on the difficulty of correlating our contemporary sociological use of "Judaism" (or "Judaisms") with first century CE usage; see my "Judaism in the Land of Israel in the First Century," in J. Neusner, ed., *Judaism in Late Antiquity, Part 2: Historical Syntheses* (Leiden: Brill, 1995) 229-61.

55. Cf. particularly 1 Macc. 1.60-63, quoted below §14.4.

more or less explicitly in terms of his eighth-day circumcision, his racial identity as an Israelite, his tribal identity as a Benjaminite, and the fact that he determinedly retained Hebrew culture (Aramaic language) even though he was (by implication) brought up in the Greek-speaking diaspora (3.5). These were four identifying features which he had previously valued but which now counted as of no value in comparison with his new knowledge of Christ (3.7-8).

b) Paul's description of his "way of life in Judaism" is also striking. "I progressed in Judaism beyond many of my contemporaries among the people, being exceedingly zealous for my ancestral traditions" (Gal. 1.14). When we correlate this with the fifth identifying marker in his self-description in Phil. 3.5-6 ("as to the law, a Pharisee . . . as to righteousness within the law, blameless"), we catch an unmistakable whiff of the factionalism of late Second Temple Judaism. For the post-Maccabean period was marked by bitter disputes among the heirs of the Maccabees, not least over the proper understanding of the Torah and particularly over purity halakhah and the calendar. This was the period in which both the Pharisees and the Essenes emerged, and both they and the literature of the time clearly indicate strongly partisan claims to maintain Torah faithfulness and equally fierce attacks on other groups.[56] The Pharisees in particular evidently stood out by their desire to separate themselves, that is, presumably, from their less faithful contemporaries,[57] and by their desire to keep the law with scrupulous accuracy and exactness *(akribeia).*[58]

Similarly when Paul speaks of his "blameless" righteousness (Phil. 3.6), he presumably is recalling the previous character of his life as lived within the terms of Israel's covenant with God. The force of the word *amemptos* ("blameless") is not wholly clear. But it is unlikely that Paul was claiming to have been sinless or never to have transgressed the law.[59] The few most relevant usages elsewhere indicate, rather, one who, like Job, held faithful to God,[60] one who stood out from the surrounding wickedness,[61] one who kept

56. See further my "Pharisees, Sinners and Jesus," *Jesus, Paul and the Law* 61-88 (here 71-77); "Jesus and Factionalism in Early Judaism," in J. H. Charlesworth, ed., *Jesus and Hillel* (Minneapolis: Fortress, 1997), and below §§14.4-5 (particularly n. 101), referring *inter alia* to *1 Enoch* 1–5, CD, 1QpHab, *Jubilees, Psalms of Solomon,* and the *Testament of Moses.*

57. "Pharisee" is generally understood to have begun as a nickname meaning "separatist"; see above §8 n. 44 and below §§14.4-5. Winninge is confident in identifying the *Psalms of Solomon* as Pharisaic *(Sinners* 170-80).

58. This is a term used by both Josephus and Acts to describe the Pharisees (Josephus, *War* 1.108-9; 2.162; *Life* 191; *Ant.* 20.200-201; Acts 22.3; 26.5).

59. The point is not usually clearly seen or stated; but see now O'Brien, *Philippians* 380; Seifrid, *Justification* 174; Thielman, *Paul* 154-55; see also n. 109 below.

60. Job 1.1, 8; 2.3.

61. Wis. 10.5, 15; 18.21.

company with the faithful,[62] one who "walked in the commandments and regulations of the Lord" (Luke 1.6). Such living within the terms of the covenant included, of course, the provision of atonement for sin through repentance and sacrifice.[63] But, given that qualification, Paul could recall his confidence in his covenant righteousness. Particularly as a Pharisee he would have endeavoured to live at a level of law-keeping which "separated" him from most of his fellow Israelites. That extra degree of faithfulness would have ensured that in the terms of covenant obligation ("righteousness") he was "without reproach."

Here again, then, we can gain some idea of what Paul converted from — from measuring righteousness primarily in terms of covenant distinctiveness, and from a competitive practice within Judaism which sought to outdo other Jews in the degree and quality of its Torah-keeping. Particularly striking is the fact that in the same breath (Gal. 1.13-14) Paul voices consciousness of separation both *of* Judaism *from the other nations* and *within* Judaism *from other Jews*.

c) A surprisingly neglected feature of both Paul's testimonies to his conversion is his use of the term "zeal." Gal. 1.14 — "I progressed in Judaism beyond many of my contemporaries among my people, being exceedingly zealous *(zēlōtēs)* for my ancestral traditions"; Phil. 3.6 — "as to the law a Pharisee, as to zeal *(zēlos)* a persecutor of the church."[64] The double usage can hardly be coincidental. "Zeal" was evidently a feature of being "in Judaism," of the competitive factionalism which marked Second Temple Judaism after the Maccabees (Gal. 1.14), of the confidence in Jewish identity which Paul expresses in Phil. 3.4-6.

In this sense we may speak of Jewish zeal as the echo of or response to divine zeal. For deeply rooted in Israel's consciousness of election was the recognition that their God was himself a "zealot" *(zēlōtēs)*. That Yahweh is "a jealous God" is firmly stated in Israel's foundation documents, typically in the form, "you shall not worship other gods, for I the LORD your God am a jealous God."[65] In each case the point being made is that Israel should therefore abstain from idolatry or following other gods. God's "zeal" was expressed in his choice of Israel to be his own, and the conclusion drawn was that Israel should maintain the exclusiveness of its devotion to Yahweh and the distinctiveness of its religion in the face of other nations and religions

62. Pss. 1.1; 101.2 (LXX v.l.).

63. Howard, *Paul* 53. See further §14.5c below.

64. Note also Rom. 10.2; see below §14.6b.

65. Exod. 20.5; 34.14; Deut. 4.24; 5.9; 6.15 — the word is the same (jealous/zealous) in both Hebrew and Greek. For what follows cf. particularly M. Hengel, *The Zealots: Investigations into the Jewish Freedom Movement in the Period from Herod I until 70 A.D.* (1961, ²1976; ET Edinburgh: Clark, 1989) 146-228.

round about. Israel's "zeal" for Yahweh and his Torah was a reflection of Yahweh's zeal for Israel.

We also know what this meant in practice. This "zeal" of Israel was exemplified in Israel's folk memory by a sequence of what we might describe as "heroes of zeal." Simeon and Levi avenged the rape of their sister Dinah by Shechem son of Hamor and defended the integrity of the family of the sons of Israel by slaughtering the Shechemites, even though the Shechemites had been circumcised (Genesis 34).[66] The greatest hero of zeal was Phinehas (Num. 25.6-13), who, on seeing an Israelite bring a Midianite woman into his tent, took his spear and pierced them both through and is remembered in conseqence as being "zealous for his God" and for thus making atonement for Israel (25.13).[67] Elijah too is recalled for his zeal, presumably not simply for his victory on Mount Carmel, when he decisively stopped the drift to syncretistic practices encouraged by Ahab and Jezebel (1 Kings 18), but also for the climax of his victory in the slaughter of the four hundred and fifty prophets of Ba'al in Wadi Kishon (18.40).[68] Jehu likewise is commended for his "zeal for the Lord," expressed particularly in wiping out Ahab's descendants in Samaria (2 Kgs. 10.16-17, 30). Not least of significance is the fact that the Maccabean revolt is recalled as an expression of that zeal: it began with a Phinehas-like killing of both Syrian and fellow Jew who apostasized (1 Macc. 2.23-26); and it was based on an appeal to such zeal (2.27, 49-68).[69]

There are three striking features of "zeal" thus understood. First, in each case the zeal was an unconditional commitment to maintain Israel's distinctiveness, to prevent the purity of its covenant set-apartness to God from being adulterated or defiled, to defend its religious and national boundaries. Second, a readiness to do this by force. In each case it is the thoroughgoing commitment expressed precisely in the slaughter of those who threatened Israel's distinctive covenant status which merited the description "zeal" or "zealot." And third, the fact that this zeal was directed not only against Gentiles who threatened Israel's boundaries, but against fellow Jews too.

It need hardly be said that this must be what Paul had in mind when he speaks of himself as a "zealot" and of his "zeal" manifested in persecution

66. The episode is recalled in Judg. 9.2-4 — Simeon and Levi "who burned with zeal for you [Yahweh] and abhorred the pollution of their blood"; also in *Jub.* 30, where the lesson drawn is that Israel is holy to the Lord and that it would be a reproach and defilement for any daughter of Israel to be given to a Gentile (30.8-14).

67. Phinehas is lauded in Sir. 45.23-24; 1 Macc. 2.54; *4 Macc.* 18.12; Pseudo-Philo 46-48. Hengel's discussion focuses on Phinehas (*Zealots* 149-77).

68. Sir. 48.2-3; 1 Macc. 2.58. See also Hengel, *Zealots* 148.

69. *Zēloō* — 1 Macc. 2.24, 26, 27, 50, 54, 58. Cf. 2 Macc. 4.2; see also Josephus, *Ant.* 12.271.

of the church (Gal. 1.13-14; Phil. 3.6).[70] First, his zeal for the ancestral traditions (Gal. 1.14) was the other side of the coin of his zeal as a persecutor (Phil. 3.6).[71] He would no doubt have understood his zeal as a reflection of God's zeal, a necessary reflection if Israel was to maintain its set-apartness to God. Second, it was certainly expressed in a physically violent way: even though we cannot deduce that the Hellenist Christians whom he persecuted were put to death, it must be significant that he can speak of persecuting the church "in excessive measure" and of "trying to destroy it" (Gal. 1.13).[72] And third, as we have already noted, his persecution seems to have been directed principally (solely?) against fellow Hellenist Jews. In other words, Paul the persecutor undoubtedly saw himself as a "zealot" in the tradition of Phinehas and the Maccabees.

From this we gain a surprisingly clear picture of Paul's motivation as a persecutor, but one too little noted in contemporary discussion of Paul's conversion. His motivation was that of earlier heroes of zeal. It was directed against the Hellenist Christians because they were seen to threaten Israel's distinctiveness and boundaries. The deduction is hard to avoid that this threat was constituted by the Hellenists taking the gospel of Messiah Jesus to the Gentiles.[73] By opening the door of this particular expression of Jewish religion and tradition to the Gentiles they were in danger of compromising Israel's integrity and purity. By failing to require of such Gentile converts circumcision and the practice of the covenant distinctives on which the Maccabeans had founded "Judaism," the Hellenists were removing the boundary markers and

70. Hengel's discussion of "zeal" fails to bring out the full significance of Paul's use of the term here (*Zealots* 180; *Pre-Christian Paul* 84); as also T. L. Donaldson, "Zealot and Convert: The Origin of Paul's Christ-Torah Antithesis," *CBQ* 51 (1989) 655-82 (despite 673).

71. The point is not that he attributes his persecuting "zeal" to his Pharisaism. Rather, his Pharisaism and his persecuting zeal were both expressions of his covenant faithfulness.

72. The verb used here, *porthein,* elsewhere always conveys the idea of material assault, destroying and ravaging cities and territories. See, e.g., Hengel, *Pre-Christian Paul* 71-72.

73. This conclusion is in some tension with the account in Acts 8.1-3. But the persecution cannot have had local Judean Nazarenes solely in view; how the Jerusalem church could be characterised as it is in Acts 21.20 and have remained as undisturbed as is indicated there would then be a major puzzle (Seifrid, *Justification* 159 n. 98, ignores this consideration). The mission to Damascus (Acts 9; implicitly confirmed by 2 Cor. 11.32) indicates a different dimension to the persecution and strongly suggests that the scattered Hellenists were the principal target. And there can be little doubt that Luke has sequenced his account out of order in order to insert the two most important events (Paul's conversion and Peter's acceptance of Cornelius — Acts 9.1–11.18) within what was otherwise an unbroken account of Hellenist mission consequent upon Stephen's death (8.4-40; 11.19-26).

tearing down the palisades and iron walls put up by Moses to hedge Israel in on all sides.[74]

It was from *this* zeal, and from "Judaism" as it called forth this zeal, that Paul converted on the Damascus road.

d) The final feature we have already touched on above (§7.4), so it need not detain us long. This is the way Paul describes his conversion as a commission from God "to preach him [God's Son] among the Gentiles" (Gal. 1.16). Given what we have now uncovered of what Paul was converted *from*, this indication of what he was converted *to* is all the more revealing. For the clear implication is that Paul was converted to the conviction of those he had previously persecuted. He had sought to "destroy" them because, we have deduced, they preached a Jewish Messiah to Gentiles and thus threatened Jewish covenant identity and distinctiveness. Whatever precisely Paul experienced on the Damascus road, it convinced him he had been wrong so to "persecute." His conclusion was understandable (however given to him or reached by him): he must do what those he had wrongly persecuted had been doing; he must take up the banner which he had tried to tear from the hands of those fellow Jews; he must press through the door which he had attempted so violently to close. The psychology of the conversion experience is easily recognizable and cannot be easily discounted.

This raises interesting questions about the development of Paul's theology, which are less appropriate for us here. Did he reach this conclusion at once?[75] Did he immediately embark on evangelistic missionary work among Gentiles in Arabia (Gal. 1.17)?[76] And so on. But so far as Paul's mature theology is concerned, the conclusion is clear. That Paul did think of his conversion as a conversion from Judaism, but from Pharisaic Judaism, a Judaism which kept itself separate from other Jews, not to mention Gentiles. And that the conversion Paul recalled was from a zealous and violent hostility to anyone who threatened to cause a breach in the palisades and iron walls of the Torah given to protect and sustain Israel.

In sum, then, we have gained a first clarification on what Paul was reacting against in his proclamation of justification by faith. He did react against his previous zeal for the law, though not as normally understood. We also begin to see more clearly that the law did become a concern for Paul, but primarily in its boundary-defining role, that is, as separating Jew from Gentile. Moreover, it now becomes more apparent how it was that justification through faith emerged

---

74. Alluding again to *Ep. Arist.* 139-42.

75. On this point my position is close to that of Räisänen, "Call Experience" (§7 n. 1).

76. An affirmative answer is given, e.g., by Bornkamm, *Paul* 27; Betz, *Galatians* 73-74; Hengel and Schwemer, *Paul between Damascus and Antioch* 109-20.

in Paul's theology, precisely as Paul's attempt to explain why and how Gentiles are accepted by God and consequently should be accepted also by their Jewish fellow believers. However, the inquiry is far from complete, and we have still to examine the key phrase in which Paul summed up what he so strongly opposed, now as a Christian: justification *by works of the law*.

§14.4 Works of the law in Judaism

The key Pauline texts we have already cited at the end of §14.2. In affirming justification from faith, Paul set it against justification *ex ergōn nomou*, "from works of the law." The traditional understanding of the phrase within Protestant theology is that it denoted good works done as an attempt to gain or achieve righteousness. The interpretation is wholly understandable, particularly in the light of Rom. 4.4-5, where the "works" in view (4.2) seem to be explained as "working for reward" and set in antithesis to "not working but [simply] believing."[77] The post-Pauline Eph. 2.8-9 looks very much like a confirmation of this: "for by grace you have been saved through faith; and that not of yourselves, it is a gift of God; not from works, lest anyone should boast" (cf. 2 Tim. 1.9 and Tit. 3.5).

The problem with the traditional view, however, emerges from "the new perspective." For as we have seen, the suggestion that Judaism typically taught that righteousness had to be *achieved* by law-keeping is a fairly fundamental misperception of "covenantal nomism."[78] And our investigation of Paul's perspective on his own pre-Christian attitudes and practice has only strengthened the view that Paul the Pharisee enjoyed a sense of participating in Israel's covenant righteousness as attested and maintained (not earned) by his devoutness and faithfulness. Presumably the resolution to the debate between the old perspective and the new lies in clarification of the distinction between *achieving* righteousness and *maintaining* righteousness. But that resolution is still some distance away. Here we must concentrate on the force of the key phrase "from works of the law."

The meaning of "works of the law" is not in much dispute. It refers

---

77. See, e.g., Hübner, *Law* 121-22; and especially Westerholm, *Israel's Law,* who sees the text as the firm rock on which all other alternative views founder (113-14, 116-17, 119, 120, etc.).

78. The point had already been made by M. Limbeck, *Die Ordnung des Heils. Untersuchungen zum Gesetzverständnis des Frühjudentums* (Düsseldorf: Patmos, 1971) 29-35: "only as a response, but not as an achievement" (173). Ziesler used the phrase "covenant keeping righteousness" (*Righteousness* 95). D. B. Garlington, *"The Obedience of Faith": A Pauline Phrase in Historical Context* (WUNT 2.38; Tübingen: Mohr, 1991), has demonstrated the pattern of "covenantal nomism" consistently through the Apocrypha.

to what the law requires, the "deeds"[79] which the law makes obligatory. To be noted at once is the fact that we are not talking about just any law here.[80] This is an observation of some importance. For the tendency in the traditional view has been to push in that direction — to see in Paul's conversion a general revulsion against the thought that any human striving or achievement can be the basis of God's acceptance. But Paul is talking about the Torah, the Jewish law. To be more precise, therefore, we should define "works of the law" as what the law required *of Israel as God's people*. Works of the law, in other words, were what Israel's righteousness consisted of, Israel's part of the covenant which Yahweh had made with Israel in first choosing Israel as his special people. "Works of the law" were Israel's response to that grace, the obedience God called for in his people, the way Israel should live as the people of God (Lev. 18.5).[81] "Works of the law" is the Pauline term for "covenantal nomism,"[82] where both words are important — law as functioning within and in relation to the covenant, law as expression of and safeguard for the covenant, law as indicating Israel's part of the agreement graciously initiated by God.

What has been too much ignored, however, are the points already developed above. That is, the way in which the law, thus understood, came to reinforce the sense of *Israel's privilege* (§6.4), the law as marking out this people in its set-apartness to God (§14.3b). As God's choice of Israel drew the corollary that God's saving righteousness was restricted to Israel, so the law's role in defining Israel's holiness to God became also its role in *separating Israel from the nations*. In this way the positive sense of "works of the law," as equivalent to Paul's talk of the obedience of faith, became the more negative sense which we find in Paul — works of the law as not only maintaining Israel's covenant status, but as also protecting Israel's privileged status and restricted prerogative.

It was for this reason that horror of idolatry was so deeply rooted in Israel's psyche. Avoidance of idolatry we might say was the supreme "work of the law."[83] And although avoidance of idolatry does not feature in Paul's references to works of the law,[84] it was just that "zeal"/"jealousy" for Israel's special relationship with God which had fueled his earlier persecuting zeal.[85]

---

79. Hebrew, *ma'aseh;* Greek, *ergon.* Contrast van Dülmen: "the doing of the law is less the fulfilment of the individual commands as the acceptance of the law as a way of salvation" (*Theologie* 135).

80. *Pace* Bultmann: " 'works of the Law' . . . represent works in general, any and all works as works-of-merit" (*Theology* 1.283).

81. See above §6.6.

82. See above §14.1.

83. Exod. 20.3-6; Deut. 5.7-10.

84. But Paul's hostility to idolatry was as implacable as any Jew's; see above §2.2 and below §24.7.

85. See above §14.3c.

There were, however, other works of the law which from early times particularly marked out Israel's set-apartness to God and separation from the nations. The terms on which *circumcision* was first required of Abraham made circumcision a fundamental identity marker of the people of the covenant (Gen. 17.9-14). Failure to circumcise a male child meant exclusion from the covenant and the covenant people.[86] No wonder, then, that Paul in his own time could boil the distinction between Jews and Gentiles down to "circumcision" and "uncircumcision."[87] Likewise, observance of the *Sabbath* became a touchstone of covenant identity and loyalty (Exod. 31.12-17).[88] Since the Sabbath was a sign of Israel's set-apartness, failure to keep the Sabbath law was a capital offence. So, for example, for Isa. 56.6, the mark of Gentile participation in the covenant would be keeping of the Sabbath.

In some ways more archetypal still were *the laws of clean and unclean,* which marked not only a separation of clean and unclean birds and beasts but also a separation of Israel from the peoples (Lev. 20.22-26).[89] According to Acts, the association (unclean foods, unclean nations) was only brought into question in emerging Christianity through Peter's encounter with Cornelius.[90] For such a mind-set the oracle of Balaam became paradigmatic: Israel, "a people dwelling alone, and not reckoning itself among the nations" (Num. 23.9). As Philo's elaboration of the text indicates: "because in virtue of the distinction of their peculiar customs they do not mix with others to depart from the ways of their fathers" (*Mos.* 1.278).[91]

---

86. "Every male among you shall be circumcised. . . . So shall my covenant be in your flesh an everlasting covenant. Any uncircumcised male who is not circumcised in the flesh of his foreskin shall be cut off from his people; he has broken my covenant" (Gen. 17.10, 13-14). "The Jew who refused to circumcise his children . . . was regarded as an apostate, above all after the Maccabaean period" (Hengel and Schwemer, *Paul between Damascus and Antioch* 71).

87. Rom. 2.25-27; 3.30; 4.9-12; Gal. 2.7-8; Col. 3.11.

88. "You shall keep my Sabbaths, for this is a sign between me and you throughout your generations, that you may know that I the LORD sanctify you. . . . everyone who profanes it shall be put to death; whoever does any work on it, that soul shall be cut off from among his people . . . a perpetual covenant . . ." (Exod. 31.13-14, 16).

89. "You shall therefore make a distinction between the clean beast and the unclean, and between the unclean bird and the clean; you shall not make yourselves abominable by beast or by bird or by anything with which the ground teems, which I have set apart for you to hold unclean. You shall be holy to me; for I the LORD am holy, and have separated you from the peoples, that you should be mine" (Lev. 20.25-26). See further Heil, *Ablehnung* Teil. 3.

90. Acts 10.10-16, 28; 11.3-12, 18; 15.8-9.

91. See again *Ep. Arist.* 139, 142 (above §14.3a). On Israel's tradition of separateness from other nations see, e.g., P. Ackroyd, *Exile and Restoration: A Study of Hebrew Thought of the Sixth Century BC* (London: SCM, 1968) 235-37; J. Neusner, *Self-Fulfilling Prophecy: Exile and Return in the History of Judaism* (Atlanta: Scholars,

As is already clear from our discussion of "Judaism" (§14.3a), the Maccabean crisis reinforced both Israel's sense of distinctiveness and the focus on particular laws as make-or-break issues in defining and defending Israel's set-apartness. It was the distinguishing features of Israel's religion which the Syrians strove to eliminate, in order to submerge the Judeans within the Hellenistic religious syncretism by which they hoped to unify their declining empire. And, as the Maccabean literature emphasizes, it was particularly the practice of circumcision and the laws on clean and unclean which became the focal point of conflict. Families which continued to practice circumcision were put to death, the infants hung from their mothers' necks (1 Macc. 1.60-61).

> But many in Israel stood firm and were resolved in their hearts not to eat unclean food. They chose to die rather than to be defiled by food or to profane the holy covenant; and they did die (1 Macc. 1.62-63).

Until recently the actual phrase "works of the law" was not attested prior to Paul, which naturally made many commentators wonder whether Paul was fighting against demons of his own creation. But the growing recognition that the Qumran sect used such a phrase[92] has been dramatically reinforced in the last few years by the publication of one of the most important of the Dead Sea Scrolls — 4QMMT. The document, *Miqsat Ma'ase Ha-Torah,*[93] is a letter in which someone, presumably a leader, or even the leader, of the sect, explains to others in Israel the sect's distinctive halakhah. It explains, in other words, the sect's interpretation of various laws which they regarded as crucial to their fulfilment of Israel's obligations under the covenant. In this case the rulings relate chiefly to the temple, priesthood, sacrifices, and purity. It is these rulings which the letter sums up towards the end as "some of the works of the law," *miqsat ma'ase*

1990) 36. That the most important of these "peculiar customs" included particularly circumcision, *kashrut,* and Sabbath observance is widely recognized. See, e.g., Meeks, *First Urban Christians* 97; Räisänen, *Paul* 167. An extreme form of the attitude is expressed in *Jub.* 22.16:

> Separate yourself from the nations, And eat not with them,
> . . . .
> For their works are unclean, And all their ways are a pollution
> and an abomination and an uncleanness. . . .

92. 4QFlor. 1.1-7; 1QS 5.20-24; 6.18. Moo, "Law," deserves more credit for drawing attention to the significance of the Qumran data for the Pauline debate.

93. E. Qimron and J. Strugnell, *Miqsat Ma'ase Ha-Torah* (DJD 10.5; Oxford: Clarendon, 1994); the text and translation were reproduced in *BAR* 20.6 (1994) 56-61; translation in García Martínez 77-85.

ha-Torah.[94] More striking still, the letter makes it clear that these "works of the law" are the reason why the sect has "separated" itself from the rest of Israel.[95] And it is these "works of the law" whose practice required them to maintain that separate existence.[96]

To sum up thus far, then, the phrase "the works of the law," does, of course, refer to all or whatever the law requires, covenantal nomism as a whole. But in a context where the relationship of Israel with other nations is at issue, certain laws would naturally come more into focus than others. We have instanced circumcision and food laws in particular.[97] In the Qumran sect the sensitive issues were not those between Jew and Gentile, but those between Jew and Jew, and so focused on internal disagreements on issues like sacrifice and purity. Elsewhere in the Jewish literature of the time we are aware of violent disagreement about how to calculate the appropriate feast days, whether by the sun or by the moon. The disagreement was so sharp that each regarded the other as failing to keep the feast, as observing the feasts of Gentiles and not those of Israel's covenant.[98] Equivalent defining issues within the history of Christianity have included believers' baptism, speaking in tongues, or apartheid. Today we might think of issues like abortion, women priests, scriptural inerrancy, or papal infallibility. None of the disputants in such internal controversies would regard the point at issue as the whole of their faith or even as the most important element in their faith. But the issues have become foci of controversy to such an extent that

94. Qimron's numbering C27 = García Martínez 113. It is this phrase from which the document has been given its name. The translation adopted by Qimron and initially by García Martínez ("the precepts of the Torah") unfortunately obscures the parallel. But at the SBL meeting in Chicago in November 1994 García Martínez acknowledged that his translation was unsatisfactory and that *ma'ase* is better rendered "works of." He has amended the second edition of his translation (1996) accordingly. See further my "4QMMT" 150-51.

95. Qimron C7 = García Martínez 92; see further below n. 100.

96. See further my "4QMMT" 147-48. Surprisingly Eckstein, *Verheißung* 21-26, seems unaware of 4QMMT, as of the more recent discussions on the "works of the law" (contrast Bachmann, *Sünder* 98-99).

97. In view of repeated misunderstanding of my initial essay on this subject (e.g., Bachmann, *Sünder* 92; Stuhlmacher, *Theologie* 264) I should perhaps underline that I do not (and never did!) claim that "works of the law" denote only circumcision, food laws, and Sabbath. A careful reading of my "New Perspective" should have made it clear that, as in Galatians 2, these were particular focal or crisis points for (and demonstrations of) a generally nomistic attitude. See also my "Yet Once More"; cf. Heiligenthal, *Werke* 133, cited below (n. 104), and Heil, *Ablehnung* 166-68. Of those who have recognized the force of my interpretation, I particularly welcome Boyarin, *Radical Jew* 53, 119-20, 210, and Nanos, *Mystery* 9-10, 177-78, 343-44.

98. *Jub.* 6.32-35; *1 Enoch* 82.4-7. See further my *Partings* 104. See also above §14.3b.

the status of the opponent's confession as a whole can in fact be called into question.

§14.5 Not of works

It is against this background that we can make best sense of Paul's use of the same phrase, "works of the law." We will look at the key passages in Galatians and Romans in turn.

a) When we turn to Paul's first use of the phrase, in Gal. 2.16, it is precisely the sort of issue just described which confronts us. Paul clearly uses the phrase to denote the attitudes he has opposed in the preceding verses (2.1-15). The "false brothers" who tried to secure Gentile Titus's circumcision (2.4) were insisting on works of the law — in this case, circumcision. For them faith in Christ was insufficient.[99] So too in the case of Peter and the other Jewish believers who "separated" themselves from the Gentile believers — presumably because the law required Israel to maintain such separation by observance of various food laws (2.12).[100] In Paul's terms they were acting as "Jews by nature," maintaining their distance from "Gentile sinners" (2.15).[101] So far as Paul was concerned, they too were insisting on works of the law. For them too faith alone was insufficient. Hence Paul's attempt to open Peter's eyes to see that "no human being is justified by works of the law, but only through faith in Jesus Christ." So too his repeated insistence in 2.16 that it is faith and not works which is the sole basis of acceptance in Christ and which therefore should be sufficient basis also for mutual acceptance by those in Christ.

Again we need not take up here the questions why the issue only emerged at Antioch, whether the principle was implicit in the revelation on the Damascus road, and whether Paul had previously formulated his gospel in these terms.[102] What is more to the point for us is that the Antioch incident

---

99. That the "false brothers" were baptized confessors of Messiah Jesus is generally recognized, despite Paul's dismissive description. See, e.g., Longenecker, *Galatians* 50-51.

100. The equivalent verb "separate" *(parash)* is clearly attested in this sense for the first time in ancient literature in 4QMMT (Qimron C7 = García Martínez 92). The echo of the Pharisees' defining characteristic *(parushim* = "separated ones"; see above §8 n. 44) would hardly be lost on Paul. See again my "4QMMT" 147-48.

101. "Sinners" was one of the terms of abuse which featured in the factional infighting of the post-Maccabean period. See my *Galatians* 132-33; also "Echoes of Intra-Jewish Polemic in Paul's Letter to the Galatians," *JBL* 112 (1993) 459-77; and above n. 56; also §8.3(3); and the fuller analysis in Winninge, *Sinners* — on Gal. 2.15-18 (246-50). Bachmann seems oblivious to this dimension of the discussion, despite his title *(Sünder oder Übertreter).*

102. See further my *Galatians* 119-24; also "Paul and Justification by Faith."

provided one of the great defining moments in Paul's theology and indeed in Christian theology. For it provoked Paul into pronouncing what was to become his most memorable and telling principle:[103] that no one is justified by works of the law, but only through faith in Christ (2.16). Evidently, however, the "works" he had in view were not deeds done to attain righteousness, but commandments of the law practised in order to maintain covenant righteousness, not least by separation from Gentiles.[104]

b) In an argument which takes off from the Antioch incident, the next two references to "works of the law" presumably have the same attitudes in mind. "Was it by works of the law that you received the Spirit, or by hearing with faith?" Paul asks his readers. And again: "He who supplies the Spirit to you and works miracles among you, is it by works of the law or by hearing with faith?" (Gal. 3.2, 5). Here too we may assume that at issue was no thought of the gift of the Spirit being earned.[105] What was at issue was whether those (Gentiles) who had already received the Spirit (by hearing with faith) needed to "judaize" (2.14), that is, to take on the distinctively Jewish lifestyle (marked not least by circumcision, food laws, and Sabbath).[106] Paul's questions obviously expect only one answer. The effectiveness of "hearing with faith"[107]

103. This claim holds however we regard the relation of 2.15-21 to 2.11-14 — whether as Paul recalling what he actually said to Peter or as Paul reflecting on what he should have said, with a view to the new crisis in the Galatian churches. See, e.g., my *Galatians* 132, and those cited by Longenecker, *Galatians* 80-81.

104. In the same year that my "New Perspective" was published, Heiligenthal also noted the socially delimiting function of "works" in Galatians 2 — "works of the law as signs of group membership" (*Werke* 127-34); followed by Boers, *Justification* 75-76, 91, 105. *Pace* particularly Schreiner, *Law* 51-57, who ignores the context which brought 2.16 to expression. But it surely cannot be denied that Paul resisted works of the law because other believers insisted on circumcision and restriction of table fellowship in respect of Gentile believers (as Bachmann, *Sünder* 100, recognizes, despite his earlier strictures [92-93]). Cf. van Dülmen, *Theologie* 24; Heiligenthal, *Werke* 133 — "when Paul speaks of the 'works of the law,' he thinks concretely of food laws and circumcision." See also Heiligenthal, "Soziologische Implikationen der paulinischen Rechtfertigungslehre im Galaterbrief am Beispiel der 'Werke des Gesetzes.' Beobachtungen zur Identitätsfindung einer frühchristlichen Gemeinde," *Kairos* 26 (1984) 38-53. For detailed exegesis of Gal. 2.15-21 see particularly E. Kok, *"The Truth of the Gospel": A Study of Galatians 2.15-21* (Durham University Ph.D. thesis, 1993).

105. It is clear from the run of the argument in 3.6-14 that "the blessing of Abraham" can be described equivalently as justification/righteousness (3.6-9) or as "the promised Spirit" (3.14). See particularly S. K. Williams, "Justification and the Spirit in Galatians," *JSNT* 29 (1987) 91-100.

106. Gal. 4.10 makes it clear that observance of feast days, including Sabbath, were also among the attractions held out to the Galatians; see further above §6 n. 84.

107. For this as the most obvious rendering of the phrase (rather than "believing the gospel message" [REB]) see S. K. Williams, "The Hearing of Faith: *AKOĒ PISTEŌS*

made taking on Jewish covenantal lifestyle ("works of the law") quite unnecessary.

c) More contentious is Gal. 3.10: "all who rely on works of the law
are under a curse; for it is written, 'Cursed is everyone who does not abide
by all that has been written in the book of the law to do it' [Deut. 27.26]."
The verse has caused more confusion than almost any other on this issue,
because of what Paul does *not* say, what he takes for granted. Most assume
that the hidden premise runs like this: the law requires perfect obedience ("all
that has been written in the book of the law"); but since that is impossible,
all are under the law's curse.[108] However, such a reading hardly makes sense
of any of our findings to date. (1) There is no evidence that the law was
understood to require "perfection" in that sense.[109] The obedience it did call
for was within the terms of the covenant, including the provision of atonement
by covenant law. That obedience was considered practicable.[110] And both Saul
the Pharisee and Paul the apostle agreed.[111]

(2) The usual reading also fails to explain why Paul specifies "all who
rely on works of the law," since it really wants to read "All (without exception)
are under a curse."[112] But the addition of our key phrase (works of the law)
presumably has in view those against whom 2.16 (its first occurrence) and
the preceding argument were directed. That is to say, it has in view those who
assumed that "works of the law" were an essential concomitant of membership of Israel's covenant, of sharing in Abraham's inheritance, and whose

---

in Galatians 3," *NTS* 35 (1989) 82-93; my *Galatians* 154-55. Note the parallel with Rom.
1.5 — "obedience of faith *(hypakoē pisteōs)*" — a more relevant parallel than is immediately obvious, since both Greek terms *(akoē, hypakoē)* reflect the Hebrew sense of "responsive hearing" *(shamaʿ);* see further below §23.3 and n. 45.

108. E.g., Hübner, *Law* 18-20; Becker, *Galater* 36; Räisänen, *Paul* 94-96, 109
(Paul was unique in his rigorism — 119-20); Schreiner, *Law* ch. 2; Thielman, *Paul* 124-26,
129-30; Eckstein, *Verheißung* 131-33, 146-47. Otherwise, Sanders, *Law* 23. It is not clear
how significant it is that the "all" ("all that has been written . . .") appears in the LXX
of Deut. 27.26 and in only a few Hebrew mss. (Stanley [§7 n. 1] 239 n. 196). See also
above §14.3b.

109. Sanders, *Paul, the Law and the Jewish People* 28; Räisänen, *Paul* 120-27,
178-79; Stowers, *Rereading* 141; M. Cranford, "The Possibility of Perfect Obedience: Paul
and an Implied Premise in Galatians 3.10 and 5.3," *NovT* 36 (1994) 242-58. This was one
of the points of consensus in Dunn, ed., *Paul and the Mosaic Law* 312.

110. Note that the clear assumption to this effect (Deut. 30.11-14: ". . . so that
you can do it") is taken up in the hope for the future (as in Ezek. 36.26-27: "I will put
my Spirit within you, and cause you to walk in my statutes and be careful to observe my
ordinances").

111. Phil. 3.6; Rom. 8.4; 13.8-10 (every commandment); Gal. 5.14 ("the whole
law").

112. Van Dülmen: "in no way only Jews, but all people . . . who stand outside
the salvation come in Christ" *(Theologie* 32).

assumption and practice involved "shutting out" Gentiles, even believing Gentiles (4.17).[113]

Against the usual view, the run of the argument in 3.6-14 provides a better solution. In this section Paul is playing on the traditional blessing and curse theme, so fundamental both in Israel's foundation promises[114] and in Deuteronomy, the classic statement of Israel's covenant theology.[115] In Gal. 3.6-9 he has focused attention on the third and most neglected strand of that promise — the promise of blessing to the nations.[116] The message of Deuteronomy was that failure to respond to God's manifested will was to court disaster. The alternative to blessing was curse. In Paul's view that is what had happened with the law devotees ("all who rely on works of the law").[117] In continuing to insist on Israel's privilege and separation from other nations, they were resisting the manifest will of God in the gospel. Consequently their understanding and practice of the law was deficient. Despite their best intentions they were not in fact "abiding by all that has been written in the book of the law to do it." Consequently, they were under the curse pronounced by Deut. 27.26.[118]

In short, Gal. 3.10 does not require any substantive modification of the picture which has been emerging throughout this and the preceding section.

d) On turning to Romans, a similar and complementary picture emerges. The equivalent to Gal. 2.16 is Rom. 3.20, where Paul sums up his indictment of "Jew first and also Gentile":[119] "By works of the law shall no flesh be justified before him." Prominent in that indictment (1.18–3.20) had

---

113. Eckstein interprets 3.10 in the light of 2.15, 17: those who seek to gain their salvation on the basis of Torah observance would be found as sinners like the Gentiles, that is, as transgressors of the law (*Verheißung* 122-31). But he misses the force of "sinners" as an expression of Jewish denial of righteousness to Gentiles. See above n. 101; and on 4.17 see my *Galatians* 237-38.

114. Gen. 9.24-27; 12.3; 27.29; Num. 23.7-8; 24.9.

115. Deuteronomy 27–30.

116. See above §6.5b.

117. The recent view that Paul was alluding to a widespread sense that Israel as a whole was still experiencing the Deuteronomic curses (the nation as a whole was still "in exile"; particularly J. M. Scott, " 'For as Many as Are of Works of the Law are Under a Curse' (Galatians 3.10)," in Evans and Sanders, eds., *Paul and the Scriptures of Israel* [§7 n. 1] 187-221; Wright, *Climax* ch. 7) neither explains why it is specifically "all who rely on the works of the law" that are specified, nor how, in that case, factions in the land of Israel, including the pre-Christian Paul, could have thought of themselves as "righteous" (e.g., *Psalms of Solomon*) and "blameless" (Phil. 3.6).

118. See further my *Galatians* 170-74. I have benefited from the research of two of my postgraduates on this passage — Jeffrey Wisdom and Andrew Carver. See also §14.5g below.

119. See above on Romans 2–3 (§5.4).

been Paul's critique of the sense of privilege and distinctiveness expressed by the "Jew" in 2.17-20. It is probable that "works of the law" here sum up that indictment, just as the same phrase summed up Paul's objection to circumcision and judaizing in Gal. 2.1-16. There is no more call here than anywhere else to conclude from the phrase that Paul suddenly, in the final summary conclusion, took up a different issue — that of self-achieved righteousness. That reading is possible only when the text is read in the context of a different debate.

e) The interpretation of 3.20 is confirmed by Paul's reversion to the issue on the other side of his central statement. For having stated how God's righteousness comes to effect (3.21-26), Paul turns back once more to the subject of boasting (3.27-30):

> [27]Where then is boasting? It has been excluded. By what kind of law? Of works? No, on the contrary, by the law of faith. [28]For we reckon that a person is justified by faith, apart from works of the law. [29]Or is he God of Jews only? Is he not also God of Gentiles? Yes, of Gentiles too, [30]since, after all, "God is one," who will justify circumcision from faith and uncircumcision through faith.

A reference back to the indictment in 2.17-24 can hardly be denied here, since it is there, and only there, that Paul has spoken of "boasting" (2.17, 23). This boasting is obviously associated with the "law of works." The "law of works" does not exclude boasting. On the contrary, the implication is, it encourages such boasting (cf. 4.2). Here again, then, the boasting associated with "works" is not thought of as boasting in self-achieved righteousness.[120] It is rather a boasting in Israel's privilege and distinctiveness (2.17-20), as attested by its distinctive privileges and practices (works).

That we are on the right lines here is surely indicated by the passage's continuing sequence of thought. The unavoidable logic of 3.28-29 is that affirmation of justification by works is tantamount to saying "God is God of Jews only." "Works of the law" are what distinguish Jew from Gentile.[121] To affirm justification by works of the law is to affirm that justification is for

---

120. It is again something of a puzzle why scholars such as Käsemann (*Romans* 102), Cranfield (*Romans* 165, 170, 219), and Hübner (*Law* 115-17) could follow Bultmann (*Theology* 1.281) in assuming that the talk of "boasting" in 3.27 was self-evidently "the act of asserting a claim upon God on the ground of one's works, of claiming to have put God in one's debt" (Cranfield 165) and effectively ignore the clear implication of 2.17, 23. See also Seifrid's critique of Bultmann (*Justification* 35-36).

121. So also Räisänen, *Paul* 170-72; cf. Nanos, *Mystery* 179-201. Heiligenthal, *Werke* 296-311, fails to carry through his earlier insight here (ignoring 3.29-30). Schreiner offers an exegesis of Rom. 3.27-28 which ignores both the preceding references to boasting (2.17, 23) and the flow of the argument in 3.27-30 (*Law* 95-103). See also §23.3 below.

Jews only, is to require that Gentile believers take on the persona and practices of the Jewish people. But if "God is one" (Deut. 6.4), justification cannot be dependent on works of the law, on adopting a distinctively Jewish lifestyle.[122] Justification cannot be dependent on the continuing separation of Jew from Gentile by the works which only Jews perform, the regulations which only Jews practise to keep themselves distinct from Gentiles.

f) Paul picks up the theme again at the beginning of Romans 4. "If Abraham was justified from works, he has something to boast about — but not before God" (4.2). The continued association of "boasting" and "works" indicates clearly that we are still in the train of thought which began at 3.27. The fact that the law had not yet been given did not prevent Paul thinking of "works of the law" in connection with Abraham,[123] for he was about to dismiss the relevance of circumcision as a factor in Abraham's being "reckoned righteous" (4.9-11).[124]

The same is presumably true of 4.6: "David speaks of the blessedness of the person to whom God reckons righteousness without works." David's righteousness was to be understood in terms of his being forgiven, of his sins not being reckoned (4.7-8),[125] rather than in terms of his being circumcised and practising the other works of the law.

In both cases the denial of justification by works (of the law) is then developed positively in terms of a promise which embraced Gentile as well as Jew and did not depend on the law (4.13-17).[126] Once again it is clear that to remove "works of the law" from the equation was to remove the blockage which prevented the gospel from reaching out beyond the boundaries of Israel marked out by the law.

g) We do not need to delay long over the remaining passages. Rom. 9.11 and 11.6 simply revert to the theme well established earlier.[127] Lest the

---

122. Seifrid criticizes me for drawing a "false dichotomy . . . between universalism (Paul) and particularism (Judaism)" (*Justification* 64). I had also warned against this danger in my *Romans* at this point (188); see also above §2.5. It should not be forgotten that an insistence on faith in Christ is another form of particularism; "in both Rabbinic literature and Paul's letters remaining in the in-group is conditional on behaviour" (Räisänen, *Paul* 186 n. 119).

123. Paul could equally think of Adam's breach of the commandment (Rom. 7.7-11; see above §4.7) and deny that Jacob's election was the result of "works" (9.11; see below §19.3a).

124. See also Cranford, "Abraham," and further below §14.7.

125. Note again, however, the unusualness of this formulation in Paul; see above §13.3, and further my *Romans* 206-7.

126. See again below §14.7.

127. We shall pick them up in outlining the argument of Romans 9–11 in §19.3a and §19.5a below.

point was insufficiently clear, Rom. 9.30-32 in effect repeats the argument of 3.27-31:

> [30]What shall we say? That Gentiles who do not pursue righteousness have attained righteousness, the righteousness which is from faith, [31]whereas Israel, pursuing the law of righteousness, has not reached the law. [32]Why so? Because they did so not from faith but as if it was from works.

Clearly the same confusion is indicated. Israel had understood the righteousness called for by God solely in terms of works. In consequence they had failed to reach the standard set by the law,[128] since it could only be attained by faith. This is an interesting confirmation of our earlier interpretation of Gal. 3.10: that an understanding of the law, and the practice of its requirements in terms of the works indicated earlier, was in fact a failure to keep the law. In other words, "works of the law" were a peculiarly Jewish problem in that they distinguished Jews from believing Gentiles.

h) One other feature of Paul's treatment of "works" should be noted. That is his assumption elsewhere that "good works" are desirable and that judgment will be in accordance with "works."[129] Had Paul's primary or even underlying polemic been directed against a prevalent view among Jews (and Christian Jews) that justification depended on works of achievement, he is hardly likely to have expressed himself so unguardedly as he does in commending good works to his readers. He is hardly likely to have spoken of a "work of faith," or of "the obedience of faith."[130] Paul evidently did not associate "works of the law" with "good works." The two phrases operated within different substructures of his thought. To both commend "good works" and rail against "works of the law" was no inconsistency for Paul.

An important corollary at once emerges. In this insight, that "works of the law" are not the same as "(good) works," we have the solution to the long-standing problem of how to correlate Paul's talk of judgment according to works in Rom. 2.6-11 with his theology of justification by faith. There is actually no problem. For "works of the law" refers primarily to the obedience

---

128. On "law" as the objective of the pursuit, see also below n. 143. Despite recognizing that the objective in 9.31 is "the law of righteousness" (*Israel's Law* 127-29), Westerholm then blurs the point on 145 ("Israel pursues 'the righteousness which is based on law'"). This serves his objective of pushing Paul into as sharp an antithesis between law and faith as he can, though here the primary distinction is clearly between "works of the law" and faith ("not from faith but as if it were from works").

129. Rom. 2.6-7; 1 Cor. 3.13-15; 2 Cor. 9.8; 11.15; Gal. 6.4; Col. 1.10; 2 Thes. 2.17; Eph. 2.10; 2 Tim. 4.14; cf. Rom. 13.12; 1 Cor. 15.58; Gal. 5.19; Col. 1.21; Eph. 5.11; 2 Tim. 4.18. The desirability of "good works" is strongly affirmed in the Pastorals (1 Tim. 2.10; 3.1; 5.10, 25; 6.18; 2 Tim. 2.21; 3.17; Tit. 1.16; 2.7, 14; 3.1, 8, 14).

130. 1 Thes. 1.3; 2 Thes. 1.11; Rom. 1.5.

to the law's requirements which most of Paul's fellow Jews regarded as their *raison d'être* as Israel in its distinctiveness among the nations. But no one disputed that all are required to do good.[131]

In sum, then, the "works" which Paul consistently warns against were, in his view, Israel's misunderstanding of what her covenant law required. That misunderstanding focused most sharply on Jewish attempts to maintain their covenant distinctiveness from Gentiles and on Christian Jews' attempts to require Christian Gentiles to adopt such covenant distinctives. Furthermore, that misunderstanding meant a misunderstanding of God and of God's promised (covenanted) intention to bless also the nations.

§14.6 Self-achieved righteousness?

We are now (not before time!) in a position to clarify the texts on which the traditional view of Paul's teaching on justification have been based.

a) *Rom. 4.4-5:*

> [4]Now to him who works, the reward is not reckoned as a favour but as a debt. [5]Whereas to him who does not work, but believes on him who justifies the ungodly, his faith is "reckoned as righteousness" [Gen. 15.6].

Whatever has been said about 3.27-31 or about the connection provided by 3.27 and 4.1,[132] the text here seems clear enough. Human effort cannot achieve righteousness. The message of justification is entirely to the contrary: that God justifies the nonworker, the ungodly, those with nothing in their favour and everything calling for their condemnation.[133]

Put like that, the principle of justification by faith is clear and its importance hardly to be questioned. But a niggling question arises. For "put like that" is a rather more polemical formulation than the text itself. In some contrast, the text is not expressed polemically but states a principle. It distinguishes a human contract from God's surprising mode of operation: he justifies the ungodly.

Furthermore, in the light of our earlier discussion of "the righteousness of God" (§14.2), an important question arises. Even put in these terms, is this not a principle which Paul's fellow Jews would also have recognized as fundamental in God's dealings with Israel? As a statement distinguishing

---

131. Cf. Snodgrass, "Justification."

132. Cf. particularly C. T. Rhyne, *Faith Establishes the Law* (SBLDS 55; Chico: Scholars, 1981); R. B. Hays, " 'Have We Found Abraham to Be Our Forefather according to the Flesh?' A Reconsideration of Rom. 4.1," *NovT* 27 (1985) 76-98.

133. See again particularly Westerholm, *Israel's Law,* here 170.

divinely given covenant from human contract, would it come as a surprise to Paul's fellow Jews or be counted as a great innovation? The answer to the two questions is probably Yes and No respectively. That presumably is why Paul could simply assert the principle without argument — because he was confident that it would not be disputed by any typically Jewish reader. That is to say, in Rom. 4.4-5 Paul probably restates a theologoumenon, not because it was contested by other (Christian) Jews, but more as a reminder of the fundamental character of all God's dealings with human beings.[134]

Paul indeed may have been simply repeating the tactic just used in the preceding paragraph. In 3.30 he had resolved the conundrum of faith versus works of the law by calling to mind the fundamental axiom that "God is one." From that agreed principle he could at once draw the corollary that God is God of Gentiles also and not of Jews only. So in 4.4-5 he probably refers to the fundamentally gracious character of all God's dealings with humans, including Israel's election. And from that agreed principle he draws the conclusion that it can only be faith which is reckoned as righteousness.

In short, it is certainly correct to draw the great Reformation principle of justification directly from Rom. 4.4-5. What is more at issue is whether it was polemically directed against a view maintained by Paul's Jewish Christian opponents. It has not been evident thus far that "works of the law" denoted a view that God's righteousness could be earned. There is of course some play between "works" *(erga),* and "the one who works/does not work *(ergazomenō)."* But the precise character of the wordplay remains unclear. Those who support the traditional understanding assume that the relation is in effect one-to-one (Paul's opponents maintain what he denies in 4.4-5). But it is quite possible that in 4.4-5 (as in 3.27-30) Paul passes allusively behind the issue in dispute (works of the law) to a point of fundamental agreement, from which he proceeds to develop his view on the issue in dispute.[135]

---

134. "To justify the ungodly" breached a primary canon of covenant law (Exod. 23.7; Prov. 17.15; 24.24; Isa. 5.23; Sir. 42.2; CD 1.19). But Israel also knew that God's covenant obligation was sustained only by grace. As the Psalmist humbly acknowledges: "If you, O LORD, should mark iniquities, LORD, who could stand?" (Ps. 130.3); note also the prominent role of Psalm 32 in the next few verses (Rom. 4.6-8) and see further above §14.2. Bultmann comments that "the paradox in 'grace' is that it is precisely *the transgressor, the sinner,* to whom it applies" (*Theology* 1.282), but then via Rom. 11.32 refers to the OT concept of "mercy" (*eleos,* translating *chesedh*). Contrast Hübner, who finds here a "new idea, revolutionary to Jewish thought" (*Law* 119, 121-22), and Martin, *Reconciliation* (§9 n. 1) 151: "the picture of a seeking, caring and forgiving God who meets the sinner before he repents is one that has no parallel in Judaism."

135. Cf. particularly Cranford, "Abraham" 79-83.

b) *Rom. 10.2-4:*

[2]I bear witness regarding them (Israel) that they have a zeal for God, but not in accordance with knowledge. [3]For, not knowing the righteousness of God and seeking to establish their own [righteousness], they have not subjected themselves to the righteousness of God. [4]For Christ is the end of the law in respect of righteousness for all who believe.

This passage regularly features in expositions of justification. The usual assumption is that Paul inveighs here against Israel for "seeking to establish their own righteousness," that is, to achieve righteousness which is "their own" as something achieved by them.[136] But this will not do. For one thing, the Greek translated "their own" *(idian)* properly denotes "theirs" as belonging to them and not to others, not "theirs" as attained by their own effort.[137] This understanding ties in with the first part of the paragraph (9.30-33). Israel's assumption that "righteousness" was a privilege granted to them and not to other nations (10.3) is of a piece with their misunderstanding of the law of righteousness in terms of works (9.32).[138]

For another, a too little noticed feature of this passage is the evocation of Israel's proud tradition of "zeal."[139] It is evident not only in the appearance of the word itself ("zeal" — 10.2). But there is also an allusion in the talk of seeking to "establish *(stēsai)*" righteousness as theirs (and not others) (10.3). For the verb *stēsai* probably reflects Hebrew *heqim* (hiphil of *qum*) and in particular the characteristic use of the verb in connection with the covenant.[140] Of marked interest is 1 Macc. 2.27, Mattathias's summons to defend the covenant: "Let everyone who is zealous for the law and would establish *(histōn)* the covenant come out after me."[141] Evidently it is this kind of zeal

---

136. "The righteousness which man exerts himself to achieve by fulfilling the 'works of the law' " (Bultmann, *Theology* 1.285); "a righteous status of their own earning" (Cranfield, *Romans* 515); similarly Hübner, *Law* 121, 128-29; others in my *Romans* 587.

137. BAGD, *idios*, "mine, peculiar to me"; "collective righteousness, to the exclusion of the gentiles" (G. E. Howard, "Christ the End of the Law: The Meaning of Romans 10.4," *JBL* 88 [1969] 331-37 [here 336]; Sanders, *Paul, the Law and the Jewish People* 38, 140; others in my *Romans* 587). Stowers' exegesis is again patchy here (*Rereading* 306-7). And Barrett is not quite to the point: "he [Paul] does not say that they were seeking to establish their own identity by emphasizing those practices that were peculiar to Jews and not shared by their Gentile neighbours" (*Paul* 83).

138. See above §14.5g.

139. As, e.g., by Westerholm, *Israel's Law* 114-15; Schreiner ignores both the *idian* and the significance of "zeal" (*Law* 106-8).

140. Usually of God "establishing" his covenant (e.g., Gen. 6.18; 17.7, 19, 21; Deut. 8.18; 29.13), but also of Israel's responsibility within the covenant (particularly Jer. 34.18). See further my *Romans* 588.

141. *Stēsai* (Rom. 10.3) and *histōn* (1 Macc. 2.27) are parts of the same verb *(histēmi)*.

and covenant loyalty which Paul had in mind here too. Once again the zeal was a determination to retain Israel's privileged status.[142] And once again that very assumption and determination was actually a misunderstanding of God's righteousness. It was the submission of the creature for which the Creator looked, not the zeal to defend privileged status.

A not irrelevant corollary is the consequence of the above line of exposition for our understanding of Rom. 10.4. For if we are right, and Rom. 10.4 speaks of the "end" of the law,[143] then we can now see more clearly in what sense the law has reached its end. Since Paul has put 10.4 as the conclusion to the exposition of 9.30–10.4, he presumably has in view the law thus misunderstood ("as if it was from works" — 9.32). That is, the law as defended by the heroes of zeal (§14.3c), as protecting Jew and excluding Gentile (10.2-3).[144] As in Galatians 3–4, the law in its temporary role now reached its end with the coming of Christ and of the possibility of faith in Christ for Gentile as well as Jew. Hence the characteristic emphasis of Paul's conclusion: "Christ is the end of the law in respect of righteousness for *all* who believe."

c) *Phil. 3.7-9:*

> [7]But whatever was gain for me I counted these things as loss on account of Christ. [8]As indeed I count everything loss on account of the surpassing worth of knowing Christ Jesus my Lord. On his account I have suffered the loss of everything and reckon it as refuse, so that I might gain Christ [9]and be found in him, not having my own righteousness which is from the law but that which is through faith in Christ, the righteousness from God to faith.

A question similar to that posed by Rom. 10.3 arises here. Did Paul mean by "my own righteousness" a righteousness attained by his own efforts? The same problem attaches to the usual affirmative answer:[145] the need to attain one's own righteousness was no part of traditional Jewish teaching; righteousness was rather the practice of the devout within the covenant. Here, however,

---

142. The "not in accordance with knowledge" (Rom. 10.2) probably expresses Paul's belief that the time of Israel's privileged standing before God is past (Gal. 3.19–4.7); see above §6.5.

143. There is an unresolved debate as to whether *telos* should be translated "end" or "goal"; see particularly R. Badenas, *Christ the End of the Law: Romans 10.4 in Pauline Perspective* (JSNTS 10; Sheffield: JSOT, 1985); there is a brief discussion in my *Romans* 589-91. What is often forgotten is that a "goal" attained is still an "end" reached. Included is the issue of whether the race imagery of 9.30-32 is carried over to 10.4 (*telos* as the finishing line), but Thielman presses the imagery too hard when he suggests that Israel has overrun the goal (*Paul* 205-8).

144. Cf. Schlier, *Grundzüge* 92-93.

145. See, e.g., Hawthorne, *Philippians* 141; O'Brien, *Philippians* 394-96.

"my own" can be more readily understood as "what I have gained." And it is possible to argue that the last items of the catalogue ("as to law, a Pharisee; as to zeal, persecuting the church; as to righteousness which is within the law, blameless") were self-chosen rather than inherited.[146]

The argument is nevertheless still dubious. It by no means follows that "my own" means "achieved by me." Any more than calling Christ Jesus "my Lord" in 3.8 means a lordship determined by Paul's efforts. If "my own" here does not mean "my own (and no one else's)," all it need mean is "my own" as "belonging to me," forgetful of its essentially gracious character ("from God"). In fact, however, the contrast with the next phrases seems to be primarily between "which is from the law" and "which is through faith in Christ, the righteousness from God."[147] So there may in fact be little difference from the contrasts in Gal. 2.16 and Rom. 3.28.

We should also beware of making a distinction in kind between the first and second halves of the catalogue in 3.5-6. It may be accurate to describe Paul's status as a Pharisee, his zeal as a persecutor, and his blameless righteousness as "self-chosen." But they were simply an intensification of the "confidence in the flesh" which sums up and characterizes the whole list (3.4).[148] They still cannot be considered "self-achieved" even if self-chosen. Rather, as we have seen, they indicate the same conviction that righteousness was Israel's, to be practised by covenant-loyal Jews and defended as Israel's by its practitioners.[149] If Paul had them particularly in mind in speaking of "my own righteousness," he was speaking qua Pharisee, qua "zealot," qua "blameless" Jew.

In all these cases, therefore, it is difficult to sustain the claim that Paul was polemicizing against "self-achieved righteousness." Of course the texts just reviewed can be read that way. The only question is whether those who read them that way have shifted the issue from one of Israel's works of the law vis-à-vis Gentile acceptability to the more fundamental one of the

146. Thielman, *Paul* 153-54, citing, but more strongly expressed than Seifrid, *Justification* 34, 173-74. Seifrid's thesis is that Paul "dissented from a Judaism in which obedience was regarded as a *necessary supplement* to God's covenantal mercies" (71). He does not explain how this differs from a Christian insistence that faith must express itself in works (see above n. 129). Schreiner simply assumes that "confidence in the flesh involves trusting in and boasting in one's effort" (*Law* 112-13).

147. "Which is from the law" is formally parallel to "which is from God" — *tēn ek nomou//tēn dia pisteōs Christou//tēn ek theou*. But see Reumann's plausible ABBA, CDDC structuring of Phil. 3.9-11 (*Righteousness* 62).

148. Note the force of the perfect in 3.3: he no longer has his previously settled confidence *(pepoithotes)* in the flesh. 3.3 thus forms an inclusio with 3.7-8: this is what he abandoned as the direct consequence of his conversion. See also §3.3b above.

149. Cf. Sanders, *Paul, the Law and the Jewish People* 43-45; Burchard, "Nicht aus Werken," 409-10.

terms of human acceptability by God. That may have happened already in Eph. 2.8-9, where the issue does seem to have moved from one of works of law to one of human effort.[150] But when the texts in the undisputed Pauline letters are read within the context of Paul's mission emerging from its Jewish matrix, the resulting picture is rather different. Within that context we gain a clear picture of Paul fiercely resisting his own earlier pre-Christian assumption that God's righteousness was only for Israel, and only for Gentiles if they became Jews and took on the distinctive obligations of God's covenant with Israel.

However much, then, we may wish theologically to press on to the further, more basic issue and to call upon Pauline texts to substantiate it, we should not lose sight of the issue which Paul himself addressed. The danger which he particularly confronted was that ethnic identity would in the event count for more than the gracious call of God or significantly determine and qualify that call.[151] And behind it was the issue of how Paul's version of the gospel should see itself in relation to Israel and Israel's covenant promises. For Christianity's self-understanding these were and are fundamental issues, whose comparative neglect has been to the cost of Christian theology and witness.

§14.7 By faith alone

Whatever precisely Paul was warning against, the thrust of his positive advocacy is clear. The means by which individuals respond to the gospel and experience its offered blessings is "faith, trust" *(pistis)*. That this was already a fundamental feature of his message, quite apart from the dispute over "works of the law," is clear from the Thessalonian correspondence. There Paul repeatedly returns to the subject of his readers' faith, commending and encouraging it.[152]

But then the issue of "works of the law" emerged in the internal Christian dispute over the terms on which the gospel could be offered to Gentiles. And in that dispute the classic antithesis was formed: "no human

150. It is this shift in the terms of the debate, and the un-Pauline use of "salvation" as something already accomplished, which adds to the very strong case for seeing Ephesians as the composition of a Paulinist (a disciple of Paul) some time after Paul's death (the view of most scholars). Cf. I. H. Marshall, "Salvation, Grace and Works in the Later Writings in the Pauline Corpus," *NTS* 42 (1996) 339-58.

151. This is the way Paul restates the issue in Rom. 9.6-13; see further below §19.3a.

152. *Pistis* — 1 Thes. 1.3, 8; 3.2, 5-7, 10; 5.8; 2 Thes. 1.3-4, 11; 2.13; *pisteuō* — 1 Thes. 1.7; 2.10, 13; 4.14; 2 Thes. 1.10.

being is justified by works of the law but only through faith in Jesus Christ"
(Gal. 2.16). To make the point clear beyond any doubt Paul repeats it another
two times: "and we have believed in Christ Jesus, in order that we might be
justified by faith in Christ and not by works of the law, because by works of
the law shall no flesh be justified" (2.16). The repeated antithesis is sharp
enough in itself to warrant the title to this section: justification by faith *alone*.
In the following elaboration of that theme we have one of the most intensive
affirmations that "faith" is of the essence of the gospel ever penned (Galatians
3). The issue was of such importance for Paul that the whole case was carefully
and fully restated in the subsequent major formulation of Paul's gospel which
is Romans (Romans 3–4).[153]

What is particularly interesting for us here is the fact that Paul expounds
justification by faith in a way which not only addresses the argument over
the terms of Gentile acceptance, but also presses beyond to provide a fundamental statement of human dependence on God.

a) If the above exposition has been sound it should be clear that Paul's
emphasis on faith was his way of combating the *restrictiveness* implicit in the
counteremphasis on works of the law. This is particularly clear in Romans.
We saw it in Rom. 3.27-31. To boast in works was tantamount to affirming
that God was God of Jews only. The counteremphasis on faith follows from
and is a fundamental expression of the alternative: the God who justifies by
faith is God of Gentile as well as Jew (3.28, 30). Similarly with the restatement
of the point in Rom. 9.30-32. Works of the law speak of Israel's restricted
conception of the law of righteousness and actually prevent Israel's attainment
of righteousness. But faith is the means by which Gentiles have attained that
righteousness.

The point comes out in a more thoroughgoing way, however, in the
thematic emphasis on "all who believe." The gospel is for "all who
believe" (1.16). The righteousness of God is "to all who believe" (3.22).
Abraham is father of "all who believe" (4.11). "Christ is the end of the
law as regards righteousness for all who believe" (10.4). "All who believe
on him shall not be put to shame" (10.11). "All" is one of the really key
words in Romans.[154] And as these same references make clear in context,
the "all" consistently means Jew as well as Gentile, Gentile as well as

---

153. In Galatians 3 *pistis* occurs 15 times (*pisteuein* twice). In Rom. 3.22–5.2
pistis occurs 20 times (*pisteuein* 7 times). This far exceeds the usage elsewhere: e.g., *pistis*
— 7 in 1 Corinthians, 7 in 2 Corinthians, 8 in Ephesians, 5 in Philippians, 5 in Colossians,
8 in 1 Thessalonians, and 5 in 2 Thessalonians. Goppelt notes that 27 of 35 faith passages
in Romans and 18 of 21 in Galatians are addressed to the issue of justification; "faith
received a special accent in Paul through the interpretation of the gospel as justification"
(*Theology* 2.126).

154. "All" occurs in Romans 71 times.

Jew.[155] In pressing this point so consistently Paul must have intended to break down the presupposition on the part of his fellow Jews that their privileged position before God involved some sort of restriction of God's grace to Israel in distinction from the other nations.

The same point comes out in Paul's exposition of what he evidently regarded as his two key proof texts — Hab. 2.4 and Gen. 15.6. Their importance is evident from the fact that they feature in both of the letters in which Paul seeks to define and defend his understanding of justification by faith.[156] The significance for us here is that we know how both texts were understood by Paul's Jewish contemporaries. So we can readily gain an insight into their function within Paul's exposition — that is, not only what Paul was arguing for, but also what he was arguing against. Knowledge of the latter is bound to help clarify the former.

b) The interesting feature of Hab. 2.4 is the different versions of the text in Hebrew, LXX, and Paul:[157]

Hebrew   the righteous [man] by his faith(fulness) shall live;
LXX   the righteous out of my faith(fulness) shall live;
Paul   the righteous out of faith/faithfulness (?) shall live.

It is evident from the personal adjective before faith(fulness) in both the Hebrew and the LXX that "faith" in Hab. 2.4 was typically understood in terms different from those of Paul. The Hebrew was in effect a restatement of Lev. 18.5 ("the one who does them shall live by them"), or as we might say, a classic statement of covenantal nomism.[158] That is, it indicated what the righteousness of the covenant member was. It was by "his faith," that is, his faithfulness[159] in regard to the law, that he lived his life. The Qumran commentary on Habakkuk took the verse in just this way: "Its interpretation

155. 1.5 ("all nations"); 1.16 ("Jew first and also Gentile"); 2.9 ("Jew first and also Gentile"); 2.10 ("Jew first and also Gentile"); 3.9 ("both Jews and Greeks"); 3.19 ("all the world"); 3.20 ("all flesh"); 3.22 ("there is no distinction"); 4.16 ("to all the seed," "father of us all"), etc.

156. Hab. 2.4 — Rom. 1.17 and Gal. 3.11; Gen. 15.6 — Rom. 4.3 and Gal. 3.6. He also uses Ps. 143.2 allusively in both Rom. 3.20 and Gal. 2.16, but Paul's insertion of "by works of the law" is a more blatant appropriation of the text for his own controversy; see my *Galatians* 140 — and below §14.8.

157. Heb. 10.38 has a further variation: "my righteous one out of faith/faithfulness (?) shall live." On the textual form see, e.g., J. A. Fitzmyer, "Habakkuk 2:3-4 and the New Testament," *To Advance the Gospel* 236-46.

158. See again above §6.6.

159. This indeed was the most natural meaning of the Hebrew *'emunah* (LXX *pistis*), denoting characteristically "firmness, steadfastness, fidelity" (BDB, *'emunah*); A. Jepsen, *TDOT* 1.316-19).

concerns those who observe the law." [160] In contrast, the LXX understood the text to speak of *God's* covenant faithfulness. It affirmed that the life of the covenant member was enabled and sustained by God's continuing faithfulness to his commitment to Israel. In other words, we have a variation here on the theme of God's righteousness. [161]

Paul, however, omitted both personal adjectives ("his," "my"), both in Rom. 1.17 and in Gal. 3.11. He thus allowed the text to be read in different ways and prevented it from being read in the restrictive way that the Hebrew implied. What the full significance of this rendering of the text is remains a matter of some dispute. Too often the debate is reduced once again to an issue of either-or exegesis. "Out of faith" either goes with "the righteous," or with "shall live," and Paul must have intended his readers to choose one rather than the other. [162] If that were so, then Paul would be going about his task in a rather ham-handed manner, since the dispute shows how readily the text can be read either way. It is more likely, then, that his wording was deliberately more open-ended. For the point he wanted to make was that human righteousness was a matter of *pistis* ("faith/faithfulness") from start to finish. The character of that *pistis* he would make clear in good time (Romans 4). In the meantime a reader who understood the text in the LXX way was not prevented from thinking gratefully of God's faithfulness, his saving righteousness to all who believe. The slightly puzzling "from faith to faith" (1.17) may be intended to be similarly open-ended: either from faith and nothing but faith, or from God's faith(fulness) to human (response of) faith, or both — and why not? [163]

In some ways the use of the same tactic in Gal. 3.11 is even bolder. For there Paul juxtaposes Hab. 2.4 with Lev. 18.5 (3.12) — two texts which, as we have just noted, functioned as nearly synonymous expressions of Israel's covenant obligation for life within the people of God. By opening the meaning of Hab. 2.4 to the more basic sense of "faith" in Paul's understanding of that word, he effectively distinguished it from Lev. 18.5. The line of thought is almost explicit in 3.12a: "the law is not 'from faith.' " That is to say, Hab. 2.4 is best understood as defining the terms on which the covenant righteousness is based (God's faithfulness and/or human faith). But Lev. 18.5, with its talk of law and not faith, is best taken as referring only to the terms in which that righteousness is then lived out. [164]

---

160. 1QpHab 7.10-11; 8.1-3. See further my *Romans* 45-46.

161. See above §14.2.

162. See, e.g., those indicated in my *Romans* 45-46.

163. Again see further the fuller discussion in my *Romans* 43-44. But see also n. 203 below.

164. See again §6.6 above.

With this last piece of the jigsaw in place we are at last in a position to follow through the train of thought in Gal. 3.10-14.[165] Paul maintains that all who restrict the promised blessing (3.8) to those who insist on works of the law have in fact breached the terms of the promised blessing and consequently have themselves fallen under the threatened curse (3.10). For the promise was of justification, and that comes to human beings by faith (3.11). The law, in contrast, was concerned primarily with how life should be lived once the promise had come into effect (3.12). The curse of the law, however, has been absorbed by Christ (3.13). So the curse has been removed. And with it both the misunderstanding of the law's role and its effect in excluding Gentiles from the promise, which had brought the curse into effect, have been declared null and void. The result is that the promised blessing can now be offered freely to Gentiles (3.14).

c) Gen. 15.6 was still more fundamental to Paul's theology of justification: "Abraham believed God and it was reckoned to him as righteousness." It forms the starting point for the main section of Paul's argument in Gal. 3.6, and a whole chapter is devoted to its exposition in Romans 4.

Here again we have a good idea of how the text was typically understood within contemporary Judaism. 1 Macc. 2.52 is in effect an exposition of Gen. 15.6: "Was not Abraham found faithful when tested, 'and it was reckoned to him as righteousness'?"[166] There can be no doubt that the allusion is to Abraham's faithfulness when tested in the offering of Isaac (Genesis 22). This was a favourite theme within Second Temple Judaism,[167] and we have already noted the emerging importance of the Aqedah in Jewish theologizing of the period.[168] It was evidently a standard hermeneutical gambit to interpret Gen. 15.6 by the subsequent episode, as Jas. 2.21-23 confirms.[169] That is to say, Genesis 22 showed what Abraham's believing involved. His *pistis* was his "faithfulness" under test, that is, his unquestioning obedience to God's command.

It should not escape notice that 1 Macc. 2.52 is part of Mattathias's role call of the heroes of zeal, given as he summed up the commitment called

---

165. Our analysis of Gal. 3.10-14 has been necessarily but unfortunately fragmentary: 3.10 (§14.5c); 3.11 (here); 3.12 (§6.6); 3.13 (§9.5); see also on 3.14 (above §14.5b and below §16.3).

166. The second half of 1 Macc. 2.52 is a verbatim quotation of Gen. 15.6 LXX.

167. Jud. 8.26; Sir. 44.19-21; *Jub.* 17.15-18; 18.16; 19.8; *m. Aboth* 5.3; see also Philo, *Abr.* 192; Josephus, *Ant.* 1.223-25; Pseudo-Philo 40.2, 5; *4 Macc.* 14.20. See also §9 n. 95.

168. See above §9.4.

169. Jas. 2.21-23 — "Was not Abraham our father justified from works, when he offered up Isaac his son on the altar? You see that faith worked with his works and was completed from his works. And the scripture was fulfilled which says, 'Abraham believed God and it was reckoned to him for righteousness' [Gen. 15.6]."

for in the Maccabean rebellion (2.49-68). It is equally noticeable that another commendation of one of the greatest of the heroes of zeal echoes the same phrase from Gen. 15.6. In Ps. 106.30-31 Phinehas is praised for his crucial intervention.[170] And then the psalmist adds the same verbatim phrase: "and it was reckoned to him as righteousness." Similarly in *Jub*. 30.17 the zealous act of Simeon and Levi in slaughtering the Schechemites[171] "was reckoned to them as righteousness."[172] Evidently Gen. 15.6 was understood within Israel's tradition of "zeal" as indicating the faithful devotion to Israel's covenant distinctiveness which God counted as righteousness. Paul, himself a former "zealot,"[173] could hardly have been unaware of this tradition. So it is likely that it forms part of the subtext of Paul's own use of Gen. 15.6.

Equally striking is the appearance of the same allusion in 4QMMT. At the end of his letter the writer hopes that "at the end of time, you may rejoice in finding that some of our words/practices are true/correct. And it shall be reckoned to you as righteousness in doing what is upright and good before him" (Qimron and Strugnell [n. 93 above] C30-31; García Martínez 116-17). Clearly in view are the practices, "the works of the Torah" just referred to (Qimron and Strugnell C27 = García Martínez 113).[174] And clearly in view is the same key text from Israel's patriarchal period (Gen. 15.6). Once again the assumption is that righteousness is reckoned in accord with one's faithfulness in observing the rulings and the works of the law which distinguished the Qumran community's halakhah.[175]

Of the two passages where Paul takes up Gen. 15.6, Romans 4 is by far the most illuminating. After drawing attention to Gen. 15:6 in Gal. 3.6, Paul does not stay long with it. He makes the point that Abraham's believing provides the pattern for the way in which God justifies (by faith, 3.7). But then he takes up another Genesis theme,[176] which provides the other principal terms around which the next section of the argument revolves — "blessing" (3.9, 14), its antonym "curse" (3.10, 13), and "promise" (3.14-29).[177]

---

170. It is also worth noting that in Ps. 106[LXX 105].30a the LXX renders Hebrew *palal* ("intervene") with *exilaskomai* ("expiate, atone") — "Phinehas stood up and made atonement."

171. See above n. 66.

172. Since Gen. 15.6 was cited more or less verbatim in *Jub*. 14.7, the allusion to Gen. 15.6 in 30.17 can hardly have been coincidental.

173. See above §14.3c.

174. See above §14.4.

175. See again my "4QMMT" 150-52.

176. "In you shall all the nations be blessed" is a mixed quotation from Gen. 12.3 and 18.8. But the promise was repeated several times within the patriarchal narratives (also 22.17-18; 26.4; 28.14). See also §20 n. 8 below.

177. "Promise," noun and verb, occurs 9 times in Gal. 3.14-29.

Possibly conscious that he had not fully exploited the potential of Gen. 15.6 for his gospel of justification in his earlier treatment, Paul returned to it in Romans 4. There he provides one of the most elegant expositions of a scriptural text available to us from antiquity, where first the text is announced, then its two main parts are expounded in turn, and the exposition is rounded off by reference back to the text.

> 4.3   "Abraham believed God and it was reckoned to him as righteousness"
> 4.3-12   The meaning of "reckoned"
> 4.13-21 The meaning of "believed"
> 4.22   Therefore, "it was reckoned to him as righteousness."

The point of the first part of the exposition in effect is to counter the current interpretation of Gen. 15.6. "Reckoned," as Paul well knew, was an accounting metaphor. So he starts by reminding his readers that when used of God's "accounting" the parallel is not with human contracts (4.4-5).[178] Rather the usage of Gen. 15.6 is better explained by the parallel provided in Ps. 32.1-2 (4.7-8): its talk of "not reckoning sin" is equivalent to "reckoning righteous" (4.6). In other words, God's accounting is a matter of divine grace, a justifying of the ungodly, a forgiving of sin.

The key question, however, is whether this blessing was reckoned to the command-keeping Abraham (4.9-10). Paul focuses the issue of Abraham's faithful law-keeping on Abraham's circumcision. Since that act of obedience (Gen. 17.23) had been subsequent to Abraham's being reckoned righteous (Gen. 15.6), it posed the same issue as the still later offering of Isaac (Genesis 22). Was Abraham reckoned righteous because of his faith, that is, his faithfulness in obeying God's command to circumcise all males of his household? The sequence of events gave Paul his answer. Abraham was "reckoned righteous" prior to his circumcision. His circumcision was simply the sign and seal of the righteous relation which he already enjoyed through faith (4.10-11). In which case, since faith prior to such works is the basis of his relation of righteousness, and since his believing was in response to God's promise of innumerable descendants (Gen. 15.5-6), faith (alone) must be the basis of his promised fatherhood (4.12).

And what then is that faith? The second part of Paul's exposition of Gen. 15.6 is important enough to be given a separate section.

d) In the second half of his exposition of Gen. 15.6 (Rom. 4.13-22) Paul gives his clearest and most powerful exposition of what he understood by *pistis,* "faith."

---

178. See above §14.6a.

In the first place he broadens out the issue from the particular case of circumcision to the issue of the law in general (4.13-16). Here in effect he is more or less repeating the fuller argument of Gal. 3.19-29. The argument amounts to pointing out that the law has a different function. That function, as we have already seen, includes the regulation of covenant life, not the more fundamental role of making alive (Gal. 3.21).[179] Paul would allude to that role again later, in his reference to Lev. 18.5 in Rom. 10.5. Here he refers to the more universal role of the law, as the measure of divine judgment on transgression (4.15).[180] More to the point, he denies outright that the law in any way determines who should be counted heirs of Abraham (4.13). Such an affirmation would not explain Gen. 15.6. Rather, it would nullify the original promise (Gen. 15.5) and render invalid the very faith by which Abraham himself had accepted that promise (4.14). That is why it had to be from faith, so that the most fundamental principle of all God's dealings with humans could be clearly seen — by grace through faith. Only so could the promise be fulfilled to all Abraham's heirs, not only those of the law (who obeyed the law as Abraham did), but also those who shared Abraham's faith independently of the law (4.16).[181]

The final phase of the exposition (4.17-21) draws upon one more text: "I have made you father of many nations" (4.17). The text is drawn, rather brazenly, from Gen. 17.5 (the circumcision passage). But as 4.18 indicates, it is because Gen. 17.5 reworded the original promise ("so shall your descendants be" — Gen. 15.5) in terms of Abraham as father of many nations that Paul was able to call it into service. More to the point, Gen. 17.5 put greater stress on the divine sovereignty which the promise expressed ("I have made/appointed you to be"). This was the promise of the Creator God, "the one who gives life to the dead, and who calls things that have no existence into existence" (4.17).[182] Before that God, the only response could be faith, simple trust.

The character of this faith is still more sharply etched by the circumstances of the promise and its fulfilment (4.18-19). Abraham's own advanced

---

179. See above §6.6.

180. See above §6.3.

181. Note the concession Paul makes here: he affirms Israel's inheritance in Abraham (this will be the theme of Romans 9–11); his protest is against that inheritance being understood in a too restrictive way. He does not replace Israel's traditional restrictiveness with a Christian restrictiveness: he does not say "not of law, but only of faith," but "not only of law but also of faith." This is the other side of Paul's concern from that expressed in Rom. 3.28 and Gal. 2.16. Such nuances in Paul's argument are often missed; see, e.g., the strained exegesis of Cranfield, *Romans* 242-43.

182. "The one who gives life to the dead" (4.17) is clearly intended to relate God's action in giving life to Sarah's dead womb (4.19) to his act in raising Jesus from the dead (4.24); see my *Romans* 217-18.

years and the barrenness of Sarah's womb made it almost impossible to envisage the promise being fulfilled in anything like the normal course of events. But Abraham believed in confident hope: that was the character of his faith — not dependent on or qualified by any legal enactment, but dependent solely on God.[183] This was the trust in the Creator God which Adam had failed to exercise. Abraham gave the glory to God (4.20) which humankind had refused to give (1.21). This was the character of a faith far more fundamental than Abraham's subsequent faithfulness, more fundamental than Israel's relation with its covenant God. This was the faith of the creature wholly reliant upon and confident in God's promise because it was God who promised (4.21).

It was this faith, Paul concludes, which "was reckoned to him as righteousness" (4.22). And he rounds off the exposition by pointing out that the faith called for in the gospel was just the same — a faith in the life-giving God who "raised Jesus our Lord from the dead" (4.23-24).

This, then, is what Paul meant by justification by faith, by faith alone. It was a profound conception of the relation between God and humankind — a relation of utter dependence, of unconditional trust. Human dependence on divine grace had to be unqualified or else it was not Abraham's faith, the faith through which God could work his own work. That was why Paul was so fiercely hostile to the qualification which he saw confronting him all the time in any attempt to insist on works of the law as a necessary accompaniment of or addition to faith. God would not justify, could not sustain in relationship with him, those who did not rely wholly on him. Justification was by faith, by faith alone.

§14.8 Faith in Christ

Despite the length of our discussion thus far, we are still not finished. For there is one other issue which has boiled up in recent years which requires some comment. This is the question whether all the *pistis* references already drawn upon should actually be taken as references to human believing in response to the gospel. Among them are a number of genitive constructions, seven in number, which speak of *pistis Christou,* literally "faith of Christ."[184]

---

183. See Käsemann's powerful reflections on the passage (*Perspectives* 92-93).
184. faith of Jesus Christ   Rom. 3.22; Gal. 3.22
    faith of Jesus   Rom. 3.26
    faith of Christ Jesus   Gal. 2.16
    faith of Christ   Gal. 2.16; Phil. 3.9
    faith of the Son of God   Gal. 2.20

A strongly held alternative view is that this phrase *(pistis Christou)* should rather be understood as referring to Christ's *own* faith, the faithfulness he displayed in his willing self-sacrifice on the cross. In some circles it is now taken for granted that the phrase should be so understood.[185]

a) Some argue that the genitive construction is determinative in itself, particularly when set beside its equivalent in Rom. 4.16 — "the faith of Abraham."[186] As "the faith of Abraham" denotes Abraham's faith, so "the faith of Christ" must denote Christ's faith.

The form however, in itself, is indeterminative. The genitive construction, in Greek still more than in English, is capable of a wide range of meanings.[187] We have already in §14.2 noted the problem of rendering *dikaiosynē theou,* "the righteousness of God" (Rom. 1.17). A similar question arises in the reference to "the love of God" in Rom. 5.5: it probably denotes God's love, but is "love for God" excluded?[188] So far as the objective genitive is concerned, we have already encountered *zēlos theou* (Rom. 10.2). The phrase translates literally as "zeal of God," but obviously from the context it denotes "zeal *for* God." Similarly, Paul speaks of "the testimony of the Christ" (1 Cor. 1.6), where the consensus is that he means "testimony to Christ." And no one takes "the knowledge of Christ Jesus" in Phil. 3.8 as anything other than knowledge which has Christ as its object.[189]

The form in itself, then, does not indicate to the reader what kind of genitive is involved. It is the function of the form within its context which is determinative. Thus, as we have already noted, in Rom. 1.2 and 9, Paul speaks in succession of "the gospel of God" and "the gospel of his Son," where context (1.2-3) points to God as the source and authority behind the gospel (subjective genitive) and to the Son as the gospel's content (objective genitive), "concerning his Son" (1.3). Outside the Pauline corpus the nearest equivalent phrase *(pistis + genitive)* speaks of *pistin theou* (Mark 11.22), where again

185. See particularly Hays, *Faith* 139-91; also *"PISTIS"*; Hooker, *"Pistis Christou"*; Wallis, *Faith*; Stowers, *Rereading* ch. 7. See Hays, *"PISTIS"* 35-36 nn.2-4 for further bibliography.

186. "The parallelism between 3:26 and 4:16 is a fatal embarrassment for all interpreters who seek to treat *Iēsou* as an objective genitive" (Hays, *"PISTIS"* 47; cf. Stowers, *Rereading* 201-2). But see also Harrisville, *"PISTIS CHRISTOU"* 241.

187. E.g., BDF §§162-68 survey examples of "genitive of origin and relationship," "objective genitive," "partitive genitive," "genitive of quality," "genitive of direction and purpose," "genitive of content and appositive genitive," and "concatenation of genitives with different meanings."

188. Cf. my *Romans* 252.

189. This is also English usage, as is a phrase like "hope of heaven." No one misunderstands the poet when he sings, "all for the love of Mary."

context indicates "faith *in* God."[190] We should therefore look to the context of Paul's usage to be determinative in the cases of *pistis Christou* in dispute.

Before passing on from grammatical considerations we should simply note the absence of the definite article in the phrase each time it occurs — "faith of Christ," rather than "the faith of Christ." Where a subjective genitive is intended we would normally expect the article — "the faith which Christ exercised." The most obvious example is Rom. 3.3 — "the faith of God," that is, "the faithfulness of God." However, the rule is by no means universal or consistent. The obvious counterexample is Rom. 4.16 — "from faith of Abraham," that is, "Abraham's faith" (contrast 4.5 — "the faith of him"). It is possible, however, that the wording of 4.16 simply draws on the thematic phrase *ek pisteōs* ("from faith").[191] And the consistent absence of the article in the *pistis Christou* phrases should perhaps be given more weight.[192]

b) When we look to context the issues become clearer. In the case of Galatians 2–3, where four of the instances of the phrase occur, it is difficult to see anything other than faith in Christ in view. The argument starts at 2.16, where the sequence of *pistis* references begins. A major consideration here for those urging the "faith of Christ" reading is what would otherwise appear to be the redundancy of the *pistis* references: human believing is indicated by the verb ("we have believed in Christ Jesus"); so the two *pistis Christou* references indicate a different aspect of the whole package ("the faithfulness of Christ").[193]

Two factors tell against this rendering, however. First, it ignores what seems to be a deliberate triple antithesis with "works of the law" (three times in 2.16). The structure of the sentence is thus as follows:

. . . *not* from works of the law	*but only* through *pistis Christou;*
	and we have believed in Christ Jesus
	in order to be justified from *pistis Christou*
and *not* by works of the law	
for by works of the law	shall *no flesh* be justified.

The point is that Paul evidently intended to repeat himself, to make himself clear beyond doubt. The antithesis to "works of the law" is *pistis,* then belief, then *pistis* again. Those who believed in Christ thus demonstrated and established the principle of *pistis Christou* as rendering works of the law unnecessary.

Second, had Paul intended *pistis Christou* as a reference to Christ's

---

190. Harrisville, *"PISTIS CHRISTOU,"* also shows that the Fathers understood the phrase consistently as an objective genitive.

191. *Ek pisteōs* — 1.17 (twice); 3.26, 30; 4.16 (twice); 5.1; 9.30, 32; 10.6; 14.23 (twice).

192. See the fuller discussion in my *"PISTIS CHRISTOU"* 66-67.

193. E.g., Longenecker, *Galatians* 87-88; Hooker, *"Pistis"* 166, 173; Wallis, *Faith* 71.

faith(fulness), it would be most odd that he makes no effort whatsoever to unpack the phrase or to restate its major theme in varied wording in what follows. 2.16 is, after all, the principal thematic statement which determines the main thrust of the letter. Were "the faithfulness of Christ" as central to Paul's argument as 2.16 would then imply, it is almost inconceivable that Paul failed to give the theme more prominence and to make clear what the otherwise somewhat enigmatic phrase meant. What was this "faith of Christ"? Did Christ also "believe" as Abraham did?[194]

In contrast, the main theme of Galatians 3 is, as we have seen, quite clear. It continues to set *pistis* over against works of the law in sharp antithesis (3.2, 5, 10-11) and to contrast the different roles of the law and *pistis* (3.10-26). It would be possible, as a somewhat desperate expedient, to take these *pistis* references as alluding to Christ's faith. And indeed the parallel between "the coming of faith" (3.23) and "the coming of the seed [Christ]" (3.19) might seem to give that suggestion some weight. But the run of the argument would then actually require *all* the *pistis* references to be so rendered.[195] For there is no obvious criterion which would enable the reader to distinguish one of the repeated *ek pisteōs* references from another.[196] This would mean that Paul's whole response to the appeal of the law was to point to the somewhat enigmatic "faith of Christ," with only the two verbal references (2.16; 3.22) to indicate the importance of the Galatians' own believing.

Much the more plausible reading of Galatians 3, however, is that the quotation of Gen. 15.6 states the theme of what follows: "Abraham believed God and it was reckoned to him as righteousness" (3.6). It certainly does so in the parallel Rom. 4.3ff., where no one disputes that the equally frequent *pistis/pisteuō* ("faith/believe") references have human believing in view. And though Galatians 3 does not treat Gen. 15.6 as its theme in the same way as the later Romans 4, the decisive consideration is that Gen. 15.6 assuredly determines the first of the crucial sequence of *ek pisteōs* references in Gal. 3.6-9. The parallel is hardly between Abraham's believing and the faith (of Jesus — not explicitly stated).[197]

---

194. 3.13 makes no attempt to relate the cursed Christ to a theme of Christ's faith; and references to "the coming of the faith" in 3.23, 25 would be no less enigmatic as references to "the faith of Christ." Otherwise the text speaks simply of "(the) faith" (see also §6 n. 82). See also my *"PISTIS CHRISTOU"* 69-71

195. Hays in effect so argues (see my *"PISTIS CHRISTOU"* 68-70); he recognizes that an understanding of how the phrase functions within the constuction of Paul's argument is crucial (*"PISTIS"* 40).

196. *Ek pisteōs* — 2.16; 3.7, 8, 9, 11, 12, 22, 24; 5.5.

197. Contrast the rather tortuous formulation of Wallis: "Abraham had faith and received the promise from God; *hoi ek pisteōs* are blessed not simply because they believe, but because in believing they participate in the faith of him to whom the promise was made (3.6-9)" (*Faith* 115).

"Those from faith" could be described as "sons of Abraham" (3.7) because they were "of (his) faith," they were in the line of descent of his faith.[198] God justifies the Gentiles "from faith" just as he justified Abraham who believed (3.8). "Those from faith are blessed with faithful Abraham" (3.9).[199] With the line of argument thus so clearly established, the subsequent *ek pisteōs* (and "through faith") references could hardly be read otherwise than as a reference to that same faith, from which and through which the blessing of Abraham was received as Abraham himself received it (3.14). In which case the double emphasis on *ek pisteōs* "those who believe" (3.22) could hardly be taken as anything other than a repeated emphasis echoing the triple emphasis of 2.16.[200]

c) The case for a "faith of Christ" rendering of *pistis Christou* is stronger in Rom. 3.21-26. For there the focus is on the redeeming, atoning action of Christ. So there is a greater plausibility in reading *pistis Christou* as a further way of stressing that the gospel stands or falls by what happened on the cross.[201]

Similar problems, however, remain. For one thing, nothing has prepared the reader to understand the abruptly introduced phrase (3.22) in this way. The "faith of Christ" reading depends on an assumption that Christ's faithfulness was a familiar theme, to which the phrase would naturally recall its Roman audiences.[202] But evidence that it was a familiar theme elsewhere in earliest Christianity is lacking. Here the grammatical point regarding the lack of the article has more weight. Were it an established theme we would have expected a reference to "the (well-known theme of) Christ's faith."[203]

In contrast it makes better sense to assume a resumption of the letter's

---

198. Rom. 4.11-12, 16 simply makes more explicit what is clearly implied in Gal. 3.7.

199. Paul does not hesitate to speak here of "faithful *(pistos)* Abraham" (3.9); he never uses a similar formulation for Christ. See also my *Galatians* 167.

200. It should be clear then that the logic of the argument does *not* require that Christ exercised Abraham's faith *(pace* Hooker, *"Pistis"* 172; see further my *"PISTIS CHRISTOU"* 71-72). Despite Hooker *("Pistis")*, an Adam or "interchange" motif is remote from this part of the argument. Elsewhere in Paul the Adam parallel is made by emphasising Christ's *obedience,* not his faith (Rom. 5.19; Phil. 2.8).

201. Note particularly B. N. Longenecker, *"Pistis* in Romans 3.25: Neglected Evidence for the 'Faithfulness of Christ'?" *NTS* 39 (1993) 478-80.

202. It is evident from Hays's original thesis that his interpretation derives from what he regards as "the narrative structure of Paul's gospel" *(Faith* ch. 4), which in effect calls for a fuller reference to the story of Christ. He has to assume that Paul's audiences hear the *pistis* references as allusions to that story.

203. The awkward "through faith," which seems to disrupt the earlier formulation (see above §7.3) in 3.25, is more likely to refer to *God's* faithfulness, since it is God's action which is being described; see my *Romans* 172-73; also *"PISTIS CHRISTOU"* 76-77, and above §14.2. Cf. Williams, "Righteousness" 268-71, 289.

theme, as announced in 1.16-17 — ". . . the power of God for salvation to all who believe . . . the righteousness of God from faith to faith, as it is written, 'the righteous from faith shall live.' " Here again we note the repeated emphasis on *pistis* — no less than four *pistis/pisteuō* references.[204] And here again we can probably assume that in resuming the theme in 3.22 Paul repeats the emphasis — "the righteousness of God through faith [now specified as faith in Jesus Christ] to all who believe."[205] The repetition also gives opportunity to reintroduce the thematic "all": "through faith . . . to *all* who believe."[206]

It is equally notable that as the *pistis* theme is developed from 3.27 there is no real room for doubt that it refers all the time and without exception to human believing.[207] "The law of faith" (3.27) is explained in terms of the individual "being justified by faith apart from works of the law" (3.28), a justifying whose coming to effect can be expressed equally as "from faith" or "through faith" (3.30-31). And then in 4.3-22 this *pistis* is explained, as we have seen, by exposition of Abraham's "believing" (4.3), his *pistis* (4.9, 11-12). The interchange of verb and noun simply reinforces the point.[208]

We need not labour the point further. The beguiling attractiveness of the "faith of Christ" reading depends too much either on an atomistic study of the key texts in isolation from their contexts[209] or on the assumption of an

204. To make his case Hays argues that Hab 2.4 is a messianic prophecy and prefigures the faith of God's Son (*Faith* 150-57; " 'The Righteous One' as Eschatological Deliverer: A Case Study in Paul's Apocalyptic Hermeneutic," in J. Marcus and M. L. Soards, eds., *Apocalyptic and the New Testament* (§12 n. 1) 191-215; *"PISTIS"* 42-44); followed by D. A. Campbell, "Romans 1.17 — A *Crux Interpretum* for the *Pistis Christou* Debate," *JBL* 113 (1994) 265-85; Stowers, *Rereading* 200; Wallis, *Faith* 81-82. Earlier support is indicated by Campbell 281 n. 47.

205. Hays's objection that since "Romans 3 is a defense of God's justice," "the objective genitive interpretation of *pistis Iēsou Christou* becomes virtually unintelligible" (*"PISTIS"* 46) seems to miss the fundamental point for Paul that faith is the only appropriate human correlate to God's gracious righteousness (see above §14.7).

206. Hardly "a peculiar redundancy" then (*pace* Hays, *"PISTIS"* 46); see also my *"PISTIS CHRISTOU"* 74-75.

207. A reference to Christ's faithfulness would rather invite a parallel with Abraham's faithfulness in offering Isaac (the normal exposition of the time); but Paul's exposition seems to run counter to that (see above §14.7; and *"PISTIS CHRISTOU"* 75-77). Contrast again Wallis's rather tortuous unpacking of "faith" in 3.27-31 as "the salvific provision of God established through the faith of Christ" (*Faith* 88-90).

208. *Pisteuō* — 4.3, 5, 11, 17, 18, 24; *pistis* — 4.5, 9, 11, 12, 13, 14, 16 (twice), 19, 20. Similarly 10.4, 6, 9-10 (despite Stowers, *Rereading* 310-11).

209. The only one of the seven texts for which such an atomistic exegesis could be justified is Phil. 3.9. But in the light of the above discussion it is more obviously read as a further variation on Paul's repeated emphasis on faith, in this case as the radical opposite to trust in the flesh (see Reumann, *Righteousness* 62 n. 72). A possible allusion to "Christ's faith" simply raises the same question: what "faith of Christ" is this? To which

underlying story of Christ's faith for which the chief evidence is the disputed texts themselves. But when these texts are read within the flow of Paul's argument in Galatians and Romans, it is hard to hear anything as intended by Paul beyond his affirmation of the central importance of "faith," now as the appropriate gospel response of "faith in Christ."[210]

Whatever the outcome of this particular debate, however, it should not be allowed to obscure two points which were clearly central for Paul. First, that the gospel centres on Christ's death and resurrection as the definitive expression of God's righteousness, by which both sins and the power of sin have been once and for all dealt with. Second, that the means by which God's saving righteousness can now be received (should we add, most fully and effectively?) is by believing in this Christ.

§14.9 The blessings of justification

All that remains is to highlight the various consequences for believers which Paul explicitly attaches or attributes to justification. So to do is not to imply that they should be linked solely to the imagery of justification, or that they should be apportioned to justification in any sort of scholastic analysis or tabulation. It is simply to observe that Paul associates several other features of his gospel with justification in particular.

a) It follows at once from the whole thrust of Paul's exposition of the theme in Rom. 1.16–4.25 that justification means acceptance by God, the God who justifies the ungodly who trust as Abraham trusted (4.5). This is no abuse of legal process or a legal fiction, as talk of justifying the ungodly (Rom. 4.5) could imply.[211] For here is where the earlier clarification and the distinction between Greek and Hebrew concepts of "righteousness" (§14.2) becomes relevant again. In fact, at this point the law court metaphor simply breaks down. For in the law court, strictly speaking, there is no place for forgiveness; the due processes of the law must take their course. But where the issue is

---

the tradition available to Paul's readers gives no clear answer (see also V. Koperski, "The Meaning of *pistis Christou* in Philippians 3.9," *Louvain Studies* 18 [1993] 198-216). Reflection on the "faith" of Jesus is a wholly appropriate interest of contemporary theology (see, e.g., O'Collins, *Christology* [§10 n. 1] 250-68), but it can hardly be said to be a preoccupation in the earliest Jesus tradition. Insofar as Paul had such a theme in mind, his chosen term was "obedience" (Rom. 5.19; Phil. 2.8). See further my *"PISTIS CHRISTOU"* 78-79.

210. It is precisely this central importance of faith, both in receiving the gospel and in daily living (see below §23.3), which prevents me from offering here a "both-and" compromise (as, e.g., Witherington, *Narrative* 270).

211. Bornkamm, *Paul* 138, raises the question of "legal fiction," an "as if."

more one of mutual obligation between partners in a relationship, there it is for the injured party to determine whether the relationship is to be ended because of the other's breach of faith or sustained despite it. It is the latter course which God in his grace follows in justifying the sinner.

The charge of legal fiction also breaks down before our earlier finding that God's sentence of death on sin is carried through in the death of Christ (§9). Were Paul's doctrine of atonement one of substitution (Jesus died and the sinner went scot-free) that would be more open to such a charge. But as we saw, Paul's teaching is of Christ's death as a representative death, the death of all, of sinful flesh. His gospel is not that the trusting sinners escape death, but rather that they share in Christ's death. The cancer of sin in the human body is destroyed in the destruction of the cancerous flesh. This is a feature of the ongoing process of salvation to which we shall have to return (§18).

For similar reasons too much weight should not be put on the aorist tense at the beginning of 5.1 — "having been justified from faith. . . ." For that simply emphasizes the *beginning* of the salvation process. As the whole conception of God's righteousness has indicated, justification is not a once-for-all act of God. It is rather the initial acceptance by God into restored relationship. But thereafter the relationship could not be sustained without God continuing to exercise his justifying righteousness with a view to the final act of judgment and acquittal.[212] Put another way, the justified do not thereby become sinless. They continue to sin. Consequently, without God's continuing exercise of his justifying righteousness, the process of salvation would be aborted. In Luther's classic formulation, *simul peccator et justus* — "sinner and justified at one and the same time." Throughout this life the human partner will ever be dependent on God justifying the ungodly. Again there are ramifications of all this to which we will have to return (§18).

b) In summing up his gospel to that point in his exposition (5.1) Paul himself indicates some immediate corollaries: Rom. 5.1-2 —

> [1]Therefore, having been justified from faith we have[213] peace in relation to God through our Lord Jesus Christ, [2]through whom we have access (by faith) into this grace in which we stand and boast in hope of the glory of God.

212. The more weight is given to the aorist tense in Rom. 5.1 and 9, the more weight should also be given to the future tense in 2.13 and 3.20, 30 (see further §§18.1-2). The aorists of 8.30 all look back on the completed process of salvation from the perspective of that end point ("glorified" as well as "called" and "justified"). Cf. also n. 150 above.

213. On the strongly attested variant reading, "let us have peace," see my *Romans* 245; in favour of that reading see particularly Fee, *Empowering Presence* (§16 n. 1) 495-96 n. 66.

If justification means God accepting the sinner (5.8), it also means God bestowing the blessing of peace on those who were formerly enemies (5.10). "Peace" here is not to be restricted to the Greek idea of cessation of war, or to be merely spiritualized (inner calm). It will certainly include the much richer Hebrew concept of *shalom,* where the basic idea is of "well-being," including social harmony and communal well-doing.[214] As the most fundamental of all human relationships, a positively interactive relationship with God is the basis of all other fruitful human relationships. Without it human community cannot fully flourish.

Justification also opens up unhindered "access" to God. The metaphor is partly cultic. For the devout worshiper no image could be more powerful than that of unhindered access to the immediate presence of the God which the centre of the cult represented.[215] But the metaphor could also denote the highly prized privilege of access through the royal chamberlain into the king's presence.[216]

More striking still, justification made possible boasting "in hope of the glory of God" (5.2). The allusion to the earlier argument is twofold. The hope[217] is that the glory which humankind at present lacks (3.23)[218] will be restored. That is to say, the justified/justifying relation is a restoration to the originally intended relation of creature to Creator (cf. 1.21). In that relationship the human creature may properly boast, in contrast to the improper boasting of Israel in its privileges and falsely conceived security.[219]

We should simply note that in winding up this section of his exposition, Paul sets in clear parallel "justification" and "reconciliation" (5.10-11):

[10]How much more then, having now been *justified* by his blood,
    we shall be saved through him from wrath.
[11]For if when we were enemies we were reconciled to God through the
    death of his Son,
    how much more, having been *reconciled,* we shall be saved by his life.

---

214. See, e.g., Deut. 23.6; 1 Kgs. 5.12; Pss. 72.3, 7; 85; 147.14; Isa. 48.18; 55.12; Zech. 6.13; 8.12; see further W. Foerster and G. von Rad, *TDNT* 2.400-420.

215. 1QS 11.13-15 constitutes quite a striking parallel (cited above §14.2); see further Wolter, *Rechtfertigung* 107-20, and §20 n. 73 below.

216. See further my *Romans* 247-48.

217. Here again Hebrew content must be allowed to prevail over Greek form. For in Greek usage "hope" had an overtone of uncertainty similar to that which pervades English usage ("I hope to see you next summer, but am by no means confident of doing so"). Whereas in Hebraic thought hope was expectation of good and (as in Rom. 4.18) closely allied to trust, hope as confidence in God (see further R. Bultmann, *TDNT* 2.519-23; Plevnik, *Parousia* [§12 n. 1] ch. 8). "Hope" continues to form a major theme in the subsequent exposition (5.2, 4, 5; 8.20, 24-25; 12.12; 15.4, 12-13). See also §16 n. 129 and §18.6 below.

218. See above §4.5.

219. 2.17, 23; 3.27. Similarly 1 Cor. 1.31. See above §§5.4(4), 6.5c, and 14.5e.

"Salvation" denotes the completed process in both verses, where "justification" and "reconciliation" serve equally to denote its beginning. Here again the metaphors are complementary[220] and should not be played off against each other.[221]

c) A third consequence of justification has also been explicit in the principal expositions in Romans 4 and Galatians 3. Justification means acceptance into a relationship with God characterized by the grace of Israel's covenant. Justification by faith means Gentiles experiencing the blessing promised to Abraham, being granted a share in Israel's inheritance. Abraham is father of *all* who believe (Rom. 4.11-12); the blessing of Abraham reaches out to Gentiles as well as Jews (Gal. 3.8-9, 14). Gentiles partaking in Israel's "inheritance" is a crucial feature of both expositions.[222] This again is an aspect of Paul's theology to which we must return (§20), not least because it poses a theological problem to which Paul's theological exposition in Romans builds up as to a climax (Romans 9–11).[223]

d) One other feature should be mentioned, since it is expressed with such intensity of feeling in Galatians. It is that justification by faith means *liberty,* and, most important of all, liberty from the law. The antithesis of Paul's gospel of justification, as equally open to Gentiles, was a divine righteousness restricted in its scope by the law and in effect to those who practised the works of the law. Hence Paul's fear in Gal. 2.4: that the Gentile Galatians' freedom might be lost if the demand for circumcision was accepted. Hence his reversion to the theme in 4.22-31: those born of promise and Spirit are the children of the free. And the explosive conclusion to the main sequence of his argument (chs. 3–4) in 5.1: "For freedom Christ has set us free. Stand firm, therefore, and do not be subject again to a yoke of slavery." Once more, then, the antithesis of faith and works is mirrored in the antithesis of freedom and circumcision (5.1-6).

Here again it simply needs to be underlined that Paul experienced his coming to faith in Christ as one of liberation. The practice of the law, which had previously been his delight, he now regarded as a kind of slavery, the slavery of the spiritually immature (4.1-3). This, of course, is the language of hindsight. But if his language resonated in any degree with his Galatian converts, they too must have experienced justification by faith as a liberation, initially at least. Paul assumes a similar resonance in his play on the metaphor of slavery and manumission in Rom. 6.16-23, and the cry of relief in Rom.

---

220. See further above §13.4.

221. As Martin, *Reconciliation* (§9 n. 1) 153-54, is in some danger of doing. See also my *Romans* 259-60; and further Wolter, *Rechtfertigung*.

222. Rom. 4.13-14; Gal. 3.18, 29; 4.1, 7, 30.

223. See below §19.

8.2 echoes that of Gal. 5.1. Not least of Paul's delights in justification by faith was that it had liberated from what he now recognized to have been a spirit of slavery, whose motivation was fundamentally one of fear (Rom. 8.15).[224] It was not least that liberating openness to the amazing richness of God's grace which for Paul was one of the chief blessings of justification by faith, and one not to be lightly let go.

---

224. This was one of Bultmann's keener insights, that "the hidden side of 'boasting' and 'putting confidence in the flesh' " is *fear* (*Theology* 1.243). Those who have come out from a fundamentalist or narrowly sectarian context know what he means.

§15 Participation in Christ[1]

§15.1 Christ mysticism

The dominance of the "justification" metaphor in traditional analyses of Paul's soteriology should be plain from the extensiveness of the discussion in §14. But for those less attracted by the judicial character attaching to it, an alternative lay close to hand. This is the imagery of participation in Christ. In fact, it is in many ways the more natural extension of Paul's christology. For we have seen how important Paul's Adam christology was for him as the essential presupposition for making sense of the saving action of God in and through Christ. Of course, as we also noted, Paul does integrate the thought of God's righteousness with that of Christ's death as sacrifice.[2] But if the rationale of Paul's theology of sacrifice is as we sketched it out above (§9.3), then its more obvious outworking would be in terms of the sinner sharing in

1. **Bibliography**: **Bousset**, *Kyrios Christos* (§10 n. 1) 153-210; **M. Bouttier**, *En Christ. Étude d'exégèse et de théologie paulinienne* (Paris: Presses Universitaires de France, 1962); *Christianity according to Paul;* **F. Büchsel**, " 'In Christus' bei Paulus," *ZNW* 42 (1949) 141-58; **Cerfaux**, *Christian* (§14 n. 1) 312-72; **Conzelmann**, *Outline* 208-12; **Davies**, *Paul* 13-15, 86-110; **A. Deissmann**, *Die neutestamentliche Formel "in Christo Jesu"* (Marburg: Elwert, 1892); *Paul,* particularly 135-57; **M. Dibelius**, "Paulus und die Mystik," *Botschaft und Geschichte: Gesammelte Aufsätze* II (Tübingen: Mohr, 1956) 134-59 = Rengstorf, ed., *Paulusbild* 447-74; **J. Dupont**, *SYN CHRISTO. L'union avec le Christ suivant saint Paul* (Bruges: Nauwelaerts, 1952); **Fitzmyer**, *Paul* 88-90; **Gnilka**, *Theologie* 96-101; *Paulus* 255-60; **O. Kuss**, "Mit Christus," *Römerbrief* 319-81; **E. Lohmeyer**, " 'Syn Chrisț,' " in *Festgabe für Adolf Deissmann* (Tübingen: Mohr, 1927) 218-57; **B. McGinn**, *The Presence of God: A History of Western Christian Mysticism* 1: *The Foundations of Mysticism: Origins to the Fifth Century* (London: SCM/New York: Crossroad, 1991); **Moule**, *Origin* (§10 n. 1) ch. 2; **F. Neugebauer**, "Das Paulinische 'in Chrisț,' " *NTS* 4 (1957-58) 124-38; *In Christus: En Chrisț. Eine Untersuchung zum paulinischen Glaubensverständnis* (Göttingen: Vandenhoeck, 1961); **Penna**, "Problems and Nature of Pauline Mysticism," *Paul* 2.235-73; **Ridderbos**, *Paul* 57-64; **Schlier**, *Grundzüge* 173-77; **A. Schweitzer**, *The Mysticism of Paul the Apostle* (London: Black, 1931); **G. Sellin**, "Die religionsgeschichtlichen Hintergründe der paulinischen 'Christusmystik,' " *TQ* 176 (1996) 7-27; **Strecker**, *Theologie* 125-32; **A. J. M. Wedderburn**, "Some Observations on Paul's Use of the Phrases 'in Christ' and 'with Christ,' " *JSNT* 25 (1985) 83-97; **A. Wikenhauser**, *Pauline Mysticism: Christ in the Mystical Teaching of St. Paul* (Freiburg: Herder/Edinburgh: Nelson, 1960); **Ziesler**, *Pauline Christianity* 49-72.

2. Especially Rom. 3.21-26 and 2 Cor. 5.21.

Christ's death (and resurrection), rather than in a judicial verdict pronounced on the basis of Jesus' sacrificial death. Moreover, as we shall shortly observe, Paul's "in Christ" language is much more pervasive in his writings than his talk of "God's righteousness."

This alternative access point into or way of ordering Paul's theology of salvation became prominent at the beginning of the twentieth century. A sharpened sensitivity to the social or "history of religions" context of Paul's teaching helped swing the focus of interest from doctrine to experience. The two most prominent and influential expositions were those of Adolf Deissmann and Wilhelm Bousset. It was Deissmann who brought the formula "in Christ" to centre stage.[3] The phrase expressed "the most intimate possible fellowship of the Christian with the living spiritual Christ," Christ being conceived as a kind of atmosphere in which Christians lived.[4] "Mysticism" was an appropriate term to use as denoting the "religious tendency that discovers the way to God direct through inner experience without the mediation of reasoning."[5]

Similarly Bousset detected in the Christ piety of Paul a new and dominant note: "the intense feeling of personal belonging and of spiritual relationship with the exalted Lord."[6] He too used the term "Christ mysticism" for the experience focused in and sustained by the cult: "for Paul Christ becomes the supra-terrestrial power which supports and fills with its presence his whole life"; Christ was "sublimated into the abstract entity of the Pneuma, into the principle of the new Christian life"; "behind Paul's mysticism of the *en Christō einai* there stands the living experience of the Kyrios Christos present in worship and in the practical life of the community"; in Paul's letters we listen in to "the development of personal mysticism out of cultic mysticism."[7]

The best-known exponent of this alternative approach to Paul has been Albert Schweitzer. He began his main study of Paul with his own definition:[8]

> We are always in the presence of mysticism when we find a human being looking upon the division between earthly and super-earthly, temporal and eternal, as transcended, and feeling himself, while still externally amid the earthly and temporal, to belong to the super-earthly and eternal.

---

3. Deissmann, *"In Christo."*
4. Deissmann, *Paul* 140; "Just as the air of life, which we breathe, is 'in' us and fills us, and yet we at the same time live in this air and breathe it, so it is also with the Christ-intimacy of the Apostle Paul: Christ in him, he in Christ" (140).
5. Deissmann, *Paul* 149.
6. Bousset, *Kyrios Christos* 153.
7. Bousset, *Kyrios Christos* 154-57.
8. Schweitzer, *Mysticism* 1.

The most distinctive feature of his study, however, is the way he presses his understanding of Paul's Christ mysticism well beyond the metaphorical.[9]

> Dying and rising with Christ is for him [Paul] not something merely metaphorical, which could be expressed also in a different metaphor, but a simple reality. . . . For him the believer experiences the dying and rising again of Christ in actual fact, not in imitative representation.

In Paul, argues Schweitzer, the concept of eschatological redemption has been already realized in the "efficacious act" of baptism.[10]

> Paul's conception is, that believers in mysterious fashion share the dying and rising again of Christ, and in this way are swept away out of their ordinary mode of existence, and form a special category of humanity.

> The original and central idea of the Pauline Mysticism is therefore that the Elect share with one another and with Christ a corporeity which is in a special way susceptible to the action of the powers of death and resurrection, and in consequence capable of acquiring the resurrection state of existence before the general resurrection of the dead takes place.

> Grafted into the corporeity of Christ, he [one who is baptized] loses his creatively individual existence and his natural personality. Henceforth he is only a form of manifestation of the personality of Jesus Christ, which dominates that corporeity.

> The Mystical Body of Christ is thus for Paul not a pictorial expression . . . but an actual entity.

> That what is in view in the Pauline mysticism is an actual physical union between Christ and the Elect is proved by the fact that "being in Christ" corresponds to and, as a state of existence, takes the place of the physical "being in the flesh."

In a characteristic and much quoted passage, Schweitzer poses this as a polemical alternative to justification by faith: "The doctrine of righteousness by faith is therefore a subsidiary crater, which has formed within the rim of the main crater — the mystical doctrine of redemption through being-in-Christ."[11]

I have cited Schweitzer at such length since the extremeness of his

9. Schweitzer, *Mysticism* 15-16.
10. Schweitzer, *Mysticism* 96-97, 115-16, 125, 127.
11. Schweitzer, *Mysticism* 225.

view helps explain why the mystical approach faded so quickly as a viable option for Pauline studies in the middle decades of the century.[12] The wider interest in mysticism, which had been a feature of the pre–World War II period,[13] had anyway been diminishing in the face of psychological critique[14] and the horror of World War I.[15] In Protestant circles its curiosity value for NT scholarship was sidetracked into the debate about pre-Christian Gnosticism — becoming another victim of the wild goose chase for a pre-Christian Gnostic redeemer myth.[16] Increasing difficulty was perceived in translating Paul's imagery of incorporation into another person into language meaningful within the intellectual context of the twentieth century.[17] The theological insights which it had brought to the fore were readily absorbed into a reinvigorated theology of baptism and of the sacramental body of Christ.[18] And in the second half of the century the focus on experience switched more to the experience of the Spirit.[19]

---

12. E.g., W. Elliger comments on "in Christ": "*En Christō* thus refers not to mystical life in Christ; it serves rather, like the related formula *en pistei*, 'in faith,' as a characterization of one's realm of existence, which is often set in contrast to the worldly realm (*en sarki*, 'in the flesh,' Phil 3:3; 1:21-22; Rom 8:8-9; 1 Tim 3:16; Phm 16)" (*EDNT* 1.448). But "in faith" is hardly a characteristic motif in Paul.

13. W. R. Inge, *Christian Mysticism* (London: Methuen, 1899); R. M. Jones, *Studies in Mystical Religion* (London: Macmillan, 1909); E. Underhill, *Mysticism* (London: Methuen, 1911); most enduring has been R. Otto, *The Idea of the Holy* (London: Oxford University, 1923). In Roman Catholic circles, however, the wider interest has been maintained through the century; see McGinn, *Foundations of Mysticism* 276-91.

14. Particularly W. James, *The Varieties of Religious Experience* (1903; London: Fontana, 1960); and J. H. Leuba, *The Psychology of Religious Mysticism* (1929; London: Routledge and Kegan Paul, 1972). See further McGinn, *Foundations of Mysticism* 291-343.

15. Existentialism in effect offered a more robust alternative which spoke with greater power to a traumatized intellectual generation in the postwar period.

16. Briefly described in Sellin, "Hintergründe" 7-11. Sellin finds the closer parallels in the Hellenistic Judaism of Philo (12-27). We should, however, note that Paul's "in Christ" (or "Christ in me") is not notably ecstatic in character; Paul's ecstasy is more apocalyptic (2 Cor. 12.1-7) or pneumatic (1 Cor. 14.18).

17. See, e.g., the quotations from which Moule begins his treatment of "The Corporate Christ" (*Origin* 48-51). During the twentieth century there has been an even more marked flight from the category of "mysticism" in studies of John's Gospel (see below n. 24).

18. See particularly Wikenhauser, *Pauline Mysticism;* Strecker, *Theologie* 127. But the early assumption that a sense of mystical identity with Christ through baptism was simply taken over from the mystery cults has likewise had to retreat before heavy criticism (see further below §17.1).

19. Sanders, who is usually named as one who refocused attention on "participation" as the more important dimension of Paul's soteriology (*Paul* 502-8; also *Paul, the Law and the Jewish People* [§14 n. 1] 5-10; also *Paul* 74-79; followed, e.g., by Winninge,

Consequently, discussion of participation in Christ has become fragmented in Pauline studies. Of studies on Paul's understanding of baptism and of the body of Christ there has been no lack, though here too the interest has more recently turned from questions of origin of concept and theology to focus more on the social dynamics involved.[20] And with the growing influence of the charismatic movement in western and Third World Christianity, interest has steadily increased in Paul's theology of the Spirit.[21] But "Christ mysticism" has become very much a "back number," the lack of clear and consensual definition for its principal term and its esoteric overtones discouraging the attention it deserves.[22] To be sure, there has been a renewed interest in the history of Christian mysticism[23] and in the Jewish mysticism of the late Second Temple period, particularly at Qumran.[24] Both have drawn attention to the same traditional "mystical" pas-

---

Sinners [§14 n. 1] 218-20), has not in fact developed the point to any extent. The shift to body of Christ and Spirit is validated to the extent that Paul speaks both of "participation in the body of Christ" (1 Cor. 10.16) and of "participation in the Spirit" (2 Cor. 13.13; Phil. 2.1); see below §20.6 and §22.6.

20. See further §§17 and 20 below.

21. See further §16 below.

22. None of the modifications to Deissmann's principal term caught on — "faith-mysticism," "hope-mysticism," "history-mysticism," "eschatological mysticism," or even the more appropriate "passion-mysticism" (details in Sellin, "Hintergründe" 9).

23. See A. Louth, *The Origins of the Christian Mystical Tradition: From Plato to Denys* (Oxford: Clarendon, 1981); but also his "Mystik II," *TRE* 23.547-80; McGinn, *Foundations of Mysticism.* The definition of "mysticism," however, remains problematic. Louth characterizes it "as a search for and experience of immediacy with God" (*Origins* xv). McGinn defines "the mystical element in Christianity [as] that part of its belief and practices that concerns the preparation for, the consciousness of, and the reaction to what can be described as the immediate or direct presence of God" (xvii). Nicholas Lash objects to the implication that "the mystical element" is only *part* of Christianity's beliefs and practices: "the 'mystical life' is really nothing other than the Christian life lived to maximum intensity" ("Creation, Courtesy and Contemplation," *The Beginning and the End of "Religion"* [Cambridge: Cambridge University, 1996] 164-82 [here 171]). Paul himself played down the significance of his most striking extraordinary experiences (2 Cor. 12.1-10). What the terms "mysticism/mystical" may properly highlight, however, is the *immediacy* of the *sense* of the presence of God as a dimension (not just a part, and not to be limited to unusual experiences) of "the Christian life" (cf. Penna, *Paul* 2.271).

24. Particularly 4Q400-405; see C. Newsom, *Songs of the Sabbath Sacrifice: A Critical Edition* (Atlanta: Scholars, 1985). The renewal of interest in Jewish mysticism was signaled by G. Scholem, *Major Trends in Jewish Mysticism* (New York: Schocken, 1946). For the light which late Second Temple Jewish mysticism can shed on John's Gospel see now J. J. Kanagaraj, *"Mysticism" in the Gospel of John: An Inquiry into the Background of John in Jewish Mysticism* (Durham University Ph.D. thesis, 1995).

sages in Paul,[25] but have cast only a sidelong glance at the "in Christ" motif. In comparison with the amazingly vigorous contemporary debate on justification by faith, interest in our present theme, even the thoroughly and distinctively Pauline "in Christ" and "with Christ" motifs, has been modest and marginal.[26]

In the following sections we will attempt to remedy this lack in some measure. It is necessary, in other words, to bring this other way of looking at Paul's understanding of God's saving work more to the fore. Not least of importance is it to reintegrate into Paul's larger theology the dimension of Christ mysticism (or whatever we call it)[27] and the experience of the Spirit and to find the best way to correlate his relatively brief teaching on baptism and the body of Christ with these major emphases. It would be misleading, therefore, to contrast the relatively brief treatment of the present section with the too lengthy treatment of justification by faith (§14), as though length of treatment were a fair guide to relative importance. For, in fact, study of participation in Christ leads more directly into the rest of Paul's theology than justification. The gift of the Spirit (§16) is closely related to our present theme, as is the ongoing process of salvation (§18). And, as already indicated, Paul's theology of baptism (§17) and the body of Christ (§20) is bound to be in substantial continuity with his understanding of participation in Christ.

At the same time we must avoid the temptation to play off one aspect of Paul's theology against another. It would be all too easy, as Käsemann, for example, demonstrates, to play off emphasis on the individual against empha-

---

25. Particularly 2 Cor. 3.17-18; 4.4-6; 12.1-4. See McGinn, *Foundations of Mysticism* 69-74; Segal, *Paul* ch. 2; C. R. A. Morray-Jones, "Paradise Revisited (2 Cor. 12.1-12): The Jewish Mystical Background of Paul's Apostolate," *HTR* 86 (1993) 177-217, 265-92; and above §2. nn. 109 and 111. There has been a recent spurt of interest in Col. 2.18 (see my *Colossians* 180-84). McGinn comments: "Naturally, there are elements of anachronism in seeing the apostle to the Gentiles as a mystic in the later classic sense, but perhaps this is no more anachronistic than viewing him as nothing more than a preacher of the contrast between law and gospel" (74). A few sentences earlier McGinn observes with regard to 1 Cor. 6.16-17 that "This formula of becoming one spirit with the Lord, while Paul does not seem to intend it in any mystical sense, was perhaps the most often-cited scriptural warrant for an understanding of mystical union that emphasizes personal intercommunion and eschews any form of identity or union of indistinction" (74).

26. The benefit of this for us is that we will not need to spend so much time engaging with contemporary literature and can therefore move forward at a greater pace.

27. In my use of the term "mysticism" I do not wish to trade upon the subsequently more familiar meaning (union with God), or to leave behind the primary *relational* character of Paul's understanding of salvation (cf. Strecker, *Theologie* 126). "Mysticism" here is simply an attempt to find a word which evokes (rather than clearly indicating) the distinctive character of Paul's "in Christ," "with Christ," "Christ in me," etc. phrases. Rather than prejudge the issue we should let Paul's own use of "in Christ" and its related motifs fill the term with their meaning.

sis on corporateness, or to regard the *extra nos* of God's saving righteousness as a protection against mysticism and religious experience.[28] Here again we must try to avoid either-or exegesis. Much the better way is to integrate the manifest features and emphases in Paul's theology, or at least to attempt to demonstrate how Paul himself held them together, whether fully integrated or not.

The obvious way to proceed in this section is to examine each of the key phrases — "in Christ," "with Christ," "into Christ," "through Christ," and so on. "The body of Christ" is obviously of a piece with them. The relative neglect of these phrases in contemporary discussion has dulled our appreciation of just how extraordinary a sequence they make. Not least of interest are their ramifications for Paul's christology as well as for his soteriology.

§15.2 In Christ, in the Lord

The phrase *en Christō* occurs 83 times in the Pauline corpus (61 if we exclude Ephesians and the Pastorals),[29] not counting the equivalent phrases using a pronoun ("in him/whom") defined by the context.[30] It usually has the form "in Christ" or "in Christ Jesus." Curious features include the fact that only the Thessalonian letters have the phrase "in the Lord Jesus Christ,"[31] perhaps indicating a stilted early usage. And the Pastorals have only "in Christ Jesus."[32] Otherwise the occurrences spread fairly evenly across the whole range of Paul's letters.[33]

More striking is the evidence that this is another distinctively Pauline feature. Elsewhere in the NT, outside the Pauline corpus, the phrase occurs only in 1 Peter, itself the most Pauline of the non-Pauline letters.[34] And subsequently, its use in the Apostolic Fathers is almost certainly a reflection of Pauline influence.[35]

28. "The Pauline doctrine of justification is a protection not only against nomism but also against enthusiasm and mysticism" (Käsemann, *Perspectives* 73-74); "faith must be rescued from the dimension of recurrent religious experience" (*Perspectives* 82-83). Contrast Deissmann's earlier protest in *Paul* 177.

29.

	Rom	1 Cor	2 Cor	Gal	Eph	Phl	Col	1 Th	2 Th	Phm	Past
in Christ —	13	12	7	7	13	10	3	4	2	3	9

30. Note particularly Colossians 1–2, where the tally has to be swollen by a further 12 "in him/whom" phrases in 1.14-19 and 2.3-15.

31. 1 Thes. 1.1; 2 Thes. 1.1; 3.12. C. F. D. Moule, in private correspondence, also notes that they alone have "in God" (1 Thes. 1.1; 2.2; 2 Thes. 1.1).

32. 1 Tim. 1.14; 3.13; 2 Tim. 1.1, 9, 13; 2.1, 10; 3.12, 15.

33. Though note the greater intensity of usage in Philippians and Ephesians.

34. 1 Pet. 3.16; 5.10, 14.

35. E.g., *1 Clem* 32.4; 38.1; Ignatius, *Ephesians* 1.1; *Trallians* 9.2.

To this list we have to add the equally distinctive Pauline phrase *en Kyriǭ*, "in the Lord" (occasionally "in the Lord Jesus")[36] — a further 47 instances (39 if we exclude Ephesians).[37] Another odd feature is the complete absence of this phrase from the Pastorals.

All this makes the current comparative neglect of the motif all the more surprising. Here if anywhere, one would have thought, we have immediate access to a characteristic and distinctive trait within Paul's theology.

The appearance of the motif in the undisputed Paulines can be analysed under three broad categories, the last two of which in particular embrace both the "in Christ" and "in the Lord" phrases.[38] It should be stressed at once that the categories are in no sense fixed or clearly discrete. On the contrary, one of the features of the motif is the way usages in different contexts blend into each other, and also into the related phrases, "with Christ," "into Christ," and "through Christ." They thus indicate a whole perspective from which Paul viewed different aspects of Christian identity and daily life.

First, there is the more objective usage, referring particularly to the redemptive act which has happened "in Christ" or depends on what Christ is yet to do.[39] So, for example, Rom. 3.24 — "They are justified . . . through the redemption which is in Christ Jesus"; 6.23 — "the gracious gift of God is eternal life in Christ Jesus our Lord"; 8.2 — "the law of the Spirit of life in Christ Jesus has set you free"; 8.39 — "neither death nor life . . . will be able to separate us from the love of God which is in Christ Jesus"; 1 Cor. 1.4 — "the grace of God given you in Christ Jesus"; 15.22 — "in Christ shall all be made alive"; 2 Cor. 3.14 — "in Christ it [the veil] is taken away"; 5.19 — "God was in Christ reconciling the world"; Gal. 2.17 — "seeking to be justified in Christ"; 3.14 — "that to the Gentiles the blessing of Abraham might come in Christ Jesus"; 5.6 — "in Christ Jesus neither circumcision nor uncircumcision counts for anything"; Phil. 2.5 — "let this mind be in you which was also in Christ Jesus";[40]

36. The three "in the Lord Jesus Christ" phrases in the Thessalonian letters are not counted twice. Note also "in Christ Jesus our Lord," as in Rom. 6.23; 8.39; 1 Cor. 15.31.

37.

	Rom	1 Cor	2 Cor	Gal	Eph	Phl	Col	1 Th	2 Th	Phm	Past
in the Lord —	8	9	2	1	8	9	4	3	1	2	0

38. It is characteristic of Paul's christology that he does not think of Christ's saving act as done by or in "the Lord," and that it is the risen and exalted Lord by which believers define themselves and under whose authority they live.

39. "Objective" — Rom. 3.24; 6.23; 8.2, 39; 15.17; 1 Cor. 1.4; 15.19, 22, 31; 2 Cor. 2.14; 3.14; 5.19; Gal. 2.17; 3.14; 5.6; Phil. 1.26; 2.5; 3.3, 9, 14; 4.19; Col. 1.28; 2.3, 9, 15; 1 Thes. 5.18; Eph. 1.20; 2.13; 4.21, 32. Is a mystical sense less prominent in this usage (cf. Wikenhauser, *Pauline Mysticism* 23-25)? But the "objective" usage includes present and future saving acts; and the past dimension is picked up in the "with" motif analysed below ("crucified with Christ," etc. — §15.3).

40. But the usage here is different; see above §11 n. 66.

4.19 — "his riches in glory in Christ Jesus"; 1 Thes. 5.18 — "the will of God in Christ Jesus."[41]

Second, there is a more *subjective* usage, where Paul speaks regularly of believers as *being* "in Christ"[42] or "in the Lord."[43] So, for example, Rom. 6.11 — "You must reckon yourselves dead indeed to sin and alive to God in Christ Jesus"; 8.1 — "There is now no condemnation for those in Christ Jesus"; 12.5 — "we all are one body in Christ"; 16.3 — "Prisca and Aquila, my fellow workers in Christ Jesus"; 1 Cor. 1.2 — "those sanctified in Christ Jesus"; 1.30 — "from him you are in Christ Jesus"; 15.18 — "those who have fallen asleep in Christ"; 2 Cor. 5.17 — "if anyone is in Christ, new creation!"; Gal. 1.22 — "the churches of Judea which are in Christ" 2.4 — "our freedom which we have in Christ Jesus"; 3.28 — "you are all one in Christ Jesus."

Similarly, with the "in the Lord" phrases. Paul regularly sends greetings to individuals "in the Lord" (Rom. 16.8-13). Timothy is his "beloved and faithful child in the Lord" (1 Cor. 4.17). He calls the Corinthians his "workmanship in the Lord" (1 Cor. 9.1). Onesimus is a beloved brother "both in the flesh and in the Lord" (Phm. 16).

Third, both "in Christ"[44] and "in the Lord"[45] phrases occur where Paul has in view his own activity or is exhorting his readers to adopt a particular attitude or course of action. For example, Paul "speaks the truth in Christ" (Rom. 9.1). He became the Corinthians' father in Christ Jesus (1 Cor. 4.15). He recalls to them his ways in Christ (4.17). He prays that his love might be with them all in Christ Jesus (16.24). Before God he speaks in Christ (2 Cor. 2.17; 12.19). His conduct as a prisoner has made it clear to all that his imprisonment is in Christ (Phil. 1.13). He commands and exhorts in the Lord Jesus Christ (2 Thes. 3.12). He calls on Philemon to refresh his heart in Christ (Phm. 20).

Again, the situation is similar with the "in (the) Lord" phrases, in which use of *kyrios* gives the observation or exhortation more authoritative force.[46] Paul is "convinced in the Lord Jesus that nothing is profane in itself,"

41. The nearest equivalent "in the Lord" phrases are 1 Cor. 1.31 and 2 Cor. 10.17, both citing Jer. 9.23.

42. "Subjective" — Rom. 6.11; 8.1; 12.5; 16.3, 7, 9, 10; 1 Cor. 1.2, 30; 4.10; 15.18; 2 Cor. 5.17; 12.2; Gal. 1.22; 2.4; 3.26, 28; Phil. 1.1; 2.1; 4.7, 21; Col. 1.2, 4; 1 Thes. 1.1, 14; 4.16; 2 Thes. 1.1; Phm. 23. See also Wikenhauser, *Pauline Mysticism* 30-31.

43. Rom. 16.2, 8, 11, 12 (twice), 13; 1 Cor. 4.17; 16.19; Col. 4.7; Phm. 16; Eph. 4.1.

44. "Active" — Rom. 9.1; 16.3, 9; 1 Cor. 4.15, 17; 16.24; 2 Cor. 2.6, 17; 12.19; Phil. 1.13; 4.13.

45. Rom. 14.14; 16.12; 1 Cor. 7.22, 39; 9.1-2; 11.11; 15.58; 2 Cor. 2.12; Gal. 5.10; Phil. 1.14; 2.19, 24; 3.1; 4.1-2, 4, 10; Col. 3.18, 20; 4.17; 1 Thes. 3.8; 5.12; 2 Thes. 3.4; Eph. 6.10, 21.

46. Cf. Bouttier, *En Christ* 55; Moule, *Origin* 59-60.

and thus feels free to eat meat (Rom. 14.14). Slaves "called in the Lord" are nevertheless free and should see themselves accordingly (1 Cor. 7.22). The fact that "in the Lord" neither gender has identity independent of the other should likewise condition attitudes (11.11). Labour done "in the Lord" is not in vain (15.58). Use of the phrase burgeons in Philippians as Paul tries to coax the recipients into more positive attitudes: "brothers made confident in the Lord to speak the word of God" (1.14); Paul "hopes in the Lord" and "trusts in the Lord" regarding future activities (2.19, 24); he urges them to receive Epaphroditus "in the Lord with all joy" (2.29); he calls on them to "rejoice in the Lord" (3.1), to "stand firm in the Lord" (4.1), to "agree in the Lord" (4.2), and to "rejoice in the Lord always" (4.4), just as he himself does (4.10).

It is worth rehearsing Paul's usage in such detail simply to bring out what a fundamental aspect of his thought and speech this "in Christ/in the Lord" motif represents. Paul's perception of his whole life as a Christian, its source, its identity, and its responsibilities, could be summed up in these phrases. No doubt some of the references indicate a kind of reflex action, added to a sentence without much forethought. But that would simply confirm how much the language and the perspective it embodied had become an integral part of the warp and woof both of his theology and, not least for Paul himself, of his living and relationships.

For us it is important to grasp what a range of Paul's theology is contained within the motif. The fact that it is used in reference to the objective saving work of Christ is certainly of major significance.[47] But the motif cannot be limited to that, nor can the rest of the usage be treated as a mere corollary. Equally it is tempting at times to regard the phrase as denoting no more than "as a Christian," or even "as a member of the community of those who believe in Christ."[48] But "in Christ" can hardly be reduced over all to a mere

---

47. See particularly Neugebauer, *In Christus*. Characteristic of the reaction to the earlier readiness to speak of Paul's mysticism has been the emphasis on this aspect. For example, Ridderbos: " 'being in Christ,' 'crucified, dead, raised, seated in heaven with him,' obviously does not have the sense of a communion that becomes reality only in certain sublime moments, but rather of an abiding reality determinative for the whole of the Christian life . . . Rather than with certain experiences, we have to do here with the church's 'objective' state of salvation" (*Paul* 59). Similarly Conzelmann: "The evidence of the text points us to the objective saving work. . . . 'In Christ' thus means that here, in him and not in me, salvation has taken place" (*Outline* 210). Schlier, *Grundzüge* 175, notes the analogy with "in Adam" (1 Cor. 15.22); Ziesler argues that the "in Adam" is modeled on the "in Christ" (*Pauline Christianity* 54). Wedderburn suggests that the background of Paul's "in Christ" and "with Christ" may be found in Paul's talk in Gal. 3.8-9 of being blessed "in Abraham" and "with (faithful) Abraham" ("Observations" 88-91).

48. Bultmann, *Theology* 1.328-29. BAGD, *en* I.5.d, list as examples of *en Christō* = "Christian" Rom. 16.10, 13; 2 Cor. 12.2; Gal. 1.22; 1 Thes. 2.14; 4.16; Eph. 4.1; 6.21; similarly "in the Lord" — Rom. 16.11; 1 Cor. 7.39; 1 Thes. 5.12. Moule offers 1 Cor. 3.1 and Rom. 9.1 as examples (*Origin* 54), and draws attention to the versatility of the preposition *en* (54-56).

label, or its significance be satisfactorily grasped in such a desiccated formulation. In particular, it would be odd to recognize the "power" character of judicial imagery like "justification," while denying the obvious implication that "in Christ" denotes transfer of lordship and existential participation in the new reality brought about by Christ.[49]

For as the earlier studies of Deissmann and Bousset rightly emphasized, at the heart of the motif is not merely a belief about Christ, but an experience understood as that of the risen and living Christ. For example, Paul uses it when he recalls the no doubt emotional experience of bringing converts to faith (1 Cor. 4.15), when conscious of his responsibility as a preacher (2 Cor. 2.17), when expressing his confidence regarding his converts (Gal. 5.10) and his own condition (Phil. 1.14), when recalling to them their common experience of encouragement (2.1), and when speaking of his hope for the future (2.19, 24) and his assurance of divine enabling (4.13). He does not hesitate to make an emotive appeal to "refresh his heart *(splanchna)* in Christ," or to express his longings "in the deep feelings *(splanchnois)* of Christ."[50] His regular dispatch of greetings "in the Lord" conveys a sense of intimacy, evoking shared memories of times past. He urges the Philippians to receive Epaphroditus in the Lord with all joy (Phil. 2.29).

Paul evidently felt himself to be caught up "in Christ" and borne along by Christ. In some sense he experienced Christ as the context of all his being and doing. We can hardly avoid some sort of locative sense in the preposition "in," at least in a number of cases.[51] What that might mean for his christology is a subject to which we must return. Here we focus more on the evident sense of Christ's presence as more or less a constant factor, from within which Paul consciously and subconsciously drew resource and strength for all his activities.

In addition, we need to recall also the complementary usage (a handful of cases) where Paul speaks of Christ as indwelling the believer,[52] and where a similar sense of a living inner resource is implied. A particularly poignant example is Gal. 2.19-20: "I have been crucified with Christ; and it is no longer I that live, but Christ lives in me."[53] Later in the same letter he uses the convoluted image of himself giving birth to Christ within the Galatians (4.19).[54]

---

49. Cf. Schlier, *Grundzüge* 174-76.

50. Phm. 20; Phil. 1.8; also 2.1. *Splanchna,* "inward parts," the seat of the emotions.

51. Moule, *Origin* 62-63.

52. Rom. 8.10; 2 Cor. 13.5; Gal. 2.20; Col. 1.27; note also Gal. 1.16 and cf. 2 Cor. 4.6; see further Moule, *Origin* 56-58.

53. Despite his later qualification (above n. 47), Conzelmann notes that "here in fact we find ourselves in the linguistic milieu of 'enthusiasm' " (*Outline* 209).

54. See further B. R. Gaventa, "The Maternity of Paul: An Exegetical Study of Galatians 4.19," in Fortna and Gaventa, eds., *The Conversation Continues* 189-201; my *Galatians* 239-41.

The tension between a present reality and a future realization is still maintained in the later Paulines. In Col. 1.27 "Christ in you" is "the hope of glory," and Col. 3.4 can also speak of the future revelation of "Christ who is our life," while the prayer of Eph. 3.17 is "that [the] Christ might dwell in your hearts through faith." Such variation is yet one more reminder that we are not dealing with literal descriptions but with emotive imagery which tapped into and expressed with differing degrees of adequacy a deeply sensed inner reality and transformation focused in Christ.

All of which makes it hard to avoid talk of something like a mystical sense of the divine presence of Christ within and without, establishing and sustaining the individual in relation to God. Likewise we can hardly avoid speaking of the community, a community which understood itself not only from the gospel which had called it into existence, but also from the shared experience of Christ, which bonded them as one.[55]

§15.3 With Christ

An equally striking feature of Paul's theology is his "with Christ" motif. Here the full weight of the motif can be lost to sight, since the phrase itself occurs infrequently and lacks a "with the Lord" parallel. Moreover, in a number of cases it may simply denote "in the company of" rather than any mystical, sacramental, or salvation-historical participation "in Christ." This certainly seems to be the case in the predominantly future reference of the phrase: to be with Christ (in heaven);[56] to appear with Christ in glory or at the parousia.[57] Only two passages speak of believers having died "with Christ."[58] 2 Cor. 4.14 speaks of being raised in the future "with Jesus."[59] 2 Cor. 13.4 presents Christ's weakness on the cross and life "from the power of God" as a paradigm for Paul's present weakness "in him" and future living "with him from the

---

55. For the double emphasis (individual and social) cf. Davies, *Paul* 86-90.

56. Phil. 1.23; 1 Thes. 4.17; 5.10; cf. Col. 3.3.

57. Col. 3.4; 1 Thes. 4.14. Both Lohmeyer, *"Syn Christǭ,"* and Dupont, *Syn Christǭ,* focused on the future aspect of the motif. Conzelmann is too schematic when he maintains that "the difference between *en* and *syn* is that life 'in him' is (dialectically) present; life 'with him' is future" (*Outline* 211).

58. Rom. 6.8; Col. 2.20; cf. Rom. 8.32; Col. 3.3. Cf. Fitzmyer: *"syn* pregnantly expresses two poles of the Christian experience, identification with Christ at its beginning, and association with him at its term. In the meantime the Christian is *en Christǭ"* (*Paul* 89).

59. Holleman, *Resurrection* (§18 n. 1) 191-94, surprisingly denies that 2 Cor. 4.14 has in view eschatological resurrection. He argues that the idea of Christians' association with Christ at his parousia and the idea of resurrection in and through Christ developed independently (ch. 14).

power of God for you."[60] But only Col. 2.13 speaks of believers as *already* having been made alive "with him."

But to focus solely on the actual "with Christ/him" references would be a mistake. For the real force of the "with Christ" motif is carried by the remarkable sequence of about forty "with" compounds which constitute yet another distinctive feature of Paul's writing.[61] He uses them both to describe the common privilege, experience, and task of believers[62] and to describe a sharing in Christ's death and life.[63] The two uses were no doubt linked in

---

60. The precise force of "for you" is unclear, but Paul presumably meant either that the power which will effect his future resurrection with Christ would be manifest in his next visit to Corinth, or that the Christ in whom he lives and with whom he will live would manifest the power of his risen life through him on that visit; but see also Martin, *2 Corinthians* 477.

61. More than half of the 40 appear only in Paul in the NT.

62. Usually nouns —

synagonizomai, "contend together with" — Rom. 15.30

synathleō, "contend together with" — Phil. 1.27; 4.3

synaichmalōtos, "fellow prisoner" — Rom. 16.7; Col. 4.10; Phm. 23

synanapauomai, "rest in company with" — Rom. 15.32

synapothnēskō, "die with" — 2 Cor. 7.3

synbasileuō, "reign with" — 1 Cor. 4.8

synbibazō, "unite" — Eph. 4.16; Col. 2.2, 19

syndesmos, "bond" — Eph. 4.3; Col. 2.19; 3.14

syndoulos, "fellow slave" — Col. 1.7; 4.7

synergeō, "work with" — 1 Cor. 16.16; 2 Cor. 6.1

synergos, "fellow worker" — 12 occurrences

synzaō, "live with" — 2 Cor. 7.3

synzygos, "yokefellow" — Phil. 4.3

synklēronomos, "fellow heir" — Eph. 3.6

synkoinōneō, "participate with" — Eph. 5.11; Phil. 4.14

synkoinōnos, "participant, partner" — Rom. 11.17; 1 Cor. 9.23; Phil. 1.7

synmimētēs, "fellow imitator" — Phil. 3.17

synoikodomeō, "build with" — Eph. 2.22

symparakaloumai, "be encouraged together with" — Rom. 1.12

synpaschō, "suffer with" — 1 Cor. 12.26

synpolitēs, "fellow citizen" — Eph. 2.19

synstenazō, "groan together with" — Rom. 8.22

synstratiōtēs, "fellow soldier" — Phil. 2.25; Phm. 2

synypourgeō, "join in helping" — 2 Cor. 1.11

synchairō, "rejoice with" — 1 Cor. 12.26; 13.6; Phil. 2.17-18

synpsychos, "united in spirit" — Phil. 2.2

synōdinō, "be in travail together with" — Rom. 8.22

63. Usually verbs —

symmorphizomai, "be conformed to" — Phil. 3.10

symmorphos, "be in the same form as" — Rom. 8.29; Phil. 3.21

symphytos, "grow together" — Rom. 6.5

Paul's mind, as with "in Christ," to express the same sense of a communality of believers rooted in its dependence upon their common experience of participation in Christ.

Particularly notable are the clustering of the compounds in several passages. Rom. 6.4-8 and 8.16-29 deserve particular attention:[64]

> [4]So then we were *buried with* him through baptism into death . . . [5]For if we have become *knit together with* the very likeness of his death, we shall certainly also be *knit together with* the very likeness of his resurrection. [6]Knowing this, that our old nature has been *crucified with* him . . . [8]But if we have died with Christ, we believe that we shall also *live with* him.

> [16]The Spirit itself *bears witness with* our spirit that we are children of God. [17]And if children, also heirs — heirs of God and *heirs together with* Christ, provided that we *suffer with* him in order that we might also be *glorified with* him. . . . [22]For we know that the whole creation *groans and suffers the pains of childbirth together* up till now. . . . [26]In the same way the Spirit *helps us* in our weakness. . . . [29]Those he knew beforehand he also predestined to be *conformed to* the image of his Son.

The prominence of the death-resurrection motif in the compounds uniting the believer to Christ underlines the distinctively Christian, that is, Pauline, character of the teaching. Paul appeals not simply to the wider sense of the appropriateness of death imagery when describing the beginning of the process of salvation. Fundamental is the eschatological claim that with Christ's death a whole epoch has passed and a new age begun. Moreover, this new age is characterized by the steady reclaiming of individuals for an ever closer conformity to the risen Christ. In some sense the event of Christ's passion and resurrection has to be reenacted in believers until the renewal of the new

---

synapothnēskō, "die with" — 2 Tim. 2.11
synbasileuō, "reign with" — 2 Tim. 2.12
syndoxazomai, "be glorified with" — Rom. 8.17
synēgeirō, "raise with" — Eph. 2.6; Col. 2.12; 3.1
synzaō, "live with" — Rom. 6.8; 2 Tim. 2.11
synzōopoieō, "make alive together with" — Eph. 2.5; Col. 2.13
synthaptomai, "be buried with" — Rom. 6.4; Col. 2.12
synkathizō, "sit with" — Eph. 2.6
synklēronomos, "fellow heir" — Rom. 8.17
synpaschō, "suffer with" — Rom. 8.17
synstauroomai, "be crucified with" — Rom. 6.6; Gal. 2.19
Note also:
synmartyreō, "bear witness with" — Rom. 8.16
synantilambanomai, "take part with" — Rom. 8.26
    64. Note also Col. 2.12-13; Eph. 2.5-6; 2 Tim. 2.11-12.

age is complete. Not only so, but the process cannot, almost by definition, be something merely individual or individualistic. Rather, by its very nature it is a shared experience which involves creation as well. The "with Christ" cannot be fully enacted except as a "with others" and "with creation." There are ramifications here for our understanding of the process of salvation and the body of Christ to which we will have to return (§18).

In the meantime we simply need to underline the tremendous sense of "togetherness" implicit in Paul's language. This again can hardly be reduced to a merely literary motif, a feature of Pauline style. Here the more mystical dimension comes to focus primarily in the decisive salvation-effecting events of Christ's death and resurrection. And here too the language cannot be reduced simply to a description of baptism or of membership in the believing community. Paul's language indicates rather a quite profound sense of participation with others in a great and cosmic movement of God centred on Christ and effected through his Spirit. Here again a term like "mysticism" is only an attempt to indicate that profundity and to signal that there are depths and resonances here which we may not be able fully to explore, but for which we need to keep our ears attuned.

§15.4 Complementary formulations

There are several other phrases which indicate the extent to which this mystical sense of being bound up with Christ overlapped with other strands of Paul's theology.

a) *Into Christ.* On several occasions Paul speaks of individuals as brought *eis Christon,* "into Christ." Those which have attracted most attention are the two descriptions of the crucial transition as "having been baptized into Christ."[65] In both cases it is difficult to avoid the basic sense of *eis,* as movement into a location.[66] This is particularly so with Rom. 6.3, where the imagery follows directly from that of Christ as the second Adam. In that context "baptized into [this] Christ" is presumably intended to convey the sense of being given participation in this Christ. This is confirmed by the closely related example, 1 Cor. 12.13 — "baptized into one body." The most obvious sense, once again, is that it was by thus being baptized that all those referred to became members of the body of Christ (12.14-27).[67] In a similar way Gal. 3.27 has to be correlated with its accompanying metaphor of "putting

---

65. Rom. 6.3; Gal. 3.27; also 1 Cor. 12.13. On 1 Cor. 10.2 see below §17 n. 34.
66. Fitzmyer: "*Eis Christon* denotes, then, the movement of incorporation" (*Paul* 89).
67. See further below §17.2.

on Christ."[68] To be baptized into Christ is complementary to or equivalent to assuming the persona of Christ.[69] In both cases some sort of identification or sense of bound-up-with-ness is implicit.

Other cases of *eis Christon* may use *eis* in the less specific sense of "towards, in reference to, for."[70] But even here we may have to allow some mystical overtone. Epaenetus was "the firstfruits of Asia *eis Christon*" (Rom. 16.5); note the conversion context. God is "the one who establishes us with you *eis Christon*" (2 Cor. 1.21); the sense of ongoing process echoes the same ambivalence noted above.[71] "The law became our custodian *eis Christon*" (Gal. 3.24), to bring us "into Christ."[72] Paul prays for Philemon "that the shared experience of your faith might be effective in the knowledge of all the good that is amongst us *eis Christon*" (Phm. 6), where the last two words may carry the sense of "bringing us into (closer) relation to Christ."[73] Even Paul's infrequent use of the phrase "believe into Christ" may have such overtones, given his other *eis Christon* usage.[74] Even if in this case he is simply reflecting a more widespread Christian usage, the sense of commitment to Christ, so as to become determined by and bound up with Christ, is not easy to escape entirely.

b) *The body of Christ.* This is a theme which we will deal with later (§20). However, its close correlation with our present theme makes some reference to it here unavoidable.[75] The two features to be noted are the obvious ones. First, the imagery describes a group of people who identified themselves by their relationship with each other. They were "individually members of one another" (Rom. 12.5), part of a larger whole, as it were, limbs and organs of a single body. Second, the body is compared with Christ, or even identified as Christ.[76] Membership in the body is also membership in Christ. In other

68. The imagery is used again in exhortation in Rom. 13.14; note also Col. 3.9-10 and Eph. 4.22-24; see further below §17.2 and n. 63.

69. See above §8 n. 58.

70. Rom. 16.5; 2 Cor. 1.21; 11.3; Gal. 3.24; Phm. 6; but 1 Cor. 8.12 (*eis* = "against").

71. E.g., Gal. 4.19 and Eph. 3.17.

72. The temporal sense ("up until and into the time of Christ") may be more dominant; but note the close following 3.27.

73. Moule, *Colossians and Philemon* 142; see also my *Colossians* 320.

74. Rom. 10.14; Gal. 2.16; Phil. 1.29; Col. 2.5.

75. Rom 12.3-8; 1 Cor. 12.12-27.

76. The variation of terminology is often lost beneath the blanket term "body of Christ": "we the many are one body in Christ" (Rom. 12.5); "as the body is one and has many members, and all the members of the body, though many, are one body, so also is Christ" (1 Cor. 12.12); "you are Christ's body and individually members of it" (12.27); Christ as the head of the body (Col. 1.18; 2.19; Eph. 4.15-16). Note also 1 Cor. 10.16-17: "the bread which we break, is it not participation in the body of Christ? Because there is one bread, we the many are one body, for we all share in the one bread."

words, the same sense of identification with Christ is present. Here most clearly there is no thought of an individualistic piety, typical of so much traditional or late medieval mystical practice. It is a sense of belonging to Christ indeed, but of belonging together with others, with the obvious implication that one without the other would make the whole unbalanced and unhealthy.[77]

c) *Through Christ.* Quite closely parallel to the range of usage of the "in Christ" and "with Christ" metaphors is Paul's use of *dia Christou,* "through Christ." His most regular formulation envisages the saving or commissioning or final action of God as happening or coming to effect "through Christ."[78] But, as we have noted earlier, Paul also speaks of believers as giving thanks to God "through Christ" or sustained by the sense of their relationship with God "through Christ."[79] And in Rom. 15.30 Paul appeals to his Roman audiences "through our Lord Jesus Christ."[80]

Here again it is worth noting that the typical Pauline usage is *dia* with the genitive — "through Christ." The alternative, *dia* with the accusative — "on account of Christ" — Paul hardly uses at all.[81] The difference in construction makes our point for us. Paul's motivation, both in his conversion and in his missionary work, was not the inspiration of a heroic tale of what Jesus taught or did two decades earlier. He was not involved in a Society to Celebrate the Memory of Jesus of Nazareth. Rather, his conception of Christ was of an open channel between God and his people, a living intermediary through whom God acted and through whom his people could approach him. Here we begin to move away from the more apparent mystical imagery. But the overlap and continuity with the earlier formulations is clear enough.

d) *Of Christ.* Finally, we need to take note of passages where the genitive *Christou,* "Christ's, of Christ, belonging to Christ," is used.[82] In most

---

77. Rom. 12.3; 1 Cor. 12.14-26; Col. 2.19; Eph. 4.13-16.

78. Rom. 2.16 (final judgment through Christ); 3.24 (through the redemption in Christ); 5.17, 21 (grace and life reign through Christ); 7.4 (you died through the body of Christ); 1 Cor. 15.57 (victory given through Christ); 2 Cor. 1.5 (encouragement through Christ); 5.18 (God reconciling through Christ); Gal. 1.1 (an apostle through Christ); Phil. 1.11 (fruit of righteousness through Christ); 1 Thes. 5.9 (salvation through Christ); Eph. 1.5 (adoption through Christ); Tit. 3.6 (Holy Spirit poured out through Christ).

79. Rom. 1.8 (giving thanks to God through Christ); 5.1 (peace with God through Christ); 5.11 (boasting in God through Christ); 7.25 (thanks to God through Christ); 16.27 (doxology through Christ); 2 Cor. 3.4 (confidence towards God through Christ); Col. 3.17 (giving thanks to God through Christ). See further §10.5c.

80. To the same effect Paul's appeal "through the name of our Lord Jesus Christ" in 1 Cor. 1.10.

81. 1 Cor. 4.10; Phil. 3.8.

82. Rom. 8.9; 14.8; 1 Cor. 1.12; 3.23; 15.23; 2 Cor. 10.7; Gal. 3.29; 5.24.

cases the context implies more than the name "Christ" functioning simply as a label. In Rom. 8.9, the motif is a variation for talk of having the Spirit, the Spirit indwelling, and Christ indwelling: "if anyone does not have the Spirit of Christ, he does not belong to him" (literally, "he is not of him"). In 1 Cor. 15.23 the resurrection of "those who are Christ's" is understood to be patterned on Christ's, and we are deep in Adam christology. In Gal. 3.29, "you are of Christ" clearly picks up the preceding clause (3.28 — "you all are one in Christ Jesus"); to be "in Christ" means also to be part of Christ, to belong to Christ. The larger context, we may recall, is of Gentile believers being able to claim descent from Abraham (3.29) by being incorporated in Christ (3.27), the singular seed of Abraham (3.16). And in Gal. 5.24, "those who belong to Christ Jesus" are defined as those who "have crucified the flesh." That is to say, and it could hardly be otherwise in Paul's scheme of things, they identify themselves with the cross of Christ (2.19); for it is only through Christ's cross that crucifixion of and to the world can be effected (6.14).

Even the more straightforwardly slogan usages cannot be reduced simply to the confession, "I am a Christian."[83] For in 1 Cor. 1.12, for example, "I am of Christ" stands in parallel to alternative slogans, "I am of Paul," "I am of Apollos," and "I am of Cephas." The identification implied is like that of an emotive bond with a contemporary leader, not simply the evocation of a past hero. The bond is of master and slave or political leader and devoted partisan. The cosmic sweep of 1 Cor. 3.21-23 is even more evocative — "All things are yours, whether Paul or Apollos or Cephas, or the world or death, or the present, or the future; all things are yours, and you are Christ's." And we should note the equivalent intensity in Rom. 14.8 — "If we live, we live for the Lord; and if we die, we die for the Lord. So whether we live or whether we die, we are the Lord's."[84] Also 2 Cor. 5.14 — "Christ's love constrains us. . . ."[85]

e) *Christ and Spirit.* We should also mention one further variation within all this — the overlap between Christ and Spirit. We have already dealt with one aspect of it (§10.6), and will have to take it up again shortly (§16). Here we need simply note the implication of one of Paul's most striking passages, already cited —

---

83. Rom. 14.8; 1 Cor. 1.12; 3.23; 2 Cor. 10.7.
84. Schlier, *Grundzüge* 174, adds "for Christ" to the "in Christ" and "of Christ" formulae, citing particularly Rom. 14.7ff.
85. The verb used here, *synechō,* probably indicates an inner compulsion to act (see discussion in Furnish, *2 Corinthians* 309-10). Deissmann talked more generally of "the mystical genitive" (*Paul* 161-64); see further Wikenhauser, *Pauline Mysticism* 33-40. In addition we might simply note Paul's experience of "the power of Christ" (2 Cor. 12.9) and his converts' experience of "the grace of Christ" (Gal. 1.6).

> You are . . . in the Spirit, assuming that the Spirit of God does indeed dwell in you — if anyone does not have the Spirit of Christ, he does not belong to him. And since Christ is in you . . . (Rom. 8.9-10).

Where "in Spirit," "have Spirit," and "Christ in you" all serve as complementary identifying descriptions, the dividing line between experience of Spirit and experience of Christ has become impossible to define in clear-cut terms. At best we may speak of Christ as the context and the Spirit as the power.[86]

In sum. Here again the point need not be pressed. As with the variation of metaphor noted earlier,[87] so in this section too the language of identification cannot be limited either to a precisely defined "mystical" sense or to a definitely "nonmystical" sense. If Paul's language represents any more than his own idiosyncratic experience, then clearly Paul and his converts must have sensed Christ as a living presence which pervaded their assemblies and their daily lives and which conditioned their response to God's grace through and through.

§15.5 The corporate Christ

Given these findings, some further christological reflection is unavoidable. Such reflection was more common when a mystical dimension to Paul's christology was more widely acknowledged.[88] But again it was sidetracked into speculation about a mythically conceived primal man or cosmic body (*makroanthrōpos*), and was rather lost to sight when that speculation proved to have the shallowest of roots in the sources of the period. The consequence

---

86. Cf. Wikenhauser, *Pauline Mysticism* 53-58; see also discussion in Bouttier, *En Christ* 61-69; Moule, *Origin* 58-62; and Ziesler, *Pauline Christianity* 63-65.

87. See above §13.4.

88. Wikenhauser, *Pauline Mysticism* 81, e.g., cites Weiss: "Christ is said to be not merely in one person but in all the faithful, and at the same time all the faithful are in Christ. This is possible only if the idea of Christ becomes vague and if his personality is dissolved in a pantheistic manner. This is expressed by describing Christ as the Spirit" (*1 Korintherbrief* 303); "in Paul's writings 'to be in Christ' means to be fully absorbed in a mystical union with the heavenly Lord; in this union the personality loses its individuality, and the thought of Christ penetrating all (2 Cor. 3:17) takes its place. In Paul's eyes Christ the Person is metaphysically identical with the impersonal Spirit. He was able to make this equation because he was trained in the thought of his time, which drew no hard-and-fast line between an abstract idea and personality; moreover, the picture which the Gospel tradition presents had not the strong influence on him which it has on us" ("Die Bedeutung des Paulus für den modernen Christ," *ZNW* 19 [1919/20] 127-42 [here 139-40]).

today is that few NT scholars seem to ask how Paul and the other first Christians actually conceptualized the exalted Christ.[89]

We have already indicated the dimensions of the issue.[90] The portrayal of a Jesus Messiah who functions severally as another Adam, firstborn from the dead and elder brother of the family of the resurrected, as divine Wisdom and life-giving Spirit, but also as co-regent with God and soon coming Lord, is bound to be confusing. Now we have also a Christ who is conceived as a "location" into which the convert is "inserted" and within which believers find themselves, or alternatively as a personal presence within believers; as God's saving action with which believers can be identified, or as the medium through whom God pours out his grace and through whom believers approach God; as a body of which believers are members, or as a leader with whom and with whose cause believers have identified; or yet again as a powerful presence equivalent to the Spirit of God.

How did Paul visualize this Jesus? Evidently our contemporary concepts of personality are quite inadequate to cope with such a range of imagery and form. How can we speak of Christ as a body consisting of human beings, or subsequently as "head" of the cosmos,[91] or think of him as somehow "inside" other individuals, and still envisage him as a person in recognizable human form who will return on clouds? To pursue such questions as though we could achieve a single answer, however, would be a false hope. It must in fact be seriously doubted whether Paul himself actually had a single conception of the risen Christ.

As with the diversity of metaphors used to describe the beginning and process of salvation (§13.4), so with the diversity in Paul's conceptualization of Christ. That is to say, in both cases we can be confident that there was a spiritual reality which came to expression through these metaphors. In this case we can be equally sure that for Paul the spiritual reality of Christ was not reducible to the faith experience of individuals or to the tangibility of the church. Christ was still a personal reality within the totality of reality, still in direct continuity with Jesus of Nazareth, still the focus of God's saving grace for both present and future. But "personal" in a sense which is no longer the

---

89. Moule's attempt to flesh out the concept of "the corporate Christ" is an exception (*Origin* ch. 2). The concept of "corporate personality" should no longer be called upon (as, e.g., by Best, *One Body* [§20 n. 1]; Ridderbos, *Paul* 61-62), since (like the pre-Christian Gnostic Redeemer myth and "the divine man") it is another twentieth-century amalgam of disparate ideas from the period (see particularly J. W. Rogerson, "The Hebrew Conception of Corporate Personality: A Re-Examination," *JTS* 21 [1970] 1-16).

90. See above §12.5(4).

91. Col. 1.18. It cannot be assumed that the addition of "the church" removes the idea of Christ as head of the cosmos, since the conceptuality is retained in 2.10. See more fully my *Colossians* 94-96.

same as the human "person," and yet is more sharply defined than talk of God as "personal."[92]

Beyond that it becomes difficult to go with human imagery and speech. Here again, as with the other diverse metaphors, there is the danger of tying Paul's language to a single image and making all the rest subordinate to it.[93] There is the still greater danger of losing the metaphor and the diversity of metaphorical image in the reductionism of human analysis and creedal (over-)definition. In this case any attempt to harmonize the diversity of Paul's imagery and to resolve the inconsistencies of different images straining against each other would be to our loss rather than our gain. Better to let the richness of the vision, its poetry and harmonies, capture heart and spirit, even if conceptual clarity remains elusive.

§15.6 The consequences of participation in Christ

As with justification (§14.9), it is of some interest to take note of those aspects of the salvation process which Paul specifically links with the theme of participation in Christ. It was, of course, easier with justification, since Paul's treatment of that theme was more concentrated. In contrast, given the pervasiveness of the "in Christ" motif in particular, it makes less sense to pick out particular features of Paul's soteriology as specifically linked with his "Christ mysticism." But some do stand out.

a) The sense of being bound up with Christ focused on two soteriological moments of particular significance. One was the event of Christ's death and resurrection. The other was the beginning of that event's impact on individual lives. The condition of "in Christ" was brought about by being brought "into Christ" and sustained by being "with Christ." The language therefore helps underscore the sense of a definite beginning to an ongoing relation. There has been a decisive transition from one context of embodiment to another, a transition which opens up new perspectives and possibilities.[94] At the same time it is important to note both soteriological moments. The two go together in Paul's theology. Paul had no thought of conversion to Christ somehow independent of the cross. Participation in Christ always included participation in his death.

---

92. Paul can of course also speak of God indwelling his people (2 Cor. 6.16), in what appears to be a merging of the LXX of Lev. 26.12 and Ezek. 37.27. Wikenhauser, *Pauline Mysticism* 75-79, refers to the contemporary attestation of experiences of inspiration — *entheos* and *enthusiasmos* as attributing such experiences to "God possession."

93. Robinson, *Body* (§3 n. 1), is vulnerable to criticism on this point.

94. See also below §20.4.

b) Still more to the fore is the sense of corporateness. It is hardly accidental that the first sequence of participation language in Romans (6.3-8) follows directly upon Paul's portrayal of Christ as the eschatological counterpart to Adam (5.12-21). Nor that the matching "into" language of 1 Corinthians (12.13) has the body of Christ in view. A sense of personal and individual participation is certainly not lacking — we need only mention Gal. 2.19-20 and Phil. 3.8-11. But the fact that the "with" language so clearly embraces fellow believers in the "with Christ" is a further reminder that participation in Christ is irreducibly corporate. Here the christological reflections (§15.5) also have their bearing. For if Christ could not be fully conceptualized apart from talk of Christ's body, so participation in Christ could not be adequately conceived independently of the body made up of many members.

c) It is also notable how in Romans 6 Paul draws immediate ethical corollaries from this being "in Christ." The conclusion of the paragraph which elaborates the "with Christ" motif (6.1-11) is: "So also you must reckon yourselves dead indeed to sin and alive to God in Christ Jesus" (v. 11). And the application follows at once (vv. 12-14):

> [12]Therefore do not let sin rule in your mortal body to obey its desires, [13]and do not give sin control of what you are or do as weapons of unrighteousness. But give God decisive control of yourselves as being alive from the dead and of what you are and do as weapons of righteousness. [14]For sin shall not exercise lordship over you; for you are not under the law but under grace. . . .

In other words, being in Christ is not any kind of mystical removal from the real world of every day. On the contrary, it becomes the starting point and base camp for a quite differently motivated and directed life. As participation in Adam had certain direct consequences (a life dominated by sin and death), so participation in Christ had direct consequences (an obedience enabled and enhanced by grace). Participation in Christ meant a change of lordship, from the lordship of law (abused by sin) to the lordship of grace (embodied in Christ). Here we may say that Paul's sense of the mystical Christ functioned in his ethical life as resource and inspiration.[95]

d) We should also observe the eschatological and cosmic dimensions in all this. We have already noted that the other most prominent clustering of "with" language comes in Rom. 8.16-29 (§15.3), with its talk of a cosmic salvation process of which individual salvation is only part. Similarly we recall

---

95. Here Elliger's reference to the contrast between "in Christ" and "in the flesh" is relevant (above n. 12; Wikenhauser, *Pauline Mysticism* 51-52, 63-64).

the correlation of 2 Cor. 5.17 — "in Christ, new creation!" And there is a similar correlation in the final summary of Gal. 6.14-15 — crucified with Christ, new creation! This is not simply what might be called a sense of "new age" resonance with the rhythms of creation. Here the sense of a disrupted, out-of-joint creation is bound up with it. "New creation" is not "new age," precisely because the former starts with the cross. The new creation is not possible without the crucifixion of me to the world and the world to me (Gal. 6.14-15). Here again the sense of participation in Christ is powerful, but the controlling thought is of participation in Christ crucified.

§16 The gift of the Spirit[1]

1. **Bibliography**: L. L. **Belleville**, "Paul's Polemic and Theology of the Spirit in Second Corinthians," *CBQ* 58 (1996) 281-304; H. **Bertrams**, *Das Wesen des Geistes nach der Anschauung des Apostels Paulus* (Münster: Aschendorff, 1913); F. **Büchsel**, *Der Geist Gottes im Neuen Testament* (Gütersloh: Bertelsmann, 1926); **Bultmann**, *Theology* 1.153-64; B. **Byrne**, *"Sons of God" — "Seed of Abraham"* (AnBib 83; Rome: Biblical Institute, 1979); **Cerfaux**, *Christian* (§14 n. 1) 239-311; Y. **Congar**, *I Believe in the Holy Spirit* 1: *The Experience of the Spirit*, 2: *Lord and Giver of Life*, 3: *The River of Life Flows in the East and in the West* (New York: Seabury/London: Chapman, 1983); J. D. G. **Dunn**, *Baptism in the Holy Spirit: A Re-Examination of the New Testament Teaching on the Gift of the Spirit in Relation to Pentecostalism Today* (London: SCM/Naperville: Allenson, 1970); "2 Corinthians 3.17 — 'The Lord is the Spirit,' " *JTS* 21 (1970) 309-20; G. D. **Fee**, *God's Empowering Presence: The Holy Spirit in the Letters of Paul* (Peabody: Hendrickson, 1994); **Gnilka**, *Theologie* 101-8; *Paulus* 260-66; **Goppelt**, *Theology* 2.118-24; H. **Gunkel**, *Die Wirkungen des Heiligen Geistes nach der populären Anschauung der apostolischen Zeit und der Lehre des Apostels Paulus* (Göttingen: Vandenhoeck, 1888); A. **Heron**, *The Holy Spirit* (London: Marshall, 1983); F. W. **Horn**, *Das Angeld des Geistes: Studien zur paulinischen Pneumatologie* (FRLANT 154; Göttingen: Vandenhoeck, 1992); M. E. **Isaacs**, *The Concept of the Spirit: A Study of Pneuma in Hellenistic Judaism and Its Bearing on the New Testament* (London: Heythrop College, 1976); F. S. **Jones**, *"Freiheit" in den Briefen des Apostels Paulus* (Göttingen: Vandenhoeck, 1987); O. **Knoch**, *Der Geist Gottes und der neue Mensch. Der Heilige Geist als Grundkraft und Norm des christlichen Lebens in Kirche und Welt nach dem Zeugnis des Apostels Paulus* (Stuttgart: KBW, 1975); D. J. **Lull**, *The Spirit in Galatia: Paul's Interpretation of* Pneuma *as Divine Power* (SBLDS 49; Chico: Scholars, 1980); J. **Moltmann**, *The Spirit of Life: A Universal Affirmation* (Minneapolis: Fortress, 1992); G. T. **Montague**, *The Holy Spirit: Growth of a Biblical Tradition* (New York: Paulist, 1976); C. F. D. **Moule**, *The Holy Spirit* (London: Mowbrays, 1978 = Grand Rapids: Eerdmans, 1979); P. **von der Osten-Sacken**, *Römer 8 als Beispiel paulinischer Soteriologie* (FRLANT 112; Göttingen: Vandenhoeck, 1975); **Ridderbos**, *Paul* 197-204, 214-23; **Schlier**, *Grundzüge* 179-85; K. L. **Schmidt**, *Das Pneuma Hagion bei Paulus als Person und als Charisma* (Eranos Jahrbuch 13; Zürich: Rhein, 1945); E. **Schweizer**, *The Holy Spirit* (Philadelphia: Fortress, 1980); E. F. **Scott**, *The Spirit in the New Testament* (London: Hodder and Stoughton, 1923); J. M. **Scott**, *Adoption as Sons of God: An Exegetical Investigation into the Background of* HUIOTHESIA *in the Pauline Corpus* (WUNT 2.48; Tübingen: Mohr, 1992); M. **Turner**, *The Holy Spirit and Spiritual Gifts Then and Now* (Carlisle: Paternoster, 1996), particularly 103-35; H. **Weinel**, *Die Wirkungen des Geistes und der Geister im nachapostolischen Zeitalter bis auf Irenäus* (Tübingen: Mohr, 1899); M. **Welker**, *God the Spirit* (Minneapolis: Fortress, 1994); **Whiteley**, *Theology* 124-29.

§16.1 The third aspect

There is a third way in which Paul describes the crucial transition — the gift of God's Spirit. Paul counted the beginning of his converts' Christian life from their personal reception of the Spirit. The imagery, we should stress at once, is complementary — not antithetical — to the imagery examined in the last two sections. For example, as we have already noted, it is clear from Gal. 3.14 in context that Paul could think of the blessing of Abraham both as justification and as reception of the Spirit.[2] And it is equally clear from the overlap of Christ mysticism and Spirit possession, as in Rom. 8.9-10, that the two went together for Paul: to be "in Christ" and to have the Spirit indwelling were two sides of the one coin.[3] Justification and being in Christ, we may say, provided the newly established context, from which and within which converts were able to "know" both themselves and the new reality of which they were now part. In turn, the gift of the Spirit provided the motivating and enabling power by which they were to live. The three images — restored status, participation in Christ, and divine enabling — together made for an integrated and mutually supportive matrix which must have been pleasing for Paul, theologian, missionary, and pastor. For it ensured a combination of intellectual appeal, embracing experience, and motivated ethic,[4] which evidently made the earliest Christian missionary outreach so attractive and compelling to a wide range of nationalities and social classes.

The history of interest in this third aspect of Christian beginnings over the past hundred years is a fascinating blend of scholarly curiosity, popular enthusiasm, and ecclesiastical reserve. The modern period of scholarship in this area was ushered in by Hermann Gunkel's famous monograph.[5] The most notable feature of the first edition was its appeal to the "popular view of the apostolic time."[6] That meant also its recognition of the experiential nature of what were regarded as manifestations of the Spirit.[7] Both features we may say were classic liberal reactions against the more traditional scholastic and ecclesiastical attempts to treat the Spirit primarily as an object of literary

---

2. See above §14 n. 105.

3. See above §15.4e.

4. By no means do I intend to exclude the impact of a welcoming and caring social group (the church); we will pick up that dimension later (§20), but see already §§15.4b and 15.6b.

5. Gunkel, *Wirkungen*.

6. The history-of-religions dimension, with which Gunkel is usually associated, only came in at the second edition.

7. "The theology of the great apostle is an expression of his experience, not of his reading. . . . Paul believes in the divine Spirit, because he has experienced it . . ." (Gunkel, *Wirkungen* 86).

analysis, theological reflection, and even ecclesiastical control.[8] This interest in the Spirit of the NT as the experienced Spirit continued to be a feature of several studies in the early decades of the twentieth century.[9] And when interest might have fallen back on older dogmatic concerns in the middle decades of the century,[10] the development of the charismatic movement ensured a new wave of interest.[11] In contrast to the current lack of interest in Paul's "Christ mysticism," the continuing fascination of the third aspect of Christian beginnings is illustrated by the three major studies which have appeared in the last two decades, by Congar (French), Horn (German), and Fee (American).[12]

The ecclesiastical reserve is hardly surprising. Talk of "mysticism," with its overtone of intense individualistic preoccupation in contemplation of or even absorption into the divine, was unnerving enough for all who recognized the irreducibly corporate and social character of Christianity. But any focus on the reception and experience of the Spirit quickly conjured up even more disturbing ecclesiastical memories of enthusiastic sects disowning traditional authority and dispensing with sacraments.[13] It should not be forgotten that classic Reformation theology and ecclesiology was formed by reaction not only to medieval Catholicism, but also to the "spiritual" or radical Reformation.[14] The safe way has always been to subordinate mysticism to ecclesiology ("in Christ" = in the church) and the gift of the Spirit to baptism properly administered. But in western Christianity a "third strand" has never

8. Summed up in the ironic repetition of Acts 15.28: "it seemed good to the Holy Spirit and to us. . . ." See also below §17.1. Cf. Congar, *Believe* 2.127-28.

9. In English-speaking scholarship we may mention particularly Scott, *Spirit,* and H. W. Robinson, *The Christian Experience of the Holy Spirit* (London: Nisbet, 1928). In contrast, it is only towards the end of his lengthy and curiously remote treatment of Paul that Büchsel begins to address our present concerns (*Geist* 429-36).

10. I recall my own surprise on consulting the *Encyclopedia Britannica* (1959) in the 1960s and discovering that the article on the Holy Spirit had only three sections: the divinity of the Holy Spirit, the procession of the Holy Spirit, and the personality of the Holy Spirit (11.684-86).

11. As examples I may instance my own *Baptism;* Knoch, *Geist;* A. Bittlinger, ed., *The Church Is Charismatic: The World Council of Churches and the Charismatic Renewal* (Geneva: WCC, 1981); Welker, *God* 7-15.

12. Congar, *I Believe;* Horn, *Angeld;* Fee, *Empowering Presence.* Contrast Conzelmann, *Outline,* who has no section on the Spirit.

13. A classic expression is Luther's alarm at the spiritualist Anabaptist who talks facilely about "Geist, Geist, Geist," and then "kicks away the very bridge by which the Holy Spirit can come . . . namely, the outward ordinances of God like the bodily sign of baptism and the preached Word of God" (cited by G. Williams, *The Radical Reformation* [London: Weidenfeld and Nicholson/Philadelphia: Westminster, 1962] 822).

14. Käsemann's reaction against enthusiasm (above §15 n. 28) is a direct echo of Luther's reaction against the *Schwärmerei* of the radical reformers.

been far from the surface, currently represented by Pentecostalism and the diverse forms of charismatic Christianity.[15] As Gunkel foreshadowed, and as we shall see, it is little wonder that Paul's teaching at this point has proved so attractive to recurrent third-stranders.

It might be said, as a curious aside, that each of the three aspects of Paul's crucial transition has characteristically appealed to one of the three strands of western Christianity — justification to Protestant Christianity, ecclesiastical or sacramental mysticism to Catholic Christianity, and reception of the Spirit to spiritual or charismatic Christianity.[16] The categorization is, of course, something of a caricature, but caricatures can often highlight prominent features or underlying tendencies. The endeavour somehow to interweave these three strands has quite properly been a feature of ecumenical concern in the second half of the twentieth century. But the contribution offered by scholarship, particularly on the latter two aspects of Paul's theology of the beginning of salvation, has been at best patchy. Here too, then, there is a need to analyse this third aspect of Paul's theology of Christian beginnings, not as against the other two aspects, but to see just how well he was able to integrate it with his other emphases. If Paul was able to hold these different dimensions together, then his writings may prove to provide still greater resources for contemporary ecumenical concerns than has so far been recognized.

§16.2 The eschatological Spirit

Paul's treatment of the gift of the Spirit is unlike his treatment of justification and Christ mysticism in one important respect. They were markedly distinctive elements within Paul's theology, both in the role they played and in the emphasis he gave them within his letters. In contrast, Paul's talk of the gift and reception of the Spirit was evidently quite characteristic across the spec-

---

15. Classic studies include N. Cohn, *The Pursuit of the Millennium* (London: Secker and Warburg/Fair Lawn: Essential, 1957), and R. A. Knox, *Enthusiasm: A Chapter in the History of Religions* (Oxford: Clarendon, 1950); but Knox failed to recognize the importance of emerging Pentecostalism. The standard text on Pentecostalism is W. Hollenweger, *The Pentecostals* (London: SCM/Minneapolis: Augsburg, 1972), a magisterial study which now needs to be supplemented by such as P. Hocken, *Streams of Renewal: The Origins and Early Development of the Charismatic Movement in Great Britain* (Exeter: Paternoster/Washington: Word Among Us, 1986), and A. Walker, *Restoring the Kingdom: The Radical Christianity of the House Church Movement* (London: Hodder and Stoughton, [2]1988).

16. The richness of Orthodox spirituality and worship would require a differently slanted analysis.

trum of earliest Christianity, at least as represented by the NT writings. This is most simply demonstrated by reference to the two key phrases — giving and receiving the Spirit — which almost assume the status of technical terms for the decisive outreach of divine grace.[17] In other words, the sect of the Nazarenes was evidently marked out within first-century Judaism by its claim to have been given the Spirit of God in a new and exceptional way.

There are two aspects of this worth highlighting, as important background to Paul's own teaching on the subject. The first is the eschatological, perhaps inevitably eschatological, character of the claim. There seems to have been a widespread belief in Second Temple Judaism that the prophetic Spirit had been withdrawn from Israel, or at least that prophecy had ceased.[18] Characteristic of the period is the sad note in 1 Macc. 4.46: when Judas Maccabeus reconsecrated the Temple, they did not know what to do with the stones of the desecrated altar, and they stored them "in a convenient place on the temple hill until a prophet should come to tell what to do with them."[19] Also the prologue of Jesus ben Sira, with its sense of having moved from a period where fresh inspiration might be expected to one of commentating on scriptures written in the past.[20] The point should not be exaggerated, for Josephus at least was prepared to speak of prophetic activity among the Essenes during the period,[21] and the experience of the Spirit at Qumran is attested by the DSS.[22] But the impact of John the Baptist suggests that he was seen to represent something which had been lacking.[23] And the first Christian claims carry the same implication.

The sense of lack, indeed, may simply have been the other side of the expectation that the age to come would be marked by fresh manifestations of

---

17. *Didonai pneuma,* "give the Spirit" — Luke 11.13; Acts 5.32; 8.18; 11.17; 15.8; Rom. 5.5; 2 Cor. 1.22; 5.5; 1 Thes. 4.8; 2 Tim. 1.7; 1 John 3.24; 4.13 — the language almost certainly reflects OT usage (particularly Ezek. 36.27 and 37.14 LXX; the same echo in 1QH 12.12); *hē dōrea tou theou,* "the gift of God" — John 4.10; Acts 2.38; 8.20; 10.45; 11.17; Eph. 4.7; Heb. 6.4. *Lambanein pneuma,* "receive the Spirit" — John 7.39; 14.17; 20.22; Acts 1.8; 2.33, 38; 8.15, 17, 19; 10.47; 19.2; Rom. 8.15; 1 Cor. 2.12; 2 Cor. 11.4; Gal. 3.2, 14; 1 John 2.27.

18. See, e.g., Horn, *Angeld* 26-36, with bibliography. But the point can be much overstated; see now J. R. Levison, "Did the Spirit Withdraw from Israel? An Evaluation of the Earliest Jewish Data," *NTS* 43 (1997) 35-57.

19. See also 1 Macc. 9.27 and 14.41. Ps. 74.9 is usually dated to the Maccabean period. Cf. also Dan. 3.38 Theodotion. Zech. 13.2-6 is usually also cited, but probably served a different function. *2 Baruch* 85.1-3 reflects the despair following the destruction of Jerusalem in 70 CE.

20. See also Horn, *Angeld* 31.

21. Josephus, *Ant.* 13.311-13; 15.373-79; 17.345-48.

22. E.g., 1QS 4.2-8, 20-26; 1QH 12.11-12; see also §4 n. 43 above.

23. Particularly Mark 6.14 pars.; Matt. 11.9/Luke 7.26; cf. Josephus, *Ant.* 18.116-19.

the revivifying Spirit, of a new spirit and new life.[24] Popular imagery was of the Spirit poured out from on high like a downpour on a parched land.[25] The Christian tradition of Pentecost (Acts 2.16-21) evidently tapped into a deep root of aspiration and longing — for the Spirit to be widely dispensed, on men and women, old and young, slave and free (Joel 2.28-29). There are echoes of the same tradition in the Pauline letters,[26] and Paul uses the same imagery of being "irrigated or watered" with the Spirit in 1 Cor. 12.13c.[27]

The claim of the first Christians, then, was that the Spirit had been dispensed as promised. The drought of the Spirit had ended. The longed for and expected new age had begun. In eschatological terms, this experience of the Spirit was as decisive for the Christians' self-understanding as was Jesus' resurrection. As the latter brought conviction that the last days were upon them (the resurrection of the dead had begun), so the gift of the Spirit brought them existential confirmation within (new heart).[28] Without that verification of God's new day, there may indeed have been a problem caused by delayed parousia.[29] But the gift of the Spirit gave them an experiential correlation with their faith conviction in Jesus as resurrected and Lord, which both confirmed the realized emphasis of their eschatology and gave the gospel of Easter and Pentecost tremendous power.

The second aspect worth highlighting is the fact that the Spirit was also given freely to Gentiles. This fact is strongly emphasized by Luke in his account of Christian beginnings.[30] And Galatians confirms the central point. It was the manifest and undeniable grace of God upon Gentiles which had convinced the pillar apostles in Jerusalem that Gentiles had also to be accepted, and without circumcision — for God had already accepted them (Gal. 2.8-9). And Paul's plea to the Galatians themselves is based on the same fact (3.1-5). Here is another point which has simply not been given sufficient attention in the reconstruction of Christian beginnings and in speculation regarding the development of a

24. Particularly Ezek. 11.19; 36.25-27; 37.1-14.

25. Isa. 32.15; 44.3; Ezek. 39.29; Joel 2.28.

26. Particularly Rom. 5.5 and Tit. 3.6; see also n. 58 below.

27. The Greek verb used (potizō) is infrequent in biblical Greek (Gen. 13.10; Isa. 29.10; Ezek. 32.6), but it was evidently a common agricultural term (MM), and is of a piece with the more familiar imagery of the Spirit likened to a downpour or cloudburst (n. 25 above).

28. This may also mean a recognition that a prior belief regarding Jesus' resurrection (Acts 1) made the first disciples psychologically receptive to experience of the Spirit (Acts 2). Note the expectation enshrined in the tradition of the Baptist's prediction of a Coming One who would baptise in the Spirit (reinforced by Acts 1.5; see below §17.2) and given pointed force in John 7.39 ("the Spirit was not yet, for Jesus had not yet been glorified").

29. See above §12.4.

30. Acts 10.44-48; 11.15-18; 15.8-9.

mission to Gentiles.[31] Something happened in the lives of Gentiles who heard the gospel, whether it was initially preached to them directly, or they overheard it as adherents in diaspora synagogues when the Nazarene missionaries began to preach there. The manifestations were such that the missionaries could only conclude: "the gift of the Spirit has been poured out even on the Gentiles" (Acts 10.45). And their testimony before the early Christian leadership was evidently such as to allow the latter no choice but to agree that God had accepted these Gentiles and that circumcision was unnecessary in their case.[32] The eschatological Spirit was indeed being poured out "on *all* flesh."[33] In this way the promise to Abraham, that he would be a blessing to the nations, was now at last being fulfilled (Gal. 3.8, 14).

§16.3 Receiving the Spirit

The prominence which Paul himself gives to his converts' reception of the Spirit is of a piece with all this. The degree to which he could take it for granted confirms that the experience of the Spirit as gift was a common — should we not say, universal? — experience of the first believers. In fact, however, Paul did not take it for granted. The action of the Spirit in entering a human life was too fundamental a feature of Christian beginings for Paul to pass it over. Indeed, of all the aspects of the crucial transition, it is this one to which Paul most frequently draws attention. What is striking not least is the constancy of the emphasis across the letters. Unlike justification, it was not an emphasis made necessary by particular situations within different churches. The centrality of the gift of the Spirit in and as the beginning of Christian discipleship is one of the foundational principles of Paul's work as evangelist, theologian, and pastor. We should pause here long enough to register the point clearly.

In 1 Thessalonians, Paul reminds his readers how they received the word "with joy of the Holy Spirit" (1.6). He characterizes God as "the one who gives his Holy Spirit to you" (4.8).[34] That this definitive statement

---

31. The failure to reflect sufficiently on what an astonishing step it was which Nazarene missionaries took, as reported in Acts 11.20-21, is a feature of most commentaries on Acts and descriptions of Christian beginnings.

32. The manifest grace of God (Gal. 2.8-9; Acts 11.23; 15.11); the manifest Spirit of God (Gal. 3.2-5, 14; 4.1-7; Acts 10.44-47; 11.15-18; 15.8-11).

33. Joel 2.28; Acts 2.17.

34. The present tense (*didonta,* "who gives") does not indicate repeated givings to the same persons (as Horn implies in *ABD* 3.271), but characterizes God as "the giver of the Holy Spirit." As is generally recognized, the language here, including the otherwise unexpected *eis hymas* ("into you"), has been determined by the echo of Ezek. 37.6, 14, part of Ezekiel's so powerfully evocative vision of spiritual renewal.

(definitive both of God and of what determines Christian relationship to God) appears in Paul's earliest letter signals a theme which remains consistent throughout Paul's letters.[35] At the end of the same letter he reminds them of the characteristically charismatic character of their worship (5.19-20); the soteriological Spirit is also the Spirit of prophecy.[36] It is worth noting that despite the strong sense of expectation of imminent parousia in 1 Thessalonians, Paul has actually to counsel against their quashing the Spirit.[37]

In Galatians, it is striking how Paul's main argument starts from the well-remembered (on both sides) fact of their reception of the Spirit (3.1-5).[38] In the event, everything stood or fell on this. In effect he says: "You remember your experience of the Spirit. How did that come about? How did you receive the Spirit?" The Spirit was that which identified them as Christ's. The Spirit was the blessing of Abraham into which they as Gentiles had already entered (3.14). As the new age began (in "the fullness of the time") with the sending of God's Son (4.3), so their entry into the experience of the new age began with the sending of the Spirit of God's Son into their hearts (4.6).[39] They, even as Gentiles, were to be recognized as Abraham's offspring, for they, like Isaac, had been born "in accordance with the Spirit" (4.29). They now were waiting expectantly in the Spirit, should be walking by the Spirit, bearing the Spirit's fruit, sowing to the Spirit.[40]

In 1 Corinthians, Paul reminds his audience that their conviction, his own poor preaching notwithstanding, was proof of the Spirit's power (2.4).[41] The Spirit which they had received stood at the heart of their spirituality; it was having the Spirit which made someone "spiritual" (2.11-14). The Spirit of God now dwelt in them (3.16; 6.19). They had been washed, sanctified, and justified in the Spirit of God (6.11), and were now united to the Lord as one Spirit (6.17).[42]

---

35. As Turner notes (*Holy Spirit* 103-13), 1 Thes. 4.8 undermines the developmental hypothesis of Horn (*Angeld* 119-57; also *ABD* 3.271-72), according to which the soteriological Spirit (the understanding that the gift of the Spirit was necessary for salvation) was a later phase in Paul's thinking.

36. *Pace* the highly dubious distinction of Luke's "prophetic" pneumatology from Paul's "soteriological" pneumatology by R. P. Menzies, *The Development of Early Christian Pneumatology with Special Reference to Luke-Acts* (JSNTS 54; Sheffield: Sheffield Academic, 1991).

37. Cf. and contrast Jewett, *Thessalonian Correspondence* (§12 n. 1) 100-104, 142-47 (see also §12 n. 37 above).

38. C. H. Cosgrove, *The Cross and the Spirit: A Study in the Argument and Theology of Galatians* (Macon: Mercer University, 1988), quite properly takes 3.1-5 as "the decisive clue to Paul's view of the 'problem at Galatia' " (2). See also Lull, *Spirit*.

39. See further below n. 121.

40. Gal. 5.5, 16, 18, 22, 25; 6.8.

41. See further below n. 102.

42. See above §10.6 and n. 158.

More strikingly than with the Thessalonians, the Spirit was at the heart of their worship (chs. 12–14). They had all been baptized in the one Spirit into the one body and all irrigated or drenched with the one Spirit (12.13).[43] That is to say, it was their reception of the Spirit which constituted each one of them members of the body of Christ.[44]

In 2 Corinthians, Paul piles up the imagery — confirmed into Christ, anointed, sealed, and given the *arrabōn* of the Spirit in their hearts (1.21-22).[45] The Spirit is the "down payment," the "first instalment" — in other words, the beginning of the salvation process.[46] So also in 5.5, the Spirit is the *arrabōn* of the process of transformation now under way in the believer, which will climax in the transformed resurrection body (4.16–5.5). In between, Paul describes the event of conversion as a letter delivered by him, but written in their hearts by the Spirit (3.3), and contrasts the deadening effect of the law reduced to "letter" with their own experience of the life-giving Spirit (3.6). We have already noted the echo of prophetic expectation in these verses.[47]

One of the most striking expressions of Paul's understanding of conversion comes in the following midrash on Exod. 34.29-35 (2 Cor. 3.7-18). For Paul the climax of the contrast between the ministries given to Moses and to him is reached in Exod. 34.34: "whenever Moses went in before the Lord to speak to him, he removed the veil until he came out." We recall Paul's interpretation of the veil as that which obscures from present Israel the fact of the old covenant's fading glory.[48] But Exod. 34.34 speaks of the veil being removed. Paul therefore rewords the verse so that it becomes a prefigurement of conversion: "but whenever anyone turns to the Lord the veil is removed" (2 Cor. 3.16). The modification does not change the essential sense, but the allusion is obvious.[49] Moses' action in entering in to the presence of the Lord and removing the veil indicated how anyone by turning to the Lord could

---

43. See above n. 27.

44. The sense is inescapably incorporative and therefore initiatory (Dunn, *Baptism* 127-29). The phrase is clearly equivalent to "baptized into Christ Jesus" (Rom. 6.4); consequently the question whether they were baptized to form one body (*eis* = so as to make one body) or to become part of a body already in existence (*eis* = so as to become members of the one body) only confuses the point. See further below §17.2.

45. See further below §17.2.

46. See also above §13 n. 70.

47. 2 Cor. 3.3, 6 — Ezek. 11.19; Jer. 31.33; see above §6.5d.

48. See above §6.5d.

49. (1) The subject is left open; it can include anyone, though the context implies that fellow Jews were primarily in view. (2) "Enter in" *(eisporeuomai)* is changed to the not too distant synonym "turn to" *(epistrephō)*, the main "conversion" word (see above §13.3). (3) The active "remove" becomes the passive "is removed," but the verb is the same. An allusion is generally recognized (see Thrall, *2 Corinthians 1–7* 268-69).

have the veil removed.[50] What is of immediate interest, however, is the explanatory addition in 3.17: "and 'the Lord' is the Spirit." Almost certainly "the Lord" is not Christ here, but "the Lord" of the text just adapted.[51] In other words, Paul was thinking here of conversion as conversion *to the Spirit*.[52] It is conversion as the experience of a veil being lifted, of eyes being opened, which he evoked for his readers.[53]

In Romans, Paul early on characterizes the true Jew as one circumcised in the heart, "in Spirit and not in letter" (2.29). In other words, he deliberately echoes the familiar Jewish recognition of the necessity of a circumcised heart,[54] with its hope of future realization.[55] It is Paul's claim in effect that this hope had been realized among the first believers (Gentiles as well as Jews). Their conversion could be described as the act of circumcising the heart by the Spirit.[56] Rom 7.6 reflects the same claim: release from the law, death to that which had confined them, and service "in newness of the Spirit" (as against "oldness of letter") were all metaphors for the same new beginning, the Spirit received and experienced as liberating, motivating, and enabling power.[57] Rom. 5.5 is another brief allusion to the gift of the Spirit, manifested as an outpouring[58] of God's love and providing a bedrock of assurance when the suffering of discipleship multiplies.

These were only brief references to the crucial function of the Spirit in marking out the new Christians' new status before God. Otherwise the silence regarding the Spirit in the first seven chapters of Romans is somewhat surprising. Surprising, that is, until we realize what Paul's tactic was. For in expounding the

50. On the question of who was the intended subject of the verb ("turns to") in 3.16, see again Thrall, *2 Corinthians 1–7* 269-71, who also notes another possible allusion to Jer. 4.1 (Israel).

51. See further my "2 Corinthians 3.17" (*pace* principally Hermann [§10 n. 1]); C. F. D. Moule, "2 Cor. 3.18b, *kathaper apo kyriou pneumatos,*" *Essays* 227-34; Thrall, *2 Corinthians 1–7* 271-74. Horn, *Angeld* 331, entirely ignores these issues.

52. The unusualness of the conceptuality is determined by the midrashic character of the identification; as Thrall notes (*2 Corinthians 1–7* 274), it is consistent with the opposite attitude of resisting, provoking, or grieving the Spirit (Acts 7.51; Eph. 4.30; Isa. 63.10).

53. See further Belleville, "Paul's Polemic"; also Turner, *Holy Spirit* 116-19.

54. Deut. 10.16; Jer. 4.4; 9.25-26; Ezek. 44.9; Philo, *Spec. Leg.* 1.305. The regular recurrence of the same motif in the DSS is particularly noticeable (1QpHab 11.13; 1QS 5.5; 1QH 2.18; 18.20).

55. Deut. 30.6; *Jub.* 1.23.

56. See further my *Romans* 124; Fee, *Empowering Presence* 492.

57. The overlap of language in 2 Cor. 3.6; Rom. 2.28-29; 7.6 (also Phil. 3.3) shows clearly that Paul's thought was all of a piece in these different contexts. There can be little doubt that in each case Paul has the Holy Spirit in view (see, e.g., Fitzmyer, *Romans* 323, 460; Fee, *Empowering Presence* 491-92). NIV is preferable to the other principal English translations here; RSV/NRSV are inconsistent between 2.29 and 7.6.

58. Note again the possible echo of the Pentecost tradition (above n. 26).

various aspects of his gospel in these first seven chapters, it is almost as though
he was holding back his trump card till the final round of exposition. He could
not restrain himself so completely, as the earlier references show. But with
amazing restraint in chs. 6–7, he was able to carry forward his discussion of the
fearful triumvirate (sin, death, and law as used by sin) with only the single
reference to the Spirit in 7.6. Consequently, when the reader reaches Rom. 8, not
least after the agonizing testimony of 7.7-25, it is almost as though a pent-up
flood has been released, and out pour Paul's convictions about the decisive role
of the Spirit in determining and shaping the believer's life. Rom. 8.1-27 is
unquestionably the high point of Paul's theology of the Spirit.[59]

He starts with the triumphant pronouncement: "So now, there is no
condemnation for those in Christ Jesus. For the law of the Spirit of life in
Christ Jesus has set you free from the law of sin and death" (8.1-2). Whatever
Paul meant by "the law of the Spirit of life,"[60] it is clearly the Spirit of God
that is intended. Equally clearly it is this Spirit which has made the decisive
difference (note the aorist tense) in countering the law abused by sin to bring
about death.[61] In the following paragraph the Roman Christians are encouraged to think of themselves (and to realize themselves) as those who
"walk in accordance with the Spirit," who have their being in terms of the
Spirit, who think the Spirit's way (8.4-6).

That the Spirit is thus to be seen as the defining mark of the Christian is
put in blunt terms in 8.9: "You are not in the flesh but in the Spirit, assuming that[62]
the Spirit of God does indeed dwell in you; if anyone does not have the Spirit of
Christ, that person does not belong to him." In this verse, in fact, Paul provides
the nearest thing to a definition of a Christian (someone who is "of Christ"). And
the definition is in terms of the Spirit. It is "having the Spirit" which defines and
determines someone as being "of Christ." A Spiritless Christian would have been
a contradiction in terms for Paul. The implication is also clear: in Paul's understanding, it was by receiving the Spirit that one became a Christian.

So also in 8.10: the Spirit is the life of the Christian, that is, the life
of God in the Christian.[63] The renewed spiritual life of the Christian is the

59. The 21 *pneuma* references in Rom. 8.1-27 (19 to the Holy Spirit) form the
most intensive focus on the Spirit in the Pauline letters.

60. See below §23.4.

61. On "the law of sin and death" see above §6.7.

62. The *eiper* ("assuming that") denotes a necessary condition for the validity of
the preceding assertion — "since" (NRSV, REB); see further my *Romans* 428.

63. "The Spirit is your life" (REB). NRSV has again improved RSV by translating
pneuma as "Spirit" rather than the quite unjustified plural "spirits." NIV and Fitzmyer,
Romans 490-91, stick with "spirit"; but note the characteristic link between Spirit and life;
Fee, *Empowering Presence* 550-51, observes that "Spirit" is the almost unanimous view
of recent commentators.

immediate effect of the life-giving Spirit, now also the indwelling Spirit. Thus has begun a process which will reach its end in the resurrection of the body, the climactic saving act of the life-giving Spirit (8.11). For the gift of the Spirit is but the firstfruits of that complete salvation, the beginning of that process and assurance of its completion (8.23). Here the harvest metaphor makes the same point as its commercial analogy (*arrabōn*, "first instalment"):[64] there has been a decisive beginning, which both prefigures what is yet to come and guarantees it.

These two references straddle the intense sequence in 8.14-16. Here, in close parallel to 8.9, membership in God's family is defined in terms of the Spirit: "as many as are led by the Spirit of God, they are sons of God" (8.14).[65] This time the implication is spelled out: you are sons of God, because "you have received the Spirit of adoption," the Spirit of the Son.[66] Where Paul the Pharisee might have identified the proselyte as one who had received the law and lived in accordance with it, Paul the apostle identifies the Christian as one who has received the Spirit and lives in accordance with it. Membership in God's family is no longer defined as being a *bar mitswah* ("son of the commandment"), but as one who has been adopted by God and shares the Spirit of God's Son. The adoption is given its existential reality by the presence and witness of the Spirit (8.16)

Of the subsequent Pauline letters, we may simply note Phil. 2.1 — the "shared experience *(koinōnia)* of the Spirit" as the basis of their common life in Christ.[67] And in 3.3 Paul takes up the same theme as Rom. 2.28-29 in a striking redefinition of "the circumcision." "The circumcision" are no longer to be identified as the nation of Israel, the Jews ethnically defined as such. "The circumcision," that is, those who have experienced what circumcision of the flesh was meant to point to (circumcision of the heart), are "those who worship by the Spirit of God, boast in Christ Jesus, and do not retain confidence in the flesh."[68]

Colossians contains allusions to such distinctive Pauline emphases — "in him you also were circumcised . . ." (Col. 1.11). And though references

64. See above §13 n. 70.

65. See my *Romans* 450. Cf. Fee, *Empowering Presence* 564: "These ["and no others" is implied] are God's children. As in Gal. 3.1-5, the Spirit alone identifies the people of God under the new covenant."

66. It is important to translate *huios* here as "son" (8.14), since it is the Spirit of the Son which is in view (as the parallel, Gal. 4.6, confirms). It is notable, however, that having implied the son/Son correlation, Paul at once switches to the gender neutral *tekna*, "children" (8.16-17).

67. On *koinōnia* see below §20.6.

68. See further above §14.4. On "the circumcision" = the Jewish people, see above §14.4 n. 87.

to the Spirit are slighter, they are not uncharacteristically Pauline.[69] In some contrast, the later Ephesians retains an authentically Pauline Spirit theology. Here we might simply note the reuse of the imagery of the Spirit as that which seals the believer and gives assurance of the complete fulfilment of the promised inheritance (Eph. 1.13-14). This seal is given to the one making the commitment of faith; it is God's mark of ownership put in and upon the one being transferred to the lordship of Christ.[70] Likewise in 2.18 and 22 the Spirit is the medium of access to the very presence of God (cf. Rom. 5.2), the mortar which bonds them as the bricks of the new temple of God. The Spirit is the bond of unity (4.3-4); it is their common share in the one Spirit which unites them as one body (cf. 1 Cor. 12.13).

In sum, this third aspect of Christian beginnings in Paul's thought is actually the most prominent of the three. Justification appears to be the more prominent, and certainly has been given more prominence. But that prominence is due in large part to the fact that Paul had to argue for his understanding of justification against many of his fellow Christian Jews. And, as we have seen, the theme is largely limited to the letters where he found it necessary to defend his Gentile mission (principally Galatians and Romans). In contrast, so far as the gift of the Spirit was concerned, Paul evidently did not need to argue the fact. That was common ground, so far as we can tell, with all the communities to which he personally wrote. In other words, it was generally recognized within the Pauline mission: that reception of the Spirit was the decisive and determinative element in the crucial transition of conversion; and that the presence of the Spirit in a life was the most distinctive and defining feature of a life thus reclaimed by God.

Likewise the action of the Spirit (gift/reception of the Spirit) is a more prominent theme in Paul's theology of the beginning of salvation than his participation "in Christ" motif. The "in Christ" motif is as widespread in Paul's letters, but mostly presumes an established condition and status — being "in Christ." The talk of participation "into Christ" is much less frequent as an aspect of the whole motif. In contrast, the Spirit motif embraces both the event of the Spirit given and received, and its consequent outworkings. It is the given/received Spirit which determines life and living as "Christian."[71]

But what did Paul have in mind when he spoke of the gift and reception of the Spirit? How did he understand "the Spirit"?

69. Col. 1.8-9; 3.16. Fee presses the point — *Empowering Presence* 638-40, 643-44.

70. On the "seal of the Spirit" see below §17.2 and n. 59.

71. Cf. Whiteley: "The teaching that the Spirit has been given to all Christians as such can be regarded as the fundamental teaching upon which all St. Paul's other utterances concerning the Spirit are based" (*Theology* 125); Cerfaux: "Participation in the Spirit of God is the first characteristic of a Christian" (*Christian* 310).

§16.4 The experience of the Spirit

How did Paul conceptualize the Spirit and the Spirit's working? The debate on the correct answer is an old one. Bultmann, for example, reflects earlier discussion stimulated by Gunkel, but stemming ultimately from patristic debate regarding the personality of the Spirit, when he distinguishes an "animistic" from a "dynamistic" conception.[72]

> In animistic thinking *pneuma* is conceived as an independent agent, a personal power which like a demon can fall upon a man and take possession of him, enabling him or compelling him to perform manifestations of power. In dynamistic thinking, on the contrary, *pneuma* appears as an impersonal force which fills a man like a fluid, so to say.

In turn, Eduard Schweizer popularized the notion of *pneuma* as denoting "the heavenly sphere or its substance."[73] More recently, Horn has offered a sixfold conceptual distinction — "functional," "substantial" *(substanzhaften),* "material" *(stofflichen),* "hypostatic," "normative," and "anthropological."[74]

There is a double danger at this point. First, such clinical analysis can easily obscure the character of the language being used — that it was the language of metaphor and imagery. The point is one made earlier:[75] the diversity of imagery was an attempt to express a reality which did not lend itself to uniform or unifaceted description. Here again it would be a mistake to play off one descriptive language against another or to accuse Paul (and the other NT writers) of inconsistent or contradictory thought. Rather, we should see in the diverse (and analytically confusing) imagery an indication of the kind and range of experiences attributed to the Spirit, and of how the first Christians struggled to find an appropriate conceptuality to describe them.

Second, as already implied, underlying these descriptions and the conceptualities involved was early Christian experience, experience understood

---

72. Bultmann, *Theology* 1.155. As examples he cites animistic conception (Rom. 8.16; 1 Cor. 2.10-16; 14.14) and dynamistic conception, the usual one, reflected in talk of the Spirit "given" or "poured out" (*Theology* 1.155-56). As Horn notes (*Angeld* 16-17), the distinction goes back to early social anthropological studies, particularly to the discussion begun by E. B. Tylor, *Primitive Culture* (1871). See also Bertrams, *Wesen;* and Schmidt, *Pneuma Hagion.*

73. Schweizer, *pneuma, TDNT* 6.416 — referring to Rom. 1.3-4.

74. Horn, *Angeld* 60: e.g., "functional" (Gal. 5.22; 1 Cor. 12.11; 14.2; 1 Thes. 1.5-6), *substanzhaften* (1 Cor. 3.16; 6.19; Rom. 8.9, 11; 1 Thes. 4.8), *stofflichen* (Rom. 5.5; 1 Cor. 1.21-22; 10.4; 12.13; 15.43; 2 Cor. 3.8), hypostatic (Rom. 5.5; 8.26-27; 1 Cor. 2.10), normative (Rom. 8.4; 15.30; 1 Cor. 4.21; Gal. 5.25; 6.1), and anthropological (Rom. 1.9; 1 Cor. 6.20 v.l.; 16.18).

75. See above §13.4. "Metaphor," of course, does not imply "unreal."

as experience of the Spirit. As Schweizer put it at the beginning of the NT section of his well-known *TDNT* article on *pneuma* — but he was simply echoing the consensus since Gunkel: "Long before the Spirit was a theme of doctrine, he was a fact in the experience of the community."[76] The most recent thorough study begins on the same note: "Whatever else, for Paul the Spirit was an *experienced* reality"; "For Paul the Spirit, as an experienced and living reality, was the absolutely crucial matter for Christian life, from beginning to end."[77]

Such an assertion of the priority of experience is, of course, open to various criticisms. For one thing, "experience" itself is far too broad and all-encompassing a term. Any closer analysis would have to start by breaking it down into more specific categories like states of consciousness, feelings, sensations, moods, perception, awareness, and so on.[78] Again, any emphasis on experience needs to recall and maintain the balance/tension in Western culture between Enlightenment and Romantic Revival, and not allow experience to be too easily played off against rationality, or "religious experience" to be defined by or limited to the extraordinary.[79] And not least is it important to remember that no experience is wholly "raw," since all experience is shaped or determined in large measure at least by physical makeup, heritage, nurture and education, social conditioning, and so on.[80] "There is always an interdependence of perception and interpretation in the experience,"[81] since any attempt to "grasp" an experience inevitably involves some sort of conceptualization — including the conceptualization of it as an "experience."

---

76. Schweizer, *TDNT* 6.396; similarly Goppelt, *Theology* 2.120; "Pneumatology deals with the most intimate, and sometimes intense, experience of the divine" (Keck, *Paul* 99).

77. Fee, *Empowering Presence* xxi, 1. Congar likewise finds it necessary to begin with "A Note on 'Experience'" (*Believe* 1.xvii). Moltmann opens with: "The simple question: when did you last feel the workings of the Holy Spirit? embarrasses us" (*Spirit* x). And Welker attempts as his starting point to take seriously "the broad spectrum of experiences of God's Spirit," "the rich reality and vitality of the Holy Spirit," "the appearance of God's reality and God's power in the midst of the structural patterns of human life" (*God* ix-xi).

78. See further, e.g., the discussion in D. Gelpi, *Charism and Sacrament* (New York: Paulist/London: SPCK, 1976), particularly ch. 1; *Experiencing God: A Theology of Human Emergence* (New York: Paulist, 1978).

79. See particularly the critique of William James in N. Lash, *Easter in Ordinary: Reflections on Human Experience and the Knowledge of God* (London: SCM, 1988). Cf. Lash's critique of McGinn in §15 n. 23 above (I owe both Lash references to my colleague Walter Moberly). See also §3.5 above.

80. See further C. F. Davis, *The Evidential Force of Religious Experience* (Oxford: Clarendon, 1989) 145-55.

81. This is Horn's repeated critique of Gunkel (*Angeld* 14-15, 20).

At the same time, however, there are experiences which come to individuals as "given," prior to conceptualization or uncontainable within available linguistic resources. The child experiences parental love before being able to talk of it. The teenager may experience an orgasm or first period without knowing what it is. The great artistic occasion provides aesthetic sensations which no words can adequately capture. There may be frightening experiences of the onset of disease or mental illness, which are frightening precisely because the sufferer has no language to describe, let alone explain, what is happening. Questionnaires followed up by personal interviews have shown that a significant proportion of the UK population have had some sort of "religious experience," but have been unable to speak of it because they lacked appropriate vocabulary.[82]

Such analogies may not be so remote as they may at first appear. For one thing, it was the unexpectedness of the experiences of the first Gentile converts (and yet also their unquestionable evidential character to the evangelists) which resulted in the breakthrough to a full-scale Gentile mission. And for another, Paul and the other first Christians did not simply conform their conceptualized experience to traditional formulations. On the contrary, it was precisely the sense of something new, the struggle to find language suitable to express a reality freshly experienced, which lies behind the diversity of Paul's imagery. Some older imagery (like "outpouring") did enable them to grasp their experience conceptually, but their experience also caused them to coin fresh images. So too, as we have seen, a mark of Paul's distinctive vocabulary is his takeover of words like "gospel," "grace," and "love" to fill them with rich new content — the content in particular of his own (and others') experience. The degree to which Paul could assume that his imagery would resonate with his audiences' own experience is itself indicative that the first Christian talk of the Spirit referred to what they all had experienced when they first believed.

What also needs to be remembered here is that "Spirit" was an experiential term from the first. In so saying, I mean that the Hebrew term *ruach* was itself the word coined to give a name or explanation to what we might call the basic experience of vitality. As we saw earlier, *ruach* denotes the breath of life, the life force from God.[83] It was conceived as an animating power, analogous to or even continuous with the force of strong wind,[84] a power which could invigorate or be invigorated in exceptional circum-

---

82. The survey was carried out by my colleague in Nottingham, Dr. David Hay; see his *Religious Experience Today* (London: Mowbray, 1990).

83. See above both §3.6 and §10.6; also Congar, *Believe* 1.5-14 ("The Action of the Breath of Yahweh").

84. E.g., Exod. 10.13, 19; 14.21; 1 Kgs. 19.11; Isa. 7.2; Ezek. 27.26; Hos. 13.15.

stances.[85] Common to such a range of usage was the sense of an invisible, mysterious, aweful force. The word itself *(ruach)* is onomatopoeic — the sound of the wind. Thus coined, *ruach* became the common denominator to denote analogous experiences of mysterious, otherly power, including a sense of the numinous quality of life itself.[86]

This basic sense continues to adhere to the Christian use of the Greek equivalent, *pneuma* — as is reflected in the fact that it too could carry a similar range of meaning. In the NT this is most evident in the wordplay of *pneuma* as "wind" and "Spirit" in John 3.8 and in the "Johannine Pentecost" of John 20.22.[87] In Paul we may simply note the ambiguity he retains when he talks of the Corinthians as "zealous for spirits" (1 Cor. 14.12)[88] or of the interface between human spirit and divine Spirit.[89] In the former, it is the sense of openness to otherly divine powers which comes to the fore. In the latter, what the reader overhears is precisely the character of *pneuma* as experienced in the innermost being, where conceptual distinction between Spirit and spirit is not of primary importance.[90] Not least we should recall that for Paul, the Spirit is preeminently "the Spirit of life," the "life-giver."[91]

Such a basic feature of biblical pneumatology probably deserves more emphasis than it has traditionally been given. In Christian tradition it has become customary to think of the gift of the Spirit as a deduction to be drawn

---

85. Judg. 3.10; 6.34; 11.29; 14.6, 19; 15.14-15; 1 Sam. 10.6; cf. Gen. 45.27 and Judg. 15.19.

86. In arguing that "the Spirit of God was originally experienced as a power that overcomes the internal disintegration of the people" *(God* 108), Welker is tendentiously schematic and ignores the more fundamental sense of *ruach*.

87. John 3.8 — "The *pneuma* blows where it will and you hear the sound of it, but you do not know whence it comes or where it goes; so is everyone who is born from the *pneuma*"; 20.22 — Jesus "breathed [on them] and said to them [the disciples]: 'Receive the Holy Spirit.' " In the latter, the use of the verb "breathed" *(enephysēsen)* no doubt was intended to recall its use in Gen. 2.7 and Ezek. 37.9 (see further my *Baptism* 180).

88. Translations consistently render *pneumata* unjustifiably as "spiritual gifts." But the reference is more obviously to eagerness for experiences of inspiration, particularly glossolalia, though not necessarily only glossolalia (Dunn, *Jesus and the Spirit* 233-34; Fee, *Empowering Presence* 227).

89. Note the unclarity evident particularly in 1 Cor. 5.3-4; 6.17; 14.14-15; Col. 2.5; see also §3 n. 16 above. Fee attempts to convey the character of such references by translating "S/spirit" *(Empowering Presence* 24-26, 123-27, 229-30, 462, 645).

90. This does not imply any reduction of the concept of Spirit to "God-consciousness" (Büchsel, *Geist* 436-38, finds that the parallel with conscience makes most sense of Paul's concept of the Spirit). Paul was conscious enough of the gift character of the Spirit. The 146 *pneuma* references in the Pauline corpus are divided between Holy Spirit and human spirit in a ratio of about 6:1.

91. See further above §6 n. 131 and §10.6.

from a correct confession or properly administered sacrament. The new church member is in effect given the assurance: "You have believed all the right things and/or received the sacrament of baptism and/or laying on of hands; therefore you have received the Spirit, whether you know it or not." With Paul it was rather different. He asks the Galatians, not "How did you receive baptism? What confession did you make?" but "How was it that you received the Spirit?" (Gal. 3.2). Their reception of the Spirit was something he could refer them to directly, not merely as a deduction from some other primary factor.[92]

The same point follows from the "definition of a Christian" in Rom. 8.9 and 14. Paul does not say: "If you are Christ's, you have the Spirit; since you are sons of God, you are led by the Spirit." In both cases, Paul puts it the other way round: "if you have the Spirit, you are Christ's; if you are being led by the Spirit, you are God's sons." The fact which was immediately discernible was not whether they were Christ's — attested by baptism or confession — a fact from which their possession of the Spirit could be deduced as a corollary. That which was ascertainable was their possession of the Spirit; that was the primary factor from which their relation to Christ could be deduced. Their Christian status was recognizable from the fact that Christ's agent was in evident control of their lives.

What then were the "evidences" of the Spirit, the "religious affections,"[93] which Paul had in mind when he recalled his readers to their first flush of discipleship? Fortunately Paul makes sufficient allusion to them for us to be able to lay them out in a sort of spectrum of experience. The procedure, of course, does not imply that the experiences indicated were neatly discrete or in the event easily distinguishable from one another.

At one end of the spectrum we would have to register various ecstatic phenomena. For example, the reminder of the Corinthian converts' beginnings — "enriched in him with all word and all knowledge . . . so that you lack in no charism" (1 Cor. 1.5, 7) — is sufficient indication that their ecstatic spirit-

---

92. Gal. 3.2 is remarkably like the account of Acts 19.2, Paul's question to "certain disciples" whom he met at Ephesus: "Did you receive the Spirit when you believed?" Given the similarity, the much quoted comment of L. Newbigin on the latter is pertinent here too: "The apostle asked the converts of Apollos one question: 'Did ye receive the Holy Spirit when you believed?' and got a plain answer. His modern successors are more inclined to ask either 'Did you believe exactly what we teach?' or 'Were the hands that were laid on you our hands?' and — if the answer is satisfactory — to assure the converts that they have received the Holy Spirit even if they don't know it. There is a world of difference between these two attitudes" (*The Household of God* [London: SCM, 1953 = New York: Friendship, 1954] 95).

93. These are traditional terms. Paul's equivalent would be "the manifestation of the Spirit" (1 Cor. 12.7).

uality (ch. 14) was a feature from the first.[94] Likewise Paul's recall of the Galatians to their beginnings (Gal. 3.1-5) includes a reminder that the "supply of the Spirit" came together with the "working of miracles" (3.5). Paul also recalls that his missionary success was marked "by the power of signs and wonders, by the power of God's Spirit" (Rom. 15.19).[95]

Moving along the spectrum we can find various memories of the gift of the Spirit as marked by strong emotional experiences. Rom. 5.5 — "the love of God poured out in your hearts," as though from an upended pitcher. 1 Cor. 12.13c — "all irrigated with or drenched in the one Spirit," like the coming of the monsoon rains.[96] 1 Thes. 1.6 — the gospel received "with joy of the Holy Spirit."[97] We should also recall that Paul envisages the identifying cry "Abba! Father!" as spoken with some intensity (*krazein,* "cry out").[98] No silent filial murmur in the innermost being this.[99] The exhilarating experience of liberation we shall return to below (§16.5a).

Closely correlated were experiences of deep conviction. 1 Thes. 1.5 — "our gospel came to you . . . in power and in the Holy Spirit and with full conviction."[100] 1 Cor. 2.4 — "my proclamation was . . . with demonstration of Spirit and power."[101]

A little further along the spectrum we could speak of experiences of intellectual illumination. Such is clearly implied in the midrash in 2 Cor. 3.12-16, already discussed (§16.3). Paul envisages conversion (to the Spirit) as an unveiling, evoking the experience of a veil being removed, of eyes being opened. Any university teacher, and, hopefully, all university students, know the experience all too well. It is quite characteristic of Paul's conception of

94. Fee draws "the Pentecostal conclusion" here when he deduces that the gift of the Spirit in Corinth was evidenced by glossolalia (*Empowering Presence* 92).

95. The more vivid account in Acts 19.6 describes manifestations of inspired speech (glossolalia and prophecy); cf. 2.4; 8.18-19 (the gift of the Spirit clearly evident and impressive to Simon the magician); 10.44-46. See further below §20.5.

96. See above n. 27.

97. See also Fee, *Empowering Presence* 46-47.

98. Rom. 8.15-16; Gal. 4.6. *Krazein* ("cry") can hardly avoid being understood as an intense or loud cry (Dunn, *Jesus and Spirit* 240; also *Romans* 453; see also Horn, *Angeld* 411). More typical of traditional exegesis is Montague — "a liturgical shout or acclamation" (*Holy Spirit* 197).

99. The traditional understanding of the *testimonium,* not least Calvin's "secret testimony of the Spirit" (*Institutes* 1.7.4), is not well rooted exegetically at this point.

100. *Plērophoria* ("full conviction/assurance"); cf. its other NT occurrences — Col. 2.2; Heb. 6.11; 10.22.

101. *Apodeixis* ("proof, demonstration"), only here in the NT, is more or less a technical term in rhetoric and denotes a compelling conclusion drawn from accepted premises (Weiss, *1 Korinther* 50-51; L. Hartman, "Some Remarks on 1 Cor. 2.1-5," *SEÅ* 39 [1974] 109-20).

the Spirit to link it with experiences of revelation and knowledge.[102] Particularly notable is 1 Cor. 2.12 — "we have received . . . the Spirit which is from God, in order that we might know what has been given to us by God." And it is worth noting that the reason why Paul preferred prophecy to glossolalia in the gatherings for worship was because prophecy was fruitful for mind as well as spirit (1 Cor. 14.14-15).

Finally, somewhere along the spectrum (if talk of a single spectrum is still meaningful) we would have to speak of the moral impact of the Spirit. Here undoubtedly the most striking passage is 1 Cor. 6.9-11:

> [9]Do you not know that the unrighteous will not inherit the kingdom of God? Do not be deceived. Neither the sexually immoral, nor idolaters, nor adulterers, nor the effeminate, nor active homosexuals, [10]nor thieves, nor the greedy, nor drunkards, nor slanderers, nor swindlers will inherit the kingdom of God. [11]And such were some of you. But you were washed, but you were sanctified, but you were justified in the name of the Lord Jesus Christ and in the Spirit of our God.

Whatever one makes of the full range of unacceptable moral practice as listed by Paul,[103] the point here is Paul's reminder of a former manner of life, now completely reversed or transformed by the Spirit received in conversion. As more recent generations have seen evidence of the Spirit's transforming power in empty taverns and reunited families, so Paul could point to lives morally transformed, often, it would appear, in quite dramatic ways ("such were some of you"). This is presumably also the sort of thing Paul had in mind when he spoke of "putting to death the deeds of the body by the Spirit" (Rom. 8.13), that is, the transformation of social ethos and lifestyle which was a consequence of "putting on the Lord Jesus Christ" (Rom. 13.13-14). Presumably also this was all of a piece with the personal transformation of which the Spirit is *arrabōn* ("first instalment") and whose end is the completion of the salvation process in resurrection (2 Cor. 4.16–5.5).

Such acceptance of religious experience, and indeed reliance on it as a sign of God's action on and in a life, has something unnerving about it.[104] Anyone familiar with the history of "enthusiastic" sects within Christianity (as in other religions and ideologies) is bound to recognize danger signals. Reliance on religious experience can easily become idealization of a particular

---

102. Especially 1 Cor. 2.10-15; 12.8; Col. 1.9; Eph. 1.17; 3.5.

103. See particularly above §5 n. 102.

104. Hence, presumably, the overreaction of Ridderbos: "What is denoted [by "being in the Spirit"] is not a subjective state of consciousness, but an 'objective' mode of being" (*Paul* 221).

experience.[105] Reliance upon experience can easily become uncritical or give rise to a leadership which is ignorant of the oft-repeated lessons of history. Reliance upon experience can easily become a means of promoting an esoteric and elitist factionalism, destructive of all community and fellowship. Fortunately Paul himself was alert to such dangers. And as we shall see later, his practical theology included several "tests" of such phenomena.[106]

Of these the most important is one we have already sketched out (§10.6). That is the redefinition, or tighter definition, of *the Spirit as the Spirit of Christ.* This in fact constitutes one of Paul's most important contributions to biblical theology, or to any theology which looks to the scriptures of Jew and Christian for its framework. For in speaking of the Spirit as the Spirit of Christ, Paul was reflecting theologically on what had been hitherto an ill-defined and vague conceptuality of the Spirit — ill-defined and vague precisely because it embraced or lay behind a wide range of experience and existential phenomena. Paul's definition, therefore, gave the conception of the Spirit a sharpness and clarity which it had been lacking.[107] The point is worth some emphasis. Paul did not speak of the Spirit uncritically in relation to all experiences of himself or his converts. On the contrary, "the Spirit of Christ" became in effect a critical conceptual tool which enabled him to evaluate experiences and to distinguish one experience from another. Only those experiences were to be recognized and welcomed which manifested the Spirit as the Spirit of Christ.[108]

What that meant in practice is indicated by several passages already referred to. 1 Cor. 12.3 — an experience of inspiration to be recognized as experience of the Spirit by the inspired confession, "Jesus is Lord." Rom. 8.15-16 — an experience of sharing in Jesus' own prayer of sonship, "Abba! Father!"[109] 2 Cor. 3.18 — the long-term experience of being shaped in accordance with the image of God in Christ.[110] Here we may also simply mention the "fruit of the Spirit" (Gal. 5.22-23) and the exaltation of love as the supreme mark of spirituality (1 Cor. 13). Paul does not say so, but the suggestion that both passages provide a "character sketch" of Christ[111] is one to which he would probably have assented wholeheartedly.

---

105. This is of a piece with the danger of reifying a particular metaphor — referred to above (§13.4).

106. See below §21.6.

107. Isaacs points out a prior phase in this process in that the authors of the LXX, in choosing to translate Hebrew *ruach* with Greek *pneuma,* "introduced Jewish theological ideas into pagan Greek concepts of *pneuma . . .* and (thus) began a process . . . whereby *pneuma* became predominantly *pneuma theou* [the spirit of God]" (*Concept* 143).

108. Luke does not show such sensitivity or discrimination; see my *Unity* 180-84.

109. See above §8.3(4).

110. Note how this motif deepens in §§18.5 and 7.

111. See my *Galatians* 309-10.

In short, Paul did not turn away from the thought of the Spirit as the experienced Spirit. It was too fundamental to his own and his churches' spirituality. The existential reality of "receiving the Spirit" was too central to his understanding of the crucial transition to Christian discipleship.[112] But he was farsighted (or experienced) enough to hedge the experiential dimension around with critical tests and to insist on Christ and the remembered character of Christ as the fundamental norm by which all claims to experience the Spirit should be measured. These are points whose ramifications shall become clearer as we proceed.[113]

§16.5 The blessings of the Spirit

As with the other two aspects of Christian beginnings, so in this case also it is worth indicating, at least briefly, the features of the Christian life which Paul specifically attributes to the Spirit given in and as the beginning of that new life. Again it is not a matter of allocating, as it were, particular blessings to particular aspects. That would be pedantic, unrealistic, and highly misleading. Again we need to recall the wholeness of what Paul had in mind and the integrated character of the beginning of salvation. Nevertheless, there is some value in noting the particular outworkings of the Spirit thus given and received. It both highlights the importance of this aspect of Christian beginnings and reminds us of how central the Spirit was in Paul's understanding of Christian spirituality and conduct.

As a preliminary we should simply recall points already made: The basic experience and manifestation of the Spirit, for Paul as for those before him, was life — the Spirit as the animating breath of life. The distinguishing mark of the Spirit and the manifestations of the Spirit was their Jesus character — the Spirit as the Spirit of Christ. Properly speaking, however, these are part of Paul's definition of the Spirit, rather than to be numbered among the Spirit's manifestations.

Given its central character in Paul's pneumatology, it is hardly surprising that the clearest indications of what the Spirit brings about in human life are given in Romans 8.

a) *Liberty.* We have already mentioned this feature (§14.9d). But we can hardly refrain from mentioning it here too. The transition from the sobering reality of Rom. 7.7-25 is described precisely in these terms. "The law of the Spirit of life in Christ Jesus has set you free from the law of sin and death" (Rom. 8.2).[114] In

---

112. Fee concludes similarly (*Empowering Presence* 854).
113. See particularly §§18.7, 21.6, and 23.4, 8.
114. Note also the foreshadowing of 8.2 in the use of *katargeomai* in 7.2, 6 with the less common sense of "released from, taken from the sphere of influence of."

a not dissimilar context, talking about the abused law *(gramma)* and misunderstood old covenant, Paul appends to his description of conversion the illuminating note: "where the Spirit of the Lord [is], [there is] freedom" (2 Cor. 3.17).[115] There could hardly be any clearer reminder that the Spirit was experienced as a liberating power. However Paul the Pharisee had experienced his devotion to Torah and traditional halakhah, Paul the convert experienced his new-found faith as liberating and attributed this powerful sense of liberation directly to the Spirit.[116]

Similarly in Galatians. For Paul the experience of the Spirit was clearly the liberating antithesis to the slavery (of the law) which his converts seemed to covet.[117] That was why Paul could scarcely credit what was happening in Galatia (Gal. 1.6; 3.3). Those "born in accordance with the Spirit" were free (4.28-31). They should not surrender that freedom, either to the law (5.1) or in irresponsible living (5.13). Only a Spirit-prompted and enabled lifestyle could resist the impulse to satisfy the desires of the flesh (5.16-18, 25) and thus maintain that liberty. Elsewhere we should simply note that Paul also considered the climax of the Spirit's saving work, in creation, but also by implication in the human body, as itself a liberation (Rom. 8.21-23).

b) *Christian conduct* is for Paul equally an outworking of the Spirit (Rom. 8.4-6, 13-14). But it will be more appropriate to discuss this later (§23.4). Here we can simply note that Paul does not hesitate to express what we might call the charismatic character of Christian daily living. Christian conduct he conceives, not simply as walking in accordance with the Spirit,[118] but as being led by the Spirit.[119] Equally characteristic of Paul is his alertness to the danger of liberty being abused.[120]

c) *Sonship/adoption* seems to have been another consequence of receiving the Spirit which Paul particularly cherished. In Rom. 8.15 he even describes the Spirit as "the Spirit of adoption." In the similar passage in Gal.

---

115. We recall that "the Spirit of the Lord" here is the Spirit of God = "the Lord" of Exod. 34.34; see above §16.3.

116. We should not forget that this has also been the experience of renewal for countless Christians: "the *libertas Ecclesiae* is becoming the freedom of the church in relation to itself in its historical and cultural forms" (Congar, *Believe* 2.130).

117. Jones's attempt to argue against the dominant view that freedom from the (Jewish) law was at the heart of Paul's concept of freedom *(Freiheit)* is thoroughly tendentious.

118. Rom. 8.4; 2 Cor. 12.18; Gal. 5.16; cf. 1 Cor. 3.1-3; 2 Cor. 10.2-4; Eph. 2.2.

119. In Rom. 8.14 and Gal. 5.18 Paul uses the same verb *(agomai)* as in 1 Cor. 12.2, which seems to be a critique of Dionysiac worship. Käsemann draws attention to the "enthusiastic" character of Paul's vocabulary in this section of Romans (*Romans* 226); but see also Bultmann, *Theology* 1.336; Pfister, *Leben* (§18 n. 1) 76-77; Deidun, *New Covenant Morality* (§23 n. 1) 79 ("*allow* themselves to be led"); my *Romans* 450; Horn, *Angeld* 397; Fee, *Empowering Presence* 563.

120. Particularly Gal. 5.13; Rom. 6.12-23.

4.5-6 it is not so clear that the sending of the Spirit into their hearts is the effectual act of adoption. However, the variant formulation in Gal. 4.4-6 is probably determined by Paul's decision to put the two sending formulae in parallel:

> [4]. . . God sent forth his Son . . .
>   in order that we might receive the adoption.
>   And in that *(hoti)* you are sons,
> God sent forth the Spirit of his Son into our hearts. . . .

In the light of Rom. 8.15 it is hard to imagine that Paul conceived of an adopted sonship antecedent to the sending of the Spirit.[121]

The metaphor of adoption is worth noting. Adoption was not a characteristically Jewish practice, and in the NT the metaphor occurs only in the Pauline literature.[122] Here is a case where Paul found that Greco-Roman law and custom provided a more immediately applicable image.[123] At the same time, it is important for the coherence of Paul's argument, particularly in Galatians 3-4, to remember that the status of sonship envisaged is entirely in Jewish categories — a sonship in Christ, which is both a sonship of Abraham and a sonship of God, and which makes it possible for even Gentiles to share in both.[124]

Several points should be noted of relevance to our present concerns. First, according to Paul, it is the Spirit which effects the new bond, no doubt because it is sonship to God which is primarily in view at this point. Since the Spirit is the outreaching, life-creating power of God in creation and society, it was natural to attribute this new status, this new existential relationship, to

---

121. On the slight puzzle of *hoti* used in an explanatory sense ("to show or prove that") see my *Baptism* 113-15; *Galatians* 219; and particularly Fee, *Empowering Presence* 406-8. Note also the characteristic Pauline variation between "us" and "you"; the implication is that Paul varied between drawing on experience that he knew (or assumed) he shared with his readers and a concern to remind them of what they themselves had personally experienced.

122. Rom. 8.15, 23; 9.4; Gal. 4.5; Eph. 1.5.

123. But see now the thorough study of the evidence by Scott, *Adoption* 3-57, with important qualification of the usual view that adoption was unknown to the OT and not practised in early Judaism (61-88).

124. See also Byrne, *Sons* — conclusion on 220. Scott, *Adoption,* pushes a much more elaborate theory, that behind Gal. 4.1-2 Israel's sojourn in Egypt is particularly in view, with the redemption from Egypt seen as a type of eschatological redemption ("New or Second Exodus"; 4.3-7), and that " 'the' (articular) *huiothesia* in Gal. 4.5b very likely alludes to the eschatological expectation in Jewish tradition which applies the promise of divine adoption in 2 Sam. 7.14 to the Messiah (4QFlor. 1.11), to Israel (*Jub.* 1.24), and to both the Messiah and Israel (*Test. Jud.* 24.3), in the time when Israel would return from Exile in the Second Exodus" (ch. 3, here 178).

the Spirit. Second, as already noted, the sonship is one shared with Christ. Hence in Gal. 4.6 the Spirit is designated "the Spirit of his [God's] Son."[125] And in Rom. 8.17 adopted son of God means also joint heir with Christ. Here the triadic relationship of Father, Son, and Spirit is particularly interesting — the Son as pattern and pioneer of a sonship to God as Father, effected by the Spirit. Third, the existential character of the sonship, as well as its character as patterned on Christ's sonship and shared with Christ, is indicated not least by the Spirit-inspired prayer "Abba! Father!"[126]

The fact that Paul makes such a similar reference in letters to two different churches (only one of which he knew personally) is a clear enough indication that the sense of sonship, both experienced in and expressed through the "Abba" prayer, was common in most churches of the diaspora. It is also important to note that this was where Paul rooted his and his fellow Christians' personal assurance that they were indeed God's children: in the "Abba! Father!" cry, "the Spirit itself bears witness with our spirit that we are children of God" (Rom. 8.16). If we can speak of a doctrine of assurance in Paul, then this is where it should start — in the experience of sonship, and not simply in formal instruction or in conformity to ecclesiastical procedures.

d) *Spiritual longing and hope.* Particularly expressive is the tension between a beginning which ensures the end and a longing for the end itself: Rom. 8.23 — "we ourselves who have the firstfruits of the Spirit, we ourselves also groan within ourselves, eagerly awaiting adoption, the redemption of our body." There is a similar sentiment in 2 Cor. 5.2: "Here indeed we groan and long to put on our heavenly dwelling." And the implication is present there too that this is groaning at the progress of the process begun by the Spirit as its first instalment (5.5). Of a piece with this is Paul's talk in Gal. 5.5 of "eagerly awaiting the hope of righteousness by the Spirit, from faith." This is a point which also requires further development in a different context (§18).

Correlated with this is the experience of hope.[127] In Rom. 8.24-25 Paul sums up the longing as an experience of hope:

> [24]For in terms of hope, we are saved. But hope which is seen is not hope; for who hopes for what he sees? [25]But if we hope for what we do not see, we await it eagerly with patience.

125. See further above §10.6.
126. See further above §§16.3-4.
127. "Hope is a form of experience and of understanding. It is the form in which faith is related to the experience of the world that is still apparently unredeemed" (Welker, *God* 245).

This correlation between the Spirit and hope recurs sufficiently frequently for us to classify hope as one of the primary blessings of the Spirit for Paul.[128] Particularly noticeable is the emphasis in Rom. 5.2-5 and 8.18-25 that this hope was experienced and sustained despite suffering and affliction. No doubt it was the experience of being buoyed up even in the most adverse circumstances which enabled Paul himself to continue his missionary work. This experience he attributed to the Spirit. Here again we should recall the difference between the Hebrew and Greek conceptions — the latter conceived as something more tentative (like typical English usage), the former as something more confident and assured.[129] No wonder, then, that in Romans 8 Paul attributes this hope to the Spirit, having just spoken of the assurance of sonship also given by the Spirit. The absence of polemic at this point should not go unnoticed.[130]

e) *Prayer.* Finally in the sequence in Romans 8, Paul's great Spirit chapter, we should note how he goes on immediately to attribute effective prayer to the Spirit (8.26-27):

> [26]In the same way also the Spirit helps us in our weakness. For we do not know what to pray for as we should, but the Spirit itself intercedes on our behalf with inarticulate groans. [27]And he who searches the hearts knows what is the Spirit's way of thinking because he intercedes as God would have it on behalf of the saints.

This is an astonishing feature of Paul's pneumatology: the Spirit experienced not in power, but in weakness;[131] the Spirit experienced not in articulate speech, but through "inarticulate groans."[132] Such a conceptuality could never

128. Rom. 5.2-5; 8.23-25; 15.13; Gal. 5.5; Phil. 1.19-20; Eph. 4.4 (one Spirit as the middle term between one body and one hope); cf. 1 Cor. 13.7, 13; 2 Cor. 3.12; Eph. 1.17-18.

129. See above §14 n. 217. This probably explains the exceptional use of the aorist here ("we were saved"); only in the later Paulines do we find comparable language (Eph. 2.5, 8; 2 Tim. 1.9; Tit. 3.5); see also §14 n. 150 above. Its use here, as explained in the following sentences, mirrors the character of hope: assured hope assures of completed salvation. The aorists of 8.29-30 reflect the same confidence: God's purpose as seen from its assured end.

130. See also my *Romans* 475-76.

131. The passage may deliberately be directed against assumptions that the "spiritual" person would be manifested as such by deeds of power (Horn, *Angeld* 413). It cuts equally across Beker's astonishing claim that "Paul often speaks of the Spirit in an inherently triumphant manner that prevents its integral relation with the weakness and suffering of the crucified Christ" (*Paul* 244). See further below §18.7.

132. The talk of "groans" echoes the groaning of 8.23. *Alalētos,* "inarticulate," occurs only here in biblical Greek. As the opposite of *lalētos* ("endowed with speech" — Job 38.14 LXX), it presumably indicates deprivation of the speech which distinguishes

have been derived from a theoretical or purely doctrinal concept of either Spirit or conversion.[133] It can only be explained out of the depths of personal experience. But integrated, no doubt, with the corresponding belief in Christ's heavenly intercession (8.34).[134] Here again the correlation between experienced Spirit and believed-in Christ was presumably important for the first Christians' understanding of their experience.

There are issues here which need to be taken up later. At this point, however, it is simply worth noting that Paul did not see his experience of physical weakness as a contradiction or denial of the Spirit's presence. On the contrary, his weakness was the prior condition for the most effective operation of the Spirit. Here we see quite clearly the complementary character of Paul's understanding of Spirit and faith. Faith in Paul's understanding is just that total reliance of human weakness on divine grace which allows the Spirit to operate most effectively within the human condition. Correspondingly, the manifestation of that effective operation is not to be measured in terms of rhetorical effect. It works precisely in, through, and as human inarticulateness. The existential character and sober realism of Paul's spirituality is nowhere so clearly indicated as here.

f) *Spiritual insight and charisms.* We need not extend this analysis further. But for completeness' sake we should simply refer to Paul's characterization of the spiritual person *(pneumatikos)* in 1 Cor. 2.13–3.1 and to his discussion of spiritual gifts *(pneumatika)* in 1 Corinthians 12–14. These, however, are more appropriately discussed in ch. 7.[135]

g) *Fruit of the Spirit.* Likewise it would hardly do to pass on from an analysis of the marks of the Spirit without mentioning "the fruit of the Spirit" in Gal. 5.22-23. But here again these are more appropriately brought into the discussion in ch. 8.[136]

---

human beings from animals. The thought is of groans not formulated in words. That Paul had glossolalia in mind (cf. Lietzmann, *Römer* 86; Käsemann, *Perspectives* 130; Gnilka, *Theologie* 104; and particularly Fee, *Empowering Presence* 580-85) is unlikely, since Paul probably conceived of glossolalia as a (or the) language of heaven (see below §20 n. 132). See further my *Jesus and the Spirit* 241-42 and *Romans* 478-79; Fitzmyer, *Romans* 518-19. Congar comments appropriately: ". . . groaning, which is quite different from complaining or whining" (*Believe* 2.107).

133. The Spirit as intercessor would then at best be a development of the more familiar motif of angelic intercession (e.g., Job 33.23-26; Tob. 12.15; see further J. Behm, *TDNT* 5.810-11).

134. See also Schlier, *Grundzüge* 181.

135. See below §21.5 and §20 n. 127.

136. §§23.5-6. See also above §16.4 and n. 111 and §21.6b below.

§16.6 Conclusion

In these three chapters we have penetrated about as far as is possible in exegetical analysis to the heart of Paul's understanding of the beginning of salvation. These three aspects — justification by faith (§14), participation in Christ (§15), and the gift of the Spirit (§16) — it should be repeated just once more, are not to be conceived as distinct and inconsistent "models" or "types." They were different ways of conceptualizing and speaking of the diverse but mutually cohering conviction and commitment which brought very different people under the single banner of Christ to adopt the single new identity of "Christian." Their complementarity comes out in different ways.

1) All three aspects were central and, so far as Paul was concerned, indispensable ways of understanding God's work in reclaiming humankind for himself. By inference, any analysis which ignores or underplays one or other of these three is in grave danger of distorting Paul's theology. It is not at all surprising that the threefold action has a triadic aspect — justified with God, bonded with Christ, gifted with Spirit. Paul's theology at this point is a reflection and expression of his concept of God as one and of the different aspects of God's working. Failure to appreciate the integrated character of his soteriology at this point is also failure to appreciate his understanding of God.[137]

2) The different functions can be categorized in a rough-and-ready way. Where justification has to do with status before God and "in Christ" speaks more of the perspective from which Christians viewed their life, the gift of the Spirit gives the whole dual relationship (with God through Christ) a dynamic quality, of which Paul's own life and work is a classic expression. But the *Ineinander* ("in-each-other-ness") of all three should not be lost sight of.

3) The distinct emphases in each aspect are not contradicted by the relatively lesser interest in these emphases in the other aspects. Paul's emphasis on faith as the only way that humans can respond to God's grace is particularly in focus with justification, but it is the presumption of all his talk of salvation. The "with Christ" of Paul's Christ mysticism helps keep alive the tension between the determinative events already past and those yet to

---

137. But does Paul's language and treatment encourage talk of the three Persons of the Godhead coming "as one . . . but according to the order and characteristics of their hypostatic being" (Congar, *Believe* 2.89)? Fee, *Empowering Presence* 827-45, is equally bold — "Paul was truly Trinitarian in any meaningful sense of that term" (840) — but without attempting any clarification of the meaning of "person" or offering any reflection on the traditional debate on the "economic" or "ontological" Trinity. Respecting Paul's theology means also respecting its time-conditioned and relatively inchoate character.

come. His treatment of the Spirit provides a constant reminder that his gospel dealt with existential realities and not just theories or principles.

4) The blessings severally linked to each of the three aspects of salvation hang together in an impressively rounded whole — peace with and access to God, liberation from an oppressive past, an identity given new meaning by integration into Israel's promises, an answer to the powers of sin and death, a sense of sonship and hope despite continuing weakness and suffering, a consciousness of shared identity in Christ with others, and a way and enabling to live responsibly and effectively.

§17 Baptism[1]

§17.1 The traditional view

In our analysis of Paul's understanding of the crucial transition, the beginning of salvation, there has been one notable omission. We have observed Paul's regular recall of his readers to the decisive event (aorist tense) from which they dated their lives as Christians. We have examined the three main aspects which make up Paul's integrated view of this beginning and its consequences — justification by faith, participation in Christ, and the gift of the Spirit. But

---

1. **Bibliography**: **G. R. Beasley-Murray**, *Baptism in the New Testament* (London: Macmillan/Grand Rapids: Eerdmans, 1963); **G. Braumann**, *Vorpaulinische christliche Taufverkündigung bei Paulus* (BWANT; Stuttgart: Kohlhammer, 1962); **R. D. Chesnut**, *From Death to Life: Conversion in Joseph and Asenath* (JSPS 16; Sheffield Academic, 1995); **E. J. Christiansen**, *The Covenant in Judaism and Paul: A Study of Ritual Boundaries as Identity Markers* (Leiden: Brill, 1995); **Conzelmann**, *Outline* 271-73; **G. Delling**, *Die Zueignung des Heils in der Taufe. Eine Untersuchung zum neutestamentlichen "Taufen auf den Namen"* (Berlin: Evangelische, 1961); **E. Dinkler**, *Die Taufaussagen des Neuen Testaments,* in K. Viering, ed., *Zu Karl Barths Lehre von der Taufe* (Gütersloh: Gütersloher, 1971) 60-153; **J. D. G. Dunn**, *Baptism* (§16 n. 1); "The Birth of a Metaphor — Baptized in Spirit," *ExpT* 89 (1977-78) 134-38, 173-75; **Fee**, *Empowering Presence* (§16 n. 1); **A. George**, et al., *Baptism in the New Testament* (London: Chapman, 1964); **Gnilka**, *Theologie* 115-20; *Paulus* 272-77; **W. Heitmüller**, *Taufe und Abendmahl* (Göttingen: Vandenhoeck, 1903); **Hengel and Schwemer**, *Paul between Damascus and Antioch* 291-300; **Horn**, *Angeld* (§16 n. 1); **Keck**, *Paul* 56-59; **Kümmel**, *Theology* 207-16; **G. W. H. Lampe**, *The Seal of the Spirit* (London: SPCK, [2]1967); **F. Lang**, "Das Verständnis der Taufe bei Paulus," in Ådna, et al., eds., *Evangelium* 255-68; **Larsson**, *Christus als Vorbild* (§11 n. 1) 1. Teil; **E. Lohse**, "Taufe und Rechtfertigung bei Paulus," *Einheit* 228-44; **L. De Lorenzi**, ed., *Battesimo e Giustizia in Rom. 6 e 8* (Roma: Abbazia S. Paolo, 1974); **K. McDonnell and G. T. Montague**, *Christian Initiation and Baptism in the Holy Spirit: Evidence from the First Eight Centuries* (Collegeville: Liturgical, 1991); **Penna**, "Baptism and Participation in the Death of Christ in Rom. 6.1-11," *Paul* 1.124-41; **M. Pesce**, " 'Christ Did Not Send Me to Baptize, but to Evangelise' (1 Cor. 1.17a)," in Lorenzi, ed., *Paul de Tarse* 339-63; **M. Quesnel**, *Baptisés dans l'Esprit* (Paris: Cerf, 1985); **Ridderbos**, *Paul* 396-414; **R. Schnackenburg**, *Baptism in the Thought of St. Paul* (Oxford: Blackwell/New York: Herder and Herder, 1964); **U. Schnelle**, *Gerechtigkeit und Christusgegenwart. Vorpaulinische und paulinische Tauftheologie* (Göttingen: Vandenhoeck, 1983); **Stuhlmacher**, *Theologie* 350-55; **G. Wagner**, *Pauline Baptism and the Pagan Mysteries* (Edinburgh: Oliver and Boyd, 1967); **A. J. M. Wedderburn**, *Baptism and Resurrection: Studies in Pauline Theology against Its Graeco-Roman Background* (WUNT 44; Tübingen: Mohr, 1987); **Whiteley**, *Theology* 166-78.

the traditional label for this beginning has been "baptism." And most studies in this area assume that Paul would have thought of it in the same way.

As in other subjects, it is not a matter of how often Paul spoke explicitly of "baptism." His actual use of the noun and verb ("baptism," "baptize") is relatively infrequent.[2] More determinative is the assumption that any reference back to conversion and initiation was bound to be a reference back to the event of baptism: the aorist tenses themselves were Paul's allusion to baptism; the metaphors he used — like washing, anointing, sealing, putting on clothes — were all images of baptism.[3] These assumptions have been operative for most of the modern period, and at such points in the text most commentators simply refer to baptismal aorists or baptismal theology without any sense of need to justify the language.[4] So with the three aspects analysed above: justification is the effect of baptism;[5] the means of union with Christ is baptism;[6] and the Spirit is mediated through or bestowed in baptism.[7]

The main research effort, indeed, has been to build on that baptismal basis by identifying baptismal liturgies, catechetical forms, baptismal hymns — or at least fragments and echoes of such,[8] the assumption again being that

2. *Baptisma* ("baptism") — Rom. 6.4; Col. 2.12; Eph. 4.5; *baptizō* ("baptize") — Rom. 6.3 (twice); 1 Cor. 1.13-17 (6 times); 10.2; 12.13; 15.29 (twice); Gal. 3.27.

3. See, e.g., D. Mollat, "Baptismal Symbolism in St Paul," in George, et al., *Baptism* 63-83, who speaks in sequence of "the baptismal bath," "baptismal circumcision," "the baptismal seal," and "the baptismal light." For details of these metaphors see above §13.4.

4. E.g., in Galatians, Schlier, *Galater,* takes it for granted that passages like 3.2; 4.6; and 5.24, as well, of course, as 3.27, are recalls to baptism and use baptismal language, or he speaks of "the sacramental sense" of the verb in 5.24.

5. This is the main thesis of Schnelle, *Gerechtigkeit,* e.g., 52, 91. Braumann, *Taufverkündigung,* proceeds by relating a lengthy sequence of Pauline motifs, including justification, to baptism.

6. Wikenhauser, *Pauline Mysticism* (§15 n. 1) 109-32; "This union is produced only by Baptism" (132); Schnelle, *Gerechtigkeit* 106-22; Strecker, *Theologie* 127. The emphasis is already there in Heitmüller, *Taufe* 11-12; and especially in Schweitzer, *Mysticism* (§15.1 above).

7. In recent treatments see, e.g., Schnelle, *Gerechtigkeit* 123-35; McDonnell and Montague, *Christian Initiation* 50-51; Horn, *Angeld* 400.

8. In 1 Thessalonians, for example, G. Friedrich suggests that 1.9-10 was "a baptismal hymn" (G. Friedrich, "Ein Tauflied hellenistischer Judenchristen 1 Thess. 1.9f," *TZ* 21 [1965] 502-16); W. Harnisch concludes that 5.4-10 contains "rudiments of a pre-Pauline baptismal tradition" (*Eschatologische Existenz* [§12 n. 1] 123-24); and U. Schnelle attempts to show that the "in Christ" of 4.16 is to be understood as the substantive communion with Christ actually begun in baptism (Schnelle, *Gerechtigkeit* 114). At the other end of the spectrum of Pauline letters J. C. Kirby argued that "when the epistolary sections of Ephesians are removed, we are left with a document complete in itself which could have been used in an act of worship" which "may have had a close connection with baptism" (*Ephesians: Baptism and Pentecost* [London: SPCK/Montreal: McGill University, 1968] 150).

baptism must have been such an important feature of earliest evangelism, theology, and church life that its importance was bound to be reflected in many features of that theology and life. So, for example, the great christological hymns in Philippians and Colossians have been designated "baptismal."[9] A currently popular suggestion is that Gal. 3.26-28 has been lifted, in whole or in part, from a pre-Pauline baptismal liturgy.[10] And it has been common to assume that the subject of Rom. 6.1-14 is "baptism," even though the language of baptism seems to function only as the first part (6.3-4) of the theme announced in 6.2 ("dead to sin").[11] In short, a typical view would be that "The whole theology of Paul can rightly be described as an exposition of baptism *(Taufauslegung)*."[12]

It would not be unfair, then, to speak of a predisposition in many commentators to recognize such baptismal allusions, a preunderstanding operative in the reading of the text.[13] This preunderstanding has been determined by two factors. One, of course, is the long tradition of sacramental theology within Christian tradition. In more or less all historic Christian traditions a sacrament is understood as a subtle interrelation of spiritual and material. The sacrament is not simply the ritual act. The sacrament, properly speaking, is the inner as well as the outward act. It denotes the spiritual reality symbolised by the ritual. And not merely symbolized — though here opinions begin to diverge — but in some sense brought to actuality in the event. That is what "baptism" means. That is why "baptism" is the most obvious single term to describe the whole.[14] And since the sacrament by definition embraces

---

9. On Phil. 2.6-11 see Martin, *Carmen Christi* (§11 n. 1]) 81-82; Käsemann designated Col. 1.12-20 "a primitive Christian baptismal liturgy" ("A Primitive Christian Baptismal Liturgy," *Essays* 149-68).

10. See particularly Betz, *Galatians* 181-85; D. R. MacDonald, *There is No Male and Female: The Fate of a Dominical Saying in Paul and Gnosticism* (Philadelphia: Fortress, 1987) 4-9.

11. See further my *Baptism* 140; *Romans* 308; Braumann calls Romans 6 "the chapter on baptism" *(Taufverkündigung* 39). Similarly with Col. 2.8-15 (see my *Colossians* 159 n. 24). In the case of Romans 6, the point is acknowledged by Dinkler, *Taufaussagen* 71; Schnelle, *Gerechtigkeit* 204 n. 386, contests but does not meet the point; see Penna, "Baptism," who notes the observation of Origen that Paul in this passage certainly meant to examine "not so much the nature of baptism as the nature of the death of Christ" (137). "The very likeness *(homoiōma)* of his [Christ's] death" (6.5a) can hardly be baptism, since the perfect tense of the verb indicates a continuing state (still immersed?!); see further my *Romans* 317 and below §18.5 and n. 100.

12. Lohse, "Taufe" 238.

13. This is not a criticism. All commentators come to the text with their own preunderstandings. Here I simply identify the preunderstanding operative in this case.

14. I attempt in these sentences to represent the consensus of Christian sacramental/baptismal theology. See, e.g., the brief summary of Reformed tradition in my *Baptism* 6.

the whole, it is natural to refer metaphors of becoming Christian to it, and natural to refer the blessings discussed above (§§14-16) to "baptism." Such I take to be the unspoken logic operating in the search for baptismal theology and liturgical fragments in the Pauline letters. The assumption is that the presupposition of centuries of Christian sacramental theology must already have been operative in the case of Paul and his first audiences.

One problem with this was indicated in my earliest study on *Baptism*. It is the fact that "baptism" thus used in reference to becoming Christian is functioning as a kind of "concertina" word.[15] That is to say, it can be extended to embrace all that was involved in the crucial transition (justification, union with Christ, the gift of the Spirit). But it can also be squeezed concertina-like until all that is really in view is the ritual act itself — "baptism" in its original sense of "immersion."[16] The problem, then, is that the spiritual reality expressed in the ritual act may become too narrowly focused on the ritual act itself. In a strict baptismal theology, the grace given, the Spirit bestowed, may be subordinated to the ecclesiastical rite, even limited to it. The potential for a church in effect claiming to control the grace of God or the Spirit of God (through its sacramental rubrics) becomes a serious danger.[17] At the very least we should beware of a question-begging concertina use of "baptism" when we turn to examine Paul's own baptismal language.

The other factor determining the preunderstanding of NT scholarship on this point, in the twentieth century at any rate, is the continuing influence of the history of religions research at the beginning of the century. One of the main features of this research was the conclusion that the earliest Christian sacraments were not simply paralleled in the contemporary mystery cults, but also influenced by their equivalent rites.[18] In particular, the deduction lay to hand that initiation into cults of dying and rising gods provided the explanation for Paul's assumption of his readers' familiarity with the motif in their own case: "Do you not know that all we who were baptized into Christ Jesus were baptized into his death?" (Rom. 6.3). The thesis has come under critical scrutiny in the interval.[19] But scholars typically have been unwilling to return

---

15. Dunn, *Baptism* 5. In the several references to my *Baptism* below I have not thought it necessary to repeat the bibliographical references contained in it.

16. LSJ, *baptizō,* "dip, plunge"; in the passive, "to be drowned," of the sinking of ships, etc. Contrast Ridderbos, *Paul* 402.

17. History shows that the danger has been succumbed to as much in enthusiastic sects as ever it may have been in the clericalism and scholasticism of the more established traditions.

18. See, e.g., those cited by Beasley-Murray, *Baptism* 127 n. 1; also Bornkamm, *Paul* 190; Kümmel, *Theology* 213.

19. Particularly H. A. A. Kennedy, *St. Paul and the Mystery Religions* (London/New York: Hodder and Stoughton, 1914); Wagner, *Pauline Baptism.*

to the idea of an early Christianity wholly isolated and distinct from the religious culture and ethos of the day. And social-anthropological appreciation of the function of rites of passage and experiences of conversion and liminality has reinforced the parallels between Christian initiation and initiation into the cults.[20]

However, there is a problem here too.[21] For one thing, we know hardly anything about the rites of the mystery cults. For the most part they, as effective secret societies, kept their "mysteries" all too secret. For another, in the case most often cited (the initiation of Lucius),[22] there is no hint of a water ritual as part of the initiation itself.[23] Moreover, the typical initiation rites to the mysteries seem to have been a good deal more complex, involving "things recited," "things shown," and "things performed."[24] And the suggestion of a mystical identification with the cult god seems to be read into the texts in question, since any implicit, let alone explicit reference seems to be wholly lacking.[25] This is not an attempt to cut Pauline Christianity off once again from its environment. There is indeed an almost inevitable similarity between experiences of radical conversion, such as that of Lucius and that of Paul, and language of death and life is a natural expression of such experiences.[26] But given that very fact, it becomes questionable whether the one need then be understood as the result of influence from the other. Analogy is not genealogy. The question remains whether the Pauline understanding, if not wholly different from, is at least distinctive within such a cultural milieu.[27]

All this, however, is by way of clarifying the factors which have influenced the exegesis of Paul's baptismal language. What of the language itself?

20. Cf. Meeks, *First Urban Christians* 156-57.

21. In what follows I briefly summarize my *Romans* 308-11. See further particularly Wedderburn, *Baptism.*

22. Apuleius, *Metamorphoses* 11. See, e.g., Schnelle, *Gerechtigkeit* 77-78; others in my *Romans* 309.

23. According to Apuleius, *Metamorphoses* 11.23 "the customary ablution" played only a preparatory role (Wagner, *Pauline Baptism* 100-103) and took place at the baths, not at the temple itself. See also Meeks, *First Urban Christians* 152-53.

24. *OCD,* "Mysteries."

25. *Pace* Schnelle, *Gerechtigkeit* 310.

26. Cf. Lucius's own report: "the very rite of dedication itself was performed in the manner of a voluntary death and of a life obtained by grace" (Apuleius, *Metamorphoses* 11.21); translation by J. G. Griffiths, *Apuleius of Madauros: The Isis-Book (Metamorphoses, Book XI)* (Leiden: Brill, 1975) 52.

27. Cf. Chesnut's findings with regard to *Joseph and Aseneth* (*Death to Life* ch. 7). We return to this question as it relates to the Lord's Supper in §22.2 below.

§17.2 Exegetical issues

a) The traditional interpretation of Paul's theology of baptism is by no means simply a case of reading in subsequent sacramental theology or of undue influence from history of religions parallels. It has a strong exegetical base in its own right.

First, we should give due weight to what must have been the social significance of baptism from the beginning. Conversion, typically, was not some private spiritual transaction. It involved baptism. In his indisputable references to the rite of baptism,[28] Paul takes it for granted that all his readers (including those unknown to him personally) had been baptized. The implication of 1 Cor. 1.13-15 is quite clearly that the Corinthians had all been baptized "in the name of Christ." In the NT, apart from Jesus' own disciples and a handful of anomalous cases (like the Ephesians in Acts 19.1-7), we do not hear of any believers who had not been baptized in the name of Jesus. But baptism involved a public act, probably a public confession (Rom. 10.9). Moreover, it constituted almost literally a "rite of passage." Those baptized were thereby renouncing old ways of life and committing themselves to a new way of life. That is precisely why Paul referred to their common baptism in Rom. 6.4 — "so we also should walk in newness of life." The social consequences of their common baptism is one of the main themes of 1 Corinthians, beginning with Paul's plea for an end to factionalism.[29] Not only so, but different nationalities were also thereby pledging allegiance to what was still seen as a Jewish messianic sect. And adoption of "Jewish ways" was a frequent cause of disparagement among Rome's intellectuals.[30] It would hardly be surprising then if baptism was in most cases an event of profound significance to which Paul and his converts could and did often revert when reflecting on the beginnings of their Christian discipleship and its consequent character.[31]

Second, Paul clearly links his talk of "baptized into Christ" with his talk of (the rite of) baptism: Rom. 6.3-4 —

> [3]Are you unaware that all we who were baptized into Christ Jesus were baptized into his death? [4]So then we were buried with him through baptism into death, in order that as Christ was raised from the dead . . . so we also should walk in newness of life.

---

28. Rom. 6.4 *(baptisma);* 1 Cor. 1.13-17.

29. See particularly Mitchell, *Paul and the Rhetoric of Reconciliation.*

30. See, e.g., the data collected in my *Romans* xlvi and xlviii, and the brief catena of vituperation from Roman authors in my *Romans* l-li.

31. So, e.g., Stuhlmacher, *Theologie* 350.

It is hardly forcing the sense to see the two phrases as equivalent: "baptized into his death" = "buried with him through baptism into death." In other words, the "into Christ" of participation in Christ was effected "through baptism."[32]

Similarly in 1 Cor. 10.2: "all were baptized into Moses in the cloud and in the sea." If the imagery of passing through the Red Sea ("under the cloud" and "through the sea")[33] is equivalent to baptismal immersion (in water), and if Moses represents Christ ("into Moses" on the analogy of "into Christ"),[34] then Paul presumably had in view the experience of being baptized (in water) into Christ.

This understanding of 1 Cor. 10.2 would also be of a piece with Paul's treatment of the Lord's Supper later in the same exposition — particularly the thought of participating in Christ's body by sharing in the "one loaf" (10.16-17) and the implication that undiscerning participation in the bread and cup can result in physical consequences, even death (11.28-30). But we shall leave further discussion of the Lord's Supper till §22.

Beyond that there is more room for dispute. In particular, is the phrase "baptized into Christ" a shortened version of "baptized into the name of Christ"? Do metaphors like "washed," "sealed," and "put off/put on clothes" reflect aspects of baptismal ceremony already at the time of Paul? In the light of the conclusions already reached a positive response to both questions has a greater degree of plausibility.

b) On the other hand, the case can be overstated, and the danger of an over-narrow focus on baptism remains.

First, we should not assume that by the time of Paul's mission baptism was an already well-developed and necessarily public ceremony. The information provided by the NT itself suggests rather that for the first half century or so at least, the inititiation ceremony was still simple and spontaneous.

---

32. So, presumably, also Gal. 3.27; cf. Dinkler, *Taufaussagen* 86 — "Becoming sons of God happens subjectively in faith, objectively through baptism."

33. The allusion to the cloud and sea may have been prompted by Wis. 19.7 in particular. That Paul saw the cloud as a symbol of the Spirit is less likely (*pace* McDonnell and Montague, *Christian Initiation* 45; I was more open to this possibility in *Baptism* 127 n. 34, with further bibliography). The implication of "under" and "through" is that Paul saw the cloud above and water on either side as prefiguring baptism by immersion. See also Fee, *1 Corinthians* 445-46.

34. 1 Cor. 10.2 ("baptized into Moses") is obviously modeled on "baptized into Christ" (Rom. 6.3-4; Gal. 3.27; 1 Cor. 12.13). It would be exegetically fallacious to derive the sense of the more common phrase elsewhere from a meaning permitted by the historical relationship between Moses and the Israelites (*pace* Delling, *Zueignung* 79-80; Wolff, *1 Korinther* 41 n. 231). In 1 Cor. 10.1-4 Moses, like the journey through the Red Sea and the food and drink in the desert, functions as a type of the eschatological reality now experienced in and through Christ. See also my *Baptism* 112, 125-26.

Certainly the testimony of Acts points firmly in that direction: three thousand received the word and were baptized the same day (Acts 2.41); both the Ethiopian eunuch and Lydia hear the gospel, respond immediately, and are baptized there and then;[35] similarly the Philippian jailor believed and was baptized — his baptism evidently taking place in the middle of the night (16.31-33); the story is repeated in Corinth, including one of the cases mentioned by Paul himself.[36] As Johannes Munck observed, "In Acts, as in the rest of the New Testament, there seems to have been no hesitation about baptizing. In a way that is remarkably casual compared with the modern formal ceremony, one baptizes and goes on one's way."[37] This ties in with the lack of any clear reference to a catechumenate before about 200 CE.[38] That there was instruction of new converts from the first can hardly be doubted.[39] What cannot be assumed, however, is that such instruction was regarded as a necessary *preparation* for baptism. Which again raises the question as to whether baptism was thought of as quite such a climactic and dramatic event in the crucial transition to membership of the new sect.

Consistent with this is the cautionary note which Paul repeatedly records in the letter which has most to say on baptism. Paul himself was evidently anxious lest the Corinthians make a false or too high evaluation of their baptism. It would appear that some of them were too ready to interpret their own baptisms in the light of similar or equivalent practices in other cults. In 1 Cor. 1.12-13 we learn that baptism by someone (or by his associate) was a ground for allegiance to that person. The logic is clear: "I am of Paul," because I was baptized by Paul; "I am of Apollos," because I was baptized by Apollos. Baptism, in other words, was thought to form some kind of mystical bond between baptized and baptizer. In 10.1-12 the implication is that baptism (and Lord's Supper) were being regarded as a kind of spiritual inoculation and guarantee against subsequent rejection by God. And in 15.29 the mysterious baptism "on behalf of the dead" presumably indicates the baptismal rite undertaken by one and regarded as effective for another already dead.[40]

35. Acts 8.36, 38; 16.14-15. The Western text adds Acts 8.37, to include a confession by the eunuch ("I believe Jesus Christ is the Son of God"), an addition which probably reflects an early sense that Luke's account was much too abrupt.

36. Acts 18.8; 1 Cor. 1.14.

37. Munck, *Paul* 18 n. 1.

38. See further my *Unity* 143-47.

39. Clearly implied in Gal. 6.6 and Paul's references to traditions passed on to and received by new established churches (see above §§7.3 and 8.3 and below §§21.3[2] and 23.5).

40. This deduction regarding the views of the Corinthians regarding baptism (1.12-13; 10.1-12; 15.29) follows the main consensus of commentators on 1 Corinthians.

In each case Paul deliberately deemphasizes baptism.[41] It was Paul himself who resisted any possible analogy between Christian baptism and equivalent cultic rites in the mysteries. Baptism provided no such bond, only with the name of Jesus. Baptism provided no such guarantee. Paul even expresses his gratitude that he baptized so few. He could recall baptizing only Crispus and Gaius, and he almost forgot to mention the household of Stephanas (1.14-16) — so, not a series of particularly significant or memorable events so far as Paul himself was concerned. So far as he was concerned, his mission was to preach the gospel, not to baptize (1.17) — an interesting comment on the role and relative importance attributed by Paul to baptism within the complex of conversion and initiation.[42]

Second, alongside Rom. 6.3-4 we have to set 1 Cor. 12.13. In contrast to the other *baptizō* references just noted, this is the only unqualifiedly positive reference to being baptized in 1 Corinthians.

> For in one Spirit we were all baptized into one body, whether Jews or Greeks, whether slaves or free, and all were irrigated with the one Spirit.

On any analysis of the tradition history lying behind this talk of being "baptized in the Spirit"[43] there is one obvious trail to be followed — though surprisingly neglected by most commentators.[44] It is the trail which begins in the tradition of John the Baptist's most striking utterance: "I baptize you with water, but he [the Coming One] will baptize you with the Holy Spirit (and fire)." The prediction is recalled in all four Gospels,[45] the only feature of the

---

41. Deemphasizes, not devalues.

42. See also my *Baptism* 118-20. The *ouk . . . alla* ("not . . . but") construction in Paul regularly expresses a sharp antithesis (Rom. 1.21; 2.13, 28-29; 3.27; 4.4, 10, 13, 20, etc.). To be noted is the fact that it is baptism which Paul sets as a lower priority than preaching, not just baptism misunderstood or the issue of *who* baptizes (as Lohse, "Taufe" 240) — a clarification Paul could have made had he thought baptism so salvation-effective as the usual interpretations of Rom. 6.3-4, etc., assume. Cf. C. K. Barrett, *Church, Ministry and Sacraments in the New Testament* (Exeter: Paternoster/Grand Rapids: Eerdmans, 1985): "I cannot understand 1 Cor. 1.14-17 as implying anything less than a relative depreciation of baptism" (66); Hengel and Schwemer speak of "Paul's relative ambivalence towards baptism" (*Paul between Damascus and Antioch* 299-300); cf. and contrast Pesce, "Christ."

43. *En* with *baptizomai* ("baptized") is most naturally taken as "baptized in," rather than "baptized by." This is the consistent usage in the NT, with *hypo* ("by") indicating the baptizer. NRSV has improved RSV at this point.

44. So, e.g., Schnackenburg, *Baptism* 26-29; Ridderbos, *Paul* 398 ("baptism is simply qualified as the baptism of the Spirit"); G. Haufe, "Taufe und Heiliger Geist im Urchristentum," *TLZ* 101 (1976) 561-66; McDonnell and Montague, *Christian Initiation* 42-43. Beasley-Murray, *Baptism* 167-71, at least raises the issue.

45. Mark 1.8; Matt. 3.11/Luke 3.16; John 1.33. In view of the antithetical form of the Baptist's words ("I in water, he in Spirit") and the fact that the Evangelists do not

Baptist's preaching for which this is true. We may deduce, then, that it was a saying particularly cherished within the communities who transmitted the tradition.[46] The trail reemerges again in Acts, where the prediction is appealed to in reference to the two most decisive events in Acts' account of Christian beginnings — Pentecost (1.5) and the crucial precedent of the Gentile Cornelius's conversion (11.16).[47] The most obvious interpretation of 1 Cor. 12.13 is that Paul himself was aware of this tradition and deliberately alludes to it at this point.

What is particularly striking about this saying, so far as it affects our present discussion, is that the imagery of "baptized in Spirit" is both coined as a metaphor from the rite of baptism and set in some distinction from or even antithesis to the rite of baptism. The consistent form of the Gospel saying contrasts John's baptizing *in water* with the Coming One's baptizing *in Spirit*. In the metaphorical adaptation, Spirit takes the place of water as that "in" which the individual is immersed. And the two Acts accounts to which the reworked metaphor is applied are both notable for their descriptions of an outpouring of the Spirit quite separate and distinct from baptism.[48] In the light of such a tradition history of the motif ("baptized in Spirit") it is at least likely that Paul, in his own use of it, likewise alluded simply to the Corinthians' experience of receiving the Spirit.[49] Too often neglected is the fact that the emphasis clearly lies on the "one Spirit" (twice repeated), rather than the verb: it was by being baptized in *one Spirit* that they had been constituted *one body* (1 Cor. 12.13).[50]

We may even have to draw in Rom. 6.3 here, with its talk of being baptized into Christ's death. We already observed the suggestions that the imagery was influenced by parallels in other cults. But here too a more obvious

---

present Jesus' anointing by the Spirit as part of his baptism (particularly Luke 3.21-22; Acts 10.37-38; John 1.32-34), it seems necessary to ask again (see my *Baptism* 32-37) whether there are any exegetical grounds for the common subsequent talk of Jesus' own "baptism with water and the Spirit" (e.g., Stuhlmacher, *Romans* 98).

46. It should not be forgotten that it was John's characteristic ministry which first gave and established the meaning of *baptizō* in a new sense as "baptize" — hence *Ioannēs ho baptizon*, "John the baptizer/the one who baptizes" (Mark 1.4; 6.14, 24).

47. That the prediction is remembered in Acts as a saying of Jesus only underlines its importance for Luke.

48. Acts 2.1-4; 10.44-48.

49. See further my *Baptism* 129-30; Fee, *Empowering Presence* 179-82, 860-63. Presumably it does not need to be said again that the term "baptize" itself means simply "baptize, immerse" (cf. n. 16 above) and not "baptize in water." Josephus, e.g., can talk of people flooding *(ebaptisen)* into a city *(War* 4.137).

50. This also has bearing on the parallel Gal. 3.27-28, since the implication there too is that it is not so much baptism which is "the soteriological principle of equality" (Stuhlmacher, *Theologie* 353) as the commonly experienced Spirit (3.2-5, 14).

tradition history suggests itself. For according to Synoptic tradition, Jesus himself is remembered as having taken up and adapted the Baptist's metaphor and applied it to his own death — his death as a baptism with which he himself was to be baptized.[51] Here too, then, we might well find the background to Paul's talk of being baptized into Christ's death. It was because Jesus was recalled as having used the metaphor of being baptized in this way that Paul felt free to adapt it afresh to his own theology. As Christ had spoken of *his death* as a *baptism,* so Paul could speak of the beginning of salvation as a *baptism* into *Christ's death.*[52] In which case it is relevant to note, once again, that the metaphor of "baptism" (a metaphor for death) had been quite far removed in conception from the actual performance of baptism in water.[53]

This also suggests a resolution to the dispute whether "baptized into Christ" is in effect an abbreviated form of the fuller "baptized into the name of Christ." For the latter is, as we have seen, a metaphor drawn from business life — baptism seen as a transfer, as we would say, "to the account of Christ."[54] But in this case the metaphor is contained in the attached phrase — "to the name of." The verb itself seems to be a straighforward reference to the act of baptism itself. In contrast, in the briefer phrase "baptized into Christ," it is the term "baptized" itself which seems to carry the metaphorical force. And its outcome is the mystical, and far from immediately public, participation in Christ. "Baptized into Christ" carries all the overtones of Adam christology (Rom. 6.3 follows directly from 5.12-21). And "baptized into his death" leads directly into the profound motif of sharing in Christ's sufferings (§18.5). In short, the two phrases function within different imagery, and, as with other metaphors of salvation, an attempt to blend or identify them may simply result in the confusion of the image conveyed by each.[55]

Third, we need to recall not least the evidence from §§16.3-4 regarding the gift and reception of the Spirit. That survey should have made two things clear: reception of the Spirit was generally a vivid experience in the remembered beginnings of Christian commitment, and Paul refers to it repeatedly, and could do so, precisely because it was such a striking highlight in that crucial transition. This is in striking contrast with the relatively few "bap-

---

51. Mark 10.38-39 pars. For more detail see my "Birth of a Metaphor."
52. Cf. Wilckens, *Römer* 2.60-61; Barrett, *Paul* 129.
53. See further my *Baptism* 139-41.
54. See §13.4 and n. 71.
55. Horrell, *Social Ethos* (§24 n. 1), cites the critique of Meeks, *First Urban Christians,* by S. K. Stowers: "Much of Meeks' discussion of ritual is brilliant. He just finds too much of it. . . . Metaphors too easily become rituals" ("The Social Sciences and the Study of Early Christianity," in W. S. Green, ed., *Approaches to Ancient Judaism* 5: *Studies in Judaism and Its Greco-Roman Context* [Atlanta: Scholars, 1985] 149-81, here 174). See again my *Baptism* 139-44, with bibliography on both sides.

tise/baptism" references, however they are interpreted. Later generations, for whom the central or even only remembered experience of Christian beginnings was their baptism, need to take care lest they assume that it was always that way. Paul's testimony is quite to the contrary. It was the experienced Spirit which made the greatest impact on their lives and in their memory. Presumably, then, the reason Paul does not refer so much to baptism is that for him, as for most of his converts, baptism was *not* the focal or most significant feature of their conversion and initiation. The focal and most memorable feature of their conversion and initiation was the gift of the Spirit.[56]

This finding also indicates the resolution to the application of some at least of the disputed metaphors. In particular, the "seal of the Spirit,"[57] despite later application to baptism,[58] should almost certainly be seen as a reference to the marked effect of the Spirit's impact on the individual life. To receive the gift of the Spirit was to be stamped with the seal of new ownership, a stamp whose effects made visible who it was to whom the individual now belonged.[59] "Anointing" likewise is more naturally linked with the Spirit.[60] In the sole Pauline occurrence of the imagery (2 Cor. 1.22) there may indeed be a further echo of the claim that Jesus himself had been anointed by the Spirit.[61] They had been anointed into the anointed one.[62]

Similarly with the imagery of "putting on Christ." There is no evidence that a change of clothes was part of the earliest baptismal ceremonies. Rather, as we have already suggested, the metaphor of "putting on Christ" gains more illumination by reference to the similar talk of an actor getting fully into his

56. This was the main finding of my *Baptism,* though the full scope of the experiential character of the gift of the Spirit only became clear to me in the further study which resulted in *Jesus and the Spirit.* Contrast the opening words of Lang, "Verständnis," 255: baptism "is 'the central "datum" of the beginning,' which determines the whole of Christian existence, so that the whole life of the Christian can be described as a constant 'recall to baptism' *(reditus ad baptismum)*." Lang cites Wilckens, *Römer* 2.23 (who spoke actually of "the experience of baptism" as "the central datum of the beginning"), and Stuhlmacher, *Romans* 99.

57. 2 Cor. 1.22; Eph. 1.13; 4.30.

58. See particularly Lampe, *Seal;* Dinkler, *Taufaussagen* 95-96; others in Fee, *Empowering Presence* 294 n. 38; Horn, *Angeld* 391-93. For Schnelle, 2 Cor. 1.21-22 make clear that "baptism and Spirit belong inseparably together" *(Gerechtigkeit* 125).

59. See my *Baptism* 133; Fee, *Empowering Presence* 294-96.

60. Indicative of the loss of the power of the metaphor in later generations is the inference by some that the reference must be to a rite of anointing (see those cited by McDonnell and Montague, *Christian Initiation* 48 n. 14); but see Dinkler, *Taufaussagen* 95.

61. The reference to Isa. 61.1-2 is most explicit in Luke 4.18, but is also implied in Luke 6.20/Matt. 5.3 and Luke 7.22/Matt. 11.5 (see also above §7.1). Luke also alludes to it in Acts 4.27 and 10.38, the latter itself an early formulation.

62. 2 Cor. 1.22 — . . . *eis Christon kai chrisas hēmas theos.*

part.[63] It is also notable that while Paul can use it for the once-for-all of becoming Christian in Gal. 3.27, he can use it also in the subsequent call to responsible living (Rom. 13.14). In other words, there is nothing inherently baptismal about the imagery. In Gal. 3.27, indeed, it is of a piece with "baptized into Christ," but perhaps primarily because the metaphor of immersion into Christ is equally close to the actor's total immersion in the character being played on stage.

The imagery of washing is more naturally seen as an allusion to baptism.[64] But even here we have to recall the extent to which Paul had spiritualized issues of ritual purity and sanctification. All believers were "saints," in complete independence of the Jerusalem cult.[65] Their bodies were now the only temple of which they need take account.[66] All things were "clean" simply because made and given by God and irrespective of Jewish tradition.[67] So, quite probably, the washing in view was that of heart and conscience, without specific reference to or dependence on the act of being baptized in water.[68]

Finally, we should note a point too often ignored in these discussions. In some ways the most obvious role for baptism in Paul's gospel was as the equivalent to and replacement for circumcision. So the assumption often runs: Paul replaced the ethnically constricted (or legalistic!) requirement of circumcision with the more universally applicable baptism.[69] However, this is precisely what we do *not* find. As we have already seen, it is faith which Paul contrasts so sharply with the works of the law, of which circumcision was a

---

63. See above §8 n. 58. Note also that the metaphor can be used to indicate an inward and spiritual change (e.g., Isa. 61.10; Zech. 3.3-5) or alternatively the Spirit's "enclothing" of human individuals (Judg. 6.34; 1 Chron. 12.18; 2 Chron. 24.20; Luke 24.49; Hermas, *Similitudes* 9.24.2; see Dunn, *Baptism* 110). Lietzmann, *Galater* 23, suggests that "put on Christ" is another expression for "receive the Holy Spirit." See further Hengel and Schwemer, *Paul between Damascus and Antioch* 294-97.

64. 1 Cor. 6.11; Eph. 5.26; Tit. 3.5. Direct reference to baptism is an almost universal assumption; cf. particularly Acts 22.16. E.g., Schnackenburg, *Baptism,* begins with the theme "baptism as a bath," referring to these texts; Ridderbos, *Paul* 397 — "That the expressions 'to wash' and 'bath of water' refer to baptism cannot be doubted."

65. See above §2 n. 90 and §13 n. 74.

66. 1 Cor. 3.16-17; 6.19; 2 Cor. 6.16.

67. *Katharos/katharizō* — Rom. 14.20; Eph. 5.26; 1 Tim. 1.5; 3.9; 2 Tim. 1.3; 2.22; Tit. 1.15; *koinos* — Rom. 14.14; cf. 1 Cor. 10.26. On these points (nn. 65-67) see further below §20.3.

68. See also my *Baptism* 121-22; similarly Quesnel, *Baptisés* 165-66; Fee, *Empowering Presence* 130-31.

69. Cf., e.g., the fairly typical handling of Col. 2.11-12. Pokorný, *Colossians* 124: "the writer explains that baptism is the true circumcision"; Wolter, *Kolosser* 130, speaks of *Taufbeschneidung* ("baptismal circumcision"); further my *Colossians* 157 n. 18.

primary obligation (§14.5). And it is the gift of the Spirit, not baptism, which provides the new covenant answer to the old covenant circumcision.[70] The eschatological newness of Christianity, the movement onto a new plane as the first Christians so experienced it, was accomplished through faith and by the Spirit. Whereas Paul says in effect to the Galatians, "You do not need circumcision because you believed, because you have received the Spirit, become part of Christ, been justified,"[71] he never says "You do not need to be circumcised because you have been baptized." Of course it is true, speaking sociologically, that Christian baptism in effect formed as effective a group boundary as circumcision. But so far as Paul's theology was concerned, the only answer to any call for circumcision which really mattered was the reality of grace through faith, of Christ through the Spirit in his converts' lives.

§17.3 An ordo salutis?

How then are we to hold together these strands in Paul's thought which seem to pull in different directions? Did Paul himself experience them as in tension? Probably not. The answer here, as in other theological issues which later commentators strive to resolve, is probably that Paul was either unaware of the ambiguities his writings would set up for later generations, or at least unconcerned by them. In this case he probably saw the event of the beginning of salvation as a complex whole. As in our analysis of the three different aspects of that beginning (justification by faith, participation in Christ, gift of the Spirit), there is a danger that we subdivide into distinct and discrete elements what Paul simply saw as the same event with differing emphases in differing cases. So too here it may be less important to give a precise location or function for baptism within Paul's theology than to recognize that it was part of the complex whole and filled an important role within the complex whole.

It is worth recalling what the differing elements within the complex whole of conversion and initiation were for Paul.[72] There is even the possibility of setting them in some sort of sequence (*ordo salutis,* "order of salvation"). Paul himself indicates a kind of sequencing in Rom. 10.14-17 and Gal. 3.1-2.

> [14]How therefore shall they call on him in whom they have not believed? And how shall they believe in him of whom they have not heard? And

70. See above §§16.2-3.
71. Gal. 3.1-5, 14; 4.6-7, 29; 5.2-6, 25; 6.13-15.
72. In my *Baptism* I coined the inelegant phrase "conversion-initiation" precisely in order to avoid an over-clinical distinction between the two elements indicated (conversion, initiation).

how shall they hear without someone preaching? [15]And how shall they preach unless they have been sent. . . . [17]So then, faith comes from hearing, and hearing through the word of Christ.

[1]You foolish Galatians! Who has bewitched you? — you before whose eyes Jesus Christ was openly portrayed as crucified. [2]This only I want to learn from you: was it by works of the law that you received the Spirit, or by hearing with faith?

The first element is the preaching of the gospel by the one duly commissioned by Christ. This does not say anything about a prior work of the Spirit in heart or conscience of those to whom the gospel is preached. It is true that Paul generally conceived of the gospel so preached as effecting a sudden opening of previously blinded eyes.[73] However, all that Paul had in view was the actual illuminating, convincing power of the gospel itself.[74]

The second element is faith, the believing response of the individual to the gospel so preached, the believing hearing of which both the above passages speak.[75] This clearly involved the double aspect of faith: believing acceptance of what has been claimed[76] and believing into, the trust like that of Abraham, the commitment to and complete reliance on the one proclaimed as Lord.[77]

Thirdly, according to Gal. 3.2 it was this believing hearing to which the Spirit was given or by which it was received.[78] Rather than a 1-2-3 sequence it is more like the 1-2-1-2 of effective engagement: the preacher sent and proclaiming, the faith response, and the Spirit given to responsive faith.

It is perhaps characteristic of our findings in the previous section (§17.2) that the place of baptism within this basic *ordo salutis* is not entirely clear. On the one hand, it evidently functioned as a metaphor for one or two of the aspects of the third element — "baptized into Christ" (§15) and "baptized in the Spirit" (§16). On the other, it can be regarded as part of the response of faith.[79] The baptisands handed themselves over to belong to the

---

73. Note particularly the extended defence of his ministry in 2 Cor. 2.14–4.6.

74. See also, e.g., Rom. 1.16; 1 Cor. 1.21; 2.4-5; 4.15; 15.1-2; 1 Thes. 1.5; 2.13; and further above (§7.1).

75. On "hearing with faith" (Gal. 3.2) see above §14 n. 107.

76. See especially Rom. 10.9-10; 1 Cor. 15.2.

77. So again Rom. 10.14; and all that is implied in the expositions of Galatians 3 and Romans 4.

78. See again §16.3 above.

79. So particularly W. Mundle, *Der Glaubensbegriff des Paulus* (Leipzig: Heinsius, 1932) 124. Kertelge, *Rechtfertigung* (§14 n. 1) 228-49, struggles to find a balance.

one named over them (1 Cor. 1.13). Otherwise Paul says nothing explicit about the correlation of faith and baptism — itself an interesting feature in one who saw the response of faith as such a crucial and sole defining element in the acceptance by God and the reception of the Spirit.

The nearest we can probably get to a definitive answer as provided by Paul's own theology is the prepositions used in the two references to baptism in Rom. 6.4 and Col. 2.12. What happened in the beginning event happened "through baptism" (Rom. 6.4) and "in baptism" (Col. 2.12). Baptism was in some sense the medium through which God brought the baptizand into participation in Christ's death and burial. There are probably echoes here (for some at least) of moving memories of the experienced symbolism of sinking below the surface of the water of baptism in immersion.[80] Alternatively expressed, baptism was the moment and context in which it all came together, so that the image of "baptized into" Christ was given its deeper resonance.

At all events, a theology drawn from Paul should be careful on two points. First, to include *all* the elements and aspects of the crucial beginning event of salvation. Otherwise, the wholeness and the richness of Paul's conceptuality and theology can be gravely diminished. Second, to observe the relative weight and emphasis Paul placed on the different elements and aspects in different contexts. That need not prevent a rich sacramental theology of baptism being drawn from Paul's letters, particularly Rom. 6.3-4 and Col. 2.11-12. But at least it would prevent later theological schemas being attributed to Paul without proper care and attention to what he actually said.

§17.4 Infant baptism

Not least of the difficulties which Paul's theology poses to later tradition is the fact that it seems to have little if any room for infant baptism. From one perspective this was almost inevitable. For Paul was a missionary and church founder. Baptism in his experience was an evangelistic rather than a pastoral act. Typically for him baptism was the initiation of newly believing adults into churches being newly formed.

The question of household baptisms remains ambiguous. There may have been young children in some at least of the households. But mention of a "household" as such did not carry that implication. A household would normally be understood to include any slaves or retainers.[81] And in the only case in point within Paul's letters — the household of Stephanas (1 Cor. 1.16)

---

80. Hence, we may suppose, the particular association of baptism with burial more than death (Rom. 6.4; Col. 2.12).
81. See, e.g., P. Weigandt, *EDNT* 2.502.

— Paul explicitly notes later that the household had "appointed themselves to ministry for the saints" (16.15).[82]

On the point of theological principle, the obvious precedent would be that baptism (new covenant) had taken the place of circumcision (old covenant). But that assumes a direct paralleling between the two covenants. And it is just at this point, as we have seen, that Paul seems to think of the new covenant as functioning on a different plane: the fulfilment of the spiritual significance of circumcision in the gift of the Spirit (§§16.2-3), membership in the people accepted by God no longer guaranteed by birth, but through faith (§14.7). Moreover, it is important to recall that circumcision did not function as a means of entry into the covenant people. Membership was received through birth. Circumcision was rather the new member's first act of law-keeping.

A more circuitous argument can be built on 1 Cor. 7.14:

> The unbelieving husband is made holy by his wife, and the unbelieving wife is made holy by the brother;[83] otherwise your children would be unclean, but now they are holy.

The argument is to the effect that the child is part of the household of faith (even if only one parent believes), and so the child should be baptized on the basis of the believing parent's faith. However, the line of argument is muddled. On the one hand it continues the un-Pauline assumption that baptism has taken the place of circumcision.[84] But on the other, there is the further assumption that baptism is somehow necessary to secure the child's status within the household of faith.[85] In contrast, the text itself seems to imply that the child's status is already secure, by virtue of being the child of a believer.

The corollary which follows more directly from 1 Cor. 7.14, then, is that Paul would *not* have considered baptism necessary in order to secure such a child's status. The child was already holy. And in the case of a household baptism the most obvious further corollary is that the conversion faith and baptism of adults would count also for any underage children who were part

---

82. Ridderbos thinks that the mention of household baptism "points clearly to infant baptism" (*Paul* 413); it is not mentioned because it was "self-evident" (414).

83. "The brother" is presumably the woman's husband — "brother" as a member of the church.

84. For the more elaborate theology in terms of the continuity of the covenant of grace, see P. C. Marcel, *The Biblical Doctrine of Infant Baptism* (London: James Clarke, 1953).

85. The fact that the *unbelieving* partner is also "made holy" hardly strengthens the suggestion that baptism is in view.

of the household.[86] That is, both the faith *and* the baptism of the believing
parent would include the child. When households were baptized, any little
children would *not* have been baptized.[87]

From our later perspective we naturally ask about children who in
growing up grew away from their parents' faith, and who may then have been
converted in their own right. Presumably they would then have been baptized
at that point. However, this is not a situation which Paul pauses to envisage.
In this, as in other aspects of Paul's sacramental theology, too little time had
elapsed for new questions to be thrown up to stimulate his further theologizing.

---

86. Cf. Beasley-Murray, *Baptism* 192-99. On the debate regarding the beginnings
of infant baptism see J. Jeremias, *Infant Baptism in the First Four Centuries* (London:
SCM, 1960); K. Aland, *Did the Early Church Baptize Infants?* (London: SCM, 1963);
Beasley-Murray, *Baptism* 306-86; and again Jeremias, *The Origins of Infant Baptism*
(London: SCM/Naperville: Allenson, 1963).

87. In characteristic style Schmithals, *Theologiegeschichte des Urchristentums*
198-205, presses this point much too far. The logic of his argument seems to be that after
the baptism of the first generation's head of household no further baptisms would be
necessary for that family in succeeding generations.

CHAPTER 6

The Process of Salvation

§18 The eschatological tension[1]

§18.1 Between the times

At the start of chapter 5 (§13.1) we noted that there were two tenses of salvation for Paul — the aorist and the continuous. These are grammatical signifiers of the two phases of salvation, the beginning and the ongoing.

1. **Bibliography**: **O. Cullmann**, *Christ and Time: The Primitive Christian Conception of Time and History* (London: SCM/Philadelphia: Westminster, revised 1962); *Salvation in History* (London: SCM/New York: Harper and Row, 1967); **J. D. G. Dunn**, *Jesus and the Spirit* ch. 10; "Rom. 7.14-25 in the Theology of Paul," *TZ* 31 (1975) 257-73; **Fee**, *Empowering Presence* (§16 n. 1); **J. M. Gundry Volf**, *Paul and Perseverance: Staying In and Falling Away* (WUNT 2.37; Tübingen: Mohr, 1990); **N. Q. Hamilton**, *The Holy Spirit and Eschatology in Paul* (*SJT* Occasional Papers 6; Edinburgh: Oliver and Boyd, 1957); **M. J. Harris**, *Raised Immortal: Resurrection and Immortality in the New Testament* (London: Marshall, Morgan and Scott, 1983); **J. Holleman**, *Resurrection and Parousia: A Traditio-Historical Study of Paul's Eschatology in 1 Corinthians 15* (NovTSup 84; Leiden: Brill, 1996); **Keck**, *Paul* 78-81; **L. De Lorenzi**, ed., *The Law of the Spirit in Rom. 7 and 8* (Rome: St. Paul's Abbey, 1976); **I. H. Marshall**, *Kept by the Power of God: A Study of Perseverance and Falling Away* (London: Epworth, 1969; Carlisle: Paternoster, [3]1995); **C. M. Pate**, *The Glory of Adam and the Affliction of the Righteous: Pauline Suffering in Context* (Lewiston: Mellen, 1993); **W. Pfister**, *Das Leben im Geist nach Paulus. Der Geist als Anfang und Vollendung des christlichen Lebens* (Freiburg: Üniversitätsverlag, 1963); **E. Schweizer**, "Dying and Rising with Christ," *NTS* 14 (1967-68) 1-14; **R. C. Tannehill**, *Dying and Rising with Christ: A Study in Pauline Theology* (Berlin: Töpelmann, 1967); **P. Tachau**, *"Einst" und "Jetzt" im Neuen Testament* (FRLANT 105; Göttingen: Vandenhoeck, 1972); **G. Theissen**, *Psychological Aspects of Pauline Theology* (Philadelphia: Fortress/Edinburgh: Clark, 1987) 177-265; **S. H. Travis**, *Christ and the Judgment of God: Divine Retribution in the New Testament* (Basingstoke: Marshall, 1986); **Ziesler**, *Pauline Christianity* 95-102.

Having looked in some detail at the event phase (ch. 5), we turn now to the process phase. That Paul thought in such terms is indicated clearly enough in one of his earlier and one of his later letters. He asks the Galatians: "Are you so foolish? Having *begun* with the Spirit, are you now *made complete* with the flesh?" (Gal. 3.3). In contrast, to the Philippians he expresses his confidence, "that the one who *began* in you a good work *will bring it to completion* up to the day of Christ Jesus" (Phil. 1.6).[2] Of course, the two phases cannot be held strictly apart. On the contrary, it is precisely Paul's point to the Galatians that the character of the beginning should also determine the continuation. Most of what we have found in ch. 5, therefore, carries forward into this chapter, particularly regarding justification by faith, participation in Christ, and the gift of the Spirit.[3] Nevertheless, there are aspects of the process phase which require special consideration and therefore deserve separate treatment. Most of the rest of this study of Paul's theology will in effect be an attempt to fill out what is involved for Paul in the process of "being saved."

It is important as the first step to get the perspective right. As we have had to remind ourselves several times, the particulars within Paul's individual letters gain their coherence as we set them in context — that is, both the context of the dialogue of which the letter itself was one part and the context of Paul's ongoing theology and theologizing. In this case the framework of his thought about the process of salvation is particularly important. For without it, the various elements we will be looking at are liable to become disconnected from each other, and the coherence of the whole is likely to be lost.[4] In this case, as elsewhere, it is the *eschatological* structure of his thought which is important.[5]

As we saw early on (§2.4), Hebraic thought typically conceived of time as a succession of ages. History was understood as an onward movement or progression, with beginning (creation) and end (final judgment), rather than as a repeating cycle.[6] It was divided into two (or more?) ages, the one to succeed the other in accordance with the predetermined plan of God. The straight line, in other words, was divided between the present age and the age

---

2. The "begin/complete" contrast is the same in each text — *enarchomai/epiteleō*. Both words were used in cultic contexts (beginning of a sacrifice, performing a religious act; see LSJ and BAGD), but were also used more generally (begin; end, complete; LSJ; G. Delling, *TDNT* 8.61).

3. To speak of "the baptismal life" makes the same point.

4. This applies particularly to the function of Rom. 7.7-25, not to mention chs. 9–11, within the flow of the letter and its exposition as a whole.

5. Cf. again particularly Beker, *Paul* 143-52.

6. Though if "end time" is in some sense a return to "primal time" (restoration of/to paradise), then we could speak of a single cycle.

to come.[7] The failures and sufferings of the present age would be put to rights by the coming of the new age. In some, though not all schemas, the transition would be effected by or coincide with the coming of the Messiah. Hence the characteristic shorthand for the age to come as "the messianic age."[8] To put it so is a simplification of more diverse and fragmentary data, but the overall eschatological perspective is fairly constant.[9] It is enough for us, however, to be able to say that Paul shared this eschatological schema. He regarded the present age as something inferior,[10] and the coming of Christ as a preplanned climax to God's plan at "the fullness of time" (Gal. 4.4). The mystery of God's purpose previously hidden from the ages and the generations had now been revealed in and as Christ (Col. 1.26-27).

The point is that the coming of Christ disrupted the previous schema and required it to be modified.[11] For Christ's coming and resurrection were indeed perceived as the eschatological climax — "the fullness of time" (Gal. 4.4), the beginning of "the resurrection of the dead" (Rom. 1.4).[12] But the end did not come: the dead were not raised; the judgment did not take place. The eschatological climax was thus incomplete; the completion of the divine purpose required a further climactic act. Christ, who had already come, must come — again! Then, and only then, the rest of the final events would unfold.[13] In other words, the single division of the time line, dividing present age from age to come, had itself been split into a two-stage division. Messiah the end point of history had become also Christ the midpoint of history.[14]

7. Both the present age and the age to come could be conceived of as a sequence of ages, without diminishing the thought of a single critical division (see again §2.4 above).

8. Schürer, *History* 2.488-554, unwisely puts the whole theme of eschatological expectation under the head of "Messianism." But we have already noted (§8.5) that an eschatological hope centred particularly on the coming of a royal messiah was probably the most common thread in that hope.

9. See, e.g., the articles on "Eschatology" (OT and Early Jewish) by D. L. Petersen and G. W. E. Nickelsburg in *ABD* 2.575-79, 579-94.

10. In §2.4 above I cite Rom. 12.2; 1 Cor. 2.6; Gal. 1.4 and refer also to Rom. 8.18; 1 Cor. 1.20; 2.8; 3.18-19; 2 Cor. 4.4; Eph. 2.2; 5.16.

11. For this whole schematization I express my gratitude especially to Cullmann, *Christ and Time* (here particularly ch. 5), which gave me the key thirty years ago to the eschatological structure of Paul's soteriology. However, I avoid use of the much disputed term "salvation history."

12. See above §10.1 and n. 23.

13. See further above §12.

14. Cf. Beker: "With the Christ-event, history has become an ellipse with two foci: the Christ-event and the Parousia, or the day of God's final victory" (*Paul* 160).

The schema can be most simply grasped in a diagram (of course, much simplified):

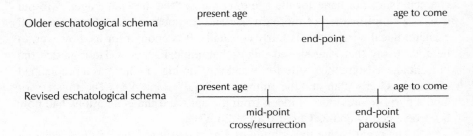

The consequences of this rather basic observation for our understanding of Paul's soteriology are profound. The key point is that in the gap opened up between the two comings of Christ, the ages overlap. The beginning of the age to come is pulled back into the present age, to begin with Christ's resurrection. But the present age has not yet ended, and will persist until the parousia:

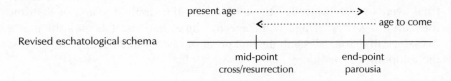

This means that for Paul those who have believed into Christ and received the Spirit live out their lives as Christ's between the midpoint and the parousia. That is, they live in the overlap of the ages, "between the times." If we refigure the schema in Adam-Christ terms, the point is equivalent:

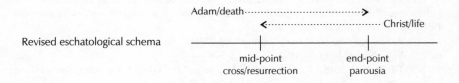

Believers are "in Adam" and continue to be "in Adam"; they have not yet died. But they are also "in Christ," and have begun to experience life, though they have yet to share in the full experience of Christ's resurrection — in the resurrection of the body. Or in the cosmic perspective to which Paul reverts at several points,[15] we could refigure the schema thus:

15. *Ktisis* ("creation") — Rom. 8.19-23; 2 Cor. 5.17; Gal. 6.15; Col. 1.15, 18;

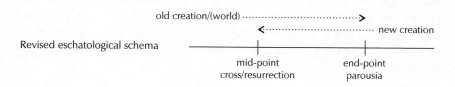

Fundamental to Paul's conception of the process of salvation, therefore, is his conviction that the believer has not yet arrived, is not yet perfect, is always *in via*, in transit. It is this which determines the experience of "being saved" as a process of "eschatological tension"[16] — the tension between a work "begun" but not "complete," between fulfilment and consummation, between a decisive "already" and a still to be worked out "not yet." The grounding for this and its consequences will become clear as we proceed.

We should, however, not pass on without underlining the importance of these observations — on two points. One is that the distinctive feature of Paul's theology at this point is *not* the eschatology, but the *tension* which his revised eschatology sets up. Eschatological hope was a common feature of Paul's religious heritage. But an eschatology split in this way between such a decisive "already" and yet still a "not yet" was a new departure.[17] It follows, secondly, that the weight of Paul's eschatology is not forward-looking, but backward-looking, or at least lies in the tension between the two. *Paul's gospel was eschatological not because of what he still hoped would happen, but because of what he believed had already happened.*[18] What had already happened (Easter and Pentecost) had already the character of the end and showed what the end would be like. Which also means that the character of

---

kosmos ("world") — particularly 1 Corinthians (1.20-21, 27-28; 2.12; 3.19; 7.31). But Paul can also speak of "the world" being reconciled (Rom. 11.15; 2 Cor. 5.19; Col. 1.20).

16. This phrase I owe also to Cullmann; see particularly his *Salvation* 202: "It is characteristic of all New Testament salvation history that between Christ's resurrection and his return there is an interval the essence of which is determined by this tension"; index "tension."

17. Cullmann, *Christ and Time* 145, 154-55; *Salvation* 172: "The *new element* in the New Testament is not eschatology, but what I call the *tension* between the decisive 'already fulfilled' and the 'not yet completed,' between present and future." Despite Beker, *Paul* 159, Qumran did not shift the weight to the "already" in the same degree. Even the already–not yet of Jesus' proclamation of the kingdom (cf., e.g., Matt. 6.10 and 12.28) does not put such a decisive weight on the already; in the Gospels, at least, the thrust is towards the climax of the passion. There was, of course, an already–not yet element in Jewish theology (e.g., Zech. 14.9).

18. Cullmann, *Christ and Time* particularly 88. Beker's shift of emphasis to the future consummation (*Paul* 176-81) is in danger of tilting the balance too far the other way; cf. Branick's critique, "Apocalyptic Paul?" (§12 n. 1).

the interim period as "eschatological" did not depend on the parousia alone, nor to any real extent on either the imminence or delay of the parousia.[19] What mattered was the fact that "the powers of the age to come" (Heb. 6.5) were already shaping lives and communities, as they would also in due course shape the cosmos.

§18.2 Already–not yet

The eschatological tension implicit in Paul's schema of salvation runs through all his soteriology. Its presence is regularly acknowledged. But its extent is rarely documented[20] and its ramifications hardly appreciated. It must be our first task to begin to remedy that defect. By consensus of usage a generally acceptable way of posing the tension is in terms of the "already" and "not yet" of Paul's theology.[21] As the terms indicate, "already–not yet" is a way of summarizing the recognition that something decisive has *already* happened in the event of coming to faith, but that the work of God in reclaiming the individual for himself is *not yet* complete. We can document its major importance in Paul's understanding of salvation by observing how the not yet qualifies the already in each of the aspects of Christian beginnings examined above (ch. 5).

A first noteworthy example of the already–not yet tension in Paul's soteriology comes in his metaphors of salvation. For in his use of many of them the tension between something already accomplished and something yet to happen is prominent. For example, "redemption" is in one sense something Paul and his readers already "have."[22] But in another sense they still await redemption, "the redemption of the body."[23] By the same token, "freedom" is something already enjoyed[24] but not yet fully experienced; for creation also waits to be "set free from the slavery of corruption into the liberty of the glory of the children of God" (Rom. 8.21). Equally powerful is the imagery of an inheritance already confirmed and entered on in part (particularly Gal. 4.1-7). But Paul also speaks, and more frequently, of the kingdom of God as an inheritance still outstanding.[25] And in 2 Cor. 11.2 Paul pictures conversion

19. See further above §12.5(3).

20. Cullmann's *Christ and Time* has been largely ignored in the last thirty years. Tachau's *Einst* is a rather isolated study. Contrast, e.g., Cerfaux, *Christian* (§14 n. 1).

21. As an alternative, Keck speaks of a "dialectic between participation and anticipation" (*Paul* 81).

22. Rom. 3.24; Col. 1.14; Eph. 1.7.

23. Rom. 8.23; Eph. 1.14; 4.30.

24. Rom. 6.18, 22; 8.2; Gal. 2.4; 5.1, 13.

25. 1 Cor. 6.9-10; 15.50; Gal. 5.21; Col. 3.24; Eph. 1.14, 18; 5.5.

as not so much a marriage as a betrothal of marriage. Alternatively, becoming Christian was like the bridal bath preparatory to the wedding ceremony itself, to be celebrated at the parousia (Eph. 5.25-27). Finally, we may recall that the classic term for the ongoing phase of the salvation process ("sanctification") is itself split between the already and not yet. Whereas the noun ("sanctification") is used in regard to the ongoing "not yet,"[26] the verb denotes the "already."[27]

When we turn to the principal metaphor of "justification by faith," the picture is the same. Certainly Paul emphasizes the aorist already, the decisive acceptance by God of the sinner, even as sinner. The triumphant opening of Romans 5 leaves no doubt of that: "Therefore, having been justified from faith . . ." (5.1).[28] But in terms of what we saw above about "the righteousness of God," it is equally important to emphasize that what has begun (by God's grace) is an ongoing relationship. In that relationship it is the righteousness of God which sustains the sinner within that relationship.[29] And the end in view is God's final vindication of his own — also an act of justification, of acquittal, in the final judgment.[30] This is clearly implied, though too much neglected, in the usual forward look of the verb "justify" *(dikaioō)*. referring to that final judgment.[31] Less typical of Paul's actual usage, but more typical of his theology, is his talk of "the hope of righteousness" (or hoped-for righteousness) as something "eagerly awaited" (Gal. 5.5). This recognition of the "not yet" dimension of justification by faith gives added force to Luther's *simul peccator et iustus.*

Similarly with participation in Christ. We noted that the "in Christ" was used typically to denote present status, including a share in the salvation-effecting events of the cross. But the "with Christ" motif (in its full scope) embraces both past and future — "with Christ" in death and burial, and "with Christ" in heaven or at the parousia.[32] In other words, the element of "Christ mysticism" in Paul's soteriology likewise extends across the already and the not yet, and emphasis on the one without the other would seriously distort Paul's theology as a whole. The point is that the split of the one coming of the Messiah into the

26. Rom. 6.19, 22; 1 Cor. 1.30; 1 Thes. 4.3, 4, 7; 2 Thes. 2.13; 1 Tim. 2.15.
27. Rom. 15.16; 1 Cor. 1.2; 6.11; Eph. 5.26; 2 Tim. 2.21.
28. Also Rom. 4.2; 5.9; 1 Cor. 6.11; Tit. 3.7.
29. See further above §14.2.
30. In the earlier phase of discussion, Kertelge, *"Rechtfertigung"* (§14 n. 1) 143-58, was surprisingly untypical in his emphasis on the future orientation of righteousness. But see now particularly Winninge, *Sinners* (§14 n. 1) 227-33.
31. Rom. 2.13; 3.20, 30, but implicit also in the present continuous tenses in Rom. 3.24, 26, 28; 4.5; 8.33; Gal. 2.16; 3.8, 11; 5.4 and aorists in Rom. 3.4; 8.30; Gal. 2.16, 17; 3.24.
32. For details see above §15.3.

two comings of Christ inevitably has to be mirrored in the salvation of those who are Christ's. Christ's death and resurrection was not the completion of his salvific work; he must come again. So those who share "in Christ" and "with Christ" are caught, as it were, between the two comings.

The same feature is reflected in what may be regarded as Paul's most basic conception of the salvation process as one of personal transformation (*metamorphōsis*),[33] that is, in particular, as transformation to become like Christ. The tenses are again present, denoting a continuing process.[34] The goal is clearly not yet.[35] Prominent in this line of thought is the language of "image" and "glory."[36] The process is one of being transformed from one degree of glory to another into the image of Christ (2 Cor. 3.18),[37] a being conformed to the image of God's Son (Rom. 8.29), "to the body of his glory."[38] Adam christology is prominent here. Paul perceives Christ as the image of the Creator, that is, the image God intended for humanity. Salvation is the completion of the original goal of creation — to renew that image, to bring humanity to that fuller share of divine glory which Adam forfeited.[39] Several of Paul's correlated images are best seen as variations on this theme. Paul can urge his audiences to "put on the Lord Jesus Christ" (Rom. 13.14)[40] or envisage "the inner person being renewed day by day," while "the outer person is deteriorating" (2 Cor. 4.16). And Col. 3.10 can speak of a stripping off of old self and putting on of new self "which is being renewed in knowledge in accordance with the image of the one who created it." Gal. 4.19 even envisages the process of pastoral care as a giving birth to Christ within the Galatians — Christ is not yet fully born within them![41] This insight sets in train a powerful sequence of thought in Paul to which we will have to return (§18.5).

33. Segal, *Paul,* makes much of this motif (see index *metamorphosis*); he sees it as drawn from mystical vocabulary (58-71).

34. *Metamorphizomai* — Rom. 12.2; 2 Cor. 3.18; *symmorphizomai* — Phil. 3.10.

35. *Symmorphos* — Rom. 8.29; Phil. 3.21. Note also Paul's view of his own progress (1 Cor. 9.26-27; Phil. 3.12-14).

36. *Eikōn* ("image") — Rom. 8.29; 1 Cor. 15.49; 2 Cor. 3.18; 4.4; Col. 3.10. *Doxa* ("glory") — Rom. 5.2; 8.18, 21; 9.23; 1 Cor. 2.7; 15.43; 2 Cor. 3.18; 4.17; Phil. 3.21; Col. 1.27; 3.4; 1 Thes. 2.12.

37. "The Lord" here (3.18), we may recall, is "the LORD" of Exod. 34.34 (3.16); see above §16.3. But "the image of God" is quickly defined as Christ (4.4). On the idea of transformation through vision see Thrall, *2 Corinthians* 290-95.

38. 1 Cor. 15.49; Phil. 3.21.

39. See above §4.5.

40. This exhortation plays a role in Romans equivalent to that of 1 Corinthians 13 and Gal. 5.22-23 in their respective letters. Hence the suggestion that the hymn to love and "the fruit of the Spirit" were modeled, consciously or unconsciously, on the remembered character of Christ (see above §16 n. 11).

41. See above §15.2 and n. 54.

The eschatological tension is no less evident in the case of the gift of the Spirit. Fundamental to Paul's gospel is the claim that the gift of the Spirit is the beginning of the process of salvation. Indeed, we can say that for Paul the gift of the Spirit is the key to the eschatological tension. For by its coming the Spirit sets up that tension.[42] The Spirit is as it were the bridge between the present and the future, between the already and the not yet. The point is most clearly seen in three more of Paul's metaphors.

One is the metaphor of "adoption." A striking feature, whose presence is noted but whose significance once again is too little reflected on, is the fact that Paul uses the metaphor twice within a few verses of each other — first for the already, and then for the not yet. The already is the reception of "the Spirit of adoption, by whom we cry 'Abba! Father!' " (Rom. 8.15). But the not yet is a further divine act of "adoption," namely "the redemption of the body" (Rom. 8.23). And that too is the work of the Spirit (8.11, 23). That Paul felt able to use the same metaphor in this way within the same sequence of thought clearly indicates that the two phases in the process of salvation were two aspects of the one whole, an adoption procedure in two stages.

The second metaphor is the business metaphor, the *arrabōn*, "first instalment, guarantee." This is what the Spirit is for Paul, the first instalment of the wholeness of salvation.[43] By linking the Spirit as *arrabōn* with the thought of inheritance, Eph. 1.13-14 simply makes explicit what was implicit in the earlier inheritance references:[44] the Spirit is the first instalment of the kingdom of God.[45]

The third metaphor is the equivalent agricultural metaphor, the *aparchē*, "firstfruits," that is, the first sheaves of harvest, the beginning of the harvest (Rom. 8.23).[46] The gift of the Spirit, then, is the first phase of the harvest which consists in the resurrection of the body. Paul here, no doubt, had in mind his description of the resurrection body as *sōma pneumatikon* (1 Cor. 15.44-46), that is, a body vivified and determined wholly by the Spirit and no longer simply by the soul *(sōma psychikon),* far less by the flesh. The gift of the Spirit is the beginning of that process. The eschatological tension, we may say, is set up precisely because the Spirit is the power of God's final purpose already beginning to reclaim the whole person for God.[47]

---

42. Similarly Turner, *Holy Spirit* (§16 n. 1) 127-30.

43. 2 Cor. 1.22; clearer in 5.5, coming as it does at the end of the sequence 4.16–5.5. In modern Greek *hē arrabōna* is used for "the engagement ring." See also §13 n. 70 above.

44. Rom. 8.17-23; 1 Cor. 6.9-11; 15.44-50; Gal. 5.21-23.

45. See also my "Spirit and Kingdom," *ExpT* 82 (1970-71) 36-40.

46. See above §13 n. 68.

47. See also Hamilton, *Holy Spirit* 26-40 ("The Spirit and the Eschatological Tension of Christian Life"); Hamilton was a pupil of Cullmann.

We should note in passing the more or less universal agreement among commentators, that by "the gift of the Spirit" Paul and his fellow first-century Christians certainly meant the Spirit itself as the gift. Paul did not think of the *arrabōn* and *aparchē* as only part of the Spirit. Nor did he think of the process of salvation as gaining or receiving an ever larger share of the Spirit. Rather, the Spirit was itself the *arrabōn* and *aparchē,* and the full "payment" or "harvest" was the wholeness of salvation which the Spirit thus given would work in and through the individual.[48]

When we turn to baptism and the imagery of baptism, the same point emerges. For it is very noticeable in Rom. 6.3-4 that Paul seems to avoid saying what most since have taken for granted. That is to say, he likens baptism to burial with Christ (6.4). But he refrains from pressing the symbolism further. He does *not* say, "in which or through which you were also raised with him." This more limited imagery would follow, of course, from the basic meaning of *baptizō* — "to plunge into or immerse in." The verb itself had probably not yet become the wholly technical term for a rite of going down and coming up. However, the very next verse indicates that there is more to this resurrection reservation than simply the actual meaning of the verb. For 6.5 is a very neat expression of the already–not yet tension. "If we have become knit together with the very likeness of his death, we shall certainly also be knit together with the very likeness of his resurrection." The future tense of the second clause could be a logical future. But in view of the future reference to living with Christ in 6.8,[49] it should almost certainly be taken as a temporal future.[50] The point then is Paul's confirmation that a share in Christ's resurrection is still part of the not yet. Believers and baptized have been given to share in his death. But there is a process of salvation to be worked through before they can also share in his resurrection. At this stage baptism represents the former, the already, but not yet the not yet.[51]

48. Hence, once again, Paul's incredulity at the Galatians' attitude and behavior (Gal. 3.3).

49. Not to mention the future references to resurrection in 8.11 and 23.

50. So most; of recent commentators see, e.g., Stuhlmacher, *Romans* 92; Barrett, *Romans*[2] 116; Moo, *Romans* 370-71; Holleman, *Resurrection* 169-71; *pace* Fitzmyer, *Romans* 435-36.

51. The *en hō̧ kai* of Col. 2.12 can be taken as either "in whom also" (referring to Christ) or "in which also" (referring to baptism). In the latter case, baptism is taken as an image of resurrection with Christ as well as an image of burial with Christ. English translations tend to follow the latter option; but it is more likely that *en hō̧ kai* was part of the sequence of "in him/whom" which is a feature of this section of Colossians (2.6, 7, 9, 10, 11, 12, 15); for the range of opinion see my *Baptism* (§16 n. 1) 154 n. 7 and *Colossians* 160. However, Col. 2.12 and 3.1 do speak of resurrection with Christ as something which has already happened. The contrast with Rom. 6.4b should not be overpressed, since Paul certainly thought of the Roman believers as sharing in Christ's

At this point we need to highlight another feature of Paul's exposition in Romans which has attracted too little attention. I refer to the way in which Paul seems deliberately to structure his exposition in the summing up of 5.1-11 and again in chs. 6–8 to bring out the reality and seriousness of the already and not yet.[52] In 5.1-5 he immediately qualifies, or, better, elaborates, his triumphant talk of justification and peace with and access to God by referring to the still future "hope of [sharing] the glory of God" (5.2). And that leads him at once to further reflection on the nature of this hope in the face of, despite, and matured by their present and ongoing afflictions (5.3-5). Clearly no scope is even envisaged for a wholly "realized" understanding of the process of salvation. Similarly he climaxes the following paragraph with the repeated "how much more" (5.9-10). Already justified, "how much more . . . we shall be saved through him from wrath" (5.9). Already reconciled, "how much more . . . we shall be saved by his life" (5.10). Here it becomes clear beyond question, if it was not already so, that "salvation" for Paul is something future, essentially an eschatological good, something still awaited, its wholeness belonging to the not yet.[53]

In Romans 6, too often the theological reflection has concentrated on the aorists of 6.2-11 and too little on the imperatives of 6.12-23, as though the imperatives had less theological weight than the indicatives.[54] But Paul presumably intended the two parts of the chapter to hang together, each to be a factor in understanding the other. Thus, the vivid imagery of 6.2-6 is assuredly intended to underscore heavily the decisive character of the beginning, of the already. But Paul can hardly have intended to imply that "the old nature" (6.6) had been totally destroyed, that there was nothing in the believer for sin to exert its influence over, that the old age was wholly past. As we have just seen, the future orientation of his talk of sharing in Christ's resurrection points away from that. And his repeated and strenuous exhortations *not* to hand themselves over to sin (6.12-23) are clear enough indication that the not yet was all too real and that the salvation process had a long way to run. The tension in Paul's teaching at this point is clear and clearly deliberate. It should not be lightly resolved by focusing on the aorists of 6.2-6 and ignoring the rest, or by attributing to Paul an idealism which runs counter to the realism of 6.12-23.

The same point will have to be made with reference to Romans 7 and

---

risen life in some degree at least (6.4, 11). Nevertheless, 6.4-5 indicates that the burial with/resurrection with tension was part of the already–not yet tension of Paul's soteriology at the time he wrote Romans.

52. See my *Romans* 302-3.

53. See also particularly Rom. 11.26; 13.11; Phil. 1.19; 2.12; 1 Thes. 5.8-9; and again the present tenses of 1 Cor. 1.18; 15.2; 2 Cor. 2.15.

54. Most notably Schweitzer, *Mysticism,* as cited above in §15.1.

8. In both cases Paul repeats the pattern — bold and sharply drawn aorists to underline the decisive already (7.4-6; 8.1-9), followed by elaboration which sets the already within the whole process, including the not yet. However, the potential contribution of these chapters to the present stage of our inquiry is so great — and so controverted! — that we will have to devote separate sections to them.

§18.3 The divided "I"

The function of Rom. 7.7-25 is one of the most disputed issues in NT studies.[55] We have seen earlier that Paul intended it to serve as a defence of the law; the real blame for human enslavement to sin and death lies with sin itself (§6.7). But what has that to do with Paul's soteriology? Not a lot, say most. Most commentators in fact regard 7.7-25 as the exposition of the state which has been described in 7.4-6 as already left behind by the believer — "man under the law."[56] The most plausible suggestion has been to see 7.7-25 as an elaboration of 7.5, and 8.1-17 as an elaboration of 7.6.[57] So far as 7.7-25 is concerned this exegesis has obvious attractions.

> [5]When we were in the flesh the sinful passions which operate through the law were effective in what we are and do so as to bear fruit for death. [6]But now we have been released from the law, having died to that by which we were confined, so that we might serve in newness of Spirit and not in oldness of letter.
> [7]What then shall we say? That the law is sin? Certainly not! Nevertheless, I would not have experienced sin except through the law; for I would not have known covetousness unless the law had said, "You shall not covet." [8]But sin, seizing its opportunity through the commandment, stirred up all manner of covetousness in me. For in the absence of the law sin is dead. [9]And in the absence of the law I was alive once. But when the commandment came, sin became alive, [10]and I died. The commandment intended for life proved for me a means to death. [11]For sin, seizing its

---

55. This is the issue (the function of Rom. 7.7-25) which should be central in the exegetical discussion. The identity of the "I" is secondary to that. Most discussions in concentrating too closely on the identity of the "I" lose focus on the more important issue. For what follows I draw on my earlier studies — "Rom. 7.14-25," *Jesus and the Spirit* 313-16, and *Romans* 376-99; these contain earlier bibliography.

56. This was the position established by the landmark study of Kümmel, *Römer 7* (§3 n. 80), and maintained consistently since then with variations by the majority of scholars. For the most recent reviews see above §4 n. 90.

57. Theissen, *Psychological Aspects* 182-83, 226, 256; Stuhlmacher, *Romans* 104, 115; Witherington, *Narrative* 23.

opportunity through the commandment, deceived me and through it killed me. [12]So that the law is holy, and the commandment holy and just and good. [13]Did that which is good, then, become death to me? Certainly not! But sin, that it might appear as sin, producing death for me through that which is good, in order that sin through the commandment might become utterly sinful.

[14]For we know that the law is spiritual; but I am fleshly, sold under sin. [15]For I do not know what I do. For what I commit is not what I want; but what I hate, that I do. [16]But if what I do is what I do not want, I agree with the law that it is admirable. [17]But now it is no longer I doing this but sin which dwells within me.

[18]For I know that there dwells in me, that is, in my flesh, no good thing; for the willing lies ready to my hand, but not the doing of what is admirable. [19]For I fail to do good as I wish, but evil which I do not wish is what I commit. [20]But if what I do not wish is what I do, it is no longer I doing it but sin which dwells within me.

[21]I find then the law, in my case wishing to do the good, to be that for me the evil lies ready to hand. [22]For I rejoice in the law of God, so far as the inner person is concerned, [23]but I see another law in my constituent parts at war with the law of my mind and making me a prisoner to the law of sin which is in my constituent parts.

[24]Wretched man am I! Who will deliver me from the body of this death? [25]But thanks be to God through Jesus Christ our Lord. So then I myself with my mind serve the law of God and with my flesh the law of sin.

My problems with the main consensus exposition begin with the amount of space Paul gives to the theme. If the experience indicated in 7.5 belongs so completely to the convert's past, why does Paul interrupt his exposition of the convert's privileges and obligations by casting such a lengthy glance back over his shoulder? If the law was so little relevant to believers, why should he spend so much time defending it?

Moreover, a feature of the second half of the passage (7.14-25) is the divided "I" and the divided law. In effect Paul begins with a statement which reflects the complexity of the situation, distancing both the law and the "I" from the real culprit, sin (7.14-17). But then he breaks down the statement into a more careful description, first of the divided "I" (7.18-20) and then of the divided law (7.21-23).[58] The "I" is divided: it is the "I" which wants to do good and to avoid

---

58. This feature — the parallel between vv. 18-20 (the divided "I") and vv. 21-23 (the divided law) — is too little noticed by commentators as a clue to Paul's line of thought. But see Theissen, *Psychological Aspects* 188-89; P. W. Meyer, "The Worm at the Core of the Apple: Exegetical Reflections on Romans 7," in Fortna and Gaventa, eds., *The Conversation Continues* 62-84 (here 76-80); and above §6 n. 154, and further below §23.4 and n. 102.

doing evil; but it is the same "I" which fails to do the good and commits the evil (7.18-19). The culprit is sin: it enslaves the fleshly "I" and thus prevents the willing "I" from achieving what it wills (7.20). Correlated with the divided "I" is the divided law. The willing "I," the inner person, the "I" as mind, approves the law as the law of God (7.21-22). But the law used by sin (as indicated in vv. 7-13) battens on the fleshly "I," the "constituent parts" of the "I."[59] And the powerful combination of sin, law, and flesh ensures the failure of the willing "I" (7.23).[60] None of this, it has to be said, reads like the description of a state or experience which is now wholly past for the writer. The existential anguish of 7.14-24 sounds like an experience Paul knew only too well.[61]

Not least of note is the conclusion to the section — 7.25b: "So then I myself with my mind serve the law of God, and with my flesh the law of sin." If that was a description of a state wholly past for believers its appearance at this point is quite simply astonishing, and entirely confusing.[62] For it comes *after* the shout of triumph (7.25a) at the solution to the frustration expressed in the anguished cry of 7.24 —

> [24]Wretched man am I! Who will deliver me from the body of this death? [25]But thanks be to God through Jesus Christ our Lord. So then I myself with my mind serve the law of God, and with my flesh the law of sin.

And the present tense of 7.25b indicates *an ongoing state* — "with my mind I go on serving the law of God, and with my flesh [I go on serving] the law of sin." It is precisely the one who knows that Jesus Christ provides the answer who goes on to observe calmly that the "I" continues to be divided between mind and flesh. As the conclusion to 7.7-25, v. 25b can hardly be read otherwise more naturally than as indicating a continuing state — a state of continuing dividedness of the "I" who says, "Thanks be to God through Jesus Christ our Lord!"

The most obvious exegetical solution is to see here a further expression of the eschatological tension. The tension of Rom. 7.7-25 is the tension of the already–not yet. It arises because the believer lives in the overlap of the ages

---

59. *Melē* denotes the limbs and organs of the body, equivalent to "the mortal body" (6.12) and the "self" (6.13) in its several parts and functions; see my *Romans* 337.

60. On the "law of sin" as shorthand for the law used by sin, see above §6.7.

61. Cf. Dahl: "The 'I' form is no doubt used as a rhetorical device, but the use of this form would hardly be meaningful unless both the speaker and his audience can in some way identify with the experience of the typical 'I' " ("The Missionary Theology in the Epistle to the Romans," *Studies* 93).

62. Which presumably is why so many have only been able to make sense of it as a gloss added later (see those cited in my *Romans* 398-99, where the amazing popularity of this sleight of hand in German scholarship is noted; cf. now Stuhlmacher, *Romans* 114-16).

and belongs to both *at the same time.* This must be why the issue arises here, in the midst of Paul's exposition of the process of salvation. The point is that the believer has not been removed from the realm of the flesh; the believer is still fleshly. But the same believer also, with the mind and in the inner person, desires to do the will of God. There is a warfare here, and the "I" as fleshly is still enslaved under sin's enticing power (7.14), still caught as a prisoner in the nexus of the sin-abused law (7.23). The "I" is still not delivered from this body of death (7.24), that is, has still to experience the resurrection of the body, the completion of the triumph of life over death, the full participation in Christ's resurrection. The point is readily illustrated in terms of the eschatological schema already outlined.

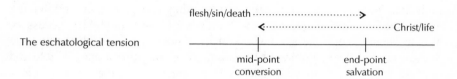

If this is on the right lines, it helps clarify what is at issue in the interpretation of this passage within the sequence of Romans 6–8. In fact, most of the differing interpretations of Rom. 7.7-25 stand on common ground. The common ground is the recognition that the passage describes humankind under the power of sin. That is why the passage appears to so many as a description of humankind apart from faith or prior to faith. The language of vv. 14 and 23 (just cited) is so bleak, without any hint of the already; quite naturally most deduce that it must surely describe a pre- or non-Christian state. How otherwise to square the clear past tense of 7.5 with the portrayal of one enslaved and imprisoned by sin?[63]

Where the difference between the line of interpretation proposed above and the larger consensus begins to emerge is with the corollary then usually drawn from the aorists and past tenses of the opening verses of chs. 6 and 7 — that "in Christ" the believer has been wholly freed from the power of sin and death. The real issue, therefore, is whether Paul saw the transition from present age to age to come, from Adam to Christ, as abrupt, totally discontinuous, and without any overlap whatsoever.[64] In other words, the real ques-

---

63. Typical again is Stuhlmacher: "The apostle's profound conception of baptism forbids one from characterizing the Christian in 7:14 as still 'sold under sin' " (*Romans* 115).

64. To be noted is the fact that posing the issue in this way allows full weight to the often noted testimony of similar-sounding moral frustration in other writers; the principal collection is in H. Hommel, "Das 7. Kapitel des Römerbriefs im Licht antiker Überlieferung," *ThViat* 8 (1961-62) 90-116, particularly 106-13; also Theissen, *Psychological Aspects* 212-19; Stowers, *Rereading* 260-63.

tion of debate is the seriousness of the "not yet" — whether Paul in fact conceived of the believer's "I" as still split between the catastrophically weak Adamic "I" and the frustrated willing "I"[65] — whether Paul saw the believer as still part of the present age, as still flesh, as one in whom death has still to have its final say. The point is not to argue for a different discontinuity: that 7.7-25 (or 7.14-25) describes only Christian experience. It is rather to ask whether in Paul's already–not yet schema the divided "I" continues to be divided into and through the process of salvation, and whether the division of the "I" cannot be entirely healed ("saved") until the resurrection of the body.[66]

The better solution, I continue to believe, is to answer that question in the affirmative. Commentators are closer to the mind of Paul and to his understanding of the salvation process when they recognize that Paul, having emphasized the decisiveness of the "already" (7.4-6), thought it necessary also to acknowledge the seriousness of the "not yet." Notwithstanding the decisiveness of the beginning of salvation, there was still an unavoidable and marked continuity with what had gone before.[67] Since the present age is characterized as being under the power of sin and death, that continues to be its character so long as it endures. And those who still are part of the present evil age, in any degree, are, to that extent, still caught in the nexus of sin and death.[68]

To take 7.5 solely as a statement of fact, then, without regard to the rhetorical and dialectical structure of these chapters, simply promotes an idealistic and unrealistic perspective, for which postbaptismal sin is impossible in theory and theologically and pastorally disastrous in practice. In contrast, Paul's exposition of an already–not yet tension has proved much more in tune

---

65. Similarly with "the inner person" (7.22): does the phrase refer only to a believer (e.g., Cranfield, *Romans* 363)? Or must we deny that it can refer to believers (despite the parallel in 2 Cor. 4.16; Eph. 3.16) (e.g., Fitzmyer, *Romans* 476)? But does Paul push us into this rather stark alternative?

66. The openness Paul allows here (does Rom. 7.7-25 describe humankind under sin in a narrow way — referring only to unbelievers?) is parallel to the openness he allows in Romans 2 (the righteous Gentile — referring only to believing Gentiles?). Here again to push for a clear exegetical choice and sharply delimited alternatives may run directly counter to what Paul had in mind.

67. This best explains the hardly indicated transition from past to present tense in 7.14 and the continuation of the present tense into 7.25b.

68. Those who find it impossible to exclude the believer from the "I" of 7.7-25 include Augustine, Luther, and Calvin and more recently Nygren, Bruce, Cranfield, and Lambrecht. In arguing that "Romans 7 embraces nothing which does not fit the Christian, or, conversely, [that] everything which Romans 7 embraces fits only the Christian" (*Paulus* 163), Laato sees in Romans 7 the continuing influence of Paul's "pessimistic anthropology" (183); I would rather say "realistic anthropology" (see above §4.1).

with personal and social reality and a much sounder theological base for pastoral counseling.[69]

§18.4 Flesh and Spirit

Romans 8 develops another facet of the eschatological tension — that between flesh and Spirit. Here again it is important to recognize the eschatological context. For in Paul the Spirit-flesh antithesis is to be understood not so much in anthropological terms[70] as in eschatological terms. The point is that the gift of the Spirit does not bring to an end a previous anthropological tension, but *begins* the eschatological tension.

As already noted (§16.3), it is almost as though Paul has held back this trump in his hand until he could play it when it would be most effective. His tactic seems to have been to concentrate in turn on each of the key factors militating against and making for salvation in each of chapters 6–8.[71] It was the confrontation of grace and sin which dominated ch. 6[72] and sin's cruel manipulation of the law in capturing the "I" which dominated ch. 7.[73] Now it is the confrontation between Spirit and flesh which dominates the first part of ch. 8.[74] We have to assume that this was the result of deliberate structuring on Paul's part. It could hardly be, for example, that he intended to imply that "grace" was not in play in chs. 7–8, simply because he last mentioned it in 6.15. And it is equally unlikely that he meant to imply that the Spirit could not be a factor in his readers' response to the exhortations of 6.12-23 simply because the Spirit is not mentioned in that chapter.

At the same time, by holding back full exposition in terms of the Spirit till this point, Paul presumably intended to indicate to his readers that the Spirit is the decisive force in the process of salvation. That is to say, not that the gift of the Spirit effects salvation there and then (when first given), but that the Spirit is the decisive key to the final resolution of the eschatological tension. Hence the imagery of Spirit as "first instalment, guarantee *(arrabōn)*" and as "firstfruits *(aparchē)*." This no doubt is why Paul held back and played

---

69. Bruce quotes the amusing comment of the great Scottish preacher, Alexander Whyte: "As often as my attentive bookseller sends me on approval another new commentary on Romans, I immediately turn to the seventh chapter. And if the commentator sets up a man of straw in the seventh chapter, I immediately shut the book. I at once send the book back and say 'No, thank you. That is not the man for my hard-earned money' " *(Romans* 151).

70. See again §§3.1, 3.

71. See my *Romans* 301-2.

72. *Charis* — 5.20-21; 6.1, 14-15; *hamartia* — 5.20–6.23 (18 occurrences).

73. *Hamartia* 15 occurrences in Romans 7; *nomos* 23 occurrences in Romans 7.

74. *Pneuma* 21 occurrences in Rom. 8.1-27; *sarx* 11 occurrences in Rom. 8.1-13.

his trump card at this point — as a counter to the potentially depressing portrayal of the continuing eschatological tension in 7.14-25. The point is not that the battle has been won, but that it has been joined. And so long as it continues, the process of salvation continues. And so long as one looks to the Spirit, the completion of salvation is assured (cf. Gal. 3.3 and Phil. 1.6).

To be sure, the decisiveness of the beginning is, once again, given the initial stress — Rom. 8.2-9:

> [2]The law of the Spirit of life in Christ Jesus has set you free from the law of sin and death. . . . [4]in us who walk not in accordance with the flesh but in accordance with the Spirit. [5]For those who exist in terms of the flesh take the side of the flesh, whereas those who exist in terms of the Spirit take the side of the Spirit. [6]For the flesh's way of thinking is death, whereas the Spirit's way of thinking is life and peace. [7]Because the flesh's way of thinking is hostility toward God, for it does not submit itself to the law of God; for it cannot. [8]And those who are in the flesh are not able to please God. [9]However, you are not in the flesh but in the Spirit, assuming that the Spirit of God does indeed dwell in you — if anyone does not have the Spirit of Christ, he does not belong to him.

If they are taken in isolation, the obvious way to understand these verses is as a contrast between two sets of people — the flesh people and the Spirit people. V. 9 in particular seems to invite the deduction that Paul thought of believers as no longer "in the flesh" and wholly "in the Spirit." The corollary would be that Christians had left the flesh entirely behind once they believed and were baptized, that "being in Christ" or "in the Spirit" had wholly replaced their "being in the flesh."[75]

But would Paul have welcomed that reading? I think not.[76] More likely he was thinking at this point in terms of what we would now call "ideal types": the flesh person is wholly cut off from God, for that is the character of the flesh; the Spirit person is wholly at one with God, for that is the character of the Spirit. The reality is that human beings partake in different measures of the two types.[77] The implied exhortation is that the readers should seek to

---

75. Precisely as Schweitzer argued in *Mysticism* (above §15 n. 1).

76. In what follows I again draw on my *Romans* 363-64, 424-25; see also below §23.4 and n. 95.

77. This is not just a feature of modern sociological analysis of "types"; cf. particularly 1QS 4.23-25 — "Until now the spirits of truth and injustice struggle in the hearts of men and they walk in both wisdom and folly. According to his portion of truth so does a man hate injustice, and according to his inheritance in the realm of injustice so is he wicked and so hates truth . . ." (Vermes). Here is where the parallels gathered particularly by Hommel, "7. Kapitel" 106-13, and Theissen, *Psychological Aspects* 212-19 (both above n. 64), gain their point.

align themselves as much as possible with the one and not the other. They should "walk in accordance with the Spirit" (8.4) — as explicitly exhorted in Gal. 5.16. Their being in terms of the Spirit should be expressed in their taking the side of the Spirit (8.5)[78] — Gal. 5.25 is again equivalent and again explicit: "if we live by the Spirit let us also order our lives by the Spirit."[79] They should think with the Spirit[80] and thus enjoy life and peace (8.6) — once again with a not very distant parallel explicit in Gal. 6.8: "those who sow to the Spirit shall from the Spirit reap eternal life."

The danger of reading the contrasts of 8.4-6 as descriptions of a wholly realized transition becomes clearer when we read on — Rom. 8.10-14:

> [10]And if Christ is in you, the body is dead because of sin, but the Spirit is life because of righteousness. [11]But if the Spirit of him who raised Jesus from the dead dwells in you, he who raised Christ from the dead will give life to your mortal bodies as well, through his Spirit which dwells in you. [12]So then, brothers, we are under no obligation to the flesh to live in accordance with the flesh. [13]For if you live in accordance with the flesh, you will certainly die; but if by the Spirit you put to death the deeds of the body, you will live. [14]For as many as are led by the Spirit of God, they are sons of God.

Verse 10 is particularly striking. First, it indicates, as clearly as anyone could wish, the reality of the continuing eschatological tension. For the believer, the Spirit[81] is life indeed, but at the same time, the body is dead. This, presumably, is the same body as was referred to in 7.24 — "the body of this death." Second, the causes of this continuing tension are clearly stated: "the body is dead because of sin, but the Spirit is life because of righteousness." That is to say, the body is not only "the body of death" (7.24) but also "the body of sin" (6.6). This confirms, third, that the aorists of 6.3-6 and

---

78. Literally "think *(phronousin)* the things of the Spirit." *Phroneō,* however, means not merely "think" but also have a settled way of understanding, hold an opinion, maintain an attitude (cf. particularly Rom. 14.6; 1 Cor. 13.11; 2 Cor. 13.11; Phil. 2.2, 5; 3.19; Col. 3.2). The fuller phrase as here was familiar in the sense "take someone's side, espouse someone's cause" (BAGD, *phroneō* 2).

79. RSV/NRSV translate *stoichōmen* by "walk," though the basic sense is "stand in line"; see further my *Galatians* 317.

80. Literally "the way of thinking *(phronēma)* of the Spirit." *Phronēma,* "way of thinking," occurs only in Rom. 8.6, 7, 27 in the NT. As is usual with *-ma* suffixes, the noun thus formed denotes the result of the action. Fitzmyer translates "concern" — "the concern of the Spirit" (*Romans* 489).

81. On *pneuma* as Holy Spirit here see above §16 n. 63. Fee, *Empowering Presence* 551: "Paul is speaking not about two constituents of the human person but about Christian existence as 'already/not yet.'"

7.4-6 are not to be taken as events finished and complete.[82] Nor can 7.14-25 be regarded as describing experiences wholly past for believers. Sin and death continue to be all too effective realities working in and through the body. Similarly we note the reappearance of the antithesis between "sin" and "righteousness" which dominated 6.13-20.[83] The implication is the same: that these two powers remain competing realities within the experience of the believer's current embodiment.

8.11 makes clear why: because deliverance from the body of sin and death will only happen at the resurrection of the body. In short, the Spirit is life and ensures life, but death has not yet been conquered. We may say, then, that in terms of perspective and paradigms, as in 8.2-9, it is a case of either-or. But in terms of the continuing eschatological tension, it is a case of both-and: both life and death (8.10), until God completes the salvation process by "giving life to their mortal bodies" (8.11).

However, the clear implications of 8.10-11 are usually ignored; and the same is true of 8.12-13. Yet if the Spirit-flesh antithesis were a thing of the past for the believer (as 8.2-9 might be taken to imply), then what meaning would there be in Paul advising his readers that they were "under no obligation to live in accordance with the flesh" (8.12)? How could he warn them that if they lived in accordance with the flesh, they would die (8.13)?[84] How could he exhort them to put to death the deeds of the body and promise them life in consequence (8.13)?[85] The only obvious answer is that the Spirit persons were still in danger of succumbing to the flesh, to its weakness and desires. They were not yet the ideal Spirit people, not yet the realized eschatological hope of resurrected bodies.[86] In the tension of the between times they had to be resolute in maintaining their alignment with the Spirit and in resisting the lure of sin in flesh.

---

82. As we shall see in a moment, the continuing state indicated in the perfect of 6.5 has to qualify the aorists of the surrounding verses (§18.5).

83. Sin/righteousness — 6.13, 16, 18-20.

84. "If you live in accordance with the flesh you will certainly *(mellete)* die." The force of *mellete* is to indicate the inevitability of death — "you are going to die, you are bound to die." Death, as typically in Romans, is understood as the due reward for sin (6.23), as the corruption of the flesh (Gal. 6.8; see above §5.7).

85. It is in this whole line of thought that Paul's use of "body" is at its most negative, overlapping with "flesh"; see above §3.4.

86. Fee, *Empowering Presence* 816-22, becomes quite muddled here. He wants to follow what he sees to be the logic of 8.4-6, that the flesh is already passé as a factor in the life of the believer (there is no constant struggle between Spirit and flesh). But he has to accept that believers do succumb to the flesh (817) — so what is it that they are succumbing to? And when he claims "that the flesh-Spirit contrast in Paul never appears in a context in which the issue has to do with 'how to live the Christian life'" (821) he seems to have forgotten 8.12-13 completely.

In short, it would appear that Romans 7 and 8 have to be taken together. 7.14-25 and 8.1-9, we might say, represent the two ends of the eschatological tension. At one end, the fleshly "I" whose continuing bondage to sin and death is ever in danger of capturing the whole "I." At the other, the Spirit as fructifying life ever threatened by death's continued hold, but ever working to transform the willing believer towards the end of resurrection and whole salvation.

An interesting confirmation that we are on the right lines is the fact that, as the implicit exhortations of 8.4-6 have their explicit parallel in Galatians 5–6, so the implication of an ongoing warfare in the life of the believer between flesh and Spirit is explicit in Gal. 5.16-17:

> [16]I tell you, walk by the Spirit and you will not satisfy the desire of the flesh. [17]For the flesh desires against the Spirit, and the Spirit desires against the flesh; for these are opposed to one another, to prevent you from doing those things you want to do.

Here Paul indicates in fairly stark terms that flesh and Spirit constitute two dimensions of the believer's present existence, that is, in the process of salvation — the two elements which most of all make for its character of tension. Quite explicit is the fact that the two dimensions run counter to each other. In terms of the eschatological tension, the believer is the battleground for the forces of the present age and the age to come, or the prize over which sin and Spirit wage war against each other.[87] Or to be more precise, the believer is involved on both sides of the cosmic struggle. In terms of Romans 7–8, "I" as flesh am at odds with "I" whose life is the Spirit. "I" am at odds with myself. The warfare is between "I" in Adam and "I" in Christ. The profoundness of the insight is indicated in the recognition that the flesh is equally as determined to frustrate the desires of the Spirit as the Spirit is to frustrate the desires of the flesh — "to prevent *(hina mē)* you from doing those things you want to do" (5.17).[88] That is, "I" as flesh am opposed to the Spirit; "I" with the fleshly side of me seek to prevent the desires of the Spirit from coming to effect. But at the same time, "I" as of the Spirit am opposed to the flesh; "I" in aligning with the Spirit seek to prevent the desires of the flesh from

---

87. Schlier, *Galater* 250.

88. *Hina* normally has a final sense ("in order that"), though many prefer to take it in a consecutive sense ("so that": NEB/REB; Lightfoot, *Galatians* 210; Lagrange, *Galates* 147-48; Oepke, *Galater* 175), which is quite possible (BAGD, *hina*). But Paul probably intended the final sense, in order to bring out the character of the tension between flesh and Spirit precisely as an adversarial contest; *hina,* in other words, expresses intention rather than accomplished fact (so Zahn, *Galater* 263; Burton, *Galatians* 301-2; Schlier, *Galater* 249; Mussner, *Galater* 377).

coming to effect. Here is a particularly poignant expression of the eschatological tension, expressive also of some depth of psychological insight.

§18.5 Sharing Christ's sufferings

But there is a still more profound feature of Paul's thought on the eschatological tension.[89] We have already touched on it in Rom. 8.10 and 13. It is that the process of salvation is a *continuing* experience not only of life, but also of death. Sanctification is a dying as well as a living. Death is at work in the believer as well as life. This is also the consequence of the believers' divided state: as members of the first Adam, they belong to this age, they are dying; as members of the last Adam, they belong to the age to come, they experience the life-giving Spirit.

This was a theme to which Paul reverted on several occasions. It is particularly prominent in 2 Corinthians. Evidently Paul's own near-death experience (1.8-11) had focused his mind on the problem of suffering, that is, on the place of suffering and death within the process of salvation.[90] And this was his conclusion: that *both* were integral aspects of that process. Hence most notably 4.7: "We have this treasure in clay jars,[91] in order that the extraordinary quality of the power might be [seen to be] of God and not from ourselves." That is precisely the character of the eschatological tension — divine power in human transience and corruptibility — not divine power obliterating or leaving behind human weakness, but *in* human weakness.

The theme comes to clearest expression at the end of the same chapter — 4.11-12, 16-17:

> [11]For while we live we are being handed over to death on account of Jesus, in order that the life of Jesus might also be manifested in our mortal flesh. [12]So then, death is at work in us, but life in you. . . . [16]Therefore we do not lose heart; even though our outer nature is wasting away, nevertheless our inner nature is being renewed day by day. [17]For this slight momentary affliction is preparing for us an eternal weight of glory beyond all measure. . . .

89. For what follows see particularly my *Jesus and the Spirit* 326-34. In that section I was particularly stimulated by Tannehill, *Dying* Part II.

90. A. E. Harvey, *Renewal through Suffering: A Study of 2 Corinthians* (Edinburgh: Clark, 1996), builds his thesis on this passage: "For the first time in his extant letters, and possibly for the first time in the entire philosophical and religious literature of the West, we find the experience of involuntary and innocent suffering invested with positive value and meaning *in itself*" (31).

91. On the background to the imagery see Furnish, *2 Corinthians* 253-54; Thrall, *2 Corinthians* 322-24.

The believer as mortal flesh, as "outer nature," is wasting away, is dying (4.16). Suffering now is a necessary preparation for and complement to future glory (4.17-18). Only when death has had its full say, only when mortality has corrupted to death, only then will the believer escape the clutches of death. Only when the bodily "home" has been renewed in the resurrection (5.1-5) will the process of salvation be complete.[92]

In another very personal experience Paul learned the same lesson even more effectively — as he relates in 2 Cor. 12.1-10.[93] As one much favoured with heavenly revelations, he was given "a thorn in the flesh, a messenger of Satan to afflict him" (12.7).[94] Three times he besought the Lord for relief (12.8). But the answer reinforced the lesson of 4.7–12.9-10:

> [9]"My grace is sufficient for you, for my power comes to complete expression in weakness." Therefore I will rather gladly boast in my weaknesses, in order that the power of Christ might dwell upon me. [10]Wherefore I am content with weaknesses, insults, hardships, persecutions, and calamities, for Christ's sake; for when I am weak, then am I powerful.

The lesson was the same: the weakness of the believer was not something which prevented the power of God from being effective; it did not have to be ended before the power of Christ could have its say. On the contrary, the implication is, out of the body experiences (12.1-6) and such like were what *prevented* the power of God from having its proper effect. Ironically, such experiences were too much of the flesh. To make too much of them actually constituted a perversion of the gospel.[95] The corollary for our present concerns is clear: it was precisely *not* experiences of power leaving behind bodily weakness which Paul saw as the mark of grace, but experiences of power in and through bodily weakness. Continuing human weakness was an integral part of the process of salvation. Human weakness was not a denial of divine

---

92. See further below §18.6.

93. It is not necessary to clarify the precise relation of 2 Corinthians 1–7 and 10–13 at this point.

94. The debate on what Paul meant by the "thorn in the flesh" is reviewed, e.g., by Martin, *2 Corinthians* 412-16. We may simply note that it was both painful and evil, and yet given by God — a unique expression of the already–not yet tension (see also §2.3 above).

95. This is the main thrust of 2 Corinthians 10–13, since it is directed against other missionaries who evidently understood the gospel and evaluated their success in the gospel in terms of powerful deeds (12.11-12), revelations, and the like. We need not seek a more precise identification of these opponents (see, e.g., Furnish, *2 Corinthians* 48-54) since the theological point being made is not dependent on a more precise identification.

power, but an unavoidable and even necessary complement to divine power in the overlap of the ages.[96]

In short, Paul regarded suffering as an integral feature of the eschatological tension. In 2 Corinthians Paul's thought was primarily of his own suffering in the course of his apostolic ministry. But the more generalized descriptions in 4.16–5.5 indicate clearly enough that Paul saw suffering as part of the already–not yet for all thus caught up in the eschatological tension. And this is confirmed by Paul's talk of affliction elsewhere.[97] Not least we should recall that the Spirit had a role in the process of death, in "putting to death the deeds of the body" (Rom. 8.13).[98]

There is, however, a still more striking feature of this strand of Paul's thought. That both the death and the life to be experienced by the believer are *Christ's*. The tension, suffering, death, and life experienced by Paul he experienced as the outworking of Christ's death and risen life. In his most systematic exposition, Paul gave a clear hint of this already in Rom. 6.5. And in Romans 8 it is the very next point of qualification to which he draws attention, following the qualification of 8.12-14 (§18.4).

What is noteworthy in Rom. 6.5 is the use of the perfect tense — a feature whose significance is again usually missed by commentators. "For if we have become knit together *(symphytos)* with the very likeness *(homoiōma)* of his death, we shall certainly also [be knit together with the very likeness] of his resurrection" (6.5). The force of the perfect is to indicate a past event establishing a state which continues to persist in the present.[99] What Paul means then, is that the believer is and continues to be in a state of having been fused with the very likeness of Christ's death.[100] That this is not a slip on Paul's part is confirmed by his use of the same tense in

96. The point is generally recognized; see, e.g., those cited in my *Jesus and the Spirit* 449 n. 136. See further §21 n. 72 below.

97. *Thlipsis* ("affliction") — 2 Cor. 1.4, 8; 2.4; 4.17; 6.4; 7.4; Phil. 1.17; 4.14; 1 Thes. 3.7; Eph. 3.13; but also Rom. 5.3; 2 Cor. 8.2; 1 Thes. 1.6; 3.3; 2 Thes. 1.4. *Pathēma* ("suffering") — Phil. 3.10; Col. 1.24; 2 Tim. 3.11; but also Rom. 8.18; 2 Cor. 1.6-7. *Paschō* ("suffer") — 2 Cor. 1.6; 2 Tim. 1.12; but also Phil. 1.29; 1 Thes. 2.14; 2 Thes. 1.5. See also my *Jesus and the Spirit* 327.

98. Tannehill, *Dying* 128; Dunn, *Jesus and the Spirit* 337-38; see further §23.4.

99. BDF §340. The best example is the use of the perfect in Greek to say "I stand," that is, "I took my stand and am still standing."

100. On the imagery of *symphytos*, "fused, knit together," see §13 n. 67. *Homoiōma*, "very likeness," denotes "the form of transcendent reality perceptible to humankind." So it denotes not Christ's death as such, nor baptism as such, but the reality and effect of Christ's death as it may be experienced by the baptizand in the here and now (for detailed discussion see my *Romans* 316-18). The reference, therefore, is not to baptism but to the state of having been baptized into Christ's death (6.3). See also particularly Tannehill, *Dying* 32-43.

similar statements earlier in Galatians. Gal. 2.19 — "I have been crucified with Christ"; 6.14 — "the world has been crucified to me and I to the world." In other words, Paul did not think of crucifixion with Christ as a once-for-all event of the past. Nor was he thinking in these passages of the believer as already taken down from the cross with Christ and risen with Christ. On the contrary, "I have been crucified with Christ"; that is, I have been nailed to the cross with Christ, and am in that state still; *I am still hanging with Christ on that cross.* The implication for the process of salvation is clear: since resurrection with Christ comes at the end point, then in a sense (in terms of soteriological effect) Christ remains the crucified one until the parousia, and those crucified with Christ continue to be crucified with Christ throughout the period of overlap.

If the point was implicit in Rom. 6.5, Paul makes it quite explicit in 8.17. The assurance of sonship through the Spirit was not in doubt (8.14-17a). But the further qualification echoes that made in 2 Cor. 4.16-17–Rom. 8.17-18:

> [17]And if children, also heirs — heirs of God and heirs together with Christ, provided that we suffer with him in order that we might also be glorified with him. [18]For I reckon that the sufferings of the present time are not to be compared with the coming glory to be revealed to us. . . .

The point is the same. Not simply that sufferings are a necessary and unavoidable preliminary ("provided that"). But that the suffering in view is precisely suffering "with him." Between the "with him" of the already ("buried with him") and the "with him" of the not yet ("raised with him"), there is the "with him" of the in-between times ("suffer with him"). This was presumably the lesson Paul learned in the crisis in Asia (2 Cor. 1.8): that the way to understand his tribulations was as the experience of the "overflow" of the sufferings of Christ (1.5a). That insight was evidently the source of his strength and resilience (1.5b).

Presumably the same line of thought is present in 2 Cor. 4.10 — "Wherever we go we carry about in our body the death/dying of Jesus *(tēn nekrōsin tou Iēsou),* in order that in this body also the life of Jesus may be revealed." *Nekrōsis* can mean either the process of being put to death ("dying") or the state of having been put to death ("death").[101] Either way, the already–not yet tension as a continued experience of death and life, and of Christ's death and life, is clear. Similarly in the more threatening terms of 2 Cor. 13.4 — "he was crucified in weakness, but lives by the power of God;

---

101. See, e.g., my *Jesus and the Spirit* 450 n. 159; Furnish, *2 Corinthians* 255-56; Fitzgerald, *Cracks in an Earthen Vessel* (§23 n. 180) 177-78; Thrall, *2 Corinthians* 331-32.

for we also are weak in him, but shall live with him by the power of God in reference to you."[102]

The most striking expression of this theme comes in the later Col. 1.24:

> Now I rejoice in my sufferings for your sake and I fill up what is lacking of the afflictions of the Christ in my flesh for the sake of his body, the church.

The words have caused puzzlement to generations of translators and commentators,[103] but they are simply an elaboration of the familiar Pauline theme — rejoicing in suffering[104] as a sharing in Christ's sufferings. The unexpected addition here is the thought that Christ's sufferings lacked something (*hysterēma,* "lack, deficiency") and needed to be completed in Paul's flesh (*antanaplēroō,* "fill up in place of"). But it is best understood simply as a spelling out of what was implicit in the perfect tenses of Rom. 6.5 and Gal. 2.19 and 6.14 (also 2 Cor. 4.10). That is, there is a sense in which Christ's passion is incomplete. Since Christ's death is the means by which the sinful flesh is killed off, it is incomplete till the whole entail of sinful flesh is brought to an end. Since Christ's death is the means by which death is conquered, it is incomplete until the final destruction of the last enemy (1 Cor. 15.26). Since believers share in Christ's sufferings, in a sense Christ's sufferings are incomplete until the last suffering of the last Christian.[105] This is of a piece with the later idea of a total sum of suffering which must be endured before the end comes,[106] the birth pangs of the messianic age (an image which Paul already echoes in Gal. 4.19).[107] The transition from old age to new age is long-drawn-out and those in transit from one to the other are caught "with Christ" in the overlap.

If there is some doubt over the authorship of Col. 1.24, then Paul's own final variation on the theme may have to be regarded as Phil. 3.10-11. The passage is particularly striking since it follows immediately on Paul's recollection of the decisive beginning of his own Christian commitment, part of a

---

102. On the interpretation of "we shall live" and "for you" see above §15 n. 60.

103. See my *Colossians* 114-15.

104. Rom. 5.3; 8.18; 2 Cor. 1.5-7; 4.17-18; 7.4; 1 Thes. 1.6.

105. The thought may be particularly of Paul also fulfilling (or completing) the Servant's role: Rom. 15.20-21 (= Isa. 52.15); 2 Cor. 6.1-2 (= Isa. 49.8); Gal. 1.15-16 (echoing Isa. 49.1-6); Phil. 2.16 (cf. Isa. 49.4). The same conviction impressed itself on the Pauline material in Acts: 13.47 (= Isa. 49.6); 26.16-18 (cf. Isa. 42.7); also 18.9-10 (cf. Isa. 41.10; 43.5).

106. Mark 13.8; John 16.21; Rev. 6.9-11; *4 Ezra* 4.33-43; see further R. Stuhlmann, *Das eschatologische Mass im Neuen Testament* (FRLANT 132; Göttingen: Vandenhoeck, 1983), here 99-101.

107. See further G. Bertram, *ōdin, TDNT* 9.669-74.

continuing sentence. Paul's whole system of values has been turned upside down (3.7-8). All he wants now is "to gain Christ and be found in him" (3.8-9),

> [10]to know him and the power of his resurrection and the fellowship of his sufferings, being conformed to his death, [11]if somehow I might attain to the resurrection from the dead.

Here again we find the same double aspect: the process of salvation as involving both an experience of the power of Christ's resurrection, and a sharing in his sufferings; the process of salvation as involving both growing conformity to Christ's death and participation in the final resurrection from the dead. What is particularly notable is the way Paul speaks of Christ's sufferings *after* he speaks of his resurrection. The process of sanctification does not consist in an initial dying with Christ followed in the course of that process by an experience of Christ's resurrection power. Paul's doctrine of salvation is quite different. The resurrection power of Christ manifests itself, and inseparably so, as also a sharing in Christ's sufferings. The process of salvation is a process of growing conformity to Christ's death. Only when that is completed (in death) can the final resurrection from the dead be attained (the resurrection of the body). Only when believers are fully one with Christ in his death will it be possible for them to be fully one with Christ in his resurrection.

In short, as we noted earlier, the process of salvation can be expressed in simple terms as "becoming like Christ" (§18.2). Integral to this process, as we have now seen so clearly, is the thought that the conformity is to Christ crucified as well as risen, that the transformation is an outworking of the cross as well as the resurrection. To be transformed into the image of Christ (2 Cor. 3.18) means also to be conformed to his death (Phil. 3.10).

§18.6 *The process completed*

The process of salvation has a goal and an end. Paul had no thought of existence as a repeating cycle of birth and rebirth. Human life climaxed in death, either as the victory of sin and death or as their defeat and destruction.[108] Except for the favoured few (only Enoch and Elijah come to mind), the process had to be worked right through. The fact of Jesus' own death made that clear: if that one died, then none could escape death.[109] The resurrection of Jesus was so central to the gospel because the good news included the fact and

---

108. See above §5.7.
109. See above §9.1.

promise of triumph over death.[110] So too with the principal aspects of salvation's beginnings in human life.[111] Justification would only be complete in the final vindication. Participation in Christ would achieve its goal in the complete transformation of believers into the image of God in Christ. The work of the Spirit would be finished when the glory lost and the image disfigured by human disobedience were wholly renewed (2 Cor. 3.18; 4.4, 6). Salvation was not, could not be, complete within this life.[112] The realization of hope lies beyond the confines of present existence: "If we have hoped in Christ only in this life, we are of all people the most pitiable" (1 Cor. 15.19);[113] the Christian hope focuses on what cannot yet be seen (Rom. 8.25);[114] it is "laid up for you in the heavens" (Col. 1.5).[115]

All this we have picked out and highlighted at various points in the preceding pages. But we could hardly end this section without gathering together the various aspects and emphases of Paul's hope of complete salvation. As with his parousia hope (§12), the individual elements are clear enough. How they hang together is less clear.

The most obvious element is what follows from §18.5 — the resurrection of the body. The importance of that hope lay not least in the fact that so many aspects of Paul's theology come together in it. It is the immediate consequence of cross and resurrection (1 Corinthians 15), is integral to the gospel (15.12-19), and confirm that victory over death is central to the gospel (15.21-22, 26, 54-57). It resolves forever the tension between flesh and body (15.42-54). It completes God's purpose in creating humanity by renewing the image of God in resurrected humanity (15.45-49). It is the final outworking of the process of inner renewal and outward decay (2 Cor. 4.16–5.5). It includes the renewal of creation as a whole (Rom. 8.19-23). And all was made possible by Christ's resurrection as the "firstborn" and prototype — resurrection "with Christ" (2 Cor. 4.14), resurrection body conformed to his glorious body[116] — and by the activity of God's Spirit, the firstfruits of the Spirit as only the beginning of the harvest of resurrected bodies (Rom. 8.23).

---

110. See above §10.1.

111. See above §18.2.

112. See above §18.2 and n. 53.

113. The wording of 1 Cor. 15.19 is slightly obscure, but the sense must be something like: there can be no hope for the future (resurrection from the dead) if there is no resurrection from the dead; in that case hope is limited to this life and the good news of Jesus' resurrection produces only a vain hope.

114. See also above §14 n. 217 and §16 n. 129.

115. This unusual Pauline formulation, using "hope" in the sense of "that which is hoped for," brings out both the forward-looking character of hope and its implication of confidence in the sureness of God's purpose (see my *Colossians* 59).

116. Rom. 6.5; 8.11; Phil. 3.11, 21.

On this subject the most intriguing paragraph composed by Paul must be 2 Cor. 5.1-5:

> [1]For we know that if the earthly tent we live in is destroyed, we have a building from God, an eternal house in the heavens, not made with hands. [2]For in this one we groan, longing to be overclothed with our heavenly dwelling, [3]so that having stripped off [or having put it on] we will not be found naked. [4]For while we are in this tent, we groan, being burdened, in that we do not wish to be unclothed, but to be overclothed, in order that what is mortal may be swallowed up by life. [5]And he who has made us for this purpose is God, who has given to us the first instalment of the Spirit.

The passage is evidently the climax of a larger unit of exposition (2 Cor. 4.16–5.5).[117] It contains a number of unresolved issues of exegesis, particularly in 5.2-4.[118] But its most obvious function is to express Paul's confidence (4.16) that the present process of wasting away ("outer nature") and renewal ("inner nature") will climax in the transformation into the resurrection body (4.17–5.4), of which the Spirit is already the first instalment and guarantee (5.5). In its basic affirmation, then, the expectation is the same as in 1 Cor. 15.53-54, though here the hope of resurrection is imaged as putting on a further garment (2 Cor. 5.2, 4).[119] Whether we should talk of a development in Paul's thought — Paul now envisaging an "intermediate state" (between death and parousia), where previously he expected to be alive at the parousia (1 Cor. 15.51-52) — is a moot question.[120] All we need note is the possibility

117. On the continuity of thought across the chapter division see Furnish, *2 Corinthians* 288.

118. See discussion in Furnish, *2 Corinthians* 295-99; Martin, *2 Corinthians* 97-101, 105-8; Thrall, *2 Corinthians* 370-82. For example, how should we translate the particles at the beginning of 5.3 — *ei ge* ("inasmuch as" — BAGD, *ge* 3a)? For the participle in 5.3 should we read "having put off" (*ekdysamenoi;* Aland[26], NRSV), or "having put on" (*endysamenoi;* NIV, REB, NJB)? And if the latter, does it refer to an earlier putting on (as in Gal. 3.27; Furnish 297), or to the putting on of the heavenly habitation (5.2; Thrall 378-79)?

119. Despite N. Walter, "Hellenistische Eschatologie bei Paulus? Zu 2 Kor. 5.1-10," *ThQ* 176 (1996) 53-64, the absence of *sōma* ("body") in 2 Cor. 5.1-5 (contrast 1 Cor. 15.35-44) has no significance, as the later Rom. 8.11, 23 confirms. See also Penna, "The Apostle's Suffering: Anthropology and Eschatology in 2 Corinthians 4.7–5.10," *Paul* 1.232-58 (particularly 246-54), who notes the absence of any reference to "soul," indicating that any echo of a more dualistic Hellenistic conceptuality is hardly more than that; and above §3.2.

120. See particularly C. F. D. Moule, "St Paul and Dualism: The Pauline Conception of Resurrection," *Essays* 200-221; Martin, *2 Corinthians* 97-101; J. Gillman, "A Thematic Comparison: 1 Cor. 15.50-57 and 2 Cor. 5.1-5," *JBL* 107 (1988) 439-54; A. Lindemann, "Paulus und die korinthische Eschatologie. Zur These von einer 'Entwicklung' im paulinischen Denken," *NTS* 37 (1991) 373-99; and further Harris, *Raised Immortal*.

that Paul envisaged an intermediate state ("naked," "unclothed" — 5.3-4) in which the groaning caused by the already–not yet tension (Rom. 8.23) might continue beyond death and up to the parousia (2 Cor. 5.2, 4).[121] Either way, however, Paul envisages an incompleteness in the process of salvation which can only be resolved by the new body of resurrection.[122]

The other most clearly set out feature of Paul's eschatological expectation is the final judgment. We have already noted that this conviction was part of Paul's Jewish inheritance.[123] Also that Paul's christology of exaltation fully embraced the thought of Christ fulfilling God's role (acting as his representative?) in that final judgment.[124] Here we need simply to observe that Paul did not envisage believers as exempt from that final judgment. "All of us must appear before the judgment seat of Christ, in order that each might receive the things done through the body, with reference to what each has done, whether good or bad" (2 Cor. 5.10).[125]

In particular, Paul seems to have been willing to affirm a tension at this point between God's saving righteousness and his wrath, between the grace/faith nexus of salvation and the moral outworkings of human choice and mind-set. Thus in Romans 1–3, the assertion both of God's righteousness (1.16-17) and of his impartiality in judging all, Jew and Greek, according to the good and evil they have done (2.1-16), lie side by side. The latter is qualified or clarified by the gospel (2.16), but believers do not escape judgment. It will happen "through Jesus Christ," but God will still "judge the secrets of all" (2.16).[126] So too the warning of divine "vengeance,"[127] of due return for deeds done,[128] applies to believers also. And likewise with the idea of reward for human action.[129] These are all images which affirm moral significance for human actions. A moral choice has moral consequences whose outcome will usually be uncontrollable by the chooser. Believers should not make the mistake for which Paul criticizes Israel (Romans 2) by thinking that because they are in process of "being saved" they will therefore be exempt from the moral consequences of their actions. The gracious God is also the impartial Judge.

---

121. Cullmann, *Christ and Time* 236-42.

122. Hence the impossibility of translating Paul's hope into a belief in "the immortality of the soul"; see also O. Cullmann, *Immortality of the Soul or Resurrection of the Dead? The Witness of the New Testament* (London: Epworth, 1958).

123. See above §2.4.

124. See above §10.5(a).

125. For what follows see also below §18.7(6) and further particularly Travis, *Christ and the Judgment of God,* and Plevnik, *Parousia* (§12 n. 1) 227-43.

126. Cf. particularly 1 Cor. 4.4-5.

127. Rom. 12.19; 1 Thes. 4.6; 2 Thes. 1.8. This reflects the fact that the prophets' warning of divine "vengeance" could be issued as much to Israel as to Israel's enemies (e.g., Jer. 5.9; 23.2; Hos. 4.9; Joel 3.21; Amos 3.2, 14; Nah. 1.2).

The nearest Paul comes to resolving the tension is in 1 Cor. 3.10-15:

[10]In accordance with the grace of God given to me, as a wise master builder I have laid a foundation, and another is building on it. Let each take care how he builds. [11]For no one can lay another foundation beside the one that is laid, which is Jesus Christ. [12]And if anyone builds upon the foundation, gold, silver, precious stones, wood, hay, straw — [13]the work of each will become evident. For the day will disclose it, because it will be revealed with fire. And the fire will test the work of each, what kind it is. [14]If the work of anyone which he has built remains, he will receive a reward. [15]If the work of anyone is burnt up, he will suffer loss. He himself will be saved, but so as by fire.

Here the point is as clear as it could be.[130] Those who have Christ as the foundation of their lives will be saved. But they will not be exempt from judgment. Justification by faith will not exclude judgment in accordance with the law and by reference to works done in the flesh.[131] And the quality of their lives, even as believers, may be such that they are saved only by a whisker. All that has been built on the foundation may be burned to the ground, and only the foundation remain.[132] The tension in this case is in the image of "salvation" where the person is saved indeed, but empty-handed of the mementos and symbols of cherished past times.

If we tie this teaching into earlier reflection on the character of the flesh and on the significance of Jesus' death,[133] it becomes possible to speak of a kind of spectrum in Paul's thought of final retribution. Those who have

---

128. This is indicated particularly by the verb *komizomai*, "get back, receive (wages)," used in 2 Cor. 5.10 and Col. 3.25; also Eph. 6.8. The idea of "measure for measure" (Matt. 7.1-2 pars.) is a strong instinct in Jewish tradition, as in the *ius talionis* (Exod. 21.23-25; Gal. 6.7-8), the fitting punishment (Prov. 22.8; 1 Cor. 3.17), and the talent with interest (Matt. 25.27; cf. Sir. 29.6). See further my *Galatians* 329-30, and *Colossians* 258.

129. Paul favours the image of a race, with a final prize (*brabeion* — 1 Cor. 9.24-27; Phil. 3.12-14; cf. Col. 2.18).

130. The warning of 3.10c is almost certainly directed to the Corinthians, rather than to Apollos or one of the missionaries who followed Paul to Corinth (see Fee, *1 Corinthians* 138-39). But even if the warning was more narrowly directed, it still expresses a principle of divine judgment which Paul presumably affirmed more widely, as the previous paragraph implies.

131. See also above §§2.4, 6.3, and 14.5.

132. Cf. H. W. Hollander, "The Testing by Fire of the Builders' Works: 1 Corinthians 3.10-15," *NTS* 40 (1994) 89-104. As we shall see below (§18.7[6]), Paul also envisages the likelihood or at least possibility that some believers will even abandon the foundation itself, so that the searching fire of judgment will burn up everything.

133. See above §§3.3-4 and 9.3.

lived solely in terms of the flesh will perish with the flesh: "if you live *kata sarka* ("in accordance with the flesh") you are sure to die" (Rom. 8.13).[134] Those, however, who have as their foundation Christ, or equivalent,[135] will be "saved," but their works will be tested by fire (1 Cor. 3.15). And those who walk *kata pneuma* ("in accordance with the Spirit") and express their faith in their lives and relationships will find that their work endures.

The most powerful of Paul's other images is that of "inheriting the kingdom." The phrase is not explicit in its meaning, and it usually appears in negative formulations — in reference to those who will *not* inherit the kingdom.[136] But it sets off a chain of resonances which give the imagery powerful effect — the promised land,[137] the banquet imagery of Jesus' parables of the kingdom,[138] and inheritance of promises and status (Gal. 4.1-7). Not least of importance here is the fact that for Paul the Spirit as such is the first instalment and guarantee of the wholeness of salvation, the *arrabōn* ("first instalment") and *aparchē* ("firstfruits") of the completeness of bodily resurrection — the *arrabōn* being the same "stuff" as the full payment, as the *aparchē* is simply the first sheaf of the whole grain harvest.[139] As with the parousia, therefore, Paul would presumably say that while we do not know just what "sharing the inheritance of the kingdom" will consist of, we do know its fundamental character — that is, by reference to the fruit and graces of the Spirit already experienced, however imperfectly.

Beyond such broad brush strokes it is difficult to go into more detail with any confidence. As with the parousia, the imagery is rich in its individuality, but difficult to build into a consistent composite whole. The talk of "appearing with Christ" (1 Thes. 4.14) and even "being with Christ" (4.17)[140] can be fitted neatly into a resurrection hope (4.15-17). But how do the incoming of the Gentiles and the salvation of "all Israel" (Rom. 11.26-27) fit in? What difference do different rewards make? And how does that imagery square

---

134. Paul's most common imagery is of being "destroyed" (*apollymi* — Rom. 2.12; 14.15; 1 Cor. 1.18; 8.11; 10.9-10; 15.18; 2 Cor. 2.15; 4.3; 2 Thes. 2.10; *katalyō* — Rom. 14.20; 2 Cor. 5.1). For the range of usage in both cases see BAGD.

135. Did Paul assume that explicit faith in Christ was necessary for salvation (cf. Rom. 10.9-17)? Or should we rather assume that he would have thought in terms also of an implicit faith, just as he thought of Gentiles who "by nature do what the law requires . . . [and] demonstrate the business of the law written in their hearts" (Rom. 2.14-15)? Contrast R. H. Bell, "Extra Ecclesiam Nulla Salus? Is There a Salvation Other Than through Faith in Christ according to Romans 2:12-16?" in Ådna, et al., eds., *Evangelium* 31-43.

136. 1 Cor. 6.9-10; 15.50; Gal. 5.21; Eph. 5.5.

137. For documentation see my *Romans* 213 and 455.

138. See above §8.3(2) and (3).

139. Rom. 8.9-23; 1 Cor. 15.50; 2 Cor. 4.16–5.5; Eph. 1.14.

140. See also 1 Thes. 5.10; 2 Cor. 5.8; Phil. 1.23.

with the imagery of being made "complete" or "perfect" "in the day of Christ" or "in Christ"?[141] The idea that the saints will participate in judging the world (1 Cor. 6.2) adds another twist. And beyond that we have the difficulty of integrating the imagery of the last Adam, the firstborn of a new humanity and elder brother of a new family, with the correlated imagery of glorification (particularly Rom. 8.29-30).

To attempt to integrate all these elements into a single, consistent whole would probably be unwise. Different metaphors cannot be blended into one without loss of something distinctive, and important, in each. As discussions, not least of the two passages we have quoted at length, well demonstrate, there is an ambiguity in Paul's treatment of these themes, which is unavoidable given their intangible character. In such cases it is better to recognize language struggling to express what language alone is incapable of expressing adequately and to cherish the fragmentary insights and principles which Paul's imagery nevertheless clearly expresses — God's faithfulness in completing what he has begun, the moral order inbuilt within humanity and society, and God's purposes embracing creation as well as human creature, divine grace, and human responsibility.

§18.7 Conclusions and corollaries

The scope of Paul's gospel of salvation should now be clear. "Salvation" properly speaking is the climax or end result of a process. The process has a decisive beginning, but it is also a lifelong process. The eschatological tension thus set up can be expressed in a number of ways.

In cosmic terms the process of salvation began with the death and resurrection of Christ, the last Adam, whose obedience has undone the disobedience of the first Adam. Salvation thus completes what creation began. The new epoch of God's final purpose, the new creation, is already under way, and with it the reclamation of humankind. But the old epoch still persists. Adam yet lives. And until all have died in Adam, the equivalent "all" cannot become fully alive in Christ.

In terms of the Pauline metaphors, the metaphors of the already must be held in tension with the metaphors of the not yet. The Pauline aorists must be balanced by the Pauline imperatives.

In terms of Paul's theology of justification, the decisive beginning has to be worked out until and in the final verdict of acquittal. The relationship with God must be sustained by God to the end. Luther's *simul iustus et peccator* is also *semper iustus et peccator* until God's final summons.

141. Gal. 3.3; Phil. 1.6; 3.12; Col. 1.28. See also below §18.7(2).

In terms of participation in Christ, the epoch of overlap is spanned by both Christ's death and his resurrection. The decisive beginning does not mean that what follows is all resurrection power and no longer crucifixion weakness. Paul's theology of salvation is not a *theologia gloriae* alone, but also a *theologia crucis*. The way to the glory of the resurrection is through the suffering of the cross, through a growing conformity to Christ's death as a continuing feature of the not yet.

In terms of the gift of the Spirit, the Spirit is the Spirit of Christ. But that also means the Spirit of Christ crucified. The gift of the Spirit, no more than the other aspects of the salvation process, does not transcend the cross or short-circuit the process of transformation that comes through sharing in Christ's suffering and death. Throughout the process of salvation the gift of the Spirit has the character of *arrabōn* and *aparchē,* first instalment and firstfruits, of the full inheritance which awaits the final resurrection. In the between times, the power of the resurrection is always experienced in the weakness of the flesh. The life-giving Spirit also bears the mark of the cross.

The corollaries are quite far-reaching in their implications.

1) Paul's pneumatology had no room for teachings which have some-times featured in high theologies of confirmation or in "second blessing" circles.[142] That is to say, his pneumatology excludes the idea that the Spirit is not given until a second phase of discipleship or commitment. For Paul the gift of the Spirit has the essential character of beginning the process of salvation. In the near-definition in Rom. 8.9 — no Spirit, no Christian. So too is excluded any thought that there is a second gift of the Spirit (which is the Spirit) which some Christians do not or may not have. The gift which is the Spirit is simply the foundation and starting point for all that follows in Paul's soteriology. This, of course, is not to question that Paul conceived of subse-quent experiences of the Spirit, and of engracings and enablings by the Spirit; on the contrary, Paul's theology of the charismatic Spirit falls wholly within this area, and we will have to return to it.[143]

2) Paul's theology of "spirituality" and "maturity" therefore has to be carefully expressed.[144] Paul's experience, particularly with the Corinthians, made him hesitant to use the terms. Some were evidently claiming to be "spritual" and "mature" on the basis of their wisdom, eloquent speech, and tongues-speaking.[145] Paul could not accept their claim since it promoted

142. For details I may refer again to my *Baptism* (§16 n. 1), one of whose main objectives was to critique such views.

143. See below §20.5.

144. *Pneumatikos* ("spiritual") — 1 Cor. 2.13, 15; 3.1; 14.37; Gal. 6.1. *Teleios* — 1 Cor. 2.6; 14.20; Phil. 3.15; Col. 1.28; 4.12.

145. 1 Cor. 2.12–3.4; 14.20, 37; cf. Phil. 3.12, 15. It is only in the later Col. 1.28 and 4.12 that *teleios* ("mature") is a wholly positive concept (see further my *Colossians* 125-26).

factionalism (elitism; 1 Cor. 3.3-4) and a disregard for others, unbelievers as well as believers (14.16-25). The mark of spirituality and maturity was rather the love described in 1 Corinthians 13, recognition of the evident authority of others (1 Cor. 14.37 — Paul himself!), pastoral sensitivity (Gal. 6.1), and a recognition of how far from being perfected one still is (Phil. 3.15).[146] In other words, for Paul, the "spiritual/mature" were those who lived in accord with the Spirit once given, not people who had been given more of the Spirit or a separate gift of the Spirit to distinguish them from others. The Paul who fought so resolutely for justification by faith was not going to give credibility to an equally divisive "us-and-them" spirituality.

3) The believer's whole life as believer is lived in the overlap of the ages, within the eschatological tension between Adam and Christ, between death and life. That means also, with the experience of the conflict between flesh and Spirit. The tension sometimes "got to" Paul: "Wretched man am I! Who will deliver me from the body of this death?" (Rom. 7.24); "we ourselves groan within ourselves, eagerly awaiting the adoption, the redemption of our body" (Rom. 8.23); "we groan, burdened in our being in this tent, wanting not to be unclothed but to be further clothed, for this mortality to be swallowed up by life" (2 Cor. 5.4). It "got to" him, we may say, precisely because he appreciated that there was no escape from this tension for the whole of his life. The cry of Rom. 7.24, the groaning of Rom. 8.23, was lifelong.[147]

The pastoral corollary here is important. For all down the centuries there has been a danger of confusing means of living *in* this tension with ways of *escaping* it. In earlier centuries practise of mysticism and asceticism, sometimes even monasticism, was liable to be thus misunderstood and abused.[148] In more recent centuries there have been teachings on sanctification, second blessing, and Spirit baptism which have been pushed in this direction. But if Paul is right, there is no escape from that tension in this life. Precisely because believers are still in some sense in the flesh, still not fully free precisely as flesh from the power of sin and death, they can enjoy the power

---

146. Phil. 3.12 is Paul's only use of the verb *teleioō,* where the imagery is obviously that of having reached the goal, but probably also reflects the belief within some of Paul's churches that "perfection" was attainable in this life. Note again the use of *epiteleō* ("complete") in Gal. 3.3 and Phil. 1.6.

147. This also means that the cry and groaning are not of despair so much as of frustration — frustration at having to live the life of the Spirit in the flesh and through the mortal body. It should not be seen as a consequence of the delay of the parousia (see also above §12.4).

148. Celibacy has also been conceived as a higher kind of spirituality which exempted the celibate from the entanglements and temptations consequent upon still living "in the flesh"!

of Christ's resurrection only as power in weakness, only as a sharing in Christ's sufferings, as life in and through death.

Equally the ongoing experience of conflict between flesh and Spirit should not unduly alarm or depress. The "I" is still divided. Death as well as life is at work in the believer. Even defeat, when flesh succeeds in thwarting Spirit, should not necessarily cause despair — so long as it is experienced as defeat.[149] On the contrary, it is the *absence* of conflict which should be a cause of concern. The presence of conflict between flesh and Spirit is a sign that the Spirit is having effect in shaping the character. The absence of conflict could indicate the absence of the Spirit.[150] The implications for pastoral theology and counseling are considerable.

4) This understanding of the process of salvation also provides the basis for a profound theology of suffering. Paul himself suffered amazing hardships and injuries.[151] His theology of suffering was no ivory tower construction. What it amounted to was a way of viewing his suffering as an integral part of the process of salvation. It reinforced awareness of his own weakness and mortality, and thus reinforced his reliance on God. And in it he saw the wasting away of his own flesh, in which sin still exercised its enticing and baleful power. In it he saw the growing conformity to Christ's death with its promise of fuller participation in Christ's resurrection beyond. Of course, a theology of suffering as friction at the interface between old age and age to come only makes sense within a theology of salvation which looks to resurrection life through and beyond death.

5) The character of the process of salvation also provides a theological foundation for a system of ethics. We will return to this subject later (§23). For the moment we may just note that a Pauline ethic inevitably starts from the already and not yet and is shot through with the eschatological tension.[152] For one thing, this would mean that the Christian life for Paul was a process which involved a continually renewed commitment. Victory in the battle between flesh and Spirit was never victory final and complete. There was another battle to be won another day, perhaps the same battle, perhaps tomor-

---

149. This is a more careful statement of my position than in *Jesus and the Spirit* 339, in response to the critique of D. Wenham, "The Christian Life: A Life of Tension? — A Consideration of the Nature of Christian Experience in Paul," in Hagner and Harris, *Pauline Studies* 80-94 (here 89).

150. "The Spirit is absent when we stop fighting, not when we lose" (H. Berkhof, *The Doctrine of the Holy Spirit* [Richmond: John Knox, 1964 = London: Epworth, 1965] 78); contrast again Fee, *Empowering Presence* 817 — "Nowhere does Paul describe life in the Spirit as one of constant struggle with the flesh."

151. Again, noticeably, it is particularly in 2 Corinthians that the extent and seriousness of his suffering come to clearest expression — 2 Cor. 1.8-9; 6.4-10; 11.23-29.

152. Recognized most recently by Sampley, *Walking* (§23 n. 1) 7-24.

row. In every moral decision there was a choice to be made, for the flesh or for the Spirit. Conversion is every day. This has been one of the strengths of an existentialist ethic. And for another, it would mean that idealistic schemes which took too little account of the continuing "not yet" would always fall under the critique of the "eschatological reservation." It is precisely his appreciation of the continuing power of sin and death and the continuing weakness of the flesh which makes Paul's ethic so realistic in regard to what may be expected from human individuals or institutions (the church not excluded).

6) A further unavoidable corollary is that *apostasy* remains a real possibility for the Pauline believer for the duration of the eschatological tension.[153] We need simply recall some of the passages which we examined above. Rom. 8.13: there is evidently the real possibility that believers may live *kata sarka;* and if they do so they will die.[154] That is to say, if they abandon the struggle and revert to a wholly fleshly existence, they will not experience the daily renewal towards wholeness, but only the daily deterioration towards the destruction of the flesh in death.[155] We are not surprised then at the equivalent warnings elsewhere where Paul envisages the possibility of "destroying" the work of salvation in a person.[156] Or at Paul's concern lest his evangelistic work might come to be in vain,[157] or lest his converts be "estranged from Christ" and "fall away from grace" (Gal. 5.4). Or at the warning to the Gentile Christians in Rome that they could be cut off from the olive tree of Israel just as easily as the unbelieving of Israel have been (Rom. 11.20-22).

We have also observed the qualifications which feature at a number of points in Paul's letters: "joint heirs with Christ, provided that we suffer with him in order that we might be glorified with him" (Rom. 8.17); the gospel "through which you are being saved, if you hold on to it" (1 Cor. 15.2); reconciled to be presented holy and blameless before God "provided that you remain in the faith established and steadfast and not shifting from the hope of the gospel" (Col. 1.22-23). As F. F. Bruce put it: "Throughout the New Testament continuance is the test of reality."[158] Hence also the calls

---

153. *Pace* the rather tendentious attempt of Gundry Volf, *Paul,* to weaken the seriousness of Paul's repeated warnings on this point. Marshall, *Kept* 99-125, better reflects the "eschatological reserve" in Paul's overall treatment.

154. Similarly Gal. 6.8 — "those who sow to their own flesh reap corruption"; cf. Phil. 3.19 — "their end is destruction."

155. Surprisingly Gundry Volf, *Paul,* seems to have ignored this verse.

156. Rom. 14.15, 20; 1 Cor. 3.17; 8.11; 10.9-11; Gal. 2.18.

157. 2 Cor. 6.1; Gal. 2.2; 4.11; Phil. 2.16; 1 Thes. 3.5.

158. *Romans* 219.

to carefulness, watchfulness,[159] and self-scrutiny[160] and Paul's recognition that discipline was still necessary if the race was to be completed.[161]

In the face of such a catalogue of concern it is hardly possible to doubt that part of Paul's pastoral theology was the real concern that faith could be once again compromised and cease to be simple trust, that commitment could be relaxed and resolve critically weakened. The result would be a critical slackening of the eschatological tension, the lapse to a life solely "in accordance with the flesh," and the loss of the prospect of resurrection life.

7) That, however, is not the note on which Paul brought his powerful exposition of the salvation process to its climax in Romans 8. Quite otherwise. His warning of 8.13, his cautionary "provided that" of 8.17, his recognition of the continuing suffering and tension of the incomplete process of salvation (8.18-23), his expression of the already and not yet of hope (8.24-25), and his acknowledgment that weakness continues to be the medium of faith (8.26-27) — all that is left behind in a growing paean of confident trust. Those who love God can trust unconditionally in God: the assurance of adoption is a firm hope, the firstfruits of the Spirit a firm guarantee of the resurrection harvest (8.14-27); those who love God are within the predetermined purpose of God, their final acquittal and glorification assured (8.28-30); no charge against them will be upheld in the final judgment (8.31-34); and nothing can separate them from God's love in Christ (8.35-39). When all clarification and qualification have been run through, the gospel once again can be reduced to its basic components — the love of God, and love for God.

---

159. 1 Cor. 3.10; 8.9; 10.12; Gal. 5.15.
160. 1 Cor. 11.29-30; 2 Cor. 13.5.
161. 1 Cor. 9.27; Phil. 3.12-14.

§19 Israel (Romans 9–11)[1]

1. **Bibliography**: M. **Barth**, *The People of God* (JSNTS 5; Sheffield: JSOT, 1983); **Becker**, *Paul* 457-72; **Beker**, *Paul* 328-47; R. H. **Bell**, *Provoked to Jealousy: The Origin and Purpose of the Jealousy Motif in Romans 9–11* (WUNT 2.63; Tübingen: Mohr, 1994); W. S. **Campbell**, "The Freedom and Faithfulness of God in Relation to Israel," *Paul's Gospel* 43-59; M. **Cranford**, "Election and Ethnicity: Paul's View of Israel in Romans 9.1-13," *JSNT* 50 (1993) 27-41; N. A. **Dahl**, "The Future of Israel," *Studies* 137-58; W. D. **Davies**, "Paul and the People of Israel," *NTS* 24 (1977-78) 4-39 = *Jewish and Pauline Studies* 123-52; E. **Dinkler**, "The Historical and Eschatological Israel in Romans 9–11: A Contribution to the Problem of Predestination and Individual Responsibility," *JR* 36 (1956) 109-27; **Eichholz**, *Theologie* 284-301; J. G. **Gager**, *The Origins of AntiSemitism* (New York: Oxford University, 1985); **Gaston**, *Paul* (§6 n. 1) chs. 5, 8, and 9; M. A. **Getty**, "Paul and the Salvation of Israel: A Perspective on Romans 9–11," *CBQ* 50 (1988) 456-69; **Gnilka**, *Theologie* 124-32; *Paulus* 281-89; E. **Grässer**, *Der Alte Bund im Neuen. Exegetische Studien zur Israelfrage im Neuen Testament* (Tübingen: Mohr, 1985); D. J. **Harrington**, *Paul on the Mystery of Israel* (Collegeville: Liturgical, 1992); G. **Harvey**, *The True Israel: Uses of the Names Jew, Hebrew and Israel in Ancient Jewish and Early Christian Literature* (Leiden: Brill, 1996); O. **Hofius**, "Das Evangelium und Israel. Erwägungen zu Römer 9–11," *Paulusstudien* 175-202; E. E. **Johnson**, *The Function of Apocalyptic and Wisdom Traditions in Romans 9–11* (Atlanta: Scholars, 1989); B. W. **Longenecker**, "Different Answers to Different Issues: Israel, the Gentiles and Salvation History in Romans 9–11," *JSNT* 36 (1989) 95-123; *Eschatology and the Covenant: A Comparison of 4 Ezra and Romans 1–11* (JSNTS 57; Sheffield: Sheffield Academic, 1991); L. de **Lorenzi**, ed., *Die Israelfrage nach Römer 9–11* (Rome: Abtei von St. Paul, 1977); H.-M. **Lübking**, *Paulus und Israel im Römerbrief. Eine Untersuchung zu Römer 9–11* (Frankfurt: Lang, 1986); U. **Luz**, *Das Geschichtsverständnis des Paulus* (Munich: Kaiser, 1968); B. **Mayer**, *Unter Gottes Heilsratschluss: Prädestinationsaussagen bei Paulus* (Würzburg: Echter, 1974); H. **Merklein**, "Der (neue) Bund als Thema der paulinischen Theologie," *TQ* 176 (1966) 290-308; J. **Munck**, *Christ and Israel: An Interpretation of Romans 9–11* (Philadelphia: Fortress, 1967); P. von der **Osten-Sacken**, *Christian-Jewish Dialogue: Theological Foundations* (Philadelphia: Fortress, 1986) 19-40; **Penna**, "The Evolution of Paul's Attitude toward the Jews," *Paul* 1.290-321; J. **Piper**, *The Justification of God: An Exegetical and Theological Study of Romans 9.1-23* (Grand Rapids: Baker, 1983); H. **Räisänen**, "Römer 9–11: Analyse eines geistigen Ringens," *ANRW* 2.25.4 (1987) 2891-2939; F. **Refoulé**, "Cohérence ou incohérence de Paul en Romains 9–11," *RB* 98 (1991) 51-79; P. **Richardson**, *Israel in the Apostolic Church* (SNTSMS 10; Cambridge: Cambridge University, 1969); **Ridderbos**, *Paul* 327-61; D. **Sänger**, *Die Verkündigung des Gekreuzigten und Israel. Studien zum Verhältnis von Kirche und Israel bei Paulus und im frühen Christentum* (WUNT 75; Tübingen: Mohr, 1994); R. **Schmitt**, *Gottesgerechtigkeit-Heilsgeschichte: Israel in der Theologie des Paulus* (Frankfurt: Lang,

§19.1 Has God's word failed (9.1-5)?

In our attempt to follow the course of Paul's own theologizing through Romans we have now reached ch. 9–11. At this point we are bound to stop short and take stock. For the function of chs. 9–11 within Romans, and so also within Paul's theology, has always been a matter of some controversy. Why did Paul turn so abruptly to express his concern for his "kinsmen in terms of the flesh" (9.3)? He had reached such a wonderful climax of Christian assurance in 8.28-39. Anything following that would inevitably appear as something of an anticlimax. But why this sudden descent to depths of existential angst: "I speak the truth in Christ, I do not lie, my conscience bearing me witness in the Holy Spirit,[2] that my grief is great and the anguish of my heart unceasing. . . ." (9.1-2)? Moreover, knowledge of the pattern followed in other letters would lead us (and perhaps some among his Roman audiences) to expect an immediate transition to ethical exhortation as the most appropriate corollary — as in 12.1-2. Why then should Paul disrupt his normal flow by inserting what almost appears like a pre-set piece (chs. 9–11)?[3]

Those seeking a theological rationale for the place of Romans 9–11 have tended to find it in different sections of the argument of these chapters. The traditional view (of both Luther and Calvin) was that having dealt with the subject of justification in Romans 1–8, Paul turns in chs. 9–11 to the subject of predestination (foreshadowed in 8.29). This view reflects not only the systematic concerns of later Christian theology, but also the powerful impact of the central section of ch. 9 (9.14-23), with its portrayal of the God who shows mercy to whom he wills and hardens whom he wills (9.18). The passage inevitably exerts a fascination for anyone striving to develop a theology — a fascination, part attraction at its theological rigour, part repulsion at the portrayal of a God so seemingly arbitrary. So it is little wonder that the issue of predestination has continued to attract attention and to put other issues in the shade.[4]

Others have found the solution in 9.30–10.17. In this passage Paul

---

1984); **Schoeps**, *Paul* 235-45; **Stowers**, *Rereading* 285-316; **Strecker**, *Theologie* 215-22; **P. Tomson**, "The Names Israel and Jew in Ancient Judaism and in the New Testament," *Bijdragen* 47 (1986) 120-40, 266-89; **N. Walter**, "Zur Interpretation von Römer 9–11," *ZTK* 81 (1984) 172-95; **Watson**, *Paul* 160-73; **Zeller**, *Juden* 108-37.

2. The triple attestation attests the solemnity of what Paul is about to say; he is speaking under oath.

3. Most often cited here are the words of Dodd: "a compact and continuous whole, which can be read quite satisfactorily without reference to the rest of the epistle"; "the epistle could be read without any sense of a gap if these chapters were omitted" (*Romans* 148, 149).

reverts, for the last time, to the theme of "righteousness" and "faith."[5] From this it can be concluded that in chs. 9–11 Paul has not after all switched the focus of his attention. The theological concern in the passage is still justification by faith.[6]

The dominant view, however, has been that chs. 9–11 are not an excursus or an appendix to an exposition otherwise complete in itself. Rather, they are to be regarded as the real climax of Paul's attempt to understand the place of Jew and Gentile within the purpose of God. In part this view stems from F. C. Baur, in his recognition that Paul's concern was not with individuals but with nations.[7] The insight did not resolve the problem of predestination posed in 9.14-23, but it decisively shifted the centre of gravity in understanding that passage. In part too the dominant view stems from a similar shift in perception of Paul's doctrine of justification — the recognition, in other words, that Paul's theology of justification emerged not as an attempt by Paul the individual to find peace with God, but as his attempt to understand how it was that Gentiles as Gentiles could be accepted by the God of Israel.[8] Particularly important has been the recognition that what was at stake was nothing less than God's own integrity, the faithfulness of God. How could Paul offer God's covenant righteousness so freely to Gentiles without calling in question God's covenant with Israel? And if God's purpose for Israel had been so frustrated, what assurance did that give to Christian believers?[9]

Since the theological rationale and the function of Romans 9–11 are so important for our own understanding of Paul's theology, it is worth documenting the grounds for this consensus position in a little detail.

The issue addressed in chs. 9–11 is posed in 9.6 and again in 11.1. 9.6 is widely recognized to provide the theme for the rest of the discussion: "Has the word of God failed?"[10] And 11.1 simply reiterates the fundamental

---

4. See particularly Dinkler, "Israel"; Mayer, *Heilsratschluss;* and Piper, *Justification.* The parallels with Qumran have revitalized the discussion; see particularly G. Maier, *Mensch und freier Wille nach den jüdischen Religionsparteien zwischen Ben Sira und Paulus* (WUNT 12; Tübingen: Mohr, 1971).

5. "Righteousness" — 9.30, 31; 10.3-6, 10; "faith/believe" — 13 occurrences.

6. So particularly Käsemann, *Perspectives* 75: "the doctrine of justification dominates Rom. 9–11 no less than the rest of the epistle" (citing Bornkamm, *Paul* 149); Bell, *Provoked* 55, who also cites Müller, *Gottes Gerechtigkeit* (§14 n. 1) 107-8, and Stuhlmacher, *Gerechtigkeit* (§14 n. 1) 91, 98.

7. See the quotations in Bell, *Provoked* 46-47.

8. The chief credit for this in recent years belongs to Stendahl, *Paul* (§14 n. 1) 3-4. See further above §14.1.

9. See, e.g., Davies, "Paul and the People of Israel"; Cranfield, *Romans* 446; Beker, *Paul* 331-32; "The Faithfulness of God and the Priority of Israel in Paul's Letter to the Romans," *HTR* 79 (1986) 10-16; Campbell, "Freedom."

10. See those cited in my *Romans* 539.

issue: "Has God repudiated his people?" But that was the issue already posed in the opening indictment of the letter. As we have seen (§5.4), central to that indictment was the claim that Jews could not escape the same indictment (2.1-29). Which inevitably raised the issue: "What then is the advantage of the Jew?" (3.1); "If some have been unfaithful, has their unfaithfulness done away with the faithfulness of God?" (3.3). That was an uncomfortable question which Paul the Jew had been unable to take up at that point in his exposition.[11] Now, however, the question can no longer be avoided. If Jews are as much in need of God's grace in Christ as any Gentiles, then what does that say about God's original choice of Israel? Is Israel still God's chosen people?

Romans, after all, is an exposition of God's righteousness (1.17). And, again as we have seen, the righteousness of God denotes the fulfilment of his obligation to the people chosen by him to be his covenant partner (§14.2). In other words, God's righteousness vis-à-vis Israel and his faithfulness towards Israel are overlapping concepts.[12] So when Paul's gospel seems to indicate that Israel's special status before God is no longer in effect or no longer effective, that puts a question mark against God's commitment to Israel — that is, against his faithfulness to Israel — that is, against his righteousness. Unless that issue can be clarified, not only does Israel's status remain in question, but Paul's own gospel (as the gospel of God's righteousness) is thrown into confusion. This was an issue which Paul simply could not avoid in what was the most sustained and systematic exposition of his theology.

Paul has also taken care in constructing the climax of the preceding section, through the second half of Romans 8, to strike notes which together build up to the swelling theme: What then of Israel? In particular, from 8.27 on he uses a cluster of terms to describe believers which are drawn immediately from Israel's own self-description — "saints" (8.27), "those who love God," "the called" (8.28), "the elect of God" (8.33).[13] To use such terms with such a transferred reference inevitably implies the question: Have the status and privileges denoted by these terms now been transferred from Israel, to be applied solely to believers in Messiah Jesus? Paul's evocation of the sacrifice of Isaac (8.32) poses a similar question: Has any significance which

11. For details see my *Romans* 128-44.

12. Note the parallel terms in 3.3-5 — God's faithfulness, God's truth, God's righteousness; details in my *Romans* 132-34; see further above §14.2.

13. "Saints *(hagioi)"* — see, e.g., my *Romans* 19-20; D. P. Wright, *ABD* 3.238-39; and above §2 n. 90. "Those who love God" — see, e.g., Mayer, *Heilsratschluss* 144-49, 152-54; my *Romans* 481; and above §2 n. 89. "The elect of God" — see, e.g., G. Schrenk, *TDNT* 4.182-84; my *Romans* 502; and above §2 n. 91. "The called" is a less prominent epithet, but the idea of a sacred feast as a "holy convocation" *(klētē hagia)* was familiar from Leviticus 23, and one of the titles for the sons of light in the final battle in the War scroll of Qumran is "the called of God" (1QM 3.2; 4.11).

has become attached to that powerfully symbolic act[14] now been absorbed wholly by the death of Jesus, with beneficial effects only for those who confessed Christ crucified?

Paul evidently takes similar care to dovetail the beginning of his discussion in chs. 9–11 into what he has just been saying about the privileges now enjoyed by believers. He begins by listing the blessings of his kinsfolk in terms of the flesh. "They are Israelites:[15] theirs is the adoption, the glory, and the covenants, the law, the service, and the promises; theirs are the fathers and from them came the Christ insofar as the flesh is concerned" (9.4-5).[16] But of course he was well aware that he had just been speaking about several of these blessings as the blessings of believers.

He starts deliberately with (1) "adoption" and (2) "glory," for it was precisely these two terms which stood at the centre of his exposition in 8.15-23.[17] (3) "Covenant" is not a term which Paul uses much, but the covenant theology of Deuteronomy and of "God's righteousness" underlay much of his earlier discussion.[18] And Paul certainly understood his gospel as the gospel of "the new covenant."[19] In view of the long running debates about Paul and the law, it is notable that Paul counts (4) "the giving of the law" as one of Israel's blessings. Again it will hardly be an accident that his very next reference to the law (9.31) indicates a goal ("the law of righteousness") missed by Israel but achieved by Gentiles (9.30). (5) "The service" *(latreia)* certainly refers to the worship in the temple cult.[20] But this too, in more spiritualized (or secularized!) form, was also something which Paul expected his readers to engage in (12.1).[21] The point is once again more obvious with (6) "the promises," since the promise stood so much at the heart of Paul's discussion of how Gentiles could count themselves sharers in Abraham's

14. See above §9.4.

15. "They *are* Israelites," not "were Israelites" (Osten-Sacken, *Dialogue* 20; Fitzmyer, *Romans* 545).

16. The list is carefully structured; see my *Romans* 522.

17. "Adoption" — 8.15, 23; 9.4; elsewhere in the undisputed Paulines only Gal. 4.5. "Glory" — 8.18, 21; 9.4, 23; "glorified" — 8.30. The use and repetition of *huiothesia* ("adoption") is particularly striking, since the term was not characteristically Jewish, but the underlying thought was — Israel chosen to be God's son(s) (e.g., Deut. 14.1; Isa. 43.6; Jer. 31.9; Hos. 1.10; Wis. 9.7); see also above §16.5c.

18. See above §14.2.

19. 1 Cor. 11.25; 2 Cor. 3.6; cf. Rom. 7.6; Gal. 3.15, 17. Note also how "covenant" reemerges at the climax of his discussion (11.27). See further Merklein, "Der (neue) Bund"; but also §6 n. 94 above and §22.3 below.

20. Cf. Josh. 22.27; 1 Chron. 28.13; 1 Macc. 2.22; Philo, *Decal.* 158; *Spec. Leg.* 2.167; Josephus, *War* 2.409; Heb. 9.1, 6.

21. These (Rom. 9.4; 12.1) are the only two uses of *latreia* in the Pauline letters. Note also the verb *latreuō* ("serve") in Rom. 1.9 and Phil. 3.3. See further below §20.3.

heritage and blessing.[22] The point is: *Gentiles* were sharers in *Israel's* promises. Even (7) "the fathers," who clearly denote the patriarchs,[23] were now
to be regarded as shared with believing Gentiles — "Abraham our forefather"
(4.1), "the father of us all," "father of many nations" (4.16-18).[24] And we
need hardly say more about (8) "the Christ" — Israel's hoped-for Messiah,
now the focus of the gospel for Jew and Gentile alike.

It can hardly be doubted that in amassing this list of Israel's blessings, Paul was deliberately posing a question: if these are Israel's blessings,
then what does the fact that others now rejoice in them say about Israel?
Equally pressing is the other side of the same question: if these are Israel's
blessings, and yet Paul's kin are in mortal peril of being "anathema from
the Christ" (9.3),[25] how secure are these same blessings for those, Gentile
and Jew, who now rejoice in them? How could Paul be so confident in
God's faithfulness to those in Christ (8.28-39), if God's faithfulness to Israel
seems to have been so ineffective and Israel's standing now caused him
such anguish (9.2)?

In short, then, the issue which confronts us in Romans 9–11 is not
simply a technical or literary one. It is not simply a question of how to make
sense of the flow and coherence of the letter to the Romans itself. The issue
is preeminently a theological one, and was so for Paul himself — which is
why we have to take proper account of it in our treatment of Paul's theology.
And as such it was so important to Paul that he devoted about one-fifth of
Romans to it, and the most lengthy single sustained discussion in all that he
wrote. Which is why we can hardly avoid giving it separate treatment.

§19.2 Who is Israel (9.6)?

The fundamental theological issue posed in Romans 9–11, therefore, is nothing
less than God, or, to be more precise, the faithfulness of God. "Has the word
of God failed?" (9.6). Paul, however, does not pose it as an issue. He simply
denies that that could be the case: "It is *not* as though the word of God has

---

22. *Epangelia,* "promise" — Rom. 4.13, 14, 16, 20; 9.4, 8, 9; 15.8 (it is no accident
that the term appears just at these point in Romans — 15.8 is the final summation of Paul's
theological exposition in Romans); Gal. 3.14, 16-18, 21-22, 29; 4.23, 28.

23. See G. Schrenk, *TDNT* 5.976-77; H. Ringgren, *TDOT* 1.10-12. Note not least
again 15.8 — "the promises of the fathers."

24. The implication is the same in 11.16, 18 ("the root"); see below §19.5b.

25. There is almost certainly an echo here of Exod. 32.32: Paul was confronted,
as Moses had been, with the real prospect of Israel's rejection — "accursed," like Achan
(Josh. 6.17-18; 7.1, 11-13; 22.20; 1 Chron. 2.7); such was his anguish at the prospect that
he offered to "stand in" for his kinspeople. See further my *Romans* 524-25.

failed" (9.6a).[26] Instead he immediately shifts the issue to Israel: "For not all those from Israel are Israel" (9.6b). It is the identity of Israel, of who makes up "Israel," which becomes the focus of his exposition. The reason is fairly obvious. Because God is the God of Israel,[27] the question of *God's* faithfulness boils down at this point to the question, Who is *Israel?*

It is important to notice, right away, the change of vocabulary. In the earlier stage of Paul's exposition in Romans, Paul developed his argument in terms of "Jews" and "Greeks" or "Jews" and "Gentiles."[28] In chs. 9–11 he does not wholly abandon that language.[29] But now a new term is introduced (9.6) and becomes the dominant term — "Israel."[30] This denotes a shift in perspective, the significance of which is usually missed.

The point is that the term "Jew" *(Ioudaios)* begins as a geographical and ethnic identifier. *Ioudaioi,* "Jews," are the people who live in or come from *Ioudaia,* "Judea";[31] as an adjective, *Ioudaios* can also be translated "Judean."[32] "Jews," as an identifier, thus lends itself to distinguishing "Jews" from peoples who come from other regions or countries.[33] Hence "Jew" is the term used when that sort of distinction is being evoked or implied. It is used by both Jews and non-Jews when referring to the Jewish people as it were from the outside, from a spectator vantage point, to distinguish the group called "Jews" from other ethnic groups. There is nothing negative or hostile as such in this usage; it is simply a matter of differentiated description.[34]

"Israel," on the other hand, denotes an "insider" perspective.[35] It

---

26. Similarly 3.3-5. On the use of scripture in Romans 9–11 see above §7 n. 33.

27. See above §2.5.

28. "Jew and Greek" — 1.16; 2.9, 10; 3.9; "Jew and Gentile" — 3.29; also "Jew" — 2.17, 28-29; 3.1; also "Gentiles" — 1.5, 13; 2.14, 24; 4.17-18.

29. "Jew and Greek" — 10.12; "Jews and Gentiles" — 9.24.

30. "Israel" — 9.6, 27 (twice); 10.21; 11.2, 7, 26; Israel and Gentiles — 9.30-31; 10.19; 11.11-12, 25.

31. See BAGD, *Ioudaia;* Harvey, *True Israel* ch. 2.

32. Mark 1.5; John 3.22. This also reminds us that the usage only developed in the postexilic period (cf. particularly Josephus, *Ant.* 11.173); see also Cohen, "Ioudaios" (§14 n. 52 above).

33. See, e.g., the usage of Philo and Josephus (Harvey, *True Israel* chs. 4-5); and the list of nations in Acts 2.9-11.

34. This point is often misunderstood, particularly in reference to Luke's use of *Ioudaioi* in Acts; but for the most part his usage is similar to that of Josephus. See further my *Partings* 144-45, 149-50.

35. Cf., e.g., Sir. 17.17; *Jub.* 33.20; *Pss. Sol.* 14.5. See further K. G. Kuhn, *TDNT* 3.359-65; Tomson, "Names." Harvey objects to such "insider" language, but recognizes that "Israel" is the name for the people chosen by God, even when many of its people fall short. Harvey's real objection is to the idea that "Israel" was limited as a title to a perceived "pure or true Israel" — which is not the point of the "insider" terminology.

indicates a *self*-understanding, a covenant understanding. It is the self-understanding of a people who identify themselves as chosen by God, the children of Israel, descendants of the patriarch (Jacob/Israel) through whom the choice and election came. In short, "Jew" defines primarily by relation to land and by differentiation from peoples of other lands, whereas "Israel" defines primarily by relation to God.[36]

Paul's shift in terminology, therefore, is significant. His concern was not to merge "Jew and Gentile." In a strict sense that would be impossible; ethnic identity cannot be so simply changed. As we saw earlier, the term "Judaism" emerged precisely as a way of reinforcing that ethnic distinction as also a religious distinction.[37] "Judaism" by definition is something which only "Jews" can practise. That was precisely at the root of the problem for Paul the Jew who believed himself called to be an apostle to Gentiles. For as long as the understanding of God's purpose was put in terms of "Jew" and "Judaism," it was almost impossible to recognize any place for Gentiles within it other than as proselytes to Judaism.[38]

By switching terms to "Israel," however, Paul opened up a different possibility. For if the function of "Israel" as a name is to identify primarily by relation to God and to God's choice, and not by differentiation from other nations and races, then the issue of whether Gentiles can be included may be resolved on a quite different basis. Strictly speaking, it is not possible to include "Greeks" within "Jews"; that is simply a confusion of identifiers. But it might be possible to include "Gentiles" within "Israel."[39] And this in effect is what Paul attempts to do in Romans 9–11.[40]

---

36. E.g., in the Gospels Jesus is called "king of the Jews" only by non-Jews; but by the chief priests he is called (derisively) "king of Israel" (Tomson, "Names" 280). Rabbis do not speak of themselves as "Jews"; "Israel" is their chosen self-designation (S. Zeitlin, *The Jews: Race, Nation, or Religion?* [Philadelphia, Dropsie College, 1936] 31-32). See further my "Judaism in Israel in the First Century," in J. Neusner, ed., *Judaism in Late Antiquity. Part 2: Historical Syntheses* (Leiden: Brill, 1995) 229-61 (particularly 232-36); also "Two Covenants or One?" (§6 n. 84) 107-13. The one or two cases cited by Harvey, *True Israel* 102, hardly disturb the weight of evidence or the argument of Tomson, "Names" 266-78.

37. See above §14.3a.

38. The tensions remain to this day. "Who is a Jew?" is a question which still racks the modern state of Israel. Are all Jews, wherever they live and have lived in the world, *de facto* citizens of the state of Israel? Are converts (proselytes) to Liberal or Reform Judaism to be recognized as "Jews"? For a discussion of the ancient issue conscious of its modern implications, see L. H. Schiffman, *Who Was a Jew? Rabbinic and Halakhic Perspectives on the Jewish-Christian Schism* (Hoboken: Ktav, 1985).

39. We may note, e.g., that Paul says "Jew and Greek," or "Jew and Gentile," but not "Israel and Gentiles." The near exceptions (9.30-31 and 11.25) arise because in these passages it is primarily unbelieving Israel that is in view, in contrast to believing Gentiles.

40. The logic of Paul's argument regarding the offspring of Abraham in Galatians

This line of reflection also brings out a further point which is frequently misunderstood. That is, that the theme of these three chapters in Romans is *not* "the church and Israel," as so often assumed.[41] The theme is simply "Israel." How is "Israel" to be understood? That also means, how is the new movement which Paul represented to be understood? Not yet as "church" in differentiation from "Israel," nor as "the true Israel," but as included in the "not my people" of Hosea (Rom. 9.24-25), as branches grafted into the tree of Israel (11.17-24). The point is that for Paul "Israel" is and remains the recipient of God's covenant blessings (9.4-5). "Israel" is the vehicle of God's saving purpose. So the theological task is to understand who is "Israel" and how "Israel" is to be defined.[42] Once that primary issue has been clarified, then the secondary issues of "Jew" and "Gentile" can be clarified in the light of that.

We should be in no doubt what is at stake at this stage in Paul's theology: not simply the identity of Israel, but the identity of Christianity also. For if church is not defined by differentiation *from* Israel, but rather by inclusion *in* Israel and identification with Israel's blessings, then Christianity's self-understanding itself is at issue. For those accustomed to centuries of confrontation of "Christianity" over against "Judaism" this can be an unnerving realization.[43] But it is unavoidable for any attempt to theologize with Paul. Not least there is the question of the full significance, not to say propriety, of Christianity taking over the scriptures of what is now another world religion — the Jewish Tanach (Torah, prophets, and writings) — and calling them its

---

3–4 suggests that Paul already had this theological argument in mind when he wrote Gal. 6.16; see further my *Galatians* 344-46. That 1 Thes. 2.14-16 is not at odds with Paul's theology of Israel in this chapter should also become clear, since Paul continues to speak here of Israel's failing (9.30-32; 10.2-3, 16, 21), and the realisation that Israel is currently filling the role of the "vessels of wrath" (9.23; 11.7-11, 15, 20-22, 25, 28-32) is one of the great moments of illumination as Paul steadily unfolds the meaning of his discourse (see also §2 n. 83 above). Similarly we may compare the use of the "hardening" motif in 2 Cor. 3.14 and Rom. 11.7. Contrast Becker, *Paul* 461-65, 469.

41. So, e.g., Eichholz, *Theologie* ch. 10; M. Theobald, "Kirche und Israel nach Röm. 9–11," *Kairos* 29 (1987) 1-22; M. Rese, "Israel und Kirche in Römer 9," *NTS* 34 (1988) 208-17; Strecker, *Theologie* 215.

42. Cf. and contrast Boyarin, *Radical Jew,* who speaks variously of "Israel according to the promise," "the Christian believers" (16), "recreation of Universal Israel" (48), "Israel according to the spirit" (74), and "the new Israel . . . ultimately the Church" (75). But note also his characterization of Romans 11: "This is an inner-Jewish discourse and an inner-Jewish controversy" (205).

43. See below n. 154. The sensitivities involved are nowhere more clearly indicated than by the hostile reactions by most Jews and some Christians to the self-styled "messianic Jews" — that is, Jews who wish to maintain their identity as "Jews" while also believing in Jesus as Messiah.

own (the Christian "Old Testament"). A Christianity which does not understand itself in some proper sense as "Israel" forfeits its claim to the scriptures
of Israel. Likewise, so long as Jewish-Christian dialogue remains a dialogue
between "Judaism" and "Christianity," it cannot really begin to engage with
the arguments of Paul. For the point is precisely that Paul, himself an Israelite
(11.1), seeks to understand his heritage as an Israelite and to claim a place
for Gentiles within that heritage. And he makes that defence in terms of the
understanding of Israel required by Israel's covenant beginnings and continuing obligations.

It is appropriate to include at this point our analysis of Paul's attempt
to make his case, since the confused identity of Israel is in effect another and
in many ways the most traumatic expression of the eschatological tension
outlined above in §18. The climax of "the process of salvation" (§18) will
be the salvation of "all Israel" (11.26). Up till the end of Romans 8 Paul's
exposition of the tension and process could have been understood in solely
individual terms. Now he makes clear what was only implicit before —
implicit in the "in Christ" (etc.) motif, and in the use of Israel terms to describe
Christian converts — that Christian identity is unavoidably corporate and
bound up with the identity of Israel. But the identity of Israel itself is now in
question, precisely because Israel too is caught up in the overlap of the ages,
caught between the times. It is no accident, then, that "Israel" appears in both
parts of the basic assertion: "not all from Israel are Israel" (9.6). For just like
the "I" (and the law) of 7.14-25, the "I" of Israel is also divided. It is divided
between the Israel of the old covenant, and, or so we might say, the Israel of
the new covenant, consisting of believing Jew and Gentile.[44] But the Israel
prior to the coming of faith (Gal. 3.19-24), the Israel over whose mind a veil
(the veil of Moses) still lies (2 Cor. 3.14), the "Jew" still boasting in privileged
status before God (Rom. 2.17-29; 3.27-29), is still the "I" of Israel. As the
individual can look for the resolution of the tension in the resurrection of the
body, so Israel can look for resolution of the tension in parousia and salvation
(11.26). But in the meantime "the elect of God" are split between Jew and
Christian, and that split will continue until Messiah, the deliverer, comes
(11.27).

To put it thus anticipates the results of the analysis of Romans 9–11,
but the preliminary overview helps clarify the theological perspective which
Paul himself brought to the task. Paul's own development of his exposition
is much more subtle.[45] His endeavour is to define the identity of "Israel," but
to do so in such a way as to make clear (a) how it can be that other nations

---

44. I should perhaps note that this is my own reformulation of Paul's argument,
as a way of bringing out Paul's own point.
45. See the analysis in my *Romans* 519.

are partaking of Israel's heritage through the gospel, (b) while his own kinsfolk are missing out on the gospel, and (c) how that anomaly will be resolved. But all this is unfolded little by little. Paul indicates at the beginning that there is something seriously wrong with regard to his kinspeople, despite all their wonderful blessings (9.1-5). But he does not make immediately clear what the problem is; that only becomes clearer through 9.31-33 and 10.21, until the clearest statement in ch. 11. Paul's tactic in chs. 9–11, in fact, is very much like his tactic in ch. 2. His exposition begins with theological affirmations which his own people would hardly dispute, but then he slowly unveils the logic which maintains the tension until its final resolution.

It is necessary to appreciate Paul's tactic and overall plan, since failure to do so too easily allows the commentator to be sidetracked into debates about predestination[46] or to be confused about the relation between chs. 9 and 11 in particular.[47] But to illuminate these greater subtleties in Paul's theology it is necessary to follow through his train of thought in more detail.

§19.3 The character of Israel's election (9.7-29)

Paul's first step is to clarify the identity of the Israel of God's purpose. He poses a conundrum: "Not all from Israel are Israel" (9.6). There is a great temptation to resolve the conundrum immediately, to jump at once to a clear distinction between "old Israel" (the Jews) and "new Israel" (Christians), as though that solved the problem addressed by Paul at a stroke — and some fall into that trap.[48] A more obvious resolution of the conundrum is that Paul was alluding to the concept of the remnant.[49] And that makes better sense, in that Paul does take up this point subsequently.[50] But neither solution is sufficiently sensitive to Paul's tactic in slowly unfolding his own answer to the conundrum. The identity of Israel, we might say, is itself part of the already–not yet. And as attempts to cut short the eschatological tension precipitately at the level of individual spirituality are usually disastrous, so here attempts to resolve the identity of "Israel" too quickly are likely to be disastrous for

---

46. It is only by limiting his discussion to 9.1-23 that Piper, *Justification*, is able to maintain his thesis that election in that passage concerns individuals and their eternal destinies.

47. Several commentators conclude that there is "a decisive contradiction between 9.6-13 and 11.1-32" (Dinkler, "Historical and Eschatological Israel" 116; similarly Walter, "Interpretation" 173-6; Watson, *Paul* 168-70; Räisänen, "Römer 9–11" 2893, 2910-12, 1927-28, 2930-35). On the unity of chs. 9–11, however, see Lübking, *Paulus* 135-56. See further my *Romans* 540.

48. See above n. 41. See also below n. 155.

49. Schoeps, *Paul* 239; Fitzmyer, *Romans* 560 ("Jewish Christians").

50. 9.27; 11.3, 5. On the idea of the "remnant" see below nn. 72 and 110.

a proper appreciation of Paul's own answer. To appreciate Paul's theology at this point we need to empathize with his way of theologizing.

a) *Rom. 9.7-13.* The key word in the first phase of Paul's exposition (9.7-29) is *kaleō,* "call."[51] It is the key term in the crucial statements of both 9.7-9 and 9.10-13. And it is the key term which brings the exposition of God's mercy and wrath (9.14-23) back to the central line of Paul's argument (9.24-26). The basic point being made in this section, then, is that the identity of "Israel" is determined by God's call. "Israel" is defined by promise (9.8) and election (9.11). Israel is the people called by God. It is important to realize that Paul is not denying Israel's election here;[52] he is defining it.

In the first part (9.7-12) of this initial phase of Paul's exposition, the two chief alternative definitions of Israel are confronted and dismissed in turn. First, Israel is defined *not* by physical descent. Not all Abraham's children are Abraham's "seed." Abraham's "seed shall be called in Isaac" (Gen. 21.12).[53] Ishmael, by implication, is not "seed," that is, not the seed which bears the promised blessings of Abraham (9.7). In other words, the children of God, "Israel," are so defined *not* by virtue of physical descent from Abraham ("the children of the flesh"); rather, "the children of promise are reckoned as seed" (9.8),[54] with specific reference to the promise that Sarah would have a son (9.9).[55]

The other alternative is dismissed in 9.10-12. As Ishmael did not constitute the promised seed, neither did Esau. What was striking in this case was the "election" (9.11) of Jacob over Esau while they were both still in the womb. So God's election did not depend on any good or evil they thereafter did (9.11). In other words, Paul reminds his readers that God's election does not operate on the same basis as his judgment. Judgment is of "good and evil" (2.9-10). But God's choice does not depend on the prior proven goodness of those chosen.[56] Nor is it "from works" (9.12). That is, it does not depend on proven fidelity to the covenant ("the works of the law"). The allusion to Paul's earlier exposition of justification is again clear.[57] God's purpose of election is determined solely by his call (9.12).

51. 9.7, 11, 24, 25, 26.

52. As Watson, *Paul* 227 n. 9; Räisänen, "Römer 9–11" 2900.

53. The LXX text of Gen. 21.12 gives Paul his first *kaleō* reference, where he obviously understands the term in a more pregnant sense than simply "named."

54. Note the strong echo of the argument in Romans 4: "promise" — 4.13-14, 16, 20; 9.4, 8-9; "reckoned" — 4.3-6, 8-11, 22-24; 9.8; "seed" — 4.13, 16, 18; 9.7-8.

55. The reference in 9.9 seems to be a combination of Gen. 18.10 and 18.14.

56. As we have seen (see above §14.6a on Rom. 4.4-5), Paul here was simply reiterating the basic covenant theology of Deuteronomy in particular.

57. See above §14.5d-g. The "works" envisaged are evidently not simply synonymous with "anything good or evil"; the range of actions envisaged could, of course, overlap, but the terms used look at and evaluate them from different perspectives. See further above §14.5.

In these two brief paragraphs, Paul has in effect summed up the earlier polemical exposition of his gospel and correlated it with the new issue of Israel's identity. The implication is plain: if Israel's identity as Israel is determined by call, promise, and election, then physical descent (ethnic identity) and covenant fidelity add nothing to that basic identity and should not be counted as integral or indispensable to that identity.[58] In effect, that is a reiteration of Paul's earlier argument in chs. 3–4. Now, however, his concern is to follow the logic of what that means for Israel. The subtleties of Paul's treatment are worth noting. They are not immediately apparent, but those who know how the exposition of chs. 9–11 finally unfolds can recognize the unfolding strategy.

For one thing, the implication is beginning to emerge that Paul is engaged in some role reversal. The traditional reading of the Isaac-Ishmael and Jacob-Esau episodes was that Israel is defined by descent from Abraham through Isaac and Jacob, and subsequently by the works of the law required of the covenant people. By pressing behind these episodes to the principle involved in them (promise and election) Paul has secured a point of critical leverage by means of which he can reinforce his earlier arguments by calling for a redefinition of Israel itself. In that redefinition, historic Israel may find itself no longer in the role of Isaac and Jacob, but in the role of Ishmael and Esau, that is, in the role of those who represent the foil to God's election of Israel!

For another, we need to note that the use of "Israel" on both sides of the opening statement (9.6) still applies. Historic Israel has not been denied or rejected. It is in effect the divided "I" of Israel which is being explored. The Israel of ethnic definition and covenant fidelity is still Israel. It may no longer as such be the Israel of God's call. But that statement can be rephrased: it is not yet as such the Israel of God's call. Israel remains caught in the eschatological tension.

b) *Rom. 9.14-23.* In this second part of the first phase of his exposition, Paul confronts boldly and without equivocation the dark side of any doctrine of election. The election of one implies as an unavoidable corollary the nonelection, that is, rejection, of another. Esau and the Pharaoh of the exodus are the prototypes. To "love" Jacob (that is, to lavish love on Jacob) means to "hate" Esau (that is, to withhold such affection from Esau; 9.13).[59] For the exodus to be a type of God's mercy it is essential that Pharaoh provide the foil as the hardened enemy of God's people. And Moses did not hesitate to attribute both roles directly to God (9.15, 17).[60] Paul con-

---

58. Cf. particularly Cranford, "Election and Ethnicity."

59. The quotation is from Mal. 1.2-3 LXX; see further my *Romans* 544-45.

60. 9.15 — Exod. 33.19: "I will have mercy on whom I have mercy, and I will show compassion to whom I show compassion." Paul would be aware that the repetition of the theme in Exod. 34.6 became one of the most cited and echoed passages in Jewish scripture and literature (for details see my *Romans* 552). 9.17 — Exod. 9.16: "For this purpose I raised you up, in order that I might demonstrate in you my power. . . ."

cludes: "so then, to whom he wills he shows mercy, but whom he wills he hardens" (9.18).[61]

Paul was quite clear that he was thereby portraying God in quite arbitrary terms. "What then shall we say? There is no injustice with God, is there?" (9.14). "You will say to me then: 'Why does he still find fault? For who has resisted his will?'" (9.19). Paul poses the questions only to deny them, of course: "Certainly not" (9.14); "Who are you, sir, who answers back to God?" (9.20). It is here that a full-blown predestinarianism seems to be the unavoidable logic, and Paul presses a little way down that road: the potter has full right to do what he wants with the clay utensils which he has made (9.21).[62] But to push further down that road is quickly to lose Paul and the thread of his argument.

There are three facets of the exposition of this troublesome section which throw light on Paul's theology, both of God and of Israel.

First, Paul does indeed stress the sovereignty and sovereign initiative of God. That was axiomatic for Paul anyway.[63] But the passage is not simply an exercise in dogmatic theology. The underlying thrust is to undercut any attempt to qualify the outworking of God's initiative by the terms within which God seems to have worked hitherto. The fact that he loved Israel/Jacob and hated Esau did not mean that God's commitment to Israel was on any terms other than divine grace. The fact that he had exercised mercy to Israel and had hardened Pharaoh meant that "Israel" was defined as the recipient of God's mercy, not that Israel determined the exercise and limits of God's mercy.

Second, it follows that Paul was attempting not so much to mount a theology of predestination as to criticize the theory which was presently in operation.[64] There was in effect a dogma of predestination which Paul had been echoing. It held that Israel was the sole beneficiary of God's electing purpose. That is, Israel defined in terms of descent from Abraham through Isaac and Jacob, Israel defined as the Israel brought out from Egypt by Moses. In terms of this dogma the dark side of election related only to Esau and Pharaoh, the non-Israel foil to Israel's election. But this is a dogma which Paul was in the process of undermining. The role reversal for which Paul's

---

61. Paul clearly echoes the language ("harden") of Exodus — 4.21; 7.3, 22; 8.15; 9.12, 35; 10.1, 20, 27; 11.10; 13.15; 14.4, 8, 17. A divine hardening, rather than a self-hardening, is clearly in view. But he also clearly anticipates the language of 11.7 and 25. See further my *Romans* 554-55.

62. The potter with his clay was a popular image for God in Jewish thought (Ps. 2.9; Isa. 29.16; 41.25; 45.9; Jer. 18.1-6; Sir. 33.13). Worth noting is the fact that the LXX of Second Isaiah uses *plassō* ("form, mould," 9.20) for God's election of Israel (Isa. 43.1, 7; 44.2, 21, 24). See again my *Romans* 556-57.

63. See above §2, particularly §2.4.

64. See my *Romans* 545-46.

definition of "Israel" was opening the way would amount to a turning upside down of that dogma. Was it so clear that the "vessels of mercy" were to be identified simpliciter with Israel, and that only the non-Israel of Esau and Pharaoh were the "vessels of wrath" (9.22-23)?[65] In short, the seeming arbitrariness attributed to God the Creator should prevent the created thing, not least Israel itself, from claiming or assuming rights before God other than as subjects of God's sovereign choice.

Third, within the light and shade of 9.14-23 the strongest note is that of mercy.[66] That is to say, Paul did not hesitate to state forthrightly the sovereign right of God over his creation, for he was confident that the ultimate purpose of God was that of mercy.[67] Again this is only implicit at this point, but Paul certainly had the final climax of his exposition in view (11.30-32)[68] when he developed this section. The negative line (Esau, Pharaoh, vessels of wrath) is thus held within a more overarching schema, the dark side of God's great composition which serves primarily to throw the positive side of God's purpose into still stronger light — God's eschatological chiaroscuro. Here again Paul prepares the way for a role reversal in which Israel has to recognize that it now fills the role of the "vessels of wrath,"[69] where it is Israel which plays the role of hardened Pharaoh (11.7, 25). And here again, therefore, we may say that Paul's theology of predestination is itself caught within the eschatological tension — the bright side of predestination as a function of the already, the dark side of predestination as a function of the not yet of God's ultimate purpose of mercy.

c) *Rom. 9.24-29.* In the final part of this phase of his exposition Paul begins to clarify whom these counters represent. He identifies first the "vessels of mercy": "By which I mean us, whom also he called, not only from Jews but also from Gentiles" (9.24). The claim of course is the one argued so carefully earlier on in chs. 1-4 — not Jews only, but also Gentiles.[70] But now the formulation is being used to identify the "vessels of mercy," and by implication, the Israel of which Isaac and Jacob were the prototypes. The Israel of God's promise and election includes both.

---

65. 9.22-23 — "But what if God, willing to demonstrate his wrath and to make known his power, bore with much patience vessels of wrath made ready for destruction, in order to make known the wealth of his glory on vessels of mercy, which he prepared beforehand for glory?" On the difficult exegetical issues of 9.22-23 see my *Romans* 558-61.

66. Verb and noun occur five times — 9.15 (twice), 16, 18, 23.

67. So particularly Cranfield, *Romans* 483-84, 496-97.

68. Verb and noun occur five times — 10.30, 31 (verb twice, noun once), 32.

69. Paul does not use the language of "wrath" again, but the thought is put variously in 11.8-10 (Deut. 29.4; Ps. 69.22-23), 11-12 (trespass, failure), 15 (rejection), 17 (broken off).

70. The reversion to the older Jew-Gentile differentiation deliberately recalls the earlier stage of the exposition; see above nn. 28-30.

And to underline the primary point — "Israel" defined by divine call — Paul then proceeds to document the character of this Israel and its constitution by citing two sets of texts. The first, from Hos. 2.23 and 1.10 (9.25-26), again indicate the character of the Israel called by God. Israel is the "not my people" called to be "my people," "the not loved" called to be loved, the "not my people" "called sons of the living God."[71] The second draw upon the concept of the "remnant" of Israel (9.27-29).[72] The Israel called of God includes also the remnant of historic Israel. The continuity and overlap of the two Israels, the divided "I" of Israel, is maintained. For the redefinition of Israel in terms of divine call does not mean a disowning of historic Israel, but simply a reminder of the character of historic Israel's call to be Israel.

§19.4 Israel's misunderstanding of its call (9.30–10.21)

Paul has now secured his base: when "Israel" is defined by God's call then it should occasion no surprise when the "not my people," the other nations, the non-Jews, are included within "Israel," the vessels of mercy. Now he begins to unfold the consequences for historic Israel. It means that the Israel which continues to define itself in the traditional terms of the law, that which separates them from other nations, is thereby failing to appreciate the role of the law. They fail to appreciate that the law is to be understood in terms of faith and in relation to Christ. And consequently they have failed to respond to the gospel. Again the argument falls into three parts.

a) *Rom. 9.30–10.4.* We have already analysed most of the argument of this paragraph. As we have seen, it summarizes much of Paul's earlier critique of Israel not only in Romans itself, but also in Galatians.[73] Here we can concentrate on grasping its function within the flow of Paul's exposition in chs. 9–11. What Paul is doing, in effect, is to argue that Israel's self-definition

---

71. The Hosea texts had in view the restoration of Israel, but enshrine the principle of God's call. The variation from the first Hosea text (2.23) is considerable, but the reference clear — Paul inserting the pregnant term "call" once again and omitting Hosea's talk of mercy.

72. The texts are from Hos. 1.10 (again) and Isa. 10.22-23. For the positive use of the remnant idea see Gen. 45.7; 2 Kgs. 19.31; Ezra 9.8; Jer. 6.9; 23.3; 24.8, etc.; Ezek. 9.8; 11.13; Mic. 4.7; 5.7-8; Sir. 44.17; 47.22; 1 Macc. 3.35; CD 1.4-5; 1QM 13.8; 14.8-9; 1QH 6.8. See further V. Herntrich and G. Schrenk, *TDNT* 4.196-214; L. V. Meyer, *ABD* 5.669-71.

73. See above particularly §§14.5g and 14.6b. Notable is the sudden concentration of the terms characteristic of the earlier discussion: *pisteuō* ("believe") — 9.33; 10.4, 9-11, 14, 16; *pistis* ("faith") — 9.30, 32; 10.6, 8, 17; *dikaiosynē* ("righteousness") — 9.30-31; 10.3-6, 10.

in terms of the works of the law (9.31-32) is a continuation of the misunderstanding of "Israel" already identified in 9.12. To continue to pursue the goal of God's requirement "as if it was from works" is to misunderstand the grounds on which Jacob was chosen and not Esau. This is the first explicit indication that Paul's anguish concerning his kinsfolk (9.2-3) has been occasioned by Israel's failure, and it begins to expose the role reversal implicit in 9.7-23.

Conversely, the reason why "not my people" Gentiles had been successful in attaining righteousness, even though they had not pursued it as a goal, was because they had done so in terms of faith (9.30). Without realizing it, they had enacted the key gospel insight that humans can only become party to God's righteousness through faith. Whereas Israel had stumbled at the call to believe in Christ (9.32-33),[74] the Gentiles found that their believing in the gospel of Christ had brought them to the goal which the law was supposed to promote.[75]

The point is restated in 10.1-4. Paul longs for Israel to become caught up in the process of salvation (10.1). But their zeal has been misdirected (10.2), and their attempt to establish righteousness as peculiarly theirs was a failure to understand how God exercised his righteousness (10.3). What Christ had done, however, left no further scope for that misunderstanding, and the success of the gospel of Christ in bringing God's righteousness to all who believe should indicate clearly enough that Israel's old self-understanding was now a hindrance to rather than an expression of God's righteousness (10.4).[76]

b) *Rom. 10.5-13*. This next part of Paul's argument is often misunderstood, primarily because it is understood in terms of a direct conflict between the law and faith, a conflict summed up in the two texts Lev. 18.5 (10.5) and Deut. 30.12-14 (10.6-9).[77] But our earlier explorations and now the flow of the argument of chs. 9–11 should help to gain a clearer picture.

First, we need to recall that Paul was not wholly antagonistic to the law. His critique was directed against the law in its role as Israel's guardian angel prolonged beyond its appointed time (Gal. 3.19–4.10).[78] And against the law as used and abused by sin (Rom. 7.7-25).[79] Here we have sufficient hints in the immediate context to reaffirm the same line: the "law of righteousness" as a proper goal for Israel's pursuit (9.31), a pursuit which had

---

74. The quotation is from Isa. 28.16 and 8.14. For details see my *Romans* 583-85.

75. Note again that the law is understood as a positive goal in 9.31 — "the law of righteousness" (see above §14.5g and below §23.3).

76. See again above §14.6b.

77. That a contrast is indicated is clear enough, but it is too quickly drawn into and interpreted in the light of later disputes; see particularly Käsemann, *Romans* 284-87.

78. I echo here the *prothesmia*, "(day) set beforehand" (LSJ, *prothesmia*) of Gal. 4.2.

79. See above §6.7.

failed not because the law was the wrong goal but because they had pursued it in the wrong way (9.32). The implication also follows that there was a proper way to pursue the "law of righteousness," namely, "from faith" (9.32). Similarly with 10.1-4. Once the force of 10.2-3 is properly understood, it should become clearer that it was the law as preserving Israel's distinctiveness which should be regarded as at an "end" (10.4).[80]

Second, when we turn to 10.5-13, we find that the first quotation is from Lev. 18.5. "For Moses writes with reference to the righteousness which is from the law, 'The man who has done the same shall live in them' " (10.5). This is a text which has also been much misunderstood.[81] As we noted earlier, it does not indicate that the law is a way to achieve or gain life; it was, rather, primarily intended to indicate the way life should be lived by the covenant people.[82] This, then, was what we might call a secondary righteousness, the righteousness which was the fruit of the primary righteousness, the righteousness from faith. Israel's failure was that it had confused the two, had given the righteousness from the law a more fundamental status — as something required of Gentile believers as much as the primary righteousness.

Third, the text which Paul then proceeds to expound in order to distinguish "the righteousness from faith" from "the righteousness from the law" (10.6-9) is Deut. 30.12-14. Now Paul would hardly have been unaware that this was a text intended to stress the relative ease of keeping the law (Deut. 30.11-14 LXX).[83]

> [11]For this commandment which I command you today is not too excessive, nor far from you. [12]It is not up in heaven saying, "Who will go up for us into heaven and get it for us; and having heard it we shall do it?" [13]Neither is it across the sea saying, "Who will go across to the other side of the sea for us and get it for us; and he will make it audible to us and shall do it?" [14]But the word is very near you, in your mouth and in your heart and in your hands, so that you can do it.

In citing just this text to expound "the righteousness from faith," it is unlikely that Paul intended a completely antithetical juxtaposition of law and faith.

80. See again above §§6.5, 14.4-5, and 14.6b.
81. Particularly when the emphasis is placed on the verb — "do" — as, e.g., Käsemann, who speaks repeatedly of "the demand for achievement" (*Romans* 284-87), echoing, no doubt, Bultmann's famous assertion that the effort to achieve salvation by keeping the law "is already sin" (*Theology* 1.264); and Schlier's well-known exegesis of the same verse in Gal. 3.12 (*Galater* 134-35); see further my *Romans* 601 and *Galatians* 176. The attempt to refer the verse to Christ (as by Cranfield, *Romans* 521-22) is still further away from the point.
82. See above §6.6.
83. The Hebrew version is cited below in §23.3.

Such an arbitrary exposition would have been too vulnerable to the rejoinder that Moses wrote these words with reference to the law. It makes better sense to assume that Paul is once again indicating a distinction between the law as characteristically understood by and within Israel and the law understood in terms of faith — the very distinction already made in 9.31-32.

In this exercise Paul was aided by the fact that other Jews before him had already expounded the same passage in a not dissimilar way. Baruch had referred it to divine Wisdom (Bar. 3.29-30),[84] which he then identified with the law (4.1). And Philo had used it with reference to "the good,"[85] with the Torah again understood as the embodiment of "the good."[86] In other words, Deut. 30.11-14 was widely understood to have a reference which transcended a simple one-to-one correlation with the Torah. Paul's exposition of the very same passage in terms of "the word of faith" (Rom. 10.8) is not so very different in character.[87] In other words, Paul here exploits the larger scope of Deut. 30.12-14 to indicate that what comes to expression in the law is not antithetical to faith. On the contrary, the law properly understood expresses that trust which is fundamental to Israel's relation with God, from beginning to end — Israel's righteousness properly understood as God's righteousness. That is what made it so different from the law understood simply as regulating life within Israel, the righteousness of daily living.

As in the two preceding paragraphs (9.30-33 and 10.1-4) Paul does not leave the contrast simply in terms of faith. The faith he is talking about is the belief that God raised Jesus from the dead and the consequent commitment to Jesus as Lord (10.9). It is that trust ("with the heart")[88] and that commitment ("with the mouth")[89] which receives both righteousness and

---

84. Bar. 3.29-20 — "Who has gone up into heaven and got it and brought it down from the clouds? Who has gone across to the other side of the sea and found it, and will gain it with choice gold?"

85. On "the good" in Greek philosophy see, e.g., W. Grundmann, *TDNT* 1.11-13.

86. Philo, *Post.* 84-85 — "What he describes as 'close by' and 'near' is the good. For it is not necessary, he says, 'to fly up into heaven' or to go 'to the other side of the sea' in searching for what is good. For it is 'near' and 'close by' for each . . . . 'For,' he says, 'it is in your mouth and in your heart and in your hands.'" Philo uses the same text also in *Mut.* 236-37; *Virt.* 183; *Praem.* 80, and alludes to it elsewhere (*Som.* 2.180; *Spec. Leg.* 1.301; *Prob.* 68).

87. Rom. 10.6-8 — "Do not say in your heart, 'Who will go up into heaven?' that is, to bring Christ down; or 'Who will go down into the abyss?' that is, to bring up Christ from the dead. But what does it say? 'The word is near you, in your mouth and in your heart,' that is, the word of faith which we preach." On the technique of adding explanatory notes, typical also of the Qumran commentaries, see my *Romans* 603.

88. For the significance of "with the heart" see above §3.5.

89. On the confession "Jesus is Lord," see above §10.4.

salvation (10.10). Repetition of the quotation of Isa. 28.16 — "Everyone who believes in him shall not be put to shame" (10.11) — locks the thought sequence into that of 9.30-33. And repetition of the thematic "all"[90] locks the thought into 10.4 — "to all who believe."

Equally important, however, is the reversion to the primary theme of chs. 9–11. What all this means for Israel is that the historical differentiation between Jew and Greek no longer amounts to anything: "there is no distinction between Jew and Greek" (10.12). The determinative category is now the "all who believe" in the one who is "Lord of all, rich to all who call upon him" (10.12). In the Adam phase of human history it was the universal sway of sin which diminished differences between Jew and Greek to insignificance (3.22-23).[91] Now it is the universal sway of Christ as Lord and the openness of God's grace to *all* who believe which leaves the Jew without historic Israel's advantage over Greek. Here God's openness in Christ to the "all who trust" corresponds to the definition of Israel in terms of God's call (9.7-13, 24-26). In the definition of Israel, the correlate to God's call is not ethnic distinctiveness or works, but faith in God's Christ. Here again the eschatological tension comes to the surface as the tension between "call" and "all."

c) *Rom. 10.14-21.* The purpose of the final part of the central section of chs. 9–11 seems to be straightforward, and we need not linger long over it. The purpose was evidently to fill out in more detail the initial contrast between Gentile belief and Israel's failure to believe (9.30-31).[92] The possibility of belief was open to Israel: the word which begets faith (10.14, 17)[93] had been widely preached, but "not all have obeyed the gospel" (10.16).[94] Israel had heard the gospel clearly enough (10.18). But while others had heard and responded (10.20 correlates closely with 9.30), Israel had remained disobedient and obstinate (10.21).[95]

The subtlety enters with 10.19. Paul had already asked "Is it the case that they have not heard?" and denied it roundly: "On the contrary . . ." (10.18). Paul seems simply to repeat the question: "But, I say, is it the case that Israel has not known?" (10.19). The repetition, however, does not simply invite the repeated answer. For Paul responds by first citing Moses: "I will provoke you to jealousy by a not nation; by a senseless

---

90. "All" — 4 times in 10.11-13.

91. The phrase used in 3.22 and 10.12 is the same: "for there is no difference (*diastolē*)."

92. The literary device of *inclusio*.

93. See above §17.3.

94. Here again we see that Paul does not hesitate to speak of obedience as an aspect of or even equivalent to faith (see below §23.3 and n. 44).

95. On the quotations used by Paul in 10.18-21 see my *Romans* 624-27.

nation I will make you angry" (10.19).[96] By thus bringing in the theme of
Israel "provoked to jealousy," Paul gives the first indication of the resolution to the problem of Israel's failure to believe. The unveiling of that
resolution awaits the climax of Paul's exposition in ch. 11 (11.11, 14, 26).
At this point, Paul is in effect indicating that the issue is not simply a matter
of Israel's hearing and disobeying. The matter is more complex. In terms
of our own theologizing with Paul, he is noting that Israel is still caught
between the times. Within God's greater purpose to extend his call to all,
historic Israel is no longer the sole or immediate beneficiary. In the process
of its salvation, Israel has still to experience the full anguish of the eschatological tension.

§19.5 Israel not abandoned (11.1-24)

In all this Paul has been walking a difficult tightrope. He has steadfastly
refused the easy solution, as we might say, of collapsing the tension. He
could not simply revert to his earlier pre-Christian position — the Israel of
God's call as ethnic Israel identified by its law works. But neither would
he resolve the issue by totally redefining "Israel" simply as those who
believe in Christ. "Israel" could not be so completely cut off from its history
and still be "Israel." But it is only now that he evidently felt able to begin
to fill out the fuller picture — a continuity through a remnant (11.1-6),
Israel's stumbling by divine providence, but with a view to a glorious
consummation (11.7-16), the olive tree of Israel with its message of hope
for historic Israel and caution for engrafted Israel (11.17-24), and the final
denouement (11.25-32).

a) *Rom. 11.1-6.* Lest the central theme has become obscured in the
interim, Paul repeats the principal question: "I ask, therefore, has God repudiated his people?" (11.1). And he responds with his characteristic "Certainly not!" The grounds for his assurance nicely document the tension within
Paul's conception of Israel on which he is playing.

We should note, first, that the wording of the question itself evokes
strong intra-Israel themes. For the only time outside a scriptural quotation,
Paul speaks of "God's people."[97] Talk of "God's people" clearly evokes

---

96. The quotation is from Deut. 32.21. Bell's principal thesis is that in citing Deut.
32.21 Paul had in view the whole Song of Moses (Deut. 32.1-43) and that Paul's
Heilsgeschichte was similar to that of the Song and of Deuteronomy as a whole (*Provoked*
ch. 7).

97. Elsewhere 9.25-26; 10.21; 11.2; 15.10-11; 1 Cor. 10.7; 14.21; 2 Cor. 6.16. But
in Rom. 11.1 Paul is probably alluding to the scriptural motif clearly echoed in the next
verse (11.2); see below n. 103.

Israel's traditional self-identification.[98] That Paul should use it here indicates clearly that Paul's line of thought is still caught (and deliberately so) within the tension of Israel recalled to its true identity as God's people. Similarly, the language of repudiation or rejection *(apōsato)* echoes the typical scriptural usage, where the thought of God rejecting his people was entertained as a prospect,[99] question,[100] or conclusion.[101] Paul's own question is posed as a question inviting the answer "No!" In effect it echoes the anguished incomprehension of those who have earlier wrestled with the same problem,[102] and the assurance that God's rejection was not after all forever.[103] The tension remains not yet resolved.

Second, Paul's immediate elaboration of his "Certainly not!" seems at first almost cavalier: God has not rejected Israel because he has not rejected me![104] But that is to miss the significance of the wording. For Paul deliberately identifies himself as "an Israelite, of the seed of Abraham, of the tribe of Benjamin" (11.1). That is to say, he identifies himself not as a "Jew" (historic Israel in its separateness from other nations). Rather, he identifies himself with the "Israelites" of 9.4. He blends his understanding of the "seed of Abraham" (Rom. 4.13-18) with his pre-Christian self-identification as "of the people of Israel, of the tribe of Benjamin" (Phil. 3.5). Paul, in other words, speaks from within "Israel," that is, as the divided "I" of Israel, caught in the already–not yet tension.

It is from within this tension, thirdly, that the second sentence of his answer gains its force: "God has not repudiated his people whom he foreknew" (11.2a). Paul could hardly be clearer: the continuity of Israel, of God's people, is unbroken. The Israel of God's call is still the Israel God called. The language of foreknowledge (8.29) and call (8.30), which undergirded the assurance of the Roman Christians, continued to give no less assurance to God's people, Israel.

98. E.g., 1 Chron. 17.21-22 — "Who is like your people Israel, one nation on the earth whom God went to redeem to be his people . . . And you made your people Israel to be your people forever; and you, O Lord, became their God." See further H. Strathmann, *TDNT* 4.32-35.

99. 2 Kgs. 23.27; Jer. 31.37; Ezek. 5.11; Hos. 9.17.

100. Pss. 60.10; 74.1; 108.11.

101. Judg. 6.13; Pss. 44.9, 23; 60.1; 78.60, 67; Jer. 7.29; Lam. 2.7; 5.22; Ezek. 11.16.

102. E.g., Ps. 44.23 — "Rouse yourself! Why do you sleep, O Lord? Awake, do not cast us off for ever"; Ps. 60.1 — "O God, you have rejected us, broken our defences; you have been angry; now restore us!"; Lam. 5.21-22 — "Restore us to yourself, O Lord, that we may be restored . . . unless you have utterly rejected us, and are angry with us beyond measure."

103. Using the same language, particularly 1 Sam. 12.22; Ps. 94.14; and Lam. 3.31.

104. See those cited in my *Romans* 635.

In this light, finally, the function of 11.2b-6 also becomes clear. It is not simply to assure the continuity of Israel in a remnant, of which the seven thousand "who had not bowed the knee to Baal" (11.4)[105] are the paradigm. It is also to remind Israel that the tension of belief and apostasy, of rejection and restoration, has been a repeated feature of Israel's history.[106] The seven thousand stand for the "now" already (11.5), over against the not yet of the rest of Israel's apostasy. Still more, it is a reminder that Israel, whether whole people or remnant, is always defined by "the election of grace," and "no longer from works" (11.5-6). The reemergence of the earlier keyword "grace"[107] underlines the character of election and the difference from an Israel defined by works.[108] It is the same grace of God, which "kept seven thousand for himself" (11.4), which is now determining this further remnant phase of Israel's history.

b) *Rom. 11.7-16.* Now at last Paul is able to bring out the full extent of the eschatological tension as it affects Israel and to explain his consequent anguish. He does so by restating the tension in terms of a triple distinction, between "Israel," "the elect," and "the rest" (11.7). "What Israel sought, that it did not obtain." That, in effect, is a rewording of 9.31. The balancing clause, in turn, echoes 9.30: "but the elect obtained it."[109] But then he adds, "And the rest were hardened." So, who are "the elect *(hē eklogē)*"? The parallel with 9.30 suggests the answer, "believing Gentiles." The contrast with "the rest" suggests the answer "believing Jews," "the remnant."[110] But the better answer is in terms of Israel caught up in the eschatological tension. For each of the terms sometimes merges into and sometimes stands

---

105. The quotation clearly has 1 Kgs. 19.18 in mind, but Paul has not bothered to give a precise quotation.

106. The tension is equally present in the factionalism of Second Temple Judaism, in the tension of the distinction in effect posed between "the righteous" and Israel (as in the *Psalms of Solomon* and the DSS), and classically in the famous affirmation of *m. Sanhedrin* 10.1 ("All Israelites have a share in the world to come"), with its subsequent qualifications. See particularly the sensitive discussion by Sanders, *Paul and Palestinian Judaism* 147-50, 240-57, 361, 367-74, 378, 388-406, 408. So here, Elijah "appeals to God against Israel" (11.2).

107. Rom. 3.24; 4.4, 16; 5.2, 15, 17, 20-21; 6.1, 14-15; see above §13.2.

108. The echo is not only of 9.11 and 32, but of the earlier 3.20 and 3.27–4.6. See above §14.5.

109.

9.30-31	11.7
Gentiles have attained righteousness,	What Israel sought for,
	that it did not obtain;
whereas Israel pursuing the law of	
righteousness has not reached it.	but the elect obtained it.

110. See the brief discussion in my *Romans* 640; on "the remnant" see above n. 72.

in distinction from the others.[111] And that reflects the character of the divided "I" of Israel — both the Israel which is currently missing out and the Israel which is already experiencing the eschatological grace in Christ through faith.

The note that "the rest were hardened" marks the beginning of the final phase, in which Paul begins to unpick the tight knots of his theology of election as developed in 9.14-23. For the term "hardened" is clearly intended to echo the equivalent language of 9.18.[112] There Paul drew the conclusion from the precedent of God's dealings with Pharaoh, that "whom he wills he hardens." Here the passive makes the same point: that the "hardening" in view was the doing of God.[113] The difference here is that it is now "the rest" (of Israel) who are in view. In the mysterious working of God's purpose of election, Israel itself is now experiencing the dark side of election.

The assertion is backed up by two striking texts.[114] The use of Deut. 29.4 (11.8) implies that Israel's present failure to respond to the gospel is simply a further example of the obtuseness which Israel displayed in the wilderness. The second quotation is more or less from Ps. 69.22-23 (11.9-10). By quoting it here Paul does what he did in Rom. 3.10-18. That is, he takes a text originally directed against David's enemies and turns David's imprecations against David's own people. This is the depth of Israel's present plight: their failure to respond to Israel's Messiah is not simply an act of disobedience (10.16, 21); it is also God's own response to David's imprecation against the enemies of Israel!

However, as in Paul's own rejoinder to 10.21 (that is, in 11.1-6), so at once Paul puts the present plight of Israel within the larger span of God's purpose. In 11.1-6 he looked back. Now he looks forward. The qualification is threefold and further clarifies the significance of Israel's role reversal.

First, their stumble is not so serious as it at first sounds. It is not a

111. Paul uses *eklogē*, "election," chiefly in Romans (otherwise only 1 Thes. 1.4) and only in Romans 9–11. In 9.11 it is part of the definition of Israel, and in 11.28 it refers to historic Israel, "beloved for the sake of the fathers." But in 11.5 it refers to the remnant, and here (11.7) it is distinguished both from "Israel" and "the rest." But "the rest" is also occasionally used for the remnant (Jer. 43.5[LXX 50.5 A]; 52.16[S]).

112. 9.18 uses the term *sklērynō*, as determined by the Exodus narrative (LXX); see above n. 61. But here Paul uses *pōroō*, in anticipation of 11.25. This latter choice of term may be determined by an allusion to Isa. 6.10, much used in earliest Christian reflection on Israel's failure to believe (Mark 4.12; Matt. 13.14-15; John 12.40; Acts 28.26-27). John 12.40 shows that Isa. 6.10 was known in a version using *pōroō*.

113. See particularly Hofius, "Evangelium" 303-4.

114. For fuller details of these quotations see my *Romans* 642-43, where I also note the considerable use made of Psalm 69 in early Christian apologetic.

complete fall, as, for example, the sprawling on one's face which puts a runner completely out of the race (11.11).[115]

Second, "by their trespass salvation is coming to the Gentiles" (11.11). The implication is clearly that Israel had to be put out of the race[116] (at least temporarily) in order that "the Gentiles" might be able to compete successfully. As we might say, Israel's early election had given historic Israel such an advantage in the pursuit of righteousness (9.30) that, had Israel smoothly taken to the new phase of the pursuit (through faith in Christ), Gentiles might have been wholly put off and missed out. Israel's disqualification was intended to open that righteousness to Gentiles more fully and more freely.

Third, but that was not all. For the further purpose was in view that the success of the gospel among Gentiles would then "provoke Israel to jealousy" (11.11). Paul elaborates the point in 11.13. This is precisely Paul's own purpose as an Israelite who is also "an apostle to the Gentiles."[117] He seeks to make a success of his ministry among the other nations, but not because he has disowned his own people. Quite the contrary. His full objective is to "provoke his kindred to jealousy" in the hope of saving some (11.14).[118] Here Paul gives a unique insight into his own self-understanding as an apostle. Once again he speaks self-consciously as both an Israelite ("my kindred") and "apostle to Gentiles." His concern was not to establish churches which were other than Israel. His concern was rather that the full scope of God's people, the Israel of grace, might be fully constituted. His own experience of being pulled in both directions was itself an expression of Israel caught in the overlap of the ages.

As one who glories in his people's identity and history, Paul delights in the prospect. The thought is so sweet that he repeats it: 11.12, 15 —

> [12]If their trespass means riches for the world, and their failure riches for the Gentiles, how much more will their fullness mean. . . . [15]If their rejection means reconciliation for the world, what will their acceptance mean other than life from the dead?

As in 5.9-10, the "how much more" nicely catches the eschatological tension — Israel caught between present failure and future fullness. Paul may have

---

115. So, e.g., W. Michaelis, *TDNT* 6.164; Cranfield, *Romans* 555; Schlier, *Römer* 327-28. See further my *Romans* 652-53.

116. Paul reverts to this imagery of the race at several points in chs. 9–11 (9.16, 31-32; 10.4; 11.11-12).

117. Paul explicitly addresses the comment to "you Gentiles." This is the first note of the warning which he will elaborate in 11.17-25.

118. We should note that Paul did not think his own mission alone was sufficient: his hope was only to save some (contrast 11.26 — "all Israel will be saved").

had in mind here the regular use of *plērōma* ("fullness") in Greek to denote the full complement of a ship's crew.[119] Without its full complement the ship of Israel cannot sail into the new age. Nor does Paul hesitate to set the whole prospect within a cosmic and eschatological framework. Israel's "already" rejection has meant "reconciliation for the world."[120] Its "not yet" acceptance will mean nothing less than "life from the dead," that is, the final resurrection.[121] The climax of God's final purpose as marked by the resurrection from the dead will be occasioned by the incoming of Israel.

The final verse of this part (11.16) provides a transition to the next part. "If the initial offering *(aparchē)* is holy, so is the mixture as a whole;[122] and if the root is holy, so also are the branches." The dispute as to whether "the initial offering" refers to the patriarchs or the first Christian converts[123] may be a further example of an either-or exegesis which has cut the tension of Israel's confused identity. The ambiguity of Paul's wording should probably be taken rather as an indication that he was functioning with both ideas. The early converts, including Gentiles, are the firstfruits of the complete harvest of Israel as a whole. The promise to the patriarchs is still at the basis of the whole programme and continues to provide assurance of God's faithfulness to his people (11.28-29).

With the second half of the verse, however, there can be little doubt that the imagery is of Israel as God's planting.[124] By "the root," then, Paul almost certainly had the patriarchs in view. "The branches" are the generations of Israel. Who all are thereby involved is what Paul will elaborate in the next paragraph. His first point, however, is to underline that the branches' holiness is dependent on that of the root. This, of course, is no reversion to a theology of sanctification by descent from the patriarchs. It is simply a way of saying that Israel's holiness is bound up with Israel's wholeness. God's call cannot have its full effect unless and until the all who are called are all included.

c) *Rom. 11.17-24*. The elaborated imagery of the olive tree is a fitting subject to serve as the immediate antecedent to the climax of 11.25-36. For the

119. LSJ, *plērōma* 3.

120. Note the variation on the eschatological tension — here between "Israel" and the "world"; cf. the more typical "Jews" and "the nations."

121. Most commentators recognize that by "life from the dead" Paul must mean the final resurrection (otherwise, Fitzmyer, *Romans* 613). Zeller, *Juden* 242-43, notes that in Jewish expectation resurrection of the dead was usually a presupposition for the restoration of Israel. Here as elsewhere Paul takes up and reworks traditional Jewish motifs.

122. Note the logic of the *aparchē,* with reference to use of the term elsewhere — particularly Rom. 8.23 and 1 Cor. 15.20, 23.

123. See my *Romans* 659.

124. Ps. 92.13; Jer. 11.17; *1 Enoch* 84.6; *Pss. Sol.* 14.3-4. See further my *Romans* 659-60.

olive tree is certainly intended as an image of Israel.[125] The use Paul makes of it is therefore highly instructive for our understanding of his theology of Israel.

First, we should note that Paul stays throughout with the imagery of a single tree. He does not even suggest that the tree might be cut down and replaced by another. There is only one Israel. The Gentile branches grafted into the tree (11.17) do not form a different or separate growth. They have status as belonging to Israel by virtue of having been given part in Israel.

Second, Paul starts from the basic distinction — Israel as the cultivated olive tree, Gentiles as from a wild olive. The identity of Israel begins, then, with the basic distinction of historic Israel from the other nations. The Gentile branches only flourish as branches by virtue of the root (11.18), that is, as we might say, by virtue of the blessings promised to the patriarchs.

Third, the principal thrust of the allegory is to warn Gentile Christians against assuming that the roles have been reversed, the tables turned.[126] The breaking off of the branches of historic Israel certainly was intended to make room for Gentiles within Israel (11.19-20). But that did not reverse the line of dependence of all branches on the historic roots (11.18).

Fourth, the basis on which branches have a place within Israel is faith. The natural branches have been broken off through unbelief. The wild branches have been grafted in and hold their place through faith (11.20). But that also means that unbelieving Gentile branches could be broken off again and newly believing natural branches could be, and will be, reengrafted (11.23-24).[127]

Fifth, sovereignly behind the whole proceedings stands God. It is God who did not spare the natural branches (11.19-21), and it is God who grafted in the branches of the wild olive "contrary to nature" (11.24). So also, it is God who may not spare the Gentile branches (11.21), and it is God who is able to graft in the former branches once again (11.23).[128] The olive tree, therefore, is a lesson in "the goodness and severity of God: to those who fell, severity; but to you the goodness of God, provided that you continue in that goodness" (11.22).[129] Here is the other side of the eschatological tension —

125. The image is not common in scripture (Jer. 11.16; Hos. 14.6), but Paul may have chosen it here because the procedures he was about to make use of allegorically were well known in olive culture (*OCD* 749-50), and the imagery of Israel as a tree was more widely established (see again my *Romans* 659-61).

126. Paul uses a more intensive form of *kauchaomai,* the term which so summed up historical Israel's sense of advantage over the nations (2.17. 23; 3.27-29); see above §14.5e. There is also a forward pointer to 12.16.

127. The allegory now strains the horticultural realities (dead branches grafted back in). But the allegory is driven theologically, not horticulturally.

128. The thought is the same in effect as that of 4.17.

129. For "goodness" see Rom. 2.4 and BAGD, *chrēstotēs;* for "severity, judicial strictness," see my *Romans* 664.

the goodness and severity of God corresponding to (Gentile and other) faith and (Israel's present) unbelief. Consequently, there is no room for pride, the antithesis to faith; only for godly fear.[130]

In a word, in Paul's hands, the olive tree (11.17-24) becomes one of the most striking and effective ways of indicating Paul's theology of Israel: that Israel was still the central subject of God's saving purpose, expressed both in his goodness and in his severity; that the identity of Israel as defined by grace and faith included both historic Israel and Gentiles; and that the process of salvation was still caught in the tension and uncertainty of the already and the not yet.

§19.6 All Israel shall be saved (11.25-36)

The final resolution, both literary and theological, comes in 11.25-27:

> [25]For I do not want you to be unaware, brothers, of this mystery, lest you be wise in your own estimation, that a hardening in part has come over Israel, until the full number of the Gentiles has come in; [26]and so all Israel will be saved, as it is written: "Out of Zion will come the deliverer; he will turn away ungodliness from Jacob. [27]And this will be my covenant with them, when I take away their sins" (Isa. 59.20-21).

The solution comes as the unveiling of a "mystery," the mystery of God's ultimate purpose.[131] That purpose, Paul can now reveal, always had in view the bringing in of the Gentiles.[132] This presumably was a conviction which

---

130. That "fear" is the appropriate attitude towards God is a strong feature of traditional Jewish wisdom (e.g., Pss. 2.11; 34.9, 11; 111.10; 112.1; Prov. 1.7; 3.7; Sir. 1.11-14, 16, 18, 20, 26-27, 30; 2.7-10, 15-17); similarly elsewhere in Paul (particularly 2 Cor. 5.11; 7.1; Phil. 2.12; Col. 3.22).

131. On "mystery" see above §12 n. 52.

132. That the "mystery" was God's purpose to draw all nations into the obedience of faith is spelled out more clearly in the addendum in Rom. 16.25-26. In the later Ephesians, this purpose to draw together Jew and Gentile as "joint heirs and joint members of the body and joint participants in the promise in Christ Jesus" is presumably understood as the means by which God will "sum up all things in Christ" (Eph. 1.9-10; 3.3-6). See further my *Romans* 678-79, 912-16; also *Colossians* 119-23. In arguing that the "mystery" here was revealed to Paul with the Damascus road revelation or soon after, S. Kim ("The Mystery of Rom. 11:25-26 Once More," *NTS* 43 [1997] 412-29) largely ignores the dramatic function of 11.25-26 as the climactic resolution of the dilemma posed at the beginning of the section (9.6); that is, the problem to which 11.25-26 was the answer only emerged with the continuing failure of the bulk of Israel to hear and believe/obey the gospel (10.14-21). Cf. Sänger, *Verkündigung* 181: the new element in the mystery "is limited to the meaning and function of Israel's *pōrōsis* (hardening)."

Paul rooted back in his conversion revelation — that God's Son had to be preached among the Gentiles (Gal. 1.16). Its scriptural foreshadowing he certainly saw in the promise to Abraham, that "in you all the nations will be blessed" (Gal. 3.8). But here it forms the resolution to the puzzle of Israel's unbelief. This was the solution to the puzzle: Israel was experiencing a "partial hardening," until "the full number of the Gentiles" had come in. Here again, then, there was no cause for Gentile self-congratulation or pride over stumbled Israel. All was in accordance with God's original and ultimate purpose.

Here at last the identity of Israel and its correlation with the elect of God are resolved. Parallel to the triple distinction of 11.7 (Israel, the elect, the rest) we now have "Israel partially hardened," "the full number of the Gentiles," and "all Israel." The first phrase indicates the whole people suffering from a partial blindness.[133] The second deliberately parallels the final full acceptance of Israel (their *plērōma* — 11.12) with the "full number *(plērōma)* of the Gentiles."[134] And the third extends the scope as widely as possible — "all Israel." There can be little doubt that by "Israel" here Paul means the historic people of that name.[135] 11.28-29 puts the issue beyond reasonable doubt.[136] But it is now Israel defined primarily by God's "election" and "call" (11.28, 29); the echo of 9.11-12 and 24 is equally clear. In other words, the split in the "I" of Israel will be healed. The division between historic Israel and those called of God will disappear in the "full number" of Israel and Gentiles. Paul continues to use "Israel" for historic Israel, but no longer in an excluding way.[137] When "all Israel" is saved, then the split in the people of God will be healed, the eschatological tension resolved, and the Israel of God made whole.

One of the most striking features of this last section of Paul's great

---

133. *Apo merous* should be taken adverbially, that is, "partial hardening or blindness" (BAGD, *meros* 1c; REB), rather than "part of Israel" (NRSV); cf. 15.15; 2 Cor. 1.14; 2.5.

134. On *plērōma* see above n. 119. But the term is imprecise. Paul's vision of the future is hardly clear in detail. All he gives expression to is his confidence in key aspects and principles informed by his basic twin conviction: God is faithful to his people; his purpose always included all the nations. But Nanos strains Paul's "Jew first, but also Gentiles" strategy too hard in arguing that "the fullness of the Gentiles" means the *initiation* of the Gentile mission (*Mystery* ch. 5, especially 272-73, 277, 287).

135. "The phrase *pas Israel* . . . occurs 148 times in the OT and always designates historic, ethnic Israel" (Fitzmyer, *Romans* 623). Against Refoulé's argument that "all Israel" = the remnant ("Coherence"), see Penna, *Paul* 1.318 n. 86.

136. "With regard to the gospel they are enemies because of you, whereas with regard to the election they are beloved for the sake of the fathers; for the gifts and the call of God are irrevocable" (11.28-29).

137. Paul continues to use "Israel" in distinction from "Gentiles" to indicate the boundaries which will no longer count for anything.

discourse on Israel is the absence of anything which is distinctively Christian. This is Paul the Israelite speaking. He does not weaken his commitment to the Gentiles in any degree. But he holds forth a hope for the final salvation of Israel which is characteristically Jewish through and through. To be sure, it focuses on the coming of "the redeemer from Zion" (11.26), on the coming of the Messiah, and not on the Torah.[138] And no doubt he has in mind the coming again of the Christ Jesus.[139] But the expression of hope is left in the vagueness of the wording drawn from Isa. 59.20-21.[140] Paul evidently wanted to word his hope for Israel in terms which would be most appealing and least offputting to those of his kinsfolk who had so far been repelled by the Christian proclamation of Jesus. In effect he invites his fellow Israelites to join with him in looking for the coming of the Messiah. In this common hope the divisive tensions of the between times, between historic Israel and the more newly called of Jews and Gentiles (9.24), can be transcended.

This note of reconciling hope is reinforced by the final passage of this great symphony (11.28-32) and the concluding chorus (11.33-36). For the theme throughout is the sovereign purpose of God. His purpose has been firm and unchanging from the beginning: "the gifts and the call of God are irrevocable" (11.29).[141] The God of Israel remains faithful to Israel; his righteousness endures to the end.[142] That purpose includes the mystery of disobedience preparatory to the reception of mercy (11.30-31).[143] And whatever the puzzlement and anguish of the period of disobedience, the assured final goal is "in

138. The suggestion that Paul had in mind an alternative way of salvation for Israel (particularly C. Plag, *Israels Wege zum Heil. Eine Untersuchung zu Römer 9 bis 11* [Stuttgart: Calwer, 1969] 49-61; F. Mussner, " 'Ganz Israel wird gerettet werden' [Röm. 11.26]. Versuch einer Auslegung," *Kairos* 18 [1976] 245-53; Gaston, *Paul* 148) mistakes Paul's tactic of deliberately imprecise definition. Similarly the reference to God's covenant leaves the matter more uncomfortably open for some. See further my *Romans* 683-84; Longenecker, "Different Answers," particularly 98-101; Fitzmyer, *Romans* 619-20.

139. Cf. particularly 1 Thes. 1.10; but also Rom. 7.24. See further my *Romans* 682. *Pace* Becker, *Paul* 471-72, Paul's hope for Israel focused on the parousia, not on a final mission (by himself) to Israel (11.14).

140. The last line of the quotation is almost certainly derived from Isa. 27.9; see above §12 n. 58. The vagueness includes the possibility of "the redeemer" being understood as Yahweh; several commentators assume this was Paul's own view (see, e.g., C. D. Stanley, " 'The Redeemer Will Come *ek Sion*': Romans 11.26-27," in Evans and Sanders, eds., *Paul and the Scriptures of Israel* [§7 n. 1] 118-42 [here 137-38]); but see n. 138 and §10 n. 11 above.

141. By "gifts" and "call" Paul presumably had in mind both the list in 9.4-5 and the "call" which was the main theme of 9.7-29.

142. See above §§2.5 and 14.2.

143. On the tight epigrammatic structure of 11.30-31 see my *Romans* 687-88. Note the "once/now" antithesis, the backward-looking eschatological "now" equivalent to the forward-looking "already–not yet."

order that he might have mercy on all" (11.32).[144] In the final paean of praise, it is God alone who is in focus (11.33-36); Christ is not mentioned. In Paul's vision of the climax to the process of salvation, this is the equivalent of the climax to christology in 1 Cor. 15.24-28 — "in order that God might be all in all."

§19.7 The final goal (15.7-13)

In assessing the function of ch. 9–11 within Romans and within Paul's theology it is often forgotten that Paul returns to the theme in what is in fact the climactic statement of the gospel and theology expounded in the letter — 15.7-13:

> [7]Therefore welcome one another, as Christ also welcomed you, to the glory of God. [8]For I declare that Christ has become servant of the circumcised for the sake of God's truth, to confirm the promises of the fathers, [9]and the Gentiles to give praise to God for his mercy. As it is written, "For this reason I will confess you among the Gentiles and sing praise to your name" (Ps. 18.49). [10]Furthermore it says, "Rejoice, Gentiles, with his people" (Deut. 32.43 LXX). [11]And again, "Praise the Lord, all the Gentiles, and let all the peoples praise him" (Ps. 117.1). [12]And again Isaiah says, "The shoot of Jesse shall come forth, even the one who arises to rule the Gentiles; in him the Gentiles shall hope" (Isa. 11.10). [13]May the God of hope fill you with all joy and peace in believing, that you may overflow in hope, in the power of the Holy Spirit.

Here we need simply note four features. (1) The linking theme to the preceding exhortation to the weak and the strong (14.1–15.6) is that of welcome. But whereas in 14.1–15.6 the primary appeal was to the strong to "welcome" the weak (14.1; 15.1), here the call is evenhanded, to both: "Welcome one another" (15.7). Since the issue addressed in 14.1–15.6 is primarily one occasioned by the sensitivities of Jewish identity,[145] the appeal for *mutual* acceptance and respect is important. Paul does not wish Christian Jewish identity to be abandoned so much as to be enlarged. The hope is that just expressed in the preceding verse: "in order that with one mind and with one voice you (together) might glorify the God and Father of our Lord Jesus Christ" (15.6).

(2) The continuity of identity with historic Israel's past is thoroughly

---

144. 11.32 is equivalent to Gal. 3.22-23: the "confining" earlier phase with a view to the fulfilment of the later phase.
145. See below §24.3.

emphasized: Christ the "servant of circumcision, for the sake of God's truth, to confirm the promises of the fathers" (15.8). That the whole letter was motivated by the objective of demonstrating God's faithfulness (= truth)[146] is clearly reaffirmed — that is, his faithfulness to his original purpose through the circumcision, in confirmation of his promises to the patriarchs.[147] The argument of Romans 11, or of 9–11 as a whole, was not an afterthought in Paul's theology according to Romans, but central to the whole. Christian continuity with Israel, but also the continuity of Israel remained fundamental to Paul's gospel.

(3) Equally central was the integration of — not assimilation to or absorption by — the other nations with God's people. It looks very much as though Paul held back from his scripture-permeated exposition in chs. 9–11 a group of scriptures which most effectively summed up his hope for the fulfilment of God's purposes. The point is subtly made. Paul reverts to the Hebrew hendiadys "truth and mercy" *(chesedh we'emeth),* so characteristic of Israel's self-understanding as God's favoured elect.[148] But just as he split the Shema in 1 Cor. 8.6 (between one God and one Lord),[149] so here he splits the hendiadys between the circumcision (15.8) and the nations (15.9); both are now embraced by the covenant mercy of God.[150] And in 15.10 the elaborated LXX version of Deuteronomy 32, the Song of Moses, such a foundational expression of Israel's self-understanding, gives Paul just the line he wanted. For the Greek turned the triumphalist Hebrew ("Praise his people, O you nations" — RSV) into something much more to Paul's point: "Rejoice, nations, with his people." The "with" provides just the note of integration which Paul evidently sought.

(4) The final sequence of texts can then sum up the inclusiveness of Paul's vision for Jew and Gentile within the community of worship and hope. "Let all the peoples praise him" (15.11), the "all" fulfilling for the last time its most characteristic role in Romans — "all," Jew first but also Gentile, Gentile as well as Jew.[151] The shoot of Jesse is one "in whom the Gentiles shall hope" (15.12). That Paul winds up his theological exposition with a triple emphasis on this "hope" (15.12-13) confirms its centrality in his theology.

---

146. See again above §§2.5 and 14.2.

147. The theme of the promises to the fathers integrates the expositions in chs. 4 and 9 (4.13-14, 16, 20; 9.4, 8-9).

148. See BDB, *chesedh* II.2.

149. See above §10.5a.

150. Paul left the connection of thought between 15.8 and 15.9 more obscure than we would have liked; see the discussion in my *Romans* 847-48.

151. See above §14.7a.

§19.8 Conclusions

In Romans 9–11 Paul bares his soul as nowhere else. His personal identity and the logic of his gospel were so intimately bound up with the call and destiny of his people.[152] Consequently, the resulting theology is more personal, and more vulnerable, than at any other point.

To be more specific, his vision of Israel's future was closely tied in to his own sense of calling as apostle to the Gentiles. His conviction and hope evidently was that his own missionary work would be a crucial trigger to the final consummation (11.13-15). His hopes of undertaking a mission to Spain (15.24, 28) did not mean that he foresaw a lengthy period of world mission still to be completed. On the contrary, he probably saw it as the final outreach to the sons of Japheth in accordance with the table of nations and its correlated geography, as originally envisaged in Genesis 10.[153] In consequence, the degree to which Paul's theology at this point was bound up with his own self-understanding as a missionary makes it difficult for the later theologian to disentangle the two. The obvious difficulty which results is that Paul's vision regarding his own part in bringing in "the full number of the Gentiles" was unfulfilled. He did not reach Spain, so far as we can tell. And the world mission of Christianity is unending. What then does that say regarding his theology of Israel and his hope for Israel?

Moreover, Paul's attempt to transform the categories has also failed. He shifted the discussion from a "Jew-Gentile" confrontation to "Israel." He attempted to redefine "Israel" as the called of God. And even when he continued to use "Israel" in reference to historic Israel he attempted to hold the category more open. But his attempt failed. Discussion quickly reverted to the more confrontational Jew/Christian, Judaism/Christianity, already in Ignatius.[154] And "Israel" became an exclusive and polemical claim, already in Barnabas and Melito — the church as the "new Israel" replacing the Israel of old.[155] When that happened, the theological hope (as well as the missionary

---

152. Rom. 9.3; 10.1; 11.1-2.

153. See further particularly W. P. Bowers, "Jewish Communities in Spain in the Time of Paul the Apostle," *JTS* 26 (1975) 395-402; Aus, "Paul's Travel Plans" (§24 n. 1); J. M. Scott, *Paul and the Nations: The Old Testament and Jewish Background of Paul's Mission to the Nations* (WUNT 84; Tübingen: Mohr, 1995); and above §12.4.

154. It is precisely as a differentiating term that "Christianity" first emerges in Ignatius (*Magnesians* 10.3; *Philadelphians* 6.1) — that is, Christianity as different from Judaism, Christianity defined as not Judaism (K.-W. Niebuhr, " 'Judentum' und 'Christentum' bei Paulus und Ignatius von Antiochien," *ZNW* 85 [1994] 218-33 [here 224-33]; Dunn, "Two Covenants or One?" [§6 n. 84]).

155. *Barnabas* 4.6-8, 13-14; Melito, *Peri Pascha* 72-99 (see again my "Two Covenants or One?" [§6 n. 84] 111-13). See also those cited by Fitzmyer, *Romans* 620.

strategy) of Romans 9–11 was already doomed, and the theology which Paul offered there was left prey to endless confusion and misunderstanding.

Nevertheless, it is there not least that the challenge of Paul's theology needs to be reevaluated and rediscovered. Here most of all Paul is and remains, like Elijah of old, a "troubler of Israel" (1 Kgs. 18.17). For on the one hand he insists to Gentile Christians that Israel still retains its prior place in the purposes of God; historic Israel is still "Israel"; they *are* Israelites (9.4). And he insists equally that Christianity cannot understand itself except as Israel, as branches of the one olive planted long ago by God. At the same time, on the other hand, he insists to his own people that Israel can understand itself only in terms of call and election, and not in terms of ethnic descent or "works." That is, "Israel" is always open to those whom God calls, who are "Israel" by virtue of that call and without further condition. The challenge is to both.

The challenge of Paul at this point, then, is precisely the reverse of what it has so often been understood to be. Traditionally Paul has been "apostle and apostate."[156] But that is the Paul of "Gentile and Jew," the Paul of separation and confrontation between "Christianity and Judaism." That is Paul as he has been interpreted by both Christian and Jew. The Paul of Romans 9–11, the Paul of "Israel," Paul the Israelite, speaks a different message and his theology offers a different potential — to build bridges rather than to sever them. The key question is whether the Paul of late Second Temple Judaism can be recognized by all concerned in this area to speak as an Israelite, as an authentic voice of Israel. The primary question is whether he can be recognized as properly representing both historic Israel's founding promise (blessing to the nations) and historic Israel's prophetic commission (as a light to the nations). Or, in a word, whether the hope he entertained for Israel (11.26), for the Gentiles to rejoice with God's people, for all the peoples to praise him (15.10-11), can be recognized as Israel's own hope. A positive answer would both revolutionize Christian theology and give fresh impulse to Jewish-Christian dialogue.

In the modern period we might cite as an example Ridderbos: "the church takes the place of Israel as the historical people of God" (*Paul* 333-34, though see also 360). Harrington, *Paul* 90, notes that Vatican II's *Nostra Aetate* 4, although presenting "a remarkably positive picture of Israel," still contains some expressions "dear to the Christian tradition . . . which [are] more at home in the 'replacement' or 'supersessionist' theologies represented by New Testament writers other than Paul."

156. I echo the subtitle of Segal's book on *Paul*.

CHAPTER 7

The Church

§20 The body of Christ[1]

1. **Bibliography**: **R. Banks**, *Paul's Idea of Community: The Early House Churches in their Historical Setting* (Exeter: Paternoster/Grand Rapids: Eerdmans, 1980; Peabody: Hendrickson, [2]1994); **S. C. Barton**, "Christian Community in the Light of 1 Corinthians," *Studies in Christian Ethics* 10 (1997) 1-15; **Becker**, *Paul* 420-30; **Beker**, *Paul* 303-27; **E. Best**, *One Body in Christ: A Study of the Relationship of the Church to Christ in the Epistles of the Apostle Paul* (London: SPCK, 1955); **L. Cerfaux**, *The Church in the Theology of St. Paul* (New York: Herder, 1959); **Conzelmann**, *Outline* 254-65; **N. A. Dahl**, *Das Volk Gottes. Eine Untersuchung zum Kirchenbewußtsein des Urchristentums* (1941; Darmstadt: Wissenschaftliche Buchgesellschaft, 1962) 209-78; **H. Doohan**, *Paul's Vision of Church* (Wilmington: Glazier, 1989); **Dunn**, *Jesus and the Spirit* (§18 n. 1) ch. 8; "'The Body of Christ' in Paul," in M. J. Wilkins and T. Paige, *Worship, Theology and Ministry in the Early Church*, R. P. Martin FS (JSNTS 87; Sheffield: Sheffield Academic, 1992) 146-62; **Fee**, *Empowering Presence* (§16 n. 1) 146-261, 604-11; **Fitzmyer**, *Paul* 90-93, 95-97; **B. Gärtner**, *The Temple and the Community in Qumran and the New Testament* (SNTSMS 1; Cambridge: Cambridge University, 1965); **Gnilka**, *Theologie* 108-15; *Paulus* 266-72; **M. Goguel**, *The Primitive Church* (London: George Allen and Unwin, 1964) 51-64; **J. Hainz**, *Ekklesia. Strukturen paulinischer Gemeinde-Theologie und Gemeinde-Ordnung* (BU 9; Regensburg: Pustet, 1972); **F. J. A Hort**, *The Christian Ecclesia* (London: Macmillan, 1897); **Jewett**, *Anthropological Terms* (§3 n. 1) ch. 5; **E. Käsemann**, *Leib und Leib Christi: Eine Untersuchung zur paulinischen Begrifflichkeit* (Tübingen: Mohr, 1933); "The Theological Problem Presented by the Motif of the Body of Christ," *Perspectives* 102-21; "Worship in Everyday Life: A Note on Romans 12," *New Testament Questions* 188-95; **Keck**, *Paul* 59-61; **W. Klaiber**, *Rechtfertigung und Gemeinde. Eine Untersuchung zum paulinische Kirchenverständnis* (FRLANT 127; Göttingen: Vandenhoeck, 1982); **H.-J. Klauck**, *Hausgemeinde und Hauskirche im frühen Christentum* (SBS 103; Stuttgart: KBW, 1981); **W. Kraus**, *Das Volk Gottes: Zur Grundlegung der Ekklesiologie bei Paulus* (WUNT 85; Tübingen: Mohr, 1996); **A. Lindemann**, "Die Kirche als Leib. Beobachtungen zur 'demokratischen' Ekklesiologie bei Paulus," *ZTK* 92 (1995) 140-65; **R. J. McKelvey**, *The New Temple: The Church in the New Testament* (London: Oxford University, 1969); **Meeks**, *First Urban Christians* 74-110; **Merklein**, "Die Ekklesia Gottes. Der Kirchenbegriff bei

§20.1 Redefining corporate identity

The sequence of Paul's thought is as much misunderstood at the end of Romans 9–11 as it is at the beginning. The key is to recognize that in chs. 9–11 Paul has in effect passed to the theme of the corporate identity of the people of God. That Christian identity is corporate was implicit in chs. 5–8 — in the Adam christology of 5.12-21, in the "in Christ" imagery of ch. 6, and in the "Israel language" of "the saints," "those who love God" and "God's elect" in 8.27-33.[2] But the predominant impression given by use of Abraham as the archetype of faith (ch. 4), and by the direct address and appeal of chs. 6–8, is that belief is something intensely personal. And so it was for Paul. That faith can never be something merely secondhand is a fundamental feature of his gospel and theology. But that does not mean that for Paul faith was only personal or that Paul thought of believers as able to enjoy a full relationship with the risen Christ on their own. The faith relationship was also corporate. And that perception is equally fundamental to Paul's theology.

But what was the corporate identity made possible by the gospel? As Paul's exposition in ch. 5–8 had raised the question, "What of God's faithfulness to Israel?"[3] so chs. 9–11 posed a crucial question in turn: If Israel is still the focus of God's electing purpose, but "Israel" not simply identical with ethnic Israel,

---

Paulus und in Jerusalem" and "Entstehung und Gehalt des paulinischen Leib-Christi-Gedankens," *Studien* 296-318, 319-44; **J. J. Meuzelaar**, *Der Leib des Messias. Eine exegetische Studie über den Gedanken vom Leib Christi in den Paulusbriefen* (Kampen: Kok, 1979; **P. S. Minear**, *Images of the Church in the New Testament* (Philadelphia: Westminster, 1960); **E. Nardoni**, "The Concept of Charism in Paul," *CBQ* 55 (1993) 68-80; **M. Newton**, *The Concept of Purity at Qumran and in the Letters of Paul* (SNTSMS 53; Cambridge: Cambridge University, 1985); **A. Oepke**, *Das Neue Gottesvolk* (Gütersloh: Gütersloher, 1950); **Penna**, "Christianity and Secularity/Laicity in Saint Paul: Remarks," *Paul* 2.174-84; **E. Percy**, *Der Leib Christi* (Sōma Christou) *in den paulinischen Homologoumena und Antilegomena* (Lund: Gleerup, 1942); **Ridderbos**, *Paul* 362-95; **Robinson**, *Body* (§3 n. 1); **J. Roloff**, *Die Kirche im Neuen Testament* (Göttingen: Vandenhoeck, 1993); **J. P. Sampley**, *Pauline Partnership in Christ: Christian Community and Commitment in Light of Roman Law* (Philadelphia: Fortress, 1980); **S. Schatzmann**, *A Pauline Theology of Charismata* (Peabody: Hendrickson, 1987); **S. Schulz**, "Die Charismenlehre des Paulus. Bilanz der Probleme und Ergebnisse," in J. Friedrich, et al., eds., *Rechtfertigung*, E. Käsemann FS (Göttingen: Vandenhoeck, 1976) 443-60; **H. Schürmann**, "Die geistlichen Gnadengaben in den paulinischen Gemeinden," *Ursprung und Gestalt* (Düsseldorf: Patmos, 1970) 236-67; **Schweizer**, "Die Kirche als Leib Christi in den paulinischen Homologoumena," *Neotestamentica* 272-92; **Strecker**, *Theologie* 190-98; **Stuhlmacher**, *Theologie* 356-63; **Turner**, *The Holy Spirit* (§16 n. 1) 261-85; **A. J. M. Wedderburn**, "The Body of Christ and Related Concepts in 1 Corinthians," *SJT* 24 (1971) 74-96; **Whiteley**, *Theology* 186-204.

2. See above §19.1.
3. See again §19.1 above.

what then is the corporate form of "the called of God," both Jew and Gentile (9.24)? If the people of God can no longer be defined simply in terms of lineal descent from Abraham (9.7-9) or identified solely by their works (9.10-12), then what are its defining features? What now marks out the Christ people?

It would be natural to assume from the flow of the exposition from chs. 9–11 to ch. 12 that the relation was one of contrast. In the modern period, from F. C. Baur at least, this contrast has been expressed in terms of national versus universal or exclusive versus inclusive. For Baur the dispute between the Petrine and Pauline parties, which dominated the development of early Christianity, was a dispute between Jewish particularism and Christian universalism. To Paul must be given the credit for delivering Christianity from the status of a mere Jewish sect and liberating "the all-commanding universalism of its spirit and aims."[4] Baur's influence on subsequent reformulations of this point has been more widespread and more sustained than most have recognized or cared to admit.[5]

But such a formulation is quite unsatisfactory. For on the one hand, Israel's foundational faith was equally universal. As Paul was able to point out in Rom. 3.29-30, the confession of God's oneness (the *Shema*) carries with it the unavoidable corollary that the one God is God of Gentiles as well as Jews.[6] Moreover, as a matter of fact, historic Israel had always been remarkably welcoming of the resident alien, the prosleyte, and the God-fearer.[7] The promise to Abraham of blessing to the nations was not forgotten,[8] Israel would be a light to the nations,[9] and the prospect of the eschatological pilgrimage of the nations to Zion to participate in worship of the Lord is a familiar theme in Jewish thought.[10] On the other hand, conversely, the new Christian movement was in effect equally restrictive and exclusive. If Judaism required of its proselytes circumcision and taking on the yoke of the law, Christianity no less required of its converts belief in Christ and baptism in his name.

---

4. F. C. Baur, *The Church History of the First Three Centuries* (1853; London: Williams and Norgate, 1878-79) 5-6, 9, 27-29, 33, 38-39, 43, 49-50, etc.

5. See particularly Ridderbos, *Paul* 333-41.

6. See also above §§2.2 and 2.5.

7. See, e.g., the data in my *Jesus, Paul and the Law* 143-47. Note the openness of the Temple to the foreigner in the consecrating prayer of Solomon (1 Kgs. 8.41-43/2 Chron. 6.32-33). See further Kraus, *Volk Gottes* 16-44.

8. In addition to Gen. 12.3; 18.18; 22.18; 26.4; and 28.14, note particularly Ps. 72.17; Jer. 4.2; and Zech. 8.13.

9. Isa. 49.6; 51.4.

10. E.g., Pss. 22.27-31; 86.9; Isa. 2.2-3; 25.6-8; 56.3-8; 66.18-23; Mic. 4.1-2; Zeph. 3.9; Zech. 2.11; 14.16; Tob. 13.11; 14.6-7; *Pss. Sol.* 17.34; *Sib. Or.* 3.710-20, 772-75. But note also 2 Kgs. 6.17; Ps. 87.4-6; Isa. 19.18-25; Jon. 3.5-10; and Mal. 1.11 (envisaging Gentile worship of Yahweh outside the land).

Discussion at this point can easily be caught in a category confusion. At a *theological* level it can be debated whether a gospel offered to all who believe is more universal than a confession of God as one. Or whether a requirement of circumcision is any more restrictive than a requirement of baptism. But at a *sociological* level it is not to be disputed that groups, however large or dispersed, have distinctive features which both identify them and mark them out from others. Groups can be classified as groups because they have some sort of boundary which distinguishes them from other groups. This is sociology's ABC. Where the category confusion bites for us is in relation, for example, to the much-cited text, "There is neither Jew nor Greek, there is neither slave nor free, there is no male and female; for you all are one in Christ Jesus."[11] For that is clearly a theological assertion rather than a sociological description. But this is a point to which we will have to return.[12]

Whatever the finer points of the issues just touched on, the question for us remains: If the called of God are not simply Israel, if "not all from Israel are Israel" (Rom. 9.6), then what is the corporate identity of the eschatological people of God? Paul Minear answered by pointing to no less than ninety-five "images of the church in the New Testament."[13] We will have to content ourselves with analysing four main categories.[14]

11. Gal. 3.28; similarly 1 Cor. 12.13 and Col. 3.11. See above §17 n. 10.
12. See below §21.1.
13. Minear, *Images*. Of those listed (not all of them properly "images of the church") the most important Pauline metaphors, apart from those examined below, are (in Minear's order): a letter from Christ (2 Cor. 3.2-3); the olive tree (Rom. 11.13-24); God's planting and God's building (1 Cor. 3.9); the bride of Christ (2 Cor. 11.1-2); citizens (Phil. 3.20*); the people of God (Rom. 9.25-26); Israel (Gal. 6.16); circumcision (Phil. 3.3); Abraham's sons (Gal. 3.29; Rom. 4.16); remnant (Rom. 9.27; 11.5-7); the elect (Rom. 8.33*); the new creation (2 Cor. 5.17); light (Phil. 2.15; 1 Thes. 5.5); slaves (e.g., Gal. 5.13); sons of God (Rom. 8.14-17* — asterisked references are my own). Kraus lists 15 images (*Volk Gottes* 111-18). It is noticeable that neither Minear nor Kraus includes "family" within his list. This is presumably because, while Paul uses the imagery of family *relationships* in writing to his churches (birthing — Gal. 4.19; father and child — 1 Cor. 4.15, 17; Phil. 2.22; 1 Thes. 2.11; brother — regularly), he evidently did not think of the assembled body of believers as *structured* as a family (father, wife/mother, children, slaves). The idea that *family* structures provide a model for *church* structures probably emerged as a corollary to the later adoption of the *Haustafel* form in Christian parenesis (see §23.7c below) and first appears in more explicit form in the Pastorals (1 Tim. 3.4-5; Tit. 1.6 and 2.5).
14. In view of Paul's limited use of the term "people of God" (all the references are in scriptural quotations or echoes — see above §19.5a and n. 97), it is questionable whether the term should be given a central role in analysis of Paul's ecclesiology (as most recently by Kraus, *Volk Gottes*), despite its value as a focal concept emphasizing continuity of and with Israel (Rom. 9.24-26; 2 Cor. 6.16).

§20.2 The church of God

The most obvious place to start is with the title "church" itself. *Ekklēsia* ("church") is the single most frequent term used by Paul to refer to the groups of those who met in the name of Christ.[15] He addresses letters specifically to "the church of the Thessalonians," to "the church . . . which is in Corinth," and to "the churches of Galatia."[16] He regularly refers to the churches, or specifically "all the churches" which came within his commission.[17] Clearly, then, "church" is the term with which Paul most regularly conceptualized the corporate identity of those converted in the Gentile mission.

Why this term? Older answers reflected on the etymology of the term — *ek-kaleō* ("call out"); so, "the church" as those "called out."[18] But although such an image would make a nice play on the idea of believers as "the called"[19] and "elect" *(eklektos,* Rom. 8.33), it is very noticeable that Paul refrains from just such an interplay of ideas. Similarly with the suggestion that Paul was influenced by the contemporary usage of *ekklēsia* for a popular assembly of citizens entitled to vote.[20] But here too the common thought is that of assembly, rather than of any particular kind of assembly. And again the absence of any playing-off of alternative ideas of "assembly" (as would have been possible, say, in 1 Corinthians 6 and 10) is indicative.

More plausible is the suggestion that Paul's usage was drawn directly from Israel's self-identity.[21] *Ekklēsia* occurs about 100 times in the LXX, where the underlying Hebrew is principally *qahal,* "assembly."[22] Most notable are the phrases *qahal Yahweh* or *qahal Israel.*[23] Since Paul speaks so

---

15. *Ekklēsia* — 62 occurrences in the Pauline corpus (most frequent in 1 Corinthians); elsewhere most common in Acts (23 occurrences) and Revelation (20) out of a total of 114 in the NT. Surprisingly Minear does not include *ekklēsia* in his list of images.

16. 1 Cor. 1.1; 2 Cor. 1.1; Gal. 1.2; 1 Thes. 1.1; 2 Thes. 1.1. Col. 4.16 refers to "the church in Laodicea."

17. Rom. 16.4, 16; 1 Cor. 4.17; 7.17; 11.16; 14.33-34; 2 Cor. 8.18, 19, 23-24; 2 Cor. 11.8, 28; 12.13; Phil. 4.15.

18. Cf. the curiously ordered article of K. L. Schmidt, *TDNT* 3.501-36 (here 530-31); Gnilka, *Theologie* 111.

19. Note the theme above in §19.3a — particularly Rom. 8.30 and 9.24.

20. So in Acts 19.39; see further LSJ and BAGD, *ekklēsia* 1. It was occasionally used also for business meetings of clubs (Meeks, *First Urban Christians* 222 n. 24).

21. Cf., e.g., Bultmann, *Theology* 1.94-98; Merklein, "Ekklesia Gottes" 303-13.

22. Reflected also in Acts 7.38 — "the *ekklēsia* in the wilderness."

23. *Qahal Yahweh* — Num. 16.3; 20.4; Deut. 23.1-3, 8; 1 Chron. 28.8; Neh. 13.1; Mic. 2.5; equivalent in Lam. 1.10 and Sir. 24.2; also Judg. 20.2 ("the assembly of the people of God"). *Qahal Israel* — Exod. 12.6; Lev. 16.17; Num. 14.5; Deut. 31.30; Josh. 8.35; 1 Kgs. 8.14, 22, 55; 12.3; 1 Chron. 13.2; 2 Chron. 6.3, 12-13.

often of "the church of God,"[24] it is hard to doubt that he had in mind this distinctive background. Similarly, his less frequent reference to "the whole church"[25] would almost certainly resonate in his mind with the frequent reference to "the whole assembly of Israel."[26] It is true that the LXX translates *qahal Yahweh* with *ekklēsia kyriou* ("the assembly of the Lord")[27] and also uses *synagōgē* for *qahal*[28] and that Paul makes no direct scriptural link between his own usage and that of the scriptures.[29] But talk of "the church of God" served Paul's purpose much better.

(1) It implied continuity with "the assembly of Yahweh," without allowing confusion over who "the Lord" might be in talk of "the assembly of the Lord."[30] Only occasionally does he bring "Christ" into the formula, and only once in the form "the churches of Christ" (Rom. 16.16). Otherwise he speaks of "the churches which are in Christ" (Gal. 1.22), or "the churches of God in Christ Jesus" (1 Thes. 2.14). The phrase "the church(es) of God" was too evocative and pregnant with meaning for Paul's deliberate use of it to be accidental. (2) There is no hint that choice of *ekklēsia* had in view some sort of polemical antithesis against the synagogue *(synagōgē)*.[31] In terms of wider Greek use *synagōgē* would have been equally as acceptable as *ekklēsia*.[32] But Paul never makes use of *synagōgē*, and the polemical thrust of Gal. 1.13 and 1 Thes. 2.14 is differently directed. So the argument is at best an argument from silence. (3) The easy way in which Paul refers to "the church(es) of God" indicates that he did not conceive of the implicit claim as polemical. It did not require scriptural proof. Allusive assumption, as with the equally key term "the righteousness of God,"[33] was sufficient for audiences and letter recipients well enough versed in the LXX.

In short, there can be little doubt that Paul intended to depict the little assemblies of Christian believers as equally manifestations of and in direct continuity with "the assembly of Yahweh," "the assembly of Israel."

24. "The church of God" — 1 Cor. 1.1; 10.32; 11.22; 15.9; 2 Cor. 1.1; Gal. 1.13; "the churches of God" — 1 Cor. 11.16; 1 Thes. 2.14; 2 Thes. 1.4; "the church in God" — 1 Thes. 1.1; 2 Thes. 1.1.

25. Rom. 16.23; 1 Cor. 14.23.

26. The bulk of the references to *qahal Israel* in n. 23 above.

27. But 1QM 4.10 uses the phrase *qahal el* ("assembly of God").

28. *Qahal = ekklēsia* — 69 or 70 times; *qahal = synagōgē* — 35 or 36 times.

29. J. Roloff, *ekklēsia*, *EDNT* 1.411.

30. We recall that *kyrios* in Paul, apart from scriptural quotations, always refers to Christ (see above §10.4 and n. 47).

31. Beker, *Paul* 315-16; against particularly W. Schrage, "Ekklesia und Synagoge," *ZTK* 60 (1963) 178-202.

32. See LSJ, *synagōgē*.

33. See above §14.2.

We can probably be more precise as to the immediate background of Paul's thought at this point. For it is noticeable how each time Paul speaks of his previous role as persecutor, it is as one who "persecuted the church of God."[34] This suggests either that the term was already in use in the pre-Pauline Christian community,[35] or that bound up with the revelation of the Damascus road was the realization that he had been persecuting what was actually God's (eschatological) assembly. Either way, the recognition was foundational for his whole ecclesiology. For on the one hand it implied the special status of the Jerusalem church as the focus and conduit of this continuity with the assembly of Yahweh and Israel.[36] And on the other, the fact that his persecution was directed chiefly against the scattered Hellenist members of that church[37] implies that from this earliest phase Paul saw "the church of God" as reaching out to draw in the other nations within its assembly.[38]

In the light of all this, Paul's own use and development of the concept becomes more illuminating. For one thing, he used the term freely for assemblies predominantly Gentile in composition. "The assembly of God" was now composed of Gentile as well as Jew. This is significant, since a not untypical concern of Jewish writings was to preserve the purity of the assembly of Israel, precisely by emphasizing its set-apartness.[39] Here, in contrast, we may speak of Paul as representing the more inclusive strand of Israel's heritage over against those who emphasized its exclusiveness,[40] though still not as an

34. 1 Cor. 15.9; Gal. 1.13; Phil. 3.6.

35. *Pace* Becker, *Paul* 427. Though usage elsewhere in the NT gives at best only allusive support for the thesis (cf. particularly Matt. 16.18; 18.17; Acts 5.11; 8.1, 3; Jas. 5.14).

36. The same inference can be drawn from Paul's use of "the saints" with special reference to the church in Jerusalem (Rom. 15.25, 31; 1 Cor. 16.1; 2 Cor. 8.4; 9.1, 12) and from his eagerness to make the collection for the poor among the saints in Jerusalem (Rom. 15.25-26; 1 Cor. 16.1-4; 2 Corinthians 8–9). Here again we note the taken-for-granted character of the belief within early Christian circles, which consequently, as with the messiahship of Jesus (§8.5 above), made further exposition or argument from scripture unnecessary.

37. See above §14.3.

38. Cf. particularly Roloff, *EDNT* 1.412; Gnilka, *Theologie* 109-11. The emphasis is already firm in 1 Thessalonians ("the church" — 1.1; "beloved" — 1.4; "elect" — 1.4; "called" — 2.12; 4.7; 5.24; Kraus, *Volk Gottes* 122-30), but is no less a feature of Paul's subsequent letters (as Kraus's analysis of 1 Corinthians, Galatians, 2 Corinthians 1–8, and Romans clearly demonstrates), so that 1 Thessalonians should not be regarded as marking out a particular phase of Paul's theology (*pace* Becker, *Paul* — above §1.4).

39. Neh. 13.1; Lam. 1.10; 1QSa 2.3-4; CD 12.3-6.

40. This is the principal thesis of Kraus, *Volk Gottes*. Thus, e.g., his comment at the end of his study of 1 Corinthians: "The 'new covenant' must not be thought of in antithesis to the 'old covenant,' but is to be understood as a renewed covenant inclusive of the Gentiles" (196).

over-simplified antithesis between "Jewish exclusiveness" and "Christian inclusiveness."

The other point of distinctiveness lies in the fact that Paul was able to speak of "the assemblies (plural) of God," whereas LXX usage is almost always singular. Paul evidently had no problem with conceiving "the assembly of God" as manifested in many different places at the same time — the churches (of God) in Judea, in Galatia, in Asia, or in Macedonia.[41] Each gathering of those baptized in the name of the Lord Jesus was "the assembly of God" in that place.[42] This is all the more striking when we recall that Paul also speaks of "the church in (someone's) house" — the church in the house of Priscilla and Aquila, of Nympha, and of Philemon.[43] The point is that wherever believers met for fellowship and worship they were in direct continuity with the assembly of Israel, they were the assembly of God.

From all this follow other points of lasting significance.

a) One is that, despite the continuity with "the assembly of Yahweh," Paul's conception of the church is typically of the church in a particular place or region. He does not seem to have thought of "the church" as something worldwide or universal — "the Church."[44]

(1) The singular usage, "the church" (as in Gal. 1.13) is sometimes read in this light. But as we have just seen, Paul's persecution of "the church" implies a recognition of the Jerusalem church's central role as the eschatological focus of the assembly of Israel, not a claim to persecute the worldwide Church. When the Hellenist believers who had been dispersed from Jerusalem met together they were still the church of God.

(2) 1 Cor. 12.28 is regularly cited as evidence that Paul already conceived of a universal Church — "God appointed in the church first apostles, second prophets, third teachers. . . ."[45] But that interpretation involves the anachronistic assumption that "apostles" was already perceived as a universal office. In contrast, Paul's own perception was of apostles appointed to found churches (1 Cor. 9.1-2), limited in the scope of their commission (2 Cor. 10.13-16), so that each church properly speaking had its own (founding)

---

41. 1 Cor. 16.1, 19; 2 Cor. 8.1; Gal. 1.2, 22; 1 Thes. 2.14. Similarly Acts 15.41; 16.5; and the seven churches of Revelation 1–3.

42. Rom. 16.1, 23; 1 Cor. 1.2; 6.4; 12.28; 14.4, 5, 12, 23; 2 Cor. 1.1; Col. 4.16; 1 Thes. 1.1; 2 Thes. 1.1.

43. Rom. 16.5; 1 Cor. 16.19; Col. 4.15; Phm 2.

44. Cf. Becker, *Paul* 422-23: "The universal element that is concretized in each congregation is not the church but the Christ at work in the gospel"; *pace* not least Ridderbos, *Paul* 328-30. For convenience I use the facility provided by the English language distinction between upper and lower case (local church, universal Church).

45. Barrett, *Paul* 121-22, thinks a universal reference here is probable, though he queries the others.

apostles[46] — just as it had its other ministries of prophets, teachers, and other charisms. In 1 Cor. 12.27-28 in particular, it is evident that Paul had in mind the church in Corinth as such: "You [the Corinthian believers] are Christ's body [in Corinth], and individually parts of it. And those whom God has appointed in the church. . . ."[47]

(3) The same is true with regard to 1 Cor. 10.32 — "Do not become an offence, whether to Jews or Greeks or to the church of God." The sequence indicates clearly enough that by "the church of God" Paul had in mind the church in Corinth (10.23-33).[48] "Jews and Greeks" could be referred to vaguely as the social groups most likely to influence and to interact locally with the believers in Christ. But as with his other uses of "the church of God," Paul's primary thought was of the local assembly as "the church of God" in the city where it met.

It is only later that *ekklēsia* is used in the Pauline letters with a more universal reference. Col. 1.18 and 24 provides the transition to the consistent use in this sense of Ephesians.[49] To recognize this as a late (or later) development in Pauline theology should not be overdramatized. Paul had no thought of his churches as a set of independent foundations. His conception of "the church of God" and regular appeal to "all the churches" would rule that out. We cannot say that Paul would have disapproved of the subsequent usage in Ephesians. What we can and should say, however, is that the "church-ness" of each individual Christian assembly did not depend for Paul on its being part of some universal entity. Its reality and vitality as church depended more immediately on its own direct continuity through Christ and its founding apostle with the assembly of Yahweh.

b) The significance of the house churches within Pauline ecclesiology should also be noted. For one thing, Paul could speak both of the whole congregation in a place as "church" and also of individual house groups within that congregation as "church" (1 Cor. 1.1; 16.19). The one was not seen as detracting from the status of the other. Wherever believers met together, they were "the church of God." The implication of 1 Cor. 16.19 set alongside 14.23 (referring to "the whole church meeting together") is probably that church gatherings consisted of more regular small house groups interspersed with less frequent (weekly, monthly?) gatherings of "the whole church."[50]

---

46. See further §21.2 below.
47. Dunn, *Jesus and the Spirit* 262-63; Hainz, *Ekklesia* 251-54; Kertelge, "Ort" (§21 n. 1) 228-29.
48. *Pace* Roloff, *EDNT* 1.413.
49. Eph. 1.22; 3.10, 21; 5.23-25, 27, 29, 32.
50. See further Banks, *Paul's Idea* 35-41.

For another, the fact that "the whole church" of Corinth could meet in a house (Rom. 16.23)[51] probably tells us something about the typical size of many of the Pauline congregations. For even a large house (we are not talking about senatorial mansions) would have been pressed to accommodate more than about forty.[52] Given the dynamic character of the Corinthian church and its tendency to factionalism, that is a salutary reminder. Historically, it is a reminder of how dependent on quite tiny groups was the development of Christianity in the northeastern Mediterranean area. Theologically, the point is that the dynamic of being "the church of God" did not require large groups in any one place.

c) Finally, it is worth noting that the focus of "church" is given by its character as "assembly." This is probably the significance of Paul's talk of believers "coming together in church."[53] For, obviously, Paul did not think of "in church" as "in a building." He thought rather of Christians coming together to be church, as church.[54] It was not as isolated individuals that believers functioned as "the church of God" for Paul. Rather, it was only as a gathering, for worship and for mutual support, that they could function as "the assembly of God."[55]

51. The consensus view is that Romans was written from Corinth.

52. See further particularly Gnilka, *Philemon* 17-33, particularly 25-33; Murphy-O'Connor, *St. Paul's Corinth* (§22 n. 1) 164-66. B. Blue, "Acts and the House Church," in D. W. J. Gill and C. Gempf, eds., *Graeco-Roman Setting,* vol. 2 of *The Book of Acts in Its First Century Setting,* ed. B. Winter, et al. (Grand Rapids: Eerdmans/Carlisle: Paternoster, 1994) 119-222, argues that a large house of the period could well accommodate a gathering of 100 people (175), but he may not give enough consideration to the presence of household furnishings and statuary, and the difficulty of holding a meeting in more than one room. Robert Jewett has also drawn attention to the likelihood that city churches met in tenements ("Tenement Churches and Communal Meals in the Early Church: The Implications of a Form-Critical Analysis of 2 Thessalonians 3.10," *BibRes* 38 [1993] 23-43), where numbers would have been still more restricted.

53. 1 Cor. 11.18; also 14.19, 28, 34-35. This may provide the reason why Paul does not speak of "the church in Rome": it was too large to meet together as a single assembly (church). The Christian presence in Rome rather thrived through a sequence of house groups. Five such may be identified in the greetings of Romans 16 — vv. 5, 10, 11, 14, 15 (see further my *Romans* 891). It is less clear why Paul did not speak of "the church in Philippi."

54. This may be reflected also in his talk of persecuting the church; that is, his strategy as a persecutor was to move against the believers in Jesus when they had gathered together (Banks, *Paul's Idea* 36-37).

55. "It is 'church' whenever individuals 'assemble as a *church (en ekklēsią)*' (1 Cor. 11.18). . . . Assembly for worship is the center and at the same time the criterion for life in the church. Here it is determined whether it really is the church 'of God.' Thus the unbrotherly behavior of the rich toward the poor in the Corinthian common meal is nothing less than 'despis[ing] the *church* of God' (11.22). What is despised here is, first, the power of the Lord's Supper to unite the church, but also what coming together should be for the Church of God" (Roloff, *EDNT* 1.413).

All this, however, does not take us much forward in our consideration of what was the corporate entity which Paul conceived of as an alternative to the historic Israel defined by birth and praxis. Indeed it is the continuity with historic Israel which underlies the thought of "the church of God" more than any discontinuity. Which may be another reason why Paul made no use whatsoever of the concept "church" in the main part of Romans before ch. 16 and why, in particular, the word is missing in the transition from ch. 11 to ch. 12. What we do find at the beginning of Romans 12 poses the issue of corporate identity in quite another way.

§20.3 Community without cult

For anyone with the sort of question in mind which, we have suggested, follows at once from a sensitive reading of Romans 9–11, the opening of Romans 12 makes a stunning impact. For Paul deliberately evokes the language of the sacrificial cult, that is, of the obligations which were characteristic of all sects and religions that focused on a temple and the worship offered there. Not least in his mind, but not exclusively so, would have been the worship carried out in the temple in Jerusalem. For that was at the heart of Jewish self-identity. Not only for those Jews actually living in Judea itself,[56] but also for Jews living in the diaspora.[57] With the question of the new churches' identity posed by his exposition in chs. 9–11 ("Israel") as much as by his usual way of conceptualizing these new groups of believers as each "the assembly of God," Paul's opening exhortation in 12.1-2 offers an unexpected answer with a radical redrawing of traditional identity markers.

> [1]I appeal to you, therefore, brothers, through the mercies of God, to present your bodies a sacrifice, living, holy, acceptable to God, which is your spiritual worship.

The reference to "the mercies of God" maintains the continuity of thought with 11.30-32.[58] But the primary thrust comes in the sacrificial language which

---

56. In Hellenistic geopolitics, Judea was properly speaking a temple state, that is, a state which existed to provide the political and financial support for a world-famous temple. Under Roman rule it is not surprising, then, that the High Priest was the chief political figure.

57. A striking feature of Rome's generally benevolent attitude towards Judea was its willingness to let very large sums be collected in the Jewish diaspora and be transported to Jerusalem as the half-shekel temple tax due every year from every Jewish male of twenty years and over.

58. Paul uses a different word *(oiktirmoi)*, but the background in Hebrew thought is the same; see further my *Romans* 709.

follows: the term "present" itself is drawn from the technical language of sacrifice;[59] "sacrifice *(thysia)*" is the normal term for a sacrifice, including sacrifices offered in accordance with the Torah;[60] and of the nine occurrences of "worship *(latreia)*" in the LXX, eight refer to Jewish cultic worship.[61] Paul implies that as much as the Israel of old, so believers now must be marked out by sacrificial worship. Only, it is worship differently conceived and differently focused. The point is not simply that Paul drew attention to the mental and spiritual attitude which must accompany any act of worship if it is to be meaningful. Something of that is implied in the metaphorical use here of the language of sacrifice and in the talk of "spiritual worship."[62] But psalmist and prophet of old had often warned against reliance on a superficial performance of the ritual act.[63]

Paul's point is indicated rather in the talk of *what* is to be sacrificed — "your bodies." Paul, of course, is not calling for self-immolation on some altar. Rather, we must suppose that he had in mind the character of human bodily existence, the corporeal nature of human society, the body as the means by which embodied beings can be in communication with one another.[64] What he calls for, then, is the offering up of oneself in one's corporeal relationships, in the relationships of every day, made possible by one's being as an embodied person. In other words, he takes the language of the cult, in its characteristic abstraction from daily living, and reverses the relationship. If "the holy place" is where sacrifice is to be offered, precisely in its set-apartness from the commonplace of everyday usage,[65] Paul in effect transforms the holy place into the marketplace. He "secularizes" the sanctuary by sanctifying the business of every day.[66]

As a Pharisee, we should recall, Paul was no stranger to the attempt to spread sanctuary holiness throughout the land. But as a Pharisee he had attempted to do that by extending the cult, or at least the purity required by the cult, throughout the land, that is, by observing the temple purity rules outside the temple.[67] Now as a Christian he was attempting to do so by

---

59. *Paristanai thysian,* "to present/offer sacrifice," is a well-established usage in Greek literature and inscriptions. See, e.g., MM; BAGD, *paristēmi* 1d; Michel, *Römer* 369; Cranfield, *Romans* 598.

60. See, e.g., J. Behm, *TDNT* 3.181-82.

61. H. Strathmann, *TDNT* 4.61.

62. See, e.g., Philo, *Spec. Leg.* 1.201, 277; and further my *Romans* 711.

63. E.g., Pss. 50.14, 23; 51.16-17; 141.2; Prov. 16.6; Isa. 1.11-17; Mic. 6.6-8; Sir. 35.1; Tob. 4.10-11; 1QS 9.3-5; *2 Enoch* 45.3; see further Behm, *TDNT* 3.186-89.

64. See above §3.2.

65. Hence the significance of *koinos* = "common, unclean" (see §8 n. 45 above).

66. Following particularly Käsemann, "Worship"; other bibliography in my *Romans* 709.

67. See, e.g., my *Partings* 41-44, 109-11 (and further above §8 n. 44).

extending the *dedication* expressed in the sanctity of the cult into everyday relationships. The objectives were similar, but the vision of what holiness involved was radically different.

This line of reflection may seem to press Rom. 12.1 overmuch. In fact, however, it is wholly of a piece with Paul's vision of Christian community as it comes to expression elsewhere in his letters. For it is a consistent feature of Paul's ecclesiology that he takes cultic language out of its context of sacred place and sacred person and uses it of "ordinary" individuals in their daily obligations in service of the gospel.

Most striking is the way Paul speaks of "the temple of God," elsewhere used to refer to the Jerusalem temple.[68] What is "the temple of God" now for believers? Paul's reply is clear: "You are God's temple" (1 Cor. 3.16-17); "your body is the temple of the Holy Spirit" (6.19). Or again, "We are the temple of the living God" (2 Cor. 6.16). The thought is not particularly new. Philo speaks of the body as "a sacred dwelling place or shrine for the reasonable soul" (*Opif.* 136-37). And the idea of the people as God's temple is already present at least in Qumran.[69] Indeed, an equivalent thought of the community gathered round Christ as "the [eschatological] temple of God" may be already implicit in Paul's reference to the three principal Jerusalem apostles as "pillars" in Gal. 2.9 (cf. Rev. 3.12) and in the tradition of Jesus' reference to (re)building the temple (Mark 14.58).[70] But with Paul at least the implication is that of a temple constituted by the immediate indwelling of God in individual and people, rather than mediately through a temple as such (2 Cor. 6.16),[71] and of such a direct indwelling that it made redundant any continuing (or for Gentile converts, new) loyalty to the Jerusalem temple.[72]

The impression is strengthened by the reference to unhindered access *(prosagōgē)* to grace in Rom. 5.2.[73] For, as already noted, the imagery may well have evoked thought of access through the royal chamberlain into the

---

68. Matt. 26.61; Luke 1.9; 2 Thes. 2.4. For more extensive use of *naos* ("temple") for the Jerusalem temple and for other temples see BAGD, *naos* 1a and 1c.

69. Gärtner, *Temple* 16-46; McKelvey, *New Temple* 46-53.

70. See further my *Galatians* 109-10.

71. Whether the *en* is translated "in" or "among," Paul's language implies an immediacy in the indwelling: "We are the temple of the living God; as God said, 'I will live in them and walk among them . . .'" (2 Cor 6.16, NRSV), with an implied shift in meaning of the text cited — Ezek. 37.27 ("My dwelling place will be among them . . .").

72. The issue of temple tax never arises in the Pauline letters. Many (most?) Jewish believers no doubt continued to pay it — as Jews. But payment by Gentiles was evidently never even considered. If the collection was considered in any sense an alternative or substitute, it was no more than that; see further below §24.8.

73. Elsewhere in the NT only in Eph. 2.18 and 3.12; but cf. use of the verb in 1 Pet. 3.18 and the near synonym, *eisodos,* in Heb. 10.19.

king's presence.[74] But the talk of access to divine grace would almost certainly evoke thought of the temple.[75] Again the implication is of an access to God's presence which no longer requires or depends on an actual temple to symbolize or facilitate such mediated access.

The same point comes through in Paul's use of the language of priesthood. For a very striking feature of Paul's letters is the absence of any reference to priests in the Pauline churches. There was evidently no distinct or separate function which required a "priest" to carry it out. In contrast, Paul refers to his own ministry in service of the gospel as priestly ministry.

In particular, in Rom. 15.16 he reminds his readers

> of the grace given me from God, so that I might be a minister *(leitourgon)* of Christ Jesus for the Gentiles, serving the gospel of God as a priest *(hierourgounta),* in order that the offering *(prosphora)* of the Gentiles might be acceptable *(euprosdektos),* sanctified *(hēgiasmenē)* by the Holy Spirit.

The language of priesthood is unmistakable: *leitourgos,* "priest";[76] *hierourgeō,* "perform the work of a priest";[77] *prosphora,* either the "act of presenting an offering" or the "offering" itself; and *euprosdektos,* "well pleasing" and *hagiazein,* "sanctify," both very apposite in reference to sacrifice.[78] It should not be deduced from this that Paul saw himself as a priest, set apart from other believers, or that he thought of apostles as having in effect taken over the characteristic intermediating roles of priests. For he also describes Epaphroditus elsewhere as a *leitourgos* (Phil. 2.25), where the ministry is that of attending to Paul's needs while in prison.[79] Likewise he describes the collection by the Gentile churches for the poor Christians in Jerusalem as an act of *leitourgein* (Rom. 15.27), of *leitourgia* (2 Cor. 9.12) — Gentiles ministering (as priests) to Jews. And when we bear in mind the previous references in Romans to unmediated access for all (5.2) and to the call to all to engage in the priestly act of offering sacrifice (12.1), the conclusion is hard to avoid: Paul saw all ministry and service on behalf of the gospel as priestly ministry, ministry which all believers could engage in and which was not limited to any special order of priests.[80]

74. See again my *Romans* 247-48.
75. See above §14 n. 215.
76. As in Neh. 10.39; Isa. 61.6; Sir. 7.30; Heb. 7.30; *1 Clement* 41.2.
77. So consistently in Philo and Josephus.
78. For further details see my *Romans* 859-61.
79. In the same verse Epaphroditus is described as an "apostle," but in the sense of "emissary" from the church in Philippi (cf. 2 Cor. 8.23).
80. Hence also his characteristic use of *hagiazō* ("sanctify") for the beginning of the process of salvation and his regular use of *hagios* ("holy, saint") for believers generally (see above §13 nn. 64-76).

The same point comes through also in Paul's use of the cultic categories of clean and unclean. He cut through the fundamental historic instinct to maintain an area of cultic purity, separated from the common *(koinos)* life by strict rules of clean and unclean *(koinos)*. He now saw, in the light of Christ, that "nothing is unclean *(koinos)* in itself"; "everything is clean *(kathara)*" (Rom. 14.14, 20). Since "the earth is the Lord's, and everything in it,"[81] the fundamental distinction between sacred and profane, holy and common no longer counted.[82] The point is analogous to that made in 12.1. This did not mean that there was no longer any such thing as impurity. What it meant was that the removal of impurity no longer depended on a cultic rite necessary for entry into the holy place. The purification in view was probably the more immediate cleansing of heart and conscience.[83] Here again Paul the apostle, like Paul the Pharisee, sought to extend the purity symbolized by the temple throughout the people of God. But where Paul the Pharisee had done so by extending rules of purity into everyday life,[84] Paul the apostle called for a purity which penetrated to the heart and which made further purity rules unnecessary or redundant.

The resulting picture is consistent and without any jarring features. Paul evidently saw the new Christian assemblies as an extension of the assembly of Yahweh, but now without any of the cultic features so characteristic of Israel's temple cult, and without any category of priest as a function different in kind from the priestly ministry of all who served the gospel. This must have marked out the house churches of Paul as very unusual, not to say odd, within the cities of the Roman Empire. They shared a common meal (the Lord's Supper)[85] and met regularly for worship. But they looked to no cult centre or temple; they had no priests, no sacrifices. In legal status they were probably regarded as equivalent to the clubs or *collegia* of the time,[86] or regarded as extensions of the Jewish synagogue.[87] But unlike such gatherings,

---

81. 1 Cor. 10.25-26, citing Ps. 24.1.

82. As noted above (§8 n. 45), *koinos* in everyday Greek meant simply "common." It gained its special Jewish sense of "profane, unclean" because it had been used in the two centuries prior to Paul to translate Hebrew *chol,* denoting the opposite of what had been withdrawn from ordinary use and set apart for cultic use, or *tame',* denoting that which rendered one unfit to enter the sanctuary.

83. Cf. the washing imagery of 1 Cor. 6.11 with Mark 7.21-22; Acts 15.9; and Heb. 9.14. And the cleansing imagery of 2 Cor. 7.1 and Eph. 5.26 with 1 Tim. 1.5; 3.9; 2 Tim 1.3; 2.22. See further my *Baptism* 120-23 and 162-65 and above §17.2.

84. See again above §8 n. 44.

85. And note the analogies drawn in 1 Cor. 10.14-22; see further below §22.

86. Formally recognized associations for shared purpose or interest — most typically trade guilds and burial societies. See, e.g., *OCD* 254-56.

87. Synagogues were able to shelter under the legislation regarding *collegia;* see, e.g., the discussion in E. M. Smallwood, *The Jews under Roman Rule* (Leiden: Brill, 1976) 134-36.

they did not meet in a temple dedicated to their God or acknowledge their dependence on their cult centre by sending an annual offering. Their meetings neither singled out any priest nor called on such to perform a priestly act like the ritual libation. For most of their contemporaries a religious association without cult centre, without priests, without sacrifices, must have seemed a plain contradiction in terms, even an absurdity.

Paul can hardly have been unaware of the strangeness of his vision of his churches at this point. On the contrary, his use of language shows that he was deliberately breaking with the typical understanding of a religious community dependent on cult centre, office of priest, and act of ritual sacrifice. Whether a community without cult was practical and sustainable, given not least that the eschatological community was itself caught in the overlap of the ages and the resulting eschatological tension, is another question.

§20.4 The body of Christ

It is noticeable that the first more extensive theme which Paul embarks on in Romans 12 is the metaphor of the Christian community as "one body in Christ" (12.5). Here again the transition can hardly have been accidental. Paul shifts within a few verses from the category of Israel for the people of God, through the transformed imagery of sacrifice (12.1), to a quite different image — that of a body, and specifically of a body defined by its relation to Christ. Evidently the implication to be drawn is that if the Gentile churches found it hard to think of themselves as Israel, even with the concept of its cult transformed, the more meaningful or realistic imagery was that of the body, and specifically of the body of Christ.

This in fact is the dominant theological image in Pauline ecclesiology. It is to this image that he immediately turns in Romans 12 (vv. 4-5). It is this image to which he turns likewise in 1 Corinthians 10, when faced with misunderstanding and abuse of the Lord's Supper, and in 1 Corinthians 12, when faced with questions about worship in the Corinthian assemblies.[88] And the image is assumed and retained in the transition to the post-Pauline letters.[89] To be noted is the fact that Paul does not speak uniformly or stereotypically of "the body of Christ." His usage is more varied: "the bread which we break is . . . participation in the body of Christ" (1 Cor. 10.16); "just as the body is one and has many members . . . so also is the Christ" (12.12); "you are

88. 1 Cor. 10.16-17; 11.24, 27, 29; 12.12-13, 14-27.
89. Col. 1.18, 24; 2.19; and 3.15 (most clearly echoing the earlier Pauline use); Eph. 1.22-23; 2.15-16; 4.4, 12, 15-16 (again clearly echoing the earlier Pauline use); 5.23, 30. See further my "Body"; also "The 'Body' in Colossians" (above §3 n. 5).

Christ's body and individually members" (12.27); "we all are one body in Christ" (Rom. 12.5). Evidently the imagery was still fresh and malleable and not yet fixed or formalized.

As with the concept "church," so with the image "body (of Christ)," we have to ask, "Why this term?" and "Where did Paul get it from?" Several answers have been offered over the years, most of them too little to the point.

Various attempts have been made to derive the imagery from other aspects of Paul's thought already examined.[90] From his Adam christology,[91] or the "in Christ" of Paul's mysticism,[92] or the related but contrived concept of "corporate personality,"[93] or as an extension of Paul's concept of the Messiah and of the people of God.[94] None of these is satisfactory since none of them really explains how and why the imagery chosen was that of the body. Equally unsatisfactory is the suggestion that Paul derived it from the words of the heavenly revelation on the Damascus road, as given in the Acts accounts — "Saul, Saul, why are you persecuting me? . . . I am Jesus whom you are persecuting."[95] This is not to deny the combined influence of at least some of such corporate features of Paul's thought; we have assumed throughout that Paul's theology formed an integrated whole. It is simply to suggest that there is a more obvious source which renders redundant such speculation as to the source of the imagery in Paul.

In the middle decades of the twentieth century a popular and much promoted view was that Paul derived the concept of the body of Christ from the Gnostic primal man myth (individuals as pieces of the body of the original heavenly man).[96] But the quest for a pre-Christian Gnostic primal man has now almost entirely been abandoned: the earlier ideas, say of a Philo, are not really "Gnostic" (in the sense intended), and to describe them as "pre-

---

90. For what follows cf. Jewett's review and critique as part of his analysis of the concept of *sōma* in Paul (*Anthropological Terms* 201-50).

91. Davies, *Paul* 53-57; Stuhlmacher, *Theologie* 358.

92. Particularly Percy, *Leib*.

93. Best, *One Body*, passim; but see Rogerson, "Hebrew Conception" (§15 n. 89 above).

94. Cf. Oepke, *Gottesvolk*, and Meuzelaar, *Leib*.

95. Acts 9.4-5; 22.7-8; 26.14-15. Robinson, *Body* 55-58, built up from this the suggestion that for Paul the community is identical with the (crucified and) resurrected body of Christ. But this makes nonsense of 1 Cor. 15.44-49 and Phil. 3.21 and runs counter to the distinctions made subsequently in Colossians, where it is clear that the crucified body of Christ is "the body of flesh" (1.22; 2.17) in distinction from the body, the church, of which Christ is head (1.18; 2.19). Note also Whiteley's critique (*Theology* 194).

96. Particularly Käsemann, *Leib;* Jewett, *Anthropological Terms* 231, notes how influential the thesis has been; still in Kümmel, *Theology* 210; Georgi, *Theocracy* (§24 n. 1) 60; and Strecker, *Theologie* 194-96.

Gnostic" is as helpful and as unhelpful as describing the medieval church as pre-Reformation.[97]

There are, in fact, only two realistic options to explain Paul's use of the metaphor. One is the sacramental usage indicated in 1 Corinthians 10 and 11.[98] In view of the interplay of "body" language in these chapters (10.16-17; 11.24-29) it can hardly be doubted that Paul saw a close connection between the broken bread (= Christ's body) and the church as one body. But does this explain why Paul should have transferred the imagery of "body" from the bread to the community? The linking thought in 1 Cor. 10.16-17 is not so much "bread" → "body of Christ" → "body (of community)," as *one* bread, therefore *one* body."[99] The body character of the community seems to be already assumed. And the more elaborated body imagery of 1 Corinthians 12 (as also Romans 12 and Ephesians 4) seems to have in view the interactive relations of the worshiping community in general, and not simply a community focused on the sacrament.

Much the most plausible source of the imagery is the use of the metaphor of the body elsewhere in precisely the way that Paul most consistently uses it[100] — the body as a vital expression of the unity of a community despite the diversity of its members.[101] The image of the city or state as a body (the body politic) was already familiar in political philosophy[102] — the famous fable of Menenius Agrippa being the best-known example.[103] And Paul's exposition in

97. See also my *Christology* 98-100, 123-26, 229-30, 248, 252-53; and further M. Hengel, "Die Ursprunge der Gnosis und das Urchristentum," in Ådna, et al., eds., *Evangelium* 190-223; also §11 n. 68 above.

98. See particularly Cerfaux, *Church* 262-82; according to Conzelmann, *Outline* 262, "The origin of the expression 'body of Christ' probably lies here, in the eucharistic tradition. There is no other model either in the history of religion or in the history of the concept"! Jewett, *Anthropological Terms* 246-48, attributes the view to A. E. J. Rawlinson, "Corpus Christi," in G. K. A. Bell and A. Deissmann, eds., *Mysterium Christi* (London: Longmans, Green, 1930) 225-44.

99. See further below §22.6.

100. So also particularly Schweizer, *TDNT* 7.1069; Fitzmyer, *Paul* 91; Lindemann, "Kirche als Leib."

101. Rom. 12.4-5; 1 Cor. 12.14-26; Col. 2.19; Eph. 4.11-16.

102. The body was "the most common *topos* in ancient literature for unity" (Mitchell, *Paul and the Rhetoric of Reconciliation* 155-62 [here 161]).

103. Livy, *Historia* 2.32; Epictetus 2.10.4-5; see further Lietzmann, *1 Korinther* (on 12.12), and Schweizer, *TDNT* 7.1038-39.

In the days when man's members did not all agree among themselves, as is now the case, but had each its own ideas and a voice of its own, the other parts thought it unfair that they should have the worry and the trouble and the labour of providing everything for the belly, while the belly remained quietly in their midst with nothing to do but to enjoy the good things which they bestowed upon it. They therefore conspired together that the hands should carry no food to the mouth, nor

1 Cor. 12.14-26 in particular closely echoes the concerns of the fable: that the unity of the state depended on the mutual interdependence of its diverse members being fully recognized.[104] This suggested origin does not explain the qualifying Christ reference ("body in Christ," "body of Christ," "so is Christ"). But that is most obviously explained precisely as Paul's adaptation of the more familiar and widely used secular metaphor. The Christian assembly is a body, like the secular body politic, but it is different precisely because its distinctive and identifying feature is that it is the body *of Christ*.[105]

The sequence of Paul's thought as he turns to an alternative corporate image for the people of God thus becomes clearer. Paul shifts the corporate image of the Christian community from that of nation state (historic Israel) to that of body politic, that is, from a community identified by ethnic and traditional boundary markers to one whose members are drawn from different nationalities and social strata[106] and whose prosperity depends on their mutual cooperation and their working harmoniously together.[107] The identity of the *Christian* assembly as "body," however, is given not by geographical location or political allegiance[108] but by their common allegiance to *Christ* (visibly expressed not least in baptism and the sacramental sharing in his body). The

the mouth accept anything that was given it, nor the teeth grind up what they received. While they sought in this angry spirit to starve the belly into submission, the members themselves and the whole body were reduced to the utmost weakness. Hence it became clear that even the belly had no idle task to perform, and was no more nourished than it nourished the rest, by giving out to all parts of the body that by which we live and thrive, when it has been divided equally amongst the veins and is enriched with digested food — that is, the blood. Drawing a parallel from this to show how like was the internal dissension of the bodily members to the anger of the plebs against the Fathers, he [Menenius Agrippa] prevailed upon the minds of the hearers (Livy 2.32.9-12).

104. We should also note the more recent observation that much of Paul's earlier vocabulary in 1 Corinthians is drawn from or shared with the language of political rhetoric (particularly L. L. Welborn, "On the Discord in Corinth: 1 Corinthians 1–4 and Ancient Politics," *JBL* 106 [1987] 85-111; and Mitchell, *Paul and the Rhetoric of Reconciliation*).

105. Cf. Ridderbos, *Paul* 376: "Believers do not together constitute one body because they are members of one another, but because they are members of Christ, and thus are one body in him (Rom. 12:5; 1 Cor. 6:15)"; the point is given too little attention by Lindemann, "Kirche als Leib."

106. That Paul was aware of this, and chose the imagery deliberately for that reason, is surely indicated by his insertion of the formula "whether Jews or Greeks, whether slaves or free" into his description of how the one body of Christ is constituted (1 Cor. 12.13).

107. The parallels are particularly clear in 1 Corinthians, where the image first appears in the Pauline letters. But if Rom. 14.1–15.6 is any guide, it was equally appropriate in Romans, even if Paul does not develop the point in Romans 12 to the extent that he did in 1 Corinthians 12.

108. Or by race, social status, or gender (Gal. 3.28; 1 Cor. 12.13; Col. 3.11).

implication is clear that only when that common allegiance is given primacy in mutual relations can the potential factional differences be transformed into the necessary mutual cooperation for the common good. This shift in identity factors and boundary markers, therefore, gives a different dynamic to the understanding of community, where the key distinguishing factor is a sense of mutual interdependence in Christ, expressed in a mutual responsibility one for another which manifests the grace of Christ.

But more can be said.

§20.5 *Charismatic community*

One of the most striking features of Paul's understanding of the body of Christ is that each of the passages in the Pauline letters in which the concept is expounded at some length envisages it as a charismatic community.[109] Rom. 12.4-8 —

> [4]For just as in one body we have many members, and all the members do not have the same function, [5]so we all are one body in Christ, and individually members of one another — [6]having charisms which differ in accordance with the grace given to us, whether prophecy in proportion to faith, [7]or service in service, or the one who teaches in teaching, [8]or the one who encourages in encouraging, the one who shares with sincere concern, the one who cares with zest, the one who does acts of mercy with cheerfulness.

1 Cor. 12.4-27 —

> [4]There are diversities of charisms, but the same Spirit. [5]There are diversities of service, and the same Lord. [6]There are diversities of activities, but the same God, who effects all things in everyone. [7]To each is given the manifestation of the Spirit for the common good. [8]To one is given a word of wisdom through the Spirit, to another a word of knowledge in accordance with the same Spirit, [9]to another faith by the same Spirit, to another charisms of healing by the one Spirit, [10]to another miraculous activities, to another prophecy, to another discernment of spirits, to another kinds of tongues, to another interpretation of tongues. [11]One and the same Spirit effects all these, distributing to each as he wills. [12]For just as the body is one and has many members and all the members of the body, though many, are one body, so also is Christ. [13]For in one Spirit we were

---

109. "Only in the context of the effects and gifts of grace does the apostle utilize the ancient world's figure of the one body and the variety of its members" (Bornkamm, *Paul* 195). Brockhaus observes quite fairly that *charisma* is not a central concept in Pauline theology (*Charisma* [§21 n. 1] 141), but then no more is the concept of "the body of Christ."

all baptized into one body, whether Jews or Greeks, whether slaves or free, and all watered with the one Spirit. [14]For the body does not have one member but many. . . .

Eph. 4.7-16 —

[7]But to each of us has been given grace in accordance with the measure of the gift of Christ. . . . [8]"He gave gifts to humans." . . . [11]And he gave some as apostles, some as prophets, some as evangelists, and some as pastors and teachers, [12]to equip the saints for the work of ministry, for the upbuilding of the body of Christ. . . .

The key word in the two undisputed Paulines is *charisma,* "charism."[110] It is another case of a word having little significance before Paul took it up, transformed it by his usage, and gave it the status of a technical term of Christian theology.[111] In fact its Pauline character is more sharply marked than in almost any other Pauline term. It is hardly attested prior to Paul, and the examples in secular usage are all much later than Paul.[112] In the NT there is only one occurrence outside the Pauline corpus.[113] And in post-Pauline Christian usage the characteristic Pauline sense seems to have been soon lost.[114] In short, "charism" as a Christian term is a concept which theology owes entirely to Paul.

Its significance for Paul's concept of the body of Christ can be easily illuminated. (a) Its very formation, *charis-ma,* indicates that it denotes the result of the act of gracious giving (*charizesthai,* "give graciously").[115] It is only a matter of shorthand to describe *charisma* as the result or effect or expression of *charis,*[116] a "concrete materialization of God's grace."[117] By

---

110. Ephesians 4 maintains the same imagery but uses the term given in the quotation from Ps. 68.19 — *domata,* "gifts."

111. This point is too often ignored in the uncritical assumption of its later sociological meaning as determined classically by Max Weber.

112. Details in my *Jesus and the Spirit* 206.

113. The rather Pauline 1 Pet. 4.10.

114. See, e.g., Schweizer, *Church Order* (§21 n. 1) nn. 377 and 519.

115. BDF §109(2). In 1 Cor. 2.12 *ta charisthenta* ("the things given to us" by God) is another way of saying *ta charismata* ("the charisms").

116. This in response to M. Turner, "Modern Linguistics and the New Testament," in J. B. Green, ed., *Hearing the New Testament: Strategies for Interpretation* (Grand Rapids: Eerdmans/Carlisle: Paternoster, 1995) 156-59; also *The Holy Spirit* 262-67. It should be clear enough that my further observations regarding Paul's theology of charisms depend not so much on the formation of the word *charisma* as on the way Paul uses it. Note the dynamic character of "grace" for Paul (above §13.2) and the way he can use *charis* as more or less synonymous with *charisma* (below §24.8a).

117. Nardoni, "Concept" 74.

definition, a charism is the result of God's gracious act; it is divine grace come to effect and expression in word or deed. Thus Paul can use it as a summary both for what Christ has accomplished[118] and for the various gifts bestowed on Israel,[119] as well as for particular blessings to or through individual believers.[120] But his most common usage is in reference to charisms for the assembly,[121] both of speaking and of doing.[122]

(b) In Rom. 12.4-6 Paul uses the synonym *praxis*, "acting, activity, function."[123] In other words, the charism is a function of the member (the limb or organ) of the body. The charism is the contribution which the individual member makes to the whole, its function within the body as a whole. The body functions charismatically.

(c) In 1 Cor. 12.4-6, in deliberately parallel formulation, Paul uses a sequence of further synonyms. The "diversity of charisms" (12.4) are, alternatively expressed, the "diversity of acts of service *(diakonia)*" (12.5), are, alternatively expressed, the "diversity of activities *(energēma)*" (12.6). Here is brought out the character of the charism, as for the benefit of others (service) and as enabled by divine power.[124]

(d) 1 Corinthians 12 contains two further synonyms. Charism is also "the manifestation *(phanerōsis)* of the Spirit for the common good" (12.7).[125] And the fact that the whole discussion is set under the head of "the spirituals" *(pneumatika)* (12.1)[126] clearly implies that *charisma*, "charism," is synony-

---

118. Rom. 5.15-16; 6.23.

119. Rom. 11.29, probably referring to or including those listed in 9.4-5.

120. Rom. 1.11 (some word or act which would benefit the Roman Christians); 1 Cor. 1.7 (referring presumably to the charisms detailed subsequently in ch. 12); 7.7 (probably the enabling to maintain self-control); 2 Cor. 1.11 (Paul's deliverance from great peril).

121. Rom. 12.6; 1 Cor. 12.4, 31; specifically "charisms of healings" (1 Cor. 12.9, 28, 30). 1 Pet. 4.10-11 has the same concept — charisms of speaking and of serving. 1 Tim. 4.14 and 2 Tim. 1.6 appear to be a development of the same sense with reference to Timothy's commissioning.

122. Rom. 12.6-8; 1 Cor. 12.8-10.

123. All the members "having a function" (12.4) is obviously the same as the members of the one body in Christ "having charisms" (12.6).

124. On *energēma* see my *Jesus and the Spirit* 209. "The emphasis seems to be on the 'effects' produced by work, not simply on activity in and of itself" (Fee, *Empowering Presence* 161 n. 279).

125. Paul uses *phanerōsis* here and in 2 Cor. 4.2, where the emphasis is on the open expression of the truth in contrast to the craftiness of Paul's adversaries. These are the only two occurrences in the NT.

126. Since the word is genitive plural *(pneumatikōn)* it could be taken as a reference to "spiritual persons" *(pneumatikoi)*. But the thrust of the whole discussion which follows, as also the clear neuter usage in 14.1 *(pneumatika)*, indicates "spiritual things," that is, spiritual gifts — as most commentators agree.

mous with *pneumatikon,* "that which is of the Spirit."[127] So Paul can say equally "Be zealous for the greater charisms" (12.31), and "Be zealous for what (plural) is of the Spirit" (14.1).

When we follow through Paul's elaboration of his concept of charismatic community several important features emerge. Basic, of course, if we are right, is the rationale for the imagery in the first place. As in its usage elsewhere, the imagery emphasizes unity (one body) despite or (better) consisting of diversity (many members). The paraenetic point of the image is to illustrate that the effective unity of community is impossible without an enacted awareness of the mutual interdependence of its members.[128] But Paul's transformation of the image from that of a body which functions by the interaction of its different trades and social groupings to one which functions through the interaction of different charisms carries several important corollaries.

1) The diversity of the charisms has its own distinct character. Paul illustrates that diversity in Rom. 12.6-8 and 1 Cor. 12.8-10, 28-30. The lists consist basically of charisms of speech and charisms of action. Charisms of speech — prophecy, teaching, encouraging (Rom. 12.6-7), "utterance of wisdom," "utterance of knowledge," prophecy, and tongues (1 Cor. 12.8-10, 28-30), with their attendant charisms (see (3) below). Charisms of action — service, sharing, caring (or leading),[129] doing acts of mercy (Rom. 12.7-8), charisms of

---

127. *Pneumatikos* — Rom. 1.11 ("spiritual *charisma*"!); 15.27; 1 Cor. 2.13; 9.11; 10.3-4; 12.1; 14.1; Col. 1.9; 3.16 ("spiritual songs" = Eph. 5.19); Eph. 1.3; 6.12; we recall Rom. 7.14 ("the law is *pneumatikos*") and 1 Cor. 15.44, 46 (*sōma pneumatikon*, "spiritual body"); "spiritual people/pneumatics" — 1 Cor. 2.13-15; 3.1; 14.37; Gal. 6.1. Elsewhere in the NT only 1 Pet. 2.5 (twice); adverb in Rev. 11.8. The use of the term in 1 Corinthians 12–14, and the inference from Rom. 12.6 that *charisma* was Paul's preferred term, suggests that *pneumatikon* was the Corinthians' term (12.1 introduces the subject in the terms which their letter used; they were "zealous for *pneumata*" — 14.12), whereas Paul preferred the term *(charisma)* which emphasized the gracious character of the gift. See further below §22.5.

128. Rom. 12.5 — "we are all one body in Christ and individually members of one another"; 1 Cor. 12.12, 14 — one body and many members, each needing the other (12.15-26); similarly Col. 2.19 and Eph. 4.16.

129. In Rom. 12.8 *ho proistamenos* could mean "the leader" (NRSV, REB), "leadership" (NIV). So most. But the verb also occurs quite frequently in the sense "be concerned about, care for, give aid" (cf. 1 Tim. 3.5; Tit. 3.8, 14), and between two other words which denote forms of aid-giving Paul probably had in mind the latter sense — three words together encompassing the earliest churches' "welfare service." So also, e.g., Cranfield, *Romans* 625-27, and Schlier, *Römerbrief* 372; see further my *Jesus and the Spirit* 250-52; also *Romans* 731. *Pace* Fitzmyer, *Romans* 649, there is no difficulty in envisaging the range of ministries suggested by the three words — e.g., distribution of food and clothing *(metadidous),* championing the cause of those who had no one to speak and act for them *(proistamenos),* giving financial aid *(eleos).*

healing and miraculous activities (1 Cor. 12.9-10, 28-30), "helpful deeds *(antilēmpseis)*," and "giving guidance" *(kybernēseis)*" (1 Cor. 12.28).[130] 1 Pet. 4.10-11 confirms the basic category distinction: "As each has received a charism, use it to serve one another . . . whoever speaks, as one speaking oracles of God, whoever serves, as out of the strength which God supplies."

2) To be noted is the fact that in his various listings Paul, no doubt deliberately, included more humdrum tasks and organizational roles,[131] as well as the more eye-catching prophecy, tongues, and miracles. The grace was in the giving, we might say, not in the form of its manifestation — the gracious gift received and enacted, however unspectacular the ministry.

3) The list in 1 Cor. 12.8-10 seems also intended to bring out the charisms' character of mutual interdependence, particularly the last three groups. The clearest instance is the association of "kinds of tongues"[132] and "interpretation of tongues" (12.10).[133] For it is evident from 1 Corinthians 14 that Paul regarded "interpretation" as some kind of control on or balance to "tongues."[134] The same is true with the association of "prophecy" and "discernment *(diakrisis)* of spirits" (12.10). Prophecy was the most valuable of all the charisms for Paul.[135] But even so, or rather for that very reason,

---

130. The terms *antilēmpseis* and *kybernēseis* in 1 Cor. 12.28 are somewhat obscure in their reference. The former means simply "help, assistance," and the latter "steering, directing, governing" (drawn from the metaphor of a helmsman — a *kybernētēs*); see further my *Jesus and the Spirit* 252-53.

131. I do not recognize Turner's attribution to me ("as Dunn would have it") of the view "that Paul is saying only the most striking acts of 'administration' or 'help' can be called *charismata*" (*The Holy Spirit* 270).

132. By "tongues" Paul probably meant "languages" (English "tongue" has the same extended meaning) — not human languages (which would undermine the argument of 14.6-11; disputed by Turner, *Holy Spirit* 227-29), but tongues of angels (13.1), the heavenly language by means of which one spoke to God (14.2). The idea that the inspired visionary would speak in the language of angels was already familiar in Jewish literature (*T. Job* 48–50; *Apoc. Abr.* 17; *Ascension of Isaiah* 7.13–9.33; *Apoc. Zeph.* 8.3-4). See further my *Jesus and the Spirit* 242-46 and n. 304. The continuing widespread interest in the subject is illustrated by Fee's bibliography in *Empowering Presence* 172 n. 336.

133. The term *hermēneia* and its cognates in biblical Greek embrace the sense of "translation" as well as "interpretation" (LSJ, BAGD) — which fits well with the understanding of "tongues" as language (n. 132 above).

134. 14.5 — "he who prophesies is greater than he who speaks in tongues, unless someone interprets, in order that the church might receive edification"; 14.13 — "let him who speaks in a tongue pray that he might interpret"; 14.26-28 — an utterance in tongues must be followed by an interpretation, and if no interpretation is forthcoming there must be no further tongue-speaking. See further my *Jesus and the Spirit* 246-48.

135. 14.1, 5, 12, 24 — precisely because it built up the church and brought its members encouragement and consolation (14.3-4) and "revelation" (14.6, 26, 30). On prophecy as "a sign for believers" (14.24-25) see my *Jesus and the Spirit* 230-32.

no inspired utterance should be accepted as a prophecy simply because it was inspired; rather, it had to be "tested" and "evaluated" *(diakrinō)* as to its source and significance (14.29).[136] We should probably make the same deduction in relation to the grouping of "faith, charisms of healing, and miraculous activities" (12.9-10). For "faith" is such a fundamental feature for Paul as that which conditions all Christian obedience (Rom. 1.5), and it is the same faith which should determine all relationships within the community (12.3)[137] and all actions which affect others within the community (14.23). So we may assume that Paul intended to indicate that healings and miracles were possible only when enacted in unqualified trust in God (cf. Gal. 3.5).[138]

In short, even the listing of the charisms in 1 Cor. 12.8-10 underlined the character of the charismatic community as one of mutual interdependence: a tongues-speaker without an interpreter was of little use to the congregation; a prophecy untested by the community could result in all sorts of misconception and error; healings and miracles attempted or claimed which did not express and promote trust in God were likely to mislead.

4) There is no suggestion that these charisms were conceived as fixed and well defined. On the contrary, the vagueness of some of the references ("service," "utterance of wisdom/knowledge," "faith") and the obvious overlap between others (prophecy/exhortation, sharing/caring/acts of mercy) assuredly indicate no attempt at precise identification but a readiness to recognize a wide range of utterances and actions as charisms. Nor is there any suggestion that the lists in Romans 12 and 1 Corinthians 12 were intended to

---

136. This is a repeated emphasis in Paul's treatment of spiritual matters (1 Cor. 2.13-15) and of prophecy in particular (also 1 Thes. 5.20-21). Indeed, recognition of the danger of false prophecy was long rooted in the tradition of Hebrew prophecy, and the need to "test" prophetic utterances was a repeated emphasis of early Christianity (1 John 4.1-3; *Didache* 11–13; Hermas, *Mandate* 11). The importance of this for Paul and early Christianity generally has often been missed in expositions of the spiritual gifts of 1 Cor. 12.8-10. See further below §21.6 and my *Jesus and the Spirit* 233-36; also "Prophetic 'I'-Sayings and the Jesus Tradition: The Importance of Testing Prophetic Utterances within Early Christianity," *NTS* 24 (1977-78) 175-98; "Discernment of Spirits — A Neglected Gift," in W. Harrington, ed., *Witness to the Spirit* (Dublin: Irish Biblical Association/Manchester: Koinonia, 1979) 79-96; "Responsible Congregation" (§21 n. 1) 216-26. See also below §23.4 and n. 109.

137. By "the measure of faith" Paul probably refers to different apportionments of faith; it is the same faith/trust, but experience then (as now) no doubt confirmed that not all trusted to the same extent. See further my *Romans* 721-22, *pace* particularly Cranfield, *Romans* 613-16. Similarly with prophecy — "in proportion to faith" (12.6); see again my *Romans* 727-28.

138. Note also Paul's misgivings about relying on "signs and wonders" as proof of apostleship (2 Corinthians 11–12; particularly 12.11-13).

be complete.[139] On the contrary, the list in 1 Cor. 12.6-8 obviously had in view the particular experiences and fascinations of the Corinthian assembly.[140] And even if the letter to the Corinthians may indicate Paul's vision of the body of Christ, the church of Corinth itself was hardly a model for Christian community.

5) The manner in which Paul speaks of charisms indicates that he understood a charism to have a certain "event" character. Properly speaking the charism is the word being spoken, the action being enacted.[141] The charism is a function (praxis), an act of service (diakonia), an activity (energēma), a manifestation (phanerōsis) of the Spirit. The point can be overpressed: Paul does speak of "having charisms,"[142] though that may just be a convenient way of speaking. At any rate, the description of the assembly's functioning in 1 Cor. 14.26-32 suggests a mixture of some prepared contribution and some spontaneous utterance. What should not be lost sight of, however, is the character of charism as something given, the result or expression of God's gracious act (Rom. 12.6)[143] — the utterance not as something rationally conceived or contrived but as a word of inspiration[144] — the action as enacted "out of the strength which God supplies" (1 Pet. 4.11). Both of the main lists emphasize the event character of the charisms in different ways — prophecy, the act of service, the one who teaches, the one who exhorts, etc. (Rom.

---

139. As some expositions within the classic Pentecostal tradition seem to assume. For the identification of a larger range of charisms in Paul see my *Jesus and the Spirit* 212-53.

140. "Wisdom" and "knowledge," particularly prominent themes in 1 Corinthians ("wisdom" — 1.17, 19-22, 24, 30; 3.1, 4-7, 13; 3.19; 12.8; "knowledge" — 1.5; 8.1, 7, 10-11; 12.8; 13.2, 8; 14.6); "miracles" — 12.10, 28-29; 2 Cor. 12.12; "prophecy" and "tongues" — 1 Corinthians 14!

141. Käsemann defines charism as "the manifestation and concretion of this power" ("the gracious power which bestows it"; "Ministry" [§21 n. 1] 65); Käsemann's treatment, as also mine in *Jesus and the Spirit* (particularly 253-56), was much influenced by the unpublished dissertation by F. Grau, *Der neutestamentliche Begriff* charisma (Tübingen University, 1946).

142. Rom. 12.6; 1 Cor. 7.7; 12.30; 14.26.

143. See also my *Romans* 725-26.

144. The old dispute as to whether "prophecy" is best described as "forth-telling" (preaching, bold, principled utterance; cf. now particularly T. W. Gillespie, *The First Theologians: A Study in Early Christian Prophecy* [Grand Rapids: Eerdmans, 1994]) or as "foretelling" (predictive) has obscured the more basic character of prophecy in the Judaeo-Christian tradition as inspired speech. The phenomenon of prophecy in the ancient world has received much attention. Of recent studies see particularly D. Aune, *Prophecy in Early Christianity and the Ancient Mediterranean World* (Grand Rapids: Eerdmans, 1983); C. Forbes, *Prophecy and Inspired Speech in Early Christianity and Its Hellenistic Environment* (WUNT 2.75; Tübingen: Mohr, 1995). For critique of Gillespie's thesis see Forbes 227-29, and Turner, *Holy Spirit* 206-12.

12.6-8)[145] — the charism given not for personal benefit but for the common good (1 Cor. 12.7) — "utterance of wisdom/knowledge" (not wisdom/knowledge itself), actual miracles and healings, etc. (12.8-10). So too it is significant that the second half of the second list in 1 Cor. 12.28 consists of "miracles, charisms of healing, helpful deeds, acts of counsel, kinds of tongues," rather than "those who perform miracles, who exercise charisms of healing, etc." However much the charism might accord with "natural ability" Paul did not conceive of it as itself something innate.[146] And at the very least, Paul would want to question any thought of a charism as a kind of private possession solely for personal benefit. As his extended counsel against speaking in tongues in the assembly makes clear (14.1-25), the test of a charism within the charismatic community is its benefit to the community at large.

6) Bound up with this is the character of charism as an enactment or embodiment of divine *charis,* "grace." It is this which makes the body of the Christian community the body of *Christ.* For Paul the archetypal *charisma* was the gracious act of Christ on the cross.[147] It was this fundamental fact which enabled Paul to transform a political image to express his vision of a community differently conceived and bonded, that is, into the body of *Christ,* the *charismatic* community. In other words, in Paul's vision as set out in Romans 12 and 1 Corinthians 12–14, the body of Christ could only function as such if the words and actions which purported to be charisms actually expressed the character of Christ's free act of grace on the cross — enacted in the strength of that grace, without selfish subplot, in service to God and for the benefit of others. A similar point follows from Paul's repeated emphasis in 1 Cor. 12.4-11 on the Spirit-given character of the charism, since the Spirit for Paul was now "the Spirit of Christ."[148]

7) A further variation in the body imagery which Paul took over is his emphasis that every member of the body should conceive of himself or herself as an active member. If the body consists in a diverse range of organs, each with its own function *(praxis),* so the body of Christ consists in diverse range of members each with her or his own charism (Rom. 12.4-6). "To each is given the manifestation of the Spirit for the common good" (1 Cor. 12.7). "One and the same Spirit effects all these, distributing to each as he wills" (12.11). The member of the body is not just the individual, but the functioning member, the member with his or her charism or charisms. Individuals are

145. The tense used in the latter half of the list (present) probably envisages repeated or regular ministries; see further below §21.3.

146. Cf. Hahn, "Charisma" (§21 n. 1) 216-17.

147. Rom. 5.15-16. See further on *charis* ("grace") above §13.2.

148. See above §10.6 and §16.4. Hence here 12.3 (inspiration identified by Christ confession), 12.4-6 (same Spirit, same Lord, same God), 12.12-13 (baptized in one Spirit into the one body which is Christ).

members of the body as charismatics. The main thrust of Paul's vivid exposition of the body in 1 Cor. 12.14-26 is to reinforce this point. He has no conception of a distinction between functioning and nonfunctioning members, between those who minister to and those who are only ministered to. No members should regard their charisms as of lesser value or of too little significance or opt out from the body's functioning (12.15-16). No members should regard the charisms of others as dispensable or unnecessary (12.21). Common respect and care for one another should rise above all diversity of function, however insignificant, however great (12.22-26).

Particularly worthy of note is Paul's insistence that ministry should not and could not (by definition of "body") be limited to a few. It was a point evidently requiring some emphasis in the Corinthian congregation. For he makes a particular point of stressing that no one member or gift could encompass the whole body (12.17-20). And he makes his point with a touch of humour by, in effect, drawing a cartoon. Imagine, he says, a body consisting solely of an eye or solely of an ear (12.17). What kind of body is that? No body at all (12.19)! Without the many and different members/organs there would be no body, or at best only fragmented bits (12.20). In short, when ministry is limited to the few the result is a grotesque parody of the body, a body eighty or ninety percent paralyzed, with only the few organs functioning, and functioning to little effect, since the effectiveness of the body depends on its diversity functioning in unity.

8) The dynamic character of the body of Christ as envisaged by Paul is also expressed in his imagery of all baptized in one Spirit into one body (1 Cor. 12.13). However the image is related to baptism as such, it is clear that the image is initiatory — "baptized into one body."[149] The point here is that Paul draws this imagery of Spirit baptism into the heart of his discussion of charisms and the body of Christ. Clearly implicit is the claim that to have been baptized in the Spirit is to have been initiated into functioning membership of the body. "Baptism in the Spirit" for Paul, we may say, was not something other than initiatory, but it was an initiation into charismatic membership of the charismatic community. As for Paul himself, conversion was also commission, initiation was also vocation, baptism in Spirit was also engracing for ministry.

More needs to be said to complete Paul's picture of the functioning church of God.[150] For the moment it is sufficient to attempt to grasp the basic character of Christian corporateness, the body of Christ. Above all it is im-

---

149. See above §16 n. 44. Ridderbos, *Paul* 372-73, puts it the wrong way around: "the Spirit . . . [is] the gift in which believers share in virtue of their incorporation into the body."

150. See below §§21.3-6.

portant to recognize the transition in conceptuality from a community identified by ethnic and traditional markers to a community where Christ and the
Spirit were the essential distinguishing features, that is, the grace of Christ
and the charisms given by his Spirit, with all that that involved.

§20.6 The shared experience of the Spirit

One other feature is implicit in what has been already said but deserves
separate notice. That is the church of God as something which grows out of
the shared experience of the Spirit. It is not something which Paul makes
explicit in Romans as such, but it is an emphasis in other letters. And I suppose
we could say that it is the correlative of the third emphasis in the beginning
of salvation: if the community without cult echoes justification by faith (§14)
and the body of Christ expresses participation in Christ (§15), so the community of the Spirit is the obvious outworking of the gift of the Spirit (§16).[151]
        The point is most straightforwardly expressed in the familiar concept
of the *koinōnia pneumatos*.[152] This is usually translated, misleadingly, as "the
fellowship of the Spirit," where the implication is of a community created by
the Spirit. But repeated studies have rightly emphasized that the basic meaning
of the phrase is better given in a translation like "participation in the Spirit."[153]
That is to say, what is in view is not a physical entity (like a congregation),
but the subjective experience of the Spirit as something shared. The point is,
then, that what draws and keeps believers together for Paul was not simply a
common membership of a congregation, but the common experience of the

---

151. Cf. Goguel: "the whole of Paul's conception of the Church may be understood
as a reflection of his doctrine of the Spirit" (*Primitive Church* 53).

152. 2 Cor. 13.13-14; Phil. 2.1. *Koinōnia* is predominantly a Pauline term within
the NT — 13 of the 19 occurrences in the NT appear in the undisputed Paulines (Rom.
15.26; 1 Cor. 1.9; 10.16 [twice]; 2 Cor. 6.14; 8.4; 9.13; 13.13; Gal. 2.9; Phil. 1.5; 2.1; 3.10;
Phm. 6).

153. J. Y. Campbell, "*KOINŌNIA* and Its Cognates in the New Testament," *JBL*
51 (1932), reprinted in *Three New Testament Studies* (Leiden: Brill, 1965) 1-28 (especially
25-27); F. Hauck, *TDNT* 3.804-8; J. Hainz, *EDNT* 2.203-5, drawing on his larger study,
KOINŌNIA. "Kirche" als Gemeinschaft bei Paulus (BU 16; Regensburg: Pustet, 1982).
The point is more obscure in G. Panikulam, *Koinonia in the New Testament: A Dynamic
Expression of Christian Life* (AnBib 85; Rome: Biblical Institute, 1979). In each case the
thought is of the act or experience of sharing, rather than of a condition or action created
by the term qualified: the act of sharing in the Lord's Supper, not the congregation which
celebrates the Lord's Supper (1 Cor. 10.16); the actual taking part in the collection, not
the generosity which prompts it (2 Cor. 8.4); the shared experience of promulgating the
gospel and of Christ's sufferings, not a quasi-title for a mission team or an order of
spirituality (Phil. 1.5; 3.10); and so on.

Spirit. It was the awareness that their experience of the Spirit (§16) was one
in which others had also shared which provided the bond of mutual understanding and sympathy.

The point is implicit in what we saw earlier about the gift of the Spirit
as constituting the basic mark and definition of the Christian for Paul (§16).
But within the material we have been looking at in §20 it is most clearly
indicated once again in 1 Cor. 12.13: it is their common experience of being
baptized in *one* Spirit which constitutes them *one* body; it is their common
experience of being watered with *one* Spirit which renders irrelevant differences of nationality and social status.[154]

The same emphasis is retained into the later Ephesians. In Eph. 4.3-4
the unity of the church is seen as the direct outworking of the unity of the
Spirit. The choice of verb is instructive: "make every effort to preserve *(tērein)*
the unity of the Spirit in the bond of peace" (4.3). The unity of the Spirit was
something given, the basis of unity, not something which they could create.
All the Ephesians could do was either preserve it or lose/destroy it.

The practical theological corollary to this is that the community of the
Spirit is in no sense a human creation. For Paul, we may fairly say, community
grew out of the shared experience of the Spirit. Or, as we might say, fellowship
(in the usual sense) grew out of common participation in the one Spirit.
Otherwise it was not the body of Christ. This, we may assume, was no
theoretical statement, but confirmed for Paul in the shared experience of many
of his churches — as most evident in the emotive appeal of Phil. 2.1-4.
Already, we may guess, he was all too conscious of the danger of the fountainhead of Christian community and unity being choked by factional disputes
and self-seeking.

§20.7 An unrealistic vision?

We should not forget that Paul expounded his vision of the body of Christ in
Romans 12 and 1 Corinthians 12 at least in part in reaction to the factionalism
and community tensions of both sets of churches. That is to say, Paul was no
mere dreamer of dreams or promoter of merely idealistic blueprints. He was
well aware of how far the churches to which he was writing were falling short
of his vision. He may well have realized that the theology expounded was
strictly speaking unrealistic in the realities of the little house churches scattered
round the Mediterranean. Someone who recognized so clearly the eschatological tension, the not yet as well as the already, in the process of personal

---

154. See further my *Jesus and the Spirit* 261-62; "Paul does not say 'one baptism,
therefore one body,' but 'one *Spirit*, therefore one body' " (261).

salvation (§18), was hardly likely to ignore the same realities at the corporate level. The church too was caught in the overlap of the ages. In its corporate existence it was as unable to throw off the weaknesses of the corporate body of this age as was the individual to escape from the weaknesses of the physical body of this age.

It is also true that Paul's own transforming vision was itself soon transformed, with many of its distinctive features lost to sight. His vision of the church of God as fully manifested in the local church was displaced by the thought of the Church universal (already in Ephesians).[155] His vision of a noncultic community, lacking any distinct order of priests, was beginning to fade already in *1 Clement*.[156] His understanding of *charisma* was already being qualified in the Pastorals and disappears in the second century.[157] His emphasis on the shared experience of the Spirit begins to be submerged beneath an understandable concern for ecclesiastical good order and sidelined as a more sectarian emphasis over the same period.[158]

Nevertheless, Paul thought it important to spell out the principles of Christian community as he saw them. He took the lessons learned by many city governments and transformed them into a model for the church of God.[159] And these principles, if they had validity in reference to the troubled churches of Paul's mission, may still have validity for churches of later times. As he called his own churches to measure themselves against his vision, so later churches could do far worse than check their own structures and operating practices against the principles he outlines.

Above all is the theological insight implicit in the very concept of "the body of Christ." The overlap with the language of "participation in Christ" (§15) can readily distract the thought into an otherworldly mysticism. But the recognition of the character of "body" as embodiment, enabling corporeal encounter and relationship (§3.2), points in quite the other direction. The point being that, as it is human embodiment which makes society possible, so the

---

155. See above §20.2. But Ephesians also shows how adaptable Paul's vision of the charismatic community was to a universal concept of the church (4.7-16).

156. See the brief discussion in my *Partings* 254-57 and note particularly the classic study of J. B. Lightfoot, "The Christian Ministry," *St Paul's Epistle to the Philippians* (London: Macmillan, 1868) 179-267. During the early centuries of the common era the other child of Second Temple Judaism, rabbinic Judaism, emerged as a different system, focused on the rabbi rather than the priest.

157. See above n. 114.

158. Particularly with regard to the Montanists.

159. Perhaps, by implication, a model of what all community should be. This thought seems to lie behind the extension of the imagery in Col. 1.18: the church as the firstfruits of the reconciled creation (1.20-22). At any rate, Klaiber's talk of an "ecclesiastical deficit" in the work of Paul (*Rechtfertigung* 9) probably does insufficient justice to the principles he expressed so clearly.

church is the means by which Christ makes actual tangible encounter with wider society. At this point there is a continuity of thought from the body language of Rom. 12.2 to that of 12.4-5. Here the vision enshrines a fundamental principle of Christian identity.

Also of importance is the recognition that in the charismatic body of Christ Paul has given the church of all times a definitive model of unity and diversity. Of a unity which grows out of the shared experience of grace (whatever the formulae and rituals which may now express it), a unity which is dynamic and not static, a unity which expresses ever anew the fresh experiences of grace of each new generation. Of a unity which recognizes the givenness of grace, the consequent and constant dependence on that grace, and that charisms are not a possession, not a right, but a responsibility, for the benefit of others, acts of service and not of self-indulgence. Of a unity which would be stifled by monoministry (the whole body an eye or an ear!) or by ministry too narrowly conceived, a unity whose effectiveness depends on the ministry of the whole people of God being fully recognized and implemented in a degree which has not been in evidence for the great bulk of Christian history. In short, Paul's vision of the body of Christ is of a unity which consists in diversity, that is, a unity which is not denied by diversity, but which would be denied by uniformity, a unity which depends on its diversity functioning as such — in a word, the unity of a body, the body of Christ.

§21 Ministry and authority[1]

1. **Bibliography**: **Barrett**, *Paul* 119-27; **N. Baumert**, "Charisma und Amt bei Paulus," in A. Vanhoye, ed., *L'Apôtre Paul* 203-28; *Woman and Man in Paul: Overcoming a Misunderstanding* (Collegeville: Liturgical/Glazier, 1996) 174-212; **A. Bittlinger**, *Gifts and Graces* (London: Hodder and Stoughton, 1967); *Gifts and Ministries* (Grand Rapids: Eerdmans, 1973); **U. Brockhaus**, *Charisma und Amt. Die paulinische Charismenlehre auf dem Hintergrund der frühchristlichen Gemeindefunktionen* (Wuppertal: Brockhaus, 1972); **J. T. Burtchaell**, *From Synagogue to Church: Public Services and Offices in the Earliest Christian Communities* (Cambridge: Cambridge University, 1992); **R. A. Campbell**, *The Elders: Seniority within Earliest Christianity* (Edinburgh: Clark, 1994); **H. von Campenhausen**, *Ecclesiastical Authority and Spiritual Power in the Church of the First Three Centuries* (1953; London: Black, 1969); **H. Doohan**, *Leadership in Paul* (Wilmington: Glazier, 1984); **Dunn**, *Jesus and the Spirit* (§18 n. 1) ch. 9; "The Responsible Congregation (1 Cor. 14.26-40)," in L. de Lorenzi, ed., *Charisma und Agape (1 Kor. 12–14)* (Rome: Abbey of St. Paul, 1983) 201-36; **E. E. Ellis**, *Pauline Theology: Ministry and Society* (Grand Rapids: Eerdmans/Exeter: Paternoster, 1989); **E. S. Fiorenza**, *In Memory of Her: A Feminist Theological Reconstruction of Christian Origins* (London: SCM/New York: Crossroad, 1983); **G. Friedrich**, "Das Amt im Neuen Testament," in J. Friedrich, ed., *Auf das Wort kommt es an* (Göttingen: Vandenhoeck, 1978) 416-30; **H. Greeven**, "Propheten, Lehrer, Vorsteher bei Paulus," *ZNW* 44 (1952-53) 1-43; **F. Hahn**, "Charisma und Amt," *ZTK* 76 (1979) 419-49 = *Exegetische Beiträge zum ökumenischen Gespräch: Gesammelte Aufsätze* (Göttingen: Vandenhoeck, 1986) 201-31; **A. Harnack**, *The Constitution and Law of the Church in the First Two Centuries* (London: Williams and Norgate, 1910); **G. Hasenhüttl**, *Charisma. Ordnungsprinzip der Kirche* (Freiburg: Herder, 1969); **B. Holmberg**, *Paul and Power: The Structure of Authority in the Primitive Church as Reflected in the Pauline Epistles* (Lund: Gleerup, 1978 = Philadelphia: Fortress, 1980); **E. Käsemann**, "Ministry and Community in the New Testament," *Essays* 63-94; **Kertelge**, "Der Ort des Amtes in der Ekklesiologie des Paulus," *Grundthemen* 216-34; **K. Kertelge**, ed., *Das Kirchliche Amt im Neuen Testament* (Darmstadt: Wissenschaftliche Buchgesellschaft, 1977); **H. Küng**, *The Church* (London: Burns and Oates/New York: Sheed and Ward, 1967); **T. M. Lindsay**, *The Church and the Ministry in the Early Centuries* (London: Hodder and Stoughton, 1902); **R. P. Martin**, *The Spirit and the Congregation* (Grand Rapids: Eerdmans, 1984); **M. Y. MacDonald**, *The Pauline Churches: A Socio-Historical Study of Institutionalization in the Pauline and Deutero-Pauline Writings* (SNTSMS 60; Cambridge: Cambridge University, 1988); **Meeks**, *First Urban Christians* 111-39; **P.-H. Menoud**, *L'Église et les ministères selon le Nouveau Testament* (Neuchâtel/Paris: Delachaux et Niestlé, 1949); **Ridderbos**, *Paul* 429-86; **J. H. Schütz**, *Paul and the Anatomy of Apostolic Authority* (SNTSMS 26; Cambridge: Cambridge University, 1975); **E. Schweizer**, *Church Order in the New Testament* (London: SCM/Naperville: Allenson, 1961); **G. Shaw**, *The Cost*

§21.1 Charism and office

Paul's exposition of the charismatic body of Christ brings in the more established ministries of apostle, prophet, and teacher in a surprisingly marginal way. They are mentioned only at the end of 1 Corintians 12 (vv. 28-29), and prophets as such likewise appear only towards the end of the lengthy discussion of the relative merits of tongues-speaking and prophecy in 1 Corinthians 14 (vv. 29-32). Similarly in Rom. 12.6-7, as we saw, the talk is of "prophecy" (rather than prophets) and of "the one who teaches" (rather than teachers). This somewhat (as it would appear to later generations) lopsided ecclesiology has been at the root of one of the classic disputes in Pauline theology. It underlay the repeated reaction against clericalism and ecclesiastical bureaucracy in church history and calls to return to the structures of the primitive church.[2] And a century ago it sparked off a long, running debate about the relation between *Charisma* and *Amt* (office).[3]

The issue crystallized in a much recalled debate between Rudolph Sohm and Adolf Harnack which spanned the turn of the century (nineteenth to twentieth). Prior to that there had been a broad consensus among Protestant theologians regarding the organization of the early church. According to this rather idealistic consensus, each local church was autonomous and governed "democratically" by the individual members acting in free association. Apostles, prophets, and teachers were functions rather than "offices."[4] Sohm,

---

of Authority: Manipulation and Freedom in the New Testament (London: SCM/Philadelphia: Fortress, 1983); **R. Sohm**, *Kirchenrecht* I (1892; Munich/Leipzig: Duncker und Humblot, 1923); *Wesen und Ursprung des Katholizismus* (Leipzig/Berlin: Teubner, [2]1912); **Strecker**, *Theologie* 198-206; **Theissen**, *Social Setting;* **W. Trilling**, "Zum 'Amt' im Neuen Testament. Eine methodologische Besinnung," in U. Luz and H. Weder, eds., *Die Mitte des Neuen Testament. Einheit und Vielfalt neutestamentlicher Theologie,* E. Schweizer FS (Göttingen: Vandenhoeck, 1983) 319-44; **A. C. Wire**, *The Corinthian Women Prophets: A Reconstruction through Paul's Rhetoric* (Minneapolis: Fortress, 1990).

2. See, e.g., E. H. Broadbent, *The Pilgrim Church* (London: Pickering and Inglis, 1931); F. H. Littell, *The Origins of Sectarian Protestantism* (New York: Macmillan, 1958).

3. In the following paragraph I follow principally Brockhaus's review (*Charisma* 7-25); but note also O. Linton, *Das Problem der Urkirche in der neueren Forschung* (Uppsala: Almquist & Wiksells, 1932); I am indebted also to the M.A. thesis by C. Clausen, *The Structure of the Pauline Churches: "Charisma" and "Office"* (Durham University, 1991). Brockhaus sums up the constitutive characteristics of "office" as: (1) duration, (2) recognition by the congregation, (3) the special status of the individual in relation to the congregation (authority, dignity), (4) a well-ordered commission (laying on of hands), (5) legal securing of the function in question (*Charisma* 24 n. 106). Clausen properly adds (6) the possibility of withdrawing the office from one person to confer it on another. For a definition of charism see above §20.5.

4. Brockhaus, *Charisma* 8.

however, sharpened the implied distinction into an antithesis — for Sohm the antithesis between *charisma* and *Kirchenrecht* ("canon law"). His principal thesis was that "canon law stands in contradiction with the nature of the Church"; "the apostolic teaching on the constitution of the *ekklēsia* is that the organization of Christendom is not a legal one ('rechtliche'), but a charismatic organization"; that is, "Christendom is organized through the distribution of spiritual gifts."[5] The church's fall ("Sündefall"), in which the charismatic organization given by God was displaced and set aside through human *Kirchenrecht,* is, for Sohm, first visible in *1 Clement.*[6]

Harnack was influenced by Sohm at various points.[7] In particular he agreed that the earliest churches were "spiritual democracies." At the same time, however, he insisted that they were not purely spiritual entities; they took a social and corporate form. Analogously he recognized with Sohm a tension in the earliest church organization between Spirit and office. The critical point of his disagreement, so far as we are concerned, was that he saw the tension not as sequential but as simultaneous (charismatic offices of the whole church, and administrative offices at the local level). These two points of disagreement in effect set the agenda for the debate which followed. We could reformulate them in our own terms thus: to what extent does Paul's vision of charismatic community have to be qualified by the realities which Paul encountered all the time in his pastoral dealings with his churches (the church in Corinth not least)? To what extent were "institution," "hierarchy," and "office" integral to Paul's vision from the first, not to say an unavoidable feature of Paul's implementation of his vision in practice?

The debate was revived in mid-century by a sequence of studies, of which the most important were those by Hans von Campenhausen, Ernst Käsemann, and the sequence of earliest contributions of Eduard Schweizer.[8] Campenhausen restated the emphasis of Sohm by insisting that for Paul the Spirit is the organizing principle of the church, and that ministry "rests in principle not on some human organisational plan . . . ; it is the employment of a gift which the Spirit bestows." Paul's vision was "of the structure of the community as one of free fellowship, developing through the living interplay of spiritual gifts and ministries, without benefit of official authority or responsible 'elders.'" It is only later on that the institution of elders, already

---

5. *Kirchenrecht* 1.1, 26 (Brockhaus, *Charisma* 15).

6. Brockhaus, *Charisma* 17. Although the resulting debate is summed up in the *Charisma-Amt* contrast, it should be noted that Sohm did not pose it so (Brockhaus 18). See further Sohm's subsequent contribution in debate with Harnack *(Wesen).*

7. The most convenient presentation of Harnack's views is his *Constitution,* with critique of Sohm in 176-258. See also the review of the debate in Ridderbos, *Paul* 439-40.

8. All three considerably influenced my *Jesus and the Spirit* chs. 8-9 on these questions.

present in the Jewish-Christian churches, appears also in the Pauline churches.[9] Käsemann attempted more vigorously than Campenhausen to transcend the antithesis of charism and office by viewing them in dialectical relationship.[10] But he still emphasised that Paul's "theory of order is not a static one, resting on offices, institutions, ranks and dignities"; in his view, "authority resides only within the concrete act of ministry as it occurs." At the same time, in characteristic vein, he recognized also that Paul's vision in practice was always vulnerable to "enthusiasm."[11] Less inhibited is Schweizer: in Paul's church order there is "no fundamental organization of superior or subordinate ranks, because the gift of the Spirit is adapted to every church member"; "the church becomes a church, not by tradition in itself, but by the repeated action of the Spirit"; "all order is an 'afterwards,' an attempt to follow what God has already designed."[12]

The discussion was characteristically Protestant in participant and content.[13] But it threw up exegetical observations and conclusions which could hardly be ignored more widely. Here the "before and after" of the Second Vatican Council is relevant. The difference is illustrated by comparison between the essentially pre-Vatican II monograph of Rudolph Schnackenburg and that of Hans Küng, reflecting as it does the two-way influence of Vatican II's dogmatic statement on the church *(Lumen Gentium).*[14] Schnackenburg has no hesitation in speaking of "offices" in connection with Paul and in putting much more emphasis on hierarchy and authority than on charisms and the freedom of the Spirit. He presupposes the primacy of Peter and stresses both Paul's status as an authorized apostle and the hierarchy implicit in 1 Cor. 12.28. Not surprisingly, then, the outcome, even for the Pauline churches, is a hierarchical structure very similar to that of subsequent Catholicism.

In contrast, Küng regards "the continuing charismatic structure" of the church as part of its "fundamental structure." Taking Paul's vision seriously, he observes: "The charism cannot be subsumed under the heading of ecclesiastical office, but all church offices can be subsumed under the charism. . . . One can speak of a charismatic structure of the Church, which

9. Campenhausen, *Authority* 68, 70-71, 76-123.

10. Cf. his much cited essay, "Sentences of Holy Law in the New Testament," *New Testament Questions of Today* 66-81, in which he posits prophetic utterances like 1 Cor. 3.17 ("If anyone destroys God's temple, God will destroy him") and argues that "it is precisely the Spirit who creates such an ordinance and makes possible in the church authoritative action and the erection of definite law" (69).

11. Käsemann, "Ministry," here 83, 93.

12. Schweizer, *Church Order* 99, 102.

13. The English-language contributions of Lindsay, *Church,* and B. H. Streeter, *The Primitive Church* (London/New York: Macmillan, 1929), were largely ignored.

14. Schnackenburg, *Church;* Küng, *Church.*

includes and goes far beyond the hierarchical structure of the Church."[15] And his analysis leaves the question of "the offices of the Church" to the end, where even there the emphasis is on "The Priesthood of All Believers" and "Ecclesiastical Office as Ministry."[16] Küng was also able to subvert to some extent the attempts of both Sohm and Käsemann to distance Paul from subsequent (early) Catholicism by insisting that the significance of the "early Catholicism" of the later Paulines be given full weight as also part of the Christian canon of scripture.[17]

We may also note that the scholarly debates were paralleled by developments at grassroots levels — particularly in the emergence of the Christian Brethren in Britain in the mid-nineteenth century and of classic Pentecostalism in the early twentieth century. Not untypically, the great bulk of scholars were oblivious to these developments. More notice has been taken of the charismatic renewal, also since the 1960s, which has given some fresh impetus to the discussion of the biblical material, though without much changing the issues.[18] One can scarcely avoid observing how frequently the charism/office debate has been played out by successive generations in practice (not just theory), usually without much awareness of the experience of former generations or of the lessons to be learned from that history.

The debate, however, has been transformed by the introduction of questions and issues which arise from viewing the Corinthian church and the Corinthian correspondence in particular from a sociological perspective. Max Weber long ago provided a potentially valuable model for interpreting Paul's theology of church structure and operation. This was the model of charismatic authority, understood as authority which is derived from a prophet's immediate contact with the supernatural or sacred, which brings disruption and innovation into the previous routine and institution, but whose transforming effect can

---

15. Küng, *Church* 187-88. "The fundamental structure of the Church" for Küng focuses on "I. The Church as the People of God, II. The Church as the Creation of The Spirit (including 'The continuing charismatic structure'), and III. The Church as the Body of Christ."

16. The same influence has shaped the WCC's statement on *Baptism, Eucharist and Ministry* (Geneva: World Council of Churches, 1982), with its similar setting of "the calling of the whole people of God" in first place.

17. H. Küng, *Structures of the Church* (New York: Nelson, 1964 = London: Burns and Oates, 1965) 135-51.

18. See particularly Bittlinger, *Gifts;* also Bittlinger, ed., *The Church Is Charismatic* (above §16 n. 11); my "Ministry and the Ministry: The Charismatic Renewal's Challenge to Traditional Ecclesiology," in C. M. Robeck, ed., *Charismatic Experiences in History* (Peabody: Hendrickson, 1985) 81-101.

be sustained only by itself being routinized or institutionalized. The correlation with the issues in the charism/office debate is obvious.[19]

John Schütz was one of the first to apply Weber's understanding of charismatic authority to Paul, by using a threefold distinction between power, authority, and legitimacy — with power understood as the source of authority, authority as the application of power, and legitimacy as the formalization of authority.[20] The more thoroughgoing use of Weber was that of Bengt Holmberg, though he drew on Weber's work only after he had analysed the distribution of power within the local Pauline churches and then related Weber's model more to the relationship between Paul and Jerusalem.[21] In his magisterial study Wayne Meeks has observed, *inter alia,* both that the house church *(kat' oikon ekklēsia)* was the "basic cell" of the Christian movement and that the structure of the household *(oikos)* was hierarchical.[22] Margaret MacDonald has analysed the early Pauline communities in terms of sect formation, though her main interest is in the process of institutionalization. Here, for example, by pointing to the leadership already evident in 1 Cor. 12.28 and 16.15-18, she is able to argue against Campenhausen for a degree of institutionalization already present in the Corinthian church.[23] Andrew Clarke in turn draws in another dimension of recent sociological analysis of the Corinthian church (its social stratification)[24] to suggest that there was indeed a religious leadership in Corinth, but the wrong kind of leadership, dependent on social status and rhetorical skill.[25]

The importance of this new dimension for the older debate needs to be appreciated. Despite the closing observations of §20, there has always been the danger of taking Paul's treatment of the charismatic community as a complete description of his ecclesiology or even as an actual description of a Pauline congregation.[26] The sociological perspective forces us to relate Paul's

---

19. A largely unsung predecessor, though he did influence Harnack, was E. Hatch, *The Organization of the Early Christian Churches* (London: Longmans, 1888), who argued that the elements of the organization of the Christian churches were already existing in human society.

20. Schütz, *Paul.*

21. Holmberg, *Paul.*

22. Meeks, *Urban Christians* 75-77.

23. MacDonald, *Pauline Churches,* particularly 51-60.

24. The credit for bringing the issue of social status effectively before NT scholarship can be given to Theissen, *Social Setting.*

25. A. D. Clarke, *Secular and Christian Leadership in Corinth: A Socio-Historical and Exegetical Study of 1 Corinthians 1–6* (Leiden: Brill, 1993); note also J. K. Chow, *Patronage and Power: A Study of Social Networks in Corinth* (JSNTS 75; Sheffield: JSOT, 1992).

26. Sohm and to some extent Campenhausen and Käsemann are vulnerable to this criticism.

vision to the reality of first-century Corinth, to take seriously the important other evidence in the Pauline letters of how his churches actually functioned and how he himself related to them as their founding apostle. In switching from a theology of church and charism to the question of what ministry actually involved for Paul and how authority (charismatic or otherwise) actually operated, we are given a unique opportunity to relate Paul's theological vision to his applied theology, to check how his theology worked out in practice and (not least of importance) how Paul reacted in turn. Here more than in almost any other sphere[27] we can gain a sense of Paul's theology as theologizing, of what the living dialogue of his theology amounted to. Paul the theologian and pastor would no doubt have appreciated the point.

The obvious place to begin is with Paul's concept and practice of his own apostleship, before we move on to the other regular ministries to which Paul refers and to the final issue of the authority which Paul attributed to the church as a whole.

§21.2 Paul's apostolic authority

The opportunity to compare Paul's theology and his practice, or, better, his theology in practice, is nowhere so promising as in the case of apostolic authority.[28] For Paul was himself an apostle. He was fiercely insistent on the point from Galatians onwards (Gal. 1.1),[29] and he did not hesitate to number his own commissioning experience of the risen Christ with the earlier resurrection appearances (1 Cor. 15.5-8).[30] Whether there was some hesitation on the part of Jerusalem-based Christians to accept this claim is not clear.[31] What was of more importance to him was that he had demonstrated his apostolic commissioning

---

27. But see also §24 below.

28. The bibliography on the subject is extensive; see, e.g., J.-A. Bühner, *apostolos, EDNT* 1.142-46; H. D. Betz, "Apostle," *ABD* 1.309-11.

29. He first registered the claim in the opening of his letter to the Galatians (the characteristic self-identification "Paul, apostle," is lacking in the two Thessalonian letters), and thereafter it became a standard feature of his letter openings (with only Philippians and Philemon as further exceptions within the Pauline corpus).

30. To be noted, however, is the fact that he saw his commissioning as "last of all" (1 Cor. 15.8). Paul did not think that there were any further appointments to apostolic rank after him (hence the "before me" of Rom. 16.7). Whether the delay of the parousia would have made any difference here, too, is hard to tell, but certainly the perspective of the later Paulines is different (cf. particularly 2 Tim. 2.2).

31. Was he echoing a factional Christian jibe when he called himself "an abortion" (*ektrōma;* NRSV's "untimely born" softens the harshness of the image) in 1 Cor. 15.8 (see above §13 n. 87)? And was the term "apostleship" withheld from the description of Paul's missionary work in the agreement reached in Jerusalem (Gal. 2.8b; so Betz, *Galatians* 98)?

by his success in founding churches. And to those churches at least he was an apostle. So to the Corinthians he could say, "If to others I am not an apostle, at least I am to you; for you are the seal of my apostleship in the Lord" (1 Cor. 9.2).[32] Paul, then, writes his letters to his churches precisely as their apostle. His letters, in other words, are themselves the exercise of his apostleship. In seeing how he deals with his churches and his converts we come to know what apostleship and apostolic authority meant in practice for Paul.

It follows that to tackle the subject properly would require analysis of more or less everything Paul wrote. Fortunately, however, Paul's concept and exercise of his authority as apostle is most explicit and overt in Galatians, the Corinthian correspondence, and Philemon. From the theologizing of these letters in particular we can see several principles of apostolic authority at work, principles in practice.

a) The central principle in Galatians is the primacy of the gospel. This comes out clearly in the letter in the fascinating interplay between, on the one hand, the gospel and, on the other, Paul's apostolic authority, the authority of the Jerusalem apostles, and his concern for the Galatians.[33]

It soon becomes clear that Paul saw his apostleship as wholly subordinate to, or better, wholly in service of the gospel. Gal. 1.1 taken in isolation can easily give the impression that Paul's primary concern was to defend his apostleship. But the first main section of the letter (chs. 1–2) shows that it was his gospel which Paul was most concerned about.[34] Even the authority of angels was subordinate to that (1.8). It is the immediate heavenly authority of his gospel which he seeks to defend in the first part of the *narratio* (1.11-24). And it is the truth of the gospel (2.4, 14), the proof of the gospel (2.7-8), and the confirmation of the gospel by Jerusalem and Peter in particular which is at stake in ch. 2. This tie-in between apostleship and gospel was obviously of first importance for Paul, both in theory and in practice. An apostle could not ride roughshod over the gospel. Apostolic authority was conditional upon the gospel and subject to the norm of the gospel.[35]

---

32. See also 1 Cor. 4.14-15; 2 Cor. 3.2-3; 11.2; 12.14; similarly 1 Thes. 2.11. In view of §7 above we need say no more here about the source of Paul's apostolic authority (see also my *Jesus and the Spirit* 276-77).

33. He did not recognize the authority of his Galatian opponents ("troublemakers, agitators" — 1.7; 5.10, 12); note the similarly dismissive "false brothers" (2.4) and "certain from James" (2.12). The real issue was whether the authority of the Jerusalem apostles could be marshalled against him.

34. *Euangelion* — 1.6-7, 11; 2.2, 5, 7, 14.

35. Schütz, *Paul,* particularly 122-23, 155-58, 284-85; see also G. Lyons, *Pauline Autobiography: Toward a New Understanding* (SBLDS 73; Atlanta: Scholars, 1985), particularly 171; B. R. Gaventa, "Galatians 1 and 2: Autobiography as Paradigm," *NovT* 28 (1986) 309-26. This is also the root of Paul's theology of suffering, including apostolic suffering (see above §18.5). See also the emphasis of Klaiber, *Rechtfertigung* (§20 n. 1) 70-85 ("Gemeinde aus dem Evangelium").

As regards the Jerusalem apostles, chs. 1–2 are again illuminating. For in these chapters Paul treads a narrow path between recognition of the Jerusalem apostles' authority (not least as "pillars") in the past, and his depreciation of their authority in the present.[36] On the one hand, Paul's anxiety to show how minimal were his early contacts with them (1.17–2.1) is itself an admission that more contact with them would have meant more influence from them. His hesitant wording in 2.2 acknowledges that their decision regarding his gospel could have rendered his mission in vain. And in the event their confirmation of his gospel was crucial: they could have "compelled" Titus to be circumcised, but did not do so; they could have "added" something to Paul, but did not do so (2.3, 6); instead they gave (as of their right) to Paul and Barnabas the right hand of fellowship (2.9).

On the other hand, Paul three times uses of them the distancing phrase "those held in repute" (2.2, 6, 9)[37] — a phrase which acknowledges the high regard in which they were held (by others), without clearly affirming their status on his own part. Still more striking is the parenthesis Paul adds in 2.6 — "what they once were makes no difference to me; God shows no partiality." The note of depreciation could hardly be clearer. And in 2.11-16 his rebuke of Peter is scathing. Here again, then, Paul evidently saw apostolic authority as wholly circumscribed by the gospel. He appeals in effect to the authority of the pillar apostles, precisely because they exercised that authority appropriately in recognizing the gospel for Gentiles as well as Jews. But where that authority came into conflict with "the truth of the gospel" (2.14) he was no longer willing to grant that recognition. In 2 Corinthians 11–12 the dismissal becomes even more scathing.[38]

As for his authority before the Galatians themselves, Paul is certainly threatening and fierce enough.[39] But there is no ordering or commanding, not even his characteristic "appeal" *(parakaleō)*.[40] Some might see his language

36. See my "The Relationship between Paul and Jerusalem according to Galatians 1 and 2," *Jesus, Paul and the Law* 108-28, where I was particularly indebted to Holmberg's observation that "the dialectic between being independent of and being acknowledged by Jerusalem is the keynote of this important text" (*Paul* 15), though much less impressed by his subsequent argument that the relation between Paul and Jerusalem in his last visit to Jerusalem was still the same as during his second visit (Gal. 2.1-10; *Paul* 56).

37. Literally, "those who are influential, recognized as being something, who have a reputation" (BAGD, *dokeō* 2b).

38. 2 Cor. 11.5, 13; 12.11-12. Note again the priority of "the truth" (of the gospel) in 2 Cor. 13.8. See also below n. 66.

39. Particularly 1.6-9; 5.2-12.

40. Rom. 12.1; 15.30; 16.17; 1 Cor. 1.10; 4.16; 16.12, 15; 2 Cor. 2.8; 5.20; 6.1; 9.5; 10.1; 12.18; Phil. 4.2; 1 Thes. 2.12; 4.1, 10; 5.14; 2 Thes. 3.12; Phm. 9-10; also Eph. 4.1. See further n. 43 below.

as bluster, some as cajoling, others simply as pleading and warning. Paul was certainly upset, anxious, and angry when he wrote the letter. But he was realistic enough to recognize that an authority overplayed was likely to be an authority repudiated. Even in this his fiercest letter[41] he was aware that the success of his appeal depended first and foremost on the effect of the gospel on his readers. Without that (3.1-5; 4.6-9) his appeal was lost. With it, his authority was best directed to reinforcing that effect.

b) On the day-to-day reality of Paul's apostolic authority, the most instructive text is undoubtedly 1 Corinthians. Here not least it is important both to remember that the letter is only one side of what was obviously a series of vigorous debates within the Corinthian church and to draw on the insights provided by recent sociological and rhetorical analysis of the letter. What emerges is a fascinating attempt on Paul's part to exercise his authority in order to encourage the Corinthians to take on fuller responsibility for themselves. Here, we may say, a second principle emerges: that apostolic authority is exercised not over the Christian community, but within it; and the authority is exercised (in the words of Ephesians) "to equip the saints for the work of ministry, for the building up of Christ's body" (Eph. 4.12).[42]

It is certainly clear enough that Paul sought to exercise authority in reference to the Corinthians as their apostle. Having stressed his apostleship (9.1-2), he proceeds to stress his authority (*exousia* — 9.4-6, 12, 18). So also throughout the letter. In the exhortation which forms the thematic statement of the letter (1.10 — the appeal for unity and for an end to factionalism), the verb used *(parakaleō)* is not a weak term, but one typical of a superior addressing inferiors.[43] He repeatedly appeals to his commission,[44] and claims to exercise the power of the Spirit.[45] He rebukes them as a mature pneumatic speaking to "people of the flesh, infants in Christ" (2.6–3.2), as their father (4.15), and assumes that he provides a model to be imitated (4.16-17; 11.1). He is dismissive of rhetorical art (in contrast to the foolishness of the cross — 1.17-25) and is emphatic on the unac-

---

41. 1.6-9 is paralleled in 2 Cor. 11.13-15, but the crudity of 5.12 is unsurpassed elsewhere.

42. Despite Lincoln, *Ephesians* (§5 n. 27 above) 253-54, the change of preposition in the three phrases *(pros . . . eis . . . eis)* suggests that the phrases are not coordinate and that the latter two ("for the work of ministry" and "for the building up of Christ's body") are dependent on the first ("to equip the saints"); but commentators are almost equally divided on the point (bibliography in Lincoln).

43. It was used in royal exhortation — diplomatic, but nevertheless forceful; see C. J. Bjerkelund, *Parakalô: Form, Funktion und Sinn der parakalô-Sätze in den paulinischen Briefen* (Oslo: Universitetsforlaget, 1967) 59-74.

44. 1.17; 3.5-10; 4.1.

45. 2.4-5; 5.4; 7.40.

ceptability of sexual license (chs. 5–6).[46] Above all, we cannot ignore his intolerance of dissent.[47]

At the same time we have to recognize also a significant degree of restraint in Paul's exercise of authority. He speaks only of "commands of God/the Lord,"[48] and distinguishes his own advice from such commands.[49] He does not call for the Corinthians' "obedience" to him.[50] He warns them against becoming "slaves of [other] human beings" (7.23), and that is not the attitude he wishes to encourage towards himself either. Campenhausen in particular has shown how careful Paul was to circumscribe his own authority by the freedom of his converts.[51] Thus at various points Paul almost seems to fall over backward to encourage the Corinthians to take responsibility for themselves, even when the desirable course of action was clear to him.[52] He tries to allow as much space as possible for different options (ch. 7), to concede and agree with catchwords even though they were being used to justify actions of which he did not approve (ch. 8). He pleads for freedom *not* to call upon their support rather than to exercise his apostolic rights (ch. 9). He presses the Corinthians to exercise proper discrimination in regard to spiritual gifts (14.29) and to acknowledge the authority of leadership when it is given (16.15-18). In some ways most striking is the fact that he *argues* against what he regards as a false view on something as crucial as the resurrection from the dead rather than simply condemning it out of hand (ch. 15).

Such evidence is, of course, open to different readings. Graham Shaw finds Paul's attempt to exercise authority blatantly manipulative and even "vindictive"[53] — demonstrating how far an unsympathetic reading or hermeneutic of suspicion can go. A fairer reading, however, would be much more sensitive to the rhetorical character of the letter and to the social factors at play in Corinth,[54] particularly when we cannot hear the other sides of the

---

46. Chs. 5–6; 10.6-12.

47. 4.18-21; 11.16; 14.37-38.

48. *Entolē* — 7.19; 14.37 (cf. Col. 4.10); *epitagē* — 7.6, 25

49. 7.6 — "as a concession not as a command"; 7.25 — "I have no command of the Lord, but I give my opinion . . ."; cf. 2 Cor. 8.8 — "not as a command."

50. Contrast 2 Cor. 7.15; 10.6.

51. Campenhausen, *Authority* 46-50.

52. 5.3-5 — they themselves must take the necessary disciplinary measures; 6.5 — surely there is someone wise enough to decide disputes without the matter being taken to court. On 1 Corinthians 7 and 8 see further below §24.5-7.

53. Shaw, *Cost, passim.*

54. E.g., E. Schüssler Fiorenza sees 1 Corinthians as a deliberative (persuasive) discourse appealing to those of higher and educational status — "Rhetorical Situation and Historical Reconstruction in 1 Corinthians," *NTS* 33 (1987) 386-403; see further Mitchell, *Paul and the Rhetoric of Reconciliation.*

debates and do not know how much the issues were caught up in the social tensions of Corinth, not least between patrons and their clients.[55]

The best example of Paul's sensitivity and skill as a mediator between individuals of different social status is in fact the little letter to Philemon. He exerts pressure on Philemon by reminding him both of his debt to Paul and of Paul's present status as a prisoner (vv. 1, 8-10, 13, 23), by complimenting him fulsomely (vv. 2, 4-7), and by indicating that he expected the letter to Philemon to be read out at a gathering of the church which met in Philemon's house (v. 2).[56] He mixes talk of obedience with talk of Philemon's consent freely given (vv. 8-9, 14, 21). His readiness to let Philemon understand the breach in the way he chose (v. 18) displays the touch of an experienced mediator, recognizing that in a master-slave dispute the master held all the cards. And the vagueness of the request and the fine mix of pressure and pleading in vv. 14-16 and 19-20 allowed Philemon to respond with dignity and generosity in a way which would both maintain and display his honour.[57]

c) 1 Corinthians articulates another principle by which Paul conditioned the exercise of his authority, one which is closely related to the second but which deserves separate mention — the principle of accommodation or adaptability. He states it clearly in 1 Cor. 9.19-23 —

> [19]For though I am free in regard to all, I have made myself a slave to all, in order that I might win more of them. [20]To the Jews I became as a Jew, in order that I might win Jews. To those under the law I became as one under the law (though I myself am not under the law), in order that I might win those under the law. [21]To those outside the law I became as one outside the law (though I am not outside the law but in-lawed to Christ), in order that I might win those outside the law. [22]To those who are weak I became weak, in order that I might win those who are weak. I have become all things to all people, in order that I might by all means save some. [23]I do it all on account of the gospel, in order that I might share its blessings.

The passage is usually taken as a missionary principle — as indeed it is. But coming where it does in 1 Corinthians 9, it clearly also functioned for Paul as a pastoral principle.[58] "Winning" and "saving" people included drawing

---

55. See further Chow and Clarke cited above n. 25.

56. Hainz, *Ekklesia* (§20 n. 1); Gnilka, *Philemon* 13.

57. On these verses see my *Philemon* (with *Colossians*); cf. particularly N. R. Petersen, *Rediscovering Paul: Philemon and the Sociology of Paul's Narrative World* (Philadelphia: Fortress, 1985).

58. S. C. Barton, " 'All Things to All People': Paul and the Law in the Light of 1 Corinthians 9.19-23," in Dunn, ed., *Paul and the Mosaic Law* (§6 n. 1) 271-85.

them into and supporting them within a community, the church, able to act responsibly as the one body of Christ.

What this meant in 1 Corinthians we have already illustrated in the previous paragraphs. But it comes to particularly clear expression in 1 Corinthians 9 itself, which indeed can be regarded as Paul's most sustained exposition of how he conceived of his authority *(exousia)*.[59] What is of interest, not least, is the way in which Paul brings the ideas of authority and freedom into interaction (9.1, 19). The issue in ch. 9 is the financial support which Paul might justifiably have claimed from his converts. He was, after all, their apostle: they owed their experience of the gospel to him (9.1-2). There was a natural justice in claiming such support (9.3-7). And the right was supported both by scripture (9.8-12) and by a command of the Lord himself (9.13-14). We may also plausibly overhear a subtext of social conventions, offended patrons, and even suspicions regarding the possibility of financial irregularities.[60] In effect Paul attempts to shift the issue of financial support away from such conventions and to resolve it in Christian terms. He does so, first, by setting out his rights *(exousia)* as an apostle, and then by justifying his refusal to exercise that authority in terms of gospel liberty (9.18-19) and self-discipline (9.24-27). His freedom as an apostle was freedom to adapt policy and practice to particular situations, even when that meant running counter to all precedent, and to both scriptural and dominical authorization.

In a famous article, Henry Chadwick defended Paul against the charge that he was a weathercock and trimmer. On the contrary, he maintained, Paul demonstrates the skill of a good apologist, displaying "an astonishing elasticity of mind, and a flexibility in dealing with situations requiring delicate and ingenious treatment which appears much greater than is usually supposed."[61] Such a pastoral sensitivity, combined with the theological and rhetorical sophistication already noted, seems closer to the Paul of 1 Corinthians than Shaw's portrayal of the vindictive manipulator.[62] It need hardly be

---

59. *Exousia* occurs more often in this chapter than in any other of the Pauline writings — 9.4-6, 12, 18.

60. Cf. P. Marshall, *Enmity in Corinth: Social Conventions in Paul's Relations with the Corinthians* (WUNT 2.23; Tübingen: Mohr, 1987), though he strains the concept of "friendship" in using it as the overarching motif in a study which also analyses concepts of flattery, *hybris,* and freedom.

61. H. Chadwick, " 'All Things to All Men' (1 Cor. 9.22)," *NTS* 1 (1954-55) 261-75 (here 275); Chadwick also notes Paul's "astonishing ability to reduce to an apparent vanishing point the gulf between himself and his converts and to 'gain' them for the Christian gospel" (275). The very fact that Paul's letters have been preserved for posterity is itself indicative of the success of Paul's pastoral strategy.

62. See also B. Hall, "All Things to All People: A Study of 1 Corinthians 9.19-23," in Fortna and Gaventa, *The Conversation Continues* 137-57.

said, however, that one who expresses his principle in dealing with diverse and seemingly antithetical situations, as Paul does in 9.19-23, inevitably leaves himself open to misunderstanding and misrepresentation. That is the character of the power and authority which Paul sought to exert.

d) The Corinthian correspondence contains another very clear statement of principle regarding apostolic authority in 2 Cor. 10.13-16:

> [13]We, however, will not boast beyond limits, but will keep within the field that God has assigned to us, to reach out even as far as you. [14]For we were not overstepping our limits when we reached you; we were the first to come all the way to you with the good news of Christ. [15]We do not boast beyond limits, that is, in the labors of others; but our hope is that, as your faith increases, our sphere of action among you may be greatly enlarged, [16]so that we may proclaim the good news in lands beyond you, without boasting of work already done in someone else's sphere of action (NRSV).

The NRSV's slightly paraphrastic translation brings out the key features well.[63] Paul conceived of his apostolic authority as a commissioning to preach the gospel within a particular sphere or field. Moreover, he saw that commissioning (and its concomitant authority) as limited to that sphere or field. He himself had been careful to work within that sphere and its limits. The implication, borne out by the context of the passage, is that other missionaries ("apostles of Christ" — 11.13) had overstepped their limits and had invaded "his territory."[64]

This is a particularly vivid statement of Paul's concept of apostolic authority. It confirms the point already drawn from 1 Cor. 9.2: Paul could address the Corinthians so forthrightly precisely (and only) because he was *their* apostle. It also confirms the point made earlier regarding 1 Cor. 12.28: that Paul regarded each church as having its own apostles (founders), who, in consequence, ranked first of the ministries within that church.[65] But it also explains another aspect of Paul's ambivalence towards Jerusalem: he regarded himself as an apostle neither *of* the Jerusalem (and Judean) churches nor *to* them. And he deeply resented any attempt from Jerusalem or its sphere of influence to draw his churches into that sphere.[66]

63. See Barrett, *2 Corinthians* 263-69, and Furnish, *2 Corinthians* 471-74, 481-82.

64. Quite how the principle relates to the division of labour agreed to in Gal. 2.9 is disputed, but the implication of Galatians itself is that Paul was fiercely resisting interference in the Galatian churches from churches elsewhere. Similarly Phil. 3.2-19.

65. See above §20.2a.

66. On the identity of the false apostles in 2 Corinthians 10–13, see, e.g., J. L. Sumney, *Identifying Paul's Opponents: The Question of Method in 2 Corinthians* (JSNTS 40; Sheffield: JSOT, 1990), with further bibliography.

In the light of the same passage we gain a better appreciation of and greater sympathy for Paul in his dealing with the congregations in Rome. For one of the most human features of the opening to Romans is the evident care Paul takes to avoid any implication that he is their apostle and therefore has apostolic rights among them. "I long to see you," he says, "that I may share with you some spiritual gift, so that you may be strengthened" (1.11).[67] But then he catches himself, "Or rather, so that there may be mutual encouragement among you through each other's faith, both yours and mine" (1.12). Evidently he wanted to avoid giving the impression that he had any kind of proprietary expectations with regard to them. Similarly, in the final section of the letter he reiterates his basic principle of apostolic mission — "my aim to preach the gospel where Christ has not been named, lest I build on another's foundation" (15.20) — before repeating with still greater care his hope to spend some time with the believers in Rome before proceeding on his mission to Spain with their support (15.23-24, 28, 32).[68]

The theological point emerging from this is important. Paul did not think of an apostle as an apostle of the universal church; this correlates with his understanding of "church" as local church.[69] Nor did he think of apostolic authority as something exercised by individuals throughout all the churches.[70] As apostolic authority was subordinate to the gospel, so it was limited by the scope of apostolic commission.

e) A final criterion is in effect given throughout 2 Corinthians. For the lesson Paul learned, to which 2 Corinthians gives such eloquent testimony, that suffering is an unavoidable and indeed necessary concomitant of the process of salvation,[71] had particular reference to his own ministry as an apostle.[72] It was precisely in his apostolic ministry that Paul learned to expe-

---

67. It was not as an apostle that Paul expected to share with them some charism, as though an apostle as apostle could assume more extensive charisms. As much as any member of the body, the apostle was dependent on the Spirit's "manifestation" (cf. 1 Cor. 2.12-16; 7.40).

68. See further my *Romans* lv-lvi, 35; and above §7 n. 3.

69. See again §20.2a above.

70. *Pace* Ridderbos, *Paul* 450.

71. See above §18.5.

72. See further E. Käsemann, "Die Legitimät des Apostels: Eine Untersuchung zu 2 Korinther 10–13," *ZNW* 41 (1942) 33-71 = Rengstorf, *Paulusbild* 475-521; E. Güttgemanns, *Der leidende Apostel und sein Herr* (FRLANT 90; Göttingen: Vandenhoeck, 1966); S. Hafemann, *Suffering and the Spirit: An Exegetical Study of 2 Cor. 2:14–3:3 within the Context of the Corinthian Correspondence* (WUNT 2.19; Tübingen: Mohr, 1986); M. Wolter, "Der Apostel und seine Gemeinden als Teilhaber am Leidensgeschick Jesu Christi. Beobachtungen zur paulinischen Leidenstheologie," *NTS* 36 (1990) 535-57; U. Heckel, *Kraft in Schwachheit: Untersuchungen zu 2 Kor. 10–13* (WUNT 2.56; Tübingen: Mohr, 1993); T. B. Savage, *Power through Weakness: Paul's Understanding of the*

rience divine consolation in his suffering and divine power in his weakness.[73] And it was precisely in his confrontation with other apostles and models of apostleship[74] that he found it necessary to insist on the real proof of apostleship. The other apostles readily claimed proof of their apostleship in such features of their ministry as their superior rhetoric (2 Cor. 11.5-6), their labours (11.23), and their "signs and wonders" (12.11-12). Such claims Paul could match, should he choose to do so — and he makes the point by boasting like a fool (11.16–12.13). But he did so only to demonstrate how untrue such criteria are to the Christ and the Spirit and the gospel they were supposed to attest (11.4). On the contrary, the true mark of apostolic ministry is the shared experience of Christ's sufferings, of divine strength in human weakness (12.9-10; 13.4). As the gospel is the gospel of the crucified, so the ministry of the gospel involves living out a *theologia crucis* rather than a *theologia gloriae*.

In sum, then, Paul held a high ideal of apostolic authority, as a specific commissioning by the risen Christ to preach the gospel and found churches. In practice, however, the exercise of that authority was always conditioned: it was always subordinate to the gospel; it worked within its churches as one of many ministries (albeit the most important) to build up the full range of responsible ministry within these churches; it was adaptable to circumstance and to Christian liberty and not determined simply by precedent or convention; it stayed within the limits of its commissioning; and it mirrored the character of its message as the proclamation of the crucified one.

§21.3 The other regular ministries

With the other chief examples we can be briefer on the interplay of ministry and authority since Paul himself is briefer. The key examples are the other two regular ministries most often mentioned as such, prophets and teachers, and the other unspecified ministries to which Paul occasionally refers.[75] It is here in particular that evidence of "official" ministries is usually found.[76]

a) *Prophets.* It is clear from 1 Corinthians 12–14 that in Corinth at

---

Christian Ministry in 2 Corinthians (SNTSMS 86; Cambridge: Cambridge University, 1996). As Fitzgerald in particular reminds us (*Cracks in an Earthen Vessel* [§23 n. 180]), suffering or adversity was widely understood in the ancient world to be the test or proof of character, as Paul was no doubt aware. But that fact neither detracts from the existential reality of Paul's own experience of suffering nor diminishes the theological significance Paul saw in it.

73. 2 Cor. 1.3-11; 4.7–5.10; 6.3-10; 7.5-7.
74. 2 Cor. 11.5, 13; 12.11-12.
75. In what follows I draw principally on my *Jesus and the Spirit* 280-91.
76. E.g., Brockhaus, *Charisma* 97-112.

least there was a fairly well-defined circle of recognized prophets.[77] We may deduce from this, from the references to regular prophecy in other churches,[78] and from the key role Paul gives to prophecy in the building up of the church,[79] that there were a number of prophets within each or most of the Pauline congregations. From the little Paul says about them we can gain a fairly clear picture of what ministry and authority meant in practice for these prophets, at least where Paul's advice was followed.

For Paul the authority of the prophet was essentially authority to prophesy under inspiration. Prophetic authority was the authority of inspiration and did not extend beyond that inspiration. This applied not only to the individual prophetic utterance: prophets should speak "in proportion to faith" (Rom. 12.6), that is, within the limits of their confidence that their words were God's words.[80] It applied also to the more established prophet: one prophet must give way to the inspiration of another (1 Cor. 14.30); "the spirits of prophets are subject to the prophets" (14.32).[81]

Moreover, the inspiration of the individual was subject to the evaluation of "the others" (1 Cor. 14.29), that is, here at any rate, the other prophets.[82] That is to say, the authority of the prophets included authority to evaluate the oracle of another prophet. The expectation, in other words, seems to have been that those most experienced in the exercise of the charism of prophecy had a primary responsibility in evaluating prophecies given within the assembly.[83]

We can immediately draw some relevant inferences even from these brief considerations for the charism/office discussion. (a) Prophetic authority for Paul did not derive from an appointment to the rank of prophet, whether

---

77. 1 Cor. 12.28-29; 14.29-32, 37. Note also Matt. 7.6; Acts 2.17-18; 11.27; 13.1; 15.32; 19.6; 21.9-10; Eph. 2.20; 3.5; 4.11; 1 Thes. 5.20; 1 Tim. 1.18; 4.14; Rev. 1.3; 10.7, 11; 11.3, 6, 10, 18, etc.; *Didache* 10.7; 13.1-6; Hermas, *Mandate* 11. Paul presumably inherited the structure from the church in Antioch (Acts 13.1). See further Greeven, "Propheten."

78. 1 Thes. 5.20; Rom. 12.6, where again we may note that Paul could assume that prophecy would be a feature of churches he had not himself established; but note also Eph. 2.20; 1 Tim. 1.18; 4.14.

79. 1 Cor. 14; cf. 1 Thes. 5.19-22; Eph. 2.20.

80. On Rom. 12.6 see above §20 n. 137.

81. Greeven, "Propheten" 12-13, thinks that two different prophets are in view, but most commentators take Paul to be speaking of each prophet's ability to control his/(her) own inspiration (cf. 14.30).

82. This seems to be the most natural way to take the Greek, the reference of "the others" being determined by the preceding noun ("two or three prophets"); cf. Luke 6.29; Rev. 17.10. Otherwise Barrett, *1 Corinthians* 328, and Fee, *1 Corinthians* 694 — "the others" = the rest of the community (as in 1 Thes. 5.19-22).

83. See further below §21.6.

by apostle or community. Prophetic authority derived from prophetic inspiration. Paul evidently did not expect the congregation to install an individual
into a prophetic office and then wait for him or her to prophesy. On the
contrary, the expectation was that the congregation would recognize the prophet because she or he had already been prophesying regularly. In a word,
prophets did not prophesy because they were prophets; they were prophets
because they prophesied.

(b) Prophetic authority was not limited to prophets. Only an apostle could
exercise apostolic authority. But anyone might prophesy. Paul clearly expected
that members of the assembly other than the recognized prophets could be
granted a prophetic charism, that is, a word of prophecy (14.1, 5, 24, 31).[84]

(c) Prophetic authority was subject to the assessment of others. The
individual's own sense of inspiration might be authority enough for a particular
prophetic utterance (Rom. 12.6). But the authority which that utterance carried
for the assembled church depended on a wider recognition of its inspiration
and significance. Properly speaking, the prophecy had not been delivered until
it had been received.

In short, while Paul clearly envisaged established prophets as well as
occasional prophecies within each of his churches, the authority of both
prophet and prophecy was primarily a charismatic authority. It was exercised
in the event of prophesying and was subject to evaluation by others.

2) *Teachers.* Several texts also imply that Paul regarded teachers as an
integral part of each church,[85] again in echo of the structure of which Paul had
himself been a part in the church in Antioch (according to Acts 13.1). These we
may presume were responsible for retaining, passing on, and interpreting the
congregation's foundation traditions, including interpretation of the prophetic
scriptures and the Jesus tradition.[86] What else would teachers teach?

Given the unavoidable expectation that such teachers would master
and be responsible for the church's traditions, it is not surprising that teachers
are the first of the regular ministries to take on a more professional aura. Such
a time-consuming responsibility might well require financial support. Hence
Gal. 6.6: "let the one who is taught the word share in all good things with
the one who teaches." As the teacher was responsible for instructing new
Christians in the congregation's distinguishing traditions, so those instructed
were expected to contribute to their teacher's upkeep. The wording, however,
suggests that the arrangement was dependent on the sense of obligation (and
no doubt the ability to pay) of the one taught, rather than (as yet) on a more
formal organization.

84. See also on 11.5 below (§21.4).
85. Rom. 12.7; 1 Cor. 12.28-29; Gal. 6.6; Eph. 4.11.
86. See above §§8.2-3; also my *Jesus and the Spirit* 282-83.

The implication of the description of the typical gathering for worship (1 Cor. 14.26) may also imply that, like prophecy, teaching was not limited to the teachers: "When you come together, each one has a psalm, a teaching, a revelation. . . ." An insight into the relevance of the church's tradition might well be given to someone not previously or formally recognized as a teacher. Indeed, according to Col. 3.16, the community as a whole had a teaching responsibility.

The authority of the teacher was much more circumscribed than that of the apostle or prophet. For the primary authority was not that of the teacher so much as of the tradition taught by the teacher. At the same time an element of interpretation would inevitably be involved in much or most of the teaching, and the line between teaching (old tradition interpreted) and prophecy (new? revelation) would often be thin. Yet it is noticeable that Paul does not speak about "discerning the spirits" in relation to teaching (as he does with prophecy). Elsewhere he is quick to discuss what he regarded as misleading teaching or to contest what he regarded as false teaching.[87] But he does so by appealing to the tradition itself,[88] and only when he goes beyond that tradition does he appeal to his own inspiration[89] and to the practice of "all the churches."[90]

In short, the fact that Paul lists prophecy and teaching in close conjunction[91] probably indicates that he saw the teaching function as an indispensable complement to prophecy. The normative role of the gospel and of the tradition common to all the churches would have provided an invaluable control on charismatic excess.[92] Yet we should also recall that he ranked prophecy above teaching. Teaching, we may say, preserves continuity; but prophecy gives life. With teaching a community will not die; but without prophecy it will not live.[93]

3) *Other regular ministries.* A striking feature of Paul's letters is the fact that he rarely seems able to address people holding formally recognized positions of authority in his churches.[94] We have already observed the absence

87. E.g., 1 Cor. 7.1; 8.1, 4a; 15.12.
88. 1 Cor. 7.10; 8.4b; 15.3-11, 14-15, 17, 20.
89. 2.16; 7.12, 40; 14.37.
90. 4.17; 7.17; 11.16; 14.33, 36.
91. Particularly 1 Cor. 12.28-29; Rom. 12.6-7.
92. Cf. Greeven: "Prophecy without teaching degenerates into fanaticism, teaching without prophecy solidifies into law" ("Propheten" 129).
93. Cf. Küng, *Church* 433.
94. Phil. 1.1's address to "bishops and deacons" (or "overseers and ministers") is exceptional (O'Brien, *Philippians* 49-50, provides a brief review of current views). Their role is also undefined, and, somewhat curiously, Paul does not seem to call on them in any of the subsequent exhortations (2.1-4; 3.17-19; 4.2-3), even in dealing with the financial gift the Philippians made to Paul (4.10-20), unless we assume that Epaphroditus was a "minister/deacon" (4.18; but 2.25 uses the term *leitourgos* — see above §20.3).

of any indication of a distinct priestly office in the letters.[95] Equally striking is the absence of any reference to "elders,"[96] who do not appear in the Pauline corpus earlier than the Pastorals.[97] And although *diakonos* ("servant, minister") is beginning to function as a title,[98] at this stage it still seems to be descriptive of an individual's sustained commitment (like "fellow worker") and not yet the title of a clearly defined "office."[99]

This is all the more astonishing when a church like that in Corinth was experiencing such disorder. The absence of an appeal to or rebuke of established leaders is very hard to explain, were there such in Corinth.[100] The implication of the text is otherwise. There was no recognized leadership group to whom Paul could appeal to give the lead in the case of an individual's immorality (5.3-5). His hope for the resolution of differences between others was that some member would be given the wisdom to judge or reconcile (6.5). There was no president of the common meal or Lord's Supper to whom appeal could be made (11.17-34), no leader to regulate the anarchic worship (14.26-40), no deacon to organize the collection (16.1-2).[101] Nor, evidently, did he expect the prophets and teachers to attempt to exercise authority beyond their prophetic and teaching function.

Leadership did emerge. As his parting shot, Paul commends to the Corinthians Stephanas and his household, and also Fortunatus and Achaicus (1 Cor. 16.15-18). But of the former Paul says explicitly that their "service of the saints" was an act/function of service which Stephanas and his house-

95. See again §20.3 above.

96. Despite Acts 14.23 and 20.17, 28; cf. Jas. 5.14; 1 Pet. 5.1, 5. Meeks notes the absence of indications that Paul imitated the organization of either the synagogue or the *collegia* (*First Urban Christians* 81, 134). The point being made in this paragraph is unaffected by the more nuanced case argued for by Campbell, *Elders*.

97. 1 Tim. 5.1-2, 17, 19; Tit. 1.5.

98. Rom. 16.1; Phil. 1.1.

99. 1 Cor. 3.5; 2 Cor. 3.6; 6.4; 11.23; Col. 1.7, 23, 25; 4.7; 1 Thes. 3.2 v.l. It is unlikely that Paul, who prized the title "apostle," would have used the term *diakonos* for his own ministry had it already been regarded as a lesser office. If there were conscious overtones of the use of the term for cultic and guild officials (LSJ, *diakonos;* H. W. Beyer, *TDNT* 2.91-92), we must assume that, as with Paul's use of priestly language elsewhere, the cult had been secularized and the terms appropriated for all ministry on behalf of the gospel (see again above §20.3). For the considerable number of Paul's coworkers and the responsibilities they undertook, see particularly W.-H. Ollrog, *Paulus und seine Mitarbeiter* (WMANT 50; Neukirchen: Neukirchener, 1979).

100. Contrast *1 Clement* 3.3; 21.6; 44; 47.6; 54.2; 57.1. The hypothesis that individuals of high status would automatically be looked to for leadership, but in this case were themselves party to the disorder (see n. 25 above), only explains some of Paul's silence.

101. Contrast Turner, *Holy Spirit* (§16 n. 1) 282: the evidence "merely shows that Corinth had ineffectual leadership."

hold had taken upon themselves (*etaxan heautous,* "appointed themselves to" — 16.15). Paul had not appointed them to it.[102] And his commendation amounts to a plea for the Corinthians to submit to such people and to recognize them (16.16, 18). That is, it was an appeal for the charismatic authority of their actions to be acknowledged. The initiatives they had taken and the hard work they had displayed[103] were so obviously good that their lead should be followed.

The earlier 1 Thes. 5.12-13 gives a similar impression: "We ask you, brothers, to acknowledge those who work hard *(kopiaō)* among you and care for you (or give you leadership)[104] in the Lord and admonish you. Esteem them highly on account of their work." Was Paul thinking of an explicit and already established leadership group? The fact that he goes on to urge the "brothers" as a whole "to admonish the idlers, to encourage the fainthearted, to help the weak, and to be patient with all" (5.14) suggests that the advice was the same as in 1 Corinthians 16. Where individuals demonstrated the strength of their concern and commitment by their hard work and were effective in admonition (the same word occurs in 1 Thes. 5.12 and 14) their de facto leadership should be recognized.[105]

Similarly with the appeal to "the spiritual ones" in Gal. 6.1 to restore the transgressing fellow believer "in a spirit of gentleness." Paul was probably putting a general challenge before all the Galatians ("brothers"), to which he expected at least some to respond.[106] That is to say, Paul evidently expected those who were led by the Spirit (5.25) to provide the spiritually sensitive leadership (rather than any rulebook formalism) which such delicate situations required.[107]

---

102. Again contrast *1 Clement* 42.2: they "appointed their firstfruits [the same term used of Stephanas in 16.15] . . . to be the bishops and deacons of future believers."

103. *Kopiaō* ("work hard") seems to indicate the quality which Paul prized in his own work (1 Cor. 15.10; Gal. 4.11; Phil. 2.16; Col. 1.29; also 1 Tim. 4.10) and looked for in church workers (Rom. 16.6, 12; 1 Cor. 16.16; 1 Thes. 5.12).

104. *Proistamenos* — the same word that Paul uses in Rom. 12.8, raising the same question: "stand before," either in the sense of "lead" or "care for" (BAGD, *proistēmi*); see above §20 n. 129.

105. "The three participles . . . name functions rather than offices" (Meeks, *Urban Christians* 134). But the question whether their ability to take initiatives (and thus their resulting authority) was a consequence of their greater wealth and social status adds a further twist to the discussion.

106. Cf. particularly Schweizer, *TDNT* 6.424 n. 605. For Paul's care in defining what "spiritual" means in such a discussion see also 1 Cor. 2.12–3.4.

107. For a fuller discussion see my *Galatians* 319-20. On the suggestion that "coworker," "brother" and "servant" *(diakonos)* all denoted special classes of workers whom Paul associated with himself in his mission (particularly E. E. Ellis, "Paul and his Co-Workers," *NTS* 17 [1970-71] 437-52; also *Theology* 92-100) see my *Jesus and the Spirit* 288.

In sum, it is clear that we can speak of an emerging leadership within the Pauline churches. But how it emerged and what its authority consisted of are questions too infrequently asked. Where Paul does provide answers to these questions it is still necessary to speak of charismatic authority more than the authority of office.[108] At the same time we cannot ignore the fact that within a generation of Paul's death the ecclesiology of the Pauline heritage (the Pastorals) was a good deal more structured and formally conceived. The question, then, would be whether the inevitable institutionalizing of the Pauline heritage could nevertheless maintain the openness to the charismatic Spirit and the primacy of gospel and of prophecy which Paul saw as fundamental to the living church.

§21.4 *The ministry and authority of women*

Although this topic as such assumes even less prominence in Paul's letters, contemporary interest in it makes a separate treatment unavoidable. The chief problem in recent discussion has been that the evidence pulls two ways: the fact of ministry is clear, but the issue of authority is more obscure.

1) So far as the ministry of women in the Pauline churches is concerned the position could hardly be clearer. Women were prominent in ministry. If we simply take the final chapter of our principal text, Romans 16, the point is made for us.[109]

There we meet first of all Phoebe (16.1-2), who is described as both a "deacon" and a "patron" of the church in Cenchreae. Phoebe, indeed, is

---

108. Despite Brockhaus's conclusion that it is not possible to make a distinction between charismatic and official functions in the communities (*Charisma* 238). Transposed into sociological terminology, MacDonald wants to speak of "institutionalization" even at this stage (*Pauline Churches* 59) and presses the argument that "there are institution building impulses inherent in the charisma itself" (*Pauline Churches* 14; already Ridderbos, *Paul* 444-46, but assuming Pauline authorship of the Pastorals; Holmberg, *Paul* 166, 175-78). While the protest against a too simple distinction is justified, and (of course) a degree of organization was unavoidable, it is nevertheless analytically confusing to speak of "institutionalization" (or "routinization of charisma") as a first-phase rather than second-phase phenomenon, however quickly the second phase supervenes upon the first. Where individuals "appoint themselves" to ministry and congregations have to be urged to "acknowledge" hard workers, it is inappropriate to speak of either "office" or "institutionalization." There can be as much idealization in the both-and thesis pioneered by Harnack as in Sohm's portrayal of the purely Spirit-led church.

109. But see also particularly Phil. 4.2-3 — Euodia and Syntyche, who fought at Paul's side in (spreading) the gospel; Col. 4.15 — Nympha, host (leader?) of the church which met in her house.

the first person within Christian history to be named "deacon."[110] As a *prostatis* ("patron, benefactor")[111] she was probably a single woman or widow of substantial means who, in part at least by virtue of her high social status, took a leading part in the church at Cenchreae.

Then we meet Prisca and Aquila (16.3-5). The fact that Paul names Prisca before her husband suggests, as do other references, that she was the more dominant of the two.[112] It is hard to doubt that she played a leading role in the churches which met in their house.[113]

In 16.7 Andronicus and Junia[114] are described as fellow prisoners of Paul, but also, more to the point, as "outstanding among the apostles, who also were in Christ before me." Such a description is most naturally linked to the wider circle of apostles who, like Paul, had been appointed to apostolic mission by the risen Christ (1 Cor. 15.7).[115] As Andronicus and Junia were the only people designated as "apostles" in relation to the congregations in Rome, the question can hardly be ignored whether they were actually the apostles (founders) of at least some of the Roman churches.

110. Assuming Romans 16 was written before Philippians. The term is *diakonos,* "deacon," not "deaconess."

111. Until recently, the persistence of translations like "helper" (RSV) has illustrated the unconscious patriarchalism against which feminist hermeneutics have justifiably reacted. We are now aware, however, of many women who in the Roman world of the time took on such leading roles in society and in patronage (see, e.g., my *Romans* 888-89; and further C. F. Whelan, "Amica Pauli: The Role of Phoebe in the Early Church," *JSNT* 49 [1993] 67-85).

112. Prisc(ill)a and Aquila (Acts 18.18, 26 — the instruction of Apollos; Rom. 16.3; 2 Tim. 4.19); Aquila and Priscilla (Acts 18.2; 1 Cor. 16.19).

113. Rom. 16.5; 1 Cor. 16.19.

114. Junia (a woman), not Junias (a man). Prosopographical studies show that "Junia" was a common female name, but have produced no example of the male name "Junias." See also R. S. Cervin, "A Note regarding the Name 'Junia(s)' in Romans 16.7," *NTS* 40 (1994) 464-70; J. Thorley, "Junia, A Woman Apostle," *NovT* 38 (1996) 18-29. Until the Middle Ages the reading "Junia" was largely unquestioned. Fitzmyer, *Romans* 737-38, notes that the first to take the name as masculine is said to have been Giles of Rome (1247-1316); but see already Epiphanius, *Index of Disciples* 125.1920 (Junias, bishop of Apameia in Syria), and Origen in Rufinus (Migne, *PG* 14.1289). More typical is Chrysostom, *Homily on Romans* 31 (I owe these references to my colleague Mark Bonnington). Here again the patriarchalism of subsequent readings of "Junias" has to be criticized for the converse (perverse!) assumption that only a man could be so described (so, e.g., Lietzmann, *Römer* 125).

115. The description would hardly be appropriate to the lesser sense of "apostles/delegates of particular churches" (2 Cor. 8.23). Fitzmyer, *Romans* 739-40, accepts that they were probably Jewish Christian apostles, from among the Jerusalem Hellenists, but then quotes Schnackenburg's gratuitous comment, "without being able to lay claim to an appearance of the risen Lord" ("Apostles before and during Paul's Time," in W. W. Gasque and R. P. Martin, eds., *Apostolic History and the Gospel,* F. F. Bruce FS [Exeter: Paternoster/Grand Rapids: Eerdmans, 1970] 287-303 [here 294]).

Finally, it should be noted that four people are picked out for their "hard working" *(kopiaō)* — the term Paul uses elsewhere in commending those whose ministry and leadership ought to be recognized.[116] In Romans 16 all four are women, and no man is so designated — Mary, Tryphaena, Tryphosa, and Persis (16.6, 12).

In addition we should simply note that Paul fully accepted the practice at least in Corinth of women leading in prayer and prophesying (1 Cor. 11.5). The discussion only makes sense if such ministry was envisaged as taking place within the assembly for worship: like the other charisms, prophecy was for the benefit of others (12.7) — prophecy above all (14.3-5). Moreover, Paul presumably included women within his general exhortations to engage in ministry addressed to church congregations as a whole.[117] We can hardly assume that Paul's vision of the charismatic community envisaged only men as members of the body of Christ, that is, as functioning members of the body (Rom. 12.4-5).

2) Against this we have to set the clear evidence that Paul was embarrassed about at least some aspects of such women's ministry. The issue focuses around two 1 Corinthians passages, 11.2-16 and 14.33b-36, reinforced by the subsequent 1 Tim. 2.12-14 ("I permit no woman to teach or have authority over a man").

In 1 Cor. 11.2-16, despite the recognition of women's role in praying and prophesying, the primary concern of the passage seems to be to hedge this function around with qualifications and restrictions. The passage begins abruptly with the first qualification, with what appears to be an unbending statement of male hierarchy: God is the head of Christ, Christ is the head of man, man is the head of woman (11.3). This is based on the creation account in Genesis 2, which is run together with the first creation account (Genesis 1), so that only man reflects the glory of God directly, while woman reflects the glory of man (11.7-9). And although the hierarchical relation is qualified by recognition that woman gives birth to man (11.12), the impression that Paul basically reaffirms female subordination to male in this passage is hard to avoid. The second restriction is that a woman should only pray and prophesy when her head is covered, though the final phase of the exhortation (11.14-15) leaves some uncertainty as to whether Paul thought long hair was a sufficient head covering in itself.[118] The final comment (11.16) reads like a rather embarrassed or indeed bad-tempered attempt to forestall further discussion on the subject.

---

116. See above §21.3c.

117. Not least 1 Cor. 14.1 and 1 Thes. 5.14. Wire, *Women Prophets,* builds her thesis regarding the importance of women prophets in Corinth on this observation.

118. See, e.g., the discussion in Fee, *1 Corinthians* 528-29, and Schrage, *1 Korinther* 2.522-23.

In this light the second passage is somewhat surprising: 14.33b-36 —

[33]As in all the churches of the saints, [34]women should be silent in the churches. For they are not permitted to speak, but should be submissive, as also the law says. [35]And if there is anything they desire to be taught, let them ask their own husbands at home. For it is shameful for a woman to speak in church. [36]Or did the word of God originate with you? Or are you the only ones it reached?

The surprise is the tension with 11.2-16: if a woman should not speak in church, how could she pray or prophesy, as 11.5 assumes? Some have felt the contradiction to be so severe that they can resolve it only by treating 14.34-35 or 14:34-36 as a later interpolation.[119] But in the absence of strong support from the textual tradition an interpolation hypothesis should always be a device of last resort.[120] The tension between the two passages may be better seen as a reflection of the tension in Paul's own thinking on the subject. Such tension is evident in 11.2-16 even without 14.34-35, not to mention 1 Tim. 2.12-14.

An important clue for exegesis is probably given in two themes which in effect link all three passages. One is, once again, the theme of authority.[121] The other is the honour-shame culture which reinforced certain social conventions.[122] In the passages in question it was not simply a matter of male-female relations, but of the social conventions governing both the way women wore their hair and the sovereign rights of the husband within the home.

Too little recognized has been the fact that Paul deals with the question of a woman ministering in the assembly as one of "authority" (1 Cor. 11.10). The point has probably been obscured by the curious way in which Paul alludes to it: "because of this [male-female interdependence — 11.8-9] a

---

119. E.g., Conzelmann, *1 Corinthians* 246; Fee, *1 Corinthians* 699-705; Stuhlmacher, *Theologie* 362-63.

120. The fact that several textual witnesses, chiefly Western, have vv. 34-35 after v. 40 probably indicates not absence of these verses from the original but scribal uncertainty as to their proper location (Metzger, 565). However, the case for seeing the passage as an interpolation has been strengthened by P. B. Payne, "Fuldensis, Sigla for Variants in Vaticanus, and 1 Cor. 14:34-5," *NTS* 41 (1995) 240-62.

121. 1 Cor. 11.10; 1 Tim. 2.12 uses the little-known *authenteō*, "have full power or authority over" (LSJ; see also BAGD). The theme is probably implicit in 1 Cor. 14.34-35.

122. *Aischros*, "shameful," is used by Paul only twice in his letters — significantly, in the two Corinthian passages (11.6; 14.35); elsewhere in the NT only in Eph. 5.12 and Tit. 1.11. The conventions which determined someone's shame are diversely illustrated in Judith 12.12 and *4 Macc.* 16.17; see further LSJ. On the importance of honour and shame in classical society see B. J. Malina, *The New Testament World: Insights from Cultural Anthropology* (Atlanta: John Knox, 1981 = London: SCM, 1983) ch. 2.

woman ought to have authority on her head on account of the angels." The last phrase ("on account of the angels") remains a puzzle;[123] but the reason why Paul speaks of a head covering as "authority" is reasonably clear.[124] If woman is the glory of man (11.7), then her head covering is there to hide *man's* glory in the presence of God and his angels. The logic is that for a woman to pray with head uncovered would reflect the glory of *man*. Therefore man's glory must be veiled, so that in her prayer and prophecy she glorifies only *God*. The head covering is what gives her the "authority" so to do. In other words, and in contrast to what many have assumed, the head covering was not intended as a symbol of woman's subjection to man. On the contrary, it was what Paul calls it, her "authority" to pray and prophesy in direct dependence on the charismatic Spirit. To be noted, then, is the fact that Paul explicitly defends a woman's right to engage in the high ministry of prophecy and does so explicitly in terms of "authority."

Somewhat conveniently this theological reasoning ties in with the prevalent social conventions regarding a woman's hairstyle. The concern seems to have focused on the practice of (some of) the Corinthian women prophets in leaving their hair unbound while prophesying. Since dishevelled hair could evoke a picture of ritual ecstasy familiar to several Greek cults,[125] the fear would be that outsiders might think the new Christian church was simply another ecstatic cult. Such practices within the gatherings of the church, open as they were to outsiders (14.16, 23-25), might well be regarded by them as "shameful," as shameful as a woman being completely shorn (11.6). The argument of 11.2-16, then, is not so much about a "creational" difference between men and women, but primarily in support of the custom of bound-up

123. The most illuminating parallel is probably Qumran's concern to preserve the holiness of the assembly because the angels participate in it or watch over it (particularly 1QSa 2.3-11); see J. A. Fitzmyer, "A Feature of Qumran Angelology and the Angels of 1 Cor. 11.10," *Essays on the Semitic Background of the New Testament* (London: Chapman, 1971 = Missoula: Scholars, 1974) 187-204.

124. Thanks particularly to M. D. Hooker, "Authority on Her Head: An Examination of 1 Corinthians 11.10," *NTS* 10 (1964), reprinted in her *Adam* 113-20. Hooker's interpretation makes better sense of v. 10 as the conclusion drawn *(dia touto)* from the connected sequence of reasoning (vv. 7-9) than the alternative rendering of *exousia epi tēs kephalēs* as "control over her head" (= "not to cast it into disorder by loosening one's hair" (e.g. Baumert, *Woman* 188; J. M. Gundry-Volf, "Gender and Creation in 1 Corinthians 11:2-6: A Study in Paul's Theological Method," in Ådna, et al., eds., *Evangelium* 151-71 [here 159-60]).

125. Unbound hair was also a feature in the cult of Isis, which may already have established a temple at Cenchreae, the Aegean port of Corinth (see below §22 n. 9). Note also the implication of 1 Cor. 12.2, that many of the Corinthian believers had previously been members of ecstatic cults (see below n. 149), and the implication of 14.12 and 14.23 that they continued to set great store on ecstatic experiences.

hair. And this not in order to restrict women prophesying, but in order that their prophesying might, with a "proper" hairstyle, not be distracting.[126]

A more weighty social convention would have been the prime importance of good management within the household. In the classic definition of Aristotle, the household was the basic unit of the state.[127] And within the household the primary fact was *patria potestas,* the absolute power of the *paterfamilias* over the other members of the family.[128] Single women and widows could have a considerable degree of independence in practice, but even so were still legally under the guardianship of the family's senior male member. Wives, however, had no choice but to be subordinate and submissive.[129]

This basic feature of social life in the cities where Paul planted his churches may give us important clues for the interpretation of the two Corinthians passages. For a potentially confusing element is the fact that Greek *gynē* can mean "wife" as well as "woman," and particularly when it is used in conjunction with *anēr,* "man, husband."[130] And it is precisely the relationship of *anēr* and *gynē* which forms the counterpoint of the principal theme in 11.2-16.[131] In speaking more generally of "man" and "woman," therefore, Paul may have had in mind primarily the socially disturbing sight of wives acting in an uninhibited way in public meetings, and the NRSV may be quite correct to translate 11.3: "the husband is the head of his wife."

The observation is even more to the point in 14.33b-36. For the severe instruction was probably directed not to all women but to wives.[132] There are several clues which point in this direction: Paul's talk of their "being subject"[133] and "at home"; and the fact that the instruction follows immediately

---

126. So particularly Fiorenza, *In Memory of Her* 227-30: "The goal of his argument . . . is not the reinforcement of gender differences but the order and missionary character of the worship community" (230).

127. See further below §23.7c. On "The Household in the Hellenistic-Roman World" see particularly D. C. Verner, *The Household of God: The Social World of the Pastoral Epistles* (SBLDS 71; Chico: Scholars, 1983) 27-81.

128. *OCD,* "patria potestas." There were variations in Greek and Jewish law, but the basic fact held true throughout the Mediterranean world that the household was essentially a patriarchal institution, with other members of the household, not least wives, children, and slaves, subject to the authority of its male head.

129. The exhortation to wives to "be subject to your husbands" (Col. 3.18; Eph. 5.24) simply conformed to current mores; cf. particularly Plutarch, *Conjugalia praecepta* 33 (= *Moralia* 142E) and pseudo-Callisthenes 1.22.4 (in Lohse, *Colossians* 157 n. 18).

130. BAGD, *anēr* 1, *gynē* 1-2.

131. *Anēr* 14 times; *gynē* 16 times.

132. See, e.g., Fiorenza, *In Memory of Her* 230-33. The same may be true of 1 Tim. 2.11-12.

133. The same word as used in Col. 3.18 and Eph. 5.24; cf. *hypotagē* in 1 Tim. 2.11.

upon Paul's further advice on the proper ordering of prophecy within the assembly (14.29-33).[134] The probability, then, is that women prophets were taking part in the process of evaluation of individual prophecies (14.29), which would presumably include their passing judgment on prophecies uttered by husbands or senior male relatives.[135] Such an apparent questioning of the authority of the *paterfamilias* would be seen by many at least to undermine both the good order of the household and so also of the church. It would be "shameful." The propriety of both home and church would be safeguarded if wives asked their questions at home (14.35).

An important factor in the tensions at this point would be the ambiguity of role and status occasioned by the fact that the church met in private homes — the tension caused by *public* gatherings in *private* space.[136] Was the senior male of the household present as *paterfamilias,* or as one member among all the rest? Was the principal woman of the household present as wife? Could she behave in church as she did in the privacy of the home, where she could exercise a certain amount of authority over other members of the household? Or alternatively, once home had become church, was she in effect in a new (Christian) family structure, with old structures of authority relativized? The tensions would be twofold: for the married woman who was both prophet and wife, and yet had to function as prophet in a space which was both church and home. If this is the correct setting for 1 Cor. 14.33b-36, then we have to conclude that in this case Paul's instruction was not only mindful of social convention but also socially conservative in character, since he instructs wives to act as wives while in church and to show by their conduct in church that they respect the authority of their husbands.[137]

To sum up. It is tempting to base a theological exposition of Paul's views on women ministry on the much quoted Gal. 3.28: "There is neither Jew nor Greek, there is neither slave nor free, there is no male and female; for you are all one in Christ Jesus."[138] But here not least it would be unwise to draw out an applied theology from the principle without regard for the way in which Paul himself actually theologized in practice. Certainly Paul's words

---

134. Cf. L. A. Jervis, "1 Corinthians 14.34-35: A Reconsideration of Paul's Limitation of the Free Speech of Some Corinthian Women," *JSNT* 58 (1995) 51-74.

135. Ellis, *Theology* 67-71.

136. S. C. Barton, "Paul's Sense of Place: An Anthropological Approach to Community Formation in Corinth," *NTS* 32 (1986) 225-46; see also Meeks, *First Urban Christians* 75-77.

137. Perhaps the compromise Paul encouraged was that while wives who were prophets could indeed prophesy in the house church, they should not take part in the process of evaluating prophecies (14.29) which had been uttered by senior male members of the church.

138. As do Fiorenza, *In Memory of Her,* and Wire, *Women Prophets,* in particular.

seem deliberately chosen to cover the full range of the most profound distinctions within human society — racial/cultural, social/economic, and sexual/gender. But his claim is that these distinctions have been relativized, not removed. Jewish believers were still Jews (Gal. 2.15). Christian slaves were still slaves (1 Cor. 7.21). And as we have seen, wives were still wives. These racial, social, and gender differentiations, which as such were often thought to indicate relative worth or privileged status before God, no longer had that significance. But, as so often with Paul's vision of ministry, the social realities conditioned the practice of the principle.

§21.5 The authority of the congregation

We have noted on several occasions that Paul encouraged the congregation to take responsibility for its own affairs and expected it to play a part in the recognition and regulation of ministry. This dimension of ministry and authority is sufficiently important for us to gather these individual points together.

a) Paul's theology on this point is clear. His understanding of the local church as the body of Christ necessarily implies each member having a function within that congregation, and a responsibility for its common life and worship. This presumably is the rationale behind his exhortations to *all* members of different churches to teach, admonish, judge, and comfort.[139]

b) Paul never addressed himself to a leadership group within a congregation (apart from Phil. 1.1). His instructions and exhortations were generally addressed to the church as a whole. This can only mean that responsibility for responding to such exhortations lay with the congregation as such and not merely with one or two individuals within it.[140] Hence the lack of mention of any leadership group, overseers or elders, in situations like those outlined in 1 Corinthians 5, 6, 11, 14, and 16. Paul did not even envisage the prophets (the most important local ministry) as giving a lead.[141] Their authority as prophets lay evidently solely in their charism of prophecy and in the evaluation of prophetic utterances.

c) The community as a whole was "taught by God" (1 Thes. 4.9). They all participated in the one Spirit *(koinōnia)*.[142] They were all in principle "spiritual people" *(pneumatikoi)*. As such they had authority to regulate and exercise judgment concerning charisms (1 Cor. 2.15). For that was why they

139. Rom. 15.14; 1 Cor. 5.4-5; 2 Cor. 2.7; Col. 3.16; 1 Thes. 5.14.
140. Lindsay, *Church* 32-33, 58-59.
141. *Pace* Greeven, "Propheten" 35-36.
142. See §20.6 above.

received the Spirit, precisely "in order that they might know/recognize all that God has graciously given them" (2.12).[143] Paul even expected them to exercise such discernment regarding his own clear conviction that his instruction was "a command of the Lord" (14.37). Hence not only prophets had responsibility to evaluate individual prophecy (1 Cor. 14.29), but the community also (and not just leaders within it) had responsibility to "test everything," prophetic utterances not least (1 Thes. 5.20-22).[144] Of a piece with this are Paul's strong warnings against any elitism in the realm of the Spirit, as being both factional and divisive (1 Cor. 3.1-4) and as disenabling the body's effectiveness (14.21).

d) Not least in importance was the congregation's responsibility to recognize and acknowledge the manifest charismatic authority of those who did not spare themselves in the service of the church and to encourage them in these more regular ministries.[145] In the light of such considerations 1 Cor. 14.16 gains a new significance. The "Amen" which the congregation uttered after a prayer or prophecy was not just a formal liturgical assent. It indicated rather the importance which Paul attached to the church's members being able to understand and to give assent to what was said in its worship.[146]

§21.6 Discerning the spirits

Something also needs to be said about the criteria by which Paul expected the authority of ministry to be recognized and heeded. We have already noted the importance Paul placed on the discerning of spirits, on the testing and evaluating of charisms, prophecy in particular.[147] And we have also already discussed the criteria by which Paul recognized the legitimate and God-approved exercise of apostolic authority (§21.2). It has not been sufficiently recognized, however, that Paul himself indicates and makes use of a sequence of criteria in his own principal treatment of charisms and community (1 Co-

---

143. On Gal. 6.1 see §21.3 above.

144. Here the exegetical base of *Lumen Gentium* §12 can be faulted, since 1 Thes. 5.14-22 is clearly addressed to the congregation as a whole, and no single exhortation or group of exhortations can be given a more limited reference without doing some violence to the text (see my "Discernment of Spirits" [above §20 n. 136] 87-89); but the interpretation is not without support (see my *Jesus and the Spirit.* 436 n. 141). It should be noted that the responsibility in testing prophecy is assumed to be that of the whole church both in 1 John 4.1-3 and in *Didache* 11. See also my "Responsible Congregation" 226-30.

145. 1 Cor. 16.15-18; 1 Thes. 5.12-13; cf. Phil. 2.29-30.

146. Cf. Schweizer, *Order* 101; Barrett, *1 Corinthians* 321 — "The responsibility of the church as a whole to hear, understand, test and control is underlined."

147. See again §20 n. 136 above.

rinthians 12–14).[148] Three in particular can be identified, which, not surprisingly, overlap with those already noted in regard to apostolic authority.

a) *The test of the gospel:* "No one speaking in/by the Spirit of God says 'Jesus is accursed'; and no one can say 'Jesus is Lord' except in/by the Holy Spirit" (1 Cor. 12.3). The circumstances calling for the application of this criterion are obscure. But in the immediate context the talk of being "led, carried away to dumb idols" (12.2) suggests that experiences of ecstatic inspiration were in view.[149] And the subsequent indication that (many of?) the Corinthians were "eager for spirits," that is, for experiences of inspiration (14.12), points in the same direction. The most plausible scenario, then, is that the letter from the Corinthians had asked Paul to advise on a situation within the church's worship where someone had in fact cried out, under inspiration, "Jesus is accursed."[150] We need not assume complete naiveté on the part of the Corinthians in the face of such inspiration (as though they assumed that all inspiration was good). It would be sufficient if the utterance had been made by a respected member of the congregation.[151]

The criterion used is the summary confession of the gospel as indicated by Paul elsewhere — "Jesus is Lord."[152] Presumably the criterion was intended in more general terms (the confession itself did not have to be repeated each time). That is, the test was whether the inspired utterance accorded with the gospel, as summarized by the confession. This suggestion fits too neatly with the first criterion of apostolic authority discussed above (§21.2a) for it to be coincidental. Which is not to say that the application of the criterion would be straightforward. Paul's own interpretation of the gospel (as freely for Gentiles) was itself a bone of contention between Paul and many Judean believers. That was why the acknowledgment of it by the Jerusalem apostles had been so crucial for Paul (Gal. 2.1-10). But Galatians also indicates how much store Paul placed on a church's initial experience of and response to the gospel.[153] The grace-giving gospel and the founding

---

148. Hahn, "Charisma" 220-25, is an exception.

149. On the ritual "madness" of the followers of Dionysus we need refer only to the classic study of E. Rohde, *Psyche: The Cult of Souls and Belief in Immortality among the Greeks* (New York: Harcourt and Brace/London: Kegan Paul, 1925).

150. There have been reports of equivalent utterances within contemporary charismatic communities, where one suggestion is that they should be regarded as cathartic — a spiritual nausea, as it were, being relieved by vomiting it up. See my *Jesus and the Spirit* 420 n. 180, and above §8 n. 73. Cf. Barrett, *Paul* 133: "it may be that we have to think of people struggling against a Spirit by which they do not wish to be overpowered."

151. In contemporary charismatic congregations a similar respect can result in the evaluation of a leading member's prophetic utterance being unduly constrained.

152. Particularly Rom. 10.9; 2 Cor. 4.5; and Col. 2.6.

153. Gal. 1.6-9; 2.7-9; 3.1-5; 4.6-11; 5.1, 4; also, e.g., 1 Cor. 15.1-2.

traditions of a church provided a criterion by which to judge its ongoing life.

b) *The test of love* — 1 Corinthians 13. The placement of ch. 13 between chs. 12 and 14 has sometimes caused puzzlement.[154] But its function could hardly be clearer. It was written in recognition that charismatic ministry and other important expressions of the Christian life and congregation could often be exercised in a selfish and uncaring manner. Not only tongues, but also the highest charism (prophecy); the most exalted and rapturous experience of worship could be loveless (13.1-2). Not only so, but even the most profound scholars, the heroes of faith, the greatest social activists, the very martyrs themselves, could be acting on baser motives than love (13.2-3). And in case the word "love" itself did not indicate what the criterion amounts to in sufficient detail Paul added the peerless description (13.4-7):

> [4]Love is patient; love is kind; love is not envious, is not boastful, is not conceited, [5]is not rude. It does not seek its own advantage; it does not become irritated; it keeps no score of wrongdoing. [6]It takes no pleasure in wickedness, but rejoices with the truth. [7]It always endures, is always trustful, always hopeful, always persistent.

It is hard to doubt that Paul in thus describing love had in mind the love of God in Christ,[155] and Jesus' own summary of the law in the command to love the neighbour.[156] A similar inference is appropriate in his naming love as the primary or all-embracing fruit of the Spirit (Gal. 5.22-23).[157] It is just this love which identifies and defines the Spirit as the Spirit of Christ, the Spirit of the self-giving and crucified Christ.[158] The point here is that this love is of more value, a mark of greater maturity, and its effects more enduring than any charism (1 Cor. 13.8-13). Paul implies that it is all too possible to experience charism without love, and he goes out of his way to stress that charism divorced from love is useless. He would no doubt have been all too well aware that living out the ideal in practice was hardly straightforward. But here too he does not hesitate to hold before his readers the vision of love, including the pattern of the love of God in Christ, as an ideal to aspire to and against which to evaluate lesser motivations.

154. See the reviews of the discussion in J. T. Sanders, "First Corinthians 13: Its Interpretation since the First World War," *Int* 20 (1966) 159-87; O. Wischmeyer, *Der höchste Weg. Das 13. Kapitel des 1. Korintherbriefes* (Gütersloh: Gütersloher, 1981).

155. Rom. 5.5, 8; 8.35, 39; 2 Cor. 5.14; see further above §13 n. 15.

156. Rom. 13.10; Gal. 5.14; see further below §23.5.

157. See further my *Galatians* 309-10. Is a contrast intended between "the *works* of the flesh" (5.19) and "the *fruit* of the Spirit" (5.22)?

158. See further above §§10.6, 16.4, and 18.7.

c) *The test of community benefit* (oikodomē) — 1 Corinthians 14. Of the three criteria used in 1 Corinthians 12–14 this is the clearest. Paul reverts to it no less than seven times in the chapter.[159] It is the test of *oikodomē* which proves prophecy superior to glossolalia, since the former benefits the church as a whole, while the latter benefits only the individual tongues-speaker (14.3-5, 12, 17). Similarly the rule about orderly procedure in the sequence of tongues and interpretation and in regard to prophecy and its evaluation is manifestly for the congregation's benefit (14.26-33). The same consideration was no doubt operative for Paul in reference to women prophesying with hair unbound and wives participating in the evaluation of prophecies; if it brought the church into disrepute with otherwise sympathetic outsiders, no one would benefit. Paul may also have intended an extension of the principle in referring to the confusion experienced by the outsider when he enters upon an assembly in which all are speaking in tongues (14.23-25).[160] Earlier on, the explicit use of the same criterion in 8.1 nicely ties together the last two criteria: "knowledge puffs up, but love builds up." And similarly in 10.23: " 'All things are lawful,' but not all things build up." Paul's own concern as an apostle for the maturity of his churches (§21.2b) is an expression of the same principle and priority.

In all this the important point of principle which emerges is that the individual's prerogative (inspiration or status) is always subordinate to the good of the whole. Even the most impressive utterances or actions are subject to being measured by the yardstick of God's love in Christ, love of neighbour. And even when the individual in question is the church's apostle, the subordination of apostolic authority to that of the gospel should provide the church itself with sufficient checks. Or in reference to the old charism/office debate (§21.1), the more we regard Paul's concept of ecclesiastical authority as essentially charismatic in character (dependent on the engracement of the Spirit), the more it has to be stressed that the only valid or effective charism is the one tested and received by the church for whom it was given. Of course, Paul's experiences with his various churches would have left him with few illusions regarding the application of such tests. It would always require spiritual people to give the lead in using them, and spirituality is easily corrupted and debased. But once again the importance of Paul's recognition of the need for critical scrutiny of claims to leadership and proffered ministry, and the potential value of the criteria he actually used himself, should not be underestimated. How much further the

159. *Oikodomeō,* "build" — 14.4 (twice), 17; *oikodomē,* "building up, edifica-tion" — 14.3, 5, 12, 26. So also earlier in 1 Corinthians (3.9; 8.1; 10.23). And elsewhere in Paul (Rom. 14.19; 15.2; 2 Cor. 10.8; 12.19; 13.10; Gal. 2.18; 1 Thes. 5.11)

160. Schweizer, *Order* 96: "For Paul . . . the one who comes from outside, the *idiōtēs,* is the most important; it is by his understanding that the preaching is to be measured, so that a church that developed a secret language unintelligible to the world would cease to be a church (1 Cor. 14:16, 23ff.)."

principle of "testing the spirits" can be pressed[161] is a question which would take us well beyond Paul's own theologizing.

§21.7 Conclusion

So far as his vision of the church of God, the body of Christ, is concerned, Paul was no armchair or ivory tower theorist. It was a vision already tempered by the social realities of community formation within hostile environments, of still inchoate forms of ministry caught in the tension between inspiration and social convention, and of emerging patterns of authority struggling to free themselves from assumptions of social status and patronal expectation. It was also a vision, we may assume, which, like Paul's vision for Israel, was in some measure at least conditioned by his own hope to complete the task of essential evangelism within his own generation. It is no surprise, then, that already in the unanticipated second-generation Pauline churches (the Pastorals) we see the familiar second-generation pattern of routinization of charisma and institutionalization of authority.

The question, theologically, however, is whether Paul's model of church, of charismatic community, of ministry and authority, with the careful balance of mutual interdependence and responsibility which he so clearly encouraged, simply expresses the idealism and unreality of a charismatic movement's first-generation enthusiasm. Or does it provide a starting point, or counterpoint, or outline of first principles which still retains a validity beyond that first generation? The fact that the NT canon includes the Pastorals as well as the earlier Paulines is a warning not to live solely with the "ideal" of 1 Corinthians 12–14. But that the canon includes the earlier Pauline letters as well as the Pastorals is an encouragement to look to Paul's earlier vision for its continuing value.

Here again we may note the significance of the developments within western Christianity over the past three decades. Prior to that the almost universal rule was in effect to treat the Pauline ecclesiologies of 1 Corinthians 12–14 and the Pastorals as divergent and in competition — two or three streams of distinct kinds of Christianity. Küng's work in particular, however, symbolizes an attempt, new in scope and potential, to take Paul's vision of the charismatic structure of the church as fundamental to the whole.[162] That potential has yet to be fully realized.

---

161. As particularly by Käsemann, *Kanon* (above §14 n. 5); "Thoughts on the Present Controversy about Scriptural Interpretation," *New Testament Questions* 260-85 (here 264).

162. Cf. *Church* 187: "In a Church or community where only ecclesiastical officials rather than all the members of the community are active, there is grave reason to wonder whether the Spirit has not been sacrificed along with the spiritual gifts."

§22 The Lord's Supper[1]

1. **Bibliography**: M. **Barth**, *Rediscovering the Lord's Supper: Communion with Israel, with Christ, and among the Guests* (Atlanta: John Knox, 1988); **Bornkamm**, "Lord's Supper and Church in Paul," *Early Christian Experience* 123-60; **Bultmann**, *Theology* 1.144-52; W. **Burkert**, *Ancient Mystery Cults* (Cambridge: Harvard University, 1987); **J. Delorme**, et al., *The Eucharist in the New Testament* (London: Chapman/Baltimore: Helicon, 1964); **Gnilka**, *Theologie* 120-24; *Paulus* 277-81; **Goppelt**, *Theology* 2.147-50; **F. Hahn**, "Herrengedächtnis und Herrenmahl bei Paulus," *Exegetische Beiträge zum ökumenischen Gespräch* (Göttingen: Vandenhoeck, 1986) 303-14; **Heitmüller**, *Taufe und Abendmahl* (§17 n. 1); **O. Hofius**, "Herrenmahl und Herrenmahlsparadosis. Erwägungen zu 1 Kor. 11.23b-25," *Paulusstudien* 204-40 = "The Lord's Supper and the Lord's Supper Tradition: Reflections on 1 Corinthians 11.23b-25," in Meyer, ed., *One Loaf* (below) 75-115; **J. Jeremias**, *The Eucharistic Words of Jesus* (London: SCM, 1966); **R. Jewett**, "Gospel and Commensality: Social and Theological Implications of Galatians 2.14," in L. A. Jervis and P. Richardson, eds., *Gospel in Paul* (§7 n. 1) 240-52; **Käsemann**, "The Pauline Doctrine of the Lord's Supper," *Essays* 108-35; **Keck**, *Paul* 61-64; **H.-J. Klauck**, *Herrenmahl und hellenistischer Kult. Eine religionsgeschichtliche Untersuchung zum ersten Korintherbrief* (Münster: Aschendorff, 1982); "Presence in the Lord's Supper: 1 Corinthians 11.23-26 in the Context of Hellenistic Religious History," in Meyer, ed., *One Loaf* (below) 57-74; **P. Lampe**, "The Eucharist: Identifying with Christ on the Cross," *Int* 48 (1994) 36-49; **X. Léon-Dufour**, *Sharing the Eucharistic Bread: The Witness of the New Testament* (New York: Paulist, 1987); **I. H. Marshall**, *Last Supper and Lord's Supper* (Exeter: Paternoster, 1980 = Grand Rapids: Eerdmans, 1981); **W. Marxsen**, *The Lord's Supper as a Christological Problem* (Philadelphia: Fortress, 1970); **Meeks**, *First Urban Christians* 157-62; **B. F. Meyer**, ed., *One Loaf, One Cup: Ecumenical Studies of 1 Cor. 11 and Other Eucharistic Texts* (Macon: Mercer University, 1993); **J. Murphy-O'Connor**, *St. Paul's Corinth: Texts and Archaeology* (Collegeville: Liturgical/Glazier, 1983); **P. Neuenzeit**, *Das Herrenmahl. Studien zur paulinischen Eucharistieauffassung* (Munich: Kösel, 1960); **A. D. Nock**, "Early Gentile Christianity and Its Hellenistic Background" and "Hellenistic Mysteries and Christian Sacraments," in *Essays on Religion and the Ancient World*, ed. J. Z. Stewart (Oxford: Clarendon, 1972) 1.49-133 and 2.791-820; **Neyrey**, *Paul in Other Words*, particularly ch. 5; **B. I. Reicke**, *Diakone, Festfreude und Zelos, in Verbindung mit der altchristlichen Agapenfeier* (Uppsala: Lundequistka, 1951); **J. Reumann**, *The Supper of the Lord: The New Testament, Ecumenical Dialogues, and Faith and Order on Eucharist* (Philadelphia: Fortress, 1985); **Ridderbos**, *Paul* 414-28; **E. Schweizer**, *The Lord's Supper according to the New Testament* (Philadelphia: Fortress, 1967); **Strecker**, *Theologie* 176-85; **Stuhlmacher**, *Theologie* 363-70; **Theissen**, "Social Integration and Sacramental Activity: An Analysis of 1 Cor. 11.17-34," *Social Setting* ch. 4; **Wedderburn**, *Baptism* (§17 n. 1); **Whiteley**, *Theology* 178-85; **W. L. Willis**, *Idol Meat in Corinth: The Pauline Argument in 1 Corinthians 8 and 10* (SBLDS 68; Chico: Scholars, 1985).

§22.1 The problem in assessing Paul's theology of the Lord's Supper

In talking of the church as the body of Christ, there can be no doubt as to the importance of the Lord's Supper for Paul.[2] The point is put beyond dispute by 1 Cor. 10.16-17:

> [16]The cup of blessing which we bless, is it not a sharing in the blood of Christ? The bread which we break, is it not a sharing in the body of Christ? [17]Because the bread is one, we though many are one body, for we all partake of the one bread.

That importance has been maintained and magnified throughout the course of Christian tradition, as any practising member of a traditional denomination will be aware. Particularly in the Orthodox and Catholic traditions, the eucharist is at the very heart of the communal life of Christianity.

It is all the more disappointing, possibly even somewhat disturbing, then, that Paul says so little on the subject, and that what he does say is limited to two chapters in one letter (1 Corinthians 10–11).

This, of course, is a consequence of Paul's theologizing by means of letters — letters which were inevitably, in one degree or other, occasional in character. Thus, where the Lord's Supper gave rise to no questions or concern, it did not need to be discussed. It belonged simply to that array of traditions and good practice with which Paul evidently endowed his churches when he first established them and to which he found it necessary to make only occasional formal allusion.[3] In this case Paul was able to refer back explicitly to the traditions in question (11.2, 23). We could justifiably be more heartened than disturbed by the thought that this feature of the common life of Paul's churches was so fundamental and so tranquil that Paul could take it so completely for granted in his other letters.

The drawbacks, however, are twofold. First, the fact that Paul does not even allude to the Lord's Supper elsewhere, even in his most systematic exposition of his theology (Romans), does raise something of a question mark: how central was the Lord's Supper in Paul's theology and in the churches to which he wrote? The issue is all the more pressing, since Romans contains a section (Rom. 14.1–15.6) closely parallel to 1 Corinthians 8–10. In what amounts to an appeal for mutual acceptance among the Roman believers (Rom. 14.1; 15.7), the absence of even an allusion to the bonding effect of the shared Supper of the Lord is surprising. Similarly with the earlier meals at Antioch,

---

2. I use Paul's own term throughout, "Lord's supper" (*kyriakon deipnon* — 1 Cor. 11.20), rather than the later "eucharist" (already in *Didache* 9.1, 5), *pascha* ("[Christian] passover" — already in Diognetus 12.9), "mass," or "holy communion."

3. See above §§8.2-3 and below §23.5.

from which Peter and the other Christian Jews separated themselves, and which most likely included the Lord's Supper at least on some occasions (Gal. 2.11-14).

The second drawback is that we become too heavily dependent on a single letter and on being able to unravel, to some extent at least, the complex background to the treatment in 1 Corinthians 10–11. As we have stressed throughout this chapter, Paul's ecclesiology was framed in reference to and tempered by the practical realities of his churches. The unavoidable issue here, then, is the extent to which Paul's theology of the Lord's Supper was adapted to the particular strains and stresses within the Corinthian church. In other cases, where references and allusions span an array of Paul's letters, we can "plot" Paul's position with some confidence by taking a "fix" on each of the separate treatments. But here we are in the position of a ship or airplane which has only one of the minimally required two directional beams to guide its course. We know roughly where we are, but we are unable to make the necessary compensatory calculations.

In this case, therefore, it is crucial to gain as much information as we can regarding the background of Paul's all too brief allusions to and exposition of the Lord's Supper. Only then will be in a position to hear Paul's theologizing in context and to make allowances for any emphases particular (or peculiar?) to the situation of the church in Corinth.

§22.2 Influence from other religions?

As in the case of baptism (§17.1), so here, the modern debate on the source of Paul's sacramental theology began with the history of religions movement.

The early history of religions school was attempting to explain the Pauline theology of an eating and drinking which purported to mediate both salvation and communion with the exalted Lord (10.16-17). In their view the pre-Pauline tradition and practice did not provide that explanation. The historicity of the Last Supper was regarded as uncertain, though the practice of a common meal in the primitive community was recognized. But in any case the scholars concerned were confident that the earlier community had not yet acquired these central features of the Pauline theology.[4] Explanation had to be sought elsewhere, and the Greek mysteries provided an inviting explanation.

A certain plausibility is added to the case by the prominence of the

---

4. See, e.g., Heitmüller, *Taufe und Abendmahl;* Bousset, *Kyrios Christos* (§10 n. 1) 138; Bultmann, *Theology* 1.147-49.

mysteries in and around Corinth.[5] The Eleusinian mysteries, the most influential and popular of the Greek mysteries, seem to have promised initiates
the conquest of death.[6] More famous and celebrated in Greece were the
mysteries of Dionysus, the more extreme forms of which took the form of
orgiastic revelry, in which feasting and drinking were prominent.[7] Of other
religious cults, the most famous was the cult of Asclepius, known as the
"Saviour," to whom was attributed many healings. We know of a major
Asclepiaeum in Corinth at this time, with accommodation for those seeking
cures and dining rooms.[8] Not least of interest is the possibility that there
may already have been a temple to Isis in the Corinthian port Cenchraea,[9]
in which we can assume the mystery of seasonal death and rebirth was
celebrated in some way.

Many of these parallels, however, are more striking than substantial.
As is usually the case, the early "parallelomania"[10] has given way to more
sober assessment.[11] Here too, as is so often the case, subsequent, more

---

5. Brief descriptions and further bibliography in *OCD*, "Asclepius," "Demeter,"
"Dionysus," "Isis"; Koester, *Introduction* 1.173-91; M. W. Meyer, "Mystery Religions,"
ABD 4.941-44. Fuller treatments in M. P. Nilsson, *Geschichte der griechischen Religion*
(Munich: Beck, 1961) 2.622-701, and of Eleusis and Dionysus in particular in Klauck,
Herrenmahl 94-118. D. G. Rice and J. E. Stambaugh, *Sources for the Study of Greek
Religion* (Missoula: Scholars, 1979), and M. W. Meyer, ed., *The Ancient Mysteries: A
Sourcebook* (San Francisco: Harper and Row, 1987), provide good selections of texts.

6. Eleusis lay less than twenty miles to the west of Athens.

7. We have already noted a possible allusion to the uninhibited Dionysiac festivals
in 1 Cor. 12.2 (see above §21 n. 149). It was in Corinth that Pausanias heard the story of
Pentheus, torn limb from limb by the female revelers (*Description of Greece* 2.6).

8. For archaeological details see Murphy-O'Connor, *Corinth* 169-74; Furnish,
2 Corinthians 17. See further MacMullen, *Paganism* (§2 n. 1) 34-42 (here 37 and n. 16).

9. For archaeological details again see Murphy-O'Connor, *Corinth* 18-21; Furnish,
2 Corinthians 19-20. It was at Cenchraea that Lucius received his vision of Isis and was
initiated into her cult (Apuleius, *Metamorphoses* 11.4-25; see also above §17 n. 26 and
§21 n. 125).

10. E.g., Kirsopp Lake's conclusion: "Christianity has not borrowed from the
Mystery Religions, because it was always, at least in Europe, a Mystery Religion itself"
(*Earlier Epistles* 215).

11. As "heir" of the History of Religions school, Strecker limits himself to noting
the possible influence of the Mystery religions on the original development which gave
the last supper "the characteristics of a sacral celebration" (*Theologie* 179). In what follows
see further particularly Klauck, who provides a full categorization with extensive documentation (*Herrenmahl* 40-91). Klauck's "Presence" emphasizes that "analogies of diverse
density between the Christian Lord's Supper and non-Christian phenomena" cannot be
denied (58) and summarizes a sequence of them. But he concludes that such analogies
"should not be allowed to create the impression that the Lord's Supper was assembled,
mosaic-like, out of the available elements, and that it owes its origin to just such a conscious
act of construction. The whole remains a creative synthesis, unique and underived" (74).

detailed research has revealed serious methodological flaws in the early hypotheses.[12]

For one thing, the earlier assumption of a clean line of distinction between Judaism and Hellenism has had to be abandoned.[13] In this case the point is well illustrated by the Hellenistic Jewish romance *Joseph and Aseneth*.[14] There we also find talk of an eating and drinking which symbolizes or mediates life and repugnance at the thought of eating and drinking at the table of idols. Joseph is a man who will "eat blessed bread of life and drink a blessed cup of immortality"; so how could he "kiss a strange woman who will bless with her mouth dead and dumb idols and eat from their table bread of strangulation and drink from their libation a cup of insidiousness"? (8.5). The parallel with 1 Cor. 10.16-17 and Paul's similar revulsion at the thought of eating food sacrificed to idols and of partaking at the table of demons (10.19-21) is striking. Subsequently the bread of life and cup of immortality are represented by a honeycomb, which is described as "the ineffable mysteries of the Most High" and as "(full of the) spirit of life," and which Aseneth eats in a kind of initiation sacrament (16.14-16).

Should we then assume that *Joseph and Aseneth* has been influenced by the Greek mysteries?[15] The problem is that we know of no similar ritual to that described in 16.14-16.[16] More striking still is the strongly Jewish character throughout. The honeycomb evidently symbolizes manna,[17] a powerful symbol from Israel's tradition of heavenly sustenance (cf. 1 Cor. 10.3-4). Moreover, the contrast of life and death is quite unlike the mystery of seasonal fertility, and is entirely bound up with traditional Jewish hostility to idolatry ("dead and dumb idols" — 8.5).[18] When so much is illuminated from the Jewish background and the postulated actual influence from the

---

12. A regrettable exception is the highly tendentious and quite uncritical argument of H. Maccoby, *Paul and Hellenism* (London: SCM/Philadelphia: TPI, 1991) chs. 3-4.

13. The principal credit for this is usually and rightly given to M. Hengel, *Judaism and Hellenism* (2 vols.; London: SCM/Philadelphia: Fortress, 1974).

14. Written probably in Egypt sometime in the first century BCE or CE (C. Burchard in Charlesworth, *OTP* 2.187-88).

15. So M. Philonenko, *Joseph et Aséneth. Introduction, texte critique, traduction et notes* (Leiden: Brill, 1968) 89-98.

16. "Such a ritual would have to be reconstructed from the very text which it is called upon to elucidate" (Burchard, *OTP* 2.193).

17. 16.8: "The comb was big and white as snow and full of honey. And that honey was like dew from heaven and its exhalation like breath of life" (cf. Exod. 16.14, 31; Wis. 19.21; *Sib. Or.* 3.746; Burchard, *OTP* 2.228 n. 16f).

18. See also Aseneth's subsequent revulsion at the thought of her mouth defiled from the table of idols and their sacrifices (11.9, 16; 12.5). On Israel's long-rooted hostility to idolatry see above §2.2.

mysteries is so obscure, the need to argue for such influence becomes itself questionable.[19]

A second weakness of the earlier theses was the assumption that analogies had to be explained genetically, by dependence of Christian practice on the wider practices of the Hellenistic cults. But here again, as with baptism, we are dealing with features which are almost universal in religions ancient and modern — rites of purification and ceremonial meals. It would be surprising, therefore, if there were not some basic similarities between earliest Christianity and contemporary religions. To repeat: analogy is not genealogy. Of the three broad categories of religious meals noted by A. D. Nock,[20] only the second (a meal at which the god was thought to preside) has any immediate relevance.[21] The first, a meal to commemorate a dead founder or benefactor, hardly fits. Christians thought of Jesus as living, not as dead. And in any event, Jeremias has pointed out that such remembrance meals were usually held on the birthday, not on the anniversary of the death, of the one so remembered.[22] And the third, the Dionysiac ritual of "eating raw meat" (omophagia), which has long fascinated Christian observers, can scarcely be thought to provide any real precedent for the Lord's Supper.[23]

Furthermore, here again our lack of knowledge of the secret practices of the mysteries makes it hazardous to draw lines of connection and dependence. We usually do not know where any symbolic act of eating or drinking happened within the mystery and what it was intended to signify.[24] That there were similarities between Christianity and Mithraism in particular was in effect acknowledged by subsequent Christian writers,[25] but it is uncertain whether Mithraism had already spread into Greece by the time of Paul.[26] Papyri invitations "to dine at a banquet of the Lord Sarapis" are of special

---

19. See further Burchard, *OTP* 2.211-12 n. 8i; also Chesnut, *Death to Life* (§17 n. 1) particularly 128-35. And on the possible relevance of *Joseph and Aseneth* to the Pauline teaching on the Lord's supper, see further C. Burchard, "The Importance of Joseph and Asenath for the Study of the New Testament: A General Survey and Fresh Look at the Lord's Supper," *NTS* 33 (1987) 102-34.

20. "Early Gentile Christianity" 107-9. Klauck, *Herrenmahl* 31-39, elaborated the analysis to eleven categories, but it is unncessary to pursue the refinements here.

21. See further below (next paragraph).

22. *Eucharistic Words* 242.

23. See further Willis, *Idol Meat* 23-32; Burkert, *Mystery Cults* 111.

24. Nock, "Early Gentile Christianity" 1.109-10; Burkert, *Mystery Cults* 110-11. Nock also notes how fluid was the use of "mystery" terminology ("Hellenistic Mysteries" 2.796-801).

25. Justin, *Apology* 1.66.4; *Dialogue* 70.1; Tertullian, *De Praescriptione Haereticorum* 940; see also Clement of Alexandria, *Protreptikos* 12.

26. Details in *OCD,* "Mithras"; Hengel and Schwemer, *Paul between Damascus and Antioch* 168.

interest, since the implication is that the god himself will be present at the banquet.[27] But Paul's language does not seem to reflect this tradition in particular. "The table of (the god)" is also used for the place where the sacrifice is made or from which it comes.[28] But Paul is as likely to have derived his talk of "the table of the Lord/demons" from the LXX, which calls gods "demons" (cf. 10.20-21) and the altar of Yahweh "the table of the Lord" (cf. 10.18).[29] Such linguistic interplay does not imply that Paul thought either of the Lord's table as an altar or of the Lord's Supper as a sacrifice.[30]

It looks from 1 Cor. 10.19-22 as though Paul had in view only the more public feasts held in temples, where it was the company of idols/demons as hosts which was the point of his objection rather than an alternative theology of salvation through eating.[31] Had the latter been the problem Paul would hardly have been so uninhibited in his subsequent advice that Christians should feel free to accept invitations to dine privately where the source of the meat was uncertain (10.25-27).[32] As in *Joseph and Aseneth,* the antipathy was more likely rooted in traditional Jewish horror at the prospect of being defiled by contact with idols (8.10).[33] The fact that Paul speaks of eating and drinking judgment against oneself only in connection with the bread and cup of the Lord (11.27-29) and not in regard to a meal eaten in a temple (8.10) also suggests that the theology of 10.16-17 is more distinctive of the Christian tradition and less likely to have been borrowed from elsewhere.

A source for Paul's theology of the Lord's Supper in the mystery and other religious cults of the time, therefore, seems unlikely. At the same time, we cannot ignore the fact that Paul does draw some sort of parallel between

27. Set out conveniently by Willis, *Idol Meat* 40-42; additional material in *NDIEC* 1.5-9. The venues include the Sarapeion itself, or a room or building attached to it, and private homes. Nock notes that the second-century orator Aristides speaks of men "inviting him [Sarapis] to their hearths and causing him to preside over their feasts" ("Early Gentile Christianity" 1.108).

28. Details in BAGD, *trapeza* 2; L. Goppelt, *TDNT* 8.214; though see also Willis, *Idol Meat* 13-17.

29. Ezek. 44.16; Mal. 1.7, 12. See also Philo, *Spec. Leg.* 1.221, cited below (n. 98).

30. Goppelt, *TDNT* 8.213-14. Wedderburn, *Baptism* 159-60, notes Nock's comment on the absence from Paul (and the NT generally) of terminology that was really distinctive of the mysteries: "any idea that what we call the Christian sacraments were in their origin indebted to pagan mysteries or even to the metaphorical concepts based upon them shatters on the rock of linguistic evidence" ("Mysteries" 2.809).

31. Cf. Wedderburn, *Baptism* 158-59.

32. See further below §24.7.

33. Though we should note that Paul's concern throughout is more with the effects of individual Christians' actions on others (8.7-13; 10.23-32; 11.17-22, 33-34) than with the issue of the reality of demons (contrast 8.4-6 and 10.19-22; see above §2.3).

partnership of the altar (of the Jerusalem temple), sharing in the table of the Lord, and sharing in the table of demons (10.18, 21). Earlier on, even though rebuking the Corinthians for their apparent assumption that participation in the Lord's Supper assured them of salvation (10.6-12), Paul speaks of "spiritual food and drink" (10.3-4). And subsequently he seems to imply that an unworthy eating and drinking of the bread and cup has resulted in illness and even death (11.30). How do these emphases find a place within his theology? The fact that we cannot simply attribute such features of Paul's argument to some influence from other Greek and Egyptian cults in the event only poses the theological questions more sharply.

§22.3 The origin of the sacrament

In contrast to the difficulties in deriving the theology of the Lord's Supper from other religions of the time, there is little difficulty in deriving the early Christian meal practice from within its own tradition. Quite apart from the meals derived from the "table" of the Jerusalem altar (10.18), fellowship meals were a particular feature of both Pharisees and Essenes. Jesus' own practice of table fellowship was criticized for its disregard for the appropriate limits.[34] The sensitivities on this score are evident also in Luke's careful telling of the story of Peter and Cornelius,[35] as well as in the incident at Antioch (Gal. 2.11-14), and directly illumine the concerns addressed by Paul both in 1 Corinthians 8–10 and Rom. 14.1–15.6.[36]

Paul himself records the tradition authorizing the Lord's Supper as the account of the last supper of Jesus with his disciples, which Paul himself received and passed on to the Corinthians at the foundation of their church (11.23).[37] A comparison of this tradition with its variant versions is instructive.[38]

34. Mark 2.16-17; Matt. 11.19/Luke 7.34; Luke 15.2; 19.7.

35. Acts 10–11, particularly 10.10-16, 28; 11.3-12.

36. See further below §§24.3. 7.

37. By attributing the tradition directly to the Lord ("I received from the Lord"), Paul himself raises the question of whether he thought of it as a personal revelation from the Lord. But the fact that he feels no need to defend it as such (contrast Gal. 1.12) and uses the traditional terminology for receiving and passing on tradition (as in 1 Cor. 15.1, 3) points firmly to the conclusion that 11.23-26 was part of the traditions also mentioned in 11.2. At such a point Paul evidently did not distinguish historical Jesus from exalted Lord: the established tradition was "received (also) from the Lord" (Bornkamm, "Lord's Supper" 131; see also O. Cullmann, "The Tradition," *The Early Church: Historical and Theological Studies* [London: SCM/Philadelphia: Westminster, 1956] 59-99 [here 67-69]). See further §8.3 above and §23.5 below.

38. The material peculiar to Matthew and Luke in the following table is indicated by brackets.

Mark 14.22-24/(Matt. 26.26-28)

22he took bread, blessed it,
broke it, and gave it to them
and said, "Take, (eat);
this is my body."

23And taking the cup, he gave
thanks and gave it to them,
. . . 24and he said to them,
"This is my blood of the covenant
which is poured out for many
(for the forgiveness of sins)."

1 Cor. 11.23-25/(Luke 22.19-20)

23he took bread, 24gave thanks,
broke it, and (gave it to them)
said (saying),
"This is my body which is (given) for
you; do this in remembrance of me."
25Likewise also the cup after dinner,

saying,
"This cup is the new covenant in my
blood (which is poured out for you)."

Two features of this common tradition call for comment.

First, there were clearly two slightly (but significantly) different versions of the form of and wording used at the last supper among the churches. One we may call the Mark/Matthew version; the other was common to Paul and Luke. It should be fairly evident even from the brief comparison above that neither can be completely derived from the other. The most obvious explanation of their otherwise striking closeness is that they come from a common source or tradition. There is a dispute as to which is likely to have been closer to the common original. But since Paul makes so little use on his own behalf of the "new covenant" tradition (the emphasis on which constitutes the most distinctive feature of the Paul/Luke version of the cup word),[39] the case for seeing the Paul/Luke version as closer to the original form probably has the edge.[40]

It also follows, secondly, that each version of the tradition constitutes some development of the original. There are indications, in turn, that Matthew has elaborated the common Mark/Matthew version and that Luke has elaborated the common Paul/Luke version. More strikingly still, Paul's version shows a further elaboration at the end. His version continues (11.25b-26):

> 25"Do this, as often as you drink it, in remembrance of me," 26for as often as you eat this bread and drink the cup, you proclaim the death of the Lord until he comes.

The addition of v. 25b parallels the Paul/Luke addition to the bread word (11.24b), so presumably Paul or his tradition simply carried through the logic of the earlier or common addition. So too Paul or his tradition has

39. See above §6 n. 94.
40. See further my *Unity* 166-68.

added and elaborated the "as often as you" element in v. 25b by adding v. 26.[41]

Both sets of elaborations probably indicate the effect of liturgical shaping. The addition of "Take, (eat)" to the bread word in the Mark/Matthew version reads like the necessary liturgical command (equivalent to Paul/Luke's "Do this in remembrance of me"). And in formulating the bread and cup word in closer parallel ("This is my body/This is my blood") the Mark/Matthew version probably reflects a form of celebration in which the two words have been brought into closer conjunction. Likewise the additions of 11.24b and 25b-26 certainly reflect a consciousness of repeated celebrations. The fact that Paul simply continues the sentence, switching almost imperceptibly from first person ("in remembrance of me") to third person ("you proclaim the Lord's death until he comes") indicates no sense of any need to distinguish clearly between tradition and commentary.

There need be little doubt, then, that Paul did indeed derive his founding tradition of the last supper from common tradition, and nothing that Paul says in 11.23-26 counts against the view that the tradition itself stemmed ultimately from the event now known as the last supper itself. The question still remains, however, whether the theology of 10.16-17 in particular can be attributed to Paul's tradition, or whether we have to look for other influences upon him. On the evidence reviewed so far, the signs point to a purely internal development. The common tradition already contained the powerful words of identification: "this (bread) is my body"; "this cup is the new covenant in my blood." And the elaboration of the tradition itself evidenced clear willingness to draw out the implications of these words, not least in terms of Jesus' death as an effective sacrifice.[42] The question, then, is whether the internal dynamic of the words themselves was not sufficient to explain the fuller theology of 10.16-17. At the very least we can easily imagine Paul interacting the tradition of the last supper with his own theology of Christ's sacrificial death (§9.2-3) and of participation in Christ (§15).

But we have still another aspect of the background to Paul's teaching in 1 Corinthians 10–11 to consider before we can begin to gain a clear picture of the function of the Lord's Supper within his theology.

---

41. Perhaps in conscious awareness of the tradition of Jesus' vow of abstinence at the last supper (Mark 14.25/Matt. 26.29/Luke 22.18); see also Klauck, *Herrenmahl* 320-23.

42. "Given for you," "poured out for you," "for the forgiveness of sins"; see further above §9.3.

§22.4 The situation in Corinth

As with other issues addressed in 1 Corinthians, so here the application of a sociological perspective has shed fresh light on old debates. Prior to the contributions of Gerd Theissen in particular, the dominant tendency was to assume that the problems tackled in 1 Corinthians 10–11 were essentially theological or religious in character — divergent doctrines of the Lord's Supper and influence from other religions or cults. But Theissen pointed out that the problems especially prominent in this section of 1 Corinthians were those of a socially stratified community.[43] Here not least it is evident that the tension was basically between rich and poor Christians, that is, between those who had enough food and drink and their own houses (11.21-22) and "those who have nothing" (11.22).[44] Presumably it was the well-to-do who were going ahead with their meal before the poorer members arrived (11.33). Since it is house churches which are always in view, we may also assume that the common meals were hosted by wealthier believers in their own homes. In accordance with the practice of the time, those of higher social status may well have kept the best food for their social peers and provided poorer quality food for their social inferiors and clients.[45]

Other features of ancient entertaining throw further light on the situation envisaged by Paul in 1 Corinthians 10–11. According to the tradition of the *eranos,*[46] either each participant brought and ate his or her own food, or all the provisions were put on a common table. The problem at Corinth would then have been that some came early and began eating (either from their own provisions or from the common stock) before the others arrived (11.21).[47] Moreover, those arriving later would probably have had insufficient time or money to prepare enough food for themselves.[48] Arriving late, they would find that most of the

43. Theissen, "Social Integration."

44. B. W. Winter qualifies "rich and poor" here as "the secure, i.e. those who are guaranteed security by reason of membership of a household, and the insecure, i.e. those who had no protection from a patron" ("The Lord's Supper at Corinth: An Alternative Reconstruction," *RTR* 37 [1978] 73-82 [here 81]).

45. Pliny, *Epistles* 2.6, provides an illuminating illustration; cited by Murphy-O'Connor, *Corinth* 167-68 (together with two of Martial's *Epigrams,* 3.60 and 4.85).

46. "Meal to which each contributed his share" (LSJ, *eranos*); "faith-supper" (Methodism); "pot-luck supper" (Marshall, *Last Supper* 109); documentation in Lampe, "Eucharist" 38-39.

47. *Prolambanō* probably retains a temporal significance here: "do something before the usual time, anticipate something" (BAGD, *prolambanō* 1a; Lampe, "Eucharist" 48 n. 13); as indicated also by the command to "wait for one another" (11.33; Wolff, *1 Korinther* 81). So 11.21 — "each goes ahead (*prolambanei*) in eating his own (*idion*) supper," the *idion* implying "his own" in disregard for others. See also next paragraph.

48. The slave or freedman still in a dependent client relationship would not be able to order his own time; still less the female slave or wife of a non-Christian husband (cf. 7.12-16).

expensive and substantial food had already been eaten.[49] Furthermore, latecomers might well find that there was insufficient room for them in the *triclinium* ("dining room") and would have had to sit in the *atrium* (the courtyard off which the dining room normally opened).[50] The picture is inevitably speculative, but nevertheless rather persuasive. It would occasion no surprise that a movement of such religious motivation operated within social conventions which were at odds with its primary inspiration, without many of its members being fully conscious of the tension. The same thing has happened often enough within the history of Christianity for it to be unremarkable in this case.

The traditional Greco-Roman dinner party often took place in two phases. A "first table," during which several courses were served, would be followed by a break. This would be followed in turn by a "symposium" (drinking party) at a "second table," often with newly arrived guests, at which some food and desserts were served. Possibly, then, the problems in the Corinthian church were caused by the richer Christians maintaining the practice of the first table and treating the Lord's Supper as the second table alone.[51] This makes some sense of the evidence in 1 Corinthians. Not least it would explain how the shared bread could come at the beginning of a single meal when people were arriving at different times after it had started.[52] The flaw in this case is that Paul seems to envisage only one common meal (the Lord's Supper). The practice he rebukes is not that of a meal separate from (preceding) the Lord's Supper, but the abuse of a single meal ("the Lord's dinner") which began with the one bread and ended with the cup "after dinner" (11.25).[53] If indeed members were arriving late for the meal,[54] it would add to the offence

---

49. Klauck, *1 Korintherbrief* 81 (for further discussion see his earlier *Herrenmahl* 291-97). D. W. J. Gill, "In Search of the Social Elite in the Corinthian Church," *TynB* 44 (1993) 323-37, notes that famine may have been a factor, since 51 CE had been a famine year (here 333).

50. Murphy-O'Connor, *Corinth* 168-69; diagrams of substantial houses on 162 and 165.

51. So particularly Klauck, "Presence" 65-66; Lampe, "Eucharist" 37-40; but see below n. 84.

52. The main consensus in German scholarship is that, although the words of tradition envisaged a single meal bracketed by the bread word and the cup word respectively, at Corinth the Lord's supper as a whole (the bread and the wine) had become separated from the meal and left till the end (e.g., Bornkamm, "Lord's Supper" 127-29, 137-38; Neuenzeit, *Herrenmahl* 70-71, 115-16; Jeremias, *Eucharistic Words* 121, 250-51; Conzelmann, *1 Corinthians* 199; Gnilka, *Theologie* 121). But in that case Paul would hardly have called the whole gathering "the Lord's supper" (11.20); see further below with nn. 84 and 87.

53. See further below (§22.6).

54. Hofius rightly insists that Paul envisaged only one meal, but pushes too hard the case that there was no rebuke of going on ahead before others arrived (11.21) and no instruction to delay the start till everyone had arrived (11.33; "Lord's Supper" 88-96;

that the late arrivals were either missing out on the breaking of the bread which opened the meal, or were having to eat it late, not as a shared act, or if, alternatively, the well-to-do who arrived early were beginning to eat before the formal beginning of the meal as a whole.[55]

Sociological analysis, therefore, suggests that what is in view in 1 Corinthians 10–11 was primarily social cohesiveness more than theological dispute. Three further features put the issue beyond reasonable dispute.

Paul introduces his exhortation by speaking of their "coming together not for the better but for the worse" (11.17). And his first ground of complaint is that their coming together in church simply reveals the "schisms" among them (11.18). This is the only time, apart from the thematic verse 1.10 and 12.25, that Paul uses this term in all his letters. It was evidently the divisiveness of the social tensions and factionalism which was his primary concern for the letter as a whole,[56] and it was evidently the Corinthians' coming together to eat the Lord's Supper at which this divisiveness was most clearly on display.

Second, in 11.19 he goes on to speak of "factions/sects *(haireseis)* among them." This is only one of two occasions on which Paul uses the word. In the other (Gal. 5.20) it is clearly a negative term (one of "the works of the flesh"),[57] though here Paul seems to acknowledge the inevitability of such factions among such a volatile group as the Corinthian church.[58]

Third, the subject is introduced in a way which suggests that the Corinthians themselves had not referred the matter to Paul (it was not part of their letter to him).[59] Rather, he had "heard" (11.18) about it independently — presumably from the group mentioned in 16.17 who had no doubt told Paul of their own concerns additional to those in the letter.[60] The implication

---

similarly Fee, *1 Corinthians* 540, 568-69; see also n. 87 below). Paul's language, however, does more naturally imply late arrivals (see above n. 47), and it would be surprising were it otherwise (see the preceding paragraph).

55. Theissen, "Social Integration" 153-55.

56. Mitchell, *Paul and the Rhetoric of Reconciliation,* rightly sees 1.10 as the "thesis statement" for the whole letter (1; see further 138-57). Notably 12.25 is also concerned about "schism in the body."

57. It is also used, of course, by Josephus and Acts for Jewish "sects/parties" (Josephus, particularly *War* 2.118; *Ant.* 13.171; Acts 5.17; 15.5; 24.5, 14; 26.5).

58. Was he making the best of a bad job in 11.19? Or possibly echoing a word of Jesus recalled elsewhere only in Justin, *Dialogue* 35.3 and *Didascalia* 6.5.2 (traced back to Jesus by J. Jeremias, *Unknown Sayings of Jesus* [London: SPCK, ²1964] 76-77)? The positive role of "divisions" (in contrast to their more obvious negative role) is equivalent to the positive role of "discipline" in contrast to "condemnation" (11.32).

59. Usually indicated by the introductory formula "Now concerning *(peri de)* . . ." (7.1; 8.1; 12.1; 16.1, 12).

60. He puts the other items which came to him apart from the letter (chs. 1–4, 5, 6) higher on his agenda.

is that the social elite in the Corinthian church were either unaware of the factionalism implicit in the typical Corinthian gathering for the Lord's Supper, or were undisturbed by it. Either way, it had not presented enough of a problem to be referred to Paul for advice.

A further point from the broader sociological perspective is also worth noting, in this case with reference to the preceding discussion (10.14-22). It is the converse of the preceding concern to note parallels with contemporary practice. For, as observed earlier,[61] the Christian house meal would have been different from the typical guest meals of the time, both private and particularly public. The lack of any reference to a cult centre, the absence of a priest, and the failure to pour a libation to some god would have set the Christian supper apart and marked it out from other apparently similar events. In other words, the Lord's Supper was a distinctive identity marker. At the same time, it presumably was not open to the public in the way that the worship service described in ch. 14 evidently was (14.22-25). Despite the lack of firm evidence, we should probably assume that the Lord's Supper was a meal shared by the baptized.[62] This fits with the implication of 10.21, that unlike the multiple loyalties possible for those willing to attend meals in honour of different gods, participation in the Lord's Supper carried with it an obligation to exclusive loyalty to the Lord. In other words, as an identity marker, the Lord's Supper functioned also as a boundary marker.[63]

A final point, to which social anthropology has drawn attention, is the concept of the holiness of the sacred. Such holiness is an almost tangible aura surrounding or attaching to the sacred object or place, which both defends those who legitimately participate in it, but which can destroy those who illegitimately breach it.[64] It is a feature of all religions, almost a defining point of religion, most obvious in "primitive" religions. Within the Jewish tradition the classic examples are the restrictions on the people to prevent them approaching or touching Mount Sinai (Exod. 19.10-25), the cautionary tales of Nadab and Abihu (Lev. 10.1-3) and of Achan (Joshua 7), and the unnerving account of Uzzah's fate when he tried to steady the ark of the covenant on its ascent to Jerusalem (2 Sam. 6.6-7). In early Christian tradition the equally unnerving story of Ananias and Sapphira in Acts 5.1-16 makes the same point,

61. See above §20.3.

62. Whether or not 1 Cor. 16.22 echoes a communion liturgy (e.g., Bornkamm, "Lord's Supper" 147-48), it is significant that *Didache* 10.6 does use the *maranatha* in that context and attaches to it an invitation to "come" (cf. Rev. 22.17; but see also C. F. D. Moule, "A Reconsideration of the Context of *Maranatha*," *Essays* 222-26).

63. Cf. Meeks, *First Urban Christians* 159-60.

64. A classic text is R. Otto, *The Idea of the Holy* (London/New York: Oxford University, 1923); see further W. G. Oxtoby, "Idea of the Holy," *The Encyclopedia of Religion* (New York: Macmillan, 1987) 6.431-38.

as is confirmed by Luke's references to the holy awe which surrounded the early Jerusalem community as a result (5.5, 11, 13). Here the point of contact is 11.30 — "for this reason many among you are weak and ill, and some have died." It is hard to escape the impression that at this point, as in Acts 5.1-11,[65] we are touching the realm of the holy.[66]

The light which all this sheds on 1 Corinthians 10–11 is unclear. Above all it is uncertain whether the light is shed on the views of the Corinthians or those of Paul. It certainly seems to be the case that (some of) the Corinthians regarded baptism as a quasi-mystical event which bonded them to their baptizers (1.12-16), and the implied effectiveness of baptism for the dead (15.29) presumably takes us into the same or a related circle of thought. To that extent at least we have to qualify any implication of the above discussion from a sociological perspective that the factionalism in Corinth was solely a matter of social incohesion. The way in which Paul elaborates his concern about their factional tendencies by immediately referring to baptism (1.11-16) indicates a more complex situation. So far as the Lord's Supper is concerned, a similar implication should probably be drawn from 10.1-12. Participation in baptism and the Lord's Supper was assumed by some to give them an assurance of divine favour and life beyond the grave.[67] To that extent we may say that (some of) the Corinthians were treating the Christian sacraments as though Christianity was a mystery cult promising immortality through its rituals.

The question for us, however, remains: What was Paul's theology of the Lord's Supper? Can we disentangle it from the above questions of influence and from views he was more criticizing than commending?

§22.5 Paul's theology of the Lord's Supper: spiritual food

To draw out Paul's theology at this point, the simplest procedure will be to look at the key passages in turn.

---

65. Possibly also 1 Cor. 5.1-5.

66. Neyrey suggests that the point behind 11.17-34 was that the selfish behavior of the Corinthians was polluting the eucharist and rendering it ineffective; it was losing its holiness (*Paul* 124). On the contrary, however, the point seems to be that the holy, when infringed, did not become ineffective; rather, its power for wholeness had become a power for destruction. Martin notes that "Paul plays with the topos linking disharmony and diseases" (*Corinthian Body* [§3 n. 1] 196). But his treatment (190-97) is in danger of reading too much into the passage: the background of "the holy" makes better sense of the passage than the idea of the *pharmakon* (both curative drug and poison); and it is unlikely that "discerning the body" included thought of "taking proper account of *one's own* bodily state" (196, my emphasis).

67. The implication of 10.5 and 12 in particular.

1 Cor. 10.3-4 — the Israelites in the wilderness "all ate the same spiritual food and all drank the same spiritual drink." As already noted, the passage provides clear enough evidence that (some of) the Corinthians were assuming that their participation in the Lord's Supper was sufficient to ensure them of salvation. Paul uses the analogy of the food and drink provided miraculously for the Israelites in the wilderness[68] to point up the Corinthians' mistake. If the Israelites had been so favoured, and yet were "struck down in the wilderness" (10.5) by reason of their lust, idolatry, sexual license, and complaining (10.6-10), the Corinthians ought to take due note (10.11-12).

Here we should note, first, that Paul uses general words for "food and drink" *(brōma, poma)*. He was thinking of the larger meal,[69] not specifically of the bread and cup *(artos, potērion)* of the Lord's Supper (10.16-17). Second, Paul's various rebukes of Corinthian views suggest that "spiritual" *(pneumatikos)* was a term of which they were particularly fond and which Paul introduced for this reason.[70] So *"spiritual* food/drink" was probably the Corinthians' way of putting it.

This suggests in turn that Paul uses this language, as with his talk of "spirituals" in 14.1, because it was nicely ambiguous. The term "spiritual" itself is unspecific.[71] The Corinthians may have meant it in the sense "conveying the Spirit."[72] But in 2.12–3.4 Paul rebukes a similar misunderstanding by insisting that the mark of the "spiritual" person is discernment and the opposite of factionalism. The echo of the wilderness miracles suggests thought of "given from or belonging to the realm of the Spirit," though nothing of what Paul says here or elsewhere implies that he thought of an invocation of the Spirit ("epiclesis") in connection with the Lord's Supper.[73] Alternatively,

---

68. Exod. 16.4-30, 35; 17.1-7; Num. 20.2-13.

69. As in his other uses of *brōma* (Rom. 14.15, 20; 1 Cor. 6.13; 8.8, 13). It also lent itself to metaphorical usage (as in 1 Cor. 3.2).

70. The implication particularly of 1 Cor. 2.13–3.1; 12.1 ("Now concerning the spirituals [about which you asked]"); and 14.37. See also above §20 n. 127.

71. See also Wedderburn's discussion (*Baptism* 241-48).

72. Käsemann, "Pauline Doctrine" 113-14, assumes that this must have been the meaning for Paul too (note also 134). Conzelmann, *1 Corinthians* 166 n. 23, prefers "containing the Spirit"; cf. Stuhlmacher, *Theologie* 365 — "the *Kyrios* imparts himself and fills his table guests with his effective power and presence in the form of the *pneuma*." If that was the point, however, did Paul think that the manna and water in the wilderness had conveyed the Spirit, and why did he not make some reference to offending or losing the Spirit thus given in the following warning (10.5-13)?

73. Hofius relates the *anamnēsis* (see below n. 101) particularly to the prayers of consecration, which he suggests could have contained an entreaty for the descent of the Spirit on the eucharistic bread and cup ("Lord's Supper" 109-11). Stuhlmacher, however, notes that the consecratory character of the eucharistic prayer is first attested in Justin, *Apology* 1.65.5 and 66.2 (*Theologie* 366).

or in addition, since the events in the wilderness are presented by Paul as "types" and "typical" (10.6, 11), "spiritual" could have the sense simply of "typological," stories expressing spiritual significance for later generations. Or again, if his subsequent equation of "spiritual" with "charism" applies here too,[74] then we would have an early expression of sacramental theology — the food and drink as the effect of grace ("means of grace"?), just like the charism of word or deed.[75]

The language used by Paul, and affirmed by Paul's own use as appropriate, therefore, is highly evocative on several fronts. But to place a precise theological significance on it is difficult, and to insist on doing so might well run counter to Paul's own intentions in using it in the first place.

§22.6 Paul's theology of the Lord's Supper: sharing in the one body

The most striking and challenging feature of Paul's theology of the Lord's Supper is undoubtedly his further understanding of the church as also the body of Christ. In particular, Paul's language here has provided the basis for all subsequent theological reflection on the correlation between sacrament and church, between the one body which is the bread and the one body which is the church. It is all the more important, then, that we pay close attention to the language which Paul used.

> *10.16-17* — "The cup of blessing which we bless, is it not a sharing in the blood of Christ? The bread which we break, is it not a sharing in the body of Christ? Because the bread is one, we though many are one body, for we all partake of the one bread";
> *11.24* — "This is my body for you";
> *11.27* — "Whoever eats the bread or drinks the cup of the Lord unworthily is *enochos,* answerable for/guilty of the body and the blood of the Lord";
> *11.29* — "for the one who eats and drinks without discerning the body eats and drinks condemnation to himself."

It is at once evident that in these passages Paul is not merely echoing or parodying the views of others in the Corinthian church. This seems to be Paul's own theology and teaching, drawing on the tradition of the last supper in particular (11.23-26). If we simply took these texts as just cited, an attractive inference would be that Paul attributed a unifying power to the bread and the

74. 12.1-4, 31; 14.1. See again §20 n. 127 above.
75. See above §20.5.

cup, and that it was disregard for the sanctity of the bread and cup which was putting the Corinthians in deadly peril. That, however, would be a lopsided reading of the texts. They need to be read more thoroughly in context. When we do so the emphasis shifts slightly but significantly. What then becomes apparent is that Paul's concern centred on the bread and the cup as the primary expressions of the unity of the congregation and as means to that unity when properly celebrated.

This comes to the fore in the first key passage (10.14-22) in the sequence of words which speak of "sharing," "partners," "partake of."[76] The concentration of these words is exceptional in Paul's letters.[77] He was evidently making a particular point here. His emphasis was not just on the one bread and the one cup, but on the sharing of the one bread and the one cup: "The cup of blessing which we bless, is it not a *sharing* in the blood of Christ? The bread which we break, is it not a *sharing* in the body of Christ?"[78] There is no hint, for example, that Paul envisaged the bread and cup being taken to absent members of the congregation, as though it was simply the bread and cup as such which made the congregation one. It was the fact that they partook of the one bread and the one cup together which made "the many" "one body," which marked and constituted their oneness as Christ's body. The reason is twofold: "*Because* there is *one bread,* we though many are *one body, for* we *all partake* of the *one bread*" (10.16-17).

The same logic underlies the continuation of the exhortation. The logic is that eating from a common sacrificial source made those who ate partners in the altar (10.18).[79] So too it was the thought of being partner with demons through drinking their cup, of partaking in other tables, which was so abhorrent

---

76. *Koinōnia* ("participation/sharing in" — see above §20.6) — 10.16 (twice); *koinōnos* ("partner, one who takes part in with someone else") — 10.18, 20; *metechō* ("share/partake in") — 10.17, 21, 30.

77. *Koinōnia* — 10 times elsewhere in Paul; *koinōnos* — 3 times elsewhere; *metechō* — 2 times elsewhere, none together as here.

78. See particularly J. Hainz, *koinōnia, EDNT* 2.304-5: " 'partnership' in the body of Christ effected at the Lord's Supper through 'participation in' the body of the exalted Christ, the Church, i.e., the partnership with the other partakers in the meal"; Merklein, *Studien* 334-35; cf. Ridderbos, *Paul* 424; Goppelt, *Theology* 2.149; Hahn, "Herrengedächtnis" 311; Marshall, *Last Supper* 120-22; Willis, *Idol Meat* 170; Mitchell, *Paul and the Rhetoric of Reconciliation* 142.

79. The phrase *koinōnoi tou thysiastēriou* (10.18) is somewhat obscure. But Paul presumably had the same thought in mind as in 9.13: "those who serve at the altar share together *(symmerizontai)* in the altar," that is, in what is sacrificed on the altar. Since *merizomai* itself means "share something with someone" (BAGD), the characteristic Pauline prefix, *syn* (see above §15.3), presumably strengthens the thought of an eating "together with" others. See further the data provided by Conzelmann, *1 Corinthians* 173 n. 31.

to Paul (10.20-21). The bond (horizontal as well as vertical) formed by the shared eating and drinking was not replicable in that way. In short, the thought connection in 10.16-17 was not just one bread → one body. There was a third or connecting element: one bread → shared → one body.

This ties in to an equivalent emphasis in the second passage (11.17-34) on their "coming together" *(synerchomai),* as well as the prominent warning against schisms and factions.[80] Paul repeats the word *(synerchomai)* at the beginning and end of the section presumably for emphasis: "you come together not for the better but for the worse" (10.17); "first, in coming together in/as church" (11.18); "when you come together . . . to eat the Lord's Supper" (11.20); "So then, my brothers, when you come together to eat" (11.33); "if you are hungry, eat at home, lest you come together for condemnation" (11.34). Evidently, then, the coming together constituted them "church." However, it was not simply a coming together, nor simply a coming to eat, but *a coming together to eat* which Paul had in mind. That was why he was so appalled at the individualism and cliqueishness of the Corinthians' practice (11.21, 33): their eating was not together; they were not really sharing their food. Their practice showed that in reality they were *not* coming together to eat the Lord's Supper (11.20). For a Lord's Supper which was not a shared supper, which was not a sharing in the one loaf and in the one cup, was not in fact the Lord's Supper.[81]

In the light of these consistent emphases, the old dispute about the meaning of the last two body references (11.27, 29) becomes clearer.[82] For almost certainly we should not allow ourselves to be caught once again into either-or exegesis. To require the commentator to make a choice between "body" referring to the bread (11.24), and "body" referring to the congregation (10.17), would assuredly run counter to Paul's whole line of exhortation.[83] We should neither ignore the obvious implication that a too casual eating and drinking could have serious spiritual and physical effects on the one who ate in unworthy manner (11.27-30), nor attribute the negative effect of the unworthy eating and drinking simply to the bread and cup as such. It is the eating and drinking as a communal act which is in view throughout. And the thrust of Paul's rebuke is clearly directed against those who ate and drank

---

80. See above §22.4.

81. In Galatians the same point emerges from a correlation of 3.28 with 2.11-16.

82. See, e.g., Neuenzeit, *Herrenmahl* 203-6; Marshall, *Last Supper* 114 and 172 n. 11.

83. Apart from anything else, a focus exclusively on *what* was eaten and drunk (rather on the communal eating and drinking) would leave the thought expressed in "discerning the body" (11.29) related only to the bread. Contrast Barrett, *1 Corinthians* 274-75, who finds difficulty with talk of "discerning the body" at this point; and Hahn, "Herrengedächtnis" 309-10.

without consideration for other members. So far as Paul was concerned, then, it would run counter to his whole point if we attempted to apportion either such positive effects (10.16-17) or such negative effects (11.27-30) to one or other aspect. Here again it is the sharing in the one bread and in the one cup which constitutes, embodies, expresses, builds up the one body.

In all this we need to recall that what Paul had in view was a whole meal, a "supper" (*deipnon*, "dinner," the main meal, eaten in the evening). There may be suggestions elsewhere that the bread and the wine had become a separate ceremony.[84] But Paul at least is clear that the bread and the cup framed the meal. The breaking of the bread would presumably begin the meal, in accordance with traditional Jewish custom.[85] Only of the cup does Paul say "after supper" (11.25).[86] In other words, a whole meal had come between.[87] Once again, then, it is the integration of bread and cup within the shared meal which Paul had in view. *The bread and the cup brought to focus the significance of the meal as a whole.*[88] This was why the selfish behavior of various individuals at the whole meal made them "answerable for *(enochos)* the body and the blood of the Lord" (11.27).

In attempting to clarify Paul's theology of the body of Christ and the one body we should not forget that Paul picks up the theme again in ch. 12. As we have already seen, his metaphor of the charismatic body of Christ (12.12-27) continues further into chs. 13 and 14. This at once poses one of the continuing puzzles in 1 Corinthians: how Paul envisaged the relation between ch. 11 and chs. 12–14; that is, how he envisaged the relation between "coming together to eat the Lord's Supper" and "coming together" for worship (14.23, 26).[89] The

---

84. Klauck follows the broad consensus opinion (above n. 52): he assumes that the implication of the Mark/Matthew form of the words (that the bread and wine came together) applies also to Paul's form of the Lord's supper; and he correlates this with the suggestion that the Lord's supper formed a second part of the meal ("Presence" 65-66; see also above §22.4 and n. 51). But he ignores the text: the implication of *deipnon* (the Lord's *dinner/main meal*); that Paul specifies the purpose of the "coming together" ("to eat the Lord's supper" — 11.20, 33); and that only of the cup does Paul say "after supper." Note the similar issues in relating the meal to the eucharist in *Didache* 9–10.

85. "Breaking the bread" is also a Lukan term for a meal (Acts 2.42, 46; 27.35; probably also 20.7, 11; cf. *Didache* 14.1).

86. "The cup of blessing" was probably already a technical term for the cup of wine drunk at the end of a meal (see, e.g., L. Goppelt, *potērion, TDNT* 6.154-55; Jeremias, *Eucharistic Words* 109-10).

87. Hofius, "Lord's Supper" 80-88, where he shows that "after supper" cannot be taken adjectively to designate one of the cups ("the cup after supper") but must be intended adverbially ("likewise [he] also [took] the cup [that is] after supper, saying").

88. Cf. Marxsen, *Lord's Supper* 5-6, 16-17; Schweizer, *Lord's Supper* 12-14.

89. Here in chs. 11 and 14 are the only occasions on which Paul uses the term "come together."

fact that he seems to specify different purposes for the "coming together" probably means that he envisaged two different comings together. One would be a gathering primarily for communal worship, a service of the word.[90] On these occasions it would appear that the outer door was left open for interested passersby to come in (14.24). The other coming together was specifically for the shared meal, the Lord's Supper, which presumably was of a more private nature, to which people came or were brought only by invitation.[91] The alternative suggestion that the two were two parts of the same gathering[92] runs aground on the absence of any clear hint from either chapter that the activities referred to in the other chapter were also in view.

It therefore remains an unresolved puzzle how Paul integrated his two portrayals of the one body of Christ. At least we can say that Paul envisaged the congregation functioning as the body of Christ whether the Lord's Supper was eaten or not. Its body-of-Christ-ness did not depend on the shared bread and cup to that extent. Where the Spirit brought charisms to functioning expression, there the congregation functioned as the body of Christ. But any suggestion of a tension or dichotomy between the two can be dismissed out of hand. Tensions there were aplenty in Paul's dealings with the church in Corinth, but none which threatened to pull apart these two aspects of the one ecclesiology. It would be farcical, for example, not to say misguided and dangerous, to set over against each other a sacramental concept and practice of the body and a charismatic concept and practice of the body, as though they were independent of each other and could somehow thrive quite separately from each other. More than in the charisma/office debate, we have to insist that charismatic body and Lord's Supper body were for Paul two sides of the one reality — the coming together to share in the one bread and the one cup, as fundamental as the body of Christ functioning as charismatic community.

A final thought relates back again to the meals (Lord's Supper?) at Antioch in reference to which Peter "separated" himself from the Gentile believers. If indeed the Lord's Supper was involved, as it must have been on at least some occasions,[93] then Peter's action was a clear expression of un-

90. See further my "Responsible Congregation" (§21 n. 1) 205-16 and those cited there, 214 n. 58. The interest throughout ch. 14 is exclusively on charisms of speaking, prophecy, and tongues and their accompanying charisms of discernment and interpretation.

91. The eucharist as a meal only for the baptized is attested as early as *Didache* 9.5 and Justin, *Apology* 1.66.1.

92. Klauck, "Presence" 66; cf. and contrast his earlier *Herrenmahl* 346-49.

93. We note again that the tradition cited by Paul (learned at Antioch?) celebrated the Lord's supper as a meal beginning with the bread and ending with the cup (1 Cor. 11.23-25).

willingness to share in the body and blood of Christ with other Christians. Paul's indignation at Peter's action focused on the issue of justification and works (Gal. 2.14-16).[94] But the principle he stood for applies equally to the sharing of the Lord's Supper: all that is needed for acceptance by God, and so also by one another, is faith in Christ alone; to require anything beyond that for a sharing in the body and blood of Christ, however hallowed the tradition cited in support, is to abandon "the truth of the gospel." Here is another case where the corollaries for contemporary ecumenical sharing have not been given sufficient consideration.[95]

§22.7 Paul's theology of the Lord's Supper: christology

The christology which is enshrined in the Lord's Supper also deserves separate mention.

In 10.4 Paul identifies Christ typologically or spiritually with the rock from which drinking water was given to Israel in the wilderness. Paul does not hesitate to use the traditional episode to present Christ as the source (the "spiritual rock") of "the spiritual drink." But he makes no attempt to identify Christ as the source of the "spiritual food." Nor does he identify Christ as the "spiritual food" itself (contrast 10.16). He was evidently content to use link points given him by his traditions,[96] rather than trying to force a point upon them. Presumably "spiritual" has the same sort of ambiguity as in the preceding references (10.3-4).

We need simply mention again that Paul identifies the blessed cup and the broken bread as a sharing in the blood of Christ and in the body of Christ (10.16-17). And we should not forget that all the body talk in §22.6 has in mind the body *of Christ*. The point of the Lord's Supper is to feed and sustain the relation with Christ, precisely as a communal/corporate relationship. Any move in eucharistic practice to isolated celebration (as though the Lord's Supper were intended simply to feed the individual with spiritual food) or which detracts from it as a shared experience runs counter to Paul's emphasis and detracts from his christology of the *body* of Christ.

The table of the shared meal is "the table of the Lord" (10.21): he is the host at the meal, as Sarapis was thought to be host at meals in his name,[97] or as Philo thought that Yahweh was host of the meals of sacrificial

94. See above §14.5a.
95. See further my "Should Paul Once Again Oppose Peter to His Face?" *HeyJ* 34 (1993) 425-28.
96. See above §22.5; also §11.3b.
97. Cf. Klauck, "Presence" 69-70.

meat.[98] We recall that it was the exclusiveness of the loyalty which the Lord was seen to require (10.21-22) which marked out "the church of God" (10.32) so sharply from other cults.[99] Paul does not hesitate to echo the Israel of old's sense of special set-apartness: the congregation of Christ must be as careful to avoid provoking God to jealousy by its idolatry as ever was the church of God in times past (10.22).[100]

11.23-25 in particular underlines the direct continuity between Jesus' hosting the last supper and the shared meals which were such an important feature of the early churches.[101] Despite the long history of dispute about the character of Christ's presence in the celebration of the Lord's Supper,[102] exegetically the meaning of "This is my body" (11.24) is as open and as ambiguous as the earlier talk of "spiritual" food (10.3).

The same passage equally underlines the importance of founding traditions about Jesus passed down to and through the new churches. The traditions of Jesus and from Jesus form a vital component in the celebration of the here-and-now relationship with Christ. Even if word gatherings and meal gatherings were separate,[103] it is clear enough that the element of word/tradition, with the shared bread and the wine, together constituted the sacrament from the beginning.

The Pauline additions to the traditional wording constitute the Lord's Supper as an occasion which forms a high point in time, from which the congregation can look both backward and forward, back to its crucial foun-

98. Philo, *Spec. Leg.* 1.221, is frequently quoted:

The sacrificial meals should not be hoarded, but be free and open to all who have need, for they are now the property not of him by whom but of him to whom the victim has been sacrificed, he the benefactor, the bountiful, who has made the convivial company of those who carry out the sacrifices partners of the altar whose board they share. He bids them not think of themselves as the entertainers, for they are the stewards of the good cheer, not the hosts. The host is he to whom the material provided for the feast has come to belong. . . .

99. See further above §22.2.

100. There is evidently a deliberate echo of the song of Moses both in 10.20 (Deut. 32.17) and 10.22 (Deut. 32.21, a verse which Paul put to key use in Rom. 10.19 and 11.11, 14).

101. Hofius, "Lord's Supper" 97-103, emphasizes the constitutive power of the words of blessing/consecration, but misses Paul's primary emphasis on the sharing of the cup and bread and on the corporate character of the meal.

102. Contrast, e.g., the strong statements by P. Benoit and M. É. Boismard in Delorme et al., *Eucharist* 83-101, 126-37 ("this bread which is precisely the real physical body of Christ" — 130), with those of Strecker, *Theologie* 183-84; and see further Reumann, *Supper* (index "presence," "real presence").

103. See above §22.6.

dation event and forward to its anticipated consummation. The precise meaning of the twice repeated "in remembrance of me" (11.24, 25) continues to occasion debate.[104] But it certainly cannot be reduced merely to an invitation to a pious remembering on the part of those who eat the bread and drink the cup.[105] The point seems rather to constitute the shared eating and drinking of what Jesus himself consecrated as symbols of his death as itself the act of remembrance, "the praise-filled 'representation' of that which happened . . . *once and for all.*"[106] The second addition — "for as often as you eat this bread and drink the cup, you proclaim the death of the Lord until he comes" — points just as firmly forward. Paul in effect here, then, makes the Lord's Supper the cord which binds the already–not yet tension together and keeps it from falling apart. Or, alternatively expressed, the Lord's Supper is presented here as a kind of bridge by which believers (again not so much individually, but precisely as the body of Christ) cross through the sometimes raging torrents of the eschatological tension.

Not least of importance is the fact that the Lord's Supper does this both by re(-)presenting the death of Christ and by proclaiming that death in and through the shared celebration. And what it enshrines not least is the "for you" character of that death, the "new covenant" graciously given. It is, above all, this "for you" character of that which lay at the heart of their shared meal which should have prevented the selfish abuse that so marred the Corinthians' coming together to eat. How could their common eating and drinking function as a remembrance of that self-giving in death unless it was an eating and drinking which showed concern for one another? "The table of the Lord" could not be a private affair, where each might do as he or she pleases. The Lord's Supper was not the *Lord's* Supper unless it bound the sharing community together in mutual responsibility for one another.[107]

The alternative, which Paul does not hesitate to formulate, is his oft-repeated warning that grace willfully refused brings judgment in its train (11.27-32). Such a blatant disregard for and denial of the "for you" of Christ's

---

104. Begun by Jeremias, *Eucharistic Words* 237-55; see especially the review of the debate in Reumann, *Supper* 27-34.

105. This weakens any parallel with the *religionsgeschichtlich* analogy of meals celebrated in memory of the dead (*pace* Lietzmann, *Korinther* 57-58); see above §22.2.

106. Hofius, "Lord's Supper" 103-9 (here 109). He also observes that there is no particular link with the Passover (as the 5 occurrences of *anamnēsis* in LXX confirm — Lev. 24.7; Num. 10.10; Pss. 38 and 70 [titles]; Wis. 16.6). Bornkamm observed earlier that, 1 Cor. 5.7 notwithstanding, Paul makes no effort to link the Lord's supper with the Passover ("Lord's Supper" 133). We could also note that "the spiritual food and drink" of 1 Cor. 10.3-4 refers to the manna and the water in the wilderness, not to the constituent elements of the Passover meal.

107. Hofius, "Lord's Supper" 113-14; Lampe, "Eucharist" 45.

death can only be maintained by a deliberate closing of eye and ear to the "for you" responsibility of the well-to-do members of the congregation for the others. Thus to abuse the Lord's Supper is to invite the Lord's judgment.[108] Here, as in all such matters, discernment is required. It is only by recognizing such differences *(diakrinō)*[109] between the Lord's Supper as it should not be celebrated and the Lord's Supper as it should be celebrated, that they could avoid being condemned *(katakrinō)*. To accept such a rebuke would transform the judgment of the Lord from condemnation to disciplining (7.32). In all this, the Lord, whose death was re(-)presented in their common participation in the bread and the cup, was also the Lord over the meal ("the *Lord's* table," "the *Lord's* Supper"). Woe betide those who forgot the latter in abusing the former.

By thus linking the Lord's Supper with judgment as well as spiritual food, with Christ's coming again as well as his death, Paul underlines the extent to which celebration of the Lord's Supper does indeed "proclaim" the whole gospel and provide instruction as well as sustenance during the long slog from the already to the not yet.

---

108. See also C. F. D. Moule, "The Judgment Theme in the Sacraments," in W. D. Davies and D. Daube, eds., *The Background of the New Testament and Its Eschatology,* C. H. Dodd FS (Cambridge: Cambridge University, 1954) 464-81.

    109. Cf. particularly 1 Cor. 6.5 and 14.29; also 12.10 *(diakrisis)*. See also above §§21.5-6.

CHAPTER 8

How Should Believers Live?

§23 Motivating principles[1]

1. **Bibliography**: **J. Barclay**, *Obeying the Truth: A Study of Paul's Ethics in Galatians* (Edinburgh: Clark, 1988); **Barrett**, *Paul* 134-41; **Becker**, *Paul* 430-40; **Beker**, *Paul* 272-94; **E. Best**, *Paul and His Converts* (Edinburgh: Clark, 1988); **Berger**, *Theologiegeschichte* 498-507; **Betz**, "Das Problem der Grundlagen der paulinischen Ethik (Röm. 12.1-2)," *Paulinische Studien* 184-205; **W. P. de Boer**, *The Imitation of Paul: An Exegetical Study* (Kampen: Kok, 1962); **Bornkamm**, *Paul* 196-219; **Bultmann**, *Theology* I, 330-45; **Conzelmann**, *Outline* 275-86; **H. Cruz**, *Christological Motives and Motivated Actions in Pauline Paraenesis* (Frankfurt: Lang, 1990); **Cullmann**, *Christ and Time* (§18 n. 1); **Davies**, *Paul* 111-46; **T. J. Deidun**, *New Covenant Morality in Paul* (AnBib 89; Rome: Biblical Institute, 1981); **M. S. Enslin**, *The Ethics of Paul* (Nashville: Abingdon, 1957); **K. Finsterbusch**, *Die Thora als Lebensweisung für Heidenchristen. Studien zur Bedeutung der Thora für die paulinische Ethik* (Göttingen: Vandenhoeck, 1996); **Fitzmyer**, *Paul* 97-107; **V. P. Furnish**, *Theology and Ethics in Paul* (Nashville: Abingdon, 1968); *The Love Command in the New Testament* (Nashville: Abingdon, 1972 = London: SCM, 1973); **D. B. Garlington**, *Faith, Obedience and Perseverance: Aspects of Paul's Letter to the Romans* (WUNT 79; Tübingen: Mohr, 1994); **B. Gerhardsson**, *The Ethos of the Bible* (Philadelphia: Fortress, 1981) 63-92; **G. Haufe**, "Das Geistmotiv in der paulinischen Ethik," *ZNW* 85 (1994) 183-91; **R. B. Hays**, *The Moral Vision of the New Testament: A Contemporary Introduction to New Testament Ethics* (San Francisco: HarperCollins, 1996); **F. W. Horn**, "Wandel im Geist. Zur pneumatologischen Begründung der Ethik bei Paulus," *KuD* 38 (1992) 149-70; **J. L. Houlden**, *Ethics and the New Testament* (Harmondsworth: Penguin, 1973); **Hübner**, *Law* (§6 n. 1); **J. L. Jaquette**, *Discerning What Counts: The Function of the* Adiaphora Topos *in Paul's Letters* (SBLDS 146; Atlanta: Scholars, 1995); **Keck**, *Paul* 88-98; also "Rethinking 'New Testament Ethics,' " *JBL* 115 (1996) 3-16; **E. Lohse**, *Theological Ethics of the New Testament* (Minneapolis: Fortress, 1991); **R. N. Longenecker**, *Paul: Apostle of Liberty* (New York: Harper and Row, 1964); **L. De Lorenzi**, ed., *Dimensions de la vie chrétienne (Rom. 12–13)* (Rome: Abbaye de S. Paul, 1979); **E. H. Lovering and J. L. Sumney**, eds., *Theology and Ethics in Paul and His Interpreters*, V. P. Furnish FS (Nashville: Abingdon, 1996); **A. J. Malherbe**, *Moral Exhortation: A Greco-Roman Sourcebook* (Philadelphia: Westminster, 1986); **W. Marxsen**, *New Testament Foundations for Christian Ethics* (Minneapolis: Fortress, 1993); **W. A.**

§23.1 Indicative and imperative

A major feature of Paul's theology is his vigorous ethical concern. As a pastor as well as theologian, Paul was inevitably concerned with the outworking of his gospel — not only in terms of the beginning and process of salvation (§§13–19) and of communal worship and ministry (§§20–22) but also in terms of how believers should live. His letters bear witness to the depth of this concern. It has been traditional to divide his letters into two parts — the theological exposition followed by the practical application. And it is true that several of them reflect this sort of structure: "since it is the case that . . . , therefore. . . ." We need only think of the transition from chs. 11 to 12 in Romans, from chs. 4 to 5 in Galatians, or from chs. 2 to 3 in Colossians.

In fact, however, the "theology followed by application" dichotomy is misleading. Paul never spoke other than as a pastor. His theology was a living theology, a practical theology through and through.[2] The application is inherent in the exposition itself, as we see, for example, implicitly in Romans

---

Meeks, *The Moral World of the First Christians* (Philadelphia: Westminster, 1986); *The Origins of Christian Morality: The First Two Centuries* (New Haven: Yale University, 1993); **O. Merk**, *Handeln aus Glauben: Die Motivierungen der paulinischen Ethik* (Marburg: Elwert, 1968); **Moule**, "Obligation in the Ethic of Paul," *Essays* 261-77; **P. von der Osten-Sacken**, *Die Heiligkeit der Torah. Studien zum Gesetz bei Paulus* (Munich: Kaiser, 1989); **R. F. O'Toole**, *Who Is a Christian? A Study in Pauline Ethics* (Collegeville: Liturgical/Glazier, 1990); **Penna**, "Dissolution and Restoration of the Relationship of Law and Wisdom in Paul" and "Problems of Pauline Morality: The Present State of the Question," *Paul* 2.135-62, 163-73; **Räisänen**, *Law* (§6 n. 1); **E. Reinmuth**, *Geist und Gesetz. Studien zu Voraussetzungen und Inhalt der paulinischen Paränese* (Berlin: Evangelische, 1985); **P. Richardson**, *Paul's Ethic of Freedom* (Philadelphia: Westminster, 1979); **Ridderbos**, *Paul* 253-326; **B. S. Rosner**, ed., *Understanding Paul's Ethics: Twentieth-Century Approaches* (Grand Rapids: Eerdmans/Carlisle: Paternoster, 1995); **J. P. Sampley**, *Walking between the Times: Paul's Moral Reasoning* (Minneapolis: Fortress, 1991); **J. T. Sanders**, *Ethics in the New Testament: Change and Development* (Philadelphia: Fortress/London: SCM, 1975); **Schnabel**, *Law and Wisdom* (§11 n. 1); **R. Schnackenburg**, *Die sittliche Botschaft des Neuen Testaments 2: Die urchristlichen Verkündiger* (Freiburg: Herder, 1988) 13-71; **W. Schrage**, *Die konkreten Einzelgebote in der paulinischen Paränese* (Gütersloh: Gütersloher, 1961); *The Ethics of the New Testament* (Philadelphia: Fortress/Edinburgh: Clark, 1988); **Schreiner**, *Law* (§6 n. 1); **S. Schulz**, *Neutestamentliche Ethik* (Zurich: Theologischer, 1987); **T. Söding**, *Das Liebesgebot bis Paulus. Die Mahnung zur Agape im Rahmen der paulinischen Ethik* (Münster: Aschendorff, 1991); **Strecker**, *Theologie* 49-54, 111-12, 206-15; **Stuhlmacher**, *Theologie* 371-91; **P. J. Tomson**, *Paul and the Jewish Law: Halakha in the Letters of the Apostle to the Gentiles* (CRINT 3.1; Assen: Van Gorcum/Minneapolis: Fortress, 1990); **C. M. Tuckett**, "Paul, Tradition and Freedom," *TZ* 47 (1991) 307-25; **Westerholm**, *Israel's Law* (§6 n. 1) 198-218; **Whiteley**, *Theology* 205-32; **M. Wolter**, "Ethos und Identität in paulinischen Gemeinden," *NTS* 43 (1997) 430-44; **Ziesler**, *Pauline Christianity* 116-26.

2. Similarly Furnish, *Theology* 110.

1–2 and 4 and explicitly in Romans 6 and 8. Even more theoretical-sounding expositions, like Romans 9–11 and 1 Corinthians 15, had immediate practical consequences, not least for himself in one case (Rom. 11.13) and for all believers in the other (1 Cor. 15.29-34). Indeed, we can hardly avoid noting that all Paul's letters were motivated by ethical concerns. And some were almost entirely taken up with the issue of how his converts should conduct themselves (1 Corinthians being the most obvious example).[3]

More characteristic, then, is the fact that Paul can sum up the double ("since . . . therefore") aspect of his theology epigrammatically. For example:

> Rom. 6.4a-b — "So then we were buried with him through baptism into death, in order that, as Christ was raised from the dead through the glory of the Father, so we should walk in newness of life."
> 1 Cor. 5.7a-b (in reverse order) — "Cleanse out the old leaven . . . as you [really] are unleavened."
> Gal. 5.1a-b — "For freedom Christ has set us free. Stand fast, therefore, and do not be subject again to a yoke of slavery."
> Gal. 5.13a-b — "For you were called to freedom, brothers; only not the freedom for opportunity to the flesh, but through love serve one another."
> Phil. 2.12-13 (in reverse order) — "So then, my beloved, . . . work out your own salvation with fear and trembling; for God is at work in you both to will and to work for his good pleasure."

These epigrams visually express the *Ineinander* ("in-each-otherness") of Paul's theology and ethics.

Paul, of course, is entirely typical of all religions which seek not so much (or simply) to escape from the world but (also) to provide resources for living in the world. But the basic components and features of his theology underscore the degree of his commitment to a theological ethic. We may think not least of his concept of "body," with its emphasis on the corporeal and corporate, the embodied person as encounterable, in community and saveable precisely as embodied[4] — in contrast to alternative ideas of salvation as the soul escaping from the material body as from a prison. The analysis of the human condition in terms of the perversion of desire in misdirected religion and self-indulgence (§§4–5) is immediately applicable as a critical warning to all human collaboration and contriving. And the metaphors of salvation, precisely as living metaphors, reflect the degree of Paul's rootedness in the real world (§13.4).

---

3. E.g., 2 Corinthians 8–9 (the collection); Philippians (mutual relations); 1 Thessalonians (interim ethics); Philemon (slavery).
4. See above §3.2 and §20.4 in particular.

Somewhat surprisingly, then, Paul's ethics have often been rather problematic for theologians. The last hundred years or so provide some instructive examples. Liberal Protestantism, in the wake of Emmanuel Kant, was deeply concerned with the question of moral living. Its reconstruction of the historical Jesus focused most characteristically on Jesus as the teacher of abiding moral values. The problem was that Paul, by contrast, was then depicted as the one who transformed the ethical teaching of Jesus into a religion of sacrifice and redemption, the very transformation which liberal Protestantism was trying to get beyond.[5] Between the wars an existentialist theology was equally, though in a different way, concerned with day-to-day living.[6] But the accompanying development of form criticism tended to promote the conclusion that Paul's paraenesis simply took over traditional material in conventional forms.[7]

Similarly, in the present phase of Pauline studies, we could note on the one hand that the sociological perspective on Paul has also been motivated in part at least by a concern to see how Paul's teaching worked out in practice, given all that we now know about the society of Paul's day and the way social groups function in relation to each other.[8] On the other hand, however, the accompanying growth of rhetorical analysis of Paul's letters ran into an immediate problem since, as Dieter Betz himself observed, "paraenesis plays only a marginal role in the ancient rhetorical handbooks, if not in rhetoric itself."[9] Not least, and especially since we are using Romans as our template, it is worth observing that only fairly recently has Romans been recognized to be a real letter, dealing with real issues among the Roman congregations, and more than an exercise in dogmatics.[10]

Despite such disincentives, there has been widespread agreement that Paul's ethics can be summed up under the rubric *indicative and imperative*. This is the major conclusion drawn by Victor Furnish in his survey of nineteenth- and twentieth-century attempts to interpret Paul's ethic, which then forms one of the

5. The classic formulation was "Fatherhood of God and brotherhood of man"; the classic statement was that of Harnack, *What Is Christianity?* (see above §8 n. 10).

6. Bultmann was, of course, the classic exponent; see, e.g., the critique in M. Parsons, "Being Precedes Act: Indicative and Imperative in Paul's Writing," in Rosner, ed., *Understanding* 217-47 (here 222-24).

7. The classic treatment was M. Dibelius, *From Tradition to Gospel* (London: Nicholson and Watson, 1934 = New York: Scribner, 1965), particularly 238.

8. See above §1 n. 31.

9. Betz, *Galatians* 254. See also above §1.2 and n. 36.

10. See, e.g., discussion in Donfried, *Romans Debate*, and A. J. M. Wedderburn, *Reasons*. Reflective of the older attitude are the commentaries of Nygren and Murray, with their relative lack of interest in Romans 12–16; and cf. now Stowers, *Rereading*. Rosner, *Understanding* 1-2, also notes the relative lack of interest in Pauline ethics, citing Hübner's "Paulusforschung seit 1945" and observing the contrast within an article of over 160 pages with only 6 devoted to ethics, as against 15 simply on "the righteousness of God."

controlling presuppositions of his own study: "the relation of indicative and imperative, the relation of 'theological' proclamation and 'moral' exhortation, is *the* crucial problem in interpreting the Pauline ethic."[11]

This certainly chimes in with the structuring of Paul's theology in the present volume, which has throughout endeavored to reflect Paul's own structuring of his theology. Thus the *indicative* has had two key moments. The first, the Christ event, that is, the life, but particularly the death and resurrection, of Christ (§§8–11). The second, the beginning of salvation, that is, all that we have analyzed in ch. 5. Both moments are nicely caught in Rom. 6.4a, cited above. Correspondingly, the *imperative* can now be seen as one of two matching emphases, the two sets of present continuous tenses which match the once-for-all aorists of the beginning. The first emphasizes the sustaining grace (righteousness) of God,[12] classically expressed in terms of sanctification, not to mention charism and sacrament.[13] The second emphasizes the correlated human responsibility, the imperative. Both elements of the ongoing process are nicely caught by Phil. 2.12-13, also cited above. Using the same language, Phil. 1.6 and Gal. 3.3 also neatly summarize the two (divine and human) sides of the process of salvation. Phil. 1.6: "he who began in you a good work will bring it to completion up to the day of Christ Jesus." Gal. 3.3: "Are you so foolish? Having begun with the Spirit are you now made complete with the flesh?"[14]

Directly relevant also is the eschatological tension, such an inescapable feature of the process of salvation, of which Paul was all too conscious (§18). For the already–not yet of life between the ages translates directly into the indicative and imperative of Paul's ethics.[15] As we observed earlier (§18.6(5)), it is precisely his appreciation of the continuing power of sin and death and the continuing weakness of the flesh which makes Paul's ethic so realistic in

---

11. Furnish, *Theology* 9, the survey on 242-79. The formula retains its popularity: see Ridderbos, *Paul* 253-58; Beker, *Paul* 275-78; Schrage, *Ethics* 167-72; Marxsen, *New Testament Foundations* 180-224; Schnackenburg, *Botschaft* 2.27-29; Parsons, "Being Precedes Act" (n. 6 above); Strecker, *Theologie* 206-8. Bultmann's essay, "The Problem of Ethics in Paul" (1924; ET now in Rosner, ed., *Understanding* 195-216), is widely regarded as decisive in establishing the theological logic of indicative-imperative in Paul (Schrage, *Ethics* 169; Rosner, ed., *Understanding* 18). See also Penna, *Paul* 2.163-73.

12. Furnish, with reference to Rom. 6.12ff.: "Righteousness is not in their power to 'do,' but righteousness is the power of God in whose service they stand" (*Theology* 196).

13. Cf. Schrage, *Ethics* 174-81.

14. See also above §18.1 and n. 2.

15. See again Sampley, *Walking* 7-24, 108-9; also "Reasoning from the Horizons of Paul's Thought World: A Comparison of Galatians and Philippians," in Lovering and Sumney, *Theology and Ethics* 114-31. The tension is well illustrated by the sequence of discussion in Romans 13 and 2 Cor. 4.16–5.10.

what may realistically be expected from human individuals or institutions (the church not excluded). In the overlap of the ages all action is bound to be flawed in greater or less degree. As there is no possibility of complete perfection in this life, so Paul's experience of his churches will have shown him that there is little realistic possibility of a policy or a decision which is universally approved by fellow Christians. Compromise (Paul would probably have preferred to say *principled* compromise) is an unavoidable feature of ethical decisions for those living between the ages. It will be one of the chief tasks in §24 to document how such compromise proved necessary, what it did not mean, and what it did involve in practice; or, alternatively expressed, how the realities of the "not yet" inevitably conditioned the ethical outworkings of the "already."

The point, widely agreed, then, is that the indicative is the necessary presupposition and starting point for the imperative. What Christ has done is the basis for what the believer must do. The beginning of salvation is the beginning of a new way of living. The "new creation" is what makes possible a walk "in newness of life."[16] Without the indicative the imperative would be an impossible ideal, a source of despair rather than of resolution and hope.[17] The imperative must be the outworking of the indicative. In Cullmann's words, "In primitive Christianity ethics without theology is absolutely inconceivable. All 'Ought' rests here upon an 'Is.' The imperative is firmly anchored in the indicative."[18] Here again[19] it is important to note that the eschatological motivation for Paul's ethics comes primarily from the already and not just the not yet.[20]

At the same time the imperative needs also to be stressed. To reduce Paul's paraenesis to an afterthought is to misunderstand Paul's theology. The imperative is the inevitable outworking of the indicative. Without the imperative the Christian ceases to be a responsible person within church and world. Without the imperative the body of Christ ceases to grow to the maturity of Christ. The most common way of expressing the imperative is in the ancient words of Pindar, "Become what you are."[21] The attempt thus to encapsulate

---

16. "New creation" — 2 Cor. 5.17; Gal. 6.15. "Newness of life" — Rom. 6.4; cf. 7.6.

17. This was why liberal moralism failed: if it is to provide a realistic model, "the ethic of Jesus" actually depends on "the gospel of Paul."

18. Cullmann, *Christ and Time* 224.

19. As in §18.1.

20. Rom. 13.11-14; 1 Cor. 7.29-31; and 1 Thes. 5.1-11 notwithstanding. Compare and contrast, e.g., Rom. 14.7-12; 1 Cor. 7.32-35; and Gal. 5.16-26. In speaking of the "eschatological basis" of Paul's ethics, Schrage defines eschatology too much in terms of future expectation (*Ethics* 181-86; cf. Schnackenburg, *Botschaft* 2.23-26). See also §18.1 above.

21. Pindar, *Pythian* 2.72; the full maxim is *genoi' hoios essi mathōn* — "become what you are having learned" (I owe the reference to my colleague Gordon Cockburn).

the indicative/imperative so concisely is praiseworthy. Whether it sufficiently expresses the eschatological tension is another question.[22] "Become what you are becoming" is probably a necessary if less elegant complementary formula, which catches the already–not yet of an exhortation like Rom. 6.11 more effectively. Or perhaps better still: "Work out what God has worked in you"[23] and continues to work in you.

At all events it will be most convenient to reflect the indicative/imperative emphasis in our own discussion. This is best done by correlating the principles on which Paul's paraenesis is based with the three aspects of the crucial transition analyzed in ch. 5 — justification by *faith,* participation in *Christ,* and the gift of the *Spirit.*[24] As the preliminary discussion has already indicated, Paul's ethics grow immediately out of his gospel and express a direct continuity with it. In §23, then, we will focus on the principles of Paul's ethics, leaving §24 for a study of how his ethical teaching worked out in practice.

§23.2 Once more, the law

There is, however, a major problem relating to Paul's ethics on which we have not yet touched. It is a problem which runs more deeply than the problem of relating indicative and imperative, a problem which has proved more troublesome and longer running than any other. It is, once again, the problem of the law, the law of Moses, the Torah. For the law obviously functioned in the religion of historic Israel in the equivalent role to Paul's paraenesis in his letters. In Israel's covenant theology, the law was Israel's part of the agreement, the directions for Israel's response to the electing grace of God. As Paul passed from indicative to imperative, so in effect does the Torah. Or as we might say, the Torah/Pentateuch was gospel before it was law. And yet Paul seems to set law and gospel in such sharp antithesis,[25] and subsequently the gospel/law antithesis came to epitomize so much that was fundamental in Reformation theology. So much so that there is a widespread impression that a continuing place for the law or the

---

22. Cf. Merk, *Handeln* 37; Schrage, *Ethics* 170.

23. Schnackenburg, *Botschaft* 2.29.

24. Cf. Hays's "three closely linked themes" which "frame Paul's ethical thought: new creation in collision with the present age, the cross as paradigm for action, and the community as the locus of God's saving power" (*Moral Vision* 19-36 [here 36]). These build into the "three focal images" by which Hays seeks to focus and guide ethical reflection in the light of the NT — "community, cross, and new creation" (196-98). Cf. also the criteria for discerning and evaluating charisms in church (above §21.6).

25. Cf. once again Rom. 3.28; 4.13-16; 10.4; Gal. 2.16, 21; 3.2, 10, 12-13; 5.4.

scriptures in Paul's ethics would have been inconceivable — particularly for Gentile converts.[26]

The new perspective on Paul, however, has raised afresh the question of whether Paul's critique of the law was not in fact more carefully targeted. And that is just what we have found in our two previous sorties into this arena.[27] Paul's critique of the law was primarily directed against its abuse by sin, and against his fellow kinsfolk's assumption that the law's protection continued to give them before God a distinctive and favoured position over the other nations, which they were responsible to maintain as such. If this is the case, and if the gospel/law contrast in Paul is not so sweeping, then once again the question of a continuing function of the law in directing Christian conduct is posed. Are the other functions of the law — defining sin and condemning transgression[28] — still in operation for believers? Alternatively posed, if "covenantal nomism" has such a Christian character, then does it not follow that Paul's ethics are themselves a kind of covenantal nomism?[29]

The debate can be nicely focused around three phrases used by Paul in Romans and Galatians — "the law of faith" (Rom. 3.27), "the law of the Spirit" (Rom. 8.2), and "the law of Christ" (Gal. 6.2).[30] The question, of course, is whether *nomos* can be properly translated "law" in all these passages and whether the positive affirmation expressed in each phrase can be credited to "the law." The fervour with which these questions are contested sheds quite an illumination on the correlation between the context in which questions are posed and the answers proffered, and on the theological presuppositions and sensitivities involved. For at this point a curious division among commentators becomes apparent. On the one hand, those who approach the issue from the standpoint of ethics have tended to find little difficulty in seeing a reference to "the law" in the "law of" phrases. But those who approach the issue from a study of Paul and the law have tended to find the idea that Paul spoke thus so positively of "the law" scarcely conceivable.

26. See the quotations from Harnack, Lindemann, and Hamerton-Kelly in Rosner, *Understanding* 5-7. Also, e.g., J. Knox, *The Ethic of Jesus in the Teaching of the Church* (London: Epworth, 1962) 97-102; Westerholm, *Israel's Law* 205-16; cf. Penna, *Paul* 2.129-30, 146, 157-62. Others in Finsterbusch, *Thora* 11 n. 3.

27. Above §§6.5, 7 and 14.4-6. Cf. particularly Finsterbusch, *Thora* chs. 3-5.

28. See above §6.3.

29. I echo Hooker's comment on Sanders's exposition of "covenantal nomism": "In many ways, the pattern which Sanders insists is the basis of Palestinian Judaism fits exactly the Pauline pattern of Christian experience: God's saving grace evokes man's answering obedience" (*Adam* 157).

30. In this and the following three sections I draw heavily on my " 'The Law of Faith,' 'the Law of the Spirit' and 'the Law of Christ,' " in Lovering and Sumney, *Theology and Ethics* 62-82;

To illustrate. On the one hand, we find Victor Furnish readily concluding that both "the law of the Spirit of life" and "the law of Christ" refer to "the sum and substance of the law of Moses."[31] Eduard Lohse likewise refers to the three "law of" phrases in terms of "the original significance of the Torah," enabling the law "once again [to] serve its original purpose of testifying to the 'holy, just and good will of God' (Rom. 7.12)."[32] Wolfgang Schrage's discussion is similarly brief and likewise takes it for granted that "the law of Christ" refers in some way to the Torah.[33] And Rudolph Schnackenburg follows the regular course of identifying "the law of Christ" with the love commandment as the "fulfilling of the law" (Rom. 13.10), though with some greater circumspection.[34]

In contrast, where the focus has been on the issue of Paul and the law, these same references have been seen as particularly problematic. Coming at them from the more characteristic antithesis between law and gospel (as it has been traditionally perceived), the tendency has been to assume either that a different law must be in view or that the term *nomos* should not be translated "law." Thus, for example, in the most recent round of discussion, Stephen Westerholm argues that for Paul the law of Moses has been replaced by the Spirit, not by another law, and deduces that the phrase "law of Christ" "is used loosely, by analogy with the Mosaic code, for the way of life fitting for a Christian."[35] And Frank Thielman argues that "the law of faith," "the law of the Spirit" is a different law from the law of Moses; it refers to Christ's atoning work — "the new covenant established by the sacrifice of Christ."[36] The most significant and influential alternative, however, has been posed in the work of Heikki Räisänen. He has argued that *nomos* in the two key Romans passages (3.27; 8.2) should be regarded as a wordplay and in the key phrases should be translated as "order of faith," "order of Spirit."[37] So too with Gal. 6.2, he thinks that *nomos* "is being used in a loose sense, almost metaphorically, much as it is used in Rom. 3:27 or 8:2. To fulfil the *nomos* of Christ is simply to live the way a life in Christ is to be lived. . . . (T)he 'law' of Christ is not literally a law."[38]

---

31. Furnish, *Theology* 235; see also 59-65, 191-94; similarly *Love Command* 100.

32. Lohse, *Theological Ethics* 161-62.

33. Schrage, *Ethics* 206-7: "the law of the Old Testament must first become the 'law of Christ' and be interpreted with respect to its true intention (Gal. 6:2); only then can it be the measure of Christian life."

34. Schnackenburg, *Botschaft* 2.43-44: the "law" of Rom. 8.2 is "law, not in the sense of the coercive law of Moses, which brings about sin and death, but in the sense of the conduct of life which is liberating, leading to the doing of God's will, and made possible through the Spirit."

35. Westerholm, *Israel's Law* 214 n. 38.

36. Thielman, *Paul* (§6 n. 1) 201-2, though note also the qualification on 210.

37. See above §6.2 n. 30.

38. Räisänen, *Law* 80-81; followed by Penna, *Paul* 2.141-42, 144-45.

Illuminating as this division of opinion is, it would be a mistake to concentrate the discussion of the possible continuing relevance of the Mosaic law for Paul's paraenesis solely on the three "law of" phrases. As we shall see, when we examine them for ourselves, they do indeed pose the larger issues rather effectively. But to focus attention on the "law of" phrases as such would be misleading and could skew the discussion too much, not least by making it overly dependent on contested exegesis. However, we have already suggested that the fundamental principles of Paul's ethic can be summed up in terms which directly reflect the emphases of his gospel — justification by *faith,* participation in *Christ,* and the gift of the *Spirit.*[39] It is unlikely to be a coincidence that the three "law of" phrases match these emphases so closely — "law of *faith,*" "law of *Spirit,*" and "law of *Christ.*" Consequently, although it will be important to summarize Paul's ethical principles simply as "faith," "Spirit," and "Christ," it will also be quite appropriate to include discussion of the corresponding "law of" phrase under each head. As we shall see, the value of the three matching "law of" phrases is that they indicate in a particularly striking way the fact that Paul saw these three emphases (faith, Spirit, Christ) as equally the key to the righteousness of ethics as to the righteousness offered in the gospel.

§23.3 Faith and "the law of faith"

Faith in the Pauline letters is usually thought of more or less exclusively as a soteriological concept, the means through which individual and church receive the saving grace of God. The dominance of the formula "justification by faith" in discussions of Paul's theology has helped reinforce that impression. As indeed Paul's own use of the term, so heavily concentrated as it is in his own discussions of justification.[40] In fact, however, faith is just as important in Paul as an ethical concept, as that out of which believers live. It could hardly be otherwise, since for Paul faith is the human response to all divine grace, the junction box, as it were, through which the transforming power of God flows into and through the life of individual and church. The point can be documented without difficulty.

It is a striking and insufficiently noted fact that Paul's first and last references to faith in Romans[41] carry precisely the connotation of a means to

---

39. §§14-16. Our ordering of the sequence differently reflects the amount of explicit teaching on the three principles. Cf. particularly Merk, *Handeln* 4-41.

40. See above §14.7 and n. 153.

41. Rom. 1.5; 14.22-23 (three times). Rom. 16.26 is part of a brief paragraph (16.25-27) generally reckoned to have been added to the letter at a later date (see my *Romans* 912-13 n. a).

responsible living. Paul introduces himself in Rom. 1.5 by describing the purpose of his apostleship as "for the obedience of faith." The term "obedience" *(hypakoē)* was a little-known word at Paul's time.[42] But its establishment in Christian terminology may be yet another case of a term which Paul in particular brought into active service through his theology.[43] Its derivation from the verb "hear" *(akouō)* means that it retains the richer meaning of the Hebrew *shamaʿ,* "hear (responsively)"[44] — "obedience" as responsive hearing. "The obedience of faith," then, characterizes faith as not merely receptive but also responsive. If the briefer form, *akoē pisteōs,* signifies "hearing with faith,"[45] the fuller form, *hypakoē pisteōs,* signifies the response which such hearing inevitably produces. By implication, that response is given not only in the immediate act of commitment, but in the obedience which follows.[46] Paul would not have cherished the image of believer as "slave"[47] if he had not also embraced its corollary: the slave obeys.[48]

The final threefold reference to faith in Romans (14.22-23) is particularly illuminating:

> [22]The faith which you have keep to yourself before God. Happy is the person who does not condemn himself by what he approves. [23]But the person who doubts is condemned if he eats, because it is not of faith *(ek pisteōs).* Everything which is not of faith *(ek pisteōs)* is sin.

This comes towards the conclusion of Paul's exhortation regarding divisive dietary practices. "The faith" in view is evidently, as usual in Paul, trust or reliance on God,[49] but here with particular reference to the individual's practice on this issue (whether one should eat only vegetables or is free to eat anything).[50] Paul thinks of faith as varying in strength from believer to believer

---

42. LSJ and MM, *hypakoē.*

43. Rom. 1.5; 5.19; 6.16 (twice); 15.18; 16.19, (26); 2 Cor. 7.15; 10.5-6; 2 Thes. 1.8; Phm. 21; elsewhere in the NT only in the more "Pauline" letters (Heb. 5.8; 1 Pet. 1.2, 14, 22).

44. BDB, *shamaʿ* 1.k-n.

45. Gal. 3.2, 5 (see above §14 n. 107). Cf. Rom. 10.16-17, where again "obedience" and "faith" are treated more or less as synonyms: "Not all have obeyed *(hypēkousan)* the gospel, for Isaiah says, 'Lord, who has believed *(episteusen)* our report *(akoē)?*' So then, faith *(pistis)* comes from hearing *(akoē).* . . ."

46. See further Furnish, *Theology* 182-87; Nanos, *Mystery* 222-37; and particularly Garlington, *Faith.*

47. Rom. 1.1; 1 Cor. 7.22; 2 Cor. 4.5; Gal. 1.10; Phil. 1.1.

48. Rom. 6.16-17; Col. 3.22; Eph. 6.5.

49. Note the almost technical phrase *ek pisteōs,* echoing its frequent use earlier (1.17; 3.26, 30; 4.16; 5.1; 9.30, 32; 10.6). This view runs counter to that of the majority (see, e.g., those cited in my *Romans* 827-29).

50. See further below §24.3.

— hence the "weak in faith" (14.1) and the "strong (in faith)" (15.1).[51] But the faith always has the same character. The point for us here is twofold. First, that it is this faith which determines the individual's conduct. Paul here emphasizes its personal and private character: one should not make a public display of the depth of one's trust in God (14.22a). Second, that this faith is the benchmark and monitor for conduct, not least on delicate or divisive issues. Conduct should be in accord with that faith. That is, it should grow out of that relationship of trust in God and should express that trust. To act in a way which contradicts that basic trust is, almost by definition, an act of self-condemnation (14.22b-23a).[52] Indeed, any conduct which does not emerge from and express that basic trust in God *(ek pisteōs)* is sin (14.23b).

This ties in immediately to Paul's earlier analysis of the human condition. For if we are right, Paul's diagnosis of the human malaise is based on an understanding that the Creator created human beings for a creaturely relationship with the Creator. At the root and heart of human sin and unrighteousness is the failure to acknowledge God as God (1.21) and to live out of that which God has provided.[53] But this is just another way of saying "faith." Adam failed because he did not believe God, did not trust God to be faithful to the Creator's responsibilities. And here again Abraham provides a contrasting model not just of saving faith but of creaturely faith: he believed in God "who gives life to the dead and calls things which have no existence into existence" (4.17).[54] What is in view once again is not just a once and for all act of believing, but an ongoing relationship which embraces the whole of living, where faith is the "port" through which the power of life flows.

This understanding of faith ties in also with what we found regarding justification in particular. For in §14 we noted that God's righteousness should not be thought of simply as a once-for-all act in regard to the believer, but also as God's sustaining and finally vindicating grace.[55] It is this recognition which enables us to integrate Paul's teaching on justification with the otherwise puzzling talk of being counted righteous at the final judgment in 2.12-16.

---

51. Similarly 12.3 — different measures of faith; see above §20 n. 137.

52. Paul is not making a general rule which would prevent individuals from acting when they entertained doubts on a certain issue; that would paralyze most actions. He has in view the danger of overbold action in delicate and divisive situations — here the particular case of the individual who is still convinced that observance of the food laws remains an integral part of his faith but who might be persuaded by others to act in defiance of that conviction (similarly 1 Cor. 8.10-12). "Doubt" *(diakrinomai),* only here and, significantly, in 4.20 in Paul, has the sense of "be at odds with oneself, hesitate, doubt" (BAGD 2b).

53. See further above §4.4.

54. See again my *Romans* 217-18.

55. See §§14.2 and 18.2.

For then the relationship of righteousness through faith can be seen more clearly to include the conduct which flows from faith ("the obedience of faith"); and judgment "according to works"[56] can be seen to correlate with justification through faith.

Moreover, it would not be inappropriate to observe that the concept of covenant righteousness in the scriptures had an integrally horizontal as well as vertical dimension. This is symbolized by the fact that the Ten Commandments included both tables — responsibility to others as well as to God.[57] And it is expressed both by the characteristic religious concern for the widow, the orphan, the stranger, and the poor[58] and by the repeated warnings of the prophets that religious and social obligation are inextricably linked.[59] Paul himself does not develop the point, but since his own concept of righteousness is so much determined by the scriptural concept, it is probably implicit in his fuller theology of righteousness through faith, as his reference to the collection as "the harvest of righteousness" (2 Cor. 9.10) indicates.[60]

If we broaden the scope for a moment to include Paul's other main treatment of justification by faith, two passages are worthy of particular note. In Gal. 2.20 Paul describes himself as "living by faith in the Son of God."[61] Since the context contrasts a lifestyle determined by works of the law (2.11-18; 3.2, 5),[62] Paul was certainly thinking of daily living. He lived his life in and by faith. The attached formula ("who loved me and gave himself for me") probably implies that Paul saw Jesus' life pattern as the pattern for his own living. To live by faith in the Son of God means to live out of the resources given by the Son of God and out of the motivation inspired by the Son of God's self-giving.[63]

At least some confirmation for such an inference is provided by Gal. 5.6 — "in Christ Jesus neither circumcision counts for anything, nor uncircumcision, but faith operating effectively[64] through love." Again the contrast is with a lifestyle characterized by circumcision and determined by the entire law (5.3). Faith contrasts with this by providing a different motivation and means for living — "faith operating effectively through love." Circumcision → entire law is answered by faith → love. We should beware of letting the two concepts stand

56. See above §§2.4, 6.3, and 18.6.

57. Exod. 20.2-17; Deut. 5.6-21.

58. E.g., Deut. 10.17-18; 24.10-22; Zech. 7.9-10.

59. E.g., Isa. 5.3-7; Ezek. 18.5-9; Amos 5.21-24; Mic. 3. See further my "Justice of God" (§14 n. 1).

60. See also below §24.8a.

61. See above §14.8.

62. See above §§14.4-5.

63. See further below §§24.5-6.

64. *Energoumenē*. We could translate "energizing" (cf. Gal. 2.8 and 3.5).

apart, as though faith were the beginning and love the outcome.[65] The phrase is more like a single concept — faith-through-love, love-energized-faith — as the close association of the two elsewhere in Paul also suggests.[66] This is not to imply (to use the terminology of later centuries) that Paul turned faith into a "work" or compromised the *sola fide*. On the contrary, it is a matter of recognizing how thoroughly the *sola fide* ran throughout Paul's theology — throughout his ethics as well. For it is precisely faith as complete reliance on and openness to God's grace which (inevitably) comes to expression in love. It is precisely this faith working through love which bridges the whole sweep of justification by faith, from the righteousness already received through faith (3.6-9) to the righteousness not yet experienced but eagerly awaited (5.5).

The reminder provided by Gal. 2.17-21 and 5.2-6 that Paul is generally remembered as one who set faith and law in antithesis raises the other major but teasing problem. Can we, should we, draw in the first of the "law of" phrases used by Paul at this point — "(the) law of faith" (Rom. 3.27)? In citing the passage again it is important to continue the quotation to the end of the chapter — 3.27-31:[67]

> [27]Where then is boasting? It has been excluded. By what kind of *nomos?* Of works? No, on the contrary, by the *nomos* of faith. [28]For we reckon that a person is justified by faith, apart from works of the *nomos*. [29]Or is he God of Jews only? Is he not also God of Gentiles? Yes, of Gentiles too, [30]since, after all, "God is one," who will justify circumcision from faith and uncircumcision through faith. [31]Do we then make the *nomos* invalid through faith? Not at all. On the contrary, we establish the *nomos*.

In the light of our previous discussion Paul's line of argument is clear.[68] By the "*nomos* of works" Paul must mean the Torah understood in terms of the works it required of Israel. The *nomos* of works did not exclude the boasting of 2.17-23 (3.27). On the contrary, it was just this narrow under-standing of Torah/*nomos* which carried with it the corollary: God is God of Jews only (3.29). But since that corollary is false (as the *Shema* confirms — 3.29-30), the premise is also false: to understand *nomos* in terms of works is to misunderstand it. The line of connection is given rather by faith, since the God of all deals with all in terms of faith (3.30). So faith does not render the

---

65. Far less faith as theory and love as practice (see Betz, *Galatians* 264 and n. 100).

66. Cf. 1 Cor. 13.13; 16.13-14; Col. 1.4; 1 Thes. 1.3; 3.6; 5.8; 2 Thes. 1.3; Phm. 5-7; Eph. 1.15; 3.17; 6.23. But Gal. 5.6 is unique in Paul in defining faith in terms of love.

67. Rom. 3.31 is clearly the conclusion to 3.27-31 and should not be separated from its preceding context to be taken as the introduction to ch. 4, a suggestion rightly rejected by Fitzmyer, *Romans* 366.

68. See above §14.5e.

nomos invalid. Rather, it establishes the *nomos* (3.31). It does not require much literary skill to recognize that 3.31 thus completes the line of argument begun in 3.27, with faith-established *nomos* answering to the "*nomos* of faith." 3.31 is in effect Paul's answer to his opening question: "by what kind of *nomos* is boasting excluded?" Paul's answer is, "By the *nomos* of faith," that is, the *nomos* established by faith. The two *nomoi* are one and the same.[69]

Moreover, Paul's argument would lose its coherence were the *nomos* on each occasion to be understood as other than the law/Torah.[70] For the question of law and faith is posed in 3.31 precisely because the rebuttal of "the law of works" might seem to leave no positive role for the law. Paul's concern, therefore, was precisely to reaffirm that faith and law were not at odds: the law is not to be understood in terms of works; but it can and should be understood in terms of faith.[71] Consequently, faith did not render the law invalid; on the contrary, it established the law. In short, Paul could speak of "the *law* of *faith*" because he believed that *faith* established the *law*.

The conclusion is strengthened by the similar line of thought in 9.30-32:

> [30]What then shall we say? That Gentiles who do not pursue righteousness have attained righteousness, the righteousness which is from faith, [31]whereas Israel pursuing the *nomos* of righteousness has not reached the *nomos*. [32]Why so? Because they did so not from faith but as if it were from works.

To be noted here is a point whose significance is often missed: that Paul can speak of Israel "pursuing the *nomos* of righteousness" and failing to reach that *nomos*. If it was not sufficiently clear that the law, the Torah, was in view, the issue is put beyond doubt by the continuing exposition through 10.4-5.[72] The point for us is twofold. First, Paul refers to the law in a wholly positive way: Israel pursued the law, and it was a good and proper goal to pursue —

---

69. The conclusion is surprisingly uncommon; but see Furnish, *Theology* 160-61, 191-94; Schnabel, *Law and Wisdom* 286-87; Osten-Sacken, *Heiligkeit* 23-33; Stuhlmacher, *Romans* 66-67; others in my *Romans* 186. Contrast Moo, *Romans* 249, who argues that Paul makes a "clear principial distinction" between faith and the Mosaic law, a claim applicable only to the law *of works,* as the comparison of 3.27 with 9.31-32 confirms.

70. *Pace* Schreiner, *Law* 34-36, who follows Räisänen (above n. 37) in rendering *nomos* here as "order," and Fitzmyer, *Romans* 363, who follows the other most popular rendering of *nomos* here as "principle."

71. Cf. Hübner, *Law* 137-44.

72. Surprisingly, NRSV has retained the RSV's misleading inverted translation of 9.31 — "Israel, who did strive for the righteousness that is based on the law, did not succeed in fulfilling that law" — making "righteousness," rather than "the law," the object of Israel's striving. For other attempts to weaken the obvious sense, see my *Romans* 581 and Fitzmyer, *Romans* 578.

"the law of righteousness." The entirely positive term "righteousness" can be complemented or expanded as "the law of righteousness." Israel failed to reach that law, but no criticism of the law is contained in that conclusion. Second, Israel's mistake was not in pursuing the law, but that they did so wrongheadedly. They did so as though the goal were to be achieved in terms of works, whereas it could only be achieved "from faith." Israel did not reach the law. Why? Because they pursued the law of righteousness not from faith but as if it were from works. Here, then, is simply an alternative way of putting the key phrase: the law pursued in terms of faith is another way of saying "the law of faith."[73]

Further confirmation comes from the continuation of the argument begun in Rom. 9.30. For in Rom. 10.6-8 Paul deliberately chose to use Deut. 30.12-14 to expound what he understood by "the righteousness from faith." But Paul would be all too well aware that Deut. 30.11-14 is all about how *easy* it is to obey the law.[74]

> [11]Surely this commandment that I am commanding you today is not too hard for you, nor is it far away. [12]It is not in heaven, that you should say, "Who will go up to heaven for us, and get it for us that we may hear it and observe it?" [13]Neither is it beyond the sea, that you should say, "Who will cross to the other side of the sea for us, and get it for us so that we may hear it and observe it?" [14]No, the word is very near to you; it is in your mouth and in your heart so that you may observe it.

In Romans 10, however, Paul takes this passage and expounds it in reference to "the word of faith" (10.8). The point is that this exposition should not be seen as totally wrenching the passage away from its original sense.[75] Paul was certainly not setting the word of faith and the law as such in antithesis. Certainly he contrasts the word of faith and the law understood

---

73. Paul's point in each of the two Romans passages can be put visually:

Rom. 3 — law of
$\begin{cases} \text{works} \rightarrow \text{boasting} \rightarrow \text{God only of Jews} (\rightarrow \text{law rendered invalid?}) \\ \\ \text{faith} \rightarrow \text{boasting excluded} \rightarrow \text{God of Gentiles too} \rightarrow \text{law established.} \end{cases}$

Rom. 9 —
$\begin{cases} \text{Israel} \rightarrow \text{works} \nrightarrow \text{law of righteousness} \\ \\ \text{Gentiles} \rightarrow \text{faith} \rightarrow \text{law of righteousness} \end{cases}$

74. The LXX version is cited above in §19.4b.

75. That Paul was probably familiar with and drawing upon a well-established line of Jewish interpretation of Deut. 30.11-14 (Bar. 3.39-40; Philo, *Post.* 84-85; *Targum Neofiti* on Deut. 30.11-14) is well known (see, e.g., my *Romans* 603-5; and above §19.4b).

"as if it were from works" (9.32; 10.5); but not the word of faith and "the law of righteousness" understood "from faith" (9.32; 10.6). Had Paul been intending to drive a wedge between the law spoken of in Deut. 30.11-14 and the word of faith, his use of the passage in this way would have left his exposition vulnerable to outright dismissal.[76] On the contrary, his very use of it confirms that for Paul the word of faith was indeed that law understood aright.

The conclusions seem to be clear. (1) The law for Paul retained its function as a measure of righteousness.[77] But (2) that measure could only be "attained" through faith. Only a living in faith and out of faith before God constituted the righteousness for which God looked. As already noted, Abraham provided the great model of what such faith involved (4.18-21). Paul clearly intended that he should: Romans 4 is obviously set up to illustrate faith-establishing law, "the law of faith" (3.31). In other words, faith for Paul meant complete trust in God, like Abraham's, total reliance on God's enabling. *That* was the root of obedience for Paul. Unless obedience sprang from that, it was misdirected. The "obedience of faith" is that obedience which lives out of the sort of trust and reliance on God which Abraham demonstrated.

The law of faith, then, is the law in its function of calling for and facilitating the same sort of trust in God as that out of which Abraham lived. This is not a reference only to sections or parts of the law but describes the function of the law as a whole. Thus we can recognize the criterion by which Paul judged the relevance of the law as a whole and in any of its particulars. Whatever commandment directed or channeled that reliance on God or helped bring that reliance to expression in daily living was the law still expressive of God's will. Conversely, whatever law required more than faith, whatever commandment could not be lived out as an expression of such trust in God alone, whatever ruling hindered or prevented such faith, that was the law now left behind by the coming of Christ. With the gospel now making it possible for *all* to express such faith in God through believing in Christ, the law which was understood to demand more than that faith was in fact the enemy of that faith and should be regarded as redundant. We should presumably add that in the continuing overlap of the ages, so long as sin and death still retain any power (§18), Paul would no doubt continue to recognize that the good purpose of the law for life can still be perverted into a force for death (Rom. 7.7-11).

76. The same Jewish line of interpretation (n. 75) shows a readiness to recognize that Deut. 30.11-14 had in view a more universal principle (divine wisdom, the good) than simply the Jewish law as such. See also above §§11.3c and 19.4b.

77. See above §§6.3 and 18.6.

In short, faith in God (in and through Christ) was for Paul as much the basis for and means to right living as it was for and to being "righteoused" (justified). This creaturely trust in and reliance on God could be expressed as "the law of faith" in that it is only living out this trust which produces the quality of living before God and for others which the law was originally intended to promote. To require more than that trust, to insist on a particular outworking of that faith, would repeat the old failure with regard to the law, to transpose the law of faith into the law of works. It is the naked faith of Abraham which both receives the promise and sustains the daily outworking of self-disinterested love.

§23.4 Spirit and "the law of the Spirit"

The most striking of Paul's ethical injunctions is undoubtedly the call to "walk by the Spirit." In the great Spirit chapter (Romans 8) the early description of Christians is of those "who walk not in accordance with the flesh but in accordance with the Spirit" (Rom. 8.3). Earlier he had talked in equivalent terms of the believers' obligation to "walk in newness of life" (6.4). The intervening 7.6 bridges the two passages in its expectation that Christians would "serve in newness of Spirit and not in oldness of letter." Similarly in Galatians Paul sums up his exhortation in the half-command, half-promise, "Walk by the Spirit and you will not satisfy the desire of the flesh" (Gal. 5.16). Another point of correlation between Romans and Galatians is Paul's description of believers as "those who are led by the Spirit."[78] And a few verses further on in Galatians Paul shows just how clearly he correlated beginning with the Spirit and the continuing ethical obligation on believers by urging, "If we live by the Spirit,[79] let us also follow[80] the Spirit" (5.25). Clearly, this is the paraenetical equivalent of the soteriological concern expressed in 3.3: those who "have begun with the Spirit" can only be "made complete" with the Spirit. That we are here in touch with a regular line of development in Pauline paraenesis is confirmed by the further parallel between Gal. 6.8 and Rom. 8.13. Gal. 6.8: "Those who sow to their own flesh reap corruption; but those who sow to the Spirit shall from the Spirit reap eternal life." Rom. 8.13: "If you live in accordance with the flesh, you

---

78. Rom 8.14; Gal. 5.18; see further above §16.5 n. 119.

79. The allusion is no doubt back to Gal. 3.2-3. NEB and REB translate "If the Spirit is the source of our life." There is, of course, no doubt expressed by the "if" (BDF §371.1).

80. The basic sense of the verb is "stand in line"; hence to "keep in step with" (NIV), "hold to, agree with, follow" (BAGD, *stoicheō*). See further my *Galatians* 317-18.

will certainly die; but if by the Spirit you put to death the deeds of the body, you will live."[81]

The metaphor of daily conduct as the "walk" of life is untypical of Greek thought,[82] but characteristically Jewish.[83] Paul uses the idiom frequently,[84] and his very use indicates the continuing Hebraic cast of his ethical thinking. Expressed quite as abruptly as such exhortations are, however, they can easily be read as encouragement to a spontaneous or charismatic or "situation ethic." Moreover, when we recall the antithesis between Spirit and *gramma* ("letter"),[85] and equate *gramma* with the law, it can readily be concluded that Paul's Spirit ethic is set in antithesis to and as a replacement for Israel's Torah ethic.[86] It is important, therefore, to be clear what is involved in Paul's Spirit ethic.

We do well to begin by recalling the moral seriousness of Israel's scriptures. For it is there that we first encounter a healthy recognition that the law could be treated in a superficial way. We need only recall the repeated warnings of the great eighth-century prophets that mere observance of festival and fast was a totally inadequate way of keeping the law.[87] Paul's own warning that "not the hearers of the law are righteous before God, but the doers of the law shall be counted righteous" (Rom. 2.13) is in fact thoroughly characteristic of scriptural and Jewish concerns.[88] Paul, in other words, was by no means the first Jew to make distinctions among attitudes to the law or among different "levels" of law-keeping.

One of the most potent ways in which this scriptural and Jewish concern was expressed was in the recognition that the law must penetrate to the heart. The obedience to the law for which Yahweh looked was obedience from the heart. Thus, for example, the repeated call to "circumcise the foreskin of your heart,"[89] and the promise that "the LORD your God will circumcise

---

81. On the eschatological tension implicit in these exhortations see above §18; cf. Schnackenburg, *Botschaft* 2.40-42.

82. BAGD, *peripateō;* H. Seesemann, *TDNT* 5.941.

83. E.g., Exod. 18.20; Deut. 13.4-5; 1 Kgs. 9.4; 2 Kgs. 22.2; Ps. 86.11; Prov. 28.18; Isa. 33.15. From the Hebrew *halakh* ("walk") comes the term used to denote the rulings and interpretations which explain and apply the law to later questions and situations, "Halakhah."

84. Rom. 6.4; 8.4; 13.13; 14.15; 1 Cor. 3.3; 7.17; 2 Cor. 4.2; 5.7; 10.2-3; 12.18; Gal. 5.16; Phil. 3.17-18; Col. 1.10; 2.6; 3.7; 4.5; 1 Thes. 2.12; 4.1 (twice), 12; 2 Thes. 3.6, 11. Here cf. particularly 2 Cor. 12.18 and Col. 1.9-10.

85. Rom. 2.28-29; 7.6; 2 Cor. 3.3, 6.

86. Westerholm, *Israel's Law* 209-16.

87. Isa. 1.12-14; Hos. 6.6; Mic. 6.8.

88. Cf., e.g., Deut. 4.1, 5-6, 13-14; 30.11-14; 1 Macc. 2.67; 13.48; Philo, *Cong.* 70; *Praem.* 79; Josephus, *Ant.* 20.44; *m. Aboth* 1.7; 5.14.

89. Deut. 10.16; Jer. 4.4; 9.25-26; Ezek. 44.9; 1QpHab. 11.13; 1QS 5.5; 1QH 2.18; 18.20; Philo, *Spec. Leg.* 1.305.

your heart and the heart of your descendants, so that you will love the LORD your God with all your heart . . ." (Deut. 30.6). The most famous expressions of this hope are, of course, the prophecies of the new covenant in Jer. 31.31-34 and of a new heart in Ezek. 36.26-27.

The point for us here is that for Paul this hope was fulfilled in the gift of the Spirit. This in fact is evidently what Paul had in mind in his distinction between *gramma* and Spirit.

> Rom. 2.28-29 — "The true Jew is not the one visibly marked as such, nor circumcision that which is performed in the flesh, but one who is so in a hidden way, and circumcision is of the heart, in Spirit and not in letter."
>
> 2 Cor. 3.3, 6 — "You show that you are a letter of Christ . . . written not with ink but with the Spirit of the living God, not on tablets of stone but on tablets of human heart . . . [so that we are] ministers of a new covenant, not of letter but of Spirit."

When we recall our earlier finding that *gramma* in Paul's usage is not simply synonymous with "law," but denotes the law understood too narrowly (in distinctive ethnic terms),[90] the point becomes clear. These passages express Paul's conviction that in the gift of the Spirit the earliest Christians had experienced the hoped-for circumcision of the heart of Deuteronomy, the hoped-for new covenant of Jeremiah, and the hoped-for new heart and new spirit of Ezekiel.[91] That presumably is why Paul was prepared to express himself with astonishing boldness at just this point: "It is we who are the circumcision, who worship in the Spirit of God and boast in Christ Jesus and have no confidence in the flesh" (Phil. 3.3).

The point can be pursued further. For it is important to recall that the hope which Paul saw as thus fulfilled in the Spirit was not hope for another law or a different Torah. The fulfilment of that earlier hope had not been perceived as dispensing individuals or communities from keeping the law. On the contrary, the hope was for a means to a more effective keeping of the law. Only a circumcision of the heart would enable an adequate keeping of the law (Deut. 30.8-10). Contrary to popular opinion, the promise of a new covenant in Jeremiah is not of a new or different law. The promise is plain: "I will put my law within them, and I will write it on their hearts" (Jer. 31.33). Likewise the new heart and spirit promised in Ezekiel has in view a more effective keeping of the law: "I will put my spirit within you, and make you

90. See above §6.5.
91. Deidun builds his whole thesis around this insight (*New Covenant Morality,* here especially 3-84). Regarding the echo of Jer. 31.31-34 in 2 Cor. 3.3, 6, see above §6.5.

follow my statutes and be careful to observe my ordinances" (Ezek. 36.27). It is this hope, precisely this hope, which Paul claims to have been fulfilled in the gift of the Spirit to those who put their faith in Messiah Jesus.[92] The coming of Christ and of faith in Christ had brought emancipation from the law in its temporary, constrictive function (Gal. 3.19–4.7).[93] That was still the case. But nothing that Paul says indicates that for him Christ had brought emancipation from the law as God's rule of right and wrong, as God's guidelines for conduct.

It is from the same sequence of Pauline thought that our second "law of" phrase emerges, "the law of the Spirit." It appears as part of Paul's defence of the law in Rom. 7.7–8.4. There, as we have seen, Paul defends the law by portraying it as the dupe of sin. And his defence proceeds by showing that both the human "I" and the law itself are split.[94] It is at this point that the controversial second "law of" phrase enters the exposition: "the law of the Spirit of life in Christ Jesus has set you free from the law of sin and death" (Rom. 8.2). Here, as with "the law of faith," most commentators find it impossible to think that Paul should refer to the law, the Torah, in such a positive way. How could Paul, after describing the law as a power for death, from which believers had been released (7.5-6), now describe it as "the law of the Spirit of life"? How, above all, could he attribute to the law the decisive role in liberating believers from the law?[95] The answer, once again, would be to read here a play on the word *nomos,* and to understand it again as "rule" or "principle."

Once again, however, such a reading simply undermines the flow of Paul's argument in Rom. 8.2-4:

> [2]The law of the Spirit of life in Christ Jesus has set you free from the law of sin and death. [3]For what the law was unable to do in that it was weak through the flesh, God sent his own Son in the very likeness of sinful flesh . . . and condemned sin in the flesh, [4]in order that the requirement of the law might be fulfilled in us who walk not in accordance with the flesh but in accordance with the Spirit.

To be noted is the way in which reference to the law is woven throughout these three verses.[96] In fact, this passage is nothing other than the climax of

---

92. On Paul's use of Deut. 30.12-14 in Rom. 10.6-8 see above §23.3.

93. See above §§6.4-5.

94. See above §§6.7 and 18.3.

95. So especially Räisänen, "Law" (§6 n. 30) 66; *Law* 51-52, followed again particularly by Moo, *Romans* 474-75. For the debate and further bibliography see Räisänen, "Law"; Dunn, *Romans* 416-18; Moo, *Romans* 473-77. As we shall see, "the law of the Spirit of life" (Rom. 8.2) is no more problematic for Paul's theology than "the law of righteousness" in 9.31.

96. In what follows cf. particularly Osten-Sacken, *Heiligkeit* 19-23; Reinmuth, *Geist und Gesetz* 48-74 (here 66-69); others in my *Romans* 417.

Paul's defence of the law, which began in 7.7. In the flow of the argument, "the law of sin and death" (8.2) is surely intended as shorthand for the law abused and misused by sin to bring about death (as described in 7.7-13).[97] The law weakened through the flesh (8.3) is the good law of God, but defeated by the combination of sin's power and the weakness of the similarly divided "I." But what then of the law freed, like the "I," from the power of sin and death? This indeed is the most obvious way to take the phrase "the law of the Spirit of life" — that is, as a reference to the law in its capacity as the law of God, but no longer caught in the nexus of human weakness and sin's power, the law freed from the power of death to serve again as a rule of life (7.10).[98] The law is "spiritual" (*pneumatikos* — 7.14) because it can be a vehicle or instrument of the Spirit (*pneuma*). As 3.31 answers to 3.27,[99] so 8.2 answers to 7.14.[100] "The law of the Spirit," in other words, is one of the ways in which Paul refers to what we might call the positive side of the divided law.[101]

Perhaps most striking of all, the purpose for which God sent his Son is explicitly stated as to bring about the fulfilment of the law's requirement (8.4).[102] For Paul, the objective of God's saving action in Christ was to make possible the keeping of the law! What has made the difference, and what has defeated the power of sin and the weakness of the flesh? The Spirit. "The requirement of the law [is] fulfilled in us who walk not in accordance with the flesh, but in accordance with the Spirit" (8.4). It would appear, then, that "the law of the Spirit" is simply a summary way of

---

97. But what seems to be an obvious deduction is much disputed (see my *Romans* 392-93 and 416-19).

98. See again above §6.6.

99. Above §23.3.

100. Hübner, *Law* 144-46, 149.

101. So particularly Hahn, "Gesetzesverständnis" (§6 n. 1) 47-49. To take *nomos* as other than "the law" here would mean that a *third nomos* was now in view in 8.2 (Fee, *Empowering Presence* [§16 n. 1] 552), which does not exactly make Paul's meaning more lucid.

102. The precise sense of "fulfill" is unclear, but Paul uses the same verb in 13.8 and Gal. 5.14. So it probably means "fulfill" in a more profound sense than simply in terms of an item-by-item correlation. The fact that Paul uses "requirement" in the singular suggests further that what is in view is the essential requirement which lies behind the individual requirements, the character and purpose which the individual requirements are intended to bring to expression (see further my *Romans* 423-24). We shall note below (§23.5) that Paul also speaks of the importance of (believers) "keeping the commandments" (1 Cor. 7.19). Compare and contrast also the various wrestlings with the otherwise problematic character of Paul's conception of Christians "fulfilling the law" — Hübner, *Law* 83-87; Räisänen, *Paul* 62-73; Barclay, *Obeying* 135-42; Westerholm, *Israel's Law* 201-5; Schreiner, *Law* 145-78; Finsterbusch, *Thora* 97-107.

speaking of the requirement of the law fulfilled by those who walk by the Spirit.[103]

In short, it is precisely as "the law of the Spirit," the law understood as guidelines for Spirit-directed conduct, the law thus freed from the misconceptions which gave the power of sin such leverage, and from the weakness of the flesh which so disempowered it, that the law can be experienced as a liberating power, as a law for living.[104] It is the law thus rightly perceived and experienced which sets free from "the law of sin and death."

And what does this mean in practice for Paul?[105] Paul presumably had in mind a conduct informed and enabled out of a direct and immediate apprehension of the divine will. This is already implied in his earliest letter: "you yourselves are being taught by God to love one another" (1 Thes. 4.9).[106]

More striking is the contrast he draws in Romans itself. On the one hand stands the claim to know God's will, as part of the Jewish boasting of which he disapproves — Rom. 2:18:

> you are called a "Jew" and rely on the law and boast in God, and know his will *(to thelēma)* and approve things that matter *(dokimazeis ta diapheronta)*, being instructed from the law.

On the other stands the knowing of God's will which comes from the renewed mind — 12:2:

> Do not be conformed to this age, but be transformed by the renewal of your mind, so that you may ascertain what is the will of God *(eis to dokimazein hymas ti to thelēma tou theou)*.

---

103. The double line of thought in Paul's defence of the law in Rom. 7.7–8.4 can be illustrated in two ways:

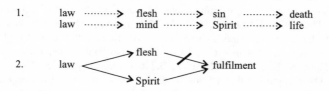

104. Though Paul still does not say as a life-giving power; see again §6.6 above.

105. The question is important since the function of the Spirit in providing guidance in specific situations is rarely explicit in Paul; Furnish regards 1 Cor. 7.40 as the only example (*Theology* 231).

106. Probably in echo of Isa. 54.13 (cf. John 6.45). See further Deidun, *New Covenant Morality* 57-58; E. J. Schnabel, "How Paul Developed His Ethics: Motivations, Norms and Criteria of Pauline Ethics," in Rosner, ed., *Understanding* 267-97 (here 278-79).

Here the contrast is between an obedience instructed by the law and an obedience instructed by the renewed mind. But it is obviously equivalent to the contrast between the law of sin preventing the will of God and the law of the Spirit enabling its fulfilment.

The same point is made, in related terms, though again without specific reference to the Spirit as such, in Paul's prayer in Phil. 1.9-10: "This I pray, that your love may overflow more and more with knowledge and full insight so that you may determine what really matters (*eis to dokimazein hymas ta diapheronta*)."[107] What Paul had in mind is what Oscar Cullmann expressed as "the capacity of forming the correct ethical judgment at each given moment,"[108] that is, the sense or instinct for what is right and appropriate in any given situation. This capacity to discern "what is really important"[109] is also to be regarded as a gift or enabling of the Spirit.[110] For Paul this knowledge of God's will was not something which could be read off from a law code or rulebook. It required much more spiritual (Spirit-enabled) sensitivity — what Col. 1.9-10 speaks of as "spiritual (*pneumatikē*) wisdom and understanding."[111] And yet in so saying, Paul had the same objective in mind as the law — the doing of God's will. So once again we can say that Paul wanted what God had intended in giving the law: that God's will be done. The law of God and the Spirit of God had the same objective, however much it had been thwarted and corrupted in the former case.[112]

We should also note the link between "the law of the Spirit" and "the law of faith." In both cases Paul presumably used the term "law" because he

107. Note how the wording of Phil. 1.10 is in effect a combination of Rom. 2.18 and 12.2.

108. Cullmann, *Christ and Time* 228; cf. also Bultmann, *Theology* 1.341-42.

109. *Ta diapheronta* — literally "the things that differ," better known by the technical term in Stoic ethics for things that do not really matter, *adiaphora*, "things neither good nor bad" (LSJ, *adiaphoros* II; K. Weiss, *TDNT* 9.63; Jaquette, *Discerning* ch. 2).

110. *Dokimazein*, "test, examine, approve," is regularly used of testing prophetic utterances (1 Thes. 5.21; 1 John 4.1; *Didache* 12.1; Hermas, *Mandate* 11.7, 16) and so overlaps with the term *diakrinein* as used in 1 Cor. 14.29 (cf. 1 Cor. 2.13-15; 12.10; *Didache* 11.7); also *diakrisis* in 1 Cor. 12.10. Note also Paul's other uses of *dokimazō* (particularly Rom. 14.22; 1 Cor. 11.28; 13.5; Gal. 6.4). See also above §20 n. 136.

111. The recognition that wisdom and understanding come from above through the Spirit is well established in Jewish theology (Exod. 31.3; 35.31; Isa. 11.2; Sir. 39.6; Wis. 9.9-10, 17-19; Philo, *Gigant.* 22-27; 4 Ezra 14.22, 39-40), and such wisdom and understanding was claimed also at Qumran, though more as a specific interpretation of the Torah (e.g., 1QH 4.9-12; 6.10-12; 11.7-10; 12.11-13; 16.11-12; 1QS 5.8-10; 9.13; 11.15-18).

112. *Pace* Schnabel, *Law and Wisdom* 331 n. 475, there was no intention in my previous formulation (*Jesus and the Spirit* [§20 n. 1] 233) to set Spirit and external norm in antithesis.

wanted to underline the vital importance of doing, obeying God's will.[113] And
in both cases the qualifier ("of faith," "of the Spirit") indicates in a summary
way how that obedience is made possible. In Paul's solution to the problem
of human weakness and sin's power, faith and Spirit are the two sides of the
same coin. The human trust is met by the power of the Spirit. The obedience
that God looks for and makes possible is, in a phrase, human responsiveness
(faith) to divine enabling (Spirit).[114]

To formulate the point from a slightly different angle, both phrases,
"the law of faith" and "the law of the Spirit," can be defined by their
contrasting phrases. As the law of faith is different from the law understood
in terms of works, so the law of the Spirit is different from the law understood
as *gramma* ("letter"). Both "works" and "letter" emphasize the visible,
public character of what is being required and done. In that situation the
tendency or danger is always for that visible element to become the dominant
feature of the obedience so expressed and for the obedience to become
divorced from obedience from the heart. As one who believed that he himself
had formerly succumbed to that danger, Paul emphasized the law of faith and
the law of the Spirit as a way of reaffirming the obedience which is required
by God. At the same time, he insists that the only obedience which actually
does God's will and fulfills the law of God is an obedience which is the
outworking of faith and enabled by the Spirit.

§23.5 Christ and "the law of Christ"

The question here is whether and in what sense Christ functioned in Paul's
ethics as a model and motivator. We have already laid the groundwork for
this section in earlier discussion. In §8 we concluded that Paul both knew
and cared about the ministry of Jesus prior to his passion; and that Paul
recalled, alluded to, and was himself influenced in his conduct as well as
his theology by important features of the Jesus tradition. In §15.2 we noted
how much the "in Christ" and "in the Lord" phrases functioned as a
leitmotiv in Paul's letters, not least in his description of his own activity
and in exhortation to his readers to adopt a particular attitude or course of
action. And in §18.2 we observed the importance of the idea of transformation in Paul's soteriology, particularly as transformation to become like
Christ, including the imagery of "putting on Christ" (Rom. 13.14) and of

---

113. Here we may recall that a more carefully delimited interpretation of Lev. 18.5
(above §6.6) is in fact quite compatible with Paul's ethics as well as his soteriology.

114. Deidun: in Paul's theology "the precise correlate of *sola fide* is the activity
of the Spirit" (*New Covenant Morality* 45).

daily renewal in knowledge in accordance with the image of God in Christ (Col. 3.10).

So far as Paul's ethics are concerned, the second and third of these have been relatively unproblematic. That Paul should see the Christian life lived out under the authority of Jesus as Lord and in conformity to him is an inevitable corollary of his gospel. What it meant in practice was presumably a combination of faith (§23.3) and immediate inspiration (§23.4), of ethos and practice determined within the body of Christ, not least by the constant measure and motivation of God's love in Christ's self-sacrificial death. The first, however, has been more problematic, particularly the issue of whether Jesus' own ethical teaching formed any sort of resource for Paul's paraenesis or model for his own conduct. Constant incentive and encouragement from the kerygma of Jesus' death and resurrection is one thing, but there has been a considerable unwillingness to recognize that appeal to the Jesus of the Jesus tradition played much if any part in Paul's own ethics.[115]

The issue can be focused around the question whether Paul's paraenesis contains any echoes of or allusions to Jesus' teaching.[116] In fact, there is widespread recognition of some eight or nine such echoes — all of them, noticeably, in Paul's paraenesis.[117] The most striking are the following:[118]

Rom. 12.14 — *"Bless those who persecute you, bless* and do not *curse"*;
Luke 6.27-28 — "Love your enemies . . . *bless* those who *curse* you";
Matt. 5.44 — "Love your enemies and pray for *those who persecute you*."

---

115. See, e.g., W. Michaelis, *mimeomai, TDNT* 4.672; H. D. Betz, *Nachfolge und Nachahmung Jesu Christi im Neuen Testament* (Tübingen: Mohr, 1967); Schrage, *Ethics* 208; Strecker, *Theologie* 111-12. On Rom. 15.7, e.g., Schrage maintains that "Christ is not primarily *exemplum* but *sacramentum*" (*Ethics* 173). However, would it not be better to say "primarily *sacramentum* but also *exemplum*"? Of course "more is involved than simple recollection" (174, referring to 2 Cor. 10.1); but does that mean we have to deny that "simple recollection" *was* involved?

116. It is a fact that only three specific traditions are attributed explicitly to Jesus — all in one letter (1 Cor. 7.10-11; 9.14; 11.23-25) — which is so surprising. On the first two see below (this section); on the third, see above §22.3.

117. Furnish, *Theology* 53-54; see further D. C. Allison, "The Pauline Epistles and the Synoptic Gospels: The Pattern of the Parallels," *NTS* 28 (1982) 1-32 (here 10), with bibliography in n. 47. Davies was confident of being able to identify 25 allusions in Romans, 1 Thessalonians, and Colossians (*Paul* 138-40). Wenham, *Paul* (§8 n. 1), now replaces A. Resch, *Der Paulinismus und die Logia Jesu in ihrem gegenseitigen Verhältnis untersucht* (TU 12; Leipzig: Hinrichs, 1904), as the maximizer of contacts between Paul and the Jesus tradition.

118. The others are Rom. 12.17 and 1 Thes. 5.15 (Matt. 5.38-48/Luke 6.27-36); Rom. 13.7 (Mark 12.17 pars.); Rom. 14.13 (Mark 9.42 pars.).

Rom. 14.14 — "I know and am persuaded in the Lord Jesus that nothing is profane *(ouden koinon)* in itself";
Mark 7.15 — "there is nothing outside a person . . . which is able to defile him *(ouden estin . . . ho dynatai koinōsai)*."

1 Cor. 13.2 — "If I *have* all *faith* so as to *move mountains*";
Matt. 17.20 — "If you *have faith* . . . you will say to this *mountain, 'Move* from here to there,' and it will *move*."

1 Thes. 5.2, 4 — "You yourselves know well that the day of the Lord is coming like a thief in the night . . . you are not in darkness that the day will surprise you like a thief";
Matt. 24.43 — "Know this that if the householder had known at what watch the thief was to come, he would have watched."

1 Thes. 5.13 — "Live at peace among yourselves *(eirēneuete en heautois);*
Mark 9.50 — "Live at peace with one another" *(eirēneuete en allēlois).*

However, the significance of these and other possible allusions is much disputed. This is partly because Paul's explicit references to Jesus are so heavily focused on his death and resurrection; that Paul was not interested in Jesus' pre-passion ministry seems self-evident.[119] Partly also because the issue becomes easily sidetracked or overwhelmed by the more pressing theological issue of whether such allusions help us to recover the *ipsissima verba* of Jesus.[120] But mostly because of Paul's failure to identify the teaching as that of Jesus. If Paul knew and alluded to Jesus tradition, why did he not identify it as such? What could have given his paraenesis more authoritative weight than a citation of Jesus as its source?[121]

Such questions, however, reveal a crucial failure to appreciate how tradition works in a community and the function of allusion. A community, almost by definition, has its shared language and metaphors and technical terms and memories. These form the common currency of conversational exchange within the community. They enable the discourse within the com-

119. But see §8 above.
120. Cf. particularly F. Neirynck, "Paul and the Sayings of Jesus," in Vanhoye, ed., *L'Apôtre Paul* 265-321.
121. See particularly N. Walter, "Paul and the Early Christian Jesus-Tradition," in Wedderburn, *Paul and Jesus* (§8 n. 1) 51-80, for whom the decisive consideration is that Paul seems to show no consciousness that he is referring to sayings of Jesus.

munity to be abbreviated to a kind of shorthand, where allusions to what is common knowledge can function as such and do not need to be spelled out every time.[122] The closer the community, the more allusive the conversations can be. Indeed, it is precisely the character of such discourse as allusive which enables it to function as a kind of glue bonding the community together. It is one's knowledge of the tradition which enables one to recognize the allusions and which thus attests one's membership of the community. Those who do not recognize the allusions thereby demonstrate that they are still outside the community. One enters the community, in effect, by "learning the language," that is, by learning the community's tradition in order to make and recognize the allusions to it, and thus to function within the community's discourse.[123]

The point should be obvious. We have already noted Paul's concern to pass on traditions to the churches he founded and the strong likelihood that they contained (if not largely consisted of) traditions about Jesus' ministry of word and deed (again §8.2).[124] In consequence Paul could assume a fair degree of knowledge about Jesus' ministry and teaching. And because it was common knowledge, he did not need to cite Jesus' authority when making such allusions. Indeed — an important point — had he cited Jesus' authority every time he referred to something Jesus said or did he would have *weakened* the force of the allusion as allusion. The allusion which has to be explained has lost its bonding effect. It no longer functions to separate those who recognize the allusion, and thus attest their competence in the Christian "language," from those who fail to recognize it, and thus attest that they are "unbelievers" or "uninstructed" (cf. 1 Cor. 14.23-24).[125]

In contrast — an equally important point — it is noticeable that in regard to the only two pieces of paraenesis which Paul did explicitly attribute to Jesus, he did so precisely because he wanted to *qualify* their authority. In the one case (1 Cor. 7.10-16), he did so to make it clear that his own instruction went *beyond* what Jesus taught (the teaching on divorce). In the other case (1 Corinthians 9), he did so to make it clear that his own practice *disregarded*

---

122. See also above §11.4 on the nature of allusion.

123. I hardly need to cite any "authority" for these observations. Anyone who is an active member of a club or college or society (or church!) will have no difficulty in thinking of examples of the abbreviations and shorthand which mark the "in-language" of such groups.

124. Note also that so many of the accepted allusions come in a letter Paul wrote to a church he had not himself founded (Romans). In other words, he could assume that his own practice of passing on traditions as part of the process of founding a church was the common practice of all church founders.

125. Again I can simply appeal to the common experience of a newcomer to a group being puzzled (or even deliberately excluded) by the allusions of the group's "in-language."

what Jesus commanded (the evangelist should be provided with financial support by the church). By way of contrast, then, the fact that all Paul's other references are allusions indicates his *acceptance* of their authority and his assumption that his readers' recognition of the allusion would likewise strengthen their authority. In other words, the allusiveness does not weaken the authority of the reference to the Jesus tradition. On the contrary, it underlines and reinforces its authority for the community of Jesus.

At this point we need to bring in the third "law of" phrase — "the law of Christ." Like the other "law of" phrases this one occurs only once or twice in Paul. In Gal. 6.2 he calls on the Galatians: "Bear one another's burdens and thus you shall fulfill the law of Christ *(ton nomon tou Christou)*."[126] And in 1 Cor. 9.20-21 he describes his personal policy:

> [20]To those under the law I became as one under the law (though I myself am not under the law), in order that I might win those under the law. [21]To those outside the law I became as one outside the law (though I am not outside the law but in-lawed to Christ [*ennomos Christou*]), in order that I might win those outside the law.

Here again, as with the other "law of" phrases discussed above, there is a widespread feeling that Paul could not be referring to the Torah when he spoke of "the law of Christ." How could he say that he had "died to the law" (Gal. 2.19), or affirm that those who had received the Spirit had been redeemed from "under the law" (Gal. 4.4-7), or warn his readers so fiercely against coming under the yoke of the law's slavery (Gal. 5.1) and then speak of the law so positively? The usual solution is that whatever the phrase means, it cannot refer to the Torah; Paul is once again playing on the term *nomos*.[127]

Once again, however, the positive strand of Paul's teaching on the law has been missed or too heavily discounted. In this case we should note particularly the striking parallel in thought between Romans and Galatians. In Rom. 13.8-10 Paul sums up his ethical teaching to that point with the words:

---

126. A natural variant was to read the imperative ("and thus fulfill"), treating the second half of the verse as a continuation of the exhortation rather than as a promise attached to the imperative of the first half; see Metzger 598.

127. See, e.g., Lietzmann, *Galater* 41, and Lührmann, *Galater* 97. Hence Betz, *Galatians* 300-301, somewhat incoherently: "Paul took over the notion from the opponents . . . and used [it] here polemically"; similarly J. L. Martyn, "A Law-Observant Mission to Gentiles: The Background of Galatians," *SJT* 38 (1984) 307-24 (here 315). E. Bammel, *"Nomos Christou,"* in F. L. Cross, ed., *Studia Evangelica* III (TU 88; Berlin: Akademie, 1964) 12-28, suggests that the phrase "the law of Christ" was coined "in an almost playful manner." See also Hübner, *Theologie* 2.103-5 and those cited above nn. 37 and 70.

⁸Owe nothing to anyone except to love one another; for he who loves the other has fulfilled the law. ⁹For the commandment, "You shall not commit adultery," "You shall not kill," "You shall not steal," "You shall not covet," and any other commandment, is summed up in this word, in the command "You shall love your neighbour as yourself." ¹⁰Love does no wrong to the neighbour; therefore the fulfilment of the law is love.

Then, a chapter and a half later, Paul again sums up, this time his extensive treatment of the problem of food laws, in a similar concern for the neighbour — Rom. 15.1-3:

¹We the strong ought to support the weaknesses of those without strength and not to please ourselves. ²Let each of us please his neighbour with a view to what is good, for upbuilding. ³For the Christ too did not please himself. . . .

Since this is the only other occasion on which Paul speaks of concern for the "neighbour,"[128] it is not too hard to see a train of thought running between the two Romans passages. Jesus' refusal to please himself was depicted by Paul as an example of pleasing the neighbour, which is another way of saying "Love your neighbour as yourself," which in turn is a fulfilment of the law.

What is noticeable for us is that Paul seems to have followed the same train of thought in Galatians. In Gal. 5.14 he says something very similar to Rom. 13.8-10: "Through love serve one another. For the whole law is fulfilled[129] in one word, in the [well-known] 'You shall love your neighbour as yourself' " (Gal. 5.13-14). And then, just half a chapter later, he calls for his audience to "Bear one another's burdens and thus you will fulfill the law of Christ" (Gal. 6.2). We can make precisely the same deduction as before. To fulfill the law of Christ is to bear one another's burdens, which is a particular example of loving the neighbour, which fulfills the law. The point should be obvious: in the parallel trains of thought "the law of Christ" (Galatians) is equivalent to Jesus' refusal to please himself (Romans).[130] Which presumably means that in Paul's mind "the law of Christ" included some reference to Jesus' own example.

A second consideration has to be added. That is the likelihood that this repeated emphasis on love of neighbour as fulfilling the whole law was a conscious echo of Jesus' own teaching on the two great commandments: " 'You shall love the Lord your God with all your heart . . .' [and] 'You shall

---

128. Except in the parallel Galatians passage — Gal. 5.14 — which is part of the present discussion.

129. See above n. 102.

130. For fuller expositions of these passages see my *Galatians* and *Romans*.

love your neighbour as yourself.' There is no other commandment greater than these" (Mark 12.30-31). Or in Matthew's version, "On these two commandments depends the whole law" (Matt. 22.40). The idea that the law could be "summed up" or encapsulated in one or a few commandments is not unique to Christianity.[131] But the evidence of the Romans and Galatians passages indicates that this emphasis on love of neighbour as summing up or fulfilling the whole law had become an established feature in Pauline paraenesis (not to say Christian paraenesis generally).[132] And given that the same emphasis is clearly established within the Jesus tradition, it would be somewhat perverse to look to another source for the earliest Christian emphasis at this point. In other words, Gal. 5.14 and Rom. 13.8-10 can be added to the list of probable allusions to Jesus' teaching.[133]

The deduction is obvious: that by "the law of Christ" Paul will have been thinking particularly of the love command. To bear the other's burden is obviously to love the burdened neighbour. And since bearing the other's burden fulfills the law of Christ, it follows that "the law of Christ" is a way of speaking of the command to love the neighbour.[134] Adding this point to the one already made, we can also make the further deduction: that by the law of Christ Paul had in mind both Jesus' teaching on the love command and Jesus' own example in living out the love command.[135]

These findings are important. First, they confirm once more that Paul did not teach that the law was to be wholly discarded or abandoned. His

131. See further my *Romans* 778-79.

132. Lev. 19.18 is one of the most quoted scriptures in the NT — Matt. 5.43; 19.19; 22.39; Mark 12.31, 33; Luke 10.27; Rom. 12.19; 13.9; Gal. 5.14; Jas. 2.8.

133. J. L. Martyn's attempt to take the law of Gal. 5.14 as "the original law of God — the pre-Sinaitic law" = "the promissory voice of the law" (4.21) = the promise of 3.8 ("The Crucial Event in the History of the Law [Gal. 5.14]," in Lovering and Sumney, *Theology and Ethics* 48-61) seems to run counter to Paul's clear distinction between the "promise" and the "law" in 3.14-29. Cf. Merklein's exposition of Rom. 8.2 (the law of the Spirit of life as a "positive antitype of the Torah") and Gal. 6.2 (the law of Christ must be understood "typologically") (*Studien* 88-89 and 104-5).

134. There is a broad consensus on this point at least; see, e.g., Hahn, "Gesetzesverständnis" (§6 n. 1) 57; Barclay, *Obeying* 126-35; and Schrage's fine exposition (*Ethics* 211-17). In his earlier study Schrage concluded that "all [Paul's] paraenesis is finally example, expression, and sharpening of the love commandment" (*Einzelgebote* 269).

135. See further particularly H. Schürmann, " 'Das Gesetz des Christus' (Gal. 6.2). Jesu Verhalten und Wort als letztgültige sittliche Norm nach Paulus," in J. Gnilka, ed., *Neues Testament und Kirche*, R. Schnackenburg FS (Freiburg: Herder, 1974) 282-300; R. B. Hays, "Christology and Ethics in Galatians: The Law of Christ," *CBQ* 49 (1987) 268-90; cf. C. H. Dodd, *"Ennomos Christou," More New Testament Studies* (Manchester: Manchester University, 1968) 134-48; Strecker, *Theologie* 154. "The Law of Christ is thus the Law transformed by Christ's crucifixion and exemplified by his behavior" (Boyarin, *Radical Jew* 134).

critique of the law was more specific and in effect peeled away from the law the functions that it no longer should serve to leave its continuing function all the clearer. In both Gal. 5.13-14 and Rom. 13.8-10 Paul talks about "fulfilling" the law as something which evidently meets the requirement of the law (Rom. 8.4) and is still desirable and necessary for believers. In so doing he indicates clearly that he had in mind the whole law. Not just the moral commands within the ten commandments, but "any other command," too (Rom. 13.9). His concern was not to abstract or separate the love command from the rest, but to emphasize the "whole law" as still obligatory for believers (Gal. 5.14). To fulfill the law of Christ was to fulfill the law.[136]

Second, the love command is the summary, epitome, condensation of the whole law. The whole law is fulfilled by loving the neighbour.[137] Particularly noticeable in Galatians is the fact that within a few verses Paul could speak both of "doing the whole law" as something entirely *un*desirable for Gentile Christians, and yet also of "fulfilling the whole law" as something entirely desirable for Christians (Gal. 5.3, 14).[138]

> 5.3 — "Everyone who is being circumcised . . . is obligated to do the whole law. You have been estranged from Christ . . .";
>
> 5.14 — "The whole law is fulfilled . . . in the [well-known] 'You shall love your neighbour as yourself.' "

If these two statements are contradictory, Paul assuredly cannot have been unaware of that contradiction. It must rather be the case that he had in mind the same twofold way of looking at and living in relation to the law to which we have now grown accustomed. The one was a misunderstanding of the role of the law in relation to Israel, all that Paul summed up under the terms "works" and "letter." But the other was a wholly acceptable and necessary appreciation of the law's continuing importance — the whole law as summed up and fulfillable in and through the command to love the neighbour. Where requirements of the law were being interpreted in a way which ran counter to the basic principle of the love command, Paul thought that the requirements could and should be dispensed with. On the other hand, it was still possible in his view for the *whole* law, and *all* its com-

---

136. Cf. Schnabel, *Law and Wisdom* 274-77.

137. We may assume that love for God was the unstated presupposition (Deidun, *New Covenant Morality* 141). The focus of Paul's concern in these passages, however, is on mutual relationships at the "horizontal" level.

138. Hübner's distinction between "the whole law" (*ho pas nomos*) in Gal. 5.14 and "the whole law (*holos ho nomos*) in 5.3 (*Law* 36-42) cannot be sustained (see my *Galatians* 290). See again above n. 102.

mandments, to be fulfilled in a way which did not run counter to the love command.[139]

A similar point emerges from another too little observed correlation between Paul's letters. Paul uses the formulation "neither circumcision nor uncircumcision is anything, but . . ." three times.[140] The comparison of the balancing clauses is instructive.

> Gal. 5.6 — "in Christ Jesus neither circumcision nor uncircumcision counts for anything, but faith operating effectively through love";
> Gal. 6.15 — "neither circumcision nor uncircumcision is anything, but a new creation";
> 1 Cor. 7.19 — "circumcision is nothing and uncircumcision is nothing, but [what matters is] keeping the commandments of God."

In the new creation, circumcision (or not) can be counted among the adiaphora, things neither good nor bad in themselves. Faith operating through love is how the commandments of God are to be kept. That is, the love command is not an alternative to the law, the commandments of God. Rather, it shows how the commandments are to be kept — including the necessity or otherwise of circumcision![141] In other words, the love command fulfills the whole law because it fulfills the spirit of the law and, in the given situation of loving the neighbour, indicates what things really matter and what can be treated as nonessentials *(adiaphora).*[142]

Third, it follows from our analysis that Jesus himself provided Paul with a model for the conduct prescribed by the law. It was Jesus' teaching which had summed up the law in the love command. But Jesus' example, as conveyed to the churches in the Jesus tradition, evidently also served to document what obeying the law through the love command meant in particular situations. There can be little doubt, for example, that the accounts of Jesus' Sabbath controversies (Mark 2.23–3.5 pars.) provided illustrations of what

---

139. Cf. Ridderbos: "Love functions here not as a new Christian ideal or as a new norm, which comes in the place of the law or makes it superfluous. It is precisely required here as the summary of the law. . . . In other words, the law does not find its criterion in love, but just the reverse, the requirement of love is so imperative because in it lies the summary of the law" *(Paul* 282).

140. See my " 'Neither Circumcision nor Uncircumcision, but . . .' (Gal. 5.2-12; 6.12-16; cf. 1 Cor. 7.17-20)," in A. Vanhoye, ed., *La foi agissant par l'amour (Galates 4.12–6.16)* (Rome: Abbaye de S. Paul, 1996) 79-110 (discussion 110-22).

141. Sanders's surprise at 1 Cor. 7.19 — "one of the most amazing sentences that he [Paul] ever wrote" *(Paul, the Law and the Jewish People* [§6 n. 1] 103) — simply indicates his failure to appreciate the nuances of Paul's view of the law.

142. See further Jaquette, *Discerning* ch. 3.

keeping the Sabbath by loving the neighbour meant. Just as Jesus' practice, as well as teaching, on clean and unclean and table fellowship[143] was no doubt also definitive for Paul.[144] The call to "welcome one another, as Christ also welcomed you" (Rom. 15.7), and to "forgive each other, . . . as the Lord also forgave you" (Col. 3.13), were informed not only by the individual's experience of acceptance and forgiveness, but presumably also by the traditions of Jesus offering acceptance and forgiveness to sinners during his own ministry. Of course, the supreme example of Jesus' own "love of neighbour" was his death "for us (sinners)" (Rom. 5.8),[145] but the Gospels remind us that the cross was not the only cherished reminiscence of Jesus' love of neighbour.[146]

In short, despite the paucity of explicit evidence, we can gain a fairly clear idea of what "living in accordance with Christ Jesus" (Rom. 15.5) and with "the law of Christ" (Gal. 6.2) meant for Paul and his addressees. Both phrases include allusion to the Jesus tradition which each church received from its founding apostle and which helped constitute it as the church of Jesus Christ. The believer seeking to live in accord with the law of Christ could refer to the Jesus tradition known widely among the churches, or in particular to the teachers of the community, whose primary function within the community was to serve as a repository for and instructors in that tradition. This tradition provided a model of what it meant to live in accord with the law as summed up in the love command. In this phrase "the law of Christ," then, we have further confirmation that the law continued to have paraenetic force for the first Christians. But it was the law as taught and as lived out by Jesus, as known to each church through its founding traditions.

§23.6 Liberty and love

The exegetical problems with which we have been dealing in this chapter can all be put down to the eschatological tension in Paul's theology of the salvation process. For they each express in turn the tension between outward rule and inward motivation, between traditional truths and fresh insight, between a

---

143. Mark 2.15-17 and 7.15-19; see above §8.3(3).

144. A corollary is that Paul here is not so distant from Matthew, who presumably intended by his account to show how Jesus "fulfilled" (the same word as in Rom. 8.4; 13.8; and Gal. 5.14) the law and the prophets (Matt. 5.17-20), though Paul's echo of Jesus' teaching on clean and unclean is closer to Mark's version (Mark 7.15/Rom. 14.14).

145. By reading the cross as "the paradigm for faithfulness to God," Hays (*Moral Vision* 197) puts more weight on the cross as a paradigm for faithful living than Paul's exposition indicates (see also §14.8 above). For Paul the cross was more an expression of *God's* faithfulness (Rom. 1.17; 3.25-26; 5.8; 8.31-39; 15.8; 2 Cor. 5.20-21).

146. See also above §21.6b.

revelation which began with creation but which now has been brought to sharper focus in Christ. Inextricably intertwined are the tensions between old nature and new, between flesh and Spirit, between Israel and church, between institution and charism, between individual and community. The tension comes to particular expression not least in the two-way tug of liberty and love. The ground has been largely covered already, but the principle of liberty and the qualification of love were of such importance for Paul that they deserve at least a brief separate mention.

The principle of Christian liberty was obviously one close to Paul's heart, as we saw at the end of §§14 and 16.[147] Who, reading Rom. 8.2 or Gal. 5.1, could doubt that? Rom. 8.2 — "the law of the Spirit of life in Christ Jesus has set you free from the law of sin and death." Gal. 5.1 — "For freedom Christ has set us free. Stand firm, therefore, and do not be subject again to a yoke of slavery." But since we first cited these texts we have seen two important qualifications.

One is, once again, the already–not yet. "Freedom from the slavery of corruption" and "the liberty of the glory of the children of God" belong to the not yet ("the redemption of our body," Rom. 8.21-23). The liberty of the Spirit of life is still constrained by the body of death (Rom. 8.10). This means that the individual believer is not yet delivered from the old nature, the flesh, and is still subject to the downward pull of desire degenerating into lust. That Paul was all too well aware of this danger is indicated clearly enough by the qualification he himself injects into Galatians 5: "You were called to freedom, brothers; only not the freedom for opportunity to the flesh, but through love serve one another" (5.13). Paul was all too well aware that freedom could easily serve as a cloak for selfish and self-seeking ends, that liberty could quickly degenerate into license. The only effective controlling factor, he implies, is love — love defined simply as the concern to serve one another.[148]

The other qualification on individual liberty is the complexity of the individual's living as part of community. Fundamental to Paul's concept of the body of Christ was both the diversity of its members and their mutual interdependence upon each other (§20.4). That also means the responsibility of the one for the whole and of the whole for the individual. Not simply in genuine care for one another,[149] but also in readiness to restrain one's own

---

147. See §§14.9d and 16.5a.

148. Note the importance of "love" throughout Paul's parenesis — Rom. 12.9; 13.8-10; 14.15; 15.30; 1 Cor. 8.1; 13.1-4, 8, 13; 14.1; 16.14; 2 Cor. 2.8; 8.7-8, 24; Gal. 5.6, 13, 22; Phil. 1.9; 2.1-2; Col. 2.2; 3.14; 1 Thes. 3.12; 5.8, 13; also Eph. 4.2, 15-16; 5.2; 1 Tim. 4.12; 6.11; 2 Tim. 2.22; Tit. 2.2.

149. See, e.g., Rom. 12.16; 1 Cor. 12.25-26; Phil. 2.2-3.

conviction of charism for the benefit of the whole (1 Cor. 14.28, 30). Here again it is important to recognize the placement of 1 Corinthians 13 between chs. 12 and 14: the only way to turn the vision of the charismatic body of Christ (ch. 12) into practice (ch. 14) is through love (ch. 13).

1 Corinthians 8–10 is a passage where Paul makes particular play on the liberty/love tension. He agrees with the theology of those who claim the right *(exousia)* to disregard idols (1 Cor. 8.9). He acknowledges the extent of their freedom — "All things are permitted *(exestin)*" (1 Cor. 10.23). But he qualifies the liberty each time by concern for the impact of that liberty on the fellow believer: it may become a stumbling block to the weak (8.9); it may not build up the church (10.23). The exercise of liberty must always be conditioned by love.[150] Nor should we forget that in the intervening chapter Paul sets up his own apostolic practice as an example of liberty conditioned by love: he emphasizes his rights (9.1-14), only to explain why he refuses to claim them (9.15-27).[151]

Paul's theology of Christian liberty as a passage between the Scylla of over-stipulative legalism and the Charybdis of self-indulgent license can be simply illustrated:

$$\text{LICENSE} \; \frac{\text{L \quad I \quad B \quad E \quad R \quad T \quad Y}}{\text{LOVE} \qquad\qquad\qquad\qquad \text{LOVE}} \; \text{LEGALISM}$$

The liberty of the Christian is itself a spectrum embracing considerable diversity. But it is ever threatened by those who find it necessary to insist on "faith plus" (that is, plus whatever their tradition counts as the essential concomitant of faith). And equally by those whose reaction against all tradition and guidelines cuts away too much that is of proven excellence and worthy of praise. The narrow margins between liberty and legalism on the one side and between liberty and license on the other can be maintained only by an active and outgoing love.

Paul, then, can be given credit for being the first to define Christian liberty. The way he does so makes an interesting and instructive comparison and contrast with one of the classic statements of individual liberty. According to John Stuart Mill,[152]

> the only freedom which deserves the name is that of pursuing our own good in our own way, so long as we do not attempt to deprive others of theirs or impede their efforts to obtain it.

---

150. For illustration of how Paul saw this as working out in practice see further below §24.7.

151. See further above §§21.2c and 23.5.

152. J. S. Mill, *On Liberty* (1859; Harmondsworth: Penguin, 1985) 72.

What is lacking in Mill's definition is the sense of liberty as something to be used *on behalf of others*.[153] In contrast, Paul saw liberty not simply as the prized right of the individual to pursue his or her own interests, but as the right of the individual in community, where rights were conditioned not only by the rights of others, but still more by active responsibility for others. It is this sense of rights married to responsibilities, of liberty exercised in love of neighbour, which marks out Paul's ethic of liberty and makes it such a powerful social, not to say political, principle.

§23.7 Traditional wisdom

One further point needs to be made, lest it be lost to sight in the various emphases which have now come to the fore. It is simply to reiterate and further elaborate the fact that Paul's new ethic of faith and Spirit, of Christ and love did not mean a wholly new and unheard-of ethos and ethic. In effect we have been underscoring the point throughout this chapter by emphasizing the continuing role of the law in Paul's ethic. But for completeness we need to recall how much of Paul's ethical teaching echoes older teaching in content and form.

a) Earlier on we noted how much of Paul's condemnation of Gentile morality was a reflection of traditional Jewish wisdom teaching.[154] We will see shortly that he drew on the same treasures of Jewish wisdom in other paraenesis (§24.2). A good case can also be made for the view that Paul's ethics were influenced by the already well-established ideas that certain fundamental laws were applicable also to Gentiles (the basis of the subsequent rabbinic doctrine of the Noahide commandments).[155] Hence Paul's unwillingness to yield on sexual immorality *(porneia)* and on food offered to idols.[156] Paul's insistence that human conduct and discharge of responsibilities will be judged by an impartial Judge is equally a motif drawn directly from his own heritage.[157] At the same time, his readiness to put the grounds

---

153. We may compare the contrast between Hillel's negative "golden rule" ("That which you hate, do not do to your fellows; this is the whole law" — *b. Shabbath* 31a) and the positive form it takes in the Jesus tradition ("In everything do to others as you would have them do to you" — Matt. 7.12). See further my brief treatment, *Christian Liberty: A New Testament Perspective* (1991 Didsbury Lectures; Carlisle: Paternoster, 1993/Grand Rapids: Eerdmans, 1994).

154. See above §4 n. 23 and §4.4.

155. Segal, *Paul* 187-223; M. Bockmuehl, "The Noachide Commandments and New Testamnent Ethics," *RB* 102 (1995) 72-101 (here 96-100).

156. See below §§24.4, 7; and Tomson, *Paul and the Jewish Law* chs. 3-5.

157. See above §§2.4 and 18.6. See also Finsterbusch, *Thora* 15-30.

of judgment in the broadest possible terms ("good" and "bad" — Rom. 2.7-10)[158] indicates a willingness to appeal to a fundamental sense in humankind of right and wrong. A similar inference can be drawn from Paul's readiness to appeal to the reaction of non-Christians as a factor influencing Christian conduct.[159]

In contrast, the resistance to any acknowledgment of Paul's dependence on his scriptures (the OT) for his paraenesis is one of the curiosities of twentieth-century exegesis.[160] The reason is, no doubt, partly the sharpness of the law/gospel antithesis, so fundamental in much Reformation theology; partly also the lack of sensitivity to the scriptural allusions and echoes which are such a feature of Paul's letters.[161] Indeed, if the above line of reflection is sound, Paul cited scriptural authority only when arguing a controversial line, whereas his paraenesis usually lacks much explicit scriptural reference precisely because the paraenesis was uncontroversial; an allusion was sufficient. In other words, the authority of scripture as a continuing criterion for Christian conduct is for the most part simply presupposed.[162] It was scripture understood in the light of Christ,[163] but it was still authoritative scripture.

b) The most obvious features of Pauline paraenesis which echo traditional formulations are his vice and virtue lists. The vice lists are more common[164] and

---

158. See further my *Romans* 85-86.

159. E.g., Rom. 14.16; 1 Cor. 10.31-33; 1 Thes. 4.11-12; 5.15. See W. C. van Unnik, "Die Rucksicht auf die Reaktion der nicht-Christen als Motiv in der altchristlichen Paränese," *Sparsa Collecta* (NovTSup 30; Leiden: Brill, 1980) 2.307-22; J. M. G. Barclay, "Conflict in Thessalonica," *CBQ* 55 (1993) 512-30 (here 520-25). See also below.

160. See above n. 26.

161. One need only follow up the many references in the margins of the Aland Greek text. See also Finsterbusch, *Thora* 108-84: the "semantic field" of Paul's parenesis is a "Torah field" (referring particularly to *peripateō, phroneō, areskō/euarestos, agathos, teleios, thelēma,* and *pneuma*); and below §24.2b.

162. So also, e.g., Furnish, *Theology* 28-44; Schrage, *Ethics* 205; T. Holtz, "The Question of the Content of Paul's Instructions," in Rosner, ed., *Understanding* 51-71; Rosner, *Paul, Scripture and Ethics* (§24 n. 1); R. B. Hays, "The Role of Scripture in Paul's Ethics," in Lovering and Sumney, *Theology and Ethics* 30-47.

163. See above §7.2.

164.

Rom. 1.29-31	Rom. 13.13	1 Cor. 5.10-11	1 Cor. 6.9-10
unrighteousness	revelry	sexually immoral	immoral
wickedness	drunkenness	greedy	idolaters
greediness	debauchery	robber	adulterers
badness	sexual excess	idolater	effeminate
jealousy	quarreling	slanderer	practising
murder	selfish envy	drunkard	homosexuals
rivalry			thieves

the virtue lists often less extensive.[165] As the references at the end of each list indicate, neither is peculiar to Paul within the New Testament, or to Christian or

Rom. 1.29-31	Rom. 13.13	1 Cor. 5.10-11	1 Cor. 6.9-10
deceit			greedy
spite			drunkards
rumour-mongers			slanderers
slanderers			robbers
God-haters			
insolent			
arrogant			
braggarts			
contrivers of evil			
disobedient to parents			
senseless			
faithless			
loveless			
merciless			

2 Cor. 12.20	Gal. 5.19-21	Col. 3.5, 8
quarreling	sexual immorality	sexual immorality
jealousy	impurity	impurity
anger	debauchery	passion
selfishness	idolatry	evil desire
backbiting	sorcery	greed = idolatry
gossip	hostile feelings/actions	anger
conceit	strife	rage
disorder	jealousy	malice
	displays of anger	slander
	selfish ambitions	abusive language
	dissensions	
	factions	
	envyings	
	drunkenness	
	excessive feasting	

See also particularly Wis. 14.25-26; *4 Macc.* 1.26-27; 2.15; 1QS 4.9-11; CD 4.17-19; Philo, *Sac.* 32; *T. Reub.* 3.3-6; *T. Levi* 17.11; *2 Enoch* 10.4-5; *3 Baruch* 8.5; 13.4; Mark 7.21-22; 1 Tim. 1.9-10; 2 Tim. 3.2-5; Tit. 3.3; 1 Pet. 4.3; Rev. 22.15; *1 Clement* 35.5; *Didache* 2–5; *Barnabas* 18-20. See further Lietzmann, *Römer* 35-36; A. Vögtle, *Die Tugend- und Lasterkataloge im Neuen Testament* (Münster: Aschendorff, 1936); S. Wibbing, *Die Tugend- und Lasterkataloge im Neuen Testament und ihre Traditionsgeschichte unter besonderer Berücksichtigung der Qumran-Texte* (BZNW 25; Berlin: Töpelmann, 1959); E. Kamlah, *Die Form der katalogischen Paränese im Neuen Testament* (Tübingen: Mohr, 1964); other illustrations of both vice and virtue lists in Malherbe, *Moral Exhortation* 138-41.

165.
2 Cor. 6.6	Gal. 5.22-23	Phil. 4.8	Col. 3.12
purity	love	true	compassion
knowledge	joy	honourable	kindness
patience	peace	just	humility

Jew or Greek.[166] This is not simply to say that the form was more or less universal across the eastern Mediterranean. It is also to recognize that the sort of ethical and moral concerns which Paul displays in these lists were also typical of those elsewhere concerned for ethical probity and moral restraint. It would simply be wrong, then, to imagine that Christianity brought an entirely new ethos and moral integrity into the world.[167] Much of its ethical teaching was conventional. And none the worse for that. It would be a peculiarly crass arrogance for Christians to believe that they had been given a unique moral sense or to be embarrassed because their ethical teaching did not mark them out completely from all others. On the contrary, Paul had no hesitation in aligning himself with the wisdom of previous generations, as it had been learned, often at bitter expense, by both Jew and Greek.

We can be more precise. Paul shared a common distaste for various vices. For example, *pleonexia* (literally "desire to have more," so "greediness, insatiableness, covetousness") was a widely condemned vice and an obvious item for inclusion in Stoic and other catalogues of vice.[168] And most if not all of the items in the list in Rom. 13.13 would have been the subject of widespread censure.[169] Equally, the list in Phil. 4.8-9 deliberately appeals to what was generally regarded as "virtue" and as "praiseworthy"; though in comparison with its prominence elsewhere, this single reference to "virtue" *(aretē)* is striking, and the complete absence of any reference to the elsewhere highly prized *eudaimonia* ("well-being, happiness") reminds us that Paul's priorities were differently directed.[170] Paul's commendation of "self-control" *(enkrateia)* would have found resonance in Greek philosophical ethics,[171] and

2 Cor. 6.6	Gal. 5.22-23	Phil. 4.8	Col. 3.12
kindness	patience	pure	gentleness
love	kindness	lovely	patience
truthful speech	goodness	gracious	putting up with others
	faith		forgiving each other
	gentleness		
	self-control		

See also, e.g., 1QS 4.2-8; Philo, *Sac.* 27; *Virt.* 182; Josephus, *Ap.* 2.146. And elsewhere in the NT, Eph. 4.2; 1 Tim. 4.12; 6.11; 2 Tim. 2.22; 3.10; 2 Pet. 1.5-7.

166. "The conventional morality of the time" (Betz, *Galatians* 282-83).

167. Furnish: "Paul's concern is not to be 'original' or to foster a morality of exclusively 'Christian' content" (*Theology* 72).

168. Rom. 1.29; 2 Cor. 9.5; Col. 3.5; 1 Thes. 2.5; also Eph. 4.19 and 5.3. See BAGD, *pleonexia;* G. Delling, *TDNT* 6.267-70.

169. *Euschēmonōs,* "decently," is an appeal to what would generally be regarded as decent, proper, presentable in responsible society (see further BAGD; H. Greeven, *TDNT* 2.771); so also in 1 Cor. 14.40 and 1 Thes. 4.12.

170. Keck, "Rethinking" 9-10.

171. *Enkrateia* was reckoned a cardinal virtue by Socrates and given full treatment

"gentleness" too was a highly prized virtue, though Greek thought typically recognized that it could be taken to extreme.[172] His condemnation of homosexual acts uses the Stoic criterion of what is "fitting,"[173] though the condemnation itself is thoroughly Jewish, as distinct from Hellenistic.[174] Similarly, his repeated abhorrence of idolatry is distinctively Jewish.[175] More distinctively Christian would be the exaltation of love to its place of prominence in 1 Corinthians 13 and Gal. 5.22[176] and the high regard for "humility."[177] Moreover, the diversity of the Pauline lists is clear enough indication that he was not simply transposing ready-made catalogues from elsewhere. Rather, the particular emphases of individual lists like Gal. 5.19-21 and Col. 3.5 strongly suggest that the items were chosen to address what were perceived as potential dangers threatening the communities in view — in Galatians divisive factionalism,[178] in Colossians sexual immorality.[179]

Much of Paul's ethical teaching, then, drew on traditional wisdom. It was presumably his awareness of a high degree of shared ethos and moral sense among people of good will which allowed him to talk of final judgment simply in terms of "good" rewarded and "evil" punished (Rom. 2.6-11). Hence also his confidence in appealing to "conscience" and in referring to those who "do by nature what the law requires" (Rom. 2.14-15).[180] He would have been sufficiently confident of a well-developed sense of right and wrong in the societies in which he mingled. At the same time, by setting love so prominently in his ethical teaching, and always with the thought of "the law of Christ" in the back of his mind, Paul no doubt looked for a quality of personal relationship and community which was only seldom achieved.

---

in Aristotle's *Ethics* (W. Grundmann, *TDNT* 2.340). Stowers sees the theme of self-mastery as central for the interpretation of Romans (*Rereading* 42-82), although the supporting evidence is at best tangential (5.3-4; 7.18; 12.3) and the thesis sits awkwardly with the stress on divine initiative (as, e.g., in 1.16-17 and 5.6-10).

172. F. Hauck and S. Schulz, *TDNT* 6.646.

173. See BAGD, *kathēkō;* and further above §2 n. 101 and §5 nn. 102 and 103.

174. See my *Romans* 65-66.

175. See again my *Romans* 61 and above §2.2.

176. See above §13 n. 15 and §21.6b.

177. Phil. 2.3; Col. 3.12. For Greek thought generally "humility" was too closely related to servility for it to serve as a positive virtue (W. Grundmann, *TDNT* 8.1-4, 11-12).

178. "Hostile actions, strife, jealousy, displays of anger, selfish ambitions, dissensions, factions, envyings." See, e.g., Barclay, *Obeying* 153, who also observes that the subsequent maxims "represent Paul's desire to give concrete instructions, to spell out for the Galatians in practical terms what it means to 'walk in the Spirit' " (167).

179. "Unlawful sex, uncleanness, passion, evil desire."

180. See further Schnackenburg, *Botschaft* 2.48-58 (with bibliography).

c) The other common form[181] which we find regularly in the paraenesis of the later letters is the table of household rules *(Haustafel)*. These letters begin to fall outside our purview, but since they correlate with emphases in the earlier Pauline teaching we should mention the tables here briefly. The first and best example in fact comes in Colossians and so may express Paul's own developing thinking on the subject — Col. 3.18–4.1:[182]

> [18]Wives, be subject to your husbands, as is fitting in the Lord. [19]Husbands, love your wives and do not become embittered toward them. [20]Children, obey your parents in everything, for this is pleasing in the Lord. [21]Fathers, do not provoke your children, that they may not lose heart.
>
> [22]Slaves, obey in everything those who are your masters in terms of the flesh, not with eye service as men-pleasers, but with sincerity of heart, fearing the Lord. [23]Whatever you do, put yourself wholly into it, as to the Lord and not to human beings, [24]knowing that you will receive from the Lord the reward of the inheritance. The master you are slave to is Christ. [25]For the wrongdoer will be paid back for the wrong done, and there is no favoritism. [1]Masters, grant your slaves what is just and fair, knowing that you also have a master in heaven.

The lengthy debate on the origin of these household rules has been recently resolved. In the past twenty years or so several scholars in quick succession have recognized that the model for the Christian household rules, insofar as there was one, was that of *oikonomia,* "household management."[183] The point

---

181. Moving beyond a specific focus on ethics we could also instance especially hardship lists; see particularly J. T. Fitzgerald, *Cracks in an Earthen Vessel: An Examination of the Catalogues of Hardships in the Corinthian Correspondence* (SBLDS 99; Atlanta: Scholars, 1988). D. Balch, et al., eds., *Greeks, Romans and Christians,* A. J. Malherbe FS (Minneapolis: Fortress, 1990), illustrates the range of discussion on the interaction of early Christians with Greco-Roman culture. Of Malherbe's contributions, see particularly *Paul and the Thessalonians: The Philosophic Tradition of Pastoral Care* (Philadelphia: Fortress, 1987) — "Paul consciously used the conventions of his day in attempting to shape a community with its own identity, and he did so with considerable originality" (109) — and " 'Pastoral Care' in the Thessalonian Church," *NTS* 36 (1990) 375-91.

182. See also especially Eph. 5.22–6.9; 1 Pet. 2.18–3.7; but also 1 Tim. 2.8-15; 6.1-2; Tit. 2.1-10; *Didache* 4.9-11; *Barnabas* 19.5-7; *1 Clement* 21.6-9; Ignatius, *Polycarp* 4.1–5.2; Polycarp, *Philippians* 4.2-3. For what follows I draw on my "The Household Rules in the New Testament," in S. C. Barton, ed., *The Family in Theological Perspective* (Edinburgh: Clark, 1996) 43-63.

183. See particularly D. Lührmann, "Wo man nicht mehr Sklave oder Frei ist. Überlegungen zur Struktur frühchristlicher Gemeinden," *Wort und Dienst* 13 (1975) 53-83 (especially 76-80); "Neutestamentliche Haustafeln und antike Ökonomie," *NTS* 27 (1980-81) 83-97; K. Thraede, "Zum historischen Hintergrund der 'Haustafeln' des NT," in

is that the household was widely recognized to be the basic unit of the state. As part of the state's good ordering, therefore, it was necessary to deal with the household's basic relationships — that is, of husband to wife, father to children, and master to slave.[184]

This is not to say that Colossians and subsequent Christian writers simply took over standard formulae. Col. 3.18–4.1 is itself the purest example of the *Haustafel* "form." And concerns for relationships within the household often feature as part of more widely ranging social concerns. Nevertheless, we can speak of common concerns regarding household management among ethical and political thinkers of the time, which early Christian writers evidently shared. Within that general concern we can also note features which would otherwise be called characteristically Stoic.[185] And the lengthy section addressed to slaves uses repeated Jewish motifs.[186] At the same time, however, we can hardly avoid noting the characteristic and distinctively Christian features, most notably the sevenfold reference to "the Lord."[187]

All this raises important questions for a critical evaluation of earliest Christian ethics. In particular, to what extent were such *Haustafeln* simply conforming to the world, compromising not least with conservative social structures, which they ought to have been questioning? We will be able to take up some of these issues when we look at how Paul's ethics worked in practice (§24). For the moment, however, it is important to realize that in the realm of household management there was also a recognition among the first Christians of "good practice" elsewhere and a readiness to support good order in both household and state.

E. Dassmann and K. S. Frank, eds., *Pietas,* B. Kötting FS (Münster: Aschendorff, 1980) 359-68; and especially D. Balch, *Let Wives Be Submissive: The Domestic Code in 1 Peter* (SBLMS 26; Chico: Scholars, 1981).

184. E.g., Aristotle, *Politics* 1.1253b 1-14; Dio Chrysostom 5.348-51 (Loeb); Seneca, *Epistles* 94.1; Dionysius of Halicarnassus, *Roman Antiquities* 2.25.4–26.4 (all cited in Balch, *Wives* [above n. 183]).

185. Again the concept of what is "fitting" (*anēken* — Col. 3.18) and what is "pleasing" (*euarestos* — Col. 3.20). On the subjection of wives see above §21.4 and n. 129.

186. "Sincerity of heart, fearing the Lord . . . you will receive from the Lord the reward of the inheritance . . . the wrongdoer will be paid back for the wrong he has done, and there is no favouritism"; see, e.g., K. Müller, "Die Haustafel des Kolosserbriefes und das antike Frauenthema: Eine kritische Rückschau auf alte Ergebnisse," in G. Dautzenberg, et al., *Die Frau im Urchristentum* (QD 95; Freiburg: Herder, 1983) 263-319 (here 273-75); and again my *Colossians* 254-59.

187. "As is fitting *in the Lord*" (3.18); "this is pleasing *in the Lord*" (3.20); "fearing *the Lord*" (3.22); "*as to the Lord*" (3.23); "you will receive *from the Lord*" (3.24); "you serve *the Lord, Christ*" (3.24); "you have *a lord in heaven*" (4.1).

§23.8 Conclusions

The principles underlying Paul's ethics are fairly easy to pick out and document. Among several notable features already discussed there is one other which deserves some mention at the end. That is the balance Paul evidently sought to maintain between what we might call internal motivation and external norm.[188]

The external norm can be variously defined. It can be defined in terms of traditional wisdom, vices and virtues commonly recognized as such, notions of what is right and wrong accepted by all those of good will, ideas of communal interdependence and good order at the heart of society. In each case, however, a Christian perspective and memory of Christ's love and self-giving adds a distinctive further element which infuses the whole. Again, given the through and through Jewish background of Pauline Christianity, the external norm, not surprisingly, may also be defined as the law. But this is the law insofar as it expresses faith, the law insofar as it has been reinforced by Christ, both his teaching and his example. That means also the law lived out in accord with the principles of faith and love of neighbour, the competing claims of the law prioritized and shown their relative importance by faith and love.[189] This does not imply a simple division of moral law from ceremonial law, for faith and love, the norm of Christ, can reinforce both and relativize both. The end result may be similar, but the principle for discerning the will of God in particular events applies to the whole law. From case to case it can result in a living "under the law" as well as a living "outside the law," but always "in-lawed to Christ" (*ennomos Christou* — 1 Cor. 9.21). Nor does such a redefinition of the law exclude or diminish the fundamental function of the law as the measure of God's judgment.[190] Within the new regime of "the law of Christ" the law still indicates responsibility for others and accountability before God. Judgment in terms of the law is also "in accordance with (Paul's) gospel" (Rom. 2.12-16).

The internal motivation combines the inner calm of trust which knows that it cannot do other than trust and the inner compulsion of the Spirit. The renewed mind, its starting point ever its dependence on God for illumination and wisdom, seeks to know the will of God, the mind of Christ. What Paul means by that process is presumably indicated by other key motifs in his

---

188. See also Schrage, *Einzelgebote* 71-93; Longenecker, *Paul* ch. 8; Deidun, *New Covenant Morality* Part IV.

189. Cf. Hays, *Moral Vision* 43: "The ethical norm . . . is not given in the form of a predetermined rule or set of rules for conduct; rather, the right action must be *discerned* on the basis of a christological paradigm, with a view to the need of the community." "The fundamental norm of Pauline ethics is the christomorphic life" (46).

190. See above §§6.3 and 18.6.

ethical thought — living "in Christ" and seeking to act "in the Lord," desiring earnestly to know the law of God written in the heart, rejoicing in one's liberty but ready equally to guard that liberty against the subtle encroachments of legalism and license. Not least he would expect his readers to recall always that the believer is not an isolated individual, with rights in the face of others and no responsibilities. On the contrary, grace received meant for Paul charism for the benefit of others, and liberty meant opportunity to serve others. To love one's neighbour as much as oneself meant in practice seeking the benefit of others before one's own.

Not least of importance was Paul's recognition that *both* the outward norm *and* the inward motivation were essential for ethical living. Without the spontaneous inward compulsion, the external norm would quickly degenerate into "letter" and thence to legalism, and the self-regulating, or better, body-regulating, principle of charism would degenerate into routine and rule. But equally, without the external norm, the internal compulsion would become a law unto itself and Christian conduct become antinomian and guru-led. Both are needed. The Christian needs to be led by the Spirit. Conduct as well as charism needs to be a manifestation of the Spirit. But unless it is also a manifestation of love, it is not the Spirit of Christ behind it. At the same time, without the Spirit the discernment of what really matters is not possible. And without love even the most self-sacrificial, spiritual, and even faithful acts can be worth nothing (1 Cor. 13.1-3).

So much for the statement of principle. How did Paul expect it to work in practice?

§24 Ethics in practice[1]

1. **Bibliography**: §24.2 — **J. D. G. Dunn**, "Romans 13.1-7 — A Charter for Political Quietism?" *Ex Auditu* 2 (1986) 55-68; **O. Cullmann**, *The State in the New Testament* (New York: Scribner/London: SCM, 1956); **J. Friedrich, W. Pöhlmann, and P. Stuhlmacher**, "Zur historischen Situation und Intention von Röm. 13.1-7," *ZTK* 73 (1976) 131-66; **V. P. Furnish**, *The Moral Teaching of Paul: Selected Issues* (Nashville: Abingdon, 1979) 115-41; **H. Merklein**, "Sinn und Zweck von Röm. 13.1-7," in H. Merklein, ed., *Neues Testament und Ethik,* R. Schnackenburg FS (Freiburg: Herder, 1989) 238-70; **F. J. Ortkemper**, *Leben aus dem Glauben: Christliche Grundhaltungen nach Römer 12–13* (Münster: Aschendorff, 1980); **P. Perkins**, *Love Commands in the New Testament* (New York: Paulist, 1982); **J. Piper**, *"Love Your Enemies": Jesus' Love Command in the Synoptic Gospels and the Early Christian Paraenesis* (SNTSMS 38; Cambridge: Cambridge University, 1979); **A. Strobel**, "Zum Verständnis von Röm. 13," *ZNW* 47 (1956) 67-93; **U. Wilckens**, "Röm. 13.1-7," *Rechtfertigung* 203-45; **W. T. Wilson**, *Love without Pretense: Romans 12.9-21 and Hellenistic Jewish Wisdom Literature* (WUNT 2.46; Tübingen: Mohr, 1991).

§24.3 — **J.-M. Cambier**, "La liberté chrétienne est et personnelle et communautaire (Rom. 14.1–15.13)," in L. de Lorenzi, ed., *Freedom and Love: The Guide for Christian Life (1 Cor. 8–10; Rom. 14–15)* (Rome: Abbey of St. Paul, 1981) 57-84; **R. Jewett**, *Christian Tolerance: Paul's Message to the Modern Church* (Philadelphia: Westminster, 1982); **R. J. Karris**, "Romans 14.1–15.13 and the Occasion of Romans," in Donfried, ed., *Romans Debate* 65-84; **W. A. Meeks**, "Judgment and the Brother: Romans 14.1–15.13," in G. F. Hawthorne and O. Betz, eds., *Tradition and Interpretation in the New Testament,* E. E. Ellis FS (Grand Rapids: Eerdmans/Tübingen: Mohr, 1987) 290-300; **M. Rauer**, *Die "Schwachen" in Korinth und Rom nach den Paulusbriefen* (Freiburg: Herder, 1923).

§24.4 — **B. Byrne**, "Sinning against One's Own Body: Paul's Understanding of the Sexual Relationship in 1 Corinthians 6.18," *CBQ* 45 (1983) 608-16; **L. W. Countryman**, *Dirt, Greed and Sex: Sexual Ethics in the New Testament and Their Implications for Today* (Philadelphia: Fortress, 1988); **G. Dautzenberg**, *"Pheugete porneian* (1 Kor. 6.18). Eine Fallstudie zur paulinischen Sexualethik in ihren Verhältnis zur Sexualethik des Frühjudentums," in H. Merklein, ed., *Neues Testament und Ethik,* R. Schnackenburg FS (Freiburg: Herder, 1989) 271-98; **B. N. Fisk**, *"PORNEUEIN* as Body Violation: The Unique Nature of Sexual Sin in 1 Corinthians 6.18," *NTS* 42 (1996) 540-58; **J. Jensen**, "Does *Porneia* Mean Fornication?" *NovT* 20 (1978) 161-84; **Martin**, *Corinthian Body* (§3 n. 1) 168-79; **B. S. Rosner**, *Paul, Scripture and Ethics: A Study of 1 Corinthians 5–7* (Leiden: Brill, 1994).

§24.5 — **D. Balch**, "1 Cor. 7.32-35 and Stoic Debates about Marriage, Anxiety and Distraction," *JBL* 102 (1983) 429-39; **N. Baumert**, *Ehelosigkeit und Ehe im Herrn.*

Eine Neuinterpretation von 1 Kor. 7 (Würzburg: Echter, 1984); *Woman and Man* (§21 n. 1) 25-131; **R. Cartlidge**, "1 Corinthians 7 as a Foundation for a Christian Sex Ethic," *JR* 55 (1975) 220-34; **W. Deming**, *Paul on Marriage and Celibacy: The Hellenistic Background of 1 Corinthians 7* (SNTSMS 83; Cambridge: Cambridge University, 1995); **Furnish**, *Moral Teaching* (as above) 30-51; **Keck**, *Paul* 112-15; **M. Y. MacDonald**, "Early Christian Women Married to Unbelievers," *Studies in Religion/Sciences Religieuses* 19 (1990) 221-34; **Martin**, *Corinthian Body* (§3 n. 1) 198-228; **Merklein**, " 'Es ist gut für den Menschen, eine Frau nicht anzufassen': Paulus und die Sexualität nach 1 Kor. 7," *Studien* 385-408; **K. Niederwimmer**, *Askese und Mysterium: Über Ehe, Ehescheidung und Eheverzicht in den Anfängen des christlichen Glaubens* (FRLANT 113; Göttingen: Vandenhoeck, 1975); **V. L. Wimbush**, *Paul the Worldly Ascetic: Response to the World and Self-Understanding according to 1 Corinthians 7* (Macon: Mercer University, 1987); **L. O. Yarbrough**, *Not Like the Gentiles: Marriage Rules in the Letters of Paul* (SBLDS 80; Atlanta: Scholars, 1985).

§24.6 — **J. M. G. Barclay**, "Paul, Philemon and the Dilemma of Christian Slave-Ownership," *NTS* 37 (1991) 161-86; **S. S. Bartchy**, *MALLON CHRESAI: First-Century Slavery and the Interpretation of 1 Corinthians 7.21* (SBLDS 11; Missoula: Scholars, 1973); **H. Bellen**, *Studien zur Sklavenflucht im römischen Kaiserreich* (Forschungen zur antiken Skaverei 4; Wiesbaden: Steiner, 1971); **R. Gayer**, *Die Stellung des Sklaven in den paulinischen Gemeinden und bei Paulus. Zugleich ein sozialgeschichtlich vergleichender Beitrag zur Wertung des Sklaven in der Antike* (Bern: Lang, 1976); **Horrell**, *Social Ethos*; **D. B. Martin**, *Slavery as Salvation: The Metaphor of Slavery in Pauline Christianity* (New Haven: Yale University, 1990); **S. C. Winter**, "Paul's Letter to Philemon," *NTS* 33 (1987) 1-15.

§24.7 — **C. K. Barrett**, "Things Sacrificed to Idols," *Essays* 40-59; **A. T. Cheung**, *Idol Food in Corinth: An Examination of Paul's Approach in the Light of Its Background in Ancient Judaism and Legacy in Early Christianity* (JSNTS; Sheffield: Sheffield Academic, 1997); **G. D. Fee**, "*Eidōlothuta* Once Again: An Interpretation of 1 Corinthians 8–10," *Bib* 61 (1980) 172-97; **P. W. Gooch**, *Dangerous Food: 1 Corinthians 8–10 in Its Context* (Waterloo: Wilfrid Laurier University, 1993); **Heil**, *Ablehnung* (§14 n. 1) 177-235; **R. A. Horsley**, "Consciousness and Freedom among the Corinthians: 1 Corinthians 8–10," *CBQ* 40 (1978) 574-89; **Jaquette**, *Discerning What Counts* (§23 n. 1) 137-53; **J. J. Meggitt**, "Meat Consumption and Social Conflict in Corinth," *JTS* (1994) 137-41; **J. Murphy-O'Connor**, "Freedom or the Ghetto (1 Cor. 8.1-13; 10.23–11.1)," in L. de Lorenzi, ed., *Freedom and Love: The Guide for Christian Life (1 Cor. 8–10; Rom. 14–15)* (Rome: Abbey of St. Paul, 1981) 7-38; **T. Söding**, "Starke und Schwache. Der Götzenopferstreit in 1 Kor. 8–10 als Paradigma paulinischer Ethik," *ZNW* 85 (1994) 69-92; **Theissen**, "The Strong and the Weak in Corinth: A Sociological Analysis of a Theological Quarrel," *Social Setting* 121-43; **Tomson**, *Paul* (§23 n. 1) 151-220; **Willis**, *Idol Meat* (§22 n. 1); **B. W. Winter**, "Theological and Ethical Responses to Religious Pluralism — 1 Corinthians 8–10," *TynB* 41 (1990) 209-26.

§24.8 — **R. D. Aus**, "Paul's Travel Plans to Spain and the 'Full Number of the Gentiles' of Rom. 11.25," *NovT* 21 (1979) 232-62; **J. M. Bassler**, *God and Mammon: Asking for Money in the New Testament* (Nashville: Abingdon, 1991) ch. 4; **D. Georgi**, *Remembering the Poor: The History of Paul's Collection for Jerusalem* (1965; Nashville: Abingdon, 1992); **Harrison**, *Paul's Language of Grace* (§13 n. 1) ch. 7; **Munck**, *Paul* 282-308; **K. F. Nickle**, *The Collection: A Study in Paul's Strategy* (London: SCM, 1966); **Zeller**, *Juden und Heiden* 224-36.

§24.1 The social context

If it was important to ask how Paul's ecclesiology worked out in practice, the same question is even more pressing in the case of his ethics. Too many ideologies claiming to promote the commonweal have failed in practice, broken on the rocks of human greed, vested interest, fear of change, or dogged intransigence. Alternatively expressed in terms of Paul's own theological critique, they have failed to appreciate the reality of the power of sin and the inescapable constraints of the eschatological tension. Both laissez-faire liberalism and eastern European Communism fell at the same hurdle. Christianity's own record is at best mixed. So how did Paul's ethical principles work in the event? Such principles will always be subject to the test of the practice they produce. And though the resulting practice may not be a fair reflection of the principles, it will certainly tell us how realistic were the principles within the social context of the age.

Paul's ethic, of course, operated with ultimate constraints, both as a promise and a threat, with his talk both of a kingdom yet to be inherited[2] and a final judgment yet to be faced.[3] But this was not a way of avoiding hard ethical issues of the time. Rather, these were inducements to present conduct.[4] And Paul's own timescale did not envisage an ethical or social programme extending across several generations.[5] So it is fair to ask how he attempted to put his ideals and principles into practice in the immediate situations with which he was confronted and in the short term. After all, it was Jesus who is recalled as giving the dictum: "You will know them by their fruits" (Matt. 7.16, 20).

A further consideration is that Paul's ethics cannot be dealt with solely under the heading of personal ethics. His concern at every turn was with social interaction. We have already observed that his understanding of the process of salvation is integrally corporate in character, that he reacted strongly against any thought of a maturity not dependent on and interdependent with the community of faith. The individual as individual, therefore, could hardly hope to live out Paul's ethical principles solely on his or her own. Too much depended on a wisdom which was corporate, whether as tradition or as fresh insight, and, either way, not least as to its interpretation. The fact that Paul put his exposition of the body of Christ at the beginning of his paraenesis in Romans 12 is itself an indication that he did not think of its imagery of mutual interdependence as applicable solely to matters of worship. And if he was

2. 1 Cor. 6.9-10; 15.50; Gal. 5.21.
3. See above §§2.4 and 18.6.
4. Note particularly 1 Cor. 3.12-15.
5. See further above §12.4. Here we should note particularly Rom. 13.11-14.

conscious of the origin of the image in political rhetoric, as is probable, he may even have thought of the church of Christ as a model of what all social (and not just religious) community should be.

In asking how Paul's ethical principles worked in practice, therefore, it is important to recall the reality of Paul's social world and that/those of his churches. In every case he was dealing with small social groups (churches) which were composed of individuals and households of diverse ethnic backgrounds, religious traditions, and social status. The identity of these groups was still in process of formation, with their boundaries usually fluid or shifting. Core beliefs, shared experience, and practice of baptism and the Lord's Supper were sufficiently consistent to provide a recognizable identity and powerful bonding factors. But as we have seen, interpretation of the beliefs and experience and diversity of the practice left the boundaries less well defined. Furthermore, the groups often functioned within large cities, themselves still more diverse in composition and character. They were very small units within a social context shaped by powerful political and economic interests. The interface between the churches and their social context, the movement across the boundaries (out and in), and the tensions within the churches themselves are all factors to be borne in mind when talking about Paul's ethics in practice.

All this comes to a head when we realize that most of the really pressing ethical questions were posed by clashes of tradition among members of traditional communities, clashes both within the churches and across their boundaries. In no case could the issue be reduced to a simple statement of principle with a straightforward application to follow. For the principle itself could not be stated without reference to both tradition and the community, and its application was often at the heart of the dispute. Nowhere more clearly than here do we see the reality of the already–not yet of Paul's theology, as principle and practice inevitably reflected the tension and often unsatisfactory compromises made unavoidable by the not yet.

The most obvious way to proceed, then, is to take a sample of hard cases with which Paul had to deal. The more concrete the better, and the more information we have on social context the better. This points us to two letters in particular — Romans and 1 Corinthians. The former has been our principal Pauline text throughout, and we know more about the social conditions of Rome than those of anywhere else in the Roman Empire during this period. 1 Corinthians, because of its character, dealing with a sequence of ethical and social issues, has given us the fullest picture of any early church within its social context. In fact, between these two letters we cover as representative a range of Pauline ethical issues as we could hope for. And as we draw in comparative material from other letters at various points, the resulting picture will be about as comprehensive as we could wish for.

§24.2 *Living within a hostile world — Rom. 12.9–13.14*

When we look at the paraenesis in Romans a certain dualism becomes apparent. The perspective is that of an embattled colony of the imminent approaching day, but still surrounded and threatened by the night and "the works of darkness" (13.11-13). Whatever other positive contacts with the surrounding world are in view, a primary consideration had to be successful survival. All the more striking, then, is the positive way Paul addresses the situation. Here we can only focus on a number of key features.[6]

a) *The social reality.* In this section Paul's paraenesis is principally concerned with relationships between the Roman congregations and the surrounding community and civic authorities (particularly 12.14–13.7). Paul himself would hardly need reminding of the political realities which confronted these new small groups of believers within the cities of the Roman Empire. In this case in particular, he was evidently well aware of the fact that the little house churches within the imperial capital itself were endangered, vulnerable to the central government's suspicions of clubs and societies and not least to further imperial rulings against Jews.[7] The very transition in identity, which is implied in the transition from chs. 9–11 to ch. 12,[8] was itself rendering the churches' position ever more hazardous. For any group which was no longer simply ethnic in composition ("Israel," Jews) could soon find itself bereft of the protection granted specifically to the synagogue. The more sharply defined the *theological* identity of the church as nonethnic in character, the more vulnerable the *political* status of the church.

The details of Paul's instruction fill out the picture still more. In 12.14-21 Paul takes it for granted that persecution and acts of malice would be directed against the small house churches of Rome. That in itself speaks eloquently of the atmosphere of threat and intimidation within which these believers had to live out their discipleship. At the same time Paul takes it equally for granted that there would be considerable actual day-to-day contact between the members of the Roman house churches and the wider community — such as would require just the advice he gives about maintaining good relationships. Paul evidently entertained no thought of the Roman Christians compartmentalizing their lives or of living their lives cut off from the wider community.

---

6. For detailed exegesis see my *Romans* 736-94.

7. Details, e.g., in my *Romans* xlvi, xlviii-li. The archaeological and inscriptional data suggest that the Jews of Rome were largely poor and of low social status (Walters, *Ethnic Issues* 53-54). Contrast the church in Corinth with its significant number of members well integrated in civic society (see below §§24.4-7).

8. See above §20.1.

Likewise, the fact that the discussion in 13.1-7 builds up to the subject of paying taxes was presumably no accident. In fact, we know from near contemporary sources that the abuses of indirect taxation were causing increasing unrest within the capital at that time.[9] Paul must have been reasonably well informed of current affairs in Rome and would be well enough aware that Christian merchants and traders associated with the Jewish "superstition" were in a particularly defenceless situation. Failure of a number of Christians to pay even an inflated tax might well draw the authorities' attention to the little congregations and put them at serious risk. The Roman authorities had a well-developed system of spies and informers. So we should certainly allow for the possibility that some at least of Paul's exhortation was framed with the thought in mind that "walls have ears."

b) *The principles.* In these circumstances what were the principles Paul drew upon in his paraenesis? Two features stand out.

First and most noteworthy is the fact that he sets the whole sequence of exhortation under the rubric of love: "Let love be without pretence" (12.9).[10] Following as it does the description of the functioning body of Christ (12.3-8), the echo of his earlier treatment of the same theme in 1 Corinthians 12–14 cannot but be deliberate. Paul recognized that the vision of the charismatic community was unrealizable without love.[11] But he equally recognized that love itself could become formalized in expression, the outward form of a judgmental or dismissive spirit, a cloak of pretence hiding an agenda of personal advancement, a pretentious claim as manipulative as any coercive claim to charismatic authority. The principle of love required a higher practice, more of the order of 1 Cor. 13.4-7.

Equally, it will be no accident that the central section (Rom. 12.14–13.7) is bracketed by the double call for love (12.9; 13.8-10). The latter, as we have seen,[12] not only reaffirms and draws upon the richness of the law as a guide for ethical conduct, but also indicates how the law is to be interpreted through love of neighbour (as taught and lived by Jesus himself). The rubric

---

9. Tacitus, *Annals* 13 (details in my *Romans* liii-liv). The suggestion that the authorities in view are the *synagogue* authorities in Rome (Nanos, *Mystery* ch. 6) is most implausible: would Paul indeed have called on Gentile believers to subject themselves (13.1) to an unbelieving Jewish leadership and to pay the Temple tax (13.7)? He could hardly attribute the right of capital punishment (13.4; see my *Romans* 764) to synagogue authorities.

10. *Anypokritos,* "without hypocrisy, genuine, sincere," is used with reference to love again in 2 Cor. 6.6 and 1 Pet. 1.22, and with reference to faith in 1 Tim. 1.5 and 2 Tim. 1.5; elsewhere in biblical Greek only in Wis. 5.18; 18.16; Jas. 3.17. The *hypocritēs* was the "play actor" who projected an image and hid his true identity behind a mask.

11. See above §21.6b.

12. On 13.8-10 see above §23.5.

of love, as the primary principle of all conduct, is therefore intended to cover the whole of the following paraenesis.

We should note also, secondly, how closely Paul correlates being "aglow with the Spirit" and "serving the Lord" (12.11). The former imagery suggests a bubbling, burning enthusiasm, emotions fully engaged.[13] The latter suggests more firmness of intention and persistence of application. Together the two indicate the importance of the two sides in determining and sustaining Christian conduct — the inner motivation channeled in accord with the outward norm.[14]

Third, the passage is also rich in illustration of how Paul sought to draw on traditional wisdom and to appeal to standards more widely recognized. The counsel of 12.14-21 is chiefly rooted in Jewish traditional wisdom regarding human relationships.[15] The unusually heavy concentration of scriptural allusions indicates a strong concern on the part of Paul to root this most demanding of ethical obligations in the tried and tested wisdom of Jewish scripture and experience.[16] Similarly in 13.1-7 the basic rationale, that political authority is from God, was one which was long familiar in Jewish wisdom.[17] More to the point in the circumstances, it was a principle to which prophet and apocalyptist had clung even when confronted by the overwhelming might of a Nebuchadnezzar or faced by Syrian oppression. As Daniel repeatedly declared: "The Most High rules the kingdom of men and gives it to whom he will."[18] Likewise the implication that "fear" is the proper response to God-appointed authority (13.7) presumably echoes consciously or unconsciously the same generations-old wisdom.[19] Such assertions must have been particularly meaningful for Jews living in the diaspora, as aliens living under a foreign power, and often as slaves and dispossessed.

The echoes of Jesus tradition through this section are also noteworthy. (1) It is particularly strong in 12.14,[20] but since that verse sets the theme for

---

13. See further my *Romans* 742.

14. See above §23.8.

15. 12.15 — Sir. 7.34; 12.16 — Prov. 3.7 and Isa. 5.21; 12.17 — Prov. 3.4; 12.18 — Pss. 34.14; 12.19 — Lev. 19.18 and Deut. 32.35; 12.20 — Prov. 25.21-22; 12.21 — *T. Ben.* 4.3.

16. Cf. Piper, *"Love Your Enemies"* 113-14; see further Wilson, *Love without Pretense.*

17. 2 Sam. 12.8; Prov. 8.15-16; Sir. 10.4; 17.17; Wis. 6.3; *Ep. Arist.* 224; Josephus, *War* 2.140.

18. Dan. 4.17, 25, 32. See also Isa. 41.2-4; 45.1-7; Jer. 21.7, 10; 27.5-6; Dan. 2.21, 37-38; 5.21; *1 Enoch* 46.5; *2 Baruch* 82.9.

19. Prov. 24.21; *Ep. Arist.* 194. The theology was evidently able to embrace the reality of hostile and oppressive government just as it was able to cope with recognition of cosmic hostility and evil (see above §2.3).

20. See above §23.5.

what follows, the echo pervades the whole — by implication 12.17 and 21, and more explicitly 12.18. (2) Similarly an echo of Jesus' teaching in 13.7 can hardly be ruled out (Mark 12.17 pars.).[21] The theme is the same: the necessity of paying tribute. The sequence of 13.7, 8-10 is paralleled by the sequence Mark 12.13-17, 18-34.[22] And Luke 20.22, 25 renders the tradition in the same terms as Paul uses here.[23] This could well be the form, then, in which this important practical counsel of Jesus was remembered in the diaspora. (3) We have already discussed the likelihood that 13.8-10 was framed in conscious echo of Jesus' teaching on the love command.[24] The fact that the echo is quickly followed and the sequence of paraenesis concluded by a final call to "put on the Lord Jesus Christ" (13.14)[25] simply confirms that the character of Jesus' own life and ministry formed a constant norm and inspiration for Paul's own conception of Christian living.

At the same time, fourthly, we should also note that Paul did not hesitate to appeal to standards much more widely recognized and lauded. The categories of "evil" and "good" (12.9, 21) are again general.[26] The virtues of "brotherly love" and "family affection" (12.10) were widely commended.[27] The obligation to provide hospitality to the stranger (12.13) was likewise deeply rooted and highly regarded in ancient society.[28] The call to "take into consideration what is noble *(kalos)*[29] in the sight of everyone" (12.17) was in effect a call for behaviour which would not leave the Roman Christians exposed to the criticisms of Stoic or Cynic. Here again Paul shows himself ready to appeal to a widespread sense of what is morally right and fitting.[30] Similarly the argument in 13.2-5 appealed to principles which commanded wide assent: regularity in nature and orderliness in society as something provided for by nature and commended by divine reason; a society needing

21. Mark 12.17 — "Render to Caesar what is Caesar's"; Rom. 13.7 — "Render to everyone their dues, tribute to whom tribute is due." For those who recognize an allusion to Jesus tradition here see my *Romans* 768.

22. Allison, "Pattern" (§23 n. 116) 16-17.

23. *Phoron (apo)didōmi* ("render tribute") — Luke 22.22, 25/Rom. 13.7.

24. See again above §23.5.

25. See also above §8.3(5) and n. 58 and §18.2.

26. See also Rom. 1.26, 28; 2.7, 10; 5.7; 13.3-4; 15.2; 16.19. Paul's use of *ponēros* ("evil") is more restricted (otherwise 1 Cor. 5.13 = Deut. 17.7; Gal. 1.4; Col. 1.21; 1 Thes. 5.22; 2 Thes. 3.2-3).

27. In nonbiblical Greek *philadelphia* always refers to "love of one's brother (or sibling)" in the literal sense (E. Plümacher, *EDNT* 3.424), though the frequent use of *philadelphos* as a title for kings (LSJ) may suggest a wider embrace. Either way the usage indicates how highly prized was the virtue of "brotherly love."

28. Details in my *Romans* 743-44.

29. *Kalos,* "beautiful, fine, good, splendid."

30. Cf. particularly Phil. 4.8 and 1 Thes. 4.12.

constraints in order to ensure "the good"; the role of the ruler in administering such constraints, commending the "good" and punishing the "bad." And the excesses outlined in 13.13 ("revelry and drunkenness," "debauchery and sexual excess," "quarreling and envy") were such as few if any would have attempted to defend.[31]

c) *The practice.* The resulting guidance is an interesting blend of principle and realism. It has several noteworthy features.

First, in 12.9–13.10 Paul makes no attempt to distinguish ethical behaviour within the church as different from that without. The same principle governs relations among believers and relations of believers with those among whom they lived.

The analysis of 12.9-21 has been thrown off balance by the questions of whether Paul is using preformed material and whether he intended a clear transition from an exhortation directed to internal church relationships (12.9-13) to one directed to external relationships (12.14-21?),[32] the problem being that while 12.14, 17-21 seem to have in view a situation of persecution and hostility, 12.15-16 seem once again to be directed to the Roman churches' internal affairs: 12.15 recalls the obligation of members of the body of Christ to each other (as in 1 Cor. 12.26);[33] and 12.16 certainly recalls the earlier warning of 11.20.[34] However, to deduce that Paul was simply failing to order the sequence of his exhortations with coherence and consistency probably misses the point. The point is rather that the obligations to "insiders" and to "outsiders" cannot be neatly pigeonholed and kept distinct. 12.15-16 should be seen rather as an indication of the degree to which Paul saw the life of the Christian churches as integrated into the wider life of the city. The call for sensitive sympathy with those caught in the ups and downs of daily life (12.15), for a proper modesty of self-esteem, and for genuine solidarity with the most lowly ranked or disadvantaged within the congregation (12.16) is of a piece with the positive will to bless the persecutor (12.14) and to do good to the malicious and spiteful (12.17). Paul evidently did not see a believer's life as divided neatly into two sets of distinguishable attitudes and obligations — one to fellow believers, the other to nonbelievers. Given the permanent state of threat under which the little churches of Rome lived, this advice is remarkable in its positive outgoing character.

31. See above §23 n. 169.

32. See, e.g., discussion in Piper, *"Love your Enemies"* 4-18, 119-22; Fitzmyer, *Romans* 651-53.

33. 12.15 — "rejoice with those who rejoice, weep with those who weep"; 1 Cor. 12.26 — "when one member suffers, all members suffer with it; when one member is honoured, all members rejoice with it."

34. 12.16 — "live in harmony among yourselves; do not cherish proud thoughts, but associate with the lowly"; 11.20 — "do not cherish proud thoughts, but fear."

Here again it is important to note that the rubric of love (12.9) covers the whole sweep of the paraenesis, however the paraenesis itself may be apportioned between obligations to insider and outsider. The same sympathetic concern and positive outgoing love should be the rule governing all cases. At the same time we should not ignore the note of realism in 12.18: "if possible, as much as it depends on you." In the face of adamant opposition, love could hope to achieve only so much. Equally the context of the bracketing call for love (13.8-10) clearly implies that the neighbour is not merely to be thought of as the Christian sister and brother, but includes also those who belong to the wider social context.[35] And here too we should note the realism of the exhortation. The neighbour was not merely the fellow believer and could be anyone. But the neighbour was not everyone. The neighbour in view was indeed the neighbour, the person encountered in the course of daily life whose need laid a claim upon the believer's resources.[36] And the output of love in action here called for included the qualification "as yourself." The call was not for a love which outran the resources of the individual, but for a love which in realistic self-esteem recognized the limits as well as the extent of the gifting and enabling from God.

Second, the policy Paul advocated was one of political realism or, alternatively expressed, political quietism. That can be expressed somewhat negatively and even dismissively — as a safety-first policy of avoiding trouble, refusal to retaliate in the face of provocation (12.14-21), recognition that the civic authorities exercise God-given authority — nothing being said of the abuse of such authority (13.1-7). This is the realism of the little people, of the powerless. But it should be put more positively, as Paul indicates. The call to respond positively to evil is in fact the linking theme in 12.14-21, being repeated with variations no less than four times (14, 17, 19, 21) and given the place of emphasis at beginning and end (14, 21). And the advice in 13.1-7 is in fact a call for good citizenship, on the assumption, no doubt partly at least, that civil disorder and strife benefits no one (least of all the little people).[37] Overall, Paul of all people will have been well aware that good citizenship

35. In the original context, Lev. 19.18 refers to the fellow Israelite. But there are some indications of greater openness elsewhere in Jewish writings: Lev. 19.34!; Prov. 6.1; Sir. 13.15; *1 Enoch* 99.15; Philo, *Spec. Leg.* 2.63; *Virt.* 116; Josephus, *War* 7.260; *T. Iss.* 7.6. See further my *Romans* 779-80; and above §2 n. 86.

36. If the prominence of the love command in Paul indicates an awareness of the Jesus tradition (see above §23.5), then Paul presumably would have welcomed an exposition of the command along the lines of the Good Samaritan (Luke 10.29-37).

37. At the same time we should note that the repeated references to God in 13.1-7 (6 occurrences) not only reinforce the authority of those responsible for the well-ordered society, but also remind them of their own accountability for that responsibility.

was also a missionary strategy which commended the gospel to those of good will.[38]

Here again we have to recognize the political realities within which these first Christian churches had to exist. There was no possibility for them to exercise political power such as the democracies of the twentieth century take for granted. The responsibilities of ancient government were exercised by a few by right of birth, connection, wealth, or ruthless self-advancement. For the rest, the great majority, there was no political power and no realistic hope of wielding it. It was hardly even thinkable for Paul, then, that his Roman readership could or should try to change social and political structures. Nor is there any indication that the unrest in Palestine was an influence on Paul or the Roman churches, or that a Zealot-like option even crossed his mind.[39] At the same time, neither did Paul advocate a policy of withdrawal from the corruption of the metropolis, as though the desert or the Qumran alternative could provide a model for Christians in general or for Roman Christians in particular. Political realism for Paul meant living *within* the political system, even if it meant to a large extent living on the terms laid down by that system.[40] This too was part of the eschatological tension.

§24.3 Living with fundamental disagreements — Rom. 14.1–15.6

In the second half of his paraenesis in Romans Paul turns from relationships with the world to relationships within the congregation. The fact that he makes this section the climax of his exhortation and gives such space to it indicates two important points. First, the situation envisaged was a real one, affecting most if not all of the Roman congregations. As is now generally

---

38. L. Schottroff, "Non-Violence and the Love of Enemies," *Essays on the Love Commandment* (Philadelphia: Fortress, 1978) 9-39 (here 23-24); R. Heiligenthal, "Strategien konformer Ethik im Neuen Testament am Beispiel von Röm. 13.1-7," *NTS* 29 (1983) 55-61. We could also observe that such a strategy is in the longer term subversive of a political system maintained by institutionalized violence, though there is no indication that Paul gave his advice with that objective in view. Cf. however the fuller but somewhat tendentious thesis of D. Georgi, *Theocracy in Paul's Praxis and Theology* (Minneapolis: Fortress, 1991).

39. *Pace* M. Borg, "A New Context for Romans 13," *NTS* 19 (1972-73) 205-18. In none of the Jewish revolts against Rome did the Jews of Rome join in.

40. Parallels with other first-century Christian documents (particularly 1 Pet. 2.13-17) indicate that this policy of political prudence was widespread among the earliest Christians (Wilckens, "Römer 13.1-7" 212-13). The repetition of key concepts — "authority" (vv. 1-3), "subject" (1, 2, 5), "good/bad" (3-4), "fear" (3, 4, 7), and "wrath" (4, 5) — "tells the reader that the Christian is willing to belong to the larger society, and that he/she is not out to subvert the social order" (Perkins, *Love* 98).

agreed,[41] here most of all we can be sure that Paul was not merely passing on generalized advice, but had in view the actual situation among the Roman churches.[42] Second, we can also justly infer that the issue was one of considerable importance for all parties, and one whose resolution was integral to Paul's own understanding of the gospel and its corporate outworking.

a) *The theological issue.* The issue which was evidently causing some deeply felt anxieties and strife among the Roman Christians is stated briefly in 14.2: "Someone has faith to eat everything; but the weak person eats [only] vegetables." As the following treatment makes clear, this was the principal bone of contention. But 14.5 indicates a secondary cause of unrest: "Someone judges one day to be more important than another; another judges every day to be alike." For twentieth-century readers such language quickly evokes thoughts of modern disagreements about healthy eating and sabbatarianism. But these modern parallels would be very misleading. What was at stake was much more profound and fundamental in character.

As most now also agree, the issue focused on Jewish perception of the importance of the traditional food laws and Sabbath. It is true that the language is not quite as specific as that, and some have argued that other or more general religious practices are in view.[43] But the whole letter has been oriented to the issue of Jew and Gentile. It would be odd, then, if this final, so full section was differently oriented. On the contrary, it is notable how natural and straightforward is the transition from this section (14.1–15.6) to the final rounding off paragraph once again on Jew and Gentile (15.7-13).[44] And the issue is put beyond reasonable doubt by the talk of "clean" and "unclean" in 14.20 and 14.14, since the former *(katharos)* is characteristically Jewish and the latter *(koinos)* distinctively Jewish terminology.[45] Almost certainly, therefore, Paul

---

41. See, e.g., those cited in my *Romans* lvii; and the discussion in Wedderburn, *Reasons*.

42. From information received no doubt through his several contacts in Rome (Rom. 16.3-15).

43. See, e.g., Rauer, *Schwachen;* Kümmel, *Introduction* 310-11; Ziesler, *Romans* 322-27.

44. Note particularly that 15.7 takes up from the plea of 14.1: "Welcome the one who is weak in faith" (14.1); "Therefore welcome one another" (15.7).

45. On *koinos* see above §8 n. 45. *Katharos* is clearly the opposite of *koinos* and again has the issue of clean and unclean foods in view — a regular usage for *katharos* in scripture, particularly the Torah (Gen. 7.2-3, 8; 8.20; Lev. 4.12; 6.11; 7.19, etc.). The maintenance of purity was a particular concern within Judaism in this period (e.g., Judith 12.7; *Jub.* 3.8-14; *Pss. Sol.* 8.12, 22; 1QS 3.5; CD 12.19-20). Whatever else the Pharisees were, they were a purity sect (see above §8 n. 44). For the Essenes see particularly Newton, *Concept of Purity* (§20 n. 1) ch. 2. Despite their living outside "the holy land," similar purity concerns are attested among diaspora Jews (Philo, *Spec. Leg.* 3.205-6; *Sib. Or.* 3.591-92), including concern regarding food laws (*Ep. Arist.* 142; Gal. 2.11-14; Col. 2.21).

had in view traditional Jewish sensitivities regarding clean and unclean as crucial laws regulating practice at the meal table.[46] Such Jewish traditional scruples were well known in the ancient world,[47] as were also the traditional Jewish festivals and the distinctively Jewish observation of one day in seven as a day of rest.[48]

All this is not to say that the parties in Rome can simply be categorized as Jewish and Gentile. For a feature of the contemporary references to such characteristic and distinctively Jewish traditions is the attractiveness of these traditions to many Gentiles.[49] And Paul was by no means the only Christian Jew who sat loose to these distinctives of traditional Judaism. Nevertheless, what was at issue and at stake in the dispute over food and special days among the Roman congregations was evidently the continuing importance of these observances, given their traditional importance as integral parts of Jewish heritage.

To grasp the seriousness of the crisis confronting the Roman house churches — and crisis is not too strong a word — it is necessary to recall just how fundamental these traditions were for Jewish identity. The laws of clean and unclean were a major part of the Torah (Leviticus 12–13), central to Israel's holiness and distinctiveness (Lev. 20.22-26), a marker of covenant identity hallowed by the blood of the martyrs (1 Macc. 1.62-63). The Sabbath was only a little less important in its role of expressing both the commitment of the covenant people and their belongingness to Yahweh.[50] What was at stake, then, was the complex issue of continuity between Israel and the church of God, of the identity of the church as defined by that continuity, of Christian Jews' loyalty to their hallowed heritage, so much part of themselves. The issue had already been at the centre of major debates within the new Christian

46. The Torah food laws, of course, envisaged the eating of meat; but to avoid the possibility of breaching the law, particularly of eating food tainted by idolatry, many Jews were practising vegetarians (e.g., Dan. 1.16; 2 Macc. 5.27; *Joseph and Aseneth* 8.5; Josephus, *Vita* 14); vegetarian practice was attributed to the Therapeutae (Philo, *Vit. Cont.* 37), to James the brother of Jesus (Eusebius, *HE* 2.23.5), and subsequently to the Ebionites (Origen, *In Matt.* 11.12). Similarly, in view of 14.21, we should note that while the consumption of wine was not forbidden in the Torah, many avoided it for similar reasons — in case it had been offered in libation to the gods before being sold in the market (cf. particularly Dan. 1.3-16; Add. Esth. 14.17; *Joseph and Aseneth* 8.5; *T. Reub.* 1.10; *T. Jud.* 15.4; *m. Abodah Zarah* 2.3; 5.2).

47. See, e.g., Philo, *Legat.* 361, and the texts cited in *GLAJJ* §§63, 196, 258, 281, and 301.

48. The attractiveness to Gentiles of the Jewish Sabbath tradition is attested in Jewish apologetic, albeit in an exaggerated way (Philo, *Mos.* 2.21; Josephus, *Ap.* 2.282), and in Gal. 4.10 and Col. 2.16; cf. particularly Juvenal, *Satires* 14.96, 105-6.

49. See again the preceding two notes.

50. See further above §14.4.

movement,[51] but it had evidently not yet been resolved in a way acceptable to all.[52] In short, the dispute was about fundamental issues of personal identity and community formation. How Paul handled it was crucial for the future of Roman Christianity.

b) *The social context.* We can fill out the social context of the dispute with the aid of a little detective work. We know that there was at this time a very substantial Jewish population in Rome.[53] It is generally agreed that the first churches would have begun within the penumbra of the various synagogues and would have been initially mainly Jewish in character.[54] We also know that many Jews, including Christian Jews, had been expelled from Rome in accordance with the decree of Emperor Claudius in 49 CE.[55] The inference to be drawn, not least from the presence of such as Priscilla and Aquila once again in Rome (16.3-5), is most probably that, following the death of Claudius (54 CE), the decree had been relaxed and Jews began to return to Rome to pick up where they had left off.

At this point we can draw in our text. For the opening sentence of Paul's exhortation is not about differences of dietary practice. It is a call to "welcome the one who is weak in faith, though not with a view to settling disputes" (14.1). The implication is that the character of the Roman churches had changed significantly during the absence of their original Jewish leadership.[56] They were now predominantly Gentile in composition and Gentile Christian in ethos.[57] In consequence, returning Christian Jews were finding it difficult to adapt to the new situation and to find what they (and Paul) regarded

51. Acts 10.1–11.18; Gal. 2.11-14; 4.10. Also Col. 2.16, 21.

52. The majority opinion is that Paul did not succeed in winning Peter over to resume his more liberal practice of table fellowship at Antioch (Gal. 2.15-21, not to say the whole of Galatians, was in effect a rerun of the argument which had been unsuccessful on that occasion) and that the "apostolic decree" of Acts 15.20, 29 did not emerge for some time after the Jerusalem council and took some time to become established practice throughout the diaspora churches.

53. Generally reckoned at about 40,000 to 50,000 (see my *Romans* xlvi).

54. In the list of greetings in Rom. 16.3-16 three are specifically named as Jews (Andronicus, Junia, and Herodion — 16.7, 11), and it is very probable that Priscilla and Aquila, Mary, and Rufus and his mother (16.3, 6, 13) were also Jews. We have already noted the possibility that Andronicus and Junia were among the founders of churches in Rome (above §21.4).

55. For details see again my *Romans* xlviii-xlix. Otherwise Nanos, *Mystery* 372-87.

56. Romans was probably written about 56 CE, give or take a year or so either way — that is, about seven years had elapsed since the expulsion of such as Aquila and Priscilla.

57. In contrast, Nanos assumes that the Gentile believers were still wholly within the orbit of the Roman synagogues (*Mystery* 30-31, 72-75); but see n. 9 above and n. 59 below.

as genuine acceptance.[58] Paul thus was dealing with a major social as well as theological problem. The issue was precisely how faith and practice interact, how and where faith should be resolute, and how and where ecclesiastical context should temper not just the expression of faith, but faith itself.

c) *The principles.* The first principle on which Paul draws becomes apparent at once — that of faith. This comes out in Paul's initial description of the different parties. These are quite often denoted summarily as "the weak" (14.1-2) and "the strong" (15.1). But in introducing them Paul takes care to describe the former more fully as "the weak in faith" (14.1) and the latter more fully as one who "has faith to eat everything" (14.2).[59] And the summary statement of the basic principle undergirding Christian conduct towards the end of his discussion makes the same point: Christian conduct grows out of and as the expression of faith (14.22-23).[60] "The strong" were not, then, as we might have expected, those who held strongly to their traditional heritage and identity markers or, as they would no doubt have said, to fundamental elements of their traditional faith and practice. On the contrary, Paul regarded such people, rather pejoratively, as "weak," that is, "weak in faith." In Paul's perspective they were trusting in something other than God alone. They were trusting in God *plus* continued observance of clean and unclean and special days. They were implying by their priorities that there could be no real trust in God apart from such observances.[61] In contrast, "the strong" were "strong in faith," like Abraham of old (4.18-21), trusting in God and his Christ alone.

A second crucial principle is the primacy of the individual's relation to his or her own Lord. Each stands before her or his own Lord in acceptance, commendation, and judgment (14.4-12). In the comparable discussion in 1 Corinthians 8–10, Paul evokes the principle of conscience.[62] But here the thought is more of the immediacy of participation in Christ and in the Spirit (14.17). The echo of the triple aspects of the beginning of salvation (faith, Lord, Spirit) is a reminder once again of the way gospel and praxis interlocked for Paul.

---

58. *Proslambanomai* (14.1; 15.7) has the force of "receive or accept into one's society, home, circle of acquaintances" (BAGD; 2 Macc. 10.15; Acts 28.2; Phm. 17). What was in view was the everyday recognition and practice of fellowship, not an official act of reception (see further my *Romans* 798).

59. The argument that "the weak in faith" were non-Christian Jews (Nanos, *Mystery* ch. 3) can hardly be accepted. For Paul the problem was not that the bulk of his fellow Jews were "weak in faith," but that they had *not* believed (Rom. 9.32-33; 10.16-21; 11.20, 23).

60. See further above §23.3.

61. It should be evident how the implied logic here echoes the explicit polemic of Gal. 2.14-16. See further above, particularly §14.7.

62. *Syneidēsis* — 1 Cor. 8.7, 10, 12; 10.25, 27-29.

Also important, thirdly, are the allusions back to Jesus' own teaching and practice. The basic axiom undergirding Paul's own conduct is clearly spelled out: "I know and am convinced in the Lord Jesus that nothing is unclean in itself" (14.14), though he also adds, anticipating 14.23, "except that to the one who reckons something unclean, to that person it is unclean" (14.14). We have already noted the echo of Mark 7.15.[63] So too the probable allusion to Jesus' teaching on the kingdom of God in 14.17.[64] The connection of thought between 14.14 and 17 most likely indicates a recollection of Jesus' own disregard of the laws of clean and unclean in his own table fellowship, as a foreshadowing of the coming kingdom, as reflected also in his own experience of the Spirit.[65] To be noted is the fact that it is just this implicit appeal to Jesus tradition and to the precedent provided by Jesus which gave Paul the justification for disregarding previously authoritative scripture and tradition (the laws of clean and unclean). Not least of importance is the climax of the exhortation in the explicit appeal to the example of Christ (15.1-3) and in the summons to "live in harmony among yourselves in accordance with Christ Jesus" (15.5)[66] and to "welcome one another as Christ also welcomed you" (15.7).

In the same connection we can hardly avoid noting the explicit appeal to the principle of love: "for if your brother is deeply upset on account of food, you are no longer conducting yourself in terms of love" (14.15). Paul continues: "Do not by your food destroy that one for whom Christ died" (14.15). So we can take it for granted that Paul saw Jesus' sacrificial death as an example of love for "the weak" (5.6).[67] Paul, in other words, would not see the several principles analysed here as distinct. In this case the two references to Christ's death and resurrection (14.9, 15) provide a note of warning against usurping Christ's role in judgment (14.10-12) as well as a motivation to self-denying action (14.15-21).

Also to be noted is the twofold appeal once again to a broader recognition of "the good." In 14.16 Paul urges: "do not let your good be brought into contempt." The implication is that insensitive conduct among the members of the Roman congregations could make a bad impression on neighbours and casual acquaintances. The vulnerability to Roman suspicions of strange cults and societies is again hinted at. But the main thought is of the bad effect of such impressions on Christian witness. Finally, in 15.2 Paul again urges:

63. See above §23.5.
64. See above §8.3(2) and (3).
65. The connection may be seen in a sequence of texts like Matt. 11.19/Luke 7.34; Matt. 12.28/Luke 11.19-20; Matt. 22.2-10/Luke 14.16-24.
66. See above §23.5.
67. Paul's talk of "weakness" in Romans is confined to the themes of "weakness" and "faith" (4.19; 14.1-2) and of the weakness met by the cross (5.6; 8.3).

"let each of us please his neighbour with a view to what is good, for upbuilding." Here the assumption is that "the good" is to be identified as the same as that which builds up the church. In the end of the day the criterion for social conduct and relationships is the same as the criterion for recognizing charisms.[68]

d) *The practice.* The threat to Christian community in Rome was the clash of two fundamentals, each held by the one group in opposition to the other — the fundamental of constitutive tradition and practice, and the fundamental of liberty of faith in Christ. The symptoms of this clash were clear. The first symptom was an unwillingness to accept, to welcome the other. This is given out initially as the primary responsibility of "the strong in faith" (14.1). But Paul's final and summary counsel is to "welcome one another, as Christ also welcomed you" (15.7). So the responsibility was mutual.

The second symptom was the attitudes of the one to the other: "Let the one who eats not despise the one who does not eat, and let not the one who does not eat pass judgment on the one who eats" (14.3).[69] The language is very striking and reveals a penetrating insight on Paul's part into the psychology of group conflict. As repeated experience within Christian history reminds us, those who stand on the fundamental of Christian liberty will be tempted to "despise," to hold in contempt the more traditional[70] — to despise them for what "the strong" regard as the narrowness of their scruples.[71] At the same time, those who stand on the fundamental of constitutive tradition will tend to "judge" or condemn the more liberal — or judge them because they regard "the strong" as having abandoned or fatally compromised the *bene esse* if not the *esse* itself of Christian tradition and identity.[72]

In response to this clear threat Paul addresses himself first primarily to "the weak in faith" (14.3-12) and then primarily to "the strong in faith" (14.13–15.6).

Paul's immediate response to the more traditionalist Christian Jews was to challenge both their condemnation of the others and its theological

---

68. See above §21.6c.

69. Paul uses *blasphemeō* ("slander, defame, bring into contempt") as equivalent to "judge, condemn" in 14.16. It is noticeable that he only uses the verb in this way three times in his undisputed letters (Rom. 3.8 and 1 Cor. 10.30, the parallel to Rom. 14.16).

70. The verb used, *exoutheneō,* implies a tone of contempt (cf. 2 Kgs. 19.21; 2 Chron. 36.16; Ezek. 22.8; Wis. 4.18; Luke 23.11).

71. Paul himself is not so far away from the same attitude in his designation of his own views as "strong in faith" and those of the others as "weak in faith"; but at least he recognizes commonality of faith.

72. This is the equivalent of Jewish factional vilification of others as "sinners," that is, as those liable to God's condemnation (see my "Jesus and Factionalism" [§14 n. 56]).

basis. That is to say, he challenged them to recognize that the faith they espoused was larger or more fundamental than their own definition of it. He challenged them to recognize that the determiner of acceptability to God was not their definition of faith, but the God in whom all believed. He challenged them to recognize that *God accepted people whose views and practices they regarded as unacceptable.* Paul pressed home the point with repeated emphasis (14.3-4):

> [3]God has welcomed him. [4]Who are you to condemn the slave of someone else? In relation to his own master he stands or falls. And he shall stand, for the master is able to make him stand.

This was the crucial step in Paul's pastoral strategy: to get the traditionalists actually to accept that someone who differed from them in something they regarded as fundamental might nevertheless genuinely believe in God's Christ and be accepted by God. The danger he clearly saw was that they were letting their own convictions shape their idea of God instead of vice versa, that they were worshiping a God made in their own image, that they were usurping a judgment proper only to Christ. The fundamental of faith alone required no further additions, and was more likely than not to be damaged rather than strengthened by such qualifications or "clarifications."

Paul's second piece of counsel was that "each should be fully convinced in his own mind" (14.5).[73] Again clearly implied is the right before God to decide what is appropriate conduct for oneself, even in regard to some cherished but controverted traditions governing social behaviour. Paul also clearly accepted the inevitable corollary: that differing praxis would be the result. His point precisely is that two believers could have contrasting or even opposing convictions regarding appropriate conduct, and *both* be acceptable to God. It was not necessary for the one to be wrong for the other to be right. The conviction of the one was the determiner of that one's conduct (14.22-23), not a rule for the other and not a stick with which to beat or coerce the other.

Paul's third piece of advice recognizes the natural suspicions of the more traditional that those who sit loose to these traditions have actually abandoned their faith. For he provides an important rule of thumb for identifying conduct determined by faith (14.6):

> The one who holds an opinion on the day does so to the Lord. And the one who eats does so to the Lord, for he gives thanks to God; and the one who does not eat does so to the Lord and gives thanks to God.

73. Note again the cross reference to Abraham as the model of faith: *plērophoreō,* "be fully convinced," occurs only here (14.5) and 4.21 in the undisputed Paulines. That there is also a cross-reference between 4.20 and 14.23 will not be accidental.

The rule of thumb is the ability to give thanks to God for the conduct followed. Only what can be received from God and offered to God in humble thankfulness counts as acceptable Christian conduct.[74] That was a limiting factor, but it was also a liberating factor. The assumption in what follows is that such living from God and "to the Lord" was the measure used in God's own judgment (14.7-12). It should therefore preempt, render unnecessary, and indeed forbid all human judgment according to other norms and traditions (14.10, 12).

If the challenge to "the weak in faith" was primarily based on the principle of faith alone, the challenge to "the strong in faith" was based more directly on the principle of love as taught and exemplified by Christ. The attitude thus inculcated was the polar opposite of the contempt of the more liberal in despising and belittling the more traditional.

In the first place, it meant not browbeating "the weak in faith": "welcome [them], though not with a view to settling disputes" (14.1).[75] Part of what it meant to respect those who had not (in the view of "the strong") sufficiently thought through the implications of their faith was to recognize that their convictions may be more instinctively held and be less clearly articulable. The instruction to the strong to keep their faith to themselves before God at the end of the chapter (14.22) matches the opening instruction, since it constitutes a further warning to all not to push their own convictions on others.

Secondly, Paul reminds "the strong in faith" of how seriously their more liberal conduct could affect the more scrupulous. The latter could be "deeply upset," even "destroyed" (14.15, 20). Paul evidently had in mind something more than hurt feelings or a sense of grievance on the part of "the weak" at seeing "the strong" acting in ways of which "the weak" disapproved. What was in view was the possibility of the conduct of "the strong" actually causing "the weak" to stumble (14.21). That is, by copying the conduct of "the strong," "the weak" might be encouraged to "eat with offence" (14.20),[76] that is, to do what they still disapproved of, to act when conviction was unclear, and so to act "not of faith" (14.23).

---

74. To be noted is the echo of 1.21: it is just the failure to "give thanks" (the same verb) which marks out human loss of God.

75. *Diakrisis dialogismōn*, literally, "distinguishing (different) opinions." What is in view is similar to the process of "discerning spirits" (1 Cor. 12.10; 14.29; see above §21.6), that is, the attempt to reach a common view on the mind of Christ (through prophecy, or otherwise) by discussion. Here the plural *(diakriseis)* implies the newcomers being subjected to a series of such discussions on their views.

76. The clause is somewhat unclear, but probably refers to "the weak" eating with an offended, bad conscience; see further my *Romans* 826. The concern is more explicitly voiced in 1 Cor. 8.10.

The strongest emphasis, however, is on the need for "the strong" to restrict their liberty by love for the other (14.13–15.3):

> [13]Let us therefore . . . decide not to put an occasion for offence or downfall in the brother's way. . . . [15]For if your brother is deeply upset on account of food, you are no longer conducting yourself in terms of love. . . . [21]It is a fine thing not to eat meat or drink wine nor do anything by which your brother stumbles. . . . [1]We the strong ought to support the weaknesses of those without strength, and not to please ourselves. [2]Let us each please his neighbour with a view to what is good, for upbuilding. [3]For the Christ, too, did not please himself. . . .

The point is clear: the more liberal must take into account not only their own convictions in determining their actual conduct, but also the way their conduct affects their more traditionalist fellow Christians. The pattern is Christ. Christian liberty expresses itself as much in self-denial as in freedom from outmoded constraint. We can thus elaborate the earlier illustration of Christian liberty:

$$
\text{LICENSE} \; \frac{ \begin{array}{ccccccc} \text{L} & \text{I} & \text{B} & \text{E} & \text{R} & \text{T} & \text{Y} \\ \multicolumn{3}{c}{\text{strong}} & & \multicolumn{2}{c}{\text{weak}} & \end{array} }{ \begin{array}{ccccc} \text{L} & & \text{O} & \text{V} & \text{E} \\ \text{F} & \text{A} & \text{I} & \text{T} & \text{H} \end{array} } \; \text{LEGALISM}
$$

To sum up. Paul would no doubt have recognized how considerable was the challenge he was putting before the Roman congregations. On the one hand, the challenge to recognize that traditions rooted in scripture and hallowed by history need not be determinative for acceptance by God. On the other, the challenge to go as far as possible in accommodating the different views of the other without compromising the most basic foundation of all — faith in God and in his Christ. In both cases the call was for genuine respect across the spectrum of faith and liberty, a respect which not only accepted those who differed on points of importance but which was also ready to defend the differing practices for the sake of the whole (as Paul was doing in this case).[77]

§24.4 Living between two worlds: sexual conduct (1 Corinthians 5–6)

There are many points of contact between the paraenesis of the two letters, Romans and 1 Corinthians. But there is a striking difference. Romans seems

---

77. Summed up in the words of 14.14: "I know and am convinced in the Lord Jesus that *nothing* is unclean in itself, except that to the one who reckons something unclean, to that person it *is* unclean."

to envisage churches which, however much they were in contact with the surrounding society and culture, were nevertheless quite distinct from them. The principal concerns of Rom. 12.9–13.14 are for a church confronted by an all too hostile world. The concerns of Rom. 14.1–15.6 are essentially for the dynamics of internal relationships within the church. In contrast, 1 Corinthians was dealing with a church where the boundaries were by no means so clear, where the ethical issues arose precisely because believers shared many of the moral values of the surrounding society or were genuinely caught between the conflicting values of church and society.[78] The ethics of living between two worlds give a different slant to Paul's paraenesis in 1 Corinthians. We need only illustrate the point from a number of examples, beginning with the issue of sexual conduct in 1 Corinthians 5–6.

We have already noted Paul's unyielding hostility to *porneia*, "unlawful sexual intercourse" (§5.5). That is not to say he was hostile to sexual relations as such, as we shall see (§24.5). It was the abuse of sex to which he was opposed, and that abuse covered the whole range of illicit sexual practice, including homosexual practice and sexual immorality in general.[79] This is significant because it was one of the points which marked out Christian churches from other religious cults and from the broader ethos of the day. Sexual mores were generally much more relaxed in the Hellenistic world.[80] Paul, however, in deliberate contrast, stood foursquare within the Jewish tradition, as indicated in Rom. 1.24-27.[81]

The question naturally arises why he should have held so firmly to Jewish tradition at this point when he qualified and abandoned it at so many others which equally affected human relationships. In this letter, in which he envisaged such lively social intercourse with the world (5.10), why did he not also accommodate more relaxed sexual behaviour? The answer presumably is that Paul retained from his Jewish upbringing a sharp sense of the danger

78. The difference is most apparent when we compare 1 Corinthians 8–10 with Rom. 14.1–15.6; for all the similarity of the issue (food and table fellowship) the situations as portrayed in the two letters are strikingly different at this point; see further below §24.7.

79. See particularly Jensen, *"Porneia,"* responding to B. Malina, "Does *Porneia* Mean Fornication?" *NovT* 14 (1972) 10-17; and further §5.5 above.

80. In the Greek view of life sexual intercourse was as natural, necessary, and justifiable for the man as eating and drinking. Only excess and overindulgence were censured. It was generally understood that husbands could indulge in casual sexual liaisons, though all extramarital intercourse was forbidden to the wife. Female slaves were particularly vulnerable to the sexual demands of their masters. The Stoic protest, as expressed particularly by Musonius, comes close to Paul's view. See F. Hauck and S. Schulz, *TDNT* 6.582-84, and further S. B. Pomeroy, *Goddesses, Whores, Wives and Slaves: Women in Classical Antiquity* (New York: Schocken, 1975) 149-89.

81. See again §5.5 above. See further particularly Rosner, *Paul, Scripture and Ethics* chs. 3-5.

of uncontrolled *epithymia,* of the legitimate "desire" which can all too quickly be corrupted into "lust."[82] Perhaps we should say that it was a realistic appreciation of the strength of the sexual drive, a power both to create life and cement relationship (7.3-5), but a power also to corrupt and destroy (cf. Rom. 7.7-11).[83]

Given this unyielding attitude, it is hardly surprising that the first' ethical issue Paul turned to in 1 Corinthians was *porneia* (5.1-5), indeed a form of *porneia* "not found even among the Gentiles" — a man living with his father's wife (5.1). Paul's attitude was clear: the person should be removed from their midst (5.2). The full circumstances are rather obscure. Paul does not identify the person. His rebuke is directed more to the church than to the individual himself. And in exercising the appropriate discipline Paul's concern was as much to encourage the church to take on the responsibility itself. This raises the intriguing possibility that the individual concerned was himself a rather prominent person, perhaps one of the congregation's initial patrons.[84] If so, Paul's refusal to countenance any thought of compromise is all the more striking. The sentence advocated is also obscure, though it purports to have the individual's best interests at heart (5.5).[85] But the ethical concerns are clear: to leave such conduct uncondemned invites a general corruption of standards. Given the mutual interdependence of the body of Christ (§20.4), one diseased member might well spread disease throughout the body; the spiritual health of the community as a whole was at stake (5.6-8).[86] And the

---

82. See again §5.5 above.

83. See further the social anthropological study of M. Douglas, *Purity and Danger: An Analysis of the Concepts of Pollution and Taboo* (London: Routledge and Kegan Paul/New York: Praeger, 1966).

84. So particularly Chow, *Patronage* 139-40, and Clarke, *Secular and Christian Leadership* ch. 7 (both cited above in §21 n. 25). If recourse to the law courts, a costly business in a legal system which markedly favoured those of higher social status (Clarke 62-68), also involved wealthy patrons in the church (Chow 123-30; Clarke ch. 5), that would explain why 6.1-8 was inserted into a discussion principally on sexual ethics. See also the discussion by B. W. Winter, "Civil Litigation in Secular Corinth and the Church: The Forensic Background to 1 Corinthians 6.1-8," in Rosner, ed., *Understanding* (§23 n. 1) 85-103.

85. 5.5 — ". . . to hand over that man to Satan for the destruction of his flesh, in order that his spirit may be saved on the day of the Lord." What is in view was presumably a kind of radical spiritual surgery which could hopefully accomplish what Paul describes elsewhere as the crucifixion of the old nature in order to do away with the body of sin (Rom. 6.6), or as the putting to death the body's deeds (8.13). See, e.g., discussion in Fee, *1 Corinthians* 210-13; G. Harris, "The Beginnings of Church Discipline: 1 Corinthians 5," in Rosner, ed., *Understanding* (§23 n. 1) 129-51 (here 144-50).

86. See particularly Martin, *Corinthian Body* 168-70; but his argument that "the pneuma which needs to be saved (5:5) is both the pneuma of the man and that of the church" is more forced (170-74).

final command is uncompromising: "Drive out the wicked person from among you" (5.13).[87]

In terms of the spectrum of Christian liberty, here was conduct which obviously went far into the realm of unacceptable license. A loving concern for the individual involved is still protested — and the policy may have succeeded (2 Cor. 2.5-11).[88] But the case went clearly beyond the liberty of practice which should be free of condemnatory judgment. The breach of the law as continuing guidelines for Christian conduct was too blatant and clear-cut.

Others of the Corinthians were evidently open to the possibility of retaining their former sexual mores (6.11) and were prepared to justify continued resort to slaves or courtesans/prostitutes for sexual release and pleasure (6.12).[89] Paul was equally adamant that such conduct was wholly unacceptable for Christians. In this case the rationale is twofold. Such self-indulgence quickly becomes a form of slavery (6.12) — slavery to flesh and once again to lust. It indicates a perspective rooted in and restricted to this ephemeral world (6.13-14). More to the point, the primary relationship for the believer was now the relationship with Christ, through the indwelling Spirit. Anything which weakened or compromised that should not even be contemplated by believers (6.15-20).

In short, in a situation where loyalties and relationships overlapped more fully than in most of Paul's other churches (so far as we can tell), Paul insisted that the Corinthian church draw a firm and distinct boundary line in terms of acceptable and unacceptable sexual practice. The criteria were the clear teaching of scripture and tradition and the character of commitment to Christ and dependence on the Spirit as ruling out any self-indulgence which compromised either.

§24.5 Living between two worlds: marriage and divorce (1 Corinthians 7)

Peter Brown observes that 1 Corinthians 7 is "the one chapter that was to determine all Christian thought on marriage and celibacy for well over a millennium."[90] It is unfortunate, then, that so much of the discussion of the

87. Paul quite properly renders the statement of Deut. 17.7 ("So shall you drive out the evil from your midst") as a command.

88. But see the discussion in Furnish, 2 Corinthians 164-68.

89. Much quoted is the statement of Apollodorus (mid-fourth century BCE): "We have courtesans for pleasure, concubines for the day-to-day care of the body, and wives to bear legitimate children and to maintain faithful guardianship of household affairs" (Pseudo-Demosthenes, Orations 59.122).

90. Brown, Body (§3 n. 1) 54.

passage, present as well as past, has been dominated by the assumption that Paul's own sexual ethic was basically ascetic in character[91] and that he promoted the idea of marriage and sexual relationships as a second best.[92]

This dominant view obviously builds on two undeniable features of the passage. One is Paul's own clearly stated preference for the unmarried state: "I wish that all were as I am" (7.6);[93] "those who marry will have affliction in regard to the flesh,[94] and I would spare you that" (7.28); "he who marries his virgin does well, and he who does not marry her does better" (7.38); "in my opinion she [a widow] is happier if she remains as she is [and does not marry again]" (7.40). The other is Paul's sense that the present age will not be long drawn out: "the time is short" (7.29);[95] "the form of this world is passing away" (7.31).[96] In the interim, "those who have wives should be as though they had none" (7.29). It is also clear from the thrust of 7.25-35 that the two concerns hang together. A large part of the reason for Paul's preference for the unmarried state is his conviction that the time is so short. The whole of that section stands under the opening statement, "I think that

91. See particularly Niederwimmer, *Askese* 80-124: the thrust behind 1 Corinthians 7 is "taboo asceticism"; cf. Wimbush, *Worldly Ascetic,* who attempts to understand 7.29-35 in terms of "spiritual detachment" = Stoic *apatheia* ("freedom from emotion").

92. See particularly Deming's critique of earlier studies (*Paul* ch. 1): "according to this view, the Apostle held a very low opinion of marriage and consequently encouraged his readers in the direction of sexual asceticism, which is the rejection of one's erotic nature in order to become more holy or closer to God" (*Paul* 1). Brown's assumption that Paul "accepted the views of his correspondents [referring to 7.1b] with gusto" (*Body* [§3 n. 1] 56) is an overstatement. Martin's treatment is similarly one-sided (*Corinthian Body* 209-12; for a start, Paul does not put the discussion in terms of "the weak" and "the strong").

93. The context and subsequent discussion indicate that Paul had in mind the celibate state, free from the anxieties which preoccupy the married person (7.32-35).

94. The phrase *(thlipsin tē sarki)* is usually taken as denoting something like "distress in this life" (NRSV). Or is the inference rather that the proper bodily function of sex often involves physical pain and even danger (particularly for the childbearing wife), or, alternatively, is always in danger of being subverted by the flesh?

95. *Kairos* ("time") probably refers to the eschatological time which began with the coming of Christ (Rom. 3.26; 8.18; 11.5; 13.11; 2 Cor. 6.2). It has been "compressed, condensed, that is, shortened" *(synestalmenos).* See further J. Baumgarten, *EDNT* 2.233; H. Balz, *EDNT* 3.313.

96. Baumert, *Ehelosigkeit* 228-36, forces the most natural sense by arguing that *schēma* should be translated "conduct" rather than "form," and that *paragein* here means "to take (spiritually) captive" rather than "to pass away." "Paul is not thinking here of some sort of *immediate* afflictions accompanying a soon-expected end of the world, but rather of the *tension-filled relation to the world* which the Christian must endure *day after day*" (Baumert, *Woman* 95-96).

on account of the present distress *(ananke)*[97] it is well for a person to continue as he is" (7.26).

However, at the same time, too little weight has been given to two other factors. One is that Paul was evidently responding to a series of questions posed by the Corinthians themselves — as indicated by the letter's first use of *peri de* ("now, concerning . . .") in 7.1 and its repetition in 7.25. This probably indicates that the Corinthians' letter put a series of questions to Paul, first with regard to the married (7.1-24) and second with regard to the virgins[98] and unmarried (7.25-38). The importance of this point is that it compels us to recognize that the scope of Paul's discussion was determined by the issues put to him.[99] In other words, he did not set out to provide a theology of marriage. No doubt this was another element of scriptural teaching which he simply took for granted (cf. 1 Cor. 6.16). That presumably is why he makes no reference to what was generally regarded as the primary purpose of marriage — to procreate — although his allusion to children in v. 14 presumably indicates that he also took that as understood.

Recognition that the agenda of Paul's treatment was given to him also carries with it the implication that Paul's discussion took up from what the letter said. In particular, the probability is now widely agreed that the opening statement ("It is well for a man not to touch a woman" — 7.1) is a quotation from the Corinthians' letter.[100] The fact that Paul's advice was probably

97. "In classical literature *ananke* stands for the *constraint* under which human beings exist and which makes free decision impossible" (see further A. Strobel, *EDNT* 1.78-79); E. Baasland, "Ananke bei Paulus im Lichte eines stoischen Paradoxes," in H. Cancik et al., eds., *Geschichte Band III Fühes Christentum* 357-85 [here 367-71]). But it is difficult to avoid the impression that the distress was in part at least a consequence of believers living in an unbelieving world, of the strain of the "already" still caught in the "not yet" (§18). Can its use in contexts of apostolic suffering (1 Thess. 3.7; 2 Cor. 6.4; 12.10) be clearly distinguished from the motif of the sufferings of the "eschatological tension" (§18.5)? But note also Paul's other usage, not least in the same chapter (1 Cor. 7.37; 9.16; 2 Cor. 9.7; Phm. 14).

98. Paul uses *parthenos* ("virgin") repeatedly in this chapter — vv. 25, 28, 34, and 36-38. He also uses *agamos* ("unmarried") in vv. 8, 11, 32, and 34, which can refer to or at least include the unmarried woman (v. 34). Since two distinct conditions are in view, we should probably assume that *parthenos* refers not simply to the unmarried woman but to one who has been betrothed; such seems to be the clear implication of 7.36 and 38. Paul's willingness for the two to become married (7.36) seems to rule out the idea of a couple already married but agreeing to live celibate lives (REB has abandoned NEB's unsatisfactory "partner in celibacy"). See fuller discussion particularly in W. G. Kümmel, "Verlobung und Heirat bei Paulus (1 Kor. 7.36-38)," *Heilsgeschehen* 310-27; see also BAGD, *gamizo;* Fee, *1 Corinthians* 325-27; Deming, *Paul* 40-47.

99. Rightly, Schrage, *Ethics* (§23 n. 1) 226-27.

100. See, e.g., those cited by Schrage, *1 Korinther* 53 n. 11, who observes that the likelihood had already been noted by Tertullian and Origen. In the context there can be no doubt that sexual intercourse is referred to (see the texts cited by Fee, *1 Corinthians* 275; also Gen. 20.6 and Prov. 6.29).

adapted to meet the views of the Corinthians themselves has to be borne in mind in determining what Paul's own views were. At the very least it may mean that the note of asceticism reflects more the Corinthians' views than Paul's.

The other factor to be borne in mind is the one alluded to at the beginning of §24.4. The community in Corinth was only in process of developing its distinctively Christian character. The networks of relationships to which its members belonged crisscrossed the still ill-formed boundaries between church and society. The strains and stresses (eschatological tension) between the new loyalty to Christ and the still continuing loyalties to (unbelieving) spouse or master were evidently quite severe and stressful. In such circumstances Paul could not simply dictate a theology of marriage unrelated to actual situations. On the contrary, it was essential that he should direct his counsel to the real and pressing difficulties put to him by the Corinthians.

Against this background we can begin to see more clearly how careful and sensitive is the advice Paul gives. He stresses again that relationship in and to the Lord is primary.[101] He refers to what authoritative Jesus tradition he has (7.10-11). He looks to the Spirit for guidance (7.40). He takes for granted the importance of "obeying the commandments of God" (7.19). He draws on the best of Stoic tradition insofar as it accords with traditional Jewish wisdom.[102] He takes account of the realities of the Corinthian situation, caught as they were "between the ages" and between two worlds. In consequence, in seeking to answer the Corinthians' questions, he does not hesitate to express his own personal views, that being unmarried had enabled him to be so devoted to the affairs of the Lord. But he makes it clear that these are "opinions"[103] and do not have the force of "commands."[104] He leans over backwards to indicate that other options are just as acceptable to the Lord. And when we look at the counsel he actually gives, it becomes clear that his primary concern is with priorities and the realism with which they should be pursued, not to promote a particular attitude to marriage or marriage relations, or to promote a policy of asceticism.

Thus in the first paragraph (7.1-7) Paul acknowledges the consequences of his own view of the dangers of *porneia* (6.12-20): in effect, that marriage is the only appropriate context for sexual activity; or, as we might say, that marriage is the medium by which *epithymia* retains its positive role as "desire"

---

101. 7.17, 22, 32, 34-35, 39.
102. On Stoic influence see particularly Deming, *Paul* ch. 3 (summary on 212-13). On Jewish influence, see Dautzenberg, *"Pheugete"*; Rosner, *Paul, Scripture and Ethics* ch. 6.
103. *Gnōmē* (7.25, 40); *syngnōmē*, "concession" (7.6).
104. *Epitagē* (7.6, 25).

and is prevented from degenerating into "lust" (7.2).[105] However, his view of marriage itself is one of genuine partnership,[106] in which active sexual relations are assumed to be the norm (7.3-4). If prayer takes priority for a time, it should be only by mutual consent and the time should be limited (7.5).[107] He recognizes explicitly that charisms are different for different people (7.7). In the case in point that amounts to the affirmation that particular dedication to prayer (a spiritual retreat?) and the concomitant self-control are enablings of the Spirit, not given to all by any means.[108] Those who lack such a charism are not at fault, any more than those not graced with the charism of prophecy.[109]

In the second paragraph (7.8-16) he first applies the same logic to the unmarried and widows contemplating (re)marriage; in the continuing present age, marriage remains the appropriate and essential setting for sexual relations (7.8-9).[110] Turning to those caught in unhappy or failing marriages,[111] he cites the norm of Jesus' own teaching: that divorce should not be countenanced, or, failing that ideal, a separated partner should not marry someone else (7.10-11). But he is quick to acknowledge that the situation of some of the Corinthian believers introduced a new factor, not obviously envisaged by

---

105. The rather limited view of marriage here, we should note again, is determined partly by the preceding line of thought in chs. 5–6 and partly by the questions of the Corinthians (that is, no doubt, by the way they put the questions to Paul). Somewhat surprisingly Martin concludes from 7.9b ("it is better to marry than to burn") that Paul wanted to preclude desire altogether (*Corinthian Body* 212-17); "Christians are to avoid desire completely . . . the function of marriage for Paul is to quench desire" (216; though the chapter does not mention *epithymia* explicitly). But the implication of 7.5, 9a, and 36 is rather that sexual desire in marriage is entirely natural and proper. In 1 Thes. 4.5 it is the doubling of the terms ("in passion of desire") which indicates the uncontrolled nature of the desire in view.

106. See also Furnish, *Moral Teaching* 35-37; Baumert, *Woman* 36-43. On Stoic parallels here see Deming, *Paul* 119-22.

107. Here it is the striking parallel with *T. Naph.* 8.7-10 which calls for notice. See also above §5 at n. 96.

108. *T. Naph.* 8.7-10 sees the "abstinence for prayer" in terms of "the commandments of the Lord," Paul as a charism; see also above §20.5 and n. 120.

109. Despite assumptions to the contrary, Paul does *not* call either the state of marriage or the state of celibacy a charism (see above on charism — §20.5; also my *Jesus and the Spirit* 206-7; Deming, *Paul* 127-28).

110. If Paul is addressing a particular question (whether various unmarried members of the Corinthian church may or should remain unmarried), then any negative overtone becomes still more diminished (Baumert, *Woman* 28-29, 48-49; "For Paul it is so natural that normally young people will get married that during the entire chapter he does not even mention this 'normal case' " [49]).

111. For the strains on Christian wives married to unbelievers, see MacDonald, "Early Christian Women."

Jesus' command. That is to say, the fact that one of the partners had not become a Christian made some difference. In those circumstances the continuation of the relationship depended on the consent of the unbelieving partner. The priority in this case was the avoidance of bitter strife between partners and across the boundaries of the church (7.15). The status of children of such partnerships within the realm of the holy (among "the saints") was not a competing priority since it was unaffected by the unbelief of the unbelieving spouse (7.14).[112]

Paul adds a reminder that present status (circumcised or uncircumcised, slave or free) is not a determining factor in standing before God (7.17-24). The priority is "keeping the commandments of God" (7.19). The primary relationship is the relationship with Christ (7.22-23) and with God (7.24). All other identity factors and relationships are relative to these primary matters. So there is no need to change from one status to another; either way the priority remains the same.[113]

In responding to the second set of questions (7.25-38) Paul follows the same line of thought. The present crisis and the shortness of the time (7.26, 29) do not change the priorities, but sharpen them.[114] The degree of relativization of present relations is increased. But that cuts both ways: marriage can be equally affirmed, or the prospect of marriage refused, without committing sin (7.27-28). Those who marry may have "trouble for the flesh" (7.28), but there is no attempt to promote ascetic views or practices as such. Nor can the ethical principle which emerges be defined solely as an "interim ethic."[115] It is the primacy of the affairs of the Lord, rather than simply the imminence of his coming, which relativizes (not abolishes or diminishes) all other concerns.

That Paul's concern is for the priority of maintaining the relationship with Christ is still clearer in 7.32-35. His anxiety is that the responsibilities attendant upon the marital relation will somehow detract from or compete with the relation to Christ. But his concern, he states explicitly, is not to lay

112. On 7.14 see above §17.4. Is there a sense here of "the holy" as an almost tangible influence, as perhaps also in 1 Cor. 11.30? See above §22.4 and cf. Hays, *Moral Vision* (§23 n. 1) 359-60. In contrast, is it enough to take the holiness as in the eyes of the believer, on the parallel of Rom. 14.14 (as Baumert, *Woman* 58-59, suggests)?

113. See further below §24.6.

114. On the *hōs mē* ("as though not") of 7.29-31, a *locus classicus* in patristic and Reformation exegesis in expounding the appropriate mode of Christian existence in the world, note particularly the parallel with the later *6 Ezra* (2 Esdras) 16.40-44; see further W. Schrage, "Die Stellung zur Welt bei Paulus, Epiktet und in der Apokalyptik. Ein Beitrag zu 1 Kor. 7.29-31," *ZTK* 61 (1964) 125-54.

115. See D. J. Doughty, "The Presence and Future of Salvation in Corinth," *ZNW* 66 (1975) 61-90 (here 68-69). The "as though not" closely resembles the Stoic ideal of *ataraxia* ("calmness, detachedness"); see the discussion in Deming, *Paul* 190-97; and cf. Penna, *Paul* 1.181-90. On *anankē* see above n. 97.

any restraint *(brochon)* on them,[116] and not to advocate any particular lifestyle, but only to ensure that their priorities as believers remain clear.[117] Similarly for the man and his betrothed (7.36-38). Of course they should marry if they so desire.[118] It is no sin to do so; they do well. Paul's personal preference would be otherwise, but he still encourages them to act according to their convictions.

It should be clear from all this that Paul speaks with the voice of the deeply caring pastor. Where he has a word from the Lord he cites it and expects it to be followed. He draws on traditional ethical insights, both Jewish and Stoic. He indicates the importance of opinions formed in accord with the Spirit (7.40), but also recognizes that believers are differently engraced (by the same Spirit, 7.7). He makes clear his own preferences as one considered trustworthy by the Lord (7.25). He senses the urgency of the times. He stresses the need to keep priorities clear and honoured. But otherwise he leans over backwards to acknowledge the complexity of the Corinthians' situation and to accommodate the proper desires of those he seeks to counsel. He does not seek to deny marriage or to constrain sexual relations within marriage or to promote any real degree of asceticism. Unlike his counsel elsewhere in the same letter,[119] his advice is remarkably nonprescriptive. Such a sensitive attempt to blend authoritative tradition, personal opinion, and pragmatic counsel which respects real-life situations, and all under the priority of faith, ought to be accorded more positive commendation.

§24.6 Living between two worlds: slavery (1 Cor. 7.20-23)

Although Paul says little on the subject in 1 Corinthians, the fact of slavery raised important questions for early Christian ethics, as other letters (particularly Philemon) indicate. Paul's treatment of the subject has also been vulnerable to criticism because it seems too accepting and unquestioning of slavery as an institution. Three points should be made at once, therefore, by way of clarification.

First, slavery had not yet come to be thought of as immoral or necessarily degrading.[120] It was simply the means of providing labour at the bottom end of

---

116. *Brochos* denotes a noose thrown or put upon *(epiballō)* someone to catch or restrain him — a metaphor from war or hunting (BAGD).

117. See also Cartlidge, "1 Corinthians 7," particularly 226-27. There are no real grounds for the view that Paul thought of the married believer as a "half-Christian" (as Niederwimmer, *Askese* 114).

118. On *hyperakmos* ("past her prime," or "with strong passions") see BAGD and Martin, *Corinthian Body* 219-26.

119. Contrast particularly 11.16 and 14.37-38.

120. It took the slave trade to bring this insight home to Western "civilization."

the economic spectrum.[121] Second, slavery was an established fact of life in the ancient world. As many as one-third of the inhabitants of most large urban centres were slaves. The economies of the ancient world could not have functioned without slavery. Consequently, a responsible challenge to the practice of slavery would have required a complete reworking of the economic system and a complete rethinking of social structures, which was scarcely thinkable at the time, except in idealistic or anarchic terms. Third, in principle slavery was antithetical to the Greek idealization of freedom,[122] and to sell oneself as a slave was a device of last resort for someone in debt. At the same time, slaves could be well educated, and, if masters were figures of substantial social status and power, their slaves could themselves be entrusted with considerable responsibility.[123] Moreover, the economic status of the freedman could well be as bad as or even worse than that of the slave: under Greek law, freedom might be only partial and limited with regard to employment and movement;[124] and the impoverished freedman in subservient client relationship to his former master might well recall with longing his former security as a slave.

We should not be surprised, therefore, that Paul's advice to slaves is as ambivalent as it seems to be. In 1 Cor. 7.20-24 Paul encourages his readers (slaves included) to "remain in that [the situation] in which [they] were called" (7.20, 24).[125] Slaves should not be "troubled" *(meletō)*[126] about their status as slaves, but if they were able to be free they should "take advantage of it" (7.21).[127] What matters is the primary relation to the Lord. That relativizes

---

121. Slaves were initially supplied from the ranks of defeated enemies, but by the time of Paul the supply was mainly through birth to slaves. See further those cited in my *Colossians* 302 n. 6.

122. See, e.g., K. H. Rengstorf, *TDNT* 2.261-64; Meeks, *First Urban Christians* 20-21. The slave was classically defined as "one who does not belong to himself but to someone else" (Aristotle, *Politica* 1.1254a.14) and as one who "does not have the power to refuse" (Seneca, *De Beneficiis* 3.19).

123. See particularly Martin, *Slavery* ch. 1. To be noted also is Paul's use of slavery as a powerful metaphor in exhortation (Rom. 6.16-17; 1 Cor. 7.22; 2 Cor. 4.5; Phil. 2.7).

124. See S. S. Bartchy, *ABD* 6.71; with further details in my *Colossians* 335 n. 30.

125. It is finally unclear whether Paul meant to include their station in life as their "calling" ("let him remain in it" — 7.25) or, more likely, limited the thought of "calling" to the summons to believe in Christ; so 7.21-22, "called *as* (while being) a slave/freeman," *not* "called to *be* a slave/freeman."

126. *Melei*, "it is a care or concern (to someone)" (BAGD). "The command is not 'Stay as you are,' but rather 'Don't let it trouble you.' . . . one could sell oneself into slavery, but slaves could not choose freedom" (Fee, *1 Corinthians* 316).

127. See particularly Bartchy, *MALLON CHRESAI;* Baumert, *Ehelosigkeit* 114-51; Fee, *1 Corinthians* 316-18; Horrell, *Social Ethos* 162-66. Manumission was the goal of every slave: "it is the slave's prayer that he be set free immediately" (Epictetus 4.1.33). And it was regularly achieved: a very substantial proportion of slaves were freed by their masters before their thirtieth birthdays (Bartchy, *ABD* 6.71).

all other relations. In relation to the Lord the slave is a free person and the freeman is Christ's slave (7.22). Neither slaves nor freemen should allow any dependency on and obligation to others to become more important than their dependency on and obligation to Christ (7.23).

We find a similar ambivalence in Paul's advice to Philemon. Did he or did he not expect Philemon to free his slave Onesimus?[128] Paul's main concern was evidently for a positive reconciliation between the two. He clearly did not expect Philemon to punish Onesimus, as Philemon might have claimed the right to do.[129] And he left the door open to Philemon to respond with dignity and generosity in a way that would both maintain and display his honour.[130] But equally clearly, the most important consideration was that the relation of both Philemon and Onesimus to the same Lord wholly relativized their relation to each other, even if that continued to be the relation of master and slave — "no longer as a slave, but more than a slave, as a beloved brother, especially to me, but how much more to you, both in the flesh and in the Lord" (Phm. 16).

The subsequent advice in the list of household rules in Col. 3.18–4.1 does not alter the picture of Paul's view of slavery in its essentials. The horizon of an imminent crisis may have lengthened. The *Haustafeln* may indicate a greater concern to demonstrate the good order of the Christian households and a consequent commitment to maintaining the orderly structure of society (§23.7c). And the appeal for humanitarian treatment of slaves was quite common in philosophical discussion.[131] But once again the clear teaching is that the primary relationship to Christ relativizes all else. The principle had already been indicated in 3.11 ("no slave, no free man, but Christ the all and in all"). In addressing slaves directly, as members equally of the church and as responsible Chirstian individuals (3.22-25), the advice goes beyond the contemporary parallels, which confine themselves to advising masters or

---

128. See above §21 n. 57.

129. If Philemon regarded Onesimus as a fugitive slave, he could quite properly have punished him with beatings, chains, branding, or worse. See particularly Bellen, *Studien* 17-31; also Bartchy, *ABD* 5.307-8 (with bibliography). But Onesimus may not have been a runaway and may simply have sought out Paul to plead on his behalf with his master, whom he had offended in some unspecified way; see particularly P. Lampe, "Keine 'Sklavenflucht' des Onesimus," *ZNW* 76 (1985) 135-37; B. M. Rapske, "The Prisoner Paul in the Eyes of Onesimus," *NTS* 37 (1991) 187-203 (here 195-203); and Bartchy, *ABD* 5.307-8.

130. See further above §21.2b. Cf. particularly Barclay, "Paul" 170-75, though his analysis is weakened by his continued assumption of the traditional hypothesis that Onesimus was a runaway slave (see further n. 129 above).

131. Cf., e.g., Seneca's well-known discourse on treating slaves as human beings (*Epistle* 47) and Philo's encouragement to masters to show "gentleness and kindness" (*Decal.* 167).

discussing what instruction should be given to slaves.[132] The call for masters to treat their slaves "with justice and equity" (4.1) assumes a higher degree of equality than was normal.[133] And, above all, the repeated reference to the primary relationship to the Lord (for both slave and free)[134] highlights a fundamental criterion of human relationships which in the longer term was bound to undermine the institution of slavery itself.

§24.7 Living between two worlds: social relations (1 Corinthians 8–10)

We have already dealt with three aspects of these chapters.[135] But the bracketing discussion (8.1-13 and 10.23–11.1) calls for further comment.

Set in context, the immediate issue is evidently the acceptability or otherwise of believers eating *eidōlothyta,* "meat offered to an idol." Some thought it acceptable: "an idol is nothing in the world" (8.4). For others it would be too much of a contradiction to their commitment (8.7-13). The reference to the latter as "the weak"[136] suggests that the situation in view was similar to that envisaged in Romans 14. And the specific and repeated reference to idolatry[137] strongly evokes the distinctively Jewish hostility to idols so much at the heart of Jewish faith and identity.[138] That is to say, "the weak" were probably those who shared what were characteristically Jewish scruples about eating anything contaminated by idolatry.[139]

Here too, however, we have to recognize that social tensions were probably involved. Many of "the weak" may well have belonged to the lower strata of society, who could not afford to include meat in their regular diet. The opportunities to eat quality meat may have been largely limited to the

---

132. The fact that four verses are addressed to the slaves of the congregation (and only one to masters) suggests that slaves made up a high proportion of the congregation in Colossae. The advice (do well what you are required to do) reflects the reality of the typical slave's powerlessness.

133. See the discussion of the term *isotēs,* "equality, equity, fairness," in my *Colossians* 259-60.

134. "Fearing the Lord" (3.22); "as to the Lord" (3.23); "you will receive from the Lord" (3.24); your master is Christ (3.24); masters also have a master in heaven (4.1). On the phrases see further my *Colossians* 252-60.

135. 8.4-6 (§§2.3c, 10.5a, 11.2a), 9 (§21.2c), 10.1-22 (§22).

136. *Astheneō* — Rom. 14.1-2; 1 Cor. 8.11-12; *asthenēs* — 1 Cor. 8.7, 9, 10; 9.22.

137. *Eidōlothytos* — 1 Cor. 8.1, 4, 7, 10; 10.19; *eidōlolatria* — 1 Cor. 10.14; *eidōlolatrēs* — 1 Cor. 10.7; *eidōlon* — 1 Cor. 8.4, 7; 10.19.

138. See above §2.2.

139. Similarly Heil, *Ablehnung* 234. Söding, "Starke und Schwache," does not give sufficient consideration to this background.

public distributions of meat at public ceremonies, at which the meat would have been dedicated to the presiding god or gods. For "the weak" the choice between a poor man's diet and acting against conscience would have been quite stark.[140] The other side of the problem was that Christians of high social status and more fully integrated into the public life of the city would have found it difficult to avoid participating in such public functions and festivities.[141] The picture was no doubt more complex. Those who were more fully integrated into public life were less likely to declare that "idols are nothing," in view of the offence it would cause. And Gentile God-fearers previously attracted *(inter alia)* by Jewish hostility to idols might already have found themselves pulled two ways. In other words, we have to allow for a more complex historical reality (including tensions of social dissonance and status inconsistency) if we are to hear Paul's instruction in relation to the actual situation in Corinth.[142]

How did Paul respond in this instance? The usual understanding of Paul's advice in the matter is that it disregarded traditional Jewish sensibilities: the Paul who counseled the Corinthians not to raise questions *(mēden anakrinontes)* about the source of the meat served (10.25, 27) was no longer governed by the characteristically Jewish antipathy to idolatry so fundamental to Jewish identity.[143] The issue of Christian liberty[144] and desirability for Christians to maintain social involvement and responsibilities (10.23-30) had taken precedent. The parallel with Romans 14 seems to settle the issue.

However, the differences between the two passages have not been given sufficient consideration. For one thing, whereas Rom. 14.1–15.6 was primarily about *unclean* food, the issue in Corinth was one of *idol* food *(eidōlothyta)*. For another, as already noted, the tensions in the Roman congregations were purely internal, within their own boundaries, confronting a threatening society; whereas those in the Corinthian church arose precisely because various members thought it important to maintain relations across the

---

140. Theissen's portrayal at this point ("Strong and Weak"), however, needs to be qualified by Meggitt's observation that poor quality meat would have been more widely available from "cookshops," wineshops, and elsewhere ("Meat Consumption").

141. Theissen, "Strong and Weak" 130, referring to Erastus, the "city treasurer" (Rom. 16.23).

142. Meeks, *First Urban Christians* 70; compare and contrast J. M. G. Barclay, "Thessalonica and Corinth: Social Contrasts in Pauline Christianity," *JSNT* 47 (1992) 48-74.

143. Often quoted is Barrett's summation: "Paul is nowhere more unJewish than in this *mēden anakrinontes*" — "an attitude of extraordinary liberalism" ("Things Sacrificed" 49, 50).

144. *Eleutheros* — 1 Cor. 9.1, 19; *eleutheria* — 10.29.

boundaries, to continue involvement within the wider society.[145] And for another, the fact that Paul uses different criteria in the two discussions may be more significant than the consensus view assumes: "faith," so central in Romans 14,[146] does not feature in 1 Corinthians 8–10; and "conscience," so determinative in 1 Corinthians 8–10,[147] does not appear in Romans 14. Why this should be so is unclear. Perhaps "conscience" was the word used in the Corinthian letter. And nothing in the preceding discussion of 1 Corinthians had prepared its recipients to understand "faith" appropriately, in the way that Romans 4 prepared for Romans 14. It is true that the role filled by "conscience" is more or less equivalent, at least to the extent that it evoked the similar awareness of a living relationship with Christ damaged by ill-considered action.[148] But it is nevertheless significant that whereas "faith" was the appropriate criterion for an internal issue, "conscience" was evidently regarded as the more appropriate court of appeal in a boundary-crossing issue (cf. Rom. 2.15).

More weighty for us, however, is the question whether the consensus view on Paul's attitude to idol food in effect constitutes an abandonment of Israel's traditional hostility to idolatry. That view should itself now be abandoned. (1) It assumes that the only meat available for believers would have come from the local temples, and therefore would have been unavoidably "contaminated" with idolatry. In these circumstances, Paul's readiness to envisage Christians eating such meat (10.25, 27) would indeed fly in the face of traditional Jewish antipathy to idolatry. But Paul's very counsel not to ask questions regarding the source of the meat offered (10.25, 27) should have been sufficient indication that meat was available from other sources, and Meggitt's summary study confirms the point.[149]

(2) It ignores Paul's hostility to idolatry, clearly attested elsewhere in his letters.[150] That is to say, elsewhere Paul clearly stands foursquare within the Jewish tradition on this point. And his attitude to idols in the main body

145. Meeks speaks of "gates" in the boundaries and contrasts the more introverted Johannine groups (*First Urban Christians* 105-7). He also observes that "the emphasis in Paul's paraenesis, however, is not upon the maintenance of boundaries, but upon internal cohesion" (100).

146. Rom. 14.1, 22-23 (4 occurrences).

147. 1 Cor. 8.7, 10, 12; 10. 25, 27-29 (8 occurrences in all). On "conscience" see further above §3 n. 16.

148. Note the parallel between Rom. 14.23 ("everything which is not of faith is sin") and 1 Cor. 8.12 ("in sinning against your brothers and wounding their weak conscience you sin against Christ").

149. "Meat Consumption." See earlier H. J. Cadbury, "The Macellum of Corinth," *JBL* 53 (1934) 134-41; Barrett, "Things Sacrificed" 47-49.

150. See above §2.2 and n. 20.

of 1 Corinthians 8–10 in fact stands within the same tradition: in particular, we have already observed the echo of Deut. 32.17, 21 in 1 Cor. 10.20-21.[151] It would be strange if his advice a few verses later ran so much counter to his otherwise consistent attitude on the subject. Certainly we have no indication anywhere else that Paul himself ever ate idol food.

(3) In some ways the most striking fact is that subsequent early church writers show no awareness that Paul condoned the eating of idol food or felt the need to defend him against those who themselves saw no problem in eating idol food.[152] In other words, there was no knowledge then of the current consensus interpretation that Paul sat light to the eating of idol food. When those closer to the thought world of Paul and closer to the issue of idol food show no inkling of the current interpretation, that interpretation is probably wrong.

How then should we characterize Paul's advice and instruction? The most straightforward exegesis is that Paul counseled the avoidance of meals at which it was known beforehand that idol food would be served.[153] That effectively ruled out public or private meals within temple precincts: to participate in a temple meal would inevitably be seen by others as consenting to the idolatrous worship of the temple.[154] Also ruled out were meals in private homes where it was clear beforehand that idol food was likely to be served.[155] At the same time, we should note that his counsel (10.25-28) envisaged the possibility of believers actually consuming idol food (unknowingly). So it was not the idol food per se which constituted "dangerous food,"[156] but eating

151. See above §2.3c. On the nothingness of idols see also Pss. 115.4-8; 135.15-18; Isa. 40.19-20; 44.9-20.

152. Cheung, *Idol Food* ch. 4. Similarly Tomson, *Paul* 177-85. Contrast J. Brunt, "Rejected, Ignored, or Misunderstood? The Fate of Paul's Approach to the Problem of Food Offered to Idols in Early Christianity," *NTS* 31 (1985) 113-24. As Cheung observes, the same evidence decisively undermines B. Witherington's attempt ("Not So Idle Thoughts about *Eidolothuton*," *TynB* 44 [1993] 237-54) to distinguish *eidōlothyton* from *hierothyton* (the former eaten in the temple, the latter coming from the temple but not eaten there).

153. Cheung, *Idol Food*.

154. Willis raises the question whether it would have been generally regarded as "pagan worship to participate in the various 'socials' held in temple precincts" (*Idol Meat* 63). Gooch, however, clearly shows that the answer should be Yes: it would have been impossible to treat meals in temples as purely secular or to dissociate them from the religious rites for which the temples primarily existed (*Dangerous Food*).

155. We recall that invitations to dine with Sarapis could have private homes as the venue (above §22 n. 27). Fee, *"Eidōlothyta,"* is a recent version of a regular attempt to resolve the issue by arguing that the issues confronted in 8.1-13 (public dining in temples) and 10.27 (private dinners) were significantly different, and that Paul forbade only the former.

156. *Pace* Martin, *Corinthian Body* 191.

it *knowing* it to be idol food. Paul's traditional Jewish antipathy to idols was qualified at least to the extent that he put no obligation on his fellow believers to avoid idol food at all costs or to parade their consciences in the matter by making scrupulous enquiry beforehand.[157] To that extent, Paul's citation of Ps. 24.1 (10.26)[158] echoes the more liberal view of Rom. 14.14, 20, as indeed the more liberal practice of diaspora Jews who maintained a lively social intercourse with non-Jews.[159] In so advising, Paul himself also in effect encouraged the Corinthian believers to maintain their social contacts within the wider community.

Other factors which evidently weighed with Paul in this tricky issue are also evident. As also the firmness and sensitivity of his pastoral concern. (1) The priority of relation with God[160] and with Christ[161] is assumed. Although the weak are never directly addressed (unlike Romans 14–15), Paul makes the giving of thanks at the meal the test of conduct which should be acceptable to all (as in Rom. 14.6).[162] Likewise he stresses that the primary basis for all human conduct is giving glory to God (10.31).[163] (2) As also in Romans, appeal is made both to the death of Christ and to the example of Christ (11.1).[164] The motivation and norm of "love" are given first place (8.1, 3). At the equivalent point in the resumption of the theme, the concern for "the other" (10.24) echoes the love command (as in Rom. 13.8). (3) Christian liberty is to be affirmed, but also to be constrained by its consequences on others.[165] He rebukes the attitude which prizes too highly its own insight, which does not seek to build up the community, and which discounts too casually the deeply felt conscientious objections of "the weak" (8.1-3, 7-13). (4) The criterion of "what builds up the community" is evoked in both sections, again as a primary consideration.[166] (5) And even more explicitly than in Romans (Rom. 14.16) the effect of Christian carping against Christian,

---

157. It is unclear by whom the issue of conscience is raised in 10.28 (see discussion in Fee, *1 Corinthians* 483-84). To this day in Jewish circles, the meal table provides opportunity to check an individual's level of devotion to the rules of clean and unclean.

158. With a probable allusion also to Ps. 50.12.

159. Cf. particularly Tomson, *Paul* 208: Paul's advice is halakhic, defining what is idol food in doubtful cases (208-20).

160. 8.3, 4-6, 8; 10.26, 31.

161. 8.6, 11-12.

162. 10.30 — "If I partake with thanks *(charis)*, why am I held in contempt *(blasphēmoumai)* over that for which I give thanks?" Note again the parallel with Rom. 14.16; see above n. 69.

163. Cf. Rom. 15.6 with its recall of 1.21.

164. 1 Cor. 8.11 = Rom. 14.15; 1 Cor. 11.1 = Rom. 15.3.

165. Again we note that the consequence in view is not simply the disapproval of "the weak" but their being encouraged to act against their conscience (8.10-12).

166. 8.1, 10; 10.23; cf. above §21.6c.

both the effect on the surrounding society and its deleterious consequences for Christian missionary work, are stressed and given the place of final, concluding consideration (10.31-33).

Theissen describes Paul's strategy here as "love-patriarchalism" which "allows social inequalities to continue but transfuses them with a spirit of concern, or respect, and of personal solicitude."[167] But that does not take sufficient account of the extent to which Paul expected the socially strong to modify their behavior in deference to the needs of the socially weak.[168] Nor does it reckon sufficiently with the dynamic of the church's own community formation, where a genuine commitment to the same Lord, the resulting bond among those who had made the same commitment,[169] and a shared concern for the church's upbuilding could be appealed to with confidence. Here not least we should recall that reference to the bonding effect of shared participation in the Lord's Supper lies at the heart of ch. 10 (10.16-17), and that it is the resulting sense of responsibility for one another as members of the same body to which Paul appeals (10.23-24) as the crucial factor in determining social relationships both within the church and across its boundaries.

§24.8 The collection

It is appropriate to round off this review of (some of) the ethical issues with which Paul dealt by referring, finally, to the collection. This was the enterprise on which he set his heart some time early in his Aegean mission, if not earlier.[170] The objective was for the mainly Gentile churches founded by Paul to make a (financial) collection to help relieve the poor fellow Christians in Jerusalem. It is appropriate to deal with it here for several reasons.

First, it was the enterprise which became more and more of a priority for Paul as his Aegean mission drew to a close. He refers to it more frequently

167. Theissen, "Strong and Weak" 139.

168. 1 Cor. 8.13; 10.28-29, 32; also 6.1-8 and 11.33-34. See further Horrell's critique of Theissen's "love-patriarchalism" (*Social Ethos,* particularly ch. 4).

169. Paul speaks repeatedly of "the brother" in 8.11-13, and begins ch. 10 with the same appeal ("brothers").

170. Gal. 2.10 is unlikely to refer to the collection as such; the references to the collection elsewhere have a similarity in language and tone which is not shared by Gal. 2.10. The collection is more likely to have been conceived by Paul as an attempt to bridge the gulf which evidently opened up between his mission and the Jerusalem or Judean churches following his failure at Antioch (Gal. 2.11-14). That the agreement mentioned in Gal. 2.10 was part of the stimulus to the collection, however, is more than likely: that he should "remember the poor" was the original request of the Jerusalem apostles; that the collection was specifically "for the poor of the saints who are in Jerusalem" was Paul's own intention (Rom. 15.26).

than any other good work he advocated.[171] It was delivery of the collection which took him back to Jerusalem for the last time, even though he was nervous regarding the outcome (Rom. 15.31). And in the event it was the reaction to that visit (and the collection?) which triggered the sequence which ended in his journey to Rome and eventual execution.[172]

Second, it is not accidental that this is the subject with which Paul closes the body of his letter to the Romans (15.25-32). That confirms its peculiar significance for Paul. And since this whole study has attempted to flesh out the structure of Paul's theology indicated by Romans, it is fitting to round off the study by thus echoing Paul's own climactic and concluding concern.

Third, and most important of all, the collection sums up to a unique degree the way in which Paul's theology, missionary work, and pastoral concern held together as a single whole. This point deserves some elaboration. In each case we should note the consistency of Paul's language and thought across the three main letters (Romans, 1 and 2 Corinthians). As might be expected, the fullest treatment (2 Corinthians 8–9) is the most illuminating.

a) Most striking is Paul's theology of "grace." The term *charis* appears no less than ten times in 2 Corinthians 8–9, and again in 1 Cor. 16.3. The range of usage is quite remarkable and highly instructive.[173] Paul uses it, of course, for "the grace of our Lord Jesus Christ" in his act of generous self-sacrifice (2 Cor. 8.9).[174] But he uses it also for the Corinthians' experience of that grace, as something which they could well recall (8.1; 9.14) and look to in the future (9.8). And he uses the same term in 8.6-7 and 19 to indicate the collection itself as "grace," a "gracious work" or "gift" (1 Cor. 16.3), where *charis* ("grace") has become more or less equivalent to *charisma* ("charism").[175] Evidently, then, for Paul it was the character of grace that it should come to expression in generous action. Grace, we might say, had only been truly experienced when it produced gracious people. In 8.4 we find what might be called the transitional usage — "begging us earnestly for the *charis* and the sharing *(koinōnia)* in the service *(diakonia)* to the saints." *Charis* here seems to signify the (sense of) engracement which prompted the Macedonians

---

171. Rom. 15.25-32; 1 Cor. 16.1-4; 2 Corinthians 8–9. It makes little difference whether 2 Corinthians 8–9 consists of two originally independent letters or two chapters of a larger letter; on the issue see, e.g., Kümmel, *Introduction* 287-93, and Betz, *2 Corinthians 8 and 9*.

172. See the final section of Acts (chs. 21–28), whose silence on the collection (apart from the allusion in 24.17) is ominous; see, e.g., Meeks, *First Urban Christians* 110; my *Partings* 85.

173. See further above §13.2.

174. See above §11.5c.

175. For the theology of charism see above §20.5.

to contribute to the collection beyond their means (8.2-3),[176] the sense both of having received grace themselves and of participation in the collection as a privilege to be earnestly requested. The complementary use of *charis* in its related sense of "thanks," that is, here, of thanks for such divine prompting (8.16) and for God's "inexpressible gift" (9.15), completes the circle of grace — from God as grace, to humans and through humans as gracious action, and back to God as thanks.[177]

The twofold emphasis on "righteousness" in 9.9-10[178] confirms that Paul shared the scriptural emphasis on the interconnection of the vertical and the horizontal: that God's righteousness as Creator produces a harvest of righteousness in kindly acts of service on behalf of others (cf. Phil. 1.11), or, as the prophets would insist, that righteous acts are the inevitable consequence and outworking of the experience of God's righteousness.[179] Worthy of note also is the fact that Paul does not hesitate to speak of the Corinthians' participation in the collection as "the obedience of your confession with respect to the gospel of Christ" (1 Cor. 9.13), where "the obedience of your confession *(hē hypotagē tēs homologias hymōn)*" is obviously another way of speaking of "the obedience of faith *(hypakoē pisteōs)*" (Rom. 1.5).

b) Equally vivid is the illustration of Paul's theology of Israel. The most consistent feature across the three passages is the reference to the recipients of the collection as "saints."[180] The intended reference is the Jerusalem church, the collection to be used for its poor members (Rom. 15.26). That Paul can refer to the Jerusalem church so consistently simply as "the saints"[181] clearly implies that the Jerusalem church held a central place among all the churches, particularly in the continuity it provided between the "saints" of Israel in the past and the "saints" of the diaspora churches.[182]

176. Note also the use of *haplotēs* ("generosity, liberality") in 8.2 and 9.11, 13, and of the less usual *authairetos* ("of one's own accord"), only in 8.3 and 17 in biblical Greek.

177. Harrison notes how effectively Paul plays on and transforms the normal benefaction ideology of the time: the grace received calls not simply for a reciprocal response to the giver ("thanks"), but for the receiver to give "grace" to others — Paul's "three dimensional" understanding of grace (*Paul's Language of Grace* §7.2).

178. 9.9-10 — "As it is written, 'He has scattered abroad, he has given to the poor; his righteousness endures for ever' [Ps. 112.9]. He who supplies 'seed to the sower and bread for food' [Isa. 55.10] will supply and multiply your seed and increase the harvest of your righteousness."

179. Cf. Rom. 6.13, 16, 19; and see above §23.3 and n. 59.

180. Rom. 15.25, 26, 31; 1 Cor. 16.1; 2 Cor. 8.4; 9.1, 12.

181. Thus in both Corinthian letters; in Romans their identity as "the saints who are in Jerusalem."

182. On the significance of Paul's use of *hagioi* ("saints") see above §2 n. 90, §13 n. 74, and §20.3.

This is all the more striking in view of the tensions between Paul and Jerusalem so marked following the incident at Antioch.[183] But that is evidently why the collection was so important for Paul. Not simply to help heal any breach; that goal is not explicitly stated, though possibly implied in the concern lest the collection not be "acceptable to the saints" (Rom. 15.31). But primarily as an expression of the Gentile churches' spiritual indebtedness to Jerusalem: "for if the Gentiles have received a share in their spiritual things, they ought also to minister to them in material things" (15.27).[184] Whereas in other circumstances Paul had been quick to emphasize the directness with which the gospel to the Gentiles had come from Christ (Gal. 1.12), here he emphasizes that Jerusalem had been an indispensable medium. This is precisely because the *pneumatika* ("spiritual blessings") which had come to the Gentile churches were the spiritual blessings of the Jerusalem church, "the spiritual things" which were an integral part of their heritage precisely as "the saints in Jerusalem."[185] Here again we may note also the complementarity which Paul saw between receiving "spiritual things" and a responsive ministering in "material things."

c) The applied theology which is Paul's ecclesiology also comes through clearly in these chapters. As with *charis,* he emphasizes the practical character of *koinōnia.* The shared "participation" in grace/Spirit (it is implied) should come to expression in the "sharing" of relative prosperity in "shared" ministry.[186] That Christians will wish to "serve" one another Paul takes for granted.[187] As elsewhere, the language of priestly ministry refers to such acts of practical service on behalf of others (9.12).[188] Here it is especially noteworthy that the sharing and service are not limited to the local church or even to the churches of the region, but reach across the ocean to another church, one regarding which feelings were somewhat mixed. The interdependence of the body of Christ is not limited to relationships within individual congregations.[189]

Not least of interest is the several times Paul alludes to a process of

---

183. See, e.g., my *Partings* 130-35.

184. It is possible that the collection was part of Paul's strategy to make Israel jealous (11.14) by demonstrating the success of the Gentile mission (particularly Munck, *Paul* 302-3; see also above §19.8). But nothing of that is clearly evident in any of the passages dealing explicitly with the collection (see also my *Partings* 84-85).

185. Cf. Rom. 9.4-5; 11.29.

186. Rom. 15.26; 2 Cor. 8.4; 9.13.

187. *Diakonia* — Rom. 15.31; 2 Cor. 8.4; 9.1, 12-13; *diakoneō* — Rom. 15.25; 2 Cor. 8.19-20.

188. See above §20.3.

189. Unusually here Paul expresses the point in terms of "equality" *(isotēs)* — apart from 8.13-14, only in Col. 4.1 (see above n. 133) in the NT; see, e.g., Furnish, *2 Corinthians* 407.

"testing" as part of the whole process.[190] He speaks of the Macedonians' "great testing of affliction" (8.2), of "testing the genuineness/sincerity *(gnēsios)*[191] of your [the Corinthians'] love" (2 Cor. 8.8), of his agent as "tested" (8.22), and of the collection itself as a "testing" (9.13). The effectiveness of even the charis(m) of welfare service depends on some measure of testing. In the same connection we note the appearance of the criteria used in Rom. 14.6 to determine the acceptability of divergent practices: the collection will "overflow in much thanksgiving to God" and in "glorifying God" (9.12-13).[192]

d) Not least of interest is the way Paul brings the various principles governing Christian conduct to bear on this final issue. As already indicated, he clearly saw the collection as the sort of concern and conduct which will inevitably flow from the experience of grace received. Here we may note also the recall of the Macedonians' joy in the Lord (8.2),[193] the reminder of the primacy of commitment to the Lord (8.5), and the repeated appeals to generosity *(haplotēs* — 8.2; 9.11, 13). As we have seen, the thought of *charis* in fact dominates all in 2 Corinthians 8–9. "Faith" is alluded to only in 8.7; but then "faith" is the assumed correlative of "grace" for Paul, and we have already noted that "the obedience of your confession" (9.13) is equivalent to "the obedience of faith." "Spirit" is not mentioned, unless alluded to in 9.15;[194] but then "Spirit" and "grace" are near synonyms in Paul. In other words, the attitude inculcated in the talk of "grace" is that elsewhere inculcated through talk of faith's outworkings and the encouragement to walk in accordance with the Spirit.

The appeal to Christ's example and its inspiration is explicit in 8.9[195] and correlated with the appeal to love (8.8; also 8.24). More noticeable is the appeal to scripture — explicitly in 8.14 and 9.9 and 10, but with allusions also in 8.20 and 9.6-7.[196] From what we have already seen we need entertain little

---

190. See above §21.6.

191. See Furnish, *2 Corinthians* 404.

192. On Rom. 14.6 see above §24.3d.

193. "Joy" is a fairly prominent feature in 2 Corinthians — 1.24; 2.3; 6.10; 7.4, 7, 9, 13, 16.

194. "The gift of God" is almost a technical term for the Holy Spirit in the NT (John 4.10; Acts 2.38; 8.20; 10.45; 11.17; cf. Eph. 3.7 and 4.7; see also §16 n. 17 above). However, the other undisputed Pauline uses (Rom. 5.15, 17) may be less specific: "the gift in grace" (5.15), "the gift of righteousness" (5.17); but Paul is deliberately varying his vocabulary in this paragraph in order to avoid overloading certain terms, particularly *charis/charisma* (7 occurrences in 5.12-21).

195. See again §11.5c above.

196. 8.14 — "The one who had much did not have too much, and the one who had little did not have too little" (Exod. 16.18); 9.9-10 — "As it is written, 'He has scattered abroad, he has given to the poor; his righteousness endures for ever' [Ps. 112.9]. He who supplies 'seed to the sower and bread for food' [Isa. 55.10] . . ."; 8.20 (Prov. 3.4); 9.6 (Prov. 11.24); 9.7 (Deut. 15.10; Prov. 22.8 LXX).

doubt that Paul saw these different appeals as all of a piece. Not to be ignored is the degree to which Paul also made use of rhetorical and literary techniques of his time[197] and his concern that his proposed plans should commend themselves as praiseworthy *(kalos)* before a wider public (8.21).

In view of our findings with regard to 1 Corinthians 7–10, not least of interest here is the pastoral sensitivity which Paul displays in encouraging the Corinthians' full and prompt participation in the collection. In ch. 8 he begins by commending to them the example of the Macedonian churches (8.1-5), as also the enthusiasm of others — particularly Titus (8.6, 16-17)[198] and the unnamed brother (8.22). To the same effect are the strong expressions of Paul's confidence in the Corinthians themselves so prominent in ch. 9 (9.1-3, 13-14). He urges them strongly (8.7, 24), encourages the right attitude (9.7), and presses home his exhortation with scriptural promises (9.6-11). At the same time, he takes care to make it equally clear that he is not writing a "command" (8.8) but simply giving his "advice/opinion" *(gnōmē —* 8.10), the same distinction as in 1 Cor. 7.25. He wants them to contribute as an act of generosity *(eulogia),* not as an act of extortion *(pleonexia)* (9.5).[199]

Throughout, Paul shows sensitivity to the Corinthians' own financial resources (8.12-15) and to the suspicions always likely to hang around such financial transactions (8.19-21; 9.5). He continues to express some qualms lest his confidence has been misplaced (9.3-5), just as elsewhere he expresses uncertainty as to the precise arrangements (1 Cor. 16.4)[200] and fear lest the whole enterprise fail in the event (Rom. 15.30-31). The resulting picture is not of a Paul striding confidently forward, riding roughshod over feelings and views of others. It is a picture rather of one with a basic conviction regarding the collection's importance, but conscious of the need to carry people with him, uncertain as to various aspects of it, and nervous about the final outcome. This final unbaring of his heart (Rom. 15.30-32) reveals to us not just Paul the theologian and pastor, but Paul the man.

§24.9 Conclusion

In this final section we have been sampling a series of ethical issues with which Paul was confronted, to test how he applied in practice the principles

197. Betz, *2 Corinthians 8–9.*
198. Note the repeated reference to *spoudē* ("eagerness") — 8.7, 8, 16.
199. The meaning of the contrasting terms is somewhat unusual for each — *eulogia* usually has the sense of "blessing," and *pleonexia* of "greed, covetousness"; see, e.g., BAGD; Furnish, *2 Corinthians* 428; Betz, *2 Corinthians 8–9* 96-97.
200. "If it is advisable *(axion)* . . ." — *axios* ("worthy") in the extended sense of "worthwhile, fitting, proper" (BAGD 1c).

outlined in §23. In the event it has been the care with which Paul applied these principles in the light of the circumstances which has been the most consistent and most impressive feature. He certainly drew on the principles all the while in the course of his paraenesis. Not in any uniform or formal way, but nonetheless clearly and carefully. The tension and balance between, on the one hand, inward insight and motivation (faith, Spirit, liberty, and love) and, on the other, outward norm (scripture, Jesus tradition, what is generally recognized as good and noble) is maintained throughout.

The eschatological tension is particularly evident and inevitably shaped the thrust of the paraenesis. That meant full awareness of the powerlessness of the little congregations within the cities of the Roman Empire, the need to demonstrate good citizenship, and the importance of bearing in mind the impressions made on outsiders by relationships within the church. In other cases it meant recognition of the sometimes delicate situations of those church members living between two worlds. Here counsel had to be directed to helping them steer a careful course between the compromises inevitable in the already–not yet stage of the process of salvation and the compromises which involved too much still belonging to and being shaped by the values and priorities of the old world.

All the while Paul sought to encourage genuine respect across the spectrum of Christian liberty. And in his own counsel he showed a considerable pastoral sensitivity to the still fragile nature of much early discipleship and many of the first churches. In some cases it was evidently important for him to draw a definite line — illicit sexual practice and idolatry being the clearest examples. But in other cases what stands out is the mix of personal opinion clearly stated, recognition of deeply felt views and established tradition, and encouragement to discern and achieve the appropriate practice for themselves. That Paul sometimes spoke with irritation and the resulting advice is sometimes complicated simply underlines the complexity of the situations and the diversity of personalities with whom he had to deal. If in the end of the day the lasting impression is not just the principles which Paul enunciated for determining Christian conduct but the care with which he sought to live them out and the complications entailed, that is probably as Paul himself would have wished it.

CHAPTER 9

Epilogue

§25 Postlegomena to a theology of Paul

§25.1 Paul's theology as dialogue

Of the models mentioned in §1 for the task of writing a theology of Paul, the one which most commended itself was that of a dialogue. Throughout the preceding pages we have in effect been attempting both to listen in on the dialogue which was Paul's theology and in some measure to participate in that dialogue. The complexity of the dialogue so conceived and the inadequacy of the model of "dialogue" itself to bring out the richness of Paul's theology should now be much clearer.

Our study has at least confirmed the usefulness of conceiving Paul's theology as a dialogue on and among three levels. The deepest level was that of Paul's inherited convictions, with all the taken-for-granteds implied. The middle, pivotal level was the faith which came to him on the Damascus road, but often referred to in formulaic or allusive terms. The most immediate level was that of the letters themselves, where the immediacy of the dialogic character of Paul's theology becomes most apparent.

It has proved to be a very personal dialogue. For it was a dialogue within Paul himself — involving, as we might say, Saul the Pharisee, Paul the Christian, and Paul the apostle. That is to say, it was a dialogue between himself as he had been and to some extent still was, and himself on the Damascus road and expressing the gospel he first received from those who instructed him, and again himself as he grew in faith and developed as missionary and teacher and pastor. Paul himself would not have been fully conscious of all the factors in that internal dialogue. But by attentive and contextual observation we may hope that our portrayal has caught at least some of the existential character of Paul's own theologizing.

The multifaceted character of the dialogue has also become clearer.

713

For at each level there were also other dialogues in process — each contributing in different measure to the dialogue of Paul's theology. His native Judaism was in dialogue with the wider culture of the Hellenistic and Roman world — we need only instance the background to passages like Rom. 1.18-32 or Col. 1.15-20. His Pharisaism was in dialogue with its religious and national heritage — hence the prominence of the issue of the law in Paul's theology. His zealotism was in a kind of dialogue with the alternative understandings of that heritage current within late Second Temple Judaism (Gal. 1.14).

In turn, Paul's Christian faith was in dialogue with the same heritage: he became a member of a different Jewish sect,[1] but the dialogue was similar in kind. So too his interpretation of his new faith ("my gospel"), or, as he himself would have said, his sense of vocation to take the gospel to the nations, was in often vigorous dialogue (altercation would be a better word) with those who were Christians and apostles before him. And as he attempted to communicate his gospel to a wider Hellenistic world he himself drew on other insights and imagery, like conscience and the body politic, and appealed to moral sensibilities and sentiments which commanded broader assent.

Most obvious of all, the topmost and most easily accessible level of his theology was the dialogue with the members of the churches to which he wrote. Or to be more precise, the several dialogues with various individuals and interest groups in these churches, Jews and Gentiles in particular, but also the factions they represented or influences which came to bear on these churches through them.

The theology which came to expression through such a dialogue was bound to be dynamic, a process of theologizing, not a settled state. Neither, on the one hand, was it a dialogue between fixed and unchanging positions, a dialogue of the deaf. Nor, on the other hand, was it a dialogue between positions in constant flux, lacking firmness and stability. In fact, it is precisely the attempt to discern what were the relatively fixed points, what were the points of transformation and innovation, and what were the points where change occurred, and the character and extent of that change, which makes the task of one who listens in on such a dialogue so fascinating.

Here in particular we have been alerted to the danger of simply assuming that the deepest level was also the most settled and that the topmost level contained the most occasional elements of Paul's theology. Certainly the features of his inherited faith which did continue through the apocalyptic revolution of his conversion had to be among the most fixed and stable of his convictions. But the dialogue between middle and deepest levels was a real dialogue which began with a radical reassessment of that heritage (Phil. 3.7-8) and clearly involved either an abandoning or downgrading of much that the

---

1. Acts 24.5, 14; 28.22.

Pharisee Saul had counted as fundamental. Similarly, at the topmost level there is always the question to be asked whether and to what extent Paul was bringing his deepest convictions to bear on a particular issue or was content with merely temporizing advice (to put the alternatives at their extreme).

All this amounts to saying that the dialogue of Paul's theology was a real dialogue — a conversation involving different partners making different contributions at different times and in different measures. In one sense we have to speak of Paul's theology as in dialogue with other theologies. But in another sense it is Paul's theology which was itself the dialogue. Or, as we might say, Paul's theology was so caught up in the dialogue at different levels that it was itself decisively shaped by that dialogue. The attempt to get that balance right has been one of our major preoccupations in the preceding chapters.

And all that we have so far described is only part of the challenge of writing a theology of Paul. For in §1 we may recall that the model of dialogue was first offered as an alternative to depicting the task of writing a theology of Paul as simply "descriptive." The point is worth repeating before we finally draw the threads together. A dialogue, almost by definition, can never be simply descriptive; it is bound to be more interactive. However much the twentieth-century observer would like to limit his or her role to overhearing and transcribing the complex dialogue of the first century, that is not possible. The listener-in is also a participant. The very questions posed to the text are our questions, not Paul's, however much we may hope that they approximate the questions which Paul sought to answer in his letters. Tradition and training, personal experience, and vested interest inevitably attune the listener's ears to catch certain motifs and themes, to fill out the allusions and blanks in accordance with a certain pattern, to filter out the notes which jar or disturb or which the listener regards as insignificant. I have pointed to several examples of this in earlier pages, particularly in the questions and challenges posed to older or alternative interpretations. And my own interpretation can hardly fail to escape similar criticism in at least some measure. But that again is the nature of dialogue. The question which others must judge is whether the above pages have allowed Paul's own voice and convictions and emphases to come through with sufficient clarity, or whether this particular dialogue partner (me!) has imposed a pattern on Paul's theology which was not Paul's, or indeed has stifled or distorted Paul's theology into a different shape.

I have also been very much aware that in any attempt to write a contemporary theology of Paul the apostle, the resulting dialogue cannot be carried on by a single twentieth-century individual alone. Over the centuries the theology of Paul has stimulated so many great theologies and theologians, and their contribution has in turn enriched subsequent perception of Paul's theology. A theology of Paul which might be fitting for the twenty-first century would have to include within its own dialogue all the Paulinists (and anti-Paulinists) of Christian history — from the post-Paulines within the NT itself, through the early church fathers (not ignoring Marcion), Augustine, Luther, Calvin, and so on.[2] But to do any justice to that agenda would have required at least another volume — and would have run the dialogue far beyond my capacity to evaluate the various key contributions to that dialogue. As it is, I am all too conscious that even the limited dialogue which I have been able to sustain with nineteenth- and twentieth-century commentators (and to some extent with the traditions of Pauline interpretation which they represent) has been far from complete.

Nevertheless, such is the stature of Paul the apostle that there must be some value even in the more limited attempt to hear again Paul in his own terms, so far as that is possible. That is the only expertise I have brought to the preceding pages: to offer the fruit of an academic but also personal dialogue with Paul and his letters which stretches back nearly forty years; to attempt to put into words a sense of empathy with Paul and what he wrote; to get inside Paul's skin, as it were, or at least inside the situations and thought processes which brought these letters into existence; to get inside the dialogue which was (and is) his theology, sensitive to the different levels of that dialogue, to take part in that dialogue on behalf of those who may read this volume, to explain it, elucidate it, even in some measure to live it. With what success I leave others to judge.

How then to sum up our findings? How to epitomize the dialogue which we have been attempting to overhear and interact with for several hundred pages? How to summarize a dialogue which is not merely an echo from the past but still demands attention from those who also theologize in classroom, church, or daily living? The obvious answer is to review the three levels of Paul's own dialogue and to clarify so far as possible how much they contributed to his theology, and what features of his theology and of his theologizing remain of enduring significance, still demanding a voice in the ongoing theological dialogue, still staking a claim to define the gospel, still providing a normative characterization for the identity of Christianity.

§25.2 The stable foundation of Paul's theology

Paul's faith remained in large measure the faith and religion of his fathers — more so than many commentators on Paul have realized. He thought of his new faith in Jesus Christ not as a departure from that older faith, but as its fulfilment. And though the practice of his religion quickly took different

2. Morgan, *Romans* 128-52, provides the most recent but very brief sketch.

shapes from his former praxis, he did not think of it as a different religion. Even as apostle to the Gentiles, he still remained Paul the Jew, Paul the Israelite. If we picture Second Temple Judaism as built on four major pillars — monotheism, election, Torah, and Temple[3] — the position can be sketched in quite quickly.

a) *God.* The conclusions drawn at the end of §2 have remained remarkably undisturbed in the chapters which followed. Throughout Paul's ongoing dialogue, God continued to be the bedrock and foundation of his theology. He never ceased to maintain the first two commandments of the Decalogue — to have no other gods beside the one God and to abhor idolatry with all his soul.

Whether Paul continued to say the *Shema* in daily confession we cannot say. But his letters clearly attest that he continued to believe it, his theology to affirm it. The issue raised by Paul's christology — whether and to what extent it modified his monotheism — was answered clearly in §10. When Jesus had been exalted as the one Lord, God the Father was still to be confessed as one (1 Cor. 8.6). When every knee was to bow to Jesus Christ as Lord, the glory would belong to God the Father (Phil. 2.10-11). When every enemy had been subjected to him, the Son himself was to be subject to the one who subjected everything to him, in order that God might be all in all (1 Cor. 15.28). The monotheism is modified, or, perhaps better, more clearly defined, by reference to Jesus. Even in the formulations just cited the point is evident. God was not simply to be known as the Creator and final Judge, not simply as the God of Israel, but also as "the God and Father of our Lord Jesus Christ."[4] But as such he was still the one God and final reference point in all Paul's theology and theologizing.

A similar feature emerged in relation to the Spirit of God. Paul's experience of God as Spirit, as mysterious vivifying and inspiring power, was of a piece with the experience of *ruach* attested by Moses (2 Cor. 3.16) and the prophets before him. That experience could be more clearly defined and recognized by reference to Christ, as the Spirit *of Christ.*[5] But it was not another Spirit which was so designated, only the Spirit of God, the Spirit given by God. If the character of Christ had now defined the character of the Spirit, it was the Spirit of God which was so defined.

Similarly with such a key concept in Paul's theology as "the righteousness of God" (§14.2) For Paul it was always *God's* righteousness, never *Christ's* righteousness. Christ was an integral part of the action and process signified by that term — he was made righteousness from God (1 Cor. 1.30),

3. See my *Partings* ch. 2.
4. See above §10 n. 100.
5. See above §10.6 and n. 157.

he would share in the final judgment (2 Cor. 5.10), believers would become the righteousness of God in him (2 Cor. 5.21) — but God was the source and measure of that righteousness from start to finish. To make the point another way, it was not Christ who turned a divine righteousness of judgment into one of justification. Rather, the death of Christ as saving act gained its definition as such from the saving righteousness which the one God displayed towards Israel from the beginning (Rom. 3.21-26). Paul did not first discover the basic principle of justification by faith (that divine acceptance is a matter of grace and not of reward) when he became a Christian; the gracious choice of a people without anything in itself to commend it was at the heart of Israel's own faith.

In short, the Paul who wrote the great doxology of Rom. 11.33-36 evidently never entertained the slightest thought or intention of abandoning his inherited faith in God as one. We see a faith more sharply (and more controversially) defined. Whether a redefinition in terms of a phrase like "christological monotheism"[6] best restates that faith remains an item for the ongoing dialogue. We see tensions within the monotheism so defined. But these were tensions which could not be coped with as beliefs in other gods had been coped with. Rather, they stimulated an elaboration of the older tension between Creator God transcendent and Spirit of God immanent, a process which eventuated in the Christian conceptualization of God as triune. The point here, however, is that the tensions were *within* the monotheism and not destructive of it. Paul, we may be confident, would never have accepted as a restatement of his theology anything which departed from or denied the fundamental affirmation that God is one.

b) *Israel.* That God had previously been known as the God of Israel highlights another in some degree surprising feature of stability in Paul's theology. Surprising, precisely because Paul the apostle saw himself as "apostle to the Gentiles" (Rom. 11.13). Moreover, he is mostly credited with breaking Christianity free from the Jewish and national mould which might otherwise have contained it. Despite all, however, the second pillar of Judaism, or, we would better say, the second pillar of Israel, remained intact for Paul's theology — as we saw in §19.

In basic terms this means that the language of Paul's thought, the currency of his theology, remained Hebraic through and through. I refer not only to his anthropological understanding (§3), but also to the analytical tools and categories which he used — not least, his use of the Adam narratives (§4), of the imagery of atoning sacrifice and redemption (§9), of divine Wisdom (§11), of God's righteousness (§14), of history in terms of apocalyptic disclosure and climax (§18), and of the church of God (§20). But also to his

6. See above §2 n. 6.

understanding of Israel itself and of Israel's destiny within the purposes of God. The poignant wrestling of Romans 9–11, we may say, was not simply a matter of national pride, or of Paul preserving his own identity as an Israelite. It was also a theological priority: to maintain faith in the God who had chosen Israel to be his special people among all the peoples of the earth; to acknowledge Israel's story as the story of God's purpose on earth. God defined in relation to Israel, Israel defined in relation to God: these are two foci around which Paul continued to circumscribe the arcs of his theology.

Of course Paul's gospel challenged the understanding of Israel then dominant among his fellow Jews. He pressed back behind Moses to Abraham, behind Abraham to Adam, and behind Israel's election to God's primal act of creation, of giving life to the dead and calling things without existence into existence (Rom. 4.17). The God of Israel was not to be defined simply as God of Jews only (Rom. 3.29). But this was not to abandon the thought of Israel's election. It was more a case of reminding Israel that their status as Israel was determined from start to finish by the gracious calling of God (Rom. 9.6-13; 11.6), more a case of recalling Israel to a fresh realization of what their calling by the one Creator God must mean for Israel's relationship with the nations.

Similarly, Paul recalled Israel to the neglected strand of the founding promise to Abraham — the promise that in Abraham all the nations would be blessed (Gal. 3.8). And his own vocation as apostle to the nations was self-consciously framed in terms of the prophet's identical summons and the Servant's own call to be a light to the nations.[7] So once again we have to insist that Paul saw his mission not as a turning of his (or God's) back on Israel, but as a fulfilment of Israel's own task.

This was an integral part of Paul's theological dialogue with his heritage. It was a dialogue which seemed to fail, soon broken off by the dominant voices in shaping rabbinic Judaism and patristic Christianity in the subsequent centuries. But it remains at the heart of Paul's own theologising (§6.3). It remains at the heart of any Christianity which defines itself in terms of Paul's theology. And it is part of the unfinished business of any theology which includes Paul as one of its dialogue partners.

c) *Torah*. If there is any subplot in Paul's theology it is his engagement with the law. Our own repeated engagement with the subject, particularly §§6, 14, and 23, reflected not only the prominence of the theme (Paul and the law) in the traditions of Reformation theology, but also the complexity of Paul's own dealings with it.

In the event we found it necessary to distinguish between different functions of the law as the clue to a proper appreciation of its role within Paul's theology. (1) The function of the law in defining sin and condemning

7. Note again the clear echo of Jer. 1.5 and Isa. 49.1-6 in Gal. 1.15-16.

transgression seems to have remained constant throughout Paul's theologising (§6.3). He was even able to extend that function to embrace the conscience-instructed Gentile (Rom. 2.12-16).

(2) To be sure, that function of the law was redefined in the light of the gospel and of experience of the gospel (§23.5). It was understood as a stimulus to faith (the law of faith), as the measure of conduct in accordance with the Spirit (the law of the Spirit), by reference to Christ's teaching and example (the law of Christ). But it could legitimately be claimed that that understanding was wholly in accordance with the prophetic hope of the law written in the heart and of a new heart and a new spirit. In this case the dialogue had a different outcome from that approved by Qumranite, Pharisee, and rabbi. But it was essentially the same dialogue. Paul saw his teaching as a full and continuing affirmation of this function of the law. He would have regretted the fact that the dialogue with his fellow Pharisees was soon to be broken off on both sides. Any restatement of Paul's theology at this point will have to strive to maintain a positive role for the law within it and to reopen the dialogue with Paul's heritage which was so fundamental to his own theologising.

(3) The complications and strains within Paul's theology of the law emerged with the third function — what we might call the law's social function in protecting and disciplining Israel in particular. The claim that that function was temporary, until the coming of Christ (§6.5), was unavoidably controversial. For in effect it put Christ in the place of the law as the primary definition and hallmark of the purpose and people of God. And it was this which gave Paul the criterion by which to discriminate between commandments of the law, allowing him to devalue or discard some while affirming the others. For in the event the commandments which were devalued and discarded in Paul's theology were those which, for good or ill, had come to mark out Israel and to maintain Israel's separation from the other nations (particularly circumcision, food laws, and feast days) (§14.4) and, less explicitly, those which Christ had rendered unnecessary (Temple sacrifice). At the same time, such a gradation or hierarchy of commandments within the Torah was hardly unusual within the Judaism of Paul's time — the clash of principles resolved by a ruling which ameliorated the harshness of one commandment in the light of another.[8] To that extent at least we can say that Paul's own halakhah was part of the dialogue already current within the Judaism of his day. The question

---

8. E.g.: (1) Hillel's *prosbul,* a legal formula designed to circumvent the Sabbath year cancellation of loans made between Israelites (Deut. 15.1-2) by turning the debt over for collection by a court (Deut. 15.1-3 being understood to refer to private, not public loans). (2) Commentators on Mark. 3.4 pars. debate on how far the Sabbath regulations had already been waived in order to save a life (cf. *m. Yoma* 8.6); and in the same connection, note the disagreement between Pharisees and the Qumranites on how far the Sabbath law could be relaxed, as reflected in Matt. 12.11, compared with CD 11.13-14.

is whether by his rulings at this point he so touched the quick of Jewish/Israel's identity that continuing dialogue became impossible for those who continued to define Israel in ethnic terms and by reference to the fence of the Torah.

(4) The most controversial function of the law in Paul's theology is its role as the cat's-paw of sin — that is, the law as taken by the power of sin beyond its role in bringing sin into consciousness, actually to bring about transgression (§6.7). Paul was well aware that to ascribe such a role to the law might seem to identify the law with sin itself and thus to damn the law altogether. He took pains, therefore, to defend the law against precisely that charge (Romans 7). His point in effect was that the law is not such a power. It is a guide for living (§6.6). It is the measure of divine wrath (§6.3). But in itself it has neither the power of life nor the power of death. Only as it is controlled by a greater power — the power of sin (the law of sin and death) or the Spirit of God (the law of the Spirit of life) — can it be a means of death or a means of life. As long as the weakness of the flesh and the power of sin endure, the law will continue to be a force for death. But under the power of the Spirit (as spiritual) it remains God's holy and good guide and yardstick. In short, Rom. 7.7–8.4 in effect attempts to draw this fourth function of the law back to its proper place within the first (1) redefined by the second (2).

d) The fourth pillar of Second Temple Judaism we identified as the *Temple* itself. If there is any pillar of his traditional religion which Paul can be said to have abandoned wholly or almost completely it is this one. As we saw in §20, Paul seems to have moved away more or less entirely from any sense that his redefined faith had to be attached to holy land or particular holy place. Categories of temple and priesthood, of holiness and purity remain elements in his theologizing, but appear only in a communalized or desacralized form — all believers as "holy ones," as temple, as priests in service of the gospel. As a defining category and religious context, the people of the holy land seem to have been replaced by the image of the body of Christ.

One of the most tantalizing questions in Paul's theology is how much this was part of Paul's fundamental theology. Did he by means of this reworking of categories of cult and holiness thereby express a sense of eschatological immediacy before God which rendered such institutions unnecessary? Or was it all part of a reaction against what now appeared to him as a too narrowly defined identity of Israel in terms of Temple and holy land? Such questions have not often been addressed and seldom dealt with satisfactorily in the ongoing dialogue of Christian theology.

So far as the dialogue with Paul's Jewish heritage is concerned, however, we should note that Paul continued to think of Jerusalem as an image of salvation and freedom (Gal. 4.26). He continued to affirm the fundamental importance of his churches' attachment to Jerusalem (the collection). He continued to share his people's hope of a deliverer to come out of Zion (Rom.

11.26). At the same time, we recall that rabbinic Judaism also had to come to terms with the loss of a living connection with Jerusalem and its temple. On this point the dialogue is painful on both sides. And the degree to which and way in which these memories of and images from former days form effective elements of stability within the theologizing of both are again part of the ongoing dialogue.

More to the point may be a shift in the focus of the fourth pillar from Temple to *scripture*. For it was certainly that shift which marked the emergence of rabbinic Judaism — a shift from priest to rabbi as the defining representative of the new phase of its own dialogue. And for Paul something of the same could be claimed. For even more than Torah, it is the scriptures of Israel (less centred on Torah as such) which provide another stable element in Paul's theology. I do not refer for the moment to Paul's way of handling and interpreting these scriptures. It is the more basic fact which is in view — the fact that Paul clearly regarded it as essential to be able to build his theology on and from the scriptures. Although we focused on this feature only briefly (§7.2), it was clear throughout that scripture served as the quarry from which Paul drew his primary ideas, terms, and themes. We need only instance his theology in the narrow sense (§2), his analysis of the human condition (§4), the categories and images he used to explicate the significance of Christ (ch. 4), his understanding and exposition of righteousness by faith alone (§14), his understanding of the life-giving Spirit (§16), his retelling of the story of Israel (§19), his exposition of the Lord's Supper (§22), and the degree to which he assumed or drew on scripture in his paraenesis (§24). At this point the rabbinic Judaism of Torah, Tanach, and Mishnah is not so far removed from the Pauline theology of law, prophets, and gospel.

Here again we may simply observe that any attempt to take Paul's theology seriously and to engage in dialogue with it will simply have to acknowledge (*pace* Marcion) the foundational significance of the scriptures of Israel for Paul's theology and so also for Christian theology. A major feature of any ongoing dialogue in Christian theology has to be the continuing status of these scriptures, a proper recognition of them as Israel's scriptures, and a continued scrutiny of the dialogue between them as Israel's scriptures and the scriptures of the new covenant, including not least the letters of Paul himself. Paul's own dialogue with his scriptural heritage is part of the ongoing dialogue his theology has provoked.

§25.3 *The fulcrum point of Paul's theology*

The middle level of Paul's theology is, of course, dominated by Christ. Here I prefer the image of fulcrum or pivot point, the point on which a whole larger mass swings round into a new plane or direction. The fact that images of dialogue, different levels, and fulcrum hardly mesh with any precision is of little moment. On the contrary, they prevent us from becoming locked into a single, inevitably inadequate image. And the friction between them helps maintain the vigour and dynamism which each image encapsulates. In this, Paul himself provides a more than adequate precedent (§13.4).

The image serves most effectively in reference to Paul's own conversion. For there most obviously his theology swung round — not out of the plane of Israel, as we have just argued (§25.2), but certainly to point in a different direction. And in that instance, beyond question, Christ was the decisive factor — as Paul's several recollections of the event clearly indicate.[9] We need not continue here the debate as to how quickly Paul's theology was reordered and in what sequence. More to the point is the fact that Christ continued to play this pivotal role in Paul's maturing and mature theology. That is to say, the fulcrum swing was not a once-for-all event in Paul's theologising. Christ continued to be the pivot in the ongoing dialogue which was Paul's theology. Alternatively expressed, bringing our imagery into closer alignment, Christ continued to function as the central criterion by which Paul made critical discrimination of what counted and what was of lesser moment. Or again, Christ was the plumb line by which Paul measured the alignment of what could and should be built on the stable foundation inherited from his past.

a) *The realignment of Paul's heritage.* We have already commented on this from the perspective of the continuity of that heritage. Here it is appropriate to remind ourselves of the way in which in Paul's theology Christ gave that heritage clearer definition.

For Paul, God was now to be known definitively by reference to Christ. If I am right, the use of Wisdom language to describe Christ, including the language of preexistence, was in the first instance an attempt to say that God's self-revelation in and through creation was now most clearly manifested in Christ (§11). God not only acted through Christ, but he revealed himself and his character most fully in terms of Christ. The debate as to whether the language of participation in creation demands thought of the personal preexistence of Christ may actually obscure this primary point: that for Paul the revelation of Christ was the revelation of God; that for Paul God so revealed himself in Christ that Christ became the definition of God (but "definition" is too scholastic a term). God as Creator, God as God of Israel, was now more clearly defined, or, better, characterized, as the Father of our Lord Jesus Christ.

In a correlated way Christ as last Adam functions in Paul's theology as the archetypal fulfilment and measure of God's purpose in creating

9. Gal. 1.15-16; Phil. 3.7-8; 2 Cor. 4.4-6.

humankind (§10.2). Here too the primary theological thrust can be diverted into details less central to the dialogue of Paul's theology — what Paul's use of the Adam myth says about Christ as first in creation or as a corporate being. The primary thrust is rather to reflect the degree to which Christ in his person and work, particularly his death and resurrection, illumines the character of humankind as it was intended to be — loving the neighbour and looking to the resurrection of the dead.

Not least of importance for an appreciation of Paul's theology is it to note also that the double imagery of Wisdom and Adam effectively interlocks creation and salvation. Paul would have had no truck with those who thought it necessary to set God apart from creation in a dualistic way or who understood salvation as salvation from the body and the bodily world. Christ as Wisdom, Christ as Adam is Christ the image of God, is Christ who in his person and work reveals both what God is like and how his good purpose embraces humankind within creation and with responsibility under God over all created things.

Similar points can be made with regard to the other two instances noted above (§25.2a). For risen Christ/last Adam as "life-giving Spirit" (1 Cor. 15.45) becomes in Paul's theology the definition also of God's Spirit (§10.6). The Spirit of God was not incarnate in Christ (Paul never hints at such a formulation). Nor did the Spirit of God simply inspire Christ. But somewhere between (and the line between inspiration and incarnation can be quite fine), the Spirit becomes known to Paul as the Spirit of Christ. The Spirit can now be recognized not only by reference to Christ (the spirit of his ministry), but even in some sense as the medium of Christ's continuing presence. Here again it is important that the ongoing theological dialogue should retain this pivotal role of Christ in characterizing the Spirit of God as well as God as Father and not lose sight of it in debates regarding substance and person.

So too with the righteousness of God. If God's righteousness also means his faithfulness as Creator and as God of Israel, then Christ as God's righteousness displays what that faithfulness means in practice — archetypally on the cross and in the resurrection. Christ's death reveals God's righteousness not for the first time, not for the only time, and not for the last time, but definitively.

As to Israel, we need simply recall Paul's argument in Galatians 3 that Christ is the seed in which the promise to Abraham is fulfilled. Here, too, we should not allow ourselves to be distracted by the apparently artificial exegesis by means of which Paul makes his point (Gal. 3.16). His point is rather that Christ so embodies and realizes the purpose of God to bless all the nations that the fulfilment of Abraham's promise can be seen as summed up in him. Faith in Christ has become the doorway through which the Gentiles enter into Abraham's inheritance. To be bound up with Christ in his death and in resurrection still to come is to be accounted Abraham's seed, full participants in Israel's heritage.

We need not rehearse here the strains which this attempt to define Israel afresh in the light of its primary calling placed upon the coherence of Paul's theology — strains which Paul himself could only resolve by appeal to the mystery of God's ultimate purpose (Rom. 11.25-32). He redefined, using our earlier imagery, the two foci of God and Israel, around which he drew the arcs of his theology, both by reference to Christ — God revealed in Christ, Israel fulfilled in Christ. He was confident that the common factor would hold all three elements together, would enable him, we might say, to fill out the arcs of his theology into a complete ellipse. The fact that that has not yet happened is simply to recognize the eschatological character of Paul's hope at this point and the ongoing nature of the dialogue which his theology began.

As to the other elements in the stable foundation of Paul's theology, we need simply note that here too Christ became for Paul the determinative measure of alignment in the case of both Torah and scripture. Christ, we might say, to vary the metaphor once again, became for Paul the decisive triangulation point from which Paul was able to assess the dimensions of Torah and scripture in their bearing on his own faith and life and on that of his churches. As already noted, Torah still had claim to guide and direct Christian living; "keeping the commandments of God" still counted for Paul (1 Cor. 7.19). But it was not the law as such which Paul had in mind, only the law as "the law of Christ" (Gal. 6.2), only as "in-lawed" to Christ (1 Cor. 9.21). Christ as the self-revelation of God in creation, Christ as the archetype of the human creature, Christ as the characterization of God's Spirit, Christ as the enactment of God's righteousness, Christ as the implementation of Israel's promise and commission, was also Christ the measure of what should still count in God's Torah, the exemplar of how the law could and should be fulfilled.

So too with scripture. "The revelation of Jesus Christ" on the Damascus road (Gal. 1.12) also lifted what he later describes as the veil which had prevented and continued to prevent a proper understanding of the old covenant and its scriptures (2 Cor. 3.14). It is almost impossible to envisage Paul, with no personal knowledge of Christ, being persuaded simply from the scriptures to look for one like the Christ proclaimed by the first Christians. But confronted with one who identified himself as that Christ, Paul found that a flood of light had been poured on the scriptures with which he had engaged himself at such length and so deeply. Here as clearly as anywhere Christ functioned as the fulcrum point on which Paul's whole theology pivoted, the key which unlocked so many of scriptures' conundrums (though setting up others), the light which illumined its dark places (though setting up a fresh pattern of light and shade).

That is not to indict Paul's hermeneutic as arbitrary; or at least it is no more arbitrary than any other reading of scripture. Nor is it to affirm that Paul's hermeneutic imposed meanings on the many scriptural passages which he drew into and by means of which he claimed validation for his theology. For Paul would have argued strenuously that his exegesis was simply drawing out and highlighting the meaning of the passage itself. And though in various cases we today find his exegetical techniques strange and less impressive, it can be justly claimed that they were fully in accord with the canons of accepted practice for his own day. Nor should we allow the impression to go unchallenged that the Christ-scripture dialogue of Paul's theology was actually a one-way monologue. For again we have seen repeatedly that the categories on which Paul drew to elucidate the significance of Jesus (not least Adam and Wisdom, Christ and sacrifice, resurrection and Lordship) were drawn directly from scripture and were only valid insofar as they continued to express their scriptural content. It was Christ who illumined the scriptures for Paul. But it was the Christ of scripture in whom he believed and whom he preached.

In short, we can indeed speak of two levels in Paul's theology, of two stories, the story of Israel and the story of Christ. The interaction (dialogue) between these two is one of the most fascinating features of Paul's theology. The one does not overwhelm the other, nor does the other undermine the one. Neither can dispense with the other, since each informs and gives meaning to the other. In Paul's theology they have a symbiotic relationship (a *syn-* compound of which Paul would no doubt have approved). That mutual enlivening is at the heart of Paul's theologizing.

b) *Christianity is Christ.* It is not only in the clarification and sharper definition of his heritage that the centrality of Christ for Paul's theology is evident. Christ is the thread which runs through all, the lens through which all comes into focus, the glue which bonds the parts into a coherent whole. The very form of the letters he wrote expresses the point for us, beginning and ending as they do most regularly by invoking on his readers the grace of Christ. And there is little difficulty in recalling how much the body and substance of Paul's theology throbs and pulses with the name of Christ and bears throughout the stamp of the impact of his life, death, and resurrection on Paul.

We need simply recall that the revelation of Christ to Paul meant a whole new world for Paul — the new epoch of resurrection life, the "new creation" already in effect (§10). This apocalyptic perspective, this eschatological shift, dictates much of what is most characteristic in Paul's theology. Not as a break with the past so much as a transformation of the past's relation to the present and the present's relation to the future. Not only personal history (§7.4), but also all human history, as Paul now perceived it, hung suspended between the midpoint of Christ's death and resurrection and the end point of Christ's parousia (§18).

Indeed, as part of this apocalyptic perspective, Paul could even envisage Christ as bracketing the whole sweep of history from beginning to end — Christ as the Wisdom of God's creation (§11.2) and Christ as the final judge of all human works (§12). To be sure, the brackets were within the still wider sweep, impossible to conceptualize in human terms, from the God who creates to God the eschatological all in all. But it is the beginning and the end seen in terms of Christ which begin to make them comprehensible to human thought, which enable theology to speak a little more meaningfully of them.

Within this all-embracing overview, the cross and resurrection of Christ are central. This was an emphasis which Paul inherited as already established in still earlier Christian tradition. But he made it his own and fundamental (or, should we say, pivotal) for his own theology. This was the christological moment par excellence for Paul. Insofar as we can talk of any thought of incarnation in Paul's theology, the mission of the Son had the saving act of his death and resurrection primarily in view.[10] And though the salvation process looked to Christ's coming (again) as a climactic point, the centre of gravity for Paul's theology still remained firmly rooted in Christ's earlier mission. It was for this reason, we observed, that the failure of Paul's imminent expectation ("the Lord is near" — Phil. 4.5) did not constitute a fatal flaw in Paul's theology (§12). Paul's theology was eschatological not because of what Christ was still to do, but because of what he had already done. As the affirmation of Christ in creation held creation and salvation together, so the affirmation of Christ in consummation gave added significance to the central act of salvation and held out the tantalizing promise of ultimate vindication for the claims made regarding it. But neither emphasis detracted from the centrality of the principal christological moment as such.

The centrality of Christ is equally evident in the gospel and process of salvation more personally perceived. The gospel called not simply for faith, but for faith in Christ. Why this should be, why faith had to be in Christ and could no longer be simply in God, Paul never properly explains. So much taken for granted by him was the conviction that Christ was the eschatological embodiment of God's saving purpose — a conviction no doubt repeatedly confirmed as both Jew and Gentile found that responding in faith to the gospel of Christ brought them realization of justification with God and the gift of his Spirit. Presumably he could have envisaged a saving faith which was not focused in Christ as such, just as he envisaged Gentiles not knowing the law but being the law for themselves. But for Paul the apostle, missionary and evangelist, teacher and pastor, the story of Christ made possible a faith which all could exercise, and that remained his focus throughout.

In the same vein we note that of the three principal aspects of the

10. Rom. 8.3; Gal. 4.4-5; Phil. 2.6-9.

727

beginning of the salvation process for Paul, the most prevalent and consistent within his letters was that of participation in Christ (§15). The "in Christ," "with Christ," "through Christ" motifs have proved themselves among the most difficult to handle within the ongoing dialogue provoked by Paul's theology. We reflected more than once in the pages above[11] on the conceptual problems posed by imagery of Christ as a corporate or representative figure for a verbal theology whose very stuff of existence is conceptualization. But here particularly the difficulty of theologizing should not be allowed to obscure the centrality of Christ in what Paul thereby affirmed. Here we should allow for the at-one-removeness of metaphorical language, and not conclude that the unavoidable "fuzziness" of such language is somehow a mark of inadequacy or a cause to renounce it. Above all, we should recognize that the language expresses an experience of grace and faith which Paul evidently felt could only adequately be described as experience of Christ — in Christ, with Christ, through Christ. The struggle thus to express a quality and character of experience in terms of Christ reminds us that the dialogue of theology has an experiential dimension, and that Christ is central in both for Paul.

It was no doubt partly the difficulty of handling such language which brought the sacraments to greater prominence in the ongoing dialogue than they seem to have had in Paul's own theology. A sacramental theology proved more manageable than one focused on "in Christ" language and experience. At the same time the most striking feature of Paul's theology of baptism (§17) and the Lord's supper (§22) is precisely that they too brought to focus the centrality of Christ in his understanding of gospel and church. Baptism was "in the name of" Christ. Individuals were baptized into Christ, into his death, into his body. The bread and cup were a sharing in the body and blood of Christ. The Supper was the Lord's. It was partaken "in remembrance" of Christ. It re(-)presented the death of Christ, and by sharing in it they proclaimed afresh Christ's death "until he comes." However Paul may have viewed the subsequent development of sacramental theology and practice, we can hardly doubt that he would not have wished these central features to be obscured.

Probably most profound of all was Paul's concept of the process of salvation as a growing conformity to Christ, and not least to his death (§18.5). Here again Paul's thought evokes a kind of mysticism, a mysticism which can be partly reenvisaged as sacramental mysticism, but only partly. And though Paul used the imagery particularly to make sense of his own apostolic suffering and hardship, he would hardly have welcomed its reworking as a purely individual mysticism. For he saw it as part of the process of salvation in which all believers shared, indeed in which the creation as a whole shared

11. See above §11.6, §12.5(4), §§20.4, 7.

(Rom. 8.17-23). The dying of the flesh and to the flesh could not be experienced solely in moments of worship, but had to be expressed also in the discipline of the daily walk in accordance with the Spirit. Within that context the theology of suffering which it enshrined, suffering as a sharing in Christ's suffering, had a powerfully positive pastoral potential. Outside that context it could appear only idealistic and lacking in seriousness.

Finally, we should just recall that the principal imagery Paul elaborated when he spoke of the corporate dimension of Christian faith was of the church as the body of Christ, as one body in Christ (§20.4). Most intriguing here is the extent to which Paul related his several uses of the body imagery. Did he indeed think of the little churches scattered round the northeastern quadrant of the Mediterranean as the embodiment of Christ in these places? He surely cannot have regarded each little church as Christ's resurrection body of glory. Did he then think the embodiment of Christ in these churches shared the same frailties as the human body, still awaiting a corporate resurrection of the body, still awaiting transformation into Christ's glorious body? Matters once again for the ongoing dialogue with Paul. Whatever the tenor of that dialogue, Paul's principal emphasis should be clear: Christian presence in the continuation of the present age was inevitably corporate, and its corporate charter was the character of Christ himself.

In short, for Paul Christianity is Christ. Any restatement of his theology, any theologizing which seeks to sustain a dialogue with Paul will simply have to recognize this. The centrality of Christ, as showing what God is like, as defining God's Spirit, as the channel of Israel's blessing for the nations, as demonstrating what obedience to Torah means, as the light which illumines Israel's scriptures, as embodying the paradigm of creation and consummation, his death and resurrection as the midpoint of time, as the magnet for faith, as the focus of all sacramental significance, as determining the personal and corporate identity of Christians, as the image to which the salvation process conforms, is simply inescapable in the theology of Paul the apostle. The difficulty which later stages of the ongoing dialogue of Christian theology have found with some of these conceptualizations cannot detract from that centrality, and besides has the benefit of driving the dialogue back to its beginnings in Paul's own formulations.

§25.4 Centre and development

To say that Christ is the focal and pivotal point of Paul's theology also in effect provides an answer to one of the questions left hanging in §1: whether we can speak of a *centre* of Paul's theology. If the imagery of "centre" is still useful for a subject like theology, then Christ has to be regarded as the centre of Paul's theology — but as a living centre of his theologising, and not just a conceptual centre of a static system. Or if a category like "coherence" is preferred (Beker), then Christ (the experience of Christ and the christology which is in symbiotic relationship with that experience) has to be seen as that which gave Paul's whole enterprise as theologian, missionary, and pastor its coherence.

None of this should detract from the points already made (§§25.2-3): it is precisely the interaction and integration of Paul's christology with and within his inherited convictions which gave Paul's theology its dynamic character as he brought it to expression in the course of his mission and letter writing. And we could, in consequence, elaborate the narrower concept of centre or coherence in a fuller formulation, in terms, for example, of God acting in Christ. But the more extensive the elaboration, the greater the diversity of formulation and more refined the nuance necessary.[12] It is probably simpler and wiser to focus on the basic factors which were at the heart of Paul's theology in the hope that the dynamic of their interaction can be illustrated in a variety of formulations. It is for this reason that I have deliberately used imagery which does not neatly fit together — dialogue, foundation, fulcrum point.

What of the other issue raised in §1.4 — whether we can speak of *development* in Paul's theology? It will be recalled that this book has attempted to fill out Paul's theology at the time he wrote Romans, using Romans as a template, and allowing for the possibility of development in Paul's theology before or after he wrote Romans. Has our study indicated moments of significant development within Paul's theologizing through his letters?

So far as this study is concerned, that question must focus on the period covered by the letters themselves — between the writing of 1 Thessalonians and the writing of Philemon or Colossians[13] — that is, a period of only about ten years. The brevity of the period cannot be counted as a determinative factor in answering the question. Theologians today may rarely change their theology dramatically over a ten-year period spanning their late 40s and 50s. But then few theologians today are engaged in such pioneer missionary work or share such traumatic experiences as Paul's letters attest.

Nevertheless, when we reflect on what we have uncovered, and allowing for diversity of circumstance and variety of expression, there does seem to be a remarkable continuity and homogeneity bonding all Paul's letters into a coherent whole. There are different emphases, certainly, but whether we should speak of significant development is doubtful. There is clarification of

12. See further my *Unity* 369-74.
13. But, of course, there is debate about the dating of the prison epistles (Philippians, Philemon, Colossians). On Colossians see above §11 n. 7.

earlier insights, an unfolding of fuller meaning and implication; but "evolution" would be a less appropriate term. At most we can probably envisage a number of events and experiences (four can be discerned) which changed the emphases and prompted the elaborations, but did not alter the main elements or overall character of his theology in a significant way.

The first is the possibility that the events in Thessalonica caused Paul to modify his preaching of the parousia. If so, again I stress, it is a matter of change of emphasis, not of content. We may also note the several unusual features in 1 and 2 Thessalonians (phrases like "in the Lord Jesus Christ" and "in God"),[14] which suggest that he was still experimenting with the formulation of some of what proved to be his characteristic motifs.

The second is the possibility that news of the threat to his churches in Galatia caused Paul to emphasize his own status as "apostle"[15] and "the truth of the gospel" as focused in "justification from faith and not from works of the law." Again, this is not to say that these elements were lacking prior to the writing of Galatians; the references back in Gal. 2.1-16 and 3.1 are sufficient testimony on that point. But it does appear that something happened to provoke the letter to the Galatians and to establish these features as a more prominent and regular feature of his theology.[16]

The third is the possibility of a major crisis in Ephesus between the writing of 1 Corinthians and 2 Corinthians — referred to most explicitly in 2 Cor. 1.8. The personal suffering involved may well have contributed to Paul's theology of suffering (particularly apostolic, but not simply apostolic suffering)[17] which is such a prominent feature of 2 Corinthians. Once again, we cannot speak of a new feature, or even a new emphasis — as passages like Gal. 2.19 and 6.17 and 1 Cor. 4.9-13 confirm. But it is true that the profoundest expressions of that theology are to be found in the later letters (2 Corinthians, Romans, and Philippians).

We may perhaps speak of a fourth transition point in Paul's ministry and theologizing. That would be the realization which lay behind the decision to write Romans itself — the realization that he had reached a significant juncture in his work. He had completed his mission in the northeastern quadrant of the Mediterranean (Rom. 15.18-23); it was time to deliver the collection to Jerusalem and to begin a new phase of his mission (15.24-29). This sense of transition did not mark a development in his theology. What it did evidently produce in Paul was the desire to set out his understanding of the gospel in

14. See above §15 n. 31.
15. See above §21 n. 29.
16. I remain convinced that Galatians must have been written soon after the Thessalonian correspondence; see my *Galatians* 5-19.
17. See above §21.2a.

a fuller and in some sense definitive or final way. Romans was the result, and subsequent generations have been in Paul's debt ever since.

As suggested in §1, the most significant developments in Paul's/Pauline theology took place before and after the letters which he dictated or penned in his own terms. The brief outline of personal history which Paul himself provides in Galatians 1–2 indicates three events of great moment for Paul's earlier theological development. The first was, of course, his conversion itself — on which enough has been said above.[18] The second was the consultation, conference, or confrontation in Jerusalem with the pillar apostles (Gal. 2.1-10). Paul, of course, was clear that the conference made no difference to his gospel (2.6). But his language also makes clear that the agreement of the Jerusalem leadership was crucial to the success of his mission (2.2) and to his hope of presenting his gospel in its continuity with the spiritual heritage represented by Jerusalem (e.g., Rom. 15.27). And the third was no doubt the incident at Antioch, with the sharpening of the issue of "works of the law" and the breach with the Jerusalem-sponsored missionary work which it seems to have triggered.[19]

Here again, however, we should not exaggerate the changes in Paul's theology involved. In particular, the extent to which Paul was able to cite already traditional Christian formulations and to allude to Jesus tradition is sufficient indication that Paul understood his theology to be in direct continuity both with the gospel of those who had believed and been called before him (cf., e.g., 1 Cor. 15.11) and with the teaching and ministry of Jesus himself. Paul himself would never have given credence to the suggestion that there was an unbridgeable gulf between Jesus and Paul, that he had distorted the message and mission of Jesus, or that he should be given credit as a second founder of Christianity in some sense comparable with Jesus.

At the other end of Paul's ministry we have also to speak of the other most significant development in Pauline theology — that is, between the theology formulated by Paul himself and that formulated in his name by his "school." Even though I regard Colossians as standing at the edge of the authentic Pauline letters,[20] there are sufficient variations from what Paul himself wrote earlier for us to speak of significant development. We may instance the full-blown cosmic christology of Col. 1.15-20 and 2.15, the equivalent development in ecclesiology as expressed in the concepts of both "church" and "body" (particularly 1.18), and the emergence of the *Haustafel* ("household rules") form as a regular feature of paraenesis (3.18–4.1). At all these points Ephesians, drawing on Colossians, takes Pauline theology forward

18. §7.4 and §14.3.
19. See above §14.5a.
20. See above §11 n. 7.

into new dimensions. The continuity is clearly evident in both cases.[21] But it becomes increasingly dubious whether we can properly talk of these letters and the Pastorals as expressions of the theology of Paul the apostle.

Development within Paul's and Pauline theology we can therefore speak of — developments of differing measure. But the character and main themes of Paul's theology as such remained remarkably consistent and coherent. The principal significance of the developments outlined above is to remind us that Paul's theology was living in quality and dynamic in character — theologizing as much as theology.

§25.5 Innovative and lasting features

Using the model of three levels in Paul's theology, we have so far concentrated on the foundation and middle levels. On the topmost level of Paul's theology, what else calls for comment? Of course, the story of Paul's own dialogue with the various churches by means of his letters is shaped in its primary theological contours by the stories of Israel and of Christ and their interaction. But not all the emphases in Paul's theology are so tightly tied to his christology, and at least some deserve separate mention. Some have made a lasting impact on Christian theology, but our indebtedness to Paul has been lost to sight. Others have become muffled or ceased to be heard in the continuing dialogue of Christian theology. But all deserve a fresh exposure.

Among the most innovative features which shaped Christian theology for all time are the key terms which Paul introduced. Above all we should think of "gospel," "grace," and "love" — gospel as the good news of Christ focusing in his death and resurrection, grace as epitomizing the character of God's dealings with humankind, love as the motive of divine giving and in turn the motive for human living. Between them, in their specialist Christian usage, these words sum up and define the scope and character of Christianity as no other three words can. And that specialist Christian usage, in each case, we owe entirely to Paul.

Other special usages which Paul introduced did not have the same lasting impact. We may think particularly of his careful distinction between "body" and "flesh" (§3.4) and of his coining of the term "charisma" (§20.5). The former should have enabled Christian theology to hold together a sense of the positiveness of the physical body with an awareness of the weakness and corruptibility of human flesh. The loss of the distinction opened a painful chapter in Christian theology which is still not closed. The latter was an

---

21. In my view Paul may even have given his approval to Timothy's penning of his message to the Colossians (Col. 4.18).

integral part of the dynamism of Paul's vision of the body, the church as charismatic community; but it seems to have lost its distinctive Pauline force almost as quickly. We shall return to the point below.

Other elements in Paul's theology deserving of mention ought to include, first of all, his analysis of the human condition — in terms both of his use of Adam and his appreciation of the powers of sin and death (§§4-5). The analysis can be easily dismissed as too dependent on primitive myth and cosmology. But that would be as much a confession of the poverty of a culture which cannot recognize the power of such myth and metaphor to inform and shape deeply felt human instincts and perceptions. The analysis has also been criticized as unduly pessimistic. I would prefer to say realistic. For a theology which takes seriously the all too real human experience of being drawn into that which is ultimately hurtful and destructive of self and community, whether as an internal or external conditioning or pressure, is hardly overpessimistic. And a theology which confronts the existential reality of death perceived as something profoundly negative is hardly out of tune with common sentiment. Above all, a gospel which addresses these realities calls for continued attention.

It need hardly be said that Paul's understanding of the spiritual dimension of human existence likewise poses a continuing challenge to all merely materialist biologies and anthropologies. But deserving of more prominence is his recognition of the essentially relational character of both the divine and the human, of both creation and salvation — that God is to be known not in himself but in his relation to creation and to the human beings he created, that human beings can only properly know themselves in relation to God as their Creator, that human beings and human society are interlocking and mutually defining terms. This came out, once again, most clearly in Paul's understanding of righteousness — both as God's faithfulness to his creation and people and as human responsibility towards God and towards others.

A further important feature emerged from the examination of Paul's theology of justification by faith (§14). That is the extent to which Paul set himself against any racialism or narrow nationalism which confused divinely granted privilege with "divine right" and saw no hope for Gentiles to share in the blessing of Abraham while remaining Gentiles. This was a dimension of Paul's teaching which was lost to sight for far too long, in a teaching on justification too much taken up with the individual's search for peace with God. To say this is not to diminish by one iota the personal character of the teaching, still less the underlying insight that no human being can (or needs to) gain acceptance with God by his or her own efforts (as already noted, a fundamental insight of Israel's own self-identity). It is simply to bring back to prominence the corporate and international character of the message as Paul first formulated it — as a defence of God's readiness to accept Gentile as well as Jew, and equally by faith alone. This dimension of the doctrine of justification by faith has more than a little to say to a world where racialism and antagonistic nationalisms remain a potent factor in international tensions.

In a similar vein the importance of theology as experienced as well as articulated was a recurring feature in the preceding chapters. It was not least Paul's own experience of grace which formed and shaped his language of grace. Not that he set experience over against rationality, "spirit" against "mind." Quite the contrary, as his treatment of prophecy and tongues speaking in 1 Corinthians 14 reminds us. But neither did he treat theology simply as an exercise in rational analysis and deduction, as a statement of dogmatic propositions. It was the character of what he and his converts experienced, through faith, in Christ, by the Spirit, which he attempted to articulate and from which he attempted to develop a soteriology and ecclesiology whose existential truth his readers could recognize and live (§16.4). The interaction and correlation between experienced theology and articulated theology remain at the heart of any theological dialogue which counts Paul a continuing partner.

Here too we ought to make special mention of Paul's conception of the process of salvation as an eschatological tension between what has already been accomplished and what has not yet been completed (§18). Paul faced with honesty the reality of believers still handicapped by the weakness of the flesh, of churches continually fractured in varying degrees by misdirected religion and self-seeking, of a world groaning with frustration as it awaits liberation and redemption. That honesty enables theology to be honest in turn as it wrestles with the problems of living between the ages. To adapt characteristic Pauline terminology: if faith, hope, and love hang so closely together, then we should not wonder that faith and love often prove imperfect so long as hope remains unfulfilled. Or as Paul himself put it: Christian existence is characterized by hope and as hope — the experience of confident hope in itself embodying the already–not yet tension of the gospel.

In Paul's ecclesiology the image of the body of Christ remains as potent as ever, in terms of all members being engraced to contribute to the benefit of the whole, the diversity of ministry as integral to the unity of the body as well as its health, the insistence that ministries are different in scope but not in kind, the refusal to allow all ministry to be focused in one member, and the recognition that authority is charismatic in character but always requires the testing and validation of the community's recognition and affirmation (§§20.5, 21.6). In addition, a corollary may follow from Paul's adaptation of the political metaphor of a "body" to represent the nature of a community composed of different individuals with different callings and interests: the church as the body of Christ should be a model of community for the wider society — a model of integration and mutual interdependence, of caring and

735

sharing, of respect and responsibility. In both cases the vision is easily stated, even if the reality then as now is almost always a very different story. Nevertheless the ideal is still worth restating, precisely as an ideal by which to measure the reality.

Also important was the balance Paul sought to achieve and maintain in his paraenesis (§23). The balance between inward motivation and outward norm. The balance between a faith which trusted wholly in God, a Spirit which stirred up love and outgoing concern, and the norm which Christ himself provided. Here too Paul would hardly have been content with, would indeed have protested vociferously against any attempt to reduce faith to formulae, to enshrine the Spirit in rubrics, to translate the law of Christ into a set of rules. The faith Paul called for was too simple and direct for that. The life-giving Spirit could not be boxed in like that. The memory of Christ epitomized in Jesus tradition and the love command could not be so tied down. The importance of Paul's theology at this point is that it should help prevent that balance between the vital experience of trust and enabling and the normative traditions of Christianity from being wholly upset.

Not least we should consider the enduring value of Paul's own example, not just as Christian and theologian, but also as teacher and pastor, or, in a word, as apostle. Here we need only instance the sensitivity with which he exercised his own apostolic authority and the way he encouraged his churches to take responsibility for their own affairs (§21.5). But also the care with which he counseled his churches in the specific situations in which they lived and the particular ethical and moral problems with which they were confronted (§24). Most striking in this latter case was the way Paul took fully into account the reality both of living in a hostile world and of living between two worlds. Also the different ways in which he wove together the various principles and precedents to provide effective patterns for conduct and antidotes to potentially damaging rifts — in some cases standing firm (on matters of sexual practice and idolatry), in others insisting on the importance of Christian liberty; in some cases sternly denouncing and instructing, in others pleading and striving to persuade. Not least of note were Paul's repeated attempts to hold together different opinions and factions within his churches by appeal to mutual faith requiring mutual respect, to liberty conditioned by responsibility, and above all to love as exemplified by Christ himself. Paul, both theologian and pastor, herein gives an enduring example of what theology in practice should mean — not necessarily so much in the advice he actually gave, but in the way he formed his opinion and gave his advice.

Last, but not least, we recall yet once again that Paul theologized by writing letters. This means that his theology was always wrapped around with the greetings, thanksgivings, and prayers of letter openings, with the travel arrangements, personal explanations, and farewells of letter closings.

Or, should we rather say, his theologizing always began and ended with the practicalities and little things of human relationships. Paul's theology, however complex and high-flown, was never of the ivory-tower kind. It was first and last an attempt to make sense of the gospel as the key to everyday life and to make possible a daily living which was Christian through and through.

Index of Subjects

Adam, 81-101, 287-88, 734
  adam = humankind, 82-83, 90, 94-95, 99, 112
  adamah, 83, 101, 112
  christology, 94, 200-204, 210-11, 219-23, 241-42, 248-49, 265, 274-76, 278n.55, 282-90, 292-93, 464, 468, 724
  in Paul's theology, 90-101
Adoption, 436, 503
Allusion, 15-19, 189-90, 283-86, 651-53
Already/not yet, 466-72, 475-77, 487-88, 493-94
  aorist/imperative, 471-72, 476-77
  divided "I," 472-77, 496
  divided law, 473-74, 646
  and ethics, 496-97, 630-31, 673
Angels, 105-6
Antichrist, 305n.54
Antioch incident, 359-60
Apocalypse, 177, 180-81, 304-5
Apocalyptic perspective, 20, 41, 179-80, 240, 297, 304-5, 318-19, 726-27
Apostasy, 497-98
Apostle, 540-41
  see also Authority, of Paul
Aqedah, 224-25, 227n.112
Assurance, 437, 498
Atheism, 34
Authority, 569-71
  apostolic, 572-74, 578-80
  of congregation, 593-94
  of Jesus-tradition, 650-53

of ministry, 583-86
of Paul, 571-80
of prophets, 580-82, 593
of teachers, 582-83
of women, 588-93

Baptism, 445, 447, 448-49, 457, 728
  into Christ, 447-48, 451-52, 456-57
  and circumcision, 454-55, 458
  at Corinth, 613
  and faith, 456-59
  household, 457-58
  infant, 457-59
  as metaphor, 331, 450-52, 456
  and mystery cults, 445-46, 449
  and resurrection, 470
  as sacrament, 444-45, 457
  and Spirit, 452-53
  in Spirit, 450-51, 560
  traditional view, 442-45, 447-48
Boasting, 119, 363-64, 372
Body, 52, 54-61
  of Christ, see Christ
  = corpse, 55-56, 61n.45
  embodiment, 56-61, 101
  and flesh, 70-73, 488, 733
  negative, 71-72, 80
  as prison, 39n.55, 71
  resurrection, 60-61, 71-72, 310, 488-90

Calendrical disputes, 358
Celibacy, 692-98

739

Index of Modern Authors

748

750

Weigandt, P., 457n.81
Weiss, B., 5n.13
Weiss, J., 62n.49, 184n.6, 408n.88, 431n.101
Weiss, K., 648n.109
Welborn, L. L., 551n.104
Welker, M., 427n.77, 429n.86, 437n.127
Wengst, K., 174n.67, 175nn.71,74
Wenham, D., 187n.20, 190n.37, 191n.43, 192n.48, 193n.52, 304n.47, 496n.149, 650n.117
Wenham, G. J., 83n.14
Werner, M., 297n.14
Wesley, C., 283
Westerholm, S., 119n.81, 130n.10, 132n.23, 139n.57, 141n.74, 152n.123, 159n.158, 339nn.18,19, 354n.77, 365n.128, 366n.133, 368n.139, 632n.26, 633, 643n.86, 646n.102
Wetter, G. P., 321n.23, 322nn.26,28
Whelan, C. F., 587n.111
Whiteley, D. E. H., 5, 28n.4, 42n.80, 54n.11, 63n.58, 97n.81, 157n.150, 223n.88, 250n.83, 272n.30, 345n.40, 425n.71, 549n.95
Whyte, A., 477n.69
Wibbing, S., 663n.164
Wicks, H. J., 35n.30
Wikenhauser, A., 393n.18, 397n.39, 398n.42, 407n.85, 408nn.86,88, 410n.92, 411n.95, 443n.6
Wilckens, U., 20, 135n.37, 139n.59, 155n.138, 168n.25, 178n.83, 216n.46, 452n.52, 453n.56, 680n.40
Williams, G., 415n.13
Williams, S. K., 214n.28, 215n.36, 345n.39, 360nn.105, 107, 383n.203
Willis, W. L., 604n.23, 605nn.27,28, 616n.78, 704n.154
Wilson, W. T., 676n.16
Wilson, S. G., 346n.45
Wimbush, V. L., 693n.91
Windisch, H., 148n.105, 210n.13, 217n.52
Winger, M., 132n.25, 133n.30, 158n.155
Wink, W., 35nn.31,32, 37n.40, 38n.47,

106nn.16,18,19, 107nn.22,23,24, 108n.30, 110nn.42,43,44, 121n.97
Winninge, M., 349n.57, 359n.101, 393n.19, 467n.30
Winston, D., 85n.23
Winter, B. W., 691n.84
Winter, R. W. 609n.44
Wintermute, O. S., 82n.7
Wire, A. C., 588n.117
Wischmeyer, O., 596n.154
Witherington, B., 4n.9, 18n.52, 191n.43, 214n.34, 223n.85, 272n.30, 280n.59, 282n.68, 286n.93, 287nn.98,100, 292n.125, 312n.93, 313n.96, 385n.210, 704n.152
Wolff, C., 184n.6,7, 193n.54, 280n.59, 448n.34, 609n.47
Wolter, M., 387n.215, 388n.221, 454n.69, 579n.72
Wrede, W., 3n.3, 7, 9n.30, 340n.22
Wright, D. F., 122n.103
Wright, D. P., 502n.13
Wright, N. T., 18n.52, 30n.6, 100n.93, 145n.90, 147n.103, 148n.112, 155n.139, 158nn.154,155, 199n.88, 216n.46, 253n.100, 285nn.86,87, 286n.96, 287n.97, 288n.106, 293n.126, 362n.117
Wuellner, W., 12n.36

Young, F. M., 233n.148
Young, N. H., 142n.75

Zahn, T., 140n.62, 481n.88
Zeitlin, S., 506n.36
Zeller, D., 524n.121
Ziesler, J. A., 4n.9, 98n.87, 115n.67, 158n.155, 278n.54, 286n.95, 337n.11, 341n.27, 354n.78, 399n.47, 408n.86, 681n.43
Zimmerli, W., 321n.19
Zobel, H.-J., 321nn.18,19, 322nn.26,29
Zwiep, A. W., 300n.28

Index of Scripture and Other Ancient Writings

759

2.1-6	**116-17**	2.17-20	**117**		373n.156,	
2.1-16	490	2.17-29	508		386n.212,	
2.1-29	502	2.18	40, 647,		467n.31, 521n.108	
2.1–3.19	115-19		648n.107	3.21	130, 180	
2.2	45n.96	2.18-20	137	3.21-26	166, **174**, **176**,	
2.2-3	41	2.20	45n.96		177, 216, 341,	
2.4	85n.23, 86n.24,	2.21-22	135n.38		343, 383,	
	327, 525n.129	2.23	123n.107, 133,		390n.2, 718	
2.5	42n.79, 52n.2,		137, 387n.219,	3.22	197, 324n.35,	
	255n.109,		525n.126		372, 373n.155,	
	307n.61	2.24	171n.43, 505n.28		379n.184, **383-84**	
2.5-8	41	2.25	133	3.22-23	518	
2.6-7	365n.129	2.25-27	356n.87	3.22–5.2	372n.153	
2.6-11	365, 665	2.26	136n.44	3.23	**93-94**, 112n.51,	
2.6-15	136	2.28	52n.2, 63n.59,		259n.134, 387	
2.7	86n.25, 677n.26		65, 69, 161, 164	3.23-26	214n.27	
2.7-10	662	2.28-29	69n.84, 149,	3.24	179n.90, 227,	
2.7-16	226n.102		422n.57, 424,		320n.12,	
2.8	42n.79, 45n.96,		450n.42,		322n.24, 397,	
	80n.4		505n.28,		406n.78,	
2.9	52n.2, 76n.114		643n.85, 644		466n.22,	
2.9-10	93, 373n.155,	2.29	52n.2, 75, 422		467n.31,	
	505n.28, 510	3.1	69n.84, **117-18**,		521n.107	
2.10	677n.26		502, 505n.28	3.24-25	183	
2.11	42	3.1-3	45	3.24-26	216	
2.12	131, 137,	3.2	170	3.25	45n.96, 111n.45,	
	492n.134	3.3	45n.96, 381,		208, **213-16**,	
2.12-13	135		424, 502		217n.55, 229,	
2.12-14	133	3.3-5	502n.12, 505n.26		231	
2.12-15	41, 165	3.3-7	344	3.25-26	196, 343n.35,	
2.12-16	**117**, 141n.70,	3.4	171n.43, 467n.31		658n.145	
	636, 668, 720	3.5	29, 42n.79, 80n.4	3.26	180n.94, 196n.71,	
2.12–8.7	134n.32	3.5-6	42		379n.184,	
2.13	136, 386n.212,	3.6	137		380n.186,	
	450n.42,	3.7	45n.96, 259n.133		381n.191,	
	467n.31, 643	3.8	686n.69		467n.31, 635n.49,	
2.14	137, 505n.28	3.9	112n.51,		693n.95	
2.14-15	492n.135, 665		373n.155,	3.27	133n.29, 364,	
2.15	52n.2, 75, 703		505n.28		387n.219,	
2.16	41, 137, 165,	3.10-12	171n.43		450n.42, 632,	
	166, 254,	3.10-18	172, 522		633, 639, 646	
	255n.109, 308,	3.10-19	118	3.27-28	363n.121, 384	
	310n.78, 381,	3.19	41, 132n.21, 137	3.27-29	508, 525n.126	
	382, 406n.78	3.19-20	135, 373n.155	3.27-30	**363-64**, 367	
2.17	**119**, 133,	3.20	52n.2, 64, 130,	3.27-31	365, 366, 372,	
	387n.219,		134, 161n.164,		**638-39**	
	505n.28, 525n.126		345, **362-63**,	3.27–4.6	521n.108	